The Handbook of British Mammals

The Handbook of British Mammals

EDITED BY GORDON B. CORBET
AND STEPHEN HARRIS

THIRD EDITION

PUBLISHED FOR THE MAMMAL SOCIETY
BY BLACKWELL SCIENTIFIC PUBLICATIONS

OXFORD LONDON EDINBURGH
BOSTON MELBOURNE PARIS BERLIN VIENNA

© 1964, 1977, 1991 by
Blackwell Scientific Publications
Editorial offices:
Osney Mead, Oxford OX2 0EL
25 John Street, London WC1N 2BL
23 Ainslie Place, Edinburgh EH3 6AJ
3 Cambridge Center, Cambridge
  Massachusetts 02142, USA
54 University Street, Carlton
  Victoria 3053, Australia

Other Editorial Offices:
Arnette SA
2, rue Casimir-Delavigne
75006 Paris
France

Blackwell Wissenschaft
Meinekestrasse 4
D-1000 Berlin 15
Germany

Blackwell MZV
Feldgasse 13
A-1238 Wien
Austria

First published 1964
Reprinted 1965
Second edition 1977
Third edition 1991

Set by Setrite Typesetters, Hong Kong
Printed and bound in Great Britain
by Butler & Tanner Ltd,
Frome and London

DISTRIBUTORS

Marston Book Services Ltd
PO Box 87
Oxford OX2 0DT
(*Orders*: Tel: 0865 791155
    Fax: 0865 791927
    Telex: 837515)

USA
Blackwell Scientific Publications, Inc.
3 Cambridge Center
Cambridge, MA 02142
(*Orders*: Tel: 800 759-6102)

Canada
Oxford University Press
70 Wynford Drive
Don Mills, Ontario M3C 1J9
(*Orders*: Tel: (416) 441-2941)

Australia
Blackwell Scientific Publications (Australia) Pty Ltd
54 University Street
Carlton, Victoria 3053
(*Orders*: Tel: (03) 347-0300)

British Library
Cataloguing in Publication Data

The Handbook of British Mammals. — 3rd ed.
  1. Great Britain. Mammals
  I. Corbet, G.B. (Gordon Barclay), *1933*–
  II. Harris, S.
  III. Mammal Society
  599.0941

  ISBN 0-632-01691-4

Library of Congress
Cataloging in Publication Data

The Handbook of British Mammals/edited by G.B.
  Corbet & S. Harris. — 3rd ed.
    p.   cm.
  ISBN 0-632-01691-4
  Mammals — Great Britain. I. Corbet. G.B.
    (Gordon Barclay) II. Harris, Stephen, *1950*–
    III. Mammal Society.
  QL727.H36   1991
  599.0941 — dc20

Contents

APPENDICES

Contributors

Alibhai, SK *Department of Biology, Royal Holloway and Bedford New College, Englefield Green, Surrey TW20 0EX* [Bank and field voles]

Anderson, SS *Sea Mammal Research Unit, c/o British Antarctic Survey, High Cross, Madingley Road, Cambridge CB3 0ET* [Grey seal]

Avery, MI *Royal Society for the Protection of Birds, The Lodge, Sandy, Beds* [Pipistrelle]

Baker, SJ *Mammal Ecology Group, ADAS Central Science Laboratory, Jupiter Road, Norwich NR6 6SP* [Coypu]

Berry, RJ *Department of Biology, University College, Gower Street, London WC1E 6BT* [House mouse]

Birks, JDS *Nature Conservancy Council, Masefield House, Wells Road, Malvern, Worcs* [Mink]

Blandford, PRS *Countryside Education Trust, John Montagu Building, Beaulieu, Brockenhurst, Hants SO42 7ZN* [Polecat, ferret]

Bonner, WN *3 Berry Lane, Godmanchester, Huntingdon PE18 8LA* [Preface, common seal]

Boyce, CCK *PO Box 2165, Glenwood Springs, Colorado 81602, USA* [Water vole]

Bullock, DJ *Department of Applied Biology and Biotechnology, Leicester Polytechnic, Scraptoft Campus, Scraptoft, Leicester LE7 9SU* [Feral goat, feral sheep]

Chanin, P *Department of Continuing and Adult Education, University of Exeter, Cotley, Streatham Rise, Exeter, Devon EX4 4PE* [Otter]

Chapman, NG *Larkmead, Barton Mills, Bury St Edmunds, Suffolk IP28 6AA* [Fallow deer, muntjac]

Cheeseman, CL *ADAS Central Science Laboratory, Ministry of Agriculture, Fisheries and Food, Tangley Place, Worplesdon, Guildford, Surrey GU3 3LQ* [Badger]

Churchfield, S *Division of Biosphere Sciences, Kings College, Campden Hill Road, London W8 7AH* [Shrews]

Clutton-Brock, J *Department of Zoology, Natural History Museum, Cromwell Road, London SW7 5BD* [Appendix: Extinct species]

Cooper, E M *35–43 Lincoln's Inn Fields, London WC2A 3PN* [British mammals and the law]

Corbet, GB *27 Farnaby Road, Bromley, Kent BR1 4BL* [Editor, Introduction, Habitats]

Cowan, DP *ADAS Central Science Laboratory, Ministry of Agriculture, Fisheries and Food, Tangley Place, Worplesdon, Guildford, Surrey GU3 3LQ* [Rabbit]

Dunstone, N *Department of Biological Sciences, University of Durham, South Road, Durham City DH1 3LE* [Mink]

Easterbee, N *Nature Conservancy Council, 12 Hope Terrace, Edinburgh EH9 2AS* [Wildcat]

Evans, PGH *Edward Grey Institute, Zoology Department, University of Oxford, South Parks Road, Oxford OX1 3PS* [Cetaceans]

Farrell, L *Nature Conservancy Council, Northminster House, Peterborough PE1 1UA* [Chinese water deer]

Fenn, MG *Department of Zoology, University of Oxford, South Parks Road, Oxford OX1 3PS* [Brown rat]

Flowerdew, JR *Department of Zoology, Downing St, Cambridge CB2 3EJ* [Wood mouse]

Gipps, JHW *Zoological Society of London, Regent's Park, London NW1 4RY* [Bank and field voles]

Gorman, MG *University of Aberdeen, Culterty Field Station, Newburgh, Ellon, Aberdeen AB4 0AA* [Mole, Orkney/Guernsey vole]

Gosling, LM *Mammal Ecology Group, ADAS Central Science Laboratory, Jupiter Road, Norwich NR6 6SP* [Coypu]

Gurnell, J *Department of Biological Sciences, Queen Mary's College, Mile End Road, London E1 4NS* [Squirrels]

Hall, SJG *Physiological Laboratory, University of Cambridge, Downing Street, Cambridge CB2 3EG* [Park cattle]

Harris, S *Department of Zoology, University of Bristol, Woodland Road, Bristol BS8 1UG* [Editor, harvest mouse, fox, vagrant seals]

Hewson, R *Department of Zoology, University of Aberdeen, Tillydrone Avenue, Aberdeen AB9 2TN* [Mountain/Irish hare]

Hills, DM *Department of Zoology, Natural History Museum, London SW7 5BD* [Appendix: Ephemeral introductions]

Hutson, AM *Winkfield, Station Road, Plumpton Green, East Sussex BN7 3BU* [Serotine]

Jewell, PA *Physiological Laboratory, University of Cambridge, Downing Street, Cambridge CB2 3EG* [Feral sheep]

Jones-Walters, LM *Nature Conservancy Council, Northminster House, Peterborough, PE1 1UA* [Fat dormouse]

King, CM *The Royal Society of New Zealand, PO Box 598, Wellington, New Zealand* [Stoat, weasel]

Lloyd, HG *Dolrhedyn, Irfon Road, Builth Wells, Powys LD2 3DE* [Fox]

Macdonald, DW *Department of Zoology, University of Oxford, South Parks Road, Oxford OX1 3PS* [Brown rat, feral cat]

Montgomery, WI *Department of Zoology, Queen's University, Belfast BT7 1NN* [Yellow-necked mouse]

Morris, PA *Department of Biology, Royal Holloway and Bedford New College, Englefield Green, Surrey TW20 0EX* [Hedgehog, common dormouse]

Neal, EG *42 Park Avenue, Bedford MK40 2NF* [Badger]

Putman, RJ *Department of Biology, Building 44, University of Southampton, Southampton SO9 5NH* [Horse, fallow deer]

Racey, PA *Department of Zoology, University of Aberdeen, Tillydrone Avenue, Aberdeen AB9 2TN* [Noctule, Leisler's and vagrant bats]

Ranft, R *National Sound Archive, 29 Exhibition Road, London SW7 2AS* [Appendix: Sound recordings]

Ransome, RD *14B Dursley Road, Woodfields, Dursley, Gloucs* [Horseshoe bats]

Ratcliffe, R *Wildlife and Conservation Research Branch, Forestry Commission, Alice Holt, Wrecclesham, Farnham, Surrey GU10 4LH* [Sika and roe deer]

Staines, BW *Banchory Research Station, Institute of Terrestrial Ecology, Hill of Brathens, Banchory AB3 4BY* [Red and roe deer]

Speakman, JR *Department of Zoology, University of Aberdeen, Tillydrone Avenue, Aberdeen AB9 2TN* [Daubenton's bat]

Stebbings, RE *74 Alexandra Road, Peterborough PE1 3DG* [Introduction to bats, barbastelle]

Stone, RD *University of Lausanne, Institute of Biology and Animal Ecology, 1016 Lausanne, Switzerland* [Mole]

Swift, SM *Drumore, Blacklunans, Blairgowrie, Perths PH10 7LA* [Long-eared bats]

Tapper, SC *Game Conservancy, Fordingbridge, Hants SP6 1EF* [Brown hare]

Taylor, KD *Warren House, Albury Heath, Albury, Guildford, Surrey GU5 9DB* [Rats]

Thompson, PM *Department of Zoology, University of Aberdeen, Tillydrone Avenue, Aberdeen AB9 2TN* [Common seal]

Trout, RC *ADAS Central Science Laboratory, Tangley Place, Worplesdon, Guildford, Surrey GU3 3LQ* [Harvest mouse]

Velander, KA *Department of Forestry and Natural Resources, University of Edinburgh, King's Buildings, Mayfield Road, Edinburgh EH9 3JU* [Pine marten]

Walton, KC *Bangor Research Unit, Institute of Terrestrial Ecology, University College of North Wales, Bangor, Gwynedd LL57 2UP* [Polecat, ferret]

Yalden, DW *Department of Environmental Biology, University of Manchester, Oxford Road, Manchester M13 9PL* [History, red-necked wallaby]

Preface

All branches of natural history need handbooks, yet it was not until 1964 that the first edition of *The Handbook of British Mammals* was published. Since the appearance of the second edition in 1977, much new material on British mammals and their ecology has accumulated, and the Council of the Mammal Society decided the time was ripe to produce an up-dated version. This extensive revision of the second edition will provide a definitive and comprehensive handbook for the study of British mammals.

The bulk of the book is taken up with the species' accounts, and the steady accretion of knowledge by professionals and amateurs alike has inevitably meant that this section is larger than before. The species accounts have been put in context by the provision of a comprehensive introduction and chapters on the history of the fauna and mammalian habitats in the British Isles. The chapter on British Mammals and the Law which appeared in the first edition, but was dropped from the second, has been entirely rewritten and up-dated. Although mammals have been subject to the laws of the chase since the earliest times of a codified legal system in these islands, it is only recently that the ordinary naturalist or researcher dealing with mammals has had to ensure that he is aware of the legal restrictions set around his activities.

The Mammal Society, and all who read and use this book, owe a great debt to the contributors, both amateur and professional. Only those who have actually experienced it know what a vast amount of work is involved in preparing what seems to be even a straightforward species account, or descriptive chapter. Even this pales into insignificance in comparison with the work done by the editors — commissioning sections, extracting the completed contributions from the authors, checking them and sending them back for revision, not to mention all the necessary liaison with the publishers. In a multi-author work of this kind the editors play the key role in ensuring that the book eventually appears. Gordon Corbet and Stephen Harris have served the Society well in this respect and we are additionally grateful to the senior editor for providing the Introduction and the chapter on Habitats.

Like its predecessors, this work will be of very great value to the increasing numbers of people who are taking an active interest in field studies and the important role played by British mammals in our countryside. Pressures on our environment have never been greater and are increasing. We hope that this volume may, by helping people to understand the biology and role of mammals, help to ensure that the diversity of our fauna is maintained.

Godmanchester   Nigel Bonner
1990   *President, The Mammal Society*

Acknowledgements

This has been a cooperative effort involving many members of the Mammal Society. Valuable comments were received from many individuals who read the accounts of particular species and these are acknowledged along with the principal author at the end of the account of each species. In addition thanks are due to the following who contributed and refereed data on a variety of species: Dr J S Fairley (Irish data); Dr T D Healing (microbial infections); Mr A M Hutson (insect ectoparasites); Mr K H Hyatt (acarine parasites); Dr J Lewis (helminth parasites).

Thanks are due to all who provided photographs, as acknowledged in the captions, and especially to Mr D Kinns and Mrs A M Kinns for supplying photographs by the late Geoffrey Kinns whose photographs so enlivened the previous editions. The senior editor is especially grateful to Mrs Shashu Lalji for her patient and expert word-processing of many of the scripts. The editors and contributors acknowledge the valuable support provided by the many university departments and other institutes that appear in the list of contributors' addresses.

List of Species

Order Insectivora: insectivores

FAMILY ERINACEIDAE
Erinaceus europaeus   Hedgehog

FAMILY TALPIDAE
Talpa europaea   Mole

FAMILY SORICIDAE: SHREWS
Sorex araneus   Common shrew
Sorex coronatus   French shrew
Sorex minutus   Pygmy shrew
Neomys fodiens   Water shrew
Crocidura russula   Greater white-toothed shrew
Crocidura suaveolens   Lesser white-toothed shrew

Order Chiroptera: bats

FAMILY RHINOLOPHIDAE: HORSESHOE BATS
Rhinolophus ferrumequinum   Greater horseshoe bat
Rhinolophus hipposideros   Lesser horseshoe bat

FAMILY VESPERTILIONIDAE: VESPERTILIONID BATS
Myotis mystacinus   Whiskered bat
Myotis brandtii   Brandt's bat
Myotis nattereri   Natterer's bat
Myotis bechsteinii   Bechstein's bat
Myotis myotis   Mouse-eared bat
Myotis daubentonii   Daubenton's bat
Vespertilio murinus   Parti-coloured bat
Eptesicus serotinus   Serotine
Nyctalus noctula   Noctule
Nyctalus leisleri   Leisler's bat
Pipistrellus pipistrellus   Pipistrelle
Pipistrellus nathusii   Nathusius' pipistrelle
Barbastella barbastellus   Barbastelle
Plecotus auritus   Brown long-eared bat
Plecotus austriacus   Grey long-eared bat

Order Lagomorpha: lagomorphs

FAMILY LEPORIDAE: RABBITS AND HARES
Oryctolagus cuniculus	Rabbit
Lepus europaeus	Brown hare
Lepus timidus	Mountain hare/Irish hare

Order Rodentia: rodents

FAMILY SCIURIDAE: SQUIRRELS
Sciurus vulgaris	Red squirrel
Sciurus carolinensis	Grey squirrel

FAMILY MURIDAE: VOLES, MICE ETC.

SUBFAMILY ARVICOLINAE: VOLES
Clethrionomys glareolus	Bank vole
Microtus agrestis	Field vole
Microtus arvalis	Orkney/Guernsey voles
Arvicola terrestris	Water vole

SUBFAMILY MURINAE: RATS AND MICE
Apodemus sylvaticus	Wood mouse
Apodemus flavicollis	Yellow-necked mouse
Micromys minutus	Harvest mouse
Mus domesticus	House mouse
Rattus norvegicus	Common rat
Rattus rattus	Ship rat

FAMILY GLIRIDAE: DORMICE
Muscardinus avellanarius	Common dormouse
Glis glis	Fat dormouse

FAMILY CAPROMYIDAE
Myocastor coypus	Coypu

Order Cetacea: whales, dolphins and porpoises

Suborder Mysticeti: baleen whales

FAMILY BALAENIDAE: RIGHT WHALES
Eubalaena glacialis	Northern right whale

FAMILY BALAENOPTERIDAE: RORQUALS ETC.
Megaptera novaeangliae	Humpback whale
Balaenoptera physalus	Fin whale
Balaenoptera musculus	Blue whale
Balaenoptera borealis	Sei whale
Balaenoptera acutorostrata	Minke whale

Suborder Odontoceti: *toothed whales*

FAMILY PHYSETERIDAE: SPERM WHALES
Physeter macrocephalus — Sperm whale
Kogia breviceps — Pygmy sperm whale

FAMILY MONODONTIDAE
Delphinapterus leucas — White whale
Monodon monoceros — Narwhal

FAMILY ZIPHIIDAE: BEAKED WHALES
Hyperoodon ampullatus — Northern bottlenose whale
Ziphius cavirostris — Cuvier's beaked whale
Mesoplodon bidens — Sowerby's beaked whale
Mesoplodon mirus — True's beaked whale

FAMILY PHOCOENIDAE: PORPOISES
Phocoena phocoena — Porpoise

FAMILY DELPHINIDAE: DOLPHINS
Delphinus delphis — Common dolphin
Stenella coeruleoalba — Striped dolphin
Tursiops truncatus — Bottle-nosed dolphin
Lagenorhynchus acutus — Atlantic white-sided dolphin
Lagenorhynchus albirostris — White-beaked dolphin
Peponocephala electra — Melon-headed whale
Pseudorca crassidens — False killer whale
Orcinus orca — Killer whale
Globicephala melas — Long-finned pilot whale
Grampus griseus — Risso's dolphin

Order Carnivora: terrestrial carnivores

FAMILY CANIDAE: DOGS
Vulpes vulpes — Fox

FAMILY MUSTELIDAE
Martes martes — Pine marten
Mustela erminea — Stoat
Mustela nivalis — Weasel
Mustela putorius — Polecat
Mustela furo — Ferret
Mustela vison — Mink
Meles meles — Badger
Lutra lutra — Otter

FAMILY FELIDAE: CATS
Felis silvestris — Wildcat
Felis catus — Feral cat

Order Pinnipedia: seals etc.

FAMILY PHOCIDAE: SEALS
Phoca vitulina   Common seal
Halichoerus grypus   Grey seal
Phoca hispida   Ringed seal
Phoca groenlandica   Harp seal
Erignathus barbatus   Bearded seal
Cystophora cristata   Hooded seal

FAMILY ODOBENIDAE: WALRUS
Odobenus rosmarus   Walrus

Order Perissodactyla: odd-toed ungulates

FAMILY EQUIDAE: HORSES
Equus caballus   Horse

Order Artiodactyla: even-toed ungulates

FAMILY CERVIDAE: DEER
Cervus elaphus   Red deer
Cervus nippon   Sika deer
Dama dama   Fallow deer
Capreolus capreolus   Roe deer
Muntiacus reevesi   Muntjac
Hydropotes inermis   Water deer
Rangifer tarandus   Reindeer

FAMILY BOVIDAE
Bos taurus   Domestic cattle
Capra hircus   Feral goat
Ovis ammon   Feral sheep

Order Marsupialia: marsupials

FAMILY MACROPODIDAE: KANGAROOS ETC.
Macropus rufogriseus   Red-necked wallaby

Chapter 1 / Introduction

Like the two preceding editions, this volume aims to provide a comprehensive account of the mammals of Britain, Ireland and the Channel Isles. The mammalian fauna of Britain, and even more that of Ireland, is considerably impoverished in comparison with that of continental Europe, even if we compare it with an area of comparable size and topographical diversity such as West Germany, as shown in Table 1.1. However, the impoverishment concerns the number of species rather than the absence of many major groups and some of the missing families were represented in the past by species that have become extinct in historical times, such as the beaver, the wild boar and the brown bear.

All species currently living in the wild in the region are dealt with in the main text, including introductions that are well established, i.e. those that have been breeding freely for more than 10 years, and also feral populations of domesticated species, i.e. those living under fairly natural conditions with respect to social organisation, reproduction and ecology. Vagrant bats, pinnipeds and cetaceans are dealt with briefly in the main text, whilst extinct species that have occurred in the region in the post-glacial period, and ephemeral introductions that have not (yet) become firmly established are dealt with in appendices. The numbers in each of these categories in each of the major groups of mammals are shown in Table 1.2.

Any deficiency in the number of species is compensated for by the intensity with which our mammals have been studied, making the British mammal fauna one of the best known in the world. That is not to say that there is little left to discover. Many factors combine to make information on how

Table 1.1. Approximate numbers of native (or possibly native), non-marine species of mammals.

Ireland	20
Britain	42
West Germany	61
Europe W of USSR	134
Palaearctic Region	450
World	4320

Table 1.2. Composition of the British and Irish mammal fauna (numbers of species).

	Indigenous or doubtfully introduced (+ certain introductions)		Additional species on small islands only	Vagrants	Feral species	Extinct (but present since Neolithic)
	Britain	Ireland				
Insectivores	5	2	3	—	—	—
Bats	15	7	—	2	—	—
Lagomorphs	2(+1)	1(+2)	—	—	—	—
Rodents	8(+6)	2(+5)	1	—	—	1
Carnivores	8(+1)	5(+1)	—	—	2	2
Pinnipeds	2	2	—	5	—	—
Ungulates	2(+4)	1(+3)	—	—	3	2
Marsupials	0(+1)	—	—	—	—	—
Cetaceans (to edge of continental shelf)	15		—	9	—	1?
Total (except cetaceans)	42(+13)	20(+11)	4	7	5	5

mammals operate in the wild difficult and time-consuming to acquire, for example their nocturnal or otherwise elusive behaviour and their use of olfaction in communication. Since the second edition of the *Handbook* was published in 1977 great advances have been made in our understanding of the spatial and social organisation of many species, especially by the use of radio-tracking which can now be applied to even the smallest of species. The study of behaviour has shifted steadily from the laboratory to the field and new syntheses have been attempted between the study of behaviour, ecology, population processes and genetics. These have provided fresh insights into the probable adaptive significance and selective value of many behavioural and physiological traits.

FORMAT OF THE SPECIES ACCOUNTS
In order to facilitate reference and to help identify gaps in our knowledge, information on each species is presented in a highly structured way. The following explanatory notes are arranged following the same sequence of headings.

CLASSIFICATION
The classification followed can be seen from the species checklist on pp. xi−xiv. It differs from that used in the second edition in the following points, and the reason for each change is given in the account of the taxon concerned.

French shrew *Sorex coronatus*, which occurs on Jersey, is accepted as specifically distinct from the common shrew *S. araneus*. The brown hare *Lepus europaeus* is accepted as specifically distinct from *L. capensis*. The subfamily Arvicolinae (voles) is included in the family Muridae. The seals, family Phocidae, and the walrus, Odobenidae are likely to be independently derived groups within the order Carnivora but are here kept in the order Pinnipedia.

A complete list of the mammals of the world is available in *A world list of mammalian species* [10]. Orders and families are described and diagnosed by Anderson & Jones [1].

NOMENCLATURE
The original citation of the species name is given, with author, date and type locality. The synonyms that follow are only those that are based on British or Irish specimens or that have been widely used for the species as a whole. Names used only for

subspecies are detailed separately under the heading Variation. The more commonly used vernacular synonyms follow, those in the celtic languages only for species occurring in the areas where the language is spoken. All synonyms, vernacular and scientific, are included in the index. In quoting scientific names of British mammals it is quite unnecessary, except when specifically discussing nomenclature, to give the author and date of the name.

RECOGNITION
This section should be read in conjunction with the diagnostic characters given in the accounts of the higher categories — genera, families, orders — or in the associated tables.

SIGN
Most of the signs mentioned are well illustrated by Bang & Dahlstrom [4] and by Lawrence & Brown [27].

DESCRIPTION
This section is normally limited to amplifying the characters most useful in recognition, pointing out the main specialisations of the species, and describing variation correlated with sex, age and season. Coloured illustrations of most species can be found in several field guides and other popular books. Colour photographs of most species are also available in a number of popular books [7, 21, 24, 25]. However, it should be noted that because of the difficulty of photographing living animals under standardised lighting conditions no existing set of photographs allows accurate comparison of colour from species to species. More detailed descriptions of external structure, skulls and teeth can be found in Miller [30]. Karyotypes of all European mammals were reviewed by Zima & Kral [42] who have been used as the principal source where British or Irish data are lacking (except in the case of bats for which Zima & Horacek [43] has been used).

MEASUREMENTS
Measurements of size can be more misleading than useful if variation with sex, age and season is not taken into account. Where figures are available with adequate qualifications they are usually tabulated. Otherwise only approximate indications of size are given in the text. Tables of cranial and dental measurements of most species were given by Miller [30].

VARIATION

Geographical variation is dealt with first, beginning with any differences between British and continental animals. Recent studies of geographical variation have generally shown that it is much less clear-cut and discrete than had previously been supposed and very few formally named subspecies can stand up to close scrutiny. Those that appear valid are diagnosed or their characters are tabulated; all other subspecific names that relate to the region are simply listed. Many aspects of variation were dealt with in *Variation in mammalian populations* [6].

DISTRIBUTION

The maps of the total range of each species are based primarily upon those in *Mammals of the Palaearctic Region* [8]. Those for Britain and Ireland are based upon the atlas published by the Biological Records Centre in 1984 (ed. HR Arnold), supplemented from other sources. Islands for which presence of a species cannot be shown clearly on the map (generally those under 100 km^2 in area) are listed in the text.

HISTORY

A general history of the British and Irish mammal faunas is given in Chapter 2 and the extinct species are dealt with in Appendix 1. In the main species accounts fossil and historical records are given only where there is little doubt as to the precise species concerned. For a general review of the Pleistocene mammals of the British Isles see Stuart [41].

HABITAT

A general account of habitats is given in Chapter 3. The habitat occupied by most species of mammal can generally be defined in terms of adequate cover as protection against predators and disturbance, and an adequate food supply.

SOCIAL ORGANISATION AND BEHAVIOUR

Information on social and individual behaviour is generally given in the following sequence: group size and composition, dispersion (home range, territory and its marking), hierarchy, communication (visual, vocal, olfactory), agonistic behaviour, seasonal pattern (including dispersal and migration), diurnal activity, burrowing, nest-building, locomotion, grooming, defence, defecation, urination, hibernation. Prominence is given to systematic studies of behaviour in natural conditions but these are scarce and for many species much of the information necessarily comes from study of captive animals or from casual observations. These last commonly consist of single observations of behaviour that are reported because they seem unusual. They are by no means irrelevant to the study of normal behaviour, but it is only when systematic observations of normal behaviour have been made that the significance of the anecdotal accounts can be appreciated.

The concept of social organisation is by no means confined to conspicuously sociable or colonial species. Even in the most 'solitary' species each individual is usually surrounded by neighbours with which it has some degree of communication and shares a characteristic pattern of spatial dispersion. A recent general text on the behaviour of mammals is *Social behaviour in mammals* [34].

FEEDING

As with behaviour there is a tendency for information on the normal diet to be swamped by records of the unusual. The 'anecdotal' literature on food is very extensive and has had to be quoted very sparingly. Normally information on feeding behaviour is given here rather than under Behaviour.

BREEDING

The sequence normally followed is: synopsis, seasonality, courtship and mating, gestation, litter size, nesting behaviour, birth, development of young to weaning. A source of general information on reproduction of mammals is Asdell [3], a comprehensive survey dealing with all groups.

POPULATION

Under this heading are presented data on population density, the age structure of the population, survival and longevity.

MORTALITY

Studies of predation that are relevant to most of the smaller species of mammals are those of Southern [39, 40] on the tawny owl, Glue [19, 20] on the barn owl and Day [13] on mustelids.

PARASITES

Rather than give exhaustive lists of parasites recorded, which would often include more stragglers than normal species, an attempt has been made to mention the species that occur frequently and regularly. All records are from Britain or Ireland unless otherwise stated. The main groups of parasites are shown in the following list which follows the sequence used in the text and includes the principal sources of information for each group.

Fleas: class Insecta, order Siphonaptera. Adults suck blood and are found in the pelage and in nests; the larvae are scavengers and live mainly in nests. Most species are not highly host-specific [17, 18, 36, 37].

Lice: class Insecta, order Phthiraptera. Two groups, both living entirely within the pelage: Mallophaga (Ischnocera) or biting lice, feeding mainly on skin debris; and Anoplura or sucking lice, feeding on blood. Many are highly host-specific. There is no compilation or identification guide for the British species.

Bugs: class Insecta, order Hemiptera. Most members of the bed-bug family (Cimicidae) occur on bats. They are blood-feeders living around the roost and with little adaptation to travel with the host [22].

Flies: class Insecta, order Diptera. The keds (Hippoboscidae) of ungulates and the bat-flies (Nycteribiidae) are highly specialised blood-feeders, remaining on their hosts for long periods [23]. The larvae of Gasterophilidae (bot-flies) and Oestridae (warble-flies) infect ungulates under the skin and in the nasal cavity [44].

Mites: class Arachnida, order Acari. Many life-styles, living on the body, in body cavities, on and in the skin, attached to hairs, and in nests. Many non-parasitic nest species may also be found in the pelage. There is no comprehensive guide to identification [14, 15].

Ticks: class Arachnida, order Acari, suborder Ixodoidea. Blood-sucking as larvae, nymphs and adults but usually attaching only temporarily to the hosts while they feed. Most are not highly host-specific [2, 38].

Tapeworms: phylum Platyhelminthes, class Cestoda. Adults live in the intestine. Immature stages (bladderworms, etc.) become encysted in intermediate hosts, in muscle, mesentery and other sites [28].

Flukes: phylum Platyhelminthes, class Trematoda. Adults in a variety of internal organs, e.g. liver, intestine, lung; immature stages usually in invertebrates [28].

Roundworms: phylum Nematoda. Adults in a variety of internal organs, e.g. stomach, intestine, lung, blood vessels; many different kinds of life-cycle, some involving invertebrate hosts [28].

Spiny-headed worms: phylum Acanthocephala. Adults in gut, immature stages in invertebrates.

Protozoans: phylum Protozoa. Microbial parasites of the gut, blood and other sites [12].

Data on parasites has been coordinated and refereed by Mr A.M. Hutson (insects), Mr K.H. Hyatt (acarines), Dr J. Lewis (helminths) and Dr T. Healing (microbial parasites).

RELATIONS WITH MAN
This section deals with the economic status of the species, its conservation and, where relevant, its maintenance in captivity.

LITERATURE
References are given here to monographs or other useful and comprehensive compilations on a particular species. References to the source of specific facts are given throughout the text and relate to the bibliographies at the end of each chapter. The following publications are important sources of information that deal with all groups (or at least more than one order) of mammals.

Anderson & Jones [1] — a concise account of each family of mammals.
Barrett-Hamilton & Hinton [5] — a very detailed account of British mammals with a great deal of historical information. Unfinished, including only the insectivores, bats, lagomorphs and rodents.
Corbet [8, 9] — a review of the taxonomy and distribution of all mammals in the Palaearctic Region.
Corbet & Hill [10] — a complete list of the mammals of the world.
Corbet & Ovenden [11] — a field guide with coloured illustrations of most species and maps showing distribution in Europe.
Fairley [16] — a bibliography of literature on mammals in Ireland with 963 references.

Fairley [17] — a detailed, but not comprehensive, account of some Irish mammals.

Kurtén, B. [26] — an account of the mammals of Europe during the Pleistocene Period.

Macdonald [24] — a highly illustrated encyclopaedia of the world's mammals, with an emphasis on behaviour and ecology.

Miller [30] — the most detailed taxonomic descriptions of European mammals, with illustrations of skulls and teeth, and tables of cranial measurements.

Niethammer & Krapp [31] — a detailed handbook of European mammals, in German, incomplete.

Nowak & Paradiso [32] — a genus-by-genus account of the mammals of the world.

Ognev [33] — very detailed accounts of the mammals of the USSR, including most species found in Britain. Includes much information on ecology and behaviour. Available in English translation.

Simpson [35] — a comprehensive classification of fossil and recent mammals.

The principal journals relating to British mammals are the following:

Mammal Review, published by Blackwell Scientific Publications for the Mammal Society. Mainly review articles covering all aspects of the study of mammals but with the emphasis on British mammals.

Journal of Zoology, London, published by Oxford University Press for the Zoological Society of London. Contains batches of 'Communications from the Mammal Society', mainly on British mammals (these are available separately to members of the Mammal Society) as well as frequent longer papers on mammals.

Journal of Animal Ecology, published by Blackwell Scientific Publications for the Ecological Society. Contains occasional papers on the ecology of British mammals.

Journal of Mammalogy, published by the American Society of Mammalogists. Mainly North American.

Mammalia, published by the Museum National d'Histoire Naturelle, Paris. Papers in French and English, many on European mammals.

Zeitschrift für Säugetierkunde, published by Paul Parey for the Deutsche Gesellschaft für Säugetierkunde. Papers mainly in German, some in English, many on European mammals.

Acta Theriologica, published by the Polish Academy of Sciences. Almost entirely on European mammals with many papers in English.

AUTHOR FOR THIS CHAPTER
G.B. Corbet.

References

1 Anderson S. & Jones J.K. eds. (1984) *Orders and families of recent mammals of the world*. New York: Wiley 686 pp.

2 Arthur D.R. (1963) *British ticks*. London: Butterworth 213 pp.

3 Asdell S.A. (1964) *Patterns of mammalian reproduction*, 2nd edn. Ithaca: Cornell University Press 670 pp.

4 Bang P. & Dahlstrom P. (1974) *Animal tracks and signs*. London: Collins 239 pp.

5 Barrett-Hamilton G.E.H. & Hinton M.A.C. (1910–1921) *A history of British mammals*. London: Gurney & Jackson 263, 748 pp.

6 Berry R.J. & Southern H.N. eds. (1970) *Variation in mammalian populations*. London: Academic Press 403 pp.

7 Burton J.A. (1982) *The Guinness book of mammals*. London: Guinness Superlatives 160 pp.

8 Corbet G.B. (1978) *The mammals of the Palaearctic Region: a taxonomic review*. London: British Museum (Natural History) 314 pp.

9 Corbet G.B. (1984) *The mammals of the Palaearctic Region: a taxonomic review: Supplement*. London: British Museum (Natural History) 45 pp.

10 Corbet G.B. & Hill J.E. (1990) *A world list of mammalian species*, 3rd edn. London: British Museum (Natural History) 254 pp.

11 Corbet G.B. & Ovenden D. (1980) *The mammals of Britain and Europe*. London: Collins 253 pp.

12 Cox F.E.G. (1970) Parasitic protozoa of British wild mammals. *Mammal Review* 1:1–28.

13 Day M.G. (1968) Food habits of British stoats (*Mustela erminea*) and weasels (*Mustela nivalis*). *Journal of Zoology* 155:485–97.

14 Evans G.O. *et al.* (1961) *The terrestrial acari of the British Isles*. London: British Museum (Natural History) 219 pp.

15 Evans G.O. & Till W.M. (1966) Studies on the British Dermanyssidae (Acarina, Mesostigmata). Part II. Classification. *Bulletin of the British Museum (Natural History), Zoology* 14:107–307.

16 Fairley J.S. (1972) *Irish wild mammals: a guide to the literature*. Galway: published by the author 127 pp.

17 Fairley J.S. (1984) *An Irish beast book*, 2nd edn. Belfast: Blackstaff Press 334 pp.

18 George R.S. (1974) *Provisional atlas of the insects of the British Isles: part 4. Siphonaptera — fleas*. Huntingdon: Biological Records Centre.

19 Glue D.E. (1967) Prey taken by the barn owl in England and Wales. *Bird Study* 14:169–83.

20 Glue D.E. (1974) Food of the barn owl in Britain and Ireland. *Bird Study* 21:200–10.

21 Haltenorth T. (1979) *British and European mammals, amphibians and reptiles*. London: Chatto & Windus 143 pp.

22 Hutson A.M. (1971) Ectoparasites of British bats. *Mammal Review* 1:143–50.

23 Hutson A.M. (1984) Keds, flat-flies and bat-flies. *Handbooks for the Identification of British Insects* 10(7):1–40.

24 Kinns G. & Grimes B. (1981) *British wild animals*. London: Hodder & Stoughton 125 pp.

25 Konig C. (1973) *Mammals*. London: Collins 256 pp.

26 Kurtén B. (1968) *Pleistocene mammals of Europe*. London: Weidenfeld & Nicolson 317 pp.

27 Lawrence M.J. & Brown R.W. (1973) *Mammals of Britain, their tracks, trails and signs.* London: Blandford 223 pp.

28 Lewis J.W. & Cox F.E.G. eds. (1987) Proceedings of a joint meeting between the Mammal Society and the British Society for Parasitology. *Mammal Review* **17**:59–147.

29 Macdonald D. ed. (1984) *The encyclopaedia of mammals,* 2 vols. London: Allen & Unwin 930 pp.

30 Miller G.S. (1912) *Catalogue of the mammals of western Europe.* London: British Museum (Natural History) 1019 pp.

31 Niethammer J. & Krapp F. (1978, 1982) *Handbuch der Säugetiere Europas,* vols 1 and 2(1): *Rodentia.* Wiesbaden: Akademische Verlagsgesellschaft 476, 649 pp.

32 Nowak R.M. & Paradiso J.L. (1983) *Walker's mammals of the world,* 4th edn, 2 vols. Baltimore & London: Johns Hopkins University Press 1362 pp.

33 Ognev S.I. (1928–50) *Mammals of the USSR and adjacent countries,* Moscow: Academy of Sciences USSR. (English translations, 1962–3, Jerusalem, Israel Program for Scientific Translations.)

34 Poole T.B. (1985) *Social behaviour in mammals.* Glasgow: Blackie 248 pp.

35 Simpson G.G. (1945) The principles of classification and a classification of the mammals. *Bulletin of the American Museum of Natural History* **85**:i–xvi, 1–350.

36 Smit F.G.A.M. (1957a) The recorded distribution and hosts of Siphonaptera in Britain. *Entomologist's Gazette* **8**:45–75.

37 Smit F.G.A.M. (1957b) *Siphonaptera. Handbook for the identification of British insects.* London: Royal Entomological Society **1**(16):1–200.

38 Snow K.R. (1978) *Identification of larval ticks found on small mammals in Britain.* Reading: Mammal Society 14 pp.

39 Southern H.N. (1954) Tawny owls and their prey. *Ibis* **96**:384–410.

40 Southern H.N. (1970) The natural control of a population of tawny owls. *Journal of Zoology* **162**:197–285.

41 Stuart A.J. (1982) *Pleistocene vertebrates in the British Isles.* London: Longman 212 pp.

42 Zima J. & Král B. (1984) Karyotypes of European mammals. *Acta Scientiarum Naturalium Academiae Scientiarum Bohemoslovacae Brno* **18**: parts 7 (51 pp), 8 (62 pp), 9 (51 pp).

43 Zima J. & Horacek I. (1985) Synopsis of karyotypes of vespertilionid bats. *Acta Universitatis Carolinae Biologica* **1981**: 311–29.

44 Zumpt F. (1965) *Myiasis in animals and man.* London: Butterworth 267 pp.

Chapter 2 / History of
the Fauna

The principal interest of fossil mammals for most mammalogists is the evidence they provide for the origin and history of the present-day mammal fauna. From this viewpoint, only the fossils from the last 15000 years are important. However, the British Isles have also yielded significant mammal faunas of Mesozoic, Eocene–Oligocene and Pleistocene ages which are worth noticing.

Mesozoic mammals

The evolution of mammals from reptiles is well documented in the fossil record [35]; so well documented, in fact, that deciding which evolutionary change heralds the emergence of the first mammal is to some extent arbitrary. It is, however, generally accepted that the evolution of a dentary-squamosal jaw joint was a key factor, and may be used to define a mammal. The earliest mammals, so defined, appear in rocks of the latest Triassic or earliest Jurassic, about 190 million years ago. Among them are *Morganucodon watsoni* and *Kuhneotherium praecursoris* from South Wales. The Middle Jurassic Stonesfield Quarries near Oxford are famous as the first site at which Mesozoic mammals, contemporary with dinosaurs, were discovered; *Phascolotherium bucklandi* was described in 1828. A few teeth of Mesozoic mammals are known from other sites of Middle Jurassic age, in Dorset, Oxfordshire and the Isle of Skye. The most diverse of the British Mesozoic mammal faunas comes from the Upper Jurassic of Durlston Bay, Dorset, from which at least 16 species have been described. From the Cretaceous, there are a very few specimens from Wealden deposits in SE England. These fossils are described, illustrated and thoroughly discussed by Lillegraven [39].

Eocene–Oligocene mammals

Lower Eocene mammals are present in the London clay and in gravels below it, notably at Abbey Wood, London; among them is the early horse *Hyracotherium*. Beds that range from Upper Eocene through to Lower Oligocene on the Isle of Wight, at both the western end of the island at Bouldner and Headon Hill, and in the east at Whitecliff Bay, have yielded large numbers of mammalian fossils, albeit mostly isolated teeth.

These faunas have not been comprehensively reviewed recently and the literature is scattered [7, 21, 29, 30] A booklet of the British Museum (Natural History) [9] provides an introduction.

Pleistocene mammals

The Pleistocene, covering the last 2 million years of the geological record, was a period of alternating cold, glacial and relatively warm, interglacial periods. The most recent of these warm periods, which began 10000 years ago, is the Flandrian in which we are living.

Pleistocene mammals occur in a variety of sediments, including marine clays, river gravels, glacial moraines and cave infills, which often constitute localised pockets that are difficult to correlate from place to place. The fossils in these sediments, including the mammals themselves but also pollen and beetles, may therefore be of major importance to geologists for stratigraphic correlation. Because they are relatively recent and closely related to or the same as existing species, they are also important to biologists for the light they shed on the evolution of existing species and the history of the present fauna and flora. There is, not surprisingly, an extensive literature on Pleistocene mammals which has fortunately been summarised by Kurtén [37] for Europe as a whole, and more specifically for the British Isles by Stuart [50]. A very readable world-wide review of Pleistocene biology is presented by Sutcliffe [52] and the question of Quaternary extinctions is dealt with by Martin & Klein [40].

Within the British Isles, there is evidence of at least three glacial periods (named Anglian, Wolstonian and Devensian), though good mammal faunas are known only from the latest, Devensian, glaciation (Table 2.1). Mammals known from the Devensian in Britain include such classic Ice Age species as mammoth *Mammuthus primigenius* and woolly rhinoceros *Coelodonta antiquitatis*, as well as reindeer *Rangifer tarandus*, lemmings, musk ox *Ovibos moschatus* and arctic fox *Alopex lagopus*. Interglacial faunas are better known, perhaps simply because more mammals were able to live here in warmer times. The early Cromerian interglacial dated about 350 000 bp (before present) has yielded an extensive fauna, principally from sites in East Anglia, including many extinct species that are ancestral to later, more modern, forms. A monkey *Macaca* sp. is one notable member of the fauna, along with the Russian desman *Desmana moschata*. The next, Hoxnian, interglacial is notable particularly for the presence of man at Swanscombe, Kent; his contemporaries included fallow deer *Dama dama* and rabbit *Oryctolagus cuniculus*, as well as both *Desmana* and *Macaca* again. The last interglacial, the Ipswichian, again saw fallow deer in Britain, and *Hippopotamus amphibus* was a characteristic member of the fauna.

One important consequence of this alternating sequence of cold and warm faunas is that identifying particular isolated fossils does not tell us much about the history of any particular species. A fallow deer antler discovered in the gravel of a river terrace could belong to Cromerian, Hoxnian or Ipswichian faunas, or could have fallen off a park deer last century. So far as we know, fallow deer are not native to Britain in the post-glacial (Flandrian) period, but were native in three previous periods. Such a history of members of our mammal fauna can only be derived from careful excavations, with particular attention paid to stratigraphy. Moreover, a complete fauna, with a range of specimens of obviously contemporary species, is much more convincing evidence than an isolated bone or two. In some cases, however, we have only such isolated records — there are, for example, only two records of saiga antelope *Saiga tatarica* in Britain from Sun Hole, Cheddar and from gravels of the Thames at Twickenham, and only one record of polar bear *Thalarctos maritimus*. The Sun Hole *Saiga* is well dated, to the Late Glacial (Younger Dryas), but the other two are of uncertain age, though probably mid-Devensian [50, 51].

ORIGIN OF THE PRESENT FAUNA

The composition of the mammal fauna of the British Isles is a consequence of three processes: natural colonisation between the end of the last glaciation and the isolation of the various isles from

Table 2.1. Occurrence of mammals in Britain in the principal periods since the Middle Pleistocene [50].

	Cromerian interglacial	Anglian glacial	Hoxnian interglacial	Wolstonian glacial	Ipswichian interglacial	Devensian glacial	Flandrian post-glacial	Present
Insectivora								
Erinaceus europaeus hedgehog	●						●	●
Talpa europaea mole	●						●	●
Talpa minor (extinct mole)	●		○					
Desmana moschata Russian desman	●		○					
Primates								
Macaca sp. (macaque monkey)	●		○					
Homo sapiens man			●		●	●	●	●
Lagomorpha								
Ochotona pusilla steppe pika						○	●	

Rodentia

Spermophilus sp. (sousliks)		●			○			
Castor fiber beaver	●		○		●		●	
Trogontherium cuvieri (extinct beaver)	●		●					
Cricetus cricetus common hamster	●							
Dicrostonyx torquatus arctic lemming					○	●		
Lemmus lemmus Norway lemming			○		○	●		
Clethrionomys glareolus bank vole	●		○		●		●	●
Mimomys savini (extinct vole)	●							
Arvicola cantiana (extinct vole)	●		○		●	●		
Arvicola terrestris water vole							●	●
Pitymys arvaloides (extinct vole)	●		○					
Pitymys gregaloides (extinct vole)	●							
Microtus arvalis common vole	●		○					
Microtus agrestis field vole			○		●	●	●	●
Microtus oeconomus northern vole	●		○	○	●	●	●	
Microtus gregalis tundra vole						●		
Apodemus sylvaticus wood mouse	●		○		●		●	●

Carnivora

Canis lupus wolf	●		○		●	●	●	
Alopex lagopus arctic fox						●		
Vulpes vulpes red fox					○		●	●
Ursus spp. (extinct bears)	●		○					
Ursus arctos brown bear					●	●	●	
Meles meles badger					●		●	●
Crocuta crocuta spotted hyaena	●				●			
Panthera leo lion			○		●			

Proboscidea

Palaeoloxodon antiquus straight-tusked elephant			●		●			
Mammuthus primigenius mammoth					●	●		

Perissodactyla

Equus ferus horse	●		●	○	●	●	●	
Dicerorhinus etruscus (extinct rhino)	●							
Dicerorhinus hemitoechus (extinct rhino)			○		●			
Coelodonta antiquitatis woolly rhino					○	●		

Artiodactyla

Sus scrofa wild boar	●		○				●	
Hippopotamus sp. (extinct hippo)	●							
Hippopotamus amphibius hippopotamus					●			
Megaloceros verticornis (giant deer)	●							
Megaloceros giganteus (giant deer)			○		●	●		
Dama dama (fallow deer)	●		○		●			●
Cervus elaphus red deer	●	●	○		●	●	●	
Alces latifrons (extinct elk)	●							
Alces alces elk					●		●	
Rangifer tarandus reindeer						●		
Capreolus capreolus roe deer	●		○				●	●
Bos primigenius aurochs			○		●		●	
Bison schoetensacki (extinct bison)	●							
Bison priscus (extinct bison)					●	●		
Ovibos moschatus musk ox					○	●		

●, Well-dated records; ○, probable occurrence based upon indirect evidence of dating.

neighbouring land (Fig. 2.1); selective extinction caused mostly by man; and selective introductions, both deliberate and accidental, by man [41, 57].

Natural colonisation

The maximum extent of ice in the last glacial (Devensian) stage and the most severe conditions appear to have been late during the period. The mammals recorded between 30 000 and 15 000 years ago include mammoth *Mammuthus primigenius*, woolly rhinoceros *Coelodonta antiquitatis*, reindeer *Rangifer tarandus* and musk ox *Ovibos moschatus*; these imply cold, open tundra, conditions, probably too severe for most of our present fauna [50].

Between 15 000 and 11 000 years ago, there was a milder interlude, the Windermere Interstadial, when the ice cap melted from the Scottish mountains. During this interstadial, both reindeer *Rangifer tarandus* and giant deer ('Irish elk') *Megaloceros giganteus* were present in Ireland as well as in Britain, while in England the elk *Alces alces* was also present though it apparently never reached Ireland. Lemmings, both *Lemmus lemmus* and *Dicrostonyx torquatus*, were also present in England during this time, along with brown bear *Ursus arctos*, the voles *Clethrionomys glareolus*, *Microtus agrestis*, *M. oeconomus* and *Arvicola terrestris*, red fox *Vulpes vulpes*, mountain hare *Lepus timidus*, wild horse *Equus ferus* and common shrew *Sorex araneus*; the wood mouse *Apodemus sylvaticus* may also have been present, though confirmation

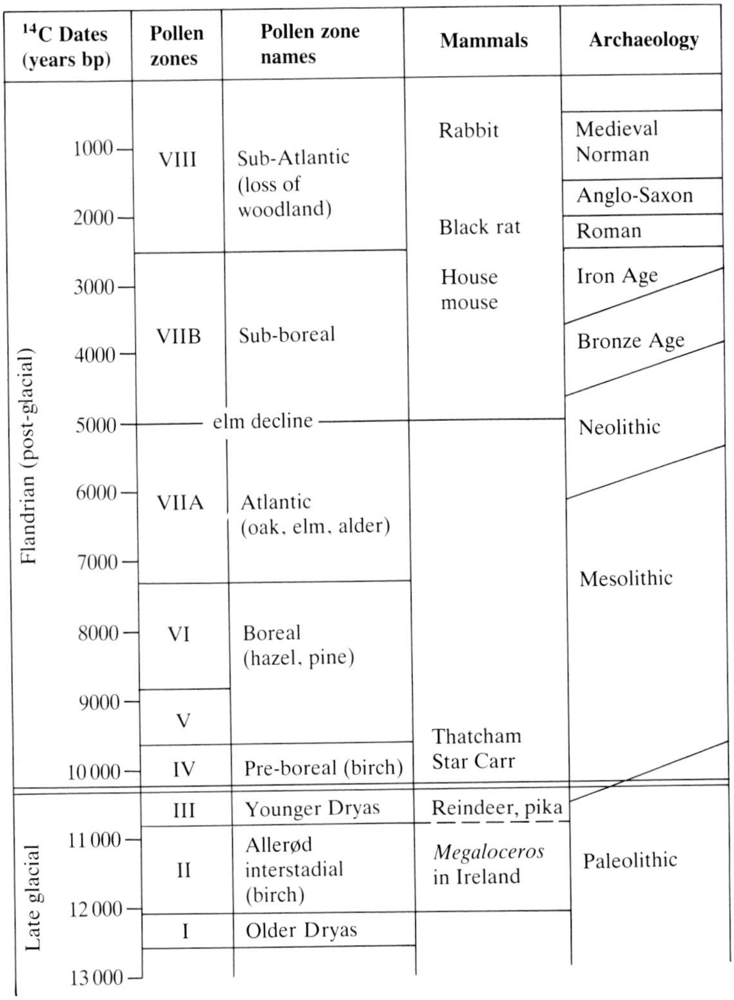

¹⁴C Dates (years bp)	Pollen zones	Pollen zone names	Mammals	Archaeology
1000 —	VIII	Sub-Atlantic (loss of woodland)	Rabbit	Medieval Norman
2000 —			Black rat	Anglo-Saxon
				Roman
3000 —			House mouse	Iron Age
4000 —	VIIB	Sub-boreal		Bronze Age
5000 —		— elm decline —		Neolithic
6000 —	VIIA	Atlantic (oak, elm, alder)		
7000 —				Mesolithic
8000 —	VI	Boreal (hazel, pine)		
9000 —	V			
10 000 —	IV	Pre-boreal (birch)	Thatcham Star Carr	
	III	Younger Dryas	Reindeer, pika	
11 000 —	II	Allerød interstadial (birch)	*Megaloceros* in Ireland	Paleolithic
12 000 —	I	Older Dryas		
13 000 —				

Flandrian (post-glacial) — *Late glacial*

Fig. 2.1. Chronological table for the late glacial and post-glacial periods in Britain [57].

(i.e. more records) would be welcome [12, 57].

The warmer conditions of the Windermere Interstadial were ended by a short reversion to cold conditions between about 11 000 and 10 000 years ago — the Younger Dryas period of archaeologists, the period of the Loch Lomond re-advance for geologists. Severe arctic conditions prevailed even in southern Britain at this time, and it is probable that many of the species which had spread into Britain during the Windermere Interstadial were unable to survive. It seems likely that *Megaloceros* was exterminated in Ireland during this cold period, for there are no convincing later records of them there [60]. In S England, however, reindeer at least survived, along with the two lemmings, voles, wild horse, stoat, weasel, red fox and, interestingly, a pika *Ochotona pusilla*; important faunas of this age are known from Ossom's Cave, Staffordshire; Robin Hood's Cave, Derbyshire and at Nazeing, Essex [8, 12, 28].

The post-glacial (Flandrian or Holocene) period began with the final retreat of the ice at about 10 000 years ago. This must have been a transitional period for both fauna and flora, but our knowledge for the mammal fauna is not precise enough to document the transition properly. Reindeer probably lingered on for a few hundred years; at least to 10 250 bp in Ireland and to 9750 bp in Yorkshire. The wild horse also lingered into Mesolithic times, at least to 9770 bp [11].

It is evident on geological grounds and from beetle faunas [43] that the change of climate and of faunas was relatively rapid, certainly more rapid than the change of flora (from the pollen record) had led us to believe. This is confirmed for mammals by the two important Mesolithic archaeological sites of Thatcham, Berkshire [36] and Star Carr, Yorkshire [24]. These sites have radiocarbon dates of 10 050–9600 bp and 9500 bp respectively. The accompanying mammal faunas include several species characteristic of temperate conditions, such as hedgehog, mole and wild boar (Table 2.2) while those indicative of arctic or tundra conditions, such as reindeer, pika, lemmings and northern voles, are not recorded. However, the small mammals were poorly represented in these sites (it is not clear whether this results from biased sampling by archaeologists or by the original Mesolithic hunters), and less reliance can be placed on evidence from them.

Two species in these faunas need discussion, rabbit *Oryctolagus cuniculus* and hare *Lepus* sp. The rabbit was recorded at Thatcham on the basis of a pelvis and tibia, whose identity is not questioned [20, 36, 42], but is not otherwise reliably recorded from any site in Britain of late glacial age, nor from any other Mesolithic, Neolithic, Bronze Age, Iron Age, Roman or Anglo-Saxon site. All the evidence, documentary and archaeological, indicates that it was introduced by the Normans; archaeological evidence of its presence begins with material dated to between the 11th and 13th centuries at Rayleigh Castle, Essex [49]. Suspicion that the rabbit at Thatcham was in fact intrusive — a relatively recent rabbit that had burrowed down into the archaeological layers — has recently been confirmed by a radiocarbon date of 270 bp [14]. This must cast doubt on the acceptance of some other species at Thatcham as the earliest post-glacial records in Britain, e.g. mole, common shrew, water vole and wildcat, although these species, unlike the rabbit, are known from other Mesolithic sites.

The situation with the hare is equally problematic. A single tibia is present at Star Carr, and was tentatively assigned to brown hare, *L. europaeus* [24]; this would not be totally incongruent with the rest of the fauna, but would represent a very early record for the species. Mayhew [42] re-examined the specimen and, while acknowledging its large size, pointed out that mountain hares, *L. timidus*, show a cline in size northwards through Europe; he felt that the Star Carr tibia could, on size, equally be a large example of *L. timidus*, and that it was more likely to be so on grounds of habitat, time and associated fauna. *L. timidus* is common in late glacial faunas in Britain, and is likely to have lingered into Mesolithic times in England. In both these cases more evidence, from carefully excavated sites, will be needed to resolve the doubts.

The subsequent history of the mammal fauna is not well documented; Grigson [26] has collated many of the useful records. Aurochs, red deer, roe deer and wild boar are regularly present at archaeological sites of Mesolithic and Neolithic age, while brown bear and beaver occur to Bronze Age times. It has been suggested that reindeer survived through to perhaps the 10th century AD (on the basis particularly of the Norse sagas) and that the elk also survived almost to historical times [45], but the lack of any archaeological evidence makes this increasingly unlikely [17, 57]. For lynx, there is evidence for its presence at a number of cave sites which, because their faunas include roe deer (and the roe was not known to have entered Britain

	Thatcham	Star Carr
Radiocarbon date	10050–9600 bp	9500 bp
Pollen zone	IV–VI	IV
Insectivora		
Erinaceus europaeus hedgehog	1	1
Talpa europaea mole	1	–
Sorex araneus common shrew	1	–
Lagomorpha		
Lepus ?timidus mountain hare	–	1
Rodentia		
Castor fiber beaver	6	8
Arvicola terrestris water vole	2	–
Carnivora		
Canis lupus wolf	1	–
Canis familiaris dog	1	2
Vulpes vulpes fox	2	2
Martes martes pine marten	1	2
Meles meles badger	3	1
Felis silvestris wildcat	3	–
Ungulates		
Equus ferus horse	1	–
Bos primigenius aurochs	2	9
Sus scrofa wild boar	7	5
Alces alces elk	1	11
Cervus elaphus red deer	8	80
Capreolus capreolus roe deer	6	33

Table 2.2. Mammals (minimum number of individuals) recorded at the Mesolithic sites of Star Carr, Yorkshire and Thatcham, Berkshire [24, 36, 42]. Thatcham, though the earlier site, belongs to rather later pollen zones, indicating the earlier immigration of hazel, etc. in the south.

in late glacial times), are believed to be of Mesolithic age [32, 33], but like reindeer and moose it seems to have died out thereafter. The wild horse is also recorded from early Mesolithic sites, e.g. at Thatcham and in the Darent gravels in Kent; it is uncertain whether it survived through to Neolithic times, to contribute perhaps to domestic horse stock, or if it had died out before Neolithic farmers arrived, bringing domestic horses with them. There is a scatter of records through Mesolithic times which suggest that it may have survived [25, 26].

Selective extinction

Of the species represented at Thatcham and Star Carr, elk, aurochs, wild horse, wild boar, brown bear, beaver and wolf are now extinct in Britain. Other species that were possibly present in Mesolithic times but are now extinct include lynx and wolverine *Gulo gulo*. Going further back to late glacial times, one can add reindeer, two lemmings (*Lemmus lemmus, Dicrostonyx torquatus*), two voles (*Microtus gregalis, M. oeconomus*) and pika *Ochotona pusilla* to the list of extinct species. The timing and causes of these extinctions are not very well established, as has been already implied. It is presumed that the late glacial species were unable to cope with the rapid climatic changes and consequent vegetational changes that took place at about 10 000 bp or could not withstand competition from new immigrants. If it is correct that a significant change in the beetle faunas took only 50 years [43], the change in mammal fauna may also have been so quick that we would be unlikely to notice transitional faunas in the archaeological record. However, we have already noted evidence that reindeer may have survived to about 9700 bp, and wild horse to somewhat later; one other species seems to have lingered much later, at least in isolation. The vole *Microtus oeconomus* has been recorded on Nornour, Isles of Scilly, in Bronze Age times (*c.* 3500 bp) [44] and it may have survived late in other refugia; it is, in Europe, less restricted to high latitudes than the other extinct late glacial British species, with a well documented relict populaton in Holland and a range spreading north and east from northern Germany and Poland. The extinction of elk and lynx may have come from overhunting in Mesolithic times, from natural habitat change (as coniferous woodland was replaced by deciduous woodland), or just possibly from human-induced habitat change in later times (Neolithic onwards). For aurochs, beaver, wild boar, brown bear and wolf, there is evidence of various sorts (documentary, place-name, archaeological) that they survived into historical times, and that direct persecution and habitat change played equally large parts in their extinction. For wolf and brown bear, protection of livestock was obviously important. The bear seems to have become extinct by Norman times, for it is mentioned as an export from Britain in Roman times, and in Anglo-Saxon documents, but not later. The wolf is mentioned in Medieval legislation, appears in many place-names, and contemporary accounts attest to its extinction in Scotland *c.* 1743 and in Ireland *c.* 1786. The beaver was probably exterminated by overhunting; it is generally believed, on the evidence of Giraldus Cambrensis, to have survived on the River Teifi, in Wales, to the 11th century [45]. For aurochs and wild boar, crop protection and protection of domesticated stock against outbreeding may have caused extinction, but it is equally possible that the wild species were in fact exterminated by being domesticated, or being diluted by domestic genotypes. If the horse survived as a wild species, perhaps in upland areas, through to Neolithic times, it is possible that it, too, was diluted out of existence. The documentary evidence suggests that aurochs survived at least to Roman times, and the wild boar to the 16th century [45].

Selective introductions

The natural colonisation of the British Isles in late glacial or post-glacial times was only possible, for land mammals, while they were in fact not isles, but a part of the mainland of Europe. This raises the important question of when the English Channel was cut, so ending immigration from the continent, and even more importantly raises the question of whether other islands were ever joined to Great Britain and when, if they were, they became isolated. This is a subject reviewed at some length by Yalden [57].

There is no doubt that at the height of the last glaciation, world sea levels were about 100 m below their present level, relative to the land, and large areas of continental shelf were exposed as land. Most of the present North Sea and English Channel were dry land, and Britain was certainly a part of Europe. The former estuaries of the Rhine and other north-flowing rivers produce clear indentations on the -100 m bathymetric contour in the sea floor between Scotland and Denmark. At present, the maximum depth on the shallowest transect of the English Channel is -37 m, and the sea floor in that area appears to be one that formed under periglacial conditions [34] rather than one that has been subsequently scoured out by marine erosion. Presumably, therefore, we may take the time at which sea level had risen from -100 m to -37 m as the time when Britain was isolated from Europe. On the basis of curves of rising sea levels in various parts of the world, this probably happened about 9500 bp, at about the time that Star Carr and Thatcham were inhabited by Mesolithic hunters. This date for the isolation of Britain is much earlier than the often quoted 5000 bp, but that is the date that sea level reached its present level; given the evaluation of the floor of the English Channel [34], it is clearly an irrelevant date for present purposes.

The situation further north, particularly in relation to the isolation of Orkney, Shetland, the Outer Hebrides and Ireland, is more complicated because, although sea level was lowered worldwide to perhaps -100 m, these northern areas were themselves depressed by the weight of ice overlying them. The relative sea level around SW Scotland seems to have been $+20$ m at 12 000 bp, and the present channel beween N Ireland and SW Scotland has a minimum depth of about -55 m. On this basis, it is unlikely that Ireland was joined to Scotland by a land bridge at any time in the post-glacial period; Yalden [56, 57] suggested that a period of relatively low sea levels at around 8000 bp might have allowed mammals to reach Ireland, but Devoy [22], reviewing the general problem of land bridges across the Irish Sea, ruled out any possibility of a post-glacial land bridge. He suggested that there may have been a short-lived, northern, bridge in late glacial times, perhaps around 11 000 bp, but that often postulated land bridges across directly from Wales to Ireland can be dismissed because of the depth and age of the deep channel down the centre of the Irish Sea [22]. Thus reindeer and *Megaloceros* presumably invaded Ireland, from SW Scotland, at around 11 000 bp. Other mammals that have been presumed to be native to Ireland (mountain hare, pygmy shrew, red fox, badger, wild horse, red deer, wild boar, brown bear, wildcat) must on this thesis either have invaded Ireland at the same time, swam across later, or been subsequently introduced by man. If they invaded at the same time, there ought to be fossil evidence of them in deposits of Windermere Interstadial age (as there is for reindeer and *Megaloceros*) but it has not so far been discovered; they also had to survive the inclement Younger Dryas. On the other hand, mountain hare, red deer and wild boar were already present at the earliest Mesolithic site of Mount Sandel in NE Ireland, at 8700 bp [54, 55], and the other species were present by Neolithic times [53]. Woodman [54] noted that red deer and wild boar were relatively uncommon at Mount Sandel, and speculated that this might be evidence of their recent introduction, to provide food, by Mesolithic hunters, or recent arrival, by swimming, from Scotland. A recently reported specimen of wood mouse from a Mesolithic site near Dublin with radiocarbon date of 7600 bp [47] suggests that this too is a native species (or very early introduction), although it had been regarded as an introduction by the Vikings.

If the likelihood of mammals reaching Ireland naturally is arguable, the situation for the more remote and smaller islands is consequently clearer. Shetland, Orkney, St Kilda and the Outer Hebrides are separated from their nearest neighbours by channels that are more than 100 m below sea level; with the added depression of the land, caused by the weight of ice, there can have been no land bridges to any of them, and their mammal faunas must have been the result of human introduction, probably accidental in many cases. Corbet [15, 16] was the first to advocate this view seriously; previous authors had developed a complicated thesis of waves of invaders and glacial relicts to explain the small mammals (in particular) that occurred on different islands (Table 2.3). Thus *Microtus arvalis* (*M. orcadensis*) in Orkney and Guernsey was assumed to be an early invader, which got to those islands first, and was then eliminated from

most of Britain by the later invading *M. agrestis*, and only survived on Orkney and Guernsey because they had been cut off from the mainland before *M. agrestis* could reach them. This thesis is clearly untenable, and the obvious explanation is that *M. arvalis* was accidentally introduced to Orkney and Guernsey by man. As Corbet [15] argued, islands have impoverished economies, and livestock, fodder, building materials, food and other goods are all likely to be the subject of regular trade to them; this would have provided ample opportunity to carry small mammals accidentally. Because they lack larger mammals, there has also been a considerable motive to introduce additional species such as rabbits and red deer for food, and hedgehogs for pleasure. For *M. arvalis* on Orkney, archaeological evidence shows that it has been present, along with *Apodemus sylvaticus*, for at least 4000 years [18, 19]; skull characteristics suggest that *M. arvalis* may have been introduced from somewhere in SE Europe [5] but Corbet [19] regards the evidence as tenuous. For the wood mouse, *Apodemus sylvaticus*, the Orkney population has not been examined, but similar evidence suggests that wood mice on St Kilda, Shetland, Outer Hebrides, Ireland and some of the Inner Hebrides are all derived from Norwegian stock, and were probably transported by the Vikings [2]; in the case of Ireland, however, this has been contradicted by more recent evidence [47]. There is contemporary evidence that hedgehogs were imported to Orkney about 1870, and brown hares about 1830 [3]; similarly, for Shetland, hedgehogs were introduced in about 1860, stoats in, probably, the 17th century, and mountain hares around 1900 and 1907 [4]. It is also recorded that moles were introduced to Skye in the late 19th century [46] where hedgehogs, mountain hares and probably brown hares are also introductions.

The most obvious introductions to mainland Britain were domestic sheep and goats, neither of which were native to western Europe. They appeared, with Neolithic farmers, at about 5400 bp [26]. The house mouse may also have been introduced by Neolithic farmers, but there seem to be no archaeological records as early as that; it was, however, certainly present by Iron Age times [10]. The black rat, so long regarded as a Mediaeval introduction, was in fact brought in by the Romans, if not before [1, 48]. The rabbit and fallow deer probably were imported by the Normans [13, 49]. Both seem to have been confined, naturally, to the

Table 2.3. Distribution of small mammals on islands [57].

	Orkney/ Guernsey vole	Field vole	Bank vole	Wood mouse	Common shrew	Pygmy shrew	White-toothed shrews	
							Lesser	Greater
British mainland	−	+	+	+	+	+	−	−
Mainland Shetland, St Kilda	−	−	−	+	−	−	−	−
Orkney Mainland	+	−	−	+	−	−	−	−
Ireland, Man	−	−	−★	+	−	+	−	−
Lewis, Barra (OH)	−	−	−	+	−†	+	−	−
N & S Uist (OH)	−	+	−	+	−	+	−	−
Coll, Tiree, Colonsay (IH)	−	−	−	+	−	+	−	−
Eigg, Muck (IH)	−	+	+	+	−	+	−	−
Raasay (IH)	−	−	+	+	+	+	−	−
Mull, Bute (IH)	−	+	+	+	+	+	−	−
Skye, Islay, Jura, Gigha, Arran (IH)	−	+	−†	+	+	+	−	−
Skomer (Wales)	−	−	+	+	+	+	−	−
Scillies	−	−	−	+	−	−	+	−
Jersey (CI)	−	−	+	+	(+)‡	−	+	−
Sark (CI)	−	−	−	+	−	−	+	−
Alderney, Herm (CI)	−	−	−	+	−	−	−	+
Guernsey (CI)	+	−	−	+	−	−	−	+

CI, Channel Islands; IH, Inner Hebrides (and Clyde Islands); OH, Outer Hebrides.
★ Now present in Ireland, presumably as a result of recent introduction.
† Single records of common shrew from Lewis and bank vole from Islay [61] need confirmation.
‡ The common shrew on Jersey is *Sorex coronatus*, elsewhere it is *S. araneus*.

Mediterranean region [6, 31], and it is unlikely that either occurred naturally in NW Europe in historical times (both had been present in the Pleistocene, Ipswichian, interglacial). Later introductions, beginning with the brown rat in the 18th century, are better documented [38, 23]. Those that have survived include the grey squirrel, edible dormouse, sika, muntjac and Chinese water deer, coypu (until recently) and American mink.

For other islands and other species, our presumption that species are present as a result of accidental introductions is speculative, and based on the erratic composition of their faunas. In particular, the Channel Isles might have been far enough south to have escaped the worst effects of the Younger Dryas period, while Jersey, at least, is near enough to France, and separated by a relatively shallow channel, that one might expect all the common small mammals to have reached it. Yet Jersey lacks any *Microtus*, *Sorex minutus*, and *Arvicola terrestris*, and has *Crocidura suaveolens* (rather than the more widespread *C. russula*) as well as *Apodemus sylvaticus*, *Sorex coronatus* and a distinctive form of *Clethrionomys glareolus*. This fauna does not seem comprehensible on any basis of natural colonisation, by comparison either with the nearest mainland or with the other Channel Isles. It seems very probable then that the fauna is the result of introduction, despite the lack of direct evidence. Likewise *Crocidura suaveolens* in the Scilly Isles, *C. russula* on Guernsey, Alderney and Herm, and bank voles on Skomer, Mull, Raasay and in SW Ireland are introductions. The most difficult species to explain this way is the pygmy shrew which, given the high susceptibility to starvation of *Sorex* sp., is not a species readily susceptible to accidental transport. It has, moreover, a very wide distribution on the Scottish Isles, as well as occurring in Ireland and the Isle of Man, which might argue for an element, at least, of natural dispersal. This is contradicted by its absence from the Channel Isles and the Scilly Isles. Perhaps it was, in fact, able to survive in some material (fodder, turves?) that was regularly shipped to the Isles. Alternatively, as Yalden [56] argued, perhaps it was more tolerant of soggy periglacial habitats than the other small mammals, or even able to disperse across frozen rivers under the snow cover of glacial times.

Conclusion

It is clear from this outline that, while we know the general pattern of post-glacial colonisation of the British Isles by mammals, we are missing much of the detail that we need for a proper understanding. In particular, we have a poor sequence of information on the smaller mammals. The dormouse and yellow-necked mouse are recorded from Neolithic sites, e.g. at Dowel Cave in the Peak District [58, 59], but this is not early enough to rule out the possibility that they are introduced species. Similarly the harvest mouse is recorded from several pre-Roman sites [27], but we do not really know if it was introduced by Neolithic farmers, or was already here as a native species. For smaller islands, the situation is even less certain. There are important opportunities for archaeologists to contribute to our understanding, but local naturalists, uncovering local documentary evidence of introductions, and interpreting place-names evidence, could help to clarify the position.

AUTHOR FOR THIS CHAPTER
D.W. Yalden.

REFERENCES

1 Armitage P. *et al.* (1984) New evidence of black rat in Roman London. *London Archaeologist* 4:375−82.

2 Berry R.J. (1969) History in the evolution of *Apodemus sylvaticus* (Mammalia) at one edge of its range. *Journal of Zoology* 159:311−28.

3 Berry R.J. (1985) *The natural history of Orkney.* London: Collins 304 pp.

4 Berry R.J. & Johnston J.L. (1980) *The natural history of Shetland.* London: Collins 380 pp.

5 Berry R.J. & Rose F.E.N. (1975) Islands and the evolution of *Microtus arvalis* (Microtinae). *Journal of Zoology* 177:395−409.

6 Biagi P. (1980) Some aspects of the prehistory of northern Italy from the final Palaeolithic to the middle Neolithic: a reconsideration of the evidence available to date. *Proceedings of the Prehistoric Society* 46:9−18.

7 Bosma A.A. (1974) Rodent biostratigraphy of the Eocene−Oligocene transitional strata of the Isle of Wight. *Utrecht Micropalaeontological Bulletin, Special Publication* 1:1−126.

8 Bramwell D. (1977) Archaeology and palaeontology. In Ford T.D. ed. *Limestone and caves of the Peak District.* Norwich: Geo Abstracts pp. 263−91.

9 British Museum (Natural History) (1975) *British Caenozoic fossils,* 5th edn. London: British Museum (Natural History).

10 Brothwell D. (1981) The Pleistocene and Holocene archaeology of the house mouse and related species. In Berry R.J. ed. *Biology of the house mouse. Symposia of the Zoological Society of London* 47:1–13.

11 Burleigh R. *et al.* (1982) British Museum (Natural History) radiocarbon measurements XV. *Radiocarbon* 24:262–90.

12 Campbell J.B. (1977) *The Upper Palaeolithic of Britain.* Oxford: Oxford University Press 264, 376 pp.

13 Chapman D. & Chapman N. (1975) *Fallow deer.* Lavenham, Suffolk: T. Dalton 271 pp.

14 Clutton-Brock J. Personal communication.

15 Corbet G.B. (1961) Origin of the British insular races of small mammals and of the 'Lusitanian' fauna. *Nature* 191:1037–40.

16 Corbet G.B. (1962) The 'Lusitanian element' in the British fauna. *Science Progress* 50:177–91.

17 Corbet G.B. (1974) The distribution of mammals in historic times. In Hawksworth D.L. ed. *The changing flora and fauna of Britain.* London: Academic Press pp. 179–202.

18 Corbet G.B. (1979) Report on rodent remains. In Renfrew C. *Investigations in Orkney.* London: Society of Antiquaries and Thames & Hudson pp. 135–7.

19 Corbet G.B. (1986) Temporal and spatial variation of dental pattern in the voles *Microtus arvalis* of the Orkney Islands. *Journal of Zoology* 208:395–402.

20 Corbet G.B. (1986) The relationships and origins of the European lagomorphs. *Mammal Review* 16:105–10.

21 Cray P.E. (1973) Marsupialia, Insectivora, Primates, Creodonta and Carnivora from the Headon Beds (Upper Eocene) of southern England. *Bulletin of the British Museum (Natural History), Geology* 23:1–102.

22 Devoy R.J. (1985) The problems of a Late Quaternary land bridge between Britain and Ireland. *Quaternary Science Review* 4:43–58.

23 Fitter R.S.R. (1959) *The ark in our midst.* London: Collins 320 pp.

24 Fraser F.C. & King J.E. (1954) Faunal remains. In Clark J.G.D. ed. *Excavations at Star Carr.* Cambridge: Cambridge University Press pp. 70–95.

25 Grigson C. (1978) The Late Glacial and early Flandrian ungulates in England and Wales — an interim review. In Limbrey S. & Evans J.G. eds. *The effect of Man on the landscape: the lowland zones.* CBA Research Report 21, pp. 46–56.

26 Grigson C. (1981) Quoted in Simmons I.G. & Tooley, M.J. eds. *The environment in British prehistory.* London: Duckworth 334 pp.

27 Harris S. (1979) History, distribution, status and habitat requirements of the harvest mouse (*Micromys minutus*) in Britain. *Mammal Review* 9:159–71.

28 Hinton M.A.C. (1952) Remains of small mammals. In Allison J. *et al.* Late-Glacial deposits at Nazeing in the Lea Valley, North London. *Philosophical Transactions of the Royal Society B* 236:169–240.

29 Hooker J.J. (1980) The succession of *Hyracotherium* (Perissodactyla, Mammalia) in the English early Eocene. *Bulletin of the British Museum (Natural History), Geology* 33:101–14.

30 Hooker J.J. (1986) Mammals from the Bartonian (middle/late Eocene) of the Hampshire Basin, southern England. *Bulletin of the British Museum (Natural History), Geology* 39:191–478.

31 Jarman M.R. (1972) European deer economies and the advent of the Neolithic. In Higgs E.S. ed. *Papers in economic prehistory.* Cambridge: Cambridge University Press pp. 125–49.

32 Jenkinson R.D.S. (1983) The recent history of the Northern lynx (*Lynx lynx* Linné) in the British Isles. *Quaternary Newsletter* 41:1–7.

33 Jenkinson R.D.S. (1984) A rapid but short-lived colonisation of the British Isles by Northern lynx. In Jenkinson R.D.S. & Gilbertson D.D. eds. *In the shadow of extinction.* University of Sheffield: Department of Prehistory & Archaeology pp. 111–15.

34 Kellaway G.A. *et al.* (1975) The Quaternary history of the English Channel. *Philosophical Transactions of the Royal Society A* 279:189–218.

35 Kemp T.S. (1982) *Mammal-like reptiles and the origin of mammals.* London: Academic Press 363 pp.

36 King J.E. (1962) Report on animal bones. In Wymer J. ed. Excavations at the Maglemosian sites at Thatcham, Berkshire, England. *Proceedings of the Prehistoric Society* 28:255–361.

37 Kurtén B. (1968) *Pleistocene mammals of Europe.* London: Weidenfeld & Nicolson 317 pp.

38 Lever C. (1977) *The naturalized animals of the British Isles.* London: Hutchinson 600 pp.

39 Lillegraven J.A. *et al.* (1979) *Mesozoic mammals: the first two-thirds of mammalian history.* Berkeley: University of California Press 311 pp.

40 Martin P.S. & Klein R.G. eds. (1984) *Quaternary extinctions, a prehistoric revolution.* Tucson: University of Arizona Press 892 pp.

41 Matthews L.H. (1982) *Mammals in the British Isles.* London: Collins 411 pp.

42 Mayhew D.F. (1975) *The Quaternary history of some British rodents and lagomorphs.* DPhil. thesis, University of Cambridge.

43 Osborne P.J. (1980) The Late Devensian–Flandrian transition depicted by serial insect faunas from West Bromwich, Staffordshire, England. *Boreas* 9:139–47.

44 Pernetta J.C. & Handford P.T. (1970) Mammalian and avian remains from possible Bronze Age deposits on Nornow, Isles of Scilly. *Journal of Zoology* 162:534–40.

45 Perry R. (1978) *Wildlife in Britain and Ireland.* London: Croom Helm 253 pp.

46 Philp B. (1981) The mammals of Skye and its islands. *Hebridean Naturalist* 5:33–8.

47 Preece R.C. *et al.* (1986) New biostratigraphic evidence of the Post-glacial colonization of Ireland and for mesolithic forest disturbance. *Journal of Biogeography* 13:487–509.

48 Rackham J. (1979) *Rattus rattus*: the introduction of the black rat into Britain. *Antiquity* 53:112–20.

49 Sheail J. (1971) *Rabbits and their history.* Newton Abbot: David & Charles 226 pp.

50 Stuart A. (1982) *Pleistocene vertebrates in the British Isles*. London: Longman 212 pp.

51 Stuart A.D. (1983) Pleistocene bone caves in Britain and Ireland. *Studies in Speleology* **4**:9−36.

52 Sutcliffe A.J. (1985) *On the track of Ice Age mammals*. London: British Museum (Natural History) 224 pp.

53 Wijngaarden-Bakker L.H. van (1974) The animal remains from the Beaker settlement at Newgrange, Co. Meath: first report. *Proceedings of the Royal Irish Academy* **76C**:313−83.

54 Woodman P.C. (1978) The chronology and economy of the Irish Mesolithic: some working hypotheses. In Mellars P.A. ed. *The early postglacial settlement of northern Europe*. London: Duckworth pp. 333−69.

55 Woodman P.C. (1978) *The Mesolithic in Ireland: hunter-gatherers in an insular environment*. Oxford: British Archaeological Reports, British Series, 58, 360 pp.

56 Yalden D.W. (1981) The occurrence of the Pigmy shrew *Sorex minutus* on moorland, and the implications for its presence in Ireland. *Journal of Zoology* **195**:147−56.

57 Yalden D.W. (1982) When did the mammal fauna of the British Isles arrive? *Mammal Review* **12**:1−57.

58 Yalden D.W. (1983) Yellow-necked mice (*Apodemus flavicollis*) in archaeological contexts. *Bulletin of the Peakland Archaeological Society* **33**:24−9.

59 Yalden D.W. (1984) The yellow-necked mouse *Apodemus flavicollis* in Roman Manchester. *Journal of Zoology* **203**:285−88.

60 Barnosky A.D. (1986) 'Big game' extinction caused by Late Pleistocene climatic change: Irish Elk *Megaloceros giganteus* in Ireland. *Quaternary Research* **25**:128−35.

61 Arnold H.R. (1978) *Provisional atlas of the mammals of the British Isles*. Abbots Ripton: Natural Environment Research Council.

Chapter 3 / Habitats and their Mammalian Communities

Before it was significantly influenced by man, the natural vegetation of most of Britain and Ireland was forest — predominantly deciduous but with extensive areas of pine in some highland areas [9]. Open communities would then have been very limited in extent, for example in exposed coastal areas, some valley wetlands, upland mires and above the tree-line on the mountains. The effect of human activity has been to diversify the landscape, most obviously by the replacement of natural vegetation by roads, buildings and cultivated crops (mostly of exotic origin), but also less obviously by the removal of forest and the maintenance of open but predominantly native vegetation by grazing, as on the chalk downs and most of the northern and western uplands, or by burning as on the grouse moors. The resultant composition of the landscape is shown in Fig. 3.1.

It follows that most native species of mammals are primarily adapted to woodland, but only a few are narrowly specialised in their habitat requirements and many are very versatile. However each habitat does have a characteristic community of mammals, reflected in the relative abundance of the widespread species as much as in presence or absence of the more restricted ones.

British habitats have been described in detail by Tansley [15], Ratcliffe [13] and Elton [6]. For practical guidance on the description and recording of habitats see Elton & Miller [7] and Anon [2].

Woodland

Native, lowland, broad-leaved forest, generally dominated by the common or pedunculate oak, *Quercus robur*, survives mainly in the form of small discrete woods, usually with a long history of management, e.g. by coppicing or pollarding. Edge effects are therefore important, not only by virtue of the long perimeters but also in the form of rides and clearings. All the common tree species — the native oak, birch, elm, beech, ash, hornbeam and hazel and the widely introduced sweet chestnut and sycamore — produce seed crops that are an important resource for mammals. Some of these trees, especially the oak and beech, are very irregular in the production of seed from year to year, a phenomenon known as masting. This has a profound effect on the population dynamics of the small seed-eating mammals and can be interpreted as a strategy evolved by the tree species to limit the consumption of seed. The dominant (and ubiquitous) small herbivores are the bank vole (wherever there is a shrub layer), the wood mouse and the introduced grey squirrel, the last two feeding primarily upon the tree seeds. Additional local species are the yellow-necked mouse, mainly in mature woodland, and the dormouse, especially where there is a dense shrub layer.

The particular species of large herbivore present in a wood, in the form of deer, depend more upon history than ecology, with roe predominating in

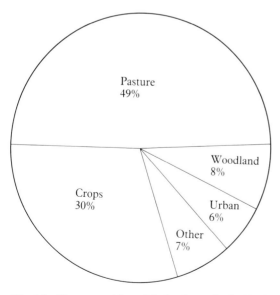

Fig. 3.1. The composition of the landscape in the UK in 1971 [3].

Pasture 49%

Woodland 8%

Crops 30%

Urban 6%

Other 7%

the north and southwest (but not in Wales) and the introduced species — fallow, sika and muntjac — in the southeast and (except for muntjac) in Ireland. The edge effect is also important. Although most deer browse to some extent upon trees and shrubs, much feeding takes place in rides, clearings and adjacent pasture or arable land. Two other herbivores, the field vole and the rabbit, are marginal in woodland since they depend upon the herbaceous field layer of clearings and edges.

Most predators are equally at home in woodland or open country. Of the shrews both common and pygmy are widespread in woodland wherever there is some ground or shrub cover, feeding upon the invertebrates of the litter, supplemented significantly in winter by pupae of arboreal insects.

Mole and hedgehog also occur in woodland but are more numerous in grassland, the hedgehog in particular favouring woodland edge, using the woodland for cover and adjacent grassland for feeding.

Most species of bats will feed in and on the edge of woodland, taking insects derived especially from the canopy. Species particularly associated with woodland, and roosting mainly in trees, are noctule, Leisler's, Bechstein's, barbastelle and brown long-eared, but whiskered, Natterer's and pipistrelles also use tree roosts in summer.

Of the carnivores, stoat and weasel are widespread, feeding mainly upon rodents and birds, the weasel in particular making use of the third dimension offered by woodland to exploit tree-nesting birds. Badger and fox will generally use woodland for cover but very often their foraging will be predominantly in adjacent open ground.

Of the avian predators, by far the most significant from the point of view of the small mammals is the tawny owl which is generally dependent upon an adequate supply of wood mice and bank voles for successful breeding [14]. A synthesis of the trophic relationships between woodland mammals, based on the long sequence of studies at Wytham Woods, Oxfordshire, was given by Hayward & Phillipson [10].

Highland oak and birch woodland has an essentially similar mammalian fauna except that dormouse and yellow-necked mouse are absent in the north and additional predators may be present — polecat and marten in Wales, marten and wildcat in the Scottish Highlands. However the absence of these species from most lowland woodland has a historical rather than an ecological explanation.

The remnant native pine forests likewise have a similar fauna but wood mouse appears to be scarce and the native red squirrel replaces the grey. Bilberry (*Vaccinium*) replaces bramble as the dominant ground shrub and constitutes an important part of the diet of bank vole and roe deer alike.

In Irish woodland the fauna is further impoverished by the absence of bank vole (except recently in the southwest), common shrew, weasel and roe deer.

Conifer plantations currently constitute about half of all British woodland and are generally grown as monocultures of exotic species, expecially spruces, pines and larches. In the young stages exclusion of large herbivores usually results in a dense grass and herb layer which can hold high densities of field voles. As a shrub layer develops bank voles and wood mice often become abundant but the voles are excluded as the canopy closes and shades out the field and shrub layers. However these, and indeed all the characteristic fauna of deciduous woodland edge, remain in rides and other edges which usually include deciduous trees and are the visible and accessible parts of such forests. Only the red squirrel, living in the canopy, remains throughout the unbroken blocks of plantation.

Farmland

The most characteristic herbivorous wild mammals of farmland are probably the hares — the brown hare in Britain and the mountain hare in Ireland — in that they can live permanently on open pasture and arable land with little need for cover. The field vole is in some respects more ubiquitous (except in Ireland) but is more dependent upon marginal cover and is generally absent from arable land and close-cropped pasture, being less subterranean than its common continental relative, *Microtus arvalis*.

Amongst the small predators the mole is widespread on pasture and the common and pygmy shrews wherever the vegetation provides concealment. Many other mammals forage in farmland from bases in adjacent woods, hedgerows, embankments and ditches, e.g. rabbits and deer amongst the herbivores, and hedgehogs, badgers and foxes amongst the predators. All of these last three forage for earthworms and other invertebrates on pasture, with the fox additionally preying upon voles, rabbits, hares and birds. Another very significant predator in farmland is the domestic and feral cat.

Wood mice colonise arable crops seasonally as cover develops but after harvest only make nocturnal forays from adjacent cover. Similarly mole runs are destroyed by ploughing and the moles recolonise each year from the periphery. They can therefore completely recolonise only very small fields, say less than 100 m wide, and occupy only the marginal fringe of large fields. Harvest mice are likewise confined to the periphery of cereal fields.

Hedgerows [12] are of major importance in providing a potentially rich habitat for mammals in farming country, with suitable conditions for many woodland species as well as for those grassland species that can forage on pasture and arable land but need more cover than these habitats can provide for nesting and breeding. Provided there is some long grass adjacent to the hedge, wood mouse, bank vole, field vole, common and pygmy shrew are ubiquitous. Where there is a good diversity of shrub species dormice may also be found and if the grass or herb cover is long enough harvest mice also. House mice frequently occur if arable land is adjacent, as do common rats, especially if there is a wet ditch. Weasels and stoats are regular and if the hedgerow is sufficiently wide and thick it may provide suitable sites for badger setts, fox earths and rabbit warrens. In arable country hedgerows, if they remain at all, are especially vulnerable to pollution from crop-spraying, which can cause problems by killing the ground vegetation that provides protective cover and food for small mammals and more directly by poisoning them.

Uplands [11]

On the non-wooded uplands the predominant land-use is as sheep pasture, with smaller areas devoted to red deer and to grouse, although these frequently share the ground with sheep. These areas are predominantly below the natural tree line but also extend above it into the alpine zone which is probably the habitat least influenced by human activity.

On upland pasture managed primarily for sheep (or cattle), grazing by other ungulates, except red deer in the Highlands, is usually only marginal, for example by roe in the vicinity of woodland and locally by feral goats, e.g. in the Cheviots. The mountain hare is a widespread grazer but few rabbits or brown hares extend above about 300 m, even in Wales where the mountain hare is absent

[5]. The field vole is a ubiquitous grazer. Although it occurs at low density on heavily grazed pasture, anything that provides extra cover, e.g. tussocks of *Molinia* and *Deschampsia* grass or patches of rushes or bracken, will encourage higher numbers. Bracken will also harbour bank voles and wood mice, and bilberry will enable bank voles to reach as high as 800 m.

Wherever the soil is reasonably well drained hill pasture is an ideal habitat for moles, which occur commonly up to 600 m and in places to 1000 m. Common shrews are also widespread.

Pure heather moor is a poor habitat for small mammals although both common and pygmy shrew can be numerous. Mountain hares on the other hand occur at higher densities than on grassy pasture. Other herbivores, such as roe deer, field and bank voles, only occur to the extent that the heather is supplemented by other shrubs and by grass.

All the species of carnivores use these lower upland pastures to some extent, although the pine marten and wildcat are predominantly woodland-based. In addition to the mammalian predators, the rodents and shrews are exposed to a considerable variety of birds of prey of which the short-eared owl, hen harrier and buzzard are the most significant. Buzzard and golden eagle are also significant predators on the hares and rabbits.

On the high plateaus and ridges above 1000 m there are few permanent residents. Field voles extend to the highest tops as long as there is cover, scree substituting for long grass wherever there is some grazing to be had. Common and pygmy shrews also reach the highest altitudes, with pygmy becoming dominant amongst the very short dwarf-shrub communities of the windswept summits whereas the common shrew predominates in the deeper cover of more sheltered slopes. Mountain hares are found on most high ground during the summer and remain even in winter wherever the wind keeps some vegetation exposed. Red deer on the other hand generally desert the highest ground in winter. Of the carnivores, fox, stoat and weasel regularly hunt on the highest ground.

Wetlands

Freshwater habitats, especially in the lowlands, have been greatly reduced and disturbed, for example by the drainage of marshes for agricultural use; by the management of rivers for flood control, navigation and industry; by the use of all kinds of water bodies for recreation, especially angling and boating; and by pollution with industrial, agricultural and sewage effluents. Of the few native species of mammals closely associated with fresh water, the water vole and water shrew remain widespread in well-vegetated waterside habitats. The otter, although in some respects more versatile in using upland and coastal habitats, has survived less well on lowland rivers because of pollution, disturbance and the removal of cover. Although not confined to wet habitats, two rodents that are very characteristic of the drier parts of marshes are the harvest mouse and the field vole.

Throughout the world many of the species most exploited for furs are aquatic. The beaver has long since been exterminated in Britain, probably through over-exploitation for furs. On the other hand the American mink and the coypu have both become established as a result of escapes from fur farms. The predatory mink is now widespread on both rivers and lakes but the coypu has been exterminated because of its potential for damage to crops and to flood banks. (A further damaging introduction, the muskrat, was successfully exterminated in the 1930s.) Wherever there is human disturbance, including arable farming, most lowland water margins, from farm ponds to the banks of major rivers, harbour common rats.

Most lowland water bodies are highly productive of insects and are therefore attractive to bats. Most British species commonly feed over water although the dominant one, as elsewhere, is usually the pipistrelle.

Highland rivers and lakes have no characteristic mammals other than the otter.

Coastal habitats

The open sea and coastal waters are the habitat of the cetaceans and seals. Both common and grey seals are frequent in inshore waters even away from breeding colonies, and both penetrate estuaries, the common seal much more regularly and deeply than the grey. Of the cetaceans the species most frequent close to the shore are the porpoise, bottle-nosed dolphin, Risso's dolphin (in the south and west), killer whale and pilot whale. Only the first two regularly enter estuaries.

The only other mammal that actually forages in the sea is the otter, especially on the north and west coasts. Otters will also hunt in the intertidal zone, taking crabs especially. The only other species regularly feeding on the shore is the common rat, although locally mink also use this habitat. The high-water tide-line can be a good habitat for all three widespread species of shrews as well as the white-toothed shrews on the Channel Isles and the Isles of Scilly, although it is not known to what extent shrews forage in the intertidal zone. Storm beaches with stable boulder fields extending above high-water mark provide ample cover for shrews and abundant food in the form of seaweed flies and sand-hoppers. Two other important resources characteristic of the tide-line and other coastal habitats are birds' eggs in summer, and carrion, especially in winter. Both of these are exploited by foxes in particular and to a lesser extent by other carnivores and hedgehogs.

It is well known that on the Orkney island of North Ronaldsay, sheep of the local endemic breed regularly feed on seaweed [1]. In view of this it is perhaps a little surprising that this abundant and widespread resource does not appear to be utilised by any wild mammalian herbivores.

Many of the more terrestrial coastal habitats are both distinctive and relatively natural in composition, for example vegetated cliffs, scrub and the mosaic of grass and scrub on stabilised sand-dunes. These provide ideal habitat for most small mammals and their predators. Rabbits in particular are often extremely abundant. Grazing marsh reclaimed from estuarine salt-marsh is a good habitat for the brown hare whilst the rough grass of the associated embankments and ditches may hold large numbers of field voles along with their mammalian and avian predators, e.g. stoat, weasel, short-eared owl, hen harrier and kestrel.

On small islands the physical and botanical components of the habitats may not differ much from those in similarly exposed mainland areas, but because of the capricious nature of colonisation the composition of the mammal fauna is usually impoverished, providing many opportunities for species to respond to the lack of competition by expanding into novel habitats. On Raasay (Inner Hebrides) for example where field voles are absent the bank voles are found in open moorland, and on many islands where both trees and voles are absent wood mice live in more open habitats than they would normally occupy on the mainland.

Urban habitats [4]

There is every intergradation between the semi-natural, but still rural, habitats already dealt with and the most drastically altered habitats such as the city centres. The more extreme urban and industrial areas are characterised by tne absence of less adaptable rural species like the dormouse, water shrew, hares and deer, but even these can and do penetrate the suburban zone in places or live closely adjacent to industrial sites. Of the small mammals the house mouse and common rat are of course especially characteristic of urban sites.

Amongst the native species the wood mouse is the dominant small mammal in parks and gardens since it can tolerate the absence of ground cover better than the shrews and voles.

Of the predators stoats and weasels are also scarce in the absence of cover, in contrast to the fox which has become increasingly common in recent years. This is probably due more to increasing tolerance of the fox than to any change in the resources available or to any change on the part of the foxes themselves although that is debatable. Another highly influential member of the urban community is the cat. All but the most pampered household pets have a significant ecological impact and the sheer numbers involved, both 'domesticated' and feral, lead to densities far beyond those reached by any population of truly wildcats or other carnivore of comparable size. Unlike the fox the badger only rarely penetrates suburban areas and is generally limited to the outer suburbs.

Cities provide an abundance of roosting sites for bats and indeed in urban or rural areas alike the great majority of bats roost in man-made sites. In urban areas it is presumably the food supply that is the limiting factor although most water bodies attract a few species of bats to feed on the adults of aquatic insects. Water courses, whether river or canal, provide one important avenue allowing essentially rural habitats and their faunas to penetrate towns. An even more ubiquitous one is provided by the railways where for many species the danger from trains is more than counterbalanced by the freedom from human disturbance and trampling. Of the terrestrial mammals it is normally only the hares and deer that are unable to take advantage of the habitats provided by railway embankments in urban areas. Rural motorways provide similar opportunities along their verges.

In the last decade there has been an increasing awareness of the potential and the desirability of managing urban open space in the interests of wildlife including mammals. With the continuing decline of traditional forms of persecution there is every prospect of urban areas becoming increasingly colonised by wild mammals and more visibly so as they acclimatise to the human presence.

AUTHOR FOR THIS CHAPTER
G.B. Corbet, with acknowledgement for comments by P.A. Morris.

REFERENCES

1 Alderson L. (1978) North Ronaldsay sheep. In *The chance to survive: rare breeds in a changing world.* London: Cameron & Tayleur, Newton Abbot: David & Charles pp. 76–9.

2 Anon. (1972) *Biological sites recording scheme.* Alford: Society for the Promotion of Nature Reserves 40 pp.

3 Best R.H. (1981) *Land use and living space.* London: Methuen 224 pp.

4 Bornkamm R. *et al.* (eds) (1982) *Urban ecology.* Oxford: Blackwell Scientific Publications 370 pp.

5 Condry W. (1981) *The natural history of Wales.* London: Collins 287 pp.

6 Elton C.S. (1966) *The pattern of animal communities.* London: Methuen 432 pp.

7 Elton C.S. & Miller R.S. (1954) The ecological survey of animal communities: with a practical system of classifying habitats by structural characters. *Journal of Ecology* **42**:460–96.

8 Gimingham C.H. (1972) *Ecology of heathlands.* London: Chapman & Hall 266 pp.

9 Godwin H. (1975) *The history of the British flora*, 2nd edn. Cambridge: Cambridge University Press 541 pp.

10 Hayward G.F. & Phillipson J. (1979) Community structure and functional role of small mammal communities. In Stoddart D.M. ed. *Ecology of small mammals.* London: Chapman & Hall pp. 131–211.

11 McVean D.N. & Lockie J.D. (1969) *Ecology and land use in upland Scotland.* Edinburgh: Edinburgh University Press.

12 Pollard E. *et al.* (1974) *Hedges.* London: Collins.

13 Ratcliffe D.A. (1977) *A nature conservation review: the selection of biological sites of national importance to nature conservation in Britain*, 2 vols. Cambridge: Cambridge University Press 401, 320 pp.

14 Southern H.N. (1970) The natural control of a population of tawny owls. *Journal of Zoology* **162**:197–285.

15 Tansley A.G. (1939) *The British Islands and their vegetation.* Cambridge: Cambridge University Press 930 pp.

Chapter 4 / British Mammals and the Law

INTRODUCTION

The prime concern of this chapter is the law relating to those species of mammal found in the wild in Great Britain. Such law includes not only that which affects free-living creatures relating, for example, to conservation, close seasons and pest control, but also the provisions such as welfare and the responsibilities of keepers which, although primarily aimed at domesticated species, also affect wildlife kept in captivity. In addition, when such animals are put to some use, such as public exhibition or scientific study, further legal controls apply.

GENERAL POINTS OF LAW

The law discussed here is primarily that of England and Wales; while that of Scotland is substantially the same, it differs in some ways, for example in respect of game. Likewise although the law of Northern Ireland generally follows that of England and Wales, it usually has its own legislation.

The law is subject to change from time to time and also, since this chapter is a simplified statement of the law, the reader who wishes to rely upon a point a law must satisfy himself or herself of the current state of the relevant law.

FREE-LIVING MAMMALS

The legislation concerned with the conservation and protection of mammals living free in the wild falls into three main categories.

Conservation: this includes year-round protection for specified species, restrictions on the use of certain methods of capturing or killing free-living animals, the provision of some habitat protection, and the control of trade.

Close-season protection: some species that have traditionally been hunted are protected during their breeding seasons and by the restriction of methods used, at any time, to kill or take them.

Pest-control: some species have no protection at all while they are free-living. Further, some are considered pests since they cause sufficient damage to warrant control measures. There are legal restrictions on the importation, keeping and release of certain species and on the methods which may be used to dispose of pests. In some cases, there is a duty to carry out control measures.

Conservation

The legislation providing year-round protection of certain free-living mammals consists of the Wildlife and Countryside Act 1981 and the Badgers Act 1973.

PROTECTED SPECIES
The Wildlife and Countryside Act 1981 (amended 1988) provides protection for the mammals listed on Schedule 5. These are shown in Table 4.1.

PROTECTION OF SCHEDULE 5 SPECIES
Section 9 provides that it is an offence intentionally to kill, injure or take a Schedule 5 mammal that is free-living at that time. Purely accidental harm

Table 4.1. Protected mammal species listed in Schedule 5.

Horseshoe bats (all species)	Rhinolophidae
Typical bats (all species)	Vespertilionidae
Cetaceans (all species)	Cetacea
Pine marten	*Martes martes*
Otter	*Lutra lutra*
Wildcat	*Felis silvestris*
Red squirrel	*Sciurus vulgaris*
Common dormouse	*Muscardinus avellanarius*
Walrus	*Odobenus rosmarus*

does not constitute an offence, although the word 'intentionally' includes not only deliberate taking, killing or injury but also acts done without regard to their consequences.

It is also an offence to have in one's possession or control a live or dead Schedule 5 mammal (or any part or derivative of one), unless it can be proved that the animal was not killed or taken from the wild (e.g. a captive-bred or legally purchased specimen) or that the killing or taking was permitted by a provision in the Act, for example, because it was obtained under licence or as a disabled animal or a road casualty.

Damaging, destroying or obstructing access to a place or structure that is being used by a Schedule 5 species for shelter or protection is an offence, as is the disturbance of such an animal while it is using the place or structure for these purposes. This provision does not apply to action taken within a dwelling house although this exemption is restricted to the living area in respect of Schedule 5 bats. Proposed interference with bats living elsewhere in a house, for example the loft, must be preceded by notification of the Nature Conservancy Council (NCC) of the proposed action, giving the NCC time to advise on whether and how it should be carried out [13, 17]. There have been several successful prosecutions for killing bats or damaging their roosts in the lofts of houses, usually in the course of timber treatment [18, 19].

The sale of a Schedule 5 wild mammal, live or dead, or any part or derivative thereof, is an offence. The term 'sale' includes equivalent transactions such as hire, barter and exchange as well as activities preliminary to sale such as advertising or transporting such animals for the purpose of sale.

EXEMPTIONS FROM PROTECTION
The *prima facie* protection afforded to Schedule 5 species does not apply in the following circumstances:
1 To captive specimens. However, there is a presumption that a Schedule 5 specimen is a wild one unless it can be proved to be captive. It is therefore extremely important to keep records and other evidence of captive-breeding or other legitimate acquisitions of Schedule 5 mammals to defend any accusation of an offence under Section 9, such as illegal taking or possession.
2 Action required by the Minister for Agriculture, Fisheries and Food or his counterpart in Wales, Scotland and Northern Ireland (MAFF) for the protection of agriculture, crops or animals.
3 An authorised person (i.e. the owner or occupier of land, a person authorised thereby or by a local authority) has a defence to the killing or injuring (but not taking) of a Schedule 5 wild animal where this was necessary urgently to prevent serious damage to property such as livestock or crops, although a licence must, if possible, be obtained in advance.
4 An action contrary to Section 9 is not an offence when it is part of an otherwise lawful activity and could not be avoided. Thus, accidentally to kill a bat or red squirrel while driving a car is not an offence providing that the driver was driving legally. (This exemption is not available in respect of actions involving bats in non-living areas of houses unless the special procedures described earlier have been followed.)
5 It is permissible to take a disabled Schedule 5 mammal from the wild in order to care for it. The animal must be released if it recovers sufficiently. If the animal's condition is in question it may be advisable to obtain a veterinary surgeon's opinion on its condition either to justify keeping it permanently in captivity or to ensure that it is fit for release. An animal may be killed (a humane method should be used, *see* Cruelty) if it is not likely to recover from its disablement. In either case the person taking advantage of this provision must be able to show that the damage to the animal was not caused by his or her own illegal action.
6 Licences are issued by the NCC to authorise activities otherwise prohibited, for example, for scientific and educational purposes, for identification, conservation or photography; by MAFF for disease control and protection of crops, property and livestock; and by the Department of the Environment (DOE) to authorise the sale of Schedule 5 species.

PROHIBITED METHODS
Section 11 of the Wildlife and Countryside Act imposes restrictions on the use of certain methods of killing or taking wild animals whether or not they are protected species, and other methods are prohibited in respect of species listed in Schedule 6. These are set out in Table 4.2. Live mammals must not be used as a decoy for killing or taking wild animals. Licences may be issued to use devices such as nets or traps for the reasons mentioned earlier. An open general licence has been issued by the NCC authorising people working with

Species	Prohibited	Permitted
Wildlife and Countryside Act 1987 (as amended)		
All	Self-locking snare, bow, crossbow, explosive, live mammal used as decoy	Free-running snare (any snare must be inspected daily)
Schedule 6[†]	Trap, snare, electrical device, poisonous or stupefying substance	Defence: placing of these articles for killing or taking unprotected species for control or conservation if reasonable precautions were taken to avoid injury to Schedule 6 species Open general licence to trap shrews
Schedule 6[†]	Net, automatic weapon, aids to night shooting, gas, smoke, sound recording	
Badgers Act 1973 (as amended)		
Badgers	Badger tongs, digging, certain firearms, cruel ill-treatment	

Table 4.2. Prohibited⋆ and permitted methods of killing and taking wild (i.e. free-living) mammals.

⋆ Prohibited methods may be authorised by a licence issued by NCC, DOE or MAFF. Protection would include domesticated or protected species that have gone feral. A licence to take would also be required to recover a Schedule 5 species which had escaped from captivity.
[†] Schedule 6 mammals: Schedule 5 species (*see* Table 4.1) plus Badger, *Meles meles*; Dormice (all species), Gliridae; Hedgehog, *Erinaceus europaeus*; Polecat, *Mustela putorius*; Shrews (all species), Soricidae.

educational and conservation bodies to trap shrews for identification and immediate release.

There are other restrictions on trapping methods which are referred to in Pest Control; *see also* [9, 27].

RELEASE OF NON-INDIGENOUS SPECIES
It is an offence to release or allow to escape into the wild any animal that is not ordinarily resident in, or a regular visitor to, Great Britain in a wild state or, because it is already established in the wild [15], is listed in Schedule 9, Part I, including the mammals listed in Table 4.3.

If a release does take place, it is a defence to show that all reasonable steps had been taken and all due diligence exercised to avoid committing an offence.

BADGERS ACT 1973 (as amended by the Wildlife and Countryside Act 1981 and Wildlife and

Table 4.3. Non-indigenous species prohibited from release into the wild.

Coypu	*Myocastor coypus*
Fat dormouse	*Glis glis*
Mongolian gerbil	*Meriones unguiculatus*
Prairie marmot or dog	*Cynomys*
American mink	*Mustela vison*
Crested porcupine	*Hystrix cristata*
Himalayan porcupine	*Hystrix hodgsonii*
Black rat	*Rattus rattus*
Grey squirrel	*Sciurus carolinensis*
Red-necked wallaby	*Macropus rufogriseus*

Countryside (Amendment) Act 1985)
This legislation provides protection for the badger comparable to that for Schedule 5 species except that the sett itself is not protected against destruction, damage or obstruction, or the animal against disturbance whilst occupying it. However, as the law has allowed additional special provisions for

this species making badger digging and cruel ill-treatment illegal [10] (*see* Table 4.2), in effect the sett is protected whilst the animal is within it. The exemptions available to an authorised person (*see* Exemptions from protection, **3**) for the protection of property also apply to any person in respect to the killing, injuring or taking of badgers but again only if there is an emergency and no time to apply for the correct licence from the Ministry of Agriculture, Fisheries and Food; digging would still be illegal. Under the 1985 amendments, any person accused of actually or attempting to kill, injure or take a badger or digging at a sett is presumed to be illegally doing so until and unless he or she can prove otherwise.

NB For further information on conservation legislation *see* [4, 6, 11, 16, 21, 22, 25].

Close-season protection

SEALS
The Conservation of Seals Act 1970 (as amended) lays down close seasons for grey seals and common seals during which it is illegal to kill, injure or take these species (Table 4.4). There are also restrictions on the use of firearms and it is illegal to use poison in the killing or taking of a seal.

These provisions are subject to exemptions for unavoidable actions and disabled seals and, in addition, it is permitted, in limited circumstances, to kill a seal in order to prevent it from causing damage to fishing nets or tackle, even within the close season.

Licences may be issued by the Home Office to authorise the killing or taking of seals for scientific or educational purposes, for zoological collections, fishery protection and seal population management.

CETACEANS
The Whaling Industry (Regulation) Act 1934 (as amended) prohibits whaling in UK waters and applies to all cetaceans in conformity with the International Convention for the Regulation of Whaling and parts of the Convention on the Conservation of Migratory Species of Wild Animals 1979 (Bonn Convention) [2].

DEER
In England and Wales close season protection is provided by the Deer Act 1963 (as amended) and in Scotland the main provisions are contained in the Deer Act 1959 (as amended). These cover red, roe, sika and fallow deer and the annual close seasons are set out in Table 4.4. Further, all species

Table 4.4. Close seasons.

Legislation	Common name	England, Wales		Scotland*	
		From	To	From	To
Seals					
Conservation of	Grey seal	1 Sept	31 Dec	1 Sept	31 Dec
Seals Act 1970	Common seal	1 June	31 Dec	1 Sept	31 Dec
Deer†					
Deer Act 1963	Red deer				
	Stag	1 May	31 July	21 Oct	30 June
	Hind	1 March	31 Oct	16 Feb	20 Oct
	Fallow deer				
	Buck	1 May	31 July	1 May	31 July
	Doe	1 March	31 Oct	16 Feb	20 Oct
Roe Deer (Close	Roe deer				
Seasons)	Buck	1 Nov	31 March	21 Oct	31 March
Act 1977	Doe	1 March	31 Oct	1 Apr	20 Oct
	Sika deer				
	Stag	1 May	31 July	21 Oct	30 June
	Hind	1 March	31 Oct	16 Feb	20 Oct

* Deer (Scotland) Act 1959 (as amended), Deer (close seasons) (Scotland) Order 1984.
† Deer Act 1987. Exception: no close season for farmed (enclosed and marked) deer.

of deer are protected at night throughout the year. Duly enclosed and marked farmed deer, however, are no longer subject to close seasons.

There are controls on the use of firearms and other methods of killing or taking deer. There are also exceptions, for example for the use of firearms, which are otherwise forbidden, in the protection of crops and for euthanasia of sick or injured deer. In England and Wales licences may authorise the use of otherwise prohibited methods, such as nets or traps and stupefying drugs to take deer alive for scientific purposes or for translocation, and in Scotland they may permit the killing or taking of deer for scientific purposes during the close seasons. In England and Wales injured or diseased deer may be taken by net or trap but not by dart gun; however in Scotland any action may be taken to prevent suffering in such circumstances.

The provisions relating to deer are complex. For greater detail see [5, 6, 22].

GROUND GAME

Hares and rabbits may be shot at night only by duly authorised persons, and spring traps may only be used in burrows. Poison must not be used although gassing is permitted (Table 4.5b).

Pest control

Many wild mammals such as the fox, weasel and hedgehog are subject to no protection beyond the prohibition of certain devices such as self-locking snares, some spring traps and crossbows. Neither are they protected by cruelty legislation while they are free-living (see Welfare, below). Some species of wild mammal cause such damage that there are special provisions requiring their control or de-

struction in the interests of, for example, agriculture or public health. Despite the desirability of pest control, the methods used are subject to restriction. The requirements for control are set out in Table 4.5a; for greater detail see [1, 3, 22, 27].

CAPTIVE MAMMALS

A wide range of legislation, though primarily concerned with domesticated species, is nevertheless applicable to non-domesticated mammals held in captivity.

Welfare

Cruelty: The Protection of Animals Acts 1911–64 (for England and Wales) and the Protection of Animals (Scotland) Act 1912 make the cruel treatment of any domestic or captive animal an offence. Several cases have examined the meaning of the term 'captive animal' and held that mere inability to escape does not constitute captivity; whether an animal in a trap is in captivity is not entirely clear. The Acts specify certain forms of cruelty but also make it an offence to cause an animal 'any unnecessary suffering'. This general phrase could apply, for example, to the failure to feed or water an animal or to provide it with veterinary attention when required; likewise, the use of an inhumane method to kill an animal could constitute an offence. In addition, the various Acts have created further offences of cruelty, notably in relation to transportation, poisons and surgical operations which are mentioned elsewhere in this chapter.

Under the Abandonment of Animals Act 1960 it is an offence of cruelty wilfully to abandon an

Legislation	Species
Pests Act 1954	Rabbits
Agriculture Act 1947	Hares
Agriculture (Scotland) Act 1948	Deer
Forestry Act 1967	Moles, other 'vermin', e.g. rats, mice, foxes
Deer (Scotland) Act 1959	Red deer, sika deer
Animal Health Act 1981	Wildlife
Rabies (Control) Order 1974	Foxes
Wildlife and Countryside Act 1981 (release prohibited)	Schedule 9 species

Table 4.5a. Pest control: requirements to control pests.

Table 4.5b. Pest control: restricted methods of control.

Legislation	Prohibited	Permitted
Wildlife and Countryside Act 1981	*See* Table 4.2	*See* Table 4.2
Pests Act 1954 Agriculture (Spring Traps) Scotland Act 1969 Spring traps (Approval) Orders 1975 Small Ground Vermin Traps Order 1958 and similar orders for Scotland	Spring traps	Approved types of spring traps, according to species (e.g. Fenn traps) Approved spring traps for rats, mice etc.
Protection of Animals Act 1911 Protection of Animals (Scotland) Act 1912	Poison	Poison used for small vermin Licensed activities
Animals (Cruel Poisons) Regulations 1963 Agriculture (Miscellaneous Provisions) Act 1972	Specified poisons	Strychnine for moles
Grey Squirrels (Warfarin) Order 1973		Warfarin for grey squirrels
Agriculture Act 1947 Agriculture (Scotland) Act 1948	Poisonous gas	Approved gas for foxes, moles, rats
Prevention of Damage by Rabbits Act 1939		Rabbits
Destructive Imported Animals Act 1932 (various orders)	Keeping, importing, releasing, e.g. mink, coypu, grey squirrel	Under licence

NB This table is a brief summary of the relevant provisions. For further details in the legislation *see also* Pest control.

animal in circumstances likely to cause it unnecessary suffering. This is applicable to the release to the wild of a mammal that had been in captivity, for example, for treatment or study. Consequently a proper assessment of ability to survive in the wild should be made prior to release (*see also* Research).

Transport: The Protection of Animals Acts provide in very general terms that no unnecessary suffering should be caused in the course of transport. The transport, by any means, of any mammal (except farm species covered by other legislation) is also covered by the Transit of Animals (General) Order 1973. An animal must be fit to travel and must be transported in a receptacle or in a manner that does not cause it unnecessary suffering. It must be given

food, water, environmental conditions and attendance appropriate to its needs. Animals that are unfit may only be transported with the authority of a MAFF veterinary inspector's certificate. Particular carriers may have specific requirements, such as those set down by the International Air Transport Association; British Rail has special requirements and mammals cannot, of course, be sent by Royal Mail.

Licensing

When certain mammals are kept in captivity the keeper (who may not necessarily be the owner) must be licensed as set out in Table 4.6. When an animal leaves licensed premises it may be necessary

Table 4.6. Requirements for licences.

Statute	Species	Purpose	Other legislation applicable on removal from premises
Zoo Licensing Act 1981 (ZLA)*	Any species not commonly domesticated in Great Britain	Kept for exhibition to public for more than 7/365 days; not in pet shop or circus	DWAA if listed, unless in care of a zoo keeper
Dangerous Wild Animals Act 1976 (as amended) (DWAA)*	Listed in Schedule, including wildcat; not fox, feral dog nor cat	Kept privately not under ZLA, PAA, A(SP)A or in a circus	Removal requires local authority permission. ZLA, if relevant
Pet Animals Act 1951 (PAA)	Vertebrates. WCA[†] licence required for sale of Schedule 5 species	Business of selling animals as pets or for ornament	DWAA, ZLA if applicable
Animals (Scientific Procedures) Act 1986 (A(SP)A)	Vertebrates	Regulated procedures	DWAA, ZLA if applicable

* Veterinary inspection obligatory.
[†] Wildlife and Countryside Act 1981. A licence is required to authorise a sale of Schedule 5 species in any circumstances.

to obtain further authorisation.

Licensing is carried out annually by local authorities together with an inspection. The Acts and the conditions imposed in licences provide for welfare of the animals concerned and for public safety.

MEDICAL

The Veterinary Surgeons Act 1966 *prima facie* restricts the practice of veterinary surgery to registered veterinary surgeons. This includes the diagnosis of disease and injury in animals, advice based on such diagnosis, medical or surgical treatment and surgical operations. This applies to all species of mammals whether captive or free-living and regardless of whether a fee is charged.

Certain exceptions are provided by the Act and the Veterinary Surgeons Act 1966 (Schedule 3 Amendment) Order 1987 which enable non-veterinarians to treat animals as follows:
1 Any person may give an animal first aid in an emergency.
2 The owner of an animal, members of his family and his employees may give minor medical treatment. This can probably be construed to extend to wild-caught animals, taken into captivity, but whether it applies to those under temporary restraint is uncertain (*see* Ownership).
3 Scientific research involving veterinary procedures may be carried out by non-veterinarians duly authorised under the Animals (Scientific Procedures) Act 1986.

Anyone who treats an animal or performs euthanasia is subject to the Protection of Animals Acts (see earlier) and must do so without causing unnecessary suffering. The same Acts require that a surgical operation be performed with due care and humanity. The Protection of Animals (Anaesthetics) Acts 1954 and 1964 require that any operation involving the sensitive tissue or bone must be carried out under anaesthesia sufficient to prevent it feeling pain. There are a number of exceptions to this provision, particularly in respect of minor procedures for which anaesthesia is not normally used or that are not normally carried out by a veterinary surgeon.

The use of medicines in animals for treatment or in the course of research are subject to the Medicines Act 1968 and the Misuse of Drugs Act 1971 [12]. Restrictions are imposed on the supply and administration of 'prescription only' medicines; they may only be supplied by a pharmacist (in accordance with the prescription of a veterinary surgeon) or by a veterinary surgeon. Institutions may also obtain such medicines, for their research or educational purposes, from a wholesale supplier. The administration of any 'prescription only' drug (including 'controlled drugs') must be carried out in accordance with the directions of a veterinary surgeon. For the application of these principles in the field *see* [23].

The Misuse of Drugs Act 1971 and Misuse of Drugs Regulations 1985 restrict the supply and possession of 'controlled drugs' (which include some of those used for the immobilisation of mammals) to limited categories such as veterinary surgeons and persons in charge of a research laboratory or to individuals for administration for veterinary purposes in accordance with the directions of a veterinary surgeon.

RESEARCH

The use of animals in research is governed by the Animals (Scientific Procedures) Act 1986 which is administered by the Home Office. The Act requires that any 'regulated procedure' carried out on a 'protected animal' (i.e. any living vertebrate, including young in the second half of gestation) must be authorised by a 'personal licence' and a 'project licence' and be carried out at a 'scientific procedure establishment' or 'other place', the latter allowing for work in the field.

A regulated procedure is defined as 'any experimental or other scientific procedure causing ... pain, suffering, distress or lasting harm'. Some indication of whether certain procedures are subject to the new Act is given in Table 4.7.

Scientific research establishments must be designated by the Home Office and have a named person (usually an animal technician) who is responsible for the day to day care of the animals and a named veterinary surgeon who is available to provide advice on their health and welfare. With Home Office approval, research such as fieldwork with wild mammals may be carried out outside a designated establishment, although the provision for a named veterinary surgeon will still apply.

The release to the wild or to a private owner of an animal used in licensed research is subject to Home Office permission and satisfactory examination by a veterinary surgeon.

The Act is complex and extensive guidance has been issued by the Home Office which must be followed meticulously. Considerable emphasis is

Table 4.7. Animals (Scientific Procedures) Act 1986 Section 5.

Regulated procedures	Not regulated procedures
'Experimental procedures', e.g. implanted telemetry 'Other scientific procedures', e.g. blood sampling or measurements	Recognised veterinary, animal husbandry or agricultural practices
Anaesthesia, analgesia, decerebration used as RP	Anaesthesia etc. when, applied for management, veterinary etc. purposes (*see* above)
Killing for RP in SPE using method not specified in Schedule 1	Killing except as opposite
Identification methods causing more than momentary pain and distress or lasting harm, e.g. toe clipping	Ringing, marking, tagging, e.g. ear notching, freeze branding, external telemetry

RP, regulated procedure; SPE, scientific procedure establishment.
NB Since the application of the Act to wildlife studies is under development, the Home Office should be consulted at an early stage in planning projects.

laid upon the limitation of pain in research animals and licensees should be conversant with current methods of its recognition and control [14, 26]. Summaries of the legislation are provided by [6, 24].

TRADE

Any person who sells animals as pets or for ornamental purposes must be licenced under the Pet Animals Act 1951 even if the animals are non-domesticated species.

The sale, for whatever purpose, of wild species listed in Schedule 5 of the Wildlife and Countryside Act is illegal unless authorised by DOE licence. A licence is not required to sell captive-bred specimens but the seller should be able to prove this, since there is a presumption that a specimen is a wild one. The term 'sale' includes hire, barter, exchange and acts associated with sale, namely transporting, advertising and possessing Schedule 5 species for trading purposes.

The international movement of endangered

Table 4.8. Species exempt from import and export regulations for endangered species.

Common domestic and laboratory species	
European mole	*Talpa europaea*
Fox (common and silver)	*Vulpes vulpes*
American mink	*Mustela vison*
Roe deer	*Capreolus capreolus*
Red deer	*Cervus elaphus*
Fallow deer	*Dama dama*
Muskrat	*Ondatra zibethicus*

species is controlled by EEC Regulation 3626/82 (as amended), which has direct effect in the UK, and the Endangered Species (Import and Export) Act 1976, as amended by the Wildlife and Countryside Act 1981, which implement the Convention on International Trade in Endangered Species of Wild Fauna and Flora (CITES or Washington Convention) and the Convention on the Conservation of European Wildlife and Natural Habitats (Berne Convention). The import and export of many species must be authorised by documentation issued by the DOE. The sale (and display for commercial, not merely sale purposes) of many of the most endangered species is also forbidden by the foregoing legislation although open general licences exist for trade in captive-bred specimens or those acquired before the legislation came into force.

Only the British mammals listed in Table 4.8 are totally free from these controls.

Details of the legal and administrative requirements for the sale, import and export of mammals are available from the DOE [7].

ANIMAL HEALTH

In order to restrict the spread of disease, orders are made under the Animal Health Act 1981 to regulate the import of animals and to control outbreaks of certain diseases. The importation of any live mammal must be authorised by a licence obtained from MAFF prior to entry into Great Britain. The licence will also require health certification and quarantine (usually 6 months) at approved premises. A licence is also required for the import of mammalian carcases, certain animal products, embryos, ova, semen and pathogenic material.

Specified diseases are designated as notifiable when they occur not only in farm animals but also in non-domesticated species, for example, foot-and-mouth in any ruminants, Aujeszky's disease in deer, anthrax in captive mammals, and rabies in any mammal. There are extensive powers to contain an outbreak of a notifiable disease. Normally this relates to farm species but can extend to others, e.g. the power to kill foxes. The control of rabies can be extended to other species and other diseases (as was formerly the case with badgers and bovine tuberculosis) [8].

RESPONSIBILITY FOR ANIMALS

Ownership

Free-living animals belong to no one, although very young animals or carcases belong to the person on whose land they are found. If a wild animal is taken into some form of permanent control or captivity, it becomes the property of the captor until ownership is transferred to another person. Ownership is lost when an animal is released, although the precise moment at which ownership ceases may be difficult to assess in cases where there is an inadvertent escape or it is intended to continue some degree of control over a released animal. An owner has the same rights in respect of theft or other unlawful interference with a captive animal as with other goods.

Liability

Any person who owns, keeps or has control over an animal is responsible for it in a number of ways in addition to those that have already been discussed regarding licensed keeping.

A person who fails to take reasonable steps to prevent some foreseeable risk, for example by permitting a person to handle an animal without appropriate precautions, may be held liable in negligence for the damage caused and be required to pay compensation (damages). By virtue of the Animals Act 1971 and Animals (Scotland) Act 1987 a person who keeps a non-domesticated species that is likely to cause severe damage is liable for any injury or damage it causes, even if there is no negligence.

The occupier of land is responsible for harm caused to visitors on the property by hazards on the land or premises; for example by an unguarded ditch or dangerous cliff face (Occupiers' Liability Act 1957). However, in some cases, under the

Occupiers' Liability Act 1984, liability can be excluded, particularly in respect of visiting fieldwork or recreational parties [6].

A person who consents to run a risk or contributes to the cause of harm may be considered not or only partly responsible and thereby entitled only to no, or reduced, compensation.

Nuisance

If animals are kept in captivity they may cause a nuisance. Excessive noise or smells, for example, which cause disturbance to a neighbourhood may constitute a nuisance and a court injunction can be obtained requiring it to be remedied.

HEALTH AND SAFETY

Those working with wild mammals as part of their employment must comply with the provisions of the Health and Safety at Work etc. Act 1974. This requires that employers, employees and the self-employed as appropriate must take reasonable steps to ensure health, welfare and safety in the course of work. This duty must be extended to visitors, assistants and students, although they are not employees. Codes of practice and guidance are normally provided for employees regarding both general and specialised aspects of work and have been considered by Nichols [20] in respect of fieldwork.

CONCLUSION

This chapter covers as widely as possible the legal requirements relating to British mammals. Depth of information has been sacrificed to breadth and the reader is strongly encouraged to look further, via the references, the legislation and standard textbooks, into the aspects of law that this chapter has introduced.

AUTHOR FOR THIS CHAPTER
M.E. Cooper, with acknowledgement to D.J. Jefferies.

REFERENCES

1 Bateman J.A. (1971) *Animal traps and trapping.* Newton Abbot: David & Charles 286 pp.

2 Birnie P. (1982) *Legal measures for the conservation of marine mammals.* Gland: International Union for Conservation of Nature and Natural Resources.

3 Britt D.P. ed. (1985) *Humane control of land mammals and birds.* Potters Bar: Universities Federation for Animal Welfare 136 pp.

4 CoEnCo (1987) *Wildlife and the law no. 3: mammals.* London: Council for Environmental Conservation and Mammal Society 2 pp.

5 Cooper M.E. (1984) The law. In Rudge A.J.B. ed. *Guidelines for the safe and humane handling of live deer in Great Britain.* Peterborough: Nature Conservancy Council pp. 251–72.

6 Cooper M.E. (1987) *An introduction to animal law.* London: Academic Press 213 pp.

7 Department of the Environment (1987) *Controls on the import and export of endangered and vulnerable species*, with Supplementary Notices 1–6. Bristol: Department of the Environment 52 pp.

8 Dunnet G. *et al.* (1986) *Badgers and bovine tuberculosis.* London: HMSO.

9 Gurnell J. & Flowerdew J.R. (1982) *Live trapping small mammals. A practical guide.* Reading: Mammal Society 24 pp.

10 Harris S. (1986) Badgers in law. *BBC Wildlife* 4:232.

11 Heap J. (1981–82) An introduction to the Wildlife and Countryside Act 1981. *Ardea* 1981–82:39–44. (Journal of the Beds and Hunts Naturalists Trust.)

12 Knifton A. & Edwards B.R. (1987) Controlled drugs and medicinal products. In *Legislation affecting the veterinary profession in the United Kingdom*, 5th edn. London: Royal College of Veterinary Surgeons, pp. 43–74.

13 Mitchell-Jones A.J. *et al.* (1986) Public concern about bats (Chiroptera) in Britain: an analysis of enquiries in 1982–83. *Biological Conservation* **36**:315–28.

14 Morton D.B. & Griffiths P.H.M. (1985) Guidelines on the recognition of pain, distress and discomfort in experimental animals and an hypothesis for assessment. *Veterinary Record* **116**:431–6.

15 Nature Conservancy Council (1979) *Wildlife introductions to Great Britain.* London: Nature Conservancy Council 32 pp.

16 Nature Conservancy Council (1982) *Wildlife, the law and you.* London: Nature Conservancy Council 14 pp.

17 Nature Conservancy Council (1984) *Focus on bats: their conservation and the law.* Peterborough: Nature Conservancy Council 16 pp.

18 Nature Conservancy Council (1988) *Bats in roofs.* Peter-borough: Nature Conservancy Council 6 pp.

19 Nature Conservancy Council (1987) *13th report, 1 April 1986 to 31 March 1987.* Peterborough: Nature Conservancy Council 164 pp.

20 Nichols D. ed. (1990) *Safety in biological fieldwork — guidance notes for codes of practice*, 3rd edn. London: Institute of Biology 46 pp.

21 Parkes C. (1983) *Law of the countryside.* Saxmundham:

Association of Countryside Rangers 189 pp.

22 Parkes C. & Thornley J. (1987) *Fair game*. London: Pelham 268 pp.

23 Porter A.R.W. (1982) Drugs for use in dart guns. *Publication of the Veterinary Deer Society* **1**(2):2−4.

24 Richards M.A. (1986) The Animals (Scientific Procedures) Act 1986. *The Society for General Microbiology Quarterly* **13**(4):102−4.

25 Sandys-Winsch G. (1984) *Animal law*. London: Shaw 260 pp.

26 Sanford J. *et al*. (1986) Guidelines for the recognition and assessment of pain in animals. *Veterinary Record* **118**:334−8.

27 Stuttard R.M. (1986) *Predatory mammals in Britain*. London: British Field Sports Society 94 pp.

Systematic Accounts

Chapter 5 / Insectivores: Order Insectivora

The insectivores are mainly small, ground-dwelling mammals that feed upon invertebrates. They are found throughout the world except in Australasia and most of South America (where they are replaced ecologically by marsupials). In spite of diverse external form they have many primitive characters: plantigrade feet, five clawed digits on each foot, small brain, continuous tooth rows with relatively few pointed cusps, long muzzle and abdominal (but ventral) testes.

In Britain three families are represented including the hedgehog, the mole and the shrews. Although superficially very different, the moles and shrews are more closely related to each other than either is to the hedgehog.

FAMILY ERINACEIDAE

The spiny hedgehogs (subfamily Erinaceinae, with four closely related genera) occur in the deciduous woodland, steppe and desert zones of Eurasia and Africa. The only other subfamily is the Echinosoricinae, or hairy hedgehogs, with six species in the evergreen forest zones of SE Asia. All members of the family are ground-dwelling, predominantly nocturnal insectivores, and the family is well represented in the fossil record. The dental formula is 3.1.3.3/2.1.2.3 in all spiny hedgehogs.

GENUS *Erinaceus*

Besides the W European *E. europaeus* the genus includes two other Palaearctic hedgehogs, *E. concolor* (*E. roumanicus*) in E Europe and W Asia, and *E. amurensis* in E Asia. Four African species commonly included in *Erinaceus* are better separated in *Atelerix* [32].

Hedgehog *Erinaceus europaeus*

Erinaceus europaeus Linnaeus, 1758; Wamlingbo, S Gothland Island, Sweden.

Urchin, hedgepig; draenog (Welsh), graineag (Scottish Gaelic), gráinneog (Irish Gaelic).

RECOGNITION
Unmistakable by virtue of spiny pelage. Tooth-rows continuous without enlarged canines. Widely flared, robust zygomatic arches (Figs 5.1, 5.2).

SIGN
Presence in area often revealed by road casualties. Animals can be found by searching after dark with a torch, especially in moist grassy areas. In winter, nests may be found by searching under low cover, e.g. bramble bushes (Fig. 5.3).

Footprints are fairly distinctive, with five claw marks, but need careful comparison with those of rats, squirrels and water vole although they are usually larger.

Faeces are characteristic, being long (15–50 mm), cylindrical (10 mm diameter), usually firmly compressed, dark grey or black and often studded with shiny fragments of insects.

DESCRIPTION
Body short, rotund and relatively unspecialised. Feet plantigrade with five well-developed and well-clawed toes. Legs quite long but normally hidden by fur on flanks. Tail short. Sexes similar, but in male penis far forward, in position of navel; in female vagina opens very close to anus. Skeleton unremarkable. Musculature of skin highly specialised to erect spines, and to enable animal to flex into ball and pull spiny part of skin down over rest of body (Fig. 5.1), chief muscle being the *orbicularis* which encircles body at limit of spines [77]. Anatomy of soft parts described by Carlier [18].

Pelage: several thousand sharply pointed spines completely replace hair on upper surface except for

Fig 5.1. Hedgehog showing how it lifts the body well clear of the ground when it is walking rapidly. When it is moving around tentatively investigating things the attitude is more crouching, while real alarm causes it to curl up.

face and a narrow median naked patch on the crown. Spines about 22 mm long, pale creamy brown with dark band near tip. Pelage on face and ventral surface sparse and coarse, usually uniform grey-brown but rather variable in intensity. No seasonal moult; spines long-lasting, replaced irregularly; individual marked spines still present after 18 months [76].

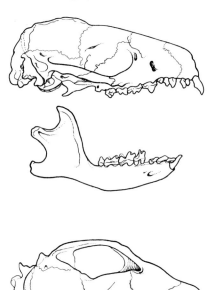

Fig. 5.2. Hedgehog: skull with permanent teeth.

Nipples: five pairs in both sexes, evenly spaced from axilla to groin. No obvious scent glands, but some individuals smelly even to human nose.

Teeth: $3.1.3.3/2.1.2.3$. I_1 procumbent, fit into gap between enlarged caniniform I^1. I^2 and I^3 resemble premolars. Canines and first premolars small, last premolars and molars larger with low-cusped crowns.

Reproductive tract: testes permanently abdominal but ventral; extremely elaborate male accessory reproductive organs enlarge to about 5% of total body weight in early summer. Female tract unremarkable; described by Deanesly [38].

Chromosomes: $2n = 48$ [149].

MEASUREMENTS
Head and body *c.* 160 mm at weaning, increasing to 260 mm or more in large adults. Condylobasal length of skull similarly increases from *c.* 40−58 mm. Males usually bigger than females, but sex differences are obscured by those due to age and growth. Body weight increases from *c.* 120 g at weaning to over 1100 g (exceptionally over 1600 g; captives can exceed 2 kg). Age and sex differences in body weight overshadowed by enormous seasonal fluctuation: massive accumulation of fat reserves in early autumn, followed by 30% loss of body weight during hibernation as reserves are depleted [86].

VARIATION
Extent to which processes of premaxillae and frontals approach each other variable (these meet

in 11 out of 16 skulls (69%) from mainland Britain and 12 out of 44 (27%) from continental Europe). This character was the basis of description of British subspecies (*E. e. occidentalis* Barrett-Hamilton, 1900, Haddington, Scotland), but British population not sufficiently distinctive to justify recognition as a subspecies.

Individuals vary in facial shape and shade of hair colour. Spine colour variable, a few all-white spines commonly present. Full albinos with pink nose and feet not infrequent, also white specimens are known with black nose and eyes. Melanics not recorded. Individuals with sparse spines sometimes reported, and one with none at all (at Luton, Bedfordshire in 1985) but not clear whether due to genetic effect or trauma.

DISTRIBUTION

In deciduous woodland and Mediterranean zones of W Europe and N Russia, replaced to the southeast by *E. concolor*.

Throughout mainland of Britain and Ireland up to tree line. Present on the following islands (known introductions marked ★, but many others probably introduced also): Shetland Mainland★, Unst★,

Map 5.1. Hedgehog.

Map 5.2. Hedgehog.

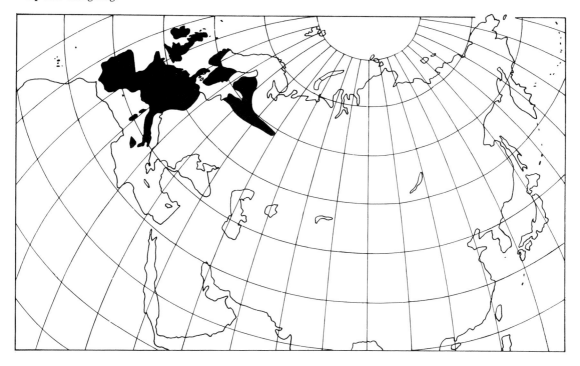

Fig. 5.3. Hedgehog nest. (Photo: P. Morris.)

Yell★, Foula★, Fetlar★, Muckle Roe★, Bressay★, Whalsay★, E Burra★, W Burra★, Vementry★; Orkney Mainland★, N Ronaldsay★; Skye, Soay, Canna★, Coll, Mull, Luing, Arran, Bute; Man (probably★), Anglesey, Wight, Alderney, Guernsey, Jersey; Beginish (Kerry). Attempted introduction (1985) to St Mary's (Isles of Scilly) and Sark. British hedgehogs introduced to New Zealand late 19th century, very abundant there now.

HISTORY
Probably indigenous in Britain; sub-fossil remains show presence since the Mesolithic period, *c.* 9500 bp at Star Carr, Yorkshire [52]. Probably introduced to Ireland — a Norman date has been suggested [175] — and to most of the small islands.

HABITAT
Most abundant where there is close proximity of grassland to woodland, scrub or hedgerow, e.g. edge of woods, hedgerows in meadowland, or sand-dunes with shrubs. Present in virtually all lowland habitats where there is sufficient cover for nesting. Notably common in suburban areas but generally scarce in coniferous wood, marshy and moorland areas. Availability of suitable site and materials for winter nest probably a factor limiting distribution.

SOCIAL ORGANISATION AND BEHAVIOUR
Essentially a solitary species but with overlapping home ranges.

Home range: normally travel between 0.5 and 1.5 km per night in open habitat (e.g. farmland), using an area of approximately 2–5 ha. Adult males travel further (up to 3 km per night) and use larger areas, *c.* 12 ha [119]. In forest-edge habitat range sizes and distances travelled seem to be reduced [118]. Total area familiar to an individual and used in course of a whole season probably at least 10 ha in farmland, up to 50 ha for adult males [119]. Total summer range sizes on suburban golf course averaged 32 ha for males and 10 ha for females, with much individual variation [138]. These data are based on intensive radio-tracking studies; mark-recapture experiments and short-duration radio-tracking result in smaller estimates of range size. Home range not significantly affected by provision of supplementary food, at least in summer [117].

Communication unlikely to be by acoustic or visual means, except perhaps at very short range. Normally silent but distressed adults can emit a loud scream; nestlings sometimes make a bird-like chirping if separated from family.

No evidence of scent marking or systematic deposition of urine or faeces. 'Self-anointing' is intriguing activity in which the hedgehog is stimulated to produce masses of frothy saliva which is liberally plastered all over its body (Fig. 5.4) [16]. Nature of stimulus and the purpose are a mystery (explanatory theories reviewed by Brockie [11]), but may be a means of spreading scent over body to facilitate individual recognition.

Aggressive behaviour: both wild and captive

Fig. 5.4. Hedgehog applying saliva to its spines — 'self-annointing'. (Photo: P. Morris.)

hedgehogs will fight to establish 'peck-order' [90]; males are especially aggressive and therefore presumed territorial, but actually do not defend exclusive territories. Many hedgehogs may visit same area, but at different times. Male's range overlaps that of several females and is also frequented by several other males. Separation perhaps temporal rather than spatial.

Activity almost entirely nocturnal but may be seen at dawn and dusk.

Hibernation in carefully built nest usually of leaves and grass under cover, e.g. bramble or brushwood, sometimes in rabbit burrow or below garden shed, etc. Some evidence of territoriality in building winter nests, which are rarely in very close proximity. More than one hibernaculum usually built; most animals move at least once during winter [113]. Arousals during winter are normal and fairly regular, though the animal often does not leave its nest before resuming torpor. Hibernation usually begins about October, induced at least partly by low temperature. Adult males begin earliest, females later; younger animals (especially late litters) may remain active until December. Hibernation ends early April in S England. Hibernation is preceded by accumulation of white fat under the skin and around the viscera, and brown fat (a thermogenetic tissue, 'hibernating gland' of earlier authors) around the shoulders. In hibernation body temperature falls from normal 34°C to match that of the environment. Optimal hibernation temperature about 4°C. Heart beat slows from 190 to about

20 beats/min; respiration reduced to about 10 intermittent breaths/min. Histological changes much studied [158].

Movement: gait rather hesitant with frequent stops to sniff the air. Snuffle and snort regularly when searching for food. Eyesight poor, smell and hearing acute. Crouch and erect spines at least sign of danger, reacting especially to noise. Roll up tightly when disturbed, with head and extremities completely protected by spines. Swim and climb surprisingly well. Some 'homing' instinct, and ability to recognise landmarks; may follow well-used paths [90]. Do not normally dig, but will use rabbit burrows for nesting.

Nest: large hibernaculum built for winter occupation may be used for up to 6 months [113]. Summer nest insubstantial (except breeding nest); often do not build nests during warm weather, but spend the day in shelter of vegetation. Summer nests often occupied for only a few days before moving to another. Males change nests more frequently than females; sometimes use nests previously occupied by other individuals [139].

Grooming: scratching of spines frequently observed during activity, especially soon after leaving nest. Fur also licked vigorously.

FEEDING

Food almost entirely ground-living invertebrates, but eat small number of birds' eggs and chicks; carrion also taken. The only detailed study in

Britain [188] from a variety of habitats, showed scarabeid beetles, caterpillars and earthworms formed 55% of the diet by weight. Carabid beetles, fly larvae, centipedes, harvestmen and spiders also frequently eaten. Slugs important food but difficult to evaluate. Average nightly intake of food believed to be about 70 g [87]. Food caught and dealt with entirely by the mouth. They do not cache food, even for winter.

Folk-tales of hedgehogs carrying fruit (usually apples) on spines frequently repeated. Validity disputed, though stories of wide currency. Similarly often repeated tales of hedgehogs taking milk from cows.

Frequently claimed to kill snakes for food but little evidence for this in Britain. Spines observed to protect skin from puncture by fangs. Hedgehogs have some degree of immunity to adder venom — macroglobulins in the blood plasma inhibit the haemorrhagic effect of the venom [183].

BREEDING

A litter of c. four to six young born usually in June, with sometimes a second litter later in the summer.

Season: males fecund early April to late August: pregnant females found May to October with early peak May to July and later peak September [109] (Fig. 5.5).

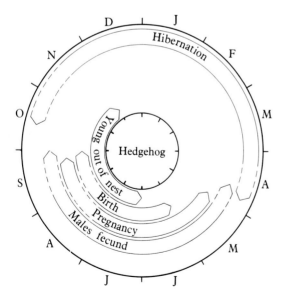

Fig. 5.5. Hedgehog: life-cycle.

Courtship consists of the male walking round and round the female with much snorting and often inconclusive results. Evidently promiscuous; both sexes may each have several partners in a season [140]. Ovulation is said to be spontaneous and early cycles are often infertile. Gestation 31–35 days; embryo number 2–7, means recorded 5.0 ($n = 10$) [38] and 4.6 ($n = 42$) [109]. Loss of embryos small (3.3%) but post-natal mortality c. 20% prior to weaning [114]. Birth in large, specially built nest. Mother eats young if disturbed soon after birth, later reacts to interference by carrying litter to safer place. Male takes no part in rearing family.

Sex ratio among juveniles 1 : 1, but excess of males observed in spring and of females in autumn probably reflecting different levels of activity and probability of being caught.

Young suckle for about 4 weeks; some females may produce second litter in same year (even a third in captivity). Young blind at birth, weighing 10–25 g; sex ratio about equal. First coat of white spines appears soon after birth, second pelage of dark spines with white tips visible by 36 hours among first white spines. Capable of rolling up from 11th day. Eyes open at 14 days, begin to leave nest at about 22 days. Replacement of milk teeth begins about 24th day, weaned at 4–6 weeks. Young disperse to lead solitary lives thereafter. Young from early summer litters are fully grown before hibernation in autumn; those from later litters must hibernate at a subadult size and are unlikely to survive the winter: a weight of 450 g or more is required to survive hibernation [116]. First breed in year following birth, at about 11 months old.

POPULATION

Densities: no systematic studies or reliable information, but must vary with habitat and season. Approximately 1 per hectare found on golf course with high population of hedgehogs. Tend to be aggregated, at least for part of the time, especially in gardens. Road mortality used as index suggests a higher density in suburban areas than in rural ones.

Population samples taken in autumn show preponderance of juveniles, but partly because adults already hibernating. At beginning of breeding season 40−45% of population comprises 1-year-old animals.

Mortality of 60−70% in 1st year is suggested by preliminary studies, with good survival over next 2 years, and decline in survival rate after 4th or 5th year [1] — age determined by growth lines in jaw [111] and epiphyseal fusion in the forefoot [112]. Live at least 7 years in captivity; 7 years certainly in wild; population turnover time probably about 8−9 years, maximum life-span may be 10 years.

Population fluctuations unknown — no accurate census method. Vermin bag records are equivocal and unreliable.

PREDATORS AND MORTALITY
Spines adequate protection against most predators, though a few young or sickly animals may be killed by foxes, badgers and dogs. Very occasionally taken by polecat, tawny owl and golden eagle. Large numbers killed on roads, perhaps a significant threat to certain populations. Many die in hibernation, especially during first winter. Mowing machines and pesticides probably kill many, but no data. Some may be incinerated through nesting or hibernating in garden bonfire heaps. Despite ability to swim many drown in garden ponds through inability to climb out. Similarly cattle grids are a potential hazard but many now fitted with escape ramps.

PARASITES AND DISEASE
The flea *Archaeopsylla erinacei* is highly specific and sometimes present in large numbers, up to 500 on one animal. Lice have not been recorded. Ticks and mites are non-specific, but the ticks *Ixodes hexagonus* and *I. ricinus* are frequent, as are the parasitic mites *Demodex canis* and *Otodectes cynotis*, the last causing 'otodectic mange' of the ears.

The parasitic nematodes *Capillaria* and *Crenosoma* ('lungworm') are often present and may result in sickness and death. A ringworm fungus, *Trichophyton erinacei*, is specific to the hedgehog, infecting the skin, especially of the head, of about 20% of British animals, more prevalent in older animals and those living at higher densities [120]. Hedgehogs carry bacteria *Leptospira* [174] and *Salmonella* [171] and the virus of foot-and-mouth disease [99]. Infection with paramyxovirus has been reported [176].

RELATIONS WITH MAN
Traditionally persecuted for predation on eggs of game-birds although damage is relatively insignificant compared to that done by foxes and crows. Formerly eaten in some areas, especially by gypsies who baked them in mud. Has been used for experimental work on viruses (foot-and-mouth disease, influenza and yellow fever). Easy to keep, will breed in captivity [110]. A popular animal, witness support given to British Hedgehog Preservation Society. Frequently kept as pets and introduced to city gardens and to islands. Often encouraged to visit food-bowls put out in gardens, an additional source of food and drink which may account for apparent abundance of hedgehogs in suburban habitats. Probably a useful predator of horticultural pests such as slugs. Afforded partial protection on Schedule 6 of The Wildlife and Countryside Act 1981; trapping requires a licence.

LITERATURE
Morris [115]: a general account. Others out of print, e.g. Herter [76]: a monograph in German. Herter [77]: English translation of a popular German work. Burton [17]: a general popular account.

SOUND RECORDINGS
(Appendix 3): A, C, F, J, P, S, V.

AUTHOR FOR THIS SPECIES
P.A. Morris.

FAMILY TALPIDAE

The mole is the only member of this family found in Britain. The family is represented throughout much of Eurasia and North America. Besides the moles it includes also several species of shrew-mole in eastern Asia and the aquatic desmans of Russia and Iberia. Related to the shrews (Soricidae), but the dentition is less specialised.

GENUS *Talpa*

The moles of the W Palaearctic, comprising about six very similar species, all highly adapted for a subterranean life. The most widespread, *T. europaea*, alone occurs in Britain. Closely related genera occur in E Asia. The dental formula is

3.1.4.3 / 3.1.4.3, i.e. the maximum found in placental mammals.

Mole *Talpa europaea*

Talpa europaea Linnaeus, 1758; S Sweden.

Moldwarp, want, taupe; famh (Scottish Gaelic), gwadd, twrch daear (Welsh).

RECOGNITION

Elongate body with uniformly short, usually black, fur. Prominent features are the broad, spade-like forelimbs, pink fleshy snout and short tail (Fig. 5.6). Ear pinnae are absent while the tapering head being deeply set into the main body gives the appearance of the absence of a proper neck. Seldom seen on the surface and unlikely to be confused with any other animal.

Skull, about 35 mm in length, has continuous tooth rows, each with 11 teeth, enlarged upper canines and very slender zygomatic arches (Fig. 5.7).

Short humerus and broad forefeet are distinctive features of the skeleton often recovered in owl pellets and mammalian scats.

SIGN

Clear evidence are the mole-hills or spoil heaps formed during the excavation of permanent tunnels. These are usually conical in shape with no opening to the surface. Beneath each mole-hill there is a vertical or sloping tunnel through which soil is pushed to the surface. Mole-hills are not permanent features but are continually eroded by the weather and animals and are rapidly colonised by vegetation. In some areas mole-hills may be

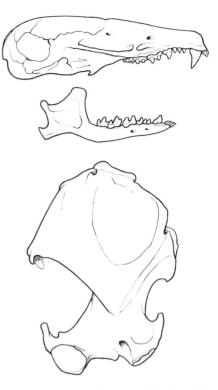

Fig. 5.7. Mole: skull and humerus. The latter is so different from the humerus of any other mammals that it is very easily recognised, e.g. in owl pellets.

confused with the more permanent, and usually larger, steep-sided hills of the yellow ant. When moles are colonising new areas, or feeding in newly cultivated fields, temporary surface tunnels, which appear as slightly raised ridges of soil, may be formed.

Under some circumstances, particularly in low-

Fig. 5.6. Mole: note the cylindrical body with heavy fossorial forelimbs and small tail carried vertically.

lying areas prone to flooding, more permanent hills may be constructed. These are often termed 'fortresses' and may contain a nest chamber above the level of the surrounding ground and several radiating tunnels. Not all moles build these structures. They are built throughout the year, but chiefly in winter, and by both sexes. They often contain large numbers of stored worms.

DESCRIPTION

Anatomy specialised for a fossorial way of life. Body is cylindrical and external features are much reduced in size to facilitate movement through the tunnels. Forelimbs are adapted for digging, being broad and flat and equipped with five large, strong claws. An extra bone, the radial sesamoid, serves to increase their surface area. The much enlarged humerus (Fig. 5.7) is strongly attached to the scapula and to the deep sternum — for details of the musculature, see Yalden [186]. In contrast, the hind limbs are slender and simple in structure. Primarily used for movement, they also serve to brace the body against the tunnel walls whilst digging. The tail is short with a constriction at the base and is usually carried erect. The eyes are reduced in size and although concealed by the thick pelage they are functional [135].

Pelage uniformly short over the whole body, *c.* 6 mm in summer, 9 mm in winter. Only the limbs and snout are largely devoid of fur. The hairs on the tail are sparse and coarse. Colour variable (*see* Variation) but usual velvet black with no sexual dimorphism. Yellow-brown secretions from skin glands form an obvious mid-ventral staining in both sexes, particularly during the breeding season. The skin on the chest is thicker than elsewhere serving to support the body while digging [160]. Short vibrissae on the snout are associated with a group of sensory receptors called Eimer's organs. Fringe hairs on the forelimbs and on the tail are also sensory.

Moult at least twice per year. In spring it begins at the posterior end of the abdomen spreading around the flanks and sides to the back and eventually to the head and shoulders. The autumnal moult proceeds in the reverse order.

External genitalia of males and non-breeding females are similar and the sexes are easily confused. The testes are located outside the abdomen, in sacs near the base of the tail, showing no external swelling. The sexes are best distinguished by the length of the prepuce — > 6 mm in males, < 6 mm in females — and by the length of the perineum — > 5 mm in males, < 4 mm in females [97]. The vagina and uterus merge to form a long, s-shaped median uterovaginal canal into which the two uterine horns open at right angles. The vulva perforates only during the breeding season. There are four pairs of nipples.

Scent glands: paired preputial glands, containing both holocrine and apocrine elements, are involved in scent-marking behaviour. Relatively larger in males than in females, they show marked seasonal changes in weight in both sexes, being largest during the breeding season and regressing thereafter [167].

Skull long and narrow, tapering forward from the middle of the brain-case, the widest point, to just behind the canines. The zygomatic arches are slender and the tympanic bullae flattened. The surface of the skull is smooth apart from a slight sagittal crest which becomes more marked in older animals. When viewed laterally, and in outline, the skull appears long and wedge-shaped and rounded off posteriorly (Fig. 5.7). The incisors are small and simple in structure, followed in the upper jaw by large canines, but in the lower jaw by smaller canines, resembling 4th incisors, and large caniniform first premolars. The other anterior premolars are small, almost rudimentary. The deciduous dentition is rudimentary, does not erupt, and is not detectable after birth except for DP_1 which persists as the functional tooth and is not replaced.

Chromosomes: $2n = 34$; $FNa = 64$ (continental data) [193].

RELATIONSHIPS
T. europaea is very similar to *T. romana* (Italy and Balkans) and the smaller *T. caeca* of S Europe. *T. caeca* has a different karyotype ($2n = 36$) from both *T. europaea* and *T. romana* ($2n = 34$ for both species) [193]. Further east, *T. europaea* is replaced by the more distinctive *T. altaica*.

MEASUREMENTS
Males are generally larger than females (Table 5.1), but body weights and sizes are highly variable and

are not recommended as characters for distinguishing between the sexes.

VARIATION

British animals not distinguishable from continental, and no evidence of clear regional variation in Britain. Abnormal coat colour, including albino, cream, apricot, rust coloured, piebald and grey or silver grey, more frequent than in other British mammals, but no figures for frequencies available.

Premolars variable: at least one upper absent in 0.3% of 8184 animals collected from throughout the range (none out of 880 from England); some lower premolars absent in 0.6% of 8653 (0.2% of 978 from England); 0.1% of 8184 had supplementary, or bicupsid, upper premolars (0.34% of 880 from England); and supplementary lower premolars were present in 2.1% of 8653 (1.7% of 978 from England) [165].

DISTRIBUTION

Throughout the mainland of Britain, wherever habitat is suitable, and on Skye, Mull, Anglesey, Wight, Alderney and Jersey. Absent from Ireland.

HISTORY

Recorded from the early Pleistocene (Cromerian interglacial), and from the last glaciation at Tornewton Cave, Devon [169]. Likely to have been a natural post-glacial colonist but records unreliable because of intrusion.

HABITAT

Highly adaptable; present in most habitats where the soil is sufficiently deep to allow tunnel construction. Originally inhabitants of deciduous woodland, moles have taken advantage of agriculture and thrive in pastures and arable land. They are uncommon in coniferous forests, on moorland and in sand-dune systems probably because of the paucity of suitable prey. Recorded at altitudes up to 1000 m in Wales [106].

Map 5.3. Mole.

SOCIAL ORGANISATION AND BEHAVIOUR

Burrow system: moles spend almost their whole lives in an extensive and elaborate system of tunnels at various depths, from just below the surface to well over a metre down. Digging is done exclusively with the fore limbs, using alternate strokes. The limb is thrust sideways and backwards, by rotation of the humerus, pushing the loosened soil into the tunnel behind the mole. While the mole is digging the hind limbs are braced against the sides of the tunnel, providing support [155]. When a quantity of earth has accumulated behind the animal the mole turns towards the displaced earth which is scooped up with the forelimbs and pushed along

	Males ($n = 42$)		Females ($n = 57$)	
	Mean	Range	Mean	Range
Head and body (mm)	143	121–159	135	113–144
Tail (mm)	33	26–40	32	25–38
Weight (g)	110	87–128	85	72–106

Table 5.1. External measurements of moles from Suffolk [62].

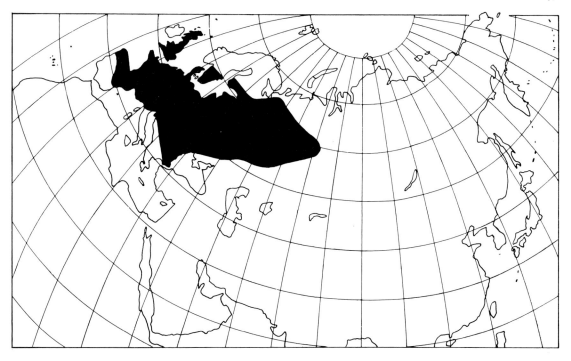

Map 5.4. Mole.

the tunnel to a previously dug vertical, or sloping shaft leading to the surface.

There is usually a single nest, which may be situated anywhere within the home range, but usually away from the periphery. Females may use two or more nests during the breeding season [167]. The nest lies in a chamber formed by enlarging a section of tunnel and is composed of dry grass, leaves or paper, gathered from the surface.

Social dispersion: males and females are solitary for most of the year, occupying largely exclusive territories [167]. If a resident is removed the territory is quickly taken over by neighbours, sometimes within a few hours. During the non-breeding season, a male's territory may overlap slightly with those of one or more females but not, at this stage of the annual cycle, with those of other males. With the onset of breeding, males tunnel over extensive areas in search of receptive females and the ranges of neighbouring males may then overlap considerably [167]. Moles are promiscuous.

Home range size of the female does not vary seasonally. During the non-breeding season, males occupy ranges about twice as large as those of females, but they increase a further three-fold during the breeding season (Table 5.2). The size of the home range is a function of habitat and of population density [167].

Scent is deposited from the preputial glands during routine daily movements. The scent advertises the presence of a resident animal, but is short-lived and must be renewed frequently. Secretions experimentally placed in tunnels will repel other moles [167].

Table 5.2. Home range sizes of moles in NE Scotland (m^2) obtained by radio-tracking [167].

	Breeding			Non-breeding		
	Mean	± SE	n	Mean	± SE	n
Males						
Pasture	7343	± 1381	6	2769	± 374	19
Woodland	7718	± 666	7	3364	± 271	5
Females						
Pasture	1314	± 374	4	1655	± 93	15
Woodland	2086	± 231	3	1945	± 99	3

Dispersal of young follows weaning and is a time of major mortality by predation. Adults rarely disperse once they have established a territory but they may do so following flooding or other disturbance [167].

Aggressive behaviour takes the form of chasing through tunnels and fighting with the forelimbs and teeth. Encounters are rarely fatal since the subordinate individual usually withdraws. Both sexes appear to be equally aggressive towards intruders. Agonistic encounters are rare because moles appear to show temporal avoidance of neighbours, with only one individual using any area of overlap between adjacent territories at any given time [167, 169].

Activity: for most of the year, both sexes have three periods of activity every 24 hours, each lasting for 3–4 hours, followed by a rest period of similar duration taken in the nest. During the breeding season, males may not return to their nests for several days at a time, sleeping at irregular intervals in the tunnel system. Lactating females return to their nests four to six times in each 24 hours, but with no change in the total time spent foraging [167]. During the autumn, males show only two active periods per 24 hours [169]. Males generally spend more time active each day than do females. Moles become active at about the same time each day, regardless of season, with no clear relationship between the onset of activity and sunrise. The onset and cessation of activity is closely synchronised between neighbouring animals [167]. However, another study [185] reported a sudden start of activity at dawn and cessation shortly before dusk, at all times of year. Differences between the two studies may be related to the fact that in the latter the moles were in captivity without competing neighbours.

Grooming involves hind feet and teeth only.

FEEDING

Food obtained almost exclusively in the tunnel system which acts as a pitfall trap for soil invertebrates. Incidental food may be obtained whilst digging and very occasionally moles are seen scavenging on the surface [67, 167]. Earthworms, particularly *Lumbricus terrestris*, are the single most important prey. Insect larvae are taken in large numbers, myriapods and molluscs less so. Diet reflects prey abundance, with earthworms predominating in winter and insects becoming more important in summer [88]. Food, particularly earthworms with their anterior segments mutilated, is commonly stored at all times of the year, but particularly in spring and autumn. Up to 470 worms (820 g) recorded in a store [46, 156]. An 80 g mole requires about 50 g of earthworms per day (*c.* 185 kJ/g per day) [62, 72].

BREEDING

A litter of usually three or four young born in spring, sometimes, especially in the south of England and Europe, followed by a second.

The breeding season is short with a rapid enlargement and regression of gonads and accessory organs. The onset of breeding varies with latitude, strongly suggesting that it is timed by changes in photoperiod. First pregnancies recorded in March in England [62] and in May–June in NE Scotland [136, 167]. The ovaries consist of two distinct parts, the gametogenic ovary and an interstitial region which is active during anoestrus and which probably produces androgens [39, 97]. Oestrus probably lasts for less than 24 hours. Gestation is *c.* 4 weeks. The average number of embryos in Britain is 3.8 [62] but means of 5.7 have been recorded in continental samples. The rate of embryo resorption is variable; in one study 6% [88], in another 25%, including 20% of litters totally resorbed [109]. Second litters occur in S England and are common in continental populations.

The young are born naked, *c.* 3.5 g. Fur starts to grow at 14 days and the eyes open at 22 days, when they weigh *c.* 40 g. Lactation lasts for 4–5 weeks. Juveniles start to leave the nest at *c.* 33 days and finally disperse at 5–6 weeks [59]. Dispersal occurs above ground. By 3 months of age juveniles are difficult to distinguish from adults on the basis of body proportions. Moles become sexually mature in the spring following their birth.

POPULATION

Sex ratio in adults is 1 : 1, but during the breeding season males outnumber females in captured samples due to their increased movements [167].

Population densities of 8 per hectare in winter and 16 in summer have been reported in English pastures [88]. In NE Scotland densities in woodland and pasture remain similar throughout the year at 4–5 per hectare [167]. The density of mole-hills is not an accurate measure of population size.

Population structure: most of the animals within a population are aged 1 year or less; most individuals do not live beyond 3 years, although some live up to 6 years. In some populations three age classes are identifiable on the basis of tooth wear [53]. Males and females live to similar ages [91]. All populations studied seem fairly stable compared to the fluctuations shown by other small mammals, particularly rodents.

MORTALITY

Predation is most severe during the surface dispersal of juveniles. Major causes of mortality are tawny owls, buzzards, stoats, domestic cats and dogs, and vehicles [67, 162, 167]. Persecution by man is still a major source of adult mortality but much less so than previously.

PARASITES AND PATHOGENS

The permanent nest is conducive to infestation by ectoparasites. The following fleas have been recorded [157]: *Palaeopsylla minor*, *P. kohauti*, *Ctenophthalmus bisoctodentatus*, *C. nobilis* and *Hystrichopsylla talpae*. No lice have been recorded. The fur mite *Labidophorus soricis* and the tick *Ixodes hexagonus* are often present.

Internal parasites include the trematodes *Ityogonimus* spp. [51], the blood protozoans *Trypanosoma talpae* and *Babesia microti* [34], and *Elleipsisoma thomsoni* [107]. The fungi *Emmonsia crescens* and *Aspergillus fumigatus* have been found in the lungs and may be pathogenic [2]. Serological evidence of bacterial infection with *Leptospira* has been reported [174]. *Mycobacterium tuberculosis* var. *bovis* was isolated from 1.3% of a sample of moles from SW England [94].

RELATIONS WITH MAN

Moles are generally regarded as a pest by farmers, horticulturists and green-keepers but usually they do little real damage. The construction of surface tunnels following cultivation damages the roots of seedlings causing them to wilt. Mole-hills produced during the construction of deeper tunnels not only cover plants, but may also damage machinery, and can lead to undesirable fermentation in silage.

Moles are beneficial in that they prey on many harmful insect larvae including those of cockchafers and carrotflies. Digging brings small archaeological artefacts to the surface and the tunnel systems may aid drainage and aeration in heavy soils.

At the beginning of the century moles were trapped in large numbers for their pelts. Current control is largely by strychnine poisoning, although less cruel alternatives are being actively sought.

Moles can be kept in captivity with relative ease.

LITERATURE

Godfrey & Crowcroft [62] and Mellanby [102] give general accounts. Quilliam [135] contains 15 research papers on many aspects of mole biology. Rudge [143] provides information on live-trapping and keeping in captivity. Basic study methods, including the use of radioactive tags are described in Godfrey [59], Meese & Cheeseman [101], and Woods & Mead-Briggs [185]. Stone & Gorman [169] and Stone [167] describe behavioural studies involving radio-telemetry. Stone [168] is a popular account of the species.

AUTHORS FOR THIS SPECIES

R.D. Stone & M.L. Gorman, with acknowledgement for comment by A.R. Mead-Briggs.

FAMILY SORICIDAE (SHREWS)

A widespread family containing a multitude of small forms, all insectivorous or carnivorous, which live mainly on the ground in leaf litter and grass. An important element in any community, breaking down animal tissue and returning materials to the soil. They are cosmopolitan except in polar regions, the Australian region and central and southern South America. Their geological range in Europe extends back to the early Oligocene, some 39 million years bp [192]. Gross form of shrews has changed little since early Tertiary.

Characterised externally by narrow pointed snout, small eyes, short rounded ears with complex lobes in the conch, short legs, plantigrade feet with five digits, slender tail and rather short, dense pelage (Fig. 5.8). There are scent glands on the flanks, marked when well-developed by a line of short white hairs.

No functional milk dentition. First incisors very large, followed in upper jaw by up to five small, single-cusped (unicuspid) teeth (Fig. 5.9). Remaining premolars and molars (P3–M3) large, with high pointed cusps. Tympanic bone annular and loosely attached to the skull, zygomatic arches lacking, mandibles with double articulating surfaces.

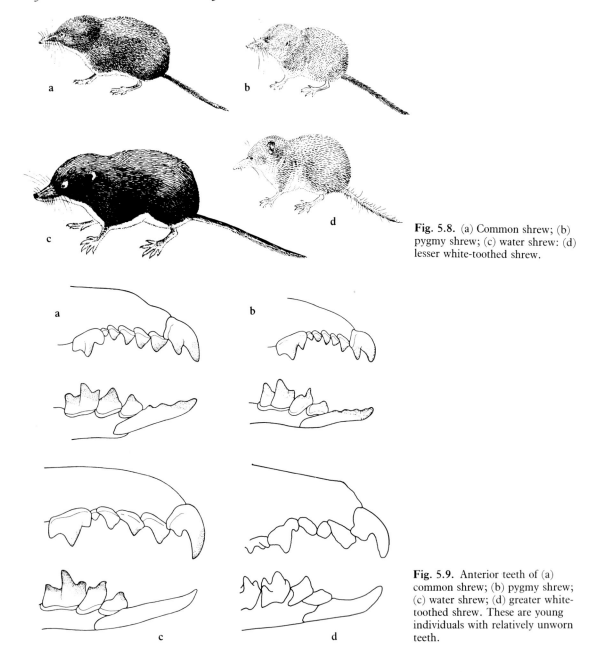

Fig. 5.8. (a) Common shrew; (b) pygmy shrew; (c) water shrew: (d) lesser white-toothed shrew.

Fig. 5.9. Anterior teeth of (a) common shrew; (b) pygmy shrew; (c) water shrew; (d) greater white-toothed shrew. These are young individuals with relatively unworn teeth.

Prominent, very large lymph-gland in abdomen — 'pancreas of Aselli' [173]. Testes ventral but internal; female tract T-shaped; no pubic symphysis.

Shrews are very voracious, with little resistance to starvation, and are active day and night and throughout the winter.

There are *c.* 250 species, in about 20 genera. The two dominant genera, *Sorex* and *Crocidura*, are both represented in Britain. Aquatic forms, represented in Britain by the water shew (*Neomys*), are also found in E Asia (*Nectogale* and *Chimarrogale*) and in North America (*Sorex palustris*). Some species are mole-like and fossorial, e.g. *Anourosorex*

Table 5.3. Identification of the genera of shrews.

	Sorex	*Neomys*	*Crocidura*
Colour of back	Brown	Black	Greyish brown
Scattered long hairs on tail	No	No	Yes
Keel of stiff hairs on underside of tail	No	Yes	No
Fringes of stiff hairs of hind feet	Slight	Prominent	Slight
Colour of teeth	Red-tipped	Red-tipped	White
Upper unicuspid teeth	5	4	3
First lower tooth (upper edge)	Wavy	Smooth	Smooth

squamipes in SE Asia. Allied to *Crocidura* is the genus *Suncus* with a large commensal species in tropical Asia as well as one of the smallest of all mammals, *S. etruscus*, in the Mediterranean region weighing under 2 g. The characters of the three genera in Britain are compared in Table 5.3.

GENUS *Sorex*

The dominant genus of shrews in the northern parts of Eurasia and North America, with about 40 species almost equally divided between the two continents. The teeth are red-tipped due to the deposition of iron in the outer layer of enamel [42] which may increase resistance to wear. There are five pairs of unicuspid teeth behind the large first incisors and the tail lacks the long, prominent tactile hairs found in *Crocidura*.

The two species found on the British mainland can be distinguished as in Fig. 5.8 and Table 5.4.

Common shrew *Sorex araneus*

Sorex araneus Linnaeus, 1758; Uppsala, Sweden.
Sorex vulgaris Nilsson, 1848.
Sorex tetragonurus Hermann, 1780; France.
Sorex grantii Barrett-Hamilton & Hinton, 1913; Islay, Inner Hebrides, Scotland.

Shrew mouse, ranny; llygoden goch, chwistl (Welsh); beathacan feior, luch shith, feornachan (Scottish Gaelic).

RECOGNITION
Easily distinguished from water shrew by brown upper surface, smaller size and, in the hand, by the evenly haired tail, lobed first lower teeth and the presence of a very small, fifth upper unicuspid tooth on each side (Fig. 5.9a). More difficult to distinguish from pygmy shrew but the sharp contrast between colour of the back and flank is distinctive and so are the relatively shorter tail and larger overall size. Length of the hind foot and the

Table 5.4. Identification of shrews of the genus *Sorex*.

	Common shrew	Pygmy shrew
Pelage	Tri-coloured, flanks contrasting with back and belly	Bi-coloured, flanks not distinctly coloured
Head and body (mm)	48–80	40–60
Tail (mm)	24–44	32–46
Tail : head and body (%)	50–60	65–70
Hind foot (mm)	12–13	10–11
Weight (g)	5–14	2.4–6.1
Length of upper tooth row (mm)	8.0–8.8	6.2–6.6
Third unicuspid tooth	Smaller than second	Larger than second

skull, and the size of the third unicuspid tooth relative to the second, are good indicators to species (*see* Table 5.4).

SIGN

Footprints: five toes on both forefeet and hind feet. Smaller than those of water shrew and of small rodents. Gait plantigrade.

Faeces almost black in colour and 3–4 mm in length. Occasionally found deposited at random or in groups in runways through the vegetation. Heterogeneous, slightly granular consistency due to chewed pieces of chitinous exoskeleton of invertebrates and snail shells.

Calls: produce a high-pitched, rapid 'chee-chee-chee' sound, just audible to the human ear, when threatened or alarmed. Often heard in summer when population density is high, particularly in hedgerows.

Burrows: make small holes for runways through ground vegetation and excavate burrows or modify those of other small mammals; not very distinctive.

DESCRIPTION

Pelage dark brown dorsally in immatures during winter and adults in summer contrasting sharply with the pale brown flanks and the grey, yellow-tinged ventral surface. Juveniles can be distinguished by their lighter brown dorsal pelage in summer before their first moult. Tail bi-coloured, of even width and, in juveniles, well-haired with a prominent terminal pencil of hairs. Tail hairs are not renewed and by the second summer the tail is almost naked, making adults and juveniles clearly distinguishable. Ears occasionally bear small tufts of white hairs after the first moult, contrasting sharply with the dark brown pelage.

Sexes very similar externally except for prominent inguinal bulges containing the testes and larger lateral flank glands in adult males, and the presence of nipples in adult females. Breeding females often have a bare or grey-haired patch on the nape of the neck where they have been held during copulation. Immature shrews can be sexed externally by the presence of a patch of intensely pigmented fur

surrounding each of the nipples in females and their absence in males [105, 147].

Moult in autumn from juvenile to winter pelage starting at the rump and moving forward to the head, dorsal surface being ahead of ventral. Two spring moults proceed in the opposite direction, starting on the head, and are completed earlier in females than in males [7]. Length of hair increases from about 3.5 mm in summer to 6–7 mm in winter [7].

Nipples: three inguinal pairs.

Scent glands: lateral flank glands situated mid-way between the forelimbs and hind limbs on a line separating the lighter belly fur from the dark upper pelage. They are small, oval areas, well-vascularised, containing many sebaceous and sweat glands and bordered by stiff hairs. They produce a slightly greasy, highly odoriferous secretion which rubs off on objects as the shrew brushes past. Present in both sexes throughout their life-time but most active in mature males at the onset of the breeding season. Those of females in breeding condition are poorly developed, possibly so as not to discourage males. Scent is also produced with the faeces.

Teeth: unicuspid teeth decreasing rather evenly in size from front to back.

Reproductive tract: in males, testes abdominal, 1.5–2.0 mm long in immatures, 7–8 mm in mature individuals when they show as large inguinal swellings. Female tract T-shaped; vagina and uterus thicken and widen greatly at maturity; combined length of uterine horns increases from 4–7 mm in immatures to over 17 mm in breeding condition.

Seasonal changes: undergo seasonal changes in size and body weight with marked decrease during winter of up to 27% brought about by shrinkage of the skeleton, notably the cranium, and of certain internal organs including the adrenal bodies, as well as reduction in body water content [24, 121, 133, 134, 152], followed by rapid gain in weight in spring as they mature.

Chromosomes: very unusual in that the number is variable, 21–33 in males, 20–32 in females, due

Fig. 5.10. Common shrew: juvenile. (Photo: P. Morris.)

to Robertsonian polymorphism affecting elements that may form metacentric and/or acrocentric chromosomes. FNa = 36; multiple sex chromosomes: females XX and males usually XYY [50, 103].

Three distinct karyotypic races have been described: an 'Aberdeen' race in the northern and western periphery of Britain, a central and eastern 'Oxford' race, and a 'Hermitage' race more intermediate in range, supporting the hypothesis that the races spread into Britain at the end of the last glaciation in successive waves [148].

RELATIONSHIPS
Closest relatives are *S. coronatus* (France, Switzerland, Jersey), *S. granarius* (NW Spain) and *S. arcticus* (Siberia) [70].

MEASUREMENTS (*see* Table 5.4).

VARIATION
British population has been distinguished subspecifically from continental on basis of duller dorsal colour, but this no longer stands up to scrutiny (*S. tetragonurus castaneus* Jenyns, 1838; Burwell

Fen, Cambridgeshire [84]). No good evidence of discrete subspecies within continental range and therefore British population can be allocated to *S. a. araneus*.

No evidence for geographical variation within British mainland except in karyotype, but some island populations show slight differentiation. Most distinctive is that on Islay, *S. a. grantii*, characterised by very grey flanks and frequent lack of fifth unicuspid teeth. Fifth unicuspids absent on at least one side in 52% of shrews on Islay (*n* = 23); 5% on island of Skomer (*n* = 126); 1.1% on British mainland (*n* = 465). On island of Bardsey (Wales), where pygmy shrew is absent, common shrew is significantly smaller than on the mainland [33].

Gross colour variation extremely rare: only one case of melanism recorded in Britain [66], albinos more frequent. Minor albinism of the ear tufts is frequent, e.g. 20% [37]; albinism of the tail tip seems to vary geographically: 4.5% in England and Wales, 8.8% in Scotland [30].

DISTRIBUTION
The whole of Europe except for the Mediterranean region, but replaced south-westwards from NE

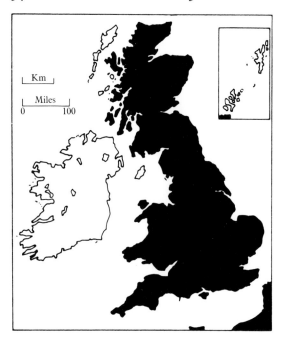

Map 5.5. Common shrew.

France through Switzerland, and on Jersey, by the closely similar French shrew *S. coronatus*. North to the Arctic coast and east into Siberia as far as the River Yenesei.

Throughout the mainland of Britain at all altitudes, and on the following islands: Raasay, Crowlin, Skye, Scalpay (Skye), Soay (Skye), Colonsay, Mull, Ulva, Lismore, Scarba, South Shuna, Luing, Jura, Islay, Gigha, Arran, Bute, Anglesey, Bardsey, Skomer and Isle of Wight. Definitely absent from the Shetlands, Orkneys, Outer Hebrides, Isles of Scilly, from the remaining larger islands of the Inner Hebrides, and from the Channel Islands.

HISTORY

Fossil remains have been found at Cat Hole, Glamorgan, dating from the Bølling Interstadial of the late Glacial Period around 12 500 – 13 000 years bp when an equable, warm temperate climate with an open type of vegetation such as birch scrub was prevalent [190]. Subsequent deterioration in climate between 11 000 and 10 000 years bp probably extinguished most, if not all, the mammal fauna including shrews.

The earliest well-dated remains in England come from the post-glacial (Flandrian) at the Mesolithic

Map 5.6. Common shrew.

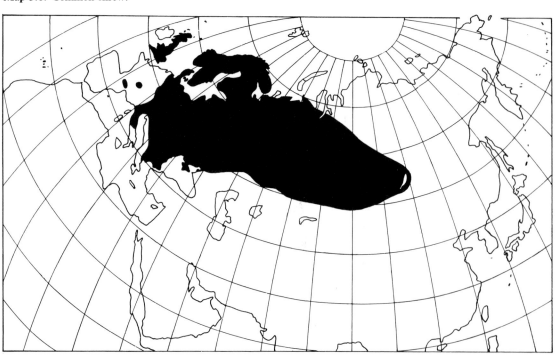

site at Thatcham, Berks which radiocarbon dating has put at 10050–9600 years bp. By this time essentially modern, temperate woodland faunas had established themselves in Britain.

Presence on some of the inner islands around Britain, e.g. Skye and Mull, is probably due to natural immigration from nearby mainland. Fossil evidence suggests that the common shrew has decreased slightly in size since the Pleistocene.

HABITAT

Found almost everywhere provided some low vegetation cover is available. Most abundant in thick grass, bushy scrub, hedgerows and deciduous woodland. At high altitudes, found occasionally amongst heather and more frequently in stable scree (to at least 1000 m). Climb quite well and have been found to occupy nests of harvest mice in bushes.

SOCIAL ORGANISATION AND BEHAVIOUR

Social Organization: essentially solitary except when mating and rearing young, and extremely aggressive towards each other. Young disperse shortly after weaning and individuals of both sexes establish their own home ranges and territories where intruders are not tolerated. Home ranges may overlap at peripheries but are largely mutually exclusive [14, 102, 148]. Some evidence that these areas are marked with scent from lateral flank glands as animals push through the vegetation [127]. Territories largely abandoned in spring with onset of breeding, particularly by males who greatly extend their home ranges in the search for females.

Home ranges vary considerably in size according to habitat and season and may decrease in winter [22, 153]. Mostly 370–630 m^2 in size but occasionally up to 1100 m^2 [105, 122]. Once established, home ranges remain quite discrete and in the same location for the remainder of the life-time.

Active both day and night, with about 10 periods of almost continuous activity alternating with shorter periods of rest. Most active during darkness and least in the early afternoon; peaks of activity at about 1000 and 2200 hours [22, 35, 83, 124]. Less active on ground surface in winter than in summer [22, 26, 152]. Periods of complete inactivity last only a few minutes at a time. Shrews usually return to the nest to rest but will cat-nap away from the nest.

Aggressive behaviour: very aggressive and pugnacious towards each other at all times once independence from the mother achieved, regardless of age or sex. Intruders are immediately rebuffed. On meeting, both individuals freeze momentarily and then commence loud squeaking and rearing on the hind legs. One may retreat and a chase ensues, sometimes resulting in a scuffle when they aim bites at each other's heads and tails, and kick out with the forelegs. One may throw itself on to its back while kicking and squeaking, and the other rushes off [37]. Often lash their tails rapidly from side to side when excited.

Movements are swift and bustling, using mobile snout to explore and probe amongst vegetation, leaf litter and soil. Occasionally rear up on hind legs and appear to sniff the air. Swim well, but do not dive underwater.

Burrowing: make their own surface runways through the vegetation, but also use those of voles and mice. Keen but rather ineffectual burrowers, and readily use and modify burrows of other small mammals plus naturally occurring crevices.

Nests: usually below ground in burrows, but also on the ground surface under logs or patches of dense cover. Nests are rounded and made of dried grass and leaves and have several entrances. Nests made for bearing young are particularly large and dome-shaped.

Groom: by scratching vigorously with hind feet and by licking the fur.

Refection: will occasionally curl up on side or back, particularly during day-time rest period, and lick the anal area and the everted rectum from which a milky-white fluid is produced [37]. This may have a similar function to coprophagy in the extraction of nutrients.

Sense: olfactory, auditory and tactile senses well-developed but sight is poor. Large vibrissae on the snout may assist prey detection by tactile means. Locate prey by probing with snout and digging using a combination of smell and touch. Able to locate prey hidden 12 cm deep in soil [23].

Vocalisation: produce soft, high-pitched but audible twitters intermittently during foraging and exploring. Use similar sounds in interactions between female and young. Very young shrews produce loud barks when separated from the mother. Characteristic raucous, high-pitched, staccato shrieks punctuated by harsh 'churls', just audible to the human ear, are emitted when alarmed or threatened, and are used in aggressive interactions between individuals; particularly evident in males.

FEEDING

Opportunistic predators feeding on a wide variety of common invertebrates, particularly beetles, earthworms, woodlice, spiders, slugs, snails and insect larvae. Over 33 different invertebrate taxa have been found in the diet. Prey range in size from small mites and springtails to large earthworms. Sixty to 82% of prey were found to be larger than 6 mm in body length and most in the range 6−10 mm, which correlated with the preponderance of small invertebrates available amongst soil and ground vegetation [1]. A positive correlation between the availability of certain prey (including beetles, earthworms, woodlice and molluscs) and their incidence in the diet has been found [25, 144]. Small quantities of plant material including seeds are also taken.

Shrews discriminate between prey and show preference for some and distaste for others. Millipedes and some molluscs (such as *Oxychilus alliarius* and *Arion hortensis*) are not favoured; amongst woodlice, *Philoscia muscorum* is highly preferred to other species [37, 126, 144]. They attack the head first to immobilise prey and usually eat it from the head down. Large wings, legs and other unpalatable parts are normally discarded. In captivity, readily cache surplus food in the nest or in a small depression in the soil which is covered by leaves.

They require 80−90% of their body weight in food daily or 6.7−9.7 kJ/g per day, rising to 1.5 times their body weight when lactating [21, 37, 72]. The high food intake has been attributed to the high water content of prey and the quantity of indigestible chitinous exoskeleton ingested.

Feeding habits are reviewed by Rudge [144]; Pernetta [126]; Churchfield [25, 27].

BREEDING (Fig. 5.11)
Gestation: 24−25 days.
Litter size: 1−10, mean six.
Weight at birth: 0.5 g.
Duration of lactation: *c.* 24 days.

Season: shrews overwintering as immatures rapidly reach maturity in March and April, males slightly earlier than females. Breeding season lasts from April to September with a peak in July and August. Number of litters per female per season is variable, commonly two but can be up to four. Initially, most females conceive at post-partum oestrus, but later, lactation dioestrus becomes more extended until the breeding season finishes. Embryo number and litter size decline as the season progresses [36, 127], first through a decrease in the ova shed and later through foetal mortality. Old adults die off at the conclusion of the breeding season. Females rarely become sexually mature in the year of their birth, although a few females from early litters may do so [132, 164] (Fig 5.11).

Mating: males seeking to mate are frequently rebuffed by females. Female is only receptive when in oestrus which may last less than 24 hours. Little courtship, and mating is brief; male mounts the female and uses his teeth to hold her by the scruff of the neck or top of the head [37]. Male shows no further interest in the female after mating. Ovulation probably follows copulation and most females become pregnant shortly after first oestrus [9].

Sex ratio is *c.* 1 : 1 but bias towards males is common in trapped samples, particularly in spring and summer.

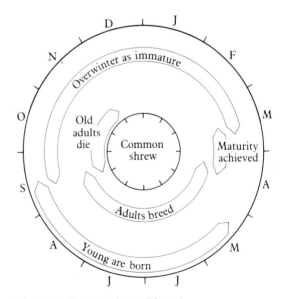

Fig. 5.11. Common shrew: life-cycle.

Young are naked and blind at birth. Growth very rapid and linear in the first 14 days. Nine days after birth pelage is evident as a soft, grey down; by 11 days the teeth have developed the characteristic red tips; by 14 days they have achieved a weight of 5−7 g and eyes are beginning to open. By 16 days the eyes are fully open, and young first venture outside the nest at about 18 days old. They take their first invertebrate prey at *c.* 21 days old, are weaned at 22−25 days old and are fully independent thereafter. Caravanning behaviour of young with the mother, just prior to weaning, has been observed, apparently resulting from disturbance of the nest [69].

POPULATION

Densities very variable but in summer peak of 42−69 per hectare reached in deciduous woodland and grassland [36, 152, 187], 7−21 in dune scrub and scrub-grassland [21, 105]. Much lower in winter, between 5 and 27 per hectare.

Age structure: young born during summer carry the population over the ensuing winter as immatures. They mature the following spring and breed during the summer, then die off in late summer and autumn. Young animals can be distinguished from the parent generation in summer by their paler colour, hairier tails and unworn teeth.

Survival: life-span is 15−18 months [9]. Life-tables and survivorship curves have been calculated [22, 26, 105, 127]. Juvenile cohort is reduced by 50% during first 2 months of life due to mortality and dispersal; *c.* 40−50% survive to 6 months and 20−30% survive to breed. Overwintering survival is relatively high, 80−100% [23, 105]. Mortality of old adults following breeding has been attributed to tooth wear, to competition with juveniles for food and nest sites, and an inability to maintain a territory.

MORTALITY

Main predators are owls, but stoats, weasels and foxes do take shrews. They constitute about 5% by weight in diets of tawny owls in woodland, being taken most frequently in summer and autumn [162], and 6−13% in diet of barn owls [13]. They are frequently killed by domestic cats, but are distasteful to them and rarely eaten. Dispersing juveniles are particularly vulnerable to predation.

Table 5.5. Ectoparasites recorded from shrews in the British Isles.

	Common shrew	Pygmy shrew	Water shrew	White-toothed shrews Lesser	Greater
Fleas					
Ctenophthalmus nobilis	+	+	+	+	+
Doratopsylla dasycnema	++	++	++		
Hystrichopsylla talpae	+	+			
Nosopsyllus fasciatus				+	+
Palaeopsylla soricis	++	++	++		
Typhloceras poppei					+
Mites					
Euryparasitus emarginatus	++	++	+		
Haemogamasus arvicolorum		+			
Haemogamasus hirsutus		+			
Haemogamasus horridus	++				
Labidophorus soricis	++		+		
Myobia blairi				+	
Myobia michaeli					+
Ticks					
Ixodes dorriensmithi				+	
Ixodes ricinus	++	+			
Ixodes trianguliceps	++	+			

+, Present; ++, particularly common.

	Common shrew	Pygmy shrew
Tapeworms (cestodes)		
Choanotaenia crassiscolex	+ +	+ +
Choanotaenia hepatica	+	+
Neoskrjabinolepis singularis	+ +	+ +
Staphylocystis furcata	+	+
Staphylocystis scalaris	+ +	+ +
Staphylocystis scutigera	+ +	+ +
Flukes (digeneans)		
Brachylaimus oesophagei	+ +	+ +
Dicrocoelium soricis	+ +	+ +
Round worms (nematodes)		
Capillaria incrassata	+ +	
Capillaria oesophagicola	+ +	+
Longistriata depressa	+ +	+
Porrocaecum talpae	+ +	+ +

Table 5.6. Helminth parasites recorded from common and pygmy shrews in Britain [193].

+, Present; + +, particularly common.

PARASITES (Tables 5.5, 5.6)

Fleas: the most abundant are *Palaeopsylla soricis* and *Doratopsylla dasycnema*, found only on shrews. The rodent flea *Ctenophthalmus nobilis* is regular and the large 'mole' flea *Hystrichopsylla talpae*, is less frequent. Several other rodent fleas are found occasionally.

Mites and ticks: the fur mite *Labidophorus soricis* is frequent, and nest mites such as *Euryparasitus emarginatus* and *Haemogamasus horridus* are commonly carried in the pelage. Larval ticks such as *Ixodes ricinus* and *I. trianguliceps* are common. Seasonal distribution of *I. trianguliceps* studied by Randolph [137].

Endoparasites: a nematode, *Porrocaecum talpae*, is very common, curled under the skin, the final hosts being owls. Tapeworms and flukes are numerous in the stomach and alimentary canal. The intermediate hosts of most of the internal parasites are invertebrate prey of shrews, particularly molluscs and beetles.

Common shrews have been found to carry the bacteria *Mycoplasma* [19, 63], *Leptospira* [174], *Mycobacterium tuberculosis* var *muris*, *Campylobacter jejuni* and *Yersinia enterocolitica* [73] and a number of other species of common enteric bacteria [74]. Infections with the virus causing louping ill in

sheep [159] and with the ringworm fungus *Trichophyton persicolor* [45] have also been detected.

RELATIONS WITH MAN

Beneficial by preying on large numbers of potential pest invertebrates, including leatherjackets (tipulid larvae), caterpillars and plant bugs.

Easy to trap but quickly die of cold, starvation and stress unless traps are visited every 2 hours or so. Quite easy to maintain in captivity on a diet of maggots, fly pupae, mealworms (or other live prey) plus fresh meat and eggs.

Common everywhere, so no special requirements for conservation. In common with all species of British shrews, it is protected by law (Wildlife and Countryside Act 1981). It is an offence to kill shrews without a special licence.

SOUND RECORDING (Appendix 3)
A.

AUTHOR FOR THIS SPECIES
S. Churchfield.

French shrew *Sorex coronatus*

Sorex coronatus Millet, 1828; Blou, Maine-et-Loire, France.
Sorex fretalis Miller, 1909; Trinity, Jersey, Channel Islands.

Map 5.7. French shrew.

'*Sorex araneus* chromosome type A', Meylan, 1964. *Sorex gemellus* Ott, 1968; Rhone Valley, Switzerland.

DESCRIPTION
An allopatric sibling species very similar to *S. araneus* but differing in karyotype. Small morphological differences have been detected. On the basis of measurements, particularly of the mandible, it is slightly smaller than *S. araneus* on the continent [70, 71], but the two species are difficult to distinguish except by karyotype. On Jersey, it differs from *S. araneus* of mainland Britain by the longer rostrum (upper tooth-row and mandible) relative to length of skull (Table 5.7).

Chromosomes: 2n = 20; FNa = 40, on Jersey [50] and continent [187]. Unlike *S. araneus*, it does not exhibit chromosome polymorphism.

MEASUREMENTS
See Table 5.7 for skull measurements.

Table 5.7 Differences in skull dimensions between *Sorex coronatus* on Jersey and *S. araneus* in mainland Britain (Oxfordshire): mature animals in May–June.

	French shrew (*n* = 13)		Common shrew (*n* = 13)	
	Mean	Range	Mean	Range
Condylobasal length (mm)	18.46	18.0–18.9	18.88	18.3–19.4
Upper tooth row length (mm)	8.40	8.0–9.2	7.68	6.7–8.2
Mandible length (mm)	7.79	7.2–8.1	7.01	6.7–8.3

DISTRIBUTION
On the Channel Islands confined to Jersey. Not recorded from mainland Britain.

HABITAT
Much as for common shrew. On Jersey, found in coastal habitats of sand dunes, heath and scrub as well as inland in deciduous woodland, hedgebanks and gardens [60].

Resembles common shrew in all its habits.

AUTHOR FOR THIS SPECIES
S. Churchfield.

Pygmy shrew *Sorex minutus*

Sorex minutus Linnaeus, 1766; Barnaul, W Siberia.
Sorex pygmaeus Laxmann, 1769; Barnaul, Siberia.
Sorex rusticus Jenyns, 1838; near Cambridge, England.

Lesser shrew; luch féir (Irish Gaelic); thollag-airhey (Manx).

RECOGNITION
Much smaller than common shrew but tail proportionately longer, thicker and more hairy (*see* Table 5.4). Lacks distinctly coloured flanks, and colour of back never as dark as in adult common shrews (Fig. 5.12).

Unicuspid teeth distinctive, third being larger than or at least as large as second (in common shrew it is smaller than second). *See* Fig. 5.9.

SIGN

Footprints as for common shrew but smaller.

Faeces similar but smaller than those of common shrew and not easily distinguishable. Apparently deposited at random.

Calls not often heard in the wild but a high-pitched, very short 'chit' when threatened or alarmed.

Burrows: use burrows of other small mammals.

DESCRIPTION

Pelage medium brown above, similar to juvenile common shrew, separated by a rather obscure dividing line from the dirty-white ventral pelage. Tail as in common shrew but longer relative to body length (see Table 5.4). Tail becomes naked in second calendar year. Adult males and females can be distinguished externally by inguinal bulges containing the testes in males, and by teat spots in females, as in common shrew. Live immatures practically impossible to sex reliably.

Moult similar to that of common shrew, but no seasonal variation in colour. Autumn moult is between August and November and proceeds from tail to head; two spring moults between March and June proceeding in the opposite direction [8, 64].

Fig. 5.12. Pygmy shrew; juvenile. (Photo: P. Morris.)

Nipples: three inguinal pairs.

Scent glands on flanks as in common shrew.

Teeth as in common shrew except for large size of third unicuspids.

Reproductive tract as in common shrew and with similar seasonal changes. Testes 6 mm in mature individuals, visible as inguinal bulges; 0.8−1.2 mm in immatures. Combined length of uterine horns 4−7 mm in immatures, up to 15 mm in breeding condition.

Seasonal changes in size and weight of body and certain internal organs as in common shrew, with marked decrease in weight in winter in order of 28% [64].

Chromosomes: 2n = 42; FNa = 54 [193].

MEASUREMENTS (*see* Table 5.4).

VARIATION
Very little geographical variation, and none between Britain and continent nor within British mainland. In Ireland and the Outer Hebrides, where common shrew is absent, the pygmy shrew is slightly larger than elsewhere [95], but not enough to justify subspecific rank. (The name *S. rusticus* var. *hibernicus* Jenyns, 1838 has been applied to the Irish form on the basis of supposedly *smaller* size and more uniform colour). Albino and cream-coloured individuals rare; albinism of the tail-tip less frequent than in common shrew — two out of 75 [30].

DISTRIBUTION
The whole of Europe except for the Mediterranean region, eastwards through Siberia to the Yenesei and in the mountains of central Asia south to the Himalayas.

Throughout the mainland of Britain and Ireland at all altitudes and very widespread on the smaller islands. Absent from the Shetlands, Isles of Scilly and Channel Islands, but present on all other islands with an area in excess of 10 km² and on the following smaller islands. Orkney: Flotta; Hebrides: S Rona, Pabay (Skye), Soay (Skye), Pabbay (Outer Hebrides), Scarba, Iona, Gigha, Sanda (Kintyre); Great Cumbrae, Ailsa Craig, Skomer, Lundy; Ireland: Rathlin, Tory Island,

Aranmore, Inishkea, Achill, Clare, Irishmore, Irishman, Great Blasket, Clear, Sherkin, Great Saltee.

HISTORY
Has the oldest fossil record of the European shrews, dating back to the beginning of the Pleistocene about 2 million years ago. At the end of the Pliocene, *S. minutus* was one of at least four species of shrew present in W Europe. Fossil evidence suggests that it has decreased in size slightly since the Pleistocene.

Its occurrence in Britain probably parallels that of the common shrew. It may have reached Ireland by a low-lying land bridge from Scotland via Islay in a short period around 8000 years bp when sea level was at its lowest [190]. It is significant that pygmy shrews outnumber common shrews on wet peaty moorland such as may have prevailed on such a land bridge. Neither do these shrews rely on earthworms and burrows as do common shrews. Yalden [189] suggests that this could have favoured the spread of pygmy shrews but not common shrews to Ireland.

Its presence on the remoter islands (in the absence of common shrew), e.g. Orkney, Lewis and Barra can only have occurred by human intro-

Map 5.8. Pygmy shrew.

duction, perhaps with shipments of fodder or live-stock, but survival of the journey would be difficult with its high metabolic rate and ease of starvation.

HABITAT

Widespread in all types of habitat, mostly wherever there is plenty of ground cover. Generally less abundant than common shrew: 12% of shrew captures in woodland and wood-edge, 35% on dunes [21, 78]; 10–18% in grassland [26, 37]. Generally shows a preference for grassland over woodland. Largely ground-dwelling but readily climbs up into shrubs.

SOCIAL ORGANIZATION AND BEHAVIOUR

Social organisation: solitary, and aggressive towards others of the same species. Territorial behaviour much as in common shrew. Territories of immatures are largely mutually exclusive but strict territoriality abandoned at sexual maturity, particularly in males as they search for mates [105].

Home ranges as in common shrew but significantly larger. Mean size 1400–1700 m² in grassland in

Britain [127]; 530–1860 m² in dunes in Netherlands [102]. Territories increased in size in winter [105, 127]. Home range size is also high in Ireland despite absence of other shrew species. Apparently no significant difference in territory sizes (or population densities) in Irish compared with Dutch habitats [44], but in some areas where common shrew is absent population densities can be higher (and so home ranges may be smaller) than in areas where they are sympatric [96].

Activity about equal by day and night. More frequent alternation of rest and activity periods than in common shrew and relatively more active during the day [36, 64]. Two main peaks of activity in captivity, at 0800–1000 hours and 2100–2300 hours [36]. They spend relatively more time on the surface of the ground than underground compared with common shrews; in the Netherlands it was found that in winter *c.* 50% of their time is spent above ground compared with only 20% for the common shrew [105].

Aggressive and intolerant of others of the same species, but not as pugnacious as common shrew.

Map 5.9. Pygmy shrew.

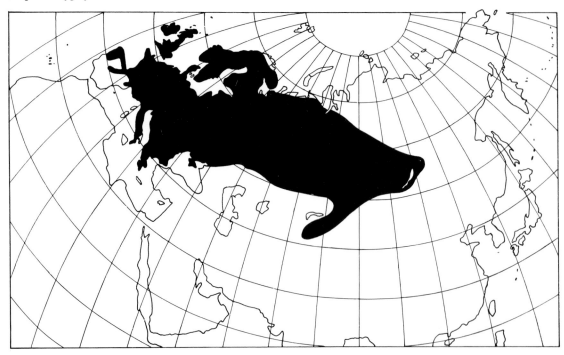

Tend to avoid contact with other individuals. On meeting, they produce a single short 'chit' sound and immediately move off in different directions. They lash the tail rapidly from side to side when angry, as in common shrew.

Locomotion: dart rapidly over the ground with movements and reactions even faster than common shrew. Use snout to probe amongst ground vegetation. Climb and swim well.

Burrowing: make surface tunnels through moss and grass, but are poor burrowers, using instead the burrows and runways of other small mammals together with natural crevices.

Nests, grooming and **refection** as for common shrew [37].

Senses: olfactory, auditory and tactile senses well-developed, as in common shrew, but do not dig for prey.

Vocalisation: much less vocal than common shrew and infrequently heard. Unlike common shrew, does not emit audible twitters during foraging and exploration. Produces a short, audible 'chit' when threatened or alarmed and on meeting another individual.

FEEDING
Feeding habits are very similar to those of common shrew. Thirty-five different invertebrate taxa were identified in the diets of Irish shrews from various habitats, including grassland, mixed woodland and sand dunes [64]. Most important in all sites were beetles (20% by composition), woodlice and adult flies (each *c.* 13%), insect larvae 10%, spiders and bugs (*c.* 8% each); all were taken consistently throughout the year. Spiders and harvestmen (particularly *Nemastoma*), beetles and woodlice were the dominant prey of English pygmy shrews [27, 126]. Earthworms are not eaten but small slugs and snails are occasionally taken, along with small amounts of plant material.

Tend to take more smaller prey than common shrews: Pernetta [126] found most prey were 2–6 mm in length; Churchfield [27] found 86% of prey were under 10 mm. Given a choice of different woodlice, captive pygmy shrews took more of the smaller ones, particularly *Trichoniscus pusillus*, than the common shrew [37]. Like common shrews, they reject millipedes.

Food intake in captivity is 1.25 times body weight or 9.7–13.0 kJ/g body weight per day [21, 72].

BREEDING
Gestation: 22–25 days.
Litter size: four to seven.
Weight at birth: *c.* 0.25 g.
Duration of lactation: *c.* 22 days.

Season: as with common shrews, pygmy shrews generally overwinter as immatures and mature in the following March and April. They breed in April to October with a peak in June and July. In Poland, 22% of breeding females have been born in the same calendar year [132] but no evidence of this in Britain. First oestrus and ovulation apparently always followed by pregnancy, but in some females a lactation anoestrus occurs. Reproduction reviewed by Brambell & Hall [10].

Mating similar to common shrew.

Sex ratio *c.* 55% females [10, 64].

Young take the same time to weaning as common shrew, but rate of growth proportionately more rapid; from 0.25 g at birth to *c.* 2.5 g at 14 days old, retaining this weight until weaning [37].

POPULATION

Densities generally considerably lower than in common shrew. Maximum 12 per hectare (mean 6) in grassland in England [127], 4–11 per hectare (mean 8) on sand dunes in the Netherlands [105] and mean 5 per hectare in forest in Czechoslovakia [122]. Peak numbers in summer and autumn, lowest in winter and spring.

Age structure: as in Common shrew; juveniles distinguished from adults by hairier tails.

Survival: peak mortality at 2–4 months of age when population reduced by *c.* 50% [105, 127]; *c.* 20% survive to breed [105]. Generally have a higher mortality rate throughout life than common shrew. Life-span *c.* 13 months in the wild, up to 16 months in captivity.

MORTALITY
High, supposedly due to predation. Main predators are owls but pygmy shrews comprised only *c.* 6%

of shrews and 0.3% of the total prey found in pellets of tawny owls over an 8-year period [162]. They comprised up to 5% of total prey of barn owls on mainland Britain [13, 57] but more in Ireland [188]. Taken occasionally by foxes, and possibly by stoats and weasels. Often killed by domestic cats but, as with common shrew, rarely eaten.

PARASITES (*see* Tables 5.5 and 5.6).

RELATIONS WITH MAN
Much as for common shrew, but encountered less frequently. Protected by law.

SOUND RECORDINGS
(Appendix 3): A, F, J.

AUTHOR FOR THIS SPECIES
S. Churchfield.

GENUS *Neomys*

A fairly distinctive genus of three Palaearctic species distinguished by black dorsal pelage, red-tipped teeth, presence of four pairs of upper unicuspid teeth and smooth, unlobed first lower incisors. The British species is quite strongly aquatic with fringes of hair on tail and feet, but in *N. anomalus*, found mainly in the montane forests of central and eastern Europe, these characters are less pronounced. *N. schelkovnikovi* (Caucasus) is close to *N. fodiens*.

Water shrew *Neomys fodiens*

Sorex fodiens Pennant, 1771; Berlin, Germany.
Sorex aquaticus Müller, 1776; France.
Sorex bicolor Shaw, 1791; Oxford, England.
Sorex ciliatus Sowerby, 1805; Norfolk, England.
Amphisorex pennanti Gray, 1838; England.
Crossopus sowerbyi Bonaparte, 1840.

Otter shrew, water ranny; labhallan (Scottish Gaelic).

RECOGNITION
Distinguished from all other British shrews by black dorsal fur, large size and habit of swimming and diving. In hand, fringe of silvery hairs on underside of tail and on margins of all feet are distinctive (although other shrews have shorter fringes on feet).

Skull distinguished from *Sorex* by absence of fifth unicuspid teeth, more strongly hooked upper incisors and absence of lobes on large lower incisor.

SIGN

Footprints as for common shrew, but larger.

Faeces similar but larger than those of common shrew and black in colour. Often found in middens on rocks beside streams, at tunnel entrances or in surface runways through vegetation.

Prey remains of invertebrates, particularly caddis fly larval cases and mollusc shells, often left at feeding sites on stream banks.

Calls: produce loud audible squeaks and rolling 'churr-churr' as a threat or alarm signal when calling to each other. Most frequently heard in summer.

Burrows made in banks of streams, rivers and drainage ditches approximately 2 cm in diameter at entrance. Burrow entrances are rounded in cross-section and, unlike those of bank voles, have little disturbance of vegetation around them, and no chopped-up plant material nearby. Also use burrows of bank voles and wood mice.

DESCRIPTION

Pelage: upper surface black, often with a small tuft of white hairs on the ears and/or white hairs around the eyes. Underside is silvery grey with a sharp line of demarcation and with a variable wash of yellow or brown in the mid-line. Tail dark brown above, white below with hairs of the mid-ventral line elongate and stiff, forming a continuous keel. Similar fringes of stiff, white hairs on the margins of the fore and hind feet probably aid in swimming.

Moult: Autumn and spring moults probably as in *Sorex araneus*, with hair changing from head to tail in spring and reverse in autumn. Also occasionally a summer moult, proceeding from head to tail [151].

Nipples: five inguinal pairs (unlike *Sorex* which only has three pairs).

Scent glands on flanks highly developed in adult

males only, fringed with white hairs. Situated on thorax, further forward than in *Sorex* spp.

Teeth: first upper incisors are large with very long, curved anterior cusps while posterior cusps are shorter than in other species (see Fig. 5.8). The large, lower incisors have a smooth upper surface with only a single, ill-defined lobe.

Reproductive tract poorly developed out of breeding season. Testes abdominal and large (7−9 mm) in breeding condition; only 2.5−3 mm in immatures. Female tract T-shaped, vagina and uterus enlarging greatly in breeding season.

Viscera: a vascular plexus in interscapular adipose tissue resembles typical, if poorly developed, *retia mirabilia* of diving mammals [82].

Seasonal changes: evidence of decrease in size and weight of body and internal organs in winter, similar to common shrew.

Chromosomes: 2n = 52; FNa = 92 on Continent [187].

MEASUREMENTS
Head and body: 67−96 mm.
Tail: 45−77 mm.
Hind foot: 15−16 mm.
Weight: 12−18 g (pregnant females up to 28 g).
Upper tooth row: 8.5−9.4 mm.

VARIATION
British population not distinguishable from continental. Colour of ventral pelage very variable, melanism being quite frequent. Few data available on insular populations, but some may be distinctive, e.g. those on Shuna (Strathclyde) are small with uniformly pale grey ventral pelage [31]. Albinos occur rarely.

DISTRIBUTION
Throughout mainland Britain but probably rather local in N Scotland. Absent from Ireland and many of the small islands, but present on Hoy (Orkney), Raasay, Skye, Pabay (Skye), Mull, S Shuna (Strathclyde), Garvellachs (all four main islands), Islay, Kerrera, Arran, Anglesey, Isle of Wight and possibly on others. Recorded at 420 m in Wales [29].

HISTORY
Probably much as for common shrew. Fossil remains of a very similar shrew found in lower Pleistocene deposits of Cromer Forest Bed Series.

HABITAT
Mainly the banks of clear, fast-flowing, unpolluted rivers and streams, but also found by ponds and drainage ditches. Especially numerous at watercress beds. In NW Scotland they occur amongst boulders on rocky beaches. Occur sporadically far from water (up to 3 km) in deciduous woodland, hedgerows and grassland. In Poland, also found in coniferous woodland [40].

SOCIAL ORGANISATION AND BEHAVIOUR
See Köhler [85] for review of behaviour.

Social organisation: essentially solitary except when mating and rearing young, but live in quite close proximity to neighbours. No evidence of hierarchies. Territorial in captivity, and may use faecal deposits to delineate territories in addition to scent from flank glands in males.

Home ranges *c*. 20−30 m^2 on land, 60−80 m^2 including water surface along brooks in West Germany [81]; overlap at peripheries. May be several water shrews inhabiting burrow systems in close proximity.

Active by day and night, but mostly during darkness. Peak activity just before dawn and least active in late morning [36]. Less active on ground surface in winter than spring and summer [27, 43]. Activities mostly restricted to a small stretch of bank and nearby water. Daily movement in order of 10−60 m, rarely 150−200 m [26, 81, 182]. Move around less in winter than summer. Appear to spend only a brief time (a few months) in one area before passing on, exhibiting intermittent nomadic existence with frequent shifts of home range [26, 129, 154].

Aggressive behaviour: more tolerant of each other than are common and pygmy shrews. Introduction of a stranger provokes strident squeaking and 'churr-churr' sound (in captivity and in wild) and may be accompanied by chases and scuffles [15, 21]. Resident usually victorious, but pugnacity gradually diminishes and they will co-exist particularly if they can establish separate nests.

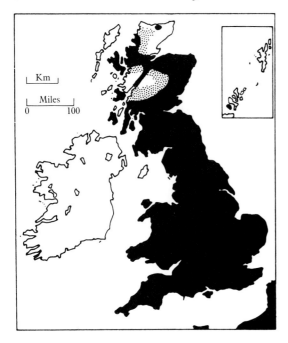

Map 5.10. Water shrew.

Map 5.11. Water shrew.

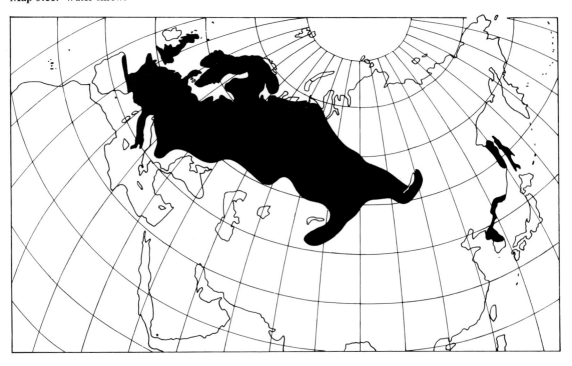

Locomotion as for common shrew on land. When swimming, use all four limbs in dog-paddle fashion. Dive frequently, when the propulsive force comes mainly from the hind feet. Can dive up to 75 cm or more in still water, but body very buoyant with air trapped in the dense coat and can only remain submerged for a few seconds. Often anchor against rocks and plant stems to remain submerged.

Burrowing: inhabit extensive burrow systems in banks of streams, usually with entrance above water, and may take over and modify burrows of other small mammals. Burrow using forefeet and teeth to loosen soil, and hind feet and mouth to remove soil and small stones [21, 37, 92, 93].

Nests usually below ground in burrows. They make rounded sleeping nests of moss, dried leaves and grass, even small stones, with one or two entrances. Nests for young are much larger.

Groom mostly after swimming. Water removed from pelage by frequent shaking, scratching with hind feet and squeezing through narrow burrows. Fur very water-repellent but may become wet with frequent dives.

Senses: olfactory, auditory and tactile senses well-developed, but sight poor. Sensitive, mobile vibrissae on snout may assist in prey detection.

Vocalisation: high-pitched twitters while exploring and foraging; loud squeaks and rolling 'churrs' in aggressive interactions.

FEEDING

They forage on land and underwater throughout the year on a wide variety of invertebrates plus small fish, frogs and newts [12, 27, 173]. Over 33 different prey taxa have been found in the diet. In Britain, 33−67% (mean 50%) of prey taken are aquatic and the dominant prey in all months are freshwater crustaceans (*Gammarus* and *Asellus*) and cased caddis larvae. Other major prey are terrestrial beetles, spiders, centipedes, molluscs and earthworms. The diet overlaps considerably with that of common and pygmy shrews, and water shrews can subsist entirely on terrestrial prey when living away from water. Feeding habits reviewed by Churchfield [27, 28]. They consume *c.* 50% of their body weight daily of 3.8−5.9 kJ/g per day [21, 72].

Aquatic prey are brought ashore to be eaten, and food caches of killed and partially-eaten prey are sometimes made [12]. Prey are usually attacked at or just behind the head. They will take prey, particularly amphibians, considerably larger than themselves. There is some evidence that immobilisation of prey may be assisted by a venom, produced in saliva by submaxillary glands, which affects the nervous, respiratory and blood systems when injected into mice [131]. A bite to man produces a burning pain and reddening of the skin which persists for a few days.

BREEDING

For account of reproduction and social behaviour see Michalak [104].
Gestation: 19−21 days.
Litter size: 3−15, mean 6.
Weight at birth: *c.* 1 g.
Duration of lactation: 38−40 days.

Breeding season extends from April to September, reaching a peak in May and June [130]. Although some females may breed in their first calendar year, most commence breeding in their second calendar year. Generally have one to two litters per breeding season (max. three). Litter size declines as season advances. They are seasonally polyoestrus; female can become pregnant at post-partum oestrus. Ovulation probably stimulated by coitus.

Mating: much as for common shrew.

Sex ratio *c.* 1 : 1, but slight bias towards males common in trapped samples.

Young are born blind and naked. Dorsal pigment is apparent by 4th day, and fur develops by 10th day. Young first leave the nest at 23−25 days old, but retain close bonds with mother. Weaned and reach independence at 27−28 days in captivity, but remain together with mother for about 40 days. First signs of aggressive behaviour within the family at *c.* 50 days old.

POPULATION

Densities vary greatly according to site and season, but always lower than those of common shrew, even on the Continent. Maximum of 3.2 per hectare recorded in water-cress beds in S England [26], but probably an underestimate. Peak numbers in summer.

Age structure: some may survive into a second winter, but the overwintering population comprises largely immatures born in the preceding summer which themselves mature and breed the following spring and summer. Juveniles have hairier tails than adults.

Survival: life-span is 14−19 months [40, 130], most adults dying at conclusion of the breeding season. Juveniles suffer high mortality during the dispersal phase in the first 2 months of life, but survival rate remains fairly steady from 3−8 months of age (equivalent to the overwintering period) followed by a steep decline in adult survival during the breeding season [26].

MORTALITY

Predators include carnivorous mammals, birds and fish. They form 3−6% of total number of shrews recovered in tawny and barn owl pellets [58, 162, 166] and only about 0.2% of the total prey.

PARASITES

See Table 5.5. In addition, known to carry *Trypanosoma* sp. [34]. Carriage of the bacteria *Campylobacter jejuni* and *Yersinia frederiksenii*, both capable of causing enteric infections in man, has recently been detected [73].

RELATION WITH MAN

As with other shrews, useful in preying upon potential pest invertebrates. May be threatened in Britain by habitat destruction, particularly in S England, through pollution of streams and disturbance and modification of banks. In common with other shrews, it is now protected by law.

SOUND RECORDINGS
(Appendix 3): A, F, J.

AUTHOR FOR THIS SPECIES
S. Churchfield.

GENUS *Crocidura* (WHITE-TOOTHED SHREWS)

A very large, homogeneous group containing *c.* 125 species distributed throughout the Afrotropical, Oriental and southern Palaearctic regions. Distinguished by unpigmented teeth, three upper unicuspids, long scattered hairs on the tail, and more prominent ears than in *Sorex* or *Neomys*. Represented in the British Isles only on the Isles of Scilly and Channel Islands. The two species concerned are rather difficult to distinguish, but so far have not been found on the same island. In Table 5.8 the more critical dental differences are placed first.

Lesser white-toothed shrew *Crocidura suaveolens*

Sorex suaveolens Pallas, 1811; Crimea, Russia.
Crocidura cassiteridum Hinton, 1924; Isles of Scilly.

Scilly shrew; garden shrew.

RECOGNITION

See Table 5.8. It is the only species of shrew on the islands on which it occurs, except for Jersey where the French shrew is also found. The lesser white-toothed shrew is slightly smaller and paler than the French shrew. It has long, scattered hairs on the tail and wholly white teeth (Fig. 5.13).

SIGN

Footprints similar to common shrew.

Faeces similar to common shrew, but have a characteristic sweet, musky odour. Often deposited in piles in prominent places.

Calls: produce high-pitched squeaks when threatened or alarmed and soft twittering sounds when exploring.

Burrows not clearly distinguishable from those of other small mammals.

Food remains of invertebrate prey, particularly littoral amphipods (sandhoppers), can sometimes be found under rocks and amongst seaweed.

Table 5.8. Identification of white-toothed shrews.

	Lesser white-toothed shrew	Greater white-toothed shrew
Length of upper unicuspids (at cingula): labial length of large premolar	< 1.3	> 1.3
Second unicuspid smaller than third (in crown view)	Markedly	Slightly
Lingual part of large upper premolar	Smaller	Larger
Length of upper tooth row (mm)	7.4–8.0	7.7–8.5
Head and body (mm)	50–75	60–90
Tail (mm)	24–44	33–46
Hind foot (mm)	10–13	10.5–14.0
Weight (g)	3–7	4.5–14.5

DESCRIPTION

Pelage greyish or reddish brown above, and slightly paler ventrally. Little seasonal variation; slightly longer and thicker in winter and in spring when ventral fur may be lighter coloured. Ears short-haired and prominent. Tail covered with short bristly hairs interspersed with fine, long, white hairs.

Sexes very similar externally except for inguinal bulges containing the testes and prominent lateral glands in adult males, and prominent nipples in oestrous and lactating females. Immature animals very difficult to sex reliably.

Moult: males tend to moult before females, and some show successive moults. Spring moult usually begins on ventral surface of head, spreading dorsally and posteriorly. Autumn moult is more rapid and proceeds in reverse direction, commencing on posterior and moving anteriorly and ventrally.

Nipples: three inguinal pairs.

Scent glands on flanks, marked by a fringe of short white hairs, are present in both sexes in all seasons, but are better developed in males. Caudal glands at the base of the tail are absent (cf. greater white-toothed shrew). Exude a sweet, musky odour.

Teeth unpigmented; three upper unicuspids, with second markedly smaller than third.

Reproductive tract similar to that of common shrew.

Seasonal changes: young born in late summer and autumn show slackening of development during winter, but body weight continues to increase, albeit very slowly. Winter decrease in size and body weight of immatures so characteristic of *Sorex* and *Neomys* is not found in *Crocidura*, but adults undergo weight reduction and slight regression of testes in autumn after breeding [141].

Chromosomes: no data from island populations; 2n = 40; FNa = 46 on the Continent [193].

RELATIONSHIPS
Most similar to *C. russula* with which it is sympatric in continental Europe.

MEASUREMENTS (*see* Table 5.8).

VARIATION
Animals from the Isles of Scilly once described as a distinct species and subsequently subspecies (*C. s. cassiteridum* Hinton, 1924) [79] on basis of darker colour; subsequent evidence suggests this separation is invalid. Populations from various Scilly

Fig. 5.13. Lesser white-toothed shrew from the Isles of Scilly. (Photo: H.N. Southern.)

Islands are more alike than those from Jersey or Sark, but, on the basis of skull and tooth-row lengths, are intermediate in size between Sark populations which are the largest and those from Jersey which are the smallest [41].

DISTRIBUTION

Apparently absent from most of Spain and NW France, but present on French offshore islands of Quessant and Yeu.

    In the Channel Islands occur on Jersey and Sark. In the Isles and Scilly, found on all but some of the smaller islands (certainly occurs on St Mary's, St Martin's, Tresco, Bryher, St Agnes, Gugh, Samson and Tean).

HISTORY

In Europe, it has essentially a southern distribution, and is likely to have been introduced to the British islands by man. Iron Age or earlier traders from France or N Spain probably introduced it to the Isles of Scilly when they came to the Cornish coast in search of tin.

HABITAT

Found in most habitats offering adequate cover, commonly in tall vegetation including bracken and also in hedgebanks and woodland. Occur amongst boulders and vegetation on the shores of the Isles of Scilly, and even amongst rotting seaweed on the tide lines. On Jersey, found mostly in coastal habitats on sand dunes, scrub, heath and in the boulder zone [61]. Common in the maquis scrub in France.

SOCIAL ORGANISATION AND BEHAVIOUR

Social organisation: essentially solitary, but not nearly as pugnacious as *Sorex*. Home ranges of individuals overlap, so probably not highly territorial. Can be kept together in groups in captivity where they generally ignore each other, but will share nests. Males are apparently dominant to females, and old to young. Indulge in 'belly marking' both in home range and, more often, in unfamiliar areas: hind feet are spread and the belly and anal area are pressed to the ground and dragged

Map 5.12. Lesser white-toothed shrew.

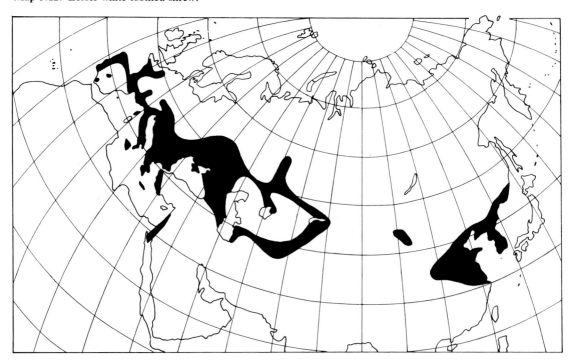

forward using forefeet. Both lateral flank glands and the anal area touch the ground during marking, so scent could be deposited from either or both. 'Chinning' has also been observed, but less frequently: underside of chin is rubbed several times against prominent objects [128]. Defaecate in prominant places, possibly also to mark out home range.

Home ranges: show low territoriality compared with *Sorex* and *Neomys* [54]. In the Isles of Scilly, males tend to have larger home ranges (average length 50 m, maximum 80 m) than females (27 m) or juveniles, although home ranges are smaller on Bryher [142, 163]. Adults have firmly established home ranges but juveniles shift theirs sometimes; individual home ranges often overlap considerably [142].

Active by day and night, but generally less diurnal than greater white-toothed shrew, with 80% of activity occurring at night [60]. In captivity, has peaks of activity at 0400–0500 hours and 1800–1900 hours [128]. Has well-marked feeding rhythms with a mean cycle length of 30–50 min [61]. Diurnal activity increases during summer months. Can be induced to reduce metabolism and become quite torpid [80].

Aggressive behaviour: when disturbed or threatened, assumes a crouched posture with head raised and teeth bared while emitting a single, sharp metallic squeak. On meeting, the intruder rears on to hind legs while resident lunges towards its neck; this results in the flight of the intruder and a chase by the resident.

Locomotion as for common shrew, but less agile and quick.

Burrowing: able to excavate their own burrows but often use those of other small mammals. Tunnel through loose humus and leaf litter, and often active under fallen logs and heaps of brushwood or stone.

Nests constructed of dried grass and twigs amongst thick grass or under logs, rocks or boulders. Spherical in shape with a tightly-woven roof and a single chamber with several exits.

Grooming: as in common shrew.

Refection observed to take place as in common shrew, in the nest while animal lies on its side.

Senses as in common shrew; vision probably not very important; smell well-developed.

Vocalisation: soft, continuous twittering is emitted while foraging and exploring. Sharp, metallic squeaks produced when threatened or alarmed.

FEEDING
On the shores of the Isles of Scilly, feed predominantly on crustaceans, especially the littoral amphipod *Talitroides dorrieni*, millipedes, adult and larval flies (particularly *Thoracochaeta zosterae* amongst rotting seaweed), adult and larval beetles (including *Cercyon littoralis*), spiders and mites [125, 163]. In captivity, will readily take various insects including grasshoppers, butterflies and moths; spiders and woodlice, fresh fish, meat and grain are also eaten. Metabolic rate is relatively low compared with *Sorex* and *Neomys*. Food intake is 4.2–8.0 kJ/g per day or 55% of body weight [21, 72].

BREEDING
Gestation: 24–32 days.
Litter size: one to six, mean three.
Weight at birth: *c.* 0.6 g.
Duration of lactation: *c.* 22 days.

Breeding season from March to September. Females have post-partum oestrus which permits lactation and pregnancy to occur simultaneously, and they give birth about once a month in captivity. May produce three to four litters per year, possibly more. Some males and females breed in calendar year of their birth [141].

Mating: much as in common shrew.

Sex ratio: significant bias towards males in trapped samples [141].

Young: litter size is significantly smaller on average than in *Sorex* and *Neomys*; young are born blind and hairless, but are slightly better developed. Young remain hairless for 7–9 days after birth, but growth is rapid and linear for 10–15 days. Eyes are open at 10–13 days, and young are fully haired by 16 days old when they take solid food. They show caravanning behaviour from 8th day, particularly when they first leave the nest [68]: the mother leads the young along in a line, each grasping the base of the tail of the one in front. This may be a response to disturbance of the nest in the wild. The young can become sexually mature by 45–50 days old, unlike *Sorex* and *Neomys*.

POPULATION

Densities are greater on Isles of Scilly than on Channel Islands; a maximum of one per 30 m^2 has been recorded on the Isles of Scilly [125]. Peak numbers occur in summer with low numbers in winter. On Jersey, where it coexists with the French shrew, neither species is very abundant [5].

Age structure: as in common shrew, juveniles swell the population in spring and summer, and replace the old adults as they die off in autumn.

Survival: life-span is longer than in *Sorex:* can live up to 4 years in captivity, but rarely survive more than 12–18 months in the wild and are unlikely to live through a second winter. Suffer greatest mortality as juveniles.

MORTALITY

On Channel Islands, owls, foxes, weasels and domestic cats are probably important predators. On the Isles of Scilly possible predators include kestrels and domestic cats. In France, occasionally taken by stoats, foxes, genets and possibly snakes [49].

PARASITES (*see* Table 5.5).

Fleas: two rodent fleas, *Nosopsyllus fasciatus* and *Ctenophthalmus nobilis*, occur on shrews in the Scilly Isles, the latter flea also on Sark specimens.

Roundworms: liver nematodes occur in shrews on St Martins, Scillies, especially those caught near the shore [125].

RELATIONS WITH MAN

Beneficial to man by preying on potential pest invertebrates. Easier to keep and breed in captivity than *Sorex* or *Neomys*, and survive better in live traps than these shrews. Protected by law.

SOUND RECORDINGS

(Appendix 3): A, T.

AUTHOR FOR THIS SPECIES

S. Churchfield.

Greater white-toothed shrew *Crocidura russula*

Sorex russulus Hermann, 1780; near Strasbourg, France.

House shrew

RECOGNITION

Slightly larger than lesser white-toothed shrew, but absolutely separable only by the dental characters shown in Table 5.8. Otherwise the two species are very similar. In Britain, it occurs only on some Channel Islands where it is the only species of shrew.

SIGN

Footprints similar to common shrew.

Faeces as for lesser white-toothed shrew.

Calls: high-pitched squeaks when threatened or alarmed; soft twitters when foraging and exploring.

Burrows not clearly distinguishable from those of other small mammals.

DESCRIPTION

Pelage: upper surface greyish or reddish brown; ventral surface is yellowish grey and duller, and not sharply demarcated from upper surface. Little seasonal variation. Ears prominent and tail furnished with long, white hairs as in lesser white-toothed shrew.

Sexes very similar. Adults can be sexed as in lesser white-toothed shrew but nipples of females are hidden by dense pelage when female is non-oestrus, making sex determination difficult. Immatures are very difficult to sex reliably.

Moult as in lesser white-toothed shrew.

Nipples: three inguinal pairs.

Map 5.13. Greater white-toothed shrew.

Scent glands on flanks as in lesser white-toothed shrew; also subcaudal and lateral caudal glands at the base of the tail, causing thickening. Exude a sweet, musky odour.

Teeth unpigmented; three upper unicuspids with second unicuspid only slightly smaller than third.

Chromosomes: no data from island populations; 2n = 42; FNa = 58 on Continent [193].

RELATIONSHIPS
Very similar to *C. suaveolens* with which it is sympatric in continental Europe.

MEASUREMENTS (*see* Table 5.8).

VARIATION
Guernsey form has been described as a subspecies (*C. r. peta* Montagu & Pickford, 1923 [108]) purely on the basis of smaller average size compared with continental animals; no longer considered a distinct subspecies, but variation between Alderney, Guernsey and continental populations has been demonstrated [41].

DISTRIBUTION
SW Europe, east to central Germany [20]. Also on some Mediterranean islands and in North Africa.

In Britain, known only on Alderney, Guernsey and Herm of the Channel Islands.

HISTORY
Fossil remains of *Crocidura* (probably *C. russula*) have been found in S Britain, for example at Tornewton Cave, Devon [145] but the dating is uncertain. *Crocidura* was widespread in Europe in interglacial times, and these remains may date from the Ipswichian interglacial. *Crocidura* could, therefore, be a glacial relict in the islands it now occupies, but only if it could have tolerated tundra conditions. It is most likely that *C. russula* was introduced to the Channel Islands. The irregular distribution of both species on the Channel Islands remains difficult to explain and points to human introduction.

HABITAT
Fairly common in woodland, hedgerows, grassland, cultivated areas and particularly around human settlements and buildings (hence its continental name of house shrew). In France, common along dry stone walls and in the maquis scrub.

SOCIAL ORGANISATION AND BEHAVIOUR

Social organisation: essentially solitary, but more social than *Sorex*. Much as for *C. suaveolens*, including nest sharing. In captivity, form pairs during breeding season and show aggression towards other individuals; male shows tendency to shelter young and crouches over them; female tolerates presence of adult male in nest with offspring even when she is out feeding [161, 178]. Defaecate in prominent places and probably mark home ranges.

Home ranges: show low territoriality compared with *Sorex* and *Neomys*; home ranges $75-395\,\text{m}^2$ with some overlap between individuals [54]. Group behaviour found in captivity, and will often live in pairs [177].

Active by day and night, but more diurnal than *C. suaveolens*, with $35-45\%$ of activity during the day [60]. Daily activity in wild remains fairly constant throughout the year, with activity periods accounting for 33% of total time. Activity polyphasic with one phase every 2 hours lasting about 35 min [56]. Distinctly less active than common shrew, with shorter activity periods and longer rest periods. Can be induced to reduce metabolism and become quite torpid [180].

Aggressive behaviour much as in *C. suaveolens*, aggressive towards strangers.

Locomotion as for common shrew, but less agile and quick.

Burrowing as for *C. suaveolens*.

Nests constructed of dried grass amongst thick grass or under logs and rocks; open and saucer-shaped, reflecting the more diurnal habits compared with *C. suaveolens*.

Grooming as for common shrew.

Senses as in common shrew; vision probably not very important; olfaction well-developed. Acquire knowledge of environment mainly by tactile exploration then orientate by spatial memory [65].

Vocalisation: soft twittering produced when exploring; high-pitched squeaks emitted when alarmed or threatened.

FEEDING
A wide range of invertebrates are taken. In West Germany over 20 different invertebrate taxa recorded in the diet but dominant items were woodlice, centipedes, lepidopteran larvae (each *c.* 9% by composition), gastropods and spiders (each 7%); less important were earthworms, beetles, aphids and millipedes; earthworms and caterpillars increased in importance in winter; small amounts of plant material were also eaten [4]. Lizards and small rodents are occasionally eaten [48]. No evidence for potent venom in saliva [3].

As with other species of *Crocidura*, characterised by a relatively low metabolic rate compared with *Sorex* and *Neomys* [181]. Food intake is *c.* 3.4 kJ/g per day or 48% of body weight [21].

Prey located chiefly by olfactory and tactile means. Easily able to locate food buried 5 cm deep in sand [146].

BREEDING
Gestation: $28-33$ days.
Litter size: $2-11$, mean four.
Weight at birth: $0.8-0.9\,\text{g}$.
Duration of lactation: *c.* 28 days.

Breeding season from February to October in Channel Islands [5]. In captivity, they reach sexual maturity at $58-71$ days old, females slightly before males, and can remain fertile for just over 1 year [179]. In wild, some reach adult weight and breed in the year of birth, at least on the Continent [19]. Females are polyoestrus with post-partum oestrus but no evidence of delayed implantation. Probably produce several litters per year as in *C. suaveolens*, and up to eight litters in a lifetime [179].

Mating as in common shrew, but in captivity they form pairs during the breeding period [179].

Litter size smaller on average than in *Sorex* and *Neomys*, and young are slightly larger at birth.

Milk has a high protein content (10%) correlated with rapid growth rate of young [75]. Show caravanning behaviour from the 7th day and when young first leave the nest. By 8–9 days old the eyes are open and pelage is fully developed. Weaned at about 20–22 days. For accounts on breeding and development see [47, 177, 178, 179].

POPULATION

Densities of 77–100 per hectare on the Continent, with peak numbers in summer and low in winter [54, 55]. Not nearly so abundant on Channel Islands.

Age structure: as in *C. suaveolens*, young appear in May and June; they dominate the population by August, replacing old adults, and grow to adulthood as they overwinter [5]. First and 2nd-year animals distinguishable by height of M^3 [6].

Survival: average life-span in captivity is 2–2.5 years, maximum 4 years. Some may survive a second winter but in the wild very few survive longer than 1.5 years [5, 179].

MORTALITY
Predators include barn owl, tawny owl, weasel and domestic cats. In France, occasionally taken by stoats, foxes and genets [49].

PARASITES (*see* Table 5.5).

Fleas: on Guernsey, the following rodent fleas have been found on these shrews: *Typhloceras poppei*, *Rhadinopsylla pentacantha*, *Ctenophthalmus nobilis*, *Nosopsyllus fasciatus* (the last also from Alderney) [5].

Tapeworms of the genus *Hymenolepis* occur in continental animals, so may also occur on shrews in the Channel Islands.

RELATIONS WITH MAN
Beneficial to man by preying on potential pest invertebrates. Often found around houses, outbuildings and gardens on the Continent. Fairly easy to maintain and breed in captivity, and survive better in live traps than *Sorex* or *Neomys*. Protected by law.

SOUND RECORDING
(Appendix 3): A.

AUTHOR FOR THIS SPECIES
S. Churchfield.

REFERENCES

1 Author's data.
2 Austwick P. (1968) Mycotic infections. *Symposia of the Zoological Society of London* **34**:249–71.
3 Bernard J. (1960) A propose de l'action predatrice des Soricidae sur les petits rongeurs. *Säugetierkundliche Mitteilungen* **8**:25–7.
4 Bever K. (1983) Zur Nährung der Hausspitzmaus, *Crocidura russula* (Hermann, 1780). *Säugetierkundliche Mitteilungen* **31**:13–26.
5 Bishop I.R. (1962) *Studies on the life histories, ecology and systematics of small mammals inhabiting the Channel Islands.* MSc. thesis, University of Southampton.
6 Bishop I.R. & Delany M.J. (1963) Life histories of small mammals in the Channel Islands in 1960–61. *Proceedings of the Zoological Society of London* **141**:515–26.
7 Borowski S. (1968) On the moult in the common shrew. *Acta theriologica* **13**:483–98.
8 Borowski S. (1973) Variations in coat and colour in representatives of the genera *Sorex* L. and *Neomys* Kaup. *Acta theriologica* **18**:247–79.
9 Brambell F.W.R. (1935) Reproduction in the common shrew (*Sorex araneus* L.). *Philosophical Transactions of The Royal Society B* **225**:1–62.
10 Brambell F.W.R. & Hall K. (1936) Reproduction of the lesser shrew (*Sorex minutus* L.). *Proceedings of the Zoological Society of London* **1936**: 957–69.
11 Brockie R.E. (1976) Self annointing by wild hedgehogs, *Erinaceus europaeus* in New Zealand. *Animal Behaviour* **24**:68–71.
12 Buchalczyk T. & Pucek Z. (1963) Food storage of the European water-shrew *Neomys fodiens* (Pennant, 1771). *Acta theriologica* **7**:376–9.
13 Buckley J. & Goldsmith J.G. (1975) The prey of the barn owl (*Tyto alba alba*) in East Norfolk. *Mammal Review* **5**:13–16.
14 Buckner C.H. (1969) Some aspects of the population ecology of the common shrew, *Sorex araneus*, near Oxford, England. *Journal of Mammalogy* **50**:326–32.
15 Bunn D.S. (1966) Fighting and moult in shrews. *Journal of Zoology* **148**:580–2.
16 Burton M. (1957) Hedgehog self annointing. *Proceedings of the Zoological Society of London* **129**:452–3.
17 Burton M. (1969) *The hedgehog.* London: André Deutsch 111 pp.

18 Carlier E.W. 1892–93. Contributions to the histology of the hedgehog (*Erinaceus europaeus*). *Journal of Anatomy and Physiology* **27**:334–46.

19 Cassell G.H. & Hill A. (1979). Murine and other small animal mycoplasmas. In G.H. Tully & R.F. Whitcomb eds *The mycoplasmas, Vol. II. Human and other animal mycoplasmas.* New York & London: Academic Press pp. 233–73.

20 Catzeflis F. *et al.* (1985) Unexpected findings on the taxonomic status of East Mediterranean *Crocidura russula* auct. (Mammalia, Insectivora). *Zeitschrift für Säugetierkunde* **50**:185–201.

21 Churchfield S. (1979) *Studies on the ecology and behaviour of British shrews.* PhD. thesis, University of London.

22 Churchfield S. (1980) Population dynamics and the seasonal fluctuations in numbers of the common shrew in Britain. *Acta theriologica* **25**:415–24.

23 Churchfield S. (1980) Subterranean foraging and burrowing activity of the common shrew. *Acta theriologica* **25**:451–9.

24 Churchfield S. (1981) Water and fat contents of British shrews and their role in the seasonal changes in body weight. *Journal of Zoology* **194**:165–73.

25 Churchfield S. (1982) Food availability and the diet of the common shrew, *Sorex araneus*, in Britain. *Journal of Animal Ecology* **51**:15–28.

26 Churchfield S. (1984). An investigation of the population ecology of syntopic shrews inhabiting watercress beds. *Journal of Zoology* **204**:229–40.

27 Churchfield S. (1984) Dietary separation in three species of shrew inhabiting water-cress beds. *Journal of Zoology* **204**:211–28.

28 Churchfield S. (1985) The feeding ecology of the European water shrew. *Mammal Review* **15**:13–21.

29 Condry W.M. (1981) *The natural history of Wales.* London: Collins 287 pp.

30 Corbet G.B. (1963) The frequency of albinism of the tail tip in British mammals. *Proceedings of the Zoological Society of London* **140**:327–30.

31 Corbet G.B. (1966) Records of mammals and their ectoparasites from Scottish islands. *Glasgow Naturalist* **18**:426–34.

32 Corbet G.B. (1988) The family Erinaceidae: a synthesis of its taxonomy, phylogeny, ecology and zoogeography. *Mammal Review* **18**: 117–72.

33 Corbet G.B. & Critchlow M. (1986) The shrews and mice of Bardsey — a comparison with mainland animals. *Bardsey Observatory Report* no. 29 **138**:141.

34 Cox F.E.G. (1970) Parasitic protozoa of British small mammals. *Mammal Review* **1**:1–28.

35 Crowcroft W.P. (1954) The daily cycle of activity in British shrews. *Proceedings of the Zoological Society of London* **123**:715–29.

36 Crowcroft W.P. (1954) *An ecological study of British shrews.* DPhil. thesis, University of Oxford.

37 Crowcroft W.P. (1957) *The life of the shrew.* London: Max Reinhardt 166 pp.

38 Deanesly R. (1934) The reproductive processes of certain mammals, Part 6. The reproductive cycle of the female hedgehog (*Erinaceus europaeus*). *Philosophical Transactions of the Royal Society B* **223**:239–76.

39 Deanesly R. (1966) Observations on reproduction in the mole (*Talpa europaea*). *Symposia of the Zoological Society of London* **15**:387–402.

40 Dehnel A. (1950) [Studies on the genus *Neomys* Kaup]. Annales Universitatis Mariae Curie −Sklodowska C **5**:1–63 (Polish, English summ.).

41 Delany M.J. & Healy M. (1966) Variation in the white-toothed shrews (*Crocidura* spp.) in the British Isles. *Proceedings of the Royal Society B* **164**:63–74.

42 Dötsch C. & Koenigswald W.V. (1978) On the reddish colouring of soricid teeth. *Zeitschrift für Säugetierkunde* **43**:65–70.

43 Efron K.M. (1962) The ecology of the water shrew (*Neomys fodiens* L.) in central Ural. *Voprosy Ekologii* **6**:1–178 (in Russian).

44 Ellenbroek F.J.M. (1980) Interspecific competition in the shrews *Sorex araneus* and *Sorex minutus* (Soricidae, Insectivora): a population study of the Irish pygmy shrew. *Journal of Zoology* **192**:119–36.

45 English M.P. & Southern H.N. (1967) *Trichophyton persicolor* infection in a population of small wild mammals. *Sabouraudia* **5**:302–9.

46 Evans A.C. (1948) The identity of earthworms stored by moles. *Proceedings of the Zoological Society of London* **118**:356–9.

47 Fairley J.S. (1975) *An Irish beast book.* Belfast: Blackstaff Press 201 pp.

48 Fons R. (1972) La musaraigne musette, *C. russula* (Hermann, 1780). *Science et Nature* **112**:23–8.

49 Fons R. (1975) Première données sur l'écologie de la pachyure étrusque *Suncus etruscus* (Savi, 1822) et comparaison avec deux autres Crocidurinae *Crocidura russula* (Hermann, 1780) et *Crocidura suaveolens* (Pallas, 1811) (Insectivora Soricidae). *Vie Millieu,* **15**:315–60.

50 Ford C.E. & Hamerton J.L. (1970) Chromosome polymorphism in the common shrew, *Sorex araneus*. *Symposia of the Zoological Society of London* **26**:223–36.

51 Frankland H.M.T. (1959) The incidence and distribution in Britain of the trematodes of *Talpa europaea*. *Parasitology* **49**:132–42.

52 Fraser F.C. & King J.E. (1954) Faunal remains. In Clark J.G.D. ed. *Excavations at Star Carr*. Cambridge: Cambridge University Press pp 70–95.

53 Funmilayo O. (1976) Age determination, age distribution and sex ratio in mole populations. *Acta theriologica* **21**:207–15.

54 Genoud M. (1978) Étude d'une population urbaine de musaraignes musettes (*Crocidura russula* Hermann, 1789). *Bulletin de la Société Vaudoise des Sciences Naturelles* **74**:25–34.

55 Genoud M. & Hausser J. (1979) Ecologie d'une population de *Crocidura russula* en milieu rural montagnard (Insectivora, Soricidae). *Terre et Vie* **33**:539–54.

56 Genoud M. & Vogel P. (1981) The activity of

Crocidura russula (Insectivora, Soricidae) in the field and in captivity. *Zeitschrift für Säugetierkunde* **46**: 222–32.

57 Glue D.E. (1967) Prey taken by the barn owl in England and Wales. *Bird Study* **14**:169–83.

58 Glue D.E. (1974) Food of the barn owl in Britain and Ireland. *Bird Study* **21**:200–10.

59 Godfrey G.K. (1957) Observations on the movements of moles (*Talpa europaea* L.) after weaning. *Proceedings of the Zoological Society of London* **128**:287–95.

60 Godfrey G.K. (1978) The ecological distribution of shrews (*Crocidura suaveolens* and *Sorex araneus fretalis*) in Jersey. *Journal of Zoology* **185**:266–70.

61 Godfrey G.K. (1978) The activity pattern in white-toothed shrews studied with radar. *Acta theriologica* **23**:381–90.

62 Godfrey G.K. & Crowcroft P. (1960) *The life of the mole*. London: Museum Press 152 pp.

63 Gourlay R.N. & Wyld S.G. (1976) Ilsley-type and other mycoplasmas from the alimentary tracts of cattle, pigs and rodents. *Proceedings of the Society for General Microbiology* **3**:142.

64 Grainger J.P. & Fairley J.S. (1978) Studies on the biology of the pygmy shrew, *Sorex minutus*, in the West of Ireland. *Journal of Zoology* **186**:109–41.

65 Grünwald, A. (1969) Untersuchungen zür Orientierung der Weisszahnspitzmause (Soricidae — Crocidurinae). *Zeitschrift für Vergleichende Physiologie* **65**:191–217.

66 Gurney J.H. (1879) Notes on shrews observed in Norfolk. *Zoologist* **3**:123.

67 Haeck J. (1969) Colonisation of the mole (*Talpa europaea*) in the Ijsselmeerpolders. *Netherlands Journal of Zoology* **19**:145–248.

68 Hanzák J. (1966) Zur Jugendentwicklung der Gartenspitzmaus, *C. suaveolens* (Pallas, 1821). *Lynx* **6**:67–74.

69 Harper R.J. (1977) 'Caravanning' in *Sorex* species. *Journal of Zoology* **183**:541.

70 Hausser J. (1984) Genetic drift and selection: their respective weights in the morphological and genetic differentiation of four species of shrews in Southern Europe (Insectivora, Soricidae). *Zeitschrift für Zoologische Systematik und Evolutionsforschung* **22**: 302–20.

71 Hausser J. & Jammot D. (1974) Étude biometrique des machoires chez les *Sorex* du groupe *araneus* en Europe continentale. *Mammalia* **38**:324–43.

72 Hawkins A.E. & Jewell P.A. (1962) Food consumption and energy requirements of captive British shrews and the mole. *Proceedings of the Zoological Society of London* **138**:137–55.

73 Healing T.D. Personal communication.

74 Healing T.D. *et al.* (1980) A note on some Enterobacteriaceae from the faeces of small wild British mammals. *Journal of Hygiene* **85**:343–5.

75 Hellwing S. (1973) The postnatal development of the white-toothed shrew *Crocidura russula monacha* in captivity. *Zeitschrift für Säugetierkunde* **38**: 257–70.

76 Herter K. (1938) Die Biologie der ëuropaischen Igel. *Kleintier und Pelztier* **14**:1–222.

77 Herter K. (1965) *Hedgehogs*. London: Phoenix House 69 pp.

78 Heydemann B. (1960) Zur Ökologie von *Sorex araneus* L. and *Sorex minutus* L. *Zeitschrift für Säugetierkunde* **25**:24–9.

79 Hinton M.A.C. (1924) On a new species of *Crocidura* from the Scilly Islands. *Annals and Magazine of Natural History* **14**(9):508–9.

80 Hutterer R. (1977) Haltung und Lebensdauer von Spitzmäusen der Gattung *Sorex* (Mammalia, Insectivora). *Zeitschrift für Angewandte Zoologie* **64**:353–67.

81 Iling K. *et al.* (1981) Freilandbeobachtungen zur Lebensweise und zum Revierberhalten der ëuropaischen Wasserspitzmaus, *Neomys fodiens* (Pennant, 1771). *Zoologische Beitrage* **27**:109–22.

82 Ivanovna E.I. (1967) New data on the nature of the rete mirabile and derivative apparatuses in some semi-aquatic mammals. *Doklady (Proceedings) of the Academy of Sciences of the USSR (Biol.)* **173**:1–3.

83 Jansky L. & Hanak V. (1960) Aktivität der Spitzmause unter natürlichen Bedingungen. *Säugetierkundliche Mitteilungen* **8**:55–63.

84 Jenyns L. (1838) Further remarks on the British shrews including the distinguishing characters of two species previously confounded. *Annals of Natural History* **1**:417–27.

85 Kohler D. (1984) Zum verhaltensinventar der Wasserspitzmaus (*Neomys fodiens*). *Säugetierkundliche Informationen* **2**:175–99.

86 Kristoffersson R. & Suomalainen P. (1964) Changes of body weight of hibernating and non-hibernating animals. *Annales Academiae Scientiarum Fennicae* Series A **76**:1–11.

87 Kruuk H. (1964) Predators and anti-predator behavior of the black-headed gull (*Larus ridibundus*). *Behavior* **11** (Suppl.):1–129.

88 Larkin P.A. (1948) *Ecology of mole* (Talpa europaea *L.) populations*. DPhil. thesis, University of Oxford.

89 Lewis J.W. (1987) Helminth parasites of British rodents and insectivores. *Mammal Review* **17**: 81–93.

90 Lindemann W. (1951) Zur Psychologie des Igels. *Zeitschrift für Tierpsychologie* **8**:224–51.

91 Lodal J. & Grue J.S. (1985) Age determination and age distribution in populations of moles (*Talpa europaea*) in Denmark. *Acta Zoologica Fennica* **173**:279–81.

92 Lorenz K.Z. (1952) *King Solomon's Ring*. London: Methuen 202 pp.

93 Lorenz K.Z. (1957) The European water shrew (*Neomys fodiens* Pennant, 1771). In Worden A.N. & Lane-Petter W. eds. *The UFAW handbook on the care and management of laboratory animals*, 2nd edn., pp. 469–72 London: University Federation for Animal Welfare.

94 Ministry of Agriculture, Fisheries, and Food (1984)

Bovine tuberculosis in badgers, eighth report, London: HMSO 17pp.

95 Malmquist M.G. (1985) Character displacement and biogeography of the pygmy shrew in northern Europe. *Ecology* **66**:372−7.

96 Malmquist M.G. (1986) Density compensation in allopatric populations of the pygmy shrew, *Sorex minutus*, in Gotland (Sweden) and the Outer Hebrides (Scotland). *Oecologia* **68**:344−6.

97 Matthews L.H. (1935) The oestrous cycle and intersexuality in the female mole (*Talpa europaea* Linn.) *Proceedings of the Zoological Society of London* **1935**:347−83.

98 McDiarmid A. & Austwick P.K.C. (1954) Occurrence of *Haplosporangium parvum* in the lungs of the mole (*Talpa europaea*). *Nature* **174**:843−4.

99 McLaughlan J.D. & Henderson W.M. (1947) The occurrence of foot and mouth disease in the hedgehog under natural conditions. *Journal of Hygiene* **54**:474−9.

100 Mead-Briggs A.R. & Woods J.A. (1973) An index of activity to assess the reduction in mole numbers caused by control methods. *Journal of Applied Ecology* **10**:837−45.

101 Meese G.B. & Cheeseman C.L. (1969) Radio-active tracking of the mole (*Talpa europaea*) over a 24 hour period. *Journal of Zoology* **158**:197−224.

102 Mellanby K. (1971) *The mole*. London: Collins 159 pp.

103 Meylan A. (1964) Le polymorphisme chromosomique de *Sorex areneus* L. (Mammalia-Insectivora). *Revue Suisse de zoologie* **71**:903−83.

104 Michalak I. (1983) Reproduction, maternal and social behaviour of the European water shrew under laboratory conditions. *Acta theriologica* **28**:3−24.

105 Michielsen N. Croin (1966) Intraspecific and interspecific competition in the shrews *Sorex araneus* L. and *S. minutus* L. *Archives Néerlandaises de Zoologie* **17**:73−174.

106 Milner C. & Ball D.F. (1970) Factors affecting the distribution of the mole (*Talpa europaea*) in Snowdonia (North Wales). *Journal of Zoology* **162**:61−9.

107 Mohamed H.A. & Molyneux D.H. (1984) *Elleipsisoma thomsoni* Franca 1912; an apicomplexan parasite in the red blood cells of the mole (*Talpa europaea*). *Parasitology* **89**:407−15.

108 Montagu I.G.S. & Pickford G. (1923) On the Guernsey *Crocidura*. *Proceedings of the Zoological Society of London* **1923**:1043−4.

109 Morris B. (1961) Some observations on the breeding season of the hedgehog and the rearing and handling of the young. *Proceedings of the Zoological Society of London* **136**:201−6.

110 Morris B. (1967) The European hedgehog. In Worden A.N. & Lane-Petter W. eds. *The UFAW handbook on the care and management of laboratory animals*, 3rd edn. London: Livingstone pp. 478−88.

111 Morris P. (1970) A method for determining absolute age in the hedgehog. *Journal of Zoology* **161**:277−81.

112 Morris P. (1971) Epihyseal fusion in the forefoot as a means of age determination in the hedgehog *Erinaceus europaeus*. *Journal of Zoology* **164**:254−9.

113 Morris P. (1973) Winter nests of the hedgehog (*Erinaceus europaeus* L.) *Oecologia* **11**:299−313.

114 Morris P. (1977) Pre-weaning mortality in the hedgehog (*Erinaceus europaeus*). *Journal of Zoology* **182**:162−7.

115 Morris P. (1983) *Hedgehogs*. Weybridge: Whittet Books 124 pp.

116 Morris P. (1984) An estimate of the minimum body weight necessary for hedgehogs (*Erinaceus europaeus*) to survive hibernation. *Journal of Zoology* **203**:291−4.

117 Morris P.A. (1985) The effects of supplementary feeding on movements of hedgehogs (*Erinaceus europaeus*). *Mammal Review* **15**:23−32.

118 Morris P.A. (1986) Movements of hedgehogs in forest edge habitat. *Mammalia* **50**:395−8.

119 Morris P.A. (1988) A study of home range and movements in the hedgehog (*Erinaceus europaeus*). *Journal of Zoology* **214**:433−49.

120 Morris P.A. & English M.P. (1969) *T. mentagrophytes* var. *erinacei* in British hedgehogs. *Sabouraudia* **7**:122−7.

121 Myrcha A. (1969) Seasonal changes in caloric value, body water and fat in some shrews. *Acta theriologica* **14**:211−27.

122 Nosek J. *et al.* (1972) Contribution to the knowledge of home range in common shrew *Sorex araneus* L. *Oecologia* **9**:59−63.

123 O'Keef D.A. & Fairley J.S. (1981) Two population studies of Irish pygmy shrews. *Irish Naturalists' Journal* **20**:269−75.

124 Pankakoski E. (1979) The influence of weather on the activity of the common shrew (*Sorex araneus*). *Acta theriologica* **24**:522−6.

125 Pernetta J.C. (1973) The ecology of *Crocidura suaveolens cassiteridum* (Hinton) in a coastal habitat. *Mammalia* **37**:241−56.

126 Pernetta J.C. (1976) Diets of the shrews *Sorex araneus* L. and *Sorex minutus* L. in Wytham grassland. *Journal of Animal Ecology* **45**:899−912.

127 Pernetta J.C. (1977) Population ecology of British shrews in grassland. *Acta theriologica* **22**:279−96.

128 Pernetta J.C. (1977) Activity and behaviour of captive *Crocidura suaveolens cassiteridum* (Hinton, 1924). *Acta theriologica* **22**:387−9.

129 Pitt F. (1945) Mass movement of the water shrew *Neomys fodiens*. *Nature* **156**:247.

130 Price M. (1953) The reproductive cycle of the water shrew, *Neomys fodiens bicolor* Shaw. *Proceedings of the Zoological Society of London* **123**:599−621.

131 Pucek M. (1967) Chemistry and pharmacology of insectivore venoms. In Bücherl W. *et al.* eds *Venomous animals and their venoms*, vol. 1. New York: Academic Press pp. 43−50.

132 Pucek Z. (1960) Sexual maturation and variability of the reproductive system of young shrews (*Sorex* L.) in the first calendar year of life. *Acta theriologica* **3**:269−96.

133 Pucek Z. (1963) Seasonal changes in the braincase of some representatives of the genus *Sorex* from the Palaearctic. *Journal of Mammalogy* **44**:523–36.

134 Pucek Z. (1965) Seasonal and age changes in the weight of internal organs of shrews. *Acta theriologica* **10**:369–438.

135 Quilliam T.A. (ed.) (1966) The mole: its adaptation to an underground environment. *Journal of Zoology* **149**:31–114.

136 Racey P.A. (1978) Seasonal changes in testosterone levels and androgen dependent organs in male moles. (*Talpa europaea*). *Journal of Reproduction and Fertility* **52**:195–200.

137 Randolph S.E. (1975) Seasonal dynamics of a host-parasite system: *Ixodes trianguliceps* (Acarina: Ixodidae) and its small mammal hosts. *Journal of Animal Ecology* **44**:425–49.

138 Reeve N.J. (1982) The home range of the hedgehog as revealed by a radio tracking study. *Symposia of the Zoological Society of London* **49**:207–30.

139 Reeve N.J. & Morris P.A. (1985) Construction and use of summer nests by the hedgehog (*Erinaceus europaeus*). *Mammalia* **49**:187–94.

140 Reeve N.J. & Morris P.A. (1986) Mating strategy in the hedgehog (*Erinaceus europaeus*). *Journal of Zoology* **210**:613–14.

141 Rood J.P. (1965) Observations on population structure, reproduction and molt of the Scilly shrew. *Journal of Mammalogy* **46**:426–33.

142 Rood J.P. (1965) Observations on the home range and activity of the Scilly shrew. *Mammalia* **29**:507–16.

143 Rudge A.J.B. (1966) Catching and keeping live moles. *Journal of Zoology* **149**:42–5.

144 Rudge M.R. (1968) Food of the common shrew, *Sorex araneus*, in Britain. *Journal of Animal Ecology* **37**:565–81.

145 Rzebik B. (1968) *Crocidura* Wagler and other Insectivora (Mammalia), from the Quaternary deposits of Tornewton cave in England. *Acta Zoologica Cracoviensia* **13**:251–63.

146 Schmidt U. (1979) Die Lokalisation vergrabenen Futters bei der Hausspitzmaus, *Crocidura russula* Hermann. *Zeitschrift für Säugetierkunde* **44**:59–60.

147 Searle J.B. (1985) Methods of determining the sex of common shrews (*Sorex araneus*). *Journal of Zoology* (A) **206**:279–82.

148 Searle J.B. & Wilkinson P.J. (1987) Karyotypic variation in the common shrew (*Sorex araneus*) in Britain — a 'Celtic Fringe'. *Heredity* **59**:345–51.

149 Searle J.B. & Erskine I. (1985) Evidence for a widespread karyotypic race of hedgehog (*Erinaceus europaeus*) in Britain. *Journal of Zoology* (A) **206**: 276–8.

150 Sebek Z. & Rosicky B. (1967) The finding of *Pneumocystis carinii* in shrews (Insectivora: Soricidae). *Folia parasitologica* **14**:263–7.

151 Shillito J.F. (1960) *The general ecology of the common shrew* (Sorex araneus L.). PhD. thesis, University of Exeter.

152 Shillito J.F. (1963) Field observations on the growth, reproduction and activity of a woodland population of the common shrew *Sorex araneus* L. *Proceedings of the Zoological Society of London* **140**:99–114.

153 Shillito J.F. (1963) Observations on the range and movements of a woodland population of the common shrew *Sorex araneus* L. *Proceedings of the Zoological Society of London* **140**:533–46.

154 Shillito J.F. (1963) Field observations on the water shrew, *Neomys fodiens*. *Proceedings of the Zoological Society of London* **140**:320–2.

155 Skoczen S. (1958) Tunnel digging by the mole (*Talpa europaea* Linne). *Acta theriologica* **2**:235–59.

156 Skoczen S. (1961) On food storage of the mole (*Talpa europaea* Linnaeus, 1758). *Acta theriologica* **5**:290–3.

157 Smit F.G.A.M. (1957) *Siphonaptera. Handbooks for the identification of British insects.* London: Royal Entomological Society of London 94 pp.

158 Smit-Vis J. (1962) Some aspects of hibernation in the European hedgehog *Erinaceus europaeus* L. *Archives Néerlandaises de Zoologie* **14**:513–97.

159 Smith C.E.G. *et al.* (1964) Isolation of Louping ill virus from small mammals in Ayrshire, Scotland. *Nature* **203**:992–3.

160 Sokolov V.E. (1982) *Mammal skin.* Berkeley: University of California Press 695 pp.

161 Soroker V. *et al.* (1982) Parental behaviour in male and virgin white-toothed shrews *Crocidura russula monacha* (Soricidae, Insectivora). *Zeitschrift für Säugetierkunde* **47**:321–4.

162 Southern H.N. (1954) Tawny owls and their prey. *Ibis* **96**:384–408.

163 Spencer-Booth Y. (1963) A coastal population of shrews *C. s. cassiteridum*. *Proceedings of the Zoological Society of London* **140**:322–6.

164 Stein G.H.W. (1961) Beziehung zwischen Bestandsdichte und Vermehrung bei der Waldspitzmaus, *Sorex araneus*, und weiteren Rotzahnspitzmäusen. *Zeitschrift für Säugetierkunde* **26**:13–28.

165 Stein G.H.W. (1963) Anomalien der Zahnzahl und ihre geographische Variabilität bei Insectivoren: 1 Maulwurf, *Talpa europaea* L. *Mitteilungen aus dem Zoologischen Museum in Berlin* **39**:223–40.

166 Stein G.H.W. (1975) Über die Bestandsdichte und ihre Zusammenhange bei der Wasserspitzmaus, *Neomys fodiens* (Pennant). *Mitteilungen aus dem Zoologischen Museum in Berlin* **51**:189–98.

167 Stone R.D. (1986) *The social ecology of the European mole* (T. europaea *L.*) *and the Pyrenean desman* (Galemys pyrenaicus *G.*): *a comparative study.* PhD. thesis, University of Aberdeen.

168 Stone R.D. (1986) *Moles.* (Mammal Society Series) Oswestry: Nelson 24 pp.

169 Stone R.D. & Gorman M.L. (1985) The social organisation of the European mole (*Talpa europaea*) and the Pyrenean desman (*Galemys pyrenaicus*). *Mammal Review* **15**:35–42.

170 Stuart A.J. (1974) Pleistocene history of the British vertebrate fauna. *Biological Reviews* **49**:225–66.

171 Taylor J. (1968) *Salmonella* in wild animals. *Symposia of the Zoological Society of London* **24**:51–73.

172 Twigg G.I. (1980) A review of the occurrence in British mammals of the major organisms of zoonotic importance. *Mammal Review* **10**:139–49.

173 Twigg G.I. & Hughes D.M. (1970) The 'Pancreas of Aselli' in shrews. *Journal of Zoology* **162**:541–4.

174 Twigg G.I. *et al.* (1968) Leptospirosis in small mammals. *Symposia of the Zoological Society of London* **24**:75–98.

175 Van Wijngaarden-Bakker L.H. (1985) Littletonian faunas. In Edwards K.J. & Warren W.P. eds. *The Quaternary history of Ireland*. London: Academic Press pp. 233–349.

176 Vizoso A.D. & Thomas W.E. (1981) Paramyxoviruses of the morbili group in the wild hedgehog *Erinaceus europaeus*. *British Journal of Experimental Pathology* **62**(1):79–86.

177 Vogel P. (1969) Beobachtungen zum intraspezifischen Verhalten der Hausspitzmaus (*C. russula*). *Revue Suisse de zoologie* **76**:1079–86.

178 Vogel P. (1972) Vergleichende Untersuchungen zum Ontogenesmodus einheimischer Soriciden (*Crocidura russula, Sorex araneus* und *Neomys fodiens*). *Revue Suisse de zoologie* **79**:1201–332.

179 Vogel P. (1972) Beitrag zur Fortpflanzungsbiologie der Gattungen *Sorex, Neomys* und *Crocidura* (Soricidae). *Verhandlungen der Naturforschenden Gesellschaft in Basel* **82**:165–92.

180 Vogel P. (1974) Kälteresistenz und reversible Hypothermie der Etruskerspitzmaus (*Suncus etruscus*, Soricidae, Insectivora). *Zeitschrift für Säugetierkunde* **39**:78–88.

181 Vogel P. (1976) Energy consumption of European and African shrews. *Acta theriologica* **21**:195–206.

182 Weissengberger J. *et al.* (1983) Observations de populations marquées de la musaraigne aquatique *Neomys fodiens* (Insectivora, Mammalia). *Bulletin de la Société Vaudoise des Sciences Naturelles* **76**:381–90.

183 Wit C.A. de & Westrom B.R. (1987) Venom resistance in the hedgehog, *Erinaceus europaeus*. *Toxicon* **25**:315–23.

184 Wolk K. (1976) The winter food of the European water-shrew. *Acta theriologica* **21**:117–29.

185 Woods J.A. & Mead-Briggs A.R. (1978) The daily cycle of activity in the mole (*Talpa europaea*) and its seasonal changes, as revealed by radio-active monitoring of the nest. *Journal of Zoology* **184**:563–72.

186 Yalden D.W. (1966) The anatomy of mole locomotion. *Journal of Zoology* **149**:55–64.

187 Yalden D.W. (1974) Population density in the common shrew, *Sorex araneus*. *Journal of Zoology* **173**:262–4.

188 Yalden D.W. (1976) The food of the hedgehog in England. *Acta theriologica* **21**:401–24.

189 Yalden D.W. (1981) The occurrence of the pygmy shrew *Sorex minutus* on moorland, and the implications for its presence in Ireland. *Journal of Zoology* **195**:147–56.

190 Yalden D.W. (1982) When did the mammal fauna of the British Isles arrive? *Mammal Review* **12**:1–57.

191 Yalden D.W. *et al.* (1973) Studies on the comparative ecology of some French small mammals. *Mammalia* **37**:257–76.

192 Yates T.L. (1984) Insectivores etc. In Anderson S. & Jones J.K. eds. *Orders and families of recent mammals of the world*. New York: Wiley pp. 117–44.

193 Zima J. & Kral B. (1984) Karyotypes of European mammals 1. *Acta Scientiarum Naturalium Academiae Scientiarum Bohemoslovacae Brno* **18**(7):1–51.

Chapter 6 / Bats:
Order Chiroptera

INTRODUCTION

Structure

Bats are the only mammals capable of true flight. Structurally they are little different from the typical mammal, but with the obvious modification of the forelimb (Figs 6.1, 6.2). The forearm consists of a single bone, the radius, with the ulna being reduced to a small slip at the elbow. Almost all bats have a relatively small clawed thumb projecting forwards from the wrist, free of membrane and used for grasping, especially in climbing upwards. Some species also hang by their thumbs while giving birth or urinating. The other four fingers are invariably attached throughout their length to the wing membrane and the bones are greatly elongated, especially the metacarpals. The third digit extends to the wingtip and the fifth finger gives rigidity to the wing breadth. Bats have by far the largest surface area/volume ratios of any group of mammals.

Bats have wing shapes that allow exploitation of differing habitats and modes of prey search and capture. Long-eared and horseshoe bats have broad, highly cambered wings; they are slow flying and highly manoeuvrable, often feeding amongst vegetation. By contrast narrow-winged noctules fly fast and feed well clear of obstacles.

Apart from wings the only other structural modification exclusive to bats is the knee which is rotated to face backwards and upwards, allowing the bat to lower the tail membrane in flight for increased manoeuvrability and to create a bag in which insects may be tucked or manipulated while in flight. It also facilitates landing and hanging head down. The tail membrane may be stiffened at the edge by the calcar, which is attached to the ankle and extends towards the tail. In adults it is usually bony and its shape and relative length can be an identification character. Other modifications are mostly around the head and often involve ela-borate development of noseleaves and ears, both associated with echolocation.

About 970 species of bat are known, divided into two suborders, Megachiroptera and Microchiroptera. The Megachiroptera are represented by one family consisting of 42 genera and about 170 species. They are almost entirely tropical and subtropical, being distributed from Africa to the Pacific islands, and have predominantly vegetable diets. The Microchiroptera comprise 17 families, 147 genera and about 800 species. They have exploited all the major land habitats with the exception of arctic regions, the highest mountains and some remote islands. They eat a wide variety of food including fruit, pollen, nectar and fish, and there are carnivorous, sanguinivorous and insectivorous bats. The last group is by far the most plentiful in numbers of species and individuals.

In cool temperate regions, including Europe, only insectivorous species occur. Three families of Microchiroptera are found in Europe (including one member of the Molossidae). Only two families reach the British Isles, where 13 species of the family Vespertilionidae are known to be resident and two Rhinolophidae. The Rhinolophidae has but one extant genus, *Rhinolophus*, the horseshoe bats, characterised by their horseshoe-shaped noseleaves.

Representatives of six genera of Vespertilionidae live in the British Isles, and a seventh occurs as a rare vagrant. Facial characters are simple and a prominent tragus is present in all species. These bats are usually crevice dwelling, but some species may be found in the open and hanging 'free'. Those hanging free hold their wings to their sides, but long-eared bats are occasionally found partially enveloped by their wings. However, they hang at an angle rather than perpendicularly like the horseshoes. Most vespertilionids are very agile quadrupedally.

The appearance of individuals of any one species is variable due to sex, age, season and inheritance. Males on average are 6% smaller than females.

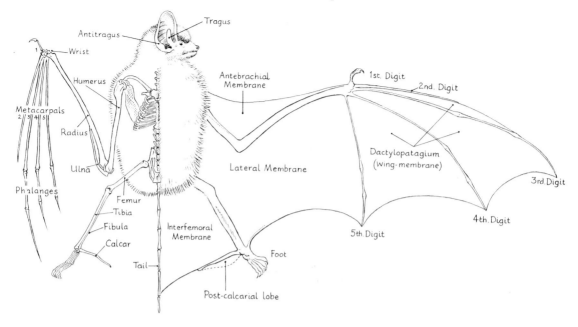

Fig. 6.1. A bat of the family Vespertilionidae illustrating some of the terms used in the text.

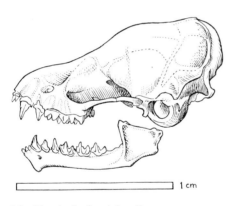

Fig. 6.2. The skull of a pipistrelle.

Young bats tend to have dull (even frizzy) greyish fur for up to 12 months, and greater horseshoes may retain some greyness for 2 years. Growth from birth is rapid with bones normally reaching full size within 60 days, but a few individuals, exceptionally born in August, may hibernate with epiphyses unfused with the bone shafts. Maximum body mass is not achieved until the 2nd or 3rd year for most species, and in the greater horseshoe only when over 5 years old. Seasonal weight changes may be as much as double the minimum. Generally, maximum body mass is reached in late October

and the minimum in early May. Average loss in hibernation is about 23%. Whereas maximum weights of individuals may be twice the minimum, linear dimensions rarely exceed 20% above minimum values.

Roosts and seasonal movements

Fifteen species are resident along the central south coast of England but only three or four species reach the north of mainland Scotland, while in Ireland eight or possibly nine species occur. Bats roost in a wide variety of sites. While most species seek seclusion and relatively dark places, others may be found in exposed sites such as crevices on trees, or walls of buildings, near the eaves or behind drain pipes. Bats very occasionally use badger setts and it is likely that a variety of animal burrows are used.

Some, but not all, bats found in exposed sites, especially if on the ground, may be injured, sick or weak through starvation.

Most bats roost in hollow trees or buildings and some species are found in caves or tunnels. Most are colonial and are creatures of habit, seasonally occupying traditional roosts. In the course of a year an individual bat may occupy many roosts in sequence and visit other members of the colony occupying nearby roost sites. These different roosts may be in the same cave or building, but more usually in a variety of places sometimes many kilometres apart. Roosts can be classified into four types: hibernacula, transitory, nursery or mating.

No species in Britain is known to migrate very long distances, although movements of up to 25 km are usual for some species, e.g. greater horseshoe between summer and winter roosts. Some long distance movements undoubtedly occur because bats are found on ships and offshore oil platforms at least 150 km from land. Also bats have been observed along the south coast of England flying with flocks of migrant birds in spring and autumn. Similarly severe cold weather in winter causes bats to awaken, presumably so that they may find less cold roost sites in which to continue hibernation. Some fly long distances, (several hundred kilometres), usually westward across northern Europe, and a few appear to reach Britain from the Continent.

Hibernation

Some species tend to be gregarious in hibernation while others are solitary, but there is wide variation.

The different species have varying strategies to cope with winter, when food is scarce. Bats of all species wake periodically and may fly and even feed in any month. Generally hibernation sites provide seclusion, safety from predators, and protection from extreme temperature fluctuation. The site must be humid but in some crevice-dwelling species evaporative losses will be minimal as the bats create their own microclimate.

The onset of hibernation is preceded by rapid weight increase, which occurs a few weeks earlier in females than in males because males feed less and remain active longer in this, the main mating season. Older females enter hibernation first but there does not appear to be any sudden change from activity to hibernation, but rather as good feeding nights become fewer so the periods of torpor lengthen. Towards the end of hibernation in late February and March the periods shorten.

During hibernation bats frequently awaken, groom and re-enter torpor or often move either within the same site, e.g. a cave, or to other places which may be many kilometres away. They appear to select their sites carefully and individual species select differing temperature regimens generally within the range 0–10°C. As winter progresses

and bats lose weight so they select lower roost temperatures.

There is no clear distinction between cave roosting species and the others but noctules, Leisler's, pipistrelles and serotines have rarely been recorded in caves. All other species are found in caves but also use buildings and hollow trees. The horseshoes are most cave-dependent but many of them hibernate in buildings, though mostly in cellars and similar cool, damp places. Species that are most cave dependent, like the horseshoes and myotis bats, are found in sites where temperature fluctuations are small, whereas the barbastelle, brown long-eared and pipistrelle tolerate wide ranges, even below freezing.

While most hibernating bats seek crevices in trees or walls of buildings or in caves hanging from walls or ceiling, Daubenton's may burrow into soft scree on the floor (a single serotine has been similarly found) and barbastelle may hang exposed in the open from vegetation.

Transition roosts in spring

In spring bats move from hibernacula and tend to form small nomadic clusters of all sex and age groups. Gradually the preponderance of females increases and for most species males move away and stay alone or in groups of two to three. In spring and up to the end of July males often remain torpid for days at a time, only feeding on the best nights, while pregnant females may feed nightly unless the weather is too cold and wet. Eventually several subgroups of females of one colony coalesce into a nursery.

Nurseries

There is much variation even within one species as to when a nursery cluster is formed and whether that group remains in the same place throughout gestation, parturition and weaning. Even for a single colony the behaviour in one year might be different from the next. However, some species such as the long-eareds and serotine tend to use the same site each year (and may live in the same building throughout the year) while noctules, and to a lesser extent pipistrelles, are often nomadic, even carrying nearly full grown juveniles between roosts. The reasons for these movements are not known but could be many, including the fact that the new sites may provide a better temperature regimen, be nearer to good feeding areas, or even the old roost may have too many ectoparasites.

Nurseries generally contain all the pregnant females of one colony with a few immature bats of both sexes and some non-breeding females. With brown long-eared and to a lesser extent Daubenton's bats, adult males may be present.

At the end of weaning the adult females leave the roost, often returning nightly to their offspring which may occupy the nursery for several weeks more, but most bats move to transition roosts again, prior to hibernation.

Mating roosts

Males of most species spend the summer away from the nurseries, but may make short visits without staying. They usually occupy a traditional site where they may remain much of the year. A small number of males may be present periodically but by August only one remains, the implication being that a dominant has driven off others.

The mating strategies are known for a few of our species; typically for noctule, Leisler's, pipistrelle and greater horseshoe males emerge at dusk making audible loud calls to attract females. Sometimes males may be found roosting with several females. It is likely that females in the wild are inseminated more than once and captive noctules may mate many times. Copulation is promiscuous.

REPRODUCTION

All species begin mating in September and some individuals continue mating throughout the winter. Like many other bats, especially in temperate regions, British species have a feature which is unique amongst mammals. Males and females may store mature sperm for many months. Sperm in the female becomes lined up against the wall of the uterus and appears to be nourished by it during hibernation. In spring (April–May) when ovulation occurs the stored sperm effects fertilisation. The early embryo implants and development proceeds. However, the gestation period is variable because females can become torpid at any time during the year. Length of gestation depends on the amount of food the female is able to catch and also the roost temperatures. In warm summers when food is plentiful gestation will be shorter than in cold wet years. During cold weather fetal growth stops but if poor conditions are experienced close to parturition abortions can occur. Also, lack of insects after birth can cause mothers to abandon their young. In general, gestation lasts about 50 days.

A single young is born between early June and late July, exceptionally to mid-August. Twins are known from several species, especially pipistrelles and noctules, and a higher incidence has been recorded in Scotland.

Vespertilionids hang head upwards by their thumbs during birth, but horseshoe bats remain hanging by their toes. The baby is washed and usually attaches to a nipple immediately and begins to suck. Young vespertilionids are usually hairless at birth but rhinolophids have short pigmented hair especially dorsally. They are about 25% of their mother's weight. Their eyes open and ears become erect after about 5 days, they are well covered in fur by 10–15 days and begin flapping their wings by 17–18 days. First flights occur around 3 weeks. Weaning is usually complete by 40 days. The mothers do not carry their young when feeding but they will carry them when changing roosts.

Some females become sexually mature in 3 months and produce young when 12 months old but males reach maturity at about 15 months. Greater horseshoe bats are exceptional with most females first giving birth at 4 years old. A few are much older and some females do not breed every year, especially when young. Greater horseshoe males generally mature in their 2nd year.

Survival rate of females is higher than for males with mean lifespans of 4–6 years and maximum longevity for both families of over 20 years.

Activity and feeding

Bats in Britain do not generally maintain a constant body temperature. Instead they have wide ranging temperatures dependent on external conditions. At any time of the year bats may be torpid, with their body temperature approximating their surroundings, often 13–15°C even in summer. Towards dusk temperatures may rise and the bats become active, usually urinating, grooming fur and oiling membranes with secretions from glands on the head prior to emergence. With body temperatures above 30°C flight is possible, and it quickly rises to 40°C (or slightly more) in flight.

Clustered pregnant females in nurseries are often

active by day, partly keeping themselves warm and frequently taking advantage of roosting in places warmed by the sun, e.g. under slates or tiles on houses. These clusters are often very noisy and noctules may be heard over 100 m away, especially on hot days.

Emergence time varies between species and from night to night. Indeed there are many factors which influence the time but there is an average for each species, related to sunset. Cloud and hot days tend to advance emergence while strong winds, cold and rain delay it. Colonies in woodland often emerge earlier than those in exposed sites.

Noctules are first to emerge, shortly after sunset, followed by pipistrelles about 15 min later. Brown long-eared and Daubenton's bats are usually very late emergers, when it is dark, but there is wide variation. Length of flight is also very variable but if food is plentiful most bats in summer will feed intermittently through the night.

Some species, like greater horseshoes which feed on large insects, may fill the stomach within 30 min but pipistrelles feeding on small ones may take four times as long. Although lactating females may return to roost several times in a night to allow the baby to suck, other bats may roost in temporary places, frequently hanging from tree branches. Long-eareds and barbastelles often use a regular perch below which insect remains accumulate.

If food is sparse, bats may return to roost within minutes and not emerge again. Although the final return to roost tends to be shortly before dawn, in mid-summer when nights are short some bats remain out until after sunrise.

Each species catches food using differing strategies. Noctules and pipistrelles generally feed clear of vegetation while the horseshoes, Bechstein's and long-eared bats catch their food amongst or off vegetation. At times, all bats land on the ground to collect food but this is most frequent in species specialising in eating big beetles or moths. Some catch food in their mouth, but many use tail membranes or cupped wings to control an insect before transfer to the mouth.

Natterer's bats specialise in locating moths resting on vegetation. These are flipped into the air with the tail and then caught in the bat's mouth.

Prey may be consumed in flight, especially small insects, but larger food is often taken to a perch, except for noctules and serotines, which eat almost all their food while in flight.

Bats make a wide range of sounds which serve various functions. Within clusters audible chattering occurs at all times, but its intensity increases before emergence. Some species such as the long-eared bats make very little sound, whereas greater horseshoes, noctules and pipistrelles are noisy. The sounds are variable especially when young are present but their purpose has been little studied. Outside the roost some bats produce audible calls, some which appear to be recognition, others aggression, and males call loudly in autumn when trying to attract females. All species produce high frequency echolocation sounds which they use to avoid obstacles and to identify, home-in on and capture prey. Each species uses sound in differing ways, which with a 'bat detector' (an instrument which in the simplest form picks up the ultrasonic sounds and reduces them to audible frequencies) can give clues to species identification.

Indeed experienced observers in the field can identify the horseshoe bats with certainty and several others with varying degrees of confidence. Individual bats produce a wide range of sounds which vary according to needs. Research is continuing to try to discover how bats use the sounds.

Populations

Historically there is little documentation on the distribution and population sizes of bats in the British Isles. From remains found at archaeological sites such as Creswell Crags, Nottinghamshire, Dowel Cave, Derbyshire [269] and Grimes Graves, Norfolk [41], it is clear that some bat distributions have changed. Lesser horseshoe bats were common around Dowel and Creswell in Neolithic times and from documentary evidence they died out in the early part of this century.

Grey long-eared bats occurred in Creswell caves a few thousand years ago as did Bechstein's in both Creswell and Grimes Graves but neither are found in those areas now.

The distribution and abundance of bats will have changed in the last 3000 years due to climate and as the landscape has been altered by man. Although bats are essentially forest dwelling animals, species such as Bechstein's declined as a result of forest clearance while pipistrelles will have increased as they favour open areas in which to feed and buildings for roosting. Modern agriculture has greatly reduced the abundance and variety of insects over large areas and that must have had a considerable effect on the numbers of bats which can be supported.

While country people state that they see only a fraction of the numbers of bats of 10 years or more ago, there is no accurate measure of these losses. Attempts have been made to estimate the former size of individual colonies of greater horseshoes. This conspicuous species is highly gregarious and in some sites where it has died out, piles of old guano allow the size of earlier clusters to be estimated. Colonies in Cornwall, Devon, Dorset and Pembrokeshire, which in the 1950s probably numbered well over 10 000 bats are now extinct or have less than 5% surviving.

Another large bat, the noctule, is now rarely seen over much of lowland Britain, but in the 1950s and earlier, it was extremely abundant and the most conspicuous bat in the dusk sky feeding with swifts and swallows.

What are the causes of these declines? Undoubtedly, catastrophes to individual clusters or colonies have resulted in sudden losses. Hollow trees containing colonies are cut down and bats killed. Colonies living in buildings have been killed by fire and particularly by remedial timber treatments.

Agricultural pesticides have caused the death of some bats and probably contributed to that of others. Bats have been deliberately killed by householders and by visitors to caves. The significance of such events is that buildings may contain all the breeding females of a colony so that destruction of those might cause the depopulation of a species from a wide area. The most widespread and abundant species in Britain, the pipistrelle, has colonies averaging about 150 bats occupying an area of about 12 km^2 but a colony of the endangered greater horseshoes in Dorset totals just 100 bats and occupies about 1500 km^2. In 1952 about 90% of that colony, which was estimated to number about 15 000 bats, was killed by a remedial timber treatment in one of four known nursery sites used by the colony [248].

Conservation

Because of the apparent decline in numbers of bats and because there are clearly identified threats to bats which are avoidable, bats have received legal protection in all European countries (excepting the Channel Islands and the Isle of Man). Northern Ireland was one of the last to enact legislation under the Wildlife (Northern Ireland) Order 1985; Great Britain gave protection with the Wildlife and Countryside Act 1981 and Eire in 1976 with the Wildlife Act.

Under all three Acts it is an offence to catch or handle wild bats and to mark them without first obtaining a licence from the appropriate authority. Bat roosts were also given protection so that nothing may be done to damage or destroy such a place without seeking advice from the Conservation Branch, DOE (Northern Ireland), Stormont, Belfast or the Nature Conservancy Council, Northminster House, Peterborough. This includes operations such as re-roofing, remedial timber treatments and also putting grilles on caves or mines to protect bats.

Different types of licence can be given for various activities such as visiting bat roosts to make counts, and research including any form of marking. Photography at a roost requires a separate licence.

In the past, research activities have contributed to local declines in numbers of bats, especially in hibernation sites. Early types of bat rings caused injuries which are believed to have contributed to the death of bats. But perhaps more important was the amount of disturbance inflicted on some bat populations which resulted in substantial loss of animals. In the 1950s it was noticed that when bats were handled or disturbed, fewer were found after each visit to a hibernaculum. If handling stopped it took c. 4 years for numbers to recover, the implication being that the bats had died.

The Mammal Society's Bat Group initiated research into the design of bat rings that would not cause injury. The current highly successful design was adopted in 1970 and refined still further in 1987.

The Bat Group provides advice on research projects. Before issuing bat rings, it needs to receive and approve a project plan and the applicant has to have an appropriate ringing licence from the Nature Conservancy Council. The Bat Group formed a partnership with the Fauna and Flora Preservation Society (FFPS) so that the research and conservation needs of local county bat groups could be met. This forum named 'Bat Groups of Britain' was formed in 1984.

LITERATURE
For general works on bats see [66, 67, 68, 78, 109, 141, 159, 206, 219, 244, 248, 268].

AUTHOR
R.E. Stebbings.

Field key to the species of bats

1 (a) Nose with horseshoe-shaped skin growth   **2**
  (b) Nose without horseshoe-shaped skin growth   **3**
2 (a) Forearm more than 45 mm   **Greater horseshoe bat**
  (b) Forearm less than 45 mm   **Lesser horseshoe bat**
3 (a) Base of ears joined over head   **4**
  (b) Ears quite separate, positioned either side of the head   **6**
4 (a) Ear more than 25 mm long when extended and nearly as long as body (the ear may be folded beneath the wing when at rest or curled like a ram's horn)   **5**
  (b) Ear less than 20 mm long, almost as wide as high, tragus more or less triangular   **Barbastelle**
5 (a) Greatest width of tragus less than 5.5 mm; face usually brown or pink   **Brown long-eared bat**
  (b) Greatest width of tragus more than 5.5 mm; face usually black   **Grey long-eared bat**
6 (a) With post-calcarial lobe (Fig. 6.1)   **7**
  (b) Without a post-calcarial lobe   **10**
7 (a) Forearm more than 37 mm   **8**
  (b) Forearm less than 37 mm   **Pipistrelle**
  NB The rare vagrant Nathusius' pipistrelle may be distinguished by its slightly broader wing: length of 5th digit (wrist to tip)/length of forearm >1.25 [245]
8 (a) Forearm more than 47 mm   **9**
  (b) Forearm less than 47 mm; fur distinctly dark brown at base with paler tips, long and shaggy; membranes opaque.   **Leisler's**
  NB Two rare vagrants may be considered here;
    (i) Northern serotine, forearm 37−44 mm, 2−3 mm of free tail, kidney-bean shaped tragus and gold tips to shaggy dark chestnut fur
    (ii) Parti-coloured bat, forearm 39−49 mm, ear shape like Leisler's, tragus curved with blunt end, whitish fur ventrally, dark brown with silver tips dorsally and thin translucent membranes
9 (a) Tragus mushroom-shaped, fur a consistent golden brown all over the body and throughout each hair, sleek; 2 mm of tail free of membrane   **Noctule**
  (b) Tragus slightly curved and finger-like, bluntly rounded at tip, fur blackish or dark brown, usually with light tips and darkest at base, 5−7 mm of tail free of membrane   **Serotine**
10 (a) Forearm less than 50 mm   **11**
  (b) Forearm more than 50 mm   **Mouse-eared bat**
11 (a) Ear less than 18 mm   **12**
  (b) Ear length more than 18 mm   **Bechstein's bat**
12 (a) Tail membrane without 1 mm stiff bristles, but perhaps some fine hairs, including some on the calcar, in which case ear length is less than 12 mm   **13**
  (b) Edge of tail membrane with a row of stiff bristles about 1 mm long from the end of calcar to tail (no bristles on calcar, but there may be some long, fine hairs); ear length 14−17 mm, tragus two thirds the length of the ear, thin, pointed and straight-sided   **Natterer's bat**
13 (a) Foot about one third the length of the shin; calcar half length from foot to tail; fur shaggy, black or dark brown, with light tips   **14**
  (b) Foot more than half the length of the shin; calcar three quarters of the length from foot to tail; fur dense, even length; hair on back uniform colour from base to tip; line of fine hairs (1 mm long) on edge of tail membrane and calcar; tragus convex on outer (posterior) edge   **Daubenton's bat**
14 (a) Tragus sharply pointed with outer (posterior) edge straight or concave; ear and nose usually black; males with thin parallel-sided penis   **Whiskered bat**
  (b) Tragus bluntly pointed with outer edge usually convex; ear and nose dark brown; males with thick club-shaped penis   **Brandt's bat**
  NB There is much variation in shape and size of many characters within whiskered and Brandt's bats and positive identification may be possible only when using skull characters [268].

FAMILY RHINOLOPHIDAE

GENUS *Rhinolophus* (HORSESHOE BATS)

A family with one genus and *c.* 68 species mainly in the tropics of the Old World. Five species reach Europe and two of these occur in Britain.

The muzzle bears a complex series of nose-leaves (Fig. 6.3) consisting of a lower *horseshoe* around the nostrils and a raised central plate or *sella* which is joined by a longitudinal connecting process, flattened in the sagittal plane, to an upper triangular lobe or *lancet* with the free tip projecting upwards against the forehead. The ears are widely spaced, lack a tragus such as occurs in all Vespertilionidae but have a broad antitragus (*behind* the basal notch).

The dental formula is 1.1.2.3/2.1.3.3. The upper incisors are carried at the tips of very slender premaxillae which frequently become detached when skulls are cleaned.

Horseshoe bats roost mainly in caves during winter, often communally. They hang freely from the roof by the claws of their feet and rest with their wings wrapped round the body and almost completely concealing it. In this they differ from all vespertilionid bats which only rarely adopt a similar, but less extreme posture. The degree to which the wings are wrapped gives some measure of control of the body microclimate within the wings. In wet weather dripping water does not wet the fur but instead runs over the membranes and drips off the wrists. A disadvantage of exposing so much membrane is the potential loss of moisture by evaporation and for this reason horseshoe bats are usually found in hibernation sites with relative humidities over 90%. Their hind limbs are long and thin with a relatively short tail, ideally suited to clasping rock projections on cave roofs when going to roost but useless for quadrupedal movement. On horizontal surfaces they progress forwards by a series of leaps in which the wings provide the thrust, or, less frequently, pull themselves backwards until they reach a vertical surface. They are amongst the most agile fliers and readily take off from the ground even in confined spaces. Echolocation pulses are emitted through the nostrils, with mouth closed, and are directed and modified by varying the shape of the 'horseshoe'.

The two species found in Britain differ greatly in size and in the shape of parts of the nose-leaf.

Greater horseshoe bat *Rhinolophus ferrumequinum*

Vespertilio ferrum-equinum Schreber, 1774; France.

RECOGNITION
Can readily be distinguished from lesser horseshoe

Fig. 6.3. Greater horseshoe bat. (Photo: S.C. Bisserôt.)

without disturbance by size. This species is about tablespoon size and the lesser teaspoon size. When active or in clusters the wings are folded alongside the body. Presence of nose-leaf, absence of a tragus and size then permits recognition (forearm 50.6– 59.0 mm in adults). Fur is fairly evenly buff brown above and below, becoming deeper, even chestnut in old females. Juveniles have greyish fur until the June moult.

Total length of skull > 20 mm compared with < 16 mm for lesser horseshoe.

SIGN
Territorial sites of males often show a yellowish brown stain on projections used for hanging, visible only on light-coloured stone.

Faeces c. 9–13 × 2.5 mm, vary in colour and texture according to diet: black after *Geotrupes* beetles, dark brown after *Aphodius* and tipulids, and light brown after most moths or *Melolontha*. Brittle after beetles are eaten; sticky after moths.

Remains of food most commonly found within a short distance of the entrance of a cave, mine, porch, etc. where a crevice allows temperatures to build up and provides suitable footholds for animals to cluster. Also found beneath trees used as nighttime perches. Remains of food most evident in spring and autumn. Only abdomen of large beetles eaten, remainder left partially or completely intact.

DESCRIPTION
Fur thick and fluffy, pale buff with darker buff tips becoming progressively darker and reddish with age. Juveniles have grey fur which may develop buff tips ventrally during their first year. Only slightly paler ventrally. Moult begins once regular

dusk and dawn feeding occurs in late May or early June and is complete by late June or early July.

Eyes small; field of view apparently partly obscured by nose-leaf. Nostrils open within the parabolic horseshoe (about 14 mm high by 8 mm wide). A few vibrissae occur beneath the horseshoe and on the lower lip. Ears large and triangular, lacking a tragus but with broad antitragus.

One pair of functional pectoral nipples; a pair of pelvic teats develop slightly anterior to the vulva during pregnancy in females breeding for the first time. They are without a milk supply, and are used by the young for holding on. They are retained, but may regress slightly during the following winter and more so if breeding is omitted for a year or more.

Chromosomes: $2n = 58$, FNa = 60, continental data [271].

Relationships: most closely related to *Rhinolophus clivosus* (Africa), *R. bocharicus* (Iran etc.) and *R. affinis* (SE Asia).

MEASUREMENTS
Head and body 56–68 mm, forearm 50.6– 59.0 mm, wingspan 330–395 mm, ear 21–26 mm, weight 13–34 g. Males about 2% smaller than females as measured by forearm: mean 54.8 mm ($n = 228$) for males and 55.5 mm ($n = 222$) for females (SD c. 1.0 mm) ([1], Gloucestershire and Somerset). Males 2–15% lighter than non-pregnant females according to age and season (Table 6.1).

VARIATION
British animals slightly smaller on average than in some continental populations, e.g. mean fore-

Table 6.1. Weights of greater horseshoe bats, Somerset 1979–1985. Means of annual means, (g ± SD) [1].	Late Oct	Late Jan	Early April
Females			
First winter	25.8 ± 0.8	20.4 ± 0.3	16.9 ± 0.2
Second winter	27.9 ± 0.6	22.4 ± 0.5	18.6 ± 0.2
Third winter	28.9 ± 0.9	23.6 ± 0.6	19.5 ± 0.1
Fourth (plus) winter	30.5 ± 0.7	25.0 ± 0.7	19.8 ± 0.1
Males			
First winter	24.4 ± 0.8	19.7 ± 0.4	16.5 ± 0.2
Second winter	26.1 ± 0.8	21.1 ± 0.3	17.5 ± 0.2
Third winter	26.8 ± 1.0	21.7 ± 0.5	17.9 ± 0.1
Fourth (plus) winter	26.0 ± 1.3	21.9 ± 0.2	18.1 ± 0.4

arm length of males 54.8 mm in England, 55.7–
56.7 mm in Italy [54], but not enough to justify
recognition as a discrete subspecies. (The name
R. f. insulanus Barrett-Hamilton, 1910 (Cheddar,
Somerset) [18] was based on this difference in
size.)

DISTRIBUTION
Possibly limited by the need to feed in winter. No
cross-channel movements have been recorded despite extensive ringing studies, in England and
France, over four decades.

HISTORY
Present in Kent and Isle of Wight until *c.* 1900.
Populations benefited from mining industries, especially limestone, ochre and metal extraction, after
mines fell into disuse early this century. However
more recently many closures for safety reasons are
thought to have seriously depressed numbers in
Dorset, and to a lesser extent in Avon, Somerset,
Wiltshire and Gloucestershire.

HABITAT
Numbers are greatest in sites with access to steep
south-facing slopes covered with mixed deciduous

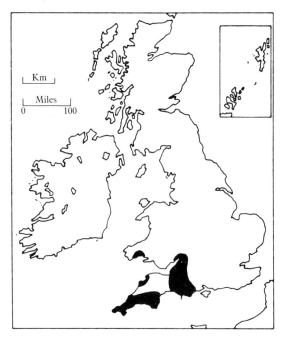

Map 6.1. Greater horseshoe bat.

Map 6.2. Greater horseshoe bat.

woodland and permanent pastures grazed by cattle, where beetles, moths and other insects are abundant. A viable population needs a series of caves, disused mines, cellars or tunnels as hibernacula which offer a range of air flow patterns and temperatures. The sites need to be dispersed among suitable feeding areas, and free from excessive human disturbance. One of these sites may be used for breeding if numbers are high, otherwise a suitable building is needed which has one or more attics warmed by the sun.

SOCIAL ORGANISATION AND BEHAVIOUR
Immature animals highly gregarious at all times, and in winter form colonies with adult males of up to 300. Adult females in winter more solitary. Adult males leave the nursery colonies in mid-summer when young are born.

Summer: in Gloucestershire some of previous year's juveniles and breeding females return to nursery site in May, but it is not until mid-June that most breeding females return. Males up to 14 years old return with the breeding females in June, and remain until mid-July when peak numbers of adults occur and births take place. Males normally leave then and remain segregated from breeding females in late summer [142, 200, 217]. During lactation only breeding females, juveniles and immatures of both sexes are present in nursery roosts in most years. In early September breeding females start to leave so that juveniles plus one or two immatures remain in late September and early October.

Preliminary studies of active bats roosting in summer have shown no evidence of hierarchy and little aggression [1]. Clusters form and disperse, largely in relation to ambient temperatures and the need to conserve energy for reproduction. Minor disputes occur as individuals enter or leave tight clusters for defaecation and urination. Communication appears to be by audible calls and movements. After leaving the roost aggressive chasing behaviour has been observed in passages nearby in late June, and similar interactions at feeding grounds may occur.

Winter: hibernacula can be broadly divided into three types based on the age and sex of the occupants.
1 Mainly 1st year animals of both sexes plus older immatures throughout the winter. Adult males may be present in midwinter. Clusters are common if numbers build up.
2 Few 1st year animals, but many 2nd and 3rd year immatures, together with surplus adult males which may also form clusters. Females up to the age of 6 years may be present but are usually solitary.
3 Single breeding male holding a territorial site, often small, and may even be a part of a type-one hibernaculum if there are several entrances. The male occupies the site in late summer, autumn and again in spring. Each is visited by up to eight breeding females in late September and October.

Females store fat, copulate and move to deeper regions of other hibernacula for most of winter. The same females return to the same sites over many years, in one case over 19 years. The male remains all winter if the site provides a suitable temperature range, otherwise he moves to larger sites as well. In spring females return to the same male territory and may remain there until mid-June, undergoing the early stages of pregnancy. Individual males have held a territory for 12 years or more. Once they are replaced, they are never seen again, and presumably are dead. Possibly territorial males and their breeding females control an area around their site for feeding in spring and autumn. Yellowish brown stain evident in territorial hibernaculum of male may assist in retaining site, but origin and use unknown.

Hibernation possible from late September to mid-May in the population as a whole, greatly affected by weather and food availability, especially in spring. It seems to start and end earliest in breeding females, and latest in the last juveniles to be born. Level of fat deposited in October varies from year to year and between individuals; lowest in adult males. April levels are much more constant and are similar in all age and sex groups [1].

Frequency of arousal depends upon environmental temperature and time of year. Occurs at *c.* 11−13°C in October falling to *c.* 7°C in February and rising again in spring [199]. Arousal frequency of once per day in autumn at 11°C falls to once in 6−10 days in February at 7°C. In Europe feeding takes place in winter if suitable mild weather occurs [111, 198, 199]. Winter movements of up to 10 km occur regularly as bats search for hibernacula with suitable temperatures and/or feeding sites [31, 111, 198, 217]. Unequal sex ratios in hibernacula do not seem to reflect composition of population, but differential site selection [1]. When hibernating they are especially prone to arousal by lights or noises when at 9°C or above, or at dusk. They show a characteristic 'knees bend' response initially.

Daily rhythm: there is an endogenous activity rhythm which continues through hibernation [71]. Activity is timed for dusk arousal and flight for feeding when possible throughout the year. A secondary dawn flight develops in spring, once insect availability permits successful feeding [201]. Between flights they may return to the breeding roost or use temporary resting places. Emergence lasts for about 30 min and peak exit time varies, according to phase of reproduction and cloud cover, between sunset and 35 min after sunset. Between May and early August bats return after feeding and spend the night in the roost. They groom themselves, digest food, defaecate and urinate over several hours before leaving for the dawn feed [201]. Similar behaviour follows the dawn return. In late August night absences develop, perhaps when juveniles start to learn the location of their hibernacula.

Movement: shifts of populations from site to site during hibernation often occur without disturbance [230] and may be a response to lack of suitable temperature for hibernation or to the need for better feeding areas. Turnover of bats from type-one sites is high from winter to winter as individuals age and move on to type-two and type-three sites.

Animals travel up to about 30 or 35 km from the breeding site and return annually to breed. This limit applies in all British populations studied, and in Italy [53] and Japan [143]. Most juveniles spend their first winter in hibernacula close to the breeding site, and may even remain in cellar systems beneath it. However, they have been recorded regularly up to 35 km away in some winters. These are often late-born animals which rarely return to the breeding site. Five movements of over 32 km were reported in Devon from 1948 to 1970 [110]. Movements of 35 to 77 km have been recorded between Somerset and Gloucestershire by four individuals in 30 years of study [1]. None were shown to return, and at least one bred in the new area. Similar movements of up to 64 km occur between Devon and Dorset, and Dorset and Wiltshire or Somerset [110, 111, 244], generally of immature animals which move between their first and second winters. Adult males originate from up to 40 km from their territories [1].

Ultrasound pulses of 83 kHz are emitted through nostrils as a narrow beam focussed by horseshoe. Relatively long pulses at constant frequency give great sensitivity to movement. Ears twitch alternately during echolocation at rest while scanning.

FEEDING
Faecal analysis, remains at feeding sites and direct observations [1] show diet consists mainly of the following insects: dor beetles (*Geotrupes* sp.) from late August to May; cockchafers (may bugs) (*Melolontha melolontha*) and moths in May and June; moths, especially the yellow underwings (*Noctua* spp.) from late June until August; large tipulid flies and dung beetles (*Aphodius*) in August. The last two are especially eaten by juveniles at weaning. Hunting flight is low, fairly slow (8.3 m/s maximum observed) and follows regular flight paths for some distance from the roost. They have been seen taking dor beetles from the ground, and hanging in trees waiting for prey to fly past [1]. Winter feeding depends upon weather, availability of suitable insects and possibly the depletion of fat reserves.

BREEDING

Season: males develop sperm during June and July from the age of 2 or 3 years. Viable sperm is stored in the epididymis from late summer until the following spring. Females normally breed at end of 3rd year, but may do so a year early or one or more years later. Females aged 3−8 years often miss breeding in some years. One female bred regularly up to the age of 24 years [1].

Copulation occurs in male territory, normally in late September or October, sometimes later in winter and possibly in spring. Male mounts female, which may be semitorpid initially, from behind and bites the nuchal fur. Copulation may last 50 min and leads to formation of vaginal plug (coagulated secretion of male urethral gland) and storage of sperm in the oviducts. Incidence of plugs rises as winter progresses, but pattern varies from year to year [1]. Spermatozoa may be trapped fortuitously within plug but this is not a site of sperm storage [188]. Plugs may be voided after autumnal copulations. Single follicle starts meiosis in October, rests during winter and completes ovum production in early April in Japan [171]. Female ovulates in mid-April, usually [217] at the time of plug ejection. Implantation follows a week later [152].

Periods of torpor in early and late pregnancy [200] delay birth until July, occasionally late June or early August. Mean of mean annual birth dates over 21 years in Gloucestershire was 15th July ±2 days (range 6th–26th), despite variation in climate and insect density. Birth occurs inside attic or cave, often at dusk. Female hangs from feet and baby emerges into overlapping wings. Babies are parked in the roost shortly afterwards while mothers leave to feed. Mature females returning to breeding site rarely fail to breed (max. 1–2% of total). Hence resorption of embryos is likely to be a rare event.

Development: young born blind with sparse short grey fur, naked abdomen, and with pink membranes. Forearm *c.* 26 mm, weight 6.2 g; increase rapidly to 50 mm and 13 g in about 17 days. Eyes open at 9 days and ultrasounds emitted. At 17 days they are just capable of flight. By 3 weeks they regularly fly from the roost and at 5 weeks begin to catch insects, usually small *Aphodius* beetles [1] but remain inside if weather is wet and windy. Steady increase in weight up to 50 days, followed by erratic changes, suggests lactation continues until then. This is supported by presence of mothers who leave immediately after this time, normally by early September. No evidence of mother–young bonds during winter, but in May adult females and last year's young return to the breeding site and the latter remain after new young are born. First time breeders often give birth late in July or early August. Their young are inclined to be stunted and have high mortality rates.

Table 6.2. Survival of female greater horseshoe bats by age; Gloucestershire, breeding site data, 1980–1983 [1].

Year age group	Number caught first year	Percentage surviving 1 year later
1	92	53
2	57	72
3	42	79
4	35	66
5	21	71
6	24	87
7	22	91
8–12	56	86
13–17	39	82
18–25	12	58
All	400	73

POPULATION

Densities: British population in 1985 thought to be about 2200 (combined estimates from author and R.E. Stebbings). Breeding site counts and captures give population data for that site but degree of overlap of breeding populations is poorly understood, even where extensive work has been attempted. Peak counts in early July plus number of juveniles born give the best simple estimate of numbers alive in summer for that population.

Sex ratio at birth 1:1. Females just outnumber males in captures made at breeding sites and in nearby hibernacula. 53% of 446 individuals captured in the breeding site and surrounding hibernacula in Gloucestershire from 1979 to 1985 were females.

Survival: perinatal deaths are rare, generally about 1–2% annually. Juveniles commonly disappear after early flights and in some years few reach the hibernacula. Juvenile survival varies according to winter climate, *c.* 40–80% of those reaching the hibernacula. Table 6.2 shows survival rates for different ages of females in Gloucestershire. Severe, prolonged, cold winters reduce survival rates, especially in adult males. Hence sex ratios fluctuate. However, both sexes can live beyond 20 years and still breed. Upper limits of 26 years for males and 24 for females in Gloucestershire [1], similar to those in Devon [110]. In France a 30-year-old male has been recorded [39].

MORTALITY
Natural predation rarely reported. Skeletal remains have been found in pellets of barn and tawny owls [244]. Rarely caught by cats. Accidental deaths from collisions with vehicles result from bats flying about 1 m above the ground. Single greatest cause of death seems to be starvation in late cold springs. Disturbance in late April and May is likely to be most crucial to bat survival. This affects all age groups and both sexes.

Diseased bats are rarely seen, and individuals have survived extensive injuries to the skin, muscles and even broken metacarpal bones.

PARASITES
The nycteribiid fly *Phthiridium biarticulatum* is principally a parasite of the lesser horseshoe bat, but occasionally occurs on this species [121]. The

flea *Rhinolophopsylla unipectinata* occurs widely in Europe but has not been recorded from Britain.

RELATIONS WITH MAN

Consumption of pest insects such as cockchafers and tipulids is beneficial. Control of insects for forestry and agriculture is likely to have been a serious factor contributing to population declines.

Difficult to keep in captivity, and no breeding success recorded. Conservation of breeding sites and hibernacula is crucial to successful survival of species. Dependence upon disused mines especially makes conservation work to maintain suitable air-flow important since they are more unstable than natural caves. Grills installed at entrances to disused mines protect bats from disturbance and owners from potential prosecutions arising from injuries to persons entering the mine.

LITERATURE

Ransome [202]: general account of its natural history intended for secondary school pupils.

AUTHOR FOR THIS SPECIES

R.D. Ransome, with acknowledgement for additional data and comment provided by P.A. Racey, P.W. Richardson and J.E. Hill.

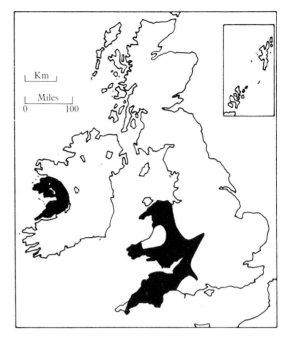

Map 6.3. Lesser horseshoe bat.

Map 6.4. Lesser horseshoe bat.

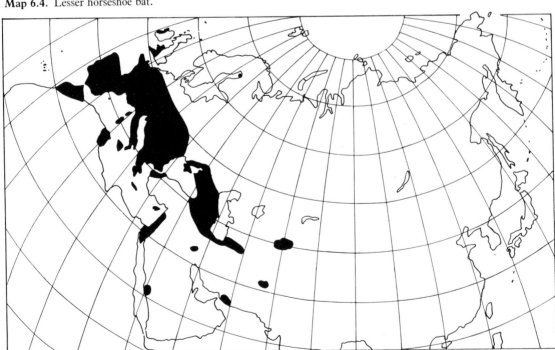

Lesser horseshoe bat *Rhinolophus hipposideros*

Vespertilio hipposideros Bechstein, 1800; France.
Vespertilio minutus Montagu, 1808; Wiltshire, England.

RECOGNITION
See Greater horseshoe. Forearm 35−42.5 mm in adults. Fur greyish in juveniles from birth to first moult in August of their 2nd year, and generally buff brown in older animals. Always fold wing membranes around the body when torpid.

SIGN
Faeces *c.* 6−8 × 1.7 mm, usually dark brown but paler when moths are eaten. Dispersed as for greater horseshoe, but in hibernacula dropping sites are often beneath low hollows in roof and are more numerous.

Feeding remains found in similar places to those of greater horseshoe, particularly porches and tunnels. Wings and legs of moths (including the lesser yellow underwing) and tipulids most often seen.

DESCRIPTION
As for greater horseshoe except for details of fur, timing of moult (August, not June) and small size. Fur is relatively longer and does not develop reddish tips with age. Nose-leaf < 12 mm long by 8 mm wide.

Chromosomes: 2n = 56, FNa = 60, continental data [271].

MEASUREMENTS
Head and body 35−39 mm, forearm 35−42.5 mm, wingspan 225−250 mm, ear 10−12 mm, weight 4.0−9.4 g. Males about 2% smaller than females as measured by forearm: mean 37.4 mm ($n = 75$) for males and 38.1 mm ($n = 53$) for females (SD *c.* 0.8 mm) ([1], Gloucestershire and Somerset).

VARIATION
British population not significantly different from continental, in spite of earlier recognition of *R. h. minutus* as British subspecies based on small size, e.g. in France mean forearm length of males 37.0 mm ($n = 171$) and females 38.0 mm ($n = 110$) [218].

DISTRIBUTION
From SW Europe and NW Africa east to the W Himalayas.

HISTORY
Recorded from Neolithic strata at Dowel Cave, Derbyshire [269]. Populations benefitted from abandoned mines in the same manner as greater horseshoes at the beginning of this century. Recent closures are likely to have depressed numbers and/ or reduced population range. However densities in forested areas have increased recently.

Fig. 6.4. Lesser horseshoe bat.
(Photo: S.C. Bisserôt.)

HABITAT

Numbers are greatest in sheltered valleys with extensive deciduous woods or dense scrub close to a range of suitable roost sites. These include attics, chimneys, boiler rooms, cellars, tunnels, sewer pipes, disused mines and caves. One site is used for breeding if it offers a range of temperature choices, e.g. cellars, chimneys and attics. If not the breeding females are likely to change site during the summer.

SOCIAL ORGANISATION AND BEHAVIOUR

Essentially similar to greater horseshoe as far as is known, except winter clusters do not occur and the deep hibernation period is shorter.

Summer: torpidity has been recorded up to 22 June and from 21 August in Gloucestershire. Gross population counts from April to September show similar patterns to those of greater horseshoes, but details of changes in population structure are not known. Site shifts are frequent, e.g. between cellars, chimneys and attics within a few hours or days. In warm sites when food is abundant they hang singly, but in cooler sites, especially during lactation when torpidity probably does not occur, dense clusters of up to 150 may develop.

In Czechoslovakia breeding females and previous year's young return in April together with a few adult males [72].

Winter: a wide range of sites are used as hibernacula from large underground pipes to extensive cave and mine systems. Each population tends to be widely scattered in mild winters, but severe weather may lead to high numbers in extensive systems. Clusters do not form in winter, but groups a few centimetres apart do occur regularly in favoured spots. Small hibernacula often contain single adult males, with or without females, in autumn, which suggests a similar territorial system to greater horseshoes.

Hibernation starts later and ends earlier than in greater horseshoes. Often they are active in hibernacula in spring and autumn during the daytime in warm weather when feeding is successful. In early hibernation adult females have most fat and adult males least (Table 6.3). Females lose c. 23% of original weight in winter, males c. 13%. Temperatures recorded near hibernating animals range from 5−11°C; higher until late December when a high proportion leave to feed on mild nights; lower in January to March when feeding is less frequent, but still occurs on mild evenings. Effect of temperature upon arousal frequency has not been investigated, but seems likely to be similar to that on greater horseshoes. The tendency for this species to select higher temperatures than greater horseshoe during winter may reflect the greater feeding efficiency of the former, the higher incidence of suitable winter food prey or different arousal frequency in response to the same temperature. Selection of higher temperatures results in deep penetration into hibernacula systems [26, 72, 111].

Daily rhythm: synchronisation of winter arousals with dusk suggests that endogenous rhythm occurs. In Czechoslovakia members of a small breeding colony were active all night even at dawn temperatures of 2°C and 3.4°C although individuals returned between dusk and dawn flights to rest. Heavy rain shortened flight activity which began at or up to 42 min after dusk [73]. In County Clare a characteristic 'light-sampling' behaviour (brief emergence/return) was noted about 25 min after sunset, earlier on cloudy nights; dawn return was half an hour before sunrise [154]. Winter movements are rare and very short, most involving < 1.5 km [1, 110]. Longer movements up to 22 km generally occur only between summer and winter sites.

Ultrasound pulses of 105−115 kHz are emitted through the nostrils; chewing insects therefore does not prevent echolocation.

FEEDING

Analysis of diet in County Clare showed main prey items to be nematoceran flies, moths, caddis flies and lacewings [154]. Craneflies and small beetles are also taken. Hunting flight is low and slow with frequent circling. Initially individuals follow

Table 6.3. Mean weight of lesser horseshoe bats (g ± SD), Somerset and Gloucestershire 1957−1963.

	Oct and early Nov	Late Dec and early Jan	Early April
Breeding females	6.93 ± 0.6 ($n = 29$)	6.27 ± 0.4 ($n = 38$)	5.34 ± 0.3 ($n = 98$)
Breeding males	5.55 ± 0.5 ($n = 58$)	5.73 ± 0.4 ($n = 144$)	4.85 ± 0.3 ($n = 98$)

regular flight paths, but soon disappear into dense vegetation. Preferred foraging sites in County Clare are over water and farmyards [154]. Great manoeuvrability, high frequency ultrasound pulses and freedom to chew without loss of echolocation ability combine to permit capture of insects in conditions in which few if any other British species can operate.

Large prey are taken back to temporary night roost sites which may include trees.

BREEDING

Females in Britain normally do not come into oestrous until they are 15 months old [152], but in Czechoslovakia a small proportion of 1st year females had already mated by January and produced young the following summer; others took 3 years before giving birth [74].

According to frequencies of vaginal plugs in females, mating mainly takes place from late September to November [74] but can occur later.

Follicle development starts in September, then rests over winter before completing oogenesis in early April. Ovulation occurs in mid-April before vaginal plug is ejected [74, 152]. Normally a single egg released but one case of two embryos recorded [74]. Calculated mean of 1.35 young per reproducing female in Holland [224] seems unlikely. Direct evidence for twins was not offered. Pregnancy lasts about 2 months and is affected by periods of torpor [1, 74]. Final weight may reach 9.4 g [1]. Mean birth date probably influenced by climate and/or food supplies.

Development: young similar to greater horseshoes, about 1.8 g at birth (mothers about 5.5 g); parked in roost whilst mothers feed [1] but often move their location so they may be difficult to find. Lactation probably lasts 4−5 weeks by which time young fly from the roost [74]. Young fly by early August in County Clare [154]. First young flying in early August, weighing 3.8−4.2 g. Period of lactation probably overlaps time of juvenile flights from roost sites as it seems to end in mid-August.

POPULATION

Densities: very difficult to estimate status of British population. An assessment in 1985 indicated a shrinkage in range, but increased densities within the range [106]. In Gloucestershire one breeding population increased from 12 in 1960 to 86 in 1985.

Populations are highly localised and variable in size. A common species throughout suitable areas in County Clare.

Sex ratio: in Czechoslovakia females formed 52% of juveniles born ($n = 234$) but only 32% of adults captured ($n = 1328$). However this was due to tendency of males to be caught in large numbers in cave hibernacula whereas females remained in buildings more frequently and were more difficult to find [72].

Survival: likely to be similar to that of greater horseshoes. Upper limit of 14 years [1] and 13 years [110] in Britain, but 18 years on the Continent [79] may reflect much larger numbers ringed.

MORTALITY

Cats are the most frequent predators reported, but starvation seems to be the major cause of death. In severe cold spells in late winter low-weight dead individuals occur, sometimes still hanging on the walls in hibernation.

PARASITES

The principle host of the nycteribiid fly *Phthiridium biarticulatum*, but apparently now much rarer than it was [121].

RELATIONS WITH MAN

Very difficult to maintain in captivity even for a few days. Have benefitted from grills installed to protect greater horseshoes from disturbance. Dependence upon buildings for breeding in many areas means they are vulnerable to timber treatment and changes in use of cellars or outhouses. Inability to travel long distances restricts potential choice of roosts, increasing vulnerability.

AUTHOR FOR THIS SPECIES

R.D. Ransome, with acknowledgement for additional data and comment provided by C. McAney, P.A. Racey and P.W. Richardson.

FAMILY VESPERTILIONIDAE

GENUS *Myotis*

The largest genus of bats, with about 100 species and a world-wide distribution. Ten species occur in Europe; five of these are known to be resident in Britain, a sixth is almost extinct.

The muzzle is narrow and unspecialised with nostrils opening outwards. Ears are well-spaced, longer than their width and all have an emargination on the outer margin, inconspicuous in most species. Tragus at least half as high as conch, generally narrow and more or less pointed. No post-calcarial lobe. The dental formula is 2.1.3.3 / 3.1.3.3.

Myotis bats are very variable in their roost preferences but, apart from the largest members, are usually found in confined spaces such as tree-holes and crevices in caves and buildings. The large species usually hang freely by their feet but hold their wings to their sides and not wrapped round the body as in horseshoe bats. Echolocation pulses are emitted through the open mouth.

Brandt's bat, *M. brandtii*, was only clearly recognised as distinct from whiskered bat, *M. mystacinus*, about 1970. Therefore some data given for whiskered bat could be based on either species and is marked with an asterisk (⋆) in the text if it has not been confirmed as applying to whiskered bat as now recognised.

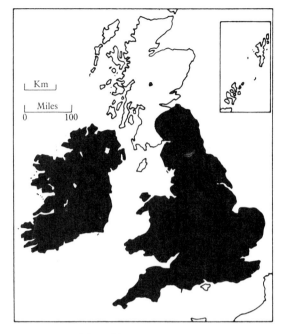

Map 6.5. Whiskered bat.

Map 6.6. Whiskered bat.

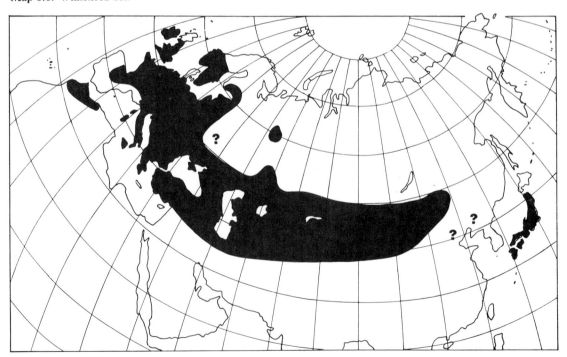

Whiskered bat *Myotis mystacinus*

Vespertilio mystacinus Kuhl, 1819; Germany.
Selysius mystacinus.

RECOGNITION

Smallest of the *Myotis* but very similar to Brandt's bat and easily confused with Daubenton's. Distinguished from latter by its small feet, very dark grey-black face, nostrils, ear and membranes, dark brown dorsal pelage and straight or concave outer margin of long pointed tragus (Fig. 6.5). Distinguished from Brandt's by its relatively longer tragus and more pointed ear and in adult males by the thin parallel-sided penis (Fig. 6.6).

The whiskered bat could also be confused with the larger, yellow-brown *M. emarginatus* which has not yet been found in Britain. This has thick opaque membranes and a deeply angular notch slightly above the middle of the posterior edge of the ear.

Skull distinguished from Brandt's by lack of conspicuous cusp on anterior inner angle of upper P³. This is visible in the living animal viewed from the side and slightly forward of perpendicular to the maxilla.

DESCRIPTION

Upper parts dark brown with lighter, golden bronze tips, under parts greyish white. Fur looks shaggy and ill-kempt. Juveniles up to 12 months are often almost black. Membranes, face and ears usually very dark brown to black. Ears moderately long, *c.* 15 mm, and narrow. Tragus a little more than half length of conch, anterior border straight and posterior border straight or slightly concave, narrowing to blunt point. Wings narrow and membranes almost translucent.

Chromosome: 2n = 44, FNa = 50−52, continental data [270].

RELATIONSHIPS

Very closely related to Brandt's bat; the two species were only clearly recognised as distinct in Europe about 1970.

MEASUREMENTS

Head and body 35−48 mm; forearm 30−37 mm; wingspan 210−240 mm; ear 14−15 mm; condylobasal length of skull 12.0−13.5 mm; weight in hibernation 4−8 g. Males smaller than females on average: mean forearm length of 36 males was 33.4 mm (range 32.0−35.3), of 11 females 33.7 mm (32.5−34.9) [1].

DISTRIBUTION

Uncertain due to confusion with Brandt's bat, but widespread in Europe and Palaearctic Asia [252]. Probably found throughout England and Wales, status in Scotland uncertain [153]. Found throughout Ireland.

Fig. 6.5. Whiskered bat. (Photo: S.C. Bisserôt.)

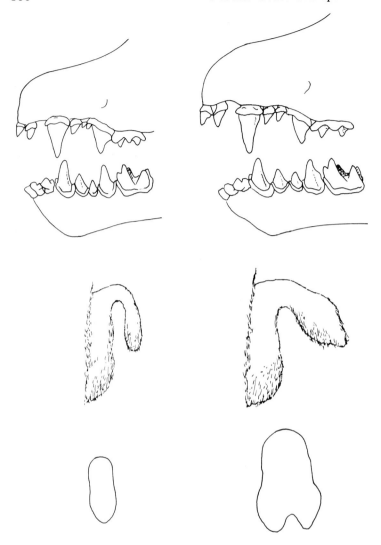

Fig. 6.6. Distinguishing characters of whiskered bat (left) and Brandt's bat (right) showing teeth (top), penis (centre) and baculum (bottom).

HABITAT

Found in wooded and open country, often near water. Roost in trees and buildings in summer and sometimes in caves in winter; use bat boxes.

SOCIAL ORGANISATION AND BEHAVIOUR

Summer: adult females segregate from adult males to form large nursery colonies, often under ridge tiles in buildings. Adult males seem to be solitary. Flight medium speed and fluttering, almost butterfly-like, up to 20 m, often along a 'beat' over a hedgerow. Flight generally level with occasional stoops. Glide for short periods especially when feeding amongst the canopy [207]. Emerge early,

often at sunset, and probably remain active intermittently throughout night. In Finland two distinct periods of activity were found in summer — after sunset and before sunrise [170].

Winter: found in caves and cellars, but probably also hibernate in trees and houses. They prefer cooler entrance regions of caves [26] and are more frequently found in caves during very cold weather. Always solitary but sometimes hang freely from roof and sometimes found in tight crevices.

Often seen flying during the day in winter and spring★.

Longest movement recorded is 1936 km, SW from Russia to Bulgaria★ [137].

FEEDING

Feed on small insects and spiders, which are sometimes picked off foliage.

BREEDING

Some females achieve sexual maturity at 3 months, majority at 15 months★ [223]. Copulation observed in Dutch cave in January★ [165] and an increasing proportion found to be inseminated as hibernation progressed [250].

POPULATION

Sex ratio in hibernation usually shows male bias★. In Suffolk 60% ($n = 68$) were males [235] and in the Netherlands 62% ($n = 1377$) [24]. In Czechoslovakia 59% males ($n = 42$) were recorded for individually roosting bats but 93% ($n = 213$) for winter colonies [75]. Several population parameters have been estimated from studies in hibernacula [26]. Adult survival rate was 0.75, giving a lifespan of 16 years and mean longevity of 4.0 years. In Surrey one was refound 23 years after banding [123] and in the Netherlands a male over 18 years old was found★ [107].

MORTALITY

Several eaten during hibernation by mouse or shrew in caves in Suffolk [1].

PARASITES

The following ectoparasites have been recorded but prior to the discovery of Brandt's bat. Therefore these will need confirmation: The flea *Ischnopsyllus simplex* is common; the mites *Spinturnix myoti*, *Steatonyssus periblepharus* and *Neomyobia mystacinalis* have been recorded.

RELATIONS WITH MAN

Has been maintained in captivity for several months on diet of moths and beetles.

AUTHOR FOR THIS SPECIES

Based upon the account in the second edition by R.E. Stebbings, with acknowledgement for additional data and comments from P.W. Richardson and A.M. Hutson.

Brandt's bat *Myotis brandtii*

Vespertilio brandtii Eversmann, 1845; Russia.
Myotis mystacinus (part).

RECOGNITION

See Whiskered bat. Adult's upper pelage is a characteristic red-brown and adult males are further distinguished by the club-shaped penis. Tragus is almost half the length of conch and has a more or less convex posterior margin. Juveniles up to 12 months old are only safely distinguishable from whiskered bats by characters of the teeth which can be seen in living bats, especially the less reduced second premolars above and below (Fig. 6.6).

DESCRIPTION

A small bat closely resembling the whiskered. Adults red-brown above and buff beneath. Membranes, face and ears are dark red-brown. Ears shorter and squarer than whiskered, *c.* 12 mm long. Penis distinctly club-shaped. Wing narrow and membranes translucent. Young bats up to 12 months old are dark grey — almost identical to whiskered.

Chromosomes: $2n = 44$; $FNa = 50$, continental data [270].

MEASUREMENTS

Head and body 37–48 mm; forearm 31–38 mm; wingspan 210–255 mm; ear 11–13 mm; condylobasal length of skull 13.0–14.5 mm. In Devon 21 adult females measured: forearm, mean 34.8 mm; wingspan, mean 240 mm.

DISTRIBUTION

Still somewhat uncertain because of confusion with whiskered bat, but widespread in England and Wales.

HABITAT

Found in wooded country, roosting in caves in small numbers (winter) and buildings (summer).

SOCIAL ORGANISATION AND BEHAVIOUR

Summer: one nursery colony found in N Devon hanging from the roof apex of a hay loft in full daylight on 16 July consisted of 49 bats. Thirteen fully grown bats escaped and of the remainder 16 were lactating adult females, five were nulliparous females at least 1 year old, and 15 were recently born babies.

Winter: usually solitary, sometimes in small groups

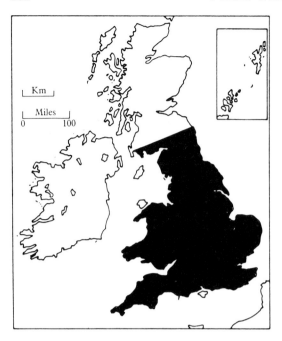

Map 6.7. Brandt's bat.

or in larger clusters of other species. Two winter movements of 2.5 km recorded in Suffolk.

POPULATION
Little known. Greatest longevity 13 years [1].

PARASITES
The flea *Ischnopsyllus simplex* is common.

AUTHOR FOR THIS SPECIES
Based upon the account in the second edition by R.E. Stebbings, with acknowledgement for additional data and comments from A.M. Hutson.

Natterer's bat *Myotis nattereri*

Vespertilio nattereri Kuhl, 1818; Germany.
Selysius nattereri.

RECOGNITION
Distinguished from the smaller whiskered and Brandt's bats by the paler face and membranes, and longer, slender tragus; and from all other species by the presence of a conspicuous fringe of stiff hairs (1 mm in length) along the outer edge of the interfemoral membrane (Fig. 6.7).

Map 6.8. Brandt's bat.

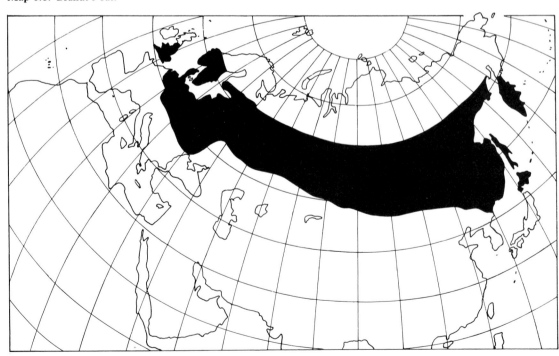

Fig. 6.7. Natterer's bat. (Photo: S.C. Bisserôt.)

DESCRIPTION

A medium-sized bat with upper parts light brown and under side white or very light buff. A clear line of demarcation from shoulder to ear. Juveniles light greyish brown for first year. Wing membranes mid-brown, face pink to light brown, ear shading from pink basally to light brown distally.

Ear fairly narrow and long, *c.* 16 mm, slightly reflexed at tip. Tragus two thirds length of ear, straight-sided, long, thin and pointed. Wings broad but pointed.

Chromosomes: 2n = 44; FNa = 50−52, continental data [270].

MEASUREMENTS

Head and body 40−50 mm; forearm 36−43 mm; wingspan 250−300 mm; ear 14−18 mm; condylobasal length of skull 14−15 mm; weight in hibernation 7−12 g; weight of females in Fife in May (pre-parturition) 6.5−8.3 g (mean 7.61, *n* = 26) [33]. Males smaller than females: mean forearm length 39.0 mm (*n* = 39) in males and 39.7 mm (*n* = 32) in females in Suffolk [1]; females also 39.7 mm (range 36.9−41.4, *n* = 42) in Northants [207] and 40.0 mm (range 38.9−41.5, *n* = 26) in Fife [33]. In Spain males 38.4 mm (*n* = 12) and females 39.6 mm (*n* = 71) [13].

DISTRIBUTION

Recent records have considerably extended the known range in Scotland [35].

HISTORY

Found in Neolithic strata at Dowel Cave, Derbyshire [269].

HABITAT

Frequently found in open woodland and park areas; in Scotland found mainly in well wooded areas of river valleys and loch sides, also in coniferous plantations. Roost in hollow trees, caves and buildings (e.g. castles, barns, old houses); in Scotland all five hibernacula have been in quarry tunnels [33].

SOCIAL ORGANISATION AND BEHAVIOUR

Summer: adult females form large nursery colonies in buildings, sometimes of 100−200 bats. Emerge 45−60 min after sunset in Fife [33]. Return an hour or two before sunrise, but when young present may return after an hour. In Czechoslovakia individual bats in a colony maintained their respective activity periods each day [147]. Flight slow to medium up to 16 m, sometimes over water but more usually around trees and amongst the canopy.

Winter: arrive into hibernation caves mostly during December and leave early March in Wiltshire and Suffolk [1]. In Poland hibernate at temperatures of 8−14°C in autumn, falling to 6−10°C in winter [100]. Show a preference for cool entrance areas and is the bat most frequent in any small exposed cave-like site. Usually solitary but small groups not

Map 6.9. Natterer's bat.

uncommon and one large colony included a cluster of *c.* 150 [245].

Longest movement in Britain 24 km but in the Netherlands 62 km [24].

FEEDING

Small insects, including moths and caddis flies, caught and eaten mostly in flight but some taken off foliage. On the Continent dipterous flies and beetles have been found to be important [23].

BREEDING

Copulation observed during December in cave [87]. Single young born at end of June or early July.

POPULATION

Little known. Sex ratio in hibernation (Suffolk) 59% males ($n = 261$) [235]. Greatest longevity in Britain over 12 years [235]; in Netherlands one refound after 17 years [107].

PARASITES

Three ectoparasites are found commonly: the flea *Ischnopsyllus simplex*, and the mites *Spinturnix myoti* and *Macronyssus ellipticus*. The rare winter flea *Nycteridopsylla longiceps* is regular.

Map 6.10. Natterer's bat.

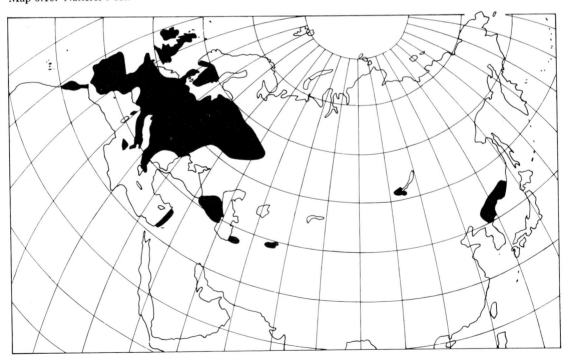

RELATIONS WITH MAN
Has survived in captivity several months [179].

AUTHOR FOR THIS SPECIES
Based upon the account in the second edition by R.E. Stebbings, with acknowledgement for additional data and comments from D.J. Bullock, A.M. Hutson and P.W. Richardson.

Bechstein's bat *Myotis bechsteinii*

Vespertilio bechsteinii Kuhl, 1818; Germany.
Selysius bechsteini.

RECOGNITION
Similar in general characters and size to Natterer's bat but with relatively long ears, extending half their length beyond the tip of the muzzle when laid forward (substantially longer than in any other British bat except the brown and grey long-eared bats in which the ears are very much longer — 75% of head and body — and meet on top of the head). Lacks fringe of hairs on interfemoral membrane.

DESCRIPTION
A medium-sized bat with upper parts light brown and lower parts greyish buff to white. Wing membranes and ears opaque, mid to dark brown. Tragus barely half the height of conch, narrow, with posterior and anterior edges more or less straight. Wings broad and slightly pointed. Face bare and pink.

Chromosomes: 2n = 44; FNa = 52, continental data [270].

MEASUREMENTS
Head and body 43—50 mm; forearm 38—45 mm (mean 40.9 mm) for males (*n* = 12) in Dorset [1]; wingspan 250—300 mm; ear 20—26 mm; condylobasal length of skull 16—17 mm; weight 7—13 g.

DISTRIBUTION
Rare in most of its range. Most records from Germany.

HISTORY
Many bones were discovered in the Neolithic flint mines at Grimes Graves, Norfolk [41]. These were about 3000—4000 years old, when forests were extensive in E Britain.

Fig. 6.8. Bechstein's bat in hibernation. (Photo: S.C. Bisserôt.)

HABITAT
A forest bat that normally roosts in trees, both summer and winter.

SOCIAL ORGANISATION AND BEHAVIOUR

Summer: most often found in tree-holes where either solitary males or small nursing colonies of adult females are found. In Germany four nursing colonies were found using artificial roost boxes placed in conifer forest with 5, 16, 21 and 47 individuals [125]. In Poland a small nursing colony of eight adults and two young was found in an ash tree on 25th July [101]. In Dorset during August and September for several years a male roosted in a hole in a house roof. Three months after finding the dead remains of the first, another male was found occupying the same hole [237, 239]. Emerges about 20 min after sunset. Flight slow, with wings held rather stiffly, up to 15 m but generally low.

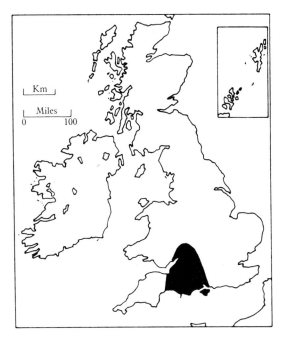

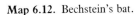

Map 6.11. Bechstein's bat.

Winter: probably hibernate in trees but occasional records of solitary hibernators in caves where they usually hang free from roof. Sometimes found in crevices but always hanging. Prefer cooler entrance areas.

FEEDING

Probably mostly moths eaten in flight. In Dorset in May a male caught a damsel fly (*Enallagma cyathigerum*) at midday [239]. A bat, almost certainly of this species, watched at close quarters, flew round an oak tree for 20 min catching moths both on the wing and resting on leaves. One in captivity also picked moths off the walls of a room [28].

POPULATION

Little known. Sex ratio in hibernation strongly biased to the males, 12 : 4 in Dorset [1], 26 : 5 in Netherlands [24]. Greatest longevity 7 years [241].

MORTALITY

One evidently eaten by a raptor [239].

Map 6.12. Bechstein's bat.

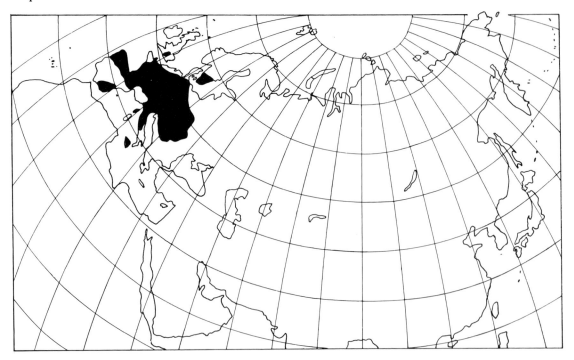

PARASITES

The nycteribiid fly *Basilia nana* is specific to Bechstein's bat and occurs on most individuals.

RELATIONS WITH MAN

One survived in captivity for 172 days and drank on the wing from a bath [28].

AUTHOR FOR THIS SPECIES

Based upon the account in the second edition by R.E. Stebbings, with acknowledgement for additional data and comments by A.M. Hutson.

Mouse-eared bat *Myotis myotis*

Vespertilio myotis Borkhausen, 1797. Germany.
Vespertilio murinus Schreber, 1774 (not of Linnaeus 1758). This name was almost universally used for this species throughout the 19th century, but is now used for a completely different species, the particoloured bat (p. 111).

RECOGNITION

A very large bat (forearm over 57 mm) distinguished from noctule and serotine by its pointed tragus and lack of post-calcarial lobe.

DESCRIPTION

Very large. Upper parts medium to light brown and under side greyish white with distinct line of demarcation along side of neck. Juveniles and sub-adults up to 12 months are much greyer. Face almost bare, pinkish or brown. Ears and membranes brown, the latter thick, leathery and broad.

Ears large, extending about 5 mm beyond tip of muzzle when laid forward. Similar in actual size and form to those of Bechstein's bat. Tragus about half the height of conch with both anterior and posterior sides more or less straight.

Chromosomes: $2n = 44$; $FNa = 50-52$, continental data [270].

MEASUREMENTS

Head and body 65–80 mm; forearm 57–68 mm; wingspan 365–450 mm; ear 20–28 mm; weight 20–45 g. Males smaller than females: length of forearm (in Sussex) — males 59.9 mm ($n = 10$), females 62.4 mm ($n = 21$) [1].

DISTRIBUTION

Effectively extinct in Britain, but perhaps never well established. Last hibernating population in

Map 6.13. Mouse-eared bat.

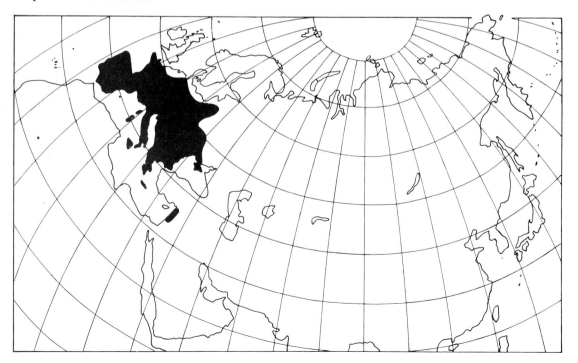

Sussex, discovered in 1969 [173], maximum of
about 30 bats and reduced to one male from 1985
to 1990.

HISTORY
Two old records from London and Epping (pre-
1850) are doubtful [18]. (Another from Cambridge
in 1888 was more likely the southern European
Myotis blythi.) A small hibernating population discovered in Dorset in 1956 [27], probably never
much exceeded 10 and was extinct by 1980. One in
Kent in the winter of 1985 [122] but extensive
subsequent search suggested that this was probably
a stray migrant.

HABITAT
Open, lightly wooded country. Roost in buildings
and caves in summer and winter.

SOCIAL ORGANISATION AND BEHAVIOUR

Summer: males solitary or in small groups, usually
in buildings with large roofs; females form large
nursery colonies in buildings or caves. Interchange
between adjacent nursery colonies seems to occur
frequently [209]. In the Netherlands 312 bats were
caught in a nursery cave roost, consisting of 156
adult females, 121 juveniles and 35 post-juvenile
males [24]. The last may have been one year old
and just reaching sexual maturity [225]. Nursing
colonies in Czechoslovakia [75] comprised 86%
adult females, 2% adult males and 12% immature
($n = 933$). Females visit solitary males for mating
in the autumn [79]. In Hungary emerge very late
when it is quite dark, and return an hour before
sunrise, again when still dark, apparently unaffected by weather conditions [261]. Flight is slow,
heavy and generally straight, medium height up to
20 m.

Winter: generally solitary but also found in small
groups. Preferred temperature 7–8°C in Poland
[100]. On the Continent preference for internal
areas of caves at beginning of winter, moving
towards the entrance by spring [50, 56]. The few
observations in Britain conform to this pattern and
most have been found hanging in high exposed
parts of tunnels. Movements of 7.5 km have been
noted in Dorset but regular movements of up to
200 km between summer and winter roosts have
been recorded in Czechoslovakia [79]. Greatest
movement 260 km [61].

FEEDING
Mostly larger moths, chafers and beetles eaten in
flight.

BREEDING
Females achieve sexual maturity at 3 months of age
[226] and males at 15 months [225]. Gestation
period 46–59 days [222].

POPULATION
During hibernation in the Netherlands a sex ratio
biased to the males — 58% ($n = 2914$) — was
found [24], but in Czechoslovakia a predominance
of females — 55% ($n = 1251$) [75]. In Sussex 32%
($n = 31$) were females [1]. Greatest longevity
recorded in Britain 15 years [124] but a male was
caught over 18 years after banding on the Continent
[175].

MORTALITY
In Poland apparently frequently taken by owls,
notably barn owls [99, 214].

PARASITES
No records from British specimens.

RELATIONS WITH MAN
Was given special protection by the Conservation
of Wild Creatures and Wild Plants Act, 1975 before
such protection was extended to all bats in the
Wildlife and Countryside Act, 1981.

AUTHOR FOR THIS SPECIES
Based upon the account in the second edition by
R.E. Stebbings, with acknowledgement for ad-
ditional comment and data from A.M. Hutson.

Daubenton's bat *Myotis daubentoni*

Vespertilio daubentoni Kuhl, 1819; Germany.
Vespertilio emarginatus Flemming, 1828 (not of
Geoffroy, 1806).
Vespertilio aedilis Jenyns, 1839; Durham, England.

Daubenton's bat, water bat

RECOGNITION
Distinguished from other species of *Myotis* by even
length of fur, uniform colour of dorsal fur from
bases to tips, long calcar (greater than half length
from foot to tail), and large feet (greater than half
length of tibia) (Fig. 6.9). Posterior margin of
tragus strongly convex.

Fig. 6.9. Daubenton's bat. (Photo: S.C. Bisserôt.)

Hunting call is frequency modulated, starting at 58–86 kHz and ending at 31–35 kHz. Calls last on average 1.8–2.3 ms and are separated by a relatively long interpulse interval of 87–216 ms [262]. On a bat detector this sounds like short sharp clicks which are evenly spaced.

SIGN
May discard parts of prey, notably wings [170] but difficult to collect. Faeces when first voided generally wetter than faeces of other British bats.

DESCRIPTION
Upper parts medium to dark brown and underside pale buffy-grey. Head blunt and rounded. Ears situated more to sides of head than pointing up on top. Pink bare skin visible around lips and eyes. Wing and tail membranes dark brown, never black.

Chromosomes: 2n = 42–44, FNa 50–52, continental data [270].

MEASUREMENTS (*see* Table 6.4).

VARIATION
Several albino/partial albino specimens have been described [18].

DISTRIBUTION
Common and widespread throughout England and

Table 6.4. Forearm lengths (mm) of Daubenton's bats in Britain. In all populations, females are larger; southerly populations tend to be smaller.

	Mean	Range	n
Inverness-shire [244]			
Males	37.3		37
Females	37.6		18
Highlands, Scotland [1]			
Males	37.1	35.8–38.4	21
Females	38.3	36.2–40.2	22
Northamptonshire [207]			
Males	36.7	33.5–40.2	65
Females	37.6	34.8–40.4	289
Suffolk [244]			
Males	36.6		87
Females	37.3		76

Wales. More scattered north of the Lake District and in Ireland.

HISTORY
Represented in Neolithic strata at Dowel Cave, Derbyshire [269]. Probably more abundant in NE Scotland in the 19th century.

HABITAT
Open wooded country. All nursery roosts ($n = 15$) at 62°N in Finland were within 200 m of water [170]. Also noted as close to water in Britain [18].

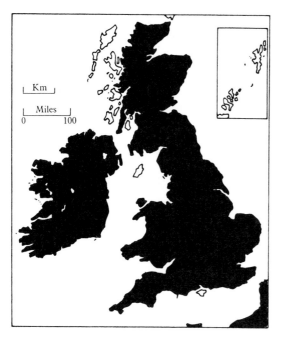

Map 6.14. Daubenton's bat.

SOCIAL ORGANISATION AND BEHAVIOUR

Summer: forms nursery colonies which may contain several hundred individuals. Of 15 roosts studied in Finland, ten were of less than 15 individuals. Maternity roosts may be in hollow trees and buildings [170] or under bridges [216]. May form cluster in open, or use a crevice [18]. In Finland most (10/15) roosts were in trees [170] but elsewhere probably prefers buildings [140].

Early workers suggested maternity roosts consisted of males and females in equal numbers [157]. More recent data suggest they consist predominantly of adult females [244, 256]. May cluster in body contact with other species: pipistrelles [132], brown long-eared bats and noctules [170].

Generally leave nursery roost to feed 30–60 min after sunset ($n = 86$ nights) [205]. Later (90–130 min after sunset, $n = 15$) from roost also occupied by brown long-eared bats [256]. Occasionally emerge in daylight. Found to fly up to 2 km from roost centered in woodland, with small ponds and a river nearby, in Scotland [256], and up to 10 km along canals in Northamptonshire [205]. Occasionally do not emerge to feed [170, 206].

Map 6.15. Daubenton's bat.

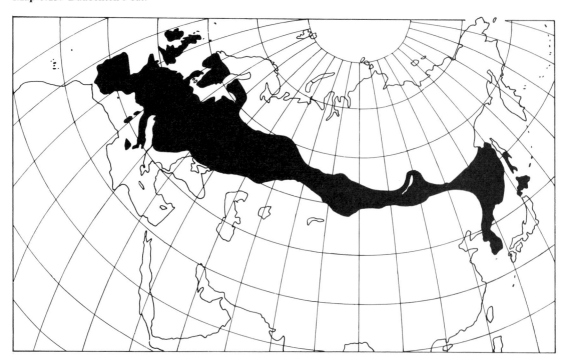

Winter: mainly in caves. Usually solitary in a crevice, often horizontal. May burrow into soft scree [59, 235]. Enter hibernacula around October [170]. May emerge during winter [138]. Males precede females into hibernacula and depart earlier in spring [64, 244]. Preferred temperature 3–8°C [76].

Longest recorded movements in Britain 19 km [207] and 14.5 km [19], but longer distances recorded on Continent, both under natural conditions (215 km) [79] or homing after displacement (132 km) [170].

FEEDING

Typically over open water in Britain [256] and normally within 1 m of surface, but may fly up to 16 m high [170]. In Finland (62°N) fed in woodland in mid-summer when almost continuously light, but shifted to over open water as nights become darker [170]. When very low over water holds wings high with shallow amplitude to beat, presumably to avoid making contact with water since may have difficulty taking off from water surface [170, 207]. This posture is also adopted by other bats flying low over water and is therefore not diagnostic.

In one study, ate mainly flies (Diptera) and caddis flies (Trichoptera) (Fig. 6.10) [256]. May occasionally eat small fish in captivity [30].

BREEDING

Copulation observed in hibernacula in October [62] and February [165]. Copulation probably initiated when males enter nursery roosts as young wean, and continues throughout winter, as increasing proportion of females in hibernation found inseminated as hibernation progressed [250]. Gestation length probably variable and dependent on weather conditions, as shown in pipistrelle [194], c. 5–7 weeks. Lactation 5–6 weeks, and young fly at 6–8 weeks [170].

POPULATION

Sex ratio in winter variable between sites: 44% male ($n = 920$) [25], 61% male ($n = 2820$) [59] and 56% male ($n = 370$) [227]. Annual survival 80% (in Netherlands) [25] which gives a predicted longevity of 20 years. Greatest recorded longevity 18 years [241].

PARASITES

Three ectoparasites are common; the fly *Nycteribia kolenatii* and the mites *Spinturnix myoti* and *Macronyssus ellipticus*. For *N. kolenatii* an infestation rate of 73% ($n = 118$) with an average 2.2 flies per bat was found in Britain [121] with a greater infestation rate and density on females. The bug *Cimex pipistrelli* is infrequently recorded.

Of 89 bats examined, 22 contained the malaria parasite *Polychromophilus murinus* and 51 the bacteria *Grahamella* sp. [81]. *P. murinus* may be transmitted to Daubenton's bats by *N. kolenatii* [121].

RELATIONS WITH MAN

Has been kept successfully in captivity for several months, fed on mealworms.

AUTHOR FOR THIS SPECIES

J.R. Speakman.

GENUS *Vespertilio*

A genus of one widespread Palaearctic species, which occurs as a vagrant in Britain, and two species in E Asia. Similar to *Eptesicus* but ears short and square, more like *Nyctalus*. Dental formula 2.1.1.3 / 3.1.2.3.

Generally found in hollow trees and in buildings, occasionally in caves. Rare throughout their range and therefore little known.

Particoloured bat *Vespertilio murinus*

Vespertilio murinus L. 1758: Sweden (in the 19th century, this name was erroneously but widely

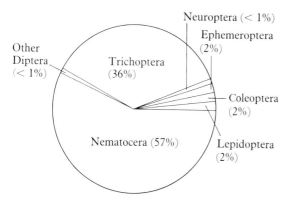

Fig. 6.10. The diet of Daubenton's bat in Speyside, Scotland: percentage occurrence of insect taxa from analysis of faeces [256].

used for *Myotis myotis*).
Vespertilio discolor Natterer, 1819.

RECOGNITION
A medium-large bat with squarish ears, small bean-shaped tragus and distinctive bicoloured dorsal fur.

DESCRIPTION
Hairs of upper parts with dark brown bases and light silver or cream tips, giving a frosted appearance. The underside is white or grey and the skin very dark brown. Ears short, slightly wider than high. Tragus short and bean-shaped, concave along anterior margin and strongly convex posteriorly. Post-calcarial lobe present but indistinct. Wings narrow and pointed.

MEASUREMENTS
Head and body 55−64 mm; forearm 40−49 mm (mean 44.5 mm for males, n = 17) [3]; wingspan 260−330 mm; condylobasal length 14.2−15.5 mm; weight 11−24 g.

DISTRIBUTION
From Central Europe to Siberia and Iran; also in S Scandinavia and as a vagrant in several other European countries (France, Holland). In Britain found at Plymouth and Yarmouth in early 19th century; Shetland in March 1927 [208], November 1981 and November 1984; Cambridge in November 1985; Brighton in March 1986. Also in North Sea 270 km east of Berwick in June 1965 [234]. A migratory species with recorded movements of 360, 800 and 850 km [251].

AUTHOR FOR THIS SPECIES
P.A. Racey.

GENUS *Eptesicus*

A genus of about 20 species throughout the Palaearctic, Africa and the Americas. It is very closely related to *Pipistrellus*, with similar short, blunt tragus, but differs in being generally larger and in having a short, broad baculum.

In addition to the serotine, *E. serotinus*, there is one other species in Europe, *E. nilssoni*. This is a highly migratory species recently reported in Britain. It is much smaller (forearm 37−44 mm) with warmer, dark chestnut brown, golden-tipped

fur contrasting with much paler underfur. Tail extending 2−3 mm beyond interfemoral membrane.

The North and Central American *E. fuscus* (big brown bat) has been recorded in Europe, having been transported accidentally by ship [263]. It has a forearm length of 42−51 mm and is uniform dark brown with blackish hair bases.

Serotine *Eptesicus serotinus*

Vespertilio serotinus Schreber, 1774: France.

RECOGNITION
A large, robust, dark brown bat, with slight post-calcarial lobe, bluntly-tipped tragus just under half height of ear, tail extending beyond margin of interfemoral membrane and conspicuously large teeth (Fig. 6.11). Leisurely flapping flight of deep wing-beats on broad wings, up to a height of 30 m. Free tip of tail sometimes visible; occasional short glides or steep descents. Forages in open pasture or in open parkland and gardens, around tree canopies and open spaces. Often flies low and sometimes takes insects from the ground.

SIGNS
Faeces often abundant in breeding roosts in buildings, at gable ends or around base of chimney, but some traditional breeding sites may exhibit few droppings. Faeces broad (3.5−4.0 mm) and blunt-ended, 8−11 mm long, giving more oval longitudinal section than in other large bats. Fresh droppings always black and glistening, quite coarse. Usually a few droppings outside the point of access, otherwise point of access not well marked.

Frequently very active chattering at roost entrance for up to half an hour before emergence. Sometimes audible during the day, including occasional short, very loud penetrating squeaks.

DESCRIPTION
Ears about twice as long as wide. Tragus blunt-tipped, less than half height of conch, widest at about a third of its length, apical half more or less parallel-sided but slightly curved anteriorly. Muzzle distinctly bulbous. Wings broad; membranes thick and opaque. Post-calcarial lobe long but narrow and ill-defined. Last and part of penultimate caudal vertebrae free from interfemoral membrane, giving about 6 mm of free tail.

Pelage: upper parts with long dark brown hair,

Fig. 6.11. Serotine. (Photo: S.C. Bisserôt.)

sometimes tinged slightly purple (plum-coloured) or chestnut, often with paler tips. Underparts paler but no clear demarcation. Face, ears and membranes very dark brown-black. Distinct glandular swellings on muzzle; gland under chin. Juveniles are very dark brown.

Teeth: canines conspicuously large; M^3 much reduced; outer incisor distinctly more than half height of inner; P_3 small, less that half the crown area of P_4. *Baculum* short and triangular, with proximal notch.

Chromosomes: $2n = 50$, $FNa = 48-50$ [270].

MEASUREMENTS
Head and body 58–80 mm; tail 34–65 mm, tail beyond membrane 5–8 mm; forearm 48–55 mm; wingspan 320–380 mm; ear length 14–21 mm; condylobasal length 19–22 mm; $C-M^3$ 7.4–8.2 mm; weight 15–35 g (adult summer non-pregnant: *c*. 20–24 g).

VARIATION
British populations not distinguishable from continental and no variation has been recognised within British range.

DISTRIBUTION
Palaearctic between *c*. 58° and 30°N in west; east to China. Recent expansion in Denmark [11] and first recorded in Sweden in 1983 [86].

Recent records from Wales [156] and Yorkshire, and increased records from Norfolk and the west of England, suggest an expanding range from its main recorded occurrence in SE England.

HISTORY
Subfossil material is known from cave deposits from late Pleistocene in Notts/Derbyshire and from Lower to Middle Pleistocene from Somerset.

HABITAT
Mainly in lowland open flat country of pasture, parkland and woodland edge or hedgerow.

Roost: mainly in buildings, frequently in those constructed around 1900 with high gable end and cavities in walls. Rarely in modern houses, often in older buildings. Access usually 6–8 m or higher, at or near gable apex or from lower eaves. Roost in crevices around chimneys, in cavity walls, between felt/boarding and tiles/slates, sometimes in open roof space at ridge ends or occasionally elsewhere along ridge. Individuals or small colonies have been found irregularly behind window shutters [113, 164]. Occasionally in tree hollows [98, 164] and in bird and bat boxes in summer [88].

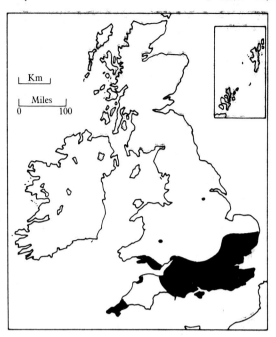

Map 6.16. Serotine.

Map 6.17. Serotine.

SOCIAL ORGANISATION AND BEHAVIOUR

Summer: some species of *Eptesicus* have a harem structure throughout the breeding season; this has not been recorded in *E. serotinus*. Colonies usually number 15−30, occasionally up to 60. Males probably solitary or in small groups (e.g. in older buildings, especially churches); occasionally with females in spring and autumn [14].

Activity starts around mid-April. Bats emerge early in evening, especially at the beginning of the season [52, 63]. Often much active squeaking prior to emergence. Main emergence within 10 min, total emergence never more than 40 min. Flight at emergence often directly towards feeding ground at about tree-top level (to *c.* 30 m), sometimes very low along lee of hedges etc. Early in the season bats return to roost about 30−40 min after emergence. As season progresses more time is spent away from roost, with some passage of bats in and out of roost at all times of night and a secondary peak of activity around dawn (often returning well after first light). On return to roost, single bats may enter without pause; others, particularly if several bats are returning at about the same time, circle around the roost entrance for several minutes before entering.

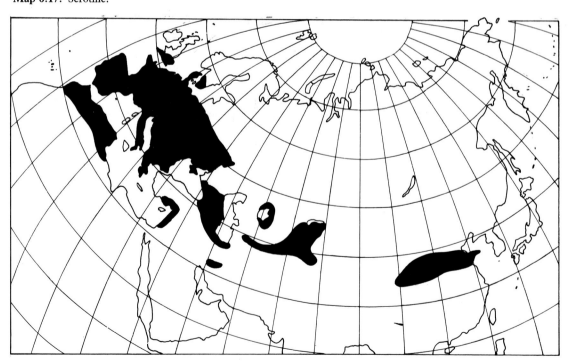

Roost building often shared with pipistrelles and/or long-eared bats [1]. Has associated with Natterer's [203], and shared access with noctules where this species was present in a building until the end of May [14].

Winter: frequently hibernate in buildings, occasionally in caves, dungeons and cellars, particularly in eastern Europe [48, 88, 251]. In caves, usually singly and close to entrance, but in European Russia recorded at 22 of 91 cave sites (17 with < 10 individuals; four with 10–50; one with 50–100) [251]. Only twice recorded from caves in UK [246]. A hardy species [105], preferring temperatures of 5–11°C in autumn and 0.5–6°C in winter [100]. Tolerant of dry air [251]. Relatively sedentary in winter, but occasionally hunt on warm winter days [99].

Movement: generally regarded as a non-migratory species, with local movements of up to 50 km, but movements of up to 330 km [105, 251] and 145 km [260] have been recorded on the Continent. The latter (one of only 20 ringed) moved NW between July 1954 and August 1955. Such movements may account for observations of serotines flying straight and purposefully at 90 m in Surrey [98].

Echolocation calls are a frequency sweep from 60–25 kHz; longer cries are produced by extending the lower frequency, and a v-shaped sweep is often used when circling outside roost during mating season [158].

Most identifiable at *c.* 28 kHz. Most typical call in cruising flight is a simple 'tock-tock-tock' (as heard through bat detector) at a rate of *c.* 4–5 pulses per second. Occasionally when cruising in the open, call slightly extended into a short 'whip-like' sound reminiscent but much shorter than that of noctule. Identifiable feeding buzzes relatively few and extremely short.

FEEDING

Fly around trees, particularly the canopy, very close to and often touching the vegetation. In open pasture etc., often fly very close to the ground or up to *c.* 10 m, with sudden steep dives. Slow and highly manoeuvrable in flight. Often feed along roads and around street lamps. Cooler weather limits feeding activity more than with noctule [46]. Occasionally feed well within beech woods [158].

Feed mainly on large beetles, e.g. *Aphodius*, Melolonthinae, *Necrophorus* and larger moths.

Many flies (Diptera, Nematocera) found in the diet in Netherlands, particularly early in the season [144]. Prey taken on wing, occasionally from the ground [55] and probably directly from vegetation. Ingestion occurs in flight, discarding legs and wings of moths and elytra of larger beetles. Feeding perches unrecorded.

BREEDING

Mating recorded (in captivity) in September and October (occasionally later). Three captive males and one female showed no sexual activity in first autumn, but yearling males developed enlarged testes and epididymides, and mating occurred in the second autumn at about 15 months. Mating can be protracted, recorded coition lasting for several hours, even during torpor [133, 192].

Nursery colonies start to build up in May, with numbers very stable in some (mainly smaller) colonies from late May; other colonies rather variable in number throughout season. Maternity colonies usually show a high level of site fidelity, but some frequently change roosts during breeding season.

The number of nulliparous individuals in breeding colonies is low, suggesting maturation in the first year; the number of non-breeding females in breeding colonies is also low, suggesting regular parturition, but samples are small. Despite high level of parturition at breeding colonies, up to 80% [88], a relatively small increase of colony size (± 30%) is seen with the weaning of young. Juvenile mortality up to 30%, mostly in first week [88]. Nothing is known of post-weaning mortality.

Females can increase weight by nearly 60% in pregnancy [133]. Single young born at about 5 g weight in early July (mid-June in Netherlands) [88]. Occasional births as late as mid-August [1]. Sex ratio at birth is 1:1 [105]. Infants possibly carried by mother for first few days [1, 45]. Young fly at 4–5 weeks. Suckling discouraged at 5–6 weeks (at *c.* 16 g weight), but may be maintained for two months [45, 133]. Development and behaviour of juvenile described from a captive animal in Germany [204]. Juvenile epiphyses fuse at 50–70 days [133]. Most of colony disperses by early September, but some bats continue to be active at breeding roosts until early October.

POPULATION

Apart from in Kent, Surrey, Sussex and Hampshire, recorded roost sites are few. Of about 50 known roost sites in Sussex, only about 10 are thought likely to be regular breeding sites, but the species appears to be widespread. Colonies are not large and so overall density is likely to be low. The suggestion that the serotine is expanding its range is not associated with any increase in density in its well established distribution. While several colonies are known to be very well established, with a history of up to 70 years, there are many sites showing evidence of this species, but no evidence of recent occupation. The insect food selected is similar to that of other large bats that are believed to be declining, e.g. noctule and greater horseshoe, and the serotine seems more dependent on occupied buildings than either of these two. If it is expanding its range, the suggested reasons for the decline of these other large species, e.g. reduction of large beetles, loss of roost sites, use of highly toxic timber treatment chemicals, may be questioned. However, the number of abandoned sites within its well established range may suggest a local decline similar to that of these other large species, but there is no clear evidence. Certainly large bats believed to be this species are still widespread and relatively common in the area of Kent and Sussex, and possibly Essex.

MORTALITY
Sharp population declines are recorded in Germany [211, 212] and UK [249], and an average decline in colony size of 15% in 10 years in the Netherlands [88, 91], where overall populations have been recorded as unaffected during last 10 years [49, 90]. Generally the little data available is conflicting, but European populations are thought to be stable [249].

The greatest recorded longevity, 6 years [78, 107], is likely to be an underestimate. Maximum longevity in captivity: 3 years [179].

One of the species more frequently taken by owls [139, 267]; no regular predators known.

PARASITES
A regular and common insect ectoparasite is the flea *Ischnopsyllus intermedius* [84, 229]. Occasionally the bug *Cimex pipistrelli* is found in the roost [1]. The tick *Argas vespertilionis* is rarely associated with this species [1] but a number of other acarines are commonly found including *Spinturnix kolenatii*, *Steatonyssus occidentalis* and *Ornithonyssus pipistrelli*. Laelapidae, other Macronyssidae, Trombiculidae and a variety of sarcoptiform mites have also been found on the Continent [65].

A rabies-like virus has been isolated in serotines in Denmark and Poland, and may be pathogenic to the bats, but there is as yet no suggestion that it is transmissible to man.

RELATIONS WITH MAN
In Britain this species appears to be dependent on buildings.

AUTHOR FOR THIS SPECIES
A.M. Hutson.

Northern bat *Eptesicus nilssonii*

Vespertilio nilssonii Kayserling & Blasius, 1839. Sweden.

RECOGNITION AND DESCRIPTION
Similar in many respects to the serotine but smaller, with a forearm length of 37–46 mm, and distinguished by the colour of its long and rather shaggy dorsal pelage. Dorsal fur with dark brown base irregularly tipped with glossy light yellowish buff or golden buff. Ventral fur is overall yellowish brown, with dark base but pale tips. This coloration extends along the sides of the head to the base of the ears, with a sharp division from the darker upperparts along the sides of the neck. The upper surface of the tail membrane is lightly furred for about half of its length and the muzzle, cheeks, ears and membranes are blackish. The tip of the tail protrudes 3–4 mm from the trailing edge of the interfemoral membrane, a little less than in the serotine [93].

DISTRIBUTION
Widely distributed from E France to central Europe and much of Scandinavia (but not yet reported from the low countries, N Germany or Denmark) and thence to Siberia and Japan. Although as a migrant it is quite likely to occur beyond its reported range, it has only been reported in Britain on one occasion at Betchworth, Surrey in a hibernaculum in January 1987 [93].

HABITAT
Mainly forest and woodland, but also in farmland and villages, with an altitudinal range sometimes extending above the timberline to 2000 m. Roosts in treeholes and buildings, and occasionally in

caves, where found between boulders on the ground [233].

AUTHOR FOR THIS SPECIES
P.A. Racey.

GENUS *Nyctalus*

A small Palaearctic genus with about six species, three of which occur in Europe. All members are characterised by narrow pointed wings (associated with fast flight and migratory habit), short squarish ears and very short tragus, wider near the tip than at the base. Calcar with post-calcarial lobe. Skull broad. Dental formula as for *Pipistrellus*: 2.1.2.3/ 3.1.2.3.

Two species occur in Britain, *N. noctula* and *N. leisleri*, broadly distinguishable by size alone but coloration also different. *N. lasiopterus* which occurs from Central Europe to Iran, and also occasionally in Western Europe (Iberia, France and Switzerland), is similar to *N. noctula* but very much larger (forearm 64–69 mm, condylobasal length 22–23 mm).

Noctule *Nyctalus noctula*

Vespertilio noctula Schreber, 1774; France.
Vespertilio magnus Berkenhout, 1789; Cambridge, England.
Vespertilio altivolans White, 1789; Selborne, Hants, England.

Great bat.

RECOGNITION

In flight: a large high-flying bat, often the first to appear in evening. Two distinct flight patterns, the first just before sunset when bats fly high, fast and straight with occasional rapid diversions; second of fast flight up to 30 m high with repeated deep dives and occasional glides.

In hand: short sleek golden, ginger or reddish fur with pronounced 'set', short, stout brown ears and mushroom-shaped tragus. Differs from Leisler's in having forearm more than 47 mm, and hair of uniform colour from base to tip. Fur quite greasy (Fig. 6.12).

With bat detector: short steep frequency-modulated sweep used when bats hunting closer to ground [5, 158], or long shallow sweep (audible to young people without detector) used together with first pulse type when hunting higher [5]. Alternation between the two explains the plip-plop sound from the detector. When only using the short FM sweep, it may be confused with serotine. Very loud.

During aerial chases and when circling the roost, social calls may be heard, sounding like an undulating whistle.

Skull: large, C–M^3 7.0–7.4 mm; second upper incisor larger in crown area than first; first upper premolar very small, invisible from side.

At roost: often betrays location of tree roosts by shrill vocalisation towards dusk. Tree roosts also recognised by black streak of faeces and urine which drains from exit hole. Faecal pellets 3.0–3.5 mm wide, 11–15 mm long.

DESCRIPTION
Dorsal fur golden, ginger or reddish, ventral fur similar but often slightly paler. Adult males brightest. Juveniles slightly darker and usually duller. Face, ears and wing membrane dark brown, almost black. Fur extends on to wing membrane.

Ears short and broad, 15 mm long and wide. Tragus mushroom-shaped, with height more or less equal to width, but broader at tip than at base. Muzzle broad and glandular, and conspicuous white glands in corners of mouth, more prominent in males than in females [103, 134], and producing a white fatty material with a conspicuous odour [162].

Post-calcarial lobe present, and tip of tail emerges about 2 mm from interfemoral membrane. Wings quite narrow and pointed with average aspect ratio [169].

Chromosomes: 2n = 42; FNa = 50, continental data [270].

MEASUREMENTS
See Table 6.5. In Suffolk mean weight of 21 adult males caught while feeding in June and July was 30.2 ± 1.7 g (range 25–34) and of 12 in October was 33.2 ± 3.2 g (range 28–38) [47]. Higher weights were recorded in captivity where food was provided *ad libitum* [163, 192]. Males slightly

Fig. 6.12. Noctule. (Photo: S.C. Bisserôt.)

smaller than females in Rumania: mean forearm length of males 53.9 mm ($n = 83$), of females 54.3 mm ($n = 145$) [16].

DISTRIBUTION
Throughout England and probably all of Wales. Colony recently (1986), recorded in SW Scotland. Vagrants recorded on Orkney (in June 1976) [189], Shetland and North Sea oil rigs, presumably blown from Europe [1].

HABITAT
Predominantly a tree bat, living mainly in rot-holes and woodpecker holes in mature deciduous trees (often beech) [115]; even roost in trees in suburban areas. On Continent roost extensively in buildings except during June and July [80, 251]. Although seldom found in caves, on Continent hibernate in crevices in rock faces [16, 80, 83], with up to 100 individuals recorded in a single fissure.

SOCIAL ORGANISATION AND BEHAVIOUR

Summer: in Europe females first appeared in their nursery roosts in March and moved between roosts throughout the summer, carrying their young during lactation [80, 227]. Nursery roosts may exceed 100 bats in Europe but are rarely this large in Britain where mean roost size in one study was 14 [115].

Males are solitary or form small groups. In August and September individual males establish territorial mating roosts between which females move. Up to 18 females found with a single male [227]. In Switzerland, males predominate for most of the year, mainly during June, July and August.

Table 6.5. Measurements of noctule and Leisler's bats (adults).

	Noctule	Leisler's
Head and body (mm)	70−82	54−64
Forearm (mm)	47−55	39−47
Wingspan (mm)	330−450	280−340
Ear length (mm)	15−18	12−13
Skull length (condylobasal) (mm)	17.6−19.0	15.2−16.0
Upper tooth-row ($C-M^3$) (mm)	7.0−7.4	5.8−6.0
Lower tooth-row ($C-M_3$) (mm)	7.2−8.2	6.0−6.2
Weight (g)	15−49	11−20

Map 6.18. Noctule.

During this time most roosts are abandoned or inhabited by males only, suggesting that although noctules mate and hibernate in Switzerland, birth and lactation occurs elsewhere, probably at lower altitudes [253]. Males predominate in all winter samples from W and C Europe [80], possibly as a result of differential migration. Two males found roosting with male Daubenton's bats in September in Yorkshire [231].

Foraging behaviour: flight activity starts 2−40 min after sunset [80, 108]. Peaks of foraging activity at dusk, for about an hour, and at dawn, for about half an hour, coinciding with flight periodicity of insects [47, 253]; where insects were attracted to mercury vapour lamps, bats foraged throughout the night. Bats mist-netted in light rain or thick mist, but not during heavy rain [47], and dawn foraging suppressed by inclement weather [253].

Migration: migratory in USSR, with ringing recoveries 500−2347 km S and SW; individuals move 20−44 km/day [95, 251]. Noctules also travelled 45 km in 24 hours in homing experiments, in one case returning to the same roost after being translocated 237 km the previous year [216]. In

Map 6.19. Noctule.

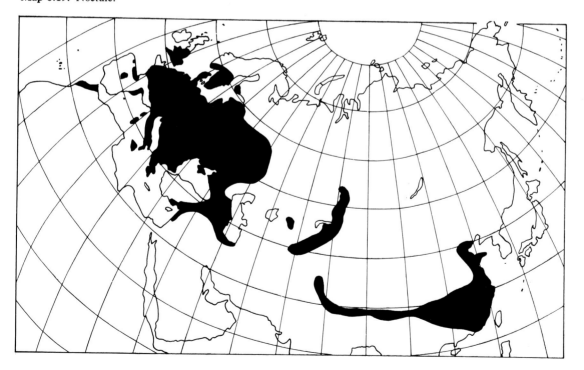

W Europe probably not migratory; in Holland most hibernated close to summer roosts but some long-distance movement recorded, up to 900 km SW from Holland to Bordeaux [227]. Not known to move out of England in winter, and recorded hibernating even in severest winters.

Winter: form large mixed-sex colonies of up to 1000 [251] in buildings or trees in Europe, although colony sizes in UK much smaller. Tree-holes occupied during winter south of the line delineating January isotherm −2 to −4°C [78].

With an ambient air temperature of −7°C, the outer individuals of a cluster of 150 were at +1°C, and those at the centre +2°C [16]. Insulating capacity of tree hole with large cavity poor [108], although the majority of a colony of 100 bats survived for 53 days when the temperature in their tree-hole was permanently below zero, occasionally falling to −16°C. The minimum recorded skin temperature was −9°C. Abrupt rises or falls in temperatures resulted in arousals [228]. Nevertheless very severe winters are thought to result in heavy mortality [251]. In England (52°N) foraging activity observed throughout winter but greatly reduced [10] and in Switzerland flight recorded in winter at an ambient temperature of +2°C [83].

FEEDING
Mostly large insects such as house crickets (*Acheta domestica*), summer chafers (*Amphimallon solstitialis*) and cockchafers (*Melolontha melolontha*), caught and eaten in flight [17, 47]. In a Russian study small flies were the main constituents of the diet, together with a wide variety of beetles. Some indication that they take food from substrate [17, 45, 249].

BREEDING (Fig. 6.13)
Single males establish mating territories in tree holes during August and September with vocalisations [80, 104, 172, 227]. Mating occurs in the wild mainly during September and October [227] but also during the winter and spring in captivity [181, 182], and spermatozoa retain their fertilising capacity after storage by both male and female bats for up to 7 months [182]. During winter, uterus distended with semen, the result of several inseminations with the same or different males [104, 182, 220].

Only European species of several maintained in captivity to breed routinely there with fertile F1

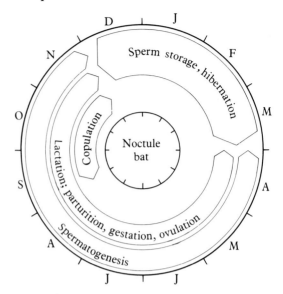

Fig. 6.13. Noctule: life-cycle.

and F2 generations [134, 179, 192]. Summer period of spermatogenesis characterised by increased aggressiveness [185]. When males are caged together at this time, one will assume dominance, drive others from the nest box and signify occupation by prolonged high-pitched vocalisations which are sometimes answered by his cage mates. He will repel intruders, but may be ousted if he loses one of the occasional but vicious fights. During winter, aggressive behaviour of caged males much reduced.

Females ovulate in spring, and after a gestation period of 70−73 days [60] give birth to a single young in June and July. Twins recorded in captivity in UK [134], rarely in the wild [129], and on the European mainland, where triplets also exceptionally occur [24, 172]. In S Bohemia most females older than 1 year have two young (mean 1.8) [80]. Segregation of sexes generally occurs when females give birth but mixed colonies are not uncommon during summer. Maternal care, growth and development of young described in captivity [133].

Young generally born first half of June to early July, and begin to fly in first half of July, but are not weaned before August [80, 227]. In England, some young do not fly until September and October [47]. A proportion of females achieve sexual maturity and mate in their first autumn and give birth as yearlings, both in the wild [47] and in captivity [134]. In males, spermatogenesis occurs first in their second summer both in the wild and in captivity as judged by distension of the epididymis with sperm in August [47, 80, 134]. Although spermatozoa were found there as early as 4 months of age in USSR, neither these individuals nor yearlings mate [80].

POPULATION

Sex ratio at birth is equal ($n = 214$) [24], but biased towards females in juvenile samples and in feeding populations. Survival rates unknown, but greatest recorded longevity 8 years [24]. In two areas of optimum habitat on Continent the average population density during summer was 0.32 per hectare.

MORTALITY

Low temperatures result in mortality in severe winters [16, 251] and bats die when roosts blown down or when trees felled. Starlings drive out (and possibly kill) noctules from roost holes [151, 115]. Remains found in pellets from both barn and tawny owls [215].

PARASITES

The following ectoparasites have been recorded: the bug *Cimex pipistrelli* (common); the fleas *Ischnopsylla elongatus* (common), *Nycteridopsylla eusarca* (a rare winter flea) and *Ischnopsylla intermedius*; the mites *Spinturnix acuminatus*, *Macronyssus flavus*, *M. kolenati*, 'Radfordia' noctulia, *Leiognathus uncinatus*, *Macrocheles glaber* and *Glycyphagus domesticus*. In captivity, a single case of phoresy by the mite *Notoedres chiropteralis* was recorded [134].

The blood protozoan *Trypanosoma vespertilionis* has also been recorded [12]. The commonest cause of death in a laboratory colony was pneumonia of unknown aetiology, which may have been the result of lack of flight [179].

RELATIONS WITH MAN

This species was the best adapted to captivity of several tried and a breeding colony was successfully maintained in close confinement for 6 years [134, 179, 191, 192]. A large outdoor flight chamber 12 m × 7 m × 4 m has also been used [104].

AUTHOR FOR THIS SPECIES

P.A. Racey, with acknowledgement for additional data and comment provided by J. Gaisler, V. Hanak, A. Mitchell-Jones, P.W. Richardson and D.W. Yalden.

Leisler's bat *Nyctalus leisleri*

Vespertilio leisleri Kuhl, 1818; Germany.

Hairy-armed bat.

RECOGNITION

Similar to noctule but distinguished by smaller size (forearm less than 48 mm) and distinctly bicolored dorsal fur with basal zone very much darker than the tips. Skull recognised by small size (condylobasal length 15–16 mm) and relatively small lower incisors. First upper premolar not so reduced as in noctule and visible from side. More shallow dives in flight than noctule. With bat-detector, similar to noctule but less strident and with distinctive rapid 'clicks' at upper part of detectable range. (Fig. 6.14.)

DESCRIPTION

Medium-large bat with upper parts varying from golden to dark rufous brown with very dark brown bases to the hairs. Under parts lighter and slightly grey brown. Facial skin, ears and patagium very dark brown, sometimes blackish. Wings narrow and pointed with thick, opaque membranes. Ears short (12 mm) and relatively narrower than those of noctule, giving the appearance of being more pointed. Tragus very short and mushroom-shaped as in the noctule. Prominent post-calcarial lobe present.

Chromosomes: 2n = 46, FNa = 50; continental data [270].

MEASUREMENTS

See Table 6.5. Mean forearm length of adult females in Ireland 43.8 mm ($n = 128$) and in Worcestershire 43.7 mm ($n = 8$) [244]. Males slightly smaller than females in Switzerland: mean forearm length of males 43.8 mm ($n = 11$), of females 44.3 mm ($n = 14$) [3].

DISTRIBUTION

Apparently rare in Britain, with a few records each year, mostly from bat boxes in conifer plantations, occasionally larger colonies in buildings but probably overlooked to some extent [266]. A vagrant recorded in Shetland in July 1968 [43]. More abundant in Ireland, where it replaces the noctule and is the third commonest bat, after pipistrelle and brown long-eared [160, 166].

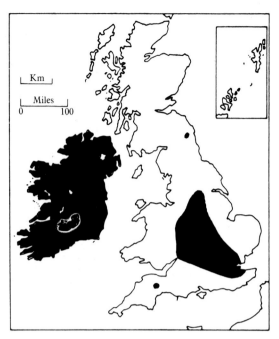

Map 6.20. Leisler's bat.

HISTORY
Represented in Neolithic deposits in Dowel Cave, Derbyshire [269].

HABITAT
Essentially forest bats roosting in tree-holes and artificial roost boxes, although often roost in buildings, both old and new, and in Britain only known colonies are in buildings, with up to 40 bats. Found in deciduous and coniferous forests, as well as parkland and urban areas.

SOCIAL ORGANISATION AND BEHAVIOUR

Summer: has been observed to emerge early, at or soon after sunset, and probably has a bimodal pattern of activity with peaks at dusk and dawn [161]. Flight straight and fairly fast with shallow dives, mostly at tree-top level but occasionally netted low over forest ponds [20] or brooks [97]. Of a total of 127 caught during three sampling periods from a colony of 400 in County Cork, 104 were adult females and 23 were immature females. There were no males [244]. Around Sheffield, apparently attracted to moths flying around

Map 6.21. Leisler's bat.

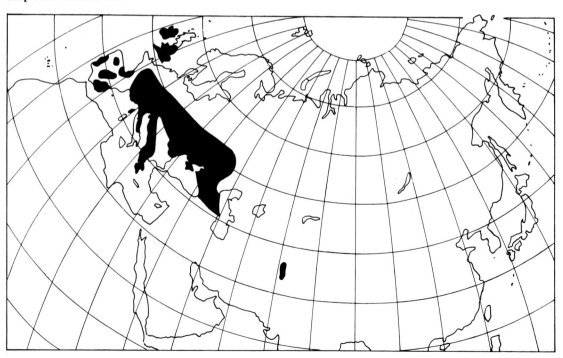

Fig. 6.14. Leisler's bat. (Photo: S.C. Bisserôt.)

mercury vapour street lights [266]. In S Bohemia, individuals sometimes found in noctule colonies.

No data for winter.

Movement: a migratory species, at least on the Continent. Longest recorded flights 418 km in Poland [137] and 810 km from Switzerland to Germany [4]; 25 individuals caught in Switzerland were probably migrating [2]. One was found dead on a glacier at 2600 m.

FEEDING
Medium to large insects eaten during flight.

BREEDING
Probably similar to noctule.

POPULATION
Nothing known but sex ratio of unweaned bats apparently unity ($n = 107$) [244].

PARASITES
Flea *Ischnopsyllus elongatus* and the bug *Cimex pipistrelli* have been recorded.

RELATIONS WITH MAN
One individual survived 372 days in captivity [28].

AUTHOR FOR THIS SPECIES
P.A. Racey, with ackowledgement for additional data and comment by J. Fairley, J. Gaisler, V. Hanak, P.W. Richardson and D.W. Yalden.

GENUS *Pipistrellus*

A genus of about 65 species with representatives world-wide except South America. Four species occur in Europe; one is common in Britain and another has occurred as a vagrant.

General characters similar to *Eptesicus* but European species with relatively shorter ears, shorter, blunt tragus, and post-calcarial lobe. Form robust as opposed to the slender, small *Myotis* with which some confusion may be experienced. Dental formula in British species as in *Nyctalus*, 2.1.2.3 / 3.1.2.3.

Pipistrelles are mostly found in trees and buildings throughout the year, but occasionally also in rock crevices and caves. Usually roost in very confined spaces in which very large numbers occur.

Due to individual variation, identification of the four European species by external characters is difficult, but is possible by comparison of teeth. *P. kuhli* and *P. savii*, both found in southern Europe, can be separated from *P. pipistrellus* and *P. nathusii* by the anterior upper premolar not being visible from the outside.

Map 6.22. Pipistrelle.

Pipistrelle *Pipistrellus pipistrellus*

Vespertilio pipistrellus Schreber, 1774; France.
Vespertilio pygmaeus Leach, 1825; Dartmoor, Devon, England.

RECOGNITION
Small size (forearm less than 35 mm), short ears, short curved blunt tragus and a post-calcarial lobe on the tail membrane separate this from all but other *Pipistrellus*. Separated from Nathusius's pipistrelle by its smaller size, short teeth and small anterior upper premolar, half hidden by the canine when viewed from the outside. Also lacks pale or white tips to dorsal hair. (Fig. 6.15.)

SIGN
Faeces cylindrical, black and about 6 mm in length, consisting of very finely ground fragments. Their presence on vertical surfaces is often the first clue to the species' presence. Faeces common around entrance/exit to roost [32]. Scratch marks often present on woodwork negotiated by bats entering their roosts. At sites of extreme longstanding these marks can be very obvious.

Map 6.23. Pipistrelle.

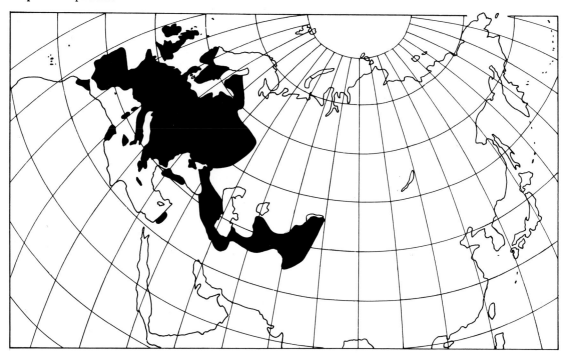

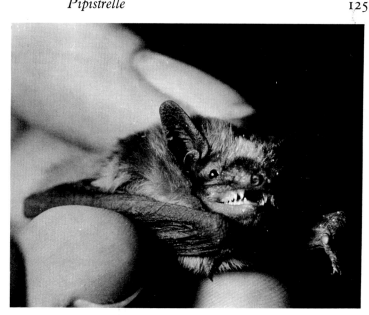

Fig. 6.15. Pipistrelle. (Photo: P. Morris.)

DESCRIPTION

Usually dark brown upperparts and slightly lighter underparts. Bare skin usually dark brown to blackish. Ear short and broad, *c.* 10 mm long. Tragus less than half the height of conch, anterior border concave, posterior almost equally convex, with round blunt tip. A post-calcarial lobe is present. Muzzle is short, and has glandular swellings of unknown function. Membranes opaque (as in whiskered bat). Wings narrow.

Chromosomes: 2n = 41−44, FNa = 48−52, continental data [270].

MEASUREMENTS

Head and body 35−45 mm; forearm 28−35 mm; wingspan 190−250 mm; ear 8−11 mm; condylobasal length 11−12 mm; weight 3−8 g. In 3-year study in E Anglia mean weights lowest at end of April (males, 4.2 g; nulliparous females, 4.7 g; parous females, 5.15 g) and highest in September (males, 5.7 g; nulliparous females, 6.1 g; parous females, 7.05 g) (*n* = 276 for males; *n* = 306 for females). Pregnant females up to 9.5 g. Linear weight loss during hibernation [7]. Males generally rise in weight during summer but show drop during the time of sperm release and mating activity [85]. Bats caught while feeding between August and October in Suffolk ranged between 5.5 and 7.5 g in both sexes (mean for males, 6.3 g, *n* = 32; females,

6.8 g, *n* = 90) [149]. Juvenile males (mean 3.98 g, *n* = 203) lighter than juvenile females (mean 4.3 g, *n* = 184) leaving nursery roost in August [240].

VARIATION

Variable in colour, more so between than within colonies. Upper parts range from orange-brown to very dark brown. Some colonies consist of bats with orange-brown fur and pink-brown bare skin, others are sleeker grey-brown furred with black skin and show an obvious black mask. Most are between these extremes [207]. Within Britain size, as measured by length of forearm (Table 6.6), varies regionally but with no obvious trends.

DISTRIBUTION

Common throughout the British Isles including Ireland and some of the outer isles. Not resident in Shetland but occasional vagrants occur, usually in autumn.

HABITAT

Feeding occurs in many habitats including farmland, open woodland, suburban gardens, marshes, riparian woodland, lakes, even in urban centres but not open moorlands. In Grampian the feeding activity of a colony was largely restricted to riparian trees [195].

Roosts often found in human habitations ranging from mediaeval churches to modern houses.

Table 6.6. Regional and sexual variation in length of forearm (mm) of adult pipistrelles [244].

	Sex	Mean	n
Wiltshire and Monmouth	♀	31.0	175
Devon	♀	31.4	83
Dorset	♀	31.7	225
Kent	♀	32.2	50
E Norfolk	♀	32.5	152
Lincolnshire	♀	32.9	75
Wigtown	♀	32.2	214
Stirlingshire	♀	32.0	412
Isle of Rhum	♀	31.2	18
Northamptonshire			
Range 29.0−33.9	♂	31.2	97
Range 29.6−34.5	♀	32.0	179

Presumably originally roosted in trees but this is now unusual. Almost always roost out of sight, in cracks and crevices, in woodwork, masonry or brickwork or under slates, usually on the outside of a building but occasionally in the apex of a roof. Will use bat boxes. Rarely found in caves. In churches often found in crevices between wooden beams, behind notices and throughout the main body and roof of the building; rarely in belfries. Nursery roosts often in modern buildings, usually S or SW facing, presumably chosen partly for their warmth. At one roost, in a laundry roof, about one hundred females roosted next to hot water pipes too hot for human touch [1]. Occasionally found roosting in the open, on walls or gates.

SOCIAL ORGANISATION AND BEHAVIOUR
During summer the sexes live mostly apart, with females occupying nursery roosts where they give birth and raise their young. Male behaviour little studied in summer although they seem to roost singly or in small numbers in cool sites. In autumn most sexual activity probably occurs, though this, too, is little studied. In winter both sexes and all age groups roost together in small numbers and most of the time is spent in torpor, at body temperatures probably close to ambient temperatures [187], but feeding occurs intermittently in winter when conditions allow. Arouse slowly from torpor, when disturbed, with faintly audible vocalisations and slow movements of wings and legs. Arousal to full activity takes up to 30 min (dependent on initial body temperature and ambient temperature). Females enter torpor during pregnancy and lactation, especially when feeding conditions are poor [193, 194].

Roost colonially throughout the year. Marked sex difference in occupation of roosts. Males studied in East Anglian churches remained in them throughout the year [7]. Females present in these roosts during the winter months (September−April, most numerous November−March) when total numbers of pipistrelles in hibernation are highest [187], but usually move out to other, nursery, roosts during March and April [244]. Few males occur in nursery roosts, and those present are almost always immature. Females begin to leave nursery roosts as soon as the young are weaned. Behaviour little studied in Britain during the period between August and November. In Scandinavia males hold territories in bat-boxes during the summer and are joined by females. Males appear to defend harems of females from July onwards [85] and insemination occurs between August and November [186, 190].

Active in all months of the year, though infrequently in winter. Winter activity occurs whenever feeding conditions allow; usually at ambient temperatures over 8°C. More bats are active on the warmer nights [7, 8].

The time of first emergence is at around 20 min after sunset throughout the year [7, 40, 254, 264]. First emergence is earliest on warmer nights [7]. Males emerge, on average, before females, from roosts holding both sexes [9]. Many emergences are initiated by a single bat followed by an interval of 3−7 minutes before the main emergence; therefore median or mean emergence times provide better comparisons [36]. Emergence pattern not disrupted by owl calls [38].

Movements between colonies are rarely detected. Of 1328 bats ringed in Yorkshire only eight were found away from their colony of origin in an 8-year study; one female was found in another breeding colony 33 km away, three years after being ringed as a juvenile [239]. Of over 200 recaptures of pipistrelles in East Anglia only one had changed colony. This female moved 19 km. A colony may consist of several roosts, and movements of colony members between these roosts is common [259]. Bats translocated in Scotland homed *c.* 80 km within a week and similar observations are well documented in Germany [213]. Longest recorded natural movement in Britain was 69 km between Bury St Edmunds, Suffolk (November) and Buxton, Norfolk (October) where it was killed by a cat 11 years later.

Behaviour within roost little studied. A variable period of audible vocalisation and movement precedes emergence from roost. Vocalising within roosts after main emergence period occurs occasionally, perhaps due to disturbance, and shows that not all individuals forage on every night but these may be youngsters or nursing mothers.

Forage up to 5 km from roost [195]. Foraging often by repeated circling around defined area (beats). May move from one beat to another and back again during course of night. Foraging period determined by weather and reproductive state [7, 8, 195]. On coldest nights bats active at feeding site for less than 5 min, but on warm nights up to 200 min. Pregnant females have one long foraging period but switch to a bimodal pattern of activity after young are born, returning to the roost in the middle of the night, presumably to enable the young to suckle but also perhaps because availability of insect food is lowest at that time [254]. Average nightly foraging period varied from 154 to 294 min [254].

Many individuals can use same foraging range, but at low levels of food availability agonistic interactions occur, with initial residents ejecting intruders after short chases involving audible vocalisations [195]. Some evidence for consistency of feeding sites for individuals and for group foraging [195].

FEEDING

Diet mostly small nematoceran Diptera and Trichoptera (caddis flies), but some mayflies, lacewing and moths [257], taken in flight and usually eaten on the wing. Detailed study in Grampian showed little selection so that in general the diet reflected variations in insect availability from night to night.

Feeding rates (as measured by rate of feeding buzzes using bat detector) rise with insect availability but level off at 10 buzzes/min at high levels of insect abundance, over 1000 insects/1000 m³ air [195]. Feeding rates over short periods can reach 20 (presumed) captures/min. Feeding activity highest at dusk during summer months. Feeding rates are directly related to ambient temperature during winter [8]. No differences in feeding behaviour between males and females but young are initially less efficient at flight and catching insects than adults [195].

In captivity pregnant females ate 3 g of mealworms (*Tenebrio*) per day [183].

BREEDING

Females copulate in their first autumn whereas males do not undergo spermatogenesis until they are about 12 months old [186]. Copulation occurs in spring [6], summer [85] autumn [180, 182, 188] — earliest recorded inseminated female in Britain on 23 September [190] — and perhaps through the winter. Most inseminations probably occur between September and November. Sperm stored throughout winter until ovulation and fertilisation occur in April and May [182, 188, 190]. Gestation about 44 days [51] but depends upon environmental conditions [178, 183]. In poor conditions pregnant females re-enter the torpid state at any stage of pregnancy, and gestation is correspondingly lengthened [178, 183, 194].

Single young (occasionally twins) born from 3rd week June until 2nd week July, with exceptional births in August. Young can first fly at 3 weeks of age. Maternal care, growth and development of young have been studied [133, 255]. Mothers recognise their young by acoustic and olfactory cues and do not suckle any young except their own. Some instances of cross fostering have been reported in captivity [34, 270], but this requires verification from the wild.

POPULATION

Maternity roosts can hold up to 1000 bats but 1−200 are much more common with an average of c. 60. Small roosts, of only a few individuals, also occur and are easily overlooked.

Sex ratio of weaned bats is near unity — 204 males: 185 females [240]. In East Anglia in winter there is a higher ratio of subadult females to adult females than would be expected from the apparent longevity of the species. This might indicate either a geographical difference in roost location or a difference in choice of site within roosts between females of different ages [1].

Long-term study at nursery roosts in Yorkshire showed annual survival rate for adult females to be 0.64 per year. Survival in first year may be lower. Two bats survived to at least 10 years of age and one to 11, the oldest recorded in Britain [250]. There is a record of 16 years 7 months in Czechoslovakia [118]. Little information for males but some live to at least 5 years [1].

MORTALITY

Vulnerable to chlorinated hydrocarbon pesticides [126] and wood preservative [196]. Some fall prey to cats, especially around houses.

PARASITES

Bugs, *Cimex pipistrelli*, and fleas, *Ischnopsyllus*

octactenus, are common; the winter flea, *Nycteridopsylla longiceps*, is regular. Ticks, *Argas vespertilionis*, recorded most commonly on ventral surface. Present on minority of hosts but maximum count from a sample of over 300 pipistrelles was 57. Females more often infested than males which appear to lose their ticks as they age. Consistent differences exist between nursery roosts in the incidence of ticks; at some roosts few bats ever have ticks. At one nursery roost the incidence of ticks and the mean parasite burden rose during the course of the spring suggesting that it is in nursery roosts that most bats acquire their ticks [1]. Mites: *Spinturnix acuminatus*, *Macronyssus kolenatii*, *M. uncinatus*, *Steatonyssus periblepharus*, *Pteracarus pipistrellia*, *Acanthophthirius etheldrae* and *Leptotrombidium russicum*.

RELATIONS WITH MAN

This is the species of bat most likely to be found in and around human habitation. Nursery colonies are particularly vulnerable to destruction by unsympathetic householders.

AUTHOR FOR THIS SPECIES

M.I. Avery, based upon the second edition text by R.E. Stebbings and with acknowledgement for additional data and comment from A.M. Hutson, P.A. Racey, P.W. Richardson, J.R. Speakman, S.M. Swift and M.J.A. Thompson.

Nathusius's pipistrelle *Pipistrellus nathusii*

Vespertilio nathusii Keyserling & Blasius, 1839; Germany.

RECOGNITION

Similar to *P. pipistrellus* but third upper premolar larger and extending well beyond the cingulum of the canine; incisors noticeably taller and thinner. Distinct gap between I_2 and I_3 [96]. Proportion of fifth digit to forearm 125% or more, less in *P. pipistrellus* [242].

DESCRIPTION

Slightly larger than *P. pipistrellus*, with longer shaggier fur with light tips on the back giving a frosted appearance. Ventral fur distinctly lighter than dorsal. On ventral surface of the wing, hair extends to the elbow, then a 5 mm band of fine hair extends to the wrist just posterior to the forearm.

MEASUREMENTS

Head and body 44−54 mm; tail 31−41 mm; forearm 31−36.5 mm; ear 10.5−16 mm; tragus 6.0−8.0 mm; weight *c.* 6.4 g.

DISTRIBUTION

From W Europe, where records are few and scattered, to the Urals, Caucasus and W Asia Minor. Reaches highest population density in central and southern areas of the European part of the USSR. In most other European countries it is rare [96]. Regarded as highly migratory [251] with general records of movement over 1000 km and the longest 1600 km.

Three individuals recorded in mainland Britain — one in Dorset in October 1969 [242], one in Hertfordshire in August 1978 [15], another 24 km away in Essex in January. Also one on a North Sea oil rig in September 1985 and three in Jersey, Channel Islands between November 1987 and March 1988 [37]. Has probably been confused with *P. pipistrellus* in the past; more may be expected in Britain and are most likely to occur during migration in autumn and winter.

Roosts: in Czechoslovakia, roosts in crevices in walls or under the roofs of isolated buildings at the periphery of woods or near ponds.

AUTHOR FOR THIS SPECIES

P.A. Racey.

GENUS *Barbastella*

A genus of two Palaearctic species, of which one occurs in Britain. Dark to black bats with very broad triangular or squarish ears joined at the bases. Dental formula 2.1.2.3 / 3.1.2.3 as in *Nyctalus* and *Pipistrellus*.

Barbastelle *Barbastella barbastellus*

Vespertilio barbastellus Schreber, 1774; France.

RECOGNITION

The black, short, broad ears joined across the forehead distinguish this from all other species (Fig. 6.16).

DESCRIPTION

A medium-sized bat with upper parts blackish

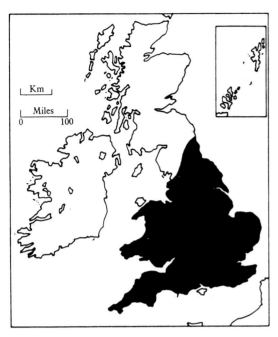

Map 6.24. Barbastelle.

brown and tips of hairs pale yellow or cream giving a frosted appearance. (Juveniles up to 12 months may not have these light tips.) Underparts grey-brown with paler tips. Face, ears and membranes very dark brown, almost black. Ears about 15 mm long and as broad. Tragus large, triangular and slightly more than half the height of conch. Muzzle short, broad and glandular. Wings broad and membranes thin.

Chromosomes: $2n = 32$, $FNa = 50-52$, continental data [270].

MEASUREMENTS
Head and body 40–52 mm; forearm 36–43 mm; wingspan 245–280 mm; ear 14–16 mm; condylo-basal length 12.9–13.8 mm; weight 6–13 g. Males are smaller than females. In Switzerland forearm means for males 38.8 mm ($n = 26$) and for females 39.9 mm ($n = 21$) [3].

HABITAT
Seem to prefer wooded river valleys. Mostly found in hollow trees and buildings but also hibernate in caves during very cold weather.

Map 6.25. Barbastelle.

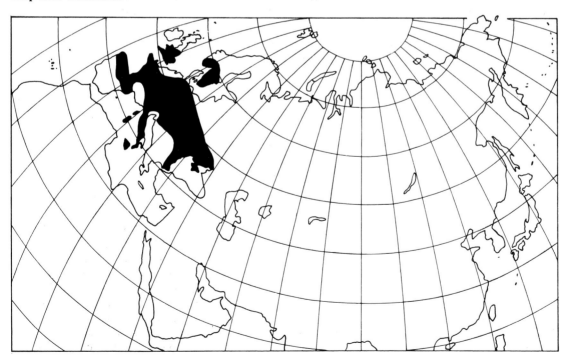

Fig. 6.16. Barbastelle. (Photo: S.C. Bisserôt.)

SOCIAL ORGANISATION AND BEHAVIOUR

Summer: little known. Females segregate from males and form small nursery colonies. Males usually remain solitary. Emergence time is rather variable, sometimes begins before sunset. Active intermittently throughout night. Flight generally low, often over water, tending to be heavy and fluttering. Flies faster when flying to feeding areas. They usually alight head up but sometimes turn somersault and hang by their feet.

Winter: in central Europe large numbers are sometimes found in hibernation but usually only in January and February when very cold. The mean experimental and natural preferred temperatures in hibernation in Poland were 4.3°C and 4.0°C. Some prefer 0°C and they are able to withstand much lower temperatures [100]. Sex ratio in hibernation shows strong bias towards the males, 67.6% ($n = 641$) [75].

It is not known whether this species is stationary or migratory, but several medium-length movements up to 290 km have been recorded in Germany [131].

FEEDING

Little known but one watched for 50 min near Bath from just before sunset feeding on swarming dipteran flies 0–30 cm above mill pond, often dipping to the water, possibly drinking. After 30 min it rested on stone bridge for 3 min before resuming feeding [1].

BREEDING AND POPULATION
No information. On the Continent two were recaptured over 18 years after initial banding. [2].

PARASITES
The flea *Ischnopsyllus hexactenus* and the mite *Neomyobia pantopus* have been recorded.

RELATIONS WITH MAN
Difficult to keep alive in captivity.

AUTHOR FOR THIS SPECIES
R.E. Stebbings.

GENUS *Plecotus* (LONG-EARED BATS)

A genus of two widespread species in the Palaearctic Region, another, *P. teneriffae*, confined to the Canary Islands, and three (sometimes separated as *Corynorhinus*) in North America. Both Palaearctic species occur in Britain. They have only been clearly recognised as distinct since 1959 [146] and since 1964 in Britain [42], and therefore many earlier records are not clearly attributable to species.

Distinguished from all other European bats by

enormous ears joined at their inner bases. Tragus is prominent and remains erect when ears are folded under wings during rest. Dental formula 2.1.2.3/3.1.3.3.

Mostly found roosting in buildings and trees but occasionally hibernate in caves, especially during cold weather. In hibernation wings usually folded loosely around body and legs held bent. Echolocation pulses are very weak and are probably related to the mode of feeding, in which most food is picked off vegetation.

Brown long-eared bat *Plecotus auritus*

Vespertilio auritus L. 1758; Sweden.
Plecotus brevimanus Jenyns, 1829; Grunty Fen, Cambridgeshire, England.

Common long-eared bat.

RECOGNITION

Distinguished from all other species except the grey long-eared bat by its very long ears (over 28 mm) which are three quarters the length of its head and body. Separated from the grey long-eared by its generally smaller size, although there may be overlap in individual measurements [238], brown-buff fur, pink to pale brown face, long slender thumb (generally over 6.2 mm), narrow tapering tragus, and by the second upper premolar being more than half the height of the first (Table 6.7).

SIGN

Faeces accumulate under roosting sites and feeding perches, 8−12 mm in length, containing a large proportion of moth scales, often shiny, looking varnished, usually black.

Feeding perches frequently used when preying on insects too large to be consumed in flight. Perches are often in porches or outbuildings [177], and may be recognised by accumulations beneath them of faeces and of moth wings and other insect remains.

DESCRIPTION

A small to medium-sized bat, of delicate build, and placid to handle. Dorsal fur usually yellow-buff or light brown, underparts buff, yellowish brown, creamy or white. An indistinct line of demarcation exists along side of neck. Juveniles less than 6 weeks old are often dark grey, and they remain greyish brown for up to 12 months. Face pink or light to mid-brown, with little hair. Snout pointed, relatively long, with nostrils on top. Wings broad, membranes thin and semi-transparent. Thumb relatively long and slender.

Eyes large and bright. Ears very large and oval, frequently folded back when the bat is at rest giving a 'ram's horn' shape lower half. Tragus almost half as high as conch, anterior border almost straight and posterior border convex proximally and becoming straight or slightly concave distally. Tragus has rounded tip (Fig. 6.17).

Upper canine small and rounded in section just below cingulum. Baculum Y-shaped, with all three limbs slender, about three times as long as wide [42].

Chromosomes: $2n = 32$; $FNa = 50−54$, continental data [270].

MEASUREMENTS

Head and body 37−48 mm; forearm 34−42 mm; wingspan 230−285 mm; ear length 29−38 mm; condylobasal length 13−16 mm (*see also* Table 6.7). Weight 6−12 g. In a colony in Dorset mean weights were 9.0 g in October, 8.0 g in January and 7.0 g in mid-April ($n = 293$), with a loss of 22% during hibernation [243].

Females slightly heavier than males, by 1 g in October but only 0.5 g in April; females also about 2.5% larger than males as measured by length of forearm (*see* Table 6.7).

VARIATION

Average size a little less in Britain than on the Continent but showing some regional differences (*see* Table 6.7).

DISTRIBUTION

In Britain, occurs everywhere except exposed regions of N and NW Scotland and the offshore islands.

HABITAT

Prefers lightly wooded areas, and is commonly found in sheltered valleys in Britain. In Central and Eastern Europe it seems to be confined to mountainous woodland areas [112, 174]. It roosts in buildings and trees throughout the year, and also uses caves in winter. Groups of this species (including nursery colonies) frequently inhabit bat boxes [77].

	Males		Females	
	Mean	n	Mean	n
Brown long-eared bats				
Dorset	37.5	38	38.3	46
Suffolk	37.6	32	38.5	35
Northamptonshire [199]	38.1	57	39.2	77
Nottinghamshire	—	—	39.3	31
Inverness	38.2	28	39.2	23
Czechoslovakia	39.5	37	40.2	58
Grey long-eared bats				
Dorset	39.9	22	41.1	35
Czechoslovakia	39.8	131	41.0	151

Table 6.7. Variation in length of forearm (mm) in long-eared bats from Britain [224] and Czechoslovakia [117].

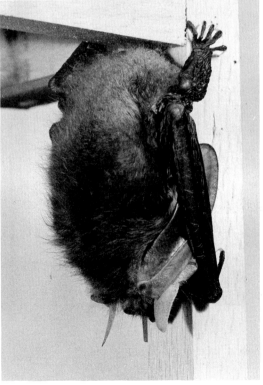

a   b

Fig. 6.17. Brown long-eared bat (a) alert, with ears erect; (b) asleep with ears folded under wing leaving erect traguses. (Photos: S.C. Bisserôt.)

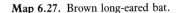

Map 6.26. Brown long-eared bat.

SOCIAL ORGANISATION AND BEHAVIOUR

Summer: nursery colonies consisting of adult females and a few immature males and females form in May or June, usually among beams in attics. Bats roost in confined spaces during the day unless air temperature exceeds about 40°C, when they hang from rafters with wings partly spread [236]. Light precipitation and wind have little effect on emergence, but heavy rain and strong wind may prevent flight [70]. Emergence begins 40 ±7 min after sunset in Scotland, and bats are active in the roost for up to 80 min before this [256]. They stretch, groom and make short flights in the roost before departing. When infants are present, females return to the roost after 1−2 hours to suckle, but at other times bats may remain outside until dawn.

Flight is slow and fluttering, usually close to trees. Wings have low aspect ratio, the bat is very agile and hovering is common [167, 168]. The slow, manoeuvrable flight, long ears and large eyes allow foliage gleaning as a method of feeding in which insects are probably located by sound and sight rather than by echolocation. The commonest echolocation pulse is a faint, short (2 ms) FM

Map 6.27. Brown long-eared bat.

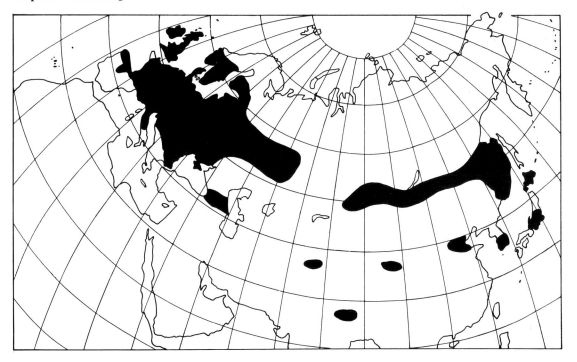

sweep which is very weak and can only be picked up on a bat detector at less than 5 m distance. However, this species also emits a loud pulse, detectable at 40 m or more, 7.1 ms long and sliding in frequency from 42 to 12 kHz. This call may be emitted irregularly, when bats are in caves, or regularly, when they are in the open [5].

Winter: hibernation begins in November and ends in late March in England and Europe [102, 243]. Bats hibernate in trees and buildings and also in caves, where they prefer the cool outer regions and where they are found in crevices [26, 50]. They may overwinter singly or in small groups [102], or may form clusters with other species which have similar thermal preferences [29]. Hibernaculum temperatures have been found to range from 4 to 7.5°C [112] and from −3 to 11°C, with most individuals choosing areas at 7°C [102]. Under experimental conditions bats occupied regions at between 1 and 8°C, with a mean of 6°C [100]. In the same experiments, bats of this species were found to be active at temperatures as low as 1°C, and this could explain why they may be found in summer roosts until well into autumn.

Generally considered to be a stationary species [79, 251], which occupies the same roost all year round in some areas. The longest flight recorded in Europe is 42 km [79]. However some immigration to Britain from the Continent is suggested by a group, apparently flying SW, that landed on a ship 70 km NE of Spurn Point, Yorkshire in November 1948 and by one found dead on a lightship 50 km E of Norfolk on 27 October 1968, coincident with a massive arrival of Scandinavian birds [43].

FEEDING
Forages in woodland, at the height of the thickest foliage (about 5−6 m above the ground) and on short, twisting beats which incorporate several trees [256]. Foliage gleaning is common, and larger prey items such as noctuid moths are taken to a feeding perch to be consumed [258]. Analyses of insect remains which are bitten off by bats and which accumulate under perches have thus led previously to the assumption that noctuids form the bulk of the diet [135, 177, 210], but in more recent studies faecal analysis has shown that many other insects are also eaten [256] (Table 6.8). Many of the moths and beetles in the diet are probably caught on trees by foliage gleaning, as are bugs, earwigs and spiders. Other insects are probably caught in free flight. Diet composition may vary throughout summer as different insects become available [265]. This species has been found to catch insects inside both summer roosts [256] and hibernacula [210].

BREEDING
Mating begins in autumn. In Britain, males are seen with epididymides distended with spermatozoa by early September [232] and copulation occurs from October until April [236, 243]. In Russia, only 14% of females were found to be inseminated on arrival at hibernacula in November, and progressively more were mated throughout winter [250]. Some males may become sexually mature in their 1st year but the majority probably achieve puberty during their second summer [232]. 75% of females give birth for the first time at the end of their 2nd year; the rest produce their first young in their 3rd year [236].

Females are palpably pregnant by late May, and birth of a single infant usually occurs in nursery colonies during the first 3 weeks of July, earlier in very warm, dry weather, or later after a cold spring. Infants cling to their mother's nipple continuously

	Percentage of total number of fragments identified
Lepidoptera (moths)	41
Coleoptera (beetles)	22
Trichoptera (caddis flies)	16
Diptera (suborder Nematocera — longhorn flies)	10
Diptera (other flies)	3
Hemiptera (bugs)	1
Neuroptera (lacewings)	1
Dermaptera (earwigs)	1
Araneae (spiders)	5

Table 6.8. The proportions of insects and spiders identified from fragments in the faeces of brown long-eared bats collected over 2 years inside a roost in Inverness-shire [256].

for the first 10 days except when the adults are foraging, at which times infants are left in groups or crèches in the roost. On her return, a female recognises her own infant by means of vocal signals and olfactory cues [255]. Lactating and post-lactating females are characterised by a sweet-smelling, oily secretion from the facial glands which stains fur and membranes [236]. This secretion is thought to aid mother–young recognition. After 10 days of age, huddling in crèches is less notice-able, and infants are rarely found attached to their mothers during the day. Young bats first leave the roost at about 30 days of age, and they make practice flights in the roost for several days before this [255]. Weaning is complete about 6 weeks after birth.

POPULATION

Colony size varies from 20 [243] to 84 [256]. Increment rate in a Dorset colony was 20% per year [243] and in this colony survival rates of 0.76 for females and 0.54 for males indicate life spans of 16 and 7 years respectively. With females sur-viving longer, the annual sex ratio was constant at 39% males. In Czechoslovakia, sex ratio during hibernation was found to be 53% males [77]. Recorded life spans vary from 6 to 22 years [4, 107] and over 13 years for a female in Dorset.

MORTALITY

In Britain, preyed upon by barn owls to a small extent — less than 0.1% of pellets examined con-tained remains of the species [92]. In Poland, skeletal remains were found in 10.9% of barn owl pellets examined ($n = 428$), and in 11.4% of tawny owl pellets ($n = 11$), although the small sample size makes the latter less significant [215]. In Yorkshire, a group was seen to be pursued by a pair of kestrels and one bat was captured [221]. Domestic cats also catch some. They are very vulnerable to poisons used for timber treatment in attics.

PARASITES

Adults harbour relatively few ectoparasites, although juveniles may suffer heavy infestations. Species most commonly occurring are the flea *Ischnopsyllus hexactenus* and the mites *Spinturnix plecotina*, *Ornithonyssus pipistrelli* and *Neomyobia plecotia*. *Nycteridopsylla longiceps* is a rare winter flea. The recorded observation of heavy infestation by nycteribiid flies [236] is either exceptional or in error [121].

RELATIONS WITH MAN

A timid bat which adapts with relative difficulty to captivity. Pregnant females have a tendency to abort during the 1st week after capture, but once established have been maintained in the laboratory for 1.5 years [179]. Young have been born and reared. Because it is active at low temperatures, it is difficult to provide ideal conditions for this species to hibernate in captivity [179].

Susceptible to pesticides, including chlorinated hydrocarbons such as HCH and Pentachlorophenol (PCP) used in remedial timber treatment, and thus colonies in attics are at risk when treatment is carried out. Less toxic chemicals are available for use in these circumstances [196].

AUTHOR FOR THIS SPECIES
S.M. Swift.

Grey long-eared bat *Plecotus austriacus*

Vespertilio auritus austriacus Fischer, 1829; Austria.

RECOGNITION

Very similar to the brown long-eared bat, but distinguished by its slightly larger size (*see* Table 6.7), overall grey colour, dark brown to black face, short thumb (generally less than 6.2 mm), broad tragus, large upper canine which is angular in sec-tion below the cingulum, and by having a very small second upper premolar, less than half the height of the first (Fig. 6.18).

SIGN

Faeces as for brown long-eared. Feeding perches are used [22], and are similar to those of brown long-eared.

DESCRIPTION

A medium-sized bat which is relatively aggressive when handled [243]. Upper parts medium to dark grey, sometimes almost black, and under parts light grey with whitish tips. Bases of hairs both dorsally and ventrally are very dark, almost black. Face dark brown to black, ears and membranes dark brown. Thumb short and relatively thick. Eyes large. Ears very large and broad, folded back when the bat is at rest. Tragus broad, with anterior edge more or less straight and posterior edge strongly convex in proximal half and concave dis-tally (Fig. 6.18). Upper canines large and angular

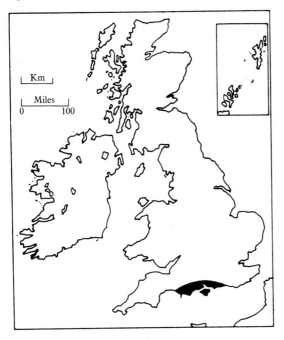

Map 6.28. Grey long-eared bat.

[238]. Baculum Y-shaped with stout proximal limbs, shorter than they are wide [42].

Chromosomes: 2n = 32, FNa = 50–52, continental data [270].

MEASUREMENTS

Head and body 40–52 mm; forearm 38–43 mm; wingspan 255–300 mm; ear length 30–38 mm; condylobasal length 15–17 mm; tragus width over 5.6 mm, usually about 6.0 mm. Weight 7–14 g; annual weight changes recorded in a Dorset colony showed males 1.0 g lighter than females pre-hibernation and 0.8 g lighter in spring. Mean weights 11.3 g in October, 10.0 g in January and 8.0 g in April, a loss of 29% during hibernation [243]. Males are also slightly smaller than females as indicated by length of forearm (*see* Table 6.7).

VARIATION

British individuals not distinguishable from continental ones, and similar in size (*see* Table 6.7).

DISTRIBUTION

Throughout central and S Europe, north to Poland as far as 53°N [214] and east to the Himalayas. It is

Map 6.29. Grey long-eared bat.

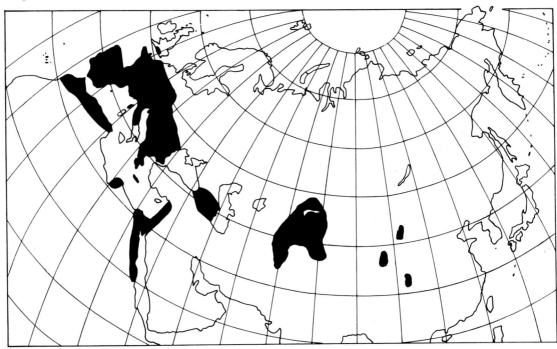

Fig. 6.18. Grey long-eared bat.
(Photo: S.C. Bisserôt.)

locally common in parts of Europe, such as low-lying areas of Belgium [130]. First recognised in Britain in 1963 [42], and has only been found in Dorset, Hampshire, Sussex and on Guernsey, Jersey and Sark in the Channel Islands.

HISTORY

In 1829 Jenyns recognised two species of *Plecotus* in England, but used the name *P. auritus* for the larger, greyer one, which he believed to be the commoner species, without giving localities [127]. It is therefore not clear whether he was dealing with *P. austriacus* as now understood. The earliest surviving British specimen of *P. austriacus* was probably collected at Netley, Hampshire in the 1870s, and there is one from Jersey in 1939 [42].

HABITAT

In England and the Channel Islands known roosts are in house roofs in open, lightly wooded country. In Europe it lives almost exclusively in cultivated lowland areas [112, 130, 214]. Nursery roosts are in attics or church lofts, often in villages or small towns. In winter, uses caves as well as cellars of buildings [112], and was never found in bat boxes, even in areas where it is common [77].

SOCIAL ORGANISATION AND BEHAVIOUR

Summer: hibernation ends in March for females

and April for males, and segregation of sexes occurs from June until September in Dorset [243]. Nursery colonies are formed in open spaces in attics [112] and in the warmest areas of church lofts [130]. Large number of healed injuries suggests a high degree of intraspecific aggression [243], and this species is also far more aggressive when handled than is the brown long-eared bat.

Emerges around dusk and forages intermittently in the vicinity of the roost until dawn [22]. Flight is straight, usually at 2–5 m above the ground, and most prey is thought to be caught in free flight, although there is some evidence of foliage gleaning [22]. Echolocation has not been studied in detail.

Winter: hibernation begins in October and takes place deep in warm caves [117] or in cellars of buildings in Czechoslovakia [112], and one bat is reported hibernating in a disused brick kiln in the Netherlands [89]. Hangs free and in exposed positions. Hibernation temperature 2–9°C in Czechoslovakia [112]. In Britain was found to hibernate at 12°C and to be relatively active during winter, but this was probably due to temperature fluctuations causing frequent arousals [243]. Hibernation weight loss was high (29%), and it is probable that unsuitable hibernating conditions in Britain confine this species to the extreme south of the country [243].

Considered to be a stationary species, with

longest recorded flight of 62 km, in Czechoslovakia [79]. One specimen was found on a lightship 18 km off the Sussex coast on 10 September 1969, followed by one found dead on the adjacent coast 11 days later, suggesting immigration from the Continent [44].

FEEDING

Piles of insect remains beneath feeding perches contain remains of moths from numerous families, as well as small to medium-sized beetles [22]. Insects are also consumed on the wing, and faecal analysis reveals Diptera, Hymenoptera, Neuroptera, Heteroptera, Homoptera and Trichoptera in the diet as well as Lepidoptera and Coleoptera [22]. Feeding is opportunistic, since large moths and chafers are selected when insects are abundant, but at other times a wide range is eaten. Over the whole year, noctuid moths form the bulk of the diet.

BREEDING

Mate in autumn, beginning mid-September and continuing for about a month [243], and probably continue to copulate during arousals in winter. Only one adult male was found per section of roost, and this could indicate territoriality [243]. Males become sexually mature at 1 year, and females first give birth in their 2nd or 3rd year [236].

Sexual segregation begins in June, when nursery colonies are formed, and young are born in July. Development of young and mother−young interaction appear to be similar to those in the brown long-eared bat.

POPULATION

Dorset colony consisted of 22, but this number fell sharply after an exceptionally cold winter and then increased again. Survival rates were 0.45 for males and 0.62 for females, giving life expectancies of 5 and 9 years [243]. Population size in a colony in Jersey has recently declined to eight, due mainly to human disturbance of the roost [145]. Sex ratio in the Dorset colony was biased, with 30% males, while in Czechoslovakia a significant predominance of males (69%) was found during hibernation [77]. Greatest longevity recorded in Britain is 11 years [244] and in Europe 12 years [79].

MORTALITY

In Europe, has been found to be preyed on by owls, particularly barn owls, 9.3% of whose pellets contained skeletal remains [215].

RELATIONS WITH MAN

Has not been kept in captivity. Colonies in Jersey and Guernsey have recently been adversely affected by the use of pesticides in a house [145].

AUTHOR FOR THIS SPECIES
S.M. Swift.

REFERENCES

1 Author's data.
2 Abel G. (1967) Wiederfund von 2 Mopfledermäusen (*Barbastella barbastellus*) nach 18 Jarhen. *Myotis* **5**: 19−20.
3 Aellen V. (1962) La baguement des chauves-souris au Col de Bretolet (Valais). *Archives des Sciences, Genève* **14**:365−92.
4 Aellen V. (1983−84) Migrations de chauves-souris de Suisse. Note complementaire. *Myotis* **21−22**: 185−9.
5 Ahlen I. (1981) *Identification of Scandinavian bats by their sounds*. Report no. 6, Department of Wildlife Ecology, Swedish University of Agricultural Sciences.
6 Aubert A. (1963) Observations sur l'accouplement des Chiroptères. *Acta theriologica* **6**:300−1.
7 Avery M.I. (1983) *The winter activity of pipistrelle bats*. PhD. thesis, University of Aberdeen.
8 Avery M.I. (1985) Winter activity of pipistrelle bats. *Journal of Animal Ecology* **54**:721−38.
9 Avery M.I. (1986) Factors affecting the emergence of pipistrelle bats. *Journal of Zoology* (A) **209**: 293−6.
10 Avery M.I. (1986) The winter activity of noctule bats (*Nyctalus noctula*). *Journal of Zoology* (A) **209**: 296−9.
11 Baagoe H.J. & Jensen B. (1973) The spread and present occurrence of the serotine (*Eptesicus serotinus*) in Denmark. *Periodicum Biologorum* **75**:107−9.
12 Baker J.R. (1974) Protozoan parasites of the blood of British wild birds and mammals. *Journal of Zoology* **172**:161−90.
13 Balcells R.E. (1956) Estudio biólogico y bioquimico de *Myotis nattereri. Publicaciones del Instituto de Biologia Aplicado* **23**:37−81.
14 Banks C. *et al.* (1980) Observations on an unusual mixed roost of serotine and noctule bats in East Hertfordshire. *Transactions of the Hertfordshire Natural History Society and Field Club* **28**:20−2.
15 Banks C. *et al.* (1983) A second Nathusius' pipistrelle (*Pipistrellus nathusii*) in Britain. *Transactions of the Hertfordshire Natural History Society* **29**:15−18.
16 Barbu P. & Sin G. (1968) Observatii asupra hibernarii speciei *Nyctalus noctula* (Schreber, 1774) in Faleza Lacului Razelm-Capul Dolosman-Dobrogea. *Studii si Cercetari de Biologie, Seria Zoologie* **20**: 291−7.

17 Barrett H.G. & Cranbrook Earl of (1961) Feeding habits of bats. *Transactions of the Suffolk Naturalists' Society* 11:528.

18 Barrett-Hamilton G.E.H. (1910–11) *A History of British mammals. I Bats*. London: Gurney & Jackson.

19 Barrington R.M. (1891) Quoted in Barrett-Hamilton 1910–1911.

20 Barta Z. (1976) Eine interessante gemeinsamjagende Fledermaus-Gesellschaft aus dem Slovenske Rudohori Gebirge. *Lynx* 18:19–25.

21 Bauer K. (1960) Die Säugetiere des Neusiedlersee-Gebietes (Osterreich). *Bonner Zoologische Beiträge* 11:141–344.

22 Bauerova Z. (1982) Contribution to the trophic ecology of the grey long-eared bat, *Plecotus austriacus*. *Folia zoologica* 31:113–22.

23 Bauerova Z. & Cerveny J. (1986) Towards an understanding of the trophic ecology of *Myotis nattereri*. *Folia zoologica* 35:55–61.

24 Bels L. (1952) Fifteen years of bat banding in the Netherlands. *Publicaties van het Natuurhistorisch Genootschap in Limburg* 5:1–99.

25 Bezem J.J. et al. (1960) Population statistics of five species of bats of the genus *Myotis* and one of the genus *Rhinolophus*, hibernating in the caves of South Limberg. *Archives Néerlandaises de Zoologie* 13:511–39.

26 Bezem J.J. et al. (1964) Some characteristics of the hibernating locations of various species of bats in South Limburg. I and II. *Proceedings, Koninklijke Nederlandse Akademie van Wetenschappen* 67:235–350.

27 Blackmore M. (1956) An occurrence of the mouse-eared bat *Myotis myotis* (Borkhausen) in England. *Proceedings of the Zoological Society of London* 127:201–3.

28 Blackmore M. (1964) Chiroptera. In Southern H. ed. *Handbook of British mammals*, 1st edn. Oxford: Blackwell Scientific Publications pp. 224–49.

29 Bogdanowicz W. (1983) Community structure and interspecific interactions in bats hibernating in Poland. *Acta theriologica* 28:357–70.

30 Brosset A. & Deboutenville C.D. (1966) Le régime alimentaire du Vespertilion de Daubenton *Myotis daubentonii*. *Mammalia* 30:247–51.

31 Brosset A. & Poillet A. (1985) Structure d'une population hibernante de grands rhinolophes *Rhinolophus ferrumequinum* dans l'est de la France. *Mammalia* 49:221–33.

32 Brown J. et al. (1983) The use of church porches by bats. *Journal of Zoology* 200:292–5.

33 Bullock D.J. Personal communication.

34 Bullock D.J. & Eales O.L. Personal communication.

35 Bullock D.J. et al. (1986) The distribution of Natterer's bat, *Myotis nattereri* (Kuhl), in Scotland. *Glasgow Naturalist* 21:137–41.

36 Bullock D.J. et al. (1987) Analysis of the timing and pattern of emergence of the pipistrelle bat (*Pipistrellus pipistrellus*). *Journal of Zoology* (A) 211:267–4.

37 Carroll J.B. (1988) Nathusius's pipistrelle *Pipistrellus nathusii* in the Channel Islands. *Bat News* 14:2.

38 Catto C. Personal communication.

39 Caubere B. et al. (1984) Un record mondial de longevité in natura pour un chiroptère insectivore? *La Terre et la Vie* 39:351–3.

40 Church H.F. (1957) The times of emergence of the pipistrelle. *Proceedings of the Zoological Society of London* 128:600–2.

41 Clarke R.B. (1963) *Grimes Graves, Norfolk*. London: HMSO 32 pp.

42 Corbet G.B. (1964) The grey long-eared bat *Plecotus austriacus* in England and the Channel Islands. *Proceedings of the Zoological Society of London* 143:511–15.

43 Corbet G.B. (1970) Vagrant bats in Shetland and the North Sea. *Journal of Zoology* 161:281–2.

44 Corbet G.B. (1971) Provisional distribution maps of British mammals. *Mammal Review* 1:95–142.

45 Cranbrook J. (1960) Birth of a serotine bat (*Eptesicus serotinus* Schreber) in captivity. *Transactions of the Suffolk Naturalists' Society* 11:387–9.

46 Cranbrook J. (1965) Notes on a foraging group of serotine bats (*Eptesicus serotinus* Schreber). *Transactions of the Suffolk Naturalists' Society* 13:14–19.

47 Cranbrook, Earl of & Barrett H.G. (1956) Observations on noctule bats captured while feeding. *Proceedings of the Zoological Society of London* 144:1–24.

48 Daan S. (1973) Activity during natural hibernation in three species of vespertilionid bats. *Netherlands Journal of Zoology* 23:1–71.

49 Daan S. (1980) Long term changes in bat populations in the Netherlands: summary. *Lutra* 22:95–105.

50 Daan S. & Wichers H.J. (1968) Habitat selection of bats hibernating in a limestone cave. *Zeitschrift für Säugetierkunde* 33:262–87.

51 Deansley R. & Warwick T. (1939) Observations on pregnancy in the common bat (*Pipistrellus pipistrellus*). *Proceedings of the Zoological Society of London* 109:57–60.

52 Degn H.J. (1983) Field activity of a colony of Serotine bats. *Nyctalus* 1:521–30.

53 Dinale G. (1966) Studi sui Chirotteri Italiani V. Esperimenti di ritorno al luogo di cattura e ricatture esterne di *Rhinolophus ferrumequinum* Schreber inanellati in Liguria. *Atti della Societe Italiana di Scienze Naturali* 105:147–57.

54 Dinale G. (1969) Studi sui Chirotteri Italiani: X. Biometria di una collezione di *Rhinolophus ferrumequinum* Schreber catturati in Liguria (Italy). *Annali del Museo Civico di Storia Naturale di Genova* 77:574–90.

55 Dobson J. (1985) Serotine feeding on ground. In Dobson, J. ed. *Essex Bat Group Report* 1985 p. 13.

56 Dorcelo J. & Punt A. (1969) Abundance and internal migration of hibernating bats in an artificial limestone cave (*Sibbergroeve*). *Lynx* 10:101–25.

57 Dulic B. (1980) Morphological characteristics and distribution of *Plecotus auritus* and *Plecotus austriacus* in some regions of Yugoslavia. In Wilson D.E. &

Gardner A.L. eds. *Proceedings of the fifth International Bat Research Conference.* Texas: Texas Technical Press, pp. 151–61.

58 Dulic B. *et al.* (1967) La formule chromosomique de la noctule, *Nyctalus noctula* (Mammalia, Chiroptera). *Experientia* 23:1–4.

59 Egsbaek W. & Jensen B. (1963) Results of bat banding in Denmark. *Videnskabelig Meddelelser fra Dansk Naturhistorisk Forening* 125:269–96.

60 Eisentraut M. (1936) Zur Fortpflanzungsbiologie der Fledermäuse. *Zeitschrift für Morphologie und Ökologie der Tiere* 31:27–63.

61 Eisentraut M. (1937) Die deutschen Fledermäuse, eine biologische Studie. *Zentralblatt für Kleintierkunde* 13:1–184.

62 Eisentraut M. (1949) Beobachtung über Begattung bei Fledermäuse in Winterquartur. *Zoologischer Jahresbericht (Syst. Oekol.)* 78:295–300.

63 Eisentraut M. (1952) Beobachtungen über Jagdroute und Flugbeginn bei Fledermäusen. *Bonner Zoologische Beiträge* 3:200–11.

64 Eliassen E. & Egsbaek W. (1963) Vascular changes in the hibernating bat *Myotis daubentonii. Arbok for Universitetet: Bergen Mat. Naturv.* 3:1–22.

65 Faveaux M.A. de (1971) Catalogue des acariens parasites et commensaux des chiroptères. *Documents de Travail, Institut Royal des Sciences Naturelles de Belgique, Studiedocumenten* 7:1–451.

66 Fenton M.B. (1983) *Just bats.* Toronto: University of Toronto Press 165 pp.

67 Fenton M.B. (1985) *Communication in the Chiroptera.* Bloomington: Indiana University Press 161 pp.

68 Fenton M.B. *et al.* (1987) *Recent advances in the study of bats.* Cambridge: Cambridge University Press 470 pp.

69 Fleming J. (1828) *A history of British animals.* Edinburgh.

70 Frylstam B. (1970) Studier over langorade fladdermusen (*Plecotus auritus* L.). *Fauna och Flora* 65:72–84.

71 Funakoshi K. & Uchida T.A. (1978) Studies on the physiological and ecological adaptation of temperate insectivorous bats. II. Hibernation and winter activity in some cave-dwelling bats. *Japanese Journal of Ecology* 28:237–61.

72 Gaisler J. (1963) The ecology of lesser horseshoe bat (*Rhinolophus hipposideros hipposideros* Bechstein, 1800) in Czechoslovakia, Part I. *Vestnik Ceskoslovenske Spolecnosti Zoologické* 27:211–33.

73 Gaisler J. (1963) Nocturnal activity in the lesser horseshoe bat, *Rhinolophus hipposideros* (Bechstein, 1800). *Zoologické listy* 12:223–30.

74 Gaisler J. (1966) Reproduction in the lesser horseshoe bat (*Rhinolophus hipposideros hipposideros* Bechstein, 1800). *Bijdragen tot de Dierkunde* 36:45–64.

75 Gaisler J. (1966) A tentative ecological classification of colonies of the European bats. *Lynx* 6:35–9.

76 Gaisler J. (1970) Remarks on the thermopreferenda of palaearctic bats in their natural habitat. *Bijdragen tot de Dierkunde* 40:33–5.

77 Gaisler J. (1975). A quantitative study of some populations of bats in Czechoslovakia (Mammalia: Chiroptera). *Acta Scientiarum Naturalium Brno* 9(59):1–44.

78 Gaisler J. (1979) Ecology of bats. In Stoddart, D.M. ed. *Ecology of small mammals.* London: Chapman & Hall pp. 281–342.

79 Gaisler J. & Hanak V. (1969) Summary of the results of bat banding in Czechoslovakia, 1948–1967. *Lynx* 10:25–34.

80 Gaisler J. *et al.* (1979) A contribution to the population ecology of *Nyctalus noctula. Acta Scientiarum Naturalium Academiae Scientiarum Bohemoslovacae. Brno* 13(1):1–38.

81 Gardner R.A. (1983–84) Blood parasites of British bats. *Myotis* 21–22:190.

82 Gardner R. Personal communication.

83 Gebhard J. (1983–84) *Nyctalus noctula* — Beobachtungen an einem traditionellen Winterquartier im Fels. *Myotis* 21–22:163–70.

84 George R.S. (1974) Siphonaptera: Fleas. In *Provisional atlas of the insects of the British Isles* 4: 12 pp + 60 maps. Huntingdon: Biological Records Centre.

85 Gerell R. & Lundberg K. (1985) Social organisation in the bat *Pipistrellus pipistrellus. Behavioural Ecology and Sociobiology* 16:177–84.

86 Gerrell R. *et al.* (1983) Sydfladdermus, *Eptesicus serotinus* Schreber 1774, ny fladdermusart i Sverige. *Fauna och Flora* 78:38–40.

87 Gilbert O. & Stebbings R.E. (1958) Winter roosts of bats in West Suffolk. *Proceedings of the Zoological Society of London* 131:321–33.

88 Glas G.H. (1981) Activities of serotine bats (*Eptesicus serotinus*) in a 'nursing roost'. *Myotis* 18–19:164–7.

89 Glas G.H. (1982) Records of hibernating barbastelle and grey long-eared bat in the Netherlands outside the southern Limburg cave areas. *Lutra* 25:15–16.

90 Glas G.H. (1986) Atlas van de Nederlandse vleermuizen 1970–1984 *Zoologischen Bijdragen* 34:1–97.

91 Glas G.H. & Braaksma S. (1980) Aantalsontwikkelingen in zomerverblijfplaatsen van vleermuizen in kerken. *Lutra* 22:84–95.

92 Glue D.E. (1970) Avian predator pellet analysis and the mammalogist. *Mammal Review* 1:53–62.

93 Greenaway F. & Hill J.E. (1987) A British record of the northern bat (*Eptesicus nilssonii*). *Bat News* 10:1–2.

94 Haffner M. & Slutz H.P. (1985–86) Abundance of *Pipistrellus pipistrellus* and *Pipistrellus kuhlii* foraging at street lamps. *Myotis* 23–24:167–71.

95 Hanak V. (1966) Ergebnisse der Fledermausberingung in der Sowjet union. *Myotis* 4:12–18.

96 Hanak V. & Gaisler J. (1976) *Pipistrellus nathusii* in Czechoslovakia. *Vestnik Ceskoslovenské Akademie Ved. Praha* 40:7–23.

97 Hanak V. & Gaisler J. (1983) *Nyctalus leisleri* (Kuhl, 1818), une éspèce nouvelle pour le continent africain.

Mammalia **47**:585−7.

98 Hancock B.D. (1963) Some observations on bats in East Surrey and recent records for the London Area. *London Naturalist* **42**:26−41.

99 Harmata W. (1962) Seasonal rhythmicity of behaviour and the ecology of bats (Chiroptera) living in some old buildings in the district of Krakow. *Zeszyty Naukowe Uniwersytetu Jagionellonskiego (Prace Zoologiczne)* **58**:149−79.

100 Harmata W. (1969) The thermopreferendum of some species of bats (Chiroptera). *Acta theriologica* **5**: 49−62.

101 Harmata W. (1969) Kolonia letnia nietoperza *Myotis bechsteini* (Kuhl) w Szymbarku kolo Gotlic w woj rzeszowskim. *Przeglad Zoologiczny* **13**:233−8.

102 Harmata W. (1973) The thermopreferendum of some species of bats (Chiroptera) in natural conditions. *Zeszyty Naukowe Uniwersytetu Jagiellonskiego* **19**: 127−41.

103 Harrison D.L. & Davies D.V. (1949) A note on some epithelial structures in Microchiroptera. *Proceedings of the Zoological Society of London* **119**: 351−7.

104 Haussler U. & Nagel A. (1983−84) Remarks on seasonal group composition turnover in captive noctules, *Nyctalus noctula* (Schreber, 1774). *Myotis* **21−22**:172−8.

105 Havekost H. (1960) Die Beringung der Breitflugelfledermaus (*Eptesicus serotinus* Schreber) im Oldenberger land. *Bonner Zoologische Beiträge* **11**:222−33.

106 Heaver S. Personal communication.

107 Heerdt P.F. van & Sluiter J.W. (1961) New data on longevity in bats. *Natuurhistorische Maandblad* **3−4**:36.

108 Heerdt P.F. van & Sluiter J.W. (1965) Notes on the distribution and behaviour of the noctule bat (*Nyctalus noctula*) in the Netherlands. *Mammalia* **29**:463−88.

109 Hill J.E. & Smith J.D. (1984) *Bats: a natural history.* London: British Museum (Natural History), 243 pp.

110 Hooper J.H.D. (1976) Bats in caves. In *The Science of Speleology.* London: Academic Press pp. 453−94.

111 Hooper J.H.D. & Hooper W.M. (1956) Habits and movements of cave-dwelling bats in Devonshire. *Proceedings of the Zoological Society of London* **127**: 1−26.

112 Horacek I. (1975) Notes on the ecology of bats of the genus *Plecotus* Goeffroy, 1818. *Vestnik Ceskoslovenske Spolecnosti Zoologiche* **39**:195−210.

113 Horacek I. (1981) Comparative notes on the population structure in several European bat species. *Myotis* **18−19**:48−53.

114 Howes C.A. (1974) Notes on the prey and feeding behaviour of the noctule bat. *Naturalist* **XX**: 107−10.

115 Howes C.A. (1979) The noctule bat, *Nyctalus noctula* in Yorkshire. *Naturalist* **104**:31−8.

116 Hurka K. (1964) Distribution, bionomy and ecology of the European bat flies with special regard to the Czechoslovak fauna (*Dip. Nycteribiidae*). *Acta Universitatis Carolinae* **XX**:167−234.

117 Hurka L. (1971) Zur Verbreitung und Okologie der Fledermäuse der Gattung *Plecotus* in Westbohmen. *Folia Musei Rerum Naturalium Bohemiae Occidentalis* **1**:1−24.

118 Hurka L. (1986) Wanderungen und Alter der Fledermaus-artenpopulationen in Westböhmen. *Zpravy Muzei Zapodoceskeho Kraje, Priroda* **32−3**: 105−9.

119 Hurka K. & Hurka L. (1964) Zum Flohbefall der beiden Europaischen *Plecotus*-Arten: *auritus* L. und *austriacus* Fischer in der Tschechechoslowakei (Aphaniptera: Ischnopsyllidae). *Vestnik Ceskoslovenske Zoologicke Spolecnosti* **28**:155−63.

120 Hutson A.M. (1964) Parasites from mammals in Suffolk. *Transactions of the Suffolk Naturalists' Society* **12**:451−2.

121 Hutson A.M. (1984) Keds, flat-flies and bat flies, Diptera, Hippoboscidae and Nycteribiidae. *Handbooks for Identification of British Insects*, vol. 10, part 7. London: Royal Entomological Society, pp. 1−40.

122 Hutson A.M. (1985) The mouse-eared bat in Britain. *Bat News* **4**:2.

123 Hutson A.M. (1987) Whiskered bats in south-east Britain. *Bat News* **11**:2−3.

124 Hutson A.M. Personal communication.

125 Issel W. (1958) Zur Okologie unserer Waldfledermäuse. *Natur Landschaft* **1**:1−4.

126 Jefferies D.J. (1972) Organochlorine insecticide residues in British bats and their significance. *Journal of Zoology* **166**:245−63.

127 Jenyns L. (1829) The distinctive characters of two British species of *Plecotus* supposed to have been confounded under the name of long-eared bat. *Transactions of the Linnean Society of London* **16**:53−60.

128 Jenyns L. (1839) *Annals of Natural History* **3**:73.

129 Jenyns L. (1846) *Observations in natural history.* London: van Voorst.

130 Jooris R. (1980) Additional data on the distribution of *Plecotus austriacus* (Fischer 1829) in the low lying districts of Belgium, with a critical assessment of biometrical data of the two *Plecotus* species. *Lutra* **23**:3−11.

131 Kepka O. (1960) Die Ergebnisse der Fledermausberingung in der Steiermark vom 1949 bis 1960. *Bonner Zoologische Beiträge* **11**:54−76.

132 Kinahan J.R. (1853) *Natural History Review* (Dublin) **1**:23−25.

133 Kleiman D.G. (1969) Maternal care, growth rate and development in bats. *Journal of Zoology* **157**: 187−211.

134 Kleiman D.G. & Racey P.A. (1969) Observations on noctule bats (*Nyctalus noctula*) breeding in captivity. *Lynx* **10**:65−77.

135 Krauss A. (1978) Materials on foodstuff of longeared bat (*Plecotus auritus* L.). *Zoologische Abhandlungen Staatliches Museum für Tierkunde in*

Dresden **34**:325−37.

136 Kristofik J. (1982) Nalezy much celade Nycteri- biidae (Diptera) na uzemi SSR. *Biologia, Bratislava* **37**:191−7.

137 Krzanowski A. (1960) Investigations of flights of Polish bats, mainly *Myotis myotis* (Borkhausen, 1797). *Acta theriologica* **4**:175−84.

138 Krzanowski A. (1961) Weight dynamics of bats wintering in the cave at Pulawy, Poland. *Acta theriologica* **4**:249−64.

139 Krzanowski A. (1973) Numerical comparison of Vespertilionidae and Rhinolophidae (*Chiroptera: Mammalia*) in the owl pellets. *Acta Zoologica Craco- viensia* **18**:133−40.

140 Kunz T.H. (1982) Roosting ecology. In Kunz T.H. ed. *The ecology of bats.* New York: Plenum, pp. 1−46.

141 Kunz T.H. (ed.) (1987) *Ecological and behavioral methods for the study of bats.* Washington DC: Smithsonian Institute Press 533 pp.

142 Kuramoto T. (1979) Nursery colony of the Japanese greater horseshoe bat, *Rhinolophus ferrumequinum nippon. Bulletin Akiyoshi-dai Science Museum* **14**: 27−44.

143 Kuramoto T. *et al.* (1985) A survey of bat-banding on the Akiyoshi-dai Plateau IV. *Bulletin of the Akiyoshi-dai Science Museum* **20**:25−44.

144 Labee A.M. & Voûte A.M. (1983) The diet of a nursery colony of the serotine bat in the Netherlands. *Lutra* **26**:12−19.

145 Laffoley D. Personal communication.

146 Lanza B. (1959) Chiroptera. In Toschi A. & Lanza B. eds. *Fauna a'Italia* IV. Bologna: Edizions Cal- derini.

147 Laufens G. (1969) Untersuchungen zur Aktivitäts- periodic von *Myotis nattereri* Kuhl, 1818. *Lynx* **10**: 45−51.

148 Lichatchev G.N. (1980) Bats of the Prioksko- terransyi Nature Reserve. In *Questions on the ecology of bats.* Moscow (in Russian) pp. 115−54.

149 Lovett W.V. (1961) A feeding population of pipis- trelle bats (*P. pipistrellus* Lin.). *Transactions of the Suffolk Naturalists' Society* **12**:39−43.

150 MacGillivray W. (1844) *Edinburgh New Philosophical Journal* **37**:392.

151 Mason C.F. *et al.* (1972) Noctules and starlings competing for roost holes. *Journal of Zoology* **166**: 467.

152 Matthews L.H. (1937) The female sexual cycle in the British horseshoe bats. *Transactions of the Zoo- logical Society of London* **23**:224−67.

153 McAney C.M. (1987) Whiskered bat in Galway. *Irish Naturalists' Journal* **22**:362.

154 McAney C. Personal communication.

155 Mein P. & Anciaux de Faveaux M. (1984) *Atlas des mammifères sauvages de France.* Societe Française pour l'Etude et la Protection des Mammifères.

156 Messenger J. (1985) The serotine (*Eptesicus serotinus*), a species new to Wales. *Bat News* **5**:7.

157 Millais J.G. (1904−05) *The mammals of Great Britain and Ireland,* I: London: Longman.

158 Miller L.A. & Degn H.J. (1981) The acoustic behav- iour of four species of vespertilionid bats studied in the field. *Journal of Comparative Physiology* **142**: 67−74.

159 Mitchell-Jones A.J. (1987) *The bat worker's man- ual.* Peterborough: Nature Conservancy Council 108 pp.

160 Moffat C.B. (1938) The Mammals of Ireland. *Pro- ceedings of the Royal Irish Academy* **44B**:61−128.

161 Moffat C.B. (1900) The habits of the hairy-armed bat, *Vesperugo leisleri. Irish Naturalist* **9**:235−40.

162 Mohr E. (1932) Haltung und Aufzucht des Abend- seglers (*Nyctalus noctula* Schrieb.). *Zoologische Garten Leipzig* **5**:106−20.

163 Nagel A. & Haussler U. (1980−81) Bemerkungen zur Haltung und Zucht von Abendseglern (*Nyctalus noctula*). *Myotis* **18−19**:186−9.

164 Natuschke G. (1960) Ergebnisse der Fledermausbe- ringung und biologischen Beobachtungen an Fleder- mausen in der Oberlausitz. *Bonner Zoologische Beiträge* **11**:77−98.

165 Nieuwenhoven P.J. van (1956) Ecological obser- vation in hibernation-quarter of cave dwelling bats in South Limberg. *Publicaties van het Naturhistorische Genootschap in Limburg* **9**:1−55.

166 Ni Lamhna E. (1979) *Provisional distribution atlas of amphibians, reptiles and mammals in Ireland,* 2nd edn. Dublin: An Foras Forbatha.

167 Norberg U.M. (1976) Aerodynamics of hovering flight in the long-eared bat *Plecotus auritus. Journal of Experimental Biology* **65**:459−70.

168 Norberg U.M. (1976) Aerodynamics, kinematics and energetics of horizontal flapping flight in the long-eared bat *Plecotus auritus. Journal of Experimen- tal Biology* **65**:179−212.

169 Norberg U.M. (1981) Allometry of bat wings and legs and comparison with bird wings. *Philosophical Transactions of the Royal Society B* **292**:359−98.

170 Nyholm E.S. (1965) The ecology of *Myotis mystacinus* (Leisl.) and *Myotis daubentoni. Annales Zoologici Fennici* **2**:77−123.

171 Oh Y.K. *et al.* (1985) Prolonged survival of the Graafian follicle and fertilization in the Japanese greater horseshoe bat, *Rhinolophus ferrumequinum nippon. Journal of Reproduction and Fertility* **73**: 121−26.

172 Panyutin K.K. (1963) Reproduction in the common noctule. *Uchenye Zapiski Moskoskovo. Obl. Pedagog. Inst.* **126**:63−6. (In Russian: from Biological Ab- stracts (1965) **46**:21. No. 96256.)

173 Phillips W.W.A. & Blackmore M. (1970) Mouse- eared bats *Myotis myotis* in Sussex. *Journal of Zoology* **162**:520−1.

174 Piechoki R. (1966) Uber die Nachweise der Langohr- Fledermäuse *Plecotus auritus* L. und *Plecotus aus- triacus* Fischer im mitteldeutschen Raum. *Hercynia* **3**:407−15.

175 Pieper H. (1968) Neues Hochstalter für die Mausohrfledermaus (*Myotis myotis*). *Myotis* **6**:

29–30.

176 Potts D.M. (1971) A light and electron microscope study of early development in the bat *Pipistrellus pipistrellus*. *Micron* 2:322–48.

177 Poulton E.B. (1929) British insectivorous bats and their prey. *Proceedings of the Zoological Society of London* 1929:277–303.

178 Racey P.A. (1969) Diagnosis of pregnancy and experimental extension of gestation in the pipistrelle bat *Pipistrellus pipistrellus*. *Journal of Reproduction and Fertility* 19:465–74.

179 Racey P.A. (1970) The breeding, care and management of vespertilionid bats in the laboratory. *Laboratory Animals* 4:171–83.

180 Racey P.A. (1972) Aspects of reproduction in some heterothermic bats. PhD. thesis, University of London.

181 Racey P.A. (1972) Viability of bat spermatozoa after prolonged storage in the epididymis. *Journal of Reproduction and Fertility* 28:171–83.

182 Racey P.A. (1973) The viability of spermatozoa after prolonged storage by male and female bats. *Periodicum Biologorum* 75:201–5.

183 Racey P.A. (1973) Environmental factors affecting the length of gestation in heterothermic bats. *Journal of Reproduction and Fertility, Supplement* 19:175–89.

184 Racey P.A. (1973) The time of onset of hibernation in the pipistrelle (*Pipistrellus pipistrellus*). *Journal of Zoology* 171:465–7.

185 Racey P.A. (1974) The reproductive cycle of male noctule bats *Nyctalus noctula*. *Journal of Reproduction and Fertility* 41:169–82.

186 Racey P.A. (1974) Aging and assessment of reproductive status in the pipistrelle bat (*Pipistrellus pipistrellus*). *Journal of Zoology* 173:263–71.

187 Racey P.A. (1974) The temperature of a pipistrelle hibernaculum, *Journal of Zoology* 173:260–2.

188 Racey P.A. (1975) The prolonged survival of spermatozoa in bats. In Duckett J.G. & Racey P.A. eds. *The biology of the male gamete*. London: Academic Press pp. 385–416.

189 Racey P.A. (1977) A vagrant noctule in Orkney. *Journal of Zoology* 183:555–6.

190 Racey P.A. (1979) The prolonged storage and survival of spermatozoa in Chiroptera. *Journal of Reproduction and Fertility* 56:391–402.

191 Racey P.A. (1987) Bats. In Poole T.B. ed. *UFAW Handbook for the Care and Management of Laboratory Animals*. Harlow: Longman pp. 240–55.

192 Racey P.A. & Kleiman D.G. (1970) Maintenance and breeding in captivity of some vespertilionid bats with special relevance to the noctule, *Nyctalus noctula*. *International Zoo Yearbook* 10:65–70.

193 Racey P.A. & Speakman J.R. (1987) The energy costs of pregnancy and lactation in heterothermic bats. *Symposia of the Zoological Society of London* 57:107–27.

194 Racey P.A. & Swift S.M. (1981) Variations in gestation length in a colony of pipistrelle bats (*Pipistrellus pipistrellus*) from year to year. *Journal of*

Reproduction and Fertility 61:123–9.

195 Racey P.A. & Swift S.M. (1985) Feeding ecology of *Pipistrellus pipistrellus* during pregnancy and lactation; 1. Foraging behaviour. *Journal of Animal Ecology* 54:205–15.

196 Racey P.A. & Swift S.M. (1986) The residual effects of remedial timber treatments in bats. *Biological Conservation* 35:205–14.

197 Racey P.A. & Tam W.H. (1974) Reproduction in the male pipistrelle (*Pipistrellus pipistrellus*). *Journal of Zoology* 172:101–22.

198 Ransome R.D. (1968) The distribution of the greater horseshoe bat, *Rhinolophus ferrumequinum*, during hibernation, in relation to environmental factors. *Journal of Zoology* 154:77–112.

199 Ransome R.D. (1971) The effect of ambient temperature on the arousal frequency of the hibernating greater horseshoe bat, *Rhinolophus ferrumequinum*, in relation to site selection and the hibernation state. *Journal of Zoology* 164:353–71.

200 Ransome R.D. (1973) Factors affecting the timing of births of the greater horseshoe bat (*Rhinolophus ferrumequinum*). *Periodicum Biologorum* 75:169–75.

201 Ransome R.D. (1978) Daily activity patterns of the greater horseshoe bat, *Rhinolophus ferrumequinum*, from April to September. *Proceedings of the fourth International Bat Research Conference, Kenya National Academy for Advancement of Arts and Sciences* 259–274.

202 Ransome R.D. (1980) *The greater horseshoe bat.* Poole: Blandford 43 pp.

203 Rapers. Personal communication.

204 Reumpler G. (1980) Handaufzucht und Jungendentwicklung einer Breitflugelfledermaus (*Eptesicus serotinus*). *Zeitschrift Kölner Zoo* 23:25–30.

205 Richardson P.W. (1985) Nightly dispersal of Daubenton's bats (*Myotis daubentoni*) from a summer roost site. *Bat Research News* 26(4):71.

206 Richardson P. (1985) *Bats*. London: Whittet Books 128 pp.

207 Richardson P.W. Personal communication.

208 Ritchie J. (1927) A long flight — the European particoloured bat (*Vespertilio murinus*) in Scotland. *Scottish Naturalist* 1927:101–3.

209 Roer H. (1968) Zur Frage der Wochenstuben — Quartrertreue weiblicher Mausohren (*Myotis myotis*). *Bonner Zoologischen Beiträge* 19:85–96.

210 Roer H. (1969) Zur Ernährungsbiologie von *Plecotus auritus* (L.) (Mamm. Chiroptera). *Bonner Zoologische Beiträge* 20:378–83.

211 Roer H. (1977) Zur Populationsentwicklung der Fledermäuse (Mammalia, Chiroptera) in der Bundesrepublik Deutschland unter besonderer Berucksictigung der Situation im Rheinland. *Zeitschrift für Säugetierkunde* 42:265–78.

212 Roer H. (1979) Zur Bestandsentwicklung der Breitflugelfledermaus (*Eptesicus serotinus* Schreber) und des Mausohrs (*Myotis myotis* Borkhausen) in Oldenburger Land. *Myotis* 17:23–30.

213 Roer H. (1981) Zur Heimkehrfahigkeit der

Zwergfledermaus (*Pipistrellus pipistrellus*). *Bonner Zoologische Beiträge* **32**:13–30.

214 Ruprecht A.L. (1971) Distribution of *Myotis myotis* (Borkhausen, 1797) and representatives of the genus *Plecotus* Geoffroy, 1818 in Poland. *Acta theriologica* **16**:96–104.

215 Ruprecht A.L. (1979) Bats (Chiroptera) as constituents of the food of Barn owls *Tyto alba* in Poland. *Ibis* **121**:489–94.

216 Ryberg O. (1947) *Studies on bats and bat parasites.* Stockholm: Svensk Naturvetenskap 318 pp.

217 Saint Girons H. *et al.* (1969) Contribution à la connaissance du cycle annuel de la chauve-souris *Rhinolophus ferrumequinnum* (Schreber, 1774). *Mammalia* **33**:357–470.

218 Saint Girons M.C. & Caubère B. (1966) Notes sur les mammifères de France. V. Sur la répartition de *Rhinolophus hipposideros hipposideros* (Bechstein, 1800) et *Rhinolophus hipposideros minimus* (Heuglin, 1861). *Mammalia* **30**:308–26.

219 Schober W. (1984) *The lives of bats.* London: Croom Helm 200 pp.

220 Schwab H. (1952) Beobachtungen über die Begattung und die Spermakonservierung in den Geschlechtsorganen bei weiblichen Fledermäusen. *Zeitschrift für Mikrosokopische-Anatomische Forschung* **58**:326–57.

221 Simms C. (1977) Kestrels hunting long-eared bats. *British Birds* **70**:499–500.

222 Sklenar J. (1963) The reproduction of *Myotis myotis* Borkh. *Lynx* **2**:29–37.

223 Sluiter J.W. (1954) Sexual maturity in bats of the genus *Myotis*. II. Females of *M. mystacinus* and supplementary data on female *M. myotis* and *M. emarginatus. Proceedings, Koninklijke Nederlandse Akademie van Wetenschappen* **57**:696–700.

224 Sluiter J.W. (1960) Reproductive rate of the bat *Rhinolophus hipposideros. Proceedings, Koninklijke Nederlandse Akademie van Wetenschappen* **63**: 383–93.

225 Sluiter J.W. (1961) Sexual maturity in males of the bat *Myotis myotis. Proceedings, Koninklijke Nederlandse Akademie van Wetenschappen* **64**:243–9.

226 Sluiter J.W. & Bouman M. (1951) Sexual maturity in bats of the genus *Myotis* I. Size and histology of the reproductive organs during hibernation in connection with age and wear of the teeth in bats *Myotis myotis* and *Myotis emarginatus. Proceedings, Koninklijke Nederlandse Akademie van Wetenschappen* **54**:594–601.

227 Sluiter J.W. & Heerdt P.F. van (1966) Seasonal habits of the noctule bat (*Nyctalus noctula*). *Archives Neerlandaises de Zoologie* **16**:423–39.

228 Sluiter J.W. *et al.* (1973) Hibernation of *Nyctalus noctula. Periodicum Biologorum* **75**:181–8.

229 Smit F.G.A.M. (1957) Siphonaptera. *Handbooks for the identification of British Insects* **1**(16):1–94.

230 Smith P. Personal communication.

231 Smith B.D.S. (1985) Co-habitation of two bat species in a single tree roost. *Imprint* **Summer 1985**:12–13.

232 Speakman J.R. & Racey P.A. (1986) The influence of body condition on sexual development of male brown long-eared bats (*Plecotus auritus*) in the wild. *Journal of Zoology* (A) **210**: 515–25.

233 Spitzenberger E. (1986) Die Nord Fledermaus (*Eptesicus nilssonii* Keyserling & Blasius, 1839) in Österreich. *Annals of the Natural History Museum, Wien* **87**:117–30.

234 Stansfield G. (1966) Parti-coloured bat (*Vespertilio murinus* L.) from a North Sea drilling rig. *Journal of Zoology* **150**:491–592.

235 Stebbings R.E. (1965) Observations during 16 years on winter roosts of bats in West Suffolk. *Proceedings of the Zoological Society of London* **144**:137–43.

236 Stebbings R.E. (1966) A population study of bats of the genus *Plecotus. Journal of Zoology* **150**:53–75.

237 Stebbings R.E. (1966) Bechstein's bat, *Myotis bechsteini* in Dorset 1960–65. *Journal of Zoology* **148**: 574–6.

238 Stebbings R.E. (1967) Identification and distribution of bats of the genus *Plecotus* in England. *Journal of Zoology* **153**:291–310.

239 Stebbings R.E. (1968) Bechstein's bat (*Myotis bechsteini*) in Dorset 1965–67. *Journal of Zoology* **155**: 228–31.

240 Stebbings R.E. (1968) Measurements, composition and behaviour of a large colony of the bat *Pipistrellus pipistrellus. Journal of Zoology* **156**:15–33.

241 Stebbings R.E. (1968) Longevity of vespertilionid bats in Britain. *Journal of Zoology* **156**:530–1.

242 Stebbings R.E. (1970) A bat new to Britain, *Pipistrellus nathusii. Journal of Zoology* **161**:282–6.

243 Stebbings R.E. (1970) A comparative study of *Plecotus auritus* and *P. austriacus* inhabiting one roost. *Bijdrogen tot de Dierkunde* **40**:91–4.

244 Stebbings R.E. (1977) Order Chiroptera. In Corbet G.B. & Southern H.N. eds *Handbook of British mammals*. Oxford: Blackwell Scientific Publications pp. 68–128.

245 Stebbings R.E. (1985) Britain's largest population of hibernating bats under threat. *Bat News* **5**:2–3.

246 Stebbings R.E. (1986) Rare cave bats — how rare are they? *Bat News* **6**:2–3.

247 Stebbings R.E. (1986) *Which bat is it? A guide to bat identification in Great Britain and Europe.* London: Mammal Society/Vincent Wildlife Trust, 48 pp.

248 Stebbings R.E. (1988) *Conservation of European bats.* London: Christopher Helm 246 pp.

249 Stebbings R.E. & Griffiths F. (1986) Distribution and status of bats in Europe. *Institute of Terrestrial Ecology.* NERC publication, 142 pp.

250 Strelkov P. (1962) The peculiarities of reproduction in bats (Vespertilionidae) near the northern border of their distribution. *International Symposium on Methods of Mammal Investigations, Brno* **1960**: 306–11.

251 Strelkov P. (1969) Migratory and stationary bats (Chiroptera) of the European part of the Soviet Union. *Acta Zoologica Cracoviensia* **14**:393–439.

252 Strelkov P.P. & Buntova E.G. (1982) *Myotis mysta-*

cinus and *M. brandti*, inter-relations of these species, part 1. *Zoologischeskii zhurnal* **61**:1227—41.

253 Stutz H.P. & Haffner M. (1985—86) The reproductive status of *Nyctalus noctula* (Schreber, 1774) in Switzerland. *Myotis* **23—24**:131—6.

254 Swift S.M. (1980) Activity patterns of pipistrelle bats (*Pipistrellus pipistrellus*) in north-east Scotland. *Journal of Zoology* **200**:249—59.

255 Swift S.M. (1981) *Foraging, colonial and maternal behaviour of bats in north-east Scotland*. PhD. thesis, University of Aberdeen.

256 Swift S.M. & Racey P.A. (1983) Resource partitioning in two species of vespertilionid bats (Chiroptera) occupying the same roost. *Journal of Zoology* **200**: 249—59.

257 Swift S.M. *et al.* (1985) Feeding ecology of *Pipistrellus pipistrellus* (Chiroptera: Vespertilionidae) during pregnancy and lactation. 2. Diet. *Journal of Animal Ecology* **54**:217—25.

258 Thompson M.J.A. (1982) A common long-eared bat *Plecotus auritus*: moth predator-prey relationship. *Naturalist* **107**:87—97.

259 Thompson M.J.A. (1987) Longevity and survival of female pipistrelle bats (*Pipistrellus pipistrellus*) on the Vale of York, England. *Journal of Zoology* **211**:209—14.

260 Topal G. (1956) The movements of bats in Hungary. *Annales Historico-Naturales Musei Nationalis Hungarici* **7**:477—88.

261 Topal G. (1966) Some observations on the nocturnal activity of bats in Hungary. *Vertebrata Hungarica* **8**:139—65.

262 Tupinier Y. & Biraud Y. (1983—84) Variabilité des signaux de croisiere de *Myotis daubentoni*. *Myotis* **21—22**:78—81.

263 Voûte A.M. (1982) First recorded accidental transatlantic bat transport. *Bat Research News* **23**:16—18.

264 Venables L.S.V. (1943) Observations at a pipistrelle bat roost. *Journal of Animal Ecology* **12**:19—26.

265 Waldhovd H. & Hoegh-Guldberg O. (1984) Nogle traek fourageringsvanerne hos Langoret Fladermus *Plecotus auritus*. *Flora och Fauna* **90**:115—8.

266 Whiteley D. & Clarkson K. (1985) Leisler's bats in the Sheffield Area. *Sorby Record* **23**:12—16.

267 Wijngaarden A. van *et al.* (1971) De verspreiding van de Nederlandse zoogdieren. *Lutra* **13**:1—41.

268 Yalden D.W. (1985) *The identification of British bats*. London: Mammal Society, 14 pp.

269 Yalden D.W. (1986) Neolithic bats from Dowel Cave, Derbyshire. *Journal of Zoology* (A) **210**: 616—9.

270 Zima J. & Horacek I. (1985) Synopsis of karyotypes of vespertilionid bats (Mammalia: Chiroptera). *Acta Universitatis Carolinae Biologica* **1981**:311—29.

271 Zima J. & Kral B. (1984) Karyotypes of European mammals 1. *Acta Scientiarum Naturalium, Brno* **18**(7):51 pp.

Chapter 7 / Lagomorphs: Order Lagomorpha

Lagomorphs are small herbivores, comprising the rabbits, hares and pikas. At one time the group was included in the order Rodentia as a suborder, named Duplicidentata because of the presence of a small second pair of upper incisors behind the large, chisel-shaped first pair (there is also a third pair which only appears as rudiments in the milk dentition). The long gap (diastema) between incisors and cheek-teeth is a further character shared with rodents but also with other herbivorous groups like ruminants and kangaroos. In other respects lagomorphs are very distinctive. The cheek-teeth as well as the incisors are rootless and grow continuously; the naked rhinarium around the nostrils is covered by flaps of skin which can be retracted; there is a very large caecum with a spiral septum; and the tail is very short. Their nutritional strategy is characterised by refection — during the day very soft faecal pellets produced in the caecum are voided and eaten, thereby passing most food through the alimentary canal twice before the production of hard fibrous faecal pellets.

There are two families, the Ochotonidae — the pikas of the mountains of Asia and western North America with short ears and legs — and the Leporidae including all the rabbits and hares.

FAMILY LEPORIDAE (RABBITS AND HARES)

This worldwide family contains one large genus, *Lepus*, including the cursorial hares living mainly in open country, along with a number of small, highly localised genera of rabbits, including *Oryctolagus*.

The most prominent characters in the family are the long ears and long hind legs and feet. All species have a large patch of soft, erect pigmented hair on the anterior part of the chest, quite different from the rest of the ventral pelage and of unknown function [53]. The dental formula is 2.0.3.3/1.0.2.3.

The characters of the three species in Britain are compared in Table 7.1.

GENUS *Oryctolagus*

A monospecific genus clearly distinct from the hares (*Lepus*) by the lack of adaptation to fast running, but very similar to other genera of rabbits such as the American *Sylvilagus* (cotton-tails) from which it differs only in its sociability and burrowing ability [54].

Rabbit *Oryctolagus cuniculus*

Lepus cuniculus Linnaeus, 1758; Germany.

Coney, conying (obsolete); cwningen (Welsh); coinean (Scottish Gaelic); coinín (Irish Gaelic).

RECOGNITION
Smaller than brown and mountain hares; ears without black tips, and hind legs shorter in relation to body than those of both species of hares (Fig. 7.1).

Skull (Fig. 7.2): distinguishable from hares by longer bony palate and narrower posterior nares, and by persistence throughout life of suture delimiting interparietal bone.

SIGN

Footprints in snow characterised by the long prints of the hind legs and small round prints of forefeet. Leaps with one foreleg ahead of the other at slow speeds, but forelimbs tending to move together as speed increases. At high speed hind prints lie ahead of those of the forefeet. Jumping mode of progression reflected in their runs from cover, through and along fences and hedges and to their grazing areas. The depressions, 'jumps' or 'beats', are 20−30cm apart. Where rabbits are

Table 7.1. Identification of lagomorphs.

	Rabbit	Brown hare	Mountain hare
Overall colour	Yellowish brown	Yellowish brown	Greyish brown, sometimes white in winter
Upper surface of tail	Black	Black	White
Tips of ears	Brown	Black	Black
Length of ears from notch (mm)	60–70	90–105	60–80
Length of hind feet (mm)	75–95	130–155	125–170

Fig. 7.1. (a) Brown hare; (b) mountain hare (summer); (c) rabbit.

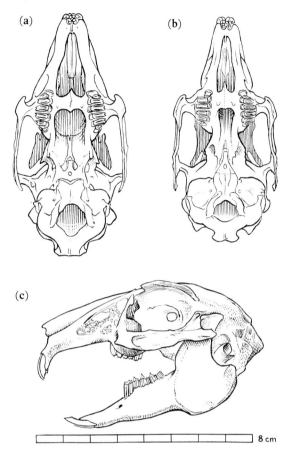

(a)   **(b)**

(c)

└───────────────────┘ 8 cm

Fig. 7.2. Skulls of (a) brown hare; (b) and (c) rabbit. Note the very wide nasal passage in the hare.

few, impressions of the jumps may be slight in short-grazed grass, and are best seen when angle of the sun is low or, if there are bare areas nearby, by smears of soil from rabbits' feet.

Fur 'flecks' frequently found on snags through fences, hedges etc.; not so much black in hair fibres as in brown hare.

Burrows especially prevalent on slopes, banks etc. where drainage is more efficient. Entrances vary from 10–50 cm in diameter, usually at a shallow angle to the horizontal from burrow; although 'bolt' or 'pop' holes may be situated vertically above burrow. Well-used burrows may be indicated by soil on jumps leading to burrows. Single entrance nesting burrows may be found and also lying-up places. Such forms may be used more than once but not puddled with hind feet as frequently as

those of hares. Annual weeds, nettles and coarse grasses such as *Brachypodium pinnatum* encouraged by the loose soil and high nitrogen levels on and around burrows. Elder a feature of well established burrow systems. Horseshoe shaped scrapes in the ground much in evidence in areas occupied by rabbits.

Faeces not always distinguishable from those of hares' — size and friability depend on diet. May be found in 'latrines', i.e. dense aggregations of pellets often on prominent features of habitat such as ant-hills [158, 159], in scrapes or elsewhere. Pellets associated with latrines and scrapes often darker than others due to coating with anal gland secretions. Distinguished from lamb faeces by absence of flat facets on surface.

Feeding: presence of rabbits also indicated by short-cropped grasses near to burrows or to surface cover, e.g. around bramble patches and field headlands. Damage to crops often seen as a series of semicircular areas of grazed plants along the field margin with radii extending up to 50 m into the field. Each area represents the activities of one social group.

DESCRIPTION

Sexes alike but female (doe) with narrower head; profile from ears to nose slightly less rounded than in male (buck). Eyes with iris not so yellow as in hares; pupil round. Ears and hind limbs long. Lumbar region heavily muscled and mobile with much of power to hind limbs derived from lower back movements. Proximal fusion of tibia used to distinguish adult from juvenile (< 9 months of age) in both live and dead animals [238]. Aging can also be based on body weight up to around 1000 g or eye lens weight [56, 246]. Five digits are present on the forelimbs but only four on the hind.

Pelage greyish brown, but much variation from sandy yellow to grey. Guard hairs banded brown and black (or grey). Nape of neck (woolly fur) and scrotum reddish, chest-patch brown, rest of underparts white or grey. Juveniles frequently with white star on forehead, rarely seen in adults. Long black vibrissae. Feet, including soles, furred and buff coloured. Ears lack the black tips of hares.

Moult once yearly; begins in March on face then

spreads over back; replacement of underfur not complete until October or November. (Sometimes moult in head region has similarities to fur replacement, in region of eyes, following recovery from myxomatosis.)

Teeth: molars and pre-molars adapted for both lateral and longitudinal grinding movements.

Genitalia: testes regress outside breeding season and become larger in dominant individuals [18, 30]. Testes lie in subcutaneous scrotal sacs and can be withdrawn into abdomen. No *os penis* nor a true glans. Penis short and points backwards in relaxed state. Female tract Y-shaped, fusiform ovaries *c.* 0.5 mm by 1.5 mm. Corpora lutea easily recognised as translucent spots on ovary surface.

Nipples: five pairs, inguinal to pectoral.

Scent glands: socially significant odours in urine, and in secretions from the submandibular (chin) gland, Harderian glands situated deep within the orbit of the eye, inguinal glands in pouches on both sides of penis/vulva, and paired anal glands [17].

Chromosomes: $2n = 44$, $FNa = 76$. Those of the domestic rabbit have been studied intensively [77].

MEASUREMENTS
Adult head and body up to 400 mm. Weight at birth 30–35 g, at weaning (*c.* 21 days) 150–200 g, adult (i.e. when skeletal growth has ceased) 1200–2000 g. Stomach and intestines represent about 20% of live weight. Growth rate from weaning to body weight of *c.* 1000 g is *c.* 10 g/day [56, 61, 203] but much lower (*c.* 5 g/day) in original range in S France and Iberia [186]. Hindfoot length: 85–100 mm; ear length (from occiput) 65–75 mm.

VARIATION
Much variation in pelage in Britain and Ireland, from light sandy colour to dark grey and totally melanic forms. Melanic forms not uncommon [194] but albinos rare on mainland. Melanism more frequent in absence of ground predators (e.g. islands/large enclosures). However, island populations often reflect introduction of domestic varieties, e.g. piebald, skewbald and long-haired forms common on Skokholm and formerly Inner Farne Island (rabbit now absent there). Island rabbits generally smaller than on mainland. Flashes of white sometimes occur, most frequently on forelimbs and over shoulders.

DISTRIBUTION
Originally Iberia, S France and possibly NW Africa but now spread or introduced into most of W Europe (but only in S Scandinavia and absent from most of Italy and the Balkans). Also introduced into Australia, New Zealand, Chile, islands off USA and elsewhere [76].

Widespread in Britain and Ireland up to the treeline and on most small islands but absent from Rhum and the Isles of Scilly. In 1970, 59% of farm holdings had rabbits on cultivable land compared with 94% before the advent of myxomatosis in 1953 [132]. Surveys of England and Wales have found increases in both distribution and abundance since 1970 [229]. Most widespread in E and SE England and Wales; most abundant in E and SE England.

HISTORY
Present at the Hoxnian (Middle Pleistocene) interglacial site at Swanscombe, Kent [209]. A single Mesolithic record from Thatcham, Berkshire [120] has been shown by radiocarbon dating to be of recent origin. Apparently absent from Neolithic, Iron Age, Roman and Anglo-Saxon sites. Introduced to England and Ireland by Normans; subsequent history documented by Sheail [198]. There were extensive warrens in N Ireland by 17th century [121]. Initially mainly confined to managed warrens, often on islands; protected from predators and supplied with additional food. Slow increase in truly wild populations mostly in coastal areas and lowland heaths, e.g. Breckland, Norfolk. Substantial increase in wild populations from *c.* 1750 onwards when changes in agriculture created favourable habitat and increasing interest in game gave rise to intensive predator control. Catastrophic decline in numbers upon advent of myxomatosis in 1953 [225].

HABITAT
Most suitable habitats are areas of short grasses, either naturally occurring as on dry heaths and machairs or closely grazed agricultural pastures, with secure refuge (burrows, boulders, hedgerows, scrub, woodland) in close proximity to feeding areas. Except in areas where erstwhile rabbit burrows exist, expanding rabbit colonies exploit areas of scrub or surface cover more readily than earth

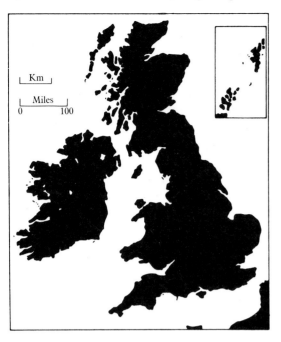

Map 7.1. Rabbit.

banks when ready-made cover is not available. Burrows in open ground not so common as formerly, partly because ploughing and seeding of pastures now widely practised but also because increased use of cyanide gas now generally limits occupation of more readily accessible warrens. Occurs up to the tree-line if land is well drained and suitable refuge available. Can make burrows on sand, shale, clay or chalk. Size and distribution of burrow systems dependent upon soil type [164, 187, 188]. Burrow systems larger (more interconnected entrances) on chalk than on sand [61]. Never abundant in large coniferous plantations, except on peripheral areas and along fire breaks and rides.

SOCIAL ORGANISATION AND BEHAVIOUR
Social behaviour [135, 151, 152, 154, 155] extensively studied in enclosures especially in Australia and in free-living populations [61, 153, 162, 203, 204]. Many populations subdivided into stable social groups based on shared access to one or more

Map 7.2. Rabbit (European distribution).

burrow systems. However, where burrow construction is relatively easy, e.g. on sand-dune systems [61] or where extensive areas of scrub are available for cover [247] discrete social groups may be absent. Within social groups linear hierarchies amongst males reflect priority of access to females. Hence, dominant males sire the majority of offspring in their group [63]. Dominant females have priority of access to best nest sites. Competition between females for access to such sites can lead to serious injury and death [152]. At high densities subordinate females may be forced to use single-entrance breeding 'stops' away from main burrow systems [85]. These stops are particularly susceptible to predation by badgers and foxes [149]. Subordinate females, usually yearlings, have shorter breeding seasons than the dominant, generally older individuals, and a higher occurrence of total loss of embryos. Juveniles born into large social groups occupying large burrow systems suffer higher levels of cat predation [162] and disease [58], although larger burrows offer increased protection against underground predators, e.g. ferrets [57].

Group territories are established during bouts of mutual paw-scraping and parallel run displays by males from adjacent groups, along territory boundaries [15, 59]. Most scrapes are created in this way, rather than as a result of feeding on roots. Hence, density of scrapes highest in areas of overlap between home ranges of bucks from adjacent social groups [59]. Territories also maintained by use of odour [15, 158, 159, 160]. Although territories are not exclusive, more than 90% of sexual interactions are within social groups [59] and up to 93% of offspring are sired by males from the social group into which they are born [63]. Females more aggressive towards juveniles than males who often protect juveniles during chases by females [157]. Adult female aggression biased towards juvenile females; adult males will also interrupt aggression between adult females [59, 159].

Home ranges generally small, 0.3–3 hectares [59, 88]. Male ranges larger than those of females. Evidence of longer movements (up to 500 m from refuge) at low densities especially after abrupt changes in environment (e.g. at harvest). Dispersal distances in excess of 4 km recorded. Juvenile males disperse more frequently than juvenile females [65, 163]. Fifty percent of females first bred in their natal social groups compared with only around 25% of males, on a chalk downland site in Oxford-shire; dispersal amongst adults was rare in this population but was also male biased [56].

Communication mainly olfactory [15, 17]. Chin and anal gland secretions particularly involved in territorial behaviour [15, 158, 159, 160]. Information concerning sexual status, individual and group recognition contained in urine and inguinal gland secretions [15, 96, 97]. Some active components of secretions have been identified, especially of anal gland [89, 98]. Female urine also shown to have 'primer' effects on growth and development of males [19]. Some visual signalling during reproductive and aggressive behaviour [204]. Flashing of white underside of tail may serve to warn other individuals during flight from a predator. Limited acoustic signalling. Evidence equivocal that distress screams upon capture by a predator or thumping of hind feet in presence of predator serve a warning function [25].

Activity crepuscular and nocturnal, but diurnal if undisturbed. Strong wind and heavy rain reduce activity.

FEEDING

Eat wide range of herbage especially grasses. Favour young succulent leaves and shoots and select more nutritious species, e.g. of *Festuca* grasses [20, 184, 202, 251]. Intensive grazing can lead to elimination of useful clovers and grasses [213] and conversion of ling heath to grassland [70]. Although exclusion of rabbits had been known to cause major changes in flora [241–244], full impact of rabbit grazing not fully appreciated until advent of myxomatosis when, for instance, large areas of chalk downland reverted to scrub [212, 219–222]. Cause damage to a wide variety of agricultural crops, including cereals, roots, pasture, horticulture and forestry [51, 52, 91, 171]. Bark of many trees eaten especially during periods of snow cover. Rabbits a major cause of failure of natural generation of forest trees [239].

BREEDING

Breeding season mainly from January to August when a succession of litters, usually of three to seven young, produced at a minimum interval of about 30 days.

Proportion of pregnant females may be high in January. Time of onset of breeding considered by many to be determined by winter weather conditions but little real evidence except in very severe winters when it may be considerably retarded. Fundamentally, onset determined by day length [27]. End of breeding season related to population density. In high-density pre-myxomatosis populations season was from January/February to June, with about 5% of females pregnant in other months. Season extended in post-myxomatosis low-density populations, with some out-of-season breeding as formerly. Premyxomatosis breeding season lasted 15−17 weeks [29]; immediately post-myxomatosis 22 weeks or more [129].

Courtship involves chases and enurination [204]. Does will copulate at approximately 7-day intervals even while pregnant [93, 114, 150]. Ovulation is induced by copulation and there is no oestrus cycle. If mating does not result in fertilisation of shed ova a 14-day pseudo-pregnancy ensues.

Gestation lasts *c*. 30 days, post-partum oestrus is normal and females are usually pregnant within 24 hours of parturition. No lactation anoestrus as is common in domestic rabbit.

Litter size: number of ova shed increases at each pregnancy (within season) until a peak in June and declines thereafter; also related to body weight of doe. Usually three to seven per litter, but seasonal mean variable according to environment. Massive pre-natal mortality of entire sets of embryos can occur through intra-uterine absorption [28, 29]. Such loss is characteristic of high-density populations (up to 60% loss), but occurs to a much smaller degree in low-density populations [130].

Productivity: 10−11 live offspring per year in high density populations [28], over 30 in 1958 following myxomatosis and about 20 in many expanding rabbit populations [133].

Parental investment: 1 : 1 pre-natal and post-natal sex ratios, although greater maternal investment in male offspring during gestation reflected in higher birth weight of males [26]. Young born in nests composed of grass or moss, lined with belly fur, situated in blind tunnels within main burrow systems or separate short burrows — 'stops'. Occasionally may breed above ground in dense vegetation. One visit per night to suckle young for only a few minutes [45]. Entrance to stop carefully sealed with soil and vegetation after suckling.

Development: young blind at birth and very sparsely furred. Eyes open around 10 days. Begin to appear at burrow entrances around 18 days old and weaned at *c*. 21−25 days. Extended maternal care up to 6 or 7 weeks of age reported for last litters in season [134]. Males fecund at about 4 months; females can breed at *c*. 3.5 months at a weight of *c*. 830 g, although breeding during season of birth is confined to young from early litters.

POPULATION

Densities vary seasonally with relatively stable overwinter numbers (< 1−15 per hectare) followed by highly variable summer peaks (< 1−40 per hectare) [226]. Summer peaks highest on sandy soils. Overwinter numbers higher on sand and chalk than on clay soils. Overall rabbit numbers in 1986 around 20% of pre-myxomatosis levels.

Age structure of populations reflects seasonal cycle with young recruited into the population during the breeding season. Sex ratios vary but may be female biased in group-living populations [59, 162]. Type of control measures may also influence sex ratio [19].

Survival: reproductive productivity high, but recruitment from 1965−73 was low in many rabbit populations [132]. Adult : juvenile ratio in November/December ranged from 1 : 0.8 to 1 : 3.0 indicating mortality of 70−92% of young of year. Mortality rate of around 95% during the first year of life calculated for a population on chalk downland [62]. Annual adult mortality varied between 45 and 65% in same population. Female life expectancy at birth calculated to be 11 weeks rising to 72 weeks at 64 weeks of age [56]. Early-born young survive significantly better than others and in general juvenile survival is highly density-dependent [56, 61, 65, 162, 252]. Lack of adequate food in terms of quality and/or quantity sometimes influences growth and survival [61, 86, 87]. Juvenile female survival higher than [56], or the same as [253], that of males. On island of Skokholm, in climax size populations, mortality rate of juveniles is about 60% per annum, adult mortality about 30%.

MORTALITY

Predation by foxes, stoats, polecats and wild cats on all ages; by badgers, buzzards, weasels and domestic cats on young animals. Predation by other species such as owls, great black-backed gull, raven and crow more occasional. Stoats favour adults while fox and cat predation is biased towards juveniles. In immediate pre-myxomatosis era unlikely that predation had significant impact on population size except possibly in marginal or less suitable habitats. Post-myxomatosis a major reduction in stoat numbers occurred, with the steady increase in the numbers taken on game estates from the early sixties onwards being attributed to recovery of rabbit population [214]. Size of buzzard population also declined after the advent of myxomatosis [230]. However, causal relationship between rabbit numbers and predator numbers difficult to establish. Rabbit abundance higher in areas where predator control practised, although, again, cause and effect have yet to be established [228].

Disease: myxoma virus appeared in Britain during 1953 and Ireland in 1954 [68], having been isolated from forest rabbit *Sylvilagus brasiliensis* of South America in which it causes a mild, non-lethal disease. Disease is highly specific and only a single, unconfirmed, infection of a brown hare reported. Spread throughout the country during the next 2 years caused more than 99% mortality [223]. Virulence of disease has since declined [192] as a result of increased transmissability of weaker strains [142]. Genetic resistance in rabbit populations confirmed [191] and increasing. Disease endemic, with major outbreaks still occurring annually in most populations especially during late summer/autumn. The best estimate of current mortality during such outbreaks is 40–60% [191]. The eventual outcome of interaction between selection pressures concerning virulence and resistance uncertain but current evidence suggests, at least in the short term, a continuing decline in levels of mortality [189]. Infection by coccidial parasites *Eimeria* spp., especially *Eimeria stiedai*, can cause high mortality amongst juveniles up to age of *c.* 4 months amongst whom the incidence of disease is highly density dependent [48, 58, 206].

PARASITES

Ectoparasites: flea *Spilopsyllus cuniculi* is specific to the rabbit and usually very abundant, especially on the ears. Seasonal variation in numbers [143] associated with the reproduction of this flea being linked to the breeding cycle of the rabbit through blood hormone levels [138]. Flea locates host using olfactory cues in hosts' urine [231]. The sucking louse *Haemodipsus ventricosus* is found regularly. Common species of mites often found abundantly in the ears and around genitalia are larval harvest mites *Trombicula autumnalis*, mange mites *Psorotes equi*, hair mites *Listrophorus gibbus* and *Cheyletiella parasitvorax* [139]. The sheep tick *Ixodes ricinus* is frequent.

Endoparasites: Apart from coccidial infections (above) endoparasites are considered to have little influence on host survival in the UK. Ubiquitous nematode infections are *Graphidium strigosum* and *Passalurus ambiguus* in the stomach and *Trichostrongylus retortaeformis* in the small intestine [21, 22, 200]. Two adult tapeworms commonly found are *Cittotaenia denticulata* and *C. pectinata*. Others include *Andrya cuniculi* and *Hymenolepis* sp. [140, 141]. The larval form of the canid tapeworm *Taenia pisiformis* (bladderworm) is common and the large cyst of *Multiceps serialis*, with the adult form again found in carnivores, can be debilitating. The sheep fluke *Fasciola hepatica* is found in rabbits, which may be responsible for the persistence of the disease in some areas.

RELATIONS WITH MAN

Pre-myxomatosis rabbits were the major vertebrate pests of agriculture with annual cost of damage estimated to be £50 million at 1952 prices [225]. Increasing numbers as a result of the decline in mortality due to myxomatosis means that they represent an increasing problem. In some situations rabbit grazing is desirable to maintain habitat (e.g. chalk downland) but management still required to prevent overgrazing/erosion. At one time rabbit trapping for food and fur was an important industry (£1.5 million contribution to agricultural economy in 1952) but now mainly pursued as a pest.

Recommended method of control is gassing with cyanide powder when access to burrows is available; population reductions following single treatment average *c.* 65% hence repetition advised [190]. Ferreting burrows, traditional method of bolting rabbits into nets or in front of guns, yields 30–50% reductions according to size of burrow systems [57]. Shooting, snares and traps also used. Limited efficacy of shooting demonstrated in New Zealand [250]. Non-lethal measures include the use of fences, both permanent and electric [144, 145] and, in forestry applications, repellents [168]. Poison baiting widely used in Australia and New Zealand but illegal in UK. Methods of management reviewed by Rees *et al.* [185]. Phillips [172] and Thompson & Armour [224] assessed effectiveness of control operations.

LITERATURE
Thompson and Worden [225]: a general account of wild rabbit biology; Lockley [136]: description of the social life of an enclosed rabbit colony; Sheail [198]: a history of the wild rabbit in Britain; Cowan [55]: popular account of the natural history of wild rabbits; Tittensor and Lloyd [227]: concise account of rabbit biology and management.

AUTHOR FOR THIS SPECIES
D.P. Cowan.

GENUS *Lepus* (HARES)

The dominant genus of lagomorphs with about 20 species occupying open habitats through most of the world. Characterised by long ears, long hind legs and very large and wide nasal passage. They are fast runners, living in the open and never making more than very simple short burrows. The young are born above ground, fully furred and with eyes open.

The characters of the two species in Britain are contrasted in Table 7.1.

Brown hare *Lepus europaeus*

Lepus europaeus Pallas, 1778; Burgundy, France.
Lepus capensis; Petter, 1961 and later authors, not of Linnaeus, 1758.

Common hare; sgwarnog, ysgyfarnog (Welsh); gearr (Scottish Gaelic).

RECOGNITION
Largest of the British lagomorphs. Distinguished from rabbit by large size and long limbs, brownish rather than grey coloration and much longer and black-tipped ears. Has a loping gait or leaping stride when running fast. The tail is held down when running so that the black dorsal surface is visible. Has longer ears and is more yellowish in colour than the mountain hare.

SIGN
May leave obvious trails on open grassland, and on agricultural land will make characteristic gaps or runs through hedges or fencerows. Use forms or shallow depressions to rest during the day. These can be in long grass or other vegetation; on cultivated land they may be dug some 10 cm into the ground. Only the back and head of the animal will be visible above ground when in such a form.

Faeces are similar to rabbit's but usually larger (1 cm) and more flattened. However, very variable and dependent on diet. Not always distinguishable from rabbit's.

Footprints in snow or soft soil show elongated side-by-side impressions with the hind feet placed ahead of the front which are normally one behind the other. Five toes visible on hind foot, four on the front. Tracks are much larger than rabbit's.

DESCRIPTION

Pelage is warm brown on the back becoming buff on the flanks and pale yellow on the cheeks and inside of limbs. The belly is white, the tail a white powder puff which is black dorsally, and the ears have a distinct black tip. The fur on the back is particularly dense consisting of three types of hair varying in length from underfur of 15 mm, a pile hair of 24–27 mm, and guard hairs of 32–35 mm in summer. In winter the fur is longer and the animal takes on a slightly redder colour with a pronounced grey area on the rump; the fur around the face and ears tends to be whiter [24, 101].

Moults in spring and autumn are preceded by a general lightening of the pelage. Spring moult, beginning at the end of March, is usually complete by the end of June. Moulting begins at the nape, mid-back, and head and spreads downwards and backwards. The course of the autumn moult, which may begin as early as July, is uncertain but probably is completed by late October or early November [24, 101].

Leveret pelage is similar to, though shorter, than adult's. There is a clear juvenile moult when the animal is about 900 g. This starts along the mid-dorsal line and moves ventrally. Subsequent moults to the first winter pelage are similar to adult's [101].

Scent glands: anal glands are smaller in proportion than the rabbit's. Inguinal glands, larger in females than males, lie in a pouch either side of the rectum and produce a brownish secretion with the characteristic 'rabbity' odour. Submandibular glands small compared to the rabbit. Lachrymal and Harderian glands found in the orbits may have a scent function — particularly if secretions are rubbed into the forepaws during face washing [156].

RELATIONSHIPS

In recent years considered to be conspecific with African *L. capensis* [169] but now generally thought to be specifically distinct mainly on the basis of differences in size, proportion and coloration in adjacent populations in Spain and Kazakhstan [54]. Closely related to *L. capensis* (Africa and SW Asia), *L. granatensis* (S Iberia), and the doubtfully distinct *L. castroviejoi* (NW Spain) [54].

MEASUREMENTS (Table 7.2).

VARIATION

Although described as a subspecies (*L. e. occidentalis* de Winton, 1898, type locality Moorhampton, Hereford, England) on the basis of darker colour, British animals are not clearly separable from those on the Continent. Colour variants include a grey form of the winter pelage caused by absence of brown and yellow pigments in the fur. Melanistic, albino, and sandy colour variants also found.

DISTRIBUTION

An animal of the open steppe which has successfully colonised farmland landscapes throughout Europe. Replaced by the mountain hare in upland Scotland, N Wales and Derbyshire where farmland or open grassland gives away to *Calluna* moorland. A similar pattern occurs on the Isle of Man where both species are present [69].

Extensively introduced into Ireland in latter part of last century by coursing clubs [12]. As a result local populations established in north-west (Donegal, Fermanagh, Londonderry, Tyrone) but detailed records lacking and always scarcer than Irish hare [68]. Unconfirmed records from elsewhere but translocations by coursing clubs possible.

Recorded from the following small Scottish islands; Gigha, Davaar, Luing (1973), Bute, Great Cumbrae, Rousay (1974) [6].

HISTORY

No definite record from Britain until the Roman period and may well have been introduced by man. Probably spread across Britain with the development of agriculture, as it appears to have done in the USSR [54].

HABITAT

Most abundant on arable areas where cereal growing predominates [123, 207, 217]. Large scale farming with a low diversity of crops seems less suitable than traditional ley farming which provides a continuity of food [80, 216] although field size *per se* does not seem to affect abundance [31]. Although grass fields are preferred feeding areas in summer when cereals no longer provide grazing [80, 216], high densities of livestock will deter hares from some pastures [10, 78].

Woods, shelterbelts, and hedgerows are frequently used as resting areas during the day particularly during winter [34, 216]. Human settlement reduces hare numbers [33].

SOCIAL ORGANISATION AND BEHAVIOUR

Social behaviour: although commonly referred to as solitary, hare distribution, even within habitat types, is significantly aggregated [43, 196]. Closely knit groupings may relate to breeding behaviour, but animals feeding within groups spend less time

Table 7.2. Measurements of brown hares.

	Mean	Range	SD	n	Locality
Head and body (mm)	544	520–595		9♂, 10♀	Norfolk [14]
Tail (with hairs) (mm)	106	85–120		9♂, 10♀	Norfolk [14]
Ear (to notch) (mm)	99	95–105		9♂, 10♀	Norfolk [14]
Weight					
Adult male (Feb) (kg)	3.23		± 0.05	723	E Anglia, Hants [9]
Adult female (Feb) (kg)	3.43		± 0.10	689	E Anglia, Hants [9]

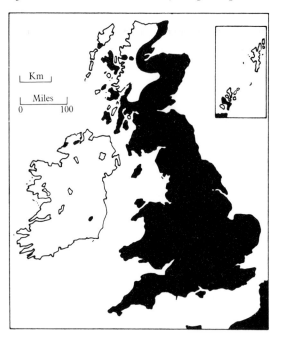

Map 7.3. Brown hare.

vigilant and more time feeding than solitary animals [43, 147]. Overall vigilance is increased in larger groups [147]. Increased group size does not normally lead to intraspecific aggression, but if the preferred food is in a small patch aggression can increase and social hierarchies may form containing both males and females [126, 147].

Under normal circumstances hares do not defend food, however males do compete for oestrus females. Dominant males guard near-oestrus females from subordinates which they chase off. Dominants also supplant other males which are guarding females. Dominants thus obtain more matings than subordinates [111]. Aggressive encounters between males consist of chases and biting. 'Boxing' is normally between males and females; typically a near-oestrus female is closely attended by a male and if unreceptive she turns and boxes him off. Chases involving several hares may be males pursuing a single female. Boxing and fighting are not confined to spring but occur throughout the summer [112].

Activity normally nocturnal, but extends into mornings and evenings during summer [112].

Map 7.4. Brown hare.

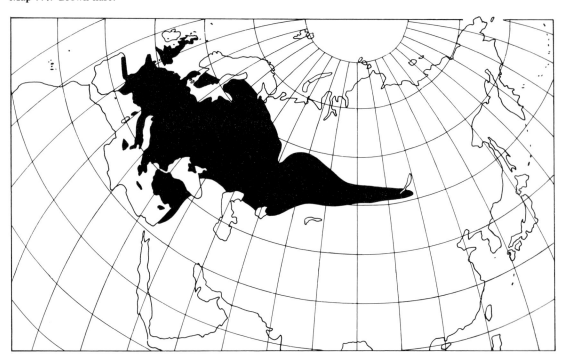

Home range: no evidence of territorial behaviour and no obvious pattern to the distribution of home ranges. Estimates of home range size based on recaptures of animals driven into nets are large [176], perhaps because animals are driven out of their normal range during netting. Results from radio-tracking suggest 20–40 hectares is average (Table 7.3).

Within home ranges activity shifts from place to place between seasons [176] and this may be related to changing food supply and cover [216]. Where cover and food are separated animals may commute between areas at dawn and dusk each day [216]. Daily movements up to 1.7 km have been recorded [109].

On bare arable land hares may dig themselves into a form during the day, which presumably provides shelter and protection from predators. Hares will re-use forms frequently if they are not disturbed [75]. They often 'back-track' along their trails several times before returning to their form [75]. This behaviour presumably reduces the risk of predation since they do not do this on leaving their forms [75]. Hares may also have a familiar 'race-track' which they may use to out-pace a pursuing predator [75]. Hares coursed by dogs will alter direction ('jink') to avoid capture.

FEEDING

Grasses, herbs and arable crops — particularly cereals during the early stages of growth. When available wild grasses and herbs are preferred to cultivated forms [83]. In summer, herbs form the bulk of the diet, whereas in winter grasses predominate [47], and if snow makes grazing difficult hares will browse shrubs [72, 113, 115]. Amongst agricultural crops hares may select between varieties, as demonstrated with turnips, but height of the crop most important, with hares preferring shorter and more open vegetation [107]. Under experimental conditions hares consume some 500 g (756 kcal : 3164 kJ) of food daily [161].

BREEDING (Fig. 7.3)

About three litters produced February to October; occasional winter pregnancies.

Gestation: 41–42 days.

Litter size: one to four with smaller litters early and late in the season.

Birth weight: *c.* 100 g.

Duration of lactation, variable, normally in excess of 23 days.

Testes reach peak weight (10 g each) between February and June, then decline until August, remain at a minimum until November when they begin to increase [125]. Viable sperm present mid-December to early September with maximum between January and June.

Ovulation is induced by mating which takes place at intervals of 7 days in non-pregnant females, every 13–14 days if pseudo-pregnancy occurs, up

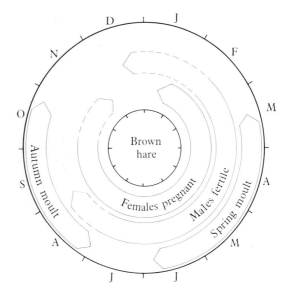

Fig. 7.3. Brown hare: life-cycle.

Table 7.3. Home ranges of brown hares determined by radio-tracking (hectares).

Habitat	Method of calculation	Months	Mean	Range	Reference
England					
Mixed farmland	90% isopleth	1–7	38	16–78	[216]
Netherlands					
Dairly farmland	Minimum polygon	1–5	26	7–59	[43]
Arable farmland	Minimum polygon	1–4	38	13–72	[43]

to 10 days before the end of a pregnancy (pre-partum oestrus), or immediately post-partum [49]. Pre-partum mating can lead to superfetation where two ages of embryos are present in the uterus [131].

Pre-natal losses are variable; early in the season in Cambridgeshire 37% of pregnancies showed pre-implantation losses and 14% of litters were lost post-implantation [131]. Throughout the season in the Netherlands only 6% of pregnancies in healthy hares showed pre-implantation losses (19% in diseased hares) and there were no post-implantation losses [42]. Pre- and post-implantation losses tend to be high at the start and middle of the breeding season [182].

Length of season, the proportion of females pregnant, and litter size vary seasonally (Table 7.4), and between years. The beginning of the breeding season is more consistent than the end and may be determined by day length [70]. In 13 years in NE Scotland first pregnancies were found 19 January to 28 February, whereas last pregnancies occurred 15 September to 30 December; thus breeding season length varied between 176 and 344 (mean 258) days [110]. Breeding success appears to be related to weather, particularly late winter/early spring, and mild autumns extend the breeding season [110]; but weather has differing effects in different geographical areas [32, 81]. Overall number of young born is negatively related to adult female density [81].

Litters per female reported to be one to four in Sweden but three is the most common, and 3-year-old hares produce more young than older or younger animals [81]. Only exceptionally do females breed in the year of their birth in Britain [125], although it may be more common elsewhere [122, 166].

Size and weight of embryos has been related to age so that conception and birth dates can be calculated from fetuses [44]. Birth weight is usually over 100 g (Netherlands: 101 g, range 80−130; Poland: 107 g, range 65−155; USSR: 100−110 g, range 80−140 [44]).

Gestation lasts 41−44 days [44]. Young are precocial.

Lactation lasts 20−30 days but may extend three times this for the last litter of the season [41]. Leverets exhibit following behaviour prior to suckling. They gather at their birthplace 1 hour after sunset and follow the female when she arrives; leverets can mistakenly follow other animals such as plovers and may even suckle from other females. Nursing normally takes as little as 5 min [41]. Females clean and remove urine and faeces from leverets, probably as an anti-predator strategy [41]. Variations in time and place of suckling can occur;

Table 7.4. Brown hare: mean litter size (based on foetal counts) and percentage of adult females pregnant in four studies.

	Norfolk [125] (n = 85)		Scotland [110] (n = 1569)		Netherlands [42] (n = 235)		Poland [182] (n = 212)	
	Mean	%	Mean	%	Mean	%	Mean	%
January	1.0	40	2.0	11	1.4	68	1.0	20
February	1.2	65	2.2	47	1.2	65	1.4	85
March	2.1	77	2.7	83	2.7	73	2.6	54
April	3.6	100	3.1	94	3.1	100	4.0	75
May	3.6	100	3.2	92	3.3	89	3.5	59
June	3.2	100	2.9	81	3.0	80	3.2	75
July	2.8	62	2.6	81	3.0	62	3.5	83
August	1.0	59	2.3	58	2.6	78	2.9	53
September			2.0	44	2.6	22	3.5	17
October			2.0	27				
November			1.8	11				
December			1.8	4				

ultrasonic communication may be used to coordinate arrival at site [46]. Leverets start grazing when 12–17 days old [41]. After 30 days they weigh 300 g, by 2 months 700 g, and they attain adult weight after 6 months [35]. Captive hares grow faster [179].

POPULATION

Density: Although easy to see on farmland they are difficult to census accurately as a proportion of the population may be hidden within cover. Census methods usually rely on either total catches from specific areas [2, 4, 249], from transects of known widths [173, 183], or spotlight counts at night [7, 82]. Total captures are considered the most reliable method but are difficult to organise and inappropriate on most British farmland. Transect methods tend to overestimate numbers due to observers including animals flushed outside the assessment belt [167, 173] and are not good where hares are hidden in thick crops or other cover [119]. Spotlight methods require less manpower and can be done when hares are actively feeding — however accuracy is affected by visibility and temperature [7, 82].

A wide range of densities on farmland in England which are similar to densities in Europe (Table 7.5). Island or semi-island populations are noticeably more dense probably due to absence of predation. Autumn densities are associated with farmland diversity [216].

Fluctuations: game-bag or shooting records provide useful evidence of changes in autumn numbers [208, 217]. Warm springs and warm late summer weather increase the size of the game-bag [3, 8, 32]. In England, some game-bag records show

evidence of quasi-cycles with an average period of 8–9 years [215]. Populations were highest around 1900 [217] and were also high during the 1960s, perhaps as a consequence of reduced rabbit abundance after the 1954 myxomatosis epizootic [8, 193], but numbers have declined significantly during the last two decades [217]. In Europe similar declines have been noted in Netherlands [37], Sweden [79], Switzerland [194], Denmark [208] and Germany [165]. The reason for the decline is not clear but modern arable farming methods may be partly responsible [8, 216].

Sex ratio at birth is close to equality (male:female ratio = 1.07:1 [202], 1.22:1 [71]). However males may predominate amongst adults (1.32:1 in an unexploited high density island population [2]). Data from hunted populations is confused by an unintentional bias towards hunting females [174].

Age determination possible by three different methods: the ossification of the distal end of the ulna which remains unossified in hares less than 7 months old [233]; eye lens weight which accurately determines age in months for hares under 1 year old, and in years for hares under 3 years old [40]; periosteal growth lines on the lower mandible are suitable for aging adult hares [84].

Adult survival varies considerably between studies (0.58 — Illumo Island, Denmark; 0.52 — Czempin, Poland; 0.51 — Sweden; 0.42 — Germany; 0.34 — Netherlands) [36]. No clear explanation for these differences exists. Males tended to survive better than females in dense Illumo Island population, and there is some evidence that animals in their first winter survive less well than older animals — otherwise survival appears constant with age.

Table 7.5. Densities of brown hares. Numbers per km^2 [216, 249].

Study area	Spring	Autumn	Method	Years
Orfordness, Suffolk	134.0	147.0	Total catch	2,3
Altcar, Lancs	28.5	21.7	Spotlight	2
Bisterne, Hants	8.3	36.0	Spotlight	2
Whitsbury, Hants	10.6	11.4	Spotlight	2
Six Mile Bottom, Cambs	46.5	53.6	Spotlight	2
Stetchworth, Norfolk	21.9	55.9	Spotlight	2,3
Westacres, Norfolk	27.3	33.6	Spotlight	2,3
North farm, Sussex	1.5	3.5	Spotlight	2
Lee farm, Sussex	–	3.2	Spotlight	2
Damerham, Hants	10.7	13.2	Spotlight	3

Life expectancy of an adult hare in the Netherlands is 1.04 years [36]. Life-span of tagged animals shows that they can live up to 7 years. Oldest animal recorded at Czempin, Poland was 12.5 years [175].

Age structure shows that typically half of an autumn population consists of young animals [118]. In Britain regularly shot populations have a rapid turnover (Table 7.6).

MORTALITY

Disease: losses can be high particularly through coccidiosis (*Eimeria* sp.) and yersiniosis (*Yersinia pseudo-tuberculosis*). Coccidiosis is most common amongst young hares [95] and reaches a seasonal peak in autumn when populations are high and humid conditions favour transmission [50]. Yersiniosis is most prevalent over winter and in France most common in north-western districts where recurrence appears to be cyclic [11]. In France 31% of disease mortalities due to yersiniosis [11], but in England only 19% of hares shot in poor condition had yersiniosis compared with 38% which had coccidiosis [195].

Predation on young leverets likely to be heavy. Fox is probably the most important predator. Impact of fox predation is unknown in Britain, but in Poland estimated that 10% of the annual natural increase is taken by foxes on an area of very low fox density and intensive predator control [177].

Agricultural hazards are numerous — particularly modern grass cutting machines and forage harvesters. Some agricultural sprays, e.g. paraquat, are known to be toxic [181] and where widely used many hares can be killed directly. Indirect effects of pesticides are unknown but herbicides are likely to have reduced the diversity of foods available to hares on farmland [205].

Road casualties may be a significant form of mortality in some areas [90].

PARASITES

Rabbit fleas, *Spilopsyllus cuniculi*, occur commonly as do sheep ticks, *Ixodes ricinus*, and sucking lice

Haemodipsus lyriocephalus.

In a survey of animals from the Berkshire Downs nematodes of the genus *Trichostrongylus* were present in all stomachs, with the nematode *Graphidium strigosum* in 63% and the tapeworm *Cittotaenia* sp. in 37% of small intestines [116]. Infestations by *G. strigosum* may be affected by rabbit abundance and may harm hares more than rabbits [38]. The tapeworms *Cittotaenia denticulata* and *C. pectinata*, and the nematode worms *Trichostrongylus retortaeformis* and *Protostrongylus terminalis* have been recorded, all from the intestine [116].

Infections with the bacteria *Yersinia enterocolitica* and *Y. pseudotuberculosis* have been recorded [137] and infections by the protozoan *Eimeria* sp. are common [195].

RELATIONS WITH MAN

A familiar farmland species that can be considered only a minor agricultural nuisance provided numbers are not excessively high. Damage to cereals and grass generally not noticed by farmers, but can be a problem on sugar beet and some horticultural crops. Young trees or shrubs may be destroyed during hard winter weather when grazing unobtainable. Damage can be reduced with chemical repellants [168]. To reduce numbers some farmers organise hare shoots in February or March which can reduce spring populations by over 50% [216]. No close season for shooting on enclosed land, but may not be offered for sale between 1st March and 31st July. Although not highly prized for shooting in Britain (as it is in much of continental Europe), it has long been a favourite quarry for hound sports such as beagles, harriers, and coursing.

Age (years)	1972		1973	
	Percentage of total	*n*	Percentage of total	*n*
<1	72.6	1372	58.6	668
1−2	22.6	428	29.4	335
2−3	4.3	81	11.0	125
3+	0.4	9	1.1	13

Table 7.6. Ages and proportions of the total numbers of brown hares taken from 22 spring shoots on estates in England during 1971 and 1972 [195]. Ages determined using eye lens weight.

AUTHOR FOR THIS SPECIES
S.C. Tapper, with acknowledgement for comments by D. Cowan and R. Hewson.

Mountain hare/Irish hare *Lepus timidus*

Lepus timidus Linnaeus, 1758; Uppsala, Sweden.
Lepus hibernicus Bell, 1837; Ireland.

Blue hare; varying hare; Arctic hare; maigheach-gheal (Scottish Gaelic); giorria (Irish Gaelic).

RECOGNITION

In summer coat distinguishable from brown hare by smaller size, shorter ears, greyer coat (except in Ireland) and absence of black top to the tail (Fig. 7.4). In winter mostly white or in transitional pelage (Fig. 7.5) (except in Ireland).

Skulls of both British hares can be distinguished from rabbit by the wider posterior nasal opening and the fusion of the interparietal and supra-occipital. In mountain hare the root of the upper incisor extends behind the suture of the maxilla and premaxilla; in brown hare it does not reach the suture.

SIGN

Conspicuous trails through heather, usually lying up and down the hill, are made and maintained by hares biting off the heather shoots.

Footprints resemble those of brown hare with the hind feet placed ahead of the front. The hind feet, being heavily furred, produce a broader print than those of brown hare, particularly in snow.

Faeces are usually brown or grey-green, often showing fibrous plant remains, about 1 cm in diameter, not distinguishable from those of brown hare and sometimes not from rabbit, although rabbit faeces are generally smaller, darker and clumped. Faeces are normally deposited at random while the animal is feeding but may be clumped at conspicuous landmarks, such as isolated boulders, where hares pause during travel.

DESCRIPTION

Pelage: the general colour in summer and autumn is dusky brown with grey-blue underfur showing through, particularly at the flanks. The pelage has three main constituents; underfur about

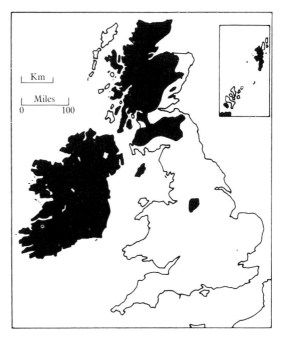

Map 7.5. Mountain hare.

15 mm long, grey proximally, brown towards the tip; pile hair about 25 mm, dark grey with a brown subterminal band 2–4 mm wide and a black tip; and guard hairs, about 40 mm, which protrude sparsely through the pile hair, particularly at the rump. Marked differences in overall colouring are due to variation in the colour and width of the sub-terminal bands of the pile hair. The underside is grey, the line of demarcation indistinct. The head, and upper surfaces of the feet are brown, although white hairs from the winter coat persist on the hind feet to June or beyond [99]. Leverets are greyer throughout. Irish hares have a generally warmer, reddish brown colouring than the Scottish race.

Moults: there are three annual moults; brown to brown (early June to mid-September); brown to white or grey-white (mid-October to January, with most of the moult completed by December); and white to brown (mid-February to late May although the summer coat may not be apparent in the field until March) [99]. Mountain hares moult faster in a warm spring than a cold one [73, 235], and hares at high altitudes turn white earlier and more completely than those lower down [235]. The winter moult is initiated by shorter day length. Its progress

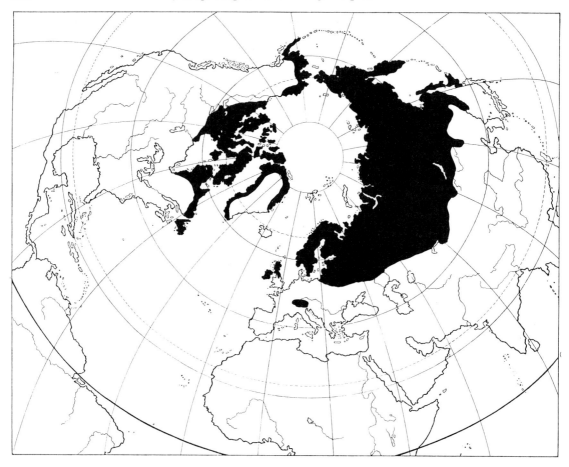

Map 7.6. Mountain hare.

during the following 10–12 weeks is strongly related to air temperature but from December to mid-February snow-lie is more important [117]. The Irish race usually moults only to a piebald coat in winter or may not whiten at all, although instances of almost total whitening are known [68].

Scent glands have not been studied but are probably similar to those of the brown hare.

MEASUREMENTS (Tables 7.7, 7.8).

VARIATION
Scottish and Irish forms are subspecifically distinct from each other and from the continental races (Table 7.9). Synonym of *L. t. hibernicus*: *L. t. lutescens* Barrett-Hamilton 1900 (Donobate, County Dublin), based upon a locally prevalent buff variety.

Colour variants include albino, black (principally a population in Caithness) and pale sandy coloured.

DISTRIBUTION
Tundra and boreal forest zones throughout the Palaearctic, and the tundra zone of N America (*L. t. arcticus* and *L. t. othus*). An isolated population in the Alps (*L. t. varronis*).

In the British Isles indigenous in the Highlands of Scotland and in Ireland. Most numerous on grouse moors in NE Scotland where heather management by rotational burning for grouse favours hares also [108]. Uncommon in W Scotland [236]. Introduced, mostly during the nineteenth century, to Shetland, Orkney (Hoy), Outer Hebrides, Skye, Raasay, Scalpay, Eigg (now extinct), Mull (including some from Ireland [12], Islay (now extinct), and Jura. Southern Scotland was colonised by intro-

Fig. 7.4. Mountain hare in winter pelage. (Photo: A. Tewnion.)

Fig. 7.5. Mountain hare in November but retaining summer pelage. (Photo: A. Tewnion.)

ductions into Ayrshire and elsewhere about the middle of the nineteenth century, and the Pennine area of S Yorkshire and Derbyshire by introductions about 1880. Irish hares were introduced into SW Scotland about 1923 and Scottish hares to Ireland (Londonderry) in the 19th century [12]. In N Wales a few may still remain from introductions near Bangor about 1885. The area occupied by

	Scotland ($n = 45$)		Ireland ($n = 27$)	
	Mean	Range	Mean	Range
Head and body (mm)	502	457−545	545	521−559
Tail (without hairs) (mm)	60	43−80	74	65−83
Hind feet (with claws) (mm)	142	127−155	156	149−168
Ear (to notch) (mm)	70	63−80	75	69−81
Weight (kg)	2.8 [103]		3.2	2.7−3.6

Table 7.7. Measurements of mountain hares [14].

Table 7.8. Weights of mountain hares in NE Scotland [103]. First winter animals weigh about 0.3 kg less than adults.

	Adult males		Adult females	
	Mean (kg)	n	Mean (kg)	n
Autumn/winter	2.7	69	2.9	59
Spring/summer	2.6	102	3.1	104

mountain hares in the Peak District appeared to have increased between 1971 and 1984 [254, 255]. Introduced to the Isle of Man, possibly since 1910 [69]. Present on the Irish islands of Rathlin (County Antrim), Mutton (County Clare), Calf (County Cork), Magee (County Down), N Bull and Lambay (County Dublin), Abbey and Valencia (County Kerry), Achill and Clare (County Mayo).

HISTORY
Present in Britain at least since the beginning of the last glaciation (Devensian) [209] and in Ireland probably since the middle of that period, c. 34 000 bp [211].

HABITAT
In Scotland heather moorland is optimum habitat, pioneer heather [240] being preferred for feeding, old heather for shelter. Many hares have access to hill pastures which are grazed quite heavily in spring in the absence of sheep and cattle [1]. Although snow may cover areas of old heather in valley bottoms, depriving hares of their forms, on exposed ridges the wind often clears away the snow providing snow-free areas for grazing, which vary from day to day according to the direction of the wind.

In the Peak District mountain hares occupy higher ground (above 130 m) than brown hares, and Calluna−Eriophorum vegetation rather than grassland [254]. Similarly mountain hares occupy higher ground than brown hares in the Isle of Man and feed in heather while brown hares feed on grasses [69].

In Ireland found in a wide range of habitats from sea level to mountain tops; very abundant on farmland, especially short grass [248].

SOCIAL ORGANISATION AND BEHAVIOUR
Largely nocturnal but much of their behaviour can be watched in daylight or at dawn and dusk, particularly during courtship between early February

	L. t. scoticus (Hilzheimer, 1906)	L. t. hibernicus (Bell, 1837)	L. t. timidus
Range	Britain	Ireland	N Eurasia (measurements for Scandinavia)
Summer coat	Greyish brown	Reddish brown	Greyish brown
Winter coat	White	Brown or partially white	White
Size	Small	Large	Large
Weight (kg)	c. 2.6	c. 3.2	
Length of skull (occipito-nasal) (mm)	83−89	91−99	89−103

Table 7.9. Subspecies of the mountain hare, Lepus timidus.

and late June. Often graze in groups, spending more time grazing and less looking around than hares feeding singly. Groups of up to 70 hares also form at the perimeter of snowfields and on sheltered slopes during strong winds with drifting snow. Groups exceeding 100 have been recorded on Irish airports [67]. Hares grazing by day in June to late August are predominantly females and probably lactating. There is a dominance order related to weight among males on the feeding grounds.

Agonistic behaviour involves interactions between males and between males and females but not between females. Cautious upwind approaches by males to females are usually rebuffed, the action varying in intensity from striking and chasing to females merely turning with ears lowered. Males occasionally box but more often flee, sometimes only for 2–3 m, where they may graze near the female. Males will approach several females, and follow scent trails of females. Dominant males may approach more females than subdominants, some of which may have been chased out of the area, but there is no clear evidence of mate-guarding [1]. Fights between males usually involve hares of similar rank [232].

Leverets are chased away by adults of both sexes but eventually succeed in feeding with groups of adult hares. Leverets spend less time grazing and much more in exploration and play. If disturbed they seek cover nearby or crouch, while adults flee.

Home range: typically comprises a night-feeding area and a day-resting place uphill and among long heather, on average about 1 km apart for both sexes but up to 2 km apart with a difference of up to 200 m in altitude. Home ranges are bigger in the breeding season than at other times of year (Table 7.10) and the area used for day-resting places is bigger than the feeding area. Several hares may feed in a relatively small area of favoured vegetation such as hill pasture or pioneer heather. The home range contains a variety of places to feed and

shelter to provide for heavy snowfall and high winds. There is a tendency to move uphill between June and October, distances varying from 200 m to 2.5 km and gains in altitude from 23 m to 370 m. There is no evidence, from capture/recapture data or from radio-tracking, of dispersal of leverets.

Forms are made in tall heather by biting off stems. They provide concealment from above, with the canopy often hiding 80–90% of the sitting hare, and wind speed within the form is reduced by about 90% compared with that 1 m above [218].

Simple burrows 1–2 m long are dug in peat, and hares often sit at the entrance during the day. If disturbed they run uphill but occasionally enter burrows. During snow hares make shallow scrapes which provide shelter from the wind, and dig tunnels through deep (>1 m) snow to reach burrows in peat [1]. In the arctic/alpine zone shallow scrapes on slopes commanding a good field of view replace forms as day resting places along with boulder fields which also provide protection against golden eagles.

FEEDING

In Scotland, heather *Calluna vulgaris* is the main food, particularly in winter, with cotton-grass *Eriophorum* spp. and grasses, both wild and in hill pastures, important at other times of year. The short, young (pioneer) heather which grows after rotational burning is preferred, but if this becomes over-grazed, or during periods of snow-lie, building heather, the next phase of the plant's development, is taken. Old heather, with woody stems and short current year's growth, is least preferred but is grazed during deep snow or if there are gaps in it big enough to accommodate a hare [100, 105]. Heavy grazing by mountain hares over 30 years maintained a Callunetum in a condition resembling pioneer heather [245]. On a smaller scale continual heavy grazing produces conspicuous short lawn-like bushes of heather. The shoots maintain a juvenile appearance and contain more nitrogen and phosphorus than the surrounding heather [148].

Table 7.10. Home range of adult mountain hares from radio-tracking (minimum convex polygon) on heather moorland in NE Scotland (hectares; mean ± SE) [1].

	Total	Breeding season	Post-breeding	Throughout year Day	Night
Males	113 ± 19	75 ± 17	54 ± 13	87 ± 18	21 ± 6
Females	89 ± 17	66 ± 13	58 ± 22	56 ± 18	16 ± 5

On high ground over 1000 m the rush *Juncus trifidus*, dwarf willow *Salix herbacea*, sedges *Carex* spp. and the grass *Deschampsia flexuosa* are available for food, with *Carex* and *D. flexuosa* preferred in tests with captive hares [104].

Heaths *Erica* spp., heath rush *Juncus squarrosus*, bilberry *Vaccinium myrtillus* and deer-sedge *Trichophorum cespitosum* are lesser constituents of the diet on moorland. During deep snow hares eat gorse *Ulex europaeus*, soft rush *Juncus effusus*, bark and twigs of willow, rowan, juniper and, least preferred, birch [100]. Soft faeces are produced and eaten (refection) from about 0900−1600 hours, and *c.* 200 hard pellets are excreted daily between 1600−0600 hours, most rapidly from 1800−2200 hours [74].

In Ireland a very limited study on uplands hinted that grasses and sedges formed more than half the diet [234]; on lowland pasture grass and dandelions were intensively grazed [248].

BREEDING

Probably three litters of one to four young born March−July in Scotland with a few August litters. Early and late litters smaller than those of mid-season. In Ireland two to three litters from January to October [66].

Gestation; 50 days, range 47−54.

Birth weight; *c.* 90 g.

Lactation; *c.* 4 weeks, longer for the final litter [74].

Most males are in breeding condition from late January to June but testis development is delayed in leverets born late in the previous year, and female hares in their first breeding season have fewer corpora lutea than older hares. There is no record of mountain hares breeding in the year of their birth [74]. Captive females were re-mated within 6−7 hours of parturition [170]. Pre-implantation loss of entire litters 6.5% with 26% of the remainder lost entirely after implantation [74]. Pre-natal mortality increases in severe weather.

Losses are higher at the beginning (February−March) and end (August) of the breeding season. All adult females pregnant March−June and some pregnant late February to mid-August [74, 102]. Leverets grow initially at about 14 g/day falling to 6.5 g/day for leverets of 2 kg or more [103].

POPULATION

Density: estimates of density in Scotland are based on counts obtained by using trained dogs over areas of 40−200 hectares. Highest densities occur on heather moors overlying base-rich rocks: mean 46/km² (95% confidence limits 30−69), with 6/km² (4.4−8.0) over intermediate and 3/km² (1.9−5.4) over poor acidic rocks [237]. Densities may however reach 300/km². The rotational burning of heather to provide new growth for red grouse also favours mountain hares, and game bags of both species are higher on well-managed moors [108]. Uncommon on arctic/alpine ground in W and NW Scotland (Table 7.11) and even scarcer on low moors there [236].

In the Peak District late winter density has been estimated at 3/km² (range 0.8−4.1 km) [255]. In County Mayo, Ireland, a density of 1/km² was recorded on blanket bog [236] and on mixed farmland in County Kildare densities increased from 5.5/km² in March to 6.8/km² in December [248].

On Swedish islands densities reached 310/km² [92], 292/km² [127] and over 400 [5] but mainland densities were much lower at 3.3/km² [128].

Survival: varies considerably with the big changes of numbers over a period of years. Over a 12 year live-trapping study in NE Scotland the number of young per adult between 1st July and 31st December varied between 0.4 and 1.8 (mean 0.74), and among large samples of shot hares between 0.3 and 0.9 per adult (mean 0.74). At high numbers and subsequent decline 75% of adults and 84% of leverets died within a year of marking. At low

Table 7.11 Densities per km² of mountain hares in NW and NE Scotland [236].

	NW Scotland			NE Scotland	
	Moors	Arctic/alpine		Moors	Arctic/alpine
Sutherland	1.0	2.5	Perth	16.7	1.7
Ross	1.2	2.5	Aberdeen	312	30
Argyll	1.0	1.2	Moray	25	
			Banff		1.2

numbers and during increase more 3-year-old adults were caught than 2-year-old, and 30% of leverets were recovered in the 3rd to 7th year after marking. Oldest hares were at least 9 years. Sex ratios did not vary significantly during population changes [104].

Population fluctuations: maximum numbers in Scotland may be 2–59 times the minimum [237], and decreases of this magnitude have been reported among high density populations in Swedish islands [5]. Peak numbers may occur at *c.* 10 year intervals in Scotland but there is no firm evidence that these are cyclical. Food shortage is the likeliest proximate factor in population crashes. Because of relatively low productivity (about six young per year) recovery is slow and probably depends upon better survival of adult females and possibly of a successful first litter. First litters are at greater risk of resorption during severe weather than later litters. Predation does not play an important part in regulating population changes [106].

A 4–5 year cycle occurs in Finland [180] and a 3–4 year cycle in the north of Sweden but not in the south [127]. On Swedish islands population crashes are likely to be due to a combination of food shortage and severe weather conditions [5].

MORTALITY
Natural mortality (predation and unknown causes) affects adults mostly between February and May, and leverets between August and October. However shooting to reduce the number of hares in winter and to provide food for dogs throughout the year may be the major cause of mortality [74]. Fox is main predator in Scotland and Ireland, but wild cats and eagles also kill adult hares in Scotland. The abundance of mountain hares on Swedish islands, compared with the mainland, is probably due to the absence of foxes [128]. In Scotland hen harriers take leverets up to 3 weeks old, buzzards and stoats take older leverets [74, 104].

PARASITES
Rabbit flea, *Spilopsyllus cuniculi*, and sheep ticks, *Ixodes ricinus* are frequent. The sucking louse, *Haemodipsus leporis* and the hair mite *Listrophorus gibbosus* occur in Scotland and Ireland [139A].

The stomach worm *Graphidium strigosum* is less common in mountain hares (21% of specimens examined) than in brown hares (68%) [116] where it may cause death [39]. Of other nematode worms

Trichostrongylus retortaeformis was found in 88% of mountain hares, *Mosgovovia pectinata* in 14%, *T. axei* in 8%, *Paranoplocephala wimerosa* in 1% and *Passalurus ambiguus* in 0.5% [23]. Coccidia, *Eimeria* spp., occurred in 93% of mountain hares and tapeworms, *Cittotaenia* spp., in 29% [116]. There is, however, no firm evidence that disease plays a large part in population changes of mountain hares.

Yersiniosis (*Yersinia pseudotuberculosis*) has been detected in the mountain hare [137]. Myxomatosis has been found sporadically in Irish hares [64].

RELATIONS WITH MAN
Not managed as a game species. Occasionally damages crops, e.g. of cereals and turnips [74], and trees, e.g. in winter in lowland Ireland [201]. In exceptional cases may compete indirectly with grouse for heather as food. Shot in large numbers (several hundred in a day) by gamekeepers in late winter. Not highly regarded as food in Britain and most carcasses are exported to Germany. Still extensively coursed in Ireland.

AUTHOR FOR THIS SPECIES
R. Hewson, with acknowledgement for additional data and comment by P. Sleeman.

REFERENCES

1 Author's data.
2 Abildgard F. *et al.* (1972) The hare population (*Lepus europaeus* Pallas) of Illumo Island, Denmark. A report on the analysis of the data from 1957–1970. *Danish Review of Game Biology* 6(5):32.
3 Andersen J. (1957) Studies in Danish hare populations. I. Population fluctuations. *Danish Review of Game Biology* 3:85–131.
4 Andrzejewski R. & Jezierksi W. (1966) Studies of the European hare XI. Estimation of population density and attempt to plan the yearly take of hares. *Acta theriologica* 11:433–48.
5 Angerbjörn A. (1983) Proximate causes of mountain hare population crashes: a review. *Finnish Game Research* 41:29–38.
6 Arnold H.R. (1978) *Provisional atlas of the mammals of the British Isles.* Abbots Ripton: Biological Records Centre 67 pp.
7 Barnes R.F.W. & Tapper S.C. (1985) A method for counting hares by spotlight. *Journal of Zoology* 206:273–6.
8 Barnes R.F.W. & Tapper S.C. (1986) Consequences of the myxomatosis epidemic in Britain's rabbit (*Oryctolagus cuniculus*) population on the numbers of

brown hares (*Lepus europaeus*). *Mammal Review* **16**:111–6.

9 Barnes R.F.W. & Tapper S.C. Personal communication.

10 Barnes R.F.W. *et al.* (1983) Use of pastures by brown hares. *Journal of Applied Ecology* **20**:179–85.

11 Barre N. *et al.* (1978) Contribution a l'étude epidemiologque de l'infection a *Yersinia pseudotuberculosis* chez les animaux sauvages en France. *Office National de la Chasse, Scientific Technical Number*: 67–82.

12 Barrett-Hamilton G.E.H. (1898) Notes on the introduction of the brown hare into Ireland. *Irish Naturalist* **7**:69–76.

14 Barrett-Hamilton G.E.H. & Hinton M.A.C. (1910–21) *A history of British mammals*. London: Gurney & Jackson, 263, 748 pp.

15 Bell D.J. (1980) Social olfaction in lagomorphs. *Symposia of the Zoological Society of London* **45**: 141–64.

16 Bell D.J. (1983) Mate choice in the European rabbit. In Bateson P.P.G. ed. *Mate choice*. Cambridge: Cambridge University Press pp. 315–27.

17 Bell D.J. (1985) The rabbits and hares: order Lagomorpha. In Brown R.E. & Macdonald D.W. eds. *Social odours in mammals*, vol. 2. Oxford: Oxford University Press pp. 507–30.

18 Bell D.J. (1986) Social effects on physiology in the European rabbit. *Mammal Review* **16**:131–7.

19 Bell D.J. & Mitchell S. (1984) Effects of female urine on growth and sexual maturation in male rabbits. *Journal of Reproduction and Fertility* **71**: 155–60.

20 Bhadresa R. (1977) Food preferences of rabbits *Oryctolagus cuniculus* at Holkham sand dunes, Norfolk. *Journal of Applied Ecology* **14**:287–91.

21 Boag B. (1972) Helminth parasites of the wild rabbit *Oryctolagus cuniculus* (L.) in North East England. *Journal of Helminthology* **46**:73–9.

22 Boag B. (1985) The incidence of helminth parasites from the wild rabbit *Oryctolagus cuniculus* (L.) in eastern Scotland. *Journal of Helminthology* **59**:61–9.

23 Boag B. & Iason G. (1986). The occurrence and abundance of helminth parasites of the mountain hare *Lepus timidus* (L.) and the wild rabbit *Oryctolagus cuniculus* (L.) in Aberdeenshire, Scotland. *Journal of Helminthology* **60**:92–8.

24 Borowski S. (1964) Studies on the European hare. I. Moulting and coloration. *Acta theriologica* **11**: 217–31.

25 Boyce J. (1985) *The defence against predation in the European wild rabbit*, Oryctolagus cuniculus. PhD. thesis, University of Aberdeen.

26 Boyd I.L. (1985) Investment in growth by pregnant wild rabbits: relation to litter size and sex of the offspring. *Journal of Animal Ecology* **54**:137–47.

27 Boyd I.L. (1986) Effects of daylength on the breeding season in male rabbits. *Mammal Review* **16**: 125–30.

28 Brambell F.W.R. (1942) Intra-uterine mortality of the wild rabbit *Oryctolagus cuniculus* (L.). *Proceedings of the Royal Society of London* (B) **130**:462–79.

29 Brambell F.W.R. (1944) The reproduction of the wild rabbit *Oryctolagus cuniculus* (L.). *Proceedings of the Zoological Society of London* **114**:1–45.

30 Bray G.C. & Bell D.J. (1984) Physiological correlates of social status in the domestic rabbit, *Oryctolagus cuniculus* L. *Acta Zoologica Fennica* **172**:23–4.

31 Bresinski W. (1976) Agrarian structure vs. the European hare population density. In Pielowski Z. & Pucek Z. eds. *Ecology and management of European hare populations*. Warsaw: Polish Hunting Association pp. 195–8.

32 Bresinski W. (1976) Weather conditions vs. European hare population dynamics. In Pielowski Z. & Pucek Z. eds. *Ecology and management of European hare populations*. Warsaw: Polish Hunting Association pp. 105–44.

33 Bresinski W. (1983) The effect of some habitat factors on the spatial distribution of hare population during winter. *Acta theriologica* **28**:435–41.

34 Bresinski W. & Chlewski A. (1976) Tree stands in fields and spatial distribution of hare populations. In Pielowski Z. & Pucek Z. eds. *Ecology and management of European hare populations*. Warsaw: Polish Hunting Association pp. 185–94.

35 Broekhuzien S. (1971) Age determination and age composition of hare populations. *Transactions of the X Congress of Game Biologists Paris* pp. 477–86.

36 Broekhuizen S. (1979) Survival in adult European hares. *Acta Theriologica* **24**:465–73.

37 Broekhuizen S. (1981) Studies on the population ecology of hares in the Netherlands. *Annual Report of The Research Institute for Nature Management*. Arnhem, Netherlands pp. 94–102.

38 Broekhuizen S. (1975) The position of the wild rabbit in the life system of the European hare. *Transactions of XII Congress of Game Biologists, Lisbon* pp. 75–80.

39 Broekhuizen S. & Kemmers R. (1976) The stomach worm *Graphidium strigosum* in the European hare *Lepus europaeus*. In Pielowski Z. & Pucek Z. eds. *Ecology and Management of European hare populations*. Warsaw: Polish Hunting Association pp. 157–71.

40 Broekhuizen S. & Maaskamp F. (1979) Age determination in the European hare (*Lepus europaeus* Pallas) in the Netherlands. *Zeitschrift für Säugetierkunde* **44**:162–75.

41 Broekhuizen S. & Maaskamp F. (1980) Behaviour of does and leverets of the European hare (*Lepus europaeus*) whilst nursing. *Journal of Zoology* **191**: 487–501.

42 Broekhuizen S. & Maaskamp F. (1981) Annual production of young in European hares (*Lepus europaeus*) in the Netherlands. *Journal of Zoology* **193**:499–516.

43 Broekhuizen S. & Maaskamp F. (1982) Movement, home range and clustering in the European hare (*Lepus europaeus* Pallas) in the Netherlands. *Zeit-*

schrift für Säugetierkunde **47**:22−32.

44 Broekhuizen S. & Martinet L. (1979) Growth of embryos of the European hare (*Lepus europaeus* Pallas). *Zeitschrift für Säugetierkunde* **44**:175−9.

45 Broekhuizen S. & Mulder J.L. (1983) Differences and similarities in nursing behaviour of hares and rabbits. *Acta Zoologica Fennica* **174**:61−3.

46 Broekhuizen S. *et al.* (1986) Variation in timing of nursing in the brown hare and the European rabbit. *Mammal Review* **16**:139−44.

47 Brull U. (1976) Nährungsbiologische Studien am Feldhasen in Schleswig-Holstein. Ein Beitrag zu Asungsverbesserung. In Pielowski Z. & Pucek Z. eds. *Ecology and management of European hare populations.* Warsaw: Polish Hunting Association pp. 93−9.

48 Bull P.C. (1958) Incidence of coccidia (Sporozoa) in wild rabbit *Oryctolagus cuniculus* (L.) in Hawke's Bay, New Zealand. *New Zealand Journal of Science* **1**:289−329.

49 Caillol M. & Martinet L. (1981) Estrus behavior, follicular growth and pattern of circulating sex steroids during pregnancy and pseudopregnancy in the captive brown hare. In Myers K. & MacInnes C.D. eds. *Proceedings of the World Lagomorph Conference.* Ontario: University of Guelph pp. 142−54.

50 Chroust K. (1984) Dynamics of coccidial infection in free living and cage-reared European hares. *Acta Veterinaria Brno* **53**:175−82.

51 Church B.M. *et al.* (1953) Surveys of rabbit damage to wheat in England and Wales 1950−1952. *Plant Pathology* **2**:107−12.

52 Church B.M. *et al.* (1956) Surveys of rabbit damage to winter cereals, 1953−1954. *Plant Pathology* **5**: 66−9.

53 Corbet G.B. (1982) The occurrence and significance of a pectoral mane in rabbits and hares. *Journal of Zoology* **198**:541−6.

54 Corbet G.B. (1986) The relationships and origins of the European lagomorphs. *Mammal Review* **16**: 105−10.

55 Cowan D.P. (1979) *The wild rabbit.* Dorset: Blandford Press, 43 pp.

56 Cowan D.P. (1983) *Aspects of the behavioural ecology of a free-living population of the European wild rabbit in southern England.* PhD. thesis, University of London.

57 Cowan, D.P. (1984) The use of ferrets *Mustela furo* in the study and management of the European wild rabbit *Oryctolagus cuniculus. Journal of Zoology* **204**: 570−4.

58 Cowan D.P. (1985) Coccidiosis in rabbits. In Mollison D. & Bacon P. eds. *Population dynamics and epidemiology of territorial animals: ITE Merlewood research and development paper no. 106.* Cumbria: ITE Merlewood pp. 25−7.

59 Cowan D.P. (1987) Aspects of the social organisation of the European wild rabbit *Oryctolagus cuniculus. Ethology* **75**:197−210.

60 Cowan D. Personal communication.

61 Cowan D.P. & Garson P.J. (1985) Variations in the social structure of rabbit populations: causes and demographic consequences. In Sibly R.M. & Smith R.H. eds. *Behavioural ecology: the ecological consequences of adaptive behaviour.* Oxford: Blackwell Scientific Publications pp. 537−55.

62 Cowan D.P. & Roman E.A. (1985) On the construction of life tables with special reference to the European wild rabbit *Oryctolagus cuniculus. Journal of Zoology* **207**:607−9.

63 Daly J.C. (1981) Effects of social organisation and environmental diversity on determining the genetic structure of a population of the wild rabbit, *Oryctolagus cuniculus. Evolution* **35**:689−706.

64 Deane C.D. (1955) Note on myxomatosis in hares. *Bulletin of the Mammal Society of the British Isles* **3**:20.

65 Dunsmore J.D. (1974) The rabbit in sub-alpine south-eastern Australia. I. Population structure of rabbits and productivity. *Australian Wildlife Research* **1**:1−16.

66 Fairley J.S. (1974) Notes on the winter breeding condition of hares in the west of Ireland. *Irish Naturalist's Journal* **18**:17−18.

67 Fairley J.S. (1975) *An Irish beast book.* Belfast: Blackstaff Press 201 pp.

68 Fairley J.S. Personal communication.

69 Fargher S.E. (1977) The distribution of the brown hare (*Lepus capensis*) and the mountain hare (*Lepus timidus*) in the Isle of Man. *Journal of Zoology* **182**:164−7.

70 Farrow E.P. (1917) On the ecology of the vegetation of Breckland. III. General effects of rabbits on the vegetation. *Journal of Ecology* **5**:1−18.

71 Flux J.E.C. (1967) Reproduction and body weights of the hare *Lepus europaeus* Pallas, in New Zealand. *New Zealand Journal of Science* **10**:357−401.

72 Flux J.E.C. (1967) Hare numbers and diet in an alpine basin in New Zealand. *Proceedings of the New Zealand Ecological Society* **14**:27−33.

73 Flux J.E.C. (1970) Colour change of mountain hares (*Lepus timidus scoticus*) in north-east Scotland. *Journal of Zoology* **162**:345−58.

74 Flux J.E.C. (1970) Life history of the mountain hare (*Lepus timidus scoticus*) in north-east Scotland. *Journal of Zoology* **161**:75−123.

75 Flux J.E.C. (1981) Field observations of behaviour in the genus *Lepus.* In Myers K. & MacInnes C.E. eds. *Proceedings of the World Lagomorph Conference.* Ontario: University of Guelph pp. 377−96.

76 Flux J.E.C. & Fullagar P.J. (1983) World distribution of the rabbit (*Oryctolagus cuniculus*). *Acta Zoologica Fennica* **174**:75−7.

77 Ford C.E. *et al.* (1980) Proceedings of the first international conference for the standardization of banded karyotypes of domestic animals, Reading 1976. *Hereditas* **92**:145−62.

78 Frylestam B. (1976) Effects of cattle-grazing and harvesting of hay on density and distribution of an European hare population. In Pielowski Z. & Pucek

Z. eds. *Ecology and management of European hare populations*. Warsaw: Polish Hunting Association pp. 199–203.

79 Frylestam B. (1976) The European hare in Sweden. In Pielowski Z. & Pucek Z. eds. *Ecology and management of European hare populations*. Warsaw: Polish Hunting Association p. 33.

80 Frylestam B. (1980) Utilization of farmland habitats by European hares (*Lepus europaeus* Pallas) in southern Sweden. *Viltrevy* **11**:271–84.

81 Frylestam B. (1980) Reproduction in the European hare in southern Sweden. *Holarctic Ecology* **3**: 74–80.

82 Frylestam B. (1981) Studies of the European hare XXXVII. Estimating by spotlight the population density of the European hare. *Acta theriologica* **26**:419–27.

83 Frylestam B. (1986) Agricultural land use effects on the winter diet of brown hares in southern Sweden. *Mammal Review* **16**:157–61.

84 Frylestam B. & Von Schantz T. (1977) Age determination of European hares based on periosteal growth lines. *Mammal Review* **7**:151–4.

85 Garson P.J. (1981) Social organisation and reproduction in the rabbit: a review. In Myers K. & McInness C.D. eds. *Proceedings of the World Lagomorph Conference*. Ontario: University of Guelph pp. 256–270.

86 Garson P.J. (1986) Intraspecific influences on juvenile recruitment rate in rabbits: observational and experimental evidence from a study in coastal duneland habitat. *Mammal Review* **16**:195–6.

87 Gibb J.A. (1979) Factors affecting population density in the wild rabbit, *Oryctolagus cuniculus* (L.) and their relevance to small mammals. In Stonehouse B. & Perrins C. eds. *Evolutionary ecology*. London: Macmillan pp. 33–46.

88 Gibb J.A. *et al.* (1978) Natural control of a population of rabbits *Oryctolagus cuniculus* (L.) for ten years in the Kourarau enclosure. *New Zealand DSIR Bulletin* **223**:1–89.

89 Goodrich B.S. *et al.* (1981) Identification of some volatile compounds in the odour of fecal pellets of the rabbit, *Oryctolagus cuniculus*. *Journal of Chemical Ecology* **7**:817–26.

90 Goransson G. & Karlsson J. (1982) Hunting and road mortality in the pheasant and the European hare in southern Sweden. *Transactions of XIV Congress of Game Biologists, Dublin* pp. 343–9.

91 Gough H.C. (1955) Grazing of winter corn by the rabbit *Oryctolagus cuniculus* (L.). *Annals of Applied Biology* **43**:720–34.

92 Hakkin I. & Jokinen M. (1981) Population dynamics of the mountain hare on an island in the outer archipelago of SW Finland. In Myers K. & MacInnes C.D. eds. *Proceedings of the World Lagomorph Conference*. Ontario: University of Guelph pp. 469–77.

93 Heath E. (1972) Sexual and related territorial behavior in the laboratory rabbit. *Laboratory Animal Science* **22**:684–91.

94 Helen W. 1965.

95 Hesterman E.R. & Kogon C. (1963) Endoparasites of the wild hare (*Lepus europaeus* Pallas) in the Australian capital territory, with a note on breeding. *CSIRO Wildlife Research* **8**:21–7.

96 Hesterman E.R. & Mykytowycz R. (1982) Misidentification by wild rabbits, *Oryctolagus cuniculus*, of group members carrying the odour of foreign inguinal gland secretion. I. Experiments with all-male groups. *Journal of Chemical Ecology* **8**:419–27.

97 Hesterman E.R. & Mykytowycz R. 1982. Misidentification by wild rabbits, *Oryctolagus cuniculus*, of group members carrying the odour of foreign inguinal gland secretion. II. Experiments with all-female groups. *Journal of Chemical Ecology* **8**: 723–8.

98 Hesterman E.R. *et al.* (1976) Behavioural and cardiac responses of the rabbit *Oryctolagus cuniculus* to chemical fractions from anal gland. *Journal of Chemical Ecology* **2**:25–37.

99 Hewson R. (1958) Moults and winter whitening in the mountain hare *Lepus timidus scoticus* Hilzheimer. *Proceedings of the Zoological Society of London* **131**: 99–108.

100 Hewson R. (1962) Food and feeding habits of the mountain hare *Lepus timidus scoticus* Hilzheimer. *Proceedings of the Zoological Society of London* **139**: 515–26.

101 Hewson R. (1963) Moults and pelages of the brown hare *Lepus europaeus occidentalis* de Winton. *Proceedings of the Zoological Society of London* **141**: 677–88.

102 Hewson R. (1964) Reproduction in the brown hare and the mountain hare in north-east Scotland. *Scottish Naturalist* **71**:81–9.

103 Hewson R. (1968) Weights and growth rates in the mountain hare *Lepus timidus scoticus*. *Journal of Zoology* **154**:249–62.

104 Hewson R. (1973) *Population changes and grazing preferences of mountain hare* Lepus timidus *L. in north-east Scotland*. MSc. thesis, University of Aberdeen.

105 Hewson R. (1976) Grazing by mountain hares *Lepus timidus*, red deer *Cervus elaphus* and red grouse *Lagopus l. scoticus* on heather moorland in north-east Scotland. *Journal of Applied Ecology* **13**:657–66.

106 Hewson R. (1976) A population study of mountain hares (*Lepus timidus*) in north-east Scotland from 1956–1969. *Journal of Animal Ecology* **45**:395–414.

107 Hewson R. (1977) Food selection by brown hares (*Lepus capensis*) on cereal and turnip crops in north-east Scotland. *Journal of Applied Ecology* **14**: 779–85.

108 Hewson R. (1984) Mountain hare, *Lepus timidus*, bags and moor management. *Journal of Zoology* **204**:563–5.

109 Hewson R. & Taylor M. (1968) Movements of European hares in an upland area of Scotland. *Acta theriologica* **13**:31–4.

110 Hewson R. & Taylor M. (1975) Embryo counts and

length of breeding season in European hares in Scotland from 1960–1972. *Acta theriologica* 20: 247–54.

111 Holley A.J.F. (1986) A hierarchy of hares: a dominance status and access to oestrous does. *Mammal Review* 16:181–6.

112 Holley A.J.F. & Greenwood P.J. (1984) The myth of the mad March hare. *Nature* 30:549–50.

113 Homolka M. (1982) The food of *Lepus europaeus* in a meadow and woodland complex. *Folia Zoologica* 31:243–53.

114 Hughes R.L. & Myers K. (1966) Behavioural cycles during pseudopregnancy in confined populations of domestic rabbits and their relation to the histology of the female reproductive tract. *Australian Journal of Zoology* 14:173–83.

115 Hyytinen T. (1974) Winter nutrition of the brown hare (*Lepus europaeus* Pallas) in Western Central Finland. *Suomen Riista* 25:42–9.

116 Irvin A.D. (1970) A note on the gastro-intestinal parasites of British hares (*Lepus europaeus* and *L. timidus*). *Journal of Zoology* 162:544–6.

117 Jackes A.D. & Watson A. (1975). Winter whitening of Scottish mountain hares (*Lepus timidus scoticus*) in relation to daylength, temperature, and snow-lie. *Journal of Zoology* 176:403–9.

118 Jezierski W. (1965) Studies on the European hare. VII. Changes in some elements of the structure and size of the population. *Acta theriologica* 10:11–25.

119 Jezierski W. (1973) Environmental conditioning of the space structure and shyness in hares (*Lepus europaeus* Pallas 1778). *Ekologia Polska* 21:1–12.

120 King J.E. (1962) Report on animal bones. In Wymer J. ed. *Excavations at the Maglemosian sites at Thatcham, Berkshire, England. Proceedings of the Prehistoric Society* 28:355–61.

121 Kirkham G. (1981) Economic diversification in a marginal economy: a case study. In Roebuck P. ed. *Plantation to partition: essays in Ulster history.* Belfast: Blackstaff Press.

122 Kovacs G. (in press). Variability of fecundity rates in a population of European hare. *Proceedings of the International Union of Game Biologists*, Czechoslovakia.

123 Kovacs G. & Heltay I. (1981) Study of a European hare population mosaic in the Hungarian lowland. In Myers K. & MacInnes C.D. eds. *Proceedings of the World Lagomorph Conference.* Ontario: University of Guelph pp. 508–28.

124 Lamhna E.Ni. (1979) *Provisional distribution atlas of amphibians, reptiles, and mammals in Ireland.* Dublin: An Foras Forbartha.

125 Lincoln G.A. (1974) Reproduction and 'March madness' in the brown hare, *Lepus europaeus. Journal of Zoology* 174:1–14.

126 Lindlof B. (1978) Aggressive dominance rank in relation to feeding in the European hare. *Viltrevy* 10:146–57.

127 Lindlof B. (1980) *Some aspects of ecology in hares.* PhD. thesis, University of Stockholm.

128 Lindlof B. & Lemnel P.A. (1981) Differences in island and mainland populations of mountain hare. In Myers K. & MacInnes C.D. eds. *Proceedings of the World Lagomorph Conference.* Ontario: University of Guelph pp. 478–84.

129 Lloyd H.G. (1963) Intra-uterine mortality in the wild rabbit, *Oryctolagus cuniculus* (L.) in populations of low density. *Journal of Animal Ecology* 32: 549–63.

130 Lloyd H.G. (1967) Variations in fecundity in wild rabbit populations. *CIBA Foundation Study Group* 26:81–8.

131 Lloyd, H.G. (1968) Observation on breeding in the brown hare (*Lepus europaeus*) during the first pregnancy of the season. *Journal of Zoology* 156:521–8.

132 Lloyd H.G. (1970) Post-myxomatosis rabbit populations in England and Wales. *EPPO Publicity Series A* 58:197–215.

133 Lloyd H.G. (1970) Variation and adaptation in reproductive performance. *Symposia of the Zoological Society of London* 26:165–88.

134 Lloyd H.G. & McCowan D. (1968) Some observations on the breeding burrow of the wild rabbit, *Oryctolagus cuniculus* on the island of Skokholm. *Journal of Zoology* 156:540–9.

135 Lockley R.M. (1961) Social structure and stress in the rabbit warren. *Journal of Animal Ecology* 30: 385–423.

136 Lockley R.M. (1964) *The private life of the rabbit.* London: André Deutsch 152 pp.

137 Main N.S. (1968) Pseudotuberculosis in free-living wild animals. *Symposia of the Zoological Society of London* 24:107–77.

138 Mead-Briggs A.R. (1964) The reproductive biology of the rabbit flea *Spilopsyllus cuniculi* (Dale) and the dependence of this species upon the breeding of its host. *Journal of Experimental Biology* 41:371–402.

139 Mead-Briggs A.R. & Hughes A.M. (1965) Records of mites and lice from wild rabbits collected throughout Great Britain. *Annals and Magazine of Natural History* (13)8:695–708.

139 Mead-Briggs A.R. & Page R.J.C. (1967) Ectoparasites from hares collected throughout the United A Kingdom, January–March, 1964. *Entomologist's Monthly Magazine* 103:26–34.

140 Mead-Briggs A.R. & Page R.J.C. (1975) Records of anoplocephaline cestodes from wild rabbits and hares collected throughout Great Britain. *Journal of Helminthology* 49:49–56.

141 Mead-Briggs A.R. & Vaughan J.A. (1973) The incidence of anoplocephaline cestodes in a population of rabbits in Surrey, England. *Parasitology* 67: 351–64.

142 Mead-Briggs A.R. & Vaughan J.A. (1975) The differential transmissibility of myxoma virus strains of differing virulence grades by the rabbit flea *Spilopsylla cuniculi* (Dale). *Journal of Hygiene* 75:237–47.

143 Mead-Briggs A.R. *et al.* (1975) Seasonal variation in numbers of the rabbit flea on the wild rabbit. *Parasitology* 70:103–18.

144 Mckillop I.G. (in press) The effectivess of barriers to exclude the European wild rabbit from crops. *Wildlife Society Bulletin.*

145 Mckillop I.G. *et al.* (1986) Specifications for wire mesh fences used to exclude the European wild rabbit from crops. In Salmon T.P. ed. *Proceedings of the 12th Vertebrate Pest Conference* Davis: University of California pp. 147–52.

146 Middleton A.D. (1934) Periodic fluctuations in British game populations. *Journal of Animal Ecology* 3:231–49.

147 Monaghan P. & Metcalfe B. (1985) Group foraging in wild brown hares: effects of resource distribution and social status. *Animal Behaviour* 33:993–9.

148 Moss R. & Hewson R. (1985) Effects on heather of heavy grazing by mountain hares. *Holarctic Ecology* 8:280–4.

149 Mulder J.L. & Wallage-Dress J.M. (1979) Red fox predation on young rabbits in breeding burrows. *Netherlands Journal of Zoology* 29:144–5.

150 Myers K. & Poole W.E. (1958) Sexual behaviour cycles in the wild rabbit, *Oryctolagus cuniculus* (L.). *CSIRO Wildlife Research* 3:144–5.

151 Myers K. & Poole W.E. (1959) A study of the biology of the wild rabbit, *Oryctolagus cuniculus* (L.) in confined populations. I: the effects of density on home range and formation of breeding groups. *CSIRO Wildlife Research* 4:14–26.

152 Myers K. & Poole W.E. (1961) A study of the biology of the wild rabbit, *Oryctolagus cuniculus* (L.) in confined populations. II: the effects of season and population increase on behaviour. *CSIRO Wildlife Research* 6:1–41.

153 Myers K. & Schneider E.C. (1964) Observations on reproduction, mortality and behaviour in a small, free-living population of wild rabbits. *CSIRO Wildlife Research* 9:138–43.

154 Mykytowycz R. (1959) Social behaviour of an experimental colony of wild rabbits *Oryctolagus cuniculus* (L.) II: first breeding season. *CSIRO Wildlife Research* 4:1–13.

155 Mykytowycz R. (1960) Social behaviour of an experimental colony of wild rabbits *Oryctolagus cuniculus* (L.). III: second breeding season. *CSIRO Wildlife Research* 5:1–20.

156 Mykytowycz R. (1966) Observations on odoriferous and other glands in the Australian wild rabbit, *Oryctolagus cuniculus* (L.), and the hare, *Lepus europaeus* P. *CSIRO Wildlife Research* 11:11–29, 49–64, 65–90.

157 Mykytowycz R. & Dudzinski M.L. (1972) Aggressive and protective behaviour of adult rabbits, *Oryctolagus cuniculus* (L.), towards juveniles. *Behaviour* 43:97–120.

158 Mykytowycz R. & Gambale S. (1969) The distribution of dung-hills and the behaviour of free-living rabbits, *Oryctolagus cuniculus* (L.) on them. *Forma et Functio* 1:333–49.

159 Mykytowycz R. & Hesterman E.R. (1970) The behaviour of captive wild rabbits, *Oryctolagus cuniculus* (L.) in response to strange dung-hills. *Forma et Functio* 2:1–12.

160 Mykytowycz R. *et al.* (1976) A comparison of the effectiveness of the odours of rabbits in enhancing territorial confidence. *Journal of Chemical Ecology* 2:13–24.

161 Myrcha A. (1968) Winter food intake in European hare (*Lepus europaeus* Pallas, 1778) in experimental conditions. *Acta theriologica* 13:453–9.

162 Parer I. (1977) The population ecology of the wild rabbit *Oryctolagus cuniculus* (L.) in a Mediterranean type climate in New South Wales. *Australian Wildlife Research* 4:171–205.

163 Parer I. (1982) Dispersal of the wild rabbit, *Oryctolagus cuniculus* (L.), at Urana in New South Wales. *Australian Wildlife Research* 9:427–41.

164 Parker B.S. *et al.* (1976) The distribution of rabbit warrens at Mitchell, Queensland in relation to soil and vegetation characteristics. *Australian Wildlife Research* 3:129–48.

165 Pegel M. (1986) *Der Feldhase* (Lepus europaeus Pallas) *in Beziehungsgefuge seiner Um- und Mitweltfaktoren.* Schriften des Justus-Liebig-Universitat Giessen. Heft 16.

166 Pépin D. (1977) Phase finale du cycle de reproduction du lièvre, *Lepus europaeus. Mammalia* 41: 221–30.

167 Pépin D. & Birkan M. (1981) Comparative total and strip census estimates of hares and partridges. *Acta Oecologica* 2:151–60.

168 Pepper H.W. (1978) *Chemical repellents.* Forestry Commission Leaflet 73, London: HMSO.

169 Petter F. (1961) Elements d'une revison des lièvres européens et asiatiques du sous-genre *Lepus. Zeitschrift für Säugetierkunde* 26:1–11.

170 Pherson A. & Lindlof B. (1984) Impact of winter nutrition in captive mountain hares (*Lepus timidus*) (Mammalia: Lagomorpha). *Journal of Zoology* 204: 201–9.

171 Phillips W.M. (1953) The effect of rabbit grazing on reseeded pasture. *Annals of the British Grassland Society* 8:16–181.

172 Phillips W.M. (1955) The effect of commercial trapping on rabbit populations. *Annals of Applied Biology* 43:247–57.

173 Pielowski Z. (1969) Belt assessment as a reliable method of determining the numbers of hares. *Acta theriologica* 14:133–40.

174 Pielowski Z. (1969) Sex ratio and weight of hares in Poland. *Acta theriologica* 14:119–31.

175 Pielowski Z. (1971) Length of life of the hare. *Acta theriologica* 16:89–94.

176 Pielowski Z. (1972) Home range and degree of residence of the European hare. *Acta theriologica* 17:93–103.

177 Pielowski Z. (1976) The role of foxes in the reduction in the European hare population. In Pielowski Z. & Pucek Z. eds. *Ecology and management of European hare populations.* Warsaw: Polish Hunting Association pp. 135–48.

178 Pielowski Z. (1981) Yearly balance of European hare population. In Myers K. & MacInnes C.D. eds. *Proceedings of the World Lagomorph Conference.* Ontario: University of Guelph pp. 538–40.

179 Pilarska J. (1969) Individual growth curve and food consumption by the European hare (*Lepus europaeus* Pallas 1778) in laboratory conditions. *Bulletin of the Polish Academy of Science (Biological Series)* **17**: 299–305.

180 Pulliainen E. (1982) Habitat selection and fluctuations in numbers in a population of the arctic hare (*Lepus timidus*) on a subarctic fell in Finnish Forest Lapland. *Zeitschrift für Säugetierkunde* **47**:168–74.

181 Quidet P. (1975) Resultats des enquètes realisées en France en 1972, 1973, 1974 sur les causes de mortalités du gibier. *Phytoma* **269**:26–32.

182 Raczynski J. (1964) Studies on the European hare V. Reproduction. *Acta theriologica* **9**:305–52.

183 Rajska E. (1968) Estimation of the European hare population density depending on the width of the assessment belt. *Acta theriologica* **13**:35–53.

184 Ranwell D.S. (1960) Newborough Warren, Anglesey, III. Changes in the vegetation on parts of the dune system after the loss of rabbits by myxomatosis. *Journal of Ecology* **48**:385–95.

185 Rees W.A. *et al.* (1985) Humane control of rabbits. In Britt D.P. ed. *Humane control of land mammals and birds.* London: Universities Federation for Animal Welfare pp. 96–104.

186 Rogers P.M. (1979) *Ecology of the European wild rabbit in the Camargue.* PhD. thesis, University of Guelph, Ontario.

187 Rogers P.M. (1981) Ecology of the European wild rabbit, *Oryctolagus cuniculus* (L.) in Mediterranean habitats. II. Distribution in the landscape of the Camargue, southern France. *Journal of Applied Ecology* **18**:355–71.

188 Rogers P.M. & Myers K. (1979) Ecology of the European wild rabbit *Oryctolagus cuniculus* (L.) in Mediterranean habitats. I. Distribution in the landscape of Coto Donana, southern Spain. *Journal of Applied Ecology* **16**:691–703.

189 Ross J. (1982) Myxomatosis: the natural evolution of the disease. *Symposia of the Zoological Society of London* **50**:77–95.

190 Ross J. (1986) Comparison of fumigant gases used for rabbit control in Great Britain. In Salmon T.P. ed. *Proceedings of the 12th Vertebrate Pest Conference* Davis: University of California pp. 153–7.

191 Ross J. & Sanders M.F. (1984) The development of genetic resistance to myxomatosis in wild rabbits in Britain. *Journal of Hygiene* **92**:255–61.

192 Ross J. & Tittensor A.M. (1981) Myxomatosis in selected rabbit populations in southern England and Wales. In Myers K. & McInness C.D. eds. *Proceedings of the World Lagomorph Conference.* Ontario: University of Guelph pp. 830–3.

193 Rothschild M. & Marsh H. (1956) Increase of hares (*Lepus europaeus* Pallas) at Ashton Wold, with a note on the reduction in numbers of the brown rat (*Rattus norvegicus* Berkenhout). *Proceedings of the Zoological Society of London* **131**:320–3.

194 Salzmann-Wandeler I. (1976) Feldhasen-Abschusszahlen in der Schweiz. In Pielowski Z. & Pucek Z. eds. *Ecology and management of European hare populations.* Warsaw: Polish Hunting Association pp. 35–40.

195 Sargent A.P. (1974) *A study of certain infectious diseases of the brown hare* (Lepus europaeus *Pallas*) *with specific reference to Yersiniosis.* MPhil. thesis, University of Reading.

196 Schneider E. (1981) Studies on the social behaviour of the brown hare. In Myers K. & MacInnes C.D. eds. *Proceedings of the World Lagomorph Conference.* Ontario: University of Guelph pp. 340–8.

197 Shatoury H.E. (1977) Genetic polymorphism in the wild rabbit in Northern Ireland. *Irish Naturalists' Journal* **19**:24.

198 Sheail J. (1971) *Rabbits and their history.* Newton Abbott: David & Charles 226 pp.

199 Shepherd R.C.H. *et al.* (1981) Observations on variations in the sex ratios of wild rabbits *Oryctolagus cuniculus* (L.) in Victoria. *Australian Wildlife Research* **8**:361–7.

200 Sibly R. *et al.* (in press). Seasonal changes in the length of the digestive tracts of wild rabbits.

201 Sleeman P. Personal communication.

202 Smith C.J. (1980) *Ecology of English chalk.* London: Academic Press.

203 Southern H.N. (1940) The ecology and population dynamics of the wild rabbit *Oryctolagus cuniculus* (L.). *Annals of Applied Biology* **26**:509–26.

204 Southern H.N. (1948) Sexual and aggressive behaviour in the wild rabbit. *Behaviour* **1**:173–94.

205 Spath V. (1985) Untersuchung zur Populationsdynamik des Feldhasen in der Ober-rheinbene. *Proceedings of the XVII Congress of the International Union of Game Biologists, Brussels* pp. 545–52.

206 Stoddart E. (1968) Coccidiosis in wild rabbits at four sites in different climatic regions in eastern Australia I. Relationship with age of rabbit. *Australian Journal of Zoology* **16**:69–85.

207 Strandgaard H. (1964) The Danish bag record I. Studies in game geography based on the Danish bag record for the years 1956–57 and 1957–58. *Danish Review of Game Biology* **4**(2):1–116.

208 Strandgaard H. & Asferg T. (1980) The Danish bag record II. Fluctuations and trends in the game bag record in the years 1941–1976 and the geographical distribution of the bag in 1976. *Danish Review of Game Biology* **11**(5):1–112.

209 Stuart A.J. (1974) Pleistocene history of the British vertebrate fauna. *Biological Reviews* **49**:225–66.

210 Stuart A. (1982) *Pleistocene vertebrates in the British Isles.* London: Longman, 212 pp.

211 Stuart A.J. (1985) Quaternary vertebrates. In Edwards K.J. & Warren W.P. eds. *The quaternary history of Ireland.* London: Academic Press pp. 221–33.

212 Sumption K.J. & Flowerdew J.R. (1985) The eco-

logical effects of the decline in rabbits (*Oryctolagus cuniculus* L.) due to myxomatosis. *Mammal Review* **15**:151–86.

213 Tansley A.G. & Adamson R.S. (1925) Studies of the vegetation of English chalk III. The chalk grasslands of the Hampshire–Sussex border. *Journal of Ecology* **13**:177–223.

214 Tapper S. (1980) The status of some predatory mammals. *Game Conservancy Annual Review* **11**: 48–54.

215 Tapper S.C. (1987) Cycles in game bag records of hares and rabbits in Britain. *Symposia of the Zoological Society of London* **58**:79–98.

216 Tapper S.C. & Barnes R.F.W. (1986) Influence of farming practice on the ecology of the brown hare (*Lepus europaeus*). *Journal of Applied Ecology* **23**: 39–52.

217 Tapper S.C. & Parsons N. (1984) The changing status of the brown hare (*Lepus capensis* L.) in Britain. *Mammal Review* **1**:57–70.

218 Thirgood S.T. & Hewson R. (1987) Shelter characteristics of mountain hare resting sites. *Holarctic Ecology* **10**:294–8.

219 Thomas A.S. (1956) Botanical effects of myxomatosis. *Bulletin of the Mammal Society of the British Isles* **5**:16–17.

220 Thomas A.S. (1956) Biological effects of the spread of myxomatosis among rabbits. *Terre et la Vie* **103**: 239–42.

221 Thomas A.S. (1960) Changes in vegetation since the advent of myxomatosis. *Journal of Ecology* **48**: 287–306.

222 Thomas A.S. (1963) Further changes in vegetation since the advent of myxomatosis. *Journal of Ecology* **51**:151–86.

223 Thompson H.V. (1956) The origin and spread of myxomatosis with particular reference to Great Britain. *Terre et la Vie* **103**:137–51.

224 Thompson H.V. & Armour C.J. (1951) Control of the European rabbit *Oryctolagus cuniculus* (L.). An experiment to compare the efficiency of gin trapping, ferreting and cyanide gassing. *Annals of Applied Biology* **38**:464–74.

225 Thompson H.V. & Worden A.N. (1956) *The rabbit*. London: Collins 240 pp.

226 Tittensor A.M. (1981) Rabbit population trends in southern England. In Myers K. & McInness C.D. eds. *Proceedings of the World Lagomorph Conference*. Ontario: University of Guelph pp. 629–32.

227 Tittensor A.M. & Lloyd H.G. (1983) *Rabbits*. Forestry Commission Record 125, London: HMSO.

228 Trout R.C. & Tittensor A.M. (in press). Predation pressure on wild rabbit *Oryctolagus cuniculus* populations.

229 Trout R.C. *et al.* (1986) Recent trends in the rabbit population in Britain. *Mammal Review* **16**:117–23.

230 Tubbs C.R. (1974) *The buzzard*. Newton Abbot: David & Charles, 199 pp.

231 Vaughan J.A. & Mead-Briggs A.R. (1970) Host finding behaviour of the rabbit flea, *Spilopsylla cuniculi*, with special reference to the significance of urine as an attractant. *Parasitology* **61**:397–409.

232 Verkaik A.J. & Hewson R. (1985) Moult and rank in male mountain hares (*Lepus timidus*). *Journal of Zoology* **207**:628–30.

233 Walhovd H. (1966) Reliability of age criteria for Danish hares (*Lepus europaeus* Pallas). *Danish Review of Game Biology* **4**:106–28.

234 Walker J. & Fairley J.S. (1968) Winter food of Irish hares in County Antrim, Northern Ireland. *Journal of Mammalogy* **49**:783–5.

235 Watson A. (1963) The effect of climate on the colour changes of mountain hares in Scotland. *Proceedings of the Zoological Society of London* **41**:823–35.

236 Watson A. & Hewson R. (1973) Population densities of mountain hares *Lepus timidus* on western Scottish and Irish moors and on Scottish hills. *Journal of Zoology* **170**:151–9.

237 Watson A. *et al.* (1973) Population densities of mountain hares compared with red grouse on Scottish moors. *Oikos* **24**:225–30.

238 Watson J.S. & Tyndale-Biscoe C.H. (1953) The apophyseal line as an age indicator for the wild rabbit *Oryctolagus cuniculus*. *New Zealand Journal of Science and Technology B* **34**:427–35.

239 Watt A.S. (1919) On the causes of failure of natural regeneration in British oakwoods. *Journal of Ecology* **7**:173–203.

240 Watt A.S. (1955) Bracken versus heather, a study in plant sociology. *Journal of Ecology* **43**:490–506.

241 Watt A.S. (1957) The effect of excluding rabbits from Grassland B (Mesobrometum) in Breckland. *Journal of Ecology* **45**:861–78.

242 Watt A.S. (1960) The effect of excluding rabbits from acidophilous grassland in Breckland. *Journal of Ecology* **48**:601–4.

243 Watt A.S. (1962) The effect of excluding rabbits from Grassland A (Xerobrometum) in Breckland 1936–1960. *Journal of Ecology* **50**:181–98.

244 Watts A.S. (1981) Further observations on the effects of excluding rabbits from Grassland A in East Anglian Breckland: the pattern of change and factors affecting it (1936–1973). *Journal of Ecology* **69**: 509–36.

245 Welch D. & Kemp E. (1973) A Callunetum subjected to intensive grazing by mountain hares. *Transactions of the Botanical Society of Edinburgh* **42**:89–99.

246 Wheeler S.H. & King D.R. (1980) The use of eye-lens weight for ageing wild rabbits *Oryctolagus cuniculus*. *Australian Wildlife Research* **7**:79–84.

247 Wheeler S.H. *et al.* (1981) Habitat and warren utilisation by the European rabbit, *Oryctolagus cuniculus* (L.) as determined by radio-tracking. *Australian Wildlife Research* **8**:581–8.

248 Whelan J. (1985) The population and distribution of the mountain hare (*Lepus timidus* L.) on farmland. *Irish Naturalists' Journal* **21**:532–4.

249 White D.A. (1969) Brown hares (*Lepus europaeus*) on Orford beach, 1964–6. *Transactions of the Suffolk Naturalists' Society* **14**:49–57.

250 Williams J.M. (1985) A possible basis for economic rabbit control. *Proceedings of the New Zealand Ecological Society* **24**:132–5.

251 Williams O.B. *et al.* (1974) Grazing management of Woodwalton Fen: seasonal changes in the diet of cattle and rabbits. *Journal of Applied Ecology* **11**: 499–516.

252 Wood D.H. (1980) The demography of a rabbit population in an arid region of New South Wales, Australia. *Journal of Animal Ecology* **49**:55–79.

253 Wood D.H. (1984). The rabbit (*Oryctolagus cunicularis* L.) as an element in the arid biome of Australia. In Cogger H.G. & Cameron E.E. eds *Arid Australia*. Sydney: Australian Museum, pp. 273–87.

254 Yalden D.W. (1971) The mountain hare (*Lepus timidus*) in the Peak District. *Naturalist* **918**:81–92.

255 Yalden D.W. (1984) The status of the mountain hare *Lepus timidus* in the Peak District. *Naturalist* **109**:55–9.

Chapter 8 / Rodents: Order Rodentia

This is the largest order of mammals with over 1700 species world-wide, the majority mouse- or rat-sized. They occupy all terrestrial and freshwater habitats and many species are individually very abundant.

The most striking characteristic of rodents is the form of the teeth. The incisors are reduced to a single pair above and below. They grow continuously from open roots and have chisel-shaped cutting edges. The lower ones in particular occupy extremely long sockets that may extend back almost to the articulation of the jaw. There is a long gap (diastema), without canines, between the incisors and the cheek-teeth which number from three to five in each row. The way in which the jaw muscles are modified for gnawing varies greatly from group to group, and influences the overall shape of the skull. The majority of rodents are seed-eaters but some are insectivorous, many are herbivorous and some are very versatile omnivores.

Fifteen species are present in Britain of which at least seven have been introduced by man. They are classified in four families to which could be added one more for the extinct beaver (p. 572). The characters of the extant families are tabulated in Table 8.1. All these characters do not apply consistently to exotic species.

FAMILY SCIURIDAE (SQUIRRELS)

The squirrels are one of the largest families of rodents with about 50 genera and 250 species, on all continents except Australia and Antarctica. The nocturnal flying squirrels, mostly in the Oriental Region, form a clearly defined subfamily (Petauristinae). The remainder are diurnal (subfamily Sciurinae) and are predominately tree squirrels, but include terrestrial species like marmots, ground squirrels and sousliks and the intermediate, semi-arboreal chipmunks. Some burrowing species hibernate but the tree squirrels do not.

Squirrels are characterised by relatively unspecialised teeth and jaw muscles compared with

Table 8.1. The principal characteristics of the families and subfamilies of rodents.

	Sciuridae squirrels	Gliridae dormice	Muridae (Murinae) rats and mice	Muridae (Arvicolinae) voles	Capromyidae coypu
Head and body (mm)	200–300	60–180	60–250	80–220	400–600
Tail					
Length relative to head and body	80–90%	80–90%	80–120%	25–60%	70–80%
Shape	Bushy	Bushy	Almost naked	Almost naked	Almost naked
Cheek teeth					
No. in each row above/below	5/4	4/4	3/3	3/3	4/4
Shape	Low-crowned, cusped	Low-crowned, transverse ridges	Low-crowned, cusped	High-crowned, alternating prisms, +/− roots	High-crowned, transverse ridges
Habitat	Woodland, arboreal	Woodland, shrubs	Woodland, scrub, commensal	Open ground, aquatic	Aquatic

the other rodents. There are one or two premolars in each tooth row in addition to three molars.

GENUS *Sciurus*

Contains three Palaearctic species, with one in Britain and Ireland, and *c*. 24 in the Americas of which one has been introduced to Britain and Ireland. The genus is fairly typical of tree squirrels including several other large genera such as *Callosciurus* in SE Asia and *Heliosciurus* in Africa. Dental formula in British species 1.0.2.3 / 1.0.1.3; first upper premolar rudimentary, absent in some other species.

Red squirrel *Sciurus vulgaris*

Sciurus vulgaris Linnaeus 1758; Upsala, Sweden

Common squirrel, brown squirrel, light-tailed squirrel, con, skug; feorag (Scottish Gaelic); iora rua (Irish Gaelic). (Note: the red squirrel of North America is a different species and genus, *Tamiasciurus hudsonicus*.)

RECOGNITION
Upper fur uniformly dark but variable in colour from deep brown to red-brown or bright chestnut to grey-brown. Ear tufts grow in late summer and are large during the winter but gradually thin to being small or absent during the summer. The larger grey squirrel may exhibit some chestnut coloration over the back and down the limbs, but it is not uniform as in the red squirrel (Fig. 8.1).

Skull shorter and deeper than the grey squirrel, with relatively smaller nasal bones (Table 8.2) (Fig. 8.2).

SIGN

Footprints: four toes on forefeet which point forwards, four closely aligned pads on palm, about 25 mm wide; five toes on hind feet, four oval plantar pads and one hind plantar pad, about 40 mm long, 35 mm wide.

Tracks characteristic with forefeet behind and inside the line of the larger hindfeet, similar to those of grey squirrel, stride about 35 cm, hops less than 1 m, tail held high therefore tail marks seldom visible [510]. Tree bark sometimes scratched in particular places, especially on frequently used pathways, up tree trunks or underneath large branches.

Faeces cylindrical or round, slightly smaller than those of rabbit (8 mm diameter), dark grey to black in colour but vary according to diet; probably deposited at random.

Food: cached during late summer and autumn; tree seeds such as hazelnuts, beech mast and acorns, as well as conifer cones, scatter-hoarded in small groups of one to four items just under the surface of the soil. Fungal fruiting bodies cut and cached singly in trees to dry.

Feeding signs: (Fig. 8.3) hazelnuts split open leaving two pieces of shell with clean edges (cf. mice

Fig. 8.1. Grey squirrel (left) and red squirrel (right).

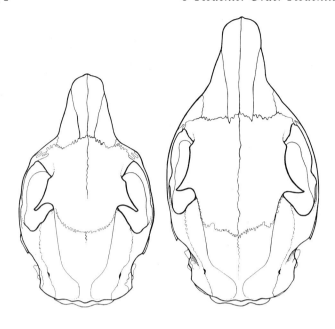

Fig. 8.2. Skulls of red squirrel (left) and grey squirrel (right).

Table 8.2. Measurements of red and grey squirrels.

	Red squirrel			Grey squirrel		
	Mean	Range	n	Mean	Range	n
Head and body (mm)	220	180−240		260*	240−285	86
Tail (mm)	180	140−195		220	195−240	
Hind feet (mm)	55	49−63		>60		
Weight (g)						
Males	279[†]	239−340	323	532[‡]	440−650	185
Females	278[†]	220−355	244	568[‡]	400−720	186
Males	300[§]	260−435	58			
Females	296[§]	260−345	70			
Condylobasal length (mm)		44−48		61.3*	58.1−64.4	337
Nasal length (mm)		13−16		20.8*	18.1−23.1	335

* Oxfordshire [218].
[†] East Scotland [809].
[‡] South England [1].
[§] East Anglia [809].

and voles). Characteristic 'cores' of conifer cones with associated piles of stripped scales with clean-cut edges rather than ragged and split edges made by birds. Feeding remains scattered but sometimes clumped, for example, on tree stumps. Bark stripped from base, stem or crown of trees, particularly pole-stage trees 10−40 years old. Stem bark often left hanging in long spiral twists. Incisor toothmarks found on fungi (larger than those of

mice and voles and not ragged like bird pecks or irregular and slimy like slug feeding). Terminal tips of branches frequently found scattered on ground in late winter/spring and summer.

Tree nests or dreys readily found, usually sited near the trunk of a tree or in a fork in the branches from *c.* 6 m upwards; *c.* 30 cm diameter. Outer twigs visible, sometimes with dead conifer needless or deciduous leaves attached.

Fig. 8.3. Cones of Scots pine stripped by red squirrel. (Photo: A.M. Tittensor.)

DESCRIPTION

Pelage: sexes similar; colour variable. Winter coat thick, deep red to brownish grey above; thick red-brown ear tufts 2.5−3.5 cm long; dark red-brown, dense tail hairs. Underside pale, white or cream. Summer coat chestnut above; ear tufts small or absent; tail thin, chestnut to creamy white. In some forms, ear tufts and tail hairs gradually bleach from winter to summer becoming white from June onwards. Juveniles darker than adults.

Four sets of vibrissae on the head: above the eyes, below the eyes, on the throat under the chin, and on the nose (whiskers). Similar hairs found on the feet, the outer sides of the forelegs, the underside of the body and at the base of the tail.

Moult: body fur moults twice a year; spring moult proceeds from front to back, autumn moult from back to front. Exact timing varies between individuals, particularly in relation to body condition. Ear tufts and tail hairs (from tip forwards) moult once, new hairs growing in late summer/autumn, and through to December in the case of ear tufts. Juveniles moult to appropriate summer or winter adult coat after weaning.

Nipples: four pairs, difficult to find in young females.

Scent glands associated with large mucous glands on side of mouth and sebacious glands in the tissues of the upper and lower lips [717]. Urine important form of olfactory signal; vaginal secretions in oestrus females may complement urine as a sign of reproductive condition.

Skull smaller than that of grey squirrel (condylobasal length < 50 mm, nasals < 16 mm); cranium deeper and post-orbital processes longer and narrower (Table 8.2).

Teeth: functional cheek-teeth rooted, low-crowned, quadrate with rounded marginal cusps and concave central area, traversed by weak transverse ridges in the upper teeth; only lower and second upper premolars deciduous and shed at 16 weeks of age. Wear of cheek-teeth and growth of cementum (as well as weight of eye lens) have been used to determine age [199, 467, 484, 517].

Post-cranial skeleton shows adaptations for climbing and leaping; bones relatively light and hind limbs disproportionately long and heavy (illustrated by Shorten) [733]. Feet plantigrade; long toes (except thumbs which are reduced to tubercles) with long curved claws. Well-developed tail used for balance, thermoregulation and as signalling device. Epiphyseal fusion of long-bones has been used to distinguish juveniles and adults [199, 517].

Sexes easy to separate by distance between genital opening and anus, very close in females, about 10 mm apart in adult males. Reproductive tract regressed in autumn and perhaps over winter if food supplies and weather poor. When active, testes large and scrotal; scrotum sometimes darkly stained. Female tract typical Y-shape, embryo post-attachment sites sometimes visible. Vulva becomes swollen at oestrus. The weight or length of the baculum in males is not an accurate method of determining age but may be used in conjunction with other techniques [199].

Chromosomes: $2n = 40$, $FNa = 70$ and 72 (continental data) [893].

RELATIONSHIPS

Closely related to the Japanese *S. lis* and more distantly to the Persian *S. anomalus* (Caucasus and Asia Minor). There is no obvious sister-species among the many American species of *Sciurus* [543].

MEASUREMENTS

See Table 8.2 — considerable individual and seasonal variation in body weight; generally an increase in weight during the autumn of about 10%, a proportionally smaller increase than the grey squirrel [477]. Weight of female not a good indicator of pregnancy.

VARIATION

Wide regional colour variation across the continental range with dorsal colour ranging from dark red to black to brown to grey to 'blue' [161, 632]. Tail, feet and ear tufts may be the same colour or contrast with the back. Underside usually white. Endemic British and Irish race, *S. v. leucourus* Kerr, 1792, characterised by bleaching of the ears and tail. However, introductions of *S. v. vulgaris* from Scandinavia into Perthshire in 1793 [393, 808] and *S. v. fuscoater* from W Europe to Lothians in 1860 (probably) and Epping Forest about 1910 [393, 730], complicate the picture; now some squirrels exhibit bleachings while others do not. Black or melanic squirrels found on the Continent are rare in Britain, as are albino forms. On the Continent, many populations are polymorphic and the relative proportion of colour phases (e.g. black, brown and red) varies geographically but is fixed for any one region.

DISTRIBUTION

Present on Brownsea Island (Dorset).

HISTORY

No datable fossil records [788] but no reason to doubt that red squirrel is native in Britain; origin in Ireland more doubtful and likely to be the result of introductions. At one time ubiquitous in woodland throughout Britain and Ireland. Historically, population numbers have fluctuated widely between years. Became extinct in Ireland and S Scotland by early 18th century, and was rare in Scottish Highlands in late 18th and early 19th centuries [393, 581]. Reintroduced to 10 sites in Scotland, mainly from England, between 1772 and 1782 [393] and to about 10 sites in Ireland from England between 1815 and 1856 [49]. Became very abundant between 1890 and 1910 throughout the British Isles, thereafter general decline and became scarce in many places in the 1920s. Some recovery by 1930 but further decline and extinctions over large areas of England and Wales as the introduced grey squirrel began to expand its range. Reasons for population declines unclear; habitat destruction and disease may have been partially responsible but direct influence of grey squirrel not likely to be a factor [358]. (Research required on possible indirect influences of grey squirrels on red squirrels, e.g. on whether high grey squirrel densities affect the reproductive performance of red squirrels.) The decline between 1910 and 1930 occurred before the spread of the grey squirrel. Since the 1960s, the red and grey squirrel have coexisted for up to 20 years in some areas such as the extensive coniferous forests at Thetford in East Anglia. The presence of grey squirrels is believed to have prevented the return of the red to many wooded areas in England and Wales, especially deciduous woodland. Red squirrels still found in deciduous woodland in the absence of the grey, e.g. Isle of Wight and Cumbria. Past and present distributions of red and grey squirrels in British Isles reviewed by Lloyd [538], and in East Anglia by Reynolds [685].

HABITAT

Across much of the Palaearctic it is found in boreal coniferous forests of Scots pine, Norway spruce and Siberian pine. In W and S Europe it is also found in broad-leaved woods. Mixtures of tree species provide a more reliable year-to-year seed food supply than single species forests. Trees also provide cover and nest sites. In Britain, populations appear to be most stable in large tracts of coniferous forest (e.g. > 100 ha) over 25 years of age. Also found in small woods and copses where grey squir-

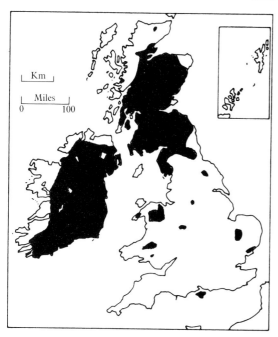

Map 8.1. Red squirrel.

rels not present. Although it has been suggested that it is more timorous than the grey squirrel it is found in urban areas on the Continent and formerly in parks in London; the last sighting of wild red squirrels in Regent's Park was in 1942; several animals experimentally introduced into Regent's Park in 1984 [92].

SOCIAL ORGANIZATION AND BEHAVIOUR

Social and spatial organisation: solitary for much of the time but communal nesting occurs especially during the winter and spring; squirrels that share dreys appear to be those that are familiar with one another [423]. Dominance hierarchies among and between sexes; males not always dominant to females. Dominant animals larger and older than subordinate animals and frequently have larger home ranges but considerable individual variation. Adult male ranges are larger than females and females similar in size to juveniles [859] but ranges of dominant animals smaller than subordinates in deciduous woods on the Isle of Wight [423]. Home ranges larger in deciduous than coniferous habitats

Map 8.2. Red squirrel.

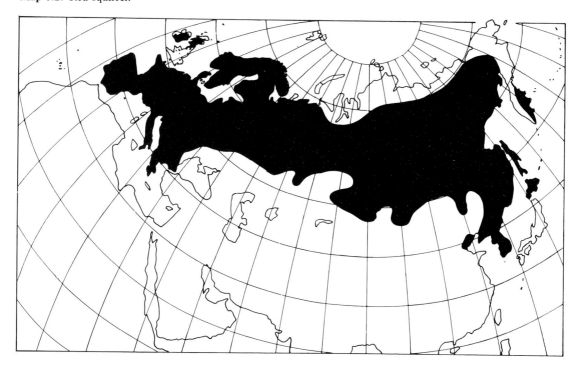

in Belgium [859]. Average home-range area from five studies in deciduous and coniferous forests 7.4 ha (± 5.26) [358]. Radio-tracking is the best way of studying home-range and spatial organisation. Home ranges overlap particularly in areas of abundant food, but overlap can be small, notably in breeding females which reduce their range and deter other squirrels when suckling young [423, 859]. Red squirrel densities are lower than grey squirrel's irrespective of habitat [477]; reasons unclear but one theory is that this may result from red squirrels maintaining larger distances between each other [358].

Aggressive acts [230] include loud chucks, vigorous tail flicking and foot stamping; aggressive encounters may include high-speed chasing, tail biting and screaming. Aggressive encounters between males occur when they congregate (from considerable distances) in 'mating chases' as they follow a female on heat. It is speculated that dominant male at head of following group of males mates with the female.

Communication and senses: wide-angled vision and probably dichromatic colour vision as in grey squirrels; the blind spot is a slender horizontal stripe above the centre of the retina giving minimum interference with vertical objects and clear upward vision. Vocal communication is associated with typical body postures and includes loud and soft chucking calls, an explosive 'wrruhh' sound and various moans and teeth chattering. Young make shrill piping calls. The sense of smell appears highly developed.

Scent marking occurs at specific places within home range (e.g. on branches or tree trunks) using urine and possibly secretions from mouth glands by face-wiping behaviour [423]. Scent marks denote occupation of home range, social status and reproductive condition. Vaginal secretions as well as urine may signal females on heat. Unclear as to whether faeces are used as markers.

Dispersal of juveniles and some adults occurs during autumn. Mass movements recorded in USSR in autumns with poor food supplies [632] but not recorded in Britain. Spring dispersal also occurs, probably of animals moving away from marginal, overwintering habitats, and summer dispersal may involve juveniles born early in the year.

Active all year (do not hibernate) but may remain in nest for several days during severe winter weather. Diurnal; onset of daily activity is related to sunrise, but termination is not related to sunset. Considerable individual variation but one main active phase during winter, peaking late morning, two phases during summer, peaking 2–4 hours after sunrise and 2–4 hours before sunset. Spring and autumn activity patterns intermediate between winter and summer. High winds, very hot or cold conditions and heavy rain reduce activity. May lie-up on a branch to keep cool during very hot weather. Food availability also greatly influences activity. Red squirrels are much more arboreal than grey squirrels irrespective of the time of the year or habitat [477]. Activity reviewed by Tonkin [812].

Movement across the ground is a scurrying, weaving run or a series of leaps with tail held out behind. Stop frequently and sit on hind legs with head held high in an 'alert' posture, ears erect and nose 'testing the air'. Agile climber, can move rapidly leaping from branch to branch and tree to tree, up to 4 m. Move down tree trunks head first with frequent pauses. Escape behaviour includes moving up the far side of a tree to the observer or predator, or 'freezing' flat against tree trunk or on a branch. Able to swim.

Nests or dreys are spherical, about 30 cm in diameter but sometimes larger, situated close to the trunk of a tree or in a fork in the branches, usually from 6 m upwards. Outer layers consist of twigs, sometimes with needles or leaves attached; inner cavity (12–16 cm diameter) lined with soft material such as moss, leaves and bark. Individuals use two, three or more dreys at one time. Drey counts may be used as crude, relative indices of population size or habitat-use [860, 881]. Hollow trees occasionally used as dens, especially in broad-leaved woods.

Grooming follows fixed sequence of events involving head and forepaw grooming, body grooming, hind leg scratching, hind foot licking and tail grooming.

FEEDING
Mainly seed but they are opportunists and take a wide variety of other foods when seed not available — hence seasonal variation in diet (Fig. 8.4). Primary foods are tree seeds, fruits, berries and

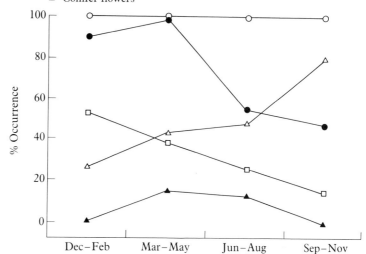

○ Conifer seed
● Conifer buds
□ Conifer shoots
△ Fungi
▲ Conifer flowers

Fig. 8.4. Diet of red squirrels in forests of Scots pine in E Scotland [583].

fungi. Secondary foods include buds, shoots and flowers of trees; bark may be eaten in any month of the year. Other green plant material, invertebrates (e.g. caterpillars), and lichen may be taken. No evidence that they are significant predators of bird eggs or nestlings. Standing water may be sought in hot weather. Tree seeds and fungi may be scatter-hoarded in the autumn. Specific cache sites not learnt although general area of caches may be; caches relocated by smell. Hoarding appears more intense in deciduous forests than cold coniferous forests [346, 812]. Exhibit feeding preferences according to species of tree and size of food item (e.g. seed cone). Bark stripped in a spiral manner from stems of coniferous trees (10–40 years old) to get at sap, usually during May–July. Reasons for bark stripping reviewed by Kenward [473]. Foods held and rotated by forefeet while squatting or hanging. Cone scales gnawed off to expose seeds, wings discarded. Between 60% and 80% of active period may be spent foraging and feeding [812]. Food and foraging behaviour reviewed by Mollar [583, 584] and energetics reviewed by Reynolds [686].

BREEDING (Fig. 8.5)
Gestation; 36–42 days.
Litter size; average three.

Lactation: 50–70 days.
Weight at birth: 10–15 g [230, 284].

Breeding season can last from December–January, when males and females that are 9–10 months old or older become sexually active, to August–September when summer litters weaned. There are two peaks in breeding within a season, with mating in winter and spring leading to spring-born (February–April) and summer-born (May–August) litters respectively. First breeding may be delayed or missed when seed food supplies poor [356], resulting in a shorter breeding season.

Males fecund for most of breeding season; period of inactivity in autumn and possibly into winter. No paternal care of young.

Females polyoestrous, in heat for only one day during each oestrous cycle. Adult females capable of producing two litters of one to six young (occasionally more) each year when breeding starts early but rarely achieve this potential. Summer litters (mean 3.6) larger than spring litters (mean 3.0) but poorer survival [735]. No post-partum oestrus until young almost weaned. Yearling females invariably produce only one litter; juveniles

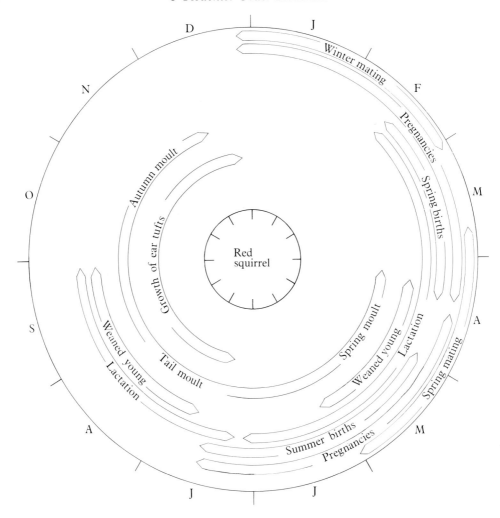

Fig. 8.5. Red squirrel: life-cycle.

rarely capable of breeding until 10–12 months old. Some females are unsuccessful in rearing any young during a season. Some intra-uterine loss; higher losses can occur during weaning. Young may be carried in mother's mouth to a new nest during suckling period.

Mating occurs with little prior courtship apart from 'mating chase' when males attracted from considerable distances to a female in heat by odour and follow her for one or more hours. Not always a chase as such; aggressive interactions may occur among males at this time. Dominant male takes position at head of following males and presumed to mate with female. Promiscuous.

Observed sex ratios *c.* 1 : 1.

Young are blind, deaf and naked at birth. Skin pigment appears on back and hairs emerge at 8–9 days. Hairs cover body by 21 days [230, 730]. Lower incisors cut 19–21 days, uppers at 31–42 days. Ears open 28–35 days, eyes open 28–30 days. Begin leaving nest and start eating solid food at *c.* 7 weeks; weaned at 8–10 weeks but maternal protective behaviour may extend beyond weaning, e.g. young may nest with mother overwinter (but more information required). Moult to adult coat at 3–4 months.

POPULATION

Densities: long term average densities of between 0.5 and 1.5 per hectare are normal for both conif-

Table 8.3. Typical red squirrel densities (mean number per hectare)

Habitat type	Location	Density (n/ha)	Reference
Coniferous	Scotland	0.8	[809]
	Scotland	0.3	[584]
	Belgium	1.3	[859]
	England	0.5	[734]
	England	1.1	[684]
	Russia	0.8	[101]
	Spain	0.1	[666]
Deciduous	England	0.7	[812]
	England	1.0	[423]
	Belgium	0.9	[859]
	Spain	0.3	[666]

erous and deciduous forests (Table 8.3), but year-to-year fluctuations can be large and are affected by seed supplies and weather. Populations are capable of recovering from very low densities in 2–3 years. Annual cycle of numbers with peaks in autumn, before autumn dispersal and overwinter losses, and troughs in spring before recruitment. Population dynamics of squirrels, particularly the affects of food availability, reviewed by Gurnell [356, 358].

Survival: year-to-year survival is positively related to availability of autumn tree seed. On average 75–85% of juveniles disappear during their first winter, average year-to-year survival improves thereafter to c. 50%. In wild, mean expectation of life at 6 months of age is about 3 years; some individuals may live to 6 or 7 years of age (in captivity up to 10 years) [808].

MORTALITY
Starvation, very cold weather, and possibly parasitic disease in undernourished animals (*see* below), believed to be responsible for many deaths. Predators, which include pine marten, wild cat, some owls, and raptors such as goshawks, do not significantly affect population numbers. Stoats may take nestlings, and foxes, cats, and dogs could take squirrels when they are on the ground. Man may influence mortalities by destroying or altering habitats, causing road casualties, or controlling populations under licence (*see* below).

PARASITES [478]

Ectoparasites: fleas, *Monopsyllus sciurorum* specific to red squirrels and common throughout the British Isles. *Orchopeas howardii*, introduced from North America with the grey squirrel, is sometimes found on red squirrels [96, 730]. *Tarsopsylla octodecimdentata* found locally in NE Scotland, probably introduced with continental squirrels in 1793 [299]. Ticks not specific; most common is the sheep tick, *Ixodes ricinus*. Little evidence of mange mites. Reports of mange more likely to be mistaken for sick, undernourished squirrels suffering from alopecia and heavy infestations of fleas and lice. Sucking lice include *Neohaematipinus sciuri* and *Enderleinellus nitzchi*.

Endoparasites: helminths are uncommon but *Enterobius* nematodes have been found in the gut.

Protozoa: the intestinal *Eimeria* spp. is common and causes coccidiosis; deaths in epidemic proportions have been ascribed to coccidiosis in Scandinavia [505], but evidence for this elsewhere is lacking. Coccidiosis may be the proximate cause of death in undernourished or stressed and overcrowded animals. *E. sciurorum* is pathogenic in Britain. Other protozoa include *Hepatozoon* and *Toxoplasma*. Bacterial infections are rare but pasteurellosis (*Pasteurella multicoda*) has been detected [478]. Ringworm fungal infections (*Trichophyton* sp., *Microsporum cookei*) have been found. Viruses isolated include parainfluenza [837], members of the encephalomyocarditis group [836] and parapox-viruses [720]. Infection with parapoxviruses in this species resembles contagious pustular dermatitis in sheep (and looks like myxomatosis), common in East Anglia; the virus is pathogenic and possibly of particular significance in undernourished animals. Reports of myxomatosis, diphtheria, distemper, 'consumption', and mange are unfounded.

RELATIONS WITH MAN
Fully protected under the Wildlife and Countryside Act (1981). Poisoning and trapping grey squirrels in areas where red squirrels are at risk are prohibited. May cause economic damage to conifer plantations by stripping bark, particularly when densities approach 2 per hectare [734]. Scots pine attacked, as well as lodgepole pine, Norway spruce and European larch. Damage may be considerable at the local level. Stem damage often heals over forming calluses and leaving low quality, scarred timber. Ring-barking, which results in die-back and wind-snap, and crown damage also occur. The causes of damage reviewed by Kenward [473].

A licence is required to control red squirrels (by cage trapping) before or during the main damage period of May–July, but poisoning is not allowed. They may be a nuisance locally to seed orchards or horticultural crops. Wild adult squirrels can suffer heavy mortality shortly after capture when confined to cages; this is probably related to stress or 'shock disease' which is associated with a reduction in body temperature, hypoglycaemia and a reduction in adrenal glucocorticoids [567].

Red squirrels are of aesthetic value, and ways of conserving them in Britain are currently being studied, such as whether it is necessary to maintain large continuous tracts of mixed conifer forests (e.g. greater than 100 hectares). Also it is suggested that clear-felling should be kept to small areas, and good seed and nest trees left behind where possible. The feasibility of translocating red squirrels as a conservation measure requires careful, detailed research. Ten squirrels introduced into Regent's Park, London, in 1984 coexisted with the resident grey squirrels aided by 'red-only' food hoppers [92]. They did not breed and most died within 20 months, mainly through motor vehicles [93]. The red squirrel is a game animal on the Continent. For reviews of squirrel management see [701, 362].

LITERATURE
Tittensor [808] — semi-popular account. Shorten [730] — first monograph on biology and history of red and grey squirrels. Laidler [503] — general semi-popular account of both species. Holm [422] popular account of both species. *Mammal Review* (1983; **13**:2–4) — symposium proceedings giving comprehensive account of ecology and behaviour of both species. Gurnell [358] — comprehensive and comparative account of natural history of Holarctic tree squirrels.

SOUND RECORDINGS
Appendix 3: A, C, E, F, J, P, V, W.

AUTHOR FOR THIS SPECIES
J. Gurnell with acknowledgement to the Forestry Commission for data on distribution.

Grey squirrel *Sciurus carolinensis*

Sciurus carolinensis Gmelin, 1788; Carolina, USA. *Neosciurus carolinensis.*

American grey squirrel; iora glas (Irish Gaelic); cat squirrel, migratory squirrel, and eastern grey squirrel in North America.

RECOGNITION
Larger than red squirrel, body predominately grey, never uniformly brown, but with some brown on the back and (in summer) on the flanks and limbs. Tail grizzled grey and ear tufts inconspicuous in winter. Another arboreal animal, the edible dormouse, has a localised distribution in Hertfordshire, and is nocturnal; also it is much smaller (*see* Fig. 8.1).

Skull longer and shallower than that of the red squirrel with relatively larger nasal bones (*see* Table 8.2).

SIGN
As in the red squirrel but stride longer (*c.* 45 cm).

DESCRIPTION

Pelage: sexes similar. In summer, upper fur grey with brown along mid-dorsal region and chestnut over flanks, limbs and feet; ears without white backs or conspicuous tufts; underside white; grey tail hairs banded with brown and black with indistinct white fringe. Winter coat thicker, grey with yellow-brown on head and along mid-dorsal region; flanks, limbs and feet grey; ears white behind with short brown, inconspicuous tufts; tail dark grey fringed with white. Juveniles are darker grey with more brown than the adult summer coat. Other pelage characteristics can be used to separate age classes [48].

Moult similar to red squirrel. Juveniles moult to appropriate winter or summer coat at about 3 months of age.

Nipples: four pairs — one inguinal, one abdominal and two pectoral. Become darkly pigmented with first pregnancy and tend to remain pigmented.

Scent glands probably as red squirrel; presence of mouth glands suggested by observations of face-wiping behaviour [794].

Teeth similar to those of red squirrel. Teeth cementum annuli, eruption, replacement and wear (as well as eye lens weight) used to determine age [219, 268, 282, 403].

Skeleton shows similar adaptations to climbing as red squirrel although larger and more heavily built

[477]. Ossification of epiphyseal cartilages used to distinguish young from old animals [219, 653]. Size of baculum may also be useful, in conjunction with other methods, as indicator of age in males [485].

Reproductive tract similar to red squirrel. Scrotum becomes heavily pigmented, almost black, in a sexually active male.

Chromosomes: 2n = 40, FNa = 76 (N America) [893].

RELATIONSHIPS
Most closely related to *S. griseus*, the western grey squirrel (W USA).

MEASUREMENTS
See Table 8.2. Wide variation in body weight in Britain influenced by season, food supply and reproductive condition; weights lowest in late spring/summer and highest in early winter; considerable increase in body weight in autumn, e.g. 23% in 1980 and 17% in 1981 in Monks Wood, Cambridgeshire; this is a much larger proportional increase in body weight than in red squirrels, e.g. 12% in 1980 and 8% in 1981 in Lawns Wood, Cumbria [477]. No sexual dimorphism although breeding females slightly heavier than males; body weight not a good indicator of pregnancy in females nor of age unless animals very young, e.g. 4 months old and less than 400 g in weight.

VARIATION
Dark-grey and melanic squirrels are common in the northern parts of their range in America, possibly associated with climate [493]. Melanics rare in Britain, but reported in Bucks, Beds, Herts and Cambs, probably from melanic grey squirrels introduced to Woburn. Albino forms rare but found in urban areas in N America, and reported from Kent, Surrey and Sussex in England. Erythristic forms with very red-brown backs occasionally found in SE England. Chestnut colouring on grey squirrels sometimes leads to confusion with red squirrels.

DISTRIBUTION
A native of NE America introduced in Britain and Ireland.

HISTORY
Introduced from USA to about 30 sites in England and Wales between 1876 and 1929, from Canada to three sites in Scotland between 1892 and 1920, and from England to one site in Ireland in 1911 [581]. Also introduced into South Africa and Australia [524]. Rapid expansion of range in England and Wales between 1930 and 1945, thereafter spread continued more slowly. The changing distribution of grey and red squirrels in British Isles has been reviewed by Lloyd [538].

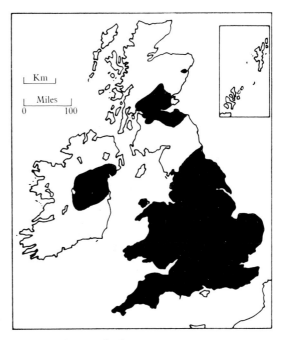

Map 8.3. Grey squirrel.

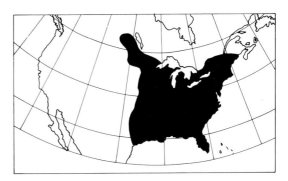

Map 8.4. Grey squirrel (original range in N. America).

HABITAT

In N America found in dense broad-leaved forests which sometimes contain up to ten or more tree species; this provides a more stable seed food supply than British broad-leaved forests containing few species. Particularly associated with mature oak-hickory forests in USA.

In Britain found in a wide range of habitats, most abundant in mature broad-leaved forests of oak, beech, sweet chestnut and hazel. Also found in broad-leaved/conifer mixtures, and mature conifer woodland, particularly when broad-leaves are available nearby, and in hedgerows, parks, gardens and urban areas with mature trees.

SOCIAL ORGANISATION AND BEHAVIOUR

Social and spatial organisation similar to red squirrel with hierarchical structure within and between the sexes [637, 793, 803], but social organisation likely to be maintained by smaller inter-individual distances; densities are much higher than those of red squirrels in comparable habitats. Considerable variation in home-range size affected by population density, food supply and habitat type [214, 215, 358, 474, 803]. Relative sizes of home range as in red squirrel, with males' ranges larger than females'. Males also increase range size during spring and summer whereas females are more stable (Table 8.4). Between 3 and 6 months of age, as young become independent, range size increases quickly and overlap between mother and young decreases to c. 50% [347]; juvenile range sizes similar to adult females [803]. Recently, methods of home-range analysis have tended to look at habitat use, and core areas where animals spend most of their time; core areas much smaller than total home-range size, e.g. 60% core areas (i.e. area occupied for 60% of time) for home ranges of grey squirrels near Oxford were 30% the size of 95% core areas [214], and 60% core areas were 28% of total home-range area in Monks Wood, Cambridgeshire [474]. Large range movements rarely recorded but range sizes of juveniles prior to dispersal increase markedly, for example to 12 hectares [474]; also distance of 3 km reported for juvenile taking up residence [796].

Female and male breeding behaviour as in red squirrel. Antagonistic behaviour described [429, 792]; fights rare but involve close contact wrestling and break off in a chase, ears may become torn and bites may occur to back, rump and tail. Peaks in

Table 8.4 Average size of range of grey squirrels in mixed deciduous woodland near Oxford, 1979–1981 (area in hectares likely to contain 95% of activity) [214].

Season	Males	Females	Spring-born juveniles
Winter	6.6	5.4	
Spring	8.8	4.7	
Summer	11.5	6.0	6.0
Autumn	5.7	6.3	

aggression at times of mating and dispersal. Adults known to huddle in nests, especially in winter [371], but the relationships of participants in the wild are not known. On one occasion, 20 squirrels escaped from a single cavity in a beech tree [185].

Communication and senses: vision similar to red squirrel; retina is a two-tiered structure with the tier towards the centre of the eye composed of rods and the outer tier of cones [440]; therefore likely to be able to see in dim light. Dichromatic colour vision, able to discriminate red or green from blue but not red from green (like human red-green colour blindness). Vocal communication has been classified into 11 different calls; namely buzz, kuk, quaa, moan; squeak, growl, scream, tooth-chatter, lip-smacking, muk-muk and mating call [35, 429, 533, 534, 535]. Tactile senses as red squirrel. Scent marking and function as red squirrel; faeces may be placed at specific points in autumn [35].

Dispersal of juveniles and some adults during autumn [804]. Road casualties increase in autumn. Mass migrations recorded in N America when densities high in autumn and food availability low [280, 726]. Also dispersal in spring (yearlings), possibly from marginal back to preferred habitats, and in summer (spring-born young). Some studies in Britain have found that dispersal is more common in June with no direct relationship with density [214].

Activity patterns and influence of weather and food similar to red squirrel. Much less arboreal than red squirrel in comparable habitats, e.g. average proportion of foraging time spent in trees throughout year for grey squirrels in Monks Wood, Cambridgeshire, was 14%, for red squirrels in Lawns Wood, Cumbria, 67% [477]. Least time spent aloft in late winter, most in mid-summer.

Movement as in red squirrel but not quite so agile.

Nests: winter nests as in red squirrel; summer dreys are shallow platforms of twigs. Drey counts may be used as crude relative indices of population size or habitat use [217]. Holes in trees such as oak and beech used as dens; centre hollowed out and entrance gnawed to 7–10 cm diameter.

Grooming as red squirrel [429, 503].

FEEDING

Mainly seeds and plant material (Fig. 8.6). Seeds preferred, including those of both deciduous and coniferous trees, but wide range of other foods taken [583]. No evidence that they are significant predators of bird eggs or nestlings. Caching behaviour as in red squirrel with scatter-hoarding of seeds when abundant in the autumn, i.e. seeds in small groups buried just under ground over wide areas; spacing of caches discussed by Kraus [497]. Location of specific caches not remembered although general area of caches may be; seeds relocated by smell; selection of sound nuts improves with experience [537]. Nutritional value of bark stripping is debatable (*see* Relations with man).

Feeding behaviour as in red squirrel but on average spend much more time foraging on the ground than red squirrels, especially during winter months. May eat 60–80 g of seed per day [545]; results from studies on energy requirements carried out in laboratory may not be applicable to free-living animals; reviewed by Knee [487].

BREEDING

Usually one or two litters of about two to four young are produced between February and July although length of season affected by food supply and weather [356, 358]. Reproductive activity in males and females reviewed by Dubock [219] and Webley & Johnson [861].
Gestation; 44 days [861].
Litter size, average three (range one to seven) [39].
Lactation; 70 days.
Weight at birth; 14 to 18 g [28].

Sexes: regression of testes (e.g. from 7 to 1 g), of paired Cowper's glands (e.g. 26 to 8 mm diameter) and prostate gland (24 to 6 mm diameter) usually occurs in autumn. Further work required on factors controlling seasonal changes in male sex organs.

Females possess twin uterine horns leading to paired ovaries; uterus in young, nulliparous females is threadlike (1.5 mm diameter) and coiled in posterior of pelvic cavity; uterus uncoils, increases in diameter and moves up into abdomen when female approaches 10 months of age [281]. Presence of a male and adequate space necessary for induction of oestrus in female [371, 861]. No evidence of post-partum oestrus. Adult females may produce two litters in a year if breeding season starts December–February; yearlings invariably produce only one litter. Uterine losses of young may be as high as 25% and further losses occur during weaning. If disturbed, mother may transfer young (by carrying individually in mouth) to another drey.

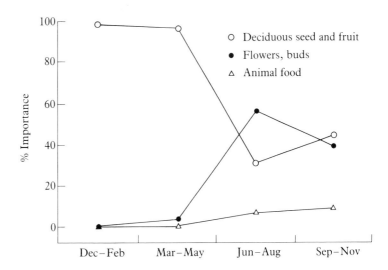

Fig. 8.6. Diet of grey squirrels in mixed deciduous woods in England [583].

Mating as in red squirrels, promiscuous.

Young: observed sex ratios vary but *c.* 1 : 1 [358].

Young are blind, deaf and naked at birth. Skin pigment appears on back and hairs emerge at 14 days. Hairs cover body by 20 days [729, 826]. Lower incisors cut 19–21 days, upper incisors cut 31–42 days. Ears open 28–35 days, eyes open 28–30 days (*c.* 90 g body weight). Begin leaving nest and start eating solid food at about 7 weeks [429]; weaned 8–10 weeks. Moult to adult coat at 3–4 months. Sexual maturity at 10–12 months, very rare in younger animals [751].

POPULATION

Densities: Long-term average densities in broad-leaved forests much higher than in the red squirrel; usually more than 2 per hectare and often much greater, e.g. 7.4 per hectare in oak wood in S England [356]. Densities greatly influenced by seed availability and weather [354, 356]. Long-term densities in pure coniferous habitat are not known. There is an annual cycle of numbers as in the red squirrel but this may be more marked with rapid changes over periods of a few months. Complete turnover of population estimated to be more than 6 years in N America [40]. Population dynamics of squirrels, including the effects of food availability, reviewed by Gurnell [356, 359].

Survival from year to year is positively related to availability of autumn tree seed. On average 75% of juveniles disappear during their first winter, average year-to-year survival improves thereafter to *c.* 50%. The shape of survival curves is similar in N American and English unexploited populations [356]. From studies in S England, the mean expectation of life is greatest in females at 6 months of age, i.e. 4–5 years, and in males at 18 months of age, i.e. 2–3 years [358]; some females survived for 7 years whereas the maximum recorded longevity in males was 5 years, but this may have reflected residency time rather than mortality. Other results show that some individuals live for up to 9 years in the wild (but < 1% of population) and up to 20 years in captivity.

MORTALITY

Predators as red squirrel; predation is not an important mortality factor. Road casualties occur particularly during the autumn. Grey squirrels are hunted extensively throughout their range in N America, but hunting has little effect on population numbers. Similarly, the control of grey squirrel numbers in England (*see* below) has only a short-term and local effect on population levels. Man has greatest effect on populations by altering or destroying habitats. Inadequate food and severe weather are important natural mortality factors and significantly influence seasonal and year-to-year population densities [356, 358]. Shock deaths occur as in red squirrels, especially in animals recently captured.

PARASITES [478]

Ectoparasites: the flea *Orchopeas howardii*, introduced from North America with the grey squirrel, is common throughout the range; the red squirrel flea *Monopsyllus sciurorum* is sometimes found [287, 730]. Ticks are not specific, the most common being the sheep tick, *Ixodes ricinus*. Autumn mite larvae, *Trombicula autumnalis*, attach themselves to exposed skin on head, elbows and underparts during the summer and autumn. Infestations by mange mites rare. Sucking lice *Neohaematipinus sciuri*, *Hoplopleura sciuricola* and *Enderleinellus longiceps* [96], most numerous on head, back and legs [639]. Drey fauna described by Twigg [821].

Protozoan parasites include *Hepatozoon* and *Eimeria* [174]. Known to carry leptospirochaete bacteria [825].

RELATIONS WITH MAN

Regarded as an attractive, mischievous animal by many people and of amenity value, but as a nuisance or a pest by others. Occasionally called a tree rat but name misleading and inappropriate. Sometimes squirrels will damage thatch or enter lofts and outhouses. Entrance holes can be blocked with wire mesh, and placing large amounts of naphthalene ('moth balls') in the entrance hole or nest can act as a repellant [551]. Other 'nuisance' activities include taking food from bird tables or bird feeders (e.g. for pheasants) [358].

Economic damage to market gardens, orchards and arable crops can occur where they are sited next to good squirrel habitats and when natural squirrel foods are in short supply. Major forest pest. Debarking damage to base, stem or crown of trees can be of economic importance and particularly occurs between May and July. Small areas of damage scar over by callus growth and the trunk may grow around them. This lowers the quality and economic value of the timber. If ring-barked or girdled, upper part of trunk or branch dies; growth can become distorted; top may be blown out of tree (wind-snap). Beech and sycamore trees at vigorous growth stage (i.e. pole-stage trees, 10–40 years old) are most vulnerable but many other species attacked. The reasons for bark stripping are unclear: two theories which are currently receiving attention are: (i) for nutritional benefit because they eat sap and damage trees with the most sap (but not the highest concentration of sugars); and (ii) as a displaced activity triggered by agonistic interaction especially when densities, particularly of juveniles from spring litters, are reasonably high [473, 476, 475]. Bark strips may also be used to line dreys. Spread of sooty bark disease on sycamore in Devon attributed to de-barking behaviour by squirrels [2].

Grey squirrels are controlled in Great Britain by cage or kill trapping (regulations laid down by the 1981 Wildlife and Countryside Act), shooting (sometimes in conjunction with drey poking) or warfarin poisoning (provisions laid down by the 1973 Squirrels (Warfarin) Order). Poisoning not allowed by law in some counties and poisoning and trapping not allowed in any areas where red squirrels are at risk (Wildlife and Countryside Act, 1981). Control methods have been described by Rowe [700]. It is illegal to import, release or keep grey squirrels in captivity without a licence from MAFF or the Secretary of State for Scotland (Destructive Imported Animals Act, 1933). Grey squirrels are an important game animal in North America where up to 40 million animals are killed annually [281].

LITERATURE
Middleton [570] — popular account of introduction and early distribution. Shorten [730] — first monograph on biology and history of red and grey squirrels. Shorten [734] — popular account. Shorten [732] — summary of biology of red and grey squirrels. Laidler [503] — general, semi-popular account of both species. Holm [422] — popular account of both species. Flyer & Gates [281] — review of biology of grey and fox squirrels in N America. *Mammal Review* (1983; **13**:2–4) — symposium proceedings giving comprehensive account of ecology and behaviour of both species. Gurnell [358]

— comprehensive and comparative account of natural history of Holarctic tree squirrels.

SOUND RECORDINGS
Appendix 3: A, F, J, V.

AUTHOR FOR THIS SPECIES
J. Gurnell.

FAMILY MURIDAE

SUBFAMILY ARVICOLINAE (VOLES AND LEMMINGS)

The arvicoline or microtine rodents form a large, clearly defined group which is variably treated as a subfamily of the Muridae, as a subfamily of the Cricetidae (along with other subfamilies including the hamsters, gerbils and New World mice) or as a separate family, the Microtidae or, more correctly, Arvicolidae. They are the dominant herbivorous rodents throughout the non-arid parts of the Holarctic region and are characterised especially by the very high-crowned cheek-teeth, which are usually rootless and continue to grow throughout life. The cusp pattern of the molars is worn off immediately the teeth erupt, revealing a complex prismatic pattern composed of areas of softer dentine surrounded by walls of hard enamel. These patterns are very characteristic of the species.

Compared with mice, voles have a rather long shaggy coat, blunt nose, small eyes and ears, short legs and short tail (under 75% of head and body). There are about 120 species in about 20 genera, of which three occur in Britain (Table 8.5).

GENUS *Clethrionomys*

Contains about seven species of red-backed voles in Eurasia and North America, in woodland and tundra habitats (Fig. 8.7). Differ from most other voles in that the molar teeth become rooted and are therefore less adapted to tough vegetation (Fig. 8.8). *C. glareolus*, the only species in Britain and Ireland, is very similar to the common N American species, *C. gapperi*. Two other species, *C. rufocanus* and *C. rutilus*, occur in northern Europe.

	Clethrionomys	Microtus	Arvicola
Colour of back	Chestnut	Brown	Brown or black
Tail : head and body	40–60%	25–40%	60–70%
Length of hind feet (mm)	15–20	16–21	27–37
Length of upper molar row (mm)	5.0–6.4	5.8–7.0	8.5–11.0
Molars develop roots	Yes	No	No
External angles of molars	Rounded	Pointed	Pointed

Table 8.5. Principal characters of the genera of voles.

Fig. 8.7. Bank vole (above) and field vole (below).

Bank vole *Clethrionomys glareolus*

Mus glareolus Schreber, 1780; Island of Lolland, Denmark.
Hypudaeus hercynicus Mehlis, 1831; Harz Mts, Germany.
Evotomys skomerensis Barrett-Hamilton, 1903; Skomer Island, Pembrokeshire, Wales.
Evotomys alstoni Barrett-Hamilton & Hinton, 1913; Tobermory, Mull, Scotland.
Evotomys caesarius Miller, 1908; St Helier, Jersey, Channel Islands.
Evotomys erica Barrett-Hamilton & Hinton, 1913; Island of Raasay, Inner Hebrides, Scotland.

Red-backed vole, wood vole, red vole.

RECOGNITION
Characteristic vole shape, with blunt nose and small eyes and ears (Fig. 8.9). Distinguished from field vole (and much larger water vole) by rich, reddish brown upper surface in adults. Young animals more greyish and easily confused, except that the tail is longer (half head and body) and ears are more prominent.

Skull less angular than that of field vole; molar teeth have angles more rounded and if extracted show signs of rooting unless the animal is quite young (< 3 months) [7].

SIGN

Footprints: four toes on forefeet and five on hind; slightly smaller than those of the wood mouse.

Faeces rounded in section, up to four times longer than wide; distinguished from those of wood mouse by their smaller diameter and from those of the field vole by the absence of a green coloration (but this depends on the foods eaten by the two species). Colour often brown to black and they may be found in small groups.

Cached food is scattered and not distinctive.

DESCRIPTION

Pelage: chestnut red upper surface, often grades into grey on flanks; ventral surface silver-grey to cream-buff. Juveniles grey-brown before the first moult.

Moult: first post-juvenile moult takes place at 4–6 weeks [459]. Moulting is predominantly sublateral

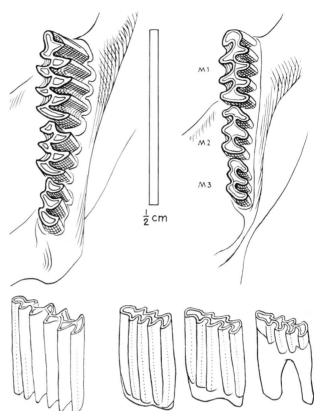

Fig. 8.8. Above: left lower tooth-row of field vole (left) and bank vole (right) showing the sharper angles and longer first tooth of the former. Below: right M₁ of field vole (left) and bank vole (remainder). Note the absence of roots in the field vole and the presence of roots, lengthening with age, in the bank vole.

Fig. 8.9. Bank vole. (Photo: P. Morris.)

(ventral to dorsal) with some older animals showing a diffuse moult; a head-to-rump moult is rare [891]. Adults moult throughout the year with peaks in spring and autumn. The post-juvenile moult leads to the seasonal moult of spring or autumn.

Teeth: open-rooted molar teeth continue to grow as the occlusal surfaces are worn away; growth of molar roots may be used as an indicator of age [7, 663, 894] but growth rate varies with season [582, 890]. Before the roots form, the growth of the constriction of the crown to form the 'neck' may be used to indicate different development stages [753].

Sexes: baculum consists of a proximal stalk and three distal processes; differences in length and width may be used to distinguish sexually mature males from immature ones [20] but there is much regional variation.

Os coxae show sexual dimorphism and changes associated with age [121] and, in females, birth [887].

Testes up to 900 mg during breeding season; those weighing more than 100 mg have mature spermatozoa [702]. Female tract Y-shaped; previous attachment sites (placental scars) show as dark spots on uterine wall. Maximum longevity of placental scars under laboratory conditions 182 days [8]. Ovaries easily distinguishable at ends of uterine horns and corpora lutea appear as large cream or pink spots in ovary.

Nipples: four pairs, two thoracic and two abdominal.

Chromosomes: $2n = 56$, FNa = 56 (on British mainland and on Skomer) [74, 394].

VARIATION
British mainland animals not distinguishable from continental form [157] (but formerly described as *Evotomys hercynicus britannicus* Miller, 1900, type locality Basingstoke, Hampshire, on basis of supposed smaller size and brighter colour). Four small island forms are subspecifically distinct (Table 8.6), but interfertile with mainland animals [772]. Shape of M^3 is variable everywhere, but predominantly simpler in south and more complex in north and especially in Scottish Highlands. A strictly local and temporary example of a population with predominantly complex M^3 has been recorded in Perthshire (Fig. 8.10) [154, 160].

Colour variants rare and not recorded in Britain. Albinism of the tail tip occurs in 0.8% in Britain [156].

MEASUREMENTS
See Table 8.7. Late summer generation overwinters at about 90 mm (head and body) and increases with onset of breeding in next spring to 100–110 mm; first generation may grow to full size in same year and breed.

DISTRIBUTION
In the north it reaches to about the edge of the tundra zone; in the south it is mainly montane, e.g. in N Iberia and Italy. Populations at exceptionally high altitude are found in S Norway (1400 m) and in the French Alps (2400 m) [770].

Throughout mainland Britain and on the islands of Handa, Raasay, Mull, Bute, Anglesey, Ramsey, Skomer, Wight, Jersey. Also in SW Ireland where first discovered in 1964; by 1982 it occurred throughout County Limerick, in large parts of Cork and Kerry, and in smaller areas of SE Clare and W Tipperary [744].

HISTORY
Recorded from all the Pleistocene interglacials since the Cromerian and in the last (Devensian) glaciation, but specific identity of these remains uncertain [787, 788]. At Ossom's Eyrie Cave, Staffordshire, it was represented at all levels from pre-Roman onwards [880]. The Irish population is almost certainly a recent introduction, but origin unknown. Populations on Raasay, Skomer, Ramsey

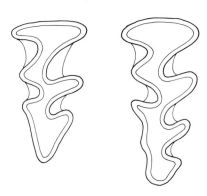

Fig. 8.10. Third upper molars of bank vole showing the simple and complex molars of the posterior, inner margin.

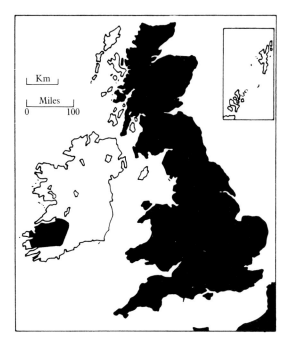

Map 8.5. Bank vole.

and Jersey very likely to be earlier introductions [153].

HABITAT
Preferred habitat mature mixed deciduous woodland with thick shrub or field layer [759]. In Britain it is also found in grassland habitats [135, 621], young deciduous plantations [6], conifer stands and hedgerows. On Skomer it is closely associated with a dense cover of bracken and bluebells (*Endymion non-scriptus*). In Europe it is also common in taiga conifer forests and spruce plantations.

SOCIAL ORGANISATION AND BEHAVIOUR [303]

Dispersion [876]: during the breeding season females are evenly dispersed in exclusive home ranges; males have larger ranges which overlap more than the females'. Immatures have smaller ranges than adults. Only adult males consistently exhibit wounds [38, 125, 126, 561, 563].

In the laboratory, sexually mature males fight, immatures do not, and mature males do not attack immatures [301, 302, 635]. Mature males and

Map 8.6. Bank vole.

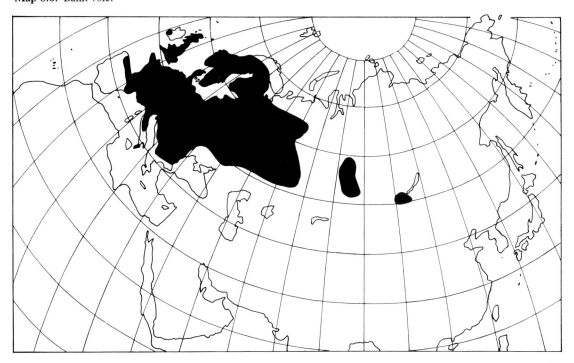

Table 8.6. Subspecies of the bank vole, *Clethrionomys glareolus*.

	C. g. glareolus	C. g. caesarius	C. g. skomerensis	C. g. alstoni	C. g. erica
Range	Mainland, etc.	Jersey	Skomer	Mull	Raasay
Dorsal colour (winter)	Dull	Dull	Bright	Dull	Dull
Ventral wash (winter)	Buff	Buff	Cream	Buff	Buff
Hind feet (mm)	Small (< 17.8)	Large (> 17.8)	Large (> 17.8)	Large (> 17.8)	Large (> 17.8)
Condylobasal length of skull (mm) (adults, spring)	Small (<24.2)	Large (> 24.2)	Large (> 24.2)	Large (> 24.2)	Large (> 24.2)
M³	Simple	Complex	Complex	Simple	Complex
Nasal bones: shape of posterior halves	Tapering	Tapering	Parallel-sided	Tapering	Tapering
Anterior palatal foramina: width as % of length	Narrow (< 30%)	Wide (> 30%)	Narrow (< 30%)	Medium (c. 30%)	Narrow (< 30%)

Table 8.7. Measurement of bank voles from Loch Tay, Tayside [164].

	First year, Aug−Nov		Second year, April	
	Mean ± SE	*n*	Mean ± SE	*n*
Head and body (mm)	90.8 ± 0.4	65	100.7 ± 0.7	38
Hind feet (mm)	16.7 ± 0.1	60	16.8 ± 0.1	57
Skull length (condylobasal) (mm)	22.1 ± 0.1	63	23.3 ± 0.1	32
Upper molar tooth row (mm)	5.38 ± 0.02	72	5.58 ± 0.02	40
Weight (g)	17.7 ± 0.3	70	♂ 26.1 ± 0.5	19
			♀ 21.9 ± 0.4	21

females defend familiar areas of a cage, females defend nest sites in large enclosures [195, 196]. Males are most aggressive in breeding season, females do not fight in laboratory tests at any season, but may defend home ranges in field [148, 579].

Dispersal [38] mostly during spring and early summer by both sexes around time of sexual maturation [753]. Proportion dispersing from natal site highest in optimal habitat [564]. Dispersers are lighter than residents [6, 654] but not genetically distinguishable [259]. More male and fewer female dispersers in breeding condition [495].

Movement is by walking or running, and homing ability after displacement is well developed [223, 708]. Tend to run for cover in the light. In the dark, older animals tend to orient better towards their home range than younger animals without a settled home range [466]. Olfactory and acoustic cues are more important than visual cues in homing [466, 708].

Juveniles are more easily caught in pitfall traps than adults, suggesting that exploratory ability improves with age and experience [17]. Sexual condition also influences the ability to trap in live traps: reproductive individuals more trappable than juveniles/subadults or post-reproductive individuals [18, 305].

Activity [23]: active throughout day and night in summer with peaks at dawn and dusk; less nocturnal activity in winter than summer [341, 479]. Variable short-term (2−6 hours) activity rhythm also observed [706]. Make runways above ground when low cover is available and are active burrowers, the tunnels being centred on a nest at 2−10 cm depth [877]. Nest in woodland made of

leaves, moss and feathers; in grassland of grass and moss. Breeding nests may be below ground or above ground in tree trunks.

Communication [784]: infants call both ultrasonically and audibly in the nest, with differences in intensity between races (e.g. mainland/Skomer) [5]. Adults sometimes emit high-pitched squeaks, particularly during aggressive interactions, as well as a sound like teeth-chattering [1, 784]. High frequency mating calls also made [784]. Males able to distinguish odour of females of their own race (e.g. mainland/Skomer) [312], and urine marking patterns differ between races [452].

FEEDING

Almost wholly herbivorous [854]. In Britain, fleshy fruits and seeds with a soft testa are eaten when available; the leaves of woody plants are preferred to those of herbs, and dead leaves are eaten in winter. Other food items include fungi, moss, roots, flowers, grass, insects and worms. The young eat less seed than adults. The diet in deciduous forests in central Europe is very similar but without the emphasis on dead leaves [379, 418]. In planted spruce forests in central Europe, there is less emphasis on seed and more on fungi [419]. In taiga coniferous forests in Scandinavia, hardly any seeds or insects are taken [375, 380]; berries are eaten in late summer, fungi in summer−autumn and lichens in winter−spring.

Peak storage activity occurs in late autumn−winter and lowest in summer−autumn, seeds with relatively thin testa being stored while those with thick testa are eaten [22]. Beechmast may be scatter-hoarded in small caches (1−10 nuts) just beneath the litter layer or into the walls of subsurface runways [448]. In captivity food is stored when day

Fig. 8.11. Hazel nuts opened by: (a) common dormouse; (b) wood mouse; (c) bank vole. Note the smooth inner edge of the hole in the case of the dormouse. (Photo: G. Barbour.)

length is reduced from 12−8 hours [574].

Hazel nuts are opened with a clean-edged hole [226] (Fig. 8.11) and only the flesh of rose hips is eaten [232]. Cocoons of forest moths (e.g. the bordered white, *Bupalus piniarias*) are also eaten [502]. In some winters they will strip the bark of elder bushes and eat the cambium below [756]. Refection has been observed in the nest [23]. The greatest daily energy demands are required by lactating females [343, 458].

BREEDING [128, 303]
Breeding is seasonal (March−October) although winter breeding is known to occur. Average litter size is around four and successive litters can be produced at intervals of 3−4 weeks.
Gestation; 18−20 days.
Litter size (laboratory); mean 3.2−4.5.
Litter size (in wild); up to seven usually three to four.
Weight at birth; 2 g.
Duration of lactation: 17−18 days.

Length of breeding season varies greatly: it usually starts in April and ends by September−October, but in some years it continues until December or does not stop at all, depending upon the abundance of seed food [272, 753]. The experimental addition of food [858] or mild temperatures [459] may bring forward the start of breeding by 2−3 weeks. However, under laboratory conditions it is photoperiod that is the crucial proximate factor controlling sexual maturation, and ambient temperature or its interaction with photoperiod plays no part [139]. There is some evidence that at high population density breeding season ends earlier [61, 202, 157]. This is also the case for cyclic populations; breeding season is extended in years of low density and curtailed in years of high density [868]. Habitat quality may also affect length of breeding season [459]. Skomer form has a very short breeding season lasting from May to September [397, 449]. In the absence of winter breeding, females remain non-parous and the testes of males regress over winter.

In the laboratory there are no oestrous cycles. Ovulation is induced by mating. Females may become pregnant post-partum, but if they do not conceive at this time they do not become pregnant until after lactation [142, 365]. Loss of pre-implantation embryos can be caused by introduction of a strange male into the cage of a pregnant female ('pregnancy block'). The failure of pregnancy is caused by a block to the release of prolactin leading to an inadequate supply of the progesterone that is necessary for implantation. The female will return to oestrus, and the formerly unfamiliar male, if still available, will mate and, in the absence of further disturbances, the eggs so fertilised will implant and later yield a litter. It seems likely that pregnancy block is caused by a urinary factor (pheromone) in males since the soiled bedding from the cage of an alien male is known to interrupt post-implantation pregnancy in several microtine rodents [713, 764]. In wild populations, females with several generations of corpora lutea have been found [106]; however, this is not sufficient evidence for pregnancy block [139].

Gestation in first pregnancy lasts 18.3 days [365]. The interbirth interval for subsequent pregnancies is dependent on the size of the suckling litter (20 days with one young to 22 days with six young), although it can go up to 27 days or more [9, 142, 365]. Mean number of corpora lutea in laboratory 4.7 (first pregnancy) to 5.5 (11—12th pregnancy) [139]; in field 3.3—3.9 [6]. Number of placental scars (in laboratory) sometimes exceeds number of young born, attributable to loss of embryos in the later stages of pregnancy or to the retention of scars from previous pregnancies [7, 171]. Maximum longevity of placental scars in the laboratory is 182 days [7]. In the wild, average number of placental scars is 3.4—3.9 depending on season and habitat.

Litter size in wild up to seven, very variable, affected by season, female body weight and age, litter succession, population density, altitude and geographical distribution [889]. Litter size also greater in optimal habitat [6]. Average litter size (in laboratory) varies from 3.2 (first litter) to 3.9 (fifth litter) in Britain [9, 139]. Sex ratio at birth is 1 : 1 (in laboratory), but female mortality is higher at birth so that sex ratio of surviving young is in favour of males [365]. In the field, sex ratio is generally in favour of males [10].

Young weigh *c.* 2 g at birth and are weaned at 17—18 days. Incisors are partially erupted at birth, all molars erupted by 28—30 days [560]. At birth they are naked and blind, the dorsal skin darkens at *c.* 3 days, pelage appears between days 4—10 and the eyes open at *c.* 12 days. Early growth in the laboratory varies with the number in the litter and temperature [641]; in the field, growth is retarded if no dispersal is allowed [562]. Thermoregulation is usually fully developed by 16—19 days [634].

In the wild, females born early in the season may reach sexual maturity and breed in the same year; however, sexual maturity of yearlings is suppressed by the presence of adult females [127, 128]. Sexual maturity is delayed in late born females until the beginning of next breeding season.

In the laboratory, females may become pregnant by the age of 31 days, although there is evidence to suggest that the fertility of young females is higher if they have experienced one or two sterile matings [363]. If young males are kept in groups of two or four, puberty is delayed in males from cyclic, but not from non-cyclic populations. If, on the other hand, young males are exposed to unfamiliar mature males, non-cyclic males are suppressed, while cyclic ones are unaffected; different mechanisms for density regulation of maturation may have evolved in cyclic and non-cyclic populations [303, 363].

POPULATION [10, 304, 406, 769]
Population fluctuations can be divided into two major types; multi-annual cycles (normally of 4-year duration) in the north (> 61°N in Scandinavia) [381] and less predictable annual changes in numbers in the south [10]. Northern cyclic populations are characterised by an increase and decline lasting approximately 3 years followed by extremely low densities for at least 1 year [382].

Non-cyclic populations do not reach very high densities, although a maximum of 137 per hectare was recorded near Oxford [621] and a maximum of 475 per hectare on Skomer [397].

Southern non-cyclic populations tend to be more variable. Most (75%) show annual cycles with spring declines; numbers increase over the summer to reach peak density in autumn followed by a decline over winter and spring [10]. However, some populations increase over spring to reach peak density in the summer [6]. In some years, numbers tend to increase from winter to summer after winter breeding [756]. Although there is no evidence for multi-annual cycles in Britain, numbers may fluctuate dramatically [760]. Densities in the south vary enormously according to season and habitat; from less than 5 to well over 130 per hectare.

Population structure and survival: the over-wintering population (young born in the latter part of the previous year and a few parous adults) grow rapidly in spring and produce the first generation. Although the young born in latter part of spring and summer have the potential for breeding themselves, mortality of these animals is very high (less than 50% survive more than 4 months) [664]. By late summer, the population is made up almost entirely of animals born that year. Animals born in the autumn grow slowly without reaching sexual maturity in the year of their birth and form the bulk of the overwintering population [10]. Winter breeding will alter this sequence of events [621].

Longevity is very variable, being dependent on a large number of factors. Spring and summer young have shorter life-span, probably due to greater intraspecific strife at this time of the year. Survival over autumn and winter is relatively better. Density may also influence longevity; at high density in Poland, mean length of life was 2.2 months compared with 3.2 months at low density [99]. In the field, animals may be followed for 18 months or more; in the laboratory survival to 40 months has been recorded [312]. In cyclic populations, survival of cohorts also depends on the phase of the multi-annual cycle [868]. Trap-revealed sex ratio usually in favour of males; an analysis of 26 non-cyclic populations showed that the ratio was in favour of males throughout the year with the greatest difference in male and female numbers over autumn and winter (high density), and lowest over spring and early summer (low density) [10].

MORTALITY [483]

Although 14 vertebrate predators are known [334], only a few of them are important in ecological terms; they include the tawny owl, which may account for 20–30% of the standing crop, and the weasel on mainland Britain [480, 483, 760]. On Skomer island, barn owls take a large proportion of juveniles but only a few adults [122]. In E Europe, one of the most important predators is the adder (*Vipera berus*) which can account for a large number of migrants, pregnant females and juveniles [657, 661]. Other predators include the stoat, polecat, mink, marten, cat and fox.

Adverse environmental factors may affect mortality either directly or indirectly; e.g. duration of snow cover may influence mortality directly [719] or indirectly through reduced predation [382].

Food conditions may also affect mortality, e.g. with reduced winter mortality in years of abundant acorn and beech mast [61, 100, 373, 447]. In years of high population density, mortality rates may increase, e.g. it was found that in spring 50% of the overwintered animals belonged to the previous autumn generation whereas in years of low density only 20% were of this generation.

PARASITES [398]

Ectoparasites: fleas are widespread, commonly found species are *Ctenophthalmus nobilis*, *Megabothris turbidus*, *M. walkeri*, *Amalaraeus penicilliger* and *Hystrichopsylla talpae*; *Rhadinopsylla integella*, *R. isacantha*, *C. congener* and *M. rectangulatus* are local (Table 8.8). *R. pentacantha* and *Peromyscopsylla spectabilis* are widespread, but less frequently recorded.

Lice; the sucking-louse *Hoplopleura acanthopus* has been recorded, but is perhaps more a parasite of the field vole.

Mites; *Haemogamasus nidi*, *H. pontiger*, *Listrophorus leuckarti*, *Trombicula autumnalis* are common. Others include *Asca affinis*, *Eugamasus magnus*, *Eulaelaps stabularis*, *Haemogamasus michaeli*, *H. hirsutus H. pygmaeus*, *Laelaps festinus*, *Microthrombidium pusillum* and *Parasitus spinipes*.

Ticks; *Ixodes trianguliceps*, *I. apronophorus*.

Endoparasites: helminths (Tables 8.9 and 8.10). The orbital fluid frequently contains many larval nematodes, possibly of a species of *Rhabditis*.

Serological evidence of infection with nine viral species has been recorded [464] and infections with three genera of Rickettsia have been detected [886]. Eleven species of bacteria have been isolated including *Mycobacterium tuberculosis* var. *muris* [862], *Mycoplasma* sp. [335], *Campylobacter fetus* [261], *C. jejuni*, *Yersinia* spp. [397] and three other species of common enteric bacteria [399]. Infection with the spirochaete bacterium *Leptospira* is widespread, highest infection rates being found in the smallest weight groups [825]. Many species of parasitic protozoa have been recorded [174, 398]. Infections with the ringworm fungus *Trichophyton persicolor* have been reported [240].

Although increased levels of disease have been found in peak or declining populations of bank voles [398], the role of disease in population fluctuations is unclear [428].

Table 8.8. Incidence of fleas on small rodents.

	Voles				Mice				Rats		Common dormouse
	Bank	Field	Orkney	Water	Wood	Yellow-necked	Harvest	House	Common	Ship	
Xenopsylla cheopis									(X)	X	
Hystrichopsylla talpae	X	X	X	X	X						
Typhloceras poppei		(X)			X			(X)			
Rhadinopsylla integella	X	X									
Rhadinopsylla isacantha	X										
Rhadinopsylla pentacantha	X	(X)			X				(X)		
Ctenophthalmus nobilis	X	X	X	X	X	X	X	(X)	X	(X)	(X)
Ctenophthalmus congener	X										
Leptopsylla segnis					(X)	(X)	.	X		X	
Peromyscopsylla spectabilis	X	(X)		(X)	(X)	(X)					
Amalaraeus penicilliger	X	X	X	(X)	(X)	(X)		(X)	(X)		
Nosopsyllus fasciatus	(X)	(X)		(X)	(X)	(X)	(X)	(X)	X	X	(X)
Nosopsyllus londiniensis					(X)			X	X	X	
Megabothris rectangulatus	X	X			X		X	(X)			
Megabothris turbidus	X	X			X		X	(X)	(X)		(X)
Megabothris walkeri	X	X		X	(X)			(X)	(X)		

X, Regular and common; (X), less frequent.

Table 8.9. Tapeworms (Eucestoda) and flukes (Digenea) recorded from some British rodents [526].

	Bank vole	Field vole	Wood mouse	Yellow-necked mouse	House mouse	Common rat
Tapeworms						
Hymenolepis diminuta			+	+	+	+ +
Rodentolepis microstoma			+		+	+
Rodentolepis straminea					+	+
Staphylocystis murissylvatici			+ +	+		
Hydatigena taeniaeformis	+ +	+ +	+ +	+ +	+ +	
Catenotaenia pusilla	+ +	+	+ +	+	+	
Skrjabinotaenia lobata	+ +		+ +	+		
Flukes						
Brachylaimus recurvum (small intestine)			+ +	+		+
Corrigia vitta (pancreas, duodenum)	+	+	+ +	+		

+, Present; + +, particularly common.

Table 8.10. Nematode worms recorded from some British rodents [526]. All are intestinal except *Pelodera strongyloides* (eyes and skin).

	Bank vole	Field vole	Wood mouse	Yellow-necked mouse	House mouse	Common rat
Capillaria murissylvatici	+ +	+	+ +	+		
Trichuris muris	+	+	+	+	+	
Pelodera strongyloides	+ +	+	+ +	+		
Heligmosomoides glareoli	+ +	+				
Heligmosomoides polygyrus	+		+ +	+ +	+	
Syphacia muris						+ +
Syphacia obvelata	+ +	+			+ +	
Syphacia stroma			+ +	+ +		
Aspiculuris tetraptera	+	+	+	+	+	

+, Present; + +, particularly common.

RELATIONS WITH MAN

On the Continent it is known as an occasional forestry pest, not only eating seeds and seedlings, but barking small trees, especially larch and elder, up to 5 m [877]. Evidence shows that bark eating occurs mainly during peak densities in winter [416, 418, 507] when the volume of bark in the diet may double. Bark may be a marginal food likely to be consumed in relatively large quantities during periods of food shortage [507]. Bark eating has also been reported in Britain [469]. The lead content has been shown to increase to 1.81 ± 0.61 ppm wet weight near main roads compared with $1.50 \pm$ 0.17 ppm in woodland and arable sites [444]. Easily takes to captivity and breeds freely; Skomer form remarkable for its docility. Can be maintained in captivity on a diet of hay and oats.

LITERATURE

Flowerdew *et al.* [279] — a volume of symposium papers on ecology and behaviour. Stenseth [769] — a volume of symposium papers on population dynamics, dispersal, reproduction and social structure.

SOUND RECORDINGS

Appendix 3: A, P.

AUTHORS FOR THIS SPECIES
S.K. Alibhai and J.H.W. Gipps.

GENUS *Microtus*

A large genus with *c.* 45 species distributed throughout the Palaearctic and Nearctic regions (*c.* 65 if the closely similar species of *Pitymys* are included). The species are superficially very similar, being small with short ears, short tail and rather long, soft pelage, usually greyish or yellowish brown. They are the dominant herbivorous rodents in many habitats and have sharply angled, rootless molar teeth capable of dealing with grass and other abrasive fodder.

Only one species, *M. agrestis*, occurs on the British mainland, but another, *M. arvalis*, probably introduced, occurs on the Orkney Islands and on Guernsey. The most clear-cut difference is in the shape of the second upper molars (Fig. 8.12).

Species of *Microtus* were well represented in the Pleistocene in Britain. The most abundant species in deposits from the Last Glaciation is *M. oeconomus*. This now has a northern and eastern distribution in Europe and has not been found living in Britain, but subfossil remains have been recorded from as late as the Bronze Age on the Isles of Scilly [650].

Field vole *Microtus agrestis*

Mus agrestis Linnaeus, 1761; Uppsala, Sweden.
Arvicola hirta Bellamy, 1839; Yealmpton, Devon.
Arvicola neglectus Jenyns, 1841; Megarnie, Perthshire.
Arvicola britannicus de Sélys Longchamps, 1847; England.
Microtus agrestoides Hinton, 1910; Grays Thurrock, Essex; Pleistocene.

Short-tailed vole, short-tailed field mouse.

RECOGNITION

A small, greyish brown vole, with small ears and eyes, a blunt snout and short tail. The colour of the back varies from greyish to yellowish brown but never shows the deep chestnut colour of the bank vole. Young may be confused except that the tail is longer in the bank vole. Young water voles similar but have larger hind feet (over 21 mm) and relatively longer tails.

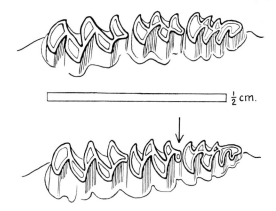

Fig. 8.12. Left upper molars of field vole (below) and Orkney vole (above) showing the additional lobe on M^2 (arrowed) characteristic of *Microtus agrestis*.

Skull more angular than that of the bank vole and recognised by the sharply angled prisms of the cheek-teeth which remain rootless. The molar tooth row never exceeds 7 mm. The additional postero-medial loop on M^2 is the most clear-cut difference between this species and *Microtus arvalis*.

SIGN

Their presence can be detected by well-formed runways at ground level amongst dense grass. Faeces oval in section and distinguished from those of the bank vole by green colour. Recent use of runs is indicated by the presence of droppings and small mounds of short nibbled grass leaves or stems.

DESCRIPTION

Greyish brown above, usually pure grey below but sometimes tinged with buff. No sexual dimorphism; juveniles darker grey than adults. No seasonal colour change, but summer coat is sparser, with coarser guard hairs and fewer fine hairs than the dense winter coat.

Moult: in S England there are a number of moults each year. Overwintered animals begin their spring moult in February and animals born during the summer have a succession of moults, ultimately producing an adult coat. This is replaced during the autumn moult, which is completed by October/November. No hair growth occurs during December and January.

Teeth: the molar teeth remain open-rooted throughout life and the column is continually renewed from the base of the tooth as it is worn away at the tip. Distinguishable from the molars of the bank vole by the sharp angles on the grinding surface and the presence of a fifth loop of enamel on M^2 (Fig. 8.12).

Chromosomes: $2n = 50$, $FNa = 50$; sex chromosomes unusually large [893].

MEASUREMENTS (Table 8.11).

VARIATION

The British form is not clearly distinguishable from continental populations, its separation as a subspecies, *hirtus*, having been based only on average differences of colour and size that are overshadowed by clinal variation within Britain.

Within the British mainland there is an increase in size and darkening of colour towards the north, the largest and the darkest animals being in the Scottish Highlands. A fourth inner ridge on M^1 is variable in all populations but increases in size and frequency towards the north with a more marked increase in Scotland between the central Highlands and the NW Highlands. It also increases significantly with altitude [151].

The following subspecific names have been proposed for Hebridean populations: *M. a. exsul* Miller, 1908; N Uist, Outer Hebrides. *M. a. mial* Barrett-Hamilton & Hinton, 1913; Island of Eigg, Inner Hebrides. *M. a. luch* Barrett-Hamilton & Hinton, 1913; Island of Muck, Inner Hebrides. *M. a. macgillivrayi* Barrett-Hamilton & Hinton, 1913; Island of Islay, Inner Hebrides. *M. a. fiona*

Montagu, 1922; Island of Gigha, Inner Hebrides.

Of these only *M. a. macgillivrayi* on Islay is sufficiently distinctive to warrant recognition as a subspecies, characterised by very dark greyish brown ventral pelage and consistently complex M^1.

Hebridean animals mostly resemble those from western mainland of Scotland in size and colour. M^1 is mainly complex (as in the NW Highlands) in the Outer Hebrides and on Skye, Scalpay, Eigg, Luing and Islay; but simpler (as in central Highlands) on Muck, Mull, Jura, Scarba, Lismore, Gigha, Arran and Bute [164].

Differences in the frequencies of 25 skeletal variants (involving skull, vertebrae, girdles and long bones), were found between populations from mid-Wales and Oxford [83].

Reported mutants in coat colour include Agouti (main alternatives black or black and tan), Pink-eye (normal pigmentation or red eye and pale coat) and Piebald (normal or white spotting on coat) [690]. Piebalds and pale-coated forms occasionally found; albinos rare and melanics very rare.

There is a widespread polymorphism for the presence or absence of a serum esterase (E1), controlled by four autosomal alleles [725]. At high population densities, animals lacking the enzyme activity (E1 negative genotype) increase in frequency, but appear to be less well adapted to winter conditions than E1 positive genotypes, which survive better in normal winters. Thus, a selective balance maintains the polymorphism. The species is also polymorphic for other enzymes [703].

DISTRIBUTION

The only species of *Microtus* on the British mainland where it is ubiquitous. It occurs on most of the

Table 8.11 Measurements of field voles from Loch Tay, Tayside [151].

| | First year, Sept–Oct (both sexes) | | Second year, April | | | | All seasons | | | |
| | | | Males | | Females | | Males | | Females | |
	Mean	n	Mean	n	Mean	n	Mean	n	Mean	n
Head and body (mm)	102	83	121	20	115	26				
Skull length (condylobasal) (mm)	23.9	118	26.1	17	25.2	21				
Weight (g)	20.8	118	39.7	20	30.9	25				
Hind feet* (mm)							17.4	101	17.0	85

*All animals with head and body over 90 mm.

Hebridean islands, but is absent from Lewis, Barra, some Inner Hebrides (S Rona, Raasay, Rhum, Colonsay, Pabay, Soay), Orkney (where it is replaced by *M. arvalis*) and Shetland. Also absent from Ireland, Isle of Man, Lundy, Isles of Scilly and the Channel Islands.

HISTORY

Well represented in British fossil sites from the penultimate (Wolstonian) glaciation onwards [494]. Subfossil teeth dated between 1500 and 2500 bp on the island of Jura, Inner Hebrides, show a slight but progressive simplification of the pattern of M^1 since that time [160].

HABITAT

Mainly rough, ungrazed grassland, including young forestry plantations with a lush growth of grass. Low population densities occur in marginal habitats such as woodlands, hedgegrow, blanket bog, dunes, scree and moorland, to over 1300 m in the Cairngorms.

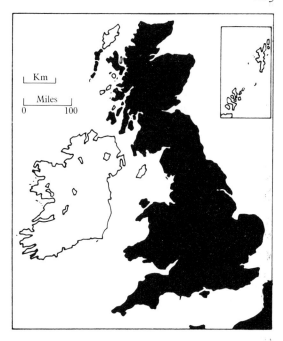

Map 8.7. Field vole.

Map 8.8. Field vole.

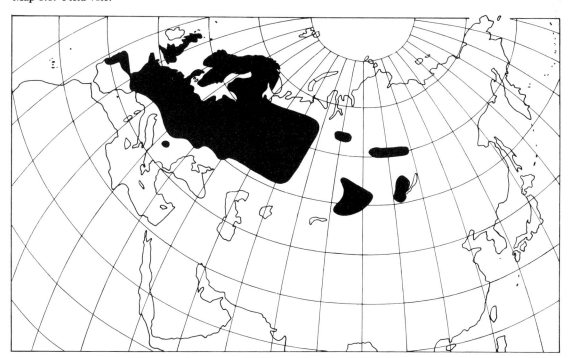

Home range: breeding females have overlapping home ranges, whereas males' ranges are more mutually exclusive [613, 832]. Adults' ranges are relatively static, subadults are more nomadic (cf. more territorial nature of breeding female bank voles).

Little data on home-range sizes, or on the variation between ages, sexes or seasons. Mean size of female home ranges in spring and summer has been estimated as 198 m^2 using radio-tracking [311]. In Finland males' ranges estimated at *c.* 600 m^2, females' *c.* 300 m^2, with females' being negatively correlated with density and food availability.

Communication and senses: olfaction is important in communication. Functional odours are found in faeces (caudal glands), urine (preputial glands) and are probably produced by flank glands. Individuals respond to strange odours (e.g. urine of predators) and can discriminate between their own odour, the odour of another conspecific and that of a closely related species [141, 195, 782, 783]. Auditory, tactile and visual communication little studied; there is evidence that new objects in a vole's cage are explored by all these senses, but most importantly by smell.

Aggression: overt aggression is shown by adult males in staged encounters in the laboratory, and by lactating and pregnant females, particularly in nest defence; juveniles of both sexes relatively immune from attack. In laboratory colonies, a single animal, usually male, becomes dominant [138, 196].

Dispersal: young females disperse from their mother's home range less often than subadult males, which are probably driven out by adult males. Dispersal of subadults particularly marked in mid-summer. Breeding females may also form a major dispersing group [374, 613, 659, 832].

Activity generally nocturnal in summer, based on trapping studies, treadle-use monitoring and passage counters in laboratory and field [53, 188, 242, 243, 513, 608, 629, 677] but more diurnal in winter [53, 242, 243]. Juveniles tend to be more nocturnal than adults [53]. Activity peaks at dawn and dusk

revealed by trapping [118]. High daytime temperatures lead to nocturnal activity in summer, cold winter nights encourage a diurnal pattern [53, 188, 242, 513]. General activity levels increase in overcast or rainy conditions, but decrease with rainfall associated with low temperatures [53, 514]. Activity levels also affected by light levels [245, 513], and circadian rhythms are entrained by daily light rhythms [513, 608]. Short-term (ultradian) activity rhythm also shown, with somewhat variable period between 2−4 hours [185] as in many other *Microtus* species [548]. Ultradian rhythm has genetical basis, associated with latitudinal and population dynamic differences [677], perhaps related to avoidance of nest fouling [513].

FEEDING

Herbivorous, feeding primarily on green leaves and stems of grasses [247, 373]. However, in S Finland, it was found that herbs were preferred to the available grasses and sedges [612] and in N Finland, bark was eaten in addition to herbaceous plants and grasses [461]. Under laboratory conditions, consumption of different grasses in autumn and winter was proportional to availability, and in spring and summer there was a preference for the more succulent species [653]. They showed an increase in preference for the more familiar diet [640].

BREEDING

Breeding is seasonal (March−October) and a succession of litters of four to six young is produced, with the young born at the beginning of the breeding season usually reproducing the same year.
Gestation: 18−20 days.
Litter size (laboratory): four to six.
Litter size (in wild): two to seven.
Weight at birth: 2 g.
Duration of lactation: 14−28 days.

Length of breeding season varies, usually from about March/April to September/October although winter breeding is known to occur [507]. Photoperiod is the principal environmental factor controlling sexual development [33, 143, 342, 763] but it may be modified by social factors. Vaginal perforation of weaned females is hastened when they are in direct contact with mature males [140], and females reared in the presence of mature males (or exposed to their bedding) have a more advanced state of sexual maturation (as indicated by uterine weight) [763].

Ovulation is induced [29, 107] but this may be by stimuli other than those associated with mating; e.g. virgin females kept in a cage containing a wire mesh maze occupied by a sexually mature male can have several separate ovulations, at intervals of about 5 days [575]. Corpora lutea formed as a result are short lived [575, 576]. The elimination of tactile, auditory and visual stimuli is accompanied by a considerable decrease in the incidence of ovulation. Laboratory experiments have shown that a strange male will block the pregnancy of a female previously mated with a stud male (Bruce effect).

Litter size may be affected by many factors including season, weight (age) of females and their parity. In Finland litter size also increases from south to north and with different phases of cyclic populations [613]. Fertility declines somewhat on days 9, 10 and 11 of a 14-day lactation [108]. Females become sexually mature at the age of about 6 weeks, dependent on photoperiod and social factors.

Plant derivatives, such as 6-MBOA, known to effect reproduction in other species such as *Microtus montanus* [60, 710], do not seem to have any effect on reproduction in *M. agrestis*.

POPULATION [304, 498, 766, 792]
Seasonal breeding pattern leads to recruitment of most young in summer/early autumn. A few individuals breed in the year of their birth, then regress; most overwinter as subadults. Very few animals survive two winters [135, 613].

Multi-annual cycles very pronounced in north of range (Scotland, N Scandinavia), weaker or sometimes absent further south [374, 382, 404 613, 792, 601, 781]. Both cyclic and annual changes in numbers associated with changes in other characteristics (e.g. body weight, survival, growth and reproduction [613, 725].

Predation thought to be important in damping cycles, and in keeping decreasing numbers low [14, 246, 377, 404]. Predator numbers follow changes in cyclic populations [246, 443, 792]; shrew and vole populations may cycle in synchrony, suggesting predator's influence. Limitations of food supply probably occurs rarely, when predator pressure is low [376]; evidence for direct link between food supply and population cycle somewhat contradic-

tory [15, 504].

Intrinsic mechanisms (genetics, behaviour) now thought insufficient, alone, to generate cycles; recent emphasis on habitat structure and quality, and the dispersal movements, mediated by social behaviour, of individuals between patches of different quality [304, 374, 768, 771]. Evolutionary aspects of microtine cycles discussed by Stenseth [767].

Success in competition with other species depends on the composition of the local rodent community, and on the structure of the habitat. Field voles generally subordinate to water voles, dominant over bank voles [405, 613, 832].

MORTALITY
Preyed upon by many birds and mammals including heron, kestrel, buzzard, eagle, harriers, barn owl, tawny owl, long- and short-eared owls, foxes, stoats, weasels, polecats, pine-martens, wildcats and badgers [14]. Foxes tend to prefer this species to other small rodents [546].

Predation rates vary with season and population density. In Sweden a high predation rate at the beginning of the breeding season delayed and reduced the annual recovery of a population [246]. It is suggested that predation is the primary factor preventing populations from cycling at intervals of 3–4 years in S Sweden [246]. Conversely, density fluctuations in this species may influence those of stoats and weasels [246, 482].

PARASITES

Ectoparasites: fleas are widespread, commonly found species are *Ctenophthalmus nobilis, Megabothris turbidus, M. walkeri, Histrichopsylla talpae,* and *Amalaraeus penicilliger. Rhadinopsylla integella* and *Megabothris rectangulatus* are local. *R. pentacantha* and *Peromyscopsylla spectabilis* are less frequent on this host. Other rodent fleas, such as *Nosopsyllus fasciatus*, are sometimes recorded.

Lice; *Haplopleura acanthopus*, a sucking louse specific to *Microtus* spp.

Ticks; *Ixodes ricinus, Ixodes triunguliceps.*

Mites; *Trombicula autumnalis, Eulaelaps stabularis, Laelaps hilaris* and *Haemogamasus nidi* commonly found as on other rodents; the hair mite *Listrophorus leuckarti* is more host-specific.

Fungus; The human ringworm fungus, *Trichophyton persicolor*, occurs in wild populations, with a 25% infection rate in voles from Berkshire [239, 241].

Endoparasites: helminths (Tables 8.9 and 8.10).

Protozoa; Several genera of protozoa are regularly encountered, as follows [174, 235, 867] — Gut: *Entamoeba* sp. (non-pathogenic); intestinal flagellates, including the genera *Chilomastix*, *Hexamita*, *Trichomonas* (non-pathogenic), the coccidian *Eimeria falciformis* (responsible for enteritis). Blood [34]: *Hepatozoon microti* (in leucocytes and infecting lungs and liver); *Babesia microti* (transmitted by ticks); *Trypanosoma microti* [586]; *Grahamella microti*. Brain: *Frankelia microti* and possibly *Toxoplasma gondii* [790]. Striped muscle: *Sarcocystis* sp.

Leptospira bacteria, the causative agent of leptospirosis in man, have been isolated from this species [114]. Serological studies revealed the following infection rates in natural vole populations: Derbyshire — 21%; Surrey — 33% [824]. *Myobacterium tuberculosis*, the cause of enzootic tuberculosis in wild populations, was isolated from a naturally infected vole. *Yersinia pseudotuberculosis*, the cause of pseudotuberculosis in man, has been isolated from this species [823]. Lung lesions due to *Corynebacterium kutscheri* have been described [50].

RELATIONS WITH MAN
At high densities, they can cause considerable damage to grassland and young plantations of fruit trees, woody-stemmed ornamental plants and forest trees. In arable land, they have been held responsible for damage to cereal crops, by cutting through the stem close to the ground and eating the stem and leaves. In 1920s and 1930s, problems of this kind were common in Britain [235], but now the problem is confined to Scandinavia [463] where populations are known to cycle, reaching very high densities at peak populations [613]. A possible source of infection of ringworm [239] and jaundice (leptospirosis).

SOUND RECORDINGS
Appendix 3: A, F, J.

AUTHORS FOR THIS SPECIES
J.H.W. Gipps and S.K. Alibhai, with acknowledgement to Dianne Evans (author in 2nd edition).

Orkney and Guernsey voles *Microtus arvalis*

Mus arvalis Pallas, 1779; Germany.

Microtus sarnius Miller, 1909; St Martins, Guernsey, Channel Islands.
Microtus orcadensis Millais, 1904; Pomona (= Mainland), Orkney Islands.

Common vole (continental Europe). Many local names in Orkney: cuttick; cutoo (East Mainland); volo (Evie); voloo (Harray); vole-mouse.

RECOGNITION
The only vole present on the Orkney Islands and Guernsey. The teeth differ from those of field vole in that M^2 lacks a terminal inward-facing loop (*see* Fig. 8.8).

DESCRIPTION
Closely resembles field vole but the coat tends to be shorter and the ears less hairy.

SIGN
Network of runs and tunnels ramifies through the vegetation and beneath the surface of the ground [843]. The same tunnels may be used over a number of years. Grass clippings are often present in the tunnels. Piles of green to black faeces are deposited at latrines which are dispersed at fairly regular intervals along the tunnels and runs, sometimes in side chambers. Usually there is only one nest, with several entrances and almost always underground.

RELATIONSHIPS
Microtus arvalis of earlier authors has recently been found to comprise two widely sympatric sibling species with distinctive karyotypes: *M. arvalis* with 2n = 46, mostly metacentric; and *M. rossiaemeridionalis* (synonyms *epiroticus*, *subarvalis*) with 2n = 54, mostly acrocentric [549]. Voles from Orkney Mainland have 2n = 46 [557, 721].

MEASUREMENTS (Table 8.12).

VARIATION
The island forms can be distinguished from continental animals (and to a lesser extent from each other) as shown in Table 8.13. The relevant subspecific names are:
M. a. orcadensis Millais, 1904. Synonyms: *M. orcadensis ronaldshaiensis* Hinton, 1913: 457 (island of South Ronaldsay); *M. orcadensis rousaiensis* Hinton, 1913: 460 (island of Rousay).
M. a. sandayensis Millais, 1905 (island of Sanday.) Synonym: *M. sandayensis westrae* Miller, 1908

Table 8.12. Measurements of adult Orkney voles from Orkney Mainland, July–August.

	Males (n = 39)		Females (n = 38)	
	Mean	Range	Mean	Range
Head and body (mm)	122	98–134	118	97–128
Tail (mm)	39	28–44	36	27–41
Weight (g)	42	29–67	36	22–55

Table 8.13. Subspecies of *Microtus arvalis*.

	M. a. orcadensis	*M. a. sandayensis*	*M. a. sarnius*	*M. a. arvalis*
Range	Orkney: Mainland, Rousay, S Ronaldsay	Orkney: Sanday, Westray	Guernsey	Lowland W Europe
Size	Large	Large	Large	Small
Max. skull length (condylobasal) (mm)	*c.* 30	*c.* 29	*c.* 28	*c.* 24
Dorsal pelage	Dark	Lighter	Lighter	Lighter
Ventral colour	Strongly suffused with orange-buff	Lightly suffused with creamy buff	Pure grey	±lightly suffused with creamy buff
M_1 anterior outer groove	Deep	Shallow	Deep	Moderately deep

(island of Westray).

M. a. sarnius Miller, 1909 (Guernsey).

Totally black individuals occur sporadically in Orkney as do examples of 'abrasion melanism' with a black patch on the back or rump due to loss of the hair tips, possibly as a result of fire (specimens in BM (NH)).

DISTRIBUTION

In the British Isles restricted to Guernsey and six of the Orkney Islands: Mainland, Westray, Sanday, Stronsay, S Ronaldsay and Rousay.

HISTORY

The population on Guernsey may have been introduced or it may have been present since the end of the Pleistocene when the island was connected to continental Europe; the fact that epigenetic polymorphisms indicate a close relationship to adjacent continental populations [82] does not resolve the question.

Probably introduced to Orkney by Neolithic settlers between *c.* 3700 BC, the earliest known human settlement, and 3400 BC, the earliest strata containing the species [163]. Radiocarbon dates derived directly from vole bones from Westray were 4800 ± 120 and 3590 ± 80 years bp (OxA−1081, 1080). Arguments have been made for a south European origin on the basis of epigenetic characteristics [82], but there is no real basis for identifying any particular European population as the ancestral one [163]. All Orkney voles are characterised by large body size, being much larger than most continental animals. However, on the basis of the size of molar teeth they appear to have *declined* in size since the Neolithic [163]. Neolithic samples from the islands of Westray and Orkney mainland show that the dental difference (in M_1) now apparent was then less pronounced [163].

Neolithic remains from the Orkney island of Holm of Papa Westray might represent an extinct population but could perhaps have been carried there by raptors [163]. They were present on the Orkney island of Shapinsay to 1906 [75], but voles appeared to be absent from there by 1943 [408].

Fossil records of *M. arvalis* from mainland Britain are all doubtful because of confusion with related species [494].

HABITAT

Present in most habitats in Orkney: coniferous and

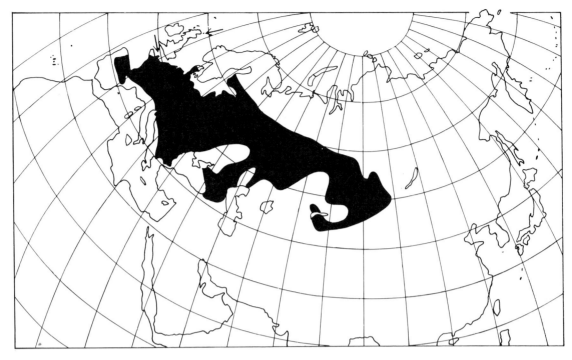

Map 8.9. Orkney/Guernsey vole.

deciduous plantations, marsh, heather moorland, hay meadows, ditches, gardens, but largely absent from arable land and short pastures [408, 689, 820]. In Guernsey appear to be more common in wet meadows than in drier hedgebanks [94].

SOCIAL ORGANISATION AND BEHAVIOUR

Social organisation: radio-tracking studies indicate that in July–August Orkney voles are associated in monogamous pairs, each pair occupying a largely exclusive range with practically no overlap between the ranges of neighbouring pairs. Ranges probably defended; when animals removed their ranges rapidly taken over by neighbours. Young animals forage with their mother for several days after leaving the nest but then disperse away from the natal area. During the winter population densities are higher, animals are not associated in pairs, and there is much overlap between the ranges of neighbours.

In captivity, Orkney voles readily live in colonies with any combination of males and females. New animals introduced to an established colony are immediately killed as are residents temporarily removed and returned.

Home-range sizes vary from habitat to habitat and from season to season. Radio-tracking in Orkney in summer has revealed ranges as large as 3700 m² for voles living in overgrown ditch systems. At the other extreme, live-trapping along a dyke suggested that animals were occupying exclusive ranges with nests only 3 m apart [843].

Activity patterns: Orkney voles have been reported to be active only during darkness [843]; in fact they are active night and day, but not continuously so. In both the wild and in captivity they show a distinct rhythm of activity comprising alternating periods of rest and foraging (Fig. 8.13). In the wild they normally return to the nest to sleep but on occasion may do so in the tunnel system. The rhythm has a clear periodicity of around 3 hours, compared with 2–2.5 hours for continental *M. arvalis* and British *M. agrestis*.

FEEDING
Herbivorous, feeding on the leaves, stems and roots of a wide variety of grasses and dicotyledons.

BREEDING
On Guernsey, mating has been recorded in

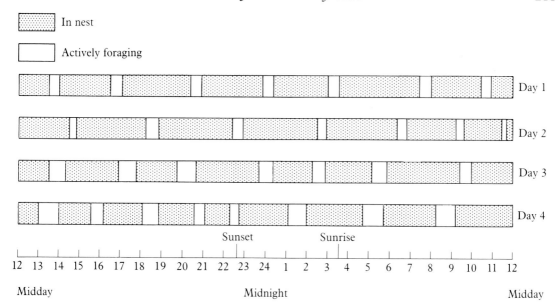

Fig. 8.13. The pattern of activity shown by a wild Orkney vole over four consecutive 24-hour periods in summer. The animal's movements were determined by radio-telemetry.

February, and young are difficult to distinguish from adults by August. Number of fetuses in eight females ranged from two to five, mean 3.3 [94].

On Orkney mainland 60–100% of females were pregnant in August and 30–50% in early September [689]. Weights of male reproductive organs and numbers of stored spermatozoa declined in early September. Reproductive output appears to vary with population density; fewer embryos are resorbed in low-density populations than in higher ones, while male reproductive organs weigh more at the low densities [689].

For captive Orkney voles, mean litter sizes are 2.7 for 508 births [520] and 2.9 (median 3, range 1–6) for 319 litters [1]. In a colony kept under ambient conditions in NE Scotland litters were born in every month of the year but most in the period April–August.

In captivity, gestation and lactation each last for about 20 days. The male spends much time in the nest with the young, grooms them and will retrieve them when displaced [184].

Crosses producing fertile young have been made between animals from Orkney and Guernsey [180] and from Orkney and Germany [895].

POPULATION

In Orkney, population densities vary widely from habitat to habitat. Densities (voles per hectare) have been measured on Orkney mainland in July–August: damp heath 273; heather moorland 102; marsh 57; coniferous plantation with grass understorey 29, with heather understorey 129; pasture 0 [689].

Animals born in one summer breed in the next and then die. The autumn population thus consists largely of young of the year. Overwinter survival and consequent breeding densities vary markedly from year to year. Major predators in Orkney are hen harriers, short-eared owls and domestic cats (100% of 1264 cat scats collected at Kingsdale, mainland contained vole remains).

PARASITES

The ubiquitous rodent fleas *Amalaraeus penicilliger*, *Ctenophthalmus nobilis* and *Hystrichopsylla talpae* occur on the Orkney vole.

SOUND RECORDINGS
Appendix 3: J, P.

AUTHOR FOR THIS SPECIES
M.L. Gorman.

GENUS *Arvicola*

A Palaearctic genus of two species, rather closely related to *Microtus*. They differ in their large size, relatively longer tail and more prominent glandular regions on the flanks. The cheek-teeth remain unrooted, as in *Microtus*, with a pattern of prisms resembling the simpler patterns found in *Microtus*, e.g. in *M. oeconomus*. Like *Microtus* they are adapted to feeding on tough vegetation including grass.

Besides *A. terrestris*, with a wide distribution from Britain to E Siberia, there is a more localised species, *A. sapidus*, in France and Iberia. The American water vole has sometimes been included in *Arvicola* but is more often allocated to *Microtus* (*M. richardsoni*).

Water vole *Arvicola terrestris*

Mus terrestris Linnaeus, 1758; Upsala, Sweden.
Mus amphibius Linnaeus, 1758; England.
Arvicola ater MacGillivray, 1832; Scotland.

Water rat.

RECOGNITION

Largest British vole (Fig. 8.14); rat-sized. Often mistaken for a common rat, but has darker fur (brown or black), a rounder body, a much shorter and chubby face with small, protuberant eyes (Fig. 8.15). The tail is shorter, the ears only just extend beyond the fur and both tail and ears are darker and more hairy than in the rat. Both species swim frequently and dive and jump well. Juvenile water voles resemble field voles, but the head and hind feet are much larger and the tail is much longer. The row of molars is longer (> 8 mm) than in all other British vole species (< 7 mm).

SIGN

Footprints show four toes on the fore and five on the hind feet. The track of the hind feet partially overlaps the imprint of the forefeet.

Faeces variable in colour and size dependent on the food eaten and the water content but usually show green when broken open. Usually $8-12$ mm in length and cylindrical with blunt ends. Deposited at latrine sites near the nest, at range boundaries, on runways and wherever they leave or enter the water [521].

Runways usually $4-9$ cm broad and within a metre of the water edge along densely vegetated banks of slow-flowing streams. Platforms develop at the water edge where voles frequently leave and enter the water. More rarely away from water when water voles tend to live exclusively below ground.

Nest usually below ground within complex burrow system. When the water table is high, water voles nest inside tussock sedges or at sites with higher ground. Nests are lined with finely shredded grasses and reeds. Exits from nursing chambers may or may not be plugged with loose soil or grass. Rarely, large balls of reed or grass are built for a nest above ground.

Fig. 8.14. Water vole.

Fig. 8.15. Water vole. (Photo: A. Bomford.)

Feeding remains frequently found on runways as neat piles of grass, reed or sedge blades. Where blades are bitten off the imprint of the two large incisors is prominent and diagnostic.

DESCRIPTION

Pelage: dorsal reddish, medium or dark brown or black. Melanic forms more typical for northern populations. Dorsal fur grading to lighter ventral fur which is brownish or greyish white. Guard hairs long and glossy, shorter and denser in juveniles. When excited guard hairs become erect giving ruffled appearance.

Moult: regular sublateral (ventral to dorsal) pattern at juvenile and adult autumn moult [499, 633]. Animals that survive one winter usually show sublateral, rarely head-to-rump spring moult. Those that survive a second winter show no signs of moult and fur appears thin [521].

Tail: terete, 55–70% of head and body length.

Head: skull of overwintered animals with definite nuchal crest. Temporal ridges unite in the interorbital region to form a low sagittal crest.

Teeth: molars are rootless (Fig. 8.16). Upper incisors are usually orthodont and on the outer surface the enamel is bright orange. Fur brushes extend from the upper lip behind the incisors downwards and close off the diastema when the vole uses its incisors for digging.

Sexes: the distance between the urinary papilla and the anus is not reliably sex specific. Sebaceous scent glands on the flanks of both sexes [778, 785], largest in breeding males (maximum in 382 males was 21×10 mm [1]) and most active during the breeding season.

Chromosomes: 2n = 36 (Edinburgh) [558], Hertfordshire [609] and Oxford [721]. No variation reported from Britain but on Continent FNa = 60–68 [893].

MEASUREMENTS
See Table 8.14. Males about 5% larger than females.

VARIATION
British animals average slightly larger than continental ones (mean condylobasal length of skull 41.1 mm ($n = 40$) in Britain, 37.5 mm ($n = 10$) in Scandinavia and 37.2 mm ($n = 14$) in Switzerland and Italy) but are not otherwise distinguishable from Scandinavian animals. Scottish animals generally smaller than English.

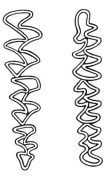

Fig. 8.16. Molar teeth of water vole; right upper (on left) and left lower (on right).

Table 8.14. Measurements of water voles.

	Males			Females		
	Mean	Range	*n*	Mean	Range	*n*
Live, breeding individuals, Woodbastwick, Norfolk [1]						
Head and body (mm)	187	121−261	327	178	119−247	296
Tail (mm)	112	82−174	327	105	80−161	296
Hind foot (mm)	31.6	26−42	327	30.9	25−41	296
Various localities						
Skull length (condylobasal) (mm) (adults with interorbital ridges fused or within 1 mm)	41.5	39.0−44.4	20	40.8	37.2−42.5	20
Overwintered adults in summer, Oxfordshire [229]						
Head and body (mm)	225	210−242	12	219	206−229	18
Tail (mm)	133	115−146	12	135	123−144	17
Hind foot (mm)	34.3	32−36	12	33.7	32.5−36	18
Weight (g) (excluding pregnant females)	311	246−386	18	272	225−310	17

The following subspecific names have been proposed but do not represent discrete subspecies: *A. amphibius reta* Miller, 1910 (Aberdeen); *A. amphibius brigantium* Thomas, 1928 (Huddersfield, Yorkshire).

Within Britain, variation is most obvious in fur colour, generally black in N and NW Scotland and brown elsewhere. However, there are melanic lowland populations in both England and Scotland and neither the distribution nor the frequency of black individuals has been studied in detail.

The name *brigantium* was based upon individuals with unusually projecting (pro-odont) upper incisors but these do not constitute a discrete race [166]. Animals on Eilean Gamhna, Argyll, have simpler molar patterns and shorter molar rows, usually < 9.2 mm.

There is a high frequency of partial albinism in the British populations investigated [1, 521, 777]. White patches of hair occur most frequently on the tail tip and forehead, but also on the chest, front paws, flanks and shoulders.

DISTRIBUTION
Generally confined to low ground and probably very local in NW and N Scotland. Absent from most islands, but present on the Isle of Wight, Anglesey, Arran and on Eilean Gamhna and Eilean Creagach near the mouth of Loch Melfort in Argyll.

HISTORY
A. terrestris probably evolved from the middle-Pleistocene *A. cantiana* [490]. *A. cantiana* already had permanently growing molars while a proposed lower Pleistocene ancestor, *Mimomys savini*, developed roots with age but shared the same complex prismatic pattern of M_1 with *A. cantiana* [491]. *Arvicola* was present in Britain at several periods during the last glacial period. During the last 12 000 years, water voles have become progressively larger and their incisors less pro-odont [587].

HABITAT
Most frequent in lowlands: on densely vegetated banks of ditches, dykes, rivers and streams, generally where the current is slow and water present throughout the year. Less frequently on ponds. Minimum depth of water seems to be a key feature affecting variations in use of habitat over short distances, sections of river bank adjoining shallow water not being used whereas the banks of nearby lengths of the river with deeper water are well used [24]. Water voles may occur completely away from water and then they burrow like moles and live

Map 8.10. Water vole.

mainly below ground, as on Read Island in the Humber estuary [757], on Eilean Gamhna, Argyll, [159] and in many continental populations [681]. In NW Scotland (Kinlochewe) a population migrated in winter to higher ground [1]. Seasonal migration from wet to dry habitats is typical for some German and Russian populations [638, 866].

SOCIAL ORGANISATION AND BEHAVIOUR

Social organisation varies seasonally and, where data are available for very high densities, also with population density [1, 521, 523]. In winter, when water voles do not breed, a female, some of her daughters and unrelated males may nest communally. In spring co-nesting females space out, engage in fights, and losers disperse. Usually by May all breeding females occupy exclusive and defended space (territories). Sons disperse from the territories by the age of 4 months and move between different territories of females until they settle. Dominant daughters settle inside the territory, others disperse. Some adult females disperse following fights with their daughters [521]. Some

Map 8.11. Water vole.

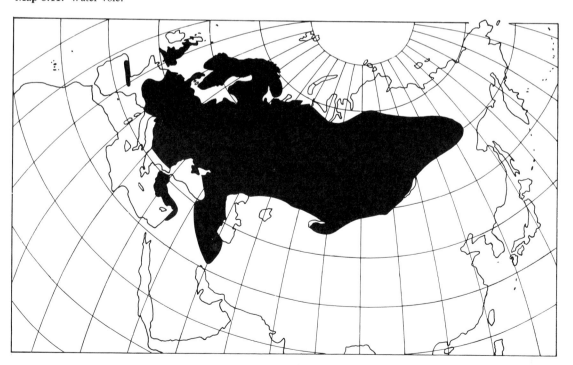

of these females were pregnant [521], as was one Scottish dispersing female [778]. In Norfolk, when population density is very high breeding females fight much less and have overlapping and undefended home ranges. In contrast, breeding males have less overlap of their home ranges when density is high than when it is low. Females have only one mate, usually for the whole breeding season. Males may have an additional one to two mates and some have none.

Home-ranges of males considerably larger than of females, and ranges of all individuals smaller at high than at low population density (Table 8.15). Ranges extend linearly along the banks of waterways, and, in Norfolk, at the boundary of females' territories large latrine sites are found where their mate scent marks. Such latrines and marking are not observed when density is high and females have overlapping ranges. Juveniles' home-ranges generally smaller than those of breeding individuals, except when young males move between territories of females. Ranges of all sexes and age classes very much smaller during the winter than during the breeding season [521].

Scent mark by actively scratching the flank glands with the hind feet [285] at latrine sites and during agonistic and sexual encounters [521]. Males respond differently to urine from oestrus as opposed to non-oestrus females [1].

Aggressive behaviour overtly by boxing with forefeet and rolling in a clinch; more severe, and involving wounding, in males than females. In females, aggressive encounters begin with teeth chattering, flank scratching and tail beating, and among unfamiliar individuals this merges into overt boxing and rolling in a clinch [521]. In Oxfordshire, but not in Norfolk, adult males were seen to seek out and attack weanlings [228].

Activity occurs both on runways and by swimming. Water voles respond to alterations of visual cues along runways with flight, to alteration of olfactory cues with urination, defaecation and scent marking; responses to changes of the course of the run show that water voles remember the course of the run by the direction itself (kinesthetically) [521]. In Aberdeenshire found to be active about every 2–4 hours and for longer during the day than the night. In winter, activity outside the burrow is very rare [521]. In Durham [25, 834] no consistent variation in activity observed between day and night nor any general limitation of activity out-side the nest in winter. The level of activity at night and during the day was generally similar, but was reduced both during the night in winter in cold weather, and during the middle of the day in summer during hot weather. The general level of activity was high, about 25% of the 24 hours being spent outside the nest throughout the non-breeding period, and a considerably higher level, reaching a peak of 38% in July, during the breeding period. When common rats were also present water voles were not active at night when the rats were foraging, but compensated for this by increased activity at dawn and dusk [488].

Table 8.15. Home range size* and density of water voles from Woodbastwick, Norfolk.

	Males		Females	
	Breeding	Juveniles	Breeding	Juveniles
Low density (1974–76, 1978, 1979)				
Mean length of range (m)	454	99	262	83
n	7	13	37	83 [sic]
Density (no. per 1.6 km)			4–10	16–22
High density (1977)				
Mean length of range (m)	161	69	92	47
n	16	6	46	17
Density (no. per 1.6 km)			46	217

* Linear extent of bank occupied in July. Each bank of water-way measured separately and measurements added. Total distance per month. Radio-tracking data [521].

Young: juvenile males, which disperse during the breeding season, usually move on runways. They occupy non-overlapping ranges in autumn on one river in Oxfordshire. Juvenile females, when on dispersal during the spring, breeding season and early autumn, usually swim [521]. They swim using fore and hind feet, and when disturbed sometimes dive and stir up mud. The respiratory properties of the blood do not reflect adaptation to oxygen shortage and excess carbon dioxide associated with diving [145].

Communication: when threatened, or in agonistic encounters, water voles voice arythmic calls lasting about 0.1 seconds at between 2.5 and 4.4 kHz; these are thought to inhibit a further approach by conspecifics [453]. Some females avoid and others approach sounds made by feeding conspecifics [521].

Grooming involves all feet, teeth and the tongue. The forefeet work from the peri-anal region and lower flanks upwards on the belly, over the shoulders and over the forehead.

FEEDING

Predominantly vegetarian [1, 417]: mainly grasses, in particular the common reed, *Phragmites*, and sedges, more rarely rushes and dicotyledons, e.g. nettles, *Urtica dioica*, and dead-nettles, *Lamium album* [25]; very exceptionally insects, molluscs, fish [407, 610, 633, 704] and locally swan mussels are taken [1]. About 80% of the body weight is eaten daily. Juveniles eat fewer reeds and rhizomes than adults [417]. Water voles usually feed sitting on their hind feet and they may eat the whole stem of young grasses; more frequently they feed only on the growth meristems, in particular the nodes and the base of the stem of reeds. Large sections of the plant then remain uneaten and can be found as piles of often similar-length pieces since nodes form at similar distances along the stem of the plant. In winter, they feed on roots and rhizomes and on bulbs of plants such as *Filipendula ulmaria* as well as hay harvested in autumn and kept quite green into the winter on the damp floors of their burrow systems [1].

BREEDING

Up to five litters, each of about six young, are born between April and September.
Gestation: 20−30 days [98, 407].

Mean number of corpora lutea: 6.4 ($n = 18$, England) [652].
Mean number of embryos: 6.4 ($n = 32$, Scotland) [778], 5.7 ($n = 18$, England) [652].
Mean litter size: 6.1 ($n = 149$, at 13−17 days, Norfolk) [1].
Weight at birth: 3.5−7.5 g.
Duration of lactation: *c.* 22 days.
Number of litters in season: one to five (mean 3.4) (Norfolk) [1].

Males are usually fecund from February. Females are poly-oestrus with post-partum oestrus and suspeñion of oestrus during lactation and in winter. They first conceive in March or April. Weaned young occur from June to October.

Young are born naked and with the eyes closed. After 14 days they weigh about 22 g or more. They make their first excursions outside the nest and are weaned about that time. They leave the nest when the mother has her next litter and when they are 22 or more days old. The rate of growth of litters can differ greatly. In one study in County Durham, the members of the first litters of the year reached an average weight of 160 g within 5 weeks of birth. Those in the second cohort took an average of 12 weeks to reach this weight [24]. Earliest sexual maturity was recorded at 77 g in females in Oxfordshire and median weight at maturity was 110 g for voles born before July [228]. However, in Britain young of the year often do not reproduce in the summer of their birth. In Norfolk only 10% of the young females of the year, at most, lactate and this occurred only when population density was exceptionally high [1, 521]. In Oxfordshire, all young born before July matured in their year of birth [228].

POPULATION

Density varies seasonally, with highest numbers in autumn and lowest in early summer before weaned young appear, and also between years: in 1974−1979, in Norfolk, the number of breeding females varied from 4 to 46 per 1.6 km of waterway in different years [1, 521]. These fluctuations are probably not regular density-limited cycles. Social behaviour, dispersal and unknown factors control density [1, 521]. Densities also vary, even over short distances, with stream and bankside condition. In a census at five sites along the Yorkshire Esk in the summer of 1984, numbers of adults trapped varied from 8 to 44/km [582], but average densities there are likely to be lower [878]. Due to the confinement of activity to a narrow zone close to the water's edge, densities can be high locally. The effective density during the year along the headwaters of the river Skerne, County Durham averaged *c*. 200 per hectare, and within this foraging area the population was eating about 20% of the primary productivity [25, 834].

Sex ratio usually 1 : 1, but an excess of males at the start of winter has been reported [780].

Survival: in Scotland, over-wintered voles disappeared by July [778]. In Norfolk, some individuals of both sexes survived two winters and, apart from their year of birth, may breed in two summers [521]. Survival of juveniles born before the end of June is significantly better than those born thereafter, and only juveniles born early in the year contribute to the next breeding season [521, 776, 778]. Survival of dispersing juvenile females and of males is significantly worse than of resident females; however, overall survival of dispersing males is much better than that of dispersing females [521].

MORTALITY
In a population study in Norfolk, main predators were herons, pike and barn owls [521]. Predation by stoats significant, but variable from year to year [1]. Rats prey upon unweaned voles in the nest. Other important predators in other areas are foxes, weasels, mink, otters, domestic cats and other owls and predatory birds [781, 869]. Mortality in dispersing individuals is greatly increased [521]. Maximum length of life recorded in laboratory was 31.5 months [869]. In the wild, rarely survive three, but frequently two winters [521, 866]. Intrauterine mortality is low [866]; post-natal mortality is very high [778].

PARASITES

Endoparasites: fleas; *Ctenophthalmus nobilis*, *Hystrichopsylla talpae* and *Megabothris walkeri* are regular. A number of other small-mammal fleas recorded [624] are undoubtedly accidentals.

Lice; the sucking louse *Polyplax spirugera* is common but not specific to water vole.

Ticks; in late summer, *Ixodes ricinus* and *I. trianguliceps*, on ears.

Ectoparasites: tapeworms; in Scotland, *Hydatigena taeniaeformis* in liver.

Diseases: *Bacillus tularense* and *Listeria monocytogenes* carried frequently by continental water voles. These pathogens cause tularaemia and listeriosis respectively in humans, but no cases of tularaemia have been recorded in Britain and *Listeria* has not been found to be carried by British water voles.

RELATIONS WITH MAN
In Britain of no economic importance. Rarely damage to canals and dams is reported.

LITERATURE
Airoldi & Meylan [4] — a bibliography of works on *Arvicola* in Europe (excepting Russia) from 1900–1972. Reichstein [681] — taxonomy, description and bibliography.

SOUND RECORDINGS
Appendix 3: A, F, J, V.

AUTHOR FOR THIS SPECIES
C.C.K. Boyce (née Leuze), with acknowledgement for additional data and comment provided by D.M. Stoddart, K.R. Ashby, G. Woodroffe and M.G. Efford.

SUBFAMILY MURINAE (MICE AND RATS)

This subfamily contains over 400 species of rats and mice, mainly in tropical Africa, Asia and Australasia. Only two genera, *Apodemus* and *Micromys*, are predominantly Palaearctic, but representatives of two others, *Mus* and *Rattus*, have become worldwide in association with man. Wherever they occur, murines are generally the dominant small rodents in woodland and forest, but many species are adapted to more open habitats.

The six species in Britain are fairly typical representatives. Compared with voles, they have long tails (at least 80% of head and body), rather pointed muzzles, large eyes, large rounded ears (least so in the harvest mouse), sleek pelage and rather long hind legs and feet. The cheek-teeth (three in each row) are low-crowned with the cusps arranged in three longitudinal rows.

Four genera are represented (Table 8.16) (Fig. 8.17).

Table 8.16. Principal characters of the genera of mice and rats.

	Micromys	*Mus*	*Apodemus*	*Rattus*
Head and body (mm)	50–70	70–90	80–130	150–270
Hind feet (mm)	13–16	16–19	19–26	30–45
Ear (mm)	8–9	12–15	15–19	20–25
Yellow spot on chest	No	No	Usually	No
Upper molar tooth row (mm)	2.6–2.8	2.9–3.4	3.7–4.6	6.4–8.0
Upper incisors notched	No	Yes	No	No
No. of roots of M^1	5	3	4 (or 5)	5

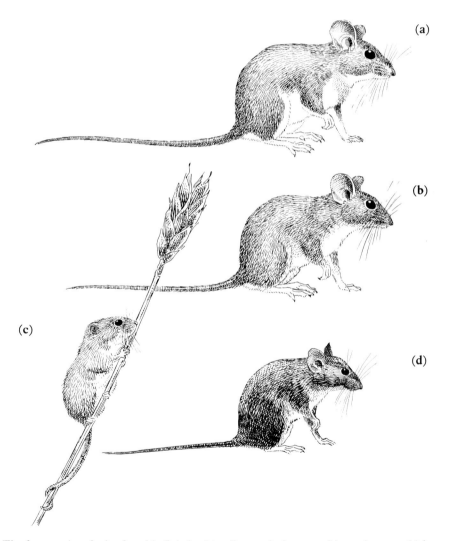

Fig. 8.17. The four species of mice found in Britain: (a) yellow-necked mouse; (b) wood mouse; (c) harvest mouse; (d) house mouse.

GENUS *Apodemus*

Contains the dominant mice of the Palaearctic Region, with 11 species, only two of which occur in Britain. They both have large ears and eyes; the dorsal pelage is dark brown mixed with yellow, which is prominent on the flanks; the ventral fur is pale grey. The tail is darker above than below and lightly haired; it is as long as the head and body. The wearing surface of each upper incisor is not notched (cf. house mouse) and the first upper molar usually has four roots with corresponding alveoli (Fig. 8.19). The first and second upper molars each have three cusps on the inner side.

The genus is replaced in woodland habitats in North America by *Peromyscus* (subfamily Hesperomyinae) which shows a remarkable convergence in appearance and ecology.

In Britain the two species, the wood mouse, *A. sylvaticus* and the yellow-necked mouse, *A. flavicollis*, are clearly distinct, but in parts of continental Europe they are so similar that they have been suspected of interbreeding although this has not been proved [626]. Of the differences detailed in Table 8.17 only the chest-spot and the colour of the ventral pelage of the adults are sufficiently clear-cut to allow individuals to be identified without doubt. The measurements given for *A. sylvaticus* refer to mainland English animals, i.e. from the areas where both species occur. On many small islands, *A. sylvaticus* is as large as *A. flavicollis*.

Wood mouse *Apodemus sylvaticus*

Mus sylvaticus Linnaeus, 1758; Upsala, Sweden.
Mus intermedius Bellamy, 1839; Devon.
Mus hebridensis de Winton, 1895; Uig, Lewis, Outer Hebrides.
Mus hirtensis Barrett-Hamilton, 1899; St Kilda, Outer Hebrides.

Long-tailed field mouse; llygoden y maes (Welsh); luch fheoir (Scottish Gaelic); luch fheir (Irish Gaelic).

RECOGNITION
Dark brown upper fur, protruding eyes, large ears and long tail distinguish this from most other British mice. (Fig. 8.18). Only lack of yellowish chest spot or, if present, its failure to join brown upper fur on either side of neck, distinguishes it from slightly larger yellow-necked mouse. Chest spot less obvious in juveniles which have greyish brown fur. Juveniles may be confused with house mice but larger eyes, ears and hind feet are distinctive, and characteristic 'acetamide' musky smell of house mouse is lacking.

Skull (Fig. 8.19) distinguishable from house mouse and harvest mouse by longer molar rows and shape of M^1 and M_1 (M^1 usually with four roots), but difficult to separate from yellow-necked mouse. Precise measurement of antero-posterior thickness of upper incisors enables most skulls to

Table 8.17. Characters of mice of the genus *Apodemus*.

	Wood mouse	Yellow-necked mouse
Yellow marking on chest	A narrow longitudinal streak, or absent	A broad collar making contact with the dark dorsal colour
Colour of underparts	Pale grey	Very pale grey
Length of hind feet, without claws (mm)	19–23	22–26
Anterior-posterior thickness of upper incisors (mm)	1.10–1.30	1.45–1.65

Skulls with the thickness of the upper incisors measuring about 1.35–1.40 mm should be treated as unidentifiable unless the molars are heavily worn, in which case they will be old wood mice, or particularly unworn, in which case they will be young yellow-necks.

Fig. 8.18. Wood mouse. (Photo: P. Morris.)

be identified (see Table 8.15), and jaw length may also be used for this purpose [883].

SIGN

Footprints: four toes on forefeet and five on hind; slightly larger than those of the bank vole and house mouse. Overprinting often occurs and prints from jumping locomotion may leave impression of tail.

Faeces variable in colour according to food; usually 3–5 mm in length, larger and darker than those of bank vole. Deposited at random within home range [875] but may sometimes be found in groups near nests, feeding sites and cached food.

Cached food commonly discovered in chambers in burrow systems, and food remains often found in sheltered feeding places or disused birds' nests. Hazel nut shells opened with a hole surrounded by tooth marks (Fig. 8.11) whereas bank vole leaves no mark on surface [226] and dormouse leaves oblique tooth marks around the opening. Achenes (pips) of rose hips opened to extract seed but flesh discarded; bank voles discard pips and eat flesh [232]. Ash fruit ('keys') have the seed extracted through a hole chewed in the side of the pericarp whereas bank voles usually split the pericarp wing

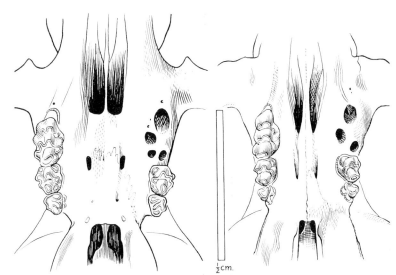

Fig. 8.19. Palate and upper molars of wood mouse (left) and house mouse (right) with left M¹ removed.

½ cm.

down the middle [275]. Coarse dust of 'kibblings' left behind after eating grain; snail shells opened by biting through shell away from spire.

DESCRIPTION

Pelage: dorsal dark brown fur grades to lighter yellow-brown on flanks; ventral fur grey-white. Juveniles show little yellow on flanks and some old individuals appear lighter brown, almost sandy in colour. Juvenile pelage grey-brown above and dark grey below. Yellow chest spot, if present, varies from small fleck to wide ventral suffusion but without meeting brown upper fur. Tail sparsely haired, not completely concealing skin which is dark above and light below.

Moult variable in pattern and occurrence. Regular sublateral (ventral to dorsal) pattern occurs in post-juvenile moult at 5−7 weeks but most adults show a 'patchy' moult with no seasonality [289]. In Cornwall and the Isles of Scilly the adult moult was found to be restricted to August−January [692].

Nipples: four pairs (three abdominal, one axillary).

Scent glands: sebaceous glands in subcaudal skin, particularly enlarged near the base of the tail of males, produce a white secretion [120, 270, 316, 779, 784]. Glandular development also found in the corners of the mouth and anus of both sexes.

Teeth: first upper molar usually has four roots, rarely five. Number of cusps prominent in the maxillary tooth row may be used as measure of age [203, 300] as may stages of wear (Fig. 8.20); twelve cusps in newly erupted tooth row are reduced in number with age. Accessory cusp recorded on third upper molar in Ireland [470].

Reproductive tract usually regressed or undeveloped in winter non-breeding season. Testes large, up to 12 mm; prominent accessory glands, lagging behind testes in development [32], include well-developed 'ram's horn' seminal vesicles bound to coagulating glands, partially external lobular prostate gland and goblet-shaped preputial glands. Female tract Y-shaped; past attachment sites (placental scars) show as dark spots on uterine wall. Ovaries easily distinguished at ends of the uterine horns; corpora lutea appear as large cream or pink spots in ovary.

Fig. 8.20. Molars of wood mouse; slightly worn (left) and heavily worn (right). Upper teeth on left in each pair [573].

Chromosomes: 2n = 48; all acrocentric (FNa = 46). Superficially similar to those of yellow-necked mouse but small differences such as absence of prominent C-band in x-chromosome, present in yellow-necked mouse [74, 238, 394].

RELATIONSHIPS
Very similar to yellow-necked mouse and to eastern European *A. microps*.

MEASUREMENTS
(Tables 8.16 and 8.18).

VARIATION
British and Irish mainland individuals not clearly distinguishable from the continental form. The following have been described as subspecies from Ireland and from small islands. Most do not justify subspecific status but there has been no comprehensive review:

Mus sylvaticus celticus Barrett-Hamilton, 1900; Caragh Lake, Co Kerry, Ireland.

Apodemus fridariensis granti Hinton, 1914; Mid Yell, Shetland.

A. f. thuleo Hinton, 1919; Foula, Shetland.

M. s. fridariensis Kinnear, 1906; Fair Isle, Shetland.

A. hebridensis nesiticus Warwick, 1940; Island of Mingulay, Outer Hebrides.

A. h. hamiltoni Hinton, 1914; Island of Rhum, Inner Hebrides.

A. h. tirae Montagu, 1923; Island of Tiree, Inner Hebrides.

A. h. maclean Hinton, 1914; Tobermory, Isle of Mull, Inner Hebrides.

A. h. larus Montagu, 1923; Island of Jura, Inner Hebrides.

A. h. tural Montagu, 1923; Island of Islay, Inner Hebrides.

Table 8.18. Measurements of adult wood mice from Perthshire.

	Males			Females		
	Mean	Range	*n*	Mean	Range	*n*
Head and body (mm)	93.6	86–103	20	91.0	81–103	13
Tail (mm)	83.2	74–95	20	82.0	71–93	13
Hind feet (mm)	22.0	20.8–23.0	20	21.6	20.2–22.8	13
Ear (mm)	15.9	14.7–17.8	17	16.1	14.6–17.3	13
Weight (g)	19.1	13–27	20	17.8	13–24	13
Condylobasal length (mm)	23.4	22.4–24.9	19	23.1	21.5–24.2	12
Upper molar tooth row (mm)	3.8	3.6–4.1	19	3.9	3.7–4.1	12

A. h. ghia Montagu, 1923; Island of Gigha, Inner Hebrides.

A. s. butei Hinton, 1914; Mountstuart, Isle of Bute, Firth of Clyde.

A. h. cumbrae Hinton, 1914; Great Cumbrae Island, Firth of Clyde.

A. h. fiolagan Hinton, 1914; Island of Arran, Firth of Clyde.

Populations on most small islands, but especially on St Kilda, Fair Isle and Rhum, are distinguished by large size [165, 204, 205]. On some islands such as St Kilda, Lewis and Channel Isles, a large proportion of population has underside heavily washed with buff. Size and pelage variation reviewed by Delany [201] and Berry [74].

Mainland variation slight but intensively studied [65, 66, 68, 85, 201, 204, 205, 206, 207, 400]. Polymorphisms of supernumary or B-chromosomes have been reported [394]. In woodland frequency of normally uncommon phosphoglucomutase genotype increased in autumn coincident with immigration from adjacent arable land [515]. Uncommon genotype was shown to be able to mobilise glycogen faster than normal genotype [516] and survived worse (or emigrated more) over winter compared with common genotypes. From a study of non-metrical variation, two distinct forms have been postulated in mainland Britain, in apparent breeding contact, but probably of different origin: an eastern type, related to French populations and a west/north type with affinities to the island forms [65, 69, 74].

Variation in time described from St Kilda [67]; collections from 1910 and 1919 differed in frequency of non-metrical variants from samples collected in 1948, 1964 and 1967 (last all homo-geneous), but samples from Barra collected 25 years apart and from Lewis 45 years apart showed no differences [65].

Silver-grey, piebald, melanistic and semi-hairless forms recorded [47, 339, 601]; albinism of tail tip in about 3% of population [156].

DISTRIBUTION

Wooded and steppe zones of western Palaearctic, but not extending far into coniferous zone. Ubiquitous in Britain and Ireland except on most open mountainous areas. Widespread on small islands. Absent only from very small islands, e.g. Lundy, Isle of May, North Rona, and from the Isles of Scilly other than Tresco and St Mary's.

HISTORY

A native species recorded in tundra faunas of Pleistocene interstadials with *Lemmus* or *Dicrostonyx*, but these records may be result of muddled excavation or late intrusion by burrowing. Probably formed part of temperate fauna of British deciduous woodland by 9500 bp before separation from Continent. In Ireland subfossil teeth recorded from Mesolithic level near Dublin dated 7600 ± 500 bp [662]. Skeletal evidence suggests that populations in the Hebrides and many smaller Scottish islands may have come from Norway [65, 74], exceptions being Mull and Colonsay which were probably colonised from Scottish mainland. Present on Orkney mainland in Neolithic times [162]. Possible survival on Channel Islands through last glaciation [68] has been disputed on geological evidence [882]. In the Isles of Scilly now only on St Mary's and Tresco but possible Bronze-Age remains have been found on Nornour [650].

Map 8.12. Wood mouse.

HABITAT

Highly adaptable, inhabiting most habitats if not too wet [276], including woodland, arable land [340, 396], grassland (ungrazed), heather, blanket bog [506] and sand dunes [210]. Common in dry-stone walls [396, 438], hedgerows [660], and gardens; also in vegetated parts of urban areas [881]. Rarely found above tree line on high moors and scree, except where stone walls or buildings give cover, but recorded at 1300 m in the Cairngorms [152] and at 1000 m in SW Ireland [250]. May show no preference [759] or some preference [167] for dense groundcover in woodland and may avoid high densities of bank voles [168, 278] or field voles. In Ireland, a preference was shown for mixed heather, grassland and bracken rather than pure grassland, despite the absence of field voles [251]. In absence of human occupation, they successfully compete with house mice in buildings and this probably caused extinction of latter on St Kilda [84].

Map 8.13. Wood mouse (also in Iceland).

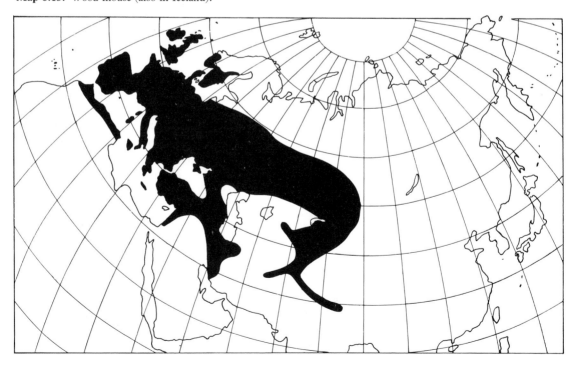

SOCIAL ORGANISATION AND BEHAVIOUR

Social organisation in winter is loose, with communal nesting of both sexes (up to three or four and possibly more). At start of breeding season some evidence of heterosexual associations from analysis of spatial organisation [675] and observations of male—female pair bonds [293]. Other studies have not found this and assume a promiscuous or polygynous mating system. Dominance hierarchy of males is likely during the breeding season but whether this is based on a group territory with dominant males patrolling it and including breeding females [119, 148] or simply on overlapping home ranges is controversial [600, 675, 874]. Male home ranges always overlap but in breeding season females maintain exclusive areas which in some studies appear to be territories [874]. Social organisation reviewed by Montgomery & Gurnell [600] and spatial organisation by Wolton & Flowerdew [876].

Home ranges initially small but increase with sexual maturity; autumn home ranges of juveniles remain small until following spring [672, 743]. Typical home-range areas shown in Table 8.19. Faecal deposition occurs throughout the home range in relation to the time spent at each place and not in particular association with the home-range boundary [875].

Communication: visual communication interpreted as important in aggressive behaviour [351] but integrated with ultrasonic and olfactory communication. Olfactory and acoustic biology reviewed by Stoddart & Sales [784]. Ultrasounds (20 kHz and above) emitted in exploration, mating, chasing, fighting, approach to a conspecific, grooming, homosexual and contact behaviour, and sonic calls (below 20 kHz) emitted by attacked individual, particularly during retaliation in male—male encounter. Ultrasonic calls of males stimulated by odour of oestrous female and inhibited by odour of strange male [784]. Infants emit few low-frequency calls in nest but high-frequency ultrasonic calls emitted on removal; intensity and rate of calling increase after days 2—4 and remain at high levels until days 12—15, ceasing by about day 19—24 [634, 750, 784]. Rate and intensity of infant calling related to degree of cold stress on removal from nest and stage in development of homeothermy.

Scent marking from subcaudal scent glands likely (particularly in males) during normal movements. Chemical differences in secretion between sexes and individuals indicate that species, sex and state of maturity are encoded [316, 784]; however, there is little direct evidence to support suggestions that subcaudal gland odour may be involved in territory or nest marking, self-advertisement or mate recognition [120]. Auditory and olfactory communication reviewed by Stoddart & Sales [784].

Dispersal recorded in adults and a few juveniles

Table 8.19. Typical home-range areas of wood mice [27, 876].

Season	Habitat	Males Area (m²)	n	Females Area (m²)	n
All	Deciduous woodland	2229	39	1812	25
All	Coniferous/deciduous woodland	1844	7	1072	11
Summer	Coniferous/deciduous woodland	13 063 D 1284 S	3 7	809	19
Summer	Deciduous woodland	4485	17	1699	10
Summer	Deciduous woodland	10 765	12	4009	12
Winter	Coniferous/deciduous woodland	299	13	242	11
Winter	Deciduous woodland	1294	63	1151	41
Apr—Nov	Sand dunes	36 499	8	15 826	9
Dec—Mar	Sand dunes	18 832	5	12 290	6

D, dominant; S, subordinate.

[857]: many adult males probably disperse through-out the year and females particularly in autumn and winter [600, 876].

Aggressive behaviour takes form of fighting and chasing while subordinates flee or avoid dominant individual [351]. Male aggression seasonal and associated with breeding season [148], increasing in spring [352]. Female aggression associated with lactation (in the laboratory) [348]; appears to be uncommon in field [148]. Encounters in laboratory and field not always aggressive [105, 148] and avoidance of dominant individuals appears to be common. Resident animals cause immigrants to disperse, and in the laboratory established males and females will isolate or kill strange juveniles [273]; food deprivation alters aggressiveness of individuals and influences outcome of encounter so that dominants become more subordinate and vice versa [348, 600].

Activity mainly nocturnal, biphasic in long nights but in short nights one peak of activity in middle of night usual [600]. Female activity above ground at mid-day in summer recorded in Scotland [872]. Start of activity well correlated with sunset [872] and controlled by photoperiod [244, 600], although light intensity also probably involved [245]. Last return to nest not related to sunrise [872]. Activity reduced by moonlight [479, 872] and apparently inhibited by combined wet and cold conditions [118, 349, 350] and by temperatures below 3°C [872].

Movement is by walking or leaping. Investigation involves slow deliberate steps or standing on hind legs and pointing nose in air. Lethargic movement has been observed during hypothermia in winter [605]; torpor is induced in the laboratory by low ambient temperatures (3°C or 12°C) following a period of food deprivation [845]. Arboreal movement is common [600]. In mixed woodland extensive use made of low level branches lying parallel to ground [592].

Burrow system can be complicated [353, 446], probably survives from one generation to next, but extensions are excavated using forefeet to dig and hind feet to clear soil [348, 446].

Nests usually below ground and especially under roots of trees or shrubs [446]; occasionally above ground in holes in trees, buildings or bird nesting boxes. Commonly made of leaves, moss and grass, but variable according to availability of material. Weight and volume of leaves used and depth of nest all increase with decrease in temperature [222]. Particularly in autumn and winter food sometimes cached in live traps and entrance blocked with earth or stones [844]; this behaviour may result in drainage pipes becoming blocked; entrances to burrows are commonly found camouflaged or blocked by debris.

Grooming involves hind and forefeet and teeth [353].

SENSES
Vision adapted for nocturnal activity with large protruding lens to eye; insensitive to infrared and red light [148, 293, 755, 761]. Sense of smell acute; individuals can discriminate between the faeces, and also the urine, of other individuals by odour alone [873]. Hearing is also acute (see 'Communication'). Orientation apparently occurs by monitoring the ambient magnetic field [554].

FEEDING
An opportunist taking seeds, green plants, fruits and animal foods, proportions greatly affected by their abundance (reviewed by Hansson [378]); see also [213, 630, 742, 854].

A study in mixed deciduous woodland showed the following foods taken: seed, including acorn and sycamore (dominant most of the year); buds (especially blackberry) and dicotyledon stems (especially in early spring); invertebrates, including lepidopterous larvae, centipedes and worms (mainly in early summer); blackberries, elderberries and fungi (in autumn) [854]. In cereal fields after harvest, sown and shed grain taken, with arthropods in spring and weed seeds and grass flowers in summer [340]; in sugar-beet fields, weed seeds eaten before harvest in autumn and arthropods, mainly larvae, also taken in winter with the addition of earthworms in late winter, together with the remains of the sugar-beet. Exceptionally vertebrate prey may be taken, e.g. frogs [580].

Differences exist in diets of different age and sex classes; e.g. in woodland juveniles eat less seed and subadults less animal food than adults, making up with greater variety of other foods [415, 854]. Females ate more green plant food and less animal food than males in spring/summer [415].

BREEDING (Fig. 8.21)

Litters of usually four to seven young in successive pregnancies from March–October; winter breeding sporadic.

Length of oestrous cycle: 4–6 days

Gestation: 19–20 days, but longer during lactation owing to delayed implantation.

Number of corpora lutea (in laboratory): young, 5.4; old, 5.2; 5th–6th pregnancy, 6.0 [139].

Litter size (in laboratory): 1st pregnancy, 4.3; 5th–6th pregnancy, 5.4 [139].

Litter size (in wild): 2–11, range of means 4.5–6.5 [276].

Weight at birth: 1–2 g.

Duration of lactation: 18–22 days.

Season: males may have fully developed testes within 28 days of weaning in laboratory [144]. Female fertility limits the breeding season as males are fecund before vaginal opening occurs in February or March [276]; most females have one or two litters but up to six have been recorded from trapping studies [276]. Last pregnancies usually occur in October or November. Winter litters probably small [753], and resorption commonly recorded [32, 645], but loss of complete sets of embryos unusual [252]. Oestrus may occur throughout breeding season but in some laboratory colonies only 15% of females show spontaneous ovulations and oestrus [139]. Breeding seasons on islands are usually shorter than on the mainland [449]. In woodland, breeding is prolonged after good autumn mast crop [373, 541, 753], but early breeding may occur without abundant seed [256]. Supplementary food in spring will advance time of vaginal opening and increase body weight [272, 858].

Mating takes place after mutual investigation of anogenital region during courtship. Several rebuffed mounting attempts occur before female accepts male [353].

Sex ratio in laboratory is 1 : 1 but in trapped samples a bias towards males is common, particularly in winter and spring [175] and in adult age classes [355]. Litter size varies with geographical location and possibly with season (or age) [276].

Young are born naked and blind. Grey-brown juvenile pelage appears at *c.* 6 days followed by whitish ventral fur. Incisors erupt at *c.* 13 days and tail and hind feet darken dorsally at *c.* 14 days; eyes open at *c.* 16 days. Growth in laboratory and field varies greatly [271, 361, 300]. Autumn-born young develop more slowly than summer-born young [340]. Reproductive biology reviewed by Clarke [139].

POPULATION

Densities vary seasonally with autumn/winter peaks and spring/summer troughs [276]. Densities of 1–40 per hectare in mixed deciduous woodland are usual, but winter increases, up to 130–200/ha after a good seed crop, have been recorded [353, 354]. In arable land seasonal variation in density was 0.5/ha in summer to 17.5/ha in winter with winter peaks as low as 8.4/ha [340]. Harvesting, straw burning and ploughing reduce densities [384]. In Irish woodlands densities in yew were 23–92 per hectare with a mean of 58; in oak 3–24, in beech 6–45, in pine 0–20 and in oak/rhododendron 4–50 [743]. Long-term fluctuations in mixed deciduous woodland [760] and in ash woodland [276, 277] show a pattern of annual fluctuations with no evidence of longer cycle.

Structure: late-born young predominate in autumn and winter and survive well into spring. Few adults survive from one summer to next. In spring mature overwintered individuals are joined

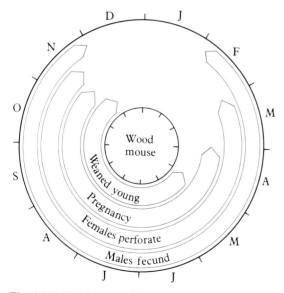

Fig. 8.21. Wood mouse: life-cycle.

by juveniles from April/May onwards but survival of latter is usually poor, forming only small part of the population until autumn when most overwintered animals disappear [276, 594].

Survival overwinter is positively related to autumn mast crop in deciduous woodland [61, 271, 274, 373, 855] but not to an index of winter severity based on minimum temperatures [276]. In ash woodland, relationship with winter food supply not so clear [277]. Increase in juvenile survival in summer or autumn results in peak densities in autumn or as late as February, according to length of breeding season and size of mast crop. Reduced survival in spring, coincident with start of breeding, increase in aggressiveness of males and formation of exclusive breeding areas by females [276, 600]. Summer densities often relatively stable and timing of increase is density-dependent (high density — late increase, low density — early increase), leading to damping of winter peak density [276, 855]. Overwintered males are aggressive to juveniles and prevent their recruitment in summer [273], but in autumn aggression is reduced and their survival is good, often coincident with cessation of breeding, increase in food supplies and decrease in home-range size [743]. One study suggested that the density of males is more important than total population density in summer for timing of increase in survival [340], and role of female behaviour in these changes in survival is still uncertain [276, 442]. In winter much dispersal of males and females occurs but immigration is not necessary for autumn increase [352, 855]. However, movement away from woodland does occur in both sexes during spring decline in some habitats [168, 384].

MORTALITY
Predators include fox, weasel, stoat, badger, marten, domestic cat, long-eared owl, tawny owl, short-eared owl, barn owl, little owl, kestrel [255, 308, 546]. Losses to avian and mammalian predators in Scandinavian mixed field and scrub habitats may be great enough to balance annual production, [246]. Tawny owls and weasels appear to take a large proportion of the population, particularly in spring in British mixed deciduous woodland, but numbers are difficult to quantify [483, 760]. Mortality from tawny owls is likely to be inversely density-dependent, becoming relatively greater at low mouse densities [760]. When wood mouse and bank vole densities are low tawny owls show reduc-

tion in number of pairs breeding and exceptionally none breeds at all [756]. In Ireland wood mouse forms about 70% of diet of long-eared owl whereas in Britain it is only 25–50% of prey [254]. In Ireland it was found to form c. 50% of the prey of barn owl where bank voles are absent but 43% where bank voles were present [741]. Mortality increases in spring probably as a result of a combination of dispersal, increased predation and intraspecific strife [276].

PARASITES
Parasites and disease were reviewed by Healing & Nowell [398].

Ectoparasites: fleas; *Ctenophthalmus nobilis*, *Hystrichopsylla talpae* and *Megabothris turbidus* are widespread and common. *Rhadinopsylla pentacantha* is also widespread, but less numerous, and *Typhloceras poppei* is closely associated through part of the host's range. A wide range of other fleas of ground nesting small mammals are recorded.

Lice; the sucking-lice *Polyplax serrata* and *Hoplopleura affinis* are common and their congeners *P. spinosula* (of rats) and *H. acanthopus* (of voles) have also been recorded.

Beetles; the beetle *Leptinus testaceus* is common, principally in the nest, and specific to this species. On the animals it is generally regarded as a scavenger [123], but there is also the suggestion that it is a predator [643].

Ticks; *Ixodes trianguliceps* adults, nymphs and larvae are common as on many small mammals [673]; also *Ixodes ricinus* larvae and nymphs.

Mites; mites found in Ireland were listed by Fairley [254]. In England, the following have been recorded: *Laelaps agilis*, *Eulaelaps stabularis*, *Radfordia lemina* and *Trombicula autumnalis*. The skin mite *Notoedres* spp. causes the skin to form dry creamy coloured scabs.

Endoparasites: helminths: *see* Tables 8.9 and 8.10. Larval rhabditid worms occur in the orbital fluid [813].

Ringworm fungi are common [240]. Infection with louping ill virus has been reported [828] as has serological evidence of infection with seven other species of viruses [464]. Infection with *Leptospira*, a spirochate bacterium, is common in Britain, especially in older individuals [825] and in damp habitats [527]. Other bacteria detected include *Mycobacterium tuberculosis* var. *muris* [869] and

Mycoplasma sp. [335] and six genera of parasitic protozoa have been recorded [174].

RELATIONS WITH MAN
The species has pest status for damage to pelleted seed of sugar beet up to time of germination; this has occurred in Britain and W Germany since early 1970s [19, 340, 649]. Control is effected by use of rodenticides, such as warfarin, or prevented by later drilling of seed in March when densities of mice are lower and germination is quicker. If drilling is carried out with damp-soil conditions occurring afterwards this helps to stop the soil blowing and exposing the seed to predation [19]. Wood mice frequently enter outhouses and buildings to become pests of stored food.

Mice may be killed accidentally by some common pesticides such as molluscicides containing methiocarb [384] and they can be contaminated by mercury and dieldrin from pesticides and dressed grain, and lead from vehicle exhausts ingested near roads [444, 445].

Satisfactory breeding occurs in the laboratory but not all females may ovulate (see 'Breeding'). The species is beneficial in preying upon harmful insects and it aids germination of tree seeds by storing fruit underground, despite eating large proportions of some mast crops.

Conservation is unnecessary as recolonisation after mortality is often rapid. May be observed by red light (see 'Senses') and have been successfully radio-tagged [874].

LITERATURE
Fairley [255] — short review of Irish literature. Gurnell [353] — a semi-popular account in the Forest Record series. Flowerdew [275] — a popular account of the species for informed amateur naturalists and older school children. Flowerdew *et al.* [279] a comprehensive account of ecology and behaviour. Gurnell & Flowerdew [360] includes a guide to live-trapping.

AUTHOR FOR THIS SPECIES
J.R. Flowerdew, with acknowledgement for additional data and comment by G.B. Corbet, J.S. Fairley and J. Gurnell.

Yellow-necked mouse *Apodemus flavicollis*

Mus flavicollis Melchior, 1834; Sielland, Denmark.

Mus sylvaticus wintoni Barrett-Hamilton, 1900; Graftonbury, Herefordshire.

RECOGNITION
In Britain, yellow collar consistently complete and discernible even in juveniles where it is suffused by grey, permitting easy separation from the wood mouse (*see* Fig. 8.18). Upper parts of adults more vivid orange-brown and lower parts paler than in wood mouse. Tail usually longer than body and proportionately thicker at base than in wood mouse. Adults on average 1.5 times the weight of adult wood mouse. Bite more readily and more vociferous than wood mice when handled.

Skull difficult to separate from that of wood mice with total accuracy. Greater antero-posterior thickness of upper incisors (Table 8.15) permits discrimination of most skulls from the smaller species [266].

SIGN
Footprints and faeces as in wood mouse.

DESCRIPTION
As for wood mouse but for features noted under 'recognition' and 'measurements'.

RELATIONSHIPS
Such is the morphological similarity between wood mice and yellow-necked mice, particularly in eastern part of their continental range, that interbreeding has often been claimed but not substantiated in wild [626]. Biochemical, cytological and morphological evidence consistently confirms that they are distinct species, at least in central and W Europe [57, 198, 298, 496, 616, 870]. Further genetic analyses [149, 181, 295] suggest that yellow-necked mouse is closely related to wood mouse and *A. microps*. These species more distantly related to *A. agrarius* and *A. mystacinus*. Divergence time of yellow-necked mouse and wood mouse has been estimated as 423 000 years bp on basis of biochemical data [181]. In Britain, breeding and biochemical studies indicate that hybridisation does not occur [460].

MEASUREMENTS (Table 8.20).

VARIATION
Chest spot variable in continental Europe, being most evident in the north-west [827]. British speci-

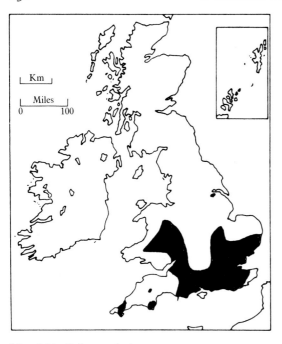

Map 8.14. Yellow-necked mouse.

mens indistinguishable from those of NW Europe. Little morphological variation within the British population.

DISTRIBUTION
Extending further north than wood mouse in Scandinavia but generally more restricted, and mainly montane in S Europe. An isolated record from Riding Mill, Northumberland, dates from before 1911 (specimen in BM (NH)).

HISTORY
Recorded from Neolithic and Roman sites in Derbyshire and Lancashire suggesting that former range was more extensive than at present [882, 883, 884].

HABITAT
In Britain occur mainly in mature deciduous woods [169, 596]. There is some evidence of association with distribution of long-established woodland in drier areas of S Britain [589]. Drink less water than wood mice when provided *ad libitum* [715]. Locally there may be an association with woods close to

Map 8.15. Yellow-necked mouse.

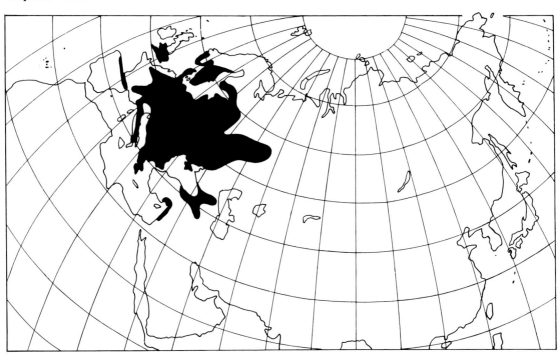

Table 8.20. External measurements of wood mice and yellow-necked mice in sympatry at Woodchester Park, Gloucestershire [885]. Material deposited in the Manchester Museum.

	Wood mice				Yellow-necked mice			
	Males (*n* = 20)		Females (*n* = 13)		Males (*n* = 9)		Females (*n* = 5)	
	Mean	Range	Mean	Range	Mean	Range	Mean	Range
Head and body (mm)	94.5	88−100	88.5	79−94	103.8	95−120	103.6	96−114
Tail (mm)	91.8	84−101	81.2	77−93	106.0	98−113	98.2	77−118
Hind foot (mm)	22.5	21−23	21.8	21−23	23.3	23−24	23.2	22−24
Ear (mm)	16.5	15−18	15.8	15−18	17.6	17−19	18.2	18−19

arable fields permitting habitat segregation of wood and yellow-necked mice during the breeding season [169]. Marginal habitats include hedges and rural gardens and buildings, but they do not extend into urban areas as much as wood mice. In woodland some preference for areas with little ground cover but with dense cover between 1 and 5 m [593, 595]. Presence has inhibitory effect on the use of space by wood mice [595, 598]. On Continent, habitat discrimination of wood mice and yellow-necked mice is inversely related to their morphological similarity along a NW to SE cline [401]. In E Europe, restricted to mature forest while wood mouse thrives in scrub or shelter-belts [28, 366, 370, 830, 889]. In central Europe, restricted to montane regions [402, 556, 611, 707]. In W and NW Europe, may share the same habitat of wood mice [182] but absent from old fields [61, 372, 413] as in Britain.

SOCIAL ORGANISATION AND BEHAVIOUR

Social organisation is poorly understood. Mother and young relationship is possibly the only strong social structure. Mating system, determined by home-range data, may be polygynous or promiscuous. Limited evidence of group formation in autumn and winter [818].

Home ranges larger than those of wood mice in shared habitats [591]. Estimates of range area vary, possibly with habitat quality, but those of males are larger on average than those of females [591, 670, 691, 884]. Range of both sexes generally less than 0.5 hectares. Home ranges overlap between and within sexes [591].

Behaviour very like wood mice [400, 590]. Visual communication integrated with ultrasonic and olfactory communication. Olfactory and acoustic biology reviewed by Stoddart & Sales [784]. Sub-caudal scent gland better developed than in wood mice, although its functions seem similar, and may be used to scent-mark branches. Secretion differs quantitatively rather than qualitatively from that of wood mice. Ultrasonic and audible calls are emitted by adults and infants. Infant calls last 60 ms and are repeated 4−5 per second. Commence at 56−60 kHz but fall to 40 kHz [896]. Calls from isolated pups elicit retrieval by lactating females [897]. Adult calls lower in frequency (40−50 kHz) and less frequent, particularly while exploring singly, and more indicative and social subordination than in wood mice [414].

Aggressive behaviour generally as in wood mice [400] but more tolerant of each other than wood mice are of conspecifics [412, 590]. Lower levels of aggression may lead to an increase in numbers in early summer [594].

Activity and movement as in wood mouse but may have a greater tendency to climb trees [158, 168, 400] though this is not apparent up to 2 m [592]. A radio-tracked male spent 2 days high in a tall tree before coming to ground [170]. Displaced mice may return to their initial place of capture from at least 1 km [104].

Residents are antagonistic towards transients which may constitute more than 30% of the population [814]. Transients are more liable to die in live traps [16]. Movements of up to 1200 m may occur throughout the year and involve both sexes [588].

Habitat: greater proportion of time spent in extensive burrow systems. Most tunnels within 50 cm of surface but some down to 150 cm. May contain stored seeds and invertebrate food [600]. One burrow (in Russia) contained 4 kg of acorns, 4 kg of hazel nuts, 150 g lime seeds and 100 g maple seeds [258]. Nests constructed of layers of leaves. Most new nests built during the breeding season, with those of females more substantial than those of males [818]. Individual mice may use several nests. In winter may nest in groups of three or four taking advantage of 'social thermoregulation' [258].

Behaviour, dispersion and movements of *Apodemus* spp. reviewed by Montgomery & Gurnell [600] and Wolton & Flowerdew [876].

FEEDING

Diet very similar to that of wood mice [378]. In sympatric populations, interspecific overlap in diet may be 80% [420]. With both wild-caught and laboratory-bred mice, yellow-necks extract beech seeds more efficiently and grass seeds less efficiently than wood mice [411], suggesting interspecific differences in foraging strategies at least between those in different habitats.

BREEDING

Litters of two to eleven young in successive pregnancies from February or later to October; winter breeding sporadic [597].

Breeding season: duration affected by food availability as in wood mouse [3]. Breed 2–8 weeks earlier than wood mice where they occur together [455, 593]. Removal of wood mice from shared woodland promotes breeding of yellow-necked mice [595]. In spring, males become reproductively active before females.

Mean number of embryos throughout breeding season 5.0–6.8 in central Europe [99, 455, 627, 646, 765]. Smaller numbers at the start and end of breeding season [646]. Losses of 12% of all oocytes or blastocysts and 5% of all embryos have been recorded [455].

Young: average birthweight is 2.8 g. Pups naked and blind. Eyes open at 13–16 days [627]. Growth rates similar to wood mouse [597]. Yellow collar visible from end of second week when juvenile pelage fully developed [290]. Post-juvenile moult progresses as in wood mouse [290]. Spring-born animals may reach sexual maturity in 2 or 3 months

[627]. Young females may attain maturity after reaching 10 g and young males after reaching 20 g [3]. Autumn-born mice usually do not reproduce until the following spring when this cohort constitutes the major part of the breeding population [594].

Sex ratio: adult sex ratio is variable but usually male biased [594, 647, 765] whereas juvenile sex ratio does not differ from unity [594] in wild-caught samples.

POPULATION

In Britain typically infrequent in woodland small mammal communities but sometimes, and in some places, may be more abundant than wood mice [357]. These localities may constitute refuges when numbers are low, and nuclei from which yellow-necked mice disperse when numbers are increasing [357, 596].

Densities: maximum densities in allopatry and sympatry are on a par with those of wood mice [594, 596]. Temporal variation in abundance of coexisting populations of wood and yellow-necked mice may be positively correlated [357] but characteristics of annual fluctuations differ [455, 588, 594, 596, 597]. Numbers typically reach a maximum in late autumn or early winter and decrease throughout winter and spring. Variation in peak abundance between years is positively related to mast production [3, 61, 100, 346, 417, 671] which may also affect numbers breeding in the following spring [61, 596]. Population growth begins with recruitment of juveniles in early summer and continues throughout the breeding season. Differences in the dynamics and regulation of wood mice and yellow-necked mice perhaps related to differences in social behaviour, habitat selection or responses to changing food availability. Interspecific differences possibly ameliorate the effects of interspecific competition.

Structure: population stucture differs from that of wood mice in that spring and summer populations have greater proportions of young of the year [594, 879].

Survival is poor during winter and good in summer and autumn [594]. Few mice survive more than 1 year. Mean life expectancy at 1 month old is between 2.9 and 3.6 months [99]. Dynamics and regulations of population size reviewed by Flowerdew [276] and Montgomery [596].

PARASITES

Ectoparasites: the flea *Ctenophthalamus nobilis* and the sucking-louse *Polyplax serrata* have been recorded, but it is likely that the yellow-necked mouse is host to a range of ectoparasites similar to wood mouse.

Endoparasites: helminths: *see* Tables 8.9 and 8.10.

RELATIONS WITH MAN
May cause annoyance in lofts and applestores etc., spoil and consume stored foods, consume seeds and interfere with electrical installations. Unlikely to damage field crops. Both inhibits and aids forest regeneration by feeding on and burying tree seeds [314, 395]. Can be bred in captivity but difficult to tame.

LITERATURE
Flowerdew *et al.* [279] is a comprehensive treatment of ecology and behaviour of woodland rodents. Montgomery [596] reviews comparative ecology of wood and yellow-necked mice.

AUTHOR FOR THIS SPECIES
W.I. Montgomery, with acknowledgement for comment by D. Corke.

GENUS *Micromys*

Contains a single species, closely related to the genera *Vandeleuria* and *Chiropodomys* of SE Asia [578].

Harvest mouse *Micromys minutus*

Mus minutus Pallas, 1771; Volga, USSR.
Mus soricinus Hermann, 1780; Strasbourg, France.
Mus tricetus Boddaert, 1785; Hampshire, England.
Mus minimus White, 1789; Selbourne, Hampshire.
Mus messorius Kerr, 1792; Hampshire.

Dwarf mouse, red mouse, red ranny.

RECOGNITION
The smallest British rodent, weighing only 6 g when adult. Easily distinguished from other murids by the blunt muzzle and small hairy ears, reminiscent of a vole's. Tail similar in length to the head and body, tip very prehensile. The tail does not strip when handled.

Pelage: sexually mature animals have a russet orange dorsal pelage and are pure white ventrally. Newly independent juveniles have a grey-brown pelage similar to that of house mice but are easily distinguishable both by their small size (*c.* 4 g as opposed to *c.* 7 g) and by the prehensile tail.

Skull: the skull is easily distinguished from other murids by the relative shortness of the rostrum and the long braincase. Distinguished from small house-mouse skulls by having five roots in the first upper molar, three in the lower, no notch in the upper incisors and the molar tooth rows less than 3 mm in length.

SIGN
The only British mouse that builds nests of woven grass leaves well above ground level, in the stalk zone of vegetation. The height depends on the vegetation; in low grasses the nests are close to ground level, but heights of 30–60 cm are more usual. In tall reeds, nests may be over a metre above ground level. The breeding nest is almost spherical and up to 10 cm in diameter; non-breeding nests are smaller and usually less than 5 cm in diameter. Both sorts of nests are built within the grass tussocks or amongst other densely growing vegetation such as cereals, rushes, herbs or brambles. Non-breeding nests may also be found at ground level amongst bales of hay or straw or on top of disused bird's nests [388]. When newly constructed the nests are difficult to find because they are built from living grass leaves, but in early winter the brown balls of withered grass stand out more clearly.

Unless present in very large numbers, there is no other obvious sign of their presence, and damage to cereal ears is rarely noticeable.

DESCRIPTION
A small, slender, delicate rodent (Fig. 8.22). The hind legs are not conspicuously large as in wood mice — hind feet 12–16 mm in length and more

Fig. 8.22. Harvest mouse. (Photo: P. Morris.)

slender than in the house mouse. Outer toes of hind feet adapted to climbing by a slight separation.

The small pubescent ears have a large triangular meatus, unlike other British murids. The tail is weakly bicoloured and sparsely haired.

Pelage: the dorsal pelage of adults consists of long dark guard hairs overlying the finer russet orange contour hairs. The ventral fur remains white in winter whilst the dorsal pelage is dark orange-brown. Juvenile animals have an overall grey-brown pelage but soon start to moult from the haunches forward into the adult phase. Thus they become bicoloured dorsally for a period.

Sexes: the anogenital distance is the best guide for determining the sex of individuals, though for recently independent juveniles this is difficult. Adult breeding males tend to have a far thicker penis than non-breeding males. Breeding females have four pairs of nipples.

Skull: the width of the brain-case is similar to that of the zygomatic breadth, 8.6–9.6 mm. The distance from the upper border of the infra-orbital foramen to tip of the nasal bone is less than a third of the distance to the posterior border of the occiput.

Teeth: the first molar of the upper jaw has five roots and that of the lower jaw three, of which the

central root is very fine. The upper incisor has no notch. Fragments from owl pellets can be identified with certainty by these features. The post-cranial skeleton is very delicate. Sex, and breeding status of females, can be determined from pelvic bones [121].

Sperm structure unlike most Muridae in that the head has no anterior hook, although the sperm head is flattened and asymmetrical [288].

Chromosomes: $2n = 68$, high for a murid [893].

MEASUREMENTS (*see* Table 8.16).

VARIATION
Study of geographical variation on the Continent has been confused by the protracted winter moult from juvenile to adult pelage when animals with bicoloured dorsal pelage are common. Russian animals are larger than British, being over twice the weight.

Individual variation in external measurements is mainly related to age, season, moult and breeding condition. At 1 week old the weight of two nestlings may vary by a factor of two, but such discrepancies disappear as adult weight is reached. Melanistic and albino forms have not been observed in the wild but individuals with white patches dorsally have been found. Variation in the incidence of some skeletal characters has been demonstrated [83].

DISTRIBUTION

In Britain, 19th century records from as far north as Banffshire have been questioned, but early records from Edinburgh southwards appear to be authentic and were confirmed in a recent survey [386]. Current records are mainly from central Yorkshire southwards, with the distribution biased towards the south-east. Records from northern English counties, southern Scotland and the coastal strip of Wales probably represent isolated populations, although the status of the species in these areas and on the Isle of Wight remains uncertain.

HISTORY

From continental Europe, fossil *Micromys praeminutus* occur in the late Pliocene as one of the steppe elements of the fauna. *Micromys minutus* recorded from the Lower Pleistocene in West Germany but thereafter there is a gap in the fossil record from Europe until the Late Pleistocene [789].

The apparent scarcity of fossils in Britain (and elsewhere) could be because the animal only became numerous in recent European faunas, perhaps as a

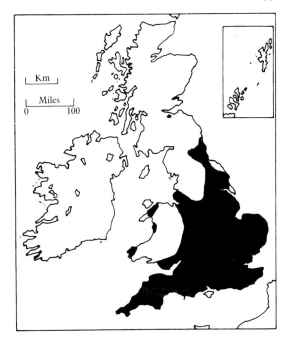

Map 8.16. Harvest mouse.

Map 8.17. Harvest mouse.

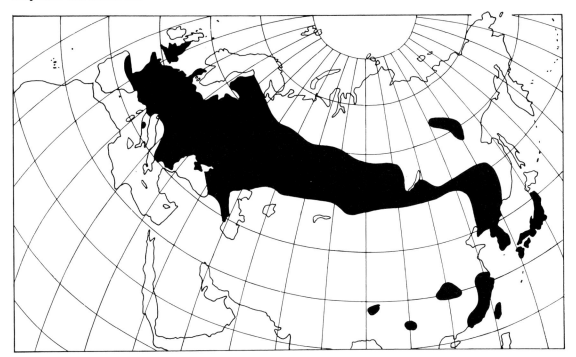

result of the clearance of woodland and the development of arable land and grasslands, which provided suitable habitats. However, many fossil rodent remains probably derive from raptor pellets [559], in which case the rarity of fossil harvest mice may merely reflect the present scarcity of harvest mice in bird pellets [386].

Whether the harvest mouse is indigenous to Britain is uncertain. Some authors consider it to be native [556], whereas others believe it to be a postglacial introduction [789]. Both suggestions are tenable, and the species may be a late post-glacial invader or an accidental introduction as a result of agricultural activities; accidental transport of the species occurs quite frequently in Britain and Europe [386, 614].

Until recently its status in Britain has been an enigma. At the end of the last century it had been recorded from most of the counties of England and parts of south and east Scotland; there were no substantiated records for Wales [386]. In the present century, the species was generally considered to be rare and in decline, until a national survey in the 1970s showed it to be widely distributed and locally common; the paucity of earlier records was attributed to the secretive nature of the species and its rarity in the pellets of predatory birds [386].

HABITAT
Favours areas of tall, dense vegetation. The breeding nests are the obvious sign of satisfactory conditions and these may be found in long grass, reedbeds, rushes, grassy hedgerows, ditches and bramble patches, cereals (with barley being least preferred) and some legume and other crops; habitats selected and species of monocotyledon used for nest building are diverse [212, 386, 451, 676]. In areas of modern agriculture, field headlands and rough grass banks act as a refuge and a reservoir during the winter. Large-scale movements are necessary from summer breeding areas such as water meadows and salt marshes, which flood in the winter [493]. Harvest mice have been recorded from young plantations but captures in coppice [409] and in mature woodland [386] may represent overspill from adjoining areas. Ungrazed meadows cut only once a year may contain considerable numbers. Occasionally recorded in rough grassy areas and waste land in urban areas [211, 386, 799].

With the dying back of vegetation in winter they appear to abandon the stalk zone and use the runway systems of other small mammals; temporary non-breeding nests are built in the bases of grass tussocks [388, 389]. There is no evidence for the normal formation of winter colonies, although concentrations of over 100 used to occur in ricks [693, 697, 762], and harvest mice occasionally overwinter in Dutch barns [388].

SOCIAL ORGANISATION AND BEHAVIOUR
An extremely active animal whose small size allows it to climb and feed in the stalk zone. When undisturbed, the mouse moves quietly amongst the vegetation, carefully testing the strength of the stems. When frightened it either 'freezes' or attempts to escape downwards into thicker vegetation.

Activity rhythms have been investigated in captivity; individual variation is large, but most studies indicate a peak of activity after dusk and close to dawn [817], although this will vary with daylength. In short days animals are primarily nocturnal, but in long days almost half the activity is in daylight [176]. Observations on captive colonies often show that some activity occurs throughout the 24 hours. Monitoring of artificial baited nests showed most activity at and after dusk [848]. Data gathered from trapping suggests that the species is more nocturnal during the summer and diurnal during winter [816].

Home ranges: in undisturbed habitats, harvest mice appear to be sedentary animals for much of the year; on the South Downs mean home-range size was $400\,m^2$ for males and $350\,m^2$ for females [816]. There is considerable movement of juveniles during the autumn, and adults may move up to $100\,m$ in spring when the population density is apparently low. Trapping data show that there is considerable overlap of home ranges for much of the year, especially for males (trap-revealed data only) [816]. Few data are available on the three-dimensional use of space but mice have been caught in traps placed high in the stalk zone in summer [848] when few can be caught at ground level [816].

Communication and senses: audible signals between individuals in the field are rare, but have been reported during courtship, mating and when the population density is high. Unlike many other rodents, blind youngsters often squeak audibly when disturbed, and produce irregular ultrasonic pulses in the range 83−114 kHz [896]. There are no published works concerning olfactory communication, but captive observations suggest that urine and faeces may be used to mark a range or territory [817].

Hearing is very acute, the animals reacting sharply to any rustling or scraping sound up to 7 m away [848]. Aided by the prehensile tail, these mice have an excellent sense of balance and judgement concerning the strength of single stems of foliage. Visual acuity is poor, but mice can detect sudden changes in silhouette from several metres.

FEEDING

Reputedly an insect and seed eater, but little published data on animals living in natural surroundings. In ricks during winter feed predominantly on cereal grains [291]. In captivity consume hard and soft bodied insects, fruits, seeds and berries. They will also pursue and catch larger insects such as butterflies and moths. In the wild they take grain from cereal heads, often eating it well above ground level and leaving characteristic sickle-shaped remains. In early spring buds are probably eaten when other food is scarce. Analysis of faecal pellets from an urban environment showed that seeds, fruit, monocotyledon and dicotyledon leaves and insects were the major dietary items, but fungi, moss, root material and other invertebrates were also consumed [211].

Food requirements are high, *c*. 2 g/day, due to the high cost of thermoregulation. Harvest mice have a surface area to volume ratio of 4.9 [344] and the daily costs of maintenance of a small harvest mouse are only slightly lower than that of a 20 g vole or mouse [315]. Mean energy budget for a 7−8 g harvest mouse has been estimated at 7.0−8.6 kcal (29.3−36.0 kJ)/day (0.97−1.07 kcal (4.06−4.48 kJ)/g/day) from both respirometry and food consumption studies [315, 817].

BREEDING

For captive British mice the gestation period was 17−19 days and litter size one to seven (mean 4.8) from 86 litters [817]. There is a post-partum oestrus and up to eight litters have been produced by a single female, though in the wild three is probably the maximum.

Mating: males pursue oestrous females on and above the ground for several minutes before mating

takes place on the ground. Mated females lose the vaginal plug quickly. Females become visibly pregnant 9−10 days after mating.

Breeding season: in England the breeding season extends from late May until October or even December depending on the weather, although in one study, 74% of litters were born in August and September [387]. Cold, wet weather, particularly in the autumn, may be a major cause of mortality, and 12% of all litters found prior to weaning were dead [387].

Litter sizes: early literature (pre-1917) gave litter sizes of four to twelve (mean 6.75 ± 0.40 from 16 published records), but in recent years eight is the maximum recorded litter size (mean 5.40 ± 1.60 from 62 wild litters); reasons for this decline in litter size are unknown [387].

Breeding nests: aerial breeding nests are built in monocotyledons by the female in late pregnancy. In the wild nests are probably built mainly at night. The female sits on a stem with her hind feet and tail, and uses her incisor teeth to split the distal ends of the grass leaf while it is still attached to the plant stalk. When enough leaves have been split longitudinally, they are woven together to form the outer framework of the nest. This is then lined by pulling more leaves through the wall and shredding their distal ends. Finally, the very centre of the nest is lined with shorter cut lengths of grass or thistle down. Usually there is no obvious entrance hole when the nest contains young mice although there may be one or two points that are regularly used for entering and leaving the nest. However, after the female abandons the young when they are 15−16 days old, they may continue to use the nest for a couple more days, and during this latter period of occupancy the nest becomes battered and obvious entrance holes may develop. Breeding nests of different females are usually spatially separated, with a minimum distance depending on the habitat type [816], and a cluster of two or three breeding nests is likely to represent successive litters from one female.

Young: in captivity birth usually occurs in early morning, but this may not be so in the wild. Development described for captive mice [286, 468, 656, 745, 817]. The young weigh 0.6 − 0.8 g at birth. Subsequent growth is extremely rapid. By the 4th day, light brown down begins to cover the back. This becomes thicker, and a dark line becomes apparent dorsally. The belly is white by the 8th and 9th days, when the eyes usually open (2.5 − 3.5 g). The position of the nipples is easily seen at this age. The young begin to leave the nest and explore at 11 days.

By the 14th day a new moult to a grey/brown coat is nearly complete and the young are capable of feeding themselves. If the mother is pregnant, the young are usually abandoned when 15 or 16 days old, and the female makes a new breeding nest, which may be close to the previous one.

POPULATION

On the basis of tooth wear, maximum life span in the wild is thought to be 18 months [500]. Data from a wild population in Britain however suggest that very few animals survive 6 months: of 454 animals marked at various ages 30% were recaptured after 6 weeks, 13.2% after 12 weeks, 4.6% after 18 weeks, 1.5% after 24 weeks and only 0.7% after 30 weeks [816]. Mice born in October survived the longest and overwintered to breed the next May or June. In captivity, several instances of non-breeding individuals living 5 years have been reported [817].

Cycles of abundance occur, particularly in continental Europe [235, 571]. In Britain, populations of 200+ per hectare may be followed by several years of low numbers [816]. Annual variations in the numbers of breeding nests may be used to compare mouse populations between years. Local populations fluctuate seasonally, and the peak numbers occur during November and fall steeply in February−March. Trapping at ground level appears to become ineffective during early and mid-summer due either to a behavioural change, perhaps associated with breeding or availability of food in the stalkzone, or to a very low density of animals. Summer samples may be biased towards males, although the average annual sex ratio is approximately equal [816]. A huge surge of juveniles is recruited into the population in September and October, and both trapping and hunting by owls are usually most successful during this period [278, 816]. Adults that have bred disappear from the population very rapidly after the termination of the breeding season. Up to four generations may reproduce within one breeding season.

MORTALITY

Predators: taken by a wide variety of vertebrates; the carnivore and bird predators include mustelids, foxes, domestic cats, owls, hawks, corvids, shrikes and even pheasants, blackbirds and toads [388]. Being active intermittently throughout 24 hours, they are liable to predation by both nocturnal and diurnal animals. However, they rarely form an important food item and most published work on predator food shows that harvest mice form less than 1% of the diet. Although nationally they occur in only 0.8% of barn owl pellets [309], a study of the food of several barn owls in West Sussex, where harvest mice are common, showed a seasonal cycle varying from a maximum of 65% of prey items in November down to less than 1% in June−July [816]. A study in Norfolk found that most of the harvest mice eaten by barn owls are young animals, and the sex ratio in pellets was 1 male : 1.2 females [124]. Remains in owl pellets can only be used as a guide to areas where harvest mice are common, and they are unlikely to be recorded by such techniques in areas where numbers are low [310, 386].

Weather: adverse weather towards the end of the breeding season causes the death of many young mice, and persistent rain, sudden drops in temperature and hard frosts can also be important causes of mortality for adult mice. Trapping data reveal that February is the month with the greatest mortality rate [816].

Others: changes in habitat management and modern methods of agriculture have probably caused a reduction in abundance, although the effects of combine harvesting, insecticide spraying, stubble burning and hedge management and clearing have not been quantified.

PARASITES

Sleptsov [740] gives lists of ectoparasites from the Continent, but there are no host-specific species. In Britain few ectoparasites were found on specimens from ricks [694], but several species of small mammal flea have been recorded on the mouse or in its nests [746, 747], and a number of mites and lice may be found in the short fur [96]. Infestation with the tick *Ixodes trianguliceps* is highest in winter, although the number of ticks is lower than on other species of small mammal that have larger home ranges [673, 674]. Infections by helminths have been reported for the Continent but not from Britain. The protozoans *Babesia microti* and a trypanosome have been recorded [174]. No fungal dermatophytes were found on ten harvest mice [240].

In continental Europe, harvest mice have been recorded as hosts to a wide variety of bacterial, viral and fungal pathogens, some of which are of economic importance. In Italian rice fields harvest mice excrete *Leptospira bataviae*, and when the mice are numerous this bacterium causes fever in rice field workers [11].

RELATIONS WITH MAN
There are no official reports of harvest mice causing damage in Britain; however, there are several instances of plague numbers of this species causing damage in USSR [740], and during occasional 'plague' periods in continental Europe harvest mice have been recorded as causing serious economic damage to stored grain [235]. They have also been reported as pests of strawberry crops in Japan [728] and may invade beet fields in Europe [456]. Even in Britain, the harvest mouse may be the most abundant small mammal species in some localities and so presumably some damage could be attributable to them. Large numbers used to occur in unthreshed ricks during the winter [697] and population estimates of up to 270 per hectare in grassland have been recorded (by trapping) [816].

Harvest mice are very easy to keep in captivity, requiring little specialised attention. They breed readily, although fighting may be a problem in captive colonies [388]. High densities of non-breeding animals live agreeably, but on lowering the density, one animal usually becomes dominant and may attack others. Mated females drive away the male, but consecutive litters have been raised successfully in captivity where the male remained in the same cage throughout. The female may consume a disturbed litter in contrast to most other rodents that simply mutilate the young. Diet does not seem to be an important factor in captive breeding, so long as dense vegetation is provided.

The conspicuous nests (particularly in the winter) facilitate locating the species, although harvest mice may be difficult to trap by conventional techniques during the summer months when they live predominantly above ground in the stalk zone. Arti-ficial baiting nests made from tennis balls with a hole cut in one side and positioned above ground level in suitable areas have been used to study the behaviour of wild harvest mice [848].

AUTHORS FOR THIS SPECIES
S. Harris and R.C. Trout.

GENUS *Mus*

A genus of about 40 species of small mice mainly in the Oriental Region and Africa (although the African species are sometimes separated in *Nannomys* or formerly in *Leggada*). They are closely related to *Rattus* and distinguished mainly by dental characters, especially the distorted shape of the first upper molars and the very reduced third molars.

The world-wide 'house mouse' group was at one time treated as a single species, *M. musculus* [718], but recent study involving both classical morphological techniques and electrophoresis of enzymes and proteins has indicated that several species were compounded in this way. Most of these species can breed together in the laboratory, but they coexist without extensive inter-breeding in the wild [552, 553, 802]. Only one species occurs wild in Britain and Ireland, and this is the same species as the domesticated laboratory and 'fancy' mice.

House mouse *Mus domesticus*

Mus musculus Linnaeus, 1758; Uppsala, Sweden (part).
Mus domesticus Rutty, 1772; Dublin, Ireland (a *nomen nudum*).
Mus muralis Barrett-Hamilton, 1899; St Kilda, Outer Hebrides (extinct).
Mus musculus domesticus; Schwarz & Schwarz, 1943.

The name *domesticus* as used by Schwarz & Schwarz (1943) has been conserved by Opinion 1607 of the International Commission of Zoological Nomenclature (1990). Grey mouse (usually in contrast to the red mouse, *Apodemus sylvaticus*).

RECOGNITION
Dull greyish-brown dorsal colour, with slightly lighter ventral surface. Juvenile wood and yellow-necked mice have very similar colouring, but can

be easily distinguished by their much longer hind feet and broader head with larger eyes (Fig. 8.23). Tail slightly thicker and more prominently scaly than that of other mice; the tail skin does not strip off easily as in the wood mouse.

Skull (Fig. 8.24) distinguished from wood and yellow-necked mice by notched upper incisors, and by three roots (rather than four) on M^1. Both M^3 and M_3 very small and occasionally absent.

SIGN

Presence revealed by faeces, runways, footprints, smears, hole scrapes, partially eaten food particles and damage.

Faeces often concentrated in favourable places, similar to those of wood mouse but smaller (about 7 mm long) and usually paler.

Runways and footprints (which are similar to but smaller than those of the wood mouse) discernible along regular routes in dusty places; small mounds of faeces, dirt, grease and urine may occur. Dirty black smears often present along well-travelled runways. 'Loop smears' similar but smaller than those of ship rats may be found around roof joists. Toothmarks on foods and other damaged com-

modities; wood mice tend to shred food and paper to a greater extent than house mice. Characteristic 'stale' smell (of acetamide).

DESCRIPTION

Pelage: rather uniform grey-brown above, and usually only slightly lighter below. The coat consists of long, straight overhairs, and shorter, kinked underhairs. The colour is effectively determined by the overhairs, although these comprise only about 20% of the total number.

Moult: periodic waves of moult spread over the body, with young hairs replacing the old ones before the latter drop out. There is no clear seasonal moult.

Nipples: usually five pairs (three thoracic and two abdominal), but variations in number are fairly common. The nipples are normally depressed, and although surrounded by folds of thickened hairless skin, are only prominent in lactating or aged females.

Scent glands: scents are produced in the preputial, coagulating (associated with the seminal vesicles) and plantar glands and in the urine. They are

Fig. 8.23. House mouse. (Photo: G. Kinns.)

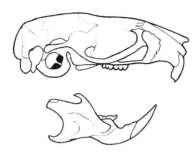

Fig. 8.24. Skull of house mouse. Note the characteristic notch in the upper incisor.

Fig. 8.25. Right upper molar teeth of house mouse showing five degrees of wear, separating ages from *c*. 2−4 months (left) to 10−14 months (right) [531].

carried particularly in the anogenital area, and may be deposited as scent marks. Marking involves placing spots of urine around the edge of an enclosure or on conspicuous objects. The male prepuce is relatively long with brush-like hairs on the tip, and a reservoir inside the tip which holds urine. The ducts of the preputial glands open near the tip.

Teeth: distinguished from other mice by distorted anterior row of cusps on M^1 and very small M^3 and M_3. Molar tooth wear seems to be a fairly accurate method of ageing mice (Fig. 8.25).

Reproductive tract: breeding can take place at any time of the year, so the reproductive tract does not regress as in many rodents. Scrotal sacs remain in contact with the body cavity, and the testes may lie in the sacs or be retracted; their situation does not indicate breeding condition in adults.

Chromosomes: 2n = 40, all acrocentric, individually recognisable by banding stains [617]. However, fusions between centromeres ('Robertsonian translocation') have been reported in a number of populations, including Caithness and several of the Orkney islands [112] (Fig. 8.26). There are clearly distinct X and Y sex chromosomes, which associate apparently end-to-end at meiosis.

RELATIONSHIPS
Of the European species previously included in *Mus musculus*, the closest relative of *M. domesticus* is *M. musculus* s.s. which replaces it in Scandinavia and northeast of a line from Denmark to the Black Sea, with little overlap and very limited interbreeding. It differs from *M. domesticus* in being paler below and having the tail shorter. This differ-

ence is by some considered only subspecific [552]. *Mus spicilegus* in S Europe (which probably includes *spretus* and forms that have, probably erroneously, been called *hortulanus* and *abbotti*) is also closely related and was formerly included in *M. musculus* [552].

MEASUREMENTS
See Table 8.21. Females tend to be slightly larger than males [66]. House mice vary greatly in both absolute size and in bodily proportions in different environments. For example, weight of mice from cold stores is *c*. 15% greater than in animals from houses and shops [508]. The tail is a heat-regulating organ, and tail length is less in mice from cold regions than warmer ones.

Overall body length and tail length continue to increase throughout life, albeit slowly in mature individuals [225]. There is considerable variation in size and weight among like-aged individuals in a population, even among older adults [179]. The length of the hind foot attains almost adult size at an early age (2−3 months after birth) and is therefore in some ways a better indication of mean size than body length.

VARIATION
Mice from Hirta, St Kilda (now extinct), were described as a distinctive species and subsequently subspecies, *M. m. muralis*, on the basis of the pale ventral colour, broad hind feet, large size (condylobasal length of skull 21−22 mm) and narrow mesopterygoid fossa on the underside of the skull [46]. This last trait also occurs in Shetland and Faroe Islands, and may imply common ancestry of these island races [87]. St Kilda race became extinct following evacuation of the human population (in 1930), apparently due to an inability to compete successfully with wood mice [84].

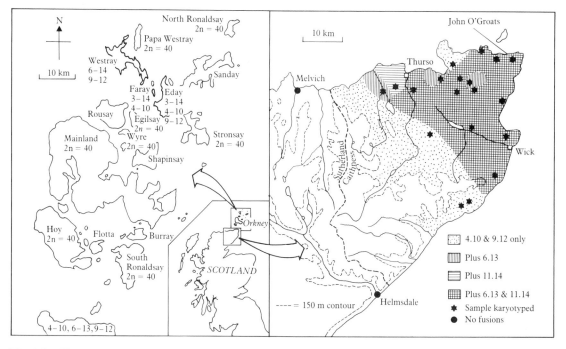

Fig. 8.26. House mouse. Distribution of Robertsonian chromosomes in Caithness and Orkney. The chromosomes are numbered from one to twenty in order of decreasing size; the numbers indicate fusions between different chromosomes [77, 720A].

Table 8.21. Measurements and litter sizes of adult house mice.

	Taunton, S England ($n = 104$)	Skokholm, Wales ($n = 117$)	Is. of May, Scotland ($n = 60$)	Orkney Mainland ($n = 331$)	Shetland Mainland ($n = 239$)
Head and body (mm)	87	93	88	75	85
Tail (mm)	74	84	71	73	75
Hind foot (mm)	16.8	17.8	17.6	17.8	18.4
Weight (g)	13.4	18.2	17.0	18.2	16.5
Mean litter size	7.2	7.5	6.7	7.7	7.6

In 1898, Jameson [441] described mice living on sand dunes on Bull Island in Dublin Bay, Ireland, ranging in colour from normal grey-brown to a light sandy hue (later named as a subspecies: *M. musculus jamesoni* Krausse, 1921). From Jameson's time, this population has been quoted as an example of natural selection for crypsis on a sandy background [e.g. 437]. There is no evidence for this: a similar colour spectrum still exists on the island, but is also found in other parts of Dublin [253]; the Bull Island itself only appeared in the early 19th century following the construction of a break-

water, and is now connected to the mainland by a causeway.

Most populations extremely variable in pelage. White ventral spotting or belly coloration common in some local groups and island races [47, 209, 705]. Other variant-coloured individuals are not infrequently found, e.g. black, black-eyed white, albino, leaden and cinnamon [146, 147, 441]. Even completely hairless adults have been described [294].

Skeletal variation (both metrical and non-metrical) is common and can be used to characterise local populations as genetically distinct [62, 63,

194, 264, 265, 511, 615, 724, 806]. Electrophoretic studies of enzyme and protein variation reveal that British mainland house mice have a mean heterozygosity per locus of about 7%, with island populations about half that value [71, 76, 81]. Evidence is lacking that local colour forms (such as *M. d. jamesoni* — see above) have spread through natural selection, but there is no doubt that some electrophoretic variants are adaptive [81, 89].

DISTRIBUTION

Besides its original range from Nepal westwards to N Africa, W and S Europe, *M. domesticus* has extended its range because of its tolerance for close association with human habitats, including ships. It is now found in the Americas, Australasia and SE Africa. It is a poor competitor in natural habitats [84, 221], and is probably restricted in its present distribution by other small mammals (particularly in Africa).

Widespread in Britain and Ireland, including most inhabited small islands.

HISTORY

Present in Britain since at least the Iron Age: the earliest well stratified record is from the pre-Roman Iron Age site at Gussage All Saints, Dorset. It formed a small (1%) but fairly constant constituent of the Peak District small mammal fauna in a bird roost cave from pre-Roman times onward [880].

HABITAT

The original habitat was probably rock crevices in the steppes of Iran and SW USSR. This niche may have pre-adapted the species for a commensal habit [705]. From this start, the species has colonised an enormous range of habitats, from coral atolls in the Pacific to near Antarctic conditions on South Georgia; from central heating ducts to refrigerated stores. In arable land in S England, the house mouse used to be the third commonest small mammal after the wood mouse and bank vole [189, 758], but its numbers have certainly decreased with the replacement of threshing by combine harvesting (corn ricks formerly protected a reservoir of mice through the unfavourable winter period). House mice avoid open fields with little cover, although in NW Scotland and the Hebrides they are caught as commonly as wood mice in agricultural land [200]. Rarely found in woodland in Britain; this is almost certainly a consequence of exclusion by other small mammals, since house mice are commonly found in woodland in other parts of the world where competitors are absent, e.g. in Hawaii [811] and New Zealand [269, 481]. House mice are not obligate commensals; they have successfully colonised many islands where there are no other small mammals, and may live completely independent of humans [90]. However, the best known habitat is in buildings and food stores [754]. Deep litter poultry houses often harbour high densities. In Ireland rarely found away from buildings on mainland, but opposite is case on offshore islands [257].

SOCIAL ORGANISATION AND BEHAVIOUR

Social organisation: direct observation, recapture studies, and genetic studies showing local concentrations of rare variants and of homozygotes have led to the assumption that house mouse populations are a collection of highly inbred family groups (or demes) with little interchange of individuals between groups. This is over-simplification: the social organisation is very flexible; in field (or feral) situations where there is a high mortality of animals at all ages, populations may approach random mating [77].

Map 8.18. House mouse.

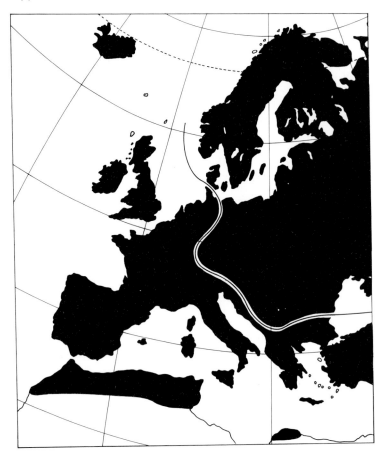

Map 8.19. House mouse (European part of range only), showing boundary between *Mus domesticus* (SW) and *M. musculus* (NE).

Home range varies enormously, and is dependent on food and cover availability, and the presence of other species. In Oxford cellars a range of *c.* 5 m² has been found [754]. This was more than twice the range in large American chicken barns [723]. In contrast, a range of 122 m² has been found in hay fields in California increasing to 365 m² where voles were absent [667].

Communication: the role of sight is not really known; sound (including ultrasound) and hearing are certainly more important in communication, both in sexual behaviour and in mother–young contacts. Mice are mainly nocturnal animals, but they use visual landmarks and are capable of visual discrimination between shapes. Uncertain whether the retina is all rods or has some cones.

Scent marking with urine is more frequent in males than females, and appears to be promoted by

changes in the environment or the presence of a strange mouse [695]. It is suppressed in behaviourally subordinate animals. Individual mice can be recognised on the basis of smell, up to a distance of at least 17 cm [117, 749]. Female oestrous cycle is very responsive to olfactory stimuli, especially urinary odours [110].

Dispersal: males move more than females, often leaving the birth area at one or two months of age. Usually little movement (*c.* 5%) between breeding groups, although over 20% of both males and females have been found to have bred at a different site to their birthplace [79].

Aggressive behaviour: mutual and immediate retreat seems to be the invariable outcome of two mice meeting on strange territory [105A]. At subsequent encounters individual differences begin to appear: one mouse holds its ground and 'freezes' and, when the other retreats, begins to make aggressive moves towards it. Fighting is frequent, particularly between territory-holding males, often leading to serious wounding. Females produce an aggression-inhibiting substance in their urine.

Activity mainly nocturnal, but exhibit periods of short-term activity (1 to 4 hours) related to feeding and stomach activity, particularly after dusk and before dawn. Out of doors, mice begin to be caught in traps within the first two hours of darkness. It is rare for mice to be caught by day, except in very dense populations. Both excess food and light (e.g. moonlit nights) reduce trapping success, presumably by restricting activity.

Movement: distances of 400 m not infrequently travelled by feral animals, and individuals have been recorded moving more than a kilometre. Little movement between separated food sources. Move away from fields and hedges into buildings in late autumn and winter; less marked reverse movement in spring. These movements are part of the characteristic tendency of the species to move in search of favourable conditions [457, 530, 699, 774]. When caged wild mice are given exercise wheels, they may achieve 60 000 revolutions in a single night (c. 20 km).

Burrow system ranges from a simple 2–3 cm diameter tunnel with one or more chambers, to a complex system with several exits and chambers (c. 10 cm in diameter), often lined with bedding material. Mice are efficient tunnellers in soft earth.

Nests vary from simple pallet to an enclosed sphere, made from any convenient material. Genetic differences between females in complexity of nest. Insulation of nest crucial to survival of young [871].

General: excellent sense of balance, and considerable climbing ability, moving up wooden or brick walls, etc., with little difficulty. Jump disconcertingly and swim capably. Mackintosh [105A, 547] has reviewed behaviour and its various components. In general, there seem to be only quantitative differences between behaviour of wild and laboratory mice.

FEEDING
Cereal grains preferred over foods containing fats and proteins. Insects form a substantial part of the diet in most wild-living populations [64, 864]. However, most foods will be taken [486, 705, 846]. Require very little free water [263]. Energy demands in the wild range from 0.42 to 1.14 kcal/g per day [665].

BREEDING
Litters of five to eight are born at about monthly intervals throughout the year (indoors) or during the summer months (outdoors).
Length of oestrous cycle; 4–5 days.
Gestation: 19–20 days (extended during lactation).
Litter size mean 6.5–7.5, normal range 5–8.
Duration of lactation c. 14 days.

Seasonality: commensal mice breed throughout the year with little reduction in winter; feral populations only during the summer months, from the end of March until the end of September. There may be rare litters born during the winter. Season is probably controlled mainly by temperature change, although food availability (including specific nutrients) may be important; house mice are unusual in that their reproduction is not affected by photoperiod [111]. However, mice living in a cold, but equable, climate may breed throughout the year [44, 88].

Mating [842, 865]: sexual maturity occurs at 5–6 weeks after birth. Copulation leaves a vaginal plug which persists for 18–24 hours. Gestation 19–20 days, but implantation may be delayed in lactating females. Little post-implantation loss, except of whole litters. [52]. The oestrous cycle is 4–5 days and there is an oestrous within 24 hours after parturition; young conceived at this time may not be born for up to 36 days due to delayed implantation. However, an average of one litter a month is normal under laboratory conditions. Females have a breeding span of 6–12 months; males about 18 months. The mean life-time production of young per fertile female is c. 40 [841].

Litter size (Table 8.21) most commonly five to eight, but varies seasonally (early litters are smaller than later ones) and in different habitats [648, 841]. Average was found to be 5.2 in houses, 5.8 in cornricks and 6.2 in cold stores [508]. Partly these differences arise because number of ova shed increases with maternal size, but this correlation disappears in large island mice, suggesting that litter size is an adaptive character in these populations [52, 688].

Sex ratio approximately equal in young animals; in most older samples, there is an excess of females [178, 648].

Young are naked, blind and bright pink at birth; after they suckle, milk becomes visible in the stomach. At 2−3 days, the eyes open; at 5−7 days, skin pigmentation becomes visible; and by 8−10 days the hair is half-grown. Weaning takes place at about 14 days when the fur is full-grown, and incisor teeth erupted. Approximately two-thirds of adult length at this time.

POPULATION

Densities: commensal populations may reach extremely high densities, much higher than when feral populations are considered to reach 'plague' numbers (Table 8.22). 'Plagues' occur almost exclusively where there is little inter-specific competition, and usually after uncommon climatic conditions (see under 'Breeding') [235, 248, 619]. Although there may be density-dependent controls on reproduction [178], these can clearly be overriden. In Britain, populations increase approximately eight-fold during the breeding season [64].

Population structure: commensal populations have a much higher proportion of older animals than wild-living ones [71, 648]. Populations living in a physically limited area may have a rather rigid structure: those in small grain storage buildings in Canada each consisted of c. 10 weaned mice of which four to seven were reproductively active, only one or two being males; population size was controlled by excluding immigrants and exporting

Table 8.22. Densities of some house mouse populations.

Habitat	No. per hectare
Artificial enclosure [532]	52 000 (max.)
Chicken barn	
Texas [723]	70 000
S Australia [620]	875 ('plague')
Open grassland, Michigan [774]	53
Rock and grassland, Skokholm, Wales [80]	60

excess young [13]. However, a proportion of emigrants establish themselves elsewhere [31, 739]. There have been many studies of the social and age structure of house mice, both in large pens and under natural conditions [70, 77, 177, 532].

Survival: commensal mice commonly live more than 2 years, but wild-living mice rarely survive two winters. The mean-life expectancy of wild mice at birth is about 100 days [78].

MORTALITY

Predation is not an important source of mortality, except when plagues occur [307]. Rats are probably as important predators as more conventional ones such as barn owls or small carnivores [191]. The greatest hazard is probably cold [86, 465, 642], and a drop in temperature may be fatal, particularly to an ageing animal [56]. A proportion of low temperature mortality is selective, and produces genetic changes in exposed populations [45, 80, 91]. Direct evidence of starvation is lacking except at very high densities [618], but food shortage is presumably a factor increasing the risk of death during cold. Although disease, most importantly ectromelia causing gangrene and loss of feet, is a recurring mortality factor in laboratory mice, the only reports of epidemic disease in wild mice are in plague populations [208, 620, 642, 658]. Infertility and uterine oedema were found in a number of adult females infected with berry bugs (*Neotrombicula autumnalis*) on the Welsh island of Skokholm [56]. Wild mice have very low titres of bacterial and viral antibodies.

PARASITES

Ectoparasites: Fleas: *Leptopsylla segnis* and *Nosopsyllus londiniensis* are specific to this species and rats, but are infrequently recorded. *Ctenophthalmus nobilis* may also be regular and *Nosopsyllus fasciatus* has been recorded.

Lice: the sucking-louse *Polyplax serrata* has been recorded, as well as the rat louse *P. spinosula*.

Mites: *Laelaps agilis*, *Myobia musculi* and *Neotrombicula autumnalis* are regular. Another seven species were reported on mice or their nesting materials from the Outer Hebrides [427].

Endoparasites: Helminths: *see* Tables 8.9 and 8.10. Very few endoparasites have been found in wild-living mice, although laboratory mice serve as experimental hosts for a great variety.

Protozoa: *Entamoeba muris, Eimeria falciformis, Cryptosporidium muris, Giardia muris, Trichomonas muris* [174].

On a world-wide scale, human cases of rickettsial pox, rat-bite fever, tularaemia and murine and scrub typhus have been linked with house mice; they can also be carriers of leptospirosis [577, 825]. Favus, a skin disease caused by the fungus *Achorion quickeanum*, can be contracted through close contact with infected mice. Despite popular belief, house mice only rarely carry *Salmonella* (food-poisoning) bacteria — only two well-documented cases of transmission to man through contamination of food, and in these the mice acquired the bacteria from rodenticide baits [115]. Infections with the enteric bacteria *Yersinia* spp. have recently been detected [397].

RELATIONS WITH MAN

A mouse only eats *c*. 4 g of food per day, but its feeding habits are very wasteful; more than 10% of the grain in corn ricks may be fragmented by mice and unsuitable for milling [754]. Moreover a mouse produces 50 or more droppings per day, and these can be difficult to remove from stored foods at economic cost [313]. In 1972 it was estimated that 9% of buildings in London were infested by house mice [683].

Active research into control was begun in the Second World War when it was realised that rat-control techniques were not reducing mouse depredations on stockpiled food stuffs. Work by Southern [754] and co-workers in the Bureau of Animal population at Oxford established the basic principles and practices of control [566, 696], and stimulated studies of the biology and behaviour of wild house mice [67, 72, 177].

Most control involves poisoning. Use of anti-coagulant poisons received serious setback with the spread of inherited resistance to warfarin [698]. Attempts to frighten mice by ultrasonic or electro-magnetic waves have failed [337, 748].

A mouse fancy was established many centuries ago in China and Japan. Some of the Japanese 'fancy' mice were brought to Europe by British traders in the mid-19th century. A national Mouse Club was established in Britain in 1895, and mouse shows continue to be held in many places. The two main groups of 'fancy' mice are 'Self' (with coats of a single colour: black, fawn, silver, champagne, etc.) and 'Marked' (dutch, tan, variegated, etc.). The number of recognised combinations is around 700 [150].

As early as 1664 Robert Hooke used a mouse to study the effects of increased air pressure. William Harvey used mice in his anatomical studies. However, the modern history of laboratory mouse breeding started in 1907 when a Harvard University student C.C. Little began to study the inheritance of coat colour under the supervision of W.E. Castle [73, 606]. Studies of mitochondrial DNA show that laboratory and 'fancy' mice are *Mus domesticus*, although they also contain traits apparently derived from other *Mus* species.

LITERATURE

Crowcroft [177] — an entertaining account of studies of house mice in grain stores. Comprehensive reference works: [12, 72, 283, 338]. General accounts with special reference to life-history and population structures: [67, 71, 705]. An introduction to 'fancy mice' [150]. A review of control techniques: [566].

SOUND RECORDINGS

Appendix 3: A, F, P.

AUTHOR FOR THIS SPECIES

R.J. Berry.

GENUS *Rattus* (RATS)

A large genus with about 60 species in the Oriental region and Australasia. A few species have become widely spread by association with man and two of these occur in Britain. Synonym: *Epimys*.

The more clear-cut differences between the two British species are listed in Table 8.23. The smaller size and more slender build of the ship rat is apparent to anyone already familiar with the common rat (Fig. 8.27), but identification can be tricky and any observation of ship rats away from their normal limited haunts should be confirmed by detailed examination whenever possible. Colour is too variable to be of much assistance.

	Common rat	Ship rat
Head and body (mm)	Up to 280	Up to 240
Tail : head and body	80–100%	100–130%
Colour of tail	Dark above, light below	Uniformly dark
Hind feet (mm)	40–44	30–38
Ear (mm)	20–22	24–27
Condylobasal length (mm)	43–54	38–43
Temporal ridges on either side of brain-case	Straight and almost parallel	Curved

Table 8.23. Distinguishing characters of adult rats.

Fig. 8.27. Ship rat (above) and common rat (below). Note the longer ears, sleeker fur and longer, thinner tail of the ship rat.

Common rat *Rattus norvegicus*

Mus norvegicus Berkenhout, 1769; Great Britain.
Mus decumanus Pallas, 1779; Europe.
Mus hibernicus Thompson, 1837; Rathfriland, Co Down, Ireland.

Brown rat, Norway rat, sewer rat.

RECOGNITION
Large size, relatively pointed muzzle and long scaly tail (a little shorter than head and body length) preclude confusion with mice, voles and squirrels. Hind feet of young much broader and a little longer than those of adult mice (over 27 mm as opposed to 22–25 mm for *Apodemus*) and tail relatively much thicker. Distinguished from ship rat by relatively smaller eyes and smaller ears which are finely furred compared with the almost hairless ears of ship rat; tail relatively shorter and thicker than that of ship rat and usually dark above and pale beneath, against the ship rat's uniformly dark tail. In water easily confused with water vole but muzzle is more pointed, ears are more prominent and tail is longer.

Skull (Fig. 8.28) very similar to that of ship rat but somewhat heavier and more angular; supra-orbital ridges tend to be less divergent over cranium than those of ship rat. Distinguishable from water vole by rooted, tuberculate molars and from squirrel by

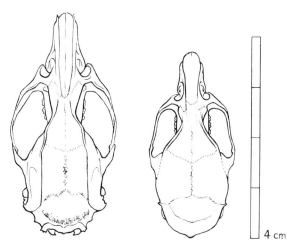

Fig. 8.28. Skulls of common rat (left) and ship rat (right). Note the more rounded braincase and temporal ridges of the ship rat.

only three cheek-teeth in each row and large infra-orbital foramen.

Footprints: four toes on forefeet, five on hind; in normal walking or trotting, impression of forefoot is always overprinted by hind foot. Tracks similar to, but much larger than, those of mice. Cannot be distinguished from ship rat and difficult to separate from water vole. Squirrel footpr... ...ow all toes pointing forward and large claws... soft mud sometimes, and in snow frequently, accompanied by tail swipes, which are also apparent in dusty environments such as grain stores.

Faeces: produce about 40 pellets a day, coarse textured; average 12 mm long, often tapering to a point at one or both ends; frequently deposited in groups (ship rat droppings are rather thinner, usually have rounded ends and tend to be deposited singly; those of water voles smaller, with rounded ends and smooth texture). Faeces of the two rats can be distinguished by microscopic examination of their hairs in the droppings [829].

Cached food such as grain or even eggs sometimes found in burrows, but large hoards uncommon.

Burrows generally 6−9 cm in diameter, often situated on sloping ground — banks or the sides of ditches — or beneath some form of cover such as flat stones, logs or tree roots. Earth dug from burrows remains in a heap close to the entrances.

Runs may show as slight linear depressions in grass or other low vegetation or as well-worn trails of bare, trampled earth. They may be 5−10 cm wide, and are continuous (rabbit runs are discontinuous, showing as series of depressions in grass). Runs in buildings show as dark, greasy smears on wood or brickwork. To a practised eye, runs are often the main clue to the presence of this secretive species.

Damage common in rat-infested areas; rats gnaw many materials (including some grades of aluminium) to gain access to food and to keep their continually growing incisors short.

DESCRIPTION

Pelage: fur of adults somewhat shaggy, grey-brown above and pale grey beneath (but melanics are common in some populations). Some individuals show white blaze or stripe mid-ventrally. Fur of juveniles from weaning to about 3 months (up to 100 g body weight) shorter, sleeker and greyer than that of adults. Clear moult patterns sometimes evident in animals reaching maturity. Sparse fur on tail (skin also) dark dorsally and pale ventrally. No sexual difference in pelage.

Nipples: six pairs (three axillary, three abdominal).

Chromosomes: $2n = 42$, $FNa = 62$ [893].

MEASUREMENTS
Head and body about 110 mm at weaning, increasing to 280 mm or more. Condylobasal length of skull up to 54 mm in large adults. Weight from 40 g at weaning to 500 g; largest recorded 794 g [519]. Males tend to be larger than females. Growth occurs throughout normal life span of 1−2 years.

VARIATION
Little variation over vast geographical range. Melanics comprise 1−2% of some populations, e.g. in London [850]. Albinism rare.

DISTRIBUTION
In urban areas throughout most of the world except in low altitude inland towns in the mainland tropics and subtropics (Africa, Asia, South America). In cultivated land and away from human habitation

Fig. 8.29. Common rat. (Photo: P. Morris.)

only in temperate regions and tropical islands where there are no or few indigenous competitors.

Found in all parts of the British Isles except in the most exposed mountain regions and on some of the smaller off-shore islands (but present on the majority of small islands).

HISTORY

Probably originated in eastern USSR or China but spread across Europe and into the British Isles during the 18th century, largely replacing the ship rat which had been present for many hundreds of years. Exact date of introduction to Britain uncertain but thought to have been around 1728–29 [47] in shipping from Russia. (Arrival in Norway considerably later, and the assumption, perpetuated in the specific name *norvegicus*, that it came to Britain from Norway is erroneous.) Spread in Scotland slow: described in 1855 as 'recently introduced' in some highland areas [555]. Still replacing ship rat in parts of United States as late as 1951 [227] and more recently in Israel [336].

HABITAT

Highly adaptable and versatile but generally limited to habitats where competing species are few or absent or where the food is augmented by human activity. Typically found associated with farms, refuse tips, sewers, urban waterways and warehouses, but occur in hedgerows around cereal crops, principally in summer and autumn, and root crops (particularly sugar beet) all the year round. Prefer areas with dense groundcover close to water.

Populations independent of man occur in many coastal habitats, particularly salt marshes; on many islands (e.g. Isle of Man, Rhum, Lundy) they occupy grassland as well as all types of coastline.

SOCIAL ORGANISATION AND BEHAVIOUR

Social organisation: tend to live in colonies, which may not be single large social groups but rather aggregations of smaller social units or 'clans' [260]. Each clan probably consists of a mated pair or a male and associated harem that defend a territory around a single burrow system or other harbourage [807], although this territory may include only runs and not the space between them [129, 800]. Some evidence suggests that some clans may be founded by several rats migrating together or within a few days of each other, rather than by a pair or single pregnant female [540]. As population density increases, territory defended by each clan decreases [539], and a dominance structure develops with high-ranking males and their harems occupying the most favourable positions close to food sources [129]. If a food source is contained within a particular clan's territory, it may be effectively unavailable to members of other clans, a possibility that has considerable implications in the field of rat control [260]. Similarly, social hierarchy has been implicated in limiting the access of subordinate rats to food (and hence to poison bait) [220].

Home range and dispersal: extent and patterns of movement largely attributable to food distribution. Longest recorded single overnight journey 3.3 km [795, 798], with 0.5 km journeys common [260] except where rats concentrated around food sources. Mean range lengths for hedgerow-dwelling males found to be 660 m (females 340 m) [795] whereas average range length of mixed-sex groups around food stores was only 65 m [383]. As well as ranging less widely, females also tend to defend smaller territories [807].

No clearly defined annual rhythm in urban situations. On agricultural land, the majority of 'transient' rats in summer and autumn are males [95], probably displaced by social pressure, whereas in winter there is a definite increase in the infestation of farm premises [436], with infestations more than 100 m away from food sources unlikely to survive [392]. End of autumn influx may be due to increased random movement but some individuals at least are familiar with areas outside their normal home ranges. Radio-tracked rats made long journeys outside their previously recorded ranges when supplementary food was discontinued [795]. Many hearsay reports of mass movements of rats, but no evidence of any regular movement of this type.

Map 8.20. Common rat.

Map 8.21. Common rat (also in many other parts of the world).

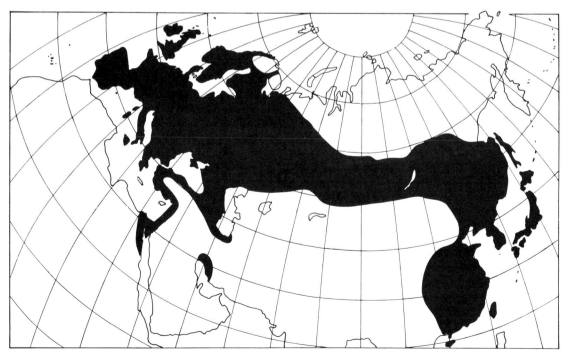

Communication: auditory and olfactory communication probably most important. Rats can hear sounds up to 100 kHz and a large part of their vocalisations are above 20 kHz, the level usually accepted as ultrasonic; most ultrasonic calls tend to be of short duration (3–300 ms) with rates of calling from 50 to 150 per minute [369]. In conflicts with other rats or predators shrill squeaks, 'grunt-squeaks' and whistles are emitted, but ultrasounds seem to be at least as important as audible sound in the areas of courtship and submission and are one of the major methods of communication between rat pups and their mother where, for example, they induce the production of prolactin [801]. Nevertheless, devices attempting to control rats by using ultrasound emissions are apparently useless [566]. Female rats can distinguish the sex of their offspring by smell [602] and olfaction has also been implicated in the induction of lactation [120]. Similarly, olfaction and ultrasonic communication have been linked in mate selection and other social interactions [369], and individual rat groups may have distinct odours or vocalisations or both. Certainly, sniffing and grooming play a large part in rat social behaviour.

Aggressive behaviour occurs within colonies as population pressure increases and is shown towards strangers entering colonies. Typically, encounters start with olfactory inspection. The antagonists may then stand on their hind legs facing each other in a 'boxing' attitude but more often they advance sideways towards each other. Vigorous scuffles are accompanied by squealing and the first rat to break off is pursued by the other. Injury from aggressive encounters is almost always on the rump. Subordinate individuals in dense colonies are often hairless and deeply scarred in this region.

Activity is mainly nocturnal but sometimes becomes diurnal in undisturbed situations, especially on frosty nights, or in response to daytime feeding opportunities. Individuals within otherwise nocturnal populations may become diurnal at times [795]. Peak activity can be at onset of darkness and again around 3 a.m. until dawn [134]. Rats in farmland showed peak of activity away from homesites 4–5 hours after sunset [795].

Movement is normally a fast trot along familiar runs but they may amble slowly, rocking body from side to side while searching for food. Will progress by repeated high bounds if chased over unfamiliar ground or when carrying large object. Swim and dive well. Climb in buildings and sometimes frequent roofs but do not often climb trees.

Burrowing: forepaws used for digging, hind feet typically kick in unison to clear loose soil from burrow entrance. Extensive systems with many exits used for generations. Individuals may use several different burrows within home range, sometimes swapping daily [795], but sometimes use same den repeatedly. Occasionally use rabbit burrows.

Nests usually below ground but can be amongst sacks or straw bales.

Senses: hearing and smell acute, sight relatively poor. Touch extremely important, especially the vibrissae or whiskers; movement patterns predictable (kinaesthesis — 'movement sense'), hence the production of well defined runs and the success of traps or sticky boards placed on these runs. Ultrasonic echolocation also apparently used [462]. Mainly use hearing to detect danger but sight sufficiently good to detect movement of potential predator. Disturbed by torchlight at night, eye reflects dull red; use of red filter on torch has little effect on degree of disturbance. Show intimate knowledge of environment and react suspiciously to any change. Unfamiliar objects placed within environment may be avoided for 48 hours or more [731].

Grooming: forepaws, hind feet, also tongue and incisors used. Rats in small well-fed populations groom meticulously. In dense populations where social order breaks down, grooming tends to be more cursory or even ignored.

FEEDING
An omnivorous opportunist but prefers starch-rich or protein-rich foods, typically cereals. In urban environments, meat, fish, bones and even soap and candles are also eaten. In agricultural land, cereals and root crops are most commonly eaten but brassicas may be attacked in the absence of more sustaining food. Many weed seeds are eaten, e.g. dock (*Rumex*) and goosefoot (*Chenopodium*); also invertebrates such as earthworms. Sea-shore colonies may feed on rice grass (*Spartina*) or crustaceans, principally crabs (*Carcinus*) and sandhoppers (Am-

phipoda) and riverside groups on molluscs [625]. Particles of food are typically picked up in the mouth and carried to a safe spot to be eaten. Food is sometimes held in the forepaws while it is gnawed.

Repeated journeys are often made from a vantage point to the food source to pick up a small item of food such as a wheat grain. Large items of food such as an apple or crab are carried in the mouth with the head held high and the animal progressing in high leaps to keep its burden clear of the ground. Larger items of food may be dragged towards safe cover. Laboratory rats, especially lactating females, hoard large amounts of food. Conflicting reports in the wild [129, 540] have led to the suggestion that hoarding of items may depend on size, larger items being cached and smaller ones being eaten immediately [625]. However, large hoards are uncommon and some apparently cached food may never be returned to. New food sources approached with caution and during first few days may be sampled only.

BREEDING

May be continuous in an unchanging environment with good food source; in these circumstances around 30% of females are pregnant throughout year [519]. In less favourable habitats breeding takes place mainly in summer and autumn. There is often a post-partum oestrus but females rarely produce more than five litters per year. Litter size related to size of mother, e.g. six at 150 g; and 11 at 500 g; average litter size seven to eight. Gestation 21–24 days; young born naked and blind; eyes open at 6 days; weaned at about 3 weeks; females mature at about 115 g (11 weeks).

POPULATION

Very dense populations, composed mostly of young individuals, may develop in favourable environments such as refuse tips. Thus of 185 rats caught on a refuse tip in November, 120 (65%) weighed 110 g or less. By the following January when food was scarce none of the 42 rats caught was under 115 g. Mortality of young in the nest and just after emergence in saturated populations was thought to be 99% per annum [186], and adult mortality may be over 90% per annum. Few rats therefore live for more than a year. Populations tend to be high in autumn and early winter and low in spring. Sex ratios in favourable environments tend to be biased towards females; percentage of male rats in corn ricks fell from 51 in juveniles (< 44 g) to 41 in adults (> 195 g), suggesting that it is sexually mature males that are displaced [519].

MORTALITY

Young rats are fair game to most predatory animals

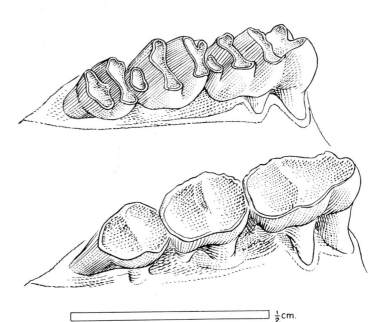

Fig. 8.30. Common rat: lower molars slightly worn (above) and heavily worn (below). Anterior on right.

½ cm.

but the aggressive nature of large rats may deter the smaller predators, such as weasels and owls; largest taken in study of barn owl predation had estimated weight of 164 g [603]. Established populations less vulnerable to predation than rats on the move. Cats may prevent invasion of farm buildings by rats but cannot eliminate an established population [237], possibly because they too will not often take rats of > 200 g [133]. Highest published incidence in fox stomachs was 13% [525]. Of 11 farmland rats that were radio-tracked, two died from poisoning, two were crushed by motor vehicles, five were killed by predators and two died from unknown causes [795].

PARASITES
See Tables 8.8, 8.9 and 8.10.

Fleas: *Nosopsyllus fasciatus* and *Ctenophthalmus nobilis* are regular. *Megabothris walkeri* and *M. turbidus* are irregular, and *Nosopsyllus londiniensis* and *Xenopsylla cheopis* have been recorded but their status on this species is not well established.

Sucking lice: *Polyplax spinosula* is common.

Mites: common mites found on 444 rats mainly from London were *Laelaps echidninus* (24%) and *Haematopinus spinulosus* (11%).

Tape worms: *Hymenolepis diminuta* and *H. longior* were found in, respectively, 28% and 25% of the rats. *Trypanosoma lewisi* was found in 19% [36].

Diseases: Leptospirosis is possibly the most common disease transmissible to man that is carried by rats in Britain. Kidney examination showed 23% infected with leptospires in 1922 [36] and 43% infected in 1958 [113]. However, this may not represent a real rise in infection, since a Canadian study showed that the incidence of rats as carriers varied from 0–46% depending on where they were caught [566]. Salmonella, the gut parasite, which causes food poisoning in man, is also commonly found in rats. Other diseases carried by rats in Britain are lymphocytic choriomeningitis and toxoplasmosis.

Common rats transmit plague and typhus in some parts of the world but they are probably not such important vectors as are ship rats because they tend to live outside rather than inside houses.

RELATIONS WITH MAN
Success and spread all over the world due to development of ability to live in close association with man. Noted as a pest of crops and stored foodstuff. Losses due to consumption of stored wheat by rats shown to be small compared with losses resulting from damage to the bags containing the wheat [41]. Contamination of foodstuff intended for human consumption with excreta and hairs important economically in most developed countries of the world [e.g. 224]. In Britain, prevention of damage by Pests Act 1949 requires notification of local authority of substantial numbers of rats. Very important as vector of some human diseases, particularly leptospirosis among rice-field workers in Spain and Italy [51] and cane-field workers in Pacific and Caribbean islands. May also be important as predator of 'desirable' wildlife, especially seabirds and their eggs on islands [585]. Almost universally hated and reviled by Western man but tolerated in the East. Stories of rats jumping at people's throats are exaggerated misinterpretations. Cornered rats jump to escape, not attack.

Earliest efforts to control rats involved traps but because rats (particularly common rat) avoid objects new to their environment trapping is largely ineffective. Rats may also react to human odour, compounding the difficulties of trapping [797]. Poisons now widely used to control rats. Initially acute poisons (e.g. arsenic, zinc phosphide) used but these produce bait shyness in rats taking sublethal quantities and generally result in less than 50% kill. They are also hazardous to operators and environment. Modern rodenticides are mostly anticoagulant poisons which are absorbed slowly by the body, requiring rats to feed for several days before lethal dose is taken and before the onset of symptoms. Bait shyness does not occur and there is less risk of accidental poisoning. First generation anticoagulants (e.g. warfarin) require rats to feed for 3–7 days before lethal dose ingested. The efficacy of these poisons is threatened by the spread of warfarin-resistance [752]. Second generation compounds (e.g. bromadiolone, brodifacoum) can kill after a single feed but onset of symptoms may still take days and so there is no bait shyness.

Secondary poisoning (i.e. effect on predators or scavengers of poisoned rats) is a serious problem with acute poisons, and far less important with anticoagulants. A predator would have to eat warfarin-poisoned rats for several days before it was affected. Second generation anticoagulants present greater risk of secondary and accidental poisoning. Vitamin K_1 an effective antidote to all anticoagulant rodenticides.

On the credit side, has served man for many decades as a laboratory animal. Laboratory rats are docile and respond to regular handling. Captive wild rats, even if hand-reared from very young, become jumpy and difficult to handle at an early age.

LITERATURE
Matheson (555) — a general, illustrated account. Twigg [822] — a sound popular account. Hart [390] — a personal account. Meehan [566] — an exceptionally well-referenced account with emphasis on control.

SOUND RECORDINGS
Appendix 3: A, F, J, P.

AUTHORS FOR THIS SPECIES
K.D. Taylor, M.G. Fenn and D.W. Macdonald.

Ship rat *Rattus rattus*

Mus rattus Linnaeus, 1758; Sweden.
Mus alexandrinus Desmarest, 1819; Egypt.
Mus frugivorus Rafinesque, 1814; Sicily.

Black rat, roof rat, house rat, alexandrine rat.

RECOGNITION
Very similar in appearance to common rat, but relatively larger eyes and ears, and longer, thinner, unicoloured tail distinguish it at close quarters (Fig. 8.27). In the hand, ears can be seen to be thinner and almost hairless compared with common rat's rather furry ears (Fig. 8.31). Guard hairs on back and flanks and vibrissae proportionately very much longer than those of common rat giving animal a somewhat spiky appearance when seen against a light background. Black fur not diagnostic, since a proportion of common rats are black and many ship rats are brown.

Skull is very similar to that of common rat; may be distinguished by flask-shaped outline of cranium and smaller, lighter construction.

Fig. 8.31. Ship rat. (Photo: P. Morris.)

SIGN

Footprints indistinguishable from common rat.

Faeces: average about 9 mm in length and tend to be smaller than those of common rat, having rounded rather than pointed ends. In large samples (over 50), droppings of the two species can be distinguished with 95% confidence on the basis of the relationship between length (l) and diameter (d), those of ship rat being proportionately thinner. If d/l is between 0.31 and 0.37 the likelihood is that the droppings are those of ship rat; if d/l is between 0.42 and 0.46 they are of common rat [193].

Burrows similar to those of common rat are made very occasionally.

Runs: greasy smears develop in places where rats pass frequently. 'Loop smears' (i.e. those left on vertical surfaces beneath joists or other obstructions where rats pass) broken rather than continuous as with common rat (Fig. 8.32). This characteristic appears diagnostic.

DESCRIPTION

Pelage is typically grey-brown above and pale grey beneath, but may also be completely black, or grey-brown above and creamy white beneath. In the last colour form there is usually a sharp demarcation between the belly and flanks, whereas in other colour forms gradation occurs. Numerous long guard hairs on flanks and dorsum. Skin and bristles on tail uniformly dark grey to black.

Nipples: variable but often two pairs axillary, three pairs abdominal.

Chromosomes: 2n = 38, FNa = 58 [893]. (A form with 2n = 42 in SE Asia should probably be considered specifically distinct, as *R. diardii*.)

RELATIONSHIPS
Very closely related species which were formerly classed as subspecies of *R. rattus* also associate with man in SE Asia, e.g. *R. argentiventer* (rice fields), *R. tiomanicus* (oil palms), *R. diardii* (urban areas).

MEASUREMENTS
Growth can continue throughout life; head and body of old individuals may reach 240 mm and tail up to 260 mm. Weight may reach 280 g but adults usually weigh 150–200 g. Males generally larger than females.

VARIATION
The colour of the pelage is polymorphic in most populations, the three forms being all black (*rattus* type), brown with grey belly (*alexandrinus* type) and brown with creamy white belly (*frugivorus* type). The frequencies of the morphs vary geographically and in different habitats, black usually being dominant in urban areas and the others in rural areas, but they do not constitute geographically definable subspecies.

In London in 1941–43, 56% were black, 24% white-bellied, 18% grey-bellied and 2% intermediate [851], but proportions fluctuate.

DISTRIBUTION
In urban areas throughout tropics and subtropics

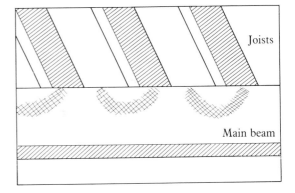

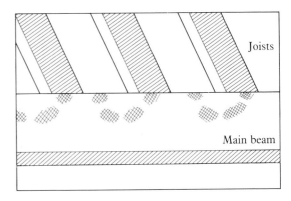

Fig. 8.32. 'Loop-smears' produced by common rats (above) and ship rats (below).

extending to many small villages and even remote farms, but do not live away from buildings except on islands where there are few or no indigenous competitors, e.g. in Caribbean and Pacific. Present in many towns in temperate regions, but tend to be restricted to ports in cooler temperate areas.

Formerly widespread in Britain but now largely replaced by common rat. On mainland recorded since 1984 only in Southwark, London, and in Avonmouth.

Colonies may occasionally develop in unexpected places following accidental translocation of individuals by road or rail. Present on the island of Lundy (Bristol Channel) in 1970 but numbers probably falling, and probably still exists on Alderney and Sark [651] and Westray in Orkney. Also present for many years on Shiant Islands, off Skye [773].

HISTORY
Probably one of the first mammals to associate with

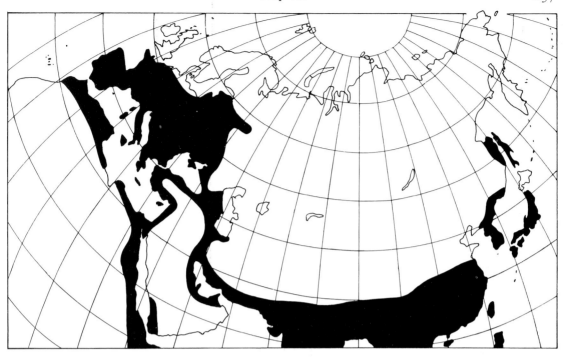

Map 8.22. Ship rat (also widespread in much of the tropics).

early man. May have spread from India to Egypt in the 4th century BC and thence along trade routes into Europe, reaching Britain during Roman times [21]. In other parts of the world, e.g. central Africa, its spread has occurred during the present century, following increasing urbanisation.

In Britain well stratified remains have been recorded in Roman sites at London, York and Wroxeter dating from the 3rd to 5th centuries AD [21]. Probably widespread in human habitation in Britain and Ireland until gradually replaced by common rat, beginning in the 18th century. By 1956 was restricted to major ports, a few inland towns and some small islands [58]; by 1961 only in a few seaports [59]. Not recorded in Manchester since 1978, Bristol since 1980, in Liverpool, Glasgow and Aberdeen since 1983. Disappearance has often coincided with demolition of dockside seed or flour mills in which rats were difficult to control with rodenticides. Elsewhere contraction has been due to habit of living only within buildings, making it more vulnerable to control measures than the common rat.

HABITAT

In Britain, mainly restricted to dockside warehouses, food-processing plants, etc., but has also occurred in supermarkets, restaurants and modern department stores. Does not live out of doors in towns. Favours buildings with cavity walls, wall panelling and false ceilings where it can move unseen. Occupies rocks and cliffs on Shiants, Lundy and Channel Islands where it is also said to live in trees [30]. Commonly nests in trees in tropical environments.

SOCIAL ORGANISATION AND BEHAVIOUR

Social organisation: live in groups each dominated by a male; more or less linear male hierarchy but less well defined female hierarchy. Intruders attacked and usually driven off but may be accepted if persistent [249].

Scent marking: observed to rub cheeks and ventral surface on branches [249].

Aggressive behaviour: agonistic encounters within groups are common, particularly after feeding. Attacks more often initiated by females than males; males inhibited from attacking females. Encounters end with appeasement or flight, physical injury rare. Most common form of attack termed 'broadsiding' in which one rat approaches another, turning sideways and pushing its opponent with hindquarters; opponent may respond with similar action. Fighting may also involve rolling and wrestling, leaping onto an opponent and 'boxing' as in common rat. Most essential component of appeasement involves mouth-to-mouth contact [249].

Activity predominantly nocturnal but may become active in daylight in undisturbed habitats or when food is scarce.

Movement similar to that of common rat but tends to move much more rapidly. Typically, sprints along ledges, overhead pipes or beams and then pauses motionless at a vantage point before sprinting again. An extremely agile climber; able to cope equally with thin wire (vertical or horizontal), brickwork and vertical pipes, provided they are sited against a wall. Can swim, but unlike common rat does not often enter water voluntarily.

Senses similar to common rat but sight better. React less strongly to unfamiliar objects than common rats and may enter traps on first night of setting.

FEEDING
Omnivorous, but often more vegetarian than common rats and notably partial to fruit. Most agricultural crops — particularly cereals — are eaten, and in the tropics sugar cane, coconuts, cocoa and even oranges and coffee berries. On Lundy, stomachs contained more vegetable matter and fewer animal remains than those of common rat.

BREEDING
Females sexually mature at about 90 g. Average litter size recorded as 6.9 on shore and 7.5 on ships in Port of London [851]. Number of embryos correlated with body weight of female. Intra-uterine mortality 25% in London. Most breeding in London from mid-March to mid-November. Litter rate about three to five per year. Gestation period 21 days [472], but 23–29 days for lactating females [249].

POPULATION
Densities vary greatly with environment. In scrubland in Cyprus 5–12 per hectare recorded [852]; in a residential area of Freetown, Sierra Leone, 52 per hectare [518]. Turnover is fast, annual mortality being of the order of 91–97% [186].

MORTALITY
In urban situations, the domestic cat is probably chief predator, but in agricultural and natural environments outside British Isles ship rats are fair game to most small mammalian, avian and reptilian predators. It has frequently been said that common rats will fight with and kill ship rats, and this has been demonstrated in confined colonies [42]. However, the two species are sympatric over much of their range (including Lundy) and it is doubtful whether the common rat under natural conditions ever preys significantly on ship rats. Replacement of the latter species by the larger common rat in many temperate regions is probably due to the common rat's greater ability to withstand cold and to hunt for food under adverse conditions. In the tropics the ship rat is well able to hold its own.

PARASITES
See Table 8.8.

Fleas such as *Nosopsyllus londiniensis*, *N. fasciatus*, *Leptopsylla segnis* and *Xenopsylla cheopis* are recorded and are all regular on this species. *Ctenophthalmus nobilis* has been recorded as a casual. Occasionally imports of ship rats have brought exotic species with them such as *Xenopsylla brasiliensis* and *X. astia*.

Lice: the sucking-louse *Polyplax spinosula* is known from this species.

Diseases: Under popular name of 'black rat' this species has been associated in people's minds for centuries with the Black Death (bubonic plague), and was responsible for transmitting the catastrophic out-breaks of the disease that occurred in Europe in the Middle Ages. But common rat can also act as vector, and both species are highly susceptible to the disease and therefore, strictly speaking, do not constitute reservoirs. The true reservoirs are species of wild rodent that are comparatively resistant to plague. Ship rats appear to carry the same diseases and parasites as common rats.

RELATIONS WITH MAN
Has developed marked ability to live in close association with man; much better adapted to living in buildings than common rat and consequently a more important urban pest in many areas. Often occurs in residential areas of tropical towns, living within the houses, and has been know to gnaw the soles of the inmates' feet while they slept. Damage and fouling in stored foodstuffs very widespread. A serious pest of agriculture on islands (notably in Pacific and Caribbean, but also Cyprus and elsewhere) attacking most crops, but particularly coconuts, sugar cane and cocoa. An important vector of plague and typhus, principally in the East.

SOUND RECORDING
Appendix 3: P.

AUTHOR FOR THIS SPECIES
K.D. Taylor.

FAMILY GLIRIDAE (DORMICE)

A small but distinctive family with eight genera, mostly monospecific, in the Palaearctic Region and Africa. Compared with the small murid rodents, dormice tend to occupy more specialised habitats. They occur at lower density, have a lower breeding potential and, except in the tropics, spend the winter in hibernation. In Britain there is one native and one introduced species, belonging to separate genera. Their characters are contrasted in Table 8.24. There is an intriguing record of a third species, the European garden dormouse *Eliomys quercinus*, in the form of subfossil mandibles from a Roman site at York [631].

Common dormouse *Muscardinus avellanarius*

Mus avellanarius Linnaeus, 1758; Sweden.

Hazel dormouse, sleeper.

RECOGNITION
Thick bushy tail is distinctive amongst mouse-sized animals. Small size and bright golden or orange-brown pelage make it very different from the fat dormouse (Fig. 8.33, Table 8.24). Juveniles greyer brown.

Skull is easily distinguished by four cheek-teeth in each row, the large ones having a unique pattern of numerous transverse ridges (Fig. 8.35).

SIGN
Possible to locate by searching for nests and especially signs of honeysuckle bark having been stripped in fine shreds for nest building in the shrub layer. (Grey squirrels and rabbits will also strip bark but more coarsely and generally high or at ground level.) Nests are most distinctive when above ground (up to 10 m), generally amongst dense undergrowth, climbing plants, in hollow branches or in the cleft of a sapling; even in gorse or bracken. Up to 15 cm in diameter, commonly made entirely of honeysuckle bark but grass, moss and leaves also used. Distinguished from birds' nests by lack of a clearly defined entrance hole. The structure is woven to surround the animal — only a few species of birds make domed nests, (e.g. the wren), sometimes found in similar situations, but then entrance hole is distinct and lower rim of hole is reinforced with grass and fibres.

Hazelnuts opened by gnawing distinctive smooth, round hole, with oblique tooth marks around cut edge; whereas wood mice and bank voles show marks of lower incisors left radially on cut surface of hole (Fig. 8.8). Characteristically opened hazelnuts provide most helpful indication of presence of dormouse [434]. Ash keys also gnawed.

Table 8.24. Characters of dormice.

	Common dormouse	Fat dormouse
Head and body (mm)	60–90	130–180
Hind feet (mm)	15–18	24–34
Colour of pelage	Orange-brown	Grey or greyish brown
Tail	Slightly bushy	Very bushy

Fig. 8.33. Common dormouse (above) and fat dormouse (below), to same scale.

Fig. 8.34. Common dormouse in hibernating attitude. (Photo: V. Almy.)

DESCRIPTION

Muzzle short, vibrissae very long, up to 30 mm. Eyes prominent, black; ears short and rounded. Feet slender with large pads; prehensile and capable of much movement at wrist and ankle. Four digits on fore and hind, plus rudimentary thumb and hallux. Tail almost as long as head and body, thickly furred with long hairs, giving thick bushy appearance.

Pelage soft and dense. Upper parts and tail uniform orange-brown, underside pale buff with pure white on throat, sometimes extending back as a narrow line to belly. Little difference between summer and winter coat. Juveniles greyer.

Moult: little information, winter pelage assumed in October.

Nipples: four pairs (one pectoral, one abdominal and two inguinal).

Scent glands near to anus in both sexes [430], but odour-free to human nose compared with other rodents.

Teeth 1.0.1.3/1.0.1.3. Premolars small and single-rooted, molars large, multiple-rooted, with flat crown bearing characteristic transverse ridges.

Chromosomes: 2n = 46 (continental data) [893].

MEASUREMENTS

Head and body of young animals in autumn 68–79 mm (8 in British Museum), of adults in summer about 80–85 mm. Tail 57–68 mm. Sub-adults at end of winter weigh 10–13 g. Adults 15–20 g, pregnant females reaching *c.* 26 g. Up to 43 g before hibernation recorded in captivity [668].

VARIATION

Description of a distinctive British race (*M.a. anglicus* Barrett-Hamilton, 1900, Bedford Purlieus, Thornhough, Northants), was based on supposedly brighter colour but this has been discredited [573]. White tail-tip not uncommon, frequency *c.* 10%. Albinos recorded but rare. Damaged ears and loss of tail tip are common.

DISTRIBUTION

Widespread but local in suitable habitats from mid-Wales, Leicestershire and Suffolk southwards

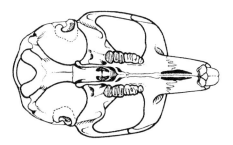

Fig. 8.35. Common dormouse: skull from below.

[434]. Apparently scarce further north and likely to have declined in the northern English counties. Records in 19th century from as far north as Carlisle and the Tyne. Evidently declined in abundance, probably due to habitat loss but also adverse climatic factors.

HISTORY

Probably a natural late post-glacial coloniser, arriving in Britain *c.* 9000 years ago, but the earliest subfossil finds date from just before the Roman period, at Ossom's Cave, Staffordshire [880].

HABITAT

Deciduous woodland with plenty of secondary growth and scrub (e.g. bramble), especially where there are trees with edible seed, e.g. hazel, sweet chestnut, beech. Frequently found in coppice, sometimes in species-rich hedgerows but also damp woods (with many mosses) and even in marshy places and reed beds with alders and bramble. Physical structure of woodland is important, especially availability of arboreal pathways formed by sprawling coppice and tangles of climbing plants such as honeysuckle [109A].

SOCIAL ORGANISATION AND BEHAVIOUR

Social organisation not known, though multiple occupancy of nests is often recorded. Older literature sometimes refers to 'colonies', i.e. several animals or nests found in close proximity. Some evidence of persistent pair-bonds [109].

Home range: an agile climber, spending majority of time high above ground in tree canopy and shrub layer. Travel about 250 m per night (radio-tracking observations); range probably about 0.5 hectare but may travel longer distances and use

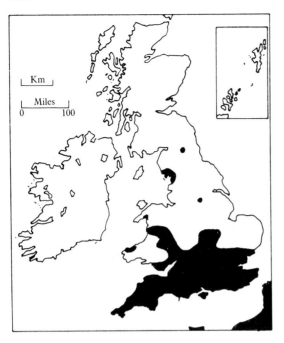

Map 8.23. Common dormouse.

larger area in course of a full season. May use several different nests in succession.

Communication: generally silent even when disturbed, but shrill squeaking noises noted during chases and aggression in captivity. Mewing and purring sounds also heard, and hibernating animals may produce a wheezing sound as they wake [431].

Dispersal: movement of marked animals in Germany recorded up to 1600 m for males and 700 m for females, but most appeared to remain close to point of first capture [716].

Activity strictly nocturnal except on rare occasions; young may be active in daylight. In summer, usually active whole night, but activity period reduced in autumn to a few hours per night [839] and probably also in bad weather. May enter facultative torpor in summer if food scarce or weather inclement.

Hibernate in nests that are usually at or below ground level. Hibernation very profound (Fig. 8.34); usually lasts from October to April but observations

Map 8.24. Common dormouse.

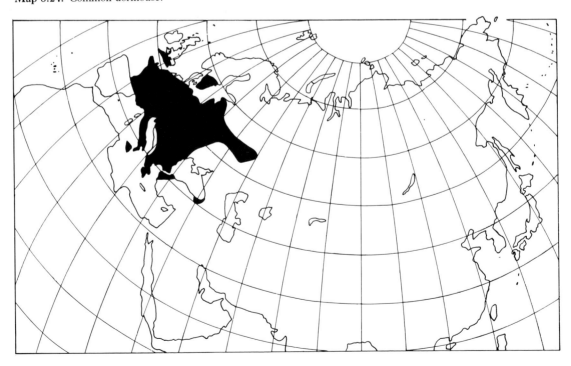

in captivity suggest that it is not normally continuous, with several days of activity alternating with several weeks of sleep. Most frequent arousals at beginning and end of winter [432, 839]. Hibernation studied in detail in Germany [231].

Onset appears to be induced by environmental temperature remaining below 15°C. Body temperature controlled during hibernation and does not fall below 0°C. Fully awake when body temperature reaches 31−32°C, normal temperature 34−38°C. Torpor during the summer has been observed at 17°C ambient temperature [109].

Movement: an agile climber, spending much time up to 5 m above ground [716]. May go higher into tree canopy, to at least 12 m.

Nests: dormice do not burrow. In summer usually occupy nests above ground, up to 10 m high but often in shrubs within a metre of the ground. Breeding nest about 15 cm diameter; newly independent young make smaller nests, up to 10 cm, often grouped only a few metres apart [432]. They will frequently use nest boxes put up for birds and are occasionally found in bat boxes. Small boxes with a 25 mm hole facing towards trunk of tree appear attractive to both sexes in suitable habitat [605A]. A high proportion of such boxes may be used during the summer, but not normally in winter. In the Forest of Dean many have been found in nest-boxes 3−3.5 m high in oaks, including six in one box on 7 October [431].

Grooming frequently watched in captivity. Rubs front paws behind head and ears, then over eyes and nose; reaches round to fur on back and sides. Finally brings tail up and forwards to comb it through mouth [431].

FEEDING

Diet varies seasonally. Flowers and pollen normally taken in early summer, more fruits (including ash keys), berries and nuts later. Also many insects [687]. Chestnuts, acorns and hazelnuts important prior to hibernation. In captivity fruit and sunflower seeds are accepted but not grain; provision of water is essential.

BREEDING

Breed first in year following birth, producing one or two litters per year, commonly of about four young.

Season: in Britain, young may be found from May to September and exceptionally October [47]. On Continent two main peaks of births, in late June/early July and in late July/early August [292]. At least two litters per year normal in Poland [736]; one per year normal in Germany [838]. Two litters known in captivity [433].

Mating: several seen in captivity were accompanied by short, high-pitched squeaks [431]. Gestation period 22−24 days. In 20 British litters median size was four, but three of seven and one of nine [109]. Litter size two to seven, mean 3.7 in Germany [838]; three to six, mean 4.7 in Czechoslovakia [292].

Young: blind at birth, pelage well developed by 13 days, eyes open at 18 days, begin to leave nest at 30 days and are independent by 40 days [838]. They may remain with mother for a further 7 weeks [109]. First pelage grey, moulted at about 18 days, second pelage more like adult but duller and greyer.

POPULATION

Density much lower than in wood mice and bank voles even in good habitat, but density relative to other rodents difficult to determine because the above-ground activity makes them more difficult to trap. However, using cage traps baited with apple and set about 2 m off the ground in trees and shrubs [604], a mark/recapture study gave estimates of 8−10 adults per hectare. On Continent may exceptionally be sufficiently abundant after a good mast crop to cause serious damage to young trees.

Population structure: ratio of young to adult in autumn probably varies from year to year (depending on breeding success). In Poland it was found to be 51:41 in 1957 and 19:36 in 1958 [736]; in France 4:18 in 1981, but 82:15 in 1982 [132]. Males predominated in nest boxes [109] and among live-trapped adults, 1.4:1 [863].

Survival: live up to 6 years in captivity [433], 4 years recorded in marked animals in wild [716]. Ridges on molar teeth more or less worn away by third year suggesting that few survive beyond that age [544].

MORTALITY
Predation by birds probably very low compared to wood mice and bank voles. Rarely found in owl pellets or discarded bottles; rarely caught by cats. Most mortality probably occurs during hibernation, owing to insufficient fat reserves, or by predation, e.g. by foxes, badgers, weasels and corvids — dormice have been seen to be dropped by crows and magpies. Nest containing hibernating mouse found in open below raven roost [435].

PARASITES

Fleas: the only flea recorded is *Ctenophthalmus nobilis*, but it is likely that some other fleas of small mammals occur and they may become infested with bird fleas.

Lice: the sucking louse *Schizophthirius pleurophaeus* is shared only with other species of dormice.

Mites: the follicle mite *Demodex muscardini* appears to be specific.

RELATIONS WITH MAN
A harmless species, vulnerable to local extinction owing to loss of its specialised habitat. Wildlife and Countryside Act of 1981 affords partial protection and proscribes trapping without a licence. Legal status upgraded to fully protected species in 1986.

LITERATURE
Hurrell [433] — a general, illustrated account.

SOUND RECORDINGS
Appendix 3: A, W.

AUTHOR FOR THIS SPECIES
P.A. Morris, with acknowledgement for additional data and comment provided by E. Hurrell and P. Bright.

GENUS *Glis*

A monospecific genus.

Fat dormouse *Glis glis*

Sciurus glis Linnaeus, 1766; Germany.

Edible dormouse, squirrel-tailed dormouse, seven-sleeper.

RECOGNITION
Very different from common dormouse, being about twice the size and lacking any suggestion of orange in the pelage. More easily confused with grey squirrel because of bushy tail and greyish colour, but much smaller. Small hind feet (under 35 mm) distinguish it from a young grey squirrel of equal size.

SIGN
Difficult to locate, but fresh signs of spiral bark-stripping in tops of conifers, especially larch, in mixed-plantations during late April and early May when animals emerge from hibernation are very characteristic.

DESCRIPTION
Squirrel-like. Head flattened, with short muzzle and long, robust vibrissae. Eyes prominent, large and black; ears rounded and relatively small. Legs short with sharply-clawed mobile toes. Tail bushy, almost as long as body, flattened dorso-ventrally, with a median parting on the underside. Short-tailed individuals are frequent.

Pelage varies considerably between individuals and at different times of year [805]. Upper parts greyish brown, darkest along the spine and lighter on the flanks. Dark ring of hair around the eyes, a dark patch at the base of the vibrissae and slightly darker stripes on the outsides of the legs. White below.

Moult: there is a single moult; the new coat is bluish grey becoming more brown with age [489].

Nipples: four to six pairs, extending from thorax to groin.

Teeth: 1.0.1.3/1.0.1.3. Premolars and molars are transversely ridged but with many fewer ridges than in the common dormouse.

Chromosomes: 2n = 62, FNa = 120 (continental data) [893].

MEASUREMENTS
Head and body up to 175 mm, mean *c.* 150 mm; tail up to 150 mm, mean *c.* 125 mm; weight up to 185 g, mean *c.* 140 g.

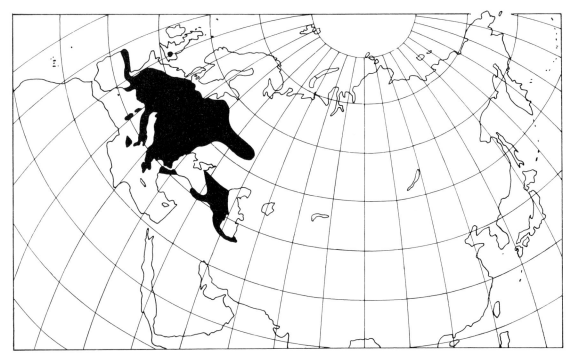

Map 8.25. Fat dormouse.

DISTRIBUTION

In Britain confined to a small area in the Chiltern Hills, although the range has been increasing steadily since its introduction.

HISTORY

A number of individuals collected in Hungary were introduced at Tring Park, Hertfordshire, in 1902 by Walter (later Lord) Rothschild (Fig. 8.36).

HABITAT

Mainly mixed and deciduous woodland of varied age, but also in orchards and gardens. Does not require a dense shrub layer. Enters houses.

SOCIAL ORGANISATION AND BEHAVIOUR

Social organisation: live together in loose groups without any strong hierarchical ranking [786]. Males become aggressive during the mating period and may exhibit a variety of threatening postures. Young animals lick the mother's mouth and ingest saliva; process repeated after nest is left. After

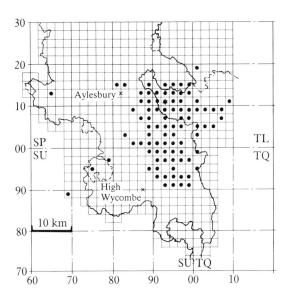

Fig. 8.36. Distribution of fat dormouse by tetrads (2 × 2 km squares), with Buckinghamshire county boundary for reference. (★ = place of introduction, Tring Park 1902.)

6 weeks family group, which can include male, begins to break up although it is common for them to remain together into hibernation [489, 831].

Communication through a variety of squeaks and snuffling noises. Threaten vocally with characteristic 'churring'.

Home range: small home range *c.* 100 m in diameter. In Germany, males dispersed 400–1700 m and females 300–1500 m [716]. In 85 years since release at Tring Park the furthest genuine record from point of origin (not the result of accidental transport or escape from captivity), is 32 km, or *c.* 380 m per year. Can have several nests in home range.

Movement: very agile climbers spending most of life in canopy of trees, although readily enter lofts of houses. Grip assisted on smooth surfaces by sticky secretion of plantar skin [489], can even climb glass. Entirely nocturnal, spending day in a tree-hole or a nest built close to the trunk, not out on a limb as is common among squirrels. May use old bird nests (especially pigeon) in which an enclosed retreat is constructed with leaves.

Nests: hibernate in nests above or below ground: in deep burrows, which they occasionally construct themselves; in rabbit warrens or fox earths [805]; tree-holes or cavities among roots and frequently in thatch or roof-spaces of buildings. Individual nests may contain 1–8 animals, but up to 69 have been caught entering the same roof space prior to hibernation [678]. Weight may increase to over 250 g before hibernation [489], which lasts from October to April; during this period weight loss can be 35–50% [831] and short spells of activity are normal. Exact time of emergence dependent on prevailing weather conditions.

FEEDING

Diet varies seasonally [786]. Will take all kinds of fruit, nuts, buds, bark (particularly of fruit trees and willow), insects, carrion, fungi and occasionally eggs or nestlings. In captivity raw meat is eaten and cannibalism may be displayed [489]. Drink large quantities.

BREEDING [489, 786, 831]

In Germany sexual maturity usually reached after the 1st winter, but animals reared from late litters do not breed until after their 2nd hibernation. Breeding starts mid-June and ends August although individuals of both sexes may be found in reproductive condition between May and October. Courtship, observed in captive animals, is characterised by the male closely following the female, emitting a diagnostic squeaking. Male driven off in early stages until ritualised behaviour is assumed. Circular dance is followed by the male mounting, biting the female's shoulders, and copulating. Peak male sexual activity in Germany is in July [292]. On the Continent, peak birth dates vary according to region.

Young: litter size is most commonly four to six but can vary between one and 11. The young are blind at birth, with ears shut. By 16 days the pelage is well developed, eyes open at 21–23 days, and by 30 days the young have left the nest.

POPULATION

Density fluctuates widely in Europe from 1–30 animals/ha; 1–5/ha is normal [786]. Population structure has been investigated by mark–recapture; most recent studies showed population composed of 23% under 1 year old, 27% 1–2 year, 42% 2–3 year and 8% over 3 years old [292]. Cool, rainy summers prevent any increase in population size. Captive animals live on average 6 years [489], with a maximum recorded age of 9 years [831].

MORTALITY

Tawny owls probably most important predator in Britain, but also taken by stoats, weasels and cats. Autotomy takes place when the tail is grasped, skin sliding easily off tail vertebrae; exposed vertebrae are then amputated by the animal [489]. Poor mast years cause high winter mortality in young animals [786].

PARASITES

The sucking louse *Schizophthirus gliris* is found on the Continent but does not appear to have been recorded from British animals.

RELATIONS WITH MAN

Were a favourite food of the Romans who reared them in oak and beech groves and fattened them for the table in special jars called *gliraria*.

Can cause serious damage to forestry plantations in the Chilterns, attacking all ages of larch and occasionally pine, spruce and beech. Damage occurs just after emergence from hibernation and takes form of bark-stripping, usually around upper part of trunk. May also cause localised damage to top-fruit crops (especially plum and apple), and to fruit trees. Readily invade lofts, cellars and outbuildings and often cause damage to property by chewing through electric cables, roofing felt, and ceiling plaster; may also feed on stored food products in houses causing fouling and risk of contamination. Regularly found drowned in drinking water cisterns. Major problem is disturbance, exceptionally numbers may reach 70 to 80 in a single roof space. Regular control has been carried out by woodland owners, fruit-growers and environmental health departments of district councils.

All Gliridae are protected under the 1979 Berne Convention on the Conservation of European Wildlife and Natural Habitats, to which the United Kingdom is signatory. The fat dormouse is included under two sections of the 1981 Wildlife and Countryside Act, precluding trapping without a license and introduction into the wild.

SOUND RECORDINGS
Appendix 3: A, E, F, J, P, T.

AUTHORS FOR THIS SPECIES
L.M. Jones-Walters and G.B. Corbet, with acknowledgements to K. Bradbury, Mrs H.C. Reason, M. Clarke, J. Robertson, the Buckinghamshire County Museum and environmental health officers of Dacorum, Aylesbury Vale, Chiltern, Wycombe, South Buckinghamshire and South Oxfordshire District Councils.

FAMILY MYOCASTORIDAE

A family of caviomorph rodents, i.e. related to guinea pigs, agoutis etc., containing only one species, the South American coypu *Myocastor coypus*. It is sometimes included with the hutias of the West Indian islands in the family Capromyidae.

Coypu *Myocastor coypus*

Mus coypus Molina, 1782; River Maipo, Chile.

Nutria.

RECOGNITION
Adults unmistakable from large size: full-grown males frequently weigh over 7 kg. Superficially rat-like with tapering cylindrical tail but nose blunt with widely spaced nostrils and hind feet webbed (Fig. 8.37); anterior surface of incisors orange.

SIGN

Footprints of hind foot up to 15 cm long with imprint of web often visible. Up to five claw marks visible in fore and hind footprints. Shallow tail scrape, up to 2 cm wide, sometimes occurs.

Faeces long, usually dark brown or green, cylindrical, often slightly curved with fine longitudinal striations, deposited in water or at random on the bank. From 2 × 7 mm at two weeks to 11 × 70 mm at full adult size.

Burrows nests and runs: excavate complex burrow systems in ditch banks; one described in South America was 6 m deep [737]. Can have several entrances at water level, 20 cm in diameter; some may open in level ground beyond the bank; nest chambers within may be empty or contain quantities of plant material. Coypus often lie up close to water, under a bush or in dense vegetation. Small shallow nests 30 cm in diameter lined with dead leaves. Larger structures, resembling swans nests, occasionally built in reedbeds. Runs, bare of vegetation when intensively used, 15 cm wide lead from regularly used 'climb-outs' at water's edge to complex network away from bank.

Fig. 8.37. Coypu.

Feeding remains usually in or near water. Distinguished from water voles by much larger amounts and the presence of paired crescentic incisor marks on food items (roots, leaf blades, etc.) up to 17 mm wide. Coypus produce short, productive 'lawns' by intensive grazing of grasses next to water courses. Excavations for roots (e.g. docks: *Rumex* spp.) and rhizomes conspicuous in winter.

DESCRIPTION
Adapted for semi-aquatic existence: webbed hind feet, valvular nostrils, small pinnae, underfur that remains dry during submersion. Long powerful claws on forefeet used for grooming, holding food and excavating burrows and food.

Pelage: glossy brown and yellow-brown guard hair, in adults dense and up to 80 mm long on dorsal surface, 35 mm long and sparse on ventral surface. Soft grey underfur 20–25 mm deep, more dense ventrally. Prominent white vibrissae up to 130 mm long.

Nipples: normally four pairs along the dorso-lateral body line; sometimes teats missing or bitten off, sometimes five pairs. High position of teats sometimes regarded as adaptation to semi-aquatic habit but young are normally suckled on nests, not in the water.

Scent glands: Males have large anal gland lying ventral to rectum and extruded during marking; female gland smaller (Table 8.25).

Genitalia [410]: in adult males, penis 4–5 cm anterior to anus; useful criterion for adulthood is whether penis can be fully everted. In females vulva immediately posterior to urinary papilla and anterior to anus, closed by a membrane in juveniles. The vulva opens at parturition and during oestrus but the membrane reforms, almost completely, during pregnancy.

Skull: large infra-orbital foramen in robust, flared zygomatic arch (Fig. 8.38).

Teeth: tooth formula: 1.0.1.3/1.0.1.3. Second molar erupts at 3 months, third at 6 months and is fully in place by 1 year. Premolar and molars wear to a uniformly flat grinding surface with complex infundibular pattern that changes as attrition pro-

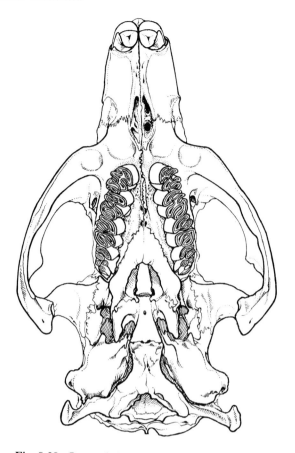

Fig. 8.38. Coypu skull from below.

ceeds. Incisors wider in males than females (Table 8.25).

Chromosomes: 2n = 42, FNa = 80 [893].

MEASUREMENTS (Table 8.25).

VARIATION
Five subspecies have been recognised in South America [636], of which *M. c. bonariensis* Geoffroy is the most widespread (Argentina, Uruguay, Paraguay, Southern Brazil) and is the one that British coypus most closely resemble. Numerous colour varieties, including albinos and black types, are bred for fur production, particularly in Poland [327]. Some variation in coat colour of wild coypus in Britain: occasional animals 'sandy' or grey; two or three out of over 30 000 seen over the past 10 years had patches of white fur and one embryo (out of many thousands) was completely white.

Table 8.25. Measurements of adult coypus over 100 weeks old [1].

	Males			Females		
	Mean	SD	*n*	Mean	SD	*n*
Total weight (kg)	6.47	0.88	646	6.02	1.06	918
Eviscerated weight (kg)	5.74	0.84	391	4.87	0.67	495
Hind foot (minus claw) (mm)	136	5	655	129	5	922
Head and body (mm)	603	29	82	593	28	99
Anal gland weight (g)	12.0	3.8	397	3.8	1.2	493
Lower incisor width (mm)	15.1	0.9	409	13.4	0.7	518
Length of molar tooth row (mm)	30.8	1.8	404	30.5	1.7	511

DISTRIBUTION

Native to the southern half of South America: Bolivia, S Brazil, Paraguay, Uruguay, Argentina, central and S Chile [636]. Feral populations from escapes and introductions in North America (mainly Louisiana), Europe, USSR, the Middle East, Africa and Japan. In Europe established populations in the Netherlands [536], Belgium, West Germany, France and Italy [712]. In Britain now restricted to East Anglia or possibly extinct. The map shows the distribution of 122 862 coypus caught in control trapping or killed in other ways, such as road deaths, between 1970 and 1987. Two isolated individuals not shown on the map were caught at Grimsby, Humberside and at Castleton, Derbyshire.

HISTORY

Imported for fur farming about 1929. At least 49 farms were established and escapes were reported from half of them. All farms discontinued by 1945 but by 1944 a feral population had become established on the River Yare near Norwich [509]. By 1965 they extended throughout East Anglia and west to Lincolnshire, Huntingdon and Peterborough (now Cambridgeshire), and Hertfordshire [190, 192, 628]. An isolated colony near Slough disappeared about 1954 [628]. The population reached a peak of an estimated 200 000 by 1962 [628]. Numbers then reduced by an extensive control campaign which started in 1962, and the very severe winter of 1962/63. In 1970 restricted to Norfolk and Suffolk [317] and numbered 2000 individuals [332]. Population changes since 1970 in 'Population' below.

HABITAT

Majority of population has always been found in extensive fen, reed swamp and other marshland communities of east Norfolk and east Suffolk and in the areas of extensive grazing marsh in these counties. Brackish coastal marshes have also supported moderate population densities. Smaller numbers also found along small streams and in isolated ponds; most lowland river valleys in Britain could support coypus.

SOCIAL ORGANISATION AND BEHAVIOUR

Social organisation: polygynous mating system. Research in Norfolk shows that at high and moderate densities females live in kin groups. These are initiated when a female colonises a patch of suitable habitat and expand as daughters establish partially overlapping ranges. At very high densities daughters disperse when kin groups meet. Males disperse as young adults and, when fully grown, compete for exclusive access to groups of females. A colonial habit with an alpha female and alpha male has also been described [847], the male was subordinate to the female except during mating; the rest of the colony was equally subordinate to these two. At low density, radio-tracking studies in Norfolk have shown that females maintain isolated home ranges. A dominant male moved between up to four females. Mothers and daughters established separate ranges following the dispersal of one or both.

Dispersal: individuals of both sexes disperse over a wide range of population densities. Out of a large sample of wild animals that were ear tagged and released, 61 males and 36 females were at large for more than 6 months. Of these, 25% of the males and 6% of the females dispersed over 4 km. Greatest distances moved were 9 km by a male and 7 km by a female. Females dispersed to isolated home ranges during a radio-tracking study of a low density population.

Home ranges initially small but increase with sexual maturity. Adult males have significantly larger ranges than adult females [325]. Ranges on grazing marsh (measured as convex polygons) where coypus stay in or near the drainage ditches, are larger than in areas, such as in wet Broadland habitat, where all the area within a home range can be utilised (Table 8.26).

Communication: eyesight appears to be poor. Mothers and offspring communicate with soft 'maaw' contact call; adults periodically make loud 'maawk' call which can be heard over large distances. Scent may be the primary mode of communication. Both sexes have a well-developed anal gland which is extruded and wiped over the ground whenever an animal gets into or out of the water. Urine is also used for scent marking. Faeces are deposited mostly in the water or at random on the bank and apparently have no social significance.

Aggressive behaviour: coypus fight by grappling with their strongly clawed forefeet then biting at the mouth and face of the opponent. Fighting is more common in males than females, as shown by a higher frequency of characteristic scars on the lips. More intense competition between males is consistent with the polygynous mating system. In captivity, females may attack males immediately after parturition and sometimes males are killed at this time: despite this, females are often mated at a post-partum oestrus.

Activity: coypus usually rest on nests or in burrows during the day and are active at night. When nights are very cold they remain in their burrows

and make up lost time by feeding during the day [330].

Locomotion: most commonly used gait is a walk which appears awkward as the large webbed hind feet are retracted. When alarmed coypus break into a bounding gallop with the hind feet making contact outside and in front of forefeet. Swim by alternate propulsive thrusts of hind legs. Dive silently or, when alarmed, with a loud splash (possible alarm signal function).

Defence: when disturbed in or near water will swim away under the surface or lie immobile under water with legs outstretched for several minutes; probably anti-predator behaviour. If cornered will grind incisors together in a threatening display; chips of enamel may be broken off the teeth in this process. However, most popular accounts of aggression to people are wildly exaggerated.

Grooming: there is extensive and prolonged grooming behaviour using teeth, forefeet and hind feet [738] especially after swimming.

FEEDING

Herbivorous except for occasional feeding on freshwater mussels. Coypus in East Anglia had a complex but ordered pattern of plant utilisation. In spring wide range of sprouting plants eaten; some selection for parts of plants, e.g. basal meristem of the tufted sedge (*Carex elata*). More selective through summer, e.g. heavy utilisation of basal meristems of burr-reed (*Sparganium erectum*) and the great pond sedge (*Carex riparia*); rest of plant usually discarded. In autumn, diet augmented by fruits of various kinds, e.g. seed pods of yellow water lily (*Nuphar lutea*). In winter most important food sources are roots and rhizomes often excavated to depths over 20 cm; rhizomes of reed mace (*Typha*

Table 8.26. Home ranges of adult coypus (ha) [325].

	Male			Female			
	Mean	SD	*n*	Mean	SD	*n*	Difference (*p*)
Calthorpe enclosure*	8.4	±3.0	55	5.5	±3.2	68	0.001
Strumpshaw Fen*	6.8	±5.5	8	3.0	±1.8	7	0.118
Cantley Marsh†	93.9	±69.5	14	46.3	±30.0	16	0.018

* Mixed aquatic, fen and carr habitat.
† Grazing marsh.

spp.) are a favourite [317]. Some plants such as pasture and salt marsh grasses are eaten throughout the year.

Complex feeding strategy allows utilisation of a wide range of crops. Can graze cereals in spring and eat mature seed heads in late summer; also brassica and root crops, especially sugar beet.

Chemical analysis suggests that these feeding patterns are linked with seasonal variation in food quality; e.g. frequency of feeding on the leaves of the reed (*Phragmites australis*), highest from mid-summer to autumn, is correlated with carbohydrate content.

Coypus are coprophagus: plant material eaten at night passes through the gut, is reingested the following day while animals are on their nests and is finally eliminated during the following night; mean retention time in the gut is thus about 24 hours [318].

Food items held in one or both forefeet while animals sits supported on hind feet. Large items held on ground until small enough to pick up. High food items, e.g. seed head of mature wheat, pulled down with forefeet or stem bitten through first. Basal meristems eaten after shallow digging using forefeet and biting through shoot below ground level.

Selective feeding by coypus caused massive reduction in the area of reedswamp fringing open water in the Norfolk Broads [102]; also alters its composition by feeding on reed mace in preference to reeds [492]. Certain plants such as cowbane (*Circuta virosa*) and great water dock (*Rumex hydrolapathum*) were all but eliminated over large areas when coypus were dense in the late 1950s [234].

BREEDING

Sexual maturity: coypus breed throughout the year in East Anglia. Age at which animals mature depends on season: earliest for animals born in late winter, greatest for those born in the autumn. This variation is presumably due to the conditions encountered as they grow. Females mature at 3−8 months, males at 4−10 months. There is a post-partum oestrus. Thereafter females are induced ovulators although they may cycle irregularly in the absence of a male; cycles recorded are between 4−47 days in length in captive coypus [306].

Litter size (Table 8.27): on average fewer females are born per litter than males. Young females give birth to smaller litters than older ones. In captivity an average of about one offspring per litter dies within a week of birth; some of these are killed when the mother lies on them or abandons them away from the nest.

Prenatal embryo losses are high: total losses between implantation and birth have been estimated at 50−60% [622]. Significant relationship between winter severity and the proportion of females that litter in the following spring: this is probably because females abort their litters after losing condition in cold weather [320]. About 28% of all litters are lost by week 6 of gestation. The average size of litters that survive this early loss is 6.5 ± 2.1 ($n = 358$ litters in week 7 of gestation). Females also resorb individual embryos and thus reduce mean litter size to 5.4 at birth. This may be a way for females to reduce litter size to a level they can support. Some losses of entire litters appear to be a mechanism for manipulating the sex ratio of offspring: young mothers in good condition, which are due to litter in the summer, abort small litters (which will thus contain large embryos) of predominantly female embryos at around week 13/14 of the 19-week gestation period. The litters which

Table 8.27. Litter size of coypus.

	Mean	SD	*n* (litters)
Males per litter at birth[*]	2.9	1.5	1107
Females per litter at birth[*]	2.6	1.6	1107
Total at birth[*]	5.5	2.0	1107
Total at birth in captivity[†]	5.4	2.2	42
Surviving 1 week after birth[†]	4.6	1.9	42
Total at birth, mothers < 15 months[*]	5.1	1.7	680
Total at birth, mothers > 15 months[*]	6.0	2.2	427

[*] From coypus dissected in late pregnancy (14−19 weeks gestation).
[†] From litters conceived in the wild but born in captivity.

they then conceive are larger than those aborted: 5.8 (SD = 2.1, $n = 97$) at a comparable gestation stage compared to 4.2 (SD = 1.7, $n = 30$). Large litters and those containing predominantly male embryos are retained. The females thus avoid investing in large female offspring and opt to produce absolutely larger numbers of young. Mothers that retain predominantly male litters are investing in a few large males which would be expected to grow into large adults and compete successfully in a polygynous mating system [322]. Embryo losses also occur, although very rarely, through the partial abortion of litters: usually all embryos in one horn of the uterus are expelled.

Young are born fully furred and with eyes open. They have functional incisors and premolars and have been artificially weaned at 5 days. Neonates are active within an hour of birth and can be swimming within a few days. Males are slightly heavier than females at birth (Table 8.28) but there is a large overlap between the sexes.

Lactation lasts for 8 weeks in the wild but up to 14 in captivity [319]. The food consumption of a sample of lactating females was 63% higher than in a control group [329]. In captivity, males grow faster than females, partly because males suck more from teats with the highest milk production (the second and third mammary glands are larger than the first and fourth). Within each sex, weight at weaning is positively correlated to birth weight [329].

Growth: maximum body size reached by 2 years (Fig. 8.40). Body size (foot length) at 2 years is positively correlated with size at weaning [326].

POPULATION

Numbers of adults in the British population between 1970 and 1987 have been estimated by population reconstruction [332] (Fig. 8.39). Population fluctuations caused mainly by the numbers of trappers employed in control and the severity of the winters [328]. Colder than average winters shown in Fig. 8.41; six trappers 1970–72, increased from 11 to 20 between 1973 and 1977, stayed at 20 over 1977–80 and was finally increased to 24 in 1981 (see relations with man for an account of the attempt to eradicate coypus). Cold winters reduce

Table 8.28. Birth weights (g) of coypus born in captivity that lived for at least 1 week.

	Mean	Range	n
Male	223	132–346	124
Female	207	111–327	105

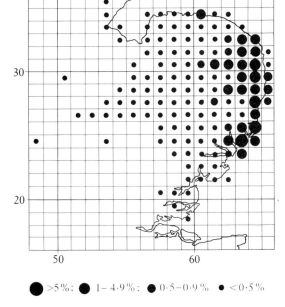

● >5%: ● 1–4·9%: ● 0·5–0·9% • <0·5%

Fig. 8.39. Distribution of coypu 1970–1987. The dots in each 10 km square represent proportions of the total number of animals caught.

breeding success and allow trapping to make larger impact on population.

Age structure of the wild population altered by intensive trapping. In a fenced study population 8.2% of males and 14.7% of females reached 3 years old, compared with 0.6 and 1.7 in the wild population. Physiological longevity 6.3 ± 0.4 years in captivity but in the wild less than 0.2% live to 4 years [323].

Sex ratio changes from 1 : 1.2 (female to male) at birth to 1.3 : 1 for adults; partly due to the greater susceptibility of males to trapping: they have larger

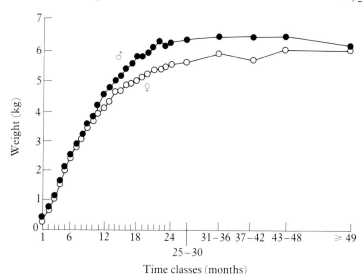

Fig. 8.40. Growth of coypus (11 575 males and 6582 females killed in control trapping) aged from the weight of the eye lens [331]. Total body weight (males); body weight minus reproductive tract (females).

Time classes (months)

home ranges and, unlike females, do not have periods of reduced activity around parturition.

MORTALITY

Predation has not been studied systematically in East Anglia. Stoats, dogs and marsh harriers have been seen killing coypus. Remains of coypus seen in heron pellets and fox faeces. Dogs are often badly bitten during attempts to kill coypus. Young coypus appear vulnerable and are probably taken by a number of predators including owls, hawks, mink, domestic cat and pike.

Juvenile survival from births in autumn and early winter usually poor and those from late winter, spring and early summer best. At most extreme, only 5% of coypus born before a cold winter survive to become adult compared with almost 90% of those born the following April. Weaned juveniles must experience difficulty in excavating roots and rhizomes, the main source of food in winter, when the ground is frozen.

Adult mortality: in Britain few native predators can kill fully grown coypus and so adult mortality is low apart from that caused directly by man (trapping, shooting, etc.). Fat reserves are reduced even in mild winters [317] but adults rarely die in spite of severe frost lesions on the feet and tail; many coypus lose all or part of their tail in cold

winters. However, adult coypus do perish in very severe winters such as 1946–47 and 1962–63. The fall in numbers trapped after the 1962–63 winter suggested 80–90% mortality [628]. Dying animals were emaciated; proximate cause of death in some cases was *Yersinia pseudotuberculosis*.

PARASITES

Ectoparasites: in East Anglia [624] 63% of coypus were infested by the host-specific sucking louse *Pitrufquenia coypus* ($n = 1861$), the only ectoparasite also recorded from South America [550]. Of 2578 coypus 76 (2.9%) carried ticks: 34 were *Ixodes ricinus*, 39 *I. arvicolae*, 1 *I. hexagonus*, and 2 *I. trianguliceps*. Fleas and mites were very rare.

Helminths: the tapeworms *Multiceps serialis* and *Hydatigena taeniformis* and the nematodes *Strongyloides papillosus* and *Trichostrongylus retortaeformis* (common in the rabbit) have been identified from coypus [623]. Up to 50% from some areas infected by liver fluke *Fasciola hepatica* [424]. Overall mean infection rate of 6.4%; infections rise from zero at weaning to 14% in those older than 1.5 years [623]. The fluke *Dicrocoelium dendriticum* also recorded.

Protozoa: 46% of coypus infected with *Eimeria* species of coccidia: *E. myopotami* (23%), *E. nutriae* (20%), *E. fluviatilis* (16%), *E. coypi* (11%), *E. seideli* (1%) [37]. Proportion of infected animals increases over first few weeks of life to 71%, then gets progressively less in older classes. Two peaks of infection in January and June/July [37]. *Sarcocystis* sp. cysts have been found in muscle samples [26]. *Toxoplasma gondii* which can cause toxoplasmosis in man and animals has been isolated from coypus [425]; can probably infect all warm blooded animals and presence in coypus does not materially increase the risk to man.

Fungi: one coypu found with hair loss caused by ringworm *Trichophyton mentagrophytes* but 15% of apparently healthy coypus were infected [623]. *Haplosporagium parvum* found in lungs of 17%; this fungus is normally associated with burrowing animals such as moles and wood mice [623].

Viruses: coypus can be infected with foot-and-mouth disease in laboratory conditions [130].

Bacteria: a small percentage of coypus in Norfolk are infected with *Yersinia pseudotuberculosis*. *Salmonella typhimurium* has been isolated from 8 out of a sample of 12 coypus. Serological studies have shown leptospira infection in 24% of samples; leptospires of *Icterohaemorrhagiae* and *Hebdomadis* serogroups prevalent, *Leptospira interrogans* serovar. *hardjo* isolated from tissue [849]. Coypu are unlikely to be a significant reservoir host for cattle-associated *L. hardjo* infection, and are probably not an important source of transmission of leptospirosis to man in Britain.

RELATIONS WITH MAN

Extensively exploited in natural range, as captive stock and in parts of feral range [327]. Over-exploited in parts of South America [636]; 10 million pelts a year exported up to 1910 [709], by 1910 only 200 000 marketed. Recent figures are again in millions but accurate information is difficult to obtain. From the 1920s increasingly bred in captivity for fur, first in Argentina then in Europe, USA and USSR. Deliberate releases in some countries, particularly the USSR to establish feral populations for the fur industry.

In late 1950s in Britain damage to dyke banks and river walls through burrowing, to agricultural crops and indigenous flora led, in 1962, to inclusion of coypus in the Destructive Imported Animals Act (1932). Systematic control started in 1962 with a campaign organised by the Ministry of Agriculture, Fisheries and Food (MAFF); nearly 40 500 coypus were trapped by the end of 1965 [628]. After 1965 control carried out by a consortium of Rabbit Clearance Societies (RCS) and Internal Drainage Boards (IDB). In 1971 a new organisation called Coypu Control was set up receiving a 50% government grant and the remainder of its finance from the Water Authority and IDBs.

In 1977 an independent group, the Coypu Strategy Group considered future control policy. Following recommendations by the group a campaign was started in 1981 with the objective of eradicating coypus from Britain within 10 years [324]. This decision took account of the fact that

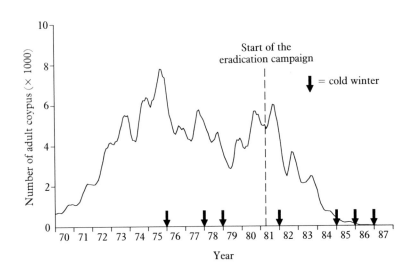

Fig. 8.41. Numbers of adult coypus present in Britain between 1970 and 1986, reconstructed using the number of animals killed in control trapping and their ages [324].

coypus are not endangered in their native range and eradication had been shown to be possible [886]. A force of 24 trappers, three foremen and a manager were employed, funded 50% by a government grant, 40% by Anglian Water and 10% by IDBs. The control method used throughout was live trapping in cage traps. Coypus were then shot and non-target species released unharmed. About 34 900 coypus were trapped or otherwise accounted for during the campaign and numbers declined rapidly (Fig. 8.41) [322A]; only 12 animals were caught in 1987 and two males found dead on roads in 1988. By January 1989 it seemed unlikely that a breeding population remained and the Coypu Control Organisation was disbanded. One male was trapped by MAFF field staff in December 1989 but no further evidence has been found despite extensive field checks. Current evidence thus suggests that coypus may have been successfully eradicated from Britain although this will not be certain for a number of years.

LITERATURE

Gosling [321] — a non-technical summary of coypu natural history. Gosling & Skinner [327] — outlines exploitation by man. Gosling [322A] — an account of the attempt to eradicate coypus from Britain.

SOUND RECORDINGS
Appendix 3: A, F, J, P.

AUTHORS FOR THIS SPECIES
L.M. Gosling and S.J. Baker.

REFERENCES

1 Author's data.
2 Abbott R.J. *et al.* (1977) Sooty bark disease of sycamore and the grey squirrel. *Transactions of the British Mycological Society* **69**:507–8.
3 Adamczewska K.A. (1961) Intensity of reproduction of the *Apodemus flavicollis* (Melchior, 1834) during the period 1954–1959. *Acta theriologica* **5**:1–21.
4 Airoldi J.P. & Meylan A. (1972) Bibliography on the genus *Arvicola*, Lacepède. Work published in Europe from 1900–1972 (excluding Russia). *EPPO publications* B78.
5 Alder E.E. (1972) *The behaviour of two races of the bank vole*, Clethrionomys glareolus. PhD. thesis, University of Edinburgh.
6 Alibhai S.K. (1976) *A study of the factors governing the numbers and reproductive success of* Clethrionomys glareolus (*Schreber*). DPhil. thesis, University of Oxford.

7 Alibhai S.K. (1980) An x-ray technique for ageing bank voles (*Clethrionomys glareolus*) using the first mandibular molar. *Journal of Zoology* **191**:418–23.
8 Alibhai S.K. (1982) Persistence of placental scars in the bank vole *Clethrionomys glareolus*. *Journal of Zoology* **197**:300–3.
9 Alibhai S.K. (1985) Effects of diet on reproductive performance of the bank vole (*Clethrionomys glareolus*). *Journal of Zoology* **205**:445–52.
10 Alibhai S.K. & Gipps J.H.W. (1985) The population ecology of bank voles. *Symposia of the Zoological Society of London* **55**:277–305.
11 Alston J.M. & Broom J.C. (1958) *Leptospirosis in man and animals*. Edinburgh: E. & S. Livingstone.
12 Altman P.L. & Katz D.D. eds. (1979) *Inbred and genetically defined strains of laboratory animals. Part 1. Mouse and Rat.* Bethesda, Maryland: Federal American Society of Experimental Biology.
13 Anderson P.K. (1964) Lethal alleles in *Mus musculus*: local distribution and evidence for isolation of demes. *Science* **145**:177–8.
14 Andersson M. & Erlinge S. (1977) Influence of predation on rodent population. *Oikos* **29**:591–7.
15 Andersson M. & Jonasson S. (1986) Rodent cycles in relation to food resources on an alpine heath. *Oikos* **46**:93–106.
16 *Andrezewski R. & Wroclawek J. (1961) Mass occurrence of Apodemus agrarius (Pallas, 1771) and variations in the numbers of associated Muridae. Acta theriologica* 13:173–84.
17 Andrzejewski R. & Rajska E. (1972) Trappability of bank vole in pitfalls and traps. *Acta theriologica* **17**:155–68.
18 Andrzejewski R. *et al.* (1971) Trappability of trap-prone and trap-shy bank voles. *Acta theriologica* **16**:401–5.
19 Anon. (1980) *Field mice and sugar beet*. Leaflet 626. Pinner: MAFF, 6 pp.
20 Artimo A. (1964) The baculum as a criterion for distinguishing sexually mature and immature bank voles. *Annales Zoologici Fennici* **1**:1–6.
21 Armitage P. *et al.* (1984) New evidence of black rat in Roman London. *London Archaeologist* **4**:375–83.
22 Ashby K.R. (1967) Studies on the ecology of field mice and voles (*Apodemus sylvaticus, Clethrionomys glareolus* and *Microtus agrestis*) in Houghall Wood, Durham. *Journal of Zoology* **152**:389–513.
23 Ashby K.R. (1972) Patterns of daily activity in mammals. *Mammal Review* **1**:171–85.
24 Ashby K.R. Personal communication.
25 Ashby K.R. & Vincent M.A. (1976) Individual and population energy budgets of the water vole. *Acta theriologica* **21**:499–512.
26 Ashford R. Personal communication.
27 Attuquayefio D.K. *et al.* (1986) Home range sizes in the wood mouse *Apodemus sylvaticus*: habitat, sex and seasonal differences. *Journal of Zoology* (A) **210**:45–53.
28 Aulak W. (1970) Small mammal communities in Bialowieza National Park. *Acta theriologica* **15**:465–515.

29 Austin C.R. (1957). Oestrus and ovulation in the field vole (*Microtus agrestis*). *Journal of Endocrinology* **15**:IV.

30 Baal H.J. (1949) The indigenous mammals, reptiles and amphibians of the Channel Islands. *Bulletin Annuel de la Société Jersiaise* **15**:101–10.

31 Baker A.E.M. (1981) Gene flow in house mice: introduction of a new allele into free-living populations. *Evolution* **35**:243–58.

32 Baker J.R. (1930) The breeding season in British wild mice. *Proceedings of the Zoological Society of London* **1930**:113–26.

33 Baker J.R. & Ranson R.M. (1933) Factors affecting the breeding of the field mouse (*Microtus agrestis*) Part 3 — Locality. *Proceedings of the Royal Society B* **113**:486–95.

34 Baker J.R. *et al.* (1963) Blood parasites of wild voles, *Microtus agrestis* in England. *Parasitology* **53**:297–301.

35 Bakken A. (1959) Behaviour of gray squirrels. *Proceedings of the Annual Conference, Southeastern Association of Game and Fish Commissioners* **13**:393–406.

36 Balfour A. (1922) Observations on wild rats in England, with an account of their ecto- and endo-parasites. *Parasitology* **14**:282–98.

37 Ball S.J. & Lewis D.C. (1983) *Eimeria* (Protozoa: Coccidia) in wild populations of some British rodents. *Journal of Zoology* **202**:373–81.

38 Bandrup-Nielsen S. & Karlsson F. (1985) Movements and spatial patterns in populations of *Clethrionomys* species: a review. *Annales Zoologici Fennici* **22**:385–92.

39 Barkalow F.S. (1967) A record gray squirrel litter. *Journal of Mammalogy* **48**:141.

40 Barkalow F.S. *et al.* (1970) The vital statistics of an unexploited gray squirrel population. *Journal of Mammalogy* **34**:48.

41 Barnett S.A. (1951) Damage to wheat by enclosed populations of *Rattus norvegicus*. *Journal of Hygiene* **49**:22–5.

42 Barnett S.A. (1958) An analysis of social behaviour in wild rats. *Proceedings of the Zoological Society of London* **130**:107–52.

43 Barnett S.A. (1975) *The rat*. Chicago: University Press, 318 pp.

44 Barnett S.A. *et al.* (1975) House mice bred for many generations in two environments. *Journal of Zoology* **177**:153–69.

45 Barnett S.A. & Dickson R.G. (1984) Changes among wild house mice (*Mus musculus*) bred for ten generations in a cold environment, and their evolutionary implications. *Journal of Zoology* **203**:163–80.

46 Barrett-Hamilton G.E.H. (1899) On the species of the genus *Mus* inhabiting St Kilda. *Proceedings of the Zoological Society of London* **1899**:77–88.

47 Barrett-Hamilton G.E.H. & Hinton M.A.C. (1910–21) *A history of British mammals*. London: Gurney & Jackson, 263, 748 pp.

48 Barrier M.J. & Barkalow F.S. (1967) A rapid technique for aging gray squirrels in winter pelage. *Journal of Wildlife Management* **31**:715–19.

49 Barrington R.M. (1880) On the introduction of the squirrel into Ireland. *Scientific Proceedings of the Royal Dublin Society* N.S. **2**:615–31.

50 Barrow P.A. (1981) *Corynebacterium kutscheri* infection in wild voles (*Microtus agrestis*). *British Veterinary Journal* **137**:67–70.

51 Barudieri B. (1953) Epidemiology of leptospirosis in Italian ricefields. *WHO Monograph Series* **19**:117–26.

52 Batten C.A. & Berry R.J. (1967) Prenatal mortality in wild-caught house mice. *Journal of Animal Ecology* **36**:453–63.

53 Baumler W. (1975) Activity of some mammals in the field. *Acta theriologica* **20**:365–79.

54 Behnke J.M. (1975) *Aspiculuris tetraptera* in wild *Mus musculus*. The prevalence of infection in male and female mice. *Journal of Helminthology* **49**:85–90.

55 Behnke J.M. & Wakelin D. (1973) The survival of *Trichuris muris* in wild populations of its natural hosts. *Parasitology* **67**:157–64.

56 Bellamy D. *et al.* (1973) Ageing in an island population of the house mouse. *Age and Ageing* **2**:235–50.

57 Benmehdi F. *et al.* (1980) Premier rapport de la genetique biochimique des populations a la systematique des mulots de France continentale et de Corse. *Biochemical Systematics and Ecology* **8**:309–15.

58 Bentley E.W. (1959) The distribution and status of *Rattus rattus* L. in the United Kingdom in 1951 and 1956. *Journal of Animal Ecology* **33**:371–3.

59 Bentley E.W. (1964) A further loss of ground by *Rattus rattus* L. in the United Kingdom during 1956–61. *Journal of Animal Ecology* **28**:299–308.

60 Berger P.J. *et al.* (1981) Chemical triggering of reproduction in *Microtus montanus*. *Science* **195**:575–7.

61 Bergstedt B. (1965) Distribution, reproduction, growth and dynamics of the rodent species *Clethrionomys glareolus* (Schreber), *Apodemus flavicollis* (Melchior) and *Apodemus sylvaticus* (Linné) in southern Sweden. *Oikos* **16**:132–60.

62 Berry R.J. (1963) Epigenetic polymorphism in wild populations of *Mus musculus*. *Genetical Research* **4**:193–220.

63 Berry R.J. (1964) The evolution of an island population of the house mouse. *Evolution* **18**:468–83.

64 Berry R.J. (1968) The ecology of an island population of the house mouse. *Journal of Animal Ecology* **37**:445–70.

65 Berry R.J. (1969) History in the evolution of *Apodemus sylvaticus* (Mammalia) at one edge of its range. *Journal of Zoology* **159**:311–28.

66 Berry R.J. (1970) Covert and overt variation, as exemplified by British mouse populations. *Symposia of the Zoological Society of London* **26**:3–26.

67 Berry R.J. (1970) The natural history of the house mouse. *Field Studies* **3**:219–62.

68 Berry R.J. (1973) Chance and change in British long-tailed field mice (*Apodemus sylvaticus*). *Journal of Zoology* 170:351–66.

69 Berry R.J. (1975) On the nature of genetical distance and island races of *Apodemus sylvaticus*. *Journal of Zoology* 176:293–6.

70 Berry R.J. (1978) Genetic variation in wild house mice: where natural selection and history meet. *American Scientist* 66:52–60.

71 Berry R.J. (1981) Town mouse, country mouse: adaptation and adaptability in *Mus domesticus* (*M. musculus domesticus*). *Mammal Review* 11:91–136.

72 Berry R.J. ed. (1981) *Biology of the house mouse.* London & New York: Academic Press, 715 pp.

73 Berry R.J. (1984) House mouse. In Mason I.L. ed. *Evolution of domesticated animals.* London: Longman pp. 273–84.

74 Berry R.J. (1985) Evolutionary and ecological genetics of the bank vole and wood mouse. *Symposia of the Zoological Society of London* 55:1–31.

75 Berry R.J. (1985) *The natural history of Orkney.* London: Collins, 304 pp.

76 Berry R.J. (1986) Genetics of insular populations of mammals with particular reference to differentiation and founder effects in British small mammals. *Biological Journal of the Linnean Society of London* 28:205–30.

77 Berry R.J. (1986) Genetical processes in wild mouse populations. *Current Topics in Microbiological Immunology* 127:86–94.

78 Berry R.J. & Jakobson M.E. (1971) Life and death in an island population of the house mouse. *Experimental Gerontology* 6:187–97.

79 Berry R.J. & Jakobson M.E. (1974) Vagility in an island population of the house mouse. *Journal of Zoology* 173:341–54.

80 Berry R.J. & Jakobson M.E. (1975) Adaptation and adaptability in wild-living house mice. *Journal of Zoology* 176:391–402.

81 Berry R.J. & Peters J. (1977) Heterogeneous heterozygosities in *Mus musculus* populations. *Proceedings of the Zoological Society of London* (B) 197:485–503.

82 Berry R.J. & Rose F.E.N. (1975) Islands and the evolution of *Microtus arvalis* (Microtinae). *Journal of Zoology* 177:395–409.

83 Berry R.J. & Searle A.G. (1963) Epigenetic polymorphism of the rodent skeleton. *Proceedings of the Zoological Society of London* 140:577–615.

84 Berry R.J. & Tricker B.J.K. (1969) Competition and extinction: the mice of Foula, with notes on those of Fair Isle and St Kilda. *Journal of Zoology* 158:247–65.

85 Berry R.J. *et al.* (1967) The relationships and ecology of *Apodemus sylvaticus* from the Small Isles of the Inner Hebrides, Scotland. *Journal of Zoology* 152: 333–46.

86 Berry R.J. *et al.* (1973) Survival in wild-living mice. *Mammal Review* 3:46–57.

87 Berry R.J. *et al.* (1978) The house mice of the Faroe Islands: a study in microdifferentiation. *Journal of Zoology* 185:73–92.

88 Berry R.J. *et al.* (1978) Sub-Antarctic house mice: colonization, survival and selection. *Journal of Zoology* 184:127–41.

89 Berry R.J. *et al.* (1979) Natural selection in mice from South Georgia (South Atlantic Ocean). *Journal of Zoology* 189:385–98.

90 Berry R.J. *et al.* (1982) Colonization by house mice: an experiment. *Journal of Zoology* 198:329–36.

91 Berry R.J. *et al.* (1987) Inherited differences within an island population of the house mouse. *Journal of Zoology* 211:605–18.

92 Bertram B.C.R. & Moltu D-T. (1986) Reintroducing red squirrels into Regent's Park. *Mammal Review* 16:81–9.

93 Bertram B.C. & Moltu D-T. (1987) *The reintroduction of red squirrels into Regent's Park.* London: Zoological Society of London, 12 pp.

94 Bishop I.R. & Delany M.J. (1963) The ecological distribution of small mammals in the Channel Islands. *Mammalia* 27:99–110.

95 Bishop J.A. & Hartley D.J. (1976) The size and age structure of rural populations of *Rattus norvegicus* containing individuals resistant to the anticoagulant Warfarin. *Journal of Animal Ecology* 45:623–46.

96 Blackmore D.K. & Owen D.G. (1968) Ectoparasites: the significance in British wild rodents. *Symposia of the Zoological Society of London* 24:197–220.

97 Blackwell J.M. (1981) The role of the house mouse in disease and zoonoses. *Symposia of the Zoological Society of London* 47:591–616.

98 Blake B.H. (1982) Reproduction in captive water voles, *Arvicola terrestris. Journal of Zoology* 198: 524–9.

99 Bobek B. (1969) Survival, turnover and production of small rodents in a beech forest. *Acta theriologica* 14:191–210.

100 Bobek B. (1973) Net production of small rodents in a deciduous forest. *Acta theriologica* 18:403–34.

101 Bobyr (1978) A contribution to the ecology of the Altaian squirrel (*Sciurus vulgaris altaicus*). *Zoologicheskii zhurnal* 57:253–9.

102 Boorman L.A. & Fuller R.M. (1981) The changing status of reedswamp in the Norfolk Broads. *Journal of Applied Ecology* 18:241–69.

103 Bostrom U. & Hansson L. (1981) Small rodent communities on mires: implications for population performance in other habitats. *Oikos* 37:216–24.

104 Bovet J. (1962) Influence d'un effet directionel sur le retour au gite des Mulots fauve et sylvestre (*Apodemus flavicollis* Melch. et *A. sylvaticus* L.) et du campagnol roux (*Clethrionomys glareolus* Schr.) (Mammalia, Rodentia). *Zeitschrift für Tierpsychologie* 19:472–88.

105 Bovet J. (1972) On the social behaviour in a stable group of long-tailed field mice (*Apodemus sylvaticus*). *Behaviour* 41:43–67.

105 Brain P.F. *et al.* eds (1989) *House mouse aggression.*
A London: Harwood Academic.

106 Brambell F.R. & Rowlands I.W. (1936) Reproduc-

tion of the bank vole *Evotomys glareolus* (Schreber). I. The oestrus cycle of the female. *Philosophical Transactions of the Royal Society of London (B)* **226**: 71–97.

107 Breed W.G. (1967) Ovulation in the genus *Microtus*. *Nature* **214**:826.

108 Breed W.G. (1969) Oestrus and ovarian histology in the lactating vole (*Microtus agrestis*). *Journal of Reproduction and Fertility* **18**:33–42.

109 Bright P. Personal communication.

109 Bright P. & Morris P. (1989) *A practical guide to*
A *dormouse conservation*. Occasional Publication No. 11. London: The Mammal Society, 31 pp.

110 Bronson F.H. (1971) Rodent pheromones. *Biology of Reproduction* **4**:344–57.

111 Bronson F.H. (1979) The reproductive ecology of the house mouse. *Quarterly Review of Biology* **54**: 265–99.

112 Brooker P. (1982) Robertsonian translocations in *Mus musculus* from NE Scotland and Orkney. *Heredity* **48**:305–9.

113 Broom J.C. (1958) Leptospiral infection rates of wild rats in Britain. *Journal of Hygiene* **56**:371–6.

114 Broom J.C. & Coghlan J.D. (1958) *Leptospira ballum* in small rodents in Scotland. *Lancet* 1041–2.

115 Brown C.M. & Parker M.T. (1957) Salmonella infections in rodents in Manchester. *Lancet* **273**: 1277–9.

116 Brown J.C. & Twigg G.I. (1965) Some observations on grey squirrel dreys in an area of mixed woodland in Surrey. *Proceedings of the Zoological Society of London* **144**:131–4.

117 Brown J.C. & Williams J.D. (1972) The rodent preputial gland. *Mammal Review* **2**:105–47.

118 Brown L.E. (1956) Field experiments on the activity of the small mammals (*Apodemus*, *Clethrionomys* and *Microtus*). *Proceedings of the Zoological Society of London* **126**:549–64.

119 Brown L.E. (1969) Field experiments on the movements of *Apodemus sylvaticus* L. using trapping and tracking techniques. *Oecologia* **2**:198–222.

120 Brown R.E. (1985) The rodents II. Suborder Myomorpha. In Brown R.E. & Macdonald D.W. eds. *Social odours in mammals, Vol 1*. Oxford: Clarendon Press pp. 345–457.

121 Brown J. *et al.* (1969) Studies on the pelvis in British Muridae and Cricetidae (Rodentia). *Journal of Zoology* **158**:81–132.

122 Brown J. *et al.* (1971) Mammalian prey of the barn owl (*Tyto alba*) on Skomer Island, Pembrokeshire. *Journal of Zoology* **165**:527–30.

123 Buckle A.P. (1976). Studies on the biology and distribution of *Leptinus testaceus* Müller within a community of mixed small mammal species. *Ecological Entomology* **1**:1–6.

124 Buckley J. (1977) Barn owl predation on the harvest mouse. *Mammal Review* **7**:117–21.

125 Bujalska G. (1970) Reproduction stabilising elements in an island population of *Clethrionomys glareolus*. *Acta theriologica* **15**:381–412.

126 Bujalska G. (1973) The role of spacing behaviour among females in the regulation of reproduction in the bank vole. *Journal of Reproduction and Fertility* **19**(Suppl.):461–72.

127 Bujalska G. (1983) Ecology of the bank vole. Dynamics and regulation of the population: Reproduction. *Acta theriologica* **28**(Suppl. 1):148–60.

128 Bujalska G. (1985) Regulation of female maturation in *Clethrionomys* species. *Annales Zoologici Fennici* **22**:331–42.

129 Calhoun J.B. (1962) *The ecology and sociology of the Norway rat*. Maryland: US Department of Health, Education and Welfare.

130 Capel-Edwards M. (1967) Foot and mouth disease in *Myocastor coypus*. *Journal of Comparative Pathology* **77**:217–21.

131 Capel-Edwards M. (1971) The susceptibility of three British small mammals to foot-and-mouth disease. *Journal of Comparative Pathology* **81**:433–66.

132 Catzeflis F. (1984) Étude d'une population de muscardins (*Muscardinus avellanarius*) lors du repos journalier. (Mammalia, Gliridae). *Revue suisse de zoologie* **91**:851–60.

133 Childs J.E. (1986) Size dependent predation on rats (*Rattus norvegicus*) by house cats (*Felis catus*) in an urban setting. *Journal of Mammalogy* **67**:196–9.

134 Chitty D. (1954) The study of the brown rat and its control by poison. In Chitty D. & Southern H.N. eds. *Control of rats and mice*, Vol. 1. Oxford: Clarendon Press pp. 160–305.

135 Chitty D. & Phipps E. (1966) Seasonal changes in survival in mixed populations of two species of vole. *Journal of Animal Ecology* **35**:313–32.

136 Chitty D. & Southern H.N. eds. (1954) *Control of rats and mice*, 3 vols. Oxford: Clarendon Press 532, 225 pp.

137 Clarke D. Personal communication.

138 Clarke J.R. (1956) The aggressive behaviour of the vole. *Behaviour* **9**:1–23.

139 Clarke J.R. (1985) The reproductive biology of the bank vole (*Clethrionomys glareolus*) and the wood mouse (*Apodemus sylvaticus*). *Symposia of the Zoological Society of London* **55**:33–59.

140 Clarke J.R. & Clulow F.V. (1973) The effect of successive matings upon bank vole (*Clethrionomys glareolus*) and vole (*Microtus agrestis*) ovaries. In Peters H. ed. *The development and maturation of the ovary and its function*. Amsterdam: Excerpta Medica (International Congress Series No. 267) pp. 160–70.

141 Clarke J.R. & Frearson S. (1972) Sebaceous glands in the hind quarters of the vole *Microtus agrestis*. *Journal of Reproduction and Fertility* **31**:477–81.

142 Clarke J.R. & Hellwing S. (1983) Fertility of the past-partum bank vole (*Clethrionomys glareolus*). *Journal of Reproduction and Fertility* **68**:241–6.

143 Clarke J.R. & Kennedy J.P. (1967) Effect of light and temperature upon gonadal activity in the vole (*Microtus agrestis*). *General and Comparative Endocrinology* **8**:474–88.

144 Clarke J.R. *et al.* (1981) Seasonal breeding in voles and wood mice: coarse and fine adjustments. In Ortavant, R. *et al.* eds. *Photoperiodism and reproduction.* Paris: INRA *(Colloq.* INRA No. 6) pp. 291–317.

145 Clausen G. *& Ersland A.* (1968) The respiratory properties of the blood of two diving rodents, the beaver and the water vole. *Respiration Physiology* 5:350–9.

146 Clegg T.M. (1963) Observations on an East Yorkshire population of the house mouse *(Mus musculus).* *Naturalist* 885:39–40.

147 Clegg T.M. (1965) *The house mouse* (Mus musculus L.) *in the South Yorkshire coal mines.* Doncaster Museum and Art Gallery.

148 Cody C.B.J. (1982) *Studies on behavioural and territorial factors relating to the dynamics of woodland rodent populations.* DPhil. thesis, University of Oxford.

149 Cooke H.J. (1975) Evolution of the long range satellite DNAs in the genus *Apodemus. Journal of Molecular Biology* 94:87–99.

150 Cooke T. (1977) *Exhibition and pet mice.* Hindhead: Saiga.

151 Corbet G.B. (1960) *The distribution, variation and ecology of voles in the Scottish Highlands.* PhD. thesis, University of St Andrews.

152 Corbet G.B. (1960) Wood mice at high altitude in Scotland. *Proceedings of the Zoological Society of London* 133:486–7.

153 Corbet G.B. (1961) Origin of the British insular races of small mammals and of the 'Lusitanian' fauna. *Nature* 191:1037–40.

154 Corbet G.B. (1963) An isolated population of the bank vole *Clethrionomys glareolus* with aberrant dental pattern. *Proceedings of the Zoological Society of London* 140:316–19.

156 Corbet G.B. (1963) The frequency of albinism of the tail tip in British mammals. *Proceedings of the Zoological Society of London* 140:327–30.

157 Corbet G.B. (1964) Regional variation in the bank vole *Clethrionomys glareolus* in the British Isles. *Proceedings of the Zoological Society of London* 143:191–219.

158 Corbet G.B. (1966) *The terrestrial mammals of Western Europe.* London: Foulis 264 pp.

159 Corbet G.B. (1966) Records of mammals and their ectoparasites from four Scottish islands. *Glasgow Naturalist* 18:426–34.

160 Corbet G.B. (1975) Examples of short- and long-term changes in dental patterns in Scottish voles. *Mammal Review* 5:17–21.

161 Corbet G.B. (1978) *The mammals of the Palaearctic region.* London: British Museum (Natural History) 314 pp.

162 Corbet G.B. (1979) Report on rodent remains. In Renfrew C. ed. *Investigations in Orkney.* London: Society of Antiquaries, Thames & Hudson pp. 135–7.

163 Corbet G.B. (1986) Temporal and spatial variation of dental pattern in the voles, *Microtus arvalis,* of the Orkney islands. *Journal of Zoology* (A) 208:395–402.

164 Corbet G.B. Personal communication.

165 Corbet G.B. & Critchlow M.A. (1986) The shrews and mice of Bardsey — a comparison with mainland animals. *Bardsey Observatory Report* 29:138–41.

166 Corbet G.B. *et al.* (1970) The taxonomic status of British water voles, genus *Arvicola. Journal of Zoology* 161:301–16.

167 Corke D. (1971) The local distribution of the yellow-necked mouse *(Apodemus flavicollis). Mammal Review* 1:62–6.

168 Corke D. (1974) *The comparative ecology of the two British species of the genus* Apodemus *(Rodentia, Muridae).* PhD. thesis, University of London.

169 Corke D. (1977) A combination of extensive and intensive survey techniques for the study of the occurrence of *Apodemus flavicollis* in Essex. *Journal of Zoology* 182:171–5.

170 Corke D. Personal communication.

171 Corthum D.W. (1967) Reproduction and duration of placental scars in the praire vole and eastern vole. *Journal of Mammalogy* 48:287–92.

172 Cotton M.J. (1970) The comparative morphology of some species of flea larvae (Siphonaptera) associated with nests of small mammals. *Entomologist's Gazette* 21:191–204.

173 Coutts R.R. & Rowlands I.W. (1969) The reproductive cycle of the Skomer vole *(Clethrionomys glareolus skomerensis). Journal of Zoology* 158:1–25.

174 Cox F.E.G. (1970) Parasitic protozoa of British wild mammals. *Mammal Review* 1:1–28.

175 Crawley M.C. (1970) Some population dynamics of the bank vole, *Clethrionomys glareolus* and the wood mouse, *Apodemus sylvaticus* in mixed woodland. *Journal of Zoology* 160:71–89.

176 Cross R.M. (1970) Activity rhythms of the harvest mouse, *Micromys minutus* Pallas. *Mammalia* 34:433–50.

177 Crowcroft P. (1966) *Mice all over.* London: Foulis 121 pp.

178 Crowcroft P. & Rowe F.P. (1958) The growth of confined colonies of the wild house mouse *(Mus musculus* L.): the effect of dispersal on female fecundity. *Proceedings of the Zoological Society of London* 131:357–65.

179 Crowcroft P. & Rowe F.P. (1961) The weights of wild house mice *(Mus musculus* L.) living in confined colonies. *Proceedings of the Zoological Society of London* 136:177–85.

180 Crowcroft W.P. & Godfrey G. (1962) Laboratory produced hybrids of the Guernsey vole *(Microtus arvalis sarnius* Miller). *Annals and Magazine of Natural History* 5(13):408–19.

181 Csaikl F. *et al.* (1980) On the biochemical systematics of three *Apodemus* species. *Comparative Biochemistry and Physiology* 65B:411–4.

182 Curry-Lindahl K. (1959) Notes of the ecology and periodicity of some rodents and shrews in Sweden. *Mammalia* 23:389–422.

183 Daan S. & Slopsema S. (1978) Short term rhythms in foraging behaviour of the common vole, *Microtus arvalis*. *Journal of Comparative Physiology* **127**: 215–27.

184 Dalgleish H.M. (1986) *Parental behaviour in Orkney voles* Microtus arvalis. Honours Thesis, University of Aberdeen.

185 Davidson A.M. & Adams W. (1973) The grey squirrel and tree damage. *Quarterly Journal of Forestry* **67**:237–47.

186 Davis D.E. (1953) The characteristics of rat populations. *Quarterly Review of Biology* **28**:373–401.

187 Davis D.E. *et al.* (1948) Studies on home range in the brown rat. *Journal of Mammalogy* **29**:207–25.

188 Davis D.H.S. (1933) Rhythmic activity in the short-tailed vole, *Microtus*. *Journal of Animal Ecology* **2**: 232–8.

189 Davis R.A. (1955) Small mammals caught near London. *London Naturalist* **35**:88–9.

190 Davis R.A. (1963) Feral coypus in Britain. *Annals of Applied Biology* **5**:345–8.

191 Davis R.A. (1979) Unusual behaviour by *Rattus norvegicus*. *Journal of Zoology* **188**:298.

192 Davis R.A. & Jenson A.G. (1960) A note on the distribution of the coypu (*Myocastor coypus*) in Great Britain. *Journal of Animal Ecology* **29**:397.

193 Davis R.A. & Rennison B.D. Personal communication.

194 Davis S.J.M. (1983) Morphometric variation of populations of house mouse *Mus domesticus* in Britain and Faroe. *Journal of Zoology* **199**:521–34.

195 De Jonge G. (1980) Response to con- and hetero-specific male odours by the voles *Microtus agrestis*, *M. arvalis* and *Clethrionomys glareolus* with respect to competition for space. *Behaviour* **73**:277–303.

196 De Jonge G. (1983) Aggression and group formation in the voles *Microtus agrestis*, *M. arvalis* and *Cethrionomys glareolus* in relation to intra- and interspecific competition. *Behaviour* **84**:1–73.

197 De Jonge G. & Ketel N.A.J. (1981). An analysis of copulating behaviour of *Microtus agrestis* and *M. arvalis* in relation to reproductive isolation. *Behaviour* **78**: 227–59.

198 Debrot S. & Mermod C. (1977) Chimiotaxonomie du genre *Apodemus* Kaup, 1829 (Rodentia, Muridae). *Revue suisse de zoologie* **84**:521–6.

199 Degn D.H. (1973) Systematic position, age criteria and reproduction of Danish red squirrels (*Sciurus vulgaris* L.) *Danish Review of Game Biology* **8**:1–24.

200 Delany M.J. (1961) The ecological distribution of small mammals in north-west Scotland. *Proceedings of the Zoological Society of London* **137**:107–26.

201 Delany M.J. (1970) Variation and ecology of island populations of the long-tailed field-mouse (*Apodemus sylvaticus* (L.)). *Symposia of the Zoological Society of London* **26**:283–95.

202 Delany M.J. & Bishop I.R. (1960) The systematics, life history and evolution of the bank vole *Clethrionomys glareolus* Tilesius in north west Scotland. *Proceedings of the Zoological Society of London* **135**:409–22.

203 Delany M.J. & Davis P.E. (1961) Observations on the ecology and life-history of the Fair Isle field mouse *Apodemus sylvaticus fridariensis* (Kinnear). *Proceedings of the Zoological Society of London* **136**: 439–52.

204 Delany M.J. & Healy M.J.R. (1964) Variation in the long-tailed field-mouse (*Apodemus sylvaticus* (L.)) in north-west Scotland. II: Simultaneous examination of all characters. *Proceedings of the Royal Society* (B) **161**:200–7.

205 Delany M.J. & Healy M.J.R. (1967) Variation in the long-tailed field-mouse (*Apodemus sylvaticus*) in the Channel Isles. *Proceedings of the Royal Society* (B) **166**:408–21.

206 Delany M.J. & Healy M.R. (1967) Variation in the long-tailed field-mouse (*Apodemus sylvaticus*) in south-west England. *Journal of Zoology* **152**:319–32.

207 Delany M.J. & Whittaker H.M. (1969) Variation in the skull of the long-tailed field-mouse, *Apodemus sylvaticus* in mainland Britain. *Journal of Zoology* **157**:147–57.

208 De Long K.T. (1967) Population ecology of feral house mice. *Ecology* **48**:611–34.

209 Deol M.S. (1970) The determination and distribution of coat colour variation in the house mouse. *Symposia of the Zoological Society of London* **26**: 239–50.

210 Deshmukh I.K. & Cotton M.J. (1970) The small mammals of a sand dune system. *Journal of Zoology* **162**:525–7.

211 Dickman C.R. (1986) Habitat utilization and diet of the harvest mouse, *Micromys minutus*, in an urban environment. *Acta theriologica* **31**:249–56.

212 Dillon P. & Browne M. (1975) Habitat selection and nest ecology of the harvest mouse *Micromys minutus* (Pallas). *Wiltshire Natural History Magazine* **70**:3–9.

213 Don B.A.C. (1979) Gut analysis of small mammals during a sawfly (*Cephalcia lariciphila*) outbreak. *Journal of Zoology* **188**:290–4.

214 Don B.A.C. (1981) *Spatial dynamics and individual quality in a population of the grey squirrel* (Sciurus carolinensis). DPhil. thesis, University of Oxford.

215 Don B.A.C. (1983) Home range characteristics and correlates in tree squirrels. *Mammal Review* **13**: 123–32.

216 Don B.A.C. (1984) Empirical evaluation of several population size estimates applied to grey squirrels. *Acta theriologica* **29**:187–203.

217 Don B.A.C. (1985) The use of drey counts to estimate grey squirrel populations. *Journal of Zoology* **206**:282–6.

218 Don B.A.C. Personal communication.

219 Dubock A.C. (1979) Methods of age determination in grey squirrels (*Sciurus carolinensis*) in Britain. *Journal of Zoology* **187**:27–40.

220 Dubock A. Personal communication.

221 Dueser R.D. & Porter J.H. (1986) Habitat use by insular small mammals: relative effects of competition and habitat structure. *Ecology* **67**:195–201.

222 Dufour B. (1972) Adaptations du terrier d'*Apodemus sylvaticus* à la température et à la lumière. *Revue*

suisse de zoologie **79**:966−9.

223 Durup M. *et al.* (1973) Quelques données sur les modalités du retour au gîte chez *Apodemus sylvaticus* et *Clethrionomys glareolus*. *Mammalia* **37**:34−55.

224 Dykstra W. (1954) Rodent filth in food. *Pest Control* **22**(7):9−14.

225 Dynowski J. (1963) Morphological variability in the Bialowieza population of *Mus musculus* Linnaeus, 1758. *Acta theriologica* **7**:51−67.

226 East K. (1965) Notes on the opening of hazel nuts (*Corylus avellana*) by mice and voles. *Journal of Zoology* **147**:223−4.

227 Ecke D.H. (1954) An invasion of Norway rats in South West Georgia. *Journal of Mammalogy* **35**: 521−5.

228 Efford M.G. (1985) The structure and dynamics of water vole populations. D.Phil thesis, University of Oxford.

229 Efford M. Personal communication.

230 Eibl-Eibesfeldt I. (1951) Beobachtungen zur Fortplanzungsbiologie und Jugendentwicklung des Eichhornchens (*Sciurus vulgaris* L.). *Zeitschrift für Tierpsychologie* **8**:370−400.

231 Eisentraut M. (1930) Beobachtungen über den Winterschlaf der Haselmaus (*Muscardinus avellanarius*). *Zeitschrift für Säugetierkunde* **4**:213−39.

232 Eldridge M.J. (1969) Observations on food eaten by wood mice (*Apodemus sylvaticus*) and bank voles (*Clethrionomys glareolus*) in a hedge. *Journal of Zoology* **158**:208−9.

233 Ellis A.E. (1963) Some effects of selective feeding by the coypu (*Myocastor coypus*) on the vegetation of Broadland. *Transactions of the Norfolk and Norwich Naturalists' Society* **20**:32−5.

234 Ellis A.E. ed. (1965) *The Broads*. London: Collins, 410 pp.

235 Elton C. (1942) *Voles, mice and lemmings*. Oxford: Clarendon Press, 496 pp.

236 Elton C.S. *et al.* (1931) The health and parasites of a wild mouse population. *Proceedings of the Zoological Society of London* **1931**:657−721.

237 Elton C. (1953) The use of cats in farm rat control. *British Journal of Animal Behaviour* **1**:151−5.

238 Engel W. *et al.* (1973) Cytogenetic and biochemical differences between *Apodemus sylvaticus* and *Apodemus flavicollis* possibly responsible for the failure to interbreed. *Comparative Biochemistry and Physiology* **44B**:1165−73.

239 English M.P. (1966) *Trichophyton persicolor* infection in the field vole and pipistrelle bat. *Sabouraudia* **4**:219−22.

240 English M.P. (1971) Ringworm in groups of wild mammals. *Journal of Zoology* **165**:535−44.

241 English M.P. & Southern H.N. (1967) *Trichophyton persicolor* infection in a population of small wild mammals. *Sabouraudia* **5**:302−9.

242 Erkinaro E. (1961) Seasonal change of the activity of *Microtus agrestis*. *Oikos* **12**:157−63.

243 Erkinaro E. (1970) The phasing of locomotory activity of *M. agrestis* (L.), *M. arvalis* (Pall) and *M. oeconomus* (Pall). *Aquilo (Zool.)* **8**:1−29.

244 Erkinaro E. (1970) Effect of the length of the day and twilight on the phase relationship of the 24 hour periodicity of the field mouse *Apodemus flavicollis* Melch. in natural light. *Oikos* **13**(Suppl.):101−7.

245 Erkinaro E. (1973) Activity optimum in *Microtus agrestis*, *Arvicola terrestris* and *Apodemus flavicollis*. *Aquilo (Zool.)* **14**:89−92.

246 Erlinge S. *et al.* (1983) Predation as a regulating factor on small rodent populations in southern Sweden. *Oikos* **40**:36−52.

247 Evans D.M. (1973) Seasonal variations in the body composition and nutrition of the vole *Microtus agrestis*. *Journal of Animal Ecology* **42**:1−18.

248 Evans F.C. (1949) A population study of house mice (*Mus musculus*) following a period of local abundance. *Journal of Mammalogy* **30**:351−63.

249 Ewer R.F. (1971) The biology and behaviour of a free-living population of black rats (*Rattus rattus*). *Animal Behaviour Monographs* **4**(3):127−74.

250 Fairley J.S. (1965) Field mice at high altitude in Co. Kerry, Ireland. *Proceedings of the Zoological Society of London* **145**:144−5.

251 Fairley J.S. (1967) Woodmice in grassland at Dundrum, County Down, Northern Ireland. *Journal of Zoology* **153**:553−5.

252 Fairley J.S. (1970) Form of the fieldmouse *Apodemus sylvaticus* (L.) in Ireland. *Irish Naturalists' Journal* **16**:281.

253 Fairley J.S. (1971) A critical reappraisal of the status in Ireland of the eastern house mouse, *Mus musculus orientalis* Cretzchmar. *Irish Naturalists' Journal* **17**: 2−5.

254 Fairley J.S. (1972) The fieldmouse in Ireland. *Irish Naturalists' Journal* **17**:152−9.

255 Fairley J.S. (1985) *An Irish beast book*, 2nd edn. Belfast: Blackstaff Press.

256 Fairley J.S. & Comerton M.E. (1972) An early-breeding population of field mice *Apodemus sylvaticus* (L.) in Limekiln Wood, Athenry, Co. Galway. *Proceedings of the Royal Irish Academy* **72B**:149−63.

257 Fairley J.S. & Smal C.M. (1987) Feral house mice in Ireland. *Irish Naturalists' Journal* **22**:284−90.

258 Fedyk A. (1971) Social thermo-regulation in *Apodemus flavicollis* (Melchior, 1834). *Acta theriologica* **16**:221−9.

259 Fedyk A. & Gebczynski M. (1980) Genetic changes in seasonal generations of the bank vole. *Acta theriologica* **25**:475−85.

260 Fenn M.G.P. & Macdonald D.W. (1987) The contribution of field studies to stored product rodent control. *Proc. BCPC Conference on stored products pest control.*

261 Fernie D.S. & Healing T.D. (1976) Wild bank voles *Clethrionomys glareolus* are possibly a natural reservoir of Campylobacters, microaerophilic vibrios. *Nature* **263**:496.

262 Ferris P.N. (1976) Diet of a *Microtus agrestis* population in south west Britain. *Oikos* **27**:506−11.

263 Fertig D.S. & Edmonds V.W. (1969) The physiology of the house mouse. *Scientific American* **221**:103−10.

264 Festing M. (1972) Mouse strain identification. *Nature* **238**:351–2.

265 Festing M. (1976) Phenotypic variability of the mandible shape in inbred and outbred mice. *Heredity* **37**:454.

266 Fielding D.C. (1966) The identification of skulls of the two British species of *Apodemus*. *Journal of Zoology* **150**:498–500.

267 Finerty J.P. (1980) *The population ecology of cycles in small mammals*. New Haven, Connecticut: Yale University Press pp. 234.

268 Fisher E.W. & Perry A.E. (1970) Estimating ages of gray squirrels by lens-weights. *Journal of Wildlife Management* **34**:825–8.

269 Fitzgerald B.M. *et al.* (1981) Spatial organization and ecology of a sparse population of house mice (*Mus musculus*) in a New Zealand forest. *Journal of Animal Ecology* **50**:489–518.

270 Flowerdew J.R. (1971) *Population regulation of small rodents in relation to social behaviour and environmental resources*. DPhil. thesis, University of Oxford.

271 Flowerdew J.R. (1972) The effect of supplementary food on a population of wood mice (*Apodemus sylvaticus*). *Journal of Animal Ecology* **41**:553–66.

272 Flowerdew J.R. (1973) The effects of natural and artificial changes in food supply on breeding in woodland mice and voles. *Journal of Reproduction and Fertility* **19**(Suppl.):257–67.

273 Flowerdew J.R. (1974) Field and laboratory experiments on the social behaviour and population dynamics of the wood mouse, *Apodemus sylvaticus*. *Journal of Animal Ecology* **43**:499–511.

274 Flowerdew J.R. (1978) Residents and transients in wood mouse populations. In Ebling F.J. & Stoddart D.M. eds. *Population control by social behaviour*. London: Institute of Biology pp. 49–66.

275 Flowerdew J.R. (1984) *Woodmice and yellow-necked mice*. Mammal Society Series. Oswestry: Nelson, 24 pp.

276 Flowerdew J.R. (1985) The population dynamics of wood mice and yellow-necked mice. *Symposia of the Zoological Society of London* **55**:315–38.

277 Flowerdew J.R. & Gardner G. (1978) Small rodent populations and food supply in a Derbyshire ashwood. *Journal of Animal Ecology* **47**:725–40.

278 Flowerdew J.R. *et al.* (1977) Small rodents, their habitats, and the effects of flooding at Wicken Fen, Cambridgeshire. *Journal of Zoology* **182**:323–42.

279 Flowerdew J.R. *et al.* eds (1985) *The ecology of woodland rodents: bank voles and wood mice*. Oxford: Oxford University Press, 418 pp.

280 Flyger V. (1969) The 1968 squirrel 'migration' in the eastern United States. *Proceedings of the Northeast Fish and Wildlife Conference* **26**:69–79.

281 Flyger V. & Gates J.E. (1982) Fox and gray squirrels, *Sciurus niger, S. carolinensis* and allies. In Chapman J.A. & Feldhammer G.A. eds. *Wild mammals of North America*. Baltimore: John Hopkins University Press pp. 209–29.

282 Fogl J.G. & Mosby H.S. (1978) Aging gray squirrels by cementum annuli in razor-sectioned teeth. *Journal of Wildlife Management* **42**:444–8.

283 Foster H.L. *et al.* (1981, 1982, 1983) *The mouse in biomedical research. I. History, genetics and wild mice. II. Diseases. III. Normative biology, immunology and husbandry*. New York & London: Academic Press.

284 Frank H. (1952) Über die Jungendentwicklung des Eichhornchens. *Zeitschrift für Tierpsychologie* **9**: 12–22.

285 Frank F. (1956) Das Duftmarkieren der grossen Wuhlmaus, *Arvicola terrestris* (L.). *Zeitschrift für Säugetierkunde* **21**:172–5.

286 Frank F. (1957) Biologie der Zwergmaus. *Zeitschrift für Säugetierkunde* **22**:1–44.

287 Freeman R.B. (1941) The distribution of *Orchopeas wickhami* (Baker) (Siphonaptera), in relation to its host the American grey squirrel. *Entomologist's Monthly Magazine* **77**:82–9.

288 Friend G.F. (1936) The sperms of British Muridae. *Quarterly Journal of Microscopical Science* **78**: 419–43.

289 Fullagar P.J. (1964) *The population structure and breeding biology of mainland and island varieties of the field mouse* Apodemus sylvaticus, *and of* Apodemus flavicollis. PhD. thesis, University of London.

290 Fullagar P.J. (1967) Moult in field mice and the variation in the chest markings of *Apodemus sylvaticus* (Linne, 1758) and *Apodemus flavicollis* (Melchior, 1834). *Säugetierkundliche Mitteilungen* **15**:138–48.

291 Gaisler J. *et al.* (1967) Mammals of ricks in Czechoslovakia. *Acta Societatis naturalium Brno* **1**: 299–348.

292 Gaisler J. *et al.* (1977) Ecology and reproduction of Gliridae (Mammalia) in Northern Moravia. *Folia Zoologica* **26**:213–28.

293 Garson P.J. (1975) Social interactions of woodmice (*Apodemus sylvaticus*) studied by direct observation in the wild. *Journal of Zoology* **177**:496–500.

294 Gaskoin J.S. (1856) On a peculiar variety of *Mus musculus*. *Proceedings of the Zoological Society of London* **24**:38–40.

295 Gemmeke H. von (1980) Proteinvariation und Taxonomie in der Gattung *Apodemus* (Mammalia, Rodentia). *Zeitschrift für Säugetierkunde* **45**:348–65.

296 Gemmeke H. von (1981) Albuminunterscheide bei Wald- und Gelbhalsmäusen (*Apodemus sylvaticus* und *A. flavicollis*, Mammalia, Rodentia) auch in getrockneten Muskeln und Balgen electrophoretisch nachweisbar. *Zeitschrift für Säugetierkunde* **46**:124–5.

297 George R.S. & Corbet G.B. (1959) A collection of fleas from small mammals in the Scottish Highlands. *Entomologist's Gazette* **10**:147–58.

298 George R.S. (1970) Ectoparasites. *Field Studies* **3**: 252–6.

299 George R.S. Personal communication.

300 Gibson D.S. & Delany M.J. (1984) The population ecology of small rodents in Pennine woodlands. *Journal of Zoology* **203**:63–85.

301 Gipps J.H.W. (1983) Maturity, castration and behaviour of male bank voles, *Clethrionomys glareolus*.

Journal of Zoology **200**:197–203.

302 Gipps J.H.W. (1984) The behaviour of mature and immature male bank voles (*Clethrionomys glareolus*). *Animal Behaviour* **32**:836–9.

303 Gipps J.H.W. (1985) Spacing behaviour and male reproductive ecology in voles of the genus *Clethrionomys*. *Annales Zoologici Fennici* **22**:343–52.

304 Gipps J.H.W. *et al.* (1986) A plague of voles: the search for a cure. *New Scientist* **1516**:48–51.

305 Gliwicz J. (1970) The relation between trappability and age of individuals in a population of the bank vole. *Acta theriologica* **15**:15–32.

306 Gluchowski W. (1954) Studies on the factors governing fertility in coypu. Part one: preliminary experiments on vaginal cycles. *Annales Universitatis Mariae Curie-Sklodowska Sect. E.* **3**:41–53.

307 Glue D.E. (1967) Prey taken by the barn owl in England and Wales. *Bird Study* **14**:169–83.

308 Glue D.E. (1970) Avian predator pellet analysis and the mammalogist. *Mammal Review* **1**:53–62.

309 Glue D.E. (1974) Food of the barn owl in Britain and Ireland. *Bird Study* **21**:200–10.

310 Glue D.E. (1975) Harvest mice as barn owl prey in the British Isles. *Mammal Review* **5**:9–12.

311 Godfrey G.K. (1954) Tracing field voles (*Microtus agrestis*) with a Geiger-Muller counter. *Ecology* **35**:5–10.

312 Godfrey J. (1958) The origin of sexual isolation between bank voles. *Proceedings of the Royal Physical Society of Edinburgh* **27**:47–55.

313 Goldenberg N. & Rand C. (1971) Rodents and the food industry: an in-depth analysis for a large British food handler. *Pest Control* **39**:24–5.

314 Golley F.B. *et al.* (1975) The role of small mammals in temperate forests, grassland and cultivated fields. In Golley P.B. *et al.* eds. *Small mammals: their productivity and population dynamics.* Cambridge University Press pp. 223–42.

315 Górecki A. (1971) Metabolism and energy budget in the harvest mouse. *Acta theriologica* **16**:213–20.

316 Gorman M. (1982) Social differences in the sub-caudal scent gland secretion of *Apodemus sylvaticus* (Rodentia: Muridae). *Journal of Zoology* **198**:353–62.

317 Gosling L.M. (1974) The coypu in East Anglia. *Transactions of the Norfolk and Norwich Naturalists' Society* **23**:49–59.

318 Gosling L.M. (1979) The twenty-four hour activity cycle of captive coypus (*Myocastor coypus*). *Journal of Zoology* **187**:341–67.

319 Gosling L.M. (1980) The duration of lactation in feral coypus (*Myocastor coypus*). *Journal of Zoology* **191**:461–74.

320 Gosling L.M. (1981) Climatic determinants of spring littering by feral coypus (*Myocastor coypus*). *Journal of Zoology* **195**:281–8.

321 Gosling L.M. (1981) The coypu. In Boyle C.L. ed. *RSPCA book of British mammals.* London: Collins pp. 129–35.

322 Gosling L.M. (1986) Selective abortion of entire litters in the coypu: adaptive control of offspring production in relation to quality and sex. *American Naturalist* **127**:772–95.

322 Gosling L.M. (1989) Extinction to order. *New A Scientist* **1654**: 44–9.

323 Gosling L.M. & Baker S.J. (1982) Coypu (*Myocastor coypus*) potential longevity. *Journal of Zoology* **197**: 285–312.

324 Gosling L.M. & Baker S.J. (1987) Planning and monitoring an attempt to eradicate coypus from Britain. *Symposia of the Zoological Society of London* **58**:99–113.

325 Gosling L.M. & Baker S.J. (1988) Demographic consequences of differences in the ranging behaviour of male and female coypus. In Putnam R.J. ed. *Mammals as pests.* London: Christopher Helm, pp. 154–67.

326 Gosling L.M. & Petrie M. (1981) The economics of social organization. In Townsend C.R. & Calow P. eds. *Physiological ecology; an evolutionary approach to resource use.* Oxford: Blackwell Scientific Publications pp. 315–45.

327 Gosling L.M. & Skinner J.R. (1984) Coypu. In Mason I.L. ed. *Evolution of domesticated animals.* Essex: Longman pp. 246–51.

328 Gosling L.M. *et al.* (1983) A simulation approach to investigating the response of a coypu population to climatic variation. *EPPO Bulletin* **13**:183–92.

329 Gosling L.M. *et al.* (1984) Differential investment by female coypus (*Myocastor coypus*) during lactation. *Symposia of the Zoological Society of London* **52**:273–300.

330 Gosling L.M. *et al.* (1980) Diurnal activity of feral coypus (*Myocastor coypus*) during the cold winter of 1978–9. *Journal of Zoology* **192**:143–6.

331 Gosling L.M. *et al.* (1980) Age estimation of coypus (*Myocastor coypus*) from eye lens weight. *Journal of Applied Ecology* **17**:641–7.

332 Gosling L.M. *et al.* (1981) Continuous retrospective census of the East Anglian coypu population between 1970 and 1979. *Journal of Animal Ecology* **50**:885–901.

333 Gosling L.M. *et al.* (1988) An attempt to remove coypus (*Myocastor coypus*) from an area of wetland habitat in East Anglia. *Journal of Applied Ecology* **25**: 49–62.

334 Goszczynski J. (1983) Predators. In Petrusewicz, K. ed. *Ecology of the bank vole. Acta theriologica* **28**(Suppl. 1):49–54.

335 Gourley R.N. & Wyld S.G. (1976) Isley-type and other mycoplasmas from the alimentary tracts of cattle, pigs and rodents. *Proceedings of the Society for General Microbiology* **3**:142.

336 Gratz N.G. (1973) Urban rodent-borne disease and rodent distribution in Israel and neighbouring counties. *Israel Journal of Medical Science* **9**: 969–79.

337 Greaves J.H. & Rowe F.P. (1969) Responses of confined rodent populations to an ultrasound generator. *Journal of Wildlife Management* **33**:407–17.

338 Green E. ed. (1966) *Biology of the laboratory mouse*, 2nd end. New York & London: McGraw-Hill.

339 Green R.E. (1978) *The ecology of bird and mammal pests of sugar beet*. PhD. thesis, University of Cambridge.

340 Green R. (1979) The ecology of wood mice (*Apodemus sylvaticus*) on arable farmland. *Journal of Zoology* 188:357–77.

341 Greenwood P.J. (1978) Timing of activity of the bank vole (*Clethrionomys glareolus*) and the wood mouse (*Apodemus sylvaticus*) in a deciduous woodland. *Oikos* 31:123–7.

342 Grocock C.A. & Clarke J.R. (1974) Photoperiodic control of testis activity in the vole, *Microtus agrestis*. *Journal of Reproduction and Fertility* 39:337–47.

343 Grodzinski W. (1985) Ecological energetics of bank voles and wood mice. *Symposia of the Zoological Society of London* 55:169–88.

344 Grodzinski W. & Gorecki A. (1967) Daily energy budgets of small rodents. In Petrusewicz K. ed. *Secondary Productivity of Terrestrial Ecosystems (Principles and Methods)* vol. 1. Warsaw: Polish Academy of Sciences pp. 295–314.

345 Grodzinski W. *et al.* (1966) Effect of rodents on the primary production of alpine meadows in Bieszczady mountains. *Acta theriologica* 11:419–31.

346 Gronwall O. Personal communication.

347 Gull J. (1977) *Movement and dispersal patterns of immature gray squirrels* (Sciurus carolinensis) *in east-central Minnesota*. MS thesis, University of Minnesota.

348 Gurnell J. (1972) *Studies on the behaviour of wild woodmice*, Apodemus sylvaticus (L.). PhD. thesis, University of Exeter.

349 Gurnell J. (1975) Notes on the activity of wild wood mice, *Apodemus sylvaticus*, in artificial enclosures. *Journal of Zoology* 175:219–29.

350 Gurnell J. (1976) Studies on the effects of bait and sampling intensity on trapping and estimating wood mice, *Apodemus sylvaticus*. *Journal of Zoology* 178:91–105.

351 Gurnell J. (1977) Neutral cage behavioural interaction in wild wood mice, *Apodemus sylvaticus* (Linné, 1758). *Säugetierkundliche Mitteilungen* 25:57–66.

352 Gurnell J. (1978) Seasonal changes in numbers and male behavioural interaction in a population of wood mice *Apodemus sylvaticus*. *Journal of Animal Ecology* 47:741–55.

353 Gurnell J. (1979) *Woodland mice*. Forest Record No. 118. London: HMSO, 22 pp.

354 Gurnell J. (1981) Woodland rodents and tree seed supplies. In Chapman J.A. & Pursley D. eds. *The worldwide furbearer conference proceedings*. Falls Chard, Virginia: Donnelly pp. 1191–214.

355 Gurnell J. (1982) Trap response in woodland rodents. *Acta theriologica* 27:123–37.

356 Gurnell J. (1983) Squirrel numbers and the abundance of tree seeds. *Mammal Review* 13:133–48.

357 Gurnell J. (1985) Woodland rodent communities. *Symposia of the Zoological Society of London* 55:377–411.

358 Gurnell J. (1987) *The natural history of squirrels*. London: Christopher Helm, 201 pp.

359 Gurnell J. (1989) Demographic implications for the control of grey squirrels. In Putnam, R.J. ed. *Mammals as pests*. London: Christopher Helm, pp. 131–43.

360 Gurnell J. & Flowerdew J.R. (1982) *Live trapping small mammals: a practical guide*. Reading: Mammal Society 24 pp.

361 Gurnell J. & Reynolls K. (1983) Growth in field and laboratory populations of wood mice (*Apodemus sylvaticus*). *Journal of Zoology* 200:355–65.

362 Gurnell J. & Pepper H. (1988). Perspectives on the management of red and grey squirrels. In Jardine D.C. ed. *Wildlife management in forests*. Edinburgh: Institute of Chartered Foresters pp. 92–109.

363 Gustafsson T.O. (1985) Sexual maturation in *Clethrionomys*. *Annales Zoologici Fennici* 22:303–8.

364 Gustafsson T.O. *et al.* (1980) Reproduction in a laboratory colony of the bank vole, *Clethrionomys glareolus*. *Canadian Journal of Zoology* 58:1016–21.

365 Gustafsson T.O. *et al.* (1983) Comparison of sensitivity to social suppression of sexual maturation in captive male bank voles, *Clethrionomys glareolus*, originating from populations with different degrees of cyclicity. *Oikos* 41:250–4.

366 Haitlinger R. (1969) Morphological variability in the Wroclaw populations of *Apodemus sylvaticus*. *Acta theriologica* 14:285–302.

367 Hall E.R. (1981) *The mammals of North America*, vol. 1. New York: Wiley.

368 Hall J. & Yalden D.W. (1978) A plea for caution over the identification of late Pleistocene *Microtus* in Britain. *Journal of Zoology* 186:556–60.

369 Halls S.A. (1981) *The influence of olfactory stimuli on ultrasonic calling in murid and cricetid rodents*. PhD. thesis, University of London.

370 Hamar M. *et al.* (1966) Biometrische und zoogeographische Untersuchungen der Gattung *Apodemus* (Kaup, 1829) in der Sozialistischen Republik Rumanien. *Acta theriologica* 11:1–40.

371 Hampshire R. (1985) *A study on the social and reproductive behaviour of captive grey squirrels* (Sciurus carolinensis). PhD. thesis, University of Reading.

372 Hansson L. (1968) Population densities of small mammals in open field habitats in south Sweden in 1964–1967. *Oikos* 19:53–60.

373 Hansson L. (1971) Small rodent food, feeding and population dynamics. *Oikos* 22:183–98.

374 Hansson L. (1977) Spatial dynamics of field voles *Microtus agrestis* in heterogeneous landscapes. *Oikos* 29:539–44.

375 Hansson L. (1979) Condition and diet in relation to habitat in bank voles, *Clethrionomys glareolus*: population or community approach? *Oikos* 33:55–63.

376 Hansson L. (1979) Food as a limiting factor for small rodent numbers. *Oecologia* 37:297–314.

377 Hansson L. (1984) Predation as a factor causing extended low densities in microtine cycles. *Oikos* 43:255–6.

378 Hansson L. (1985) The food of bank voles, wood

mice and yellow-necked mice. *Symposia of the Zoological Society of London* 55:141–68.

379 Hansson L. (1985) Personal communication.

380 Hansson L. & Larsson T-B. (1978) Vole diet on experimentally managed reforestation areas in northern Sweden. *Holarctic Ecology* 1:16–26.

381 Hansson L. & Henttonen H. (1985) Regional differences in cyclicity and reproduction in *Clethrionomys* species: are they related? *Annales Zoologici Fennici* 22:277–88.

382 Hansson L. & Henttonen H. (1985) Gradients in density variations of small rodents: the importance of latitude and snow cover. *Oecologia* 67:394–402.

383 Hardy A.R. & Taylor K.D. (1979) Radio tracking of *Rattus norvegicus* on farms. In Amalner C.J. & Macdonald D.W. eds. *A Handbook on biotelemetry and radio tracking.* Oxford: Pergamon Press pp. 657–65.

384 Hare R. Personal communication.

385 Harris S. Personal communication.

386 Harris S. (1979) History, distribution, status and habitat requirements of the harvest mouse (*Micromys minutus*) in Britain. *Mammal Review* 9:159–71.

387 Harris S. (1979) Breeding season, litter size and nestling mortality of the harvest mouse, *Micromys minutus* (Rodentia: Muridae), in Britain. *Journal of Zoology* 188:437–42.

388 Harris S. (1979) *The secret life of the harvest mouse.* London: Hamlyn, 77 pp.

389 Harris S. (1980) *The harvest mouse.* Poole: Blandford Press, 43 pp.

390 Hart M. Unpublished data.

391 Hart M. (1982) *Rats.* London: Allison & Busby 171 pp.

392 Hartley D.J. & Bishop J.A. (1979) Home range and movement in populations of *Rattus norvegicus* polymorphic for warfarin resistance. *Biological Journal of the Linnean Society* 12:19–43.

393 Harvie-Brown J.A. (1880–81) The squirrel in Great Britain. *Proceedings of the Royal Physical Society of Edinburgh* 5:343–8; 6:31–63, 115–82. (Also in book form: (1881) Edinburgh: Macfarlane & Erskine.)

394 Hassan N. (1984) *Chromosomal investigations on some British wild rodents.* PhD. thesis, University of London.

395 Hayward G.P. & Phillipson J. (1979) Community structure and functional role of small mammals in ecosystems. In Stoddart D.M. ed. *Ecology of small mammals.* London: Chapman and Hall pp. 135–211.

396 Healing T.D. (1980) The dispersion of bank voles (*Clethrionomys glareolus*) and wood mice (*Apodemus sylvaticus*) in dry stone dykes. *Journal of Zoology* 191: 406–11.

397 Healing T.D. Personal communication.

398 Healing T.D. & Nowell F. (1985) Diseases and parasites of woodland rodent populations. *Symposia of the Zoological Society of London* 55:193–218.

399 Healing T.D. *et al.* (1980) A note on some Enterobacteriaceae from the faeces of small wild British

mammals. *Journal of Hygiene* 85:343–5.

400 Hedges S.R. (1966) *Studies on the behaviour, taxonomy, and ecology of* Apodemus sylvaticus (*L.*) *and* Apodemus flavicollis (*Melchior*). PhD. thesis, University of Southampton.

401 Hedges S.R. (1969) Epigenetic polymorphism in populations of *Apodemus sylvaticus* and *A. flavicollis* (Rodentia, Muridae). *Journal of Zoology* 159: 425–42.

402 Heinrich G. (1951) Die deutschen Waldmäuse. *Zooligische Jahrbucher (Systematik)* 80:99–122.

403 Hench J.E. *et al.* (1984) Age classification for the grey squirrel based on erruption, replacement, and wear of molariform teeth. *Journal of Wildlife Management* 48:1409–14.

404 Henttonen H. (1985) Predation causing extended low densities in microtine cycles: further evidence from shrew dynamics. *Oikos* 45:156–7.

405 Henttonen H. *et al.* (1977) Interspecific competition between small rodents in subarctic and boreal ecosystems. *Oikos* 27:581–90.

406 Henttonen H. *et al.* (1985) Comparisons of amplitudes and frequencies (spectral analyses) of density variations in long term data sets of *Clethrionomys* species. *Annales Zoologici Fennici* 22:221–8.

407 Herfs A. (1939) Über die Fortpflanzung und Vermehrung der Grossen Wuhlmaus *Arvicola terrestris* (L.). *Nachrichten für Schadlingsbekampfung* 14:91–193.

408 Hewson R. (1951) Some observations on the Orkney vole *Microtus o. orcadensis* (Millais). *Northwestern Naturalist* 23:7–10.

409 Hicks M.J. (1986) The effects of coppicing on small mammal populations. *Bulletin of the British Ecological Society* 17:78–80.

410 Hillemann H.H. *et al.* (1958) The genital system of nutria (*Myocastor coypus*). *Anatomical Record* 139: 515–28.

411 Hoffmeyer I. (1976) Experiments on the selection of food and foraging sites by the mice *Apodemus sylvaticus* (Linné, 1758) and *A. flavicollis* (Melchior, 1834). *Säugetierkundliche Mitteilungen* 24:112–24.

412 Hoffmeyer I. (1983) *Interspecific behavioural niche separation in wood mice* (Apodemus flavicollis *and* A. sylvaticus) *and scent marking relative to social dominance in bank voles* (Clethrionomys glareolus). PhD. thesis, University of Lund.

413 Hoffmeyer I. & Hansson L. (1974) Variability in number and distribution of *Apodemus flavicollis* and *A. sylvaticus* in S. Sweden. *Zeitschrift für Säugetierkunde* 39:15–23.

414 Hoffmeyer I. & Sales G.D. (1977) Ultrasonic behaviour of *Apodemus sylvaticus* and *A. flavicollis*. *Oikos* 29:67–77.

415 Holisova V. (1960) Potrava mysice krovinne *Apodemus sylvaticus* L. na Ceskomoravske vrchovine. *Zoologicke Listy* 9:135–58.

416 Holisova V. (1966) Food of an overcrowded population of the bank vole, *Clethrionomys glareolus* Schreber, in a lowland forest. *Zoologicke Listy* 15: 207–24.

417 Holisova V. (1970) Trophic requirements of the water vole, *Arvicola terrestris*, Linn., on the edge of stagnant waters. *Zoologicke Listy* **19**:221–33.

418 Holisova V. (1971) The food of *Clethrionomys glareolus* at different population densities. *Acta Scientiarum Naturalium Academiae Scientiarum Bohemoslovacae* **5**:1–43.

419 Holisova V. & Obrtel R. (1979) The food eaten by *Clethrionomys glareolus* in a spruce monoculture. *Folia Zoologica* **28**:219–30.

420 Holisova V. & Obrtel R. (1980) Food resource partitioning among four myomorph rodent populations coexisting in a spruce forest. *Folia Zoologica* **29**:193–207.

421 Holland S.C. (1967) Mammal notes and records. *Journal of the North Gloucestershire Naturalists' Society* **18**:225–6.

422 Holm J. (1987) *Squirrels*. London: Whittet Books 127 pp.

423 Holm J. Personal communication.

424 Holmes R.G. (1962) Fascioliasis in coypus (*Myocastor coypus*). *Veterinary Record* **74**:1552.

425 Holmes R.G. *et al.* (1977) Toxoplasmosis in coypu. *Veterinary Record* **101**:74–5.

426 Homolka M. (1983) On the problem of exanthropic occurrence of *Rattus norvegicus*. *Folia Zoologica* **32**:203–11.

427 Hora A.M. (1934) Notes on mites collected from the Isle of Lewis, Outer Hebrides. *Parasitology* **26**:361–5.

428 Hornfeldt B. (1978) Synchronous population fluctuations in voles, small game, owls and tularemia in northern Sweden. *Oecologia* **32**:141–52.

429 Horwich R.H. (1972) The ontogeny of social behaviour in the gray squirrel, *Sciurus carolinensis*. *Advances in Ethology*, 8. Hamburg: Paul Parey.

430 Hrabe V. (1971) Circumanal glands of central European Gliridae (Rodentia). *Zoologicke Listy* **20**:247–58.

431 Hurrell E. Personal communication.

432 Hurrell E. (1962) *Dormice*. London: Sunday Times Publications, 24 pp.

433 Hurrell E. (1980) *The common dormouse*. Poole: Blandford Press 43 pp.

434 Hurrell E. & McIntosh G. (1984) Mammal Society dormouse survey, January 1975 to April 1979. *Mammal Review* **14**:1–18.

435 Hurrell H.G. Personal communication.

436 Huson L.W. & Rennison B.D. (1981) Seasonal variability of Norway rat (*Rattus norvegicus*) infestation of agricultural premises. *Journal of Zoology* **194**:257–60.

437 Huxley J.S. (1942) *Evolution, the modern synthesis*. London: Allen & Unwin.

438 Hynes J.A. & Fairley J.S. (1978) A population study of fieldmice in dry-stone walls. *Irish Naturalists' Journal* **19**:180–4.

439 Innes S. & Lavigne D.M. (1979) Comparative energetics of coat colour polymorphisms in the eastern grey squirrel, *Sciurus carolinensis*. *Canadian Journal of Zoology* **57**:585–92.

440 Jacobs G.H. (1981) *Comparative color vision*. New York: Academic Press.

441 Jameson H.L. (1898) On a probable case of protective coloration in the house mouse (*Mus musculus* L.). *Zoological Journal of the Linnean Society of London* **26**:465–73.

442 Jamon M. (1986) The dynamics of wood mouse (*Apodemus sylvaticus*) populations in the Camargue. *Journal of Zoology* (A), **208**:569–82.

443 Jarvinen A. (1985) Predation causing extended low densities in microtine cycles: implications from predation on hole-nesting passerines. *Oikos* **45**:157–8.

444 Jefferies D.J. & French M.C. (1972) Lead concentration in small mammals trapped on roadside verges and field sites. *Environmental Pollution* **3**:147–56.

445 Jefferies D.J. *et al.* (1973) The ecology of small mammals in arable fields drilled with winter wheat and the increase in their dieldrin and mercury residues. *Journal of Zoology* **171**:513–39.

446 Jennings T.G. (1975) Notes on the burrow systems of wood mice (*Apodemus sylvaticus*). *Journal of Zoology* **177**:500–4.

447 Jensen T.S. (1982) Seed production and outbreaks of non-cyclic rodent populations in deciduous forest. *Oecologia* **54**:184–92.

448 Jensen T.S. (1985) Seed–seed predator interactions of European beech, *Fagus sylvatica* and forest rodents, *Clethrionomys glareolus* and *Apodemus flavicollis*. *Oikos* **44**:149–56.

449 Jewell P.A. (1966) Breeding season and recruitment in some British mammals confined on small islands. *Symposia of the Zoological Society of London* **15**:98–116.

450 Jewell P.A. & Fullagar P.J. (1965) Fertility among races of the field mouse (*Apodemus sylvaticus*) and their failure to form hybrids with the yellow-necked mouse (*Apodemus flavicollis*). *Evolution* **19**:175–81.

451 Johnson M. (1977) The harvest mouse (*Micromys minutus*); current distribution and nesting habitats in Lincolnshire. *Transactions of the Lincolnshire Naturalists Union* **19**:75–7.

452 Johnson R.P. (1975) Scent marking with urine in two races of the bank vole (*Clethrionomys glareolus*). *Behaviour* **55**:81–93.

453 Johst V. (1973) Struktur und Funktion akustischer Signale der Schermaus, *Arvicola terrestris* (L.). *Forma et Functio* **6**:305–22.

454 Jones P.W. & Twigg G.I. (1976) Salmonellosis in wild mammals. *Journal of Hygiene* **77**: 51–4.

455 Jüdes U. von (1979) Untersuchengen zur Ökologie der Waldmaus (*Apodemus flavicollis* Linne, 1758) und der Gelbhalsmaus (*Apodemus flavicollis* Melchior, 1834) im Raum Kiel (Schleswig-Holstein). *Zeitschrift für Säugetierkunde* **44**:81–95;185–95.

456 Jüdes U. (1981) Some notes on population density of *Micromys minutus* in secondary biotope. *Zeitschrift für Säugetierkunde* **46**:266–8.

457 Justice K.E. (1962) Ecological and genetical studies of evolutionary forces acting on desert populations

of *Mus musculus*. Tucson, Arizona: Arizona-Sonora Desert Museum.

458 Kaczmarski F. (1966) Bioenergetics of pregnancy and lactation in the bank vole. *Acta theriologica* **11**:409–417.

459 Kaikusalo A. (1972) Population turnover and wintering of the bank vole, *Clethrionomys glareolus* (Schreber) in southern and central Finland. *Annales Zoologici Fennici* **9**:219–24.

460 Kalela O. (1957) Regulation of reproduction rate in subarctic populations of the vole *Clethrionomys rufocanus*. *Annales Academiae Scientiarum Fennica, A IV* **34**:1–60.

461 Kalela O. (1962) On the fluctuations in numbers of arctic and boreal small rodents as a problem of production ecology. *Annales Academiae Scientiarum, Fennica A IV* **66**:1038.

462 Kaltwasser M.T. & Schnitzler H.U. (1981) Echolocation signals confirmed in rats. *Zeitschrift für Säugtierkunde* **46**:394–5.

463 Kanervo V. & Myllymäki A. (1970) Problems caused by the field vole, *Microtus agrestis* (L.) in Scandinavia. *EPPO Publications* (A) **58**:11–26.

464 Kaplan C. *et al.* (1980) Evidence of infection by viruses in small British field rodents. *Journal of Hygiene* **84**: 285–95.

465 Kaplan H.M. *et al.* (1983) Physiology. In Foster H.L. *et al.* eds. *The mouse in biomedical research*, vol. 3. New York & London: Academic Press pp. 247–92.

466 Karlsson A.F. (1984) Age-differential homing tendencies in displaced bank voles, *Clethrionomys glareolus*. *Animal Behaviour* **32**:515–9.

467 Karpukhin I.P. & Karpukhina N.M. (1971) Eye lens weight as a criterion of age of *Sciurus vulgaris*. *Zoologicheskii zhurnal* **50**:274–7.

468 Kästle W. (1953) Die Jugendentwicklung ·der Zwergmaus, *Micromys minutus soricinus*. *Säugetierkundliche Mitteilungen* **1**:49–59.

469 Keeler B. (1961) Damage to young plantations by the bank vole at Bernwood Forest 1958–60. *Journal of the Forestry Commission* **30**:55–9.

470 Kelly P. & Fairley J.S. (1982) An accessory cusp on the third upper molar of wood mice *Apodemus sylvaticus* from the west of Ireland. *Journal of Zoology* **198**:532–3.

471 Kelly P.A. *et al.* (1982). An analysis of morphological variation in the field mouse *Apodemus sylvaticus* (L.) on some Irish islands. *Proceedings of the Royal Irish Academy* **82**(B):39–51.

472 Kenneth J.G. & Ritchie G.R. (1953) *Gestation periods*, 3rd edition. Edinburgh: Bureau of Animal Breeding.

473 Kenward R.E. (1983) The causes of damage by red and grey squirrels. *Mammal Review* **13**:159–66.

474 Kenward R.E. (1985) Ranging behaviour and population dynamics of grey squirrels. In Sibly R.M. & Smith R.H. eds *Behavioural ecology*. Oxford: Blackwell Scientific Publications, pp. 319–30.

475 Kenward R. (1989) Bark stripping by grey squirrels in Britain and North America. In Putman R.J. ed. *Mammals as pests*. London: Christopher Helm, pp. 144–54.

476 Kenward R.E. & Parish T. (1986) Bark stripping by grey squirrels. *Journal of Zoology* (A) **210**:473–81.

477 Kenward R.E. & Tonkin M. (1986) Red and grey squirrels; some behavioural and biometric differences. *Journal of Zoology* (A) **209**:279–81.

478 Keymer I.F. (1983) Diseases of squirrels in Britain. *Mammal Review* **13**:155–8.

479 Kikkawa J. (1964) Movement, activity and distribution of the small rodents, *Clethrionomys glareolus* and *Apodemus sylvaticus* in woodland. *Journal of Animal Ecology* **49**:259–99.

480 King C.M. (1980) The weasel, *Mustela nivalis* and its prey in an English woodland. *Journal of Animal Ecology* **49**:127–60.

481 King C.M. (1982) Age structure and reproduction in feral New Zealand populations of the house mouse (*Mus musculus*) in relation to seedfall of southern beech (*Nothofagus*). *New Zealand Journal of Zoology* **9**:467–80.

482 King C.M. (1983) The life-history strategies of *Mustela nivalis* and *M. erminea*. *Acta Zoologica Fennica* **174**:183–4.

483 King C.M. (1985) Interactions between woodland rodents and their predators. *Symposia of the Zoological Society of London* **55**:219–47.

484 Kiris I.D. (1937) (Method and technique of age determination of the squirrel and analysis of the age-group composition of squirrel populations). *Byulleten Moskovskovo Obshchestva. Ispytatelei Prirody* **46**: 36–42. (Russian, French summary).

485 Kirkpatrick C.M. & Barnett E.M. (1957) Age criteria in male grey squirrels. *Journal of Wildlife Management* **21**:341–7.

486 Knapka J.J. (1983) Nutrition. In Foster H.L. *et al.* eds. *The mouse in biomedical research*, vol. 4. New York & London: Academic Press pp. 51–67.

487 Knee C. (1983) Squirrel energetics. *Mammal Review* **13**:113–22.

488 Knight D.A. (1975) *Some aspects of activity of the water vole* Arvicola terrestris *and the brown rat* Rattus norvegicus. Dissertation, University of Durham.

489 Koenig L. (1960) Das Aktionssystem des Siebenschläfers (*Glis glis* L.) *Zeitschrift für Tierpsychologie* **17**:427–505.

490 Koenigswald W. von. (1970) Mittelpleistozäne Kleinsäugerfauna aus der Spaltenfullung Petersbuch bei Eichstatt. *Mitteilungen der Bayerischen Staatssammlung für Palaontologie und historische Geologie* **10**:407–32.

491 Koenigswald W. von. (1980) Schmelzstruktur und Morphologie in den Molaren der Arvicolidae (Rodentia). *Abhandlungen der Senckenbergischen Naturforschenden Gesellschaft* **539**:1–129.

492 Kohli E. (1981) *Untersuchung zum Eingfluss der Nutrias (*Myocastor coypus *Molina) auf die natürliche Vegetation der Camargue*. PhD. thesis, University of Bern.

493 Koskela P. & Viro P. (1976) The abundance, autumn migration, population structure and body dimensions of the harvest mouse in northern Finland. *Acta theriologica* 21:375−87.

494 Kowalski K. & Sutcliffe A.J. (1976) Pleistocene rodents of the British Isles. *Bulletin of the British Museum (Natural History) Geol.* 27:31−147.

495 Kozakiewicz M. (1976) The weight of eye lens as the proposed age indicator of the bank vole. *Acta theriologica* 21:314−6.

496 Kral B. (1970) Chromosome studies in two subgenera of the genus *Apodemus*. *Zoologike Listy* 19:119−34.

497 Kraus B. (1983) A test of the optimal density-model for seed scatterhoarding. *Ecology* 64:608−10.

498 Krebs C.J. & Myers J.H. (1974) Population cycles in small mammals. *Advances in Ecological Research* 8:267−399.

499 Kryltzov A.I. (1964) Moult topography of Microtinae, other rodents and Lagomorpha. *Zeitschrift für Säugetierkunde* 29:1−17.

500 Kubik J. (1952) [The harvest mouse − *Micromys minutus* Pall. − in the Bialowieza National Park.] *Annales Universitalis Mariae Curie-Sklodowska* 7: 449−82. (British Library Translation no 7692).

501 Kulicke H. (1962) Home range and territorial behaviour in the field vole and the bank vole. Brno: *Proceedings of International Symposium of Mammal Investigation*, 1960:195.

502 Kulicke H. (1963) Kleinsäuger als Vertilger forstschadlicher Insekten. *Zeitschrift für Säugetierkunde* 28:175−83.

503 Laidler K. (1980) *Squirrels in Britain*. Newton Abbot: David & Charles, 192 pp.

504 Laine K. & Henttonen H. (1983) The role of plant production in microtine cycles in northern Fennoscandia. *Oikos* 40:407−18.

505 Lampio T. (1967) Sex ratios and the factors contributing to them in the squirrel, *Sciurus vulgaris*, in Finland. *Finnish Game Research* 29:5−67.

506 Lance A.N. (1973) Numbers of wood mice (*Apodemus sylvaticus*) on improved and unimproved blanket bog. *Journal of Zoology* 171:471−3.

507 Larsson T.B. & Hansson L. (1977) Vole diet on experimentally managed afforestation areas in northern Sweden. *Oikos* 28:242−9.

508 Laurie E.M.O. (1946) The reproduction of the house mouse (*Mus musculus*) living in different environments. *Proceedings of the Royal Society of London* (B) 133:248−81.

509 Laurie E.M.O. (1946) The coypu (*Myocastor coypus*) in Great Britain. *Journal of Animal Ecology* 15: 22−34.

510 Lawrence M.J. & Brown R.W. (1967) *Mammals of Britain: their tracks trails and signs*. London: Blandford Press 298 pp.

511 Leamy L. (1977) Genetic and environmental correlations of morphometric traits in random bred house mice. *Evolution* 31:357−69.

512 Lehmann E. von. (1962) Vorubergehende Verandurungen im Haar der Rotelmaus, *Clethri-*

onomys glareolus. *Bonner Zoologische Beiträge* 12: 235−40.

513 Lehmann U. (1976) Short-term and circadian rhythms in the behaviour of the vole, *Microtus agrestis* (L.). *Oecologia* 23:185−99.

514 Lehmann U. & Sommersberg C.W. (1980) Activity patterns of the common vole, *Microtus arvalis* − automatic recording of behaviour in an enclosure. *Oecologia* 47:61−75.

515 Leigh Brown A.J. (1977) Genetic changes in a population of fieldmice (*Apodemus sylvaticus*) during one winter. *Journal of Zoology* 182:281−9.

516 Leigh Brown A.J. (1977) Physiological correlates of an enzyme polymorphism. *Nature* 269:803−4.

517 Lemnell P.A. (1973) Age determination in red squirrels (*Sciurus vulgaris* L.). *International Congress of Game Biology* 11:573−80.

518 Leslie P.H. & Davis D.H.S. (1939) An attempt to determine the absolute number of rats on a given area. *Journal of Animal Ecology* 8:94−113.

519 Leslie P.H. *et al.* (1952) The fertility and population structure of the brown rat (*Rattus norvegicus*) in cornricks and some other habitats. *Proceedings of the Zoological Society of London* 122:187−238.

520 Leslie P.H. *et al.* (1955) The longevity and fertility of the Orkney vole *Microtus orcadensis* as observed in the laboratory. *Proceedings of the Zoological Society of London* 125:115−25.

521 Leuze C.C.K. (1976) *Social behaviour and dispersion in the water vole*, Arvicola terrestris (*L.*). PhD. thesis, University of Aberdeen.

522 Leuze C.C.K. (1979) Social behaviour and dispersion in the water vole, *Arvicola terrestris* (L.). *Abstracts of the XVIth International Ethological Conference*. Section 1: Invited Plenary Papers.

523 Leuze C.C.K. (1980) The application of radio-tracking and its effect on the behavioural ecology of the water vole, *Arvicola terrestris* (L.). In Amlaner C.J. & Macdonald D. eds. *The handbook of biotelemetry and radio-tracking*. Oxford: Pergamon, pp. 361−6.

524 Lever C. (1985) *Naturalized mammals of the world*. London: Longman 487 pp.

525 Lever R.J. *et al.* (1957) Myxomatosis and the fox. *Agriculture*, 64:105−11.

526 Lewis J.W. (1987) Helminth parasites of British rodents and insectivores. *Mammal Review* 17: 81−93.

527 Lewis J.W. & Twigg G.I. (1972) A study of the internal parasites of small rodents from woodland areas in Surrey. *Journal of Zoology* 166:61−77.

528 Lewis J.W. (1968) Studies on the helminth parasites of voles and shrews from Wales. *Journal of Zoology* 154:313−31.

529 Lidicker W.Z. (1985) Dispersal. In Tamarin, R.H. ed. *Biology of New World Microtus*. American Society of Mammalogists, Special Publication 8:420−54.

530 Lidicker W.Z. (1965) Comparative study of density regulation in confined populations of four species of rodents. *Research in Population Ecology* 7:57−72.

531 Lidicker W.Z. (1966) Ecological observations on a feral mouse population declining to extinction. *Ecological Monographs* **36**:27—50.

532 Lidicker W.Z. (1976) Social behaviour and density regulation in house mice living in large enclosures. *Journal of Animal Ecology* **45**:677—97.

533 Lishak R.S. (1982) Grey squirrel mating calls: a spectrographic and ontogenic analysis. *Journal of Mammalogy* **63**:661—3.

534 Lishak R.S. (1982) Vocalizations of nestling gray squirrels. *Journal of Mammalogy* **63**:446—52.

535 Lishak R.S. (1984) Alarm vocalizations of adult gray squirrels. *Journal of Mammalogy* **65**:681—4.

536 Litjens B.E.J. (1980) De beverrat, *Myocastor coypus* (Molina), in Nederland. I. Het verloop van de populatie gedurende de periode 1963—1979. *Lutra* **23**: 43—53.

537 Lloyd H.G. (1968) Observations on nut selection by a hand reared squirrel (*Sciurus carolinensis*). *Journal of Zoology* **155**:240—4.

538 Lloyd H.G. (1983) Past and present distributions of red and grey squirrels. *Mammal Review* **13**:69—80.

539 Lore R. & Flannelly K. (1977) Rat societies. *Scientific American* **236**:106—16.

540 Lore R. & Flannelly K. (1978) Habitat selection and burrow construction by wild *Rattus norvegicus* in a landfill. *Journal of Comparative Physiology and Psychology* **92**:888—96.

541 Louarn H. Le & Schmitt A. (1972) Relations observées entre la production des faines et la dynamique de population du mulot, *Apodemus sylvaticus* L. en forêt de Fontainebleau. *Annales des Sciences Forestières* **30**:205—14.

542 Lowe V.P.W. (1971) Root development of molar teeth in the bank vole. *Journal of Animal Ecology* **40**:49—61.

543 Lowe V.P.W. & Gardiner A.S. (1983) Is the British squirrel (*Sciurus vulgaris leucourus* Kerr) British? *Mammal Review* **13**:57—67.

544 Lozan M.N. (1961) Age determination of *Dryomys nitedula* Pall. and of *Muscardinus avellanarius* L. *Zoologicheskii zhurnal* **40**:1740—3.

545 Ludwick R.L. *et al.* (1969) Energy metabolism of the eastern gray squirrel. *Journal of Wildlife Management* **33**:569—75.

546 Macdonald D.W. (1977) On food preference in the red fox. *Mammal Review* **7**:7—23.

547 Mackintosh J.H. (1981) Behaviour of the house mouse. *Symposia of the Zoological Society of London* **47**:337—65.

548 Madison D. (1985) Activity rhythms and spacing. In Tamarin R.H. ed. *Biology of New World* Microtus. American Society of Mammalogists, Special Publication **8**:373—419.

549 Malygin V.M. (1983) *Systematics of the common voles.* Moscow: Izdat. Nauka 208 pp.

550 Marelli C.A. (1932) El nuevo y especie, *Pitrufquenia coypus* de Malofago de la Nutria Chilena. *La Charca* **3**:7—9.

551 Marsh R. & Howard W.E. (1977) Vertebrate control manual: tree squirrels. *Pest Control Manual* **45**: 36—48.

552 Marshall J.T. (1986) Systematics of the genus *Mus*. *Current Topics in Microbiology and Immunology* **127**: 12—18.

553 Marshall J.T. & Sage R.D. (1981) Taxonomy of the house mouse. *Symposia of the Zoological Society of London* **47**:15—25.

554 Mather J.G. & Baker R.R. (1981) Magnetic sense of direction in woodmice for route-based navigation. *Nature* **291**:152—5.

555 Matheson C. (1962) *Brown rats.* London: Sunday Times Publications, 24 pp.

556 Matthews L.H. (1952) *British mammals.* London: Collins, 410 pp.

557 Matthey R. (1951). La formule chromosomique de *Microtus orcadensis* Mill. *Revue suisse de zoologie* **58**:201—13.

558 Matthey R. (1956) Cytologie chromosomique comparée et systematique des Muridae. *Mammalia* **20**: 93—123.

559 Mayhew D.F. (1977) Avian predators as accumulators of fossil mammal material. *Boreas* **6**:25—31.

560 Mazak V. (1963) Notes on the dentition in *Clethrionomys glareolus* Schreber, 1780 in the course of postnatal life. *Säugetierkundliche Mitteilungen* **11**: 1—11.

561 Mazurkiewicz M. (1971) Shape, size and distribution of home ranges of *Clethrionomys glareolus* (Schreber, 1780). *Acta theriologica* **16**:23—60.

562 Mazurkiewicz M. (1972) Density and weight structure of populations of the bank vole in open and enclosed areas. *Acta theriologica* **17**:455—65.

563 Mazurkiewicz M. (1981) Spatial organisation of a bank vole, *Clethrionomys glareolus*, population in years of large and small numbers. *Acta theriologica* **26**:31—46.

564 Mazurkiewicz M. & Rajska E. (1975) Dispersion of young bank voles from their place of birth. *Acta theriologica* **20**:71—81.

565 McLaren A. & Walker P.M.B. (1970) Rodent DNA: comparisons between species. *Evolution* **24**: 199—206.

566 Meehan A.P. (1984) *Rats and mice. Their biology and control.* East Grinstead: Rentokil 383 pp.

567 Merson M.H. *et al.* (1978) Characteristics of captive gray squirrels exposed to cold and food deprivation. *Journal of Wildlife Management* **42**:202—5.

568 Meyer M.N. *et al.* (1972) On the nomenclature of 46- and 54-chromosome voles of the type *Microtus arvalis. Zoologicheskii zhurnal* **51**:157—61.

569 Middleton A.D. (1930) The ecology of the American grey squirrel (*Sciurus carolinensis* Gmelin) in the British Isles. *Proceedings of the Zoological Society of London* **1930**: 809—43.

570 Middleton A.D. (1931) *The grey squirrel.* London: Sidgwick & Jackson, 107 pp.

571 Migula P. *et al.* (1970) Vole and mouse plagues in south-eastern Poland in the years 1945—1967. *Acta theriologica* **15**:233—52.

572 Millar J.C.B. (1980) *Aspects of the ecology of the American gray squirrel* Sciurus carolinensis *Gmelin in South Africa.* MS thesis, University of Stellenbosch.

573 Miller G.S. (1912) *Catalogue of the mammals of western Europe.* London: British Museum (Natural History), 1019 pp.

574 Miller R.S. (1955) Activity rhythms of the wood mouse, *Apodemus sylvaticus* and the bank vole, *Clethrionomys glareolus. Proceedings of the Zoological Society of London* 125:505–19.

575 Milligan S.R. (1974) Social environment and ovulation in the vole, *Microtus agrestis. Journal of Reproduction and Fertility* 41:35–7.

576 Milligan S.R. (1975) Mating, ovulation and corpus luteum functions in the vole, *Microtus agrestis. Journal of Reproduction and Fertility* 42:35–44.

577 Minnette H.P. (1964) Leptospirosis in rodents and mongooses on the island of Hawaii. *American Journal of Tropical Medicine and Hygiene* 13:826–32.

578 Misonne X. (1969) African and Indo-Australian Muridae: evolutionary trends. *Annales du Musée Royal de l'Afrique Centrale, Sciences Zoologiques* 172: 1–219.

579 Mitchell-Jones A. (1979) *Population dynamics of* Clethrionomys glareolus *and* Apodemus sylvaticus *in relation to aggressive behaviour and genetic variation.* PhD. thesis, Durham University.

580 Moffat C.B. (1928) The field mouse. *Irish Naturalists' Journal* 11:106–9.

581 Moffat C.B. (1938) The mammals of Ireland. *Proceedings of the Royal Irish Academy* (B) 44:61–128.

582 Moffat M. Personal communication.

583 Mollar H. (1983) Foods and foraging behaviour of red (*Sciurus vulgaris*) and grey (*Sciurus carolinensis*) squirrels. *Mammal Review* 13:81–98.

584 Mollar H. (1986) Red squirrels (*Sciurus vulgaris*) feeding in a Scots pine plantation in Scotland. *Journal of Zoology* 209:61–84.

585 Moller A.P. (1983) Damage by rats (*Rattus norvegicus*) to breeding birds on Danish islands. *Biological Conservation* 25:5–8.

586 Molyneux D.H. (1969) The morphology and life history of *Trypanosoma* (*Hespetosoma*) *microti* of the field vole *Microtus agrestis. Annals of Tropical Medicine and Parasitology* 63:229–44.

587 Montgomery W.I. (1975) On the relationships between sub-fossil and recent British water voles. *Mammal Review* 5:23–9.

588 Montgomery W.I. (1977) *Studies on the ecology of two sympatric species of* Apodemus (*Rodentia: Muridae*). PhD. thesis, University of Manchester.

589 Montgomery W.I. (1978). Studies on the distributions of *Apodemus sylvaticus* (L.) and *A. flavicollis* (Melchior) in Britain. *Mammal Review* 8:177–84.

590 Montgomery W.I. (1978) Intra- and interspecific interaction of *Apodemus sylvaticus* (L.) and *A. flavicollis* (Melchior) under laboratory conditions. *Animal Behaviour* 26:1247–54.

591 Montgomery W.I. (1979) Trap-revealed home range in sympatric populations of *Apodemus sylvaticus* and

A. flavicollis. Journal of Zoology 189:535–40.

592 Montgomery W.I. (1980) The use of arboreal runways by the woodland rodents, *Apodemus sylvaticus* (L.), *A. flavicollis* (Melchior) and *Clethrionomys glareolus* (Schreber). *Mammal Review* 10:189–95.

593 Montgomery W.I. (1980) Spatial organisation in sympatric populations of *Apodemus sylvaticus* and *A. flavicollis* (Rodentia: Muridae). *Journal of Zoology* 192:379–401.

594 Montgomery W.I. (1980) Population structure and dynamics of sympatric *Apodemus* species (Rodentia: Muridae). *Journal of Zoology* 192:351–77.

595 Montgomery W.I. (1981) A removal experiment with sympatric populations of *Apodemus sylvaticus* (L.) and *A. flavicollis* Melchior (Rodentia: Muridae). *Oecologia* 51:123–32.

596 Montgomery W.I. (1985) Interspecific competition and the comparative ecology of two congeneric species of mice. In Cook L.M. ed. *Case studies in population biology.* Manchester: Manchester University Press pp. 126–87.

597 Montgomery W.I. (1989) *Peromyscus and Apodemus: patterns of similarity in ecological equivalents.* In Kirkland G.L. & Layne J.N. eds *Advances in the study of* Peromyscus. Texas Technical University Press, pp. 293–365.

598 Montgomery W.I. (1989) Population parameters, spatial division and niche breadth in two *Apodemus* species sharing a woodland habitat. In Morris D.W. *et al.* eds *Patterns in the structure of mammalian communities.* Texas Technical University Press, pp. 45–57.

599 Montgomery W.I. Personal communication.

600 Montgomery W.I. & Gurnell J. (1985) The behaviour of *Apodemus. Symposia of the Zoological Society of London* 55:89–115.

601 Montgomery S.S.J. & Montgomery W.I. (1985) A new semi-hairless mutant of the wood mouse, *Apodemus sylvaticus. Journal of Zoology* (A) 207: 626–8.

602 Moore C.L. (1981) An olfactory basis for maternal discrimination of sex of offspring in rats (*Rattus norvegicus*). *Animal Behaviour* 29:383–6.

603 Morris P. (1979) Rats in the diet of the barn owl (*Tyto alba*). *Journal of Zoology* 189:540–5.

604 Morris P. & Whitbread S. (1986) A method for trapping the dormouse (*Muscardinus avellanarius*). *Journal of Zoology* 210:642–4.

605 Morris P.A. (1968) Apparent hypothermia in the wood mouse (*Apodemus sylvaticus*). *Journal of Zoology* 155:235–6.

605 Morris P.A. *et al.* (1990) Use of nestboxes by the
A   dormouse *Muscardinus avellanarius. Biological Conservation* 51:1–13.

606 Morse H.C. ed. (1978) *Origins of inbred mice.* New York: Academic Press.

607 Mosby H.S. (1969) The influence of hunting on the population dynamics of a woodlot gray squirrel population. *Journal of Wildlife Management* 33:59–73.

608 Mossing T. (1975) Measuring small mammal loco-motory activity with passage counters. *Oikos* **26**: 237–9.

609 Muldal S. (1950). A list of vertebrates observed at Bayfordbury, 1949–50. *Report, John Innes Horticultural Institution* **41**:39–41 (*see also* p. 24).

610 Müller-Bohme H. (1939) Beiträge zur Anatomie, Morphologie und Biologie der grossen Wuhlmaus (*Arvicola terrestris* L., *Arvicola terrestris sherman* Shaw). Gleichzeitig ein Versuch zur Losung ihrer Rassenfrage. *Arbeiten der Kaiserlichen Biologischen Reichsanstalt — Land-Fortwirtschaft* **21**:363–453.

611 Müller J.P. von (1972) Die Verteilung der Klein-säuger auf die Lebensraume an einen Nordhang im Churer Rheintal. *Zeitschrift für Säugetierkunde* **37**: 257–86.

612 Myllymäki A. (1959) Bedeütung und Ursachen der Mausefrasschaden in Finland. *Valtion Maatalouskoetoiminnan Julkaisuya* **178**:75–100.

613 Myllymäki A. (1977) Interspecific competition and home range dynamics in the field vole, *Microtus agrestis*. *Oikos* **29**:553–69.

614 Naber F. (1982) Eerste vondst van de dwergmuis *Micromys minutus* (Pallas, 1771) op Terschelling. *Lutra* **25**:95–6.

615 Nash H.R. *et al.* (1983) The Robertsonian translocation house mouse populations of north east Scotland: a study of their origin and evolution. *Heredity* **50**:303–10.

616 Nascetti G. & Filipucci M.G. (1984) Genetic variability and divergence in Italian populations of *Apodemus sylvaticus* and *Apodemus flavicollis* (Rodentia, Muridae). *Supplemento alle Ricerche di Biologia della Selvaggina* **9**:75–83.

617 Nesbitt M.N. & Francke U. (1973) A system of nomenclature for band patterns of mouse chromosomes. *Chromosoma* **41**:145–58.

618 Newsome A.E. (1969) A population study of house mice. *Journal of Animal Ecology* **38**:341–77.

619 Newsome A.E. & Corbett L.K. (1975) Outbreaks of rodents in semi-arid and arid Australia: causes, preventions, and evolutionary considerations. In Prakash I. & Ghosh P.K. eds. *Rodents in desert environments*. The Hague: Junk pp. 117–53.

620 Newsome A.E. & Crowcroft W.P. (1971) Outbreaks of house mice in South Australia in 1965. *CSIRO Wildlife Research* **16**:41–7.

621 Newson R. (1963) Differences in numbers, reproduction and survival between two neighbouring populations of the bank vole (*Clethrionomys glareolus*). *Ecology* **44**:111–20.

622 Newson R.M. (1966) Reproduction in the feral coypu (*Myocastor coypus*). *Symposia of the Zoological Society of London* **15**:323–34.

623 Newson R.M. (1968) Parasites occurring on the coypu since its introduction to Britain. *Bulletin of the Mammal Society of the British Isles* **29**:13–14.

624 Newson R.M. & Holmes R.G. (1968) Some ecto-parasites of the coypu in eastern England. *Journal of Animal Ecology* **37**:471–81.

625 Nieder L. *et al.* (1982) Burrowing and feeding behaviour in the rat. *Animal Behaviour* **30**:837–44.

626 Niethammer J. (1969) Zur Frage der Introgression bei den Waldmäusen *Apodemus sylvaticus* und *A. flavicollis* (Mammalia, Rodentia). *Zeitschrift für Zoologische Systematik und Evolutionforschung* **7**: 77–127.

627 Niethammer J. & Krapp P. eds. (1978) *Handbuch der Säugetiere Europas*, Vol. 1. Wiesbaden: Akademische Verlagsgesellschaft.

628 Norris J.D. (1967) A campaign against feral coypus (*Myocastor coypus*) in Great Britain. *Journal of Applied Ecology* **4**:191–9.

629 Nygren J. (1978) Individual influence on diurnal rhythms of activity in cycling and non-cycling populations of the field vole, *Microtus agrestis* L. *Oecologia* **35**:231–9.

630 Obrtel R. & Holisova V. (1979) The food eaten by *Apodemus sylvaticus* in a spruce monoculture. *Folia Zoologica* **28**:299–310.

631 O'Connor T.P. (1986) The garden dormouse *Eliomys quercinus* from Roman York. *Journal of Zoology* (A), **210**:620–2.

632 Ognev S.I. (1940) *Animals of the USSR and adjacent countries. 4 Rodents.* Moscow, Leningrad. English translation (1966) Jerusalem: Israel Program for Scientific Translations.

633 Ognev S.I. (1950) *Animals of the USSR and adjacent countries.* Moscow, Leningrad. English translation (1964) Jerusalem: Israel Program for Scientific Translations.

634 Okon E.E. (1972) Factors affecting ultrasound production in infant rodents. *Journal of Zoology* **168**: 139–48.

635 Oldfield C.J. (1968). *A study of the agonistic behaviour of the long-tailed field mouse* (Apodemus sylvaticus) *and the bank vole* (Clethrionomys glareolus). MSc. thesis, University of Durham.

636 Osgood W.H. (1943) Mammals of Chile. *Field Museum Natural History Publications Zoology Series* **30**:131–4.

637 Pack J.C. *et al.* (1967) Influence of social hierarchy on gray squirrel behaviour. *Journal of Wildlife Management* **31**:720–8.

638 Panteleyev P.A. (1968) *Population ecology of the water vole.* Moscow. [In Russian; English translation National Lending Library, 1971].

639 Parker J.C. & Holliman R.B. (1972) A method of determining ectoparasitic densities on gray squirrels. *Journal of Wildlife Management* **36**:1227–34.

640 Partridge L. (1981) Increased preferences for familiar foods in small mammals. *Animal Behaviour* **29**:211–16.

641 Pearson A.M. (1962) Activity patterns, energy metabolism and growth rate of voles *Clethrionomys rufocanus* and *Clethrionomys glareolus* in Finland. *Annales Societas Zoologique–Botanicae Fennicae Vanamo* **24**:1–58.

642 Pearson O.P. (1963) History of two local outbreaks of feral house mice. *Ecology* **44**:540–9.

643 Peck S.B. (1982) A review of the ectoparasitic *Leptinus* beetles of North America (Coleoptera: Leptinidae). *Canadian Journal of Zoology* 60:1517–27.

644 Pefaur J.E. *et al.* (1979) Biological and environmental aspects of a mouse outbreak in the semi-arid region of Chile. *Mammalia* 43:313–22.

645 Pelikan J. (1967) Resorption rate in embryos of four *Apodemus* species. *Zoologicke Listy* 16:325–42.

646 Pelikan J. (1967) Analysis of three population dynamical factors in *Apodemus flavicollis* (Melch). *Zeitschrift für Säugetierkunde* 31:31–7.

647 Pelikan J. (1970) Sex ratio in three *Apodemus* species. *Zoologicke Listy* 19:23–34.

648 Pelikan J. (1974) On the reproduction in the house mouse. *Symposia of the Zoological Society of London* 47:205–29.

649 Pelz H.-J. (1979) Die Waldmaus, *Apodemus sylvaticus* L., auf Ackerflächen: Populationsdynamik, Saatschäden und Abwehrmöglichkeiten. *Zeitschrift für Angewandte Zoologie* 66:261–80.

650 Pernetta J.C. & Handford P. (1970) Mammalian and avian remains from possible bronze age deposits on Nornour, Isles of Scilly. *Journal of Zoology* 162:534–40.

651 Perrin M.R. & Gurnell J. (1971) Rats on Lundy. *Annual Report, Lundy Field Society* 22:35–40.

652 Perry J.S. (1943) Reproduction in the water vole, *Arvicola amphibius* Linn. *Proceedings of the Zoological Society of London* 112:118–30.

653 Petrides G.A. (1951) Notes on age determination in squirrels. *Journal of Mammalogy* 32:111–12.

654 Petrusewicz K. ed. (1983) Ecology of the bank vole. *Acta theriologica* 28(Suppl. 1):242 pp.

655 Phillipson J. *et al.* (1983) Food consumption by *Microtus agrestis* and the unsuitability of faecal analysis for the determination of food preference. *Acta theriologica* 28:397–416.

656 Piechoki R. (1958) *Die Zwergmaus* Micromys minutus *Pallas.* (*Die neue Brehm Bucherei*, 222) Wittenberg Lutherstadt: Ziemsen, 56 pp.

657 Pielowski Z. (1962) Untersuchungen über die Ökologie der Kreuzotter (*Vipera berus* L.). *Zoologische Jahrbucher (Systematik)* 89:479–500.

658 Piper S.E. (1928) The mouse infestation in Buena Vista Lake Basin, Kern County, California, September 1926 to February 1927. *Department of Agriculture, State of California, Monthly Bulletin* 17:538–60.

659 Pokki J. (1981) Distribution, demography and dispersal of the field vole, *Microtus agrestis*, in the Trarminne archipelago, Finland. *Acta Zoologica Fennica* 164:1–48.

660 Pollard E. & Relton J. (1970) Hedges V: A study of small mammals in hedges and cultivated fields. *Journal of Applied Ecology* 7:549–57.

661 Pomianowska-Pilipiuk I. (1974) Energy balance and food requirements of adult vipers *Vipera berus* (L.). *Ekologia Polska (A)* 22:195–211.

662 Preece R.C. *et al.* (1986) New biostratigraphic evidence of the post-glacial colonization of Ireland and for Mesolithic forest disturbance. *Journal of Biogeography* 13:487–509.

663 Pucek Z. & Zejda J. (1968) Technique for determining age in the red-backed vole *Clethrionomys glareolus* (Schreber). *Small Mammals Newsletters* 2:51–60.

664 Pucek Z. *et al.* (1969) Estimation of average length of life in bank vole, *Clethrionomys glareolus* (Schreber 1780). In Petrusewicz K. & Ryszkowski L. eds. *Energy flow through small mammal populations*. Warsaw: Polish Scientific Publications, pp. 137–201.

665 Pulliam H.R. *et al.* (1969) Bioelimination of tracer zinc-65 in relation to metabolic rates in mice. In Nelson D.J. & Evans F.C. eds. *Radioecology*. Springfield, Virginia: US Department of Commerce, pp. 125–730.

666 Purray F.J. & Rey J.M. (1974) Estudio ecologico y sistematico de la ardilla (*Sciurus vulgaris*) en Novarra. *Boletin de la Estacion Central de Ecologia* 3:71–82.

667 Quadagno D.M. (1968) Home range size in feral house mice. *Journal of Mammalogy* 49:149–51.

668 Rabus A. (1881) Beiträge zur Kenntnis über den Winterschlaf der Siebenschläfer. *Zoologiche Garten, Frankfurt*, 321–5 (translation in *Zoologist* (1882) 6:161–4).

669 Raczynski J. (1983) *Clethrionomys glareolus*. In Pucek Z. & Raczynski J. eds. *Atlas of Polish mammals*. Warsaw, pp. 1–88.

670 Radda A. (1969) Untersuchungen über den Aktionsraum von *Apodemus flavicollis* (Melchior). *Zoologicke Listy* 18:11–22.

671 Radda A. *et al.* (1969) Bionomische und ökologische Studien an österreichischen Populationen der Gelbhalsmaus (*Apodemus flavicollis* (Melchior, 1834)) durch Markierungsfang. *Oecologia* 3:351–73.

672 Randolph S.E. (1973) A tracking technique for comparing individual home ranges of small mammals. *Journal of Zoology* 170:509–20.

673 Randolph S.E. (1975) Seasonal dynamics of a host-parasite system: *Ixodes trianguliceps* (Acarina, Ixodidae) and its small mammal hosts. *Journal of Animal Ecology* 44:425–49.

674 Randolph S.E. (1975) Patterns of distribution of the tick *Ixodes trianguliceps* Birula on its hosts. *Journal of Animal Ecology* 44:451–74.

675 Randolph S.E. (1977) Changing spatial relationships in a population of *Apodemus sylvaticus* with the onset of breeding. *Journal of Animal Ecology* 46:653–76.

676 Rands D.G. (1979) The distribution of the harvest mouse (*Micromys minutus*) in Bedfordshire. *Bedfordshire Naturalist* 33:13–16.

677 Rasmuson B. *et al.* (1977) Genetically controlled differences in behaviour between cycling and non-cycling populations of field vole (*Microtus agrestis*). *Hereditas* 87:33–42.

678 Reason H.C. Personal communication.

679 Reichstein H. (1963) Beitrag zur systematischen Gliederung des Genus *Arvicola* Lacepede 1799. *Zeitschrift für Zoologische Systematik und Evolutions-*

forschung 1:155–204.

680 Reichstein H. (1978) *Mus musculus* Linnaeus, 1758 – Hausmaus. *Handbuch der Säugetiere Europas* Vol. 1. Wiesbaden: Akademische Verlagsgesellschaft, pp. 421–5.

681 Reichstein H. (1982) Genus *Arvicola* Lacepede, 1799 – Schermause. In Niethammer J. & Krapp F. eds. *Handbuch der Säugetiere Europas* Vol. 2. Wiesbaden: Akademische Verlagsgesellschaft, pp. 209–52.

682 Renaud P. (1938) La formule chromosomiale chez sept éspèces de Muscardinidae et de Microtinae indigènes. *Revue suisse de zoologie* 45:349–83.

683 Rennison B.D. & Shenker A.M. (1976) Rodent infestation in some London boroughs in 1972. *Environmental Health* 84:9–10,12–13.

684 Reynolds J.C. (1981) *The interaction of red and grey squirrels.* PhD. thesis, University of East Anglia.

685 Reynolds J.C. (1985) Details of the geographic replacement of the red squirrel (*Sciurus vulgaris*) by the grey squirrel (*Sciurus carolinensis*) in eastern England. *Journal of Animal Ecology* 54:149–62.

686 Reynolds J.C. (1985) Autumn/winter energetics of Holarctic tree squirrels: a review. *Mammal Review* 15:137–50.

687 Richards C.G.J. *et al.* (1984) The food of the common dormouse, *Muscardinus avellanarius*, in South Devon. *Mammal Review* 14:19–28.

688 Roberts R.C. (1981) Genetical influences on growth and fertility. *Symposia of the Zoological Society of London* 47:231–54.

689 Robertson J.G.M. (1977) *Population density and reproduction in* Microtus arvalis orcadensis. Honours thesis, University of Aberdeen.

690 Robinson R. (1970) Homologous mutants in mammalian coat colour variation. *Symposia of the Zoological Society of London* 26:251–69.

691 Rodl P. (1974) Beitrag zur Kenntnis der Raumaktivität von *Apodemus flavicollis* Melch. und *Clethrionomys glareolus* Schreb. *Lynx* 16:46–60.

692 Rood J.P. (1965) Observations on the life cycle and variation of the longtailed field mouse *Apodemus sylvaticus* in the Isles of Scilly and Cornwall. *Journal of Zoology* 147:99–107.

693 Rowe F.P. (1958) Some observations on harvest mice from the corn ricks of a Hampshire farm. *Proceedings of the Zoological Society of London* 131:320–3.

694 Rowe F.P. (1961) Ectoparasites found on harvest mice. *Proceedings of the Zoological Society of London* 137:627.

695 Rowe F.P. (1970) The response of wild house mice (*Mus musculus*) to live-traps marked by their own and by a foreign mouse odour. *Journal of Zoology* 162:517–20.

696 Rowe F.P. (1981) Wild house mouse biology and control. *Symposia of the Zoological Society of London* 47:575–89.

697 Rowe F.P. & Taylor E.J. (1964) The numbers of harvest-mice (*Micromys minutus*) in corn-ricks. *Pro-*

ceedings of the Zoological Society of London 142:181–5.

698 Rowe F.P. & Redfern R. (1965). Toxicity tests on suspected warfarin resistant house mice (*Mus musculus* L.) *Journal of Hygiene* 63:417–25.

699 Rowe F.P. *et al.* (1963) The numbers and movements of house mice (*Mus musculus* L.) in the vicinity of four corn-ricks. *Journal of Animal Ecology* 32:87–97.

700 Rowe J. (1980) *Grey squirrel control.* Forestry Commission Leaflet No. 56. London: HMSO.

701 Rowe J. (1983) Squirrel management. *Mammal Review* 13:173–82.

702 Rowlands I.W. (1936) Reproduction of the bank vole (*Evotomys glareolus* Schreber). II. Seasonal changes in the reproductive organs of the male. *Philosophical Transactions of the Royal Society of London B* 226:99–120.

703 Russell M.A. & Semeonoff R. (1967) A serum esterase variation in *Microtus agrestis*. *Genetical Research* 10:27.

704 Ryder S.R. (1962) Water voles. London: The Sunday Times, 24 pp.

705 Sage R.D. (1981) Wild mice. In Foster H.L. *et al.* eds. *The mouse in biomedical research*, vol. 1. New York: Academic Press pp. 39–90.

706 Saint Girons M.C. (1960) Le rythme nycthéméral d'activité du campagnol roux, *Clethrionomys glareolus* (Schreber) 1780. I. Les males. *Mammalia* 24:516–32.

707 Saint Girons M.C. (1973) *Les mammifères de France et du Benelux.* Paris: Doin.

708 Saint Girons M.C. & Durup M. (1974) Retour au gîte chez le mulot, *Apodemus sylvaticus* et de campagnol russâtre, *Clethrionomys glareolus*. *Mammalia* 38:389–404.

709 Samkow J.A. & Trubezkoij G.W. (1974) Nutriazucht jenseits der Grenzen. *Deutsche Peltztierzuchter* 48:130–2.

710 Sanders E.H. *et al.* (1981) 6-Methoxybenzoxazolinone: a plant derivative that stimulates reproduction in *Microtus montanus*. *Science* 214:67–9.

711 Sanderson H.R. *et al.* (1976) Gray squirrel habitat and nest tree preference. *Proceedings of the Annual Conference, Southeastern Association of Game and Fish Commissioners* 30:609–16.

712 Santini L. (1980) La nutria *Myocastor coypus* (Molina) allo stato selvatico in Toscanna. *Frustula Entomologica* (new series) 1:273–88.

713 Schadler M.H. (1981) Post-implantation abortion in pine voles (*Microtus pinetorum*) induced by strange males and pheromones of strange males. *Biology of Reproduction* 25:295–7.

714 Schiller E.L. (1956) Ecology and health of *Rattus* at Nome, Alaska. *Journal of Mammalogy* 37:181–8.

715 Schropfer R. von (1974) Comparative ecological studies on water requirement of *Apodemus tauricus* (Pallas, 1811) and *Apodemus sylvaticus* (Linné, 1758). *Zoologische Jahrbucher, Abteilung für Systematik, Okologie und Geographie der Tiere* 101:236–48.

716 Schulze W. (1970) Beitrage zum Vorkommen und zur Biologie der Haselmaus (*Muscardinus avellanarius* L.) und des Siebenschläfers (*Glis glis* L.) in Sudharz. *Hercynia* 7:354−71.

717 Schumacher (1924) Eine Lippenplatte beim Eichhornchen (*Sciurus vulgaris* L.) *Anatomischer Anzeiger* 58:75−80.

718 Schwarz E. & Schwarz H.K. (1943) The wild and commensal stocks of the house mouse, *Mus musculus* Linnaeus. *Journal of Mammalogy* 24:59−72.

719 Schwarz S.S. *et al.* (1964) Biological peculiarities of seasonal generations of rodents with special reference to the problem of senescence in mammals. *Acta theriologica* 8:11−43.

720 Scott A.C. *et al.* (1981) Parapoxvirus infection of the red squirrel (*Sciurus vulgaris*). *Veterinary Record* **109**: 202.

720 Scriven P. & Brooker P. C. (1990) Caithness revisited:
A Robertsonian chromosome polymorphisms in Caithness house mice. *Heredity* **64**:25−7.

721 Searle J.B. Personal communication.

722 Seebeck J.H. (1984) The eastern gray squirrel, *Sciurus carolinensis*, in Victoria. *Victorian Naturalist* **101**:60−6.

723 Selander R.K. (1970) Behaviour and genetic variation in natural populations. *American Zoologist* **10**: 53−66.

724 Self S.G. & Leamy L. (1978) Heritability of quasicontinuous skeletal traits in random bred population of house mice. *Genetics* 88:109−120.

725 Semeonoff R. & Robertson W. (1968) A biochemical and ecological study of plasma esterase polymorphism in natural populations of the field vole, *Microtus agrestis* L. *Biochemical Genetics* 1:205−27.

726 Seton E.I. (1920) Migrations of the gray squirrel (*Sciurus carolinensis*). *Journal of Mammalogy* 1: 53−8.

727 Shillito E.E. (1963) Exploratory behaviour in the short-tailed vole *Microtus agrestis*. *Behaviour* **21**: 145−54.

728 Shiraishi S. (1964) Damage of mice and voles on the fruits of strawberries under the plastic-cover culture and their control. *Science Bulletin of the Faculty of Agriculture, Kyushu University* 21:89−96.

729 Shorten M. (1951) Some aspects of the biology of the grey squirrel (*Sciurus carolinensis*) in Great Britain. *Proceedings of the Zoological Society of London* **121**:427−51.

730 Shorten M. (1954) *Squirrels*. London: Collins, 212 pp.

731 Shorten M. (1954) The reaction of the brown rat towards changes in its environment. In Chitty D. & Southern H.N. eds. *Control of rats and mice*, Vol. 2. Oxford: Clarendon Press pp. 307−34.

732 Shorten M. (1962) *Red squirrels. Animals in Britain*, vol. 6. London: The Sunday Times.

733 Shorten M. (1962) *Grey squirrels. Animals in Britain*, vol. 5. London: The Sunday Times.

734 Shorten M. (1962) Squirrels, their biology and control. *MAFF Bulletin* 184:1−44.

735 Shorten M. & Courtier F.A. Personal communication.

736 Sidorowicz J. (1959) Über Morphologie und Biologie der Haselmaus (*Muscardinus avellanarius* L.) in Polen. *Acta theriologica* 3:75−91.

737 Sierra De Soriano B. (1960) Elementos constituvos de una habitacion de *Myocastor coypus bonariensis* (Geoffroy). *Revista de la Facultad de Humanidades y Ciencias, Universidad de la Republica, Uruguay* 18:257−76.

738 Sierra De Soriano B. (1961) Algunos modelos de las actividitades en *Myocastor coypus bonariensis* Geoffroy ('nutria') en cautiverio. *Revista de la Facultad de Humanidades y Ciencias, Universidad de la Republica, Uruguay* 19:261−9.

739 Singleton G.R. & Hay D.A. (1983) The effect of social organization on reproductive success and gene flow in colonies of wild house mice, *Mus musculus*. *Behavioral Ecology and Sociobiology* 12:49−56.

740 Sleptsov M.M. (1948) The biology of *Micromys minutus ussuricus* Barr.-Ham. *Fauna i Ekologiya Gryzunov* 2:69−100. (Translation British Lending Library No. RTS 7767.)

741 Smal C.M. (1990) The diet of the barn owl *Tyto alba* in southern Ireland with reference to a recently introduced prey species − the bank vole (*Clethrionomys glareolus*). *Bird Study* 34:113−25.

742 Smal C.M. & Fairley J.S. (1980) Food of wood mice (*Apodemus sylvaticus*) and bank voles (*Clethrionomys glareolus*) in oak and yew woods in Killarney, Ireland. *Journal of Zoology* 191:413−18.

743 Smal C.M. & Fairley J.S. (1982) The dynamics and regulation of small rodent populations in the woodland ecosystems of Killarney, Ireland. *Journal of Zoology* **196**:1−30.

744 Smal C.M. & Fairley J.S. (1984) The spread of the bank vole *Clethrionomys glareolus* in Ireland. *Mammal Review* **14**:71−8.

745 Smirnov P.K. (1959) The postembryonic development of the harvest mouse (*Micromys minutus* Pallas). *Nauchnye Doklady Vysshei Shkoly, Biologi Nauki* 3:76−8.

746 Smit F.G.A.M. (1957) Siphonaptera. *Handbook for the Identification of British Insects* 1(16):1−94.

747 Smit F.G.A.M. (1957) The recorded distribution and hosts of Siphonaptera in Britain. *Entomologist's Gazette* 8:45−75.

748 Smith J.C. (1976) Responses of adult mice to models of infant calls. *Journal of Comparative Physiology* 90:1105−15.

749 Smith J.C. (1981) Senses and communication. *Symposia of the Zoological Society of London* 47: 367−93.

750 Smith J.C. & Sales G.D. (1980) Ultrasonic behaviour and mother−infant interactions in rodents. In Smotherman W. & Bell R. eds. *Maternal influences and early behaviour*. New York: Spectrum Publications pp. 105−33.

751 Smith N.B. & Barkalow F.S. (1967) Precocious breeding of the gray squirrel. *Journal of Mammalogy* 48:326−30.

752 Smith R.H. & Greaves J.H. (1986) Resistance to anticoagulant rodenticides: the problem of its management. Tel Aviv, Israel: 4th International Conference on stored-product protection.

753 Smyth M. (1966) Winter breeding in woodland mice, *Apodemus sylvaticus*, and voles, *Clethrionomys glareolus* and *Microtus agrestis*, near Oxford. *Journal of Animal Ecology* **35**:471−85.

754 Southern H.N. (1954) *Control of rats and mice*, vol. 3. *House mice*. Oxford: University Press, 255 pp.

755 Southern H.N. (1955) Nocturnal animals. *Scientific American* **193**:88−98.

756 Southern H.N. (1970) The natural control of a population of tawny owls (*Strix aluco*). *Journal of Zoology* **162**:197−285.

757 Southern H.N. & Crowcroft P. (1956) Terrestrial habits of the water vole. *Proceedings of the Zoological Society of London* **126**:166−7.

758 Southern H.N. & Laurie E.M.O. (1946) The house mouse (*Mus musculus*) in corn ricks. *Journal of Animal Ecology* **15**:135−49.

759 Southern H.N. & Lowe V.P.W. (1968) The pattern of distribution of prey and predation in tawny owl territories. *Journal of Animal Ecology* **37**:75−97.

760 Southern H.N. & Lowe V.P.W. (1982) Predation by tawny owls (*Strix aluco*) on bank voles (*Clethrionomys glareolus*) and wood mice (*Apodemus sylvaticus*). *Journal of Zoology* **198**:83−102.

761 Southern H.N. *et al.* (1946) Watching nocturnal animals by infra-red radiation. *Journal of Animal Ecology* **37**:75−97.

762 Southwick C.H. (1956) The abundance and distribution of harvest mice (*Micromys minutus*) in corn ricks near Oxford. *Proceedings of the Zoological Society of London* **126**:449−52.

763 Spears N. & Clarke J.R. (1986) Effect of male presence and of photoperiod on the sexual maturation of the field vole (*Microtus agrestis*). *Journal of Reproduction and Fertility* **78**:231−8.

764 Stehn R.A. & Jannett F.J. (1981) Male induced abortion in various microtine rodents. *Journal of Mammalogy* **62**:369−72.

765 Steiner H.M. (1968) Untersuchungen über die Variabilität und Bionomie der Gattung *Apodemus* (Muridae, Mammalia) der Donau-Auen von Stockerau (Niederösterreich). *Zeitschrift für Wissenschaftliche Zoologie* **177**:1−96.

766 Stenseth N.C. ed. (1977) Population dynamics of the field vole *Microtus agrestis*: a modelling study. *Oikos* **29**:447−62.

767 Stenseth N.C. (1977) Evolutionary aspects of demographic cycles: the relevance of some models of cycles for microtine fluctuation. *Oikos* **29**:525−38.

768 Stenseth N.C (1977) On the importance of spatio-temporal heterogeneity for the population dynamics of rodents: towards a theoretical foundation for rodent control. *Oikos* **29**:545−52.

769 Stenseth N.C. ed. (1985) *Clethrionomys* biology: population dynamics, dispersal, reproduction and social structure. *Annales Zoologici Fennici* **22**: 205−395.

770 Stenseth N.C. (1985) Geographic distribution of *Clethrionomys* species. *Annales Zoologici Fennici* **22**:215−19.

771 Stenseth N.C. *et al.* (1977) General models for the population dynamics of the field vole, *Microtus agrestis*, in central Scandinavia. *Oikos* **29**:616−42.

772 Steven D.M. (1955) Untersuchungen uber die britischen Formen von *Clethrionomys*. *Zeitschrift für Säugetierkunde* **20**:70−4.

773 Steventon D. Personal communication.

774 Stickel L.C. (1979) Population ecology and house mice in unstable habitats. *Journal of Animal Ecology* **48**:871−87.

775 Stoddart D.M. (1969) Daily activity cycle of the water vole (*Arvicola terrestris*). *Journal of Zoology* **159**:538−40.

776 Stoddart D.M. (1970) Individual range, dispersion and dispersal in a population of water voles (*Arvicola terrestris* (L.)). *Journal of Animal Ecology* **39**: 403−25.

777 Stoddart D.M. (1970) Tailtip and other albinisms in the voles of the genus *Arvicola* Lacepède 1799. *Symposia of the Zoological Society of London* **26**: 271−82.

778 Stoddart D.M. (1971) Breeding and survival in a population of water voles. *Journal of Animal Ecology* **40**:487−94.

779 Stoddart D.M. (1973) Preliminary characterisation of the caudal organ secretion of *Apodemus flavicollis*. *Nature* **246**:501−3.

780 Stoddart D.M. (1974) Recruitment and sex ratio in a semi-isolated population of *Arvicola terrestris* (L.). In Kratochvil J. & Obital R. eds. *Proceedings of the International Symposium on Species and Zoogeography of European Mammals*. Prague, pp. 345−65.

781 Stoddart D.M. (1977) Genus *Arvicola*. In Corbet G.B. & Southern H.N. eds. *The handbook of British mammals*, 2nd edn. Oxford: Blackwell Scientific Publications pp. 196−204.

782 Stoddart D.M. (1982) Does trap odour influence estimation of population size of the short-tailed vole, *Microtus agrestis*? *Journal of Animal Ecology* **51**: 375−86.

783 Stoddart D.M. (1982) Demonstration of olfactory discrimination by the short-tailed vole, *Microtus agrestis*. *Animal Behaviour* **30**:293−4.

784 Stoddart D.M. & Sales G. (1985) The olfactory and acoustic biology of wood mice, yellow-necked mice and bank voles. *Symposia of the Zoological Society of London* **55**:117−39.

785 Stoddart D.M. *et al.* (1975) Evidence for social differences in the flank gland organ secretion of *Arvicola terrestris* (Rodentia: Microtinae). *Journal of Zoology* **177**:529−40.

786 Storch G. (1978). *Glis glis* (Linnaeus, 1766) — Siebenschläfer. In Niethammer J.B. & Krapp F. eds *Handbuch der Säugetiere Europas* I (1). Wiesbaden: Akademische Verlagsgesellschaft

pp. 243−58.

787 Stuart A.J. (1974) Pleistocene history of the British vertebrate fauna. *Biological Reviews* **49**:225−66.

788 Stuart A.J. (1982) *Pleistocene vertebrates in the British Isles*. London & New York: Longman 212 pp.

789 Sutcliffe A.J. & Kowalski K. (1976) Pleistocene rodents of the British Isles. *Bulletin of the British Museum (Natural History) Geology* **27**:31−147.

790 Tadros W.A. (1968) The rediscovery of Findlay and Middleton's organism (the so-called *Toxoplasma microti*) in voles in the type locality in Wales. *Transactions of the Royal Society for Tropical Medicine and Hygiene* **62**:7.

791 Tamarin R.H. ed. (1985) The biology of New World *Microtus. American Society of Mammalogists*, Special Publication 8, 893 pp.

792 Tapper S.C. (1976) Population fluctuations of field voles (*Microtus*): a background to the problems involved in predicting vole plagues. *Mammal Review* **6**:93−117.

793 Taylor J.C. (1966) Home range and agonostic behaviour in the grey squirrel. *Symposia of the Zoological Society of London* **18**:229−35.

794 Taylor J.C. (1977) The frequency of grey squirrel (*Sciurus carolinensis*) communication by use of scent marking points. *Journal of Zoology* **183**:534−45.

795 Taylor K.D. (1978) Range of movement and activity of common rats (*Rattus norvegicus*) on agricultural land. *Journal of Applied Ecology* **15**:663−77.

796 Taylor K.D. *et al*. (1971) Movements of the grey squirrel as revealed by trapping. *Journal of Applied Ecology* **8**:123−46.

797 Taylor K.D. *et al*. (1974) The responses of captive wild rats to human odour and to the odour of other rats. *Mammalia* **38**:581−90.

798 Taylor K.D. & Quy R.J. (1978) Long distance movements of a common rat (*Rattus norvegicus*) revealed by radio-tracking. *Mammalia* **42**:63−71.

799 Teagle W.G. (1964) The harvest mouse in the London area. *London Naturalist* **43**:136−49.

800 Telle H.J. (1966) Beitrage zur Kenntnis der Verhaltenswerise von Ratten verfleichend dargestellt bei *Rattus norvegicus* und *R. rattus*. *Zeitschrift für Angewandte Zoologie* **53**:129−96.

801 Terkel J. *et al*. (1979) Ultrasonic cries from infant rats stimulate prolactin release in lactating mothers. *Hormones and Behavior* **12**:95−102.

802 Thaler L. *et al*. (1981) Process of speciation and semi-speciation in the house mouse. *Symposia of the Zoological Society of London* **47**:27−41.

803 Thompson D.C. (1978) The social system of the grey squirrel. *Behaviour* **64**:305−28.

804 Thompson D.C. (1978) Regulation of a northern grey squirrel (*Sciurus carolinensis*) population. *Ecology* **59**:708−15.

805 Thompson H.V. (1953) The edible dormouse (*Glis glis* L.) in England, 1902−1951. *Proceedings of the Zoological Society of London* **122**:1017−24.

806 Thorpe R.S. (1981) The morphometrics of the mouse: a review. *Symposia of the Zoological Society of London* **47**:85−125.

807 Timmermans P.J.A. (1978) *Social behaviour in the rat*. PhD. thesis, Catholic University of Nijmegen.

808 Tittensor A.M. (1975) The red squirrel. *Forest Record*, No. 101. London: HMSO, 36 pp.

809 Tittensor A. (1977) Red squirrel *Sciurus vulgaris*. In Corbet G.B. & Southern H.N. eds. *Handbook of British mammals*, 2nd edn. Oxford: Blackwell Scientific Publications pp. 153−64.

810 Tittensor A. (1977) Grey squirrel *Sciurus carolinensis*. In Corbet G.B. & Southern H.N. eds. *Handbook of British mammals*, 2nd edn. Oxford: Blackwell Scientific Publications pp. 164−72.

811 Tomich P.Q. (1969) *Mammals in Hawaii*. Honolulu: Bishop Museum 238 pp.

812 Tonkin J.M. (1983) Activity patterns of the red squirrel (*Sciurus vulgaris*). *Mammal Review* **13**: 99−111.

813 Trapido H. Personal communication.

814 Trojan P. (1965) Intrapopulation relations and regulation of numbers in small forest rodents. *Ekologia Polska* (A) **13**:143−68.

815 Trout R.C. (1976) *An ecological study of wild populations of harvest mice*. PhD. thesis, University of London.

816 Trout R.C. (1978) A review of studies on populations of wild harvest mice (*Micromys minutus* (Pallas)). *Mammal Review* **8**:143−58.

817 Trout R.C. (1978) A review of studies on captive harvest mice (*Micromys minutus* (Pallas)). *Mammal Review* **8**:159−75.

818 Truszkowski J. (1974) Utilisation of nest boxes by rodents. *Acta theriologica* **19**:441−52.

819 Tupikova N.V. *et al*. (1968) A method of age determination in *Clethrionomys. Acta theriologica* **13**: 99−115.

820 Turner D.T.L. (1965) A contribution to the ecology and taxonomy of *Microtus arvalis* on the island of Westray, Orkney. *Proceedings of the Zoological Society of London* **144**:143−50.

821 Twigg G.I. (1966) Notes on the invertebrate fauna of some grey squirrel dreys. *Entomologist* **99**: 51−3.

822 Twigg G.I. (1975) *The brown rat*. London: David & Charles 150 pp.

823 Twigg G.I. (1980) A review of the occurrence in British mammals of the major organisms of zoonotic importance. *Mammal Review* **10**:139−49.

824 Twigg G.I. & Cuerdon C.M. (1966) Leptospirosis in British mammals: initial survey results. *Journal of Zoology* **150**:494−8.

825 Twigg G.I. *et al*. (1968) Leptospirosis in British wild mammals. *Symposia of the Zoological Society of London* **24**:75−98.

826 Uhlig H.G. (1955) The gray squirrel. Its life history, ecology and population characteristics in West Virginia. *Pitman-Robertson Project* 31-R, Commission of West Virginia.

827 Ursin E. (1956) Geographical variation in *A. sylvaticus* and *A. flavicollis* (Rodentia, Muridae) in Europe with special reference to Danishard Latvian populations. *Biologiske Skrifter Kongelige Dansk*

Videnskabernes Selskabs 8:1−46.

828 Varma M.G.R. & Page R.J.C. (1966) The epidemiology of louping ill in Ayrshire, Scotland: ectoparasites of small mammals I. (Siphonaptera). *Journal of Medical Entomology* 3:331−5.

829 Vasquez A.W. (1961) Structure and identification of common food contaminating hairs. *Journal of the Association of Official Analytical Chemists* 44:754−79.

830 Vereschagin N.K. (1959) *Mammals of the Caucasus. History of the Formation of the Fauna.* Leningrad: Izdatelstvo Akademii Nauk.

831 Vietinghoff-Riesch A. von (1960) Der Siebenschläfer *(Glis glis L.) Monographien der Wildsäugetiere* 14:1−196.

832 Viitala J. (1977) Social organisation in cyclic, subarctic population of the voles *Clethrionomys rufocanus* (Sund.) and *Microtus agrestis* (L.). *Annales Zoologici Fennici* 14:53−93.

833 Viitala J. & Hoffmeyer I. (1985) Social organisation in *Clethrionomys* compared with *Microtus* and *Apodemus*. *Annales Zoologici Fennici* 22:359−71.

834 Vincent M.A. (1974) *Energy utilisation and activity patterns of the vole* Arvicola terrestris amphibius *(L.).* PhD. thesis, University of Durham.

835 Viopio P. (1970) Polymorphism and regional differentiation in the red squirrel (*Sciurus vulgaris*). *Annales zoologici Fennici* 7:210−15.

836 Vizoso A.D. *et al.* (1964) Isolation of a virus resembling encephalomyocarditis from a red squirrel. *Nature* 201:849−50.

837 Vizoso A.D. *et al.* (1966) Isolation of unidentified agents capable of morphologically transforming hamster cells *in vitro*. *Nature* 209:1263−4.

838 Wachtendorf W. (1951) Beitrage zur Ökologie und Biologie der Haselmaus (*Muscardinus avellanarius*) im Alpenvorland. *Zoologische Jahrbucher Abteilung Systematik* 80:189−203.

839 Walhovd H. (1971) The activity of a pair of common dormice *Muscardinus avellanarius* in conditions of captivity. *Oikos* 22:358−65.

840 Walhovd H. (1974) Hibernation of a pair of confined dormice, *Muscardinus avellanarius*, in three successive winters. *Natura Jutlandica* 17:9−24.

841 Wallace M.E. (1981) The breeding, inbreeding and management of wild mice. *Symposia of the Zoological Society of London* 47:183−204.

842 Wallace M.E. & Hudson C.A. (1969) Breeding and handling small wild rodents: a method study. *Laboratory Animals* 3:107−17.

843 Wallis S.J. (1981) Notes on the ecology of the Orkney vole (*Microtus arvalis orcadensis*). *Journal of Zoology* 195:532−6.

844 Wallis S.J. (1983) Note on the movement of stones by the Common shrew (sic), *Apodemus sylvaticus*. *Journal of Zoology* 200:300−2.

845 Walton J.B. & Andrews J.F. (1981) Torpor induced by food deprivation in the wood mouse *Apodemus sylvaticus*. *Journal of Zoology* 194:260−3.

846 Ward R.J. (1981) Diet and nutrition. *Symposia of the Zoological Society of London* 47:255−66.

847 Warkentin M.J. (1968) Observations on the behaviour and ecology of the nutria in Louisiana. *Tulane Studies in Zoology* 15:10−17.

848 Warner L.J. & Batt G.T. (1976) Some simple methods for recording wild harvest mouse (*Micromys minutus*) distribution and activity. *Journal of Zoology* 179:226−9.

849 Watkins S.A. *et al.* (1985) The coypu as rodent reservoir of Leptospira infection in Great Britain. *Journal of Hygiene* 95:409−17.

850 Watson J.S. (1944) The melanic form of *Rattus norvegicus* in London. *Nature* 154:334−5.

851 Watson J.S. (1950) Some observations on the reproduction of *Rattus rattus* L. *Proceedings of the Zoological Society of London* 120:1−12.

852 Watson J.S. (1951) *The rat problem in Cyprus.* London: HMSO, (Colon. Res. Publ. no. 9).

853 Watts C.H.S. (1966) *The ecology of woodland voles and mice with special reference of movement and population structure.* DPhil. thesis, Oxford University.

854 Watts C.H.S (1968) The foods eaten by wood mice (*Apodemus sylvaticus*) and bank voles (*Clethrionomys glareolus*) in Wytham Woods, Berkshire. *Journal of Animal Ecology* 37:25−41.

855 Watts C.H.S. (1969) The regulation of wood mouse (*Apodemus sylvaticus*) numbers in Wytham Woods, Berkshire. *Journal of Animal Ecology* 38:285−304.

856 Watts C.H.S. (1970) A field experiment on intraspecific interactions in the red-backed vole, *Clethrionomys glareolus*. *Journal of Mammalogy* 51:341−7.

857 Watts C.H.S. (1970) Long distance movement of bank voles and wood mice. *Journal of Zoology* 161:247−56.

858 Watts C.H.S. (1970) Effect of supplementary food on breeding in woodland rodents. *Journal of Mammalogy* 51:169−71.

859 Wauters L.A. & Dhondt A.A. (1985) Population dynamics and social behaviour of red squirrel populations in different habitats. Brussels: *XVII Congress of the International Union of Game Biologists* pp. 311−18.

860 Wauters L.A. & Dhondt A.A. (1988) The use of red squirrel (*Sciurus vulgaris*) dreys to estimate population density. *Journal of Zoology* 214:179−87.

861 Webley G.E. & Johnson E. (1983) Reproductive physiology of the grey squirrel (*Sciurus carolinensis*). *Mammal Review* 3:149−54.

862 Wells A.Q. (1946) The murine type of tubercle bacillus (the vole acid-fast bacillus). *Special Report Series, Medical Research Council* 259:1−48.

863 Whitbread S. & Morris P. Personal communication.

864 Whittaker J.O. (1966) Food of *Mus musculus, Peromyscus maniculatus bairdi* and *Peromyscus leucopus* in Vigo County, Indiana. *Journal of Mammalogy* 47:473−86.

865 Whittingham D.G. & Wood M.J. (1983) Reproductive physiology. In Foster H.L. ed. *The mouse in biomedical research*, vol. 3. New York & London: Academic Press pp. 137−64.

866 Wieland H. (1973) Beiträge zur Biologie und zum Massenwechsel der grossen Wuhlmaus (*Arvicola terrestris* L.). *Zoologisches Jahrbuch, Abteilung Sys-*

tematik **100**:351–428.

867 Wiger R. (1977) Some pathological effects of endo-parasites on rodents with special reference to the population ecology of microtines. *Oikos* **29**:598–606.

868 Wiger R. (1982) Roles of self-regulating mechanisms in cyclic populations of *Clethrionomys* with special reference to *Clethrionomys glareolus:* a hypothesis. *Oikos* **38**:68–71.

869 Wijngaarden A. van. (1954) *Biologie en bestrijding von de woelrat, Arvicola terrestris (L.) in Nederland.* Dissertation, University of Eindhoven.

870 Williams S.L. *et al.* (1980) Glans penes and bacula of five species of *Apodemus* from Croatia, Yugoslavia. *Mammalia* **44**:245–58.

871 Wolffe J.L. & Barnett S.A. (1977) Effects of cold on nest-building by wild and domestic mice, *Mus musculus* L. *Biological Journal of the Linnean Society of London* **9**:73–85.

872 Wolton R.J. (1983) The activity of free-ranging wood mice, *Apodemus sylvaticus. Journal of Animal Ecology* **52**:781–94.

873 Wolton R.J. (1984) Individual recognition by olfaction in the wood mouse, *Apodemus sylvaticus. Behaviour* **88**:191–9.

874 Wolton R.J. (1985) The ranging and nesting behaviour of wood mice, *Apodemus sylvaticus* (Rodentia, Muridae), as revealed by radio-tracking. *Journal of Zoology* (A) **206**:203–24.

875 Wolton R.J. (1985) A possible role for faeces in range-marking by the wood mouse, *Apodemus sylvaticus. Journal of Zoology* (A) **206**:286–91.

876 Wolton R.J. & Flowerdew J.R. (1985) Spatial distribution and movements of wood mice, yellow-necked mice and bank voles. *Symposia of the Zoological Society of London* **55**:249–75.

877 Wrangel H.V. von (1939) Beiträge der Rötelmause, *Clethrionomys glareolus* (Schreber). *Zeitschrift für Säugetierkunde* **14**:54–93.

878 Woodroffe G. Personal communication.

879 Yalden D.W. (1971) A population of the yellow-necked mouse. *Journal of Zoology* **164**:244–50.

880 Yalden D. (1977) Small mammals and the archaeologist. *Bulletin of the Peakland Archaeological Society* **30**:18–25.

881 Yalden D.W. (1980) Urban small mammals. *Journal of Zoology* **191**:403–6.

882 Yalden D.W. (1982) When did the mammal fauna of the British Isles arrive? *Mammal Review* **12**: 1–57.

883 Yalden D.W. (1983) Yellow-necked mice (*Apodemus flavicollis*) in archaeological contexts. *Bulletin of the Peakland Archaeological Society* **33**:24–9.

884 Yalden D.W. (1984) The yellow-necked mouse, *Apodemus flavicollis*, in Roman Manchester. *Journal of Zoology* **203**:285–8.

885 Yalden D.W. & Hounsome M.V. Personal communication.

886 Young A.S. (1970) *Studies of blood parasites of small mammals with special reference to piroplasms.* PhD. thesis, University of London.

887 Zarrow M.X & Wilson E.D. (1963) Hormonal control of the pubic symphysis of the Skomer bank vole (*Clethrionomys skomerensis*). *Journal of Endocrinology* **23**:103–6.

888 Zejda J. (1966) Litter size in *Clethrionomys glareolus* Schreber. *Zoologicke Listy* **15**:193–206.

889 Zejda J. (1966) Habitat selection in *Apodemus agrarius* (Pallas, 1778) (Mammalia: Muridae) on the border of the area of its distribution. *Zoologicke Listy* **16**:15–30.

890 Zejda J. (1971) Differential growth of three cohorts of the bank vole, *Clethrionomys glareolus. Zoologicke Listy* **20**:229–45.

891 Zejda J. & Mazak V. (1965) Cycle de changement du pelage chez le compagnol roussâtre, *Clethrionomys glareolus* Schreber, 1780 (Microtidae, Mammalia). *Mammalia* **29**:577–97.

892 Zedja J. & Pelikan J. (1969) Movements and home ranges of some rodents in lowland forests. *Zoologicke Listy* **18**:143–62.

893 Zima J. & Kral B. (1984) Karyotypes of European mammals, 2. *Acta Scentiarum Naturalium Academiae Scientiarum Bohemoslovacae* **18**(8):62.

894 Zimmerman K. (1937) Die markische Rötelmaus, Analyse einer population. *Markishe Tierwelt* **3**: 24–40.

895 Zimmermann K. (1959) *Taschenbuch unserer wildle-benden Säugetiere.* Leipzig-Jena; Urania-Verlag.

896 Zippelius H.M. (1974) Ultraschall-laute nestjunger Mäuse. *Behaviour* **49**:197–204.

897 Zippelius H.M. & Schleidt W. (1956) Ultraschall-Laute bei jungen Mausen. *Naturwissenschaften* **43**:502.

Chapter 9 / Whales, Dolphins and Porpoises: Order Cetacea

INTRODUCTION

Although their lives are conducted within water, cetaceans share with their terrestrial counterparts the major mammalian features of giving birth to live young and suckling these with milk produced by mammary glands. Unlike fish (including sharks) which some may superficially resemble, they are warm-blooded and breathe air with the aid of lungs. However, their aquatic lives have produced a number of important adaptations which make them a most distinctive order.

The general form of all cetaceans is torpedo-shaped, streamlined for ease of movement through water with the minimum of resistance. External hind limbs are absent altogether and forelimbs are modified to form flippers with fingers enclosed within a common integument. Ear pinnae are also absent and external sexual organs usually hidden, the penis of the male retracted and the teats of the female within slits on either side of the genital area. Hair has been virtually lost and to help maintain a stable body temperature, cetaceans have an insulating layer of blubber.

The skeleton shows a number of simplifications usually with a reduction of vertebrae (except in lumbar region). The neck vertebrae are often fused into a single mass so that the neck region has an ill-defined external appearance. The nostrils or 'blow-hole' are situated on top of the head. In toothed cetaceans, the upper lip is often hypertrophied to form a large bulbous mass of fat referred to as the 'melon'. The back frequently bears an extension of the integument forming a triangular or sickle-shaped dorsal fin. There is also a lateral expansion of the integument of the tail to form a pair of large fibrous 'flukes'. These serve as the main propulsive surface.

When diving, a cetacean holds its breath; the small but elongated, elastic lungs compress and force the air into the windpipe and its branches and also into the extensive nasal passages. Here oxygen is exchanged via a rich network of capillaries, and the relatively little amount of nitrogen contained therein is returned swiftly to the lungs. When returning to the surface, the lungs gradually expand and the nasal plug that closes the blowholes is forced open. The used air is expelled appearing as a cloud of spray, and fresh air taken in once more. The size and shape of the blow varies between species and in a number of cases helps their identification.

Present-day cetaceans are divided into two sub-orders: Mysticeti or baleen whales, and Odontoceti or toothed whales. Mysticetes have no teeth (except in fossil representatives) but instead a series of transverse plates of comb-like baleen made of keratin which descend from the roof of the mouth into the buccal cavity and serve to strain plankton. In odontocetes, teeth may be very numerous in upper and lower jaws or they may occur only in the lower jaw and sometimes (for example, in the family Ziphiidae) be reduced to a single pair. Other major differences between the two sub-orders include a symmetrical skull with no melon, and a pair of nasal openings in mysticetes, compared with an asymmetrical skull (except in fossil representatives) with a melon, and a single external nasal opening in odontocetes.

There are currently considered to be at least 77 living species of cetaceans. Sixty-six species are odontocetes, including one large whale (sperm whale) but otherwise medium-sized whales, and smaller dolphins and porpoises; 11 species are mysticetes and these comprise the great whales, traditionally the source of protein and oil for generations of humans. Many species, particularly some of the beaked whales (Ziphiidae), are very poorly known, in some cases only from skeletal material washed up on some lonely beach. Others show very small external differences and their taxonomy remains unresolved. Many species (particularly of larger whale) are cosmopolitan in distribution, occurring in all the world's oceans and often at a whole range of latitudes. Others have much more restricted distributions.

Thirty-three cetacean species have been recorded in European seas. Twenty-three of those (six mysticetes, 17 odontocetes) occur in British and Irish waters. Although some species remain in our coastal waters throughout the year, a number undergo seasonal movements either from offshore regions or from other latitudes. Most of the great whales breed in the tropics or subtropics during the northern winter and then move northwards in spring to spend the summer months in N European waters. These latitudinal migrations appear to be made primarily in deep waters along the continental shelf edge, west of Britain and Ireland. Individuals or small groups may then travel eastwards towards the Atlantic coasts of Ireland and Scotland, some entering the northern North Sea.

During the summer months, the longer days with greater hours of sunshine, warmer sea temperatures and calmer seas allow concentrations of planktonic plants to build up, so providing abundant food for predators ranging from zooplankton to marine mammals and humans. After 5 or 6 months of extensive feeding (perhaps 50−60 percent above normal intake), a great whale greatly increases its layer of blubber. This serves as an energy store during the rest of the year when it is in relatively unproductive waters. Seasonal movements from summer feeding grounds to winter mating/calving grounds are intimately connected with the reproductive cycle of baleen whales. The gestation period lasts from 10−12 months with the single calf weaned over a period commonly of 5−7 months. The lactation period is thought to provide a relatively high energy cost to the mother so that she usually rests for 6−18 months before mating once more. For most of the great whales, the calving interval is therefore probably 2 to 3 years. Those baleen whales, such as minke whale and some fin whales, that feed upon fish in addition to plankton, may not have a reproductive cycle so seasonally constrained. They may be able to feed over a greater period and to reduce the calving interval perhaps even to a single year.

Some of the toothed whales (such as sperm and pilot whales) feed primarily upon squid which are of low-energy content. This may account for their longer gestation periods of 15−17 months, and often extended lactation periods (which may go to 2 years or even longer). For those species, a seasonal reproductive cycle may be less important so that breeding need not necessarily occur at a particular time of year. There are still usually periods of peak food abundance so that those species may give birth to their young primarily at a particular time of year.

Some medium-sized whales and most of the smaller dolphins (including the harbour porpoise) have fairly catholic diets which may include a variety of fish species (see Table 9.1) as well as sometimes squid and crustaceans. It is likely that they are able to feed over a greater part of the year, although food abundance is almost certainly much higher during the middle to late summer. Although the larger species give birth either in late winter or spring, the smaller dolphins and the harbour porpoise calve mainly in summer with a gestation period of 10−12 months but a lactation period varying from *c.* 8 months in the harbour porpoise to 18−19 months in many delphinids. During the summer months, sea surface temperatures are highest so assisting body temperature maintenance for a small calf, and food is abundant. Where seasonal movements occur they are usually of an offshore onshore nature, in some cases associated with concentrations of fish. Together with the greater frequency of calm sea conditions, these help to account for most small cetacean species being seen in coastal waters primarily between April and October.

Until little more than a decade ago, most of our knowledge of the status and distribution of cetaceans in British and Irish waters came from records of animals stranded on the coast. In a statute enacted in the 14th century *De Praerogativa Regis* the sovereign was given entitlement for any whale or dolphin stranded on, or caught near the coasts of the United Kingdom. These were designated *Fishes Royal* and reported to H.M. Receivers of Wreck by coastguards and others, usually with a view to the disposal of the carcases.

In 1912 a recording scheme was instigated whereby Receivers of Wreck send reports of cetaceans to the British Museum (Natural History). The first Report on Cetacea stranded on British coasts covering the year 1912 was published in 1914 [60], and since then there have been further reports by Harmer [61] and Fraser [47, 49−52] with shorter reviews by Sheldrick [110, 111]. A list of Irish strandings was published by O'Riordan [94], whilst strandings since then have been noted by Fairley [42] and various observers in recent issues of the *Irish Naturalists' Journal*.

The role of the British Museum's strandings scheme cannot be over-emphasised. Important bio-

Table 9.1. Diet of porpoise, dolphins and small toothed whales in W European waters.

Food species	Porpoise	Common dolphin	Striped dolphin	Bottle-nosed dolphin	White-sided dolphin	White-beaked dolphin	Killer whale	Pilot whale	Risso's dolphin
Fish									
Clupea herring	+	+		+	+	+	+		
Sprattus sprat	+	+							
Sardina pilchard	+	+	+	+					
Engraulis anchovy		+		+					
Salmo salmon								+	
Osmerus smelt					+				
Anguilla eel				+				+	
Mugil mullet				+					
Trachurus horse mackerel	+	+	+					+	
Ammodytes/Hyperoplus sandeel	+					+			
Scomber mackerel	+	+	+	+	+	+	+	+	
Dicentrarchus bass								+	
Gadus cod	+			+	+	+	+	+	+
Trisopterus Norway pout	+	+	+	+	+	+		+	
Pollachius pollack	+							+	
Micromesistius blue whiting	+	+	+	+	++				
Merlangius whiting	+	+	+		+	+			
Merluccius hake	+	+	+		+			+	
Melanogrammus haddock						+			
Pleuronectes plaice						+			
Limanda sole						+			
Cephalopods									
Loligo	+	+	+	+	+	+	+	+	+
Alloteuthis		+	+						
Histioteuthis			+					+	
Brachioteuthis								+	
Gonatus			+					+	+
Sepiola			+					+	
Rossia									+
Sepietta									+
Todarodes							+	++	+
Illex			+				+		
Ommastrephes								+	
Eledone								+	+
Sepia				+			+	+	+
Marine mammals									
Phocoena harbour porpoise							+		
Globicephala pilot whale							+		
Halichoerus grey seal							+		
Birds									
Fratercula puffin							+		
Cepphus black guillemot							+		
Rissa kittiwake							+		

+, present in diet; ++, common in diet.

logical information can often be obtained only from dead animals. These include precise data on diet and on calving seasons, on rates and causes of mortality, growth and reproductive rates, and on population parameters, such as age distribution. Studies of live animals can usually give only rough measures, and, in some cases, even these are not possible. Some species, for example True's beaked and Sowerby's beaked whales, are scarcely known except from strandings, the majority of which have been British and Irish specimens. Other commoner species, such as white-beaked dolphin, are recorded more frequently in our waters than anywhere else and yet biological information of the above nature has yet to be collected.

In order to complement information from strandings, the Cetacean Group was formed within the Mammal Society in 1973, to collect information from free-living animals. A network of observers was set up which now numbers around 700 individuals. These include not only professional biologists working primarily with marine birds, seals or fisheries, but also amateurs, such as merchant seamen, yachtsmen and holidaymakers, birdwatchers, lighthouse keepers, and personnel from oil platforms and ocean weather ships. Coverage includes the NE Atlantic, Irish Sea, North Sea and English Channel.

A preliminary analysis was carried out [33] and with the publication of standardised recording forms and an identification guide [36], the amount of useful and interpretable data increased enormously. This enabled a more detailed analysis to be published [34] and led to a 3-month research cruise in summer 1980 with transects across the continental shelf, in coastal waters of western Britain and Ireland, and in the northern North Sea [35]. Other smaller scale cruises have also been conducted.

Two problems of obtaining biological data from sightings are the difficulties of specific identification, particularly for certain groups; and the inevitable biases resulting from uneven coverage and varying viewing conditions. Much progress has now been made to partially overcome both these problems. The number of trained observers has increased greatly as has the quality of sightings records, many including photographs as additional documentation. The volume of data is such that it has to be coded and stored on a computer where basic analyses may be carried out. By 1986, the date of the latest analyses, around 10 000 records

had been logged [40] and the number has steadily increased since then. However, uneven coverage remains the greatest difficulty when using the data for monitoring temporal and geographical variation in numbers. Dedicated cruises, which quantify effort and environmental conditions, overcome many of these problems but of necessity their coverage is limited in space and time. Two approaches have therefore been adopted: (i) the setting up of as many sites as possible which are manned at regular intervals with observer effort quantified; and (ii) a major expansion of the network of opportunistic observers so as to provide more even coverage, at least geographically.

With the formation of a European Cetacean Society in 1987, coordinated sightings schemes are developing throughout Europe, with the prospect of producing quantified distribution maps for a number of commoner species using data collected by several countries in a uniform manner.

As field studies of cetaceans proliferate around the world, new techniques develop for collecting information from live cetaceans. Animals may be marked and re-sighted, radio transmitters attached to follow their movements and study their diving patterns, and individuals recognised by a combination of natural markings. Photography has helped greatly not only towards unambiguous identification of species and individuals, but also in recording the sex of individuals and measuring size and growth patterns. Now, the collection of a small sample of tissue or blood may additionally be used to obtain genetic information either by isozyme analysis or techniques such as DNA fingerprinting.

Cetaceans presently face many pressures both directly and indirectly from humans. From prehistoric times, they have been exploited by man either for meat or for oil. As populations of slow-moving coastal species, such as the northern right whale and humpback, declined because of overhunting, British whalers travelled farther afield towards arctic waters. However, in the early years of the 20th century (mainly from 1904—14 and 1920—29) some commercial whaling took place in coastal waters, operating from shore stations in Shetland (two in Ronas Voe, one each in Colla Firth and Olna Firth), the Outer Hebrides (West Loch Tarbert) and Western Ireland (Inishkea, and Blacksod Bay near Belmullet). These concentrated upon the large rorqual whales — blue, fin and sei whales — and sperm whales, although small numbers of humpback and right whales were also taken. By this time, populations of the two latter species were almost certainly reduced to mere remnants of their former size, and this additional exploitation provided further nails to the coffin. When whaling recommenced in the Outer Hebrides for two seasons (1950–51), no right or humpback whales were obtained. These populations are presently much smaller than those on the western side of the North Atlantic and, unlike those, they show little sign of recovery.

Smaller cetaceans have also been hunted, either primarily for subsistence by local coastal communities or more recently commercially, after the demise of the great whales. Small-whale coastal drive fisheries for pilot whales persisted for centuries on an opportunistic basis in certain regions, notably Shetland and Orkney. Although ceasing there in the latter part of the 19th century, they continue further north in the Faroe Islands. In recent decades, Norwegian vessels have operated in the NE Atlantic (including around the Northern Isles), taking minke whales, northern bottlenose, pilot and killer whales. Since 1986 a ban on the commercial exploitation of all of these species has been put into effect by the International Whaling Commission. However, this has not meant the end of all whaling. In the NE Atlantic, both Norway and Iceland continue taking minke whales for scientific reasons; Iceland additionally takes some sei whales for the same reason, and the Faroe Islanders continue pilot whaling.

Many major status changes experienced by cetacean species in British and Irish waters can be explained by the effects of human exploitation. However, in the last 30 years, two coastal species, the harbour porpoise and bottle-nosed dolphin, have undergone widespread declines in Europe, particularly along the North Sea and Channel coasts. Those declines cannot have been caused by direct takes since neither species has been hunted in the region. We must therefore look elsewhere to other potential threats facing cetaceans.

With increased industrialisation, a number of heavily populated coastal areas of Western Europe have discharged a wide range of pollutants into the sea. Those most likely to affect cetaceans include heavy metals such as mercury, pesticides such as DDT, and industrial chemicals such as PCBs. Untreated sewage also may have indirect effects by making coastal areas uninhabitable for a variety of marine life, some of which are prey to cetaceans. Most polluted areas include southern North Sea coasts, and parts of the English Channel and Irish Sea coasts.

The present century has also seen the over-exploitation of a number of fish species. Most notable of these for cetaceans has probably been the demise of North Sea herring by the 1950s, and, more recently, the often excessive exploitation of mackerel (Outer Hebrides and SW England) and sand-eels (Shetland Islands).

Alongside fisheries developments since the 1940s has been the widespread use of inconspicuous and highly durable nylon monofilament netting. A wide variety of fishing gear is involved and many of these (for example, drift nets) pose important threats, such as entangling cetaceans and causing them to drown. The harbour porpoise appears to be the most affected but other species known to have drowned in this way include white-beaked and bottle-nosed dolphins, and pilot whales. The problem appears to be greatest in parts of the North Sea where the Danish wreck fishery is involved, but also in the Kattegat and Skagerrak. Along the Western Irish coast, the extensive salmon drift-net fishery is an important threat, whilst in Britain, numbers of cetaceans drown in nets within coastal waters of E Scotland, NE England and SW England. However, the extent of mortality in all these regions is still poorly known.

Finally, the southern North Sea coasts and eastern portion of the Channel, in particular, receive enormous amounts of marine traffic. Besides the additional pollution often associated with this volume of traffic, there are much greater opportunities for accidental collision leading to the maiming or death of a cetacean (as witnessed from wounds on an increasing number of animals washed ashore). Furthermore, these vessels (and particularly fast-moving pleasure craft) may cause sound disturbance to a number of cetacean species.

There is no up-to-date regional account of the cetaceans of Northern Europe, although Tomilin [117] remains an important source of data. Regional guides to identification include that of Fraser [50] to stranded animals, and that of Evans [36] to sightings at sea. For a more detailed field guide to all the world's cetaceans, the Sierra Club Handbook of Whales and Dolphins [75] is to be recommended whilst general reviews of the natural history of whales and dolphins may be found in Bonner [12] and Evans [37]. Most general biological data contained in the following species accounts derive from the last book, which the reader should consult for more detailed information and further reference sources.

SUBORDER MYSTICETI (BALEEN WHALES)

This group, including all the large whales with the exception of the sperm whale, comprises two families, Balaenidae and Balaenopteridae, dealt with here, along with a third, Eschrichtiidae, containing only the grey whale *Eschrichtius robustus*. The last no longer exists outside the Pacific although sub-fossil remains have been found in England and elsewhere in Europe, as well as in the south-eastern United States. The North Atlantic population is thought to have gone extinct in recent historical times, possibly in the 17th or early 18th century.

FAMILY BALAENIDAE (RIGHT WHALES)

A family of three species, of which one has occurred in British waters. Some authorities consider the pygmy right whale (*Caperea marginata*) to belong to a separate family Neobalaenidae [37]. Compared with the rorquals (Balaenopteridae), right whales are slow swimmers with very large heads, highly arched upper jaws with very long baleen, no grooves on the throat, no dorsal fin and broad, rounded flippers.

GENUS *Eubalaena*

Contains the northern right whale, *E. glacialis*, and southern right whale. *E. australis*, and sometimes included with the bowhead or Greenland right whale in the genus *Balaena*. The southern right whale, which occurs only in the southern hemisphere, has previously been considered conspecific with its northern counterpart and its status is still uncertain.

Northern right whale *Eubalaena glacialis*

Balaena glacialis Müller, 1776; North Cape, Norway.
Balaena britannica Gray, 1870, Dorset, England.

RECOGNITION
With its finless back and huge head marked by distinctive white callosities, the Northern right whale (Fig. 9.1) is unlikely to be confused with any other species in European waters. The blow is highly characteristic: the blowholes are widely separated and produce two distinct spouts, which may rise to 5 m, in a V-shaped mist. During respiration the body is held high, and on diving the flukes are nearly always shown. When the animal swims, mouth agape near the surface, the baleen sometimes appears pale, even white.

DESCRIPTION
No dorsal fin; large head 30% of body length; strongly arched upper jaws and strongly bowed lower jaws; narrow rostrum; white, grey or yellowish callosities on the rostrum, near the blowholes, and on the chin and lower lips, usually infested with barnacles and cyamid crustaceans (whale lice); baleen plates long (usually 2.2−2.6 m), narrow, ranging in colour from dark brownish through dark grey to black, some of the anterior plates sometimes white; body generally black to brown, sometimes mottled, with white patches on throat and belly, and less frequently on other parts of the body; no grooves on throat. The arrangement of callosities is idiosyncratic and can be used to recognise individuals.

Fig. 9.1. Northern right whale.

Tail broad, deeply notched tail flukes, with concave trailing edge. Tail often lifted in air before dive.

MEASUREMENTS

Length *c.* 15–18 m and weight *c.* 50–56 (occasionally up to 90) tonnes. Females larger than males. Newborn calf *c.* 4.4–4.8 m length. Length at sexual maturity *c.* 13.0–16.0 m. Fully-grown skull usually 3.8–4.2 m length.

DISTRIBUTION

In both cold and warm temperate regions of the northern hemisphere. Now very rare in eastern North Atlantic, between Azores and Spitsbergen; a more viable population in western North Atlantic. Together they make up a total North Atlantic population of somewhere between 200 and 500 individuals. There have been no strandings on British and Irish coasts since 1913, but three well-documented sightings in recent years in British and Irish waters, one off S Ireland in August 1970, the second in the Northern Irish Sea in May 1979 and a third in the Outer Hebrides in August 1980 [40]. Two other sightings have occurred *c.* 600 km west of Scotland, in September 1974 [40], one off the north coast of Spain in September 1977 [2], whilst a female was harpooned near Madeira in February 1967 [86]. In any event, the population in the region must be very small indeed.

HISTORY

Formerly abundant from the Azores, Madeira, and NW Africa to Iceland, SE Greenland, and Spitsbergen. The Bay of Biscay was an important wintering area and formed the centre for a flourishing whaling industry up to the middle of the 19th century. During the Middle Ages there is some evidence that whaling for this species occurred also in the Channel and North Sea [114]. As the first stock to experience commercial whaling, and as a readily accessible prize in those waters, the eastern North Atlantic stock has been reduced to an extremely low level.

The Outer Hebrides appears to have been a centre of concentration with 94 animals taken in the region (mostly within the continental shelf) between 1903–28 compared with six in Shetland during the same period [146]. None was obtained when whaling resumed between 1950–1951 [14]. In W Ireland, 18 were caught between 1908–14 but none in 1920 and 1922 [42].

Records in British and Irish waters are all from May to October. During whaling activities peak numbers were caught in June [116].

SOCIAL ORGANISATION AND BEHAVIOUR

Most sightings are of single individuals. The southern right whale which exists in larger numbers and is better studied, occurs singly, as mother–calf pairs or in larger groups (usually less than 12) of mixed age and sex. Slow swimmer rarely exceeding 12 km/hour. Typically blows once a minute during surface cruising for 5–10 min before dive lasting 10–20 min. Vocalisations well studied only in related southern right whale where include low-frequency (50–500 Hz) tonal moans and pulsed belches (50–200 Hz), both of 0.5–3.5 (6) seconds duration.

FEEDING

Mainly copepod crustaceans, also euphausiids; apparently do not feed on larger invertebrates or fish. Most feeding takes place in northern waters in summer.

BREEDING

Single young thought to be born mainly between November and January in tropical or subtropical waters. Gestation period 10 months. Lactation possibly 12 months. Calving interval 2–4 (mainly 3) years. These data based primarily upon related southern right whale populations. Age at sexual maturity not known.

PARASITES/COMMENSALS

Heavily infested with barnacles *Coronula biscayensis* and whale lice, especially *Cyamus ovalis* which is particularly abundant on the 'bonnet' (the top of the head in front of the blowholes).

RELATIONS WITH MAN

One of the earliest whale species to be hunted by man, possibly from Neolithic times, and the main species taken in temperate regions during the Middle Ages. After serious overexploitation by man, completely protected since 1935.

FAMILY BALAENOPTERIDAE

The largest family of baleen whales, including the humpback (*Megaptera*) and the rorquals (*Balaenoptera*).

GENUS *Megaptera*

Contains a single species, *M. novaeangliae*.

Humpback whale *Megaptera novaeangliae*.

Balaena Novae Angliae Borowski, 1781; New England, USA.
Megaptera longimana moorei Gray, 1866; Dee Estuary, Cheshire.

RECOGNITION

From a distance can be confused with any of the other large rorquals, but have a habit of raising the flukes high into the air when starting a long dive, although in shallow water they may not raise the flukes at all. At close range the knobs on the head and long flippers are diagnostic (Fig. 9.2). The blow is 'bushy', 2.5−3 m tall, generally wide relative to height and distinct from the V-shaped blow of the right whale, or the blow of the sperm whale, which comes from the front of the head and is angled forwards and to the left. The back is arched at the start of a dive, accentuating the dorsal fin. Both humpback and sperm whales frequently raise their tail flukes before diving, but the humpback is distinguished by the fluke having a serrated rear margin and often white underside.

DESCRIPTION

Flippers very long (to nearly one third body length), often white or partly white, with knobs on the leading edge; head in front of blowholes flat and covered with knobs; 270−400 relatively narrow baleen plates (up to 70 cm long by 30 cm wide), generally all black, with black or olive-black bristles. Flukes and flippers scalloped on the trailing edge. Dorsal fin variable in size and shape from small triangular knob to larger distinctly sickle-shaped, placed nearly two-thirds along back.

Viewed from above, the head is broad and rounded. In profile, the head is slim, with a rounded protuberance near the tip of the lower jaw. The body is more robust than other balaenopterids. There are 14−35 broad ventral grooves, up to 38 cm wide, extending at least to the navel.

Tail flukes are broad and butterfly shaped, distinctly notched, and commonly scalloped with knobs along the rear margin. The undersides can be completely or partially white. The shape, and markings of the undersides of the fluke are idiosyncratic, and can be used for individual identification. There is now a large catalogue of photographs of different individuals identified by their tail flukes (in combination with dorsal fin shape).

Skin black or grey, with a white region of varying extent on the throat and belly. The skin is frequently infested with barnacles and cyamid crustaceans.

MEASUREMENTS

Female 12.0−15.0 m length; male 11.5−15.0 m length. Weight *c*. 65 tonnes. Newborn calf *c*. 4.1 m length. Length at sexual maturity *c*. 12.0 m (female), *c*. 11.5 m (male).

DISTRIBUTION

World-wide, but rarely to ice edge. Strongly migratory. In the eastern North Atlantic winter around the Cape Verde Islands and off NW Africa, and in summer particularly around Iceland, in the Greenland Sea, and north and west of Norway. Some mixing with the western Atlantic population may occur since a whale tagged off Iceland was later re-sighted in the Caribbean [83].

The western North Atlantic stock now shows signs of recovery after earlier over-exploitation, comprising most of the North Atlantic population

Fig. 9.2. Humpback whale.

of somewhere between 4000–10 000 individuals. In contrast the eastern North Atlantic stock remains very low. There may be some slight sign of a recent recovery with four sightings and two strandings records since 1966 in coastal waters of the British Isles (mainly in the Outer Hebrides or west coast of Scotland; otherwise Shetland, SW coast of Ireland, and W Wales), and three sightings in mid-Atlantic, 700 km west of Scotland. Those records mainly of single individuals, all but one being in the months June to August.

HISTORY
Because of their tendency to congregate on both summer and winter grounds, often near coasts in easily accessible areas, humpbacks were easy prey for shore-based whalers and were severely depleted everywhere. Some stocks do not seem to have increased appreciably since protection in 1966.

Catches in the Scottish whale fishery amounted to 51 (Shetland) and 19 (Outer Hebrides) between 1903–28 [116] and none in the Outer Hebrides between 1950–51 [14]. In W Ireland six humpbacks were taken between 1908 and 1914, but with none in 1920 and 1922 [42]. Indeed, there were no records of the species in the region until those since 1966, noted above.

SOCIAL ORGANISATION AND BEHAVIOUR
Not fast swimmers, travelling at between 6 and 12 km/hour. Despite their size, they are acrobatic, often leaping clear of the water. They frequently raise a flipper and slap it against the water, or 'lobtail', raising the tail high into the air and bringing it down on the water with a loud report. They may be seen lying on the side with a long flipper in the air or on the back with both flippers in the air. Often found alone or in groups of two or three, but throughout the breeding and feeding ranges may congregate in groups of up to 20. Female and calf is commonest association, but singing males may temporarily join as escort to form triad. If accepted, male may then mate with female. Vocalisations very varied consisting of moans, snores and groans in frequency range 40 Hz to 5 kHz, repeated in ordered sequence of themes. Songs are almost confined to breeding grounds and may change throughout population from year to year. However, different populations show distinct dialects.

FEEDING
Mainly euphausiid krill (of genera *Meganyctiphanes*, *Thysanoessa*, *Euphausia* and *Pseudoeuphausia*), and schooling fish (particularly *Clupea*, *Mallotus*, *Gadus*, *Ammodytes*, *Osmerus* and *Pollachius*). Feeding methods vary with prey type from formation of bubble-nets (air released as a vertical stream of bubbles from the blowhole which may entrap plankton), to flick-feeding (using tail to generate wave concentrating plankton) and lunge-feeding when herding fish shoals. Feeding primarily in summer after coastal migration west of Britain and Ireland.

BREEDING
Births mainly in January to February, in equatorial waters off NW Africa. Gestation period 10–12 months. Lactation period 10–11 months with calving interval 2+ years (occasionally possibly one year). Age at sexual maturity now thought to be 4–5 years.

POPULATION
Longevity at least 30 years. Annual adult mortality *c.* 12%.

PARASITES/COMMENSALS
Heavily infested with barnacles, *Coronula* and *Conchoderma* spp., and by whale lice, *Cyamus* spp.

RELATIONS WITH MAN
Greatly reduced in numbers by whaling but totally protected since 1966.

GENUS *Balaenoptera* (RORQUALS)

Whales belonging to this genus distinguished from humpback by flipper being much less than one third of total body length and not irregularly outlined. Trailing edge of tail without serrations. Grooves on throat and chest more numerous, averaging 85 to 90. Five species, of which four are widely distributed and have been recorded in British and Irish waters.

Fin whale *Balaenoptera physalus*

Balaena physalus Linnaeus, 1758; Spitsbergen.
Balaena sulcata Neill, 1811; Firth of Forth.
Balaenoptera tenuirostris Sweeting, 1840; Dorset.
Physalus duguidii Heddle, 1856; Orkney.

Common rorqual.

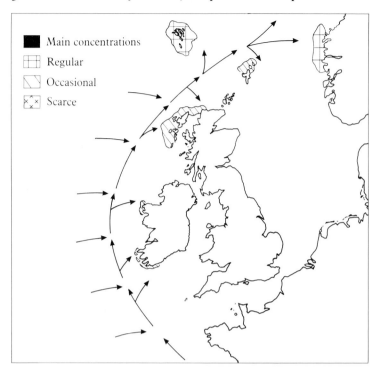

■ Main concentrations
⊞ Regular
⬙ Occasional
⬙ Scarce

Map 9.1. Fin whale.

RECOGNITION

The second largest of all whales, females up to 24 m in length. Uniform slate grey (Fig. 9.3). Does not generally show tail flukes when diving. Relatively small dorsal fin with little curvature. White on right lower lip and palate diagnostic. Tall blow (4–6 m high) shaped like inverted cone, followed by long shallow roll showing fin, repeated four to five times at intervals of 10–20 s before dive, commonly of 5–15 min. Slender head, V-shaped and flattened from above but with prominent median ridge.

DESCRIPTION

General form slender in relation to length. Baleen plates relatively short (maximum 72 cm long, 30 cm wide), 260–480 on each side of upper jaw. Plates on right side usually white for 75–100 cm from front end. Remaining plates of right side and

all of left side slaty grey alternating with longitudinal yellowish bands. Fringes of the plates are brownish grey to greyish white. General body colour grey above, white below including lower surface of flukes and inner surfaces of flippers (cf. Sei whale). Fairly slender pointed flippers, about one-seventh body length. Throat grooves 56–100, ending posterior to maximum cross-section of body (i.e. around navel). Dorsal fin one-third along back from tail, *c.* 60 cm tall (i.e. taller than in much larger blue whale) though appears relatively small compared with that of smaller rorqual species. Behind fin, back is ridged to tail flukes, which are broad, triangular with slight median notch.

MEASUREMENTS

Female length *c.* 20.0 m; male *c.* 18.5 m. Weight *c.* 80 tonnes. Newborn calf *c.* 6.4 m long. Length at

Fig. 9.3. Fin whale.

sexual maturity *c.* 20.0 m (female), *c.* 19.0 m (male).

VARIATION
Northern hemisphere animals average *c.* 1 m smaller than those of southern hemisphere.

DISTRIBUTION
World-wide, though less prevalent in low latitudes. Less distinct latitudinal seasonal migrations than most other rorquals, though tend to occupy cooler waters in summer and warmer waters in winter. Although probably the commonest large whale species in the NE Atlantic (and Mediterranean), this species has clearly been much reduced by whaling. Present North Atlantic population estimated at somewhere between 9000 and 14 000. Between 1913–48, 34 strandings were recorded on the British coasts, compared with only six between 1949 and 1987. Twenty-one documented sightings have been made since 1968 but ten of those were from weather ships 700 km west of Scotland [1, 40]. The rest are from either N Scotland or SW Ireland. A number of sightings have also been made of unidentified large whales that probably belong to this species.

All but two of the documented sightings are of single individuals, between the months of April and November, one of the exceptions being a herd of 20 fin whales off the coast of County Cork in July 1979. In British and Irish waters, there may be an offshore movement in the autumn since no sightings have occurred in coastal waters (indeed within 500 km) during the winter period.

HISTORY
Between 1903 and 1928, Scottish catches of fin whales amounted to 4356 (Shetland) and 1492 (Outer Hebrides) [116] with a further 46 caught in the Outer Hebrides in 1950–51 [14]. Irish catches totalled 435 fin whales between 1908–14 and 157 in 1920 and 1922 [42]. Those catches almost certainly seriously depleted stocks in the region and it is only in the last 10 years that there has been any sign of a recovery.

SOCIAL ORGANISATION AND BEHAVIOUR
Usually seen singly or in small groups up to ten individuals. Aggregations usually associated with feeding. Fast swimmer travelling on average between 4 and 15 km per hour although can show bursts of speed exceeding 32 km per hour. May breach clear of the water, re-entering with loud splash. Vocalisations include low frequency moans around 20 Hz lasting 1 second and regularly repeated over 2–20 min periods with a short (1–3 min) pause before continuing often over several hours, probably serving mainly for communication between widely spaced individuals. Other sounds include single moans of 40–75 Hz frequency, chirps and whistles of 1.5–5 kHz frequency, and high (16–28 kHz) frequency clicks.

FEEDING
Diet more generalist than other large rorquals, including planktonic crustaceans (euphausiids of genera *Thysanoessa*, *Meganyctiphanes*, and *Euphausia* and calanoid copepods) and fish (particularly *Clupea*, *Mallotus*, *Ammodytes*, *Gadus* and *Pollachius*). Like humpback, may use variety of feeding methods from engulfing prey from behind by distending the throat grooves and taking in a large gulp of water and prey, to side- and lunge-feeding which may involve some herding of the prey into a tight concentration.

BREEDING
Peak births occur in November and December in warm temperate and subtropical regions (possibly mainly around Canaries and Cape Verde Islands, and in the western Mediterranean). Gestation period 11–12 months. Lactation about 7 months. Calving interval 2–3 years. Sexually mature at about 8 years (previously 11 years but reduced during this century after fewer competitors due to human exploitation).

POPULATION
Can live to 85–90 years [73]. Adult annual mortality *c.* 10%.

PARASITES
External parasites, e.g. the copepod crustacean *Penella* sp. and the barnacle *Coronula* sp., occur only in warmer waters and are lost in polar regions. Often infected by nematodes of the genus *Crassicauda*, and severe infections thought to cause congestion of the kidney and renal failure [74].

RELATIONS WITH MAN
Heavily exploited by man since the invention of steam catcher boats and the explosive harpoon gun in mid-19th century but given full protection from commercial whaling in 1986.

Blue whale *Balaenoptera musculus*

Balaena musculus Linnaeus, 1758; Firth of Forth, Scotland.
Physalus sibbaldii Gray, 1847; Yorkshire.

RECOGNITION

Largest whale, reaching 28 m length. Pale bluish grey over most of body, mottled with grey or greyish white (Fig. 9.4). Very small dorsal fin, variable in shape but usually with little curvature, distinctly more than two-thirds along back so that seen only just prior to dive, some time after blow. Vertical, tall, slender blow (to 9 m high). Typically makes several shallow dives at intervals of *c.* 20 seconds. Very broad long body with broad, flat U-shaped head with single ridge extending from raised area forwards of blowholes towards tip of snout.

DESCRIPTION

Largest and heaviest mammal. Body form robust with broad snout and large head up to 25% of total length. Baleen plates relatively short (90 cm long by 50 cm wide), 260−400 on each side of upper jaw, stiff and coarsely fringed, and jet black in colour. General body colour bluish grey, mottled with grey or greyish white, sometimes with mustard yellow coloration mainly on belly (caused by diatoms from periods spent in high latitudes). Flippers long, slim with underside and pointed tips white or pale greyish blue. Throat grooves 55−68, extending more than halfway along body to navel. Dorsal fin less than one-third along back from tail, very small, usually less than 33 cm high, but variable in shape from nearly triangular to moderately sickle-shaped. Tail flukes broad, triangular with slight median notch, lifted only slightly before diving.

MEASUREMENTS

Female length *c.* 26.0 m; male *c.* 24.0 m. Weight *c.* 150 tonnes. Newborn calf *c.* 7.0 m long. Length at sexual maturity *c.* 24.0 m (female), *c.* 22.6 m (male).

VARIATION

Northern hemisphere animals a few metres smaller than those of southern hemisphere. Separate small subspecies recognised, pygmy blue whale *B. m. brevicauda*, in certain tropical areas of southern hemisphere (for example southern Indian Ocean).

DISTRIBUTION

World-wide, but populations everywhere seriously depleted by whaling. North Atlantic population now reduced to *c.* 300−500, but most of those are in western portion where there are some signs of a recent recovery. Previous whaling records indicate that small numbers pass west of Britain and Ireland, in deep waters off the edge of the continental shelf. There were four strandings on the British coasts between 1913−23, but none since then [51, 111]. The only recent well-documented sighting is of an individual off the NW coast of Ireland in May 1977 [40]. There have also been a few sightings during recent cruises off the Spanish coast [3, 106].

HISTORY

Evidence for the presence in British and Irish waters of blue whales in small numbers comes from the whale fisheries of the early part of this century. The Scottish whale fishery took 85 between 1903−28 from Shetland and 310 from the Outer Hebrides [116]. In 1950−51, a further six were captured in Outer Hebridean waters [14]. The Irish whale fishery captured 98 blue whales between 1908−14, and 27 in 1920 and 1922. Most captures were made in deep waters off the edge of the continental shelf.

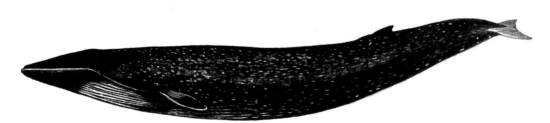

Fig. 9.4. Blue whale.

SOCIAL ORGANISATION AND BEHAVIOUR

Usually seen singly or in pairs, though larger aggregations may occasionally occur. Very fast swimmer with recorded speeds up to 55 km per hour. When diving, lifts tail stock only slightly and generally dives at a shallow angle. Rarely if ever breaches clear of water. Vocalisations include 20–30 Hz moans lasting 15–38 seconds sometimes with higher pitched pulses, and clicks at 6–8 or 21–31 kHz.

FEEDING

Almost exclusively planktonic crustaceans, either euphausiids (*Thysanoessa*, *Nematoscelis* and *Meganyctiphanes*) or copepods (*Temora*). Feeding methods similar to those of fin whale, capturing plankton by gulping, side- or lunge-feeding.

Feeding occurs in deep waters primarily during summer after extensive latitudinal migration from wintering grounds in equatorial regions.

BREEDING

Birth is thought to be mainly between November and December. Breeding grounds are not known but thought to be somewhere in the tropical Atlantic off NW Africa. Gestation period is 11 months. Lactation period 7 months with calving interval of 3 years. Sexual maturity in southern hemisphere population reached at 5 years.

POPULATION

Longevity *c.* 80 years. Annual adult mortality possibly *c.* 10–12%.

PARASITES/COMMENSALS

The copepod crustacean *Penella balaenopterae* is found embedded in the skin and a commensal crustacean, *Balaenophilus unisetus*, is found on the baleen.

RELATIONS WITH MAN

Nearly brought to extinction by whaling operations particularly during the early part of this century. Despite total protection since 1967, there are few signs of recovery, at least for NE Atlantic population.

Sei whale *Balaenoptera borealis*

Balaenoptera borealis Lesson, 1828; Germany.

RECOGNITION

Dark steely grey back, often with grey or white round scars. The sei whale (Fig. 9.5), unlike the fin whale, has right lower lip and mouth cavity usually uniformly grey and no white on undersides of flippers or tail flukes. Prominent dorsal fin, strongly sickle-shaped, often visible simultaneously with blow. Moderately tall blow (*c.* 3 m high), shaped like an inverted cone. Along with dorsal fin, remains in view for relatively long periods before typically making shallow dive. May blow two to three times at 20-second intervals followed by dive of 5–6 min duration, or five to six times at 30–40 second intervals before longer dive of 15–30 min. Slender head with slightly arched forehead, though not as rounded as blue whale, with single prominent median ridge.

DESCRIPTION

Slender, streamlined body. Baleen plates relatively short, 300–410 on each side of upper jaw, uniformly grey-black but with fine almost silky white fringes. General body colour dark grey on back and sides, and rear part of belly, but greyish white on middle part of throat grooves. Relatively small pointed flippers, about one-eleventh body length. Throat grooves 32–60, all ending well before navel. Dorsal fin fairly erect, usually between 25 and 60 cm high, strongly sickle-shaped and located a little more than one-third along back from tail (i.e. slightly further forward than in fin whale and much further forward than in blue whale). Relatively small tail flukes, broad and triangular with slight median notch.

MEASUREMENTS

Female length *c.* 14.5 m; male *c.* 14.0 m. Weight *c.* 30 tonnes. Newborn calf *c.* 4.4 m long. Length at sexual maturity *c.* 14.0 m (female), *c.* 13.6 m (male).

Fig. 9.5. Sei whale.

VARIATION

Northern hemisphere animals average about 0.5−1.0 m smaller than those found in the southern hemisphere.

DISTRIBUTION

World-wide, mainly offshore in deep waters. Seasonal migrations from polar and cold temperate regions (mainly around Iceland, in the Greenland Sea and W Barents Sea) in summer, to tropical or warm temperate waters (off Spain, Portugal and NW Africa) in winter. No population estimate for North Atlantic but probably somewhere in low thousands.

Rarely seen in coastal waters of Britain and Ireland, though probably under-recorded because of difficulties of specific identification. Only nine strandings between 1913 and 1987, the last being in Lewis, Outer Hebrides, in May 1975, and in Lancashire in September, 1980. Six documented sightings have been made since 1973, all off the coast of W Scotland and Outer Hebrides, mainly involving single individuals between June and August. However, three of those sightings were far offshore, from weather ships, 700 km west of Scotland.

HISTORY

Catches in Scottish and Irish waters earlier this century suggest that sei whales were, as at present, not as abundant as fin whales. Scottish catches of sei whales amounted to 1839 (Shetland) and 375 (Outer Hebrides) between 1903−28 [116] and three in 1950−51 (Outer Hebrides) [14]. In W Ireland, 88 sei whales were caught between 1908−14, and a further three in the years 1920 and 1922 [42]. Catches off the Outer Hebrides were particularly along the shelf edge near St Kilda, and occurred mainly in June; those north of Shetland were mainly in July and August.

SOCIAL ORGANISATION AND BEHAVIOUR

Most sightings are of single individuals or small groups of up to five animals. Aggregations usually associated with feeding. Very fast swimmer (possibly fastest of all rorquals), attaining speeds of 55 km/hour, though usually 3.6−30 km/hour. Usually does not dive very deeply, and so generally surfaces and dives again at shallow angle. Often breaches clear of water. Vocalisations little studied but include 3 kHz pulsed clicks each of less than 1 second duration.

FEEDING

Diet in North Atlantic mainly copepods (*Calanus*, *Eucalanus*, *Metridia*, and *Temora*); also euphausiids (*Thysanoessa and Meganyctiphanes*). Feed either by taking large mouthfuls of water with plankton, or swimming near the surface, skimming plankton swarms with half-open mouth, and head above water.

BREEDING

Peak births in November and December, possibly offshore from NW Africa or west of Iberian peninsula. Gestation period c. 11 months. Lactation period possibly 6 months. Calving interval 2−3 years. Sexual maturity reached around 8 years.

POPULATION

Longevity c. 65 years [77]. Annual adult mortality c. 9−10% in exploited Icelandic population [78].

PARASITES/COMMENSALS

White scars in skin may be caused by copepod crustaceans of genus *Penella*, or lesions made by the shark *Isistius* or by lampreys.

RELATIONS WITH MAN

Heavily exploited by whaling industry particularly in second half of 19th and first half of 20th centuries. Total commercial protection in 1986, but recent scientific take in Iceland.

Minke whale *Balaenoptera acutorostrata*

Balaenoptera acutorostrata Lacepede, 1804; Cherbourg, France

Lesser rorqual.

RECOGNITION

The smallest of the baleen whales in British and Irish waters (Fig. 9.6). Blow low (2 m high), inconspicuous, usually seen at same time as relatively tall sickle-shaped dorsal fin. Typical breathing sequence five to eight blows at intervals of less than 1 min. Flippers have diagonal white band on upper surface. Slender, pointed triangular head with straight rather than curved borders to rostrum.

DESCRIPTION

General form similar to fin and sei whales but with sharply pointed snout. Baleen plates short (maximum 20 cm long, 12 cm wide), yellowish

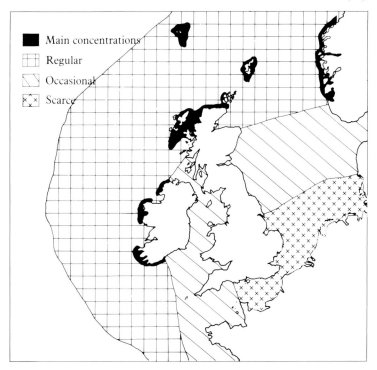

Map 9.2. Minke whale.

Legend:
- Main concentrations
- Regular
- Occasional
- Scarce

Fig. 9.6. Minke whale.

white, 230–360 on each side of upper jaw; plates sometimes have black streaking, and all are fringed with fine white bristles. General body colour dark grey to black on back, lightening to white on belly and undersides of flippers. Occasionally light chevron on back behind head, and may have two light grey regions, one just above and behind flippers, the other just below and in front of dorsal fin. Flippers one-eighth of body length, relatively short and narrow with distinctive white band. Throat grooves 50 to 70, ending just behind the flippers but in front of the navel. Dorsal fin a little more than one-third along back from tail flukes, relatively tall (compared with fin and blue whales), usually distinctly sickle-shaped. Broad tail flukes with small median notch.

MEASUREMENTS
Female length *c.* 8.5 m; male *c.* 8.0 m. Weight *c.* 10 tonnes. Newborn calf *c.* 2.6 m long. Length at sexual maturity *c.* 7.3–7.45 m (female), 6.9 m (male).

VARIATION
Northern hemisphere animals average *c.* 0.5 m smaller than those of southern hemisphere.

DISTRIBUTION
Commonest of all rorquals both world-wide and in British and Irish waters. North Atlantic population estimated to be between 50 000 and 100 000, mainly in temperate and polar regions. Widely distributed along the Atlantic seaboard of Britain and Ireland, W and N Norway, the Faroes and Iceland, often close to the coast. Also occurs in northern and central North Sea regularly as far south as the Yorkshire coast, but virtually absent from the Channel. This is the species of baleen most likely to be observed from land, particularly from headlands along the coasts of W Scotland and the Northern Isles. Most sightings occur in August although the species can be seen anytime between May and October. In the autumn there appears to be an offshore movement, possibly associated with breeding. Little evidence for substantial latitudinal migrations as in some of larger rorquals.

HISTORY
Because of its small size, the minke whale was not a target of the Scottish and Irish whale fisheries in the early part of this century. It has only been exploited recently when stocks of other larger rorquals became depleted and, in some cases, received protection. Since the 1920s, whaling for this species was carried out along the Norwegian coast, expanding just before the Second World War to Spitsbergen, and Shetland–Faroe Islands, and later moving also to the Barents Sea and Iceland. Most whaling was by Norway, but more recently Iceland has had a limited minke whale fishery.

SOCIAL ORGANISATION AND BEHAVIOUR
Usually seen singly or in pairs, though may sometimes aggregate into larger groups when feeding. Some evidence from recognisable individuals that exclusive home ranges are occupied from one season to next [30]. Moderately fast swimmer cruising at 5–26 km/hour. When beginning a long dive, often arch tail stock but without raising flukes above surface. Occasionally breaches clear of water. Vocalisations include grunts (80–140 Hz frequency), trains of thumps (mainly at 100–200 Hz frequency), and very short ratchet-like pulses at 850 Hz frequency, and high frequency (mainly 4–7.7 kHz) clicks.

FEEDING
Most catholic feeder of the rorquals taking more fish (*Clupea, Gadus, Mallotus, Eleginus, Pollachius* and *Ammodytes*) than others. Euphausiids and pteropods also taken. Like humpback and fin whales, minke whales use a variety of feeding methods depending on nature of prey, from engulfing prey with open mouth from behind, to side- and lunge-feeding. Surface of water often used to trap fish shoals.

Feeding occurs often in upwelling areas around headlands and small islands, primarily during summer.

BREEDING
Birth mainly around December, probably in temperate offshore waters. Gestation period is 10 months. Lactation period less than 6 months with calving interval 1–2+ years. Sexual maturity reached at *c.* 7 years.

POPULATION
Longevity *c.* 40–50 years [73]. Annual adult mortality 9–10%.

PARASITES/COMMENSALS
Ectoparasites rare but the crustacean *Penella balaenopterae* is found embedded in the skin, especially near the urinogenital opening.

RELATIONS WITH MAN
This is the latest of the baleen whales to be exploited by the whaling industry, mainly in Norwegian and Icelandic waters. Since 1986 the species has been given total protection from commercial whaling although Norway continues a small take for scientific purposes.

SUBORDER ODONTOCETI (TOOTHED WHALES)

FAMILY PHYSETERIDAE

Contains two genera, *Physeter*, the sperm whale, and *Kogia*, the pygmy and dwarf sperm whales. Only the first two species have been recorded from British and Irish waters.

GENUS *Physeter*

Contains only one species.

Sperm whale *Physeter macrocephalus*

Physeter macrocephalus Linnaeus, 1758.
Physeter catodon Linnaeus, 1758; Orkney.

RECOGNITION
Huge square head (one-quarter to one-third of body length). Distinct dorsal hump about two-thirds along back followed by knuckles along spine. Conspicuous bushy blow (to height of *c.* 1.5 m) projecting from anterior of snout forward sharply to left. Numerous large teeth in lower jaw only. Skull with high occipital crest and in general form shaped like a chariot.

DESCRIPTION
Largest of all the toothed whales (Fig. 9.7). Large blunt head (proportionately larger in adult males), with single blowhole placed at left anterior limit of snout. Lower jaw not extending to anterior limit of head and very narrow, the two rami being fused together for most of their length. In lower jaw, 20 to 25 large conical teeth in male, fewer and smaller teeth in female; in upper jaw, up to ten frequently

Fig. 9.7. Sperm whale.

curved teeth in male which remain virtually concealed below the gums. General body colour dark grey or brownish grey, paler at front of head and on belly, with white fringes to mouth, particularly at corners. Juveniles overall much lighter grey. Skin often has a corrugated or shrivelled appearance. Short ill-defined grooves in throat region, diagnostic of Physeteridae. Rounded flippers. No dorsal fin but distinct triangular or rounded hump two-thirds along body followed by spinal ridge to broad triangular and deeply notched tail flukes. Unlike humpbacks, these are black in colour with straight rear margin. Keel along underside of tail stock. Tail flukes thrown high into the air before a deep dive. Head and anterior part of body generally marked by numerous scratches and circular scars said to be inflicted by the tentacles of large squid which form the main diet. The pointed extremities of the lower teeth fit into sockets on the sides of the palate when the mouth is closed. Disproportionate size of head due to development of a large sac of fat, the spermaceti organ, unique to the Physeteridae.

MEASUREMENTS
Female length 11 m (rarely up to 12 m); male length 15.8 m (rarely up to 18 m). Weight 15–20 tonnes in female; 45–70 tonnes in male. Newborn young *c.* 3.5–4.0 m long. Length at sexual maturity *c.* 8.8 m (female), *c.* 11.9 m (male).

DISTRIBUTION
World-wide in deep waters of all seas, except close to ice edge. Females undergo less extensive seasonal migrations than males, rarely going north of 40°N. The commonest of large whales with North Atlantic population somewhere in the region of 20 000–30 000. Feeding areas include deeper waters along continental slope west of British Isles, north to Iceland; breeding areas around Azores and Madeira but also in the Mediterranean.

In British and Irish waters, the sperm whale mainly occurs off the edge of the continental shelf. Of 25 sightings recorded since 1965, 21 have been at least 300 km west of the British Isles, the remaining being in the vicinity of the Shetland and Orkney islands, or west of Ireland [34, 40]. In the past, it was virtually only lone males that came as far north as the British Isles. However, although most sightings are of single individuals, groups numbering three to six (including young) have occurred recently on several occasions.

There has been a clear increase in the number of strandings on British and Irish coasts this century, with nine between 1913–48, and 28 between 1949–85 (20 since 1973) [51, 111]. Together with sightings data, they suggest that an increasing number of females and young are now moving into high latitudes. Furthermore, there is no obvious seasonal pattern of occurrence and a number of sightings have occurred between October and December.

HISTORY
The Scottish whale fishery took 19 sperm whales in Shetland and 76 in the Outer Hebrides between 1903–29 [14, 116]. One individual was taken in the latter region in 1950–51 [14]. In Ireland, 48

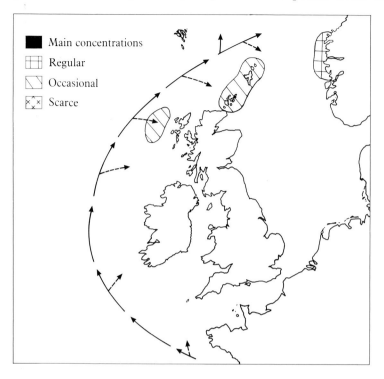

Map 9.3. Sperm whale.

sperm whales were taken between 1908–14 and a further 15 in 1920 and 1922 [42]. Most catches occurred in deep waters just off the edge of the continental shelf.

SOCIAL ORGANISATION AND BEHAVIOUR
Matriarchal society with groups comprising adult females with their calves and immatures; adult males associate to form temporary harem groups. Immature males form bachelor groups often of larger group size. Solitary males tend to penetrate colder waters than maternity/nursery groups. Group size may vary from 1–50+ individuals, although in NE Atlantic most observations are of single individuals or small groups numbering six or less.

Relatively slow swimmer, with average cruising speed of *c.* 5–12 km/hour. May remain at surface for extended period, blowing about 40 times in 7–10 min, before diving for 30–60 min to depths sometimes exceeding 1000 m. Vocalisations include high frequency (mainly 10–16 kHz) pulsed sonar clicks which may last from 1–10 seconds to 20 minutes or more. Clicks repeated at very regular intervals, some with characteristic repetition rates, and may have a communication function in addition to their uses for navigation or food-finding.

FEEDING
Diet mainly medium-sized squid (particularly of families Onychoteuthidae and Ommastrephidae). Inshore populations may take proportionately more fish: stomachs of sperm whales taken from coastal waters of Iceland comprised mainly fish such as *Sebastes*, *Raja*, *Lophius* and *Cyclopterus*.

BREEDING
Males probably mate with more than one female. Young born mainly between July and September after a gestation period of *c.* 16–17 months. Lactation period uncertain ranging between 19–42 months. Males may suck at least occasionally up to age of 13 years and females to 7.5 years. Solid food taken for first time after 1 year. Calving interval probably around 5–6 years (based on South African populations). Sexual maturity reached around 18–19 years in male, and 7–12 years in female.

POPULATION
Longevity 65–70 years [77]. Annual adult mortality *c.* 6%.

PARASITES/COMMENSALS
Cyamid crustaceans (notably *Neocyamus physeteris*) usually occur on calves, young males and adult

females. Remora fish frequently attach to skin of juvenile sperm whales (up to 6 m length).

Fig. 9.8. Pygmy sperm whale.

RELATIONS WITH MAN

Since early 18th century, sperm whales have been especially valuable to whaling industry for waxy spermaceti (used originally as a fuel for lamps, later as a lubricant in engineering and textile industries), blubber, meat for fertilizer, and ambergris (an intestinal deposit highly valued as a fixative in cosmetic industry). After populations of most baleen whale species had become depleted, sperm whales formed main target of whaling industry. Recent whaling for this species occurred around Iceland, Spain, Madeira and the Azores, but total commercial protection received from 1985.

GENUS *Kogia*

Contains two closely related species, only one of which has been recorded from British and Irish waters.

Pygmy sperm whale *Kogia breviceps*

Physeter breviceps Blainville, 1838; South Africa.

RECOGNITION

Superficial dolphin-like appearance with conical or square-shaped head and underslung lower jaw, and small mouth, resembling shark. False gill on side of head. Low, slightly recurved dorsal fin, placed just behind centre of back. Skull resembles that of miniature sperm whale, with similar marked asymmetry of bony nares and numerous teeth confined to lower jaw.

Smaller dwarf sperm whale *Kogia simus* only recently recognised as separate species. Best distinguished externally by taller more erect dorsal fin, more centrally placed, and by an additional one to three pairs of teeth sometimes present in upper jaw. Stranding record from French coast in 1986, but not yet from British Isles.

DESCRIPTION

The head is only one-sixth of the body length as opposed to one-third in the sperm whale (Fig. 9.8). Conical shaped head becomes squarer with age. No beak. The blowhole is situated on top of the head as in most other toothed whales. No functional teeth in upper jaw but (10) 12 to 16 pairs of narrow inward-curving pointed teeth in lower jaw. Short,

ill-defined grooves in throat region. Flippers relatively long (up to 14% of body length), wide at the base tapering to rounded point. Body colour dark blue-grey on back, outer margin of flippers and upper surface of tail flukes, lightening to pale grey on flanks and dull white belly (sometimes with pinkish tinge). Skin may have wrinkled appearance (cf. sperm whale). Tail has concave trailing edge with distinct median notch. Low and inconspicuous blow during slow sluggish roll. May bask on surface with head and back exposed.

MEASUREMENTS

Female length 3.03 m; male 3.07 m. Weight 318−408 kg. Newborn young 120 cm long. Length at sexual maturity 260−280 cm (female), 270−300 cm (male).

DISTRIBUTION

Poorly known but apparently world-wide in deep waters. Rarely sighted so that most information comes from beached animals. In North Atlantic, strandings more frequent along coast of the United States than European coasts. There have been two strandings of pygmy sperm whales on the Atlantic coasts of British Isles: one in County Clare in April 1966, one in S Wales in October 1980. There have also been three sightings thought to be of this species, one in August 1979 in the North Sea off NE England, and the other two on successive days in June 1982 in deep waters off NW Ireland.

SOCIAL ORGANISATION AND BEHAVIOUR

Poorly known. Apparently not gregarious with most sightings either of single individuals or small groups numbering up to six animals. Apparently not a fast swimmer.

FEEDING

Diet predominantly squid (*Histioteuthis* spp., *Chiroteuthis*, *Ommastrephes*, *Loligo*), octopus (*Octopoteuthis*, *Eledona* sp.) and sepiolids (*Sepiola*), but also deep-water fish (for example *Micromesistius*) and crabs [22, 28, 85].

BREEDING

Breeding season unknown. Gestation period *c.* 11 months (based on individuals stranded on coast of South Africa). Lactation period and age at sexual maturity unknown.

FAMILY MONODONTIDAE

Currently considered to comprise three mono-specific genera — *Orcaella*, *Delphinapterus* and *Monodon*, of which the last two have been record-ed from British waters. The first, the Irrawaddy dolphin *Orcaella brevirostris* occurs in coastal waters of the Indo-Pacific.

GENUS *Delphinapterus*

White whale *Delphinapterus leucas*

Delphinapterus leucas Pallas, 1776; Mouth of River Ob, Siberia.

Beluga.

RECOGNITION

Adults pure white (juveniles slate-grey to reddish brown becoming blue-grey at 2 years old). Stout body with small head and rounded melon. No dorsal fin. Upper profile of skull slightly convex rather than concave as in all other odontocetes except narwhal, but distinguished from latter by having teeth in both upper and lower jaws.

DESCRIPTION

The head of the white whale (Fig. 9.9) is relatively small with well-defined neck, prominent, rounded melon with short but distinct beak. Eight to 11

pairs of irregular, often curved teeth in upper jaw, eight to nine pairs in lower jaw. Teeth *c.* 60 mm in diameter. Body rather robust, white in adult. The grey colour of calf may lead to confusion in narwhal. Short, paddle-shaped flippers. No dorsal fin though slightly darker back with narrow ridge along spine just before midpoint. The ridge may be notched laterally to form a series of small bumps. Broad tail flukes with deeply notched centre and obliquely truncated lobes.

MEASUREMENTS

Female length *c.* 360 cm; male *c.* 420 cm. Weight 500–1500 kg. Newborn young 150–160 cm long. Length at sexual maturity *c.* 300 cm (female), *c.* 360 cm (male).

DISTRIBUTION

Entire Arctic Ocean, rarely penetrating into more temperate waters. The only record of a stranding on the British coast was in October 1932 in River Forth near Stirling. There have been seven accept-able sightings, mainly in the northern North Sea. These include singles off Clare Island, County Mayo in September 1948; off the island of Soay, near Skye, in 1950; between Orkney and Burray in October 1960; in Gourock Bay during late summer 1964, and possibly the same individual at Arrochar, Loch Long; off the Yorkshire coast east of Whitby in June 1987, and possibly the same individual off the coast of Northumberland in March 1988.

Recent sightings of single white whales have also been made from the Danish, German and Dutch coasts. Some of these may involve the same indi-viduals but they suggest that a small number have come south from the Barents Sea (where they are now regularly seen along the north Norwegian coast) and remained within the North Sea.

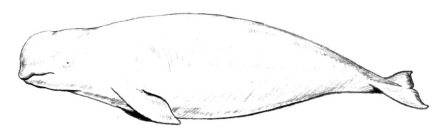

Fig. 9.9. White whale.

SOCIAL ORGANISATION AND BEHAVIOUR

Although vagrants in temperate waters are usually seen singly, typical group sizes in Arctic are between five and 20 animals, and aggregations of 1000 or more white whales may occur during summer breeding and on migration.

Relatively slow swimmer, generally not more than 10 km per hour. Often beaches on sand banks. Shallow diver, and virtually never leaps clear of water. Vocalisations very varied including yelps, chirps and whistles (0.26–20 kHz), and high frequency (1.2–1.6, 40, 80 and 120 kHz) echolocating clicks.

FEEDING

Mainly squid but also shallow water fish (including *Cyclopterus*, *Eleginus*, *Mallotus*, *Ammodytes*, *Melanogrammus*, *Osmerus*, *Boreogadus* and *Salmo*) and crustaceans.

BREEDING

Young born in Arctic Ocean in summer, mainly in July and August. Gestation period 14.5 months. Lactation period 20–24 months. Calving interval 3 years. Males reach sexual maturity at 8–9 years, females at 4–7 years.

POPULATION

Longevity *c*. 25–30 years. Average annual mortality 12%.

RELATIONS WITH MAN

Has been heavily exploited by native peoples of the Arctic.

Products include meat, blubber (muktuk) and oil, although 'porpoise hide' bootlaces were made in England from the skins during the early part of this century.

Frequently displayed in dolphinaria, and an individual kept in an aquarium in Brighton in 1878 was one of the first cetaceans in captivity.

GENUS *Monodon*

Narwhal *Monodon monoceros*

Monodon monoceros Linnaeus, 1758; Arctic seas.

RECOGNITION

Body shape of Narwhal (Fig. 9.10) similar to white whale, lacking dorsal fin and with small rounded head, but males (occasionally also females) have spiralled tusk extending from left upper jaw giving 'unicorn' appearance. Skull similar to white whale but having no teeth in lower jaw.

DESCRIPTION

Stout body with small, rounded head, bulbous forehead and very slight beak. One pair of teeth in upper jaw only, left tooth in male greatly extended as spiralled tusk (up to 3 m long). Rarely are both teeth thus elongated. In female, tusks embedded in bone of rostrum and not erupted. Body mottled grey-green, cream and black but old animals can appear almost white, causing potential confusion with white whales. However, these are usually male narwhal and so possess tusk. Newborn are blotchy slate grey or bluish grey but juveniles appear darker through lack of mottling. Short, broad flippers with upturned tips. No dorsal fin but ridged back. Fan-shaped tail flukes with deep notch in centre.

MEASUREMENTS

Female length *c*. 350 cm; male length *c*. 410 cm

Fig. 9.10. Narwhal.

(excluding tusk). Weight 800–1600 kg (males larger than females). Newborn young 150–170 cm long. Length at sexual maturity *c.* 340 cm (female), *c.* 390 cm (male).

DISTRIBUTION

Entire Arctic Ocean, only occasionally penetrating into temperate waters. Recorded only six times in British waters. All but one of these were strandings of single individuals — in 1648, 1800, 1808, and two separate ones in 1949 (both in Thames Estuary). The exception was a sighting of two individuals off Orkney in late June 1949, suggesting that the last two may have been part of a larger group. No records since then.

SOCIAL ORGANISATION AND BEHAVIOUR

Vagrants in temperate waters lone individuals, though possibly part of larger dispersed group. In Arctic Ocean, groups usually comprise 5–20 animals but as with white whale, aggregations sometimes exceeding 1000 animals may occur at breeding areas or on migration. Relatively fast swimmer. Vocalisations include whistles of 0.3–10 kHz frequency, often rising or falling in pitch, and lasting 0.5–1.0 seconds; pulsed tones of 0.5–5.0 kHz; and echolocating clicks of 0.5–24.0 kHz frequency. The pulsed tones are thought to vary individually so having a signature function.

FEEDING

Mainly squid and shallow bottom-living fish (such as *Raja, Platichthys, Gadus, Boreogadus, Hippoglossus, Reinhardtius* or *Salmo*); also crustaceans (decapods and euphausiids).

BREEDING

Calf born in summer, mainly in July and August. Gestation period 14–15 months. Lactation period 20 months. Calving interval possibly 3 years. Sexual maturity reached around 11–13 years in male, 5–8 years in female.

RELATIONS WITH MAN

Native hunting in arctic Canada and Greenland mainly for its ivory, but also for meat and skin (which contains a lot of vitamin C). The tusk has been of great commercial value (with supposed medicinal properties) to European and American whalers and traders for many centuries.

FAMILY ZIPHIIDAE (BEAKED WHALES)

Whales belonging to this family are medium in size, 3.7–12.8 m in length, with a distinct beak extending from skull. Teeth usually very reduced in number and entirely absent from upper jaw; on each side of lower jaw of adult males, one or two comparatively large teeth projecting from mouth as small tusks (usually not erupted in females and juveniles). Two characteristic V-shaped grooves under throat. Single crescentic blowhole concave towards snout and rather larger than in most toothed whales. No notch in middle of tail flukes. Three genera are represented in British and Irish waters.

GENUS *Hyperoodon*

World-wide. Two species, one confined to Southern Ocean.

Northern bottlenose whale *Hyperoodon ampullatus*

Balaena ampullata Forster, 1770; Maldon, Essex, England.
Delphinus bidentatus Bonnaterre, 1789; River Thames.
Delphinus diodon Lacepède, 1804; Near London.
Hyperoodon bidens Fleming, 1828; Essex.
Hyperoodon latifrons Gray, 1846; Orkney.

RECOGNITION

Large, bulbous head (particularly in male) and short bottle-nosed beak. Usually one pair of teeth in lower jaw (of male), no teeth visible in mouth of female. Solid bony maxillary crests on rostrum becoming larger and heavier with age.

DESCRIPTION

The largest of the British beaked whales (Fig. 9.11) distinguished from other members of the family by large bulbous forehead and distinct short dolphin-like beak (15–17.5 cm long). Older males have single pair of pear-shaped teeth (up to 45 mm long and 19 mm in diameter), erupting at tip of lower jaw; in females, rarely appear through gum. Minute vestigial teeth embedded in gums of upper and lower jaws. Pair of V-shaped throat grooves.

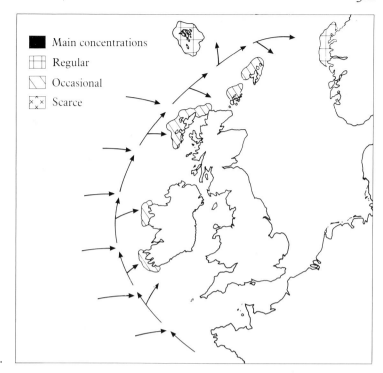

Main concentrations
Regular
Occasional
Scarce

Map 9.4. Northern bottlenose whale.

Fig. 9.11. Northern bottlenose whale.

Coloration very variable from chocolate brown to greenish brown above, often lighter on flanks and belly, and with irregular patches or blotches of greyish white; lightens to buff or cream all over with age. Calves uniform chocolate brown. Long, fairly robust cylindrical body. Single crescent-shaped blowhole in depression behind forehead giving single low (to 2 m) bushy blow, slightly forward-pointing. Short tapering flippers. Dorsal fin of moderate height (30 cm), often strongly hooked, situated one third along back from tail. Broad unnotched tail flukes with deeply concave trailing edge.

MEASUREMENTS
Males larger than females. Female length 7.0–8.5 m; male 8.5–9.5 m. Weight *c.* 7.5 tonnes in male and *c.* 5.8 tonnes in female. Newborn calf *c.* 360 cm. long. Length at sexual maturity *c.* 690 cm (female), *c.* 750 cm (male).

DISTRIBUTION
Temperate and arctic North Atlantic, particularly in deep waters. Main regions of concentration, identified from former whaling activities, appear to be west of Norway, in the Greenland Sea west of Spitsbergen, and north of Iceland [10]. The species

is thought to migrate off the edge of the continental shelf, passing northward west of Britain and Ireland in spring, and returning south again in autumn, but with some onshore movement between July and September [34, 40]. Some individuals very probably winter in arctic or subarctic latitudes.

There is some indication of a decline in NE Atlantic in recent years. The number of strandings on British and Irish coasts has declined from 55 between 1913–48 to 44 between 1949–85 [51, 111]. Sightings records also show a decline with 149 animals sighted between 1960–72 compared with 66 animals between 1973–85 despite much better coverage in the latter period [40]. Most records in fact come from deep waters, 500–700 km west of Scotland and Ireland. Those in coastal waters are concentrated in the southwest approaches to the British Isles and around the Outer Hebrides, with some also in the northern North Sea.

HISTORY
Small numbers were taken in the Scottish whaling industry early this century, though preference was given to the larger rorquals. Between 1903 and 1928, 25 were captured around Shetland and one in the Outer Hebrides (none in 1950–51) [14, 116]. None was taken off W Ireland [42]. Most catches in deep waters off edge of continental shelf.

Between 1939–69, more than 5000 were taken by Norwegian whalers who also hunted the species in the late 19th and early 20th centuries (ceasing in the 1920s). Although that fishery has ceased now, it appears that the NE Atlantic population is much depleted.

SOCIAL ORGANISATION AND BEHAVIOUR
Usually seen either solitarily or in small groups of up to ten individuals, occasionally up to 30–40. Groups may segregate by sex and age during migration [10]. Females with their calves may form basic social unit, and large males associating with groups of females with young could be polygynous though this needs verification.

Often known to approach vessels, and to remain beside wounded companions, making them vulnerable to hunting. Deep diver (making vertical dives and taking out up to 1000 m of line when harpooned); may remain submerged for up to 2 hours. After a long dive they usually remain at surface for 10 minutes or more, blowing regularly. When making a dive, sometimes shows tail flukes above

water. Occasionally seen breaching or lobtailing. Vocalisations poorly known but include high frequency echolocation clicks.

FEEDING
Diet mainly squid (particularly *Gonatus fabricii*, also *Loligo* sp. and *Sepia* sp.) but fish recorded from specimens include *Clupea harengus* (Norway) and *Brosmius*, *Cyclopterus* and *Sebastes* sp. (Iceland) [10, 22, 117].

BREEDING
Males possibly mate with more than one female. Young born mainly April and May after a gestation period of *c.* 12 months. Lactation period uncertain but at least 12 months. Calving interval probably 2 (−3) years. Sexual maturity reached at 7–11 years in male, *c.* 11 years in female.

POPULATION
Longevity at least 37 years [19].

RELATIONS WITH MAN
Previously hunted from Norwegian shore stations (mainly from 1882 to late 1920s and 1938–1972), for oil and animal food.

GENUS *Ziphius*

Cuvier's beaked whale *Ziphius cavirostris*

Ziphius cavirostris Cuvier, 1823; Mouth of Rhone, France.

Cuvier's whale.

RECOGNITION
Rarely seen at sea but best recognised by sloping (rather than bulbous) forehead, often pale (even white in older animals) indistinct beak, pair of usually conical teeth at tip of lower jaw in males, and often scarred body. Skull without bony maxillary crests on rostrum.

DESCRIPTION
Long stout body with small slightly concave head (likened to goose beak) (Fig. 9.12). Beak ill-defined particularly in older individuals, with slightly protruding lower jaw. Single pair of conical teeth (57 mm long and *c.* 32 mm in diameter) at tip of lower jaw, usually erupt only in males. V-shaped pair of throat grooves. Coloration grey or blue-

Fig. 9.12. Cuvier's beaked whale.

grey, paler grey or white head (particularly in older males) with linear pale scars often on back and sides and cream or white oval blotches on sides and belly. Distance from snout to blowhole less than in northern bottlenose. Low, inconspicuous blow directed forwards and obliquely to left. Small rounded flippers with pointed tip. Dorsal fin variable from small, triangular to relatively tall (up to 38 cm high), sickle-shaped, about two-thirds along back. Somewhat concave tail flukes, like other beaked whales lacking distinct median notch.

MEASUREMENTS
Female length *c.* 7.0 m, male *c.* 6.7 m. Weight *c.* 6.5 tonnes in female, *c.* 5.6 tonnes in male. Newborn young *c.* 270 cm long. Length at sexual maturity *c.* 5.8 m (female), *c.* 5.5 m (male).

DISTRIBUTION
Poorly known but probably world-wide except perhaps polar waters. Like other beaked whales, appears to be mainly deep-water species. In British and Irish waters, the species is probably more common than records suggest. There have been only three well-documented sightings, in the northern North Sea east of Orkney in August 1980, off the coast of County Cork, S Ireland, in August 1984, and southwest of Ireland in July 1987 [1, 40]. There were 39 strandings between 1913 and 1985, with 15 of these since 1963 [51, 111]. Most of these come from the Atlantic seaboard, in N and W Scotland and W Ireland. Records have occurred in every month of the year but particularly between January and March and between June and July.

SOCIAL ORGANISATION AND BEHAVIOUR
Rarely seen but most sightings either of single individuals or small groups of three to ten (occasionally up to 25) animals. Social organisation unknown.

May dive for at least 30 min, and probably dives deeply. Rarely breaches. Vocalisations not known.

FEEDING
Diet mainly squid (*Brachioteuthis*, *Histioteuthis*,

Octopoteuthis, *Enoploteuthis*) and deep-sea fish (*Micromesistius*) [22, 28].

BREEDING
No information.

POPULATION
Longevity *c.* 36 years [87].

GENUS *Mesoplodon*

A large genus of poorly differentiated species, often scarcely known, in some cases only from stranded animals. Two species of *Mesoplodon* occur in British and Irish waters, although one other (Gervais' beaked whale *Mesoplodon europaeus*) recorded once from English Channel in 1840, whilst Gray's beaked whale *Mesoplodon grayi* stranded on Dutch coast in 1927.

Sowerby's beaked whale *Mesoplodon bidens*

Physeter bidens Sowerby, 1804; Moray, Scotland.

Sowerby's whale.

RECOGNITION
Rarely seen at sea, when it would be difficult to distinguish from other *Mesoplodon* species. Like others of genus, may have a prominent bulge on forehead, with moderately long slender beak. Diagnostic feature is one pair of triangular teeth (exposed above gum only in male) at mid-point of lower jaw.

DESCRIPTION
Long slender tapering body with small head and well-defined slender beak (Fig. 9.13). Pair of teeth extruding outside of mouth from middle of beak in adult males. Teeth project backwards then slightly forwards. In females and young these are smaller, and may be concealed beneath gum. Dark grey coloration which may be sandy-coloured around head, paler grey on belly, and light spots scattered

Fig. 9.13. Sowerby's beaked whale.

over back and flanks. Young animals have lighter bellies and fewer spots. Relatively small flippers, one-seventh to one-ninth of body length, and often tucked into 'flipper pockets'. Dorsal fin triangular or slightly sickle-shaped, almost two-thirds along back. Unnotched tail flukes have trailing edge slightly concave.

MEASUREMENTS
Length *c.* 5 m; weight *c.* 3.4 tonnes. Newborn calf *c.* 2.4 m long.

DISTRIBUTION
Known only from the temperate North Atlantic, mainly in European waters. Distribution appears to be centred upon North Sea (possibly Norwegian trench north to Faroe–Shetland channel and Norwegian basin). Rarely seen, but many strandings in Britain and Ireland. There have been 43 strandings between 1913–85, with 23 of these since 1963 [111]. These have occurred mainly in the Northern Isles and along the coast of eastern Britain although there are a number of records also from English Channel, some from W Ireland and from those European countries bordering the North Sea. Strandings have generally been of single individuals, occurring in most months but particularly July to September. The only documented sighting has been of one off the west coast of Scotland in August 1977, soon after which two individuals stranded separately on the Isle of Skye and neighbouring Raasay [40].

SOCIAL ORGANISATION AND BEHAVIOUR
Virtually unknown. All records are of single individuals or 'pairs'. Fast swimmer, often at surface, and clearly mainly pelagic. Echolocating sound pulses recorded from young animal kept in a dolphinarium for a few hours. A specimen which stranded alive was reported as lowing like a cow.

FEEDING
Diet is squid (for example Ommastrephidae) but very poorly known. Oral musculature indicates a suctorial action when feeding.

BREEDING
Virtually unknown. Mating and birth possibly occurs mainly in late winter and spring.

True's beaked whale *Mesoplodon mirus*

Mesoplodon mirus True, 1913; North Carolina, USA.

RECOGNITION
Not yet identified at sea, when it would be very difficult to distinguish from other *Mesoplodon* species. Best feature to separate from Sowerby's beaked whale is placement of single pair of teeth at extreme tip of lower jaw (extruded only in males).

DESCRIPTION
Long tapering body, more robust than Sowerby's beaked whale (more similar to Cuvier's beaked whale) (Fig. 9.14). Slight bulge on forehead and slight depression in area of blowhole. Pronounced, slender beak. Single pair of teeth directed forward, at extreme tip of lower jaw of males, and exposed outside mouth in older animals. Teeth flattened, oval in cross-section, 25 × 13 mm. In females, pair of teeth is concealed below gum. Coloration dark grey to grey-black on back, lighter slate grey on sides, grey on belly, with scratches and light spots usually present, particularly in anal and genital regions. Relatively small narrow flippers often tucked into 'flipper pockets' and triangular or slightly sickle-shaped dorsal fin situated almost two-thirds along back. Unnotched tail flukes have trailing edge slightly concave.

Fig. 9.14. True's beaked whale.

MEASUREMENTS
Length *c*. 4.9–5.5 m; weight *c*. 3.2 tonnes. Length of shortest reported calf is 233 cm.

DISTRIBUTION
Range very poorly known but may be widespread in deep waters of temperate Atlantic extending to southwestern Indian Ocean with records from eastern N America, NW Europe and South Africa. Of nine strandings records from Europe, six are from W Ireland (Killadoon, County Mayo to Ballinskelligs Bay, County Kerry) and one from Outer Hebrides. Three strandings occurred between 1913–37 and the other three since 1973, with no higher frequency at any particular time of the year.

SOCIAL ORGANISATION AND BEHAVIOUR
No information.

FEEDING
Presumably deep-water squid as others in genus, but no data.

BREEDING
No information.

PARASITES/COMMENSALS
A male stranded in County Mayo in November 1987 had many *Conchoderma* growing around its teeth [120].

FAMILY PHOCOENIDAE

True porpoises, never more than 2.1 m in length and all having flattened spade-shaped teeth. Now divided into four genera: *Phocoena*, *Neophocaena*, *Phocoenoides* and *Australophocaena*. Only one species (of genus *Phocoena*) occurs in European waters.

GENUS *Phocoena*

Harbour porpoise *Phocoena phocoena*

Delphinus phocoena Linnaeus, 1758; Swedish Seas.
Delphinus ventricosus Lacepède, 1804; River Thames.
Phocoena tuberculifera Gray, 1865; Margate, Kent.

RECOGNITION
Smallest British cetacean, not more than 2 m in length (Fig. 9.15). Rarely leaps clear of water as do dolphins. Short blunt head, no beak, and dorsal fin small, triangular, situated in centre of back. Upper and lower jaws containing spade-shaped teeth (conical in all dolphins).

DESCRIPTION
Small rotund body with small head, no forehead or beak. 19–28 pairs of small, spade-shaped teeth in each jaw. Dark grey back with paler grey patch on flanks and white belly, though coloration of back and sides variable. Grey line from flippers to jawline. Short, slightly rounded flippers. Upper and lower jaws, chin, flippers and flukes black. Low, triangular dorsal fin centrally placed on back. Central notch in tail flukes.

MEASUREMENTS
Length *c*. 170 cm (female), *c*. 145 cm (male); weight 54–65 kg. Newborn calf 67–80 cm long. Length at sexual maturity *c*. 145 cm (female), *c*. 135 cm (male).

VARIATION
Skeletal material from Denmark and Holland indi-

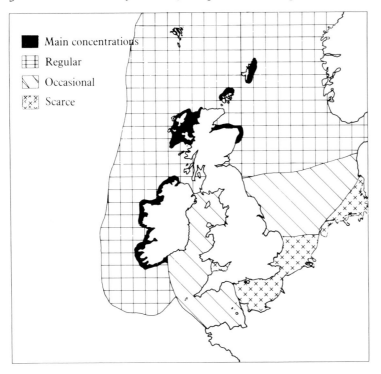

Main concentrations
Regular
Occasional
Scarce

Map 9.5. Harbour porpoise.

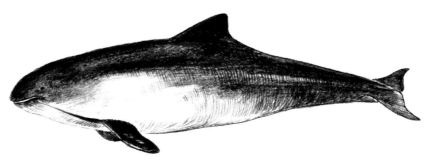

Fig. 9.15. Harbour porpoise.

cates some geographical segregation of Baltic and North Sea populations [70].

DISTRIBUTION

Widely distributed in coastal waters of temperate and subarctic North Atlantic. Although the most frequently observed (and stranded) cetacean in British and Irish waters, this species appears to have declined in the last 30 years along southern North Sea and Channel coasts [34, 40, 112]. Present distribution is concentrated along the Atlantic coasts of S and W Ireland and W Scotland, and in the northern North Sea around NE Scotland [40].

Most sightings are within 10 km of land but with an offshore movement in winter involving at least a portion of the population [40]. Porpoises are seen in coastal waters in all months but with a distinct seasonal peak between July and October [40].

SOCIAL ORGANISATION AND BEHAVIOUR

Most sightings are of single individuals or small groups of up to 10 animals [33, 40]. Sometimes (probably mainly associated with rich feeding conditions), these may form aggregations numbering up to 200–300. However, these are most likely to be only temporary coalitions of those smaller groups. Basic social unit probably female with calf, which may sometimes be accompanied by a yearling. Segregation by sex and age may also occur in larger groups.

Slow swimmer, though when pursued, can attain speeds of up to 22 km/hour. Does not normally leap clear of water. Difficult to observe for extended periods, showing little curiosity to boats unlike many dolphin species. Does not bow-ride. Surfacing frequency varies according to behaviour (generally highest during travel), with submergence periods between 2 and 169 seconds. Basic pattern of four shorter dives (up to 30 sec) usually followed by a long dive (more than 30 sec) [72].

Distances moved by radio-tagged adult male in E Canada over 4-day period amounted to at least 40 km though not exceeding 20 km per day [56]. Studies of activity patterns suggest within 24 hour period, 76% of time spent feeding, 21% time in travel, and 3% in rest [122].

Vocalisations include pulses mainly of 1–2 kHz frequency and others of 10–15 kHz frequency, both types of very short duration (up to 5 ms).

FEEDING
Wide variety of fish including *Clupea*, *Ammodytes*, *Sprattus*, *Scomber*, *Sardina*, *Micromesistius*, *Trisopterus*, *Merluccius*, *Trachurus*, *Pollachius*, *Gadus* and *Merlangius*, and also crustaceans and cephalopods (*Loligo*) [28, 34, 40, 103].

BREEDING
Young born mainly between May and August though some as early as March [40, 44, 72, 89]. Although parturition may start offshore before spring movement towards coast, most births probably occur in coastal waters during the summer. Gestation period *c.* 11 months (possibly as short as 8). Lactation period *c.* 8 months. Calving interval 1–2 years.

POPULATION
Longevity relatively short, *c.* 15 years [55, 118]. Age at sexual maturity *c.* 5 years (male), *c.* 6 years (female).

PARASITES/COMMENSALS
Circular lesions frequently occur on skin, attributed to lamprey. Internal parasites include the nematodes *Anisakis simplex* (stomach), *Stenurus minor* (cranial sinuses), *Pseudalius inflexus* (bronchi, lungs, and heart), and *Torynurus convolutus*

(bronchi); and trematode *Campula oblonga* (bile and pancreatic ducts) [7, 28, 58].

RELATIONS WITH MAN
Formerly hunted in Baltic and off coast of Holland, herded by slapping surface of water with sticks. Now, a major threat is incidental drowning in a variety of fishing gear (fixed nets or traps for cod or salmon, drift nets and purse seines for cod, herring or plaice). Most important appears to be Danish fisheries around wrecks in the North Sea and also in the Kattegat and Skagerrak [5, 71] although small numbers are also caught at scattered localities along the coast of E Scotland and England [1, 93].

High levels of PCBs (max. 260 ppm lipid weight) and DDT (560 ppm lipid weight) have been recorded from stranded specimens on Swedish west coast [98]; levels also high in Baltic but generally lower on Scottish North Sea coast [90, 98]. Mercury levels low (max. 16 ppm in liver) from Scottish specimens [43] but much higher in three Dutch specimens (mean 70 ppm, max. 192 ppm in liver) [73].

Causes of declines in southern North Sea and Channel not known with certainty but three principal factors probably involved: coastal pollution, changes in fish stocks (particularly herring) and, in certain regions, accidental drowning in fishing nets.

FAMILY DELPHINIDAE

Contains the great majority of cetaceans. Worldwide and divided into 16 genera, eight of which are known in British and Irish waters.

GENUS *Delphinus*

Common dolphin *Delphinus delphis*

Delphinus delphis Linnaeus, 1758; European seas.

RECOGNITION
Small swift dolphin (Fig. 9.16) with long, slender beak. Often gregarious, frequently leaps clear of water revealing distinctive hourglass pattern of yellow and white intersecting patches on flanks.

DESCRIPTION
Slender torpedo-shaped body with long (11–12 cm) dark beak. In each jaw, 40 to 55 pairs of small

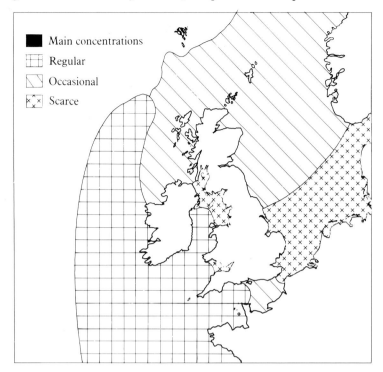

- ■ Main concentrations
- ⊞ Regular
- ⧄ Occasional
- ⊠ Scarce

Map 9.6. Common dolphin.

Fig. 9.16. Common dolphin.

(diameter 3 mm), sharp-pointed teeth. Chevron-shaped groove separates beak from low, receding forehead. Coloration variable, black or brownish black on back and upper flanks, creamy white to white chest and belly. On flanks, conspicuous hour-glass pattern of cream or yellowish tan forward of dorsal fin becoming less conspicuous paler grey behind where it may reach dorsal surface. Black stripe from flipper to middle of lower jaw, and from eye to base of beak. Tapering light grey to white flippers, and slender, sickle-shaped to erect dorsal fin, centrally placed on back. Fin ranges in colour from black (often with grey central spot) to mostly white but with dark border. Dark grey or black tail flukes with distinct median notch.

MEASUREMENTS
Length 2.1 m (female), 2.4 m (male). Weight *c.* 75–85 kg. Newborn calf *c.* 80 cm long. Length at sexual maturity 1.9 m (female), 2.0 m (male).

DISTRIBUTION
World-wide in temperate and tropical waters. Widely distributed in British and Irish waters but with a primarily western and southern component, small numbers entering southern Irish Sea and

North Sea [34, 40]. Mainly offshore, particularly associated with Gulf Stream west of continental shelf edge. Most sightings are between July and October when there may be a slight onshore movement [34, 40].

SOCIAL ORGANISATION AND BEHAVIOUR
Group sizes commonly between 10 and 20 individuals but may number in the hundreds [34, 40]. Social structure poorly known but can form groups of mixed age and sex, often with equal numbers of males and females. Fast swimmer, usually travelling at 15–24 km/hour, but can exceed this when alarmed. Commonly engages in a variety of breaching activities, also tail-smacking of water. Blowing and sounding may be synchronised between members of group.

Vocalisations vary from whistles of 1–12 kHz frequency to echolocation clicks of 4–9 kHz. Clicks and whistles may be given simultaneously.

FEEDING
Diet includes variety of fish and squid. Fish species recorded from French specimens mainly pelagic forms including *Micromesistius*, *Trisopterus*, *Merluccius*, *Trachurus*, *Sardina*, *Engraulis* and *Merlangius* [24, 28]. Cephalopods included mainly *Loligo*, *Alloteuthis* and *Sepiola* and were apparently more important in winter [24, 28].

Food-herding behaviour commonly observed with apparent co-operation between school members [1, 35].

BREEDING
Births mainly between June and September [24, 34, 40, 51]. Gestation period *c.* 10–11 months. Lactation period *c.* 19 months. Calving interval 1–2 years.

POPULATION
Longevity *c.* 30 years.

PARASITES/COMMENSALS
Internal organs sometimes infested with nematode worms (notably *Anisakis simplex*) and cestodes (*Phyllobothrium delphini* and *Monorygma grimaldii* [28]). Whale lice and barnacles, *Xenobalanus globicipites*, have also been observed on some specimens.

RELATIONS WITH MAN
Has been kept in captivity but does not train easily. Hunted in Southern European waters (including Mediterranean) either opportunistically or in response to perceived threat to local fisheries. In Black Sea, a major fishery for the species, involving Soviet Union and Turkey, existed until recently, causing substantial declines. May also be drowned accidentally in fishing gear, for example in mackerel fishery off SW Cornwall [99].

High levels of mercury (max. 604 ppm wet weight in liver) found in specimens from W Mediterranean [119]; also in an individual that died at Zeebrugge, Belgium [68]. Moderately high levels of PCBs and DDT found also in livers of specimens from W Mediterranean [4].

GENUS *Stenella*

A genus widely distributed, mainly in warmer waters, with a number of poorly differentiated forms. Only one species in European waters.

Striped dolphin *Stenella coeruleoalba*

Delphinus coeruleo-albus Meyen, 1833; east coast of S America.
Delphinus styx Gray, 1846; South Africa.
Delphinus euphrosyne Gray, 1846.

Euphrosyne or blue-white dolphin.

RECOGNITION
Small, swift dolphin (Fig. 9.17) with long, slender beak, superficially resembling common dolphin. Often gregarious. Frequently breaches clear of water, showing black lateral stripes from eye to flipper and eye to anus, and distinctive white or light grey V-shaped blaze on flanks, originating above and behind eye. No yellow pigment as in common dolphin. Skull lacking deep palatal grooves of the common dolphin.

DESCRIPTION
Slender, torpedo-shaped body with elongated beak (to *c.* 13 cm). In each jaw, 45–50 pairs of sharp, slightly incurved teeth (*c.* 3 mm diameter). Distinct groove separates beak from forehead. Coloration variable, dark grey to brown or bluish grey on back, lighter grey flanks, and white belly. Two distinct black bands on flanks, one from near eye down side of body to anal area (with short secondary stripe originating with this band, turning downwards towards flippers) and second from eye to flippers. Conspicuous white or light grey V-shaped blaze originating above and behind eye with one

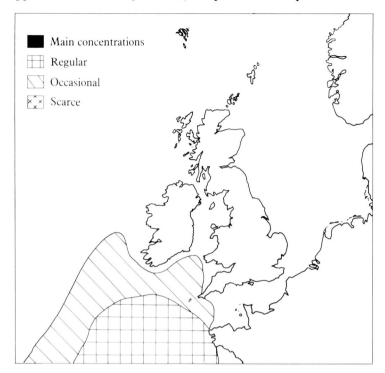

Map 9.7. Striped dolphin.

Fig. 9.17. Striped dolphin.

finger narrowing to a point below the dorsal fin and the lower one extending back towards tail (sometimes upwards over dorsal surface of tail stock). Tapering, black flippers inserted in white region, and slender sickle-shaped, centrally-placed dorsal fin. Narrow tail stock with no obvious keel; dark tail flukes with median notch.

MEASUREMENTS
Length *c.* 2.0–2.25 m (female), *c.* 2.05–2.4 m (male). Weight *c.* 100 kg. Newborn calf *c.* 100 cm long. Length at sexual maturity *c.* 1.95–2.2 m (male slightly longer than female).

VARIATION
Some intraspecific variation in pigmentation patterns [53].

DISTRIBUTION
World-wide mainly in tropical and warm temperate waters. In NE Atlantic, mainly offshore west of Spain, Portugal and France (also in W Mediterranean). In British and Irish waters, the species is rare, recorded almost exclusively from the south-west [40]. There are a few records further north, 700 km west of Scotland, suggesting that the distribution is extended northward offshore by the Gulf Stream [1, 40]. Between 1913 and 1962 there had been only four strandings on British and Irish coasts, but since then (to 1988) a further 16 have been added, all from Atlantic or Irish Sea coasts [15, 51, 111 and issues of *Irish Naturalists' Journal* since then]. These suggest that the species may be occurring further north than previously, although some earlier specimens may have been misidentified as *Delphinus*, as may have occurred with some Irish specimens [95].

No particular seasonal pattern to sightings with some occurring between July and September and others in December and February [1, 40].

SOCIAL ORGANISATION AND BEHAVIOUR
Sightings in British and Irish waters involve either single individuals (sometimes in mixed herds with common dolphins) or groups up to 30 individuals

[40]. Elsewhere, group size may number hundreds or even low thousands of animals. Basic social unit probably female and calf. However, groups may show strong segregation by age, some schools entirely comprising immatures, and others mixed with mature and immature males and females. Some evidence of segregation of sexes outside breeding season. Often seen in association with schools of common dolphins. Fast swimmer, and frequently breaches clear of water. May also bow-ride.

FEEDING

Variety of fish (including *Micromesistius*, *Trisopterus*, *Gadiculus*, *Merlangius*, *Merluccius* and *Trachurus*) and squid (including *Chiroteuthis*, *Loligo*, *Alloteuthis*, *Todarodes*, *Illex* and *Histioteuthis*) [28].

BREEDING

Breeding season may be extended and variable, but with births probably mainly in July to September. Reproductive parameters found to vary with exploitation pressure. Gestation period *c.* 12–13 months, but lactation period between 8 and 20 (probably usually 12–14) months. Calving interval *c.* 1–4 years. Sexual maturity reached at *c.* 9 years (both sexes).

POPULATION

Longevity *c.* 30 years. Overall sex ratio (male : female) 1.06 but varies with age (1.05 in animals less than 4 years old; 1.54 in animals from 4 to 11 years old; 0.75 in animals greater than 11 years old) [88].

PARASITES/COMMENSALS

Frequently infested with nematode worms (notably *Anisakis simplex*) in middle ear and other cavities. Other internal parasites include tapeworms (*Phyllobothrium delphini* and *Monorygma grimaldii*) and trematode *Pholeter gastrophilus* [28]. Oval or circular scars on skin caused by lampreys or remoras.

RELATIONS WITH MAN

Hunted (either by hand harpoon or driving ashore) in large numbers off coast of Japan, also in Solomon Islands and Papua New Guinea, and occasionally in Southern Europe (including Mediterranean). Has until recently also experienced some mortality by drowning in eastern Pacific tuna purse seine fishery, and sometimes in Mediterranean [81]. High pollutant levels (max. 833 ppm wet weight PCBs and 706 ppm wet weight total DDT) found in blubber of striped dolphins from French Mediterranean [4]. Often depicted in ancient Greek and Roman art. The species has not been maintained successfully in captivity.

GENUS *Tursiops*

A widely distributed genus with a number of poorly differentiated forms (presently considered within same species), one of which occurs in European waters.

Bottle-nosed dolphin *Tursiops truncatus*

Delphinus truncatus Montagu, 1821; River Dart, Devon, England.

RECOGNITION

Generally unmarked, robust dolphin (Fig. 9.18) with relatively short but distinct beak. Brown or dark grey on back and upper flanks, paler lower flanks and belly. Moderately tall, but slender, sickle-shaped dorsal fin, centrally placed.

DESCRIPTION

Stout torpedo-shaped body, robust head with distinct short beak (often with white patch on tip of lower jaw). In each jaw, 18–26 pairs of teeth (10–13 mm diameter). Coloration variable but usually brown or dark grey on back, lighter grey on lower flanks, grading to white on belly. Indistinct cape from apex of melon broadening from blowhole to dorsal fin, then narrowing to a thin line behind dorsal fin. Fairly long, pointed flippers, dark in colour. Centrally-placed dorsal fin, fairly tall, slender and sickle-shaped. Margins of dorsal fin remain dark, but centre may be pale. Moderately keeled tail stock and curved tail flukes with deep median notch.

MEASUREMENTS

Length *c.* 2.5–2.6 m (female), *c.* 2.7 m (male). Weight *c.* 150–275 kg. Newborn young 98–130 cm long. Length at sexual maturity 2.2–2.35 m (female), 2.45–2.6 m (male).

VARIATION

Coastal and offshore populations often differ in size, and there are also geographical variations in external pigmentation.

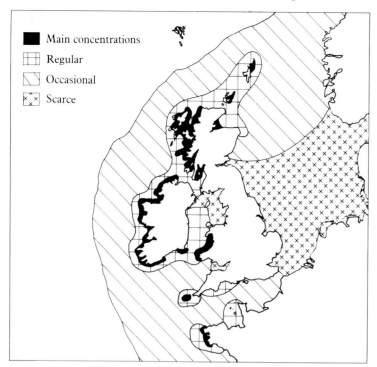

Map 9.8. Bottle-nosed dolphin.

Fig. 9.18. Bottle-nosed dolphin.

DISTRIBUTION

World-wide in mainly coastal waters, but with (possibly separate) offshore populations. In NE Atlantic, locally common in S Europe, with small populations in scattered localities in bays and estuaries around Britain and Ireland (mainly west and north). Most important concentrations appear to be on west coast of Ireland (for example Galway and Clew Bays), in Cardigan Bay (Dyfed), and in Cromarty and Moray Firths (NE Scotland) [1, 34, 40]. Although once amongst the commonest of inshore cetacean species in Britain and Ireland, this species has declined in the last 20 years, particularly in the southern North Sea and English Channel [1, 40].

Essentially an inshore species with most sightings from within 10 km of land, although may also occur in offshore waters, often associated with other cetaceans, notably pilot whales. Most sightings occur in July to September although the species has been seen in most months [40]. A possible offshore movement between December and February, although some populations more or less resident [1, 40] as found elsewhere in Europe (France and Portugal) [31, 64].

SOCIAL ORGANISATION AND BEHAVIOUR

Sightings are usually either of single individuals or small groups of up to 25 animals [1, 40]. Sometimes, probably in association with rich concentrations of food, these may combine to form large aggregations of up to 1000 individuals, although this has been seen only off the Atlantic coast of Ireland. The social structure has been studied intensively in a number of geographical regions, and groups of the following composition recognised: females with calves; subadult males; adult females; and, less commonly, subadult females; and adult males. Group membership may change from day to day although long term (up to at least 8 years) affiliations also occur, involving particularly mother and calf or females with other adults. Captive studies indicate a dominance hierarchy system with dominance displayed in form of jaw claps, biting, ramming or tailslaps against subordinates. In the wild, also displayed by positioning within group, mothers and small calves occupying the centre. Attentive and helpful towards young and wounded, and adult females ('aunts') may remain with unrelated calves whilst their mother is away feeding.

Home range of group in Florida was *c.* 85 km², but smaller for individuals, varying with age and sex. Females with calves had largest ranges (*c.* 40 km² followed by subadult males, adult males, adult females (without calves), and subadult females (between 15 and 20 km²) [123]. Home-range size and social structure can vary geographically, with some individuals (Argentina) moving 300 km before returning to original location [125]. Inshore groups tend to have definable home ranges that may be used over extended periods in some cases to 6+ years [31, 64].

Generally slower swimmer (*c.* 4 km/hour) than smaller dolphins, though can attain speeds briefly of 54 km/hour [79]. Offshore groups often associate with pilot whale herds. Often bow-ride moving vessels or even large whales. Frequently engage in aerial breaching, particularly during feeding activities, and sometimes remain vertical for short periods with head above surface [1, 31].

Vocalisations intensively studied and include short barks (0.2–16 kHz), a variety of whistles between 2 and 20 kHz, and echolocation clicks of 0.1–30 kHz frequency.

FEEDING
Diet consists of wide variety of fish including particularly *Mugil*, but also *Anguilla*, *Engraulis*, *Phoxinus* and *Alosa* (coastal), and *Micromesistius*, *Trisopterus*, *Sardina*, *Clupea*, *Gadus* and *Scomber* (offshore), squid (for example *Loligo* — mainly offshore) and cuttlefish (*Sepia* — coastal) [22, 28, 31, 117].

Tends to feed singly or in small groups either semi-independently or sometimes cooperatively, herding fish schools into tight concentrations close to water surface, sometimes even throwing fish onto the beach [31].

BREEDING
Births over an extended period but with a peak in March to May, and possibly a second one in August to September. Gestation period *c.* 12(−13) months. Lactation period *c.* 19 months. Calving interval probably mainly 2−3 years. Age at sexual maturity *c.* 11 years (males) and *c.* 12 months.

POPULATION
Longevity *c.* 25 years [108]. Sex ratio (male : female) usually *c.* 1.0 (though obviously varies within segregated groups).

PARASITES/COMMENSALS
Frequently infested with nematode worms (notably *Anisakis simplex*, *Crassicauda* sp.) [28] in gut, middle ear and other cavities. Oval or circular scars on skin caused by lampreys or remoras.

RELATIONS WITH MAN
The best known and most widely exhibited of all dolphins in aquaria. Wild, lone individuals sometimes associate with bathers and small vessels. Coastal populations face threats of inshore pollution with high levels of DDT, PCBs and heavy metals in specimens from western Mediterranean [119] and accidental drowning in fishing nets [1, 92].

GENUS *Lagenorhynchus*

A widespread genus with six species, two of which occur in European waters.

Atlantic white-sided dolphin
Lagenorhynchus acutus

Delphinus (Grampus) acutus Gray, 1846; Orkney.

RECOGNITION
Similar in appearance to white-beaked dolphin. Large robust dolphin (Fig. 9.19) with short beak, black back and distinctive long white patch on flanks extending backwards as narrow yellow-ochre band. Large often erect sickle-shaped dorsal fin, centrally placed. Skull distinguished from that of white-beaked dolphin by having more numerous

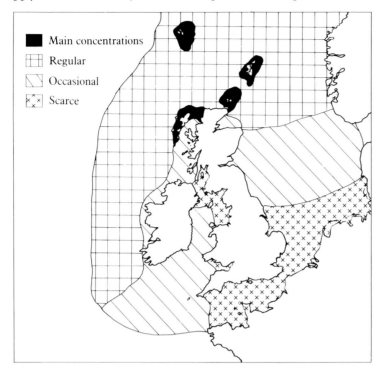

Map 9.9. Atlantic white-sided dolphin.

Fig. 9.19. Atlantic white-sided dolphin.

DESCRIPTION

Stout torpedo-shaped body, rounded snout with short black beak (*c.* 5 mm long), 29–40 pairs of small (*c.* 5 mm diameter), sharp-pointed teeth in each jaw. Coloration black on back, dark grey flanks but with long white oval blaze from below dorsal fin (not extending over back as often in white-beaked dolphin) to area above anus; an elongated yellow-ochre band extends backwards from upper edge of white blaze towards tail, white and smaller teeth. Also no bony bridge between pterygoid and squamosal in skull.

belly. Pointed black sickle-shaped flippers with narrow dark stripe extending from angle of mouth to flipper insertion. Also, black eye patch from which a thin line extends forward to the dark rostrum, though neither of these features are easy to see in the wild. Centrally placed sickle-shaped dorsal fin, relatively tall and more erect in adult males. Very thick tail stock narrowing close to slightly notched tail flukes with strongly concave trailing edge.

MEASUREMENTS

Length *c.* 2.25 m (female), 2.5 m (male). Weight

c. 165 kg. Newborn young *c.* 110 cm long. Length at sexual maturity 2.0–2.2 m (female), 2.3–2.4 m (male).

DISTRIBUTION

Restricted to northern North Atlantic, in mainly offshore waters from central West Greenland, Iceland and southern Barents Sea south to Cape Cod and SW Ireland. Less common than white-beaked dolphin in coastal waters of Britain and Ireland, though nevertheless reasonably abundant. Although concentrated in North Scottish waters (including northern North Sea) extends down the Atlantic seaboard to SW Britain and Ireland [34, 40].

Not particularly coastal but will occur within 10 km of land. Numbers are greatest between August and October with very few records in winter when there is a possible offshore movement [34, 40].

SOCIAL ORGANISATION AND BEHAVIOUR

Most sightings in British and Irish waters are of groups of less than ten individuals but some herds number 50–100 individuals, particularly offshore [34, 40]. Elsewhere, groups of up to 1000 animals have been recorded. Groups are of mixed age and both sexes, possibly with some age segregation, immatures and young adults largely absent from breeding groups. Otherwise, social structure poorly known.

Fast swimmer which only occasionally bow-rides. Engages in breaching activities but not to extent of white-beaked, bottle-nosed or common dolphins. Sometimes associates with pilot whales.

Vocalisations include whistles of 8–12 kHz frequency and echolocation clicks.

FEEDING

Diet consists of variety of fish (including *Micromesistius, Clupea, Gadus, Scomber, Merlangius, Osmerus, Trisopterus* and *Merluccius*), squid (*Loligo*) and gammarid crustaceans [1, 28, 34, 54, 113, 121].

BREEDING

Births mainly in early summer (May–July) [34, 40, 51, 109]. Breeding areas not known precisely but sightings data suggest they are offshore in northern North Sea and in Atlantic to north and west of there. Gestation period 10–12 months. Lactation period *c.* 18 months. Calving interval

possibly 2–3 years. Age at sexual maturity uncertain but limited data suggest 4–6 years (male) and 5–8 years (female) [109].

POPULATION

Longevity *c.* 27 years.

PARASITES/COMMENSALS

Internal parasites include nematode worms *Anisakis simplex* (stomach) and cestodes *Monorygma grimaldii*) (abdominal, peritoneum and testes), *Phyllobothrium* sp. (abdominal blubber), and *Pseudalius inflexus* (bronchi and lungs) [28, 58, 121].

RELATIONS WITH MAN

Not hunted commercially though taken opportunistically by small whale fisheries (for example Faroe Islands), which previously killed numbers in coastal drives in W Norway.

White-beaked dolphin *Lagenorhynchus albirostris*

Lagenorhynchus albirostris Gray, 1846; Great Yarmouth, England.

RECOGNITION

Large stout dolphin (Fig. 9.20) with short beak (often white in colour), black back, except behind dorsal fin where pale grey to white area extends from flanks; also grey to white oblique blaze on flanks forward of dorsal fin. Large, often erect, sickle-shaped dorsal fin, centrally placed. Skull distinguished from white-sided dolphin by having fewer and larger teeth. A bridge of bone stretches from pterygoid to squamosal, though frequently lost during maceration.

DESCRIPTION

Very stout torpedo-shaped body with rounded snout and short light grey or white beak (though poor identification feature because it is not always easy to see and may, in fact, sometimes be absent). In each jaw, 22–28 pairs of small (*c.* 6 mm diameter), sharp-pointed teeth. Dark flippers broad at base and pointed at tip. Coloration dark grey or black over most of back but pale grey to white area over dorsal surface behind fin (less distinct in young animals), commonly dark grey to white blaze from near dorsal surface behind eye, across flanks and downwards to anal area. Sometimes has

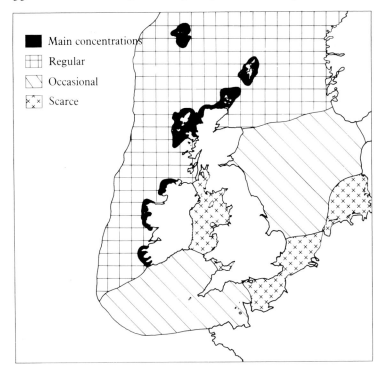

Map 9.10. White-beaked dolphin.

Fig. 9.20. White-beaked dolphin.

dark flecks behind eyes and a dark grey stripe between angle of mouth and flipper insertion. Centrally placed, tall sickle-shaped dorsal fin which is more erect in adult males. Very thick tail stock and dark, slightly notched tail flukes with concave trailing edge.

MEASUREMENTS
Length *c.* 2.5–2.7 m (male slightly larger than female). Weight *c.* 180 kg. Newborn young *c.* 120 cm.

DISTRIBUTION
Restricted to northern North Atlantic, from central W Greenland, Greenland Sea and the southern Barents Sea south to Newfoundland, Cape Cod, and SW Ireland. Common in British and Irish waters, with a similar distribution to white-sided dolphin though less pelagic and apparently more abundant at least in coastal waters [34, 40]. Distribution centred mainly upon the North Sea (mainly in the north but extending down towards Netherlands coast), N and NW Scotland and ex-

tending southwards towards SW Britain and Ireland [34, 40].

Although recorded in most months, most sightings are in summer, particularly August [34, 40]. There appears to be an inshore movement at this time, probably associated with concentrations of food fishes in those areas [40].

SOCIAL ORGANISATION AND BEHAVIOUR

Most groups are of less than 10 individuals but herds of 30 to 50 not uncommon and there are a few sightings of groups of 100 to 500 animals off NW Scotland. Social structure presently being studied but still poorly known. Herds apparently of mixed age and both sexes.

Moderately fast swimmer. Frequently approaches boats and bow-rides. Often breaches clear of water, particularly during feeding activities.

FEEDING

Diet consists of variety of fish (*Clupea*, *Gadus*, *Scomber*, *Merlangius*, *Trisopterus*, *Melanogrammus*, *Pleuronectes*, *Limanda*, *Eleginus* and *Hyperoplus*), squid and octopus, and benthic crustaceans [1, 34, 54, 113].

Engages in cooperative herding of food fishes, bunching fish shoals into tight clusters and then trapping them at water surface [1, 37].

BREEDING

Births mainly in late spring to summer (May to August) [34, 40, 51]. Breeding grounds not known but sightings of small young suggest that they are offshore in northern North Sea, and north and west in Atlantic. Gestation period probably *c*. 10 months. Lactation period and calving interval unknown.

POPULATION

No data.

RELATIONS WITH MAN

Not hunted commercially, though taken opportunistically in small whale fisheries (for example, Faroe Islands) and previously in Norwegian coastal fishery. Small numbers drown accidentally in drift nets set for cod, salmon or herring (mainly off coast of NE England, E Scotland and W Ireland) [1, 93].

GENUS *Peponocephala*

Contains a single species.

Melon-headed whale *Peponocephala electra*

Lagenorhynchus electra Gray, 1846; North Pacific.

RECOGNITION

Almost all black, form slender. Triangular-shaped head with rounded forehead but very indistinct beak and often white lips. Centrally-placed sickle-shaped dorsal fin. Skull resembles those of members of genus *Lagenorhynchus* with similar number of small pointed teeth, but with a more rounded cranium, much larger antorbital arches, and a much shorter tooth row relative to the total length of the rostrum. There are also other small differences in the skulls of the two genera.

DESCRIPTION

Slender torpedo-shaped body with triangular-shaped head and rounded forehead, and slightly underslung jaw presenting a very indistinct beak. On each side of each jaw 21–25 small, sharply-pointed teeth. Coloration almost all black but with paler belly, particularly around anus and genital region, and lips often white. Indistinct pale grey anchor-shaped throat patch, and sometimes indistinct downward-pointing darker triangle below dorsal fin; in the face tapers towards the eyes. Long, black narrow tapered flippers. Slender tail stock. Tall centrally-placed sickle-shaped dorsal fin.

MEASUREMENTS

Length *c*. 2.3–2.7 m (males slightly larger than females). Weight *c*. 160 kg. Size of newborn young somewhere between 65 cm (largest fetus) and 112 cm (smallest individual recorded) [17].

DISTRIBUTION

This very poorly-known species has an apparently world-wide distribution, in offshore tropical and subtropical waters. In the North Atlantic it has been recorded from deep waters near St Vincent, and off Senegal and in the Gulf of Guinea. However, a skull from Charlestown, Cornwall (September 1949), previously identified as *Lagenorhynchus albirostris* [14] has been re-examined recently and found to be *Peponocephala electra* [87A]. This represents not only the first record for Britain but also for Europe.

SOCIAL ORGANISATION AND BEHAVIOUR

Little information, but group sizes often very large, between 150 to 1500 individuals. Social organisation not known, but groups examined have included animals of both sexes and varying ages.

Relatively inconspicuous at sea, the species has been recorded swimming just under the surface with dorsal fins exposed, occasionally coming above the surface sufficiently to expose the head and upper body. On diving, the tail stock is strongly arched. Like pilot whales, the species may sometimes spy-hop with head above the water.

FEEDING

Diet unknown but dentition suggests small fish and squid [75].

BREEDING

Season poorly-known but conceptions and calving thought to occur around June—August, with a gestation period of *c.* 12 months [17, 27, 91]. Lactation period unknown. Males mature somewhere between 3 to 7 years (= dentinal/cemental growth layers); females between 4 to 12 years (growth layers) [17].

POPULATION

Longevity up to 47 years (growth layers) [17].

PARASITES

No information.

RELATIONS WITH MAN

Rarely encountered by humans, but when a herd of *c.* 500 animals came into Suruga Bay, Japan in March 1965, half of these were driven ashore and consumed [91]; in 1980, a further 200 animals were trapped in Taiji Bay. Four animals were landed in the small whale fishery on St Vincent, Lesser Antilles [18]. A male calf was caught in a tuna net off Guatemala, eastern tropical Pacific [100]. Specimens from a mass-stranding in eastern Australia in 1973 were used as bait in lobster pots [16].

GENUS *Pseudorca*

Contains a single species.

False killer whale *Pseudorca crassidens*

Phocaena crassidens Owen, 1846; Lincolnshire Fens (subfossil).

RECOGNITION

Almost all black, form slender. No beak. Small slender, tapered head with snout projecting beyond extremity of lower jaw. Tall, sickle-shaped dorsal fin, centrally placed. Skull with large teeth somewhat smaller proportionately than those of killer whale and circular in cross-section (Fig. 9.21).

DESCRIPTION

Long slender body with small tapered head and underslung jaw, which contains 8–11 pairs of large (25 mm diameter) teeth, circular in cross-section. Coloration all black except for a blaze of grey (variable from indistinct to nearly white) on belly near flippers. Sometimes also light grey area on sides of face. Black, narrow tapered flippers (onetenth of body length) with broad hump on front margin near middle. Tall (to 40 cm), sickle-shaped (rounded to sharply pointed) dorsal fin just behind midpoint of back.

MEASUREMENTS

Length *c.* 4.5 m (female), *c.* 5.4 m (male). Weight

Fig. 9.21. False killer whale.

c. 1200–2000 kg. Newborn young *c.* 193 cm long. Length at sexual maturity *c.* 3.6–4.3 m (female), *c.* 3.9–4.6 m (male).

DISTRIBUTION

World-wide, but mainly in tropical and warm temperate offshore waters. In NE Atlantic, only occasional north of the British Isles. Indeed, in Britain and Ireland, strandings were confined to a few mass strandings: in 1927 (*c.* 150 at Dornoch Firth, NE Scotland); 1934 (*c.* 25 in S Wales); 1935 (*c.* 75 in S Wales). There have been no strandings since 1935 [51, 111]. Being pelagic, usually occurring in deep waters off the continental shelf edge, the species has rarely been observed at sea. There are four sightings since 1976, at between 5 and 54 km from land, two off W Scotland, one south of Cornwall towards the French coast, and the fourth off NE Scotland [1, 40]. The first three involve single individuals but the last sighting was of a herd of 100–150 animals. All sightings were between July and November.

SOCIAL ORGANISATION AND BEHAVIOUR

Mass strandings and observations at sea suggest the species may form large herds up to *c.* 300 animals, though groups of 10 to 30 individuals are more commonly recorded. Herds are of mixed age and both sexes.

Very fast swimmer up to 30 knots, and very manoeuvrable. May breach clear of water and may bow-ride vessels.

FEEDING

Diet primarily consists of squid and large fish (for example *Seriola*, *Thunnus*) though has been known to prey on dolphins (*Stenella*, *Delphinus*), for example during tropical E Pacific tuna purse seine fishery.

BREEDING

Season apparently protracted with no obvious calving peak. Gestation period 15.5 months (but possibly down to 11). Lactation period uncertain, but previously estimated at 6 months with calving interval of 3 years. Sexual maturity at *c.* 8–14 years (both sexes) [101, 102].

POPULATION

Longevity 30–40 years [101, 102]. Age structure possibly indicates fairly high immature mortality rate.

PARASITES/COMMENSALS

Scars caused by shark-suckers (*Remora*), a commensal fish, are frequently found on the body.

RELATIONS WITH MAN

Kept as display and performing animal in many dolphinaria.

GENUS *Orcinus*

Contains only one species.

Killer whale *Orcinus orca*

Delphinus orca Linnaeus, 1758; European seas.

Orca, grampus.

RECOGNITION

Striking black and white pattern (white patch above and behind eye, large white patch extending from belly to flanks, and less distinct pale grey saddle behind dorsal fin). Tall, triangular or sickle-shaped dorsal fin, centrally placed. Broad, rounded flippers. Teeth large, pointed and anterio-posteriorly compressed.

DESCRIPTION

Powerfully built robust torpedo-shaped body with conical-shaped head, and indistinct beak (Fig. 9.22). Ten to 13 pairs of large conical teeth. Coloration very striking black on back and sides, white belly extending as a rear-pointing lobe up the flanks and less markedly at head and around throat, chin and undersides of flippers, and a distinctive, conspicuous white oval patch above and behind eye. Indistinct grey saddle over back behind dorsal fin. Large rounded, paddle-shaped flippers and centrally placed conspicuous dorsal fin, sickle shaped in adult female and immatures, but very tall (to 1.8 m high) and erect (triangular, sometimes tilted forwards) in adult male. Tail flukes black above, white below with shallow median notch and concave trailing edge.

MEASUREMENTS

Length 5.6–5.7 m (female), *c.* 9.4–9.5 m (male). Weight 2500–3000 kg in female and 4000–5000 kg in male. Newborn young 208–220 cm long. Length at sexual maturity *c.* 4.5–4.9 m (female), *c.* 5.7–5.8 m (male).

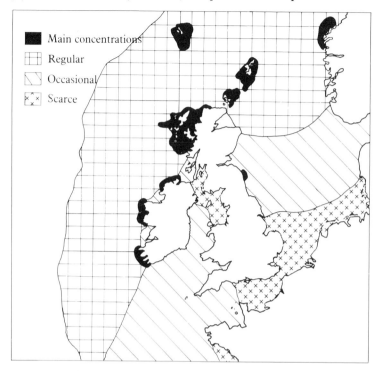

Main concentrations
Regular
Occasional
Scarce

Map 9.11. Killer whale.

Fig. 9.22. Killer whale.

VARIATION
Geographical differences observed in size, shape and position of lateral markings [41].

DISTRIBUTION
World-wide from tropical to polar seas. In NE Atlantic, apparently most numerous around Iceland, Faroes, and in localised regions off W

Norway. Although widely distributed in small numbers in British and Irish waters, mainly occur along the Atlantic seaboard and in the northern North Sea [38, 40]. The species is rare or absent from the southern North Sea and English Channel. Sightings occur in all months, but in coastal waters the species is mainly found between April and September. There is some evidence of an offshore movement, possibly associated with mating/calving in late autumn and winter [38, 40].

SOCIAL ORGANISATION AND BEHAVIOUR
Sightings in British and Irish waters are mainly of single individuals or small herds numbering less than eight individuals, although one group sighted in the northern North Sea numbered 80 to 100 animals [38, 40]. Elsewhere, herds commonly number up to 40, and sometimes over 100, though these probably represent temporary coalitions. Social structure has been intensively studied along Pacific coast of Washington and British Columbia [8, 11]. They indicate a matriarchal system with basic social unit being mothers with their calves, those groups usually including immatures of both sexes and one or more adult males which are probably either polygynous or promiscuous. Other groups may comprise only immature males or adult males. Single animals are mainly subadults and adult males [11, 38, 63]. It has been suggested that these groups form extended family units; certainly members have been shown to remain within the group (or pod as often termed) for many years [8]. Other evidence that pods remain stable from one generation to the next comes from presence of distinct vocal dialects between groups (even in localised area), with sharing of sounds only when pods have split up as group size increases [45, 46]. These results apply to resident herds but smaller transient herds with migratory nature also observed in the region [8, 11].

Resident killer whale pods apparently maintain communal territories with large home ranges that may extend for 320−480 km, and even within a single day can be 120−160 km [9]. No particular diurnal pattern of behaviour observed but foraging activities related to tidal cycle, and amounted to 53% of time. 20% of time spent in playful foraging; 13% in more obvious play; 12% in rest or sleep; 2% in intermingling behaviour [13, 96, 97].

Fast swimmer, travelling at 14−22 km per hour but can attain speeds of 50 km per hour.

Vocalisations well studied and include a variety of whistles of variable duration mainly of 6−12 kHz frequency, a pulsed call primarily in frequency range 1−6 kHz, and very short echolocation clicks mainly of 12−40 kHz.

FEEDING
Very varied diet including fish, squid, marine mammals and even occasionally turtles and birds [34, 38, 75, 78, 117, 124]. Fish species include *Salmo*, *Clupea*, *Gadus*, *Scomber*, *Pleurogrammus*, *Hippoglossus*, *Sardinella* and *Sarda*. Marine mammals include minke whale, humpback whale, long-finned pilot whale, harbour porpoise and various seal species including grey seal. Auks and kittiwakes have also been taken by killer whales in Faroese waters. Squid include members of Loliginidae (for example, *Loligo*).

Often use tidal rips in which to capture salmon, cooperatively herding them into tight clusters, at the same time breaching, lobtailing and slapping the water with their flippers [25, 62, 67, 80]. Cooperative feeding upon a grey seal also seen off N Scotland, with adult male making the kill then moving aside for remaining herd members to feed [34].

BREEDING
Births probably mainly in late autumn and winter (October to January) and may be associated with offshore movement at this time [38, 40]. Fetal lengths from Norwegian specimens suggest that mating peaks around October to November [20, 21]. Precise breeding areas not known. Gestation period *c.* 12 (possibly up to 16) months. Lactation period unknown, but at least 12 months. Calving interval at least 3, maybe sometimes up to 8−9 years. Age at sexual maturity 15−16 years in male, 8−10 years in female [11, 20, 21, 69].

POPULATION
Longevity 50+ years in male and 80+ years in female [37]. Individuals of up to 35 years estimated age found off Norway [20]. Annual mortality estimates uncertain but suggest relatively low rate, perhaps 2.8% in male and as low as 0.7% in female [11].

RELATIONS WITH MAN
Hunted opportunistically in eastern Canadian Arctic, W Greenland and the Faroes (in latter case using similar driving methods as used on pilot whales). Commercial catches primarily by Norway both in coastal waters and offshore. Total catch between 1938 and 1981 was 2455 whales [65, 66]. A live capture fishery also has been conducted sporadically off Iceland since 1975, with animals going into dolphinaria [26]. Sometimes perceived as fisheries threat to herring, halibut, tuna and salmon, but no evidence for any serious effects on fisheries.

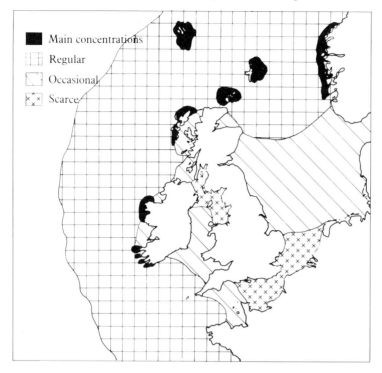

Map 9.12. Long-finned pilot whale.

Fig. 9.23. Long-finned pilot whale.

GENUS *Globicephala*

Two closely related species, only one of which occurs in British and Irish waters, the other being of tropical to warm temperate distribution.

Long-finned pilot whale *Globicephala melas*

Delphinus melas Traill, 1809; Scapa Bay, Orkney.
Globicephala melaena Thomas, 1898.

Pilot whale, blackfish, caaing whale, pothead whale.

RECOGNITION
Black or dark grey medium-sized whale (Fig. 9.23)

with square bulbous head and low dorsal fin, sickle-shaped in subadults and females and flag-shaped in adult males, situated slightly forward of centre of back. Long slender flippers. Male larger than female. Skull similar in shape but differing from that of killer and false killer by having much smaller teeth.

DESCRIPTION
Long, slender body becoming more robust with age, with square bulbous head, particularly in old males, slightly protruding upper lip. In each jaw, 8 to 12 pairs of small (less than 13 mm diameter) peglike teeth. Flippers long (to one-fifth body length, i.e. much longer than in false killer), pointed and sickle-shaped. Coloration black or dark

grey on back and flanks with anchor-shaped patch of greyish white on chin and grey area on belly, both variable in extent and intensity (lighter in younger individuals). Some older animals have grey saddle behind dorsal fin. Fairly low dorsal fin, slightly forwards of midpoint, with long base, sickle-shaped (in adult females and immatures) to flag-shaped (in adult males), usually black but sometimes grey. With changing shape of dorsal fin as animal grows older, form of dorsal fin becomes more rounded and less dolphin-like. Thick keel on tail stock. Tail flukes have concave trailing edge and are deeply notched in centre.

MEASUREMENTS

Length *c.* 4.0–5.0 (6.0) m (female), *c.* 5.5–6.0 (8.5) m (male). Weight *c.* 1800–2500 kg in female, 3000–3500 kg in male. Newborn young *c.* 175–178 cm long, weighing 60–80 kg. Length at sexual maturity *c.* 3.0–4.0 m (female), *c.* 5.0 m (male).

VARIATION

Northern and southern hemisphere populations show some morphological variation and are recognised as different subspecies, separated by the tropical short-finned pilot whale *Globicephala macrorhynchus*. Variation in dorsal fin shape and isozyme frequencies suggest that there may be restricted gene flow between certain pods [6].

DISTRIBUTION

Widespread in temperate regions of world, in mainly offshore waters. Common and widely distributed in NE Atlantic from the Iberian Peninsula to the Faroes and Iceland and common in Mediterranean. In British and Irish waters, it is the most commonly observed whale species [34, 40]. There is evidence from both sightings and strandings data that the species increased substantially in the region in 1970s and early 1980s though with an apparent decline since then [39, 41]. Though mainly pelagic, pilot whales are seen in all coastal areas except the southernmost part of the North Sea [40]. The coastal populations are greatest in northern Britain, in NW and N Scotland, and along the continental shelf edge west of Ireland. The species is common in the northern North Sea southward to the central sector.

Sightings occur in all months of the year, but numbers in coastal waters are highest between September and January, possibly associated with an autumn onshore movement following their prey [40]. Sightings offshore from weather ships, 700 km

west of Scotland, show lowest numbers over this period.

SOCIAL ORGANISATION AND BEHAVIOUR

Gregarious with herds of 20–40 commonly recorded and sometimes these may number in the hundreds or even low thousands (though probably representing temporary coalitions of social groups) [34, 40]. Examination of specimens from mass-strandings and coastal drive fisheries have yielded information on herd structure [82, 84, 107]. Most groups comprise females with calves, immatures and one or more adult males. Sex ratio of groups often biased in favour of females. Mating system assumed to be polygynous; otherwise probably promiscuous. Adult male often positions himself between a vessel approaching a herd and females with young.

Relatively slow swimmer, travelling at *c.* 5–15 km/hour, though may attain speeds of *c.* 40 km/hour. Rarely bow-ride although may allow boats to approach. Usually move through water in undemonstrative manner, scarcely ever breaching clear of water (generally only young animals), though may slap surface with tail. Frequently lie vertically in water with head and top of flippers above surface. On occasions observed resting motionless on surface. Dolphins (mainly bottle-nosed and Atlantic white-sided) may associate with pilot whale herds.

Vocalisations include variety of whistles mainly between 3.4–4.7 kHz of between 0.65 and 1.0 second duration, and echolocation clicks of between 0.1 and 100 kHz frequency.

FEEDING

Mainly squid (notably *Todarodes*, but also *Ommastrephes*, *Gonatus*) but also variety of fish (*Gadus*, *Scomber*, *Pollachius*, *Molva*, *Dicentrarchus*, *Conger*, *Anguilla*, *Merluccius* and *Trisopterus*) [22, 28, 29, 34].

BREEDING

No distinct breeding season although some evidence for slight peak in births in late winter to early spring (January to March) [40, 84]. Further north in Faroe islands, conceptions peak between April and July whilst births occur most often between July and September [82] though differences may only reflect variation between pods. Gestation period *c.* 14–16 months. Lactation period *c.* 22 months. Calving interval 3–4 years. Various estimates of age at sexual maturity: 10–12 years (male) and 6–7 years (female) for shore drive specimens from Newfoundland [107]; 9–14 years (male) and *c.* 7 years (female) from British mass-strandings [84]; and 15–20 years (male) and 9–10 years (female) for shore drive specimens in Faroe islands [82].

POPULATION

Longevity at least 20 years (male) and 25 years (female), possibly higher due to difficulty in reading dentine layers in teeth of older animals [84]. Life span estimates elsewhere are between 40–50 years [107]. Although segregation of sexes in herds may possibly occur, skewed sex ratios (*c.* 60% females) suggest higher annual mortality rate for males than for females.

PARASITES/COMMENSALS

Recently studied intensively in 125 Faroese specimens [105], where 15 species recorded: two crustacean species (*Isocyamus delphini* — common; *Xenobalanus globicipitis* — rare) on skin, either around natural openings, wounds (former) or on edge of dorsal fin and flukes (latter); three trematode species (mainly *Pholeter gastrophilus*, also *Leucasiella* sp., and rarely *Odhneriella* sp. in stomach and intestine); four cestodes (*Trigonocotyle* sp., *Phyllobothrium delphini*, *Diphyllobothrium* sp., *Monorygma grimaldii*) either within blubber or in intestine; five nematodes (mainly *Anisakis simplex* and three *Stenurus* spp., also *Crassicauda* sp.) in gut (*Anisakis*), lungs, air sinuses, and tympanic bullae (*Stenurus* spp.), and within mammary glands (*Crassicauda* sp.); one acanthocephalan species (*Bolbosa* sp.) in intestine.

RELATIONS WITH MAN

Organised drives have taken place for at least 11 centuries in the Faroe islands, where they continue to present day. Other drive fisheries have operated in an opportunistic manner mainly in Shetland and Orkney, but also in Outer Hebrides and W Ireland, until the early part of present century. Between 1947 and 1972, there was also an extensive coastal drive pilot whale fishery in Newfoundland, Canada. Otherwise, small numbers have been taken by the coastal Norwegian small whale fishery, off W Greenland and Iceland.

Relatively high levels (up to 95 ppm wet weight in blubber) of PCBs have been found in stranded animals in Britain [84] and up to 995 ppm PCBs in an immature from western Mediterranean [4]. High levels of DDT and mercury also recorded from Faroese specimens [76, 90].

GENUS *Grampus*

Contains only one species.

Risso's dolphin *Grampus griseus*

Delphinus griseus Cuvier, 1812; Brest, France.
Grampus cuvieri Gray, 1846; Isle of Wight, England.

RECOGNITION

Robust large dolphin (Fig. 9.24) with blunt, rounded head, slight melon but no beak, greyish colour (whitening with age) often with numerous, white scars on flanks, and tall sickle-shaped dorsal fin in midpoint of back. Few teeth, all in lower jaw.

DESCRIPTION

Stout torpedo-shaped body narrowing behind dorsal fin to quite narrow tail stock, blunt snout, rounded with slight melon and no beak. Deep, V-shaped furrow present in area of forehead, seen only at close range. Two to seven (but usually four) peglike teeth at tip of each lower jaw, often badly worn and sometimes lost; no teeth in upper jaw. Coloration dark to light grey on back and flanks, palest in older individuals so that head may be pure white; many conspicuous white scars on flanks of adults; white belly enlarging to oval or anchor-shaped patch on chest and chin (cf. pilot whale). Newborn young are overall light grey changing to chocolate brown as juveniles. Long (one-sixth body length), pointed flippers usually dark in colour. Tall centrally placed sickle-shaped dorsal fin (taller, more erect in adult males), dark in colour but may lighten with age, particularly along leading edge. Dark tail flukes with median notch and concave trailing edge.

MEASUREMENTS

Length *c.* 3.3–3.8 m (male slightly larger than female). Weight 350–400 kg. Newborn young *c.* 150 cm long.

DISTRIBUTION

World-wide in tropical to temperate waters of all seas. In NE Atlantic reaches northern limits of its range in Northern Isles of Scotland. Widely distrib-

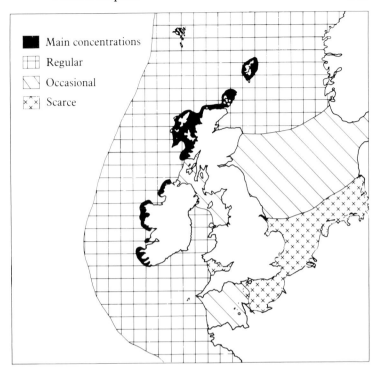

Map 9.13. Risso's dolphin.

Legend:
- ■ Main concentrations
- ⊞ Regular
- ◨ Occasional
- ⊠ Scarce

Fig. 9.24. Risso's dolphin.

uted in coastal waters of Britain and Ireland, primarily on Atlantic seaboard but also in northern North Sea [34, 40]. Rare in English Channel and rare or absent from central and southern North Sea. Most sightings come from within 10 km of the coast although the species probably occurs regularly in deeper offshore waters, as noted elsewhere in its range. The species is nowhere common but is seen most frequently in the summer months, particularly August and September, when there may be a movement towards the coast.

SOCIAL ORGANISATION AND BEHAVIOUR
Most sightings are of less than 10 individuals although herds of between 10 and 30 individuals are not uncommon and one herd of 50 animals was

recorded in June [34, 40]. Long-term studies of recognisable individuals in NW Scotland suggest the species forms very stable groups which occupy the same areas from one summer to the next (over at least 3 years) [1, 40]. Groups commonly comprise a mature male, four to six females and young of both sexes. Mating system is probably polygynous and adults observed to spar with one another, possibly competing for mates. Such aggressive activities may give rise to some of body scars frequently found on flanks and around head [1, 40].

Young animals may breach repeatedly clear of water (as if in play), but this activity becomes rare in older animals though they will slap water surface with flippers, tail flukes or sides of body [1]. Commonly remain vertical in water with head exposed above surface, similar to pilot whales. Do not bow-ride. Sometimes associate with pilot whales.

Usually fairly slow swimmer, travelling at *c.* 10–12 km/hour but when frightened, can speed at 20–25 km/hour [1].

Vocalisations little studied but include a variety of whistles, buzzes and grunts as well as high frequency echolocation clicks.

FEEDING

Diet primarily squid (*Todarodes, Loligo, Gonatus, Histioteuthis*), octopus (*Eledone*), cuttlefish (*Sepia*) and sepiolids (*Rossia, Sepietta*), but also sometimes fish (*Gadus*) [23, 28, 32, 126].

BREEDING

Sightings of small juveniles and fetal records from strandings suggest that births are mainly in early spring–summer (March to June) [34, 40, 51]. Reproductive parameters poorly known with no data on gestation and lactation periods, or age at sexual maturity. Suspected hybrids of mating with bottle-nosed dolphin found on Irish coast [48], and hybrid calf of the two species successfully produced in captivity in Japan.

PARASITES/COMMENSALS

Internal parasites include the cestode *Monorygma grimaldii* and nematodes *Stenurus* sp. and *Crassicauda* sp. [28].

RELATIONS WITH MAN

Not hunted commercially though occasionally drown accidentally in fishing gear. Measurement of mercury levels of stranded animal indicated more than 50% of mercury in liver and kidney in inorganic form, suggesting species can detoxify organic mercury [126]. Sometimes kept in dolphinaria.

AUTHOR FOR THIS CHAPTER
P.G.H. Evans.

REFERENCES

1 Author's data.
2 Aguilar A. (1981) The black right whale, *Eubalaena glacialis*, in the Cantabrian Sea. *Report of International Whaling Commission* **31**:457–9.
3 Aguilar A. *et al.* (1983) Report of the 'Ballena 1' whale marking and sighting cruise in the waters off western Spain. *Report of the International Whaling Commission* **33**:649–55.

4 Alzieu C. & Duguy R. (1979) Teneurs en composes organochlores chez les cétacés et pinnipèdes frequentant les côtes françaises. *Oceanologia Acta* **2**(1): 107–20.
5 Andersen S.H. & Clausen B. (1985) Bycatches of the harbour porpoise *Phocoena phocoena* in Danish waters 1980–1981, and evidence for overexploitation. *International Whaling Commission* SC/32/35/SM14:1–8.
6 Andersen L.W. (1988) Genetic differences among local populations of the long-finned pilot whale, *Globicephala melaena*, off the Faroe Islands and its karyotype. In Evans, P.G.H. ed. *European research on Cetaceans.* Proceedings of 2nd Annual Conference of European Cetacean Society, Troia, Portugal, 5–7 February 1988.
7 Balbuena J.A. *et al.* (1987) Some data on parasites of the harbour porpoise *Phocoena phocoena* in French Atlantic waters. In Broekema J.W. & Smeenk C. eds. *The European Cetacean Society Report of the 1987 Meeting,* Hirtshals, Denmark, 26–28 January 1987 pp. 56–8.
8 Balcomb K.C. & Bigg M.A. (1986) Population biology of the three resident killer whale pods in Puget Sound and off Southern Vancouver Island. In Kirkevold B.C. & Lockard J.S. eds. *Behavioral biology of killer whales.* New York: Alan R. Liss pp. 85–95.
9 Balcomb K.C. *et al.* (1980) *Observations of killer whales* (Orcinus orca) *in greater Puget Sound, state of Washington.* U.S. Department of Commerce, NTIS PB80–224728.
10 Benjaminsen T. & Christensen I. (1979) The natural history of the bottlenose whale *Hyperoodon ampullatus.* In Winn, H.E. & Olla B.L. eds., *Behavior of marine animals, Vol. 3: Cetaceans,* New York: Plenum pp. 143–64.
11 Bigg M.A. (1982) An assessment of killer whale (*Orcinus orca*) stocks off Vancouver Island, British Columbia. *Report of International Whaling Commission* **32**:655–66.
12 Bonner W.N. (1980) *Whales.* Poole: Blandford Press 278 pp.
13 Boran J.R. *et al.* (1981) Habitat use of Puget Sound killer whales (Abstract). In Proceedings of 4th Biennial Conference on the Biology of Marine Mammals, Dec 14–18, 1981, San Francisco, CA.
14 Brown S.G. (1976) Modern whaling in Britain and the north-east Atlantic Ocean. *Mammal Review* **6**: 25–36.
15 Bruton T. & Greer J. (1985) Euphrosyne dolphin *Stenella coeruleoalba* (Meyen). *Irish Naturalists' Journal* **21**:538–40.
16 Bryden M.M. *et al.* (1977) Melon-headed whale, *Peponocephala electra*, on the east coast of Australia. *Journal of Mammalogy* **58**:180–7.
17 Bryden M.M. *et al.* (1977) Some aspects of the biology of *Peponocephala electra* (Cetacea: Delphinidae). *Australian Journal of Marine and Freshwater Research* **28**:703–15.

18 Caldwell D.K. *et al.* (1976) First records for Fraser's dolphin (*Lagenodelphis hosei*) in the Atlantic, and the melon-headed whale (*Peponocephala electra*) in the western Atlantic. *Cetology* 25:1–4.

19 Christensen I. (1973) Age determination, age distribution and growth of bottlenose whales, *Hyperoodon ampullatus* (Forster), in the Labrador Sea. *Norwegian Journal of Zoology* 21:331–40.

20 Christensen I. (1982) Killer whales in Norwegian coastal waters. *Report of International Whaling Commission* 32:633–42.

21 Christensen I. (1984). Growth and reproduction of killer whales, *Orcinus orca*, in Norwegian coastal waters. *Report of International Whaling Commission* (special issue 6):253–8.

22 Clarke M.R. (1986) Cephalopods in the diet of odontocetes. In Bryden M.M. & Harrison R.J. eds. *Research on dolphins.* Oxford: Clarendon Press pp. 281–322.

23 Clarke M.R. & Pascoe P.L. (1985) The stomach contents of a Risso's dolphin (*Grampus griseus*) stranded at Thurlestone, South Devon. *Journal of Marine Biological Association UK* 65:663–5.

24 Collet A. (1981) *Biologie du dauphin commun Delphinus delphis L. en Atlantique Nord-Est.* PhD. thesis, University of Poitiers, Poitiers.

25 Condy P.R. *et al.* (1978) The seasonal occurrence and behaviour of killer whales *Orcinus orca*, at Marion Island. *Journal of Zoology* 184:449–64.

26 Dahlheim M.E. (1981) A review of the biology and exploitation of the killer whale, *Orcinus orca*, with comments on recent sightings from Antarctica. *Report of International Whaling Commission* 31: 541–6.

27 Dawbin W.H. *et al.* (1970) Observations on the Electra Dolphin *Peponocephala electra. Bulletin British Museum (Natural History) Zoology* 20: 173–201.

28 Desportes G. (1985) *La nutrition des odontocetes en Atlantique Nord-Est.* PhD. thesis, University of Poitiers, Poitiers.

29 Desportes G. (1988) Preliminary results on the diet of the pilot whale exploited off the Faroe Islands. In Evans P.G.H. ed. *European research on Cetaceans.* Proceedings of 2nd Annual Conference of the European Cetacean Society, Troia, Portugal, 5–7 February, 1988, pp. 59–63.

30 Dorsey E.M. (1983) Exclusive adjoining ranges in individually identified minke whales (*Balaenoptera acutorostrata*) in Washington state. *Canadian Journal of Zoology* 61:174–81.

31 dos Santos M.E. & Lacerda M. (1987) Preliminary observations of the bottlenose dolphin (*Tursiops truncatus*) in the Sado estuary (Portugal). *Aquatic Mammals* 13:65–80.

32 Eggleton J. (1905) The occurrence of Risso's Dolphin, *Grampus griseus* Cuv., in the Forth. *Transactions of Natural History Society of Glasgow* 7: 253–7.

33 Evans P.G.H. (1976) An analysis of sightings of Cetacea in British waters. *Mammal Review* 6:5–14.

34 Evans P.G.H. (1980) Cetaceans in British waters. *Mammal Review* 10:1–52.

35 Evans P.G.H. ed. (1981) *Report of NE Atlantic scientific cruise, 1981.* Occasional publication, Mammal Society, London.

36 Evans P.G.H. (1982) *Guide to identifications of cetaceans in the North east Atlantic.* London: The Mammal Society.

37 Evans P.G.H. (1987) *The natural history of whales and dolphins.* Bromley: Christopher Helm 360 pp.

38 Evans P.G.H. (1988) Killer whales (*Orcinus orca*) in British and Irish waters. *Rit Fiskideildar* 11:42–54.

39 Evans P.G.H. & Sheldrick M.C. (in prep.) Status changes of the long-finned pilot whale (*Globicephala melaena*) in British and Irish waters.

40 Evans P.G.H. *et al.* (1986) *Analysis of cetacean sightings in the British Isles, 1958–1985,* Unpublished report to Nature Conservancy Council, Peterborough, 71 pp.

41 Evans W.E. *et al.* (1982) Geographic variation in the color pattern of killer whales (*Orcinus orca*). *Report International Whaling Commission* 32:687–94.

42 Fairley J.S. (1981) *Irish whales and whaling.* Dublin: Blackstaff Press 218 pp.

43 Falconer C.R. *et al.* (1983) Trace elements in the common porpoise *Phocoena phocoena* in the North Atlantic. *Journal of Zoology* 161:471–86.

44 Fisher H.D. & Harrison R.J. (1970) Reproduction in the common porpoise (*Phocoena phocoena*) of the North Atlantic. *Journal of Zoology* 161:471–86.

45 Ford J.K.B. & Fisher H.D. (1982) Killer whale (*Orcinus orca*) dialects as an indicator of stocks in British Columbia. *Report of International Whaling Commission* 32:671–9.

46 Ford J.K.B. & Fisher H.D. (1983) Group-specific dialects of killer whales (*Orcinus orca*) in British Columbia. In Payne R. ed., *Communication and behavior of whales,* AAA Selected Symposium 76, Boulder, Colorado: Westview Press pp. 129–61.

47 Fraser F.C. (1934) *Report on cetacea stranded on the British coasts from 1927 to 1932,* No. 11. London: British Museum (Natural History) 41 pp., 6 maps.

48 Fraser F.C. (1940) Three anomalous dolphins from Blacksod Bay, Ireland. *Proceedings of Royal Irish Academy (B)* 45:413–55.

49 Fraser F.C. (1946) *Report on cetacea stranded on the British coasts from 1933 to 1937,* No. 12. London: British Museum (Natural History) 56 pp., 7 maps.

50 Fraser F.C. (1953) *Report on cetacea stranded on the British coasts from 1938 to 1947,* No. 13. London: British Museum (Natural History) 48 pp., 9 maps.

51 Fraser F.C. (1974) *Report on cetacea stranded on the British coasts from 1948 to 1966,* No. 14. London: British Museum (Natural History) 65 pp., 9 maps.

52 Fraser F.C. (1976) *British whales, dolphins and porpoises/A guide for the identification and reporting of stranded whales.* London: British Museum (Natural History) 34 pp.

53 Fraser F.C. & Noble B.A. (1970) Variations of

pigmentation pattern in Meyen's Dolphin, *Stenella coeruleoalba* (Meyen). *Investigations on Cetacea* 2: 147–63.

54 Gaskin D.E. (1982) *The ecology of whales and dolphins.* London: Heinemann, 459 pp.

55 Gaskin D.E. & Blair B.A. (1977) Age determination of harbour porpoise, *Phocoena phocoena* (L.), in the western North Atlantic *Canadian Journal of Zoology* 55:18–30.

56 Gaskin D.E. & Watson A.P. (1985) The harbor porpoise, *Phocoena phocoena*, in Fish Harbour, New Brunswick, Canada: occupancy, distribution, and movements. *Fishery Bulletin, US* 83:427–42.

57 Gaskin D.E. *et al.* (1975) Preliminary study of movements of harbour porpoises (*Phocoena phocoena*) in the Bay of Fundy using radiotelemetry. *Canadian Journal of Zoology* 53:1466–71.

58 Gibson D.I. & Harris E.A. (1979) The helminth parasites of cetaceans in the collection of the British Museum (Natural History). *Investigations on Cetacea* 10:309–24.

59 Hancock J. (1965) Killer whales kill and eat a minke whale. *Journal of Mammalogy* 46:341–2.

60 Harmer S.F. (1914) *Report on cetacea stranded on the British coasts.* London: British Museum (Natural History) 12 pp.

61 Harmer S.F. (1927) *Report on cetacea stranded on the British coasts from 1913 to 1926,* No. 10. London: British Museum (Natural History) 91 pp.

62 Heimlich-Boran J.R. (1986) Fishery correlations with the occurrence of killer whales in Greater Puget Sound. In Kirkevold B.C. & Lockard J.S. eds. *Behavioral biology of killer whales.* New York: Alan R. Liss pp. 113–31.

63 Heimlich-Boran S.L. (1986) Cohesive relationships among Puget Sound killer whales. In Kirkevold B.C. & Lockard J.S. eds. *Behavioral biology of killer whales.* New York: Alan R. Liss pp. 251–84.

64 Hussenot E. (1980) Le grand dauphin *Tursiops truncatus* en Bretagne: types de frequentation. *Penn ar Bed* 12:355–80.

65 International Whaling Commission (1982) *Thirty-third report of the International Whaling Commission.* Cambridge: International Whaling Commission.

66 International Whaling Commission (1987) *Report of the Meeting on North Atlantic Killer Whales.* International Whaling Commission SC/39/SM 18.

67 Jacobsen J.K. (1986) The behavior of *Orcinus orca* in the Johnstone Strait, British Columbia. In Kirkevold B.C. & Lockard J.S. eds. *Behavioral biology of killer whales.* New York: Alan R. Liss pp. 135–85.

68 Joiris C. *et al.* (1987) Contamination by stable pollutants (organochlorines and heavy metals) of a common dolphin *Delphinus delphis* found dying in Belgium. In Broekema J.W. & Smeenk C. eds. *The European cetacean society Report of the 1987 Meeting, Hirtshals, Denmark, 26–28 January 1987* pp. 30–1.

69 Jonsgard A. & Lyshoel P.B. (1970) A contribution to the knowledge of the biology of the killer whale

Orcinus orca (L.). *Norwegian Journal of Zoology* 18:41–8.

70 Kinze C.C. (1985) Intraspecific variation in Baltic and North Sea porpoises. *Videnskabelige Meddelelser fra Dansk Naturhistorisk Forening* 146:63–74.

71 Kinze C.C. (1987) Hvad ved vi om marsvinet? Økologisk status over Danmarks truede ynglehval. *Kaskelot* 75:14–23.

72 Kinze C.C. (1988) Studies on behaviour and ecology of the harbour porpoise (*Phocoena phocoena*): preliminary results from a series of sighting cruises in Danish waters, April–August 1987. In Evans P.G.H. ed. *European research on cetaceans.* Proceedings of 2nd Annual Conference of European Cetacean Society, Troia, Portugal, 5–7 February 1988, pp. 91–7.

73 Koeman J.H. *et al.* (1972) Persistent chemicals in marine mammals. *TNO-nieuws* 27:570–8.

74 Lambertson R.H. (1986) Disease of the common fin whale (*Balaenoptera physalus*): crassicaudiosis of the urinary system. *Journal of Mammalogy* 67:353–66.

75 Leatherwood S. *et al.* (1983) *Sierra Club handbook of whales and dolphins.* San Francisco: Sierra Club Books 302 pp.

76 Lehman J.W. & Peterle T.J. (1971) DDT in Cetacea. *Investigations in Cetacea* 3:349–51.

77 Lockyer C.H. Personal communication in Evans P.G.H. (1987).

78 Lockyer C.H. & Martin A.R. (1983) The sei whale off western Iceland. II. Age, growth and reproduction. *Report of International Whaling Commission* 33:465–76.

79 Lockyer C.H. & Morris R. (1987). Observations on diving behaviour and swimming speeds in a wild juvenile *Tursiops truncatus. Aquatic Mammals* 13: 27–30.

80 Lopez J.C. & Lopez D. (1985) Killer whales (*Orcinus orcinus*) of Patagonia, and their behavior of intentional stranding while hunting inshore. *Journal of Mammalogy* 66:181–3.

81 Magnaghi L. & Podesta M. (1987) An accidental catch of 8 striped dolphins, *Stenella coeruleoalba* (Meyen, 1833), in the Ligurian Sea. *Atti Societa Italiana di Scienze Naturali Museo Civico Storia Naturale Milano* 128:235–9.

82 Martin A.R. & Desportes G. (1988) Preliminary studies of pilot whales from Faroese waters since 1986: Reproduction and foetal growth. In Evans P.G.H. ed. *European research on cetaceans.* Proceedings of 2nd Annual Conference of European Cetacean Society, Troia, Portugal, 5–7 February 1988, p. 52.

83 Martin A.R. *et al.* (1984) Migration of humpback whales between the Caribbean and Iceland. *Journal of Mammalogy* 65:333–6.

84 Martin A.R. *et al.* (1987) Aspects of the biology of pilot whales (*Globicephala melaena*) in recent mass strandings on the British coast. *Journal of Zoology* 211:11–23.

85 Martins H.R. *et al.* (1985) A pygmy sperm whale, *Kogia breviceps* (Blainville, 1838) (Cetacea:

Odontoceti) stranded on Faial Island, Azores, with notes on cephalopod beaks in stomach. *Ciencias Biologicas* 63–70.

86 Maul G.E. & Sergeant D.E. (1977) New cetacean records from Madeira. *Bocagiana* 43:1–8.

87 Mead J.G. (1984) Survey of reproductive data for the beaked whales (Ziphiidae). *Report of International Whaling Commission* (special issue 6):91–6.

87 Mikkelsen A.M. & Sheldrick M. Personal com-
A munication.

88 Miyazaki N. (1984) Further analyses of reproduction in the striped dolphin, *Stenella coeruleoalba*, off the Pacific coast of Japan. *Report of International Whaling Commission* (special issue 6):343–53.

89 Møhl-Hansen U. (1954) Investigations on repro-
duction and growth of the porpoise (*Phocaena phocaena* (L.)) from the Baltic. *Videnskabelige Meddelelser fra Danske naturhistorisk Forening i København* 116:369–96.

90 Natural Environment Research Council (1983). Contaminants in marine top predators. *NERC Publications. Series C* 23:1–30.

91 Nishiwaki M. & Norris K. (1966) A new genus *Peponocephala*. *Scientific Report, Whales Research Institue* 20: 95–100.

92 Northridge S. (1984) *World review of interactions between marine mammals and fisheries*. FAO Fisheries Technical Paper 251. Rome: Food and Agriculture Organization, 190 pp.

93 Northridge S. (1987) *Interactions between marine mammals and fisheries in Britain*. London: Unpubl. report to Wildlife Link.

94 O'Riordan C.E. (1972) Provisional list of cetacea and turtles stranded or captured on the Irish coast. *Proceedings of Royal Irish Academy* 72B:253–74.

95 O'Riordan C.E. & Bruton T. (1986) Notes on the crania of the Euphrosyne Dolphin *Stenella coeruleoalba* (Meyen) in the collections of the National Museum of Ireland. *Irish Naturalists' Journal* 22: 162–3.

96 Osborne R.W. (1981) Social behavior of Puget Sound killer whales; sequencing, budgeting and circadian independence (Abstract). *Proceedings of 4th Biennial Conference on the Biology of Marine Mammals*, Dec 14–18, 1981, San Francisco, CA.

97 Osborne R.W. (1986) A behavioral budget of Puget Sound killer whales. In Kirkevold B.C. and Lockard J.S. eds. *Behavioral biology of killer whales*. New York: Alan R. Liss pp. 211–49.

98 Otterlind G. (1976) The harbour porpoise (*Phocoena phocoena*) endangered in Swedish waters. *International Council for Exploration of the Sea*, Doc. C.M. 1976/N:16: 1–7.

99 Pascoe P.L. (1986) Size data and stomach contents of common dolphins, *Delphinus delphis*, near Plymouth. *Journal of Marine Biological Association, UK* 66:319–22.

100 Perrin W.F. (1976) First record of the melon-headed whale, *Peponocephala electra*, in the eastern Pacific, with a summary of world distribution. *Fisheries Bulletin* 74:457–8.

101 Purves P.E. (1977) Order Cetacea. Whales, dolphins and porpoises. In Corbet G.B. & Southern H.N. eds. *The handbook of British mammals*. Oxford: Blackwell pp. 266–309.

102 Purves P.E. & Pilleri G. (1978) The functional anatomy and general biology of *Pseudorca crassidens* (Owen) with a review of the hydrodynamics and acoustics in Cetacea. *Investigations on Cetacea* 9: 67–227.

103 Rae B.B. (1965) The food of the common porpoise. *Journal of Zoology* 146:114–22.

104 Rae B.B. (1973) Additional notes on the food of the common porpoise (*Phocoena phocoena*). *Journal of Zoology* 169:127–31.

105 Raga J.A. *et al.* (1988) Preliminary Report on para-
sitological research on pilot whales in the Faroe Islands. In Evans P.G.H. ed. *European research on cetaceans*. Proceedings of 2nd Annual Conference of European Cetacean Society, Troia, Portugal, 5–7 February 1988, pp. 65–7.

106 Sanpera C. *et al.* (1984) Report of the 'Ballena 2' whale marking and sighting cruise in the Atlantic waters off Spain. *Report of the International Whaling Commission* 34:663–6.

107 Sergeant D.E. (1962) The biology of the pilot or pothead whale *Globicephala melaena* (Traill) in Newfoundland waters. *Bulletin of Fisheries Research Board of Canada* 132:1–84.

108 Sergeant D.E. *et al.* (1973) Age, growth and maturity of bottlenosed dolphin (*Tursiops truncatus*) from northeast Florida. *Journal of Fisheries Research Board of Canada* 30:1009–11.

109 Sergeant D.E. *et al.* (1980) Life history and northwest Atlantic status of the Atlantic white-sided dolphin, *Lagenorhynchus acutus*. *Cetology* 37:1–12.

110 Sheldrick M.C. (1976) Trends in the strandings of Cetacea on the British coasts. *Mammal Review* 6: 15–23.

111 Sheldrick M.C. (1979) Cetacean strandings along the coasts of the British Isles 1913–1977. In Geraci J.R. & St. Aubin D.J. eds, *Biology of marine mammals: insights through strandings*. Washington DC: US Marine Mammal Commission pp. 35–53.

112 Smeenk C. (1987) The harbour porpoise *Phocoena phocoena* (L., 1758) in the Netherlands: stranding records and decline. *Lutra* 30:77–90.

113 Smeenk C. & Gaemers P.A.M. (1987) Fish oto-
liths in the stomachs of white-beaked dolphins *Lagenorhynchus albirostris*. In Broekema J.W. & Smeenk C. eds. *The European Cetacean Society Report of the 1987 Meeting, Hirtshals, Denmark, 26–28 January 1987* pp. 12–13.

114 Smet W.M.A. de (1981) Evidence of whaling in the North Sea and English Channel during the Middle Ages. *FAO Fisheries Series (5) [Mammals in the Seas]* 3:301–10.

115 Taylor W. (1913) Risso's Dolphin in the Moray Firth. *Scottish Naturalist* 1913:40–1.

116 Thompson D'A.W. (1928) On whales landed at the

Scottish whaling stations during the years 1908–1914 and 1920–1927. *Scientific Investigations, Fishery Board of Scotland* **3**:1–40.

117 Tomilin A.G. (1967) *Mammals of the USSR and adjacent countries*. Vol. 9. *Cetacea*. Jerusalem: Israel Program for Scientific Translations, 717 pp.

118 van Utrecht W.L. (1978) Age and growth in *Phocoena phocoena* Linnaeus, 1758 (Cetacea, Odontoceti) from the North Sea. *Bijdragen tot de Dierkunde* **48**:16–28.

119 Viale D. (1978) Evidence of metal pollution in cetacea of the western Mediterranean. *Annales Institut oceanographique, Paris* **54**:5–16.

120 Viney M. Personal communication.

121 Waller G.H. & Tyler N.J.C. (1979) Observations on *Lagenorhynchus acutus* stranded on the Yorkshire coast. *The Naturalist* **104**:61–4.

122 Watson A.P. (1976) *The diurnal behaviour of the harbour porpoise* (Phocoena phocoena *L.*) *in the coastal waters of the Bay of Fundy*. Ontario: MSc. thesis, University of Guelph.

123 Wells R.S. *et al.* (1980) The social ecology of inshore odontocetes. In Herman L.M. ed. *Cetacean behavior*. New York: Wiley Interscience pp. 263–318.

124 Whitehead H. & Glass C. (1985) Orcas (killer whales) attack humpback whales. *Journal of Mammalogy* **66**:183–5.

125 Wursig B. & Wursig M. (1979) Behavior and ecology of bottlenose porpoises, *Tursiops truncatus*, in the South Atlantic. *Fisheries Bulletin, U.S.* **77**:399–442.

126 Zonfrillo B. *et al.* (1988) Notes on a Risso's dolphin from Argyll, with analyses of its stomach contents and mercury levels. *Glasgow Naturalist* **1988**:297–303.

Chapter 10 / Carnivores:
Order Carnivora

INTRODUCTION

This order includes most of the truly carnivorous mammals — predators feeding predominantly on vertebrate prey. World-wide it includes seven families and about 240 species. All the species in Britain are indeed carnivorous except for the badger. The pinnipeds (seals, sealions) are sometimes included in the order Carnivora but they are also sometimes treated as a separate order and that course is followed here.

Carnivores vary enormously in outward form, from the tiny sinuous weasels to the heavy lumbering bears. The dentition is characterised by enlarged conical canine teeth and by the specialisation of one upper and one lower cheek-teeth on each side (p^4 and M_1) for cutting and shearing — the carnassial teeth. The articulation of the jaw allows little movement other than direct opening and closing. Most species have a characteristic technique of hunting — pouncing and snapping with the long jaws in the case of the fox; pouncing and striking with the paws and sharp, retractile claws in the cat; fast pursuit in confined spaces in the case of the weasel and stoat. However, most carnivores are very adaptable with regard to the species of prey taken, being able to concentrate on species that are temporarily or locally abundant.

Eight indigenous species occur in Britain, a further two (wolf and brown bear) have been exterminated in historic times whilst one introduction, the American mink, is well established. Most of the native species have suffered severely from exploitation for fur and persecution in the interests of game preservation. However, all but the otter are now either widespread or expanding their range.

Our carnivores belong to four families, if the extinct bear is included: Canidae (fox, wolf), Ursidae (bears), Mustelidae (weasel, marten, badger, otter, etc.) and Felidae (cats). However, if they are clearly seen all species are individually distinctive and easily recognised by superficial appearance. Any problems of identification arise within the Mustelidae and are dealt with under that family.

FAMILY CANIDAE (DOGS)

A clear-cut family with a world-wide distribution and about 38 species including the wolves, jackals and foxes. The members of the family are described in [82]. In general they are long-legged and cursorial, hunting their prey largely by sight and mainly in open country. The muzzle is long and the canine and carnassial teeth well developed. Now represented in Britain by only the fox (and domestic dogs) but formerly also by the wolf (p. 573).

GENUS *Vulpes*

A widespread genus comprising about 12 species of foxes; for a recent review of classification see reference [82]. They are distributed throughout the N hemisphere and S Africa, and introduced to Australia. Most are adapted to open habitats — the sole species in Britain probably frequents woodland to a greater extent than any other species. Dental formula 3.1.4.2 / 3.1.4.3, although 3rd molar vestigial and often absent [596].

Fox *Vulpes vulpes*

Canis vulpes Linnaeus 1758; Sweden.
Canis crucigera Bechstein 1789; Germany.

Tod.
Male — dog; female — vixen; young — cub.

RECOGNITION
Conspicuous characters are the erect, black-backed ears, slender muzzle, long horizontally held bushy tail, white muzzle, usually white bib of throat and often white tail tip, and the black socks and ears (Fig. 10.1).

Fig. 10.1. Fox.

Skull dog-like but narrower (Fig. 10.2), with more sharply pointed, prominent, slender canine teeth; the concavity of the upper surfaces of the post-orbital processes distinguishes it readily from that of dog.

SIGN

Footprints with four toes on fore and hind feet readily observed in mud or snow. In soft mud, hairs between toes may register, especially in winter when fur thicker. Typically print is more oval in shape than in most small dogs, with the two centrally placed toes extending well ahead of others. Forefoot larger (5 cm long, 3–4 cm wide) than hind foot, which is more slender. When walking or trotting, overprinting of fore prints by hind feet usually occurs, and may sometimes give mistaken impression of five toes being in contact with ground. The prints of a trotting fox form a straighter line than those of a dog, although this is not an infallible identification. When walking, prints are about 30 cm apart; when galloping, groups of prints can be up to 250 cm apart. Runs through hedges smaller than those of badger, and larger than brown hare and without the jump pattern of the latter. Regular passage through hedges, rusty fences, bramble patches, under chestnut palings, etc., can usually be recognised by hairs adhering to snags.

Faeces variable according to food; if much indigestible remnants, e.g. fur or feathers, usually pointed and may be linked together by hairs; length 5–20 cm. When fresh, usually black with characteristic odour. Faeces containing fur or feather may persist for several months after small inclusions have been leached. In absence of indigestible hard parts, faeces may be indistinguishable from dogs', except, if fresh, by odour. Faeces often deposited on prominent objects — stones, fallen branches, molehills. Other scent stations, which occur where drops of urine have been sprinkled on prominent objects, even long stalks of grass, can be detected by smell. At all times of year wind-borne characteristic smell of fox may be detected but apparently not by everyone.

Dens occupied by cubs indicated by unconsumed food remnants inside and outside den. Outside breeding season, use of dens erratic and, except in the worst weather, foxes will lie out above ground in thick cover. Even in breeding season, vixen progressively spends less time below ground with cubs. In winter, many earths or disused rabbit burrows may be 'cleaned out' with fresh soil in evidence, and possibly with strong smell of fox in earth, but this is not indicative of occupancy of the earth. May share sett with badgers, sometimes emerging from same entrance.

Cached food items, buried singly, may be found. Eggs frequently cached and cached food often buried with legs or wings projecting [165].

Other signs of foxes are the characteristic vocalisations, most frequently heard during rut, and indications of kills. Primary wing feathers sheared close to bases are indicative of fox. Manner of killing and subsequent treatment also often characteristic (in lambs, teeth marks over shoulder and crushed cervical vertebrae) and lambs and poultry often decapitated, heads sometimes buried. Gap

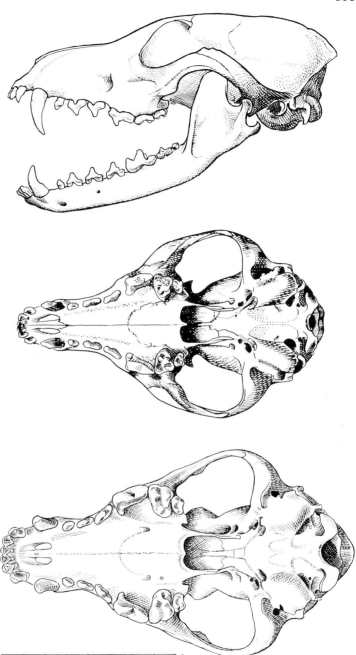

Fig. 10.2. Skulls of fox (top and centre) and dog (bottom). Note the wider muzzle and more crowded teeth of the dog, although some foxes also have crowded teeth.

between upper canines 30 mm, between lower canines 26 mm, equivalent to that of a medium-sized dog [661] and so cannot be used as sole evidence of fox predation. Skins of mammals, such as rabbits and hedgehogs, picked clean and turned inside out; similar signs also left by badgers. At night fox eyes highly reflective, blue/white when viewed head-on, but pink when not looking directly at light source. Eye shine difficult to distinguish from that of domestic cat.

DESCRIPTION

Pelage: overall colour yellow-brown, but much variation from sandy colour to (rarely) henna red. White foxes with normal coloured eyes and albinos have been reported very rarely; melanic forms common in North America, where called black, silver or cross foxes, depending on degree of blackness, but very rarely observed in Britain. Guard hairs composed of black, yellow-brown and white bands, but much variation in proportions of these according to parts of body. Underfur grey. The backs of ears, socks and sometimes the entire leading edge of the limb, usually black, but black on limbs may be much reduced; also a black stripe from eye to muzzle; lips and nose dark brown; the belly may be white, pale or deep slate grey; there is no age distinction. The tail is less colourful than the shoulders and back, with a white tip that may be conspicuous or reduced to a few white hairs; white tag is not confined to dog foxes. Caudal scent gland usually marked by a conspicuous black patch. Mandible, upper lips and throat white. White flecking may occur throughout pelage, even in juveniles. Pads naked, but much interdigital fur. Scrotum covered in cream-coloured hair, which is usually lost during the rut. Belly fur of vixens, and to a lesser extent dog foxes, assumes pinkish tinge in March–April, and in vixens may be brick red during lactation. Many colour mutants bred commercially; genetics of fox coat colours described in [605].

Moult: two moulting periods, but only that of spring is clearly visible. During autumn moult only fine hair growth takes place and this thickens the summer coat [509]. From April onwards, significant loss of guard and fine hairs; at end April new coat appears on extremities of legs and progresses dorsally. At end of June summer coat covers legs, abdomen and flanks; elsewhere guard hairs still being shed. Finally reaches tail late August to early September. In October and November further growth of fine hairs, again in ventro-dorsal direction. Moult coincides with seasonal decrease in testicular endocrine function and seasonal hyperthyroidism [507].

Anatomy: eyes blue until 4 weeks old, thereafter yellow; pupil, when contracted, a vertical slit. Nictitating membrane present but only moves when eye is closed. Fox has binocular vision. Vibrissae on snout black, with a total span of 255–280 mm; also shorter vibrissae on underside of lower jaw and elsewhere on head, and also on forelimbs just above the dew claw. Five digits on forefeet, but only four in contact with ground; four on hind feet, which lack a dew claw. Seasonal changes in thymus gland in [704].

Scent glands: paired anal sacs on either side of anus and each opening through a single duct; the two openings are clearly visible on the circumanal skin. Lined by sebaceous glands. Anal sac acts as fermentation chamber in which aerobic and anaerobic bacteria convert sebum into aliphatic acids and other odorous compounds [8, 10]. Caudal gland about 75 mm from root of tail on dorsal side; gland oval in shape, 25 mm long, 13 mm wide. Reported to smell of violets. Evidence of increased secretory activity in males during spermatogenesis, which may tie in with reported steroid metabolising properties [7, 9, 478]. Presence of foot glands equivocal; interdigital cavities deep, have reddish tinge to skin, strong smell and heavily glandular [478], but difficult to decide if the feet have a scent-marking function [456]. Skin of angle of jaw and mandible richly endowed with sebaceous glands, and this maxillary gland may be important in females foxes in the rut [478].

Skull of adult males and females differentiated in about 70% of cases by prominent sagittal crest in male. Skulls of males up to 10 months old resemble females in this respect. Frontal silhouette of head and ears has been used to identify sex in the field [53]. Sequence and timing of closure of cranial sutures described by Churcher and by Harris [76, 268]. Sequence and timing of eruption of permanent teeth described by Harris [268].

Reproductive tract: testes scrotal at all times, but with marked (six-fold) seasonal increase in testicular size associated with spermatogenic activity [268, 508]. Cowper's gland and seminal vesicles absent; prostate gland not large. Primitive bicornuate uterus with direct continuity between two horns; ovaries in bursa. Vulva swollen and often pinkish at oestrus; corpora lutea large and persistent throughout pregnancy. Placenta zonary, endotheliochorial, with prominent lateral haematomata. Placental scars persist from birth to next oestrus, and can be used to estimate litter size. Embryos visible at 20 days as delicate streak of cells within fetal membranes, and can be aged from 33 days by weight or crown-rump length [456].

Nipples: usually four pairs, but some variation, and seven, nine or 10 not uncommon.

Chromosomes: 2n = 34 [767].

RELATIONSHIPS
Considered conspecific with *V. fulva* of N America. [75]. Although the type species of the genus, using a numerical taxonomy it was found to bear a rather low similarity to the rest of the foxes on all characters [82]. By this means *V. bengalensis* considered to be the species most similar to *V. vulpes*.

MEASUREMENTS
Body measurements Table 10.1. Males slightly larger than females (ratio approximately 1.2 : 1) but considerable overlap and not reliable as a means of identifying sex. There are seasonal variations of body weight [456], and of fat deposits [272A, 406].

Suggestions that foxes from Scotland should be regarded as a distinct subspecies or race [293, 679] on basis of larger size not accepted. Skull measurements in Table 10.2. Multivariate analysis used to show sex differences in skull measurements [342].

VARIATION
British foxes formerly ascribed to subspecies *V. v. crucigera* Bechstein 1789 (Thuringia, Germany); this subspecies was said to be slightly smaller, with distinctly smaller teeth, and the premolars widely spaced and seldom, if ever, in contact [519]. However, many British skulls can show a high degree of tooth compaction, particularly in some populations [1]. Continuity of range of red fox is such that it is doubtful whether any discrete, definable subspecies can be recognised [92].

Northern animals in Europe and N America have larger white tip to tail and longer coat than southern animals. In Scotland, foxes become larger from south to north and this variation is independent of the climate, prey taken or productivity of

Table 10.1. Body measurements of British foxes.

	England [293]				Scotland [404]			
	Males (*n* = 34−41)		Females (*n* = 31−35)		Males (*n* = 39)		Females (*n* = 30)	
	Mean	Range	Mean	Range	Mean	Range	Mean	Range
Head and body (mm)	671	600−755	627	570−700	712	659−750	679	574−732
Tail (mm)	412	375−470	385	335−420	436	388−493	411	277−491
Hind foot (mm)	152	135−170	141	125−150	167	143−178	159	143−168
Ear (mm)	93	85−100	89	90−95	96	87−106	94	89−102
Weight (kg)	6.7	5.5−8.2	5.4	3.5−6.7	7.3	5.7−9.3	6.2	4.2−7.8

	Wales [456]				Northern Ireland [191]			
	Males (*n* = 50; weight *n* = 463)		Females (*n* = 50; weight *n* = 610)		Males (*n* = 42; weight *n* = 207)		Females (*n* = 42; weight *n* = 281)	
	Mean	Range	Mean	Range	Mean	Range	Mean	Range
Head and body (mm)	666	570−747	622	560−730	723	635−777	677	614−744
Tail (mm)	411	350−465	380	330−420	367	222−429	348	289−410
Hind foot (mm)	154	130−172	142	130−155	161	109−173	151	134−166
Ear (mm)	90	83−102	86	82−98	104	94−113	99	56−110
Weight (kg)	6.4	−	5.5	−	6.9	4.0−9.2	5.8	4.0−6.9

Table 10.2. Skull measurements (mm) of British foxes [456].

	SE England				Wales			
	Males (*n* = 16)		Females (*n* = 12)		Males (*n* = 10)		Females (*n* = 10)	
	Mean	Range	Mean	Range	Mean	Range	Mean	Range
Condylobasal length	144.7	137.8−152.8	136.2	129.6−141.1	146.4	135.4−154.0	136.0	132.2−139.8
Zygomatic width	84.1	79.7−90.7	78.5	74.8−81.8	82.0	75.9−86.5	76.1	70.3−80.0
Inter-orbital width	31.3	27.9−34.5	28.9	27.4−31.4	29.8	27.2−35.0	27.6	24.6−30.2
Post-orbital width	21.4	18.6−24.2	21.9	18.3−24.6	22.4	18.5−27.9	21.9	20.5−24.1
Mandible length	112.2	104.6−117.2	105.2	99.8−109.8	112.6	103.1−119.0	104.5	100.8−108.8
Length mandibular tooth row	78.3	74.3−81.8	73.4	69.5−75.9	79.0	74.4−84.0	74.2	72.5−77.3
Length of upper tooth row	76.6	73.0−83.8	72.2	67.3−77.4	77.9	71.4−83.0	72.8	71.2−75.0

areas in which each population lives; suggested that N−S cline in size is the result of increased hunting hours at higher latitudes during winter [400]. Hill foxes of Westmorland said to be larger than lowland foxes, but opposite tendency in Wales. Using material from Israel, foxes were found to increase in size towards the end of the Pleistocene, with a reduction in size thereafter [114, 115]. Geographical variation in cranial measurements of red fox populations from six counties in Wales described [344]; comparative figures for Irish skulls described [197].

Non-metrical variation has been described [637], but genetic polymorphisms not described from British foxes. Syndactyly with two different genetic origins described [265], and three cases with a 3rd genetic origin reported from vixens caught at the same earth in different years [1]. Sporadic individuals lack guard hairs locally (often only on tail) or completely, giving a woolly appearance; called 'Samson' foxes.

DISTRIBUTION
Present throughout most of N hemisphere. Introduced from Britain to E USA in mid-18th century, from whence spread westward and interbred with native stocks, and to Australia about 1850 [436].

Almost ubiquitous on British mainland and in Ireland; absent or uncommon until recently in many parts of Norfolk, and coastal areas of

Aberdeenshire, Nairn and Moray [315]. However, in recent years a general increase in areas where previously rare. Common in many urban areas in S England and parts of Scotland [282, 484], and spread into those areas in the late 1930s/1940s to

Map 10.1. Fox.

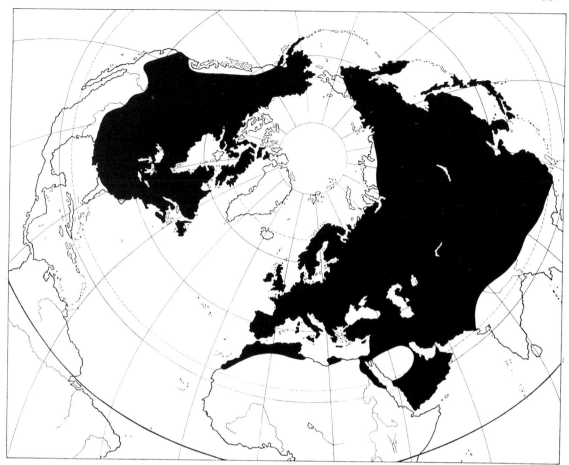

Map 10.2. Fox (also introduced into Australia).

colonise the new low-density residential suburbs [277, 282]. Occurs at over 1300 m in Cairngorms. Absent from all Scottish islands except Skye (present some years on Scalpay). Absent from Anglesey until 1962. Absent from Scilly Isles and Channel Isles; until recently absent from Isle of Man but several reliable reports and extensive debate in Manx press in 1988 suggest that a recent illegal introduction may have occurred; whether foxes have or will become established on the island is unknown at present.

HISTORY
Antecedent of red fox probably *Vulpes alopecoides*, which appeared in middle Villafranchian [429]. *V. vulpes* found in middle Pleistocene deposits 400 000 years old; foxes were probably an important food item for Neolithic hunters.

Bounty payments recorded in churchwardens' accounts in 1700s and first half of 1800s, suggest foxes were uncommon [456]. In latter part of the 19th century foxes were introduced from Europe to reinforce local populations for hunting [436, 603]. No detailed information on population changes in recent history, but has been increasing in numbers in East Anglia and parts of north-east Scotland since 1950 [456].

HABITAT
A highly adaptable, unspecialised, versatile species, and lack of specific habitat requirements is one of the keys to success. Most abundant in fragmentary habitats offering wide variety of cover and food, but also found on large expanses of hill land, sand dunes, etc. Small woodlands, especially conifers, afford good shelter in upland areas; large coniferous

plantations are good habitat while ground vegetation remains, but not highly desirable foraging areas subsequently. Most movements and foraging on habitat edges, hence most abundant in areas of habitat diversity. Habitat requirements of urban foxes determined from surveys of seven cities [280], and these habitat data used to devise a model to predict numbers of foxes in different types of urban habitat [281]. Habitat use by radio-tracked foxes in Edinburgh [402].

SOCIAL ORGANISATION AND BEHAVIOUR
Great deal of information in recent years and much of this has come from studies in Britain — popular account [479] and reviews in relation to spread of rabies [472, 485].

Territories: foxes live in family groups which share a joint territory, and in areas of higher population density (i.e. more favourable habitats) and/or low hunting pressure, female cubs may remain on parental range [472]. The number of additional females may be as high as six, but one to two is more common [271, 472]. These extra females are usually young of the previous year, and have been described as 'helpers' who play a role in rearing the dominant vixen's cubs. However, has also been argued that these groups are a response to a temporary resource surplus, and so may not help the breeders in their reproductive effort [728]. Captive studies show that the non-breeding vixens will guard, groom, play with and retrieve cubs that stray, and provision them. Same thought to occur in wild [469]. The role of these extra vixens in terms of kin selection discussed in [474, 483].

Size of territory varies with habitat type; in hill areas of Scotland territories may be as large as 4000 hectares [460]; in urban areas territories may be as small as 20 hectares, although the mean in Bristol and Oxford was 45 hectares [271, 472] and in Edinburgh about 100 hectares [403].

In areas of very high population density it would appear that there is a minimum size below which territories do not fall, and that there is an increase in the degree of overlap between adjacent territories [696]. Nor is there any significant relationship between territory size and fox family group size [476], and in urban Bristol the mean fox family group size was found to remain constant in areas of different population density [284].

Fox social systems variable and have been shown to be adaptable to habitat type [476]. Resource

dispersion used to explain group living strategies in foxes [475, 476]. Alternative explanations have been proposed [448, 728].

Many parts of territory will only be used infrequently, mainly for travel between key foraging areas [456]. In Edinburgh, railway lines used as travel routes between foraging areas by dog foxes [401, 402]. Core areas of activity may include only a small proportion of territory; in Bristol, core areas encompassing 60% of radio fixes often only 10% of total territory [758].

Scent marking: territories marked with urine and faeces. Small urine marks left on conspicuous objects at nose height, and both sexes may cock leg to do this but vixens normally have a more convex back and elevated tail [470]. Urine marks left on main travel routes in proportion to frequency with which each path travelled irrespective of location of path within range. Number of sites marked rapidly drops to zero as fox reaches border of range; socially dominant animals in group mark more frequently than do subordinates [470, 473]. Foxes may urine-mark inedible food remnants or empty caching holes where odour of food still lingers to avoid wasting search time on unproductive sites [299]. Faeces usually single, almost exclusively on or near conspicuous objects, and scattered throughout territory [473]. Foxes may mark some site with urine and faeces, and may rub perioral region along site before/after urinating.

Other communication: wide range of facial and body postures used to describe dominant/ submissive status, and many of these — threat gape, for example — visible in young cubs. There is also a range of visual cues [213].

Aggressive behaviour: when fighting, animals will stand with forelegs on each others' chest/shoulders, and use open-mouthed threats. Such fights usually between juveniles or adults of the same sex.

Vocalisation: wide range; 28 groups of sounds based on 40 forms of sound production [675]. Most characteristic are the triple bark and 'scream' heard particularly during the rut. Still little known about seasonal variations in types of vocalisation or their biological significance.

Dispersal: occurs principally in animals 6–12 months old, but some older or younger animals will disperse [286]. Tagging study in Bristol showed that by end of December in first year, 59% of males and 33% of females had dispersed; by end of March figures were 67% and 32%, and by end of following March figures were 73% and 32%. Proportion of animals dispersing depends on density of population, and possibly also level of control; in some populations up to 100% of males and 77% of females disperse [694]. Factors affecting whether an individual fox disperses or not are unknown; for males, small cubs from large litters more likely to disperse, and females that disperse come from larger litters [286]. For males that disperse, life expectancy only 85% that of non-dispersers, and for both males and females those that disperse further have shorter life expectancy [286].

Most animals in a population disperse relatively small distances, but a few can move very long distances; occasional movements over 300 km recorded in USA, over 100 km in Europe, but in Britain most dispersal distances much lower; for Bristol mean and maximum for males 2.3 and 18.0 km, for females 0.8 and 6.3 km [286]. For mid-Wales comparable figures for males are 13.7 and 52.0 km, for females 2.3 and 24.0 km [456], for Ireland mean distances for males and females 14.8 and 7.5 km [189, 190, 191]. Distance moved positively correlated with home-range size and negatively with population density; equations to predict mean and maximum dispersal distances from simple population parameters have been calculated [696], and used to develop a simulation model to predict pattern of dispersal in urban fox populations [694].

Disturbance, particularly by fox hunts, may be important in stimulating an animal to disperse [456]. Actual pattern of movements very variable; animals may make a number of exploratory movements before finally moving, slowly drift into a neighbouring range, or make a sudden one-off movement [726].

Dispersal may last only a few days or, exceptionally, several weeks or even months [1]. Few barriers deter a dispersing fox; tidal stretches of River Avon swum regularly by dispersing foxes [277], and in urban areas foxes will disperse across gardens, etc., and not necessarily follow railways or other corridors [695]. Direction of dispersal random, although there is a tendency for littermates to disperse in the same general direction [286].

Activity mainly nocturnal and crepuscular, with amount of diurnal activity dependent on degree of persecution. In summer may remain active long after dawn, especially if vixen trying to feed young cubs. In urban areas, most active after midnight [758], but great deal of individual variation, and even in city centres daylight sightings quite frequent. Activity influenced by weather, and reduced activity on cold, wet nights, although warm, wet weather provides an ideal opportunity for 'worming'. Influence of other weather conditions on activity not quantified.

Denning behaviour very variable. Outside breeding season many (perhaps most) animals prefer to lie up above ground in dense cover, and only use earths in periods of particularly bad weather. Earths dug in wide variety of habitats: extensive earths dug in banks; old rabbit burrows enlarged; disused or occupied badger setts utilised; natural holes in rock crevices, drains and turbaries (peatlands) used as earths, when often very little signs of occupation by foxes. In urban areas, under sheds, under buildings, etc., are favoured sites for earths, and foxes may spend the day on roofs of buildings if they can gain access by sloping roofs or walls [266, 277].

In breeding den no bedding used, and cubs born on bare ground. Vixen stays with cubs when very young, but progressively lies up above ground nearby, only returning to feed cubs. Dog fox rarely remains in natal earth, but occasionally one or two dog foxes may be in earth with young cubs, sometimes without the vixen, or usually with one or more adult vixens also present [1]. Except in urban areas, cubs will be moved to another earth at slightest disturbance from man or dogs, and several earths available to vixen on each territory.

Earths occupied by cubs recognised by fresh food debris around and inside earth, often accompanied by putrid smell and flies in hot weather. As well as food, play items, such as food wrappings, balls and clothes brought back to earth [272A]. With onset of hot weather in late May or June, most litters of cubs moved away from earth, and lie up above ground in dense vegetation. At this stage, or sometimes while still living underground, litter of cubs split into groups of one or two and only come together at night to play.

Occasional reports of more than one litter of cubs on a territory, sometimes in earths only a few metres apart, refer to more than one vixen in some family groups breeding, and this probably also accounts for pooling of litters; more than one litter may be found sharing an earth, and they may stay together semi-permanently, or for only a few days before being separated again [1].

Locomotion usually at a walk when hunting or investigating; when moving unhurriedly, travels at slow trot of 6–13 km per hour, at slightly greater speed uses a lope or canter, and when pursued will gallop; speeds of over 65 km per hour have been reported but a lower figure is probably more realistic [456].

FEEDING

A highly adaptable omnivore, and lack of specialised food requirements one of keys to success. Many British food studies in rural environments [53, 191, 209, 217, 309, 311, 312, 316–318, 329, 331, 333, 347 405, 407, 437, 438, 458, 468, 602, 604, 639, 740], and in urban environments [272A, 287]. Most rural studies based on percentage occurrence of food items in scats or stomachs, and lack of uniformity in presenting results makes direct comparisons between studies difficult; some rural studies summarised in Table 10.3. Urban studies based on percentage of diet by volume and these are summarised in Table 10.4.

Most show that mammals, e.g. lagomorphs, wood mice or field voles, most frequently eaten; bank voles and insectivores are uncommon, and this the result of a food preference [468].

Cannibalism of littermates [575], or predation by vixens on other litters, may occur [1, 468]. Of birds, passerines, pigeons and various galliformes (hens, game birds) most frequent, but in coastal areas scavenged or predated gulls and waders common [331, 333]. Beetles and a wide variety of invertebrates common, as is fruit (windfall apples, pears and plums and blackberries) frequent in autumn. In most habitats scavenging is important; in upland areas sheep and deer carcasses are main food supply in winter. Any item likely to occur; non-food items frequent in stomachs (e.g. [272A]) and fish may be caught in warm weather when active near the surface [361]. Few quantified data but usually assumed that food reflects prey availability, but studies on black-headed gull and eider duck colonies show that these species when nesting are not used in proportion to their abundance, probably because they are not a preferred food item [217, 415]. Following myxomatosis [660], importance of rabbits in diet decreased, and field voles increased [438] (in Ireland brown rats —

[187]), but in recent years importance of rabbit increased in most areas. In Scotland, availability of field voles in winter shown to be the most likely factor associated with population fluctuations [406]. In W Scotland, breeding delayed when compared with NE Scotland, and this attributed to more intermittent food supply in west [406, 407].

Hunting behaviour very variable [479]. Predation at nesting colonies of gulls and anti-predator behaviour described in [415, 418], results of sand tracking foxes through colonies in [165]. Earthworms, in some months, could provide over 60% of the average fox's calorific intake [471]. Earthworms hunted probably by hearing, grasped by incisor teeth, and dislodged from burrow by slow but accelerating head movement. Young may be taught to hunt earthworms and low status or younger foxes may exploit earthworms more frequently than adults [471].

Impact of predation still little studied in this country. Foxes can be a major pest of nesting colonial birds, e.g. terns, and electric fences used to reduce depredations [513, 524]. In urban Bristol in area of high fox density, it is estimated that 0.7% of cats and 7% of other pets killed by foxes each year [272A]. Foxes can be a significant predator of brooding hen partridges, although post-hatching fox predation may not be important [583]. Recent work by Game Conservancy suggests that impact of fox predation on harvestable pheasant population can be significant [601]. However, in hill areas, foxes do not limit the numbers of breeding grouse or the numbers available for shooting, and non-territorial birds were most vulnerable to predation [354].

Surplus killing: Foxes occasionally kill large numbers of easy prey, e.g. ground nesting birds and captive hens, and leave many uneaten [417]. In one breeding season about 200 black-headed gulls were killed by each of four foxes, with 230 killed in one night. Gulls most likely to be killed on dark nights. Biological significance of behaviour discussed by Kruuk [416].

Food caching is an important strategy; food may be cached even when fox is still hungry as a means of protecting it from competitors or of increasing time available for food capture. Surplus food scatter-hoarded and more likely to be cached if it is a preferred food item; caches probably found by memory and most likely to be found by the fox that

Table 10.3. Summary of some British fox food studies. The figures are percentage occurrence in either scats or stomachs and only the main food items are shown. In some studies the figures were presented in broad groupings, in others they were presented by orders, families or species; combining these into the headings used for this table may have produced a slight over-estimate of percentage occurrence.

	S Devon [602]: Adult scats (n = 186)	Gibralter Point, Lincs [331]: Scats (n = 111)	Spurn Peninsula, Yorks [333]: Scats (n = 165)	Kent [456]: Adult stomachs, winter only (n = 64)	Wales [456]: Adult stomachs, winter only (n = 67)	NE Scotland [405]: Adult stomachs (n = 272)	W Scotland [405]: Adult stomachs (n = 137)	NE Ireland [191]: Adult stomachs (n = 340)
Lagomorphs	24	88	55	39	30	62	14	45
Small rodents	36	16	24	47	54	20	70	23
Other wild mammals	5	2	–	14	3	2	4	–
Passerines	6	4	16	14	9	} 48	} 48	4
Galliformes	3	–	4	19	15			16
Columbiformes	1	–	4	8	2			–
Other birds	8	9	21	5	5			22
Beetles	78	1	} 5	6	15	} 6	} 12	–
Other insects	37	–		6	3			–
Earthworms	14	–	–	–	2	–	–	–
Fish	–	1	2	–	–	–	–	–
Crabs	–	7	12	–	–	–	–	–
Sheep carrion	2	–	–	13	51	7	45	9
Deer carrion	–	–	–	–	–	4	13	–
Fruit	11	–	–	9	–	?	?	–

	London [272a]		Bristol [287]	
	Adults (n = 313)	Cubs (n = 258)	Adults (n = 642)	Cubs (n = 344)
Earthworms	12.2	11.1	6.5	9.2
Pet mammals	2.9	4.2	0.6	0.7
Wild mammals	13.1	10.0	4.5	3.5
Pet birds	5.8	3.4	1.8	0.8
Wild birds	14.4	27.5	6.5	11.5
Insects	9.2	15.4	16.3	26.9
Fruit and vegetables	7.6	8.2	13.6	11.2
Scavenged meat and fat	24.1	13.8	26.6	19.2
Other scavenged items	10.7	6.4	23.6	17.0

Table 10.4. Food of two urban fox populations. The figures are percentage of diet by volume; adults are animals over 6 months old, cubs animals less than 6 months old.

makes them, although may be found by other foxes [360, 467, 689].

Food requirements for captive adult foxes estimated as 121 kcal (507 kJ) per kg of body weight; requirements of carbohydrates, fats, proteins and vitamins for growth and various stages of life history for captive foxes given in [18], as are main features of deficiency diseases. For captive pups 13−14 weeks old, estimated that mean daily ingestion 223 kcal (934 kJ) per kg body weight, with 91% assimilation efficiency [725].

BREEDING (Fig. 10.3)
Monoestrous, mating December−February, spontaneous ovulation, pregnancy 53 days, peak birth March, mean litter size four to five, breed when 10 months old. Largely monogamous.

Males seasonally fecund with a peak of spermatogenesis in December−February, but some males fecund in November and March [456]. Onset of breeding later with increasing latitudes and this correlated with daylength [457]. During quiescent period, testes still scrotal, but scrotum far less conspicuous than during breeding season. During first breeding season, growth of testes of juveniles slightly delayed when compared with older males. Seasonal variations in plasma testosterone, LH and prolactin [508]. Average volume of semen ejaculated by adult males 6 ml, 2.5 ml in young animals, and total number of spermatozoa on average in excess of 300 million [456].

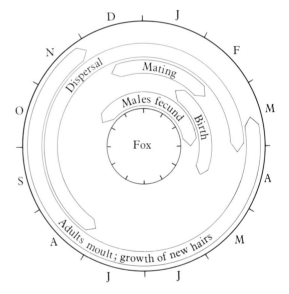

Fig. 10.3. Fox: life-cycle.

Females have a single oestrus period lasting 3 weeks but fertilisation possible only during 3 days, although mating may occur outside this period [456]. During oestrus male closely attends female, and as peak receptivity approaches male shadows every move of female, with his tail held higher than usual. First attempts to mate usually rejected by female, and mating may occur during day or night. Successful mountings may last only a few seconds, with ejaculation occurring quickly, or the pair may 'tie' or 'lock' back to back, with their tails curved over each other's rump. Once tied, the male cannot withdraw his penis, and pair may stay tied for up to 90 min. Pair may mate several times, and between matings lie close together.

During oestrus, cervix very firm and round, and vulva swollen and slightly pink. In anoestrus, uterus thin-walled and flaccid; following oestrus, uterus rapidly elongates and becomes round and turgid. Implantation between 10 and 14 days; implantation sites evenly spaced throughout two horns of uterus and transmigration of ova from one horn of uterus to other occurs. Swelling of uterine horns follows implantation; pregnancy lasts 52−53 days, and age of embryos can be determined from 33 days [456]. There are variations in circulating hormone levels in anoestrus and pregnancy [42, 528].

Polyovular follicles common in cubs, but frequency decreases at approach of oestrus, and functional polyovular follicles probably uncommon in wild foxes [456]. In London, 3.6% of follicles released two ova [266]. Corpora lutea develop rapidly and persist throughout pregnancy. Pseudopregnancy lasts for *c.* 40 days; corpora lutea develop, and uterus becomes turgid in condition similar to that at implantation. There may be development of mammary glands, and milk may even be visible microscopically in glands [610].

In later stages of pregnancy, vixen digs out several earths before selecting one as natal den. Cubs born on bare soil; soon after birth fur lost from belly and peak lactation lasts an average of 7 weeks [100], but cubs will try to suck up to 14 weeks. At 28 to 35 days, milk 18.1% dry matter, 5.8% fat, 6.7% protein, 4.6% sugar, 0.9% ash [551]. At end of lactation nipples regress but usually still possible to recognise breeding from barren animals on size of regressed nipple [568]. Ovarian activity during anoestrus described in [527].

Productivity: mean number of corpora lutea 5.5 in Kent, 5.7 in Wales [456]; losses from ovulation to birth calculated to be 10.2% in London [266], but no data to show whether loss pre- or post-implantation. Mean number of placental scars in London 4.77, mean litter size of cubs less than 6 weeks old 3.97, hence 16.8% natural mortality in cubs below ground [266]. Similar figures calculated for other populations. Mean litter size four to five, with litters of up to 10 reported from placental scars (e.g. [270]); larger litters of cubs are reported but these may represent the pooling of litters. In London, litter size significantly reduced in vixens over 4 years old [270], but no such observations in Bristol [284]. Number of barren vixens very variable in some regions, such as northern Sweden, where food supply very variable [164], but in most of Britain such marked annual variations in number of barren vixens not observed. In London and Bristol, animals with no placental scars most frequently 1st year vixens and those over 4 years old; for 2nd to 4th years, number of vixens with no scars lowest [284]. In addition to those animals with no placental scars, some vixens undergo a full-term pregnancy but do not produce viable cubs; mechanisms of this late-term reproductive failure unknown but occurs in 17.6% of vixens in London, and 22.7% in Bristol; including all vixens in population, mean productivity per vixen 3.22 in London, 2.61 in Bristol [284], 3.70 in Wales [456].

For most British populations, variations in productivity between populations result from changes in the proportion of non-breeding vixens rather than changing mean litter size. Barren vixens are most common in populations subject to low levels of control; in areas where mortality rates are high, very few barren vixens occur. In boreal Sweden, where food supplies fluctuate, yearly ovulation rate correlated with abundance of voles in coming year [449].

Young: cubs born blind and deaf, with short black fur, but with white tag to tail evident from birth; birth weight 80−120 gms. For first 2−3 weeks unable to thermoregulate effectively, and vixen stays with cubs, nursing them all the time, and is fed by the dog fox or possibly a barren vixen. From 3 weeks onwards, vixen spends an increasing amount of time away from cubs, and by 4−5 weeks often only comes back to earth to feed cubs. Eyes and ears open 11−14 days; eyes slate-blue in colour, and change to adult amber colour at 4−5 weeks.

Coat colour starts to change at 3 weeks, when black eye streak appears. White muzzle and red patches on face apparent at 4 weeks. At same age, ears change from lying flat to erect, and muzzle starts to elongate from previous snub shape. By 6 weeks fur colour becoming more similar to adult, but with a woolly appearance. Facial proportions much more fox-like, and full complement of milk teeth by 7−8 weeks. By 8 weeks, woolly coat begins to be covered by shiny guard hairs, and colour and pattern very like that of adult. Thereafter, growth rapid but no significant changes in appearance, and reach adult size by end of September, although weight will continue to increase slightly until the end of the year [1].

Sexual dimorphism in average body proportions evident from 6 weeks, but considerable overlap between sexes. In large litters growth rates lower, and may find considerable variation in both size and developmental age between littermates; such variations in speed of development may produce some erroneous reports of pooled litters.

Cubs suckled until 4 weeks, when progressively weaned onto solids. First emerge above ground at this age. By 5−6 weeks cubs eating wide variety of solid items, and may even be catching earthworms and insects for themselves. During summer, cubs become progressively independent, but may hunt with vixen until July or August. How cubs learn to hunt unclear, but probably largely by trial and error.

POPULATION

Density very variable, and dependant on habitat. In hill areas of Scotland, one pair per 40 km^2 [460]. Area per breeding den in various Scottish habitats: 32 km^2 in deer forest, 23 km^2 on grouse moors and 10 km^2 on agricultural land [313]. For mid-Wales one breeding pair per 1.2−4.8 km^2, for parts of Pembrokeshire 0.4−0.8 per km^2 [456]. In New Forest, 0.76 family groups per km^2 [346]. In farmland areas of lowland Britain, density variable but one family group per km^2 typical. In rural areas, density estimated in different land types from maps [486]; this gave a total adult fox population in spring for England, Scotland and Wales of 250 000.

In urban areas mean fox density in 14 cities ranged from 0.19 family groups per km^2 (in Wolverhampton) to 2.24 (in Cheltenham) [283], although in urban areas locally densities can be as high as 5.0 family groups per km^2.

Number of foxes killed in a small area in late autumn/early winter does not represent population density since large numbers of itinerant foxes may be killed (e.g. in Pembrokeshire over 8 weeks in winter on 3.2 km^2 an average of one fox per 4 hectare was killed [1]. Effects of control on population density unknown; locally snaring may be effective in reducing fox numbers. By comparing fox population in Bristol (uncontrolled) and London (some control), appears that control operations did not significantly reduce number of fox family groups in an area, but did reduce total number of adult foxes and cubs in the population, and hence mean family group size [284].

If number of foxes known to be killed annually reflects the population density, there is evidence of a periodic fluctuation in numbers [188, 189, 315], and a trend towards an increase in numbers in Scotland from 1953 to 1978 [310, 315].

Sex ratio at birth in most populations 1 : 1 [694], but caught samples invariably have a preponderance of males, especially in the winter months, and samples from heavily controlled areas show a large excess of itinerant males. In Bristol, in a high density urban fox population, birth sex ratio in whole population 1 male : 0.83 females, and in highest density parts of city 1 male : 0.76 females [694]. In adult population in Bristol, sex ratio 1 male : 0.81 females [284]; the city has 211 fox family groups [272], which comprise 333 adult females, 383 adult males, i.e. 1.6 adult females, 1.8 adult males per family group. The role of these excess males in the adult population is unknown.

Age determination: most techniques, such as eye lens weight, baculum weight, epiphyseal and suture closure, can be used to differentiate young of the year from older animals, but thereafter only reliable method of age determination from incremental lines in cementum of teeth [268, 359]. Incremental lines laid down in later part of winter; formation associated with physiological changes during sexual cycle [399]. By using known-age animals from the same population as a standard, incisor tooth wear can be a useful guide to the age of an adult fox [268]. Age related variability in skull measurements described in [343]; skulls of male foxes appear to change more with age than females, but no relationship adequate for age determination.

Age structure of various samples shown in Table 10.5; no significant differences between sexes, although very old animals more likely to be males. Maximum survival in wild 10 or 11 years, but in captivity animals up to or even over 14 years not unusual [1]. Proportion of animals less than a year old in sample reflects intensity of control, and varies from 0.98 to 5.6 per adult [266], although most British samples towards the low end of this range, and annual mortality rates for both adults and juveniles vary between 50 and 60% per annum.

Survival low; including an estimate for mortality of cubs less than 4 weeks old, mean life expectancy in London, where level of control low, 12.1 months for males, 12.4 months for females; for Bristol

Table 10.5. Age distribution of several British fox populations, both sexes combined. The figures are percentages; ages were determined from incremental lines in the teeth.

Age in years	Bristol [284]	London [284]	NE Scotland [406]	W Scotland [406]	W Wales [456]	Mid-Wales [456]	Isle of Skye [456]
0–1	50	57	62	56	43	59	67
1–2	24	24	21	27	23	25	19
2–3	13	10	9	6	13	11	10
3–4	7	5	5	6	11	5	3
4–5	4	3	1	1	3	2	1
5–6	2	1	1	2	5	1	
6–7	1	<1	1	1	1		
7–8	<1	<1	<1	1	1		
8–9	<1		<1	1	1		
9–10	<1						

where no control, comparable figures 16.6 and 17.8 months [284]. Mortality of vixens highest in April to June when cubbing, and January to February during rut; for dog foxes mortality highest in the rut [284].

High rate of annual turnover means that survival of both members of a pair unlikely; in mid-Wales adult mortality 57% and so probability of both members of pair dying is 32.5%, of one member dying 49%, and of both members surviving 18.5% [456].

MORTALITY

Few natural predators; some cubs killed at earths by golden eagles, and some cubs and (rarely) adult foxes killed by badgers. In urban areas, dogs are a significant predator of young cubs, and occasionally kill adult foxes [272]. However, most mortality believed to be man-induced, although few samples of foxes thought to represent true causes of mortality. Probably most comprehensive sample from urban Bristol, where for adults road accidents 61%, man (shot, snared, etc.) 18%, disease 10%, fights 3%, parturition deaths <1%, trains 1%, misadventure (trapped in fences, falling into pits, etc.) 2%, and unknown causes 5%. There was a significant increase in the number of foxes dying from disease and fights with other foxes as population density increased [284].

In early 1960s large numbers of foxes died in East Anglia as a result of secondary poisoning, eating birds killed by seed dressings [38]. Of 60 foxes examined, 23 had died from insecticide poisoning, and remainder from a variety of diseases [38].

Number of foxes killed by man each year estimated to be 100 000 [456], but this may be a conservative estimate. Number killed by fox hunts each year about 12 500 [1], and each year 1965–1980 the number of foxes killed by the Forestry Commission and the 221 fox destruction societies in England, Wales and Scotland was 22 000 [456]. It is impossible to obtain an accurate estimate of number of foxes killed by gamekeepers, farmers, etc., but no evidence that this high level of mortality has reduced fox numbers, and in fact they have been increasing in some areas (e.g. [313]). In Northern Ireland, fox population probably limited by high cub mortality as a result of various diseases; disease and hunting by man may reduce population further in autumn and winter, but hunting (encouraged by a bounty system) did not limit fox population [192].

PARASITES

Ectoparasites: fleas; most are stragglers, and mean infestation is low [50, 608]. Some fleas, e.g. *Spilopsyllus cuniculi*, are probably obtained from prey, whilst others, e.g. *Archaeopsylla e. erinacei*, may be collected while travelling around range. Some fleas feed on fox, and these believed to include *Pulex irritans*, *Ctenocephalides canis* and *Paraceras melis*, although no host specific flea in Britain [50].

Ticks; *Ixodes ricinus* and *I. hexagonus* most common, and particularly frequent on nursing vixens and juveniles still using earths [285]; very large infestations only rarely recorded, when extensive fur loss from scratching may occur. *I. canisuga* more frequent in north.

Lice; *Trichodectes vulpis*, which is specific to the fox, recorded infrequently and very little known about its ecology. It is rare, e.g. only three foxes infested in over 3000 examined in Bristol [1] but these three infestations each numbered many hundreds or thousands of lice. It is possible that small infestations may be overlooked. *T. melis* occurs as a straggler from badgers.

Mites; *Sarcoptes scabiei* is most important, and causes sarcoptic mange. This disease prevalent in a few areas; mites burrow into skin and cause extensive hair loss, first on base of tail and hind feet, then rump, and finally spreading forward to cover whole body [1]. Animal also scratches at infected areas, causing excessive tissue fluid exudation which dries on body as thick crust, exceptionally over 1 cm thick. In final stages there may be many millions of mites on fox [1], which loses up to 50% of body weight, most of fur, and may gnaw at infested limbs and tail. Mean time from infestation until death is 4 months [649]. Locally sarcoptic mange may exterminate fox populations, and mange in southern England at the end of last century resulted in some hunts restocking with healthy foxes [666]. Mange may be transferred from foxes to domestic dogs and humans [649, 650].

Other skin mites (*Demodex folliculorum* and *Notoedres* sp.) have been reported but their frequency of occurrence in Britain unknown. *Otodectes cyanotis* is frequent in the ear canal with, for example, over 70% of foxes in Bristol infested [1]. The pentastomid mite *Linguatula serrata*, which infects the nasal passages, has been recorded twice in Britain [456]. Ringworm *Microsporum* recorded occasionally [608].

Endoparasites: variety of helminths reported in Britain; nine nematodes and 11 cestodes listed in [456]. Of the gut nematodes, *Toxocara canis*, *Toxascaris leonina* and *Uncinaria stenocephala* most common; *Capillaria aerophila* and *Crenosoma vulpis* occur in the lungs and *Capillaria plica* in bladder. *Trichinella spiralis* only recorded infrequently in British foxes. Of tapeworms, *Taenia serialis* and *T. pisiformis* most common, and *Echinococcus granulosus* recorded particularly in sheep-rearing areas. Eleven species of trematodes recorded [456], but little known about their frequency of occurrence or effects on host.

Of infectious diseases, little information from Britain. No record of distemper in a wild fox, although it can be locally common in Europe [456]. In urban areas, antibodies to various pet diseases (e.g. parvo virus) recorded, but no information on the effects of such diseases on the fox population [1]. Various infections are discussed in [456], but these are all sporadic reports. *Brucella abortus* recorded from Ireland [511]. *Salmonella infantes* recorded in British foxes [672]. Ten of the 15 serotypes of *Leptospira* recorded [703], and a further one by Blackmore [38]. Of these, *L. icterohaemorrhagiae* and *L. canicola* most common, and in old foxes extensive nephritis thought to be associated with former, and may be an important cause of mortality, but no firm data [1, 608]. *Mycobacterium bovis* found in six of 776 foxes examined, but they were not infectious [523].

Most important disease rabies, and throughout much of range fox is main vector of the disease; see [366] for a review of the disease, and [485] for a review of fox biology as it affects transmission of rabies. The Government has plans for dealing with a rabies event [522] in Britain.

Foxes prone to a number of traumatic injuries. Of all foxes in London over 6 months of age, 32.4% had one or more broken bones, and these were probably the result of road accidents. These had all healed naturally, although often involved shortening or distortion of long bones [269]. Other frequent injuries include loss of part or all of the tail, and some or all of a limb; three-legged foxes are reported infrequently, particularly in urban areas where their mobility and reproductive capabilities seem to be little impaired [1].

In London, arthritis was frequent, particularly in the spine, where fusion of whole lengths could occur in badly affected animals [267]; there was some evidence that badly affected animals were in poorer condition, and debilitating levels of affection could be an important cause of mortality in older age groups.

RELATIONS WITH MAN
Very mixed. A lot of mythology and folklore surrounds the fox [719]. A beast of the chase, with over 200 packs of hounds in Britain killing about 12 500 foxes a year [1]. In 1982, estimated that nearly 200 000 people hunted foxes with hounds at a total annual expenditure of about £80 million [83].

Generally, foxes have a bad reputation with rural communities, and are unwelcomed by gamekeepers, shepherds, and many farmers. One survey of 867 farmers found that 90% thought that foxes needed to be controlled for depredations on stock, usually on the grounds that there were too many or because they were suspected of spreading disease [477]. Lamb killing is the main cause of complaint against foxes, despite studies that show that most losses are small, e.g. [188, 192]. A survey of 80% of farms in Radnorshire, Breconshire, and Montgomeryshire in 1967 estimated losses to foxes as 0.53% [456]; in Scotland over 4 years, lamb losses were 0.6−1.8% [311]. Similarly, a survey of nearly 400 farms with sheep showed that approximately 70% each year lose no lambs to foxes, and killing of large numbers of lambs is infrequent [477].

Average value of pelt increased dramatically in 1970s, reaching a peak of £27.80 in 1979, and trade in UK pelts via major auctioneers in London up to 30 000 a year in late 1970s [481]. Some sources put total UK figure at that time nearer 100 000 pelts, although this was speculative. In 1980s, price of pelts decreased considerably, and number of pelts traded now believed to be lower. Effects of trade on fox population unknown, but decrease of foxes in Ireland was reported [753].

In urban areas, foxes are generally welcomed by most residents [276, 287] and popular pressure, particularly in London, has reduced the number of foxes killed by local authorities. Damage caused by foxes in urban areas is generally slight [272A, 482].

Techniques for study: a medium-sized elusive carnivore that was difficult to study until the advent of radio-tracking and night-viewing equipment; for application of the techniques see [479]. Other techniques include capture−mark−recapture [286]; studies on captive foxes [468]; urban fox survey techniques [275]. Habituation of foxes to an observer has been used very successfully to study detailed aspects of behaviour in remote areas where foxes probably less wary of humans [300]. Field and laboratory techniques [456]; methods of rearing orphaned fox cubs [279].

SOUND RECORDINGS
Appendix 3: A, C, E, F, J, M, P, S, V.

LITERATURE
Extensive review of literature by Lloyd [456], but now a little dated; symposium on behaviour and ecology [768]. Urban foxes [277]; results of a long-term study [479]; photographic study in Japan [665]; and long-term field study in N America [300].

AUTHORS FOR THIS SPECIES
S. Harris and H.G. Lloyd.

FAMILY MUSTELIDAE (WEASELS, ETC.)

INTRODUCTION
One of the largest families of carnivores, found throughout the world except for Australasia. The dominant family of small carnivores in the north temperate region but outnumbered by the Viverridae and Herpestidae in the Tropics of the Old World. Most species are fairly small with long slender bodies and short legs and constitute the subfamily Mustelinae (Fig. 10.4); other subfamilies are the Melinae (badgers), Lutrinae (otters), Mellivorinae (honey badger) and Mephitinae (skunks); the last two not represented in Britain or Europe.

The jaws of mustelids are intermediate in relative length between those of dogs and cats, and the dental formula is also intermediate, being 3.1.3−4.1/3.1.3−4.2. All species have prominent scent glands adjacent to the anus, and the smell is sometimes pungent, as in the polecat.

Four genera are represented in Britain, three of them each with one species (*Martes* − marten, *Meles* − badger, and *Lutra* − otter), the other (*Mustela*) with four. The characters of the genera are given in Table 10.6.

SUBFAMILY MUSTELINAE

GENUS *Martes*

A genus of eight species, in the Palaearctic and Nearctic, with one extending to S. Asia. *M. martes* in northern Europe is replaced by the Sable, *M. zibellina*, in Siberia and by the American marten, *M. americana*, in North America. The beech or stone marten, *M. foina*, is a more southern species overlapping extensively with the pine marten in Europe. Last century it was commonly believed to occur also in Britain, but there is, in fact, no evidence that it has ever occurred here. Martens are agile, mainly arboreal animals with a longer muzzle, and more teeth than species of *Mustela*: dental formula 3.1.4.1/3.1.4.2. Most species provide valuable pelts for the fur trade.

(a)

(b)

(c)

(d)

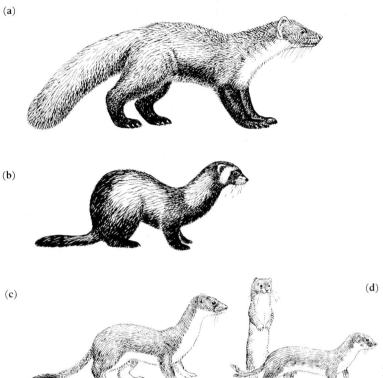

Fig. 10.4. (a) Pine marten; (b) polecat; (c) stoat; (d) weasel.

Pine marten *Martes martes*

Mustela martes Linnaeus, 1758, Upsala, Sweden.

Pine marten, marten cat, sweet mart; bele (Welsh), taghan (Scottish Gaelic), cat crainn (Irish Gaelic).

RECOGNITION
A beautiful, almost cat-like, animal (Fig. 10.5)

with a flatter head and more pointed face characteristic of the Mustelidae, dark brown fur, a cream or orange chest and throat patch, large rounded ears and long fluffy tail. Usually seen loping across the road at night or bounding along the edge of a clearing. Can be distinguished from cat, mink or polecats by characteristic loping gait, throat patch, colouring, large ears, bushy tail and more upright

Table 10.6. Some characters of the genera of Mustelidae.

	Martes	*Mustela*	*Meles*	*Lutra*
Upper teeth	3. 1. 4. 1	3. 1. 3. 1	3. 1. 4. 1	3. 1. 4. 1
Lower teeth	3. 1. 4. 2	3. 1. 3. 2	3. 1. 4. 1	3. 1. 3. 2
Upper carnassial teeth	Long and narrow	Long and narrow	Small and triangular	Large and triangular
Upper molars (last upper teeth)	Transversely elongate	Transversely elongate	Large and square	Transversely elongate
Toes	Unwebbed	Unwebbed	Unwebbed	Webbed
Tail	Long and bushy	Moderately long	Short	Long and tapering

Fig. 10.5. Pine marten. (Photo: G. Kinns.)

body carriage (Fig. 10.6). In trees, may be confused with squirrels, but has a longer body and tail, darker coat and is much larger.

Skull (Fig. 10.7): differs from other mustelids except badger by having four pairs of premolars in upper and lower jaw. Smaller and has less prominent sagittal crest than adult badger.

SIGN

Footprint (Fig. 10.8): five toes per foot although fifth toe does not always register, making it possible to confuse with dog or fox (cat more rounded print so can be distinguished). Claws may not show unless print on soft ground. Footprints appear larger than expected for animal's size due to hair around pads on feet. In winter, this hair gives an indistinct imprint in snow. Prints found in groups of two when bounding; stride when running 60−90 cm.

Faeces: shape varies depending on content, usually long (4−12 cm), black, cigar shaped with convolutions. If fur, feather and/or bones are present, held together by mucus and will remain intact, otherwise breakdown very easily into piles or flattened mounds of insect cuticle, berries, fungus or a black gelatinous substance. Heaps of partially digested rowan berries can also be found. Faeces deposited throughout the home range in prominent places (tracks, paths, cliff ledges, boulders).

Food caching has been reported in snow in Finland, but food is usually eaten at site of kill or taken back to den [590, 626].

Fig. 10.6. Pine martens on a bird table. (Photo: Lady McKissock.)

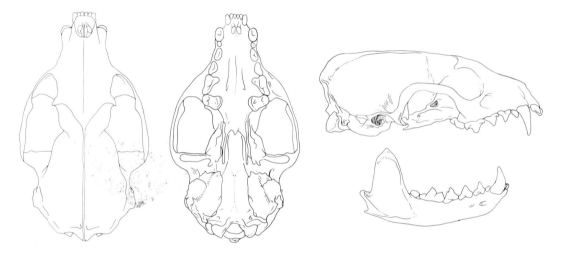

Fig. 10.7. Pine marten: skull. [519]

DESCRIPTION

Pelage: rich dark brown guard hairs with more reddish undercoat on main body, tending towards black on limbs and tail. Coat appears paler as animal approaches the moult. Summer coat short and very dark brown with winter pelage beginning growth in September, reaching its prime in October [339]. Tail less bushy in summer due to loss of guard hairs during moult [1]. Ears large, upright, rounded, pale at edges and over 40 mm long. Undivided throat patch varying from cream to orange fades over year. The pattern of brown and cream or orange in patch is unique and can be used to recognise individual animals.

Moult occurs annually in spring, beginning at limbs, ending on back [339].

Nipples: two pairs.

Scent glands: anal glands are used for setting scent by rubbing against the item being marked [339, 626]. Young animals start depositing scent at about 4 months [254]. Abdominal glands present in both males and females, although become more

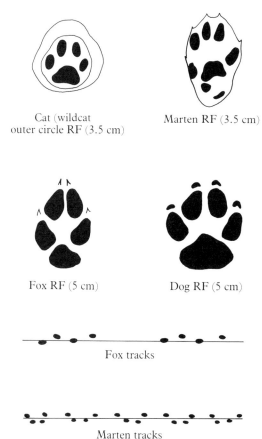

Cat (wildcat
outer circle RF (3.5 cm)

Marten RF (3.5 cm)

Fox RF (5 cm)

Dog RF (5 cm)

Fox tracks

Marten tracks

Fig. 10.8. Pine marten footprints and tracks, compared with those of wild cat, fox and dog.

apparent just before and during breeding season [1].

Teeth: typically sharp canines and cutting carnassials of the mustelids. Upper jaw less than half length of skull, upper incisors very small, large canines, four premolars increasing in size from front to back with 1, 2, 2, 3 roots respectively, molar with three roots. Lower pattern similar with addition of small second molar with one root. In young martens milk teeth erupt at 7 weeks, are replaced by permanent teeth at 4 months [653] with the carnassials erupting last [376]. As yet no consistent relationship has been found with the formation of incremental lines in cementum and age or sex [250]. Abrasion of the enamel has been used in the Soviet Union to age animals up to 3 years with some success [765].

Chromosomes: $2n = 38$, FNa $= 64$ [767].

RELATIONSHIPS

Very similar to beech marten (*Martes foina*) with which some overlap occurs in Europe, and to the American marten (*Martens americana*) which it closely resembles in appearance and behaviour. Differs from beech marten by slightly smaller size, lighter build and undivided throat patch of cream or orange colouring versus white of beech marten.

MEASUREMENTS

About the size of a domestic cat with slightly shorter legs in relation to its body length. Females approximately two-thirds size of males (Table 10.7). Cranial measurements have been used for age determination [376].

VARIATION

No apparent variation between populations of Britain and the Continent or within British Isles.

DISTRIBUTION

Throughout forest areas of Europe except Spain, Greece and in parts of NW USSR. East of River Yenesei replaced by the sable (*Martes zibellina*). In Scotland, martens can be found as far north as Cape Wrath and Tongue, south to Appin and Dalmally in Argyll, Rannoch in Tayside, and Perthshire. Populations occur all along the W Highland coast and eastwards to Speyside with some animals being reported as far east as Grampian. In 1981–82, seven animals were released into Dumfries by the Forestry Commission, and martens are still present. There are also populations in the Lake District and Yorkshire in England and in mid and North Wales, but these populations appear to be small and fragmented. In Ireland it is mainly confined to wood and scrub areas of the midwestern region [559].

HISTORY

Native to both mainland Britain and Ireland. Bones found on sites dating to 10 050 bp in Mesolithic archaelogical sites in England, presumably arriving before Britain was cut off from the Mainland around 9000 bp [761]. Animals may have reached Ireland via a land bridge 8000 bp or earlier. Marten bones have been recorded from a late Neolithic/early Bronze Age site on Westray, Orkney [466]. These could represent a native population or animals imported and traded for their skins.

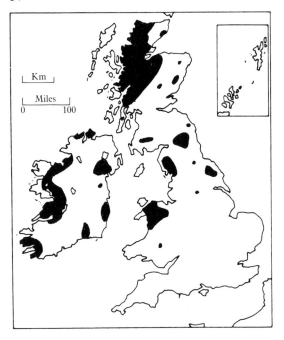

Map 10.3. Pine marten: since 1977 (Britain); since 1960 (Ireland).

Until the 19th century, widespread throughout mainland Britain, the Isles of Wight, Jura and Lewis and Ireland, although large-scale deforestation and changes in land use were already exerting pressures on marten habitat [430, 559].

In the middle of the 19th century a rapid decline in the marten population took place through intensive persecution that was closely associated with the invention of the breach-loading firearm and the development of the sporting estate and gamekeeping profession. 'Vermin' control methods were largely indiscriminate with heavy use of steel traps, snares and poisoned bait. 'Hunting the mart' in areas where it was sufficiently numerous was a recognised field sport.

By the turn of the 20th century, the marten survived only in NW Scotland, N Wales, Lake District and parts of Northumberland, N Yorkshire and Ireland, being forced to retreat into areas of remote upland forest and rocky moorland [200, 430, 518, 559].

By 1959, martens had spread south and east with the main population still north and west of Loch Ness. Animals were also reported in Speyside and Argyll. This pattern continued so that by 1976 the

Map 10.4. Pine marten.

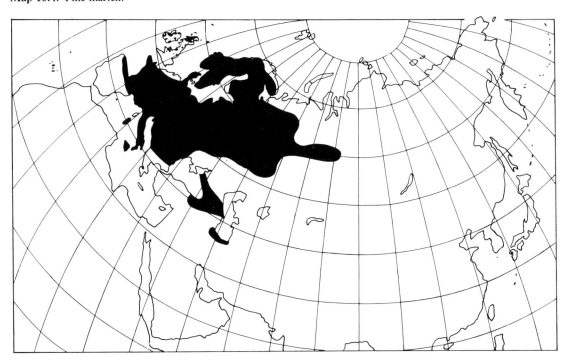

Table 10.7. Measurements of pine martens.

	Ireland [376]				Scotland [1]				USSR [302]			
	Males		Females		Males		Females		Males		Females	
	Range	n	Range	n	Range	n	Range	n	Range	n	Range	n
Head and body (mm)	460–510	31	410–450	38	510–540	3	460–540	4	405–473	93	365–420	102
Tail (mm)	200–220	31	200–210	38	260–270	3	180–240	4	185–228	104	170–210	100
Weight (g)	1500–1950	31	1100–1450	38	1630–1680	3	1285–1480	4	670–1050	59	484–850	49

distribution was similar, but with a greater density of sightings outside their main range. By 1982, the range had extended further south and east stretching into Argyll and Grampian. However, at that time, there was little evidence of animals in the far north [720]. By 1987, martens were again being seen in the northern areas as far east as Borgie (by Bettyhill) [1].

HABITAT
Found in a wide variety of habitats, including conifer and deciduous woodland, clear felled areas within forest, pasture, scrub, coastal sites, moorland and open treeless fells [133, 559, 593, 720, 721]. Density of animals varies with habitat type and prey availability, with preference shown for areas with some cover (e.g. trees, scrub), while the more open areas (e.g. clear fell, moorland, open ground with small patches of cover) underused [592, 593, 721]. In a Scottish study ground with older conifer cover was preferred for hunting [721]. Similar work in Sweden showed that older mixed conifer was favoured along with young forest pine or spruce 10–19 years old [119]. In Finnish Lapland 98% of tracks were found in forest with conifers, nearly 80% of which was spruce [593]. Spruce forest was also selected in the Caucasus [764].

SOCIAL ORGANISATION AND BEHAVIOUR
Solitary, with mother–young group being main extended period of social contact. Encounters occur through home range due to overlap with neighbours of both sexes and chance meetings with transients, and during courtship and mating.

Home-range size varies depending on habitat, season and sex (Table 10.8). Males on average

occupy larger areas than females and overlap between animals occurs [592, 721]. Studies on *M. americana* supports this information [294, 640, 646] and suggests that adult animals do not use areas of overlap simultaneously [646, 673]. Home-range boundaries in both species may coincide with vegetation boundaries or topographical features, e.g. meadows, clearfells, waterways [721], and in *M. americana* may remain stable for many years and during more than one marten's residence [294]. Complete shifts in range have been reported for hunting [550]. Territorial defence (e.g. fighting) has not been noted as yet. Faeces act as markers with the highest intensities of droppings occurring near the boundaries and in the central parts of the range [592].

Communication: faeces may act as visual stimuli to other individuals, particularly when other scent marks may be less strong due to weather conditions [592]. Urine, faeces and secretions from the anal and abdominal glands are used to mark objects in their area, [186, 590, 721].

Dispersal: young disperse in autumn.

Aggressive behaviour: threat is shown by a low growl progressing to a deep huffing noise when extremely agitated. Growling may be followed by fighting, which may involve biting and a high-pitched squealing/screaming noise. Aggression reaches its peak during the breeding season both between the same and opposite sexes [625, 626]. No actual instances of fighting in territorial defence have been recorded; mutual avoidance seems more likely to be the method by which home ranges are maintained. In trapped martens, growling may rise to huffing when extremely agitated.

Table 10.8. Pine marten home-range sizes in various habitats.

Location	Pure conifer	Mixed conifer/ broadleaf	Mixed habitats*	Unspecified habitat	Techniques and source
Fort Augustus, Scotland			0.19–1.32 km²		Radio-tracking [721]
Republic of Ireland		♂ 0.19–0.44 km² ♀ 0.14–0.80 km²			Trapping [560]
Finnish Lapland			14–93 km²		Trapping [592]
European Russia	5–10 km²				Trapping [764]
N Russia				30–50 km²	Trapping [550]
Bucin, Czechoslovakia			0.93–1.39 km²		Inhabited dens [567]

* Mixed woodland, clear felled, open hill, pure conifer.

Activity: mostly nocturnal [550, 593, 721] with first and last emergences from den usually between sunset and sunrise, although daytime emergences have been recorded. In NW Scotland, Lockie noted one out of four sightings during the day, three out of four between sunset and sunrise. Near Fort Augustus, Scotland, two peaks of activity were found between these periods in the summer, while four occurred in the winter [721]. In Ireland, daytime sightings were most frequent in May and June, and were mostly of females carrying food [560].

Movement: a very agile animal well adapted for climbing and capable of short bursts of speed. Walks or bounds along the ground, the latter producing a very recognisable pattern of footprints. Well built for climbing with long, well-muscled limbs, strong claws and a long tail to aid balance. Climbs using claws and clutching the surface of the tree with one pair of legs while moving the other [338]. Have been reported making leaps of 4 m using tail to aid balance and falling 20 m, landing on all fours safely [339].

Nests/dens found in a variety of places including rock falls, hollow or fallen trees, amongst tree roots or stumps, squirrel nests and nest boxes set up for owls [338, 567, 721]. Outbuildings, lofts and even airing cupboards are also used by some animals living near or in human habitation [1]. Several main dens may be found within a home range; these are used frequently. There are also numerous subsidiary dens that are inhabited only occasionally as temporary lying-up sites [591, 721]. Favourite resting places may be visited by the same or different individuals during successive winters [591].

Grooming: similar to cat with stroking or scratching with fore and hind feet accompanied by licking and biting motions. Following grooming, fur balls may be coughed up [634].

FEEDING

A wide variety of foods taken, the percentages of which vary with seasonal availability. Main prey includes small rodents and birds, beetles and berries (Table 10.9). Similar data for Ireland, but rabbits and hares more frequent, occurring in 9% of scats [739]. In some studies in Finland and Sweden, squirrel was the main mammal in the diet [119, 550], although Russian data suggests that predation on squirrels is an idiosyncrasy shown by certain individuals only [365]. Although martens are very agile climbers, most hunting occurs on the ground [550, 593]. In Finland, small rodents and lemmings are pursued on the surface of the snow where their tracks are found and animals are dug out of hiding places under fallen trees and between stones. Berries, mushrooms and eggs are also dug up out of snow, while birds are tracked to roosting places and killed there [550, 593]. Martens will eat on average 140–160 g food/night [590] or approximately 10% of body weight [626].

BREEDING (Fig. 10.9)

Mate in July–August, with one litter born in March–April. In American marten, oestrous cycle with two or three periods of heat (3–4 days) separated by short quiescent intervals of 7–10 days [496].

Table 10.9. Mean percentage occurrence of food items in pine marten faeces.

	March−June			July−Oct			Nov−Feb		
	Scotland [721]	Scotland [459]	Finland [590]	Scotland [721]	Scotland [459]	Finland [590]	Scotland [721]	Scotland [459]	Finland [590]
Small rodents and shrews	49	45	69	50	25	60	77	50	66
Squirrels	0	NRF	5	<1	NRF	8	0	NRF	6
Other mammals	0	NRF	8	2	NRF	3	4	NRF	4
Carrion	10	NRF	14	1	NRF	2	0	NRF	15
Birds	26	8	18	14	6	4	19	14	15
Berries	0	0	3	29	42	44	1	NRF	11
Mushrooms	0	NRF	1	0	NRF	29	0	NRF	6
Insects	48	34	NR	40	19	NR	4	9	NR
Eggshell	1	NRF	NR	0	NRF	NR	0	NRF	NR

NR, not recorded; NRF, not recorded in format suitable for inclusion.

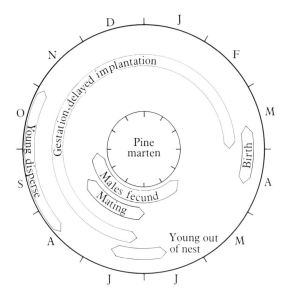

Fig. 10.9. Pine marten: life-cycle.

Implantation delayed 5.5−6.5 months; post-implantation gestation 30 days [625, 626]. Total gestation controlled by photoperiod in American marten [566].

Litter size for captive martens, 1−5 in Britain [338], 2−5 from 41 litters in Germany [626]. At birth young weigh 30 g [625, 626]. Lactation lasts 5−6½ weeks [626].

Martens show an increase in scent marking (both urine and abdominal gland) and obvious changes in external genitalia when coming into breeding condition. Male testis and penis enlarge in early June and remain so until September when recede again [625].

Males and females reach adult weight in first summer, but no sexual activity is evident until the second season (15+ months) [338]. In captivity, males show no obvious development of testes during the first season [625]; in American marten, they produce sperm and may show mating behaviour in second season [364], but may not succeed in fertilising a female until the third [496]. Females have a similar pattern, showing breeding behaviour in second season, but only a few succeed in producing young before third year. In American martens, oldest breeding female reported was 9 years [496].

Mating: precopulatory behaviour includes following and playful chasing, with purring and growling vocalisations. The female is then restrained by a neck bite and dragged about by the male. She assumes the mating posture (presentation) and copulation lasts from 15−75+ minutes. Females emit a clucking or piping noise as they approach oestrous [625, 626]. Martens are promiscuous and females can mate many times during an oestrous cycle [626]. Mating usually occurs on the ground, but has been reported in the branches of a tree [633].

Young are born with whitish fur, blind and deaf

and emit a call similar to tearing of cloth or like the call of a snipe [338]. Milk teeth reported at around 3 weeks (Germany, [254]), 4–5 weeks (Russia, [376]). Eyes open at approximately 40 days, but young do not go far from den for another 4 weeks [338]. By 3 months are out and very active with full juvenile coat which is similar in colouring to adults. Tail originally thin and tapering, becomes bushier with new adult growth in autumn. For growth rates see Table 10.10. Sexes show size differentiation from 8 weeks.

POPULATION

Densities vary with habitat and food availability. Changes in population numbers occur between seasons and years [460]. In American martens, when populations are put under pressure, adult females and juveniles succumb more quickly, possibly due to greater food requirements during production and care of young and while reaching adult size [748].

Sex ratio from trapping results slightly weighted towards males. Life expectancy in captive martens up to 17 years [338]. Longevity of 17–18 years reported in Lithuania in the wild with 45% of animals under 1 year, 29% 1–3 years, 26% over 3 years [376].

MORTALITY
Main predator man; killed by cars, trapping, shooting and general keepering. Eagles will take martens in Finland [550]; also observed in Scotland [26]. No information available on natural mortality or death resulting from indiscriminate use of poisons.

PARASITES
In Scotland wild caught animals are relatively free of external parasites [1]. The biting louse *Trichodectes salfii* is recorded from the Continent. The nematode *Skrjabingylus nasicola*, which infects the nasal cavity, occurs frequently in Russia, being found in up to 90% of animals under 1 year and up to 50% of animals over 3 years [376]; less frequent in Scandinavia (mean 5%) [262]. A lungworm, *Filaroides* sp., is also frequent in Russia.

RELATIONS WITH MAN
Previously hunted for pelts, sport and as general vermin in Britain [460, 518], but now given legal

Table. 10.10. Weights(g) of young pine martens.

Age in days	Males [626]	Males [254]	Females [496]
28		200	183
54–66	680		
74–77	820		
82–84	1040	950–1150	800–900
105	1360		
182		1700	1350

protection. Can live and breed in quite close association with man with few unfavourable results. In forestry, around crofts and farms consumption of small rodents and insects species may be of benefit. However, will take chickens if given the opportunity. Unlike other members of Mustelidae, not farmed commercially for its pelt due to late maturity, low breeding success in captivity, small litter size and only one litter per year.

Added to Schedule 5 of the Wildlife and Countryside Act in 1988. Present increase in distribution aided by the decrease in persecution and the additional habitat available from reafforestation (providing cover and food). Plantings providing a variety of habitats (verges, scrub, cliff, riverbank and different stages of canopy closure) are more suitable. Clear felling in patches is preferable as open areas were used less frequently [720, 721].

SOUND RECORDINGS
Appendix 3: A, F, J, P, S.

LITERATURE
Popular account in Hurrell [338, 339, 340].

PRINCIPAL AUTHOR FOR SPECIES
K.A. Velander.

GENUS *Mustela*

In its wider sense, as used here, this genus contains about 15 species and is represented throughout the N hemisphere. Three species, stoat (*M. erminea*), weasel (*M. nivalis*) and polecat (*M. putorius*), are native to Britain, whilst a fourth, American mink (*M. vison*), has been introduced. To these must be added a feral domestic form, the ferret (*M. furo*). The polecat and mink are sometimes separated from the stoat and weasel in distinct genera,

Putorius and *Lutreola* respectively. Although this may seem reasonable when considering the species represented in Britain, such a separation has very little basis when the entire genus is considered. The distinguishing characters of the four species are given in Table 10.11. Dental formula 3.1.3.1 / 3.1.3.2. Strong canine and carnassial teeth, and reduced premolars, reflect meat diet.

Stoat *Mustela erminea*

Mustela erminea Linnaeus 1758; Sweden.
Putorius hibernicus Thomas & Barrett-Hamilton, 1895; Enniskillen, Co. Fermanagh, Ireland.

Clubtail, royal hunter, hob, white weasel, stot; whittret (Scotland), weasel (Ireland).

RECOGNITION
Long slender body (20–30 cm) and short legs, as in weasel, but stoat has relatively longer tail (6–12 cm) with distinctive black tip present at all seasons. Live animals usually seen only fleetingly, bounding with characteristic arched-back gallop across a road, but it is sometimes possible to entice either species (both are characteristically very curious and may respond to squeaking noises or imitation of rabbit squeal) close enough to observe the tail. Both habitually sit up on hind legs to investigate strange sounds. Males much larger than females in both.

Skull flattened, with five lower cheek-teeth, width across slender cheek bones little more than across the brain case; distinguishable from that of weasel only by larger size (total length greater than 42 mm, lower jaw over 22 mm); but the smallest female stoats may be as small or smaller than the largest male weasels, even in sympatric populations.

SIGN

Footprints: five toes on each foot: tracks of front foot about 2.0 × 2.2 cm, hind foot about 4.2 × 2.5 cm. Stride when bounding about 30–50 cm between each group of four prints (average 30 cm in female, 56 cm in male) [549].

Droppings long (4–8 cm), thin, covered in hard black mucilage when dry; contain hair, feathers and bone fragments of prey, often drawn out into characteristic twists of fur at each end. May be piled up in dens [203], occasionally found deposited on prominent stones in the middle of a track.

Dens are usually the nests of former prey; in cold climates the walls are lined with rodent fur [493]. Dens may contain the remains of many days' meals [203] — teeth, feet and tails of rodents, flight feathers or beaks of birds, whole shrews. Territories of resident stoats contain several (2–10) dens and temporary resting places, used in turn [549, 584].

DESCRIPTION

Pelage: summer pelage russet to ginger brown above, white to cream below; margin dividing

Table 10.11. Characteristics of the species of *Mustela*.

	M. nivalis weasel	*M. erminea* stoat	*M. putorius* polecat	*M. vison* mink
Colour of upper parts	Reddish brown	Reddish brown	Dark brown	Dark brown
Colour of under parts	White	White	Brown	Brown
Colour of tail	Uniform	Black-tipped	Uniform	Uniform
Head and body (mm)	165–230	240–310	320–450	320–460
Tail (mm)	20–75	95–140	125–190	130–220
Greatest width of skull (mm)	32–42	42–53	58–71	60–72
Width of post-orbital constriction (mm)	7–9	9–12	16–18	10–13

upper from lower colour always straight, except in Ireland where only 13.5% of 170 *M. e. hibernica* had the straight colour pattern [638]; the rest were irregularly marked, like British weasels.

Moult: twice a year. Spring moult slow, progressing from head across back to belly; autumn moult faster, progressing in reverse direction [219, 712]. Initiation of the moult is controlled by day length; stoats from higher latitudes start the moult cycle earlier in autumn and later in spring, regardless of weather or altitude [394]. Winter pelage in north of range, including northern Scotland, entirely white except for black tip of tail ('ermine' condition); further south, winter coat brown but denser and sometimes paler than in summer. Across narrow intermediary zone of variable temperate climates, including England and New Zealand, various halfway stages can be observed, depending on minimum temperature and snowlie [319] and frost and altitude, but not daylength [394]. In USSR, ermine do not turn white in regions where stable snow cover last for < 40 days/year [219]. Females are more often found in full ermine than males [207, 255, 535]; hence the process of winter whitening might be controlled by a rare type of sex-linked genetic polymorphism [345]. Histology of moult and colour change illustrated in [627].

Anatomy and Physiology: eyes round, black, slightly protruding; whiskers brown or white, very long; muzzle black, dog-like; ears rounded, short, almost flat to head; feet furred between small pads. Large (8.5 × 5 mm in males, smaller in females) anal glands under tail emit a strong musky scent produced by several sulphur-containing compounds, identified as mixtures of thietanes and dithiolanes [45, 104]. Histology and anatomy of the anal glands described by [655]. Body temperature 38−40°C, oxygen consumption 3−4 ml/g per hour, respiration rate 86−100 breaths/min, average resting pulse 402 (range 360−480) in male, 421 (360−510) in female [698]. Small size, long thin shape and short fur make thermoregulation in cold climates very expensive in energy, as in weasel [60]; however, there are compensating advantages in small size for both weasels and stoats [391], which are especially important in the far north.

Reproductive tract: scrotum furred, testes regressed but still visible in adults from October to March; scarcely visible in 1st-year males. Nipples usually four or five pairs, visible only in adult females. Uterus simple shape, uniform colour (no placental scars); ovaries with prominent yellow corpora lutea of delay for 9−10 months of the year.

Teeth highly specialised for an almost exclusively carnivorous diet. Baculum long and slender, gently curved; increasing in weight and developing a smooth proximal knob in adults; length 20−30 mm, weight 10−80 mg according to age.

Chromosomes: $2n = 44$, $FNa = 60$ — data from Sweden, Japan and Ontario [767].

RELATIONSHIPS
Similar in general appearance to *M. nivalis*, but very different in ecology [395]; also similar to *M. frenata*, with which it co-exists in parts of N America [595].

MEASUREMENTS
See Table 10.12. Males about 50% larger than females; ratio of male to female adult mean body weights in five countries ranges from 1.4 to 1.8 : 1 [533] with great local and individual variation. In Britain, males grow to *c.* 260 g by July and reach adult weight of *c.* 320 g only in the following spring; females to 190 g and 220 g in same periods [122].

VARIATION
Size largest in Britain but not sufficient to justify recognition as subspecies (formerly named as *Putorius erminea stabilis* Barrett-Hamilton 1904; Blandford, Dorset): mean weights of adult males in other European countries range 208−283 g; Russia 134−191 g, N America 56−206 g [208, 255, 302, 412, 713], tending to be smaller in the north and east of Eurasia, south and west of N America. Intraspecific geographical variation in size and sexual dimorphism thoroughly investigated in both Russia [569, 570, 763] and N America [595]. Bergmann's Rule (correlation of large size with cold environment) does not explain the observed patterns in size (tending in opposite directions) on either continent. Two possible explanations for geographical variation in body size of stoats are body size of the local prey [181] or ecological energetics [616].

Irish subspecies, *M. e. hibernica*, distinguishable by irregular dividing line on flank, leaving only a narrow white ventral stripe in majority of individuals. Size increases from north to south in Ireland (Table 10.12). Form on Islay and Jura, described as subspecies (*Putorius erminea ricinae* Miller, 1907; Islay) mainly on basis of small size, is not distinguishable from mainland British form.

DISTRIBUTION

Present through the northern Holarctic. Introduced from Britain to New Zealand. Absent from Mediterranean lowlands south of N Spain and Portugal.

Throughout mainland Britain and Ireland at all altitudes, and now or formerly on many offshore islands larger than 60 km², including Jersey, Guernsey, Islay, Jura, mainland Shetland (introduced in 17th century or before), Wight, Skye, Anglesey, Sheppey, Man, Mull. Smaller islands, and some remote larger ones (e.g. Orkney, Outer Hebrides), apparently have too few mammalian prey to support a permanent population of stoats [395], though transient animals may visit smaller islands up to about 1 km offshore.

HISTORY

The immediate ancestor of *M. erminea* was *M. palerminea*, which was common in Europe from the Villafranchian until the Cromerian interglacial [429]. Fossil *M. erminea* dating from the last (Devensian) glacial period common in Europe [429] and recorded from Castlepook Cave, Ireland, at 33 500 years bp [652]; presumably also lived in Britain then, certainly throughout the post-glacial Flandrian period. Elaborate theories have been constructed to explain the variation in body size of stoats in Britain, Ireland and Europe, on the assumption that the local races of different body size have colonised post-glacial areas from different refugia [412] but *cf.* [761]; but mean body size of local populations descended from a common stock can show significant differences in only 100 years, as shown by stoats in New Zealand [394]. Total range in historical time not reduced by persecution from gamekeepers; artificially extended to various previously unattainable islands (e.g. mainland Shetland) on the assumption that stoats would help control small mammal pests [395].

HABITAT

Found in any habitat, at any altitude, that offers cover and prey; includes farmland, woodland, moors, marshes, mountains. Avoids open spaces

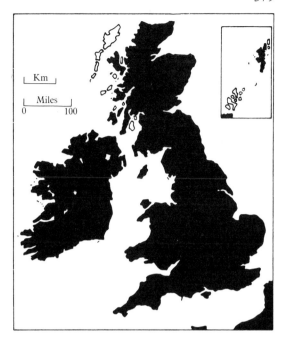

Map 10.5. Stoat.

by travelling along hedgerows and stone walls [174, 175, 584]; concentrates on piles of brush or timber that might harbour small mammals [706], marshes inhabited by water voles [174], or meadows and early successional communities favoured by field voles, rather than mature forests with little ground cover and fewer small mammals [203, 636].

SOCIAL ORGANISATION AND BEHAVIOUR

Most information comes from Sweden [174–177, 184], Switzerland [130, 132], Scotland [462, 584] and Canada [636].

Territories: sexes live separately. Territories of males may include those of one or more females [636]: resident animals of each sex defend territory, if necessary, against intruders of same sex [174]. Size of territory and pattern of use depends on distribution and density of prey: certain areas intensively used and repeatedly visited, others ignored.

One male in homogenous habitat (young plantation in Stirlingshire, with field voles 110–540 per hectare) occupied ⩾ 20 hectares [462]. In agricultural land near Aberdeen the figure for overall size of home range (e.g. minimum of 254 hectares for

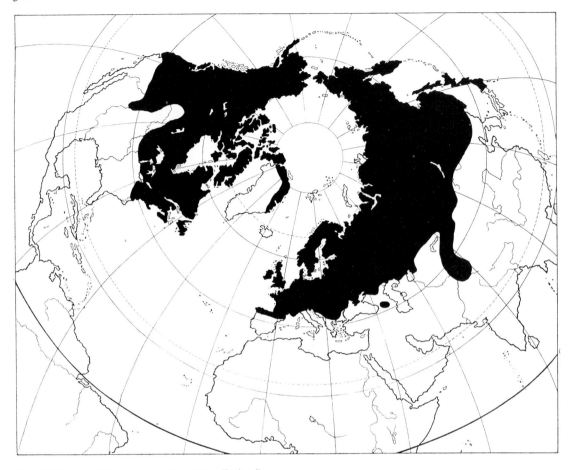

Map 10.6. Stoat (also introduced into New Zealand).

one male, mean of 114 hectares for three females) from radio-tracking [584] includes open fields never visited by stoats; 'exploitable' area (total length of dikes plus adjacent verges) nearer Stirlingshire figure. In open pastureland with scattered marshes in S Sweden, stoats concentrate on the marsh areas and connecting streams and stone walls: males occupied 8−13 hectare, females 2−7 hectare [174], estimated from trapping, snow- and radio-tracking. Trapping in Switzerland found home ranges of 8−40 hectare for males, 2−7 hectare for females [130]. Live trapping in Killarney unsuccessful [686]; in Cork, found home ranges of 2−22 hectares in females, 11 hectares in a male [638]; live trapping apparently never attempted in England/Wales.

In spring, the territorial system of the males breaks down, and dominant males range much farther than usual in search of mates. This rapid change from mainly nocturnal territorial behaviour in autumn and winter to mainly diurnal wide-ranging behaviour in spring [132], probably has evolved because the decisive resource for males in spring (receptive females) is more widely dispersed and less predictable and defensible than the decisive resource in the non-breeding season, usually food [182]. Females are also more diurnal in summer, but make the change later than males. Structure of retina suggests vision good both night and day, possibly including colour perception [226].

Distance travelled in one hunt depends on temperature and prey density; capable of 1−2 km in a few hours [584]; usually work along hedgerows, walls and banks, following familiar and regularly reused routes [175, 537, 549]: in extremely cold climates, remains under snow [410]. Families may hunt together into autumn and, since families can

Table 10.12. Measurements of British and Irish stoats (adults only).

| | Britain (general) [122, 206, 394] | | | | | | Aberdeenshire [584] | | | | | |
| | Males | | | Females | | | Males | | | Females | | |
	Mean	Range	n	Mean	Range	n	Mean	SD	n	Mean	SD	n
Head and body (mm)	297	275–312	4	264	242–292	8	275	± 16.7	31	240	± 11.5	23
Tail (mm)	110	95–127	4	117	95–140	8	—	—		—	—	
Weight (g)	321	200–445	204	213	140–280	99	296	±50.9	28	188	±26.9	23
Condylobasal length (mm)	49.61	± 0.283 SE	45	44.83	±0.283 SE	23	—			—		

| | Ireland, Co. Down [196] | | | | | | Ireland, Co. Waterford [196] | | | | | |
| | Males | | | Females | | | Males | | | Females | | |
	Mean	± SE	n	Mean	± SE	n	Mean	± SE	n	Mean	± SE	n
Head and body (mm)	252	± 3.7	24	208	± 7.0	13	278	± 4.7	11	230	± 8.7	9
Tail (mm)	—			—			—			—		
Weight (g)	233	± 12.9	24	123	± 9.1	13	334	± 15.5	11	165	± 19.9	9
Condylobasal length (mm)	45.9	± 5.89	15	39.4	±6.1	12	49.3	± 5.1	11	43.1	± 9.6	8

be large (5−8 young), reports arise of stoats hunting in packs.

Activity: spells of activity, usually 10−45 min long, interrupted by periods of rest; retreats and dens distributed throughout the territory; active throughout the 24 hours but relatively more at night during winter and in daylight during summer; ranges further and active periods longer, when prey scarce. Climbs easily and well even to great heights, running fearlessly along branches and down trunks head first [330, 539]; sometimes poked out of squirrel dreys [660].

Scent marking: territories of both males and females marked by scent marks of two distinct kinds, deposited by anal drag or body rubbing, which apparently carry different messages (body rubbing associated with threat signals during agonistic interaction, anal drag used to mark a resident's ground with its own individual scent). Scent marking certainly conveys complex information including not only the identity of the resident but also the probable asymmetry of a potential conflict between resident and intruder. Dominant individuals of both sexes mark more frequently than subordinates; dominance in males increases with length of residence, age and size, and high-ranking males dominate all younger or intruding males, and all females except those with young: between females, social status is less likely to be related to age and size. Various forms of offensive behaviour (approach, thrusting gestures, threat vocalisations, chasing, rarely actual fighting), less common than defensive behaviour (mutual avoidance, retreat into nest, escape, submissive vocalisation). Resident males may or may not 'patrol' their ranges, depending on the season and the amount of 'pressure' from neighbours; scent marks normally renewed in the course of hunting.

Voice: usually silent, but can produce range of sounds similar to weasel [176, 239].

FEEDING
Food mainly small mammals of rabbit/water vole size or less, of whatever species locally available, although not necessarily in direct proportion to availability (Fig. 10.10). In British Isles before myxomatosis, rabbit was staple food; studies in following 10−20 years found rabbits still comprised about one-third of the diet of the remaining stoats,

but supplemented with small rodents, brown rats, squirrels, birds and other less usual items [660]. In Europe, USSR and N America stoats small, ideally sized for hunting in tunnels [635], and are specialists on voles. When food is short, stoats turn to secondary foods, e.g. earthworms [557] and fruit; a road casualty in Devon was found to have its stomach full of blackberries [341].

Food preferences in the wild explicable in terms of optimal foraging theory [179]; stoats hunt in the most profitable microhabitats, and tend to become more selective as prey becomes more abundant, preferring larger prey (watervoles, young rabbits) that give the best return in energy for the effort spent in catching them. Shrews may be killed, especially in cold climates where they are active under snow all winter, but not often eaten; more usually ignored. Killing behaviour is independent of satiation, and the caching of large numbers of surplus prey should be seen as a positive strategy for small carnivores dependent on unstable resources [554].

Foraging behaviour and hunting tactics observed in enclosures [538] and by radio-tracking in the field [179, 584]. Prey located mainly by sound or sight (motionless vole or mouse may remain undetected until it moves) during active searching throughout likely habitat; stoat never lies in wait (cf. [549]). Systematically examines every patch of cover, zig-zagging from one to next or running straight between hunting areas along easiest route, e.g. along wall tops, paths or roads [584]. Kill always made by a swift and accurate bite at back of neck [239, 760]; large prey, such as rabbits, gripped at nape, enfolded by forelegs and scratched with hind claws. If necessary, stoat may leap on to rabbit's back from up to 2 m away, not always successfully. If blood extrudes from wound, stoat will lick it first before beginning to eat, which may have given rise to false idea that stoats suck blood. Well-grown rabbits and hares and large birds, e.g. ptarmigan, are too large to be killed at once by neck bite; these probably die of shock [314].

Birds on ground stalked from cover, though stoat often gives itself away too soon; birds may be attracted by 'dancing displays' and pounced on if close enough, but this behaviour not always related to presence of potential prey (13 cases observed [584]); the possibility that such displays are less a deliberate hunting policy than a response stimulated by intense irritation caused by skrjabingylosis

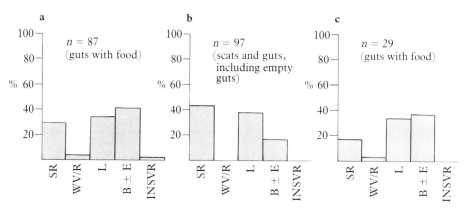

Fig. 10.10. Food of stoats (a) in Britain generally (recalculated from [116]); (b) in Scotland [584]; (c) in Ireland (recalculated from [116]). SR = small rodents; WV/R = water voles, rats; L = lagomorphs; B±E = birds with/without eggs; INSVR = insectivores.

(see below) not disproved. May pursue a single rabbit through a colony whose other members continue to feed, and victim may eventually act in panic-stricken way (a 'stoated' rabbit) and lie down squealing without further resistance [211]. Swims well, across streams and in seawater to inshore islands up to 1 km away [395, 674]. The large British stoats freely enter underground tunnels of water voles and rabbits, but are excluded from those of voles and mice.

Impact of predation by stoats on their prey depends on the local circumstances. The small Californian ermine removed 6–54% of the over-wintering population of voles (*Microtus montanus*) from their subnivean winter nests [203] and may have a substantial influence on the 3–4 year *Microtus* cycle; mustelids (mostly stoats) in one New Zealand study area robbed many nests of native and introduced birds, reducing the birds' reproductive success [534]; losses of partridge eggs and chicks to predators, including stoats, may significantly influence the size of partridge populations in good nesting habitats, especially the size of the exploitable surplus [582]; six to nine stoats introduced to the Dutch island of Terschelling (110 km²) in 1931 exterminated a large population of water voles by 1937 [715]; the same result was achieved, but more quickly, by six stoats released on the Danish island of Strynoe Kalv (46 hectares) in 1980 [369]; on the other hand, in Britain the number of rabbits controls the number of stoats, not *vice versa* [660], so it is not surprising that

stoats failed to check the spread or numbers of rabbits introduced into New Zealand [387].

Daily food requirements of British stoats calculated as: males, 57 g/day (23% body weight), females 33 g/day (14%) (minimum estimates) [116]. German males in captivity required 19–32% of body weight and females 23–27%/day [535]. Food requirements of a female during lactation two to three times higher than normal; whilst providing for weaned but still dependent young, five to ten times higher [535]. Elongate shape allows pursuit of prey into burrows, but at a high cost in energetic inefficiency [46].

BREEDING (Fig. 10.11)
Mate in summer, but implantation is delayed until the following spring when a single litter of *c.* 6–12 is born.

Males become sexually mature at 10–11 months old: weight of baculum remains at 20–30 mg until that age, then almost doubles with the onset of puberty, and continues slowly to increase for at least 4 years [251, 713]. During the period of rapid spring enlargement of the testes of both 1st year and older males (February to April), there is a massive increase in concentration of plasma testosterone [252]. Adults have a well defined fertile season from May to July [122]; then testes regress rapidly and are quiescent until November, although the regressed testes of adults in autumn and winter are still distinctly larger than the undeveloped testes

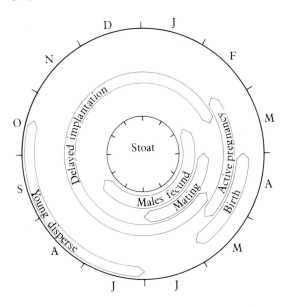

Fig. 10.11. Stoat: life-cycle.

marked seasonal increase in activity and trapping rate, while younger ones remain close to a resident female and attempt to retain priority of access to at least one mate [615]. By midsummer virtually all females, of all ages, are impregnated.

Initial development of the corpora lutea and blastocysts is rapid, but is interrupted after 2–3 weeks by an obligate delay in implantation of 9–10 months, lasting until March, during which time the corpora lutea remain small and plasma progesterone levels low [122, 123, 253]. Implantation is controlled by increasing spring daylength, and mediated by a rise in plasma progesterone, produced by the reactivated corpora lutea [253]. The critical daylength stimulating implantation is reached earlier in lower latitudes, hence the season of births is earlier, e.g. a difference of about 10 days between northern and southern populations in New Zealand, seven degrees of latitude apart [394]. Active gestation is 4 weeks [609] and the young are born in April or May.

Productivity: mean ovulation rate in Britain 10, range 6–17 [609]; in New Zealand 10, range 3–20, with an inverse correlation between counts for the two ovaries of one individual [394]. Fecundity tends to be higher in 1st year females than older ones [394, 677], and in seasons when small rodents are abundant [382]. The number of young produced depends on the extent of intra-uterine (resorption) and pre-independent (nestling) mortality, which may vary from 0–100% of available blastocysts depending on food supplies during the season of implantation and lactation. The highest reproductive success is recorded in areas [179] or in years [382, 386] with the highest density of favoured prey.

Embryo counts average nine ($n = 12$, range 6–13, [122]; $n = 17$, of which 25% showed some resorptions, [609]). Sex ratio at birth 1 : 1 [535, 677].

of subadults at the same season [394]. Spermatogenesis begins in December, but spermatozoa are not found in the cauda epididymidis until May [252].

Females: juveniles become sexually mature at about 2.5–3 weeks old, and even though at that age they are still immature in every other respect, they enter a normal oestrus and are mated by the adult males. In captivity a 17–day-old female, which weighed 18 g and was blind, deaf, helpless and almost immobile, was mated for 1 min and after 337 days gave birth to 13 kits and fed them successfully [677]. In the wild, the lack of a year-round pairbond and the rapid turnover of population [127, 636] reduces the chances that the male is serving his own young.

Adult females have a post-partum oestrus and induced ovulation [609] facilitated by repeated and vigorous mating [535, 677]. Artificial insemination always unsuccessful even after injection of gonadotropin [609]; corpora lutea not found in un-mated females. Males take no part in rearing the young [177]; rather, they attempt to maximise the number of matings they can obtain. Has been suggested that they use different strategies depending on their age and social status; the older, dominant males search for multiple mates over extensive areas during the season, contributing to a

Young: newborn young are blind, deaf, toothless and covered with fine white or pinkish down. At 3 weeks the neck region develops a prominent but temporary brown mane. Birth weight in Britain about 3–4 g [122]. When the female is away, kits under 5–7 weeks old are unable to maintain body temperature; they huddle together, and below 10–12°C will enter into reversible cold rigor with reduced sensitivity, cardiac and respiratory function; full homoiothermy at environmental temperatures down to 0°C attained only when fur fully grown at about 8 weeks old [629].

Eyes open at 5−6 weeks (females first); black tail tip appears at 6−7 weeks; milk teeth erupt at 3 weeks, solid food taken from 4 weeks on, lactation lasts 7−12 weeks [155, 257, 535]. The female feeds and cares for the litter unaided [322]. Permanent carnassial teeth Pm and M_1, last in place; typical prey killing behaviour pattern innate, but improves with practice from 10 weeks to full development at 12 weeks [239]. Young females usually remain near their natal area [174]; 16 of 18 did so for life [180]; but young males capable of very long (20 km+) dispersal within a few weeks of independence [393].

Male and female stoats have different reproductive strategies, and their breeding success is controlled by different criteria (males by competition for mates, females by the energy demands of solo parenthood); the optimal body size for each sex is not exactly the same, hence the pronounced sexual dimorphism observed (Table 10.12) [177, 533, 616]. The problem of why stoats have delayed implantation, whereas weasels do not, is the subject of current debate [385, 388, 587, 614, 617, 643].

POPULATION

Both stoats and weasels have the attributes of opportunistic or r-selected species, by comparison with other British mustelids [396]. Density and local distribution of stoats closely related to those of their favourite prey [384], e.g. the water vole in Eurasia [25, 125, 126, 180], the rabbit in Britain [660], and *Microtus* in Germany [599]. Annual variations in density are controlled mainly by breeding success; substantial local increases in favoured prey in spring increase survival of the already fixed number of young available to be born that season, by reducing mortality either in the uterus or in the nest or both [382, 386]; hence the numerical response observed after a glut of prey is due mainly to an unusually large cohort of young animals [382, 597].

Density: mean density of several studied populations: Sweden (autumn) 0.3−1.0 stoats per 10 hectares, up to 2.2 per 10 hectares in favoured areas [180]; Switzerland, average of five to six adults present every month from January to June, and two to three adults plus three to eight young each month from July to December, on 616 hectares [127]. Density indices (captures per 100 trapnights) simple to calculate from kill trapping records, and

when calibrated against known density do give valid results [180]; the range of density indices commonly < 1−7 captures/100 trapnights, depending on season (highest in late summer and autumn), habitat (prey density), and year [130, 180, 386, 636, 670].

British stoat populations severely reduced for 15−20 years after myxomatosis almost cleared the countryside of rabbits in 1953−56 [660]. Numbers caught annually on 1600 hectares in Hampshire were 136−302 in 1947−53, 13−58 afterwards [17]; on 9300 hectares in Norfolk, the annual kill was 409−1013 in 1927−1954, 40−257 in 1955−1969, 168−448 in 1970−1976 [379]. The gradual return of stoats since 1970, closely following that of rabbits [669], is best documented in Sussex but detectable all over the country. A similar short-term decline in density of stoats in S Sweden, correlated with a decline in rabbits observed from 1975−1979 by [180], was not directly attributed to the loss of the rabbits, but to the consequent increased competition for voles from other generalist predators living in the same area. The Swedish stoat is smaller and eats fewer rabbits than the British; on the other hand, it is possible that this explanation might apply in Britain as well. Less drastic variations normal following fluctuations in prey; capable of startling population increase if introduced into favourable habitat: nine multiplied to 180 in 3 years on Terschelling Island, Holland [715].

Sex ratio at birth 1 : 1, but kill-trapping normally produces an excess (60−65%) of males, even higher in spring; however, observation of undisturbed live animals sometimes shows an excess of females [549, 597]. Live-traps may, over a period (especially in autumn), record males and females about equally often, but the individuals most often recaptured are always males [180, 393], probably because the home ranges of females are much smaller than those of males. The number of females caught in any kind of trap is strongly influenced by trap spacing [381]: live traps are commonly set closer than spring traps.

Age determination by skull characters and baculum [394, 713], relative width of canine pulp cavity [408] or canine cementum layering (confirmed to be annual on 20 known-aged stoats in [251]). Minimum baculum weight of adults in Holland 32 mg [713]; in New Zealand 38 mg [394];

in Britain unknown but probably within this range. In living animals, young of the year can be distinguished from adults only in summer. Over 99% of adult males have enlarged testes in summer, but young of the year do not; adult females have visible nipples, small if they have not borne young, larger if they have, but nipples of young of the year are invisible. These distinctions 100% correct when checked from canine pulp cavity widths or cementum annuli [180, 393]. Skull shape and pulp cavity width can be determined on living animals by X-ray [128].

Age structure of any particular year's catch depends on the breeding success of the previous year; proportion of young (0−1 year old) can vary from 90% to 0%; average lifespan short, especially where kill-trapping pressure is continuous [127]. Data on undisturbed populations obtainable only by live trapping. In 5 years data from southern Sweden, the proportion of young varied from 31% to 76%; average life expectancy from the age of independence (3−4 months old), 1.4 years in males, 1.1 years in females; maximum age observed 4.5 years (1 of 47) in males, 3.5 years (1 of 48) in females [180]. In 3 years data from Switzerland, the proportion of juveniles from August to December was 55−67%, mean age 14.4 months [127]. Maximum age attained (infrequently) by wild stoats in temperate countries about 6−8 years [251], less in the far north [408].

Survival: juvenile survival from blastocyst to independence clearly correlated with food supplies [384, 386]; recruitment independent of spring density [180]; overwinter survival similar in all years, regardless of autumn density, sex or food supplies [180, 382]. A hypothetical model of a constantly cropped population in Holland, assuming sex ratio 1 : 1, litter size six and constant mortality of 0.75 (all later shown to be more or less correct) predicted the observed age structure very well [713]. Actual mortality rates in undisturbed populations measured in the field slightly lower: 0.40−0.78 (males) and 0.54−0.83 (females), according to age and year, in Sweden [180], 0.68 (both sexes) in Switzerland [127]; i.e. two-thirds of all live adults in one year will die before the next year. Population turnover very high (0.93/year) [127], i.e. only 7% of adults remained resident a 2nd year, but the study area was rather small relative to the dispersal capabilities of stoats.

Competition: stoats co-exist with weasels over most of the Holarctic, even though both species depend on virtually the same resources: in theory, this should lead to intense competition and local exclusion of one or the other [588]. The relative proportion of the two does vary between places and years, especially since myxomatosis, but long-term co-existence can be observed in game records both in Britain [503, 669] and Europe (e.g. [14]). This is probably because each species has one competitive advantage over the other; the weasel in hunting rodents (exploitation competition) and the stoat in social dominance (interference competition), and the shifting balance of these advantages makes complete exclusion of one by the other temporary only [395]. Later work has confirmed the superior tunnel-hunting ability of the weasel [584], and the aggressive advantage of the stoat [183]; local and temporary extinctions and returns do seem to be characteristic of both species.

MORTALITY

Shortage of food is probably the primary agent of mortality for stoats, especially those under 1 year old; other causes of death include predation and trapping. Hawks, owls and larger carnivores all kill stoats occasionally, and whether or not predation affects population density, it may have a significant selective effect on the biology of small mustelids. Experiments with tame hawks showed that the black tip of the tail of *M. frenata* deflects the raptor's strike, so has survival value as a predator-confusion device [586].

The steel spring trap, set with or without bait, often in tunnels, runways and holes, catches individual stoats very effectively, though not all are equally catchable [127, 180, 393] and some can learn to avoid traps [56]; the proportion of the total population caught depends on the arrangement, spacing and frequency of inspection of the traps [381]. Trapping of stoats (for fur or protection of game) less intensive now than formerly, and probably never did have any effect on the density of stoat populations generally: trapping must remove >75% of the population in order to exceed the high natural mortality rate, and this is probably impossible over any large area [381]. Intensive local and seasonal trapping on a game estate in Sussex removed most resident stoats for a few months each spring, but these were quickly replaced as soon as the keepers turned to other work [670]; a century of trapping on British game estates has had no long-term effects on stoats [396]. Trapping may, however, affect age structure and longevity [127].

Mortality due to disease scarcely documented. Skrjabingylosis is probably less damaging than it appears (see below).

PARASITES

Stoats commonly suffer invasion of the nasal sinuses by the nematode *Skrjabingylus nasicola* causing recognisable deformity of the skull. Calculated rate of infestation in Britain varies from 17% ($n = 12$, [439]) to 31% ($n = 46$, [714]). Obligate intermediate hosts are terrestrial snails. Paratenic hosts once thought to be shrews [261], but this is likely to vary geographically. Recent experimental work has demonstrated invasive 3rd stage *S. nasicola* larvae encapsulated in *Apodemus*, which readily eat molluscs both in the wild and in captivity, and can induce skrjabingylosis in an uninfected stoat within 24 days [747]. Shrews may well contribute to the level of damage by adding re-invasions, but cannot account for the general rate of infestation.

Heavy infestations believed adversely to affect skull size on Terschelling [714] and density and fertility in Russia [432, 581], but stunting of infested individuals not detected in sample of 1492 in New Zealand, and density more likely to be affected by prey resources [394].

Fleas are scarce, and always comprise the species stoats can acquire directly or indirectly from their prey, or by sleeping in nests taken over from prey, including fleas specific to animals rarely eaten by stoats, e.g. mole fleas. European records of stoat fleas total 26 species [129]. The fleas of British stoats have not been examined systematically, but two male stoats from Aberdeenshire were carrying two *Rhadinopsylla pentacantha*, an uncommon flea specific to vole nests, and one *Megabothris rectangulatus* [495]. The biting louse, *Trichodectes ermineae*, appears to be uncommon.

Other diseases recorded are few, e.g. distemper and tularaemia [581].

RELATIONS WITH MAN

Stoats are among the traditional vermin regularly killed by gamekeepers and poultry farmers, most obviously because a single stoat in a pen or enclosure can cause great damage, destroying every bird in sight. Recent research by the Game Conservancy supports the traditional view that stoats can help to substantially reduce the harvestable surplus population of gamebirds in the field [582, 670], and keepers are advised to control them [19], even though the effect is only temporary [670].

Stoats are legally protected in Eire, but not in Britain. They are probably not in need of active conservation in any country. Their reputation as destroyers of rodents and rabbits is often exaggerated [455].

Techniques for field study (Fenn-trapping, live trapping, footprint recording) reviewed in [392]. Stoats can survive injuries ranging from bruises to loss of toes, foot or whole leg in gin traps; Fenn traps are much more humane and should be used even where gin traps are still legal [383]. Radio-telemetry methods for stoats well developed [178, 584] and very effective.

SOUND RECORDINGS
Appendix 3: A, J, P, S, V.

LITERATURE
[390] — a monograph on stoats and weasels.

AUTHOR FOR THIS SPECIES
C.M. King.

Weasel *Mustela nivalis*

Mustela nivalis Linnaeus, 1766. Vesterbotten, Sweden.
Mustela vulgaris Erxleben, 1777. Central Europe.

Kine, cane, beale, rassel, mousehunter, grass-weasel, finger weasel; whittret (Scotland), bronwen (Wales).

RECOGNITION
Very small size, short legs and long slender body (13−23 cm) distinguish it from all other species except stoat. Usually difficult to distinguish live weasels from stoats when seen at any distance (e.g. bounding across road, sitting upright on hind legs), but in the hand, weasels easily identified by the lack of a black tip to the short (3−6 cm) tail.

Skull very small (total length under 42 mm, jaw under 22 mm) and distinguishable from that of stoat only by size; but even in Britain the range of sizes of the largest male weasels may overlap that of the smallest female stoats, and weasels in southern Europe are larger than stoats in Scandinavia. Severe distortions of the postorbital area of the skull caused by skrjabingylosis relatively more common in weasels than in stoats.

SIGN

Footprints show five toes on each foot: tracks of front foot about 1.3 × 1.0 cm, hind foot about 1.5 × 1.3 cm. Stride when bounding about 20–30 cm between each group of four prints.

Droppings very similar to those of stoat but smaller (3–6 cm long). Feeding sign likely to be found only in dens, then indistinguishable from stoat.

Dens: Weasels do not make their own runways or dens but take over those of prey, complete with nest parasites [374]. Each home range includes many dens and resting places visited at intervals [584], which in cold climates may be thickly lined with accumulated fur of prey [103].

DESCRIPTION

Pelage: summer pelage russet to ginger-brown above, white to cream below; margin dividing upper from lower colour irregular in Britain and West European subspecies, straight in N Scandinavian [648], Russian and N American subspecies [255]. Those with the irregular markings usually also have a large brown spot at the corner of the mouth, entirely or partially separate from the brown of the head, and often also spots and blotches of brown on the belly. This variable pattern allows recognition of individuals [453].

Moult twice a year, in same manner as stoat [377]. In N and E Eurasia turns entirely white in winter [220, 648]. Southern limit of winter whitening further north than for stoat, seldom including British Isles, but winter fur paler; at a certain stage of spring moult the incoming summer fur may appear as a distinct dark stripe [377].

Anatomy and physiology: general appearance very similar to that of stoat, but smaller. Anal glands 7 × 5 mm [655]; chemistry of contents distinctly different from that of stoat [45]. Long thin shape, short fur and small size give weasels higher mass specific rate of heat loss than in other mammals of similar body mass in all seasons; body temperature is 39–40°C, and the energy cost of thermoregulation in cold climates is very high, so winter is a time of severe energetic stress [60]; the ability to retreat under insulating snow blanket and into fur-lined nests crucial to survival [391]; activity pattern maximising time in nest is a positive strategy even in cool temperate climates [49]. Normal oxygen consumption 4–7 ml/g per hour, respiration rate 96–104 breaths per minute, pulse 451 (range 420–480) in male, 468 (420–510) in female [698].

Reproductive tract: scrotum furred, testes regressed but still visible in adults from November to January. Uterus similar to stoat, but smaller; ovaries show corpora lutea only in breeding season.

Nipples usually three or four pairs, visible only in adult females.

Baculum short and thick, with strong hook at distal end, increasing in weight and developing spiny proximal knob in adults; length 16–20 mm, weight 10–60 mg according to age.

Chromosomes $2n = 42$ on the Continent and in N America [767].

RELATIONSHIPS
Previously considered distinct from the N American least weasel, *M. rixosa*, which was believed by some also to co-exist with *M. nivalis* in N and E Eurasia; but these now usually regarded as conspecific [13, 30, 92].

MEASUREMENTS
See Table 10.13. Males about twice the size of females (ratio of male to female adult mean body weights in three countries ranges from 1.8 to 2.2: [533]) with huge local and individual variation, not only between local British populations but also between years in the same population and even between days in the same individual [372].

VARIATION
In continental Europe there is a very substantial north–south increase in mean size from N Scandinavia (mean head and body length 166 mm male, 148 mm female [648] to Egypt (278, 242 mm) [556]. Variation in condylobasal lengths in W Europe [411], also shows north–south increase in size; mean for Britain falls within this pattern, but trend within Britain is in opposite direction (Table 10.13). Smallest weasels found in N and E Eurasia, Alps and N America.

British form indistinguishable from W European (*M. n. vulgaris*). Distinguished from *M. n. nivalis* (N Scandinavia and Siberia) by irregular flank line and lack of winter whitening [648]. These have been considered separate species but are in fact interfertile [215].

DISTRIBUTION

Sympatric with stoat throughout the northern Holarctic, except that weasel extends further south than stoat into Mediterranean countries, including N Africa and Egypt, and is absent from Ireland. Introduced from Britain to New Zealand, but much less common and widespread there than stoat [395].

Throughout British mainland and on offshore islands, larger than 380 km² including Wight, Skye, Anglesey and Sheppey, together with stoat, but not on smaller islands or without stoat [395].

HISTORY

Descended from *M. praenivalis* by a gradual transition, completed by the Cromerian interglacial stage [429]. Modern form recorded among a forest fauna of that age at West Runton, Norfolk [652], and common in European cave deposits dating from the last glaciation [429]. Date of recolonisation of Britain uncertain; in fact, a high-arctic mammal fauna, including both weasel and stoat, could live near to ice front, and might not ever have been completely expelled from southern England [761] and the exposed land south of the present coast. Absence of weasel from Ireland and northern islands previously taken to mean weasel returned later than stoat, after Ireland was cut off, but modern distributions not likely to be explicable from events so far back. An alternative hypothesis [395] is that weasels and stoats both reached Ireland in the early Holocene, together with a varied cold-adapted fauna including lemmings, but not voles (*Microtus* or *Clethrionomys*); then weasels died out when the lemmings became extinct and were not replaced by voles. Total range in historical times not reduced by persecution from gamekeepers.

HABITAT

Very wide range of habitats, as stoat, though less common where small mammals are scarcer, e.g. on higher mountains or in woodland if with sparse ground cover [172, 372]. In severe climates, woodland preferred to open ground in winter [540], if available, otherwise weasels capable of living entire season under snow [514]. In temperate open country, restricted to hedgerows, stone dykes and other cover [530, 584].

SOCIAL ORGANISATION AND BEHAVIOUR

Territories: sexes live on separate territories, much larger in males than in females; social hierarchy, mutual avoidance and territory-marking behaviour much like that of stoat [49, 216, 236, 722]. Size of male's territory, as revealed by trapping, depends on season and food supplies. In thick ungrazed grassland (young plantation) in Stirlingshire, where prey (field vole) density was 110–540 per hectare, 10 males occupied 1–5 hectares each [462]; in mature deciduous woodland near Oxford, where prey (wood mouse and bank vole) density in 1968–70 was 21–39 per hectare, seven males occupied 7–15 hectares each, three females 1–4 hectares [372]; in the same area in 1978–80, when density of bank voles (the weasel's main prey in this habitat) was especially low, there were no resident weasels [295]. In Aberdeenshire farmland in 1971–73, total winter ranges of five males were 9–16 hectares, summer ranges of three males 10–25 hectares, ranges of two females about 7 hectares [530]; in same area in winter/spring 1977–78, total ranges

Map 10.7. Weasel.

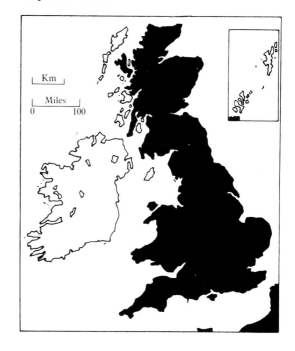

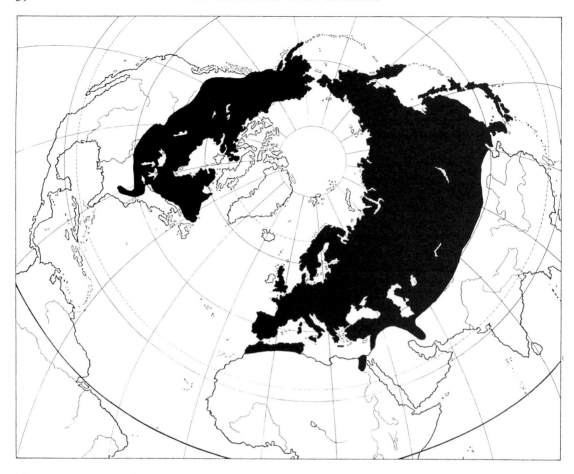

Map 10.8. Weasel (also introduced into New Zealand).

of seven males estimated by radio-tracking averaged 34 hectares, of two females 38 and 12 hectares [584]. As in stoat, large parts of total range in farmland (i.e. open fields) normally unused; when these excluded, exploitable area reduced to average of 2.4 hectares for males, 1.2 hectares for females [584]; however, one male observed in turnip field during harvest, working along rows hunting for wood mice disturbed by labourers. Males extended their ranges in spring [172, 530]. Distance travelled in one hunt variable: as in stoat, pattern is of localised foraging in favourable areas interrupted by longer straightline excursions between them, which can be very rapid (e.g. 1.3 km in 55 minutes [530], [584]).

Activity: active both day and night in the wild, usually in bouts of 10–45 minutes separated by

rest periods including one to three of 4 hr+ each day; radio-tracked excursions away from nest mainly by day [584] and hence trapping success greater by day [372, 530], but in captivity, activity pattern often more or less nocturnal, and easily influenced by feeding regime [589]. In spring, females less active, saving energy for pregnancy by remaining in nest and feeding from cache, but males are more active in spring, as in stoat [49]. Time spent out of nest strongly influenced by ambient temperature (more in summer) [295].

Voice described and analysed in [239, 337]. Four basic sounds: two threatening, a guttural hiss when slightly alarmed and a short screaming bark or chirp when provoked; a shrill defensive wail or squeal; and an excited, high-pitched trilling during friendly encounters between mates or between

Table 10.13. Measurements of British weasels.

Locality	Head and body (mm)				Tail (mm)				Weight (g)				Source
	Mean	SD	Range	n	Mean	SD	Range	n	Mean	SD	Range	n	
Aberdeenshire*													
Males	210	10	185–229	54	50	4	39–58	54	129	27	73–202	194	[530]
Females	174	4	167–180	8	37	3	34–42	8	62	7	52–74	22	[530]
Wigtownshire													
Males	210	10	180–225	24	44	5	33–57	24	131	24	72–174	30	[370]
Females	173	—	168–181	3	28	—	18–36	3	55	—	53–57	3	[370]
Northumberland													
Males	209	12	183–226	38	46	6	35–60	38	122	26	80–189	38	[370]
Females	181	4	169–185	15	40	6	29–54	15	61	10	47–77	14	[370]
Berkshire*													
Males	214	9	202–229	13	46	8	36–59	13	112	17	55–138	262	[370]
Females	177	1	176–179	5	40	4	34–44	5	63	7	50–77	38	[370]
Hertfordshire†													
Males	205	—	194–216	27	47	—	42–52	27	117	—	109–125	26	[730]
Females	177	—	171–183	12	39	—	34–44	12	69	—	56–82	10	[730]
Sussex													
Males	204	10	175–219	34	44	5	32–55	34	106	19	68–161	104	[370]
Females	180	5	172–192	20	40	3	32–44	20	63	7	45–80	61	[370]
Devonshire													
Males	—	—	—	—	—	—	—	—	95	—	71–115	25	[116]
General (Mostly Wales)													
Males	202	—	175–220	46	60	—	40–75	46	115	—	70–170	162	[320]
Females	178	—	165–190	12	50	—	40–65	12	59	—	35–90	36	[124]

* Weights of live animals, measurements from carcases. Figures include juveniles and pregnant females.
† Gives medians, not means.

mother and young. Vision is good, and includes detailed form-discrimination [304].

FEEDING

Normal diet summarised in Fig. 10.12. In general, weasels are specialists on small rodents, and are strongly adapted in every respect of their biology to exploitation of, and dependence on, this feast-or-famine resource; however, in Britain and other mild climates, birds and their eggs are very acceptable additional prey; shrews are generally avoided, although occasional individuals may actually prefer them [173]. Seasonal and local variation in prey may or may not reflect local availability. Among six individual male weasels in Oxfordshire, bank voles were the staple prey of the woodland residents, and the number of field voles eaten increased in proportion to the extent of the grassland habitat in each males' territory [378]; in Aberdeenshire, wood

mice comprised 3% of the diet of farmland weasels in spring, 33% after harvest, and bank voles were much less often taken than would be expected from their abundance [531]; in Sweden in autumn and winter rodents were almost the only food for weasels of both sexes (94%), and were taken in proportion to abundance, but in spring and summer, when these were scarce, male weasels (but not females) turned to the newly available young rabbits (40%) [173]. In farmland in Sussex there was a spring shift to young lagomorphs (especially by male weasels) in March–May, followed by a brief period in June when weasels of both sexes concentrated on birds, especially in years when field voles were scarce [668]. By contrast, few birds were eaten by the weasels on the Swedish study area, where the density of breeding birds in that year (1972–73) was low but rabbits were available. In Oxfordshire (birds abundant, rabbits scarce in 1968–70),

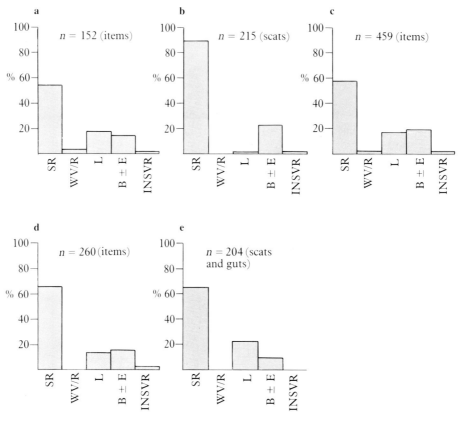

Fig. 10.12. Food of weasels (a) in Britain generally [117]; (b) in Oxford [378]; (c) in Sussex [668]; (d, e) in Aberdeen [531, 584]. SR = small rodents; WV/R = water roles, rats; L = lagomorphs; B±E = birds with/without eggs; INSVR = insectivores.

weasels took a large number of birds and eggs in spring, and no rabbits [378]; they do so in many years, especially since myxomatosis [140].

Males tend to take more larger prey (lagomorphs, rats) than females [47, 668], though the difference is not always significant [375, 531], since, for example, it disappears when small rodents are abundant [173], or it may reflect different hunting strategies by males and females (e.g. females spending longer in rodent burrows and hence less likely to meet rabbits on the surface than males). When introduced on to islands where voles are absent, weasels are at a disadvantage [395].

Foraging behaviour of weasel similar in style to that of stoat, except that weasels concentrate on searching through tunnels and runways of voles and mice too small to admit stoats, whereas stoats will enter rabbit burrows avoided by weasels. Female weasels move freely through all but smallest field-vole burrows (20–25 mm diameter); males get through the largest with a squeeze [584], and also use mole runs [374], and are occasionally caught in mole traps [330]. In Aberdeenshire, male weasels spent about 50% active time under matted grass, females about 90% [584]. Access to tunnels means that weasels may forage at any time independent of the activity rhythm of prey; rodents have no effective refuge or defence, even if aware of the predator [647], other than familiarity with their home range, freezing, and demographic compensation [389]. Weasels capable of living for months together in a mouse-infested corn rick or in lemming burrows under snow.

Observations of weasels hunting in an enclosure [173] showed that males and females had no particular preferences, but caught voles and mice in about the same numbers and generally ate them in the order they were caught; but males were more efficient as hunters, and caught more of the prey offered, than did females. Prey located by sound, sight or smell [105, 584]. Rodents always killed by a well-aimed, stereotyped bite at the back of the neck [239, 297]. Attacks on larger animals unusual, but records include brown hares [51], even tawny owls [688]: however, possibly these were not intended prey, but were attacked while defending their leverets or attempting to prey on the weasel. Climbs and swims as well as stoat [330]. Often raids bird nestboxes [631] and may have a substantial effect on these bird populations [140, 201]; will also kill birds caught in mistnets [22], even small mammals caught in Longworth traps [445]. Weasels need to eat frequently (five to ten meals of 2–4 g each per day) and have a high metabolic rate, so cannot survive starvation beyond *c.* 24 hours; part-eaten prey are cached [232, 554].

Impact of predation by weasels on the density or population biology of their prey difficult to calculate and results seldom (so far) totally convincing. In Wytham Woods, Oxford, weasels apparently removed 8–10% per month each of the population of bank voles and wood mice present, much less than the calculated total disappearance rate of 12–64% in the same months, and there was no correlation between the local patterns of density and survival of weasels and rodents [378]; however, when predation by weasels and by tawny owls was considered together, the combined impact could have been substantial [389]. Weasels are also by far the most important cause of breeding failure of tits (Paridae) nesting in boxes in Wytham Wood, especially in years when rodents are few [140]. Weasels could, in theory, account for the entire known loss of gamebird chicks in an average summer on a Sussex game estate [667].

Daily food requirements of weasels is about a third of body weight per day (males 0.33 g/g per day, females 0.36 g/g per day: [532]; mean assimilation efficiency is about 80%, higher for the least bulky foods (i.e. larger prey from which weasels can take mostly meat and avoid the fur and feathers). Meals (dyed mouse) pass through gut in 3–4 hours [632]. Most of the energy absorbed goes on respiration, although reproduction is also very expensive; even at 12–13°C, two captive breeding females required an additional 6–7% of their normal intake during gestation, plus 80–100% during lactation [295].

BREEDING (Fig. 10.13)
One or two litters, each of usually four to six young, born each season without delayed implantation.

Males and females can become mature at 3–4 months old, and may mate in the year of their birth, though usually unsuccessfully. Most do not produce young until the following year [124]. In Britain, adult males fecund from February to October, though early stages of spermatogenesis present throughout winter [320]. In adult females, anoestrus lasts from September to February; heat

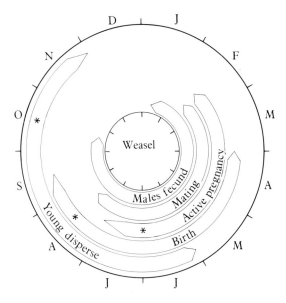

Fig. 10.13. Weasel: life-cycle. ⋆ Secondary peaks of activity in vole peak years only (not every year).

Productivity: in Britain mean ovulation rate 7.1, range 4−11 ($n = 32$); embryo rate 5.6 ($n = 12$) to 6.4 ($n = 5$); number of young born 6.2, range four to eight (17 litters) [124, 379].

Growth: birth weight 1.5−4.5 g, slightly heavier in male kits [295], increasing rapidly to 70−90 g in males, 50−55 g in females, by two months old; sex ratio at birth 1:1 [373]. Development of young in captivity well documented [41, 154, 290, 295, 296]. Deciduous teeth erupt at 2−3 weeks, weaned at 3−4 weeks, though lactation may last to 12 weeks; eyes open at 4 weeks (females first); kill efficiently at 8 weeks; permanent dentition completed at 10 weeks; family group breaks up at 9−12 weeks; adult weight attained at 12−16 weeks, later in males. Growth in second litters (if any) slower than in those produced in spring, 'minivers', or exceptionally small weasels, may represent these late-born young [90].

POPULATION

The weasel is the most strongly r-selected (opportunistic) of the British mustelids [396]. Weasel populations are very unstable, varying over a wider range than those of stoat, and closely related to fluctuations of rodents [384, 385].

Density: Correlation between local density and distribution of weasels and small rodents well established [134, 379, 668]. Immediate effect of 1st myxomatosis outbreak dramatic: the flush of vegetation released by removal of rabbits led to great abundance of small rodents in 1957−58, followed by record catches of weasels on game estates [660], a sudden reversal of the usual ratio (2−3:1) of stoats to weasels [307], and a steadily increasing population of weasels at least to the early 1970s [669]; the removal of rabbit trapping, and of interference competition from stoats, may have helped. The gradual recovery of the stoat, accelerated after 1970, has been accompanied by a substantial decline in weasels, though not as yet to the pre-myxomatosis ratio. Capable of sudden massive population increases in response to vole peaks, not only because of improvements in survival, but also because of the capacity (unique among carnivores) to produce additional litters in summer [379, 385]. Conversely, in vole-poor years, weasels may become locally extinct [295], but they have high dispersal ability and will probably recolonise in due course. On the possible effect of competition with stoats on

(indicated by a swollen vulva; implantation is direct), and pregnancies may be observed at any time between March and August [124, 379]. During vole peaks, adult females may produce a second litter, and early born young can also breed for the first time. By mid to late summer of a good vole year, the 1st year females have several times the numbers and only half the mortality rate of the adults, hence most of the large number of young weasels born in July and August of such years are produced by the early born young females [379]. Even though breeding is very demanding in energy, it is such a high priority for weasels that they are able to continue pregnancy through moult (after a temporary pause during oestrus [377]) and at below-zero temperatures (subnivean temperature data given by [514]). Conversely, during very poor vole years, adult females may fail to rear any young at all [668]. The minimum density of voles necessary for successful breeding calculated as 10/ha [172], 14/ha [667], 15/ha [135]; if voles scarcer than this, weasels cannot breed on *Apodemus* alone even if these are at 35/ha [135].

No delay in implantation; gestation period 34−37 days [41, 290, 296]; rearing takes at least 9 weeks, hence the full cycle takes about 3−4 months.

distribution and density of weasels, *see* Stoat (p. 385).

Sex ratio at birth 1 : 1, but in trapped samples almost always a surplus of males (mean 75%, range 65−86%, in 12 local samples, total *n* = 2211 [373]). There is no evidence of differential mortality between sexes, and sex ratio does not change significantly with season or age, so the excess of males trapped is probably due to a bias in sampling. Males have much larger territories, so are more likely to find traps, and females may well be less active and more trap shy, especially in spring [373].

Age of living animals extremely difficult to determine. There is a method of classifying ages of skulls, based on known-age material and suitable for use on dated museum material which must not be damaged [380]. There is no definable minimum baculum weight distinguishing adults. More precise results can be obtained from counting cementum annuli [250] but these not so far proved to be annual from known-aged material; periosteal zonation in the mandibles is not satisfactory [380].

Greatest part of population at any one time composed of weasels < 1 year old (range 68−83% in samples from five British game estates (total *n* = 455) [379]; not significantly lower in small sample not previously trapped (59%, *n* = 22). Mean age of males 0.86 year, females 0.93 year; range in different samples 0.79−1.16 year, mean 0.88 year; maximum age attained about 3 years. Similar figures reported from Denmark [358].

Survival: mean expectation of life at independence usually < 1 year; turnover of the population very rapid; mean mortality rate from independence in 1st year 75−80%, in 2nd 80−90%; only one in 80−90 young survive to over 2 years old in the wild, but can live up to 10 years in captivity [379]. None of the live animals observed by Lockie [462] lived longer than 3 years.

MORTALITY

Predators: weasels are small enough to be regarded as, or confused with, prey by almost all other predators, including hawks, owls, foxes, cats and mink; even stoats are best avoided [183], but weasels can sometimes fight back [52]. Even when dead, they are regarded as distasteful by, for example, foxes [468]. From experiments with tame hawks [586], it was shown that model *M. nivalis* with black-tipped tails were easily caught by hawks, and suggested that the tail of *M. nivalis*, in contrast to that of *M. frenata*, is too short to carry an effective predator-deflection mark. Hence predation may exert a selective effect on the appearance of weasels, even though populations of weasels are much less likely to be controlled by predation [585], than by food [384].

Trapping: traditional gamekeepering probably incapable of having any long-term effect on weasel populations, although it does introduce a seasonal peak in the mortality rate in spring, when most trapping is done [379]; but that does not imply that keepers affect the annual level of mortality. The weasels removed in March−May are rapidly replaced in July−September [668]. However, stress is generally higher during the spring breeding season even in undisturbed populations: several resident male weasels at Wytham died after drastic loss of weight in spring [372].

PARASITES

Prevalence of the nematode parasite *Skrajabingylus nasicola* in the nasal sinuses ranged from 69−100% in seven samples of British weasels (*n* = 614) [375]. The degree of damage to the skull is a good indicator of the number of worms carried per host [440]. Infestation increases with age, probably by repeated invasions; on average, 1st year weasels carried 5.7 female worms averaging 143 mm long, plus 2.2 males, 84 mm; older weasels carried 7.5 (145 mm) and 3.3 (93 mm) [440]. Although the incidence of *S. nasicola* is high in Britain compared with Europe, N America and Russia (26−56% in seven samples [136, 262, 432, 714, 724]), and the damage can be extremely severe, especially in damper areas, there was no evidence that infested weasels were smaller, lighter, leaner, or died sooner than others [375].

Fleas picked up from the runways and dens of small rodents which weasels have hunted through or slept in. Eleven species recorded at Wytham, Oxford [374]; six of these plus an additional two species recorded from Aberdeen [495]. Of the 13 species, eight are normally found on voles and mice, or in their nests; two are monoxenous on moles (*Ctenophthalmus bisoctodentatus* and *Palaeopsylla m. minor*), one on shrews (*P. s. soricis*), one on rats and other rodents (*Nosopsyllus fasciatus*) and one on birds (*Dasypsyllus gallinulae*). Weasels seldom eat moles, shrews or rats, so would have less opportunity to acquire these fleas, or the specifically nest fleas, such as *Rhadinopsylla pentacantha*, by direct contact with the normal hosts, than indirectly, by borrowing infested nests. Conversely, frequently eaten prey with uninviting nests, e.g. birds, seldom passed their fleas to weasels. The host specific biting louse, *Trichodectes mustelae*, has been recorded.

Diseases recorded from weasels are few, but they are susceptible to sarcosporidiosis [664] and perhaps also to distemper and tularaemia, as stoat.

RELATIONS WITH MAN

Gamekeepers have traditionally made no distinction between stoats and weasels as enemies of game; weasels certainly capable of killing gamebird chicks, and, in some years, could have a substantial effect [583, 667], but they are probably less important in the long run than foxes, stoats and other predators, which can kill the sitting hens, because the losses of these are more directly density-dependent than are the losses of chicks [582].

The weasel's ability to control rodents is commonly overstated; local people attributed the Scottish vole plague of 1892 to widespread removal of weasels for export to New Zealand [289].

Can make excellent pets [137]. Methods of live trapping weasels described in [371, 497, 612]; handling under anaesthesia in [463]; Fenn trapping and footprint tracking in [392]. Radio telemetry has been applied successfully to weasels [584].

SOUND RECORDINGS
Appendix 3: A, J, P, S.

LITERATURE
[390] — a monograph on stoats and weasels.

AUTHOR FOR THIS SPECIES
C.M. King.

Polecat *Mustela putorius*

Mustela putorius Linnaeus, 1758; Sweden.
Putorius vulgaris Griffith, 1827.
Putorius foetidus Gray, 1843.

Foul marten, fulimart, foumart, foumaire, fummet (English vernaculars); fitchuke, fitchew, fitcher, fitchet, fitch (in fur trade); ffwlbart (Welsh).

Male — hob; female — jill or jen; young — kits or (pole) kittens.

RECOGNITION
Distinguished from mink by creamy underfur over most of body, bicoloured guard hairs which are pigmented almost to base in summer coat but conspicuously divided into light basal half and dark tip in winter, facial mask and white ear margins; from escaped ferrets by (usually) much darker appearance and more restricted white facial band (Fig. 10.14), though some feral ferrets and polecat—ferret hybrids probably indistinguishable on external features.

Skull distinguished from mink's by greater absolute and proportional width of postorbital constriction ($\geqslant 15$ mm in polecat, < 15 mm in mink); similarly with ferret skull (postorbital constriction < 15 mm) but absolute separation from ferrets and polecat—ferret crosses difficult [23, 24].

SIGN

Footprints (Fig. 10.15) rarely seen and may be confused with those of mink. Commonest gait arched-back gallop, in which hind feet placed in same position as forefeet and tracks in groups of two. Average stride at this gait 40—60 cm. When walking, feet placed singly astride median line with 20—25 cm between each track. When bounding at speed, body stretches out more and pattern of four prints rectangular, rhomboid or irregular. Tail drag may show. Polecat uses regular paths and runways, including man-made tracks, but keeps under cover where possible.

Faeces: scats long, cylindrical, twisted and taper to one end, coiling slightly as dropped, 5—9 mm in diameter and up to 70 mm long; looser if polecat fed on frogs. Blackish, especially when fresh, but colour varies with diet. Fresh droppings bear characteristic musky odour but not used as markers. Deposited inconspicuously in latrine associated with den [39]. Pungent anal scent marks (sometimes visible as smears) of independent origin. Distinguished from faeces of stoats and weasels by size, and from mink by usually not containing fish bones (mink scats almost always do).

Fig. 10.14. Heads of wild Welsh polecat (left) and polecat-ferret (right).

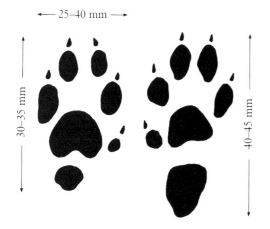

Fig. 10.15. Polecat: fore and hind footprints.

Feeding remains: cranium of prey often bitten through at base. Heads of toads not eaten because of poison glands. Frog ovary masses also rejected. Birds' eggs opened in characteristic way (large, jagged, square opening bitten in side) and egg shells may bear marks of canines. Prey usually carried by polecat to nearest burrow but may be cached among vegetation.

Dens vary from casual resting places above ground to self-excavated lairs with compartments [236]. Usually simple and occupied opportunistically. In winter, polecat may seek shelter in or under buildings.

DESCRIPTION

Long, sinuous, cylindrical body, relatively short legs, long neck, small, flattish head, blunt face and small, broadly rounded ears. During autumn/early winter lays down subcutaneous fat and appears tubby. Marked sexual dimorphism in size (male larger) and some difference in shape of muzzle (thicker in male) but otherwise sexes alike. Eyes small with dark brown iris; facial vibrissae long; tail furry, slightly bushy and comparatively short. Hind toes long, slightly webbed and bear weakly curved, non-retractile claws 4 mm long; front claws 6 mm long, strongly curved and partially retractile. Plantar and palmar tubercles bare in summer and furred in winter; soles always thickly furred.

Pelage: coat contains both underfur and guard hairs. Proportion of these types of hairs varies between juvenile and summer coats, when density of underfur and guard hairs reduced, and adult winter coat. Underfur buff over most body but greyish over shoulders and forelimbs, rump and hind limbs and on tail. Coarser guard hairs pigmented (dark brown to purplish black with iridescent sheen) almost to base. Fine structure illustrated by [131]. Guard hair width 100–125 μm (cf. 8–20 μm for underfur), with medullary index of 0.70–0.85.

In winter, coat underfur much longer (25 mm vs 15 mm), denser and whiter, except over extremities. Guard hairs much longer (up to 40 mm) with distal half pigmented and basal half white. Also denseness of wool forces guard hairs to stand out and expose underfur. Back assumes whitish hue which may have camouflage value.

Greyish white face markings distinct features. All polecats have white ear margins, white chin patch extending onto muzzle and white cheek patches. Mask appears in young about 9th week, firstly as two white patches between eyes and ears which elongate towards jaw angle as animal grows older. In winter, both adults and juveniles show varying degrees of development of white frontal band which appears across forehead to unite cheek patches. Sometimes cheek patches join but more often remain separated by grizzled area. May also develop downwards to join up with chin patch and form complete ring. Winter coat fully moulted May–June, when animal reverts to juvenile pattern of face patches.

Skull (Fig. 10.16) robust and rather flat, with short rostrum, short, broad braincase and long, nearly parallel-sided postorbital constriction [519]. Juvenile cranium pear-shaped, with greater cranial capacity, slight postorbital constriction, short nasal region, small tympanic bullae, rough surface, poorly developed crests and obvious sutures. May not reach final dimensions until 3rd year [302].

Teeth: upper canines long, narrow and almost straight; lower canines recurved at front. A proportion of adult skulls have asymmetrical dentition, most often supernumerary incisors [611], perhaps due to recent addition of ferret genes [29]. Tooth-wear can be severe in older animals and may prevent feeding properly. Two patterns of attrition have been identified [31].

Baculum (Fig. 10.17) weight and shape used to separate male juveniles up to age 7 months from adults [734]. Adult baculum consists of expanded knobbly base, tapering shaft and hooked tip. Shape and size of baculum differs considerably in juveniles but above about 300 mg becomes indistinguishable from that of adults.

Scent glands: anal glands are paired spherical bodies at base of tail: secrete foetid creamy musk.

Chromosomes: 2n = 40, FNa = 64 [767].

RELATIONSHIPS
Very similar to steppe polecat *M. eversmanni* apart from colour. Ecology and behaviour also very similar, except where dictated by differences in habitat preference. Formerly regarded as conspecific.

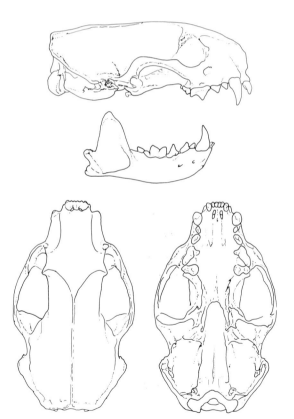

Fig. 10.16. Polecat: skull of adult [519].

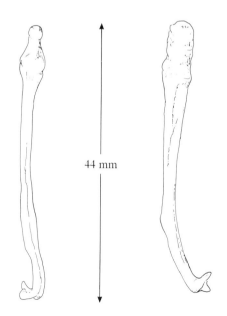

44 mm

Fig. 10.17. Polecat: baculum of adult [734].

Steppe and European polecat largely separated but possible crosses with intermediate characteristics [548] and diploid chromosome number 39 [241]. In Finland, polecats known to interbreed with European mink (*M. lutreola*) [242].

MEASUREMENTS

See Table 10.14. Body weight varies seasonally in males; males are in poorest condition from April to June, females lightest from July to September [746]. Weights up to 1815 g recorded in captivity. Mean male:female sexual dimorphism in body weight is 1.61. Marked changes in female body weight caused by pregnancy/lactation [39]. Further skull dimensions and proportions quoted in [24, 519, 574].

VARIATION

May be characterised locally by considerable variation in dimensions and proportions [48] but geographic variability overall slight and subspecies not recognised. Some differences in average sizes between British and continental samples [732], cf. [111, 233]. Two forms described from British Isles as endemic subspecies: *Putorius p. anglius* Pocock, 1936; Llangammarch Wells, Breconshire (Powys), for England and Wales; and *P. p. caledoniae* Tetley, 1939; Lochinvar, Sutherland (Highland), for Scotland. Validity of both recently questioned [109].

Occasionally black pigment in guard hairs replaced by reddish one ('red' or erythristic variety). Degree of redness variable; most British records

from a restricted, mainly coastal area of W Wales. First record 1903 [210]; several reported by 1950s [504] but few since. Erythristic animals noted in other parts European range, e.g. W Russia [687]. Red and normal colour varieties may occur together in same litter [571]; red genetically recessive to normal black [573].

Only other variation in coat pattern seen in a few animals that show slight flare-shaped extensions of white chin patch onto black throat, usually associated with a scattering of white hairs on limbs. Probably acquired from breeding in wild with escaped ferrets. The situation is further complicated by man's producing 'fitch ferrets' by crossing true ferrets with wild polecats. In polecat's main range, external features of animals of mixed blood are quickly absorbed by the wild population, although evidence of cross-breeding detected in Mid Wales [39]. On perimeters of range traces of polecat–ferret crosses more common.

DISTRIBUTION

Range on continent extended towards N, E and S during recent decades, though densities often sparse and polecat under pressure from land-use changes over much of W Europe. Overlaps with and replaced by steppe polecat in E. Europe and European Russia.

Despite earlier claims [55], European polecat does not appear to occur in Africa [561]. Successfully introduced to New Zealand in 19th century.

In British Isles formerly widespread range currently restricted to Wales and adjacent English

Table 10.14. Measurements of adult polecats in Britain.

	Males			Females		
	Mean	Range	*n*	Mean	Range	*n*
Body weight (g)	1111	800–1710	28	689	530–915	14
Head and body (mm)	398	330–450	28	367	335–385	14
Tail (mm)	149	125–165	28	133	125–145	14
Neck circumference (mm)	146	125–180	28	123	115–130	14
Ear (mm)	26.1	22–29	28	22.7	21–24	14
Hind foot (mm)	60.4	53–68	28	53.1	51–58	14
Condylobasal length (mm)	67.0	–	31	60.4	–	7
Zygomatic width (mm)	41.4	–	25	34.8	–	7
Minimum frontal breadth (mm) (= postorbital constriction)	16.5	–	31	15.8	–	7

External measurements from mid Powys [39]; skeletal measurements from Wales [732].

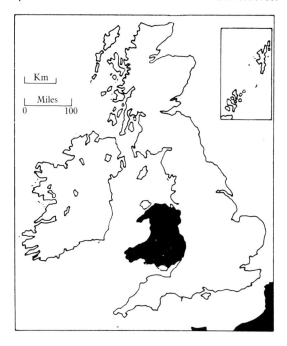

Map 10.9. Polecat.

counties but has been increasing since relaxation of persecution by man. Apparently never present in Ireland.

HISTORY

Probably entered Britain during the early post-glacial but earliest genuine subfossils Neolithic [249]. History prior to 1800 poorly documented but evidently widespread and common throughout England, Scotland and Wales. Despite various pressures, continued to maintain itself until middle 19th century, when numbers fell and range reduced. This decline was correlated with the development of sporting estates [430] rather than decline in woodland. Last definite record for Scotland 1912 [603]. Few possibly survived in isolated parts of England until the 1930s. Population minimum probably reached 1915. Continued to flourish in Central Wales and Marches, where little keepering. Even there suffered from widespread gin-trapping when rabbits were trapped commercially. First World War relieved gamekeeper pressure and marked the beginning of a period of decreased keepering activity, to which polecat responded rapidly with increase in numbers and range [502].

Map 10.10. Polecat.

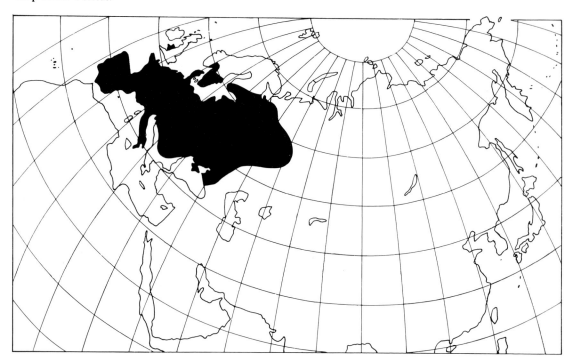

Most recent expansions traceable to changes in 1950s. Commercial rabbit trapping was no longer economical after the introduction of myxomatosis. Trapping out-of-ground predators also stopped, reinforced by 1958 legislation banning the use of gin traps, and this allowed the polecat to recover. The Wildlife & Countryside Act 1981 afforded extra protection to polecat.

Future seems to be assured. Extensive drainage, hedge removal or agricultural improvement could constitute serious threat to survival. Increased forest planting probably assisted recovery. Predicted large-scale forestry development (replacing some upland agriculture) in Wales unlikely to affect status in short term. Present distribution in Britain half as large again as 20 years ago [731, 733]. No reason for expecting reversal of trend but unrealistic to expect a full recovery to former position. Some successful reintroductions in Scotland.

HABITAT
In Britain, polecats occupy a variety of habitats: woodland, forest plantations, wide hedgebanks, farmland, marginal land, marsh, river banks, sea cliffs and sand dunes, generally in thinly populated areas. Less common on high ground in mountainous areas, though plantations may enable exploitation of higher ground. Generally from sea level to 520 m but recorded at 920 m. Many records (mostly road casualties) in Britain from river valleys. This may simply be because roads tend to follow valleys, although it may reflect prey distribution.

Often associated (especially in winter) with farm buildings and houses on the edges of settlements, where adequate shelter and prey (rats and mice) often abundant. Rubbish tips similarly favoured habitat. Will tolerate the presence of small numbers of people. Found near the centre of Aberystwyth [578], Bangor [1] and Llandrindod Wells [39] and even found in cities on the Continent.

SOCIAL ORGANISATION AND BEHAVIOUR
European polecat, ferret and hybrids differ in behaviour [579]. Polecats are quick, nervous and easily frightened, whereas ferrets are easy to handle and resemble juvenile polecats in behaviour. Hybrids show intermediate characteristics.

Home range and denning: home-range behaviour and social system dynamics studied by live-trapping and radio-tracking in Mid Wales [39]. Home-range characteristics very variable according to season,

habitat (prey availability) and polecat's sex and social status (Table 10.15). Breeding females settled into discrete home range, whilst rutting males and dispersing juveniles more mobile, with fluid home ranges. Dispersal movements up to 10 km recorded. Mean home-range area for all polecats studied 101 hectares. Average male:female dimorphism in home-range size 1.84 (Table 10.15). Home-range shape variable, covering various habitat types, but always two-dimensional rather than linear (cf. mink). Strong habitat selection exhibited with respect to core areas (primary foraging areas) exploited but nature of this preferred habitat varied individually. A diversity of dens (Table 10.16) formed important foci of activity. Much time spent resting in them or foraging in their vicinities; dens occupied either temporarily or for longer periods. Breeding females limited to single den when rearing young.

Intrasexual territorial spacing; territorial overlap ascribed to breeding factors. Otherwise solitary with no direct contact. Limited cohesive behaviour established in captivity but no hierarchy. Territorial behaviour only weakly developed when densities are low. Territories vacated voluntarily and often not refilled [39]. Play, fighting and other interactions well studied in captives (e.g. [576, 577]).

Movements and activity: movements categorised into short foraging excursions (usually concentrated around one den), inter-den movements and more extensive shifts/expansions of range. Most stays at one den about one day (mean 26.6 hours). Males undertook longer inter-den movements. Nightly foraging routes typically covered 3–4 km (maximum about 8 km). Average 85% time spent in core area occupying about 20% of range, and ranges rarely regularly patrolled. Radio-tracked polecats predominantly or exclusively nocturnal with crepuscular activity peaks, although many reports of diurnal behaviour elsewhere [303]. Activity correlated principally with that of prey and suppressed by availability of food surpluses but also modified by weather. Average time spent by females in foraging (4.2 hours/day) greater than that for males (mean 3.0 hours/day). Both sexes became more diurnal and exhibited reduced activity in winter [39].

Normally walks with ambling gait, body fully stretched out, almost level, and head held low. Heels placed flat on ground, tail trails downwards

	Males ($n = 14$)		Females ($n = 7$)	
	Mean	Range	Mean	Range
Home range area (ha)	119	18–355	64	29–83
Perimeter length (km)	4.65	1.9–8.1	4.0	2.7–5.0
Maximum linear distance within home range (km)	1.8	0.7–4.3	1.3	1.1–1.5
Core area (ha)	13.4	3.6–22.8	10.9	6.6–17.6
Number of dens	5.3	2–11	4.6	1–6
Inter-den distances (m)	715	30–3350	475	0–1100
Mean daily inter-den movement distance (m)	523	138–943	393	80–802
% nocturnal movements	92	67–100	93	85–100

Table 10.15. Home-range characteristics of polecats radio-tracked in mid Powys [39].

	Males ($n = 74$)	Females ($n = 32$)	Total ($n = 106$)
Rabbit burrow	53	41	49
Badger sett/other burrow	22	28	24
Log/brushwood pile	11	16	12
Couch in vegetation	5	6	6
Tree base/rock crevice	5	3	5
Human artefact	4	6	5

Table 10.16. Percentage of den types used by 20 radio-tracked polecats in mid Powys [39].

and pelvic region is highest point of body. When moving faster back repeatedly arched, giving sinuous appearance to gait. When hunting moves with large jumps. Can penetrate relatively small openings owing to flexibility of body. Can climb but rarely does; has little springing agility and judges distance poorly. Sometimes described as semi-aquatic and good swimmer, but in Britain at least rarely ventures directly into water.

Olfaction: relative amount of the active constituents of anal gland secretions species-specific to polecat [45]. Odour strong and unpleasant and used for setting scent, presumably to mark territory [159]. Musk also extruded as reflex action if frightened or enraged.

Vocalisation: adults normally silent but possess wide variety of calls. Divided into threat and molesting calls, squeal/shriek defensive/submissive calls and begging, greeting and appeasement calls [239]. Make clucking and chattering sounds when relaxed. Hiss and scream when frightened to disconcert enemy. Young emit distress calls.

Senses: capable of localising sounds very accurately and reacts quickly to slight noises. Keen sense of smell used in hunting, recognising territory and finding mate [760]. Although picks up and follows scent trails on ground, also sensitive to windborne scents [536]. Eyesight in daytime not good but better at night, particularly in relation to moving objects [536, 630]. More sensitive to light intensity than colour but can distinguish red from blue or green [226]. Fifteen rods per cone [578].

FEEDING
Prey selection and predatory behaviour of known (radio-tracked) individuals studied in Mid Wales by scat analysis [39]. Food very varied but mainly vertebrate. Bulk of diet comprised lagomorphs (37%), small rodents (32%), birds (19%) and amphibians (6%), and included notable semi-aquatic component but no fish (Table 10.17). Relative importance of lagomorphs (mainly rabbits) increases to 63% when corrected for handling/digestibility. Some food taken as carrion. Birds' eggs and a variety of invertebrates occurred as traces. Plant material taken only incidentally. In

Table 10.17. Diet of polecats in Wales, based on 558 scats collected from 20 polecats.

Prey category	% bulk estimate in diet
Lagomorphs	36.5
Wood mice	14.8
Bank vole	10.6
Field vole	5.7
Other mammals (each < 2%)*	6.9
Galliformes	7.6
Passeriformes	4.2
Columbiformes	2.3
Other birds (each < 2%)†	5.2
Amphibians	6.0
Invertebrates	0.3

* Includes hedgehog, shrew, mole, house mouse, rat, squirrel.
† Includes Anseriformes, Gruiformes, waders, gulls.

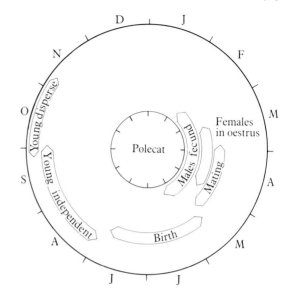

Fig. 10.18. Polecat: life-cycle.

Europe, eat fish as well [111]. Eels may be caught by polecats in Britain. Feeding strategy opportunistic, and prey taken roughly in proportion to seasonal and relative abundance. Variations in diet of different age classes of polecats insignificant. There is a high degree of association between male and female diets but dietary overlap varies seasonally, being greatest in spring and least in summer [39]. Various European studies confirm catholic and opportunistic nature of diet, different prey items predominating according to habitat and season.

Predatory behaviour: movement of prey is important stimulus to predatory behaviour [20]. Smell may also serve as stimulus for prey selection [21]. Prey stalked and seized in fangs, then killed by neck bite which is instinctive [235, 760] but perfected by practice [160]. When rabbits and rodents taken these are often young from the nest, although the polecat is capable of killing animals as large as a goose or hare. Caches food [594], often large numbers of frogs or toads, in times of excess [236]; these are bitten at base of skull so that they are paralysed but not killed and so remain fresh; this may be a special technique [760] or a chance effect.

BREEDING

Seasonal, breeding once a year (Fig. 10.18). Both sexes sexually mature and begin to breed in the year following birth. Wild females probably in oestrus from late March. Captive females have

remained in oestrus for up to 6 weeks when unmated, but this is unlikely to happen in the wild. Climate and latitude may affect the timing of breeding [110]. Lips of vulva become engorged. Testes heaviest and sperm most abundant from March to May [736]. There is no courtship.

Mating behaviour is vigorous, the male grasping the female by the neck and dragging her about. This acts as a stimulus to induced ovulation. Copulation lasts up to 1 hour. Probably promiscuously polygamous, the male mating with several females. No delayed implantation. Gestation 42 days [305]. Most animals born late May/June. Although only one litter usual, in Russia there is the potential to reproduce again if litter lost [676] but this is unlikely in Britain.

Nipples difficult to locate in non-lactating animals. Number of active nipples (maximum 10) does not correspond to number of offspring [39]. Litter size 2–12 (usually 5–10), seven or fewer on average surviving to weaning.

Young: usually first observed occurrence of young is appearance of 'families' of mother and dependent young. Males known to stay in vicinity of breeding den but do not assist in rearing young [39]. At birth young weigh 9–10 g and have head and body length 55−70 mm and tail length 14−15 mm [254]. Eyelids and ears closed. Week-old kits have thin covering of silky, white hair. Replaced when 3−4 weeks old with cinnamon brown-greyish woolly coat. Ear tips and parts of muzzle retain whiteness. By 50 days young have assumed more typical appearance with characteristic facial markings.

Weaning begins at 3 weeks. Eyes open at beginning 5th week, when litter mates of both sexes are of equal size. Subsequently, the males grow faster. Eruption of permanent dentition begins at 7−8 weeks and completed by 11−13 weeks [254]. Juveniles reach adult proportions in the late autumn of the year of birth. Achieve independence when 2−3 months old.

POPULATION

Densities in Mid Wales and elsewhere apparently not great. Distribution of territories clumped for no obvious reason. Low breeding rate and high juvenile mortality coupled with past persecution may explain present spatial organisation [39]. Life expectation of males at birth 8.1 months [732]. Observed adult sex ratio based on captures/corpses heavily male-biased [39]; males survive better as juveniles but observed sex ratio due mainly to behavioural differences. Life span 8−10 years, rarely 13−14 years, in captivity but 4−5 years more probable in wild. Some suggestion that polecats are particularly susceptible to cold but not supported by thermoregulatory properties: polecat's reaction to cold similar to that of mink and stoat, which have more northerly distributions [409]. Populations may also fluctuate markedly in response to abundance of small mammals [548].

MORTALITY

Ferocity and powerful scent protect polecat from most larger predators. Sometimes killed by dogs, possibly also by foxes and raptors [214]. Man chief predator. In one sample of British polecats 86% were killed by road traffic or trapping, the remaining 14% by dogs, snares or shooting [734]. Secondary poisoning by anticoagulants probably common. Natural disease accounts for the deaths of an unknown number of polecats: 52% of polecats in one sample recorded in 4 months August−November [735], a period when young recruited to population and suffer heavy mortality. Smaller peak in deaths caused by rutting males in spring.

High incidence of road casualties in Britain (even on minor roads) surprising considering the low density of traffic in Wales during autumn and the lack of foraging activity near roads [39].

PARASITES

Fleas: the cat flea, *Ctenocephalides felis*, is very common on captive animals, including ferrets. *Archaeopsylla erinacei*, *Nosopsyllus fasciatus*, *Paraceras melis* are among several species recorded infrequently but none specific [737].

Tick *Ixodes hexagonus* is commonest ectoparasite, sometimes in large numbers, especially on neck and behind ears; *I. canisuga* also recorded [737].

Lice: the biting louse *Trichodectes jacobi* is known from polecat, but not in Britain.

Cestodes: *Taenia tenuicollis*, *T. martis* (stomach and intestine).

Nematodes: *Molineus patens*, *Strongyloides papillosus*, *Capillaria putorii* (intestine/stomach), *Filaroides martis* (lungs), *Skjrabingylus nasicola* (nasal and ethmoid sinuses, causing death through abnormal bone growth) [439].

Suffers from distemper, influenza, colds and pneumonia. Occasionally has malignant tumours [234] and hydrocephaly [323]. Broken teeth commonly found. Abscesses on jaw and around head and neck rarer but often fatal. In Europe, carrier of trichinosis [491], leptospirosis [199], toxoplasmosis [642] and adiaspiromycosis [413]. High incidence of rabies in polecats in localised areas of Europe [2].

RELATIONS WITH MAN

Its reputation as vermin and a wanton killer of poultry dates back to Chaucer. In 1566 this prejudice led to bounty payments for polecats and other predators, and many records appear in parish accounts [326]. Methods of killing or taking now severely restricted, although there is no ban on disturbing the animal or destroying dens. All trapping and all methods of killing, except shooting, illegal without licence, although polecats still trapped by many estates. Polecats can cause much damage if they enter poultry houses or pheasant pens. Conversely, they are efficient controllers of agricultural and forestry pests.

Formerly hunted with hounds in Wales, Devon and Westmorland. Large numbers were once caught in Britain for the fur trade and in Europe to supply London auctions [603]. Pelts highly valued when polecat made scarce. Fitch farming currently practised in Scotland and New Zealand.

'Polecats' in zoos are mostly hydrids with ferrets

but true polecats take well to captivity if caught young and can be bred easily [39].

SOUND RECORDINGS
Appendix 3: J.

LITERATURE
Comprehensive bibliography and review of all aspects of biology [40]. Semi-popular illustrated account of polecat in Wales [578].

AUTHORS FOR THIS SPECIES
P.R.S. Blandford and K.C. Walton.

Feral ferret *Mustela furo*

Mustela furo Linnaeus, 1758; 'Africa'.

'Polecat' (sometimes) when dark-coloured; polecat-ferret when dark or hybrid with *M. putorius*; fitch, etc. (*see* section on Polecat); ffured (Welsh); feòcullan (Scottish gaelic).

Male — dog or hob; female — bitch or jill; young — kits.

RECOGNITION
Proportions and external measurements as for polecat. Darkest forms may be indistinguishable from polecat but generally the pelage is either albino or like that of polecat but lighter, as if the pigment has been partially washed out, and with more extensive white or cream on face and throat.

Skull has more distinct post-orbital constriction than in polecat (minimum frontal breadth usually < 15 mm).

SIGN AND DESCRIPTION
As for polecat with the exception of pelage and skull characteristics given above.

RELATIONSHIPS
A domesticated form of uncertain taxonomic status [520]. Present-day ferret was derived either from the European polecat (*Mustela putorius*), with which it is fully interfertile, or from the steppe polecat (*M. eversmanni*), which it resembles more closely in certain cranial characteristics, or possibly from both [600]. The ferret closely resembles the European polecat in overall size and shape of skull, position of the postorbital constriction, proportions of the pre- and postzygomatic parts of skull, shape of the nasal bones and hooking of the hamular processes. It resembles the steppe polecat more closely in the degree of constriction of the post-orbital region. Skull of ferret more variable than that of either European or steppe polecat. The changed breeding system and selective forces which operate on captive animals may explain the origin of the differences observed. Karyotype of ferret identical to that of European polecat and differs from that of steppe polecat [727]. There is no significant difference in morphology of the chromosomes between European polecat and ferret; Robertsonian rearrangement results in decreased diploid number (2n = 36) in steppe polecat [738]. Ferret treated provisionally as distinct species [94] but could be treated as domesticated form of the European polecat, and the differences between ferrets and polecats are probably due entirely to selective breeding.

VARIATION
Feral populations very variable in pelage but little information available as to whether long-standing colonies in Britain develop greater uniformity, as has happened in New Zealand [510]. Supernumerary upper incisors are not unusual [32].

DISTRIBUTION
Since ferrets are widely kept, escaped animals can be encountered almost anywhere and make it difficult to detect well-established feral populations. Many such populations on islands in Mediterranean, e.g. Sardinia and Sicily, and in New Zealand [499]. In Britain, feral ferrets occur, or once occurred, in significant numbers on Mull [680], Lewis [108], Bute [229], Arran [230] and the Isle of Man, as well as in several places on the mainland [328, 332].

HISTORY
Ferrets may have been brought to Britain by the Romans but probably arrived later, either with the Normans or possibly as late as the 14th century [561, 685].

HABITAT
Little information for Britain. On Mull mainly found on open moorland.

SOCIAL ORGANISATION AND BEHAVIOUR
Trapping used to investigate population dynamics of feral ferrets in New Zealand [431]. No British

data; probably not significantly different from wild polecat.

FEEDING
No information in Britain.

BREEDING
Two litters per year normal for domestic ferrets but feral ferrets in New Zealand produce a single litter per breeding season [431]. Life-cycle similar to that of the polecat, except where human intervention changes it. For example, female ferrets may come into heat and mate as late as the end of June, if confined with a male. This results in a litter in late July. Such events are unlikely to occur in wild polecats.

RELATIONS WITH MAN
Ferrets have been bred for bolting rabbits for at least 2000 years. First description by Aristotle in 4th century BC. Mentioned 350 years later by Strabo as having been introduced into Balearic islands to counter a plague of rabbits [685]. Possibly originated in S Europe but might have been known in Palestine before 1000 BC [766].

Ferrets were introduced to New Zealand in an attempt to control rabbits; the first animals arrived before 1870 and many thousands were shipped over from London between 1882 and 1884. Although these animals are referred to as ferrets, it is unlikely that all were domesticated animals and some polecats from continental Europe were probably included [510]. The feasibility of using ferrets to control rabbits in New Zealand has been investigated [227, 228], but it was concluded that this means of control was unlikely to solve an enormous pest problem at anything other than the local level.

SOUND RECORDINGS
Appendix 3: F, P.

AUTHORS FOR THIS SPECIES
P.R.S. Blandford and K.C. Walton.

Mink *Mustela vison*

Mustela vison Schreber, 1777; eastern Canada.

RECOGNITION
Medium-sized mustelid, dark chocolate brown, may appear almost black at times. Usually a white chin patch and white patches on chest, belly and in groin. Tail slightly bushy, approximately half body length (Fig. 10.19). Semi-aquatic. Cannot be easily distinguished from European mink (*Mustela lutreola*) in those countries with sympatric populations.

Skull (Fig. 10.20) similar to polecat. Width of post-orbital constriction less than 15 mm in the mink, greater in the polecat.

SIGN

Footprints most useful indicator of presence, due to the animal's habit of following soft margins of waterways: 2.5—4.0 cm long, and 2—4 cm wide, depending upon softness of substrate and sex of animal (males leave a larger print than females). The toes radiate from a lobed, central pad, giving prints a characteristic splayed 'star' shape, best seen in soft mud (Fig. 10.21). Often only four of the five toes leave an impression. Each toe pad, with the associated claw mark, leaves a slim, pear-shaped impression. Bounding gait often results in over-printing. Prints are similar to those of the polecat, but usually more splayed.

Faeces cylindrical, with tapered ends, 5—8 cm long and usually 1 cm or less in diameter. Colour and consistency of faeces (known as scats) varies according to freshness and food taken; many are a dark green or brown. Fresh scats have an unpleasant foetid odour due to a covering of secretions from the proctodeal glands [44]. Scats deposited at dens and on prominent objects (rocks, tree roots, etc.). Otter faeces (spraints) found at similar sites, but have a looser consistency and a sweeter smell. Faeces of polecats very similar to those of mink, but unlikely to contain fish remains.

Prey remains: larger prey items (e.g. birds, rabbits, fish) often stored in hollow trees or beneath rocks by the waterside. Dens may contain partly-eaten remains of several prey items [35]. Vertebrate prey usually killed by a bite to the back of the head or neck. The upper canines leave puncture marks 9—11 mm apart.

DESCRIPTION

Pelage dark brown, appearing almost black, in wild type. Dark guard hairs protrude through slightly lighter underfur. White patches, spots,

Fig. 10.19. Mink.

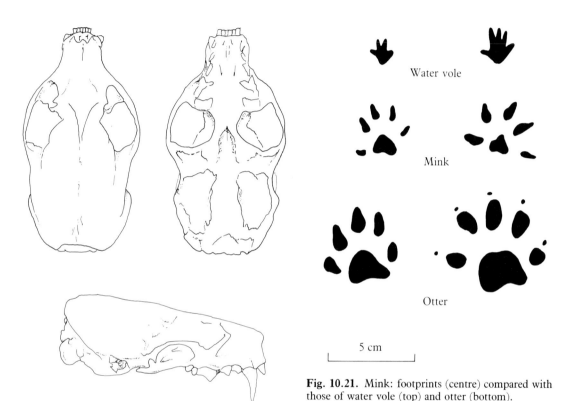

Fig. 10.20. Mink: skull.

Water vole

Mink

Otter

5 cm

Fig. 10.21. Mink: footprints (centre) compared with those of water vole (top) and otter (bottom).

and sometimes only a few white hairs at chin, throat and on ventral surface. Experimental breeding from mutated individuals on fur farms has produced a variety of pelage colours such as Aleutian (white), Breath of Spring, Black Cross, light and dark Pastel, Palomino, Pearl, Platinum, Silver-Blue and Topaz. Offspring of later generations of wild mink vary in colour but most approximate to the wild, dark-brown type. The second most common colour in feral populations is the Silver-Blue, a pale silvery grey colour (comprising 3% of a population trapped in Devon and 9% of

a population trapped in southern Scotland [34]). Older animals may develop areas of white flecking amongst the darker fur around the cheeks and nape of the neck, thought to grow from the sites of scars received during fighting and mating activity.

Morphometric details have been presented for ranch-bred specimens [564] and for feral animals [750].

Moult twice per year, regulated by photoperiod. Development of summer pelage begins late March and completed mid-July; shorter, less dense fur remains intact until mid-August when development of winter pelage initiated. During succeeding three month period summer coat is shed and the animals reach winter prime by about mid-November [28, 139].

Nipples difficult to detect outside breeding season; one to eight palpable teats detected in lactating wild mink and number is related to number of kits being suckled [1, 64].

Scent glands: anal glands with paired sacs opening just inside the anus, and proctodeal glands which open into the rectum [44]. Suggested that odour of faeces due to secretion of proctodeal glands since ducts from anal sacs close during defaecation. Behaviour during scent-marking suggests ventral glands also present.

Teeth can show considerable variation in wear, particularly in coast-living populations; hence not a useful indicator of age.

Chromosomes: $2n = 30$, $FNa = 54$ [767].

RELATIONSHIPS
Forms a superspecies with the Siberian weasel, *Mustela sibirica*, and the European mink, *M. lutreola*. Although the geographical extremes, i.e. the American and European species, are superficially very similar, a recent study [762] indicated that *M. lutreola* is more closely related to *M. sibirica* than to *M. vison*. Hybridisation (in captivity) with *M. lutreola* and with the polecat, *M. putorius*, has been reported [762].

MEASUREMENTS
Data from two rivers in SW England and a site in southern Scotland are presented in Tables 10.18 and 10.19. Males are larger than females with sexual dimorphism ratio of approximately $1.66 - 1.86 : 1$.

Can be approximately aged using bacula [161], dentition [565] and osteology [247].

VARIATION
Feral mink in Britain are derived from those bred on fur farms in N America which are thought to represent six or possibly more subspecies so intermingled and interbred that no separation is now possible.

DISTRIBUTION
Native range covers most of N America, including the deciduous and coniferous zones and extending into the tundra. Translocations associated with the fur trade have led to the establishment of feral populations in several areas in the Palaearctic, including Iceland, Britain, Ireland, France, Spain, Germany, all Scandinavian countries and USSR.

Widespread in mainland Britain and Ireland, though some areas remain incompletely colonised. Occurs on a few islands, e.g. Lewis and Arran.

HISTORY
Imported to Britain and bred on fur farms from 1929 onwards [34, 144, 683]. Escapes or releases led to establishment of a self-sustaining feral population in Devon by the late 1950s [454] and others elsewhere by the early 1960s [106, 683]. Not farmed in Ireland until the early 1950s, so feral populations established later there than on mainland Britain [121, 195]. The history of mink farming and the establishment of feral populations have been documented elsewhere [34, 144].

Map 10.11. Mink.

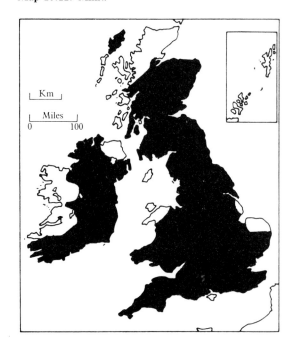

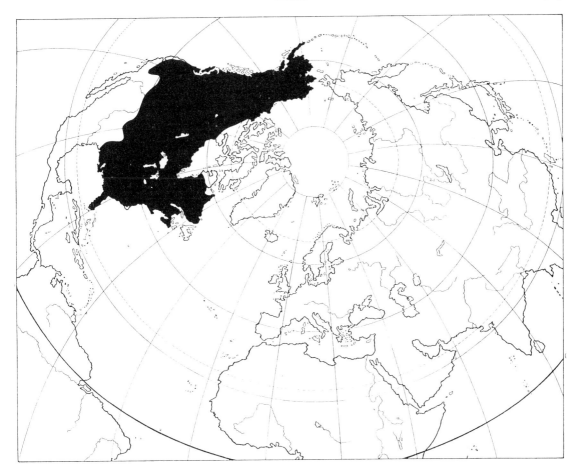

Map 10.12. Mink (original range).

HABITAT

Normally associated with a wide range of aquatic habitats (Fig. 10.22), but may spend some time away from water where suitable prey, such as rabbits, are abundant [450]. Favours eutrophic streams and rivers with abundant bankside cover, and eutrophic lakes fringed with reedbeds and carr [12, 33, 61]. Less abundant on oligotrophic waters or where waterside cover sparse or absent [12, 34, 61]. Relatively dense populations may occur in undisturbed rocky coastal habitat with a broad littoral zone and nearby cover [146]. Also may occur on estuaries [34], and on rivers and canals near urban areas if sufficient cover and prey available [33, 37]. Habitat requirements have been reviewed and evaluated by Allen [12].

SOCIAL ORGANISATION AND BEHAVIOUR

Based upon individual territories with minimal intrasexual overlap but often much overlap of territories held by animals of opposite sex [33, 62, 145]. The territorial system appears to be unstable in suboptimal habitat [33, 61, 62]. Non-territorial transient individuals especially common during the spring mating season when many males vacate territories [33, 62, 225]. The mating system is promiscuous, with an absence of pair-bonding [498]. Fighting between males is common during the mating season, and it has been suggested that this may result in a loose, temporary dominance hierarchy governing access to receptive females [33].

	River Otter/Teign, SW England [64]							
	Males				Females			
	Mean	SD	Range	n	Mean	SD	Range	n
Head and body (mm)	397	23.8	330−450	39	338	10.1	320−360	29
Tail (mm)	193	15.5	150−220	39	168	12.1	135−190	29

Table 10.18. Measurements of mink (excluding kits).

	Ross Peninsula, S Scotland [151]							
	Males				Females			
	Mean	SD	Range	n	Mean	SD	Range	n
Head and body (mm)	395	17.8	360−430	43	343	11.3	330−370	20
Tail (mm)	181	18.7	150−220	43	157	9.9	140−180	20

Location	Age	Mean	SD	Range	n
River Otter, SW England [64]					
Males	Adults	1232		1024−1439	2
	Juveniles	1009	187	685−1329	14
Females	Adults	665	94	559−778	7
	Juveniles	605	98	437−738	8
River Teign, SW England [64]					
Males	Adults	1153		850−1805	48
Females	Adults	619		450−810	32
Ross Peninsula, S Scotland [151]					
Males	Adults	1121	172	840−1500	23
	Juveniles	987	157	690−1220	17
Females	Adults	676	62	560−805	13
	Juveniles	630	66	500−745	11

Table 10.19. Weights of mink (g) from three sites in Britain.

Home ranges tend to be linear in shape (Fig. 10.22) because activity is concentrated on the water's edge [37, 145]. Linear ranges 1−6 km in length, with those occupied by males generally larger than those of females (Table 10.20) [37, 62, 146]. Home ranges largest where social environment unstable due to absence of, or frequent removal of, neighbouring territory holders [37, 224]. There is evidence to suggest that home-range size is inversely related to habitat productivity [146]. Use of the home range is uneven, with activity concentrated in those parts where prey are seasonally abundant [33, 37].

Mink may utilise several dens within the home range, often located close to foraging area [37]. Dens commonly situated within or beneath waterside trees, in rabbit burrows, amongst rocks or above ground in scrub or brushpiles; mink rarely excavate their own dens [34, 37]. Most dens within 10 m of water [33].

Activity predominantly nocturnal or crepuscular, but may occur at any time [37, 146, 223]. In one study, mink spent only 16% of time outside dens, though there were seasonal deviations from this mean value [146]. Frequency and timing of foraging activity probably influenced by the activity and

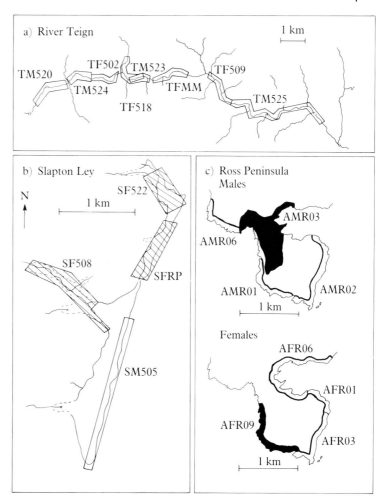

Fig. 10.22. The territorial system of mink in three habitat types: (a) riverine; (b) lacustrine; (c) rocky coast [146].

Table 10.20. Home-range distances (km) of adult mink.

Location	Habitat	Mean	Range	n	Source
Devon, England					
Males	River	2.5	1.6–4.4	5	[61]
Females	River	2.0	1.2–3.2	5	[61]
Males	River/lake	2.5	1.9–2.9	3	[37]
	River/lake	(5.6)	(5.0–5.9)	(3)	[37]
Females	River/lake	2.2	1.5–2.9	2	[37]
SW Scotland					
Males	Coastal	1.5	—	4	[146]
Females	Coastal	1.1	—	4	[146]
Sweden					
Males	River/lake	2.6	1.8–5.0	4	[224]
Females	River/lake	1.8	1.0–2.8	2	[224]

Data in parentheses are from animals occupying socially unstable areas.

availability of prey [37, 223]. The level of activity is generally depressed in winter relative to summer [37, 224].

Movements within the home range tend to show a patrolling pattern, with regular visits to the boundaries [37, 224]. Insufficient data exists to determine dispersal distances accurately. However, one American study recorded a movement of more than 50 km by a juvenile in less than 4 months [3], and studies in Britain suggest that juveniles commonly disperse further than 10 km from their birth places from August onwards [33, 61]. Movements made by rutting males during January–March also poorly understood, but available information suggests they may be extensive [33].

Communication largely achieved by scent-marking involving jelly-like anal gland secretions which coat the faeces, and may also be deposited alone either as a blob or as a smear by anal dragging [33, 44]. Behavioural observations suggest that glands in the skin of the throat and chest may also play a scent-marking role [33]. Volatile odours released from anal glands of alarmed animals may serve as an antipredator defence mechanism [44] and as a means of intimidating conspecifics during aggressive interactions [33].

Vocalisations normally confined to close encounters with conspecifics or threatening predators. Basic vocalisations have been analysed [231], and include piercing shrieks (fundamental frequency 325 Hz with overtones rising to 2 kHz, mean duration 1 second, maximum intensity 20 dB) and hisses (fundamental frequency 600 Hz, mean duration 0.8 seconds) in response to threat [33, 231, 492]. During the mating season both sexes may emit a muffled 'chuckling' sound (ranging up to 800 Hz; [231]) when they meet [163]. Juvenile mink squeak repeatedly when separated from their mothers [33].

Aggressive behaviour: a range of threatening behaviour patterns shown during aggressive interactions have been described, including back-arching, erecting hairs on tail ('bottle-brushing') and lashing of the tail, stamping and scraping of the feet, 'broadside' threat postures and an open-mouth display [33, 492]. If dominance not established by threat displays a fight may result, especially between males during the mating season when

aggression levels are high [492]. Fights may result in wounds to the head and neck region [33, 64] but are only rarely fatal (e.g. [464]).

Locomotion: commonest form on land is a bounding gait with speeds of up to 6.5 km/hour being attained [752]. Mink also climb and swim well. Fish and other aquatic prey are caught during underwater dives with chases of 5–20 seconds duration [143, 580]. Underwater foraging efficiency has been investigated in laboratory studies [143, 148, 149]. Aquatic locomotion involves alternate use of all four limbs when swimming underwater and of the forelimbs only when surface swimming; speeds of up to 2.7 km/hour have been recorded [580, 751]. Heart rate and gas exchange have been measured in freely diving mink to give an estimate of the metabolic costs of underwater hunting [645].

SENSES

Terrestrial vision is superior to that underwater in bright light [150] whilst the ability to perceive moving stimuli is not impaired by submergence [81]. Psychophysical studies [226] suggest mink have colour discrimination ability, and histological examination of the retina [142, 306] has demonstrated the presence of rods and cones in the proportion of 20 : 1. Little is known concerning other sensory abilities although, undoubtedly, olfaction and hearing are of considerable importance.

FEEDING

An opportunistic predator taking a wide variety of mammal, bird, fish and invertebrate prey (Table 10.21). Composition of the diet shows spatial and seasonal variations in response to changing availability of prey [36, 67, 107, 118, 147, 222, 754, 755, 756]. Rabbits, where common, are the most heavily predated mammal (especially in summer), and often most important food overall [147, 352, 756]. A range of small rodents and insectivores are predated to a lesser degree [67, 756] and brown hares are occasionally taken [35].

Several bird species eaten, but ducks, moorhens and coots are most heavily predated on rivers and lakes [67, 756]. In coastal habitat, gulls are commonest avian prey, mostly taken as juveniles or as carrion from the seashore [35, 36, 107]. Birds were marginally the most important food in one study area [756], but in others mammals [352, 756] or fish [67, 107] assumed greatest importance. Birds' eggs not commonly recorded in diet, and

Table 10.21. Diet of mink from three habitat types in Britain; values given are % frequency occurrence in scats.

	Fish	Invertebrates	Lagomorphs	Other mammals	Birds	Amphibians	Minor items	*n*
River Dart/Webben, SW England [756]	25	2	30	12	5	10	9	448
Lacustrine Slapton Ley [756]	32	1	15	14	37	< 1	< 1	513
Rocky coast Ross Peninsula [36]	29	24	32	6	9	0	0	1024

when present, quantities are small [118, 756].

Differences in predation upon fish species may be governed by relative availability, with eels (*Anguilla anguilla*), for example, predated selectively because of great susceptibility to capture [67, 756]. Coastal mink feed on rock-pool fish such as blenny (*Lipophrys pholis*), and onshore crabs (*Carcinus maenas*) [36, 107, 147]. Crayfish (*Austropotamobius pallipes*) may be heavily predated on rivers where they occur [195]. Other foods eaten infrequently include amphibians, snakes, beetles, earthworms and molluscs [67, 107, 756]. Studies indicate that the diets of the two sexes may differ significantly, with males preying upon larger foods than do females [36, 628].

Although there is still popular concern to the contrary, detailed studies indicate that mink predation has had little overall effect upon prey populations in mainland Britain [67, 756], although some local reductions in prey numbers may have occurred in suboptimal habitats [34, 62]. Initial fears as to the importance of mink as an agricultural pest were exaggerated; several studies show that poultry and game birds make up less than 1% of the diet, e.g. [36, 67, 107].

Studies of the interaction between mink and otters suggest that, although the diets of the two predators may overlap significantly, there is no evidence of competition [63, 352, 756]. It was concluded, however, that competition may occur when a shared resource, such as fish, becomes scarce [756], as may happen during severe winters in Sweden [171].

The mink's successful colonisation of Britain and Ireland, in the apparent absence of both a shift in its feeding ecology or extermination of populations of prey or competitors, suggests that it is exploiting a niche which was previously unoccupied [34, 67, 121, 756].

BREEDING (Fig. 10.23)
One litter of *c.* four to six per year, usually in May. Following the winter solstice and throughout January, females may exhibit some vulval swelling, but will not mate, and males experience moderate testis growth [64]. The breeding season *per se* is the 3–4 week period around the time of the vernal equinox throughout which females appear to be continually receptive (oestrus) [139, 572]. Ovulation is induced by copulation. Implantation may be delayed by a variable length of time and gestation may last from 39–76 days [163], with birth *c.* 28 days after implantation.

The normal litter size is four to six but larger numbers (up to 17, [619]) recorded in captivity. Throughout the 6–8 weeks of lactation and subsequent 5–6 months anoestrus there are no externally visible or behavioural manifestations of reproductive activity. Weaning starts at *c.* 5–6 weeks, adult size attained at approximately 4 months; young can breed following year. Females are fecund for 7 years or more [163].

Various aspects of the annual reproductive cycle of ranch mink have been reviewed in detail [163, 572, 723]. In the northern hemisphere under normal ranch management they are mated, initially once or on two successive days, and then again after an interval of 7–10 days, during March.

POPULATION
In Britain highest recorded density is one territory holder per 0.5 km of rocky coastline in SW Scotland

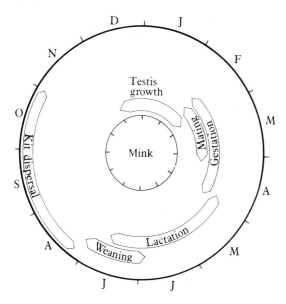

Fig. 10.23. Mink: life-cycle.

[145, 146]. On an acid river average population density varied in time between one territory-holder per 3.8 km and one per 1.9 km of river, with the higher density recorded when rabbits more abundant [33, 61]. In Sweden, a disease-induced elimination of crayfish from a river was thought to result in a three-to-four-fold reduction in population density [225]. Seasonal variations in density of territory holders influenced by vacation of territories by rutting males in spring and resettlement after mating season, and by settlement of juveniles following dispersal in August [33]. Non-territorial, transient population peaks in spring (rutting males) and autumn (dispersing juveniles) [33, 62, 225].

The sex ratio of trapped populations often shows a male bias resulting from their greater mobility when compared with females, e.g. [61, 195]. Outside the mating season, however, the sex ratio of trapped mink is often close to unity [61], and studies of the resident sector of the population often reveals a preponderance of females, e.g. [33, 225].

There is little information on the age structure and survivorship of populations in Britain. 81% of mink trapped in late summer on one river were juvenile [61]. A similar preponderance of juveniles was also noted in a Swedish population, in which only 15% of all individuals remained on the study area for longer than 18 months [225]. Female territory holders most sedentary sector of population:

44% of those present initially in one study remained for 2 years, and one held a territory for over 5 years [33]. The results of an American study revealed an almost complete turnover of the population every 3 years [526].

MORTALITY
Relative importance of different mortality factors not well known. In many places large numbers trapped or shot by man [33, 62]; smaller numbers are killed by minkhounds [34], and some are drowned in traps or nets set for fish [225]. Occasional predators include the otter (in Russia — [248]), badger [34] and golden eagle (in Sweden — [690]). Mink occasionally kill each other as a result of fighting (e.g. [464]); females may die from exhaustion or injuries during the mating season, e.g. [34, 292]. Examination of corpses suggests that kidney disease may afflict mink in some areas [64], and in Sweden, mercury poisoning and starvation were recorded in trapped mink [225]. High levels of organochlorines and PCBs have been reported from the USA [298]. Most natural mortality may be a consequence of the territorial system, which forces non-territorial animals to adopt a riskier, transient lifestyle [34].

PARASITES
Feral mink commonly carry light infestations of ticks and fleas none of which are specific to mink. Two species of tick have been identified from feral mink: *Ixodes hexagonus* and *I. ricinus*. The six species of fleas collected were *Palaeopsylla minor*, *Malaraeus penicilliger*, *Ctenophthalmus nobilis*, *Megabothris walkeri*, *Typhloceras poppei* and *Nosopsyllus fasciatus* [64, 195]. The biting louse of mink, *Trichodectes larseni*, has not yet been recorded from feral mink in Britain.

Cranial damage resulting from the presence of the nematode worms *Skrjabingylus nasicola* [138] and *Troglotrema acutum* [262] has been recorded.

Diseases of ranched animals are well documented and include botulism, steatitis, Aleutian disease and distemper. Afflictions of wild animals poorly documented but include jaw abscesses, gastric ulcers, renal failure and a distemper-like disease that reduced numbers on one Devon river.

RELATIONS WITH MAN
Much publicity initially given to predation by mink upon domestic ducks and poultry, game birds and pets. Regarded as a pest by fish-farmers, game and

poultry keepers, though its overall commercial impact is negligible. Easily trapped, but difficult to eradicate except where populations small and isolated [33, 62, 684]. Hunting with hounds is practised, with about 20 packs covering most of England, Wales and parts of southern Scotland [34].

The nature of the mink's impact upon Britain's native wildlife has been the subject of lively debate amongst scientists and naturalists, e.g. [434, 435, 451, 452].

Field-study techniques employed in Britain include live-trapping and ear-tagging [33, 61], faecal and stomach contents analysis, e.g. [6, 67, 118, 756], and radio-tracking [37, 145].

SOUND RECORDINGS
Appendix 3: J.

LITERATURE
[34] and [144] — readable accounts of the biology of this species. [37] — particularly useful account of the species' behavioural ecology. [163] — reproductive biology comprehensively covered.

AUTHORS FOR THIS SPECIES
J.D.S. Birks and N. Dunstone.

SUBFAMILY MELINAE

GENUS *Meles*

The Palaearctic badger is the only member of this genus. Other badgers are very distinctive and are placed in separate genera — *Taxidea* (North America), *Arctonyx*, *Mydaus*, *Suillotaxus* (included with *Mydaus* [465]) and *Melogale* (from SE Asia). Although very similar to *Meles* in form and behaviour, the honey badger *Mellivora capensis*, is not included in this subfamily. Dental formula of *Meles* 3.1.3.1/3.1.3.1 but an additional minute vestigial (1st) premolar may occur just behind one or more canines; they are more often found in the lower jaw.

Badger *Meles meles*

Ursus meles Linnaeus, 1785; Upsala, Sweden.
Meles taxus Boddaert, 1785.

Brock, grey pate, bawson, baget; brochlach (Scottish gaelic); broc (Irish gaelic); mochyn daeaar, broch, pryf penfrith, pryf llwyd (Welsh).

Male — boar; female — sow; young — cub.

RECOGNITION
Unlike any other British mammal in having a white head with a conspicuous dark strip on either side which includes the eye (Fig. 10.24). Skull of adult has prominent interparietal ridge, prominent canines and flattened molars (Fig. 10.25).

SIGN
Burrow system or sett is extensive. Typically has three to ten large entrances at least 25 cm in diameter (often much greater). The large spoil heaps outside contain discarded bedding — plant debris, hay, bracken, straw, etc. (A fox's earth contains no plant material incorporated in the spoil heap.) Underground there is a labyrinth of tunnels and chambers, sometimes of considerable size and complexity.

Paths: those leading from the sett are well marked and may be followed for long distances; they are very conspicuous where they cross hedgebanks. Hairs often get caught in the lowest strand of barbed wire where a badger passes under it.

Footprints (Fig. 10.26): these typically show five toes and the broad impression of the fused plantar pads; the longer claw marks of the forefeet show up well in soft ground, and in mud and snow the heel (normally raised slightly) may leave an impression. Print of forefoot is broader than hind and the inner toe is set further back. Overprinting often occurs, but not when travelling fast.

Faeces looser than those of dog, but consistency varies with food eaten; they appear muddy when earthworms have been consumed. Beetle elytra and corn husks may be conspicuous and a purplish colour is often an indication of blackberries. Faeces are usually placed in shallow pits which are not covered after use, but occasionally are deposited on the ground surface. Aggregations of pits are referred to as latrines.

DESCRIPTION
Powerfully built with a rather small head, thick short neck, stocky wedge-shaped body and short tail. The body is low-slung and carried on short but powerful limbs. Feet are digitigrade with five toes

Fig. 10.24. Badger.

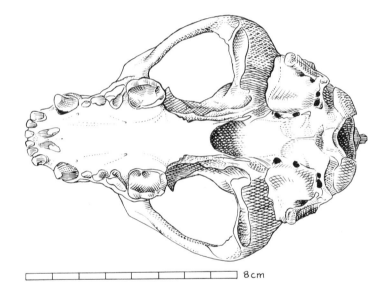

Fig. 10.25. Skull of badger. Note the sagittal crest and the flat-crowned and rectangular last molars.

8cm

Left hind foot

Fig. 10.26. Badger: footprint.

on each foot with especially large claws on the front feet. The snout is flexible and muscular, an aid to probing and digging. Eyes are small, ears short and tipped with white. Vibrissae occur on the snout and above the eye.

Sex difference: the majority are difficult to sex in the field, although the more extreme cases are easily distinguished. Typically, a boar has a broader head, thicker neck and a rather pointed, narrow, white tail, whilst sows are sleeker, have a narrower less domed head and a more tufty tail. The tail is not a reliable feature on its own.

Pelage: badgers appear grey from a distance owing to the colour of the guard hairs which in dorsal and lateral regions of the body are light at the base and tip with a dark patch between, but nearer to the tip of the hair. The legs and underside of the body are covered by uniformly dark hairs which are often sparse on the ventral surface. Underfur is thick in winter and pale in colour.

Moult: there is a single prolonged moult which begins in the spring when the underfur is shed, followed by the guard hairs. The process begins in the withers and shoulders, spreading along the back and flanks. New guard hairs grow in the late summer followed by new underfur [509, 548].

Genitalia: scrotal sacs of adult males are conspicuous when they sit up and scratch. The penis is not visible as it lies under the skin in a forward projecting position, but when in use protrudes through an aperture in the skin. Both sexes have three pairs of nipples, well-developed in adult females.

Scent glands: the subcaudal gland occurs as an invagination of skin just below the base of the tail. It secretes a cream-coloured fatty substance with a faint musky smell. A pair of anal glands are situated just below the skin on either side of the tail region; they open by short ducts just internal to the anus. They secrete a yellowish brown fatty fluid with a powerful rank musky odour.

Skull has prominent interparietal ridge which starts growth at 10 months and may reach a height of 15 mm in old males. Juvenile skulls have no interparietal ridge but show temporal ridges (lines) on the skull surface marking the upper limit of the temporalis muscles on the sides of the cranium. These lines gradually migrate with age nearer to the mid-line and coalesce to form the interparietal ridge. The lower jaw of adult skulls articulates in such a way that dislocation is impossible without fracturing the skull.

Teeth: the dentition is well suited for an omnivorous diet: the incisors are small and chisel-like, the canines are prominent, there are no specialised carnassial teeth and the molars are considerably flattened for grinding. Tooth wear has been used as a criterion for age [4].

The deciduous teeth are 3.1.3 / 3.1.3, sometimes with additional first premolars as in the permanent dentition. The incisors are sometimes reduced in numbers and I_1 and I_2 often never penetrate the gums — an adaptation for suckling.

Baculum: length and weight attain adult proportions during the 2nd year of life, but as time of maturity varies considerably the baculum is an unreliable indicator for age determination [240].

Reproductive tract: weights of paired testes in mature males reach a mean maximum of 11 g in February–March, decreasing slowly to a mean minimum of 5 g in October–November; thereafter a rapid increase [5].

Uterus is bicornuate, the mean length of each horn in mature females during the period of delayed implantation is 86 mm [562] with a mean flat diameter of 6.6 mm [1]. The ovaries are partly embedded in fat and their state can only be determined by removing the wall of the bursa. They may reach a maximum of $15 \times 10 \times 8$ mm. The surface is smooth up to the time of maturity. Corpora of delay are cream coloured and nearly flush with the surface, those during pregnancy may project prominently and are well vascularised. The tube is much convoluted. Placental scars persist as dark patches for a considerable length of time so that it is sometimes difficult to distinguish between old and new scars.

Viscera: the gut is longer than that of the fox. Mean length of small intestine 5.36 m [641]. There is no caecum.

Chromosomes: 2n = 44; FNa = 72 — (continental data) [767].

MEASUREMENTS

See Table 10.22. The wide range of weights of adults is mainly due to the accumulation of fat in late summer and autumn giving maximum weights during October–January. Minimum weights occur in the period from March to May when surplus fat has been used up. Greatest weight changes occur in adult sows probably because of the long lactation: September–February, average 12.2 kg ($n = 22$), March–May, 8.8 kg ($n = 25$). Average weight attained by cubs in their 1st year, 8.8 kg ($n = 14$) in SW England.

VARIATION

Recognition of British population as subspecies (*M. m. britannicus* Satunin, 1906, based on cranial measurements) is not justified. A number of colour variations have been described, the genetics of which are not clear. These include albinos (no melanin), semi-albinos (eye-stripes visible), erythristic (gingery), and melanistic (very dark). Much staining of the fur from the soil in which the setts are dug also occurs, e.g. in red sandstone regions [543].

DISTRIBUTION

Very widespread in Britain and Ireland, being absent only in regions of high altitude (usually above 500 m), most (although not all) large conurbations, some intensively farmed areas, extensive lowlands liable to flooding and offshore islands apart from Anglesey, Arran, Wight and possibly Mull. Attempts to introduce badgers to islands including Jura and Ailsa Craig failed [291].

HISTORY

Meles appears to have evolved in temperate forests of Asia and spread into Europe. Primitive forms

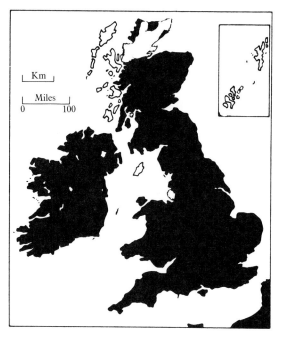

Map 10.13. Badger.

Map 10.14. Badger.

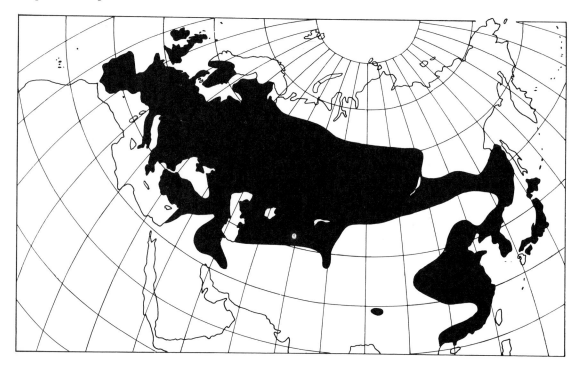

were present in the Early Pleistocene. Thoral's badger, *Meles thorali*, was the earliest fossil found in Europe of genus *Meles* about a million years ago. By the early Middle Pleistocene, badgers in Europe were very similar to modern forms. The earliest record for Britain is a fossil from Barrington in Cambridgeshire estimated at about 250000 years old.

Badgers were widespread in Britain in 17th and 18th centuries, but suffered much persecution in 19th century and numbers dropped considerably. Since the First World War numbers steadily increased, reaching a peak in about 1960. After that, in some regions, numbers fell (road accidents, persecution, keepering). Legislation (1973 and later) helped recovery, but in recent years an increase in persecution has caused a dramatic drop in some regions, particularly in parts of Yorkshire, the Midlands, Essex and S Wales. However, in some southern and south-western counties numbers have remained high.

HABITAT

Setts are dug in a wide variety of places including woodland, scrub, hedgerows, quarries, sea cliffs, moorland and open fields and, occasionally, in embankments, Iron-Age forts, mines, caves, coal tips, rubbish dumps and under buildings. They may also occur in some urban situations [274]. The sett survey carried out by the Mammal Society (1963 onwards) showed that for the whole of Britain there was a marked preference for deciduous and mixed woodland and copses (52%), 19% were in hedgerows and scrub, 9% in coniferous woods and 8% in open situations [80]. The favourable factors influencing choice were the presence of adequate cover, soil which was well drained and easy to dig, little disturbance by man and his animals and a varied and plentiful food supply (particularly

earthworms) nearby. The latter is assured where deciduous woodland, pasture and arable land occur within the territory [542, 544]. Low-lying marshy areas and regions of high altitude are avoided.

SOCIAL ORGANISATION AND BEHAVIOUR

Structure: badgers form social groups comprising an average of six (range 2–23) individuals [72, 278, 419, 425]. About 70% of badger latrines are located on or near the territorial boundary. Territory size ranges from *c.* 30 hectares in optimal habitat to more than 150 hectares in marginal habitat, and territorial behaviour is less pronounced in areas of low density [101].

There is usually a dominant boar in each group but it has not been established whether there is a dominance hierarchy within groups. Boars tend to play a more active role in the demarcation of territory than sows and have correspondingly larger ranges within the territory [69, 419]. Territorial activity reaches a peak in the early spring, coinciding with the period when mating activity is also at a peak [543, 544, 607]. Although most cubs are fathered by the resident boars in their group there is evidence that boars will visit neighbouring groups and successfully mate with sows [185]. This, together with the dispersal of badgers away from their natal social group [73] ensures gene flow in the population. Group living in badgers is postulated to be the most efficient way to exploit irregularly dispersed food resources [325, 423].

Scent marking: scent is probably the most important means of communication, both within and between social groups. The large subcaudal gland is important in the maintenance of territory as well as individual recognition within a social group [238, 425]. Anal glands are also present, which

Table 10.22. Measurements of badgers over 1 year old from SW England [543].

	Males			Females		
	Mean	Range	*n*	Mean	Range	*n*
Head and body (mm)	753	686–803	31	724	673–787	31
Tail (mm)	150	127–178	31	150	114–190	31
Weight (kg)	11.6	9.1–16.7	33	10.1	6.6–13.9	84
Skull length (condylobasal) (mm) [259]	120	116–130	28	119	111–125	26

impart a powerful musky odour to the faeces, as are interdigital glands, the function of which is less well known but appears to be important in marking territory. Vocal repertoire quite extensive [544].

Aggressive behaviour is mainly associated with territorial defence and mating activity. The greatest frequency of bite wounding occurs in the spring and is mostly seen in boars [221]. Badgers typically bite each other around the neck and rump, while running and chasing and uttering low 'kekkering' sounds. Wounding can be severe and occasionally fatal [221]. Sows aggressively defend cubs against potential predators such as foxes [543].

Dispersal: in rural habitats it is uncommon for badgers to disperse from their natal social group. Of those which do, the majority are sexually mature males [74, 425]. Disturbance to a population increases the likelihood of movements occurring. Dispersal is more common in urban habitats with boars showing a greater tendency to disperse than sows.

Activity mainly crepuscular and nocturnal. Emergence from the sett usually around dusk, but the time varies according to sex, age, season and environmental conditions [544]. Emergence usually before dark in May–August, usually after dark at other times, but much less regular in November–February. Emergence and activity is reduced in winter, especially in the north [212], but no true hibernation. Effects of weather on activity of suburban badgers have been described [102]. Badgers can go without food for long periods and may remain below ground for many days at a time particularly during periods of severe frost. Disturbance, such as the practice of earthstopping by foxhunts, causes a delay in emergence and may sometimes prevent emergence [447].

Diurnal activity is not unusual in secluded places. Badgers will sometimes lie out away from the sett in bracken, brambles or cereal crops, particularly in August and September. Shortage of food, as in times of drought, is a common cause of diurnal behaviour.

Setts and tunnels: digging and bedding collection may be carried out during any month of the year, but particularly in autumn and spring. Setts consist of a complex system of tunnels and chambers typically with three to ten entrances (range 1–80). A large sett excavated in the Cotswolds extended over an area of 35×15 m with 12 entrances and tunnels totalling 310 m in length; the volume of the system was 15.28 m^3, equivalent to 25 tonnes of soil [521]. Tunnels are known to run along a hillside up to 100 m, but typically 10–20 m; tunnels may be at several levels. Chambers are frequently lined with large amounts of bedding brought in on dry nights. Bedding may consist of grass, bracken, straw, leaves or moss and 20 to 30 bundles may be brought in on a single night, the badger working its way backwards to the sett keeping the bundle in place with chin and forepaws. Periodically, old bedding is discarded, and in winter bedding may be taken outside near the entrance on sunny mornings and retrieved later.

Locomotion: when travelling, a badger moves at an ambling trot, head down with hindquarters swaying from side to side, pausing frequently to listen. Movement is at a slow walk when foraging, but when alarmed, badgers can travel at up to 30 km/hour over short distances. They may climb sloping trees, gripping the bark like a bear. Badgers can swim, but avoid having to do so if possible.

Grooming: frequently this is done after emergence with great thoroughness using claws and teeth. Mutual grooming occurs and may have a social function. Sows groom their cubs. Badgers will also lick their fur and mutual licking has been observed [525].

Defence: the black and white mask is probably a warning coloration. A cub's defence is to face the attacker showing the facial pattern to best advantage, fluff up its fur and make menacing noises. An adult also faces an aggressor in the same way but keeps its body and head low. If attacked, it will slash upwards with its teeth or use its front claws with rapid raking movements.

Defaecation takes place in shallow pits, several pits forming a latrine. Some pits are dug near the sett; in a region of Kent more than 50% of these occurred within 10 m of an entrance [547]. Latrines also occur at strategic places near the perimeter of the territory and where a food source is abundant. Faeces may also be deposited underground in a side chamber and occasionally on the spoil heap. Urination occasionally takes place in empty dung pits, but is usually random.

SENSES

Sense of smell and hearing are very acute. Eyesight is poor and, because rods predominate in the retina, is best in poor light. A tapetum is present. Cubs are very short-sighted.

FEEDING

Badgers are primarily opportunistic foragers; they are omnivorous and exploit a wide range of animal and plant food. Earthworms are the most important item in the diet. These and other foods are taken according to availability, hence their diet varies according to geographical location, the types of habitat present within their territory, the season of the year and the weather conditions prevailing at any particular time. Apart from earthworms, the main food categories exploited are larger insects, small mammals (mainly their young), carrion (particularly in winter), cereals, fruit and underground storage organs. Mammals include rabbits, rats, mice, voles, shrews, moles and hedgehogs; insects: chafers, dung and ground beetles, caterpillars, leatherjackets, wasps' and bumble bees' nests; cereals: wheat, oats and maize, occasionally barley; fruit: windfall apples, pears, plums, blackberries, bilberries, raspberries, acorns and beechmast; pignut and wild arum corms. Other foods taken when available include birds, mainly ground nesters and ground roosters; frogs, toads and newts; snakes and lizards; snails and slugs; fungi; green food such as clover and grass, which is occasionally taken in winter and in times of drought. Recent studies have shown the badger to be a highly adaptable species in terms of its feeding behaviour. Detailed analysis of diet in Britain — see [43, 274, 324, 423, 424]. Continental studies summarised by Neal [544].

BREEDING (Fig. 10.28)

Mating usually in spring, implantation delayed until December, one to four young born about February, emerge in April.

Most boars mature at 12–15 months but some take up to 2 years [5]. Boars are normally fecund in the early months of the year, but high concentrations of sperm in the epididymis may be found in some animals throughout the year [240]. Sows usually begin to ovulate in the spring of their 2nd year when 12–15 months old, some animals taking a few months longer [5]. Exceptionally, some females become mature at around 9 months [72, 198, 202].

Badgers are induced ovulators. Mating can take place during any month of the year but mostly between February and May, when mature sows are in oestrus, post-partum, and when younger animals may have their first oestrus. Matings at other times may involve sows which did not conceive at earlier matings, and those late in maturing. Some sows may have a second oestrus during the period of delay before implantation of the blastocysts causing further matings [5, 545]. Subsequent matings may stimulate further ovulations and though there may be an increase in the number of corpora lutea, no

Fig. 10.27. Badger foraging. (Photo: Hans Kruuk.)

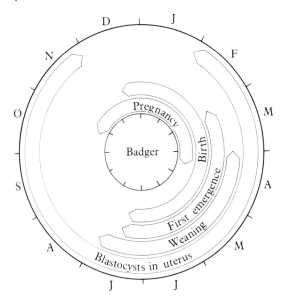

Fig. 10.28. Badger: life-cycle.

additional conceptions result [545]. Mating is prolonged (15–60 min), although short duration copulations (under 2 min) also occur when a sow is not in full oestrus. Oestrus lasts 4–6 days and frequent copulations may occur during this period, sometimes with more than one boar involved.

There is a long period of delay before implantation (2–9 months) with the probable exception of December matings when implantation may follow at once [202]. Implantation usually occurs during December followed by a true gestation of about 7 weeks. The physiological control of delayed implantation remains largely unresolved, although it has been established that decreasing daylengths are important in triggering blastocyst implantation [57, 58, 59], and there is limited evidence of a possible relationship between seasonal changes in body temperature and implantation [212].

Births usually occur between mid-January and mid-March with a peak in the first 3 weeks of February (slightly later in the north). Birth occurs in an underground chamber containing bedding. Breeding above ground, sometimes in buildings, has been recorded where surrounding countryside was waterlogged [544]. Litter size is one to five. The average for Europe based on fetuses and placental scars is 2.7 [15]. Litter size deduced from observations on families seen above ground in SW

England averaged 2.3 (50 families) containing nine singles, 23 twins, 11 triplets, seven quadruplets [544]. Both litter sizes and pregnancy rates tend to be lower in yearlings.

The new born cub has a pink skin covered with greyish, silky fur; the darker eye stripe is usually visible. Eyelids are fused — usually open at around 5 weeks. Average head and body length 120 mm; weight variable (75–132 g), those from large litters being smaller.

Eruption of milk teeth occurs over a period of 2 weeks when about 4–6 weeks old. First permanent incisors appear at about 10 weeks and full transition to a permanent dentition occurs during the following 6 weeks. Some milk teeth may be present and functional after the corresponding permanent teeth have come through. This is possible because canines and premolars do not emerge through the same sockets as their milk precursors [543, 544].

Cubs emerge above ground for the first time at about 8 weeks. Weaning usually starts at 12 weeks, but some suckling may continue until 4–5 months [544]. The nipples of sows which have produced cubs are always longer than those of non-breeding sows. During weaning the sow has been observed to provide cubs with solid food [327, 544]. Growth rate during 1st year varies according to food availability. When earthworms have been abundant weights of 10 kg may be attained by December.

POPULATION
Densities vary from 20 adults per km^2 in the better habitats where social groups are contiguous, to only one or two, or less, per km^2 in less favourable areas with a discontinuous, patchy distribution of badgers [70, 71, 72, 278, 419]. A typical density where badgers are common is around 10 adults per km^2. The sex ratio is equal at birth but a higher mortality of boars gives a predominance of sows in the adult population [72, 278]. Mortality of cubs is high, with between 50% and 65% dying in their 1st year from birth [72, 278, 544]. The mortality is about 30–35% per year in the adult population. Few badgers exceed 6 years in the wild, although some have reached 11 years; in captivity badgers live up to 19 years [72, 544].

MORTALITY
Adult badgers have no natural enemies apart from man in Britain. Territorial fights between boars may result in death. It is not unusual for young

cubs to be killed by dogs, foxes and sometimes even by adult badgers.

The major cause of death in many parts of Britain is road traffic [74, 544].

PARASITES

The following parasites have been recorded: fleas *Paraceras melis* (very common), *Chaetopsylla trichosa* (very rarely), *Pulex irritans* (occasional) [682]; biting lice *Trichodectes melis* (very common) [682]; ticks *Ixodes ricinus* (occasional), *Ixodes canisuga* (common), *Ixodes hexagonus* (common), *Ixodes reduvius* (occasional), *Ixodes melicola* (occasional) [681]; roundworms *Molineus patens* (intestinal). *Uncinaria stenocephala* (intestinal), *Capillaria erinacei* (stomach), *Aelurostrongylus falciformis* (lungs) [363]; tapeworms *Mesocestoides lineatus*, *Dilepis undula* [363]; flukes *Itygonimus lorum* [363].

Mange has been reported in badgers (e.g. [544]) but there are no confirmed cases in the literature. Bovine tuberculosis (*Mycobacterium bovis*) has been found in badgers and they are suspected of transmitting this disease to cattle [141]. However, tuberculosis has not been found to be a major cause of mortality in badgers [74]. Rabies has been found in badgers in Europe but badgers are not believed to be a primary host [258]. Badger parasites and diseases reviewed in [258].

RELATIONS WITH MAN

Badgers should not be regarded as pests and rarely do any damage of economic importance [97]. In places of high density near habitation, poultry killing can sometimes be a nuisance but this is usually confined to individuals which acquire the habitat. Some flattening of cereals occurs and grain is eaten, the amount varying according to location and weather conditions, but resultant losses are seldom serious. Damage to high-value crops such as grapes, sweetcorn and strawberries can be a problem, but it is possible to prevent badgers gaining access to such crops by the use of electric fencing. Occasionally badgers open up holes in fields. This can be a hazard, especially with heavy machinery, as the roofs of the tunnels may collapse. Badgers do not trouble foresters, indeed they destroy many small rodents, wasps' nests and other pests. They may force up wire netting around plantations and let rabbits in, but this problem can be alleviated by the use of badger gates [397]. Game-bird eggs are occasionally eaten, but losses

are insignificant [19]. Badgers are subject to control by the Ministry of Agriculture, Fisheries and Food in areas where they are suspected of transmitting bovine tuberculosis to cattle. This occurs mainly in parts of SW England [141].

Persecution: badger digging and baiting, shooting with the use of lamps at night and gassing all occur although the badger is fully protected by law (Badgers Act 1973, amended by the Wildlife and Countryside Act 1981, further amended 1985). Any unauthorised killing or taking of badgers is illegal and it is an offence to keep them as pets.

Conservation: the best way to conserve badgers is to leave them alone. With an increasing number of reports of persecution in recent years many badger protection societies have been formed to protect setts from diggers and report persecution to the police.

Techniques for study: radio-telemetry and or infrared/image intensifying binoculars are invaluable aids in behavioural and ecological studies, although a powerful torch with a red filter can be effective for observation near the sett. Capture—mark—recapture techniques are of great value in population studies. Coloured markers presented in food at main setts and recovered in perimeter latrines help to delineate territories.

SOUND RECORDINGS
Appendix 3: A, F, J, S, V.

LITERATURE
[465, 544] — recent reviews. [79] — popular account. [288] — guide to dealing with badger problems.

AUTHORS FOR THIS SPECIES
E.G. Neal and C.L. Cheeseman.

SUBFAMILY LUTRINAE

GENUS *Lutra*

The subfamily Lutrinae has a world-wide distribution and otters of the genus *Lutra* are found on all continents except Antarctica and Australia. Subfamily subject to recent revision, with 8 out of 13 species placed in *Lutra* [94]. Species of *Lutra* are typically fish eating river otters. Some otters feed mainly on invertebrates (*Enhydra* — the sea otter; *Aonyx* — clawless otters). There is only one species of *Lutra* in Britain and Europe. Dental formula 3.1.4.1/3.1.4.2.

Otter *Lutra lutra*

Mustela lutra Linnaeus, 1758; Sweden.
Lutra vulgaris Erxleben, 1777.
Lutra roensis Ogilby, 1834; Roe Mills, near Newton Limnavaddy, Londonderry, Ireland.

Balgaire, Cudoun (Burn dog), Matadh (Hound) (Scottish Gaelic); Tek, Dafi, Dratsi (Shetland); Madrirga (Water dog), Maclaidh uisce, Dobharchu (Irish Gaelic); Dwr-gi (Water dog) or Dyfrigi (Welsh).
Male — dog; female — bitch; young — kits.

RECOGNITION
In water, the otter (Fig. 10.29) is distinguished from mink and aquatic rodents by large size, flattened head and long, tapering tail, very thick at base. A large V-shaped wake is usually produced. Swimming movements are not jerky like aquatic rodents. On land it is much larger than mink (otter larger than domestic cat, mink smaller); mid-brown coat compared to dark brown almost black coat of mink; tail of mink cylindrical and fluffy, of otter, stout and tapering.

Skull distinguished from all other mustelids by large size, narrow post-orbital constriction and five upper post-canine teeth. (Fig. 10.30)

SIGN

Footprints show four or five toes, 5—7 cm across in adults; web and claw marks sometimes visible; outline rounded, not bilaterally symmetrical. Stride about 36 cm at walk, 50 cm at gallop and 90—100 cm when bounding.

Faeces (known as spraints) deposited at regularly used places, often on prominent features such as logs, rocks, under bridges and at bases of trees; also where bank has been eroded under tree roots. May scrape soil, gravel or vegetation to form 'sign heaps' and spraint on top. Scraping also occurs without formation of heaps; areas up to a metre across scraped bare of vegetation; spraints also found at these sites. Faeces dark and mucilaginous, with musky smell when fresh; pale and crumbly when dry. Size varies from small tarry smear containing a few or no bones to cylindrical faeces 1 cm in diameter and up to 10 cm long; contain mainly fish scales and bones, shells of crustacea, feathers or fur.

Trails and hauling out places sometimes seen on rivers, especially cutting across meanders. More often noticed on lakes and in coastal regions where interconnecting trails link the shore with freshwater pools, resting and rolling places. Several regularly used spraint sites are found at each of these 'spraint stations' which, in Scotland, were dispersed along the coast, usually at intervals of 40—70 m [697].
  Partially eaten remains of large prey sometimes found; difficult to distinguish from those of other

Fig. 10.29. Otter.

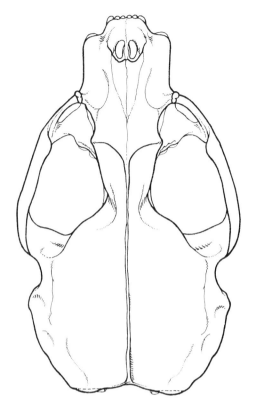

Fig. 10.30. Otter skull. The post-orbital constriction in the adult is narrower than in the skull of any other British carnivore.

predators, particularly mink, unless other signs present.

DESCRIPTION

Body elongate, legs short, head flat with small eyes and ears, and broad muzzle with prominent whiskers. Tail long, flattened and tapering evenly from a thick base. Feet webbed, five digits on each. Pelage appears glossy when wet (spiky after shaking); dense underfur remains dry when animal is in water. Colour uniform brown except for paler throat, sometimes with white patch on chin; may be used to recognise individuals [741]. One extended moult per year [548].

Scent glands: pair of anal glands discharge on either side of the anus [237], and proctodeal glands discharge into rectum [654, 697].

Nipples: two or three pairs.

Teeth: wear on teeth not usually apparent until 3rd year of life [654]. Full development of skull not until over 2 years old [654]. Jaw hinged to move in one plane only. Baculum more than 60 mm long in adult, weighing 2 g or more [710]; curved upwards at distal end.

RELATIONSHIPS

Closely related to other Old World *Lutra*, i.e. *L. maculicollis* (Africa), *L. perspicillata* and *L. sumatrana* (SE Asia) but not to the American river otters (*L. canadensis* etc.), which are sometimes placed in a separate genus *Lontra* [718].

MEASUREMENTS

See Table 10.23. Some authors have reported weights of specimens which had been skinned or were otherwise incomplete [194, 356, 644], and so a formula was derived for predicting whole body weight with correction factors for missing parts such as head, feet or tail [348].

VARIATION

Irish population has been recognised as distinct on the basis of darker colour, especially above, and lesser extent of white on the throat [109]. However, no significant variation has been substantiated in the European part of the range and no subspecies are currently recognised [501].

DISTRIBUTION

In Oriental region sympatric with smooth-coated otter *Lutra perspicillata* and Asian small-clawed otter *Aonyx cinerea*. Populations have declined in some areas and otters now scarce or absent in many parts of their range.

Still found throughout Ireland and much of Scotland although much reduced near areas of intense agriculture and industry in the central lowland belt. Absent from S Wales (Glamorgan), Anglesey [16], and from central England. Populations low in N, S and E England but present in reasonable numbers in the SW and in counties bordering mid-Wales [488].

HISTORY

At the beginning of the century numbers believed to be low, though population widespread, owing to persecution. May have recovered as gamekeeping pressures declined [506]. Hunting records in some areas suggest an increase during first half of the century [66]. In the early 1950s, otter considered to

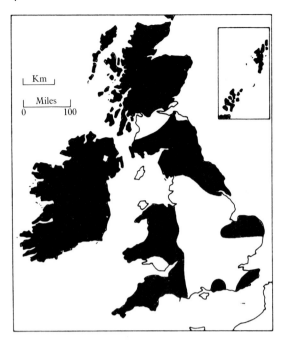

Map 10.15. Otter: since 1980 in Britain.

be 'very numerous' in 10 river-board areas in England and Wales; 'numerous' in 12; 'fairly small population' in nine; 'scarce' in two; also considered to be 'very numerous' throughout Scotland [644].

Severe decline occurred in England and S Wales starting *c.* 1957. Introduction of Dieldrin and related pesticides suggested as cause [66]. Organo-chlorine pesticides, including Dieldrin and DDT, as well as PCBs and heavy metals, were found in otter tissues and spraints collected in the 1980s, and these substances may still adversely affect otter populations in some areas [501]. Surveys carried out between 1977 and 1979 indicated that in some areas populations had continued to decline, to extinction in parts of Wales and in central England [98, 433]. Populations in Scotland and Ireland apparently unaffected during initial decline. Similar surveys in these countries showed otters to be present and abundant except for the central belt of Scotland [68, 244].

Repeat surveys carried out between 1984 and 1986 in England, Scotland and Wales indicate further changes (Table 10.24). In England, western populations increased in range, while in East Anglia

Map 10.16. Otter (also in Sri Lanka, Malaysia, Sumatra and Java).

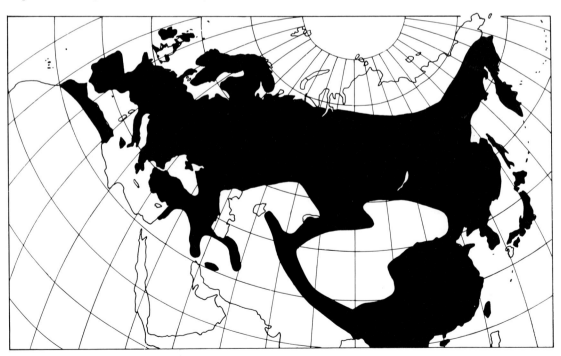

Table 10.23. Measurements of otters [1, 194, 644, 701].

	Males			Females		
	Mean	SD	n	Mean	SD	n
Head and body (mm)	720	33.2	18	636	25.9	24
Tail (mm)	446	22.5	18	398	20.0	24
Weight (kg)	10.1	1.37	433	7.0	1.03	220
	9.1	0.97	22	6.5	0.79	25

Female otters lighter than 5.0 kg and males lighter than 7.25 kg were considered to be juvenile and excluded from calculations. Where appropriate, the formulae in [348] were used to correct for missing parts of bodies.

Table 10.24. Summary of otter surveys in Britain and Ireland.

Area	Date	Sites visited	Sites positive (%)	Source
Wales	1977−78	1030	20	[98]
	1984−85	1097	38	[16]
England	1977−79	2940	6	[433]
	1984−86	3188	9	[651]
Scotland	1977−79	4636	73	[244]
Ireland	1980−81	2323	92	[68]

Positive sites were those at which signs of otters were found. At each site 600 m of river bank was searched.

the range continued to contract [651]. In Wales, otters probably became extinct on Anglesey between 1978 and 1984 [16]. In Scotland, the second survey was confined to areas S of the Highland Region, and otters showed an increased range in the East (particularly Fife), in the Clyde valley and along the margins of the central belt [245].

HABITAT

Lakes, rivers, streams and marshes; capable of overland journeys between watersheds. In coastal areas may alternate between marine and freshwater habitats or live entirely on the coast. Dependence on water makes otters vulnerable to interference from river management, human recreational activities and water pollution. Availability of secure lying-up and breeding sites may influence distribution [489].

SOCIAL ORGANISATION AND BEHAVIOUR

Essentially solitary, groups of otters usually consist of female plus young of the year; sexes normally remain separate except during courtship.

Home ranges vary greatly in size, depending partly on food supply; may be only a few hundred metres

across for some females in productive coastal regions [702]. In Shetland, 12 radio-tracked otters had ranges covering between 2 and 13 km of coast [420]; three otters radio-tracked on a river in Perthshire had ranges of 16 and 22 km (females) and 39 km (male). In Sweden, otters living on a system of lakes and interconnecting streams were followed by snow tracking; females with young had ranges between 4 and 8 km across ($n = 6$) and adult males home ranges of 11−21 km ($n = 8$) [167].

On South Uist, otters fish for eels in freshwater lochs near the coast during summer but during winter activity is confined to the coast [702]. Suggestions that otter might migrate to follow spawning runs of salmonids have not been substantiated in Europe. Juveniles probably disperse at 8−12 months of age [167, 351]. One young male first left natal area at 7 months; area travelled gradually increased until at 12 months range included 68 km of river after which contact was lost [351].

Males' ranges much larger than females'; extensive overlap in ranges between sexes; degree of overlap within sexes varies. In Sweden, ranges of females with young generally separate and exclusive but male ranges partially overlapped [167]. In

Perthshire, female ranges overlapped greatly, male rather less; some evidence of territoriality in males. Females with cubs may be dominant to other otters [246, 558]; evidence of dominance hierarchy in males, with subordinate animals found in peripheral, less favourable habitats [169, 321].

Mean overnight distances for male otters in Sweden, 9.5 km ($n = 36$; maximum 16 km); travels of family groups increased from 2.7 km ($n = 8$) in autumn when cubs were small to 6.9 km ($n = 9$) in spring [167]. In Scotland, mean daily distance of a male was 5.4 km (maximum 16.2 km) and two females without cubs were estimated to cover distances of a quarter and two thirds of this [246].

Faeces may be important in communication; otter can discriminate between spraints of different individuals [697]. Home ranges marked with spraint; much more frequently by males [321]. Males mark throughout their range, females mainly in areas of greatest activity. At parturition, marking close to the natal den ceases [246]; captive females have been observed to defaecate in water at this time [558]. In Shetland, where coastal otters breed seasonally, there is a seasonal variation in the number of spraints found, most occurring in the autumn and winter, least in the summer when the cubs are born [88].

Vocalisation: vocal repertoire limited; well-known otter 'whistle' is a contact call; 'hah!' sound is an anxiety call; other more complex sounds used in social interaction [743]. Otters are particularly vocal during courtship [246].

Aggressive behaviour: fights between wild otters not recorded; a captive male otter was bitten in the inguinal region during a fight with another male [170]. Fractured bacula recorded on a number of occasions [194, 644, 710] and were familiar to otter hunters [644].

Activity: on rivers, activity mainly noctural; bimodal patterns revealed during radio-tracking in two studies on inland streams, first period lasting 3–5 hours after dusk and the second, shorter, before dawn [246, 350]. Coastal otters mainly active during the day, particularly in the early morning and late evening during the summer [427].

In remote areas and on coasts may rest for short periods in the open [517] but usually lie up in dense cover or use burrows (holts). Of 45 resting sites used by three otters in Perthshire, 24 were

above ground (couches) ranging from substantial piles of sticks or scrub covered islets to depressions in bankside vegetation (bedding found at only two of 15 examined). Twenty of the remainder were in natural cavities, mainly under the roots of bankside trees, one was a rabbit burrow. Female dens less accessible than those of the male [246]. In Welsh borders, dens were disproportionately frequently associated with the spreading roots of ash and sycamore [490].

Movement: terrestrial locomotion consists of walking, running and bounding. Swimming at surface consists of kicking with all four feet in no fixed pattern; during fast swimming, below surface, hind legs lie alongside tail and dorso-ventral flexion in the lumbar region provides thrust [671]. Maximum swimming speed probably *c.* 1 m/s [65].

FEEDING

Opportunistically feed on a wide range of prey but mainly fish [355, 745, 756]; in a few areas crayfish or frogs may predominate [168, 248, 512]. These, together with waterfowl, are more usually seasonal and of secondary importance. Waders and passerines taken in some areas [355]; starlings and hirundines seasonally frequent when they roost in reedbeds (over winter or during migration) [168]. Mammals taken rarely, rabbit and water vole more than other species [355, 756]. Aquatic insects occasionally recorded as deliberately eaten (rather than ingested with other prey) [168]. Fish also dominate the diet of coastal otters; crabs are of secondary importance accounting for up to 20% of items identified in spraints [500, 741].

Proportions of different species of fish depend on swimming speed as well as abundance; slower moving species, such as eels, apparently favoured. Coastal otters feed mainly on eel-like or benthic species. In Shetland, eel pout (*Zoarces viviparus*), rocklings (Gadoidea) and butterfish (*Pholis gunnellus*) formed more than 75% of items taken [428]. Size of fish taken also dependent on availability; small individuals usually predominate. In a Devon river, 74% of salmonid fish taken were under 12 cm long [756]; in coastal marshes of Norfolk during one month, only stickleback remains were found in spraint [749]. Predation on pike and salmon up to *c.* 10 kg has been reported [264].

Seasonal variation in diet affected by prey activity as well as abundance. In S England eels taken less frequently in winter when less active [745, 756], and pike taken more frequently during spawning season when most active [63]. Daily food consumption probably *c.* 12–15% of body weight in adult males [501].

Allegations of damage to fishing interests have declined with declining otter populations. In Sweden it was not possible to demonstrate any effect on a crayfish populations or on population of fish in a lake fishery [168].

In clear, well-lit water, hunt by sight but when visibility is poor, vibrissae are used to detect fish movements [243]. Fish are searched for and chased underwater; otter often approaching from below and behind. Otters usually submerge for short periods (means for series of dives range from 4.7 to 28.5 seconds) [89, 308, 351, 421, 741]. In shallow water, prolonged chases may occur when otter breaks surface to breathe without interrupting pursuit. In deeper water, search and pursuit times may be constrained by time taken to travel to and from the bottom [421]. Single dives of up to 70 seconds have been recorded [428]. In marine habitats, otters caught more (smaller) prey and spent more time hunting than in freshwater lochs [89]. Fish usually caught in mouth.

BREEDING

In mainland Britain, breeding probably normally aseasonal [264]. In Scotland, survival of young born on inland lochs in autumn or winter was poor when winters were severe [351] and in coastal areas of NW Scotland most cubs are born in summer [428]. In Shetland, peak of births May to August (29 out of 34 recorded litters). Females therefore lactating during periods of highest food availability. Of five adult females observed in two consecutive years, four bred in both years [428].

Courtship involves much vigorous chasing and play [246, 263, 743]; mating may take place on land or in water. In the wild, pairs of otters stay together for about a week [169, 246]. Gestation 62–63 days, no delay in implantation. Litter size normally two or three, range 1–5. Populations in coastal areas tend to have smaller litters than those inland (Table 10.25). Mean of 70 wild litters in East Germany, 2.3 [656]; mean of 26 captive litters, 2.4 [65].

Young: cubs 12 cm long at birth and furred [743]. Crawl at 2–3 weeks; eyes open at 4–5 weeks. Solid food first taken at 7 weeks; permanent molars

Table 10.25. Litter sizes of otters.

Litter size	Area	Source
Coastal		
1.8	Shetland	[428]
1.95	Norway	[428]
1.55	NW Scotland	[428]
Inland		
2.8	Netherlands	[716]
2.3	East Germany	[657]
2.4	Poland	[757]
2.3	Czechoslovakia	[27]

erupt at 8 weeks [541]; suckling continues until 14 weeks. Cub increasingly active from 7 weeks, when they begin to run and first venture outside the natal den to defaecate. First swim at 3 months [742, 743].

At 36 days, two female cubs weighed 591 g and 647 g; at 75 days, 716 g and 998 g; a solitary male cub weighed 1540 g at 36 days [742]. Growth of a male and female cub charted over one year in [644] but ages uncertain.

Young stay with female for 7–12 months; daily travels of family groups increase as cubs get older [167, 351]. Sexual maturity reached in 2nd year of life. Testes of a captive male reached maximum size at 20–22 months [353]. Earliest recorded breeding in captivity 17 months for male and 22 months for female; average age of first breeding for eight captive females, 3 years 8 months [743].

POPULATION

Density difficult to determine; sprint density is not a reliable guide to population density [88, 427]. In Perthshire, seven or eight breeding females estimated along 98 km of waterway [246]. Suitable coastal regions may have much higher densities; in Shetland one otter per 1.1 km of coastline recorded [741]. In Sweden, estimates of one otter per 5 km of river and one per 2–3 km of lakeshore in good habitat [169]. Sex ratio 1:1 in young and adults [654].

Young of the year may be recognised by size in the wild, and formed 25–38% of the population in parts of Sweden [169]. Corpses aged by bacular morphology [356], skull shape and tooth wear [654] and (in *L. canadensis*) from annular rings in teeth [662]. Proportion of immature animals (less than 2 years) ranges from 32–41% [709] to 75% [654]. Variation may be due to different sampling and ageing techniques. In East Germany, 42% of 91 otters were in their 1st year and 33% in their 2nd [656]. Analysis of trapping returns for *L. canadensis* indicate lower survival in the 2nd year of life (46%) than the 1st (68%) and later years (73%) [662]. In this sample, the oldest animal (aged by cementum rings) was in its 12th year.

MORTALITY

Very few natural predators in Britain. In Shetland, very small young may be vulnerable to attacks by skuas. In Europe, reports of sea eagles, wolves and lynx attacking otters [501]. Man is responsible directly or indirectly for most of known mortality (Table 10.26). Of dead otters recorded in Shetland 35 of 65 died a violent death (mainly road traffic accidents). The remainder died from starvation or disease. Natural deaths were most frequent from March to June (73%) when prey biomass was at its lowest; otters were significantly lighter at this time of year [428].

Between 1975 and 1984, 88 otters are known to have drowned in fish or crustacean traps in Britain [349], most of these in the Outer Hebrides (23 killed in fyke nets, 22 in lobster traps on South Uist).

Annual cull by otterhunts during 1930s was 400 otters with no discernible effect on population. Mean for period 1950–59, 199 otters per year; as population declined hunts progressively reduced both total kill and proportion killed. Mean for 1960–69, 100 otters and for 1970–76, 11 otters. Hunting ceased after 1977. [1, 65, 66]. In Shetland, otters are still trapped illegally for their fur [87].

PARASITES

No systematic studies. The biting louse, *Lutridia exilis* is specific to otters and occurs in Britain. Ticks are frequent [644]. Of 32 otters examined in Ireland, six had intestinal parasites which were probably parasitic on ingested fish rather than the otters [194]. Many of the species listed in [644] probably fall into the same category. Parasitism of Swedish otters by tapeworm has been reported [168] but species uncertain [65]. *Dioctophyme renalis* (nematode) and *Euparyphium melis* (digenean fluke) are found in otters [529]. Captive otters may suffer from canine distemper, pneumonia, leptospirosis, renal calculi and dental abscesses [152, 153, 264, 743]. The last two of these also recorded in wild otters as well as tuberculosis, endocarditis and cirrhosis of the liver [356, 644].

RELATIONS WITH MAN

In Britain, exploitation for fur, although occurring over a long period never as intense as in some continental European countries; most otters killed for control or sport. Shetland was probably an exception, and several hundred otters were probably trapped each year in the large, specially constructed 'otter houses'.

Otters long branded as pests of fisheries but unlikely that wild fish stocks have been depleted. Fish hatcheries and farms may be vulnerable if otters are not excluded; increases in fish farming in Scotland during the 1980s may lead to more complaints about otters [501].

Hunting with dogs dates back to the 13th century but has probably always been as much for sport as for control. During the 1950s up to 13 otter hunts were active in Britain covering most of England and Wales and SW Scotland. Each pack hunted for 40–50 days/year finding 30–40 otters and killing about half of these. Hunting activity declined as otters became scarce and ceased after legal protection was given to otters in England and Wales in 1978. Since 1982, otters have been protected throughout Britain under the Wildlife and Countryside Act (1981). Also protected in N Ireland.

Habitat protection is principal method of conser-

Cause	Britain (%) (n = 165) [65]	East Germany (%) (n = 486) [656]
Killed on roads	34	11
Killed deliberately	37	33
Found dead, cause unknown	16	14
Caught in fish traps	10	36
Killed by dogs	2	4
Other causes	1	2

Table 10.26. Mortality records for otters in Britain and East Germany.

Other causes includes electrocution and drowning under ice.

vation although the need to reduce pollutants and deaths in fish traps also considered important. Areas of land have been designated as Otter havens in which management is carried out in sympathy with the otter's needs and by agreement with land-owners and water authorities [501]. Further information is needed on the effectiveness and, particularly, on the size of the areas needed.

Captive-bred otters have been released into selected areas in East Anglia to restock depleted areas and reintroduce otters to areas in which they are absent [349]. Five groups of either one male and one female or one male and two females (totalling 13 otters) were released up to the end of 1986 and a number of these have bred [744]. Assessment of rivers for pollution levels is a priority in any programme for otter conservation [501].

SOUND RECORDINGS
Appendix 3: A, F, J, S, W.

LITERATURE
[65, 501] provide comprehensive reviews.

AUTHOR FOR THIS SPECIES
P. Chanin.

FAMILY FELIDAE (CATS)

The cat family, comprising the 'big cats' in the genus *Panthera*, the cheetah (*Acinonyx jubatus*), and the 'small cats' (including, however, the puma), which are variously classified in a single genus *Felis* or in a number of separate genera. Cats are characterised especially by their powerful paws with retractile claws and very short muzzles with reduced number of cheek-teeth.

GENUS *Felis*

In its most restricted sense includes about four species of cats in Eurasia and Africa but many more are frequently included. Although the domestic cat is agreed to have been derived from the wildcat (Fig. 10.31), *Felis silvestris*, it is best treated as a separate species to avoid confusing problems of nomenclature. Dental formula 3.1.3.1 / 3.1.2.1.

Wildcat *Felis silvestris*

Felis (catus) silvestris Schreber, 1777; Germany.
Felis grampia Miller, 1907; Invermoriston, Inverness-shire, Scotland.

Cath gwyllt, cath y coed (Welsh); cat-fiadhaich (Scottish Gaelic).

RECOGNITION
Similar to domestic 'tabby' cat but typically larger and more robust. Wildcats have seven to 11 dark body stripes and no substantial areas of white (e.g. on paws) or ginger markings. The tail is usually slightly more than half the combined head and body length; it is thickly furred and appears relatively short and club-like. It has three to five distinct rings and terminates in a blunt, black tip. Domestic and hybrid cats invariably have more tapering tails, often with less distinct rings.

Skull (Fig. 10.32) distinguishable from domestic cat by greater cranial volume: $> 35 \, \text{cm}^3$ for wildcat, $< 32 \, \text{cm}^2$ for domestic cat and also by cranial index: skull length/cranial volume for wildcat < 2.75, for domestic cat > 2.75 [620]. Wildcat's skull more robust, and sagittal suture more convoluted compared with domestic cat. Skull morphometrics have been used to distinguish wild and domestic cats and their hybrids [218].

SIGN

Footprints (Fig. 10.33): four toes and a tri-lobed main pad; fifth toe on front foot and metacarpal pad do not register. Print roughly circular in outline, larger than that of domestic cat, more delicate than that of fox; overprinting often occurs. Claws retractile and do not usually register.

Faeces dark and variable in colour from brown to grey-green, with a strong musty odour when fresh. Roughly cylindrical in shape 1.5−6.0 cm in length [95], but may be formless depending on diet. Sometimes buried, but usually left exposed and often deposited in conspicuous areas on rocks, tussocks of vegetation and along animal trails [95, 309].

Communication: scratch marks left on trees and saplings when removing cornified layers on claws, which are probably also visual and olfactory cues for other cats.

Fig. 10.31. Wildcat (top) and domestic cat (bottom). Note the bushy, truncated tail of the wildcat. some blotchy markings as shown completely striped but most show some blotchy markings as shown here.

Feeding remains: lagomorph feeding remains typically have skin everted, with muscle cleaned from bones, and ribs and scapulae chewed [95]. However, same signs left by domestic cats when feeding on similar prey. Caching of uneaten prey has been observed, with remains being hidden under vegetation and covered with debris [95, 692].

DESCRIPTION

Fur thick, about 50 mm long on sides and 60 mm along the back. Background coat colour is buff grey or yellowish brown (the agouti pattern) with seven to 11 dark brown or black body stripes, four to seven transverse bands on the hind legs and two to three less distinct bands on the forelegs. The tail is thickly furred and club-like, with three to five distinct black rings and a blunt black tip. Four narrow longitudinal stripes extend from the nape up and over the forehead, where they may become confused, and down onto the shoulders where they

disappear. In this region there are two usually well-defined longitudinal stripes about 60 mm in length and 10−20 mm apart [519]. The dorsal stripe begins behind the shoulder stripes and terminates at the base of the tail. On the cheeks there are three stripes, two of which are fused. There are small patches of white fur at the umbilicus and occasionally on the chest and throat, and the chin is off-white [95]. The ears are the same colour as the body with ochre coloured fur along the posterior margin. Underparts lighter in colour with ochrous fur in groin, inside hind legs and underside of tail base. Kittens are darker and more distinctly marked than adults, with a less bushy tail.

Moult: little information available. Seasonal moults have been recorded, with fairly heavy moult in spring and a lighter moult in late summer [692].

Senses: eyes amber in colour; pupil narrows to

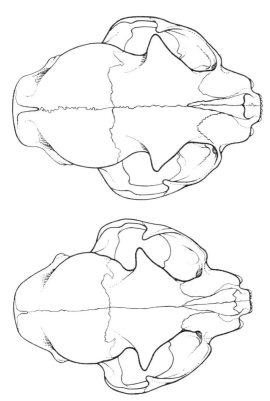

Fig. 10.32. Skulls of wildcat (above) and domestic cat (below).

Hind pad

Fig. 10.33. Footprint of wildcat.

vertical slit in bright light. Good vision in poor light with rods outnumbering cones by a factor of 25 (in domestic cat) and presence of tapetum. Nose pink; sense of smell keen, and under favourable conditions have been reported to detect meat at up to 200 m [692]. Vibrissae mostly white. Majority on upper lips with a few on each cheek and over the eyes. Short bristle-like whiskers found on the chin.

Ears erect, cone shaped and able to be moved through 180° to locate source of sound. Hearing very sensitive and in domestic cat extends from 30 Hz – 65 kHz [759].

Nipples: four pairs, axillary pair sometimes absent [505].

Scent glands: apocrine and sebaceous scent glands on head, chin and base of tail, and sebaceous glands between toes.

Teeth: incisors small and rather weak; canines and carnassials (pm^4 and M_1) well developed. First upper pre-molar (pm^2) vestigal or absent; pm_2 occasionally present.

Chromosomes: $2n = 38$, $FNa = 68$ (continental data) [767], as in domestic cat.

RELATIONSHIPS
Most closely related to *Felis chaus*, the jungle cat of S. Asia, *F. margarita*, the sand cat of the Sahara etc., and *F. bieti*, the Chinese desert cat [92].

MEASUREMENTS (Table 10.27).

VARIATION
Wildcats occurring in Scotland have been considered as a subspecies (*F. s. grampia*) on the basis of general darker coloration, with extensive, well-defined dark markings on sides and legs [519]. However, there is considerable variation within the Scottish population and a distinction between British and mainland European forms may not be justified [398].

Hybridisation with domestic cats can occur producing fertile offspring. Hybrids can closely resemble *F. silvestris* making identification difficult. However, tails of hybrids tend to resemble those of *F. catus*, being tapered and less distinctly marked [95]. *F. silvestris* is distinguishable from *F. catus* on the basis of cranial volume [620] and gut length [622], but hybrids can usually be distinguished with some certainty using skull morphometrics [218].

Melanistic forms have been reported from Scotland but their status, i.e. *F. silvestris*, *F. catus* or hybrid, remains in doubt. The status of appar-

	Males			Females			
	Mean	Range	n	Mean	Range	n	Source
Head and body	564	485–628	28	515	488–542	10	[1]
(mm)	564	515–650	26	543	507–595	16	[398]
	574	547–632	9	563	521–580	7	[95]
Tail (mm)	295	242–338	28	283	265–305	10	[1]
	307	235–356	26	293	240–360	16	[398]
	293	267–315	9	289	258–300	7	[95]
Hind foot (mm)	127	120–140	25	122	116–127	8	[1]
	134	115–147	26	126	105–140	16	[398]
	134	127–147	9	125	117–135	7	[95]
Weight (kg)	5.2	4.2–6.3	26	4.5	3.5–5.5	13	[1]
	4.7	3.5–7.1	26	3.9	2.5–5.6	16	[398]
	4.4	3.8–5.0	9	4.0	3.5–4.6	7	[95]

Table 10.27. Measurements of adult Scottish wild cats.

ently similar forms in E Europe is also unclear [11, 552, 618].

DISTRIBUTION
Woodland, savanna and steppe zones from Europe to W China and central India, and throughout Africa, except in desert and tropical forest areas. In Britain, the range is confined to central and northern Scotland; absent from Scottish islands. A recent survey of the wildcat in Scotland [156, 157] failed to find any evidence that this species was present south of the central industrial belt of Scotland. Reports of wildcats further south probably refer to feral cats, although the possibility of an unofficial release of this species cannot be ruled out. The central industrial belt appears to be acting as a physical barrier to the natural southward movement of the wildcat in Scotland.

HISTORY
Present as part of post-glacial temperate fauna of mainland Britain; recorded at Mesolithic site at Thatcham, Berkshire [761]. Some evidence [717] for its possible occurrence in Ireland in Neolithic times, but if so it became extinct early on, and confusion with domestic cat is possible.

More recent history of this species has been documented in [430]. The wildcat in Britain experienced a steady reduction in range from the Middle Ages through hunting and habitat destruction. Disappeared from S England probably during the 16th century. It was lost from N England and Wales by 1880, and at about this time it was also last heard of from S Scotland. Population minimum occurred about 1914, when it was confined to

Inverness-shire, parts of Argyllshire, Ross-shire and Sutherland. Freedom from persecution during the first World War (1914–18) and reduced persecution levels since then have allowed the wildcat to expand its range, aided by the increased planting of coniferous woodland.

HABITAT
Found in upland forests and woodlands, moorland

Map 10.17. Wildcat.

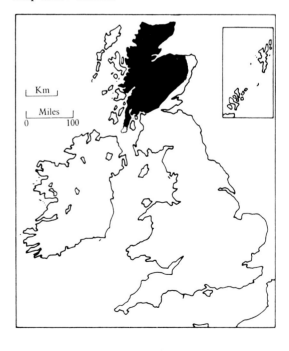

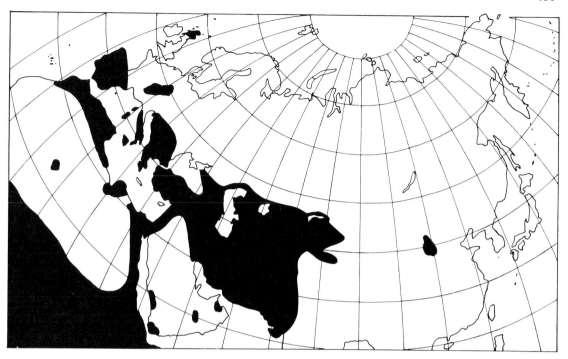

Map 10.18. Wildcat (also to southern Africa).

and hill ground. Recorded from over 800 m, but usually found below 500 m. Onset of bad weather in winter drives wildcats from exposed moorland and hill ground to areas containing more woodland and scrub [95]. Forestry plantations, especially in the early years after planting, are an important habitat, offering shelter and prey such as small mammals and rabbits [95].

SOCIAL ORGANISATION AND BEHAVIOUR
Except when mating, wildcats are solitary and territorial [95]. Male ($n = 2$) and female ($n = 2$) ranges similar in size in NE Scotland with mean annual area of 175 hectares [95], but likely to vary in relation to quality of habitat. Overlap of range between male and female, but the core areas of an individual's range are avoided by other cats; least overlap of range between animals of same sex. Females more sedentary and exclusively territorial, probably related to the need for exclusive hunting areas when raising young. Young animals have smallest ranges (females ($n = 3$) average 77 ha; males ($n = 3$) average 54 ha). Many males, particularly young animals, are nomadic [95].

Scent marking: territorial marking achieved by spraying urine on trees, vegetation and boulders and by depositing faeces in prominent places, e.g. tussocks of vegetation. Scratching of trees and saplings may also serve as a visual marker and as an olfactory sign by the deposition of scent from interdigital glands on paws. Exhibit Flehmen reaction. Little information on hierarchy, but older cats dominant to young animals [95].

Vocal communication: little information; mostly silent, but wildcats have been heard to scream during the mating season [624, 692], and vocalisation frequent between mother and kittens. Purring by mother and kittens has been recorded during suckling [85].

Aggressive behaviour: rarely recorded except between males during mating season over access to females. Aggressive encounters possibly not common because of mutual avoidance. Young animals failed to settle in areas that were already occupied [95], but whether this was a result of direct aggression is not known.

Activity: mainly crepuscular and nocturnal, although during the course of year may be active at any hour of the day [95]. More strictly nocturnal in summer, but in winter active over more of the day, probably in response to food shortage. Remained inactive for periods up to 28 hours during heavy snowfall and rain [95]; also inactive during strong winds which upset their ability to hunt [692].

Dens situated amongst large rocks and boulders and rocky cairns on hill ground, old fox earths, badger setts and amongst tree roots. Little attempt at nest building in den, though some effort may be made by female to rake in dry grass and heather before giving birth [692].

Locomotion by walking, running and leaping. Swim well when necessary and climb well, but usually descend trees backwards unlike true arboreal animals.

Grooming involves use of barbed tongue and forepaws with the use of teeth and claws to remove debris in fur.

FEEDING

Carnivorous, taking small rodents, lagomorphs and birds. Composition of diet related to availability of prey. Hunting organised in circuit, with different habitats visited [95]. Small rodents taken by cat sitting in wait or 'hunting' through suitable habitat [624]. Larger prey, e.g. lagomorphs, stalked from behind cover when possible, before final rush and seizure of prey, which is killed by bite to back of neck, severing spinal cord. May also sit over rabbit holes waiting for prey to emerge [95]. Carrion (sheep and deer) rarely taken [95, 309, 692]; scavenge road casualties, e.g. lagomorphs. Other species taken include: amphibians, reptiles, insects and a variety of small mammals and birds. Vegetation, including grass and bracken, also eaten possibly as a source of roughage [692].

BREEDING (Fig. 10.34)

One litter produced, usually in May, but kittens can be born through until August. Oestrous cycle 5–8 days, gestation 66 days (range 63–69.5) [86]. Mean litter size in captivity 3.4, range one to eight [86], mean litter size in wild 3.7, range two to six [624]. Weight at birth 100–163 g [621], duration of lactation 2.5–3.5 months [692].

In captivity, females able to breed at 1 year of

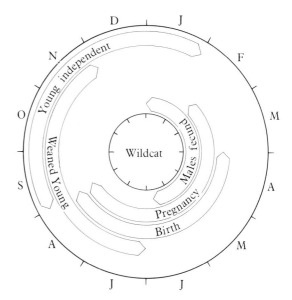

Fig. 10.34. Wildcat: life-cycle.

age, and males begin to show signs of sexual activity from age of 9–10 months [86]. Females come into oestrus in spring, usually in March in Scotland [505]. Single litter produced, usually in May; reports of repeated breeding in same year [505], but this may result from confusion with late-born litters. Reports of several males attending oestrus female, but also records of male and female alone together, having formed temporary pair [624]. Male and female observed to share same range and occasionally to move about together over 2-week period at mating time [95]. Sex ratio equal at birth [86], but trapped and shot samples usually show bias towards males.

Young are blind at birth but covered in fur. Pads pink, darkening almost to black at 3 months [95]. Eyes open at 10–13 days, blue at first, but change from 7 weeks to final golden colour at about 5 months [95]. Milk teeth all erupted by 6–7 weeks [516], and permanent dentition complete at 175–195 days [86]. Four upper canines present for limited period as permanent canines erupt before deciduous ones are lost [86]. Largely grown by 10 months, with skeletal growth continuing to 18–19 months, when epiphyses of long bones close [623].

Family breaks up at about 5 months [120, 446], and young enter roaming stage while attempting to establish home range [95].

POPULATION

In NE Scotland one cat per 3.3 km² [95], but density will vary with quality of habitat and is likely to be much lower in poorer areas of NW Scotland. In Europe, estimates vary from one cat per 0.7 to 10 km² [624].

Age structure little known, but two samples of cats from NE Scotland indicated essentially young population, containing 15% and 25% adult animals respectively [95].

MORTALITY

Persecution is major cause of death in many areas of Scotland. Golden eagles and foxes may take kittens, and there are reports from Europe of stoats taking young kittens from the den, and martens taking young cats [624]. Starvation during winter has been recorded in Scotland [95] and in Germany [120]. Road accidents also contribute to mortality.

PARASITES

Mites — *Otodectes* sp. recorded from captive bred animals in Britain [166], and a probable case of *Notodectes cati* has been recorded [1]. Fleas — probably the cat flea, *Ctenocephalides felis*, occurs, but other recorded species, e.g. *Spilopsyllus cuniculi* (from rabbits) and *Hystrichopsylla talpae* (from small rodents) are casual from prey items [95]. Ticks — *Ixodes ricinus*. Lice — *Felicola subrostratus*. Roundworms — *Toxacara cati* [54]. Tapeworms — *Taenia taeniaeformis* (intermediate hosts small rodents, shrews and lagomorphs), *Taenia pisiformis* (intermediate hosts lagomorphs and occasionally rodents), *Mesocestoides litteratus* (intermediate hosts mites followed by birds and rodents) [54], *M. lineatus* (intermediate hosts mites followed by rodents and possibly birds).

Very little known about diseases. Chronic infection of unknown cause recorded in three wild cats in Glen Tanar, two of which subsequently died [95]. Injuries from snares and illegal gin traps have been reported. May receive burns during heather burning [95].

RELATIONS WITH MAN

More enlightened attitudes have reduced overall persecution this century. Although they take many rabbits and small rodents which are considered pests of forestry and agriculture, still regarded by gamekeeping interests (pheasant, red grouse) as vermin, and many killed every year.

Legislation: included within Schedule 5 of the Wildlife and Countryside Act 1981, which grants full protection since animals on Schedule 5 may only be 'taken' under licence if causing serious damage or for scientific purposes.

Conservation: the survival of the wildcat as a species in Britain may be threatened by hybridisation with domestic cats. All local and isolated populations should be safeguarded to conserve this species and maintain its genetic integrity.

Techniques for study: a difficult animal to study, but radio-tagging has been successful [95]. Faeces analysis a useful technique for dietary information [95, 309].

SOUND RECORDINGS

Appendix 3: A, F, P.

LITERATURE

[624] reviews the ecology of this species. [95] most recent major work in Scotland; brief report in [96]. [692] popular account of wildcats in semi-captivity. Two monographs in German [120, 256].

AUTHOR FOR THIS SPECIES

N. Easterbee.

Feral cat *Felis catus*

Felis catus Linnaeus, 1758.

Domestic cat 'gone wild'. Male — tom; female — queen, puss, she-cat; young — kitten.

RECOGNITION

A domestic cat living, at least partly, independently of humans. The legal and biological distinctions between a household or pet domestic cat and a feral one are sometimes hazy, since many pet cats live partly (even largely) independent of their 'owners'. The distinction may lie more in the attitude of the owner than in the behaviour of the cat. It is convenient to use the adjective dependent (on people) to describe those domestic cats that are not feral (or independent).

Domestic cats are best distinguished from wildcats by the latter's thick tail which ends in a blunt, rounded tip. In contrast, the tabby domestic cat's tail tends to taper to a pointed end. Also, the wildcat's tail is circled by three to five clearly separate broad black rings, whereas those of domestic tabbies are often less distinct and usually joined into a dorsal stripe. The blotched tabby pattern (circular whorls on the flanks) is a domestic variant — the wild type being a striped tabby pattern (vertical stripes or spots on the flanks). Striped domestic tabbies may have more stripes on both tail and body than wildcats. Typically, wild cats are larger than domestic ones, but there is much variation. Hybrids are difficult, or impossible, to distinguish externally, but their tails are reputedly more like those of *F. catus* than *F. silvestris* [96].

Skull: width of brain case (mastoid width) > 75% of zygomatic width. Domestic and wildcat skulls very similar, but differ in the frontal region — in the wildcat the medial junction of the nasals and frontal is in one plane; in the domestic cat it is usually in a pit, and the hindmost tips of the nasals in the wildcat project further back relative to the ends of the maxillae than in the domestic cat [659]. There is also a difference in an index of cranial volume and overall length (*see* Wildcat, p. 433). Hybrids cannot be identified conclusively by skull measurements, but historical changes in such measurements may indicate that rate of hybridization has increased during the past century [218].

Chromosomes: 2n = 38; FNa = 68 as in wildcat [767].

SIGN

Tracks are readily distinguishable due to four toes, lack of claw marks and similarly rounded shape of both fore- and hindpaw prints. Toe prints compact, arranged in an arc, and all four point forward. Great size variation, but print on soft ground about 3.5 cm long × 4.0 cm wide. Hind pad three lobed. Track distinguished from canids by very different shape and, generally, absence of claw marks, and from mustelids by absence of claw marks and four rather than five toes. When walking, hind foot placed in front of corresponding forefoot track; stride 30 cm and straddling the mid-line (cf. fox). When trotting, stride lengthens to 35–40 cm and becomes straighter.

Will use paths and tracks such as those of fox, badger, rabbits, but does so with less regularity than either of these species, and does not normally form its own network of trails. Generally travels along hedgerows, woodland edges and other bor-

ders. Characteristically coloured fur caught on barbed wire fences at crossing places. Dens often in outbuildings, haystores, woodpiles, rockpiles or other natural shelters in the countryside; in urban areas dens in crevices in buildings. Claw sharpening scratch marks sometimes on trees (often elder), fenceposts and other wooden uprights.

Faeces and scent: pungent urine sprayed backwards by adult males onto upright surfaces, e.g. fenceposts and grassy tussocks; this behaviour much less frequent in females. Those associated with farms tend to bury faeces when in vicinity of farmyard, as do house cats, but leave them atop conspicuous objects along trails when further afield in their home ranges, as do wildcats [487, 563]. Faeces 6–8 cm long, 1–5 cm diameter.

Food remains difficult to distinguish from other carnivores. Chews through feather quills, as does fox, but unlike fox tends not to break bones of larger prey such as rabbits and rarely chews off heads of rabbits or birds. Bite marks of upper canine teeth approx 1.8 cm apart. Food sometimes, but not often, cached beneath loose covering of leaf litter, or dragged into cover and off the ground, but never buried as by fox.

MEASUREMENTS

Females: 2.5–4.5 kg, males: 3.5–7.0 kg. Newborn: 80–140 g, 5 weeks *c.* 450 g, 8 weeks *c.* 1 kg.

VARIATION

Selective breeding has produced a large number of varieties. Coat colours may be associated with other qualities (pleiotropic effects) affecting survival of feral cats; blotched tabby and black gene are common in urban feral populations [606], and the dark mutant that occurs commonly among feral cats on Marion Island is associated with small adrenal glands [708]. Distribution of some varieties (e.g. blotched tabby) reflect ancient shipping routes [691].

DISTRIBUTION

Feral cats in various degrees of dependence upon man probably numerous throughout the British Isles, but in unknown numbers and distribution. Most conspicuously associated with urban development, especially hospitals, warehouses, and dockyards and urban centres, but also found in the countryside. Introductions to many islands, e.g. St

Kilda in 1930, and to Noss, South Havra and Holm of Melly in the Shetlands in the 1890s to control rats. In 1950, 36 cats released on Great Saltee Island off Ballyteige Bay, Co. Wexford, for rabbit control [436]. Wherever there are crofters, e.g. Outer Hebrides, there are cats living feral in some degree, and there are feral populations on some uninhabited islands, e.g. Monach Isles, where they were initially released to control rabbits [95]. The distribution of feral cats in urban areas is reviewed in [705], but little is known on the extent of their independence from provisioning by people. There are probably over six million cats in Britain, of which about 20% have been classed as feral [663].

HISTORY

Ancient Egyptian paintings dating to 2000 BC are the earliest records of cats in domestic circumstances, which appear subsequently in the art of India and China [691]. Domestic cats introduced to Europe by the Romans, and possibly did not arrive in Britain until brought by the Normans in the 11th century [766]. Wild ancestor probably *Felis silvestris lybica* [84], which may have begun its own domestication by exploiting the rodents associated with early grain stores.

HABITAT

Found at various degrees of dependence on people, in wide variety of habitats. These range from urban dockland [112, 113] to wooded valleys [205] and farmland [442, 480].

SOCIAL ORGANISATION AND BEHAVIOUR

Structure: social organisation varies between habitats from more solitary where food dispersed and fluctuating in abundance to more sociable where it is clumped and abundant, e.g. farms and rubbish tips [367]. Social relationships within a group of farm cats have been described in [487]. It appears that groups develop as matrilines, successive generations of daughters sharing a home range with broadly amicable relationships. The social structure of these groups involves a net flow of social greetings from socially peripheral, and perhaps subordinate, females to a central one which is perhaps the original female of the matriline. Larger colonies are probably not integrated social units, but composed of a central, and reproductively successful, matriline which monopolise the re-

source, and peripheral, unsuccessful matrilines [367]. Younger males live within the female group until about 12 months old when attacked by older males. At 2–3 years young males begin to challenge established breeding males, who occupy larger home ranges which may embrace several groups of females [442].

Home-range sizes vary enormously with habitat and dispersion of food [487]. Males' home ranges generally bigger than females by five-fold or more. On British lowland farmland females 13.1 hectare, male 83.0 hectare [480]. Home-range sizes may vary considerably with season and status [95, 443]. Where food clumped, females' ranges overlap as group territories; male ranges overlap each other widely and those of several females [442, 700].

Predation: predominantly sit-and-wait predators. On farmland, generally hunt by travelling hedgerows, so hunting range equivalent to travel route. Elsewhere travel rapidly between good hunting areas (e.g. barns, rabbit warrens, feeding sites).

FEEDING

Many populations of feral cats are dependent upon offal from humans [112]. The remainder fit into two broad categories: either they are principally predators of colonial seabirds [362, 707], or they are principally predators of rodents and lagomorphs. The cats living on the uninhabited Monach Islands (Hebrides) fed mainly on rabbits [95] whereas on farmland they tend to eat rodents [487] or to alternate seasonally between the two [442]. Around farms, cats are thought to suppress the recovery of rat populations following poisoning, but they are unable to reduce established infestations unaided [162].

A national survey concluded that birds comprised 21% of the wild prey taken by house cats, with mammals comprising most of the remainder [334, 335]. Birds accounted for 35% of the prey items brought to homes by cats in a Bedfordshire village, the annual catch comprising 22 species of birds and 15 species of mammals [77]. The same study found that house cats killed about one-third of the total breeding population of house sparrows. The proportion of birds in the diet appears to be higher in residential areas than in rural ones, but in general country cats appear to kill more prey than do suburban ones [663]. Other surveys of the numbers of house cats and their predatory behaviour include

[515, 598]. However, the extent to which predation by these largely 'dependent' cats reflects that by more 'independent' ones is unknown.

BREEDING

Gestation: 55–65 days. Induced ovulation; reproductive physiology as for domestic cat. Mating in groups sometimes monopolised by one or a few breeding males [442], but other observations of several males mating same female [699]. One to three litters per annum, probably determined by mother's nutritional state. Breeding season in Europe, January to August, occasionally year-round.

Development: at 8–13 days eyes open; at 18 days crawling and ears straighten; 21 days stand unsteadily; at 8 weeks have full set of milk teeth; at 12 weeks start to shed milk teeth and eye colour begins to change from blueish to yellow.

POPULATION

Wide variation with habitat. Cats living independently of people on a Hebridean island had a population density of $3.7/km^2$ [95]. One survey on English farmland revealed an average of 6.3 cats per property or $13.9/km^2$. Considering the differences in sizes of male and female home ranges, effective densities of 30 cats/km^2 around farms with cats, and densities closer to 2 cats/km^2 further from farmsteads where only males roamed [487].

MORTALITY

Little is known of mortality, but in cat groups viral disease is often of obvious importance. Feline panleucopaenia (also known as feline distemper, feline infectious enteritis or cat flu) is widespread.

PARASITES

The flea *Ctenocephalides felis* is common; the many other flea species found on feral cats are of accidental occurrence. The biting louse *Felicola subrostrata* is probably common.

RELATIONS WITH MAN

Domestic cats live at various levels of independence of man, and this may vary for an individual cat not only within its lifetime but on a regular seasonal basis. Cats which a farmer regards as his property are generally seen as an asset. In one survey, 81% of English farms had cats; modal number was two, mean colony size four [487]. Of these farmers, 87%

claimed to keep cats primarily for rodent control, and only 21% of them believed that they provided their cats with sufficient food. The implication was that cats on almost two thirds of surveyed English farms were, to varying extents, independent or semi-feral, and studies of the diet of such farm cats indicates that they do not confine their hunting to farmyard rodents [487].

Cats whose circumstances differ little from the foregoing, but which nobody claims, are generally regarded as pests. Indeed, even among farmers who keep cats, some 6.6% of farmers questioned in one survey regarded cats as pests on their land. Feral cats are widely held, but not proven, to be an important predator of game birds, and occasionally of poultry. It is debatable whether a domestic cat which goes wild thereby loses the protection of the Protection of Animals Acts and is then entitled to the same treatment as a genuine wildcat [658]. Alternatively, and more likely, a feral cat's status in the UK is probably analogous to that of mink, and therefore enjoys no protection.

On many oceanic islands feral cats have proven disastrous to the conservation of endemic birds [436]. They are generally regarded as damaging to the interests of birds and birdwatchers [515]. In general, feral cats prove very difficult to eliminate or control. Most attempts in remote areas have been by shooting. In urban areas, cage trapping is the norm, but recent attention by those concerned for cat welfare has focused on castration of breeding males [546, 705]. On Marion Island (Southern Ocean), cats were virtually eliminated by the controlled, but controversial, introduction of the virus feline panleucopaenia [711].

LITERATURE
[699] — extensive review of behaviour and ecology.

AUTHOR FOR THIS SPECIES
D.W. Macdonald.

REFERENCES

1 Author's data.
2 Adamovich V.L. (1978) Landscape–ecological foundations of the local foci of rabic infection. *Zoologicheskii zhurnal* 57:260–71.
3 Adams A.W. (1965) Mink movement study. *North Dakota State Game and Fish Department Report* No. 524.

4 Ahnlund H. (1976) Age determination in the European badger, *Meles meles* L. *Zeitschrift für Säugetierkunde* **41**:119−25.

5 Ahnlund H. (1980) Sexual maturity and breeding season of the badger, *Meles meles* in Sweden. *Journal of Zoology* **190**:77−95.

6 Akande M. (1972) The food of feral mink (*Mustela vison*) in Scotland. *Journal of Zoology* **167**:475−9.

7 Albone E.S. (1975) Dihydroactinidiolide in the supracaudal scent gland secretions of the red fox. *Nature* **256**:575.

8 Albone E.S. & Fox M.W. (1971) Anal gland secretion of the red fox. *Nature* **233**:569−70.

9 Albone E.S. & Flood P.F. (1976) The supracaudal scent gland of the red fox *Vulpes vulpes*. *Journal of Chemical Ecology* **2**:167−75.

10 Albone E.S. *et al.* (1974) The anal sac secretion of the red fox (*Vulpes vulpes*); its chemistry and microbiology. A comparison with the anal sac secretion of the lion (*Panthera leo*). *Life Sciences* **14**:387−400.

11 Aliev F. (1972) The Caucasian black cat, *Felis silvestris caucasica* Satunin, 1905. *Säugetierkundliche Mitteilungen* **22**:142−5.

12 Allen A.W. (1983) Habitat suitability index models: mink. *United States Department of Interior, Fisheries, and Wildlife Service Report* No. FWS/OBS-83/10.61; 19 pp.

13 Allen G.M. (1933) The least weasel a circumboreal species. *Journal of Mammalogy* **14**:316−9.

14 Anderson J. (1978) [Numerical aspects of the occurrence of the weasel (*Mustela nivalis*) in relation to the stoat (*Mustela erminea*) in Denmark.] *Natura Jutlandica* **20**:123−8.

15 Anderson R.M. & Trewhella W. (1985) Population dynamics of the badger (*Meles meles*) and the epidemiology of bovine tuberculosis (*Mycobacterium bovis*). *Philosophical Transactions of the Royal Society of London B* **310**:327−81.

16 Andrews E. & Crawford A.K. (1986) *Otter survey of Wales 1984−85*. London: Vincent Wildlife Trust 74 pp.

17 Anon (1960) Vermin bag records. *Imperial Chemical Industries Game Services Annual Report for 1959* p. 56.

18 Anon (1968) *Nutrient requirements of mink and foxes*. Washington, DC: National Academy of Sciences Publication 1676 46 pp.

19 Anon (1981) *Predator and squirrel control*. Fordingbridge, Hampshire: Game Conservancy 68 pp.

20 Apfelbach R. (1973) Woran erkennt ein Raubtier seine Beute? *Umschau* **73**:453−7.

21 Apfelbach R. (1973) Olfactory sign stimulus for prey selection in polecats (*Putorius putorius* L.). *Zeitschrift für Tierpsychologie* **33**:270−3.

22 Armitage J.S. (1980) Notes on the hunting techniques and prey of the weasel. *Sorby Record* **18**:83.

23 Ashton E.H. (1955) Some characters of the skulls of the European polecat, the Asiatic polecat and the domestic ferret. (Addendum). *Proceedings of the Zoological Society of London* **125**: 807−9.

24 Ashton E.H. & Thomson A.P.D. (1955) Some characters of the skulls and skins of the European polecat, the Asiatic polecat and the domestic ferret. *Proceedings of the Zoological Society of London* **125**: 317−33.

25 Aspisov D.I. & Popov V.A. (1940) [Factors determining fluctuations in the numbers of ermines.] *Trudy Obshchestva estestvoispytatelei pri Imperatorskom kazanskom universitetê* **6**:41−64.

26 Balharry, D. Personal communication.

27 Baruš V. & Zejda J. (1981) The European otter (*Lutra lutra*) in the Czech Socialist Republic. *Prírodovédné Práce ústavu Ceskoslovenske Akademie Véd v Brné* **15**(12):1−41.

28 Bassett C.F. & Llewellyn L.M. (1949) The moulting and fur growth pattern in the adult mink. *American Midland Naturalist* **42**:751−5.

29 Bateman J.A. (1970) Supernumerary incisors in mustelids. *Mammal Review* **1**:81−6.

30 Beaucournu J.C. & Grulich I. (1968) A propos de la belette de Corse. *Mammalia* **32**:341−71.

31 Berkovitz B.K.B. & Poole D.F.G. (1977) Attrition of the teeth in ferrets. *Journal of Zoology* **183**:411−18.

32 Berkovitz B.K.B. & Thomson P. (1973) Observations on the aetiology of supernumerary upper incisors in the albino ferret (*Mustela putorius*). *Archives of Oral Biology* **18**:457−63.

33 Birks J.D.S. (1981) *Home range and territorial behaviour of the feral mink* (Mustela vison *Schreber) in Devon*. PhD. thesis, University of Exeter.

34 Birks J. (1986) *Mink*. Oswestry, Shropshire: Anthony Nelson 24 pp.

35 Birks J.D.S. & Dunstone N. (1984) A note on prey remains collected from the dens of feral mink (*Mustela vison*) in a coastal habitat. *Journal of Zoology* **203**:279−81.

36 Birks J.D.S. & Dunstone N. (1985) Sex-related differences in the diet of the mink *Mustela vison*. *Holarctic Ecology* **8**:245−52.

37 Birks J.D.S. & Linn I.J. (1982). Studies of home range of the feral mink, *Mustela vison*. *Symposia of the Zoological Society of London* **49**:231−57.

38 Blackmore D.K. (1964) A survey of disease in British wild foxes (*Vulpes vulpes*). *Veterinary Record* **76**: 527−33.

39 Blandford P.R.S. (1986) *Behavioural ecology of the polecat* Mustela putorius *in Wales*. PhD. thesis, University of Exeter.

40 Blandford P.R.S. (1987) Biology of the polecat *Mustela putorius*: a literature review. *Mammal Review* **17**:155−98.

41 Blomquist L. *et al.* (1981) Breeding the least weasel (*Mustela rixosa*) in Helsinki Zoo. *Zoologische Garten, Jena* **51**:363−8.

42 Bonnin M. *et al.* (1978) Oestrogen and progesterone concentrations in peripheral blood in pregnant red foxes (*Vulpes vulpes*). *Journal of Reproduction and Fertility* **54**:37−41.

43 Bradbury K. (1974) The badger's diet. In Paget R.J.

& Middleton A.L.V. eds *Badgers of Yorkshire and Humberside*. York: William Sessions pp. 113–25.

44 Brinck C. *et al.* (1978) Anal pouch secretion in mink *Mustela vison*. *Oikos* 30:68–75.

45 Brinck C. *et al.* (1983) Anal sac secretion in mustelids: a comparison. *Journal of Chemical Ecology* 9:727–45.

46 Brown J.H. & Lasiewski R.C. (1972) Metabolism of weasels: the cost of being long and thin. *Ecology* 53:939–43.

47 Brugge T. (1977) [Prey selection of weasel, stoat and polecat in relation to sex and size.] *Lutra* 19:39–49.

48 Buchalczyk T. & Ruprecht A.L. (1977) Skull variability of *Mustela putorius* Linnaeus, 1758. *Acta theriologica* 22:87–120.

49 Buckingham C.J. (1979) *The activity and exploratory behaviour of the weasel*, Mustela nivalis. PhD. thesis, University of Exeter.

50 Buckle A. & Harris S. (1980) The flea epifauna of a suburban fox (*Vulpes vulpes*) population. *Journal of Zoology* 190:431–9.

51 Bullock D. & Pickering S. (1982) Weasels (*Mustela nivalis*) attacking a young and an adult brown hare (*Lepus capensis*). *Journal of Zoology* 197:307–8.

52 Burnham P.M. (1970) Kestrel attempting to prey on weasels. *British Birds* 63:338.

53 Burrows R. (1968) *Wild fox*. Newton Abbot: David & Charles 203 pp.

54 Burt M.D.B. *et al.* (1980) Helminth parasites of wild cats in north-east Scotland. *Journal of Helminthology* 54:303–8.

55 Cabrera A. (1932) Los mamiferos de Marruecos. *Trabajos del Museo nacional de ciencias naturales, Madrid* 57:1–361.

56 Cahn A.R. (1936) A weasel learns by experience. *Journal of Mammalogy* 17:286.

57 Canivenc R. (1966) A study of progestation in the European badger (*Meles meles*, L.). *Symposia of the Zoological Society of London* 15:15–26.

58 Canivenc R. & Bonnin M. (1975) Les facteurs écophysiologiques de regulation de la fonction lutéale chez les mammifères à ovo-implantation différée. *Journal de physiologie, Paris* 70:533–8.

59 Canivenc R. & Bonnin M. (1981) Environmental control of delayed implantation in the European badger (*Meles meles*). *Journal of Reproduction and Fertility, Supplement* 29:25–33.

60 Casey T.M. & Casey K.K. (1979) Thermoregulation of arctic weasels. *Physiological Zoology* 52:153–64.

61 Chanin P.R.F. (1976) *The ecology of the feral mink* (Mustela vison *Schreber*) *in Devon*. PhD. thesis, University of Exeter.

62 Chanin P. (1981) The feral mink — natural history, movements and control. *Nature in Devon* 2:33–54.

63 Chanin P. (1981) The diet of the otter and its relations with the feral mink in two areas of south-west England. *Acta theriologica* 26:83–95.

64 Chanin P. (1983) Observations on two populations of feral mink in Devon, U.K. *Mammalia* 47: 463–76.

65 Chanin P. (1985) *The natural history of otters*. Beckenham, Kent: Croom Helm 179 pp.

66 Chanin P.R.F. & Jefferies D.J. (1978) The decline of the otter *Lutra lutra* L. in Britain: an analysis of hunting records and discussion of causes. *Biological Journal of the Linnean Society* 10:305–28.

67 Chanin P.R.F. & Linn I. (1980) The diet of the feral mink (*Mustela vison*) in southwest Britain. *Journal of Zoology* 192:205–23.

68 Chapman P.J. & Chapman L.L. (1982) *Otter survey of Ireland 1980–81*. London: Vincent Wildlife Trust 40 pp.

69 Cheeseman C.L. & Mallinson P.J. (1980) Radio tracking in the study of bovine tuberculosis in badgers. In Amlaner C.J. & Macdonald D.W. eds. *A handbook on biotelemetry and radio tracking*. Oxford: Pergamon Press pp. 649–56.

70 Cheeseman C.L. *et al.* (1981) The population structure, density and prevalence of tuberculosis (*Mycobacterium bovis*) in badgers (*Meles meles*) from four areas in south-west England. *Journal of Applied Ecology* 18:795–804.

71 Cheeseman C.L. *et al.* (1985) Population ecology and prevalence of tuberculosis in badgers in an area of Staffordshire. *Mammal Review* 15:125–35.

72 Cheeseman C.L. *et al.* (1987) Badger population dynamics in a high-density area. *Symposia of the Zoological Society of London* 58:279–94.

73 Cheeseman C.L. *et al.* (1988) Comparison of dispersal and other movements in two badger (*Meles meles*) populations. *Mammal Review* 18:51–9.

74 Cheeseman C.L. *et al.* (1988) Dynamics of tuberculosis in a naturally infected badger population. *Mammal Review* 18:61–72.

75 Churcher C.S. (1959) The specific status of the New World red fox. *Journal of Mammalogy* 40:513–20.

76 Churcher C.S. (1960) Cranial variation in the North American red fox. *Journal of Mammalogy* 41: 349–60.

77 Churcher J.B. & Lawton J.H. (1987) Predation by domestic cats in an English village. *Journal of Zoology* 212:439–55.

78 Ciampalini B. & Lovari S. (1985) Food habits and trophic niche overlap of the badger (*Meles meles* L.) and the red fox (*Vulpes vulpes* L.) in a Mediterranean coastal area. *Zeitschrift für Säugetierkunde* 50: 226–34.

79 Clark M. (1988) *Badgers*. London: Whittet 128 pp.

80 Clements E.D. *et al.* (1988) The national badger sett survey. *Mammal Review* 18:1–9.

81 Clements F.A. & Dunstone N. (1984) Comparative aerial and underwater motion perception capability of the mink (*Mustela vison*) as a function of stimulus radiant intensity and discrimination distance. *Animal Behaviour* 32:790–7.

82 Clutton-Brock J. *et al.* (1976) A review of the family Canidae, with a classification by numerical methods. *Bulletin of the British Museum (Natural History) Zoology* 29:119–99.

83 Cobham Resource Consultants 1983. *Countryside*

sports — *their economic significance. Summary report.* Reading: Standing Conference on Countryside Sports 45 pp.

84 Collier G.E. & O'Brien S.J. (1985) A molecular phylogeny of the Felidae: immunological distance. *Evolution* **39**: 473–87.

85 Condé B. (1970) Ronronnement et empreinte chez un félidé sauvage. *Compte rendu des séances de la Société de biologie* **164**:1392–4.

86 Condé B. & Schauenberg P. (1969) Reproduction du chat forestier d'Europe (*Felis silvestris* Schreber) en captivité. *Revue suisse de zoologie* **176**:183–210.

87 Conroy J.W.H. Personal communication.

88 Conroy J.W.H. & French D.D. (1987) The use of spraints to monitor populations of otters (*Lutra lutra* L.). *Symposia of the Zoological Society of London* **58**:247–62.

89 Conroy J.W.H. & Jenkins D. (1986) Ecology of otters in northern Scotland. VI. Diving times and hunting success of otters (*Lutra lutra*) at Dinnet Lochs, Aberdeenshire and in Yell Sound, Shetland. *Journal of Zoology* **209**(A):341–6.

90 Corbet G.B. (1966) *The terrestrial mammals of western Europe.* London: Foulis & Co. 264 pp.

91 Corbet G.B. (1971) Provisional distribution maps of British mammals. *Mammal Review* **1**:95–142.

92 Corbet G.B. (1978) *The mammals of the Palaearctic region: a taxonomic review.* London: British Museum (Natural History) 314 pp.

93 Corbet G.B. & Clutton-Brock J. (1984) Appendix: taxonomy and nomenclature. In Mason, I.L. ed. *Evolution of domesticated animals.* London: Longman pp. 434–8.

94 Corbet G.B. & Hill J.E. (1980) *A world list of mammalian species.* London: British Museum (Natural History) 226 pp.

95 Corbett L.K. (1979) *Feeding ecology and social behaviour of wildcats* (Felis silvestris) *and domestic cats* (Felis catus) *in Scotland.* PhD. thesis, University of Aberdeen.

96 Corbett L.K. (1981) The wildcat. In Boyle C.L. ed. *The RSPCA book of British mammals.* London: Collins pp. 185–9.

97 Council for Nature 1973. *Predatory mammals in Britain.* London: Council for Nature 56 pp.

98 Crawford A. *et al.* (1979) *Otter survey of Wales 1977–78.* Lincoln: Society for the Promotion of Nature Conservation 70 pp.

99 Creed R.F.S. (1960) Observations on reproduction in the wild red fox (*Vulpes vulpes*) — an account with special reference to the occurrence of fox–dog crosses. *British Veterinary Journal* **116**:419–26.

100 Creed R.F.S. (1972) *Aspects of reproduction and early development in* Vulpes vulpes. PhD. thesis, University of London.

101 Cresswell W.J. & Harris S. (1988) Foraging behaviour and home-range utilization in a suburban badger (*Meles meles*) population. *Mammal Review* **18**:37–49.

102 Cresswell W.J. & Harris S. (1988) The effects of weather conditions on the movements and activity of badgers (*Meles meles*) in a suburban environment. *Journal of Zoology* **216**:187–94.

103 Criddle S. (1947) A nest of the least weasel. *Canadian Field Naturalist* **61**:69.

104 Crump D.R. (1980) Thietanes and dithiolanes from the anal gland of the stoat (*Mustela erminea*). *Journal of Chemical Ecology* **6**:341–7.

105 Cushing B.S. (1985) Estrous mice and vulnerability to weasel predation. *Ecology* **66**:1976–8.

106 Cuthbert J.H. (1973) The origin and distribution of feral mink in Scotland. *Mammal Review* **3**:97–103.

107 Cuthbert J.H. (1979) Food studies of feral mink *Mustela vison* in Scotland. *Fish Management* **10**: 17–25.

108 Cuthbert J.H. Personal communication.

109 Dadd M.N. (1970) Overlap of variation in British and European mammal populations. *Symposia of the Zoological Society of London* **26**:117–25.

110 Danilov P.I. & Rusakov O.S. (1969) [Peculiarities of the ecology of *Mustela putorius* in the north-west districts of the European part of the USSR.] *Zoologicheskii zhurnal* **48**:1383–94.

111 Danilov P.I. & Tumanov I.L. (1976) [*Mustelids of northwestern USSR.*] Leningrad.

112 Dards J.L. (1978) Home ranges of feral cats in Portsmouth dockyard. *Carnivore Genetics Newsletter* **3**:242–55.

113 Dards J. (1981) Habitat utilisation by feral cats in Portsmouth dockyard. In *The ecology and control of feral cats.* Potters Bar, Hertfordshire: UFAW pp. 30–46.

114 Davis S. (1977) Size variation of the fox, *Vulpes vulpes* in the palaearctic region today, and in Israel during the late Quaternary. *Journal of Zoology* **182**: 343–51.

115 Davis S.J.M. (1987) *The archaeology of animals.* London: Batsford 224 pp.

116 Day M.G. (1963) *An ecological study of the stoat* (Mustela erminea *L.*) *and the weasel* (Mustela nivalis *L.*) *with particular reference to their food and feeding habits.* PhD. thesis, University of Exeter.

117 Day M.G. (1968) Food habits of British stoats (*Mustela erminea*) and weasels (*Mustela nivalis*). *Journal of Zoology* **155**:485–97.

118 Day M.G. & Linn I. (1972) Notes on the food of feral mink *Mustela vison* in England and Wales. *Journal of Zoology* **167**:463–73.

119 de Jounge J. unpublished.

120 de Leuw A. (1957) *Die Wildkatze.* Munich: Merkblatt Niederwildaussschuss Deutschland Jagdschutzverband 334 pp.

121 Deane C.D. & O'Gorman F. (1969) The spread of feral mink in Ireland. *Irish Naturalists' Journal* **16**: 198–202.

122 Deanesly R. (1935) The reproductive processes of certain mammals. Part 9 — Growth and reproduction in the stoat (*Mustela erminea*). *Philosophical Transactions of the Royal Society of London B* **225**:459–92.

123 Deanesly R. (1943) Delayed implantation in the stoat. *Nature* **151**:365–6.

124 Deanesly R. (1944) The reproductive cycle of the female weasel (*Mustela nivalis*). *Proceedings of the Zoological Society of London* **114**:339–49.

125 Debrot S. (1981) Trophic relations between the stoat (*Mustela erminea*) and its prey, mainly the water vole (*Arvicola terrestris* Sherman). In Chapman J.A. & Pursely D. eds. *Proceedings of the first worldwide furbearer conference*. Frostburg, Maryland: Worldwide Furbearer Conference Inc. pp. 1259–89.

126 Debrot S. (1983) Fluctuations de populations chez l'hermine (*Mustela erminea* L.). *Mammalia* **47**: 323–32.

127 Debrot S. (1984) Dynamique du renouvellement et structure d'age d'une population d'hermines (*Mustela erminea*). *Terre et la vie* **39**:77–88.

128 Debrot S. & Mermod C. (1978) Morphométrie crânienne par radiographie. 2: Application à une population d'hermines (*Mustela erminea*). *Revue suisse de zoologie* **85**:738–44.

129 Debrot S. & Mermod C. (1982) Quelques siphonaptéres de mustélides dont *Rhadinopsylla pentacantha* (Rothschild, 1897), nouvelle espéce pour la Suisse. *Revue suisse de zoologie* **89**:27–32.

130 Debrot S. & Mermod C. (1983) The spatial and temporal distribution pattern of the stoat (*Mustela erminea* L.). *Oecologia* **59**:69–73.

131 Debrot S. *et al.* (1982) *Atlas des poils de mammifères d'Europe*. Neuchâtel: Institut de Zoologie, Université de Neuchâtel.

132 Debrot S. *et al.* (1985) The day and night activity pattern of the stoat (*Mustela erminea* L.). *Mammalia* **49**:13–17.

133 Degn H.G. & Jensen B. (1977) Skovmaren (*Martes martes*) i Denmark. *Dansk Vildtundersøgelser* **29**: 3–20.

134 Delattre P. (1983) Density of weasel (*Mustela nivalis* L.) and stoat (*Mustela erminea* L.) in relation to water vole abundance. *Acta zoologica fennica* **174**: 221–2.

135 Delattre P. (1984) Influence de la pression de prédation exercée par une population de belettes (*Mustela nivalis* L.) sur un peuplement de Microtidae. *Acta Oecologica, Oecologia Generalis* **5**: 285–300.

136 Dougherty E.C. & Hall E.R. (1955) The biological relationships between North American weasels (genus *Mustela*) and nematodes of the genus *Skrjabingylus* Petrov 1927 (Nematoda: Metastrongylidae), the causative organisms of certain lesions in weasel skulls. *Revista Ibérica de Parasitología, tomo extraordinaro*: 531–76.

137 Drabble P. (1977) *A weasel in my meatsafe*. London: Michael Joseph 187 pp.

138 Dubnitskii A.A. (1956) [A study of the development of the nematode *Skrjabingylus nasicola*, a parasite of the frontal sinuses of mustelids.] *Karakulevodstvo i Zverovodstvo* **1**:59–61.

139 Duby R.T. & Travis H.F. (1972) Photoperiodic control of fur growth and reproduction in the mink (*Mustela vison*). *Journal of Experimental Zoology* **182**: 217–25.

140 Dunn E. (1977) Predation by weasels (*Mustela nivalis*) on breeding tits (*Parus* spp.) in relation to the density of tits and rodents. *Journal of Animal Ecology* **46**:633–52.

141 Dunnet G.M. *et al.* (1986) *Badgers and bovine tuberculosis — review of policy*. London: HMSO 71 pp.

142 Dunstone N. (1976) *Vision in relation to subaquatic predatory behaviour in the mink*. PhD. thesis, University of Wales.

143 Dunstone N. (1978) The fishing strategy of the mink (*Mustela vison*); time-budgeting of hunting effort? *Behaviour* **67**:157–77.

144 Dunstone N. (1986) Exploited animals: the mink. *Biologist, Institute of Biology* **33**:69–75.

145 Dunstone N. & Birks J.D.S. (1983) Activity budget and habitat usage by coastal-living mink (*Mustela vison* Schreber). *Acta zoologica fennica* **174**:189–91.

146 Dunstone N. & Birks J.D.S. (1985) The comparative ecology of coastal, riverine and lacustrine mink *Mustela vison* in Britain. *Zeitschrift für Angewandte Zoologie* **72**:59–70.

147 Dunstone N. & Birks J.D.S. (1987) The feeding ecology of mink (*Mustela vison*) in coastal habitat. *Journal of Zoology* **212**:69–83.

148 Dunstone N. & O'Connor R.J. (1979) Optimal foraging in an amphibious mammal. I. The aqualung effect. *Animal Behaviour* **27**:1182–94.

149 Dunstone N. & O'Connor R.J. (1979) Optimal foraging in an amphibious mammal. II. A study using principal component analysis. *Animal Behaviour* **27**:1195–201.

150 Dunstone N. & Sinclair W. (1978) Comparative aerial and underwater visual acuity of the mink, *Mustela vison* Schreber, as a function of discrimination distance and stimulus luminance. *Animal Behaviour* **26**:6–13.

151 Dunstone N. *et al.* unpublished.

152 Duplaix-Hall N. (1972) Notes on maintaining river otters in captivity. *International Zoo Yearbook* **12**: 178–81.

153 Duplaix-Hall N. (1975) River otters in captivity: a review. In Martin R.D. ed. *Breeding endangered species in captivity*. London: Academic Press pp. 315–27.

154 East K. & Lockie J.D. (1964) Observations on a family of weasels (*Mustela nivalis*) bred in captivity. *Proceedings of the Zoological Society of London* **143**: 359–63.

155 East K. & Lockie J.D. (1965) Further observations on weasels (*Mustela nivalis*) and stoats (*Mustela erminea*) born in captivity. *Journal of Zoology* **147**: 234–8.

156 Easterbee N. (1988) The wild cat *Felis silvestris* in Scotland: 1983–1987. *Lutra* **31**:29–43.

157 Easterbee N. *et al.* (in press). *Survey of the status and distribution of the wildcat* (Felis silvestris) *in Scotland*. Peterborough: Nature Conservancy Council.

158 Eiberle K. (1969) Vom Iltis (*Mustela putorius*) in der

Schweiz. *Schweizerische Zeitschrift für Forstwesen* **120**:99−107.

159 Eibl-Eibesfeldt I. (1956) Zur Biologie des Iltis (*Putorius putorius* L.). *Verhandlungen der Deutschen zoologischen Gesellschaft* **19**:304−14.

160 Eibl-Eibesfeldt I. (1956) Angeborenes und Erworbenes in der Technik des Beutetötens (Versuche am Iltis, *Putorius putorius* L.). *Zeitschrift für Säugetierkunde* **21**:135−7.

161 Elder W.H. (1951) The baculum as an age criterion in mink. *Journal of Mammalogy* **32**:43−50.

162 Elton C.S. (1953) The use of cats in farm rat control. *Journal of Animal Behaviour* **1**:151−5.

163 Enders R.K. (1952) Reproduction in the mink (*Mustela vison*). *Proceedings of the American Philosophical Society* **96**:691−755.

164 Englund J. (1970) Some aspects of reproduction and mortality rates in Swedish foxes (*Vulpes vulpes*), 1961−63 and 1966−69. *Viltrevy* **8**:1−82.

165 Ennion E.A.R. & Tinbergen N. (1967) *Tracks*. Oxford: Clarendon Press 63 pp.

166 Ensley P.K. (1979) *Otodectes* sp. infection in Scottish wildcats − a case report. *Journal of Zoo Animal Medicine* **10**:92−3.

167 Erlinge S. (1967) Home range of the otter *Lutra lutra* L. in southern Sweden. *Oikos* **18**:186−209.

168 Erlinge S. (1967) Food habits of the fish-otter, *Lutra lutra* L. in south Swedish habitats. *Viltrevy* **4**:371−443.

169 Erlinge S. (1968) Territoriality of the otter *Lutra lutra* L. *Oikos* **19**:81−98.

170 Erlinge S. (1968) Food studies on captive otters *Lutra lutra* L. *Oikos* **19**:259−70.

171 Erlinge S. (1972) Interspecific relations between otter *Lutra lutra* and mink *Mustela vison* in Sweden. *Oikos* **23**:327−35.

172 Erlinge S. (1974) Distribution, territoriality and numbers of the weasel *Mustela nivalis* in relation to prey abundance. *Oikos* **25**:308−14.

173 Erlinge S. (1975) Feeding habits of the weasel *Mustela nivalis* in relation to prey abundance. *Oikos* **26**:378−84.

174 Erlinge S. (1977) Spacing strategy in stoat *Mustela erminea*. *Oikos* **28**:32−42.

175 Erlinge S. (1977) Home range utilisation and movements of the stoat, *Mustela erminea*. *International Congress of Game Biologists* **13**:31−42.

176 Erlinge S. (1977) Agonistic behaviour and dominance in stoats (*Mustela erminea* L.). *Zeitschrift für Tierpsychologie* **44**:375−88.

177 Erlinge S. (1979) Adaptive significance of sexual dimorphism in weasels. *Oikos* **33**:233−45.

178 Erlinge S. (1980) Movements and daily activity pattern of radio tracked male stoats, *Mustela erminea*. In Amlaner C.J. & Macdonald D.W. eds. *A handbook on biotelemetry and radio tracking*. Oxford: Pergamon Press pp. 703−10.

179 Erlinge S. (1981) Food preference, optimal diet and reproductive output in stoats *Mustela erminea* in Sweden. *Oikos* **36**:303−15.

180 Erlinge S. (1983) Demography and dynamics of a stoat *Mustela erminea* population in a diverse community of vertebrates. *Journal of Animal Ecology* **52**:705−26.

181 Erlinge S. (1987) Why do European stoats *Mustela erminea* not follow Bergmann's Rule? *Holarctic Ecology* **10**:33−9.

182 Erlinge S. & Sandell M. (1986) Seasonal changes in the social organization of male stoats, *Mustela erminea*: an effect of shifts between two decisive resources. *Oikos* **47**:57−62.

183 Erlinge S. & Sandell M. (1988) Coexistence of stoat, *Mustela erminea*, and weasel, *Mustela nivalis*: social dominance, scent communication, and reciprocal distribution. *Oikos* **53**:242−6.

184 Erlinge S. *et al.* (1982) Scent-marking and its territorial significance in stoats, *Mustela erminea*. *Animal Behaviour* **30**:811−18.

185 Evans P.G.H. *et al.* (1989) Social structure of the Eurasian badger (*Meles meles*): genetic evidence. *Journal of Zoology* **218**:587−95.

186 Ewer R.F. (1973) *The carnivores*. London: Weidenfeld and Nicolson, 494 pp.

187 Fairley J.S. (1966) An indication of the food of the fox in Northern Ireland after myxomatosis. *Irish Naturalists' Journal* **15**:149−51.

188 Fairley J.S. (1969) The fox as a pest of agriculture. *Irish Naturalists' Journal* **16**:216−19.

189 Fairley J.S. (1969) Tagging studies of the red fox *Vulpes vulpes* in north-east Ireland. *Journal of Zoology* **159**:527−32.

190 Fairley J.S. (1970) More results from tagging studies of foxes *Vulpes vulpes* (L.). *Irish Naturalists' Journal* **16**:392−3.

191 Fairley J.S. (1970) The food, reproduction, form, growth and development of the fox *Vulpes vulpes* (L.) in north-east Ireland. *Proceedings of the Royal Irish Academy B* **69**:103−37.

192 Fairley J.S. (1971) The control of the fox *Vulpes vulpes* (L.) population in northern Ireland. *Scientific Proceedings of the Royal Dublin Society B* **3**:43−7.

193 Fairley J.S. (1971) New data on the Irish stoat. *Irish Naturalists' Journal* **17**:49−57.

194 Fairley J.S. (1972) Food of otters (*Lutra lutra*) from Co. Galway, Ireland, and notes on other aspects of their biology. *Journal of Zoology* **166**:469−74.

195 Fairley J.S. (1980) Observations on a collection of feral Irish mink *Mustela vison* Schreber. *Proceedings of the Royal Irish Academy B* **80**:79−90.

196 Fairley J.S. (1981) A north-south cline in the size of the Irish stoat. *Proceedings of the Royal Irish Academy B* **81**:5−10.

197 Fairley J.S. & Bruton T. (1984) Some observations on a collection of fox skulls from north-east Ireland. *Irish Naturalists' Journal* **21**:349−51.

198 Fargher S. & Morris P. unpublished.

199 Farina R. & Andreani E. (1970) Leptospirosi degli animali selvatici in Italia. *Archivio veterinario italiano* **21**:127−41.

200 Fergusson E.J. (1939) The pine marten in northern

Scotland. *Journal of the Society for the Preservation of the Fauna of the Empire* **36**:27–30.

201 Ferns P.N. (1974) Predation by weasels of eggs laid in nestboxes. *Bird Study* **21**:218–19.

202 Ferris C. (1986) Mating and early maturity of badgers in Kent. *Journal of Zoology* **209** (A):282.

203 Fitzgerald B.M. (1977) Weasel predation on a cyclic population of the montane vole, *Microtus montanus* in California. *Journal of Animal Ecology* **46**:367–97.

204 Fitzgerald B.M. (1981) Predatory birds and mammals. In Bliss L.C. *et al*. eds. *Tundra ecosystems: a comparative analysis*. Cambridge: University Press pp. 485–508.

205 Fitzgerald B.M. & Karl B.J. (1979) Food of feral house cats (*Felis catus* L.) in forest of the Orongorongo Valley, Wellington. *New Zealand Journal of Zoology* **6**:107–26.

206 Flintoff R.J. (1935) The weights and measurements of stoats and weasels. *Northwestern Naturalist* **10**:29–34.

207 Flintoff R.J. (1935) Stoats and weasels, brown and white. *Northwestern Naturalist* **10**:214–29.

208 Fog M. (1969) Studies on the weasel (*Mustela nivalis*) and the stoat (*Mustela erminea*) in Denmark. *Danish Review of Game Biology* **6**(2):1–14.

209 Forbes T.O.A. & Lance A.N. (1976) The contents of fox scats from western Irish blanket bog. *Journal of Zoology* **179**:224–6.

210 Forrest H.E. (1904) Varieties of polecat and badger. *Zoologist, fourth series* **8**:227.

211 Forsyth J.F. (1967) Stoated rabbits. *Shooting Times* **March**:327.

212 Fowler P.A. & Racey P.A. (1988) Overwintering strategies of the badger, *Meles meles*, at 57°N. *Journal of Zoology* **214**:635–51.

213 Fox M.W. (1971) *Behaviour of wolves, dogs and related canids*. London: Jonathan Cape 214 pp.

214 Fozzer F. (1981) *Distribuzione e biologia di 22 specie di mammiferi in Italia*. Pubblicazioni AQ/1/142–164 del Consiglio Nazionale delle Ricerche — Collana del Progetto Finalizzato 'Primozione della qualita' dell'ambiente': 89–94. Roma.

215 Frank F. (1974) Wurfzahl und Wurffolge beim nordischen Wiesel (*Mustela nivalis rixosa* Bangs, 1896). *Zeitschrift für Säugetierkunde* **39**:248–50.

216 Frank F. unpublished.

217 Frank L.G. (1979) Selective predation and seasonal variation in the diet of the fox (*Vulpes vulpes*) in N.E. Scotland. *Journal of Zoology* **189**:526–32.

218 French D.D. *et al*. (1988) Morphological discriminants of Scottish wildcats (*Felis silvestris*), domestic cats (*F. catus*) and their hybrids. *Journal of Zoology* **214**:235–59.

219 Gaiduk V.E. (1977) [Control of moulting and winter whitening in the ermine, (*Mustela erminea*).] *Zoologicheskii zhurnal* **56**:1226–31.

220 Gaiduk V.E. (1980) [Seasonal and geographical variations in the time of moult and change of hair cover colour in the weasel (*Mustela nivalis*).] *Zoologicheskii zhurnal* **59**:113–19.

221 Gallagher J. & Nelson J. (1979) Causes of ill health and natural death in badgers in Gloucestershire. *Veterinary Record* **105**:546–51.

222 Gerell R. (1967) Food selection in relation to habitat in mink (*Mustela vison* Schreber) in Sweden. *Oikos* **18**:233–46.

223 Gerell R. (1969) Activity patterns of the mink *Mustela vison* Schreber in southern Sweden. *Oikos* **20**:451–60.

224 Gerell R. (1970) Home ranges and movements of the mink *Mustela vison* Schreber in Sweden. *Oikos* **21**:160–73.

225 Gerell R. (1971) Population studies on mink (*Mustela vison* Schreber) in southern Sweden. *Viltrevy* **8**:83–114.

226 Gewalt W. (1959) Beiträge zur Kenntnis des optischen Differentzierungsvermögens einiger Musteliden mit besonderer Berücksichtigung des Farbensehens. *Zoologische Beiträge* **5**:117–75.

227 Gibb J.A. *et al*. (1969) An experiment in the control of a sparse population of wild rabbits (*Oryctolagus c. cuniculus* L.) in New Zealand. *New Zealand Journal of Science* **12**:504–34.

228 Gibb J.A. *et al*. (1978) Natural control of a population of rabbits, *Oryctolagus cuniculus* (L.), for ten years in the Kourarau enclosure. *New Zealand Department of Scientific and Industrial Research Bulletin* **223**:1–89.

229 Gibson J.A. (1970) The mammals of the Island of Bute. *Transactions of the Buteshire Natural History Society* **18**:5–20.

230 Gibson J.A. (1970) Additional mammal notes from the Island of Arran. *Transactions of the Buteshire Natural History Society* **18**:45–7.

231 Gilbert F.F. (1969) Analysis of basic vocalizations of the ranch mink. *Journal of Mammalogy* **50**:625–7.

232 Gillingham B.J. (1984) Meal size and feeding rate in the least weasel (*Mustela nivalis*). *Journal of Mammalogy* **65**:517–9.

233 Glas G.H. (1974) Over lichaamsmaten en gewichten van de bunzing *Mustela putorius* Linnaeus, 1758, in Nederland. *Lutra* **16**:13–19.

234 Glas G.H. (1977) [Two unusual polecats from the Netherlands.] *Lutra* **19**:64–5.

235 Goethe F. (1940) Beiträge zur Biologie des Iltis. *Zeitschrift für Säugetierkunde* **15**:180–223.

236 Goethe F. (1964) Das Verhalten der Musteliden. *Handbüch der Zöologie* (Band 8), **10**(19):1–80.

237 Gorman M.L. *et al*. (1978) The anal scent sacs of the otter (*Lutra lutra*). *Journal of Zoology* **186**:463–74.

238 Gorman M.L. *et al*. (1984) Social functions of the sub-caudal scent gland secretion of the European badger *Meles meles* (Carnivora: Mustelidae). *Journal of Zoology* **203**:549–59.

239 Gossow H. (1970) Vergleichende Verhaltenstudien an Marderartigen 1. Über Lautäusserungen und zum Beuteverhalten. *Zeitschrift für Tierpsychologie* **27**:405–80.

240 Graf M. & Wandeler A.I. (1982) Der Ge-

schlechtszyklus mannlicher Dachse (*Meles meles* L.) in der Schweiz. *Revue suisse de zoologie* **89**: 1005–8.

241 Grafodatskii A.S. *et al.* (1978) [Cytogenetics of albinism in ferrets of the genus *Putorius* (Carnivora, Mustelidae).] *Genetika* **14**:68–71.

242 Granqvist E. (1981) [European mink (*Mustela lutreola*) in Finland and the possible reason for its disappearance.] *Memoranda Societatis pro fauna et flora fennica* **57**:41–9.

243 Green J. (1977) Sensory perception in hunting otters, *Lutra lutra* L. *Journal of the Otter Trust* 1977:13–16.

244 Green J. & Green R. (1980) *Otter Survey of Scotland 1977–79*. London: Vincent Wildlife Trust 46 pp.

245 Green J. & Green R. (1987) *Otter Survey of Scotland 1984–85*. London: Vincent Wildlife Trust 40 pp.

246 Green J. *et al.* (1984) A radio-tracking survey of otters *Lutra lutra* on a Perthshire river system. *Lutra* **27**:85–145.

247 Greer K.R. (1957) Some osteological characters of known-age ranch minks. *Journal of Mammalogy* **38**: 319–30.

248 Grigor'ev N.D. & Egorov Y.E. (1969) [On the biocenotic connections of the mink with the common otter in the Bashkirian SSR.] *Sbornik trudov Nauchno-issledovatel' skogo instituta zhivotnovodstva Syr'ya Pushniny* **22**:26–32.

249 Grigson C. (1978) The Late Glacial and Early Flandrian ungulates in England and Wales — an interim review. In Limbrey S. & Evan J.G. eds. *The effect of man on the landscape: the lowland zone*. CBA Research Report no. 21, pp. 46–56.

250 Grue H. & Jensen B. (1979) Review of the formation of incremental lines in tooth cementum of terrestrial mammals. *Danish Review of Game Biology* **11**(3): 1–48.

251 Grue H.E. & King C.M. (1984) Evaluation of age criteria in New Zealand stoats (*Mustela erminea*) of known age. *New Zealand Journal of Zoology* **11**: 437–43.

252 Gulamhusein A.P. & Tam W.H. (1974) Reproduction in the male stoat, *Mustela erminea*. *Journal of Reproduction and Fertility* **41**:303–12.

253 Gulamhusein A.P. & Thawley A.R. (1974) Plasma progesterone levels in the stoat. *Journal of Reproduction and Fertility* **36**:405–8.

254 Habermehl K.H. & Röttcher D. (1967) Die Möglichkeiten der Alterbestimmung beim Marder und Iltis. *Zeitschrift für Jagdwissenschaft* **13**:89–102.

255 Hall E.R. (1951) American weasels. *University of Kansas Publications Museum of Natural History* **4**: 1–466.

256 Haltenorth T. (1957) *Die Wildkatze*. Wittenberg-Lutherstadt: A. Ziemsen 100 pp.

257 Hamilton W.J. (1933) The weasels of New York. *American Midland Naturalist* **14**:289–344.

258 Hancox M. (1980) Parasites and infectious diseases of the Eurasian badger (*Meles meles* L.): a review. *Mammal Review* **10**:151–62.

259 Hancox M. unpublished data.

260 Hanell H. Personal communication.

261 Hansson I. (1967) Transmission of the parasitic nematode *Skrjabingylus nasicola* (Leuckart 1842) to species of *Mustela* (Mammalia). *Oikos* **18**:247–52.

262 Hannson I. (1970) Cranial helminth parasites in species of Mustelidae. 2. Regional frequencies of damage in preserved crania from Denmark, Finland, Sweden, Greenland and the northeast of Canada compared with the helminth invasion of fresh mustelid skulls from Sweden. *Arkiv för zoologi* **22**: 571–94.

263 Harper R.J. & Jenkins D. (1981) Mating behaviour in the European otter (*Lutra lutra*). *Journal of Zoology* **195**:556–8.

264 Harris C.J. (1968) *Otters: a study of the recent Lutrinae*. London: Weidenfeld & Nicolson 397 pp.

265 Harris S. (1975) Syndactyly in the red fox, *Vulpes vulpes*. *Journal of Zoology* **176**:282–7.

266 Harris S. (1977) Distribution, habitat utilization and age structure of a suburban fox (*Vulpes vulpes*) population. *Mammal Review* **7**:25–39.

267 Harris S. (1977) Spinal arthritis (spondylosis deformans) in the red fox, *Vulpes vulpes*, with some methodology of relevance to zooarchaeology. *Journal of Archaeological Science* **4**:183–95.

268 Harris S. (1978) Age determination in the red fox (*Vulpes vulpes*) — an evaluation of technique efficiency as applied to a sample of suburban foxes. *Journal of Zoology* **184**:91–117.

269 Harris S. (1978) Injuries to foxes (*Vulpes vulpes*) living in suburban London. *Journal of Zoology* **186**: 567–72.

270 Harris S. (1979) Age related fertility and productivity in red foxes, *Vulpes vulpes*, in suburban London. *Journal of Zoology* **187**:195–9.

271 Harris S. (1980) Home ranges and patterns of distribution of foxes (*Vulpes vulpes*) in an urban area, as revealed by radio tracking. In Amlaner C.J. & Macdonald D.W. eds. *A handbook on biotelemetry and radio tracking*. Oxford: Pergamon Press pp. 685–90.

272 Harris S. (1981) An estimation of the number of foxes (*Vulpes vulpes*) in the city of Bristol, and some possible factors affecting their distribution. *Journal of Applied Ecology* **18**:455–65.

272 Harris S. (1981) The food of suburban foxes (*Vulpes*
A *vulpes*) with special reference to London. *Mammal Review* **11**:151–68.

273 Harris S. (1982) Activity patterns and habitat utilization of badgers (*Meles meles*) in suburban Bristol: a radio tracking study. *Symposia of the Zoological Society of London* **49**:301–23.

274 Harris S. (1984) Ecology of urban badgers *Meles meles*: distribution in Britain and habitat selection, persecution, food and damage in the city of Bristol. *Biological Conservation* **28**:349–75.

275 Harris S. (1985) Surveying the urban fox. *Biologist, Institute of Biology* **32**:259–64.

276 Harris S. (1985) Pest control in urban areas: humane control of foxes. In Britt D.P. ed. *Humane control of land mammals and birds*. Potters Bar, Hertfordshire: UFAW pp. 63–74.

277 Harris S. (1986) *Urban foxes*. London: Whittet 128 pp.

278 Harris S. & Cresswell W. (1987) Dynamics of a suburban badger (*Meles meles*) population. *Symposia of the Zoological Society of London* 58: 295–311.

279 Harris S. & Macdonald D. (1987) *Orphaned foxes — guidelines on the rescue and rehabilitation of fox cubs*. Horsham, West Sussex: RSPCA 16 pp.

280 Harris S. & Rayner J.M.V. (1986) Urban fox (*Vulpes vulpes*) population estimates and habitat requirements in several British cities. *Journal of Animal Ecology* 55:575–91.

281 Harris S. & Rayner J.M.V. (1986) Models for predicting urban fox (*Vulpes vulpes*) numbers in British cities and their application for rabies control. *Journal of Animal Ecology* 55:593–603.

282 Harris S. & Rayner J.M.V. (1986) A discriminant analysis of the current distribution of urban foxes (*Vulpes vulpes*) in Britain. *Journal of Animal Ecology* 55:605–11.

283 Harris S. & Smith G.C. (1987) The use of sociological data to explain the distribution and numbers of urban foxes (*Vulpes vulpes*) in England and Wales. *Symposia of the Zoological Society of London* 58: 313–28.

284 Harris S. & Smith G.C. (1987) Demography of two urban fox (*Vulpes vulpes*) populations. *Journal of Applied Ecology* 24:75–86.

285 Harris S. & Thompson G.B. (1978) Populations of the ticks *Ixodes* (*Pholeoixodes*) *hexogonus* and *Ixodes* (*Pholeoixodes*) *canisuga* infesting suburban foxes, *Vulpes vulpes*. *Journal of Zoology* 186:83–93.

286 Harris S. & Trewhella W.J. (1988) An analysis of some of the factors affecting dispersal in an urban fox (*Vulpes vulpes*) population. *Journal of Applied Ecology* 25:409–22.

287 Harris S. & Woollard T. (1990) Bristol's foxes. *Proceedings of the Bristol Naturalists' Society*, in press.

288 Harris S. *et al.* (1988) *Problems with badgers?* Horsham: RSPCA 48 pp.

289 Harting J.E. (1894) The weasel. *Zoologist* 52: 417–23, 445–54.

290 Hartman L. (1964) The behaviour and breeding of captive weasels (*Mustela nivalis* L.). *New Zealand Journal of Science* 7:147–56.

291 Harvey Brown J.A. (1882) The past and present distribution of the rarer animals of Scotland. *The Zoologist, third series* 6:41–5.

292 Hatler D.F. (1976) *The coastal mink of Vancouver Island, British Columbia*. PhD. thesis, University of British Columbia.

293 Hattingh I. (1956) Measurements of foxes from Scotland and England. *Proceedings of the Zoological Society of London* 127:191–9.

294 Hawley V.D. & Newby F.E. (1957) Marten home ranges and population fluctuations. *Journal of Mammalogy* 38:174–84.

295 Hayward G.F. (1983) *The bioenergetics of the weasel, Mustela nivalis L.* DPhil. thesis, University of Oxford.

296 Heidt G.A. (1970) The least weasel, *Mustela nivalis* L.: developmental biology in comparison with other North American *Mustela*. *Publications Michigan State University, Museum (Biological Series)* 4:227–82.

297 Heidt G.A. (1972) Anatomical and behavioral aspects of killing and feeding by the least weasel, *Mustela nivalis* L. *Proceedings of the Arkansas Academy of Science* 26:53–4.

298 Henry C.J. *et al.* (1981) PCBs and organochlorine pesticides in wild mink and river otters from Oregon. In Chapman J.A. & Pursely D. eds. *Proceedings of the first worldwide furbearer conference*. Frostburg, Maryland: Worldwide Furbearer Conference Inc. pp. 1763–80.

299 Henry J.D. (1977) The use of urine marking in the scavenging behaviour of the red fox (*Vulpes vulpes*). *Behaviour* 61:82–106.

300 Henry J.D. (1985) *Red fox — the catlike canine*. Washington, D.C.: Smithsonian Institution Press 174 pp.

301 Heptner V.G. (1964) Über die morphologischen und geographischen Beziehungen zwischen *Mustela putorius* und *Mustela eversmanni*. *Zeitschrift für Säugetierkunde* 29:321–30.

302 Heptner V.G. & Naumov N.P. eds. (1967) [*Mammals of the Soviet Union. Vol. 2. Sirenia and Carnivora*.] Moscow: Vysshaya Shkola 1004 pp.

303 Herrenschmidt V. (1982) Note sur les désplacements et le rhythme d'activité d'un putois, *Mustela putorius* L., suivi par radiotracking. *Mammalia* 46:554–6.

304 Herter K. (1939) Psychologische Untersuchungen an einem Mauswiesel (*Mustela nivalis* L.). *Zeitschrift für Tierpsychologie* 3:249–63.

305 Herter K. (1959) *Iltisse und Frettchen*. Wittenburg-Lutherstadt: A. Ziemsen 112 pp.

306 Herter K. & Klaunig J.R. (1956) Untersuchungen an der Retina amerikanischer Nerze (*Mustela lutreola vison* Schreb.). *Zoologische Beiträge* 2:127–43.

307 Hewson R. (1972) Changes in the number of stoats, rats and little owls in Yorkshire as shown by tunnel trapping. *Journal of Zoology* 168:427–9.

308 Hewson R. (1973) Food and feeding habits of otters *Lutra lutra* at Loch Park, north-east Scotland. *Journal of Zoology* 170:159–62.

309 Hewson R. (1983) The food of wild cats (*Felis silvestris*) and red foxes (*Vulpes vulpes*) in west and north-east Scotland. *Journal of Zoology* 200:283–9.

310 Hewson R. (1984) Changes in the numbers of foxes (*Vulpes vulpes*) in Scotland. *Journal of Zoology* 204: 561–9.

311 Hewson R. (1984) Scavenging and predation upon sheep and lambs in west Scotland. *Journal of Applied Ecology* 21:843–68.

312 Hewson R. (1985) Lamb carcasses and other food remains at fox dens in Scotland. *Journal of Zoology (A)* **206**:291–6.

313 Hewson R. (1986) Distribution and density of fox breeding dens and the effects of management. *Journal of Applied Ecology* **23**:531–8.

314 Hewson R. & Healing T.D. (1971) The stoat *Mustela erminea* and its prey. *Journal of Zoology* **164**:239–44.

315 Hewson R. & Kolb H.H. (1973) Changes in the numbers and distribution of foxes (*Vulpes vulpes*) killed in Scotland from 1948–1970. *Journal of Zoology* **171**:345–65.

316 Hewson R. & Kolb H.H. (1975) The food of foxes (*Vulpes vulpes*) in Scottish forests. *Journal of Zoology* **176**:287–92.

317 Hewson R. & Kolb H.H. (1976) Scavenging on sheep carcases by foxes (*Vulpes vulpes*) and badgers (*Meles meles*). *Journal of Zoology* **180**:496–8.

318 Hewson R. & Leitch A.F. (1983) The food of foxes in forests and on the open hill. *Scottish Forestry* **37**:39–50.

319 Hewson R. & Watson A. (1979) Winter whitening of stoats (*Mustela erminea*) in Scotland and northeast England. *Journal of Zoology* **187**:55–64.

320 Hill M. (1939) The reproductive cycle of the male weasel (*Mustela nivalis*). *Proceedings of the Zoological Society of London B* **109**:481–512.

321 Hillegaart V. *et al.* (1985) Area utilisation and marking behaviour among two captive otter (*Lutra lutra* L.) pairs. *Journal of the Otter Trust* **1984**: 64–74.

322 Hirschi R. (1985) A mother's work is never done. *BBC Wildlife* **3**:222–6.

323 Hoekstra B. (1975) Een geval van hydrocephalie bij de bunzing, *Putorius putorius* (Linnaeus, 1758). *Lutra* **17**:1–6.

324 Hofer H. (1986) *Patterns of resource dispersion and exploitation of the red fox* (Vulpes vulpes) *and the Eurasian badger* (Meles meles): *a comparative study.* DPhil. thesis, University of Oxford.

325 Hofer H. (1988) Variation in resource presence, utilization and reproductive success within a population of European badgers (*Meles meles*). *Mammal Review* **18**:25–36.

326 Hope Jones P. (1974) Wildlife records from Merioneth parish documents. *Nature in Wales* **14**: 35–43.

327 Howard R.W. & Bradbury K. (1979) Feeding by regurgitation in the badger (*Meles meles*). *Journal of Zoology* **188**:299.

328 Howes C.A. (1973) Historical records of mammals in southeast Yorkshire and the Doncaster district. *Naturalist, Leeds* **98**:41–50.

329 Howes C.A. (1974) Notes on the food of foxes on Spurn Peninsula. *Naturalist, Leeds* **99**:131–3.

330 Howes C.A. (1977) A survey of the food habits of stoats (*Mustela erminea*) and weasels (*Mustela nivalis*) in Yorkshire. *Naturalist, Leeds* **102**:117–21.

331 Howes C.A. (1978) Notes on the food of foxes

at Gibralter Point, Lincolnshire. *Naturalist, Leeds* **103**:25–6.

332 Howes C.A. (1980) Aspects of the history and distribution of polecats and ferrets in Yorkshire and adjacent areas. *Naturalist, Leeds* **105**:3–16.

333 Howes C.A. (1980) The seasonal food of foxes on Spurn Peninsula. *Spurn Bird Observatory Report for 1980*:74–5.

334 Howes C. (1981) What the cat brought in. *Bird Life* **March–April 1981**:18–19.

335 Howes C. (1982) What the cat brought in. *Bird Life* **January–February 1982**:26.

336 Howes C. (1984) *Changes in the status of some Yorkshire Mammals 1600–1900.* MPhil. thesis, University of Bradford.

337 Huff J.N. & Price E.O. (1968) Vocalizations of the least weasel, *Mustela nivalis. Journal of Mammalogy* **49**:548–50.

338 Hurrell H.G. (1968) *Pine martens.* London: HMSO 24 pp.

339 Hurrell H.G. (1968) *Wildlife: tame but free.* Newton Abbot: David and Charles 188 pp.

340 Hurrell H.G. (1981) *Fling, the pine marten.* Plymouth: Westway Publications 55 pp.

341 Hurrell H.G. Personal communication.

342 Huson L.W. & Page R.J.C. (1979) A comparison of fox skulls from Wales and south-east England. *Journal of Zoology* **187**:465–70.

343 Huson L.W. & Page R.J.C. (1980) Age related variability in cranial measurements in the red fox (*Vulpes vulpes*). *Journal of Zoology* **191**:427–9.

344 Huson L.W. & Page R.J.C. (1980) Multivariate geographical variation of the red fox (*Vulpes vulpes*) in Wales. *Journal of Zoology* **191**:453–9.

345 Hutchinson G.E. & Parker P.J. (1978) Sexual dimorphism in the winter whitening of the stoat *Mustela erminea. Journal of Zoology* **186**:560–3.

346 Insley H. (1977) An estimate of the population density of the red fox (*Vulpes vulpes*) in the New Forest, Hampshire. *Journal of Zoology* **183**:549–53.

347 Jefferies D.J. (1974) Earthworms in the diet of the red fox (*Vulpes vulpes*). *Journal of Zoology* **173**: 251–2.

348 Jefferies D.J. (1986) Estimation of complete body weights for skinned European otters *Lutra lutra* (L.). *Journal of Zoology* (A)**209**:282–5.

349 Jefferies D.J. *et al.* (1984) *Commercial fish and crustacean traps: a serious cause of otter* Lutra lutra (L.) *mortality in Britain and Europe.* London: Vincent Wildlife Trust 31 pp.

350 Jefferies D.J. *et al.* (1986) Reinforcing the native otter *Lutra lutra* population in East Anglia: an analysis of the behaviour and range development of the first release group. *Mammal Review* **16**:65–79.

351 Jenkins D. (1980) Ecology of otters in northern Scotland I. Otter (*Lutra lutra*) breeding and dispersion in mid-Deeside, Aberdeenshire in 1974–79. *Journal of Animal Ecology* **49**:713–35.

352 Jenkins D. & Harper R.J. (1980) Ecology of otters

in northern Scotland II. Analyses of otter (*Lutra lutra*) and mink (*Mustela vison*) faeces from Deeside, N.E. Scotland in 1977−78. *Journal of Animal Ecology* 49:737−54.

353 Jenkins D. & Harper R.J. (1982) Fertility in European otters (*Lutra lutra*). *Journal of Zoology* 197:299−300.

354 Jenkins D. *et al.* (1964). Predation and red grouse populations. *Journal of Applied Ecology* 1:183−95.

355 Jenkins D. *et al.* (1979) Analyses of otter (*Lutra lutra*) faeces from Deeside, N.E. Scotland. *Journal of Zoology* 187:235−44.

356 Jensen A. (1964) Odderen i Danmark. *Danske Vildtundersogelser* 11:1−48.

357 Jensen A. & Jensen B. (1972) Ilderen (*Putorius putorius*) og Ilderjagten i Danmark 1969/70. *Danske Vildtundersogelser* 18:1−32.

358 Jensen B. (1978) [Results of catches using cage traps.] *Natura jutlandica* 20:129−36.

359 Jensen B. & Nielsen L.B. (1968) Age determination in the red fox (*Vulpes vulpes* L.) from canine tooth sections. *Danish Review of Game Biology* 5(6):1−15.

360 Jeselnik D.L. & Brisbin I.L. (1980) Food-caching behaviour of captive-reared red foxes. *Applied Animal Ethology* 6:363−7.

361 Johnson C.E. (1980) An unusual food source of the red fox (*Vulpes vulpes*). *Journal of Zoology* 192:561−2.

362 Jones E. (1977) Ecology of the feral cat, *Felis catus* (L.), (Carnivora: Felidae) on Macquarie Island. *Australian Wildlife Research* 4:249−62.

363 Jones G.W. *et al.* (1980) The helminth parasites of the badger (*Meles meles*) in Cornwall. *Mammal Review* 10:163−4.

364 Jonkel C.J. & Weckwerth R.P. (1963) Sexual maturity and implantation of blastocysts in the wild pine marten. *Journal of Wildlife Management* 27:93−7.

365 Jurgenson P.B. (1954) [On the influence of marten (*M. martes*) on the numbers of squirrels (*Sciurus vulgaris*) in the northern Taiga.] *Zoologichesiï zhurnal* 33:166−73.

366 Kaplan C. (1985) Rabies: a worldwide disease. In Bacon P.J. ed. *Population dynamics of rabies in wildlife*. London: Academic Press pp. 1−21.

367 Kerby G. & Macdonald D.W. (1988) Cat society and the consequences of colony size. In Turner D.C. & Bateman P. eds. *The domestic cat: the biology of its behaviour*. Cambridge: University Press pp. 67−81.

368 Kharchenko V.I. & Minoranskii V.A. (1967) [New and rare mammals of the Rostov district and Eastern Priazovje.] *Zoologicheskii zhurnal* 46:781−3.

369 Kildemoes A. (1985) The impact of introduced stoats (*Mustela erminea*) on an island population of the water vole, *Arvicola terrestris*. *Acta zoologica fennica* 173:193−5.

370 King C.M. (1971) *Studies on the ecology of the weasel* (Mustela nivalis *L.*). DPhil. thesis, University of Oxford.

371 King C.M. (1973) A system for trapping and handling live weasels in the field. *Journal of Zoology* 171:458−64.

372 King C.M. (1975) The home range of the weasel (*Mustela nivalis*) in an English woodland. *Journal of Animal Ecology* 44:639−68.

373 King C.M. (1975) The sex ratio of trapped weasels (*Mustela nivalis*). *Mammal Review* 5:1−8.

374 King C.M. (1976) The fleas of a population of weasels in Wytham Woods, Oxford. *Journal of Zoology* 180:525−35.

375 King C.M. (1977) The effects of the nematode parasite *Skrjabingylus nasicola* on British weasels (*Mustela nivalis*). *Journal of Zoology* 182:225−49.

376 King C.M. (1977) Pine marten *Martes martes*. In Corbet G.B. & Southern H.N. eds. *The handbook of British mammals*. Oxford: Blackwell Scientific Publications pp. 323−30.

377 King C.M. (1979) Moult and colour change in English weasels (*Mustela nivalis*). *Journal of Zoology* 189:127−34.

378 King C.M. (1980) The weasel *Mustela nivalis* and its prey in an English woodland. *Journal of Animal Ecology* 49:127−59.

379 King C.M. (1980) Population biology of the weasel *Mustela nivalis* on British game estates. *Holarctic Ecology* 3:160−8.

380 King C.M. (1980) Age determination in the weasel (*Mustela nivalis*) in relation to the development of the skull. *Zeitschrift für Saügetierkunde* 45:153−73.

381 King C.M. (1980) Field experiments on the trapping of stoats (*Mustela erminea*). *New Zealand Journal of Zoology* 7:261−6.

382 King C.M. (1981) The reproductive tactics of the stoat (*Mustela erminea*) in New Zealand forests. In Chapman J.A. & Pursely D. eds. *Proceedings of the first worldwide furbearer conference*. Frostburg, Maryland: Worldwide Furbearer Conference Inc. pp. 443−68.

383 King C.M. (1981) The effects of two types of steel traps upon captured stoats (*Mustela erminea*). *Journal of Zoology* 195:553−4.

384 King C.M. (1983) Factors regulating mustelid populations. *Acta zoologica fennica* 174:217−20.

385 King C.M. (1983) The life history strategies of *Mustela nivalis* and *M. erminea*. *Acta zoologica fennica* 174:183−4.

386 King C.M. (1983) The relationships between beech (*Nothofagus* sp.) seedfall and populations of mice (*Mus musculus*), and the demographic and dietary responses of stoats (*Mustela erminea*), in three New Zealand forests. *Journal of Animal Ecology* 52:141−166.

387 King C. (1984) *Immigrant killers: introduced predators and the conservation of birds in New Zealand*. Auckland & Oxford: Oxford University Press 224 pp.

388 King C.M. (1984) The origin and adaptive advantages of delayed implantation in *Mustela erminea*. *Oikos* 42:126−8.

389 King C.M. (1985) Interactions between woodland rodents and their predators. *Symposia of the Zoological Society of London* **55**:219–47.

390 King C.M. (1989) *The natural history of weasels and stoats.* London: Christopher Helm 253 pp.

391 King C.M. (1989) The advantages and disadvantages of small size to weasels, *Mustela* species. In Gittleman J.L. ed. *Carnivore behavior, ecology and evolution.* Cornell: University Press, pp. 302–40.

392 King C.M. & Edgar R.L. (1977) Techniques for trapping and tracking stoats (*Mustela erminea*); a review and a new system. *New Zealand Journal of Zoology* **4**:193–212.

393 King C.M. & McMillan C.D. (1982) Population structure and dispersal of peak-year cohorts of stoats (*Mustela erminea*) in two New Zealand forests, with especial reference to control. *New Zealand Journal of Ecology* **5**:59–66.

394 King C.M. & Moody J.E. (1982) The biology of the stoat (*Mustela erminea*) in the national parks of New Zealand. *New Zealand Journal of Zoology* **9**:49–144.

395 King C.M. & Moors P.J. (1979) On co-existence, foraging strategy and the biogeography of weasels and stoats (*Mustela nivalis* and *M. erminea*) in Britain. *Oecologia* **39**:129–50.

396 King C.M. & Moors P.J. (1979) The life-history tactics of mustelids, and their significance for predator control and conservation in New Zealand. *New Zealand Journal of Zoology* **6**:619–22.

397 King R.J. (1958) The training of badgers in Pershore Forest. *Journal of the Forestry Commission* **2**:45–50.

398 Kolb H.H. (1977) Wildcat *Felis silvestris*. In Corbet G.B. & Southern H.N. eds. *Handbook of British mammals.* Oxford: Blackwell Scientific Publications pp. 375–82.

399 Kolb H. (1978) The formation of lines in the cementum of premolar teeth in foxes. *Journal of Zoology* **185**:259–63.

400 Kolb H.H. (1978) Variation in the size of foxes in Scotland. *Biological Journal of the Linnean Society* **10**:291–304.

401 Kolb H.H. (1984) Factors affecting the movements of dog foxes in Edinburgh. *Journal of Applied Ecology* **21**:161–73.

402 Kolb H.H. (1985) Habitat use by foxes in Edinburgh. *Terre et la vie* **40**:139–43.

403 Kolb H.H. (1986) Some observations on the home ranges of vixens (*Vulpes vulpes*) in the suburbs of Edinburgh. *Journal of Zoology* **210**(A):636–9.

404 Kolb H.H. & Hewson R. (1974) The body size of the red fox (*Vulpes vulpes*) in Scotland. *Journal of Zoology* **172**:253–5.

405 Kolb H.H. & Hewson R. (1979) Variation in the diet of foxes in Scotland. *Acta theriologica* **24**:69–83.

406 Kolb H.H. & Hewson R. (1980) A study of fox populations in Scotland from 1971 to 1976. *Journal of Applied Ecology* **17**:7–19.

407 Kolb H.H. & Hewson R. (1980) The diet and growth of fox cubs in two regions of Scotland. *Acta theriologica* **25**:325–31.

408 Kopein K.I. (1967) [Analysis of the age structure of ermine populations.] *Trudy Moskovskogo obshchestva ispytatelei prirody* **25**:33–9.

409 Korhonen H. *et al.* (1983) Thermoregulation of polecat and raccoon dog: a comparative study with stoat, mink and blue fox. *Comparative Biochemistry and Physiology* (A) **74**:225–30.

410 Kraft V.A. (1966) [Influence of temperature on the activity of the ermine in winter.] *Zoologicheskii zhurnal* **45**:148–50.

411 Kratochvíl J. (1977) Sexual dimorphism and status of *Mustela nivalis* in central Europe (Mammalia, Mustelidae). *Acta Scientia Naturale, Brno* **11**:1–42.

412 Kratochvíl J. (1977) Studies on *Mustela erminea* (Mustelidae, Mammalia) I. Variability of metric and mass traits. *Folia Zoologica* **26**:291–304.

413 Krivanec K. *et al.* (1975) The role of polecats of the genus *Putorius* Cuvier, 1817 in natural foci of adiaspiromycosis. *Folia Parasitologica* **22**:245–9.

414 Kruisinga D. (1965) Enige winterwaarnemingen aan Dassen en andere Masterachtigen te St Michielsgestel. *Levende Natuur* **68**:73–83.

415 Kruuk H. (1964) Predators and anti-predator behaviour of the black-headed gull (*Larus ridibundus* L.). *Behaviour, Supplement* **11**:1–130.

416 Kruuk H. (1972) Surplus killing by carnivores. *Journal of Zoology* **166**:233–44.

417 Kruuk H. 1972. The urge to kill. *New Scientist* **54**:735–7.

418 Kruuk H. (1976) The biological function of gulls' attraction towards predators. *Animal Behaviour* **24**:146–53.

419 Kruuk H. (1978) Spatial organization and territorial behaviour of the European badger *Meles meles*. *Journal of Zoology* **184**:1–19.

420 Kruuk H. (1985) Ecology of otters in a marine environment. *IUCN Otter Specialist Group (European Section) Bulletin* **3**:7–8.

421 Kruuk H. & Hewson R. (1978) Spacing and foraging of otters (*Lutra lutra*) in a marine habitat. *Journal of Zoology* **185**:205–12.

422 Kruuk H. & Parish T. (1981) Feeding specialization of the European badger *Meles meles* in Scotland. *Journal of Animal Ecology* **50**:773–88.

423 Kruuk H. & Parish T. (1982) Factors affecting population density, group size and territory size of the European badger, *Meles meles*. *Journal of Zoology* **196**:31–9.

424 Kruuk H. & Parish T. (1985) Food, food availability and weight of badgers (*Meles meles*) in relation to agricultural changes. *Journal of Applied Ecology* **22**:705–15.

425 Kruuk H.H. & Parish T. (1987) Changes in the size of groups and ranges of the European badger (*Meles meles* L.) in an area of Scotland. *Journal of Animal Ecology* **56**:351–64.

426 Kruuk H. *et al.* (1984) Scent-marking with the subcaudal gland by the European badger, *Meles meles* L. *Animal Behaviour* **32**:899–907.

427 Kruuk H. *et al.* (1986) The use of spraints to survey

populations of otters *Lutra lutra*. *Biological Conservation* 35:187−94.

428 Kruuk H. *et al.* (1987) Seasonal reproduction, mortality and food of otters (*Lutra lutra* L.) in Shetland. *Symposia of the Zoological Society of London* 58:263−78.

429 Kurtén B. (1968) *Pleistocene mammals of Europe*. London: Weidenfeld & Nicolson, 317 pp.

430 Langley P.J.W. & Yalden D.W. (1977) The decline of the rarer carnivores in Great Britain during the nineteenth century. *Mammal Review* 7:95−116.

431 Lavers R.B. (1973) Aspects of the biology of the ferret *Mustela putorius* forma *furo* L. at Pukepuke Lagoon. *Proceedings of the New Zealand Ecological Society* 20:7−12.

432 Lavrov N.P. (1944) [Effect of helminth invasions and infectious diseases on variations in numbers of the ermine, *Mustela erminea* L.] *Trudy Tsentral' noĭ nauchno-issledovatel'skoi laboratorii biologii okhotnich'ego promȳsla i tovarovedeniya zhivotnogo sȳr'ya*, 1944 (6):151−63.

433 Lenton E.J. *et al.* (1980) *Otter Survey of England 1977−79*. Shrewsbury: Nature Conservancy Council 75 pp.

434 Lever C. (1978) The not so innocuous mink? *New Scientist* 78:812−14.

435 Lever C. (1978) Are wild mink a threat? *New Scientist* 80:712.

436 Lever C. (1985) *Naturalized mammals of the world*. Harlow, Essex: Longman 487 pp.

437 Lever R.A. (1957) Two records of foxes eating larval hover flies and dor beetles. *Proceedings of the Zoological Society of London* 128:596−7.

438 Lever R.J.A.W. (1959) The diet of the fox since myxomatosis. *Journal of Animal Ecology* 28:359−75.

439 Lewis J.W. (1967) Observations on the skull of Mustelidae infected with the nematode, *Skrjabingylus nasicola*. *Journal of Zoology* 153:561−4.

440 Lewis J.W. (1978) A population study of the metastrongylid nematode *Skrjabingylus nasicola* in the weasel *Mustela nivalis*. *Journal of Zoology* 184:225−9.

441 Liberg O. (1980) Spatial patterns in a population of rural, free-roaming, domestic cats. *Oikos* 35:336−49.

442 Liberg O. (1981) *Predation and social behaviour in a population of domestic cats — an evolutionary approach*. PhD. thesis, University of Lund.

443 Liberg O. (1983) Home range and territoriality in free-ranging cats. *Acta zoologica fennica* 171:283−5.

444 Liberg O. (1984) Food habits and prey impact by feral and house-based domestic cats in a rural area of southern Sweden. *Journal of Mammalogy* 65:424−32.

445 Lightfoot V.M.A. & Wallis S.J. (1982) Predation of small mammals inside Longworth traps by a weasel. *Journal of Zoology* 198:521.

446 Lindeman W. (1955) Über die Jugendentwicklung beim Luchs (*Lynx* L. *lynx* Kerr) und bei der Wildkatze (*Felis s. silvestris* Schreber). *Behaviour* 8:1−45.

447 Lindsay I.M. & Macdonald D.W. 1985. The effects of disturbance on the emergence of Eurasian badgers in winter. *Biological Conservation* 34:289−306.

448 Lindström E. (1986) Territory inheritance and the evolution of group-living in carnivores. *Animal Behaviour* 34:1825−35.

449 Lindström E. (1988) Reproductive effort in the red fox, *Vulpes vulpes*, and future supply of a fluctuating prey. *Oikos* 52:115−19.

450 Linn I.J. & Birks J.D.S. (1981) Observations on the home ranges of feral American mink (*Mustela vison*) in Devon, England, as revealed by radio-tracking. In Chapman J.A. & Pursely D. eds. *Proceedings of the first worldwide furbearer conference*. Frostburg, Maryland: Worldwide Furbearer Conference Inc. pp. 1088−102.

451 Linn I. & Chanin P. (1978) Are mink really pests in Britain? *New Scientist* 77:560−2.

452 Linn I. & Chanin P. (1978) More on the mink 'menace'. *New Scientist* 80:38−40.

453 Linn I. & Day M.G. (1966) Identification of individual weasels *Mustela nivalis* using the ventral pelage pattern. *Journal of Zoology* 148:583−5.

454 Linn I. & Stevenson J.H.F. (1980) Feral mink in Devon. *Nature in Devon* 1:7−27.

455 Lippincott J.W. (1940) I trap no more weasels. *Pennsylvania Game News* 10:6, 25.

456 Lloyd H.G. (1980) *The red fox*. London: Batsford 320 pp.

457 Lloyd H.G. & Englund J. (1973) The reproductive cycle of the red fox in Europe. *Journal of Reproduction and Fertility*, Supplement 19:119−30.

458 Lockie J.D. (1956) After myxomatosis. *Scottish Agriculture* 36:65−9.

459 Lockie J.D. (1961) The food of the pine marten *Martes martes* in west Rosshire, Scotland. *Proceedings of the Zoological Society of London* 136:187−95.

460 Lockie J.D. (1964) The breeding density of the golden eagle and fox in relation to food supply in Wester Ross, Scotland. *Scottish Naturalist* 71:67−77.

461 Lockie J.D. (1964) Distribution and fluctuations of the pine marten, *Martes martes* (L.), in Scotland. *Journal of Animal Ecology* 33:349−56.

462 Lockie J.D. (1966) Territory in small carnivores. *Symposia of the Zoological Society of London* 18:143−65.

463 Lockie J.D. & Day M.G. (1963) The use of anaesthesia in the handling of stoats and weasels. In Jones O.G. ed. *Symposium on small mammal anaesthesia*. Oxford: Pergamon Press pp. 187−9.

464 Long C.A. & Howard T. (1976) Intra-specific overt fighting in the wild mink. *Reports on Fauna and Flora of Wisconsin* 11:4−5.

465 Long C.A. & Killingley C.A. (1983) *The badgers of the world*. Springfield, Illinois: Charles C. Thomas 404 pp.

466 MacCormack F. unpublished data.

467 Macdonald D.W. (1976) Food caching by red foxes and some other carnivores. *Zeitschrift für Tierpsychologie* **42**:170–85.

468 Macdonald D.W. (1977) On food preference in the red fox. *Mammal Review* **7**:7–23.

469 Macdonald D.W. (1979) 'Helpers' in fox society. *Nature* **282**:69–71.

470 Macdonald D.W. (1979) Some observations and field experiments on the urine marking behaviour of the red fox, *Vulpes vulpes* L. *Zeitschrift für Tierpsychologie* **51**:1–22.

471 Macdonald D.W. (1980) The red fox, *Vulpes vulpes*, as a predator upon earthworms, *Lumbricus terrestris*. *Zeitschrift für Tierpsychologie* **52**:171–200.

472 Macdonald D.W. (1980) *Rabies and wildlife — a biologist's perspective*. Oxford: University Press 151 pp.

473 Macdonald D.W. (1980) Patterns of scent marking with urine and faeces amongst carnivore communities. *Symposia of the Zoological Society of London* **45**:107–39.

474 Macdonald D.W. (1980) Social factors affecting reproduction amongst red foxes (*Vulpes vulpes* L., 1758). In Zimen E. ed. *The red fox — symposium on behaviour and ecology*. The Hague: W. Junk pp. 123–75.

475 Macdonald D.W. (1981) Resource dispersion and the social organization of the red fox (*Vulpes vulpes*). In Chapman J.A. & Pursley D. eds. *Proceedings of the first worldwide furbearer conference*. Frostburg, Maryland: Worldwide Furbearer Conference Inc. pp. 918–49.

476 Macdonald D.W. (1983) The ecology of carnivore social behaviour. *Nature* **301**:379–84.

477 Macdonald D.W. (1984) A questionnaire survey of farmers' opinions and actions towards wildlife on farmlands. In Jenkins D. ed. *Agriculture and the environment*. Cambridge: Institute of Terrestrial Ecology pp. 171–7.

478 Macdonald D.W. (1985) The carnivores: order Carnivora. In Brown R.E. & Macdonald D.W. eds. *Social odours in mammals*. Oxford: Clarendon Press pp. 619–722.

479 Macdonald D. (1988) *Running with the fox*. London: Unwin Hyman 224 pp.

480 Macdonald D.W. & Apps P.J. (1978) The social behaviour of a group of semi-dependent farm cats, *Felis catus*: a progress report. *Carnivore Genetics Newsletter* **3**:256–68.

481 Macdonald D.W. & Carr G.M. (1981) Foxes beware: you are back in fashion. *New Scientist* **89**:9–11.

482 Macdonald D. & Doncaster P. (1985) *Foxes in your neighbourhood?* Horsham, West Sussex: RSPCA 16 pp.

483 Macdonald D.W. & Moehlman P.D. (1982) Cooperation, altruism, and restraint in the reproduction of carnivores. *Perspectives in Ethology* **5**:433–67.

484 Macdonald D.W. & Newdick M.T. 1982. The distribution and ecology of foxes, *Vulpes vulpes* (L.), in urban areas. In Bornkamm R. *et al*. eds. *Urban ecology*. Oxford: Blackwell Scientific Publications pp. 123–35.

485 Macdonald D.W. & Voigt D.R. (1985) The biological basis of rabies models. In Bacon P.J. ed. *Population dynamics of rabies in wildlife*. London: Academic Press pp. 71–108.

486 Macdonald D.W. *et al*. (1981) Fox populations, habitat characterization and rabies control. *Journal of Biogeography* **8**:145–51.

487 Macdonald D.W. *et al*. (1987) Social dynamics, nursing coalitions, and infanticide among farm cats, *Felis catus*. *Advances in Ethology* **28**:1–66.

488 Macdonald S.M. (1983) The status of the otter (*Lutra lutra*) in the British Isles. *Mammal Review* **13**:11–23.

489 Macdonald S.M. & Mason C.F. (1983) Some factors influencing the distribution of otters (*Lutra lutra*). *Mammal Review* **13**:1–10.

490 Macdonald S.M. *et al*. (1978) The otter and its conservation in the River Teme catchment. *Journal of Applied Ecology* **15**:373–84.

491 Machinskii A.P. & Semov V.N. (1973) [Trichinellosis of wild animals in Mordovia.] *Meditsinskaya Parazitologiya i Parazitarnye Bolezni* **40**:532–4.

492 MacLennan R.R. & Bailey E.D. (1969) Seasonal changes in aggression, hunger, and curiosity in ranch mink. *Canadian Journal of Zoology* **47**:1395–404.

493 Maher W.J. (1967) Predation by weasels on a winter population of lemmings, Banks Island, North West Territories. *Canadian Field Naturalist* **81**:248–50.

494 Mal'dzhyunaite S.A. (1957) [Age determination and age structure of pine martens in Lithuania.] *Trudy Akademii nauk Litovskoĭ SSR series B* **3**:169–77.

495 Mardon D.K. & Moors P.J. (1977) Records of fleas collected from weasels (*Mustela nivalis* L.) in north-east Scotland (Siphonaptera: Hystrichopsyllidae and Ceratophyllidae). *Entomologist's Gazette* **28**:277–80.

496 Markley M.H. & Bassett C.F. (1942) Habits of captive marten. *American Midland Naturalist* **28**:604–16.

497 Marsh R.E. & Clark W.R. (1968) An effective weasel trap. *Journal of Mammalogy* **49**:157.

498 Marshall W.H. (1936) A study of the winter activities of the mink. *Journal of Mammalogy* **17**:382–92.

499 Marshall W.H. (1963) The ecology of mustelids in New Zealand. *Information Series of the New Zealand Department of Scientific and Industrial Research* **38**:1–32.

500 Mason C.F. & Macdonald S.M. 1980. The winter diet of otters (*Lutra lutra*) on a Scottish sea loch. *Journal of Zoology* **192**:558–61.

501 Mason C.F. & Macdonald S.M. (1986) *Otters: ecology and conservation*. Cambridge: University Press 236 pp.

502 Matheson C. (1932) *Changes in the fauna of Wales within historic times*. Cardiff: National Museum of Wales 88 pp.

503 Matheson C. (1959) The stoat and the weasel in the

British Isles. *Bulletin of the Mammal Society of the British Isles* **11**:26–9.

504 Matheson C. (1963) The distribution of the red polecat in Wales. *Proceedings of the Zoological Society of London* **140**:115–20.

505 Matthews L.H. (1941) Reproduction in the Scottish wild cat, *Felis silvestris grampia* Miller. *Proceedings of the Zoological Society of London B* **111**:59–77.

506 Matthews L.H. (1952) *British mammals*. London: Collins 410 pp.

507 Maurel D. & Boissin J. (1983) Comparative mechanisms of physiological, metabolical and eco-ethological adaptation to the winter season in two wild European mammals: the European badger (*Meles meles* L.) and the red fox (*Vulpes vulpes* L.). In Margaris N.S. *et al*. eds. *Adaptations to terrestrial environment*. New York: Plenum Press pp. 219–33.

508 Maurel D. *et al* (1984) Seasonal reproductive endocrine profiles in two wild mammals: the red fox (*Vulpes vulpes* L.) and the European badger (*Meles meles* L.) considered as short-day mammals. *Acta Endocrinologica* **105**:130–8.

509 Maurel D. *et al*. (1986) Seasonal moulting patterns in three fur bearing mammals: the European badger (*Meles meles* L.), the red fox (*Vulpes vulpes* L.), and the mink (*Mustela vison*). A morphological and histological study. *Canadian Journal of Zoology* **64**:1757–64.

510 McCann C. (1956) Observations on the polecat (*Putorius putorius* Linn.) in New Zealand. *Records of the Dominion Museum, Wellington* **2**:151–65.

511 McCaughey W.J. & Fairley J.S. (1969) Serological reactions to *Brucella* and *Leptospira* in foxes. *Veterinary Record* **84**:542.

512 McFadden Y.M.T. & Fairley J.S. (1984) Food of otters *Lutra lutra* (L.) in an Irish limestone river system with special reference to the crayfish *Austropotamobius pallipes* (Lereboullet). *Journal of Life Sciences, Royal Dublin Society* **5**:65–76.

513 McKillop I.G. & Sibley R.M. (1988) Animal behaviour at electric fences and the implications for management. *Mammal Review* **18**:91–103.

514 McLean S.F. *et al*. (1974) Population cycles in Arctic lemmings: winter reproduction and predation by weasels. *Arctic and Alpine Research* **6**:1–12.

515 Mead C.J. (1982) Ringed birds killed by cats. *Mammal Review* **12**:183–6.

516 Meyer-Holzapfel M. (1968) Breeding the European wild cat *Felis s. silvestris* at Berne Zoo. *International Zoo Yearbook* **8**:31–8.

517 Miles H. (1984) *The track of the wild otter*. London: Elm Tree Books 160 pp.

518 Millais J.G. (1905) *The mammals of Great Britain and Ireland*, vol. II. London: Longmans, Green & Co. 299 pp.

519 Miller G.S. (1912) *Catalogue of the mammals of western Europe (exclusive of Russia) in the collections of the British Museum*. London: British Museum (Natural History) 1019 pp.

520 Miller G.S. (1933) The origin of the ferret. *Scottish Naturalist* **1933**:153.

521 Ministry of Agriculture, Fisheries and Food (1977) *Bovine tuberculosis in badgers: second report*. London: MAFF 16 pp.

522 Ministry of Agriculture, Fisheries and Food (1985) *Rabies prevention and control — the risk to Great Britain from rabies. Government policy*. London: HMSO 16 pp.

523 Ministry of Agriculture, Fisheries and Food (1987) *Bovine tuberculosis in badgers: eleventh report*. London: MAFF 36 pp.

524 Minsky D. (1980) Preventing fox predation at a least tern colony with an electric fence. *Journal of Field Ornithology* **51**:180–1.

525 Mitchell D. Unpublished.

526 Mitchell J.L. (1961) Mink movements and populations on a Montana river. *Journal of Wildlife Management* **25**:48–54.

527 Mondain-Monval M. *et al*. (1977) Ovarian activity during the anoestrus and the reproductive season of the red fox (*Vulpes vulpes* L.). *Journal of Steroid Biochemistry* **8**:761–9.

528 Mondain-Monval M. *et al*. (1979) Androgens in peripheral blood of the red fox (*Vulpes vulpes* L.) during the reproductive season and the anoestrus. *Journal of Steroid Biochemistry* **11**:1315–22.

529 Mönnig H.O. (1950) *Veterinary helminthology and entomology*. London.

530 Moors P.J. (1974) *The annual energy budget of a weasel* (Mustela nivalis *L.*) *population in farmland*. PhD. thesis, University of Aberdeen.

531 Moors P.J. (1975) The foods of weasels (*Mustela nivalis*) on farmland in north-east Scotland. *Journal of Zoology* **177**:455–61.

532 Moors P.J. (1977) Studies on the metabolism, food consumption and assimilation efficiency of a small carnivore, the weasel (*Mustela nivalis* L.). *Oecologia* **27**:185–202.

533 Moors P.J. (1980) Sexual dimorphism in the body size of mustelids (Carnivora): the roles of food habits and breeding systems. *Oikos* **34**:147–58.

534 Moors P.J. (1983) Predation by mustelids and rodents on the eggs and chicks of native and introduced birds in Kowhai Bush, New Zealand. *Ibis* **125**:137–54.

535 Müller H. (1970) Beiträge zur Biologie des Hermelins, *Mustela erminea* Linné 1758. *Säugetierkundliche Mitteilungen* **18**:293–380.

536 Murphy M.J. (1985) *Behavioural and sensory aspects of predation in mustelids*. PhD. thesis, University of Durham.

537 Musgrove B.F. (1951) Weasel foraging patterns in the Robinson Lake area, Idaho. *Murrelet* **32**:8–11.

538 Nams V. (1981) Prey selection mechanisms of the ermine (*Mustela erminea*). In Chapman J.A. & Pursely D. eds. *Proceedings of the first worldwide furbearer conference*. Frostburg, Maryland: Worldwide Furbearer Conference Inc. pp. 861–82.

539 Nams V.O. & Beare S.S. (1982) Use of trees by ermine, *Mustela erminea. Canadian Field Naturalist* **96**:89–90.

540 Nasimovich A.A. (1949) [The biology of the weasel in Kola Peninsula in connection with its competitive relations with the ermine.] *Zoologicheskiĭ zhurnal* **28**:177–82.

541 Neal E.G. (1962) *Otters*. London: The Sunday Times 24 pp.

542 Neal E. (1972) The national badger survey. *Mammal Review* **2**:55–64.

543 Neal E.G. (1977) *Badgers*. Poole: Blandford Press 321 pp.

544 Neal E. (1986) *The natural history of badgers*. Beckenham, Kent: Croom Helm 238 pp.

545 Neal E.G. & Harrison R.J. (1958) Reproduction in the European badger (*Meles meles* L.). *Transactions of the Zoological Society of London* **29**:67–131.

546 Neville P.F. & Remfrey J. (1984) Effect of neutering on two groups of feral cats. *Veterinary Record* **114**: 447–50.

547 Newcombe M.J. (1982) Some observations on the badger in Kent. *Transactions of the Kent Field Club* **9**:16–30.

548 Novikov G.A. (1962) *Carnivorous mammals of the fauna of the USSR*. Jerusalem: Israel Program for Scientific Translations 284 pp.

549 Nyholm E.S. (1959) [Stoats and weasels and their winter habitats.] *Soumen Riista* **13**:106–16.

550 Nyholm E.S. (1970) [On the ecology of the pine marten (*Martes martes*) in Eastern and Northern Finland.] *Suomen Riista* **22**:105–18.

551 Oftedal O.T. (1984) Milk composition, milk yield and energy output at peak lactation: a comparative review. *Symposia of the Zoological Society of London* **51**:33–85.

552 Ognev S.I. (1962) *The mammals of the USSR and adjoining countries, vol. III: Carnivora*. Jerusalem: Israel Program for Scientific Translations.

553 Oksanen L. & Oksanen T. (1981) Lemmings (*Lemmus lemmus*) and grey-sided voles (*Clethrionomys rufocanus*) in interaction with their resources and predators on Finnmarksvidda, northern Norway. *Annales Universitatis turkuensis (Biologica, Geographia, Geologia)* **66**(17):7–31.

554 Oksanen T. *et al.* (1985) Surplus killing in the hunting strategy of small predators. *American Naturalist* **126**:328–46.

555 Oppenheimer E.C. (1980) *Felis catus*: population densities in an urban area. *Carnivore Genetics Newsletter* **4**:72–7.

556 Osborn D.J. & Helmy I. (1980) The contemporary land mammals of Egypt (including Sinai). *Fieldiana: Zoology* **5**:1–579.

557 Osgood F.L. (1936) Earthworms as a supplementary food of weasels. *Journal of Mammalogy* **17**:64.

558 Ostman J. *et al.* (1985) Behavioural changes in captive female otters (*Lutra lutra* L.) around parturition. *Journal of the Otter Trust* **1984**:58–63.

559 O'Sullivan P.J. (1983) The distribution of the pine marten (*Martes martes*) in the Republic of Ireland. *Mammal Review* **13**:39–44.

560 O'Sullivan P.J. unpublished.

561 Owen C. (1984) Ferret. In Mason I.L. ed. *Evolution of domesticated animals*. London: Longman pp. 225–8.

562 Page R.J.C. Personal communication.

563 Panaman R. (1981) Behaviour and ecology of free-ranging female farm cats (*Felis catus* L.). *Zeitschrift für Tierpsychologie* **56**:59–73.

564 Park A.W. & Nowosielski-Slepowron B.J.A. (1981) Aspects of the skull and dentition morphology of the mink, *Mustela vison. Acta morphologica* **18**:47–65.

565 Pascal M. & Delattre P. (1981) Comparaison de différentes méthodes de détermination de l'âge chez le vison (*Mustela vison* Schreber). *Canadian Journal of Zoology* **59**:202–11.

566 Pearson O.P. & Enders R.K. (1944) Duration of pregnancy in certain mustelids. *Journal of Experimental Zoology* **95**:21–35.

567 Pelikán J. & Vačkař J. (1978) Densities and fluctuations in numbers of red fox, badger and pine marten in the 'Bucin' Forest. *Folia Zoologica* **27**: 289–303.

568 Petrides G.A. (1950) The determination of sex and age ratios in fur animals. *American Midland Naturalist* **43**:355–82.

569 Petrov O.V. (1956) [Sexual dimorphism in the skull of *Mustela erminea* L.] *Vestnik Leningradskogo Universiteta* **15**:41–56.

570 Petrov O.V. (1962) [The validity of Bergmann's rule as applied to intraspecific variation in the ermine.] *Vestnik Leningradskogo Universiteta* **9**:144–8.

571 Phillips E.C. (1921) The red polecat of Cardiganshire. *Transactions of the Woolhope Club* 1918–1920: LXXVIII and 60–1.

572 Pilbeam T.E. *et al.* (1979) The annual reproductive cycle of mink (*Mustela vison*). *Journal of Animal Science* **48**:578–84.

573 Pitt F. (1921) Notes on the genetic behaviour of certain characters in the polecat, ferret and in polecat–ferret hybrids. *Journal of Genetics* **11**: 99–115.

574 Pocock R.I. (1936) The polecats of the genera *Putorius* and *Vormela* in the British Museum. *Proceedings of the Zoological Society of London* **1936**: 691–723.

575 Polis G.A. *et al.* (1984) A survey of intraspecific predation within the class Mammalia. *Mammal Review* **14**:187–98.

576 Poole T.B. (1966) Aggressive play in polecats. *Symposia of the Zoological Society of London* **18**:23–44.

577 Poole T.B. (1967) Aspects of aggressive behaviour in polecats. *Zeitschrift für Tierpsychologie* **24**:351–69.

578 Poole T.B. (1970) *Polecats*. London: HMSO 19 pp.

579 Poole T.B. (1972) Some behavioural differences between the European polecat, *Mustela putorius*, the ferret, *M. furo*, and their hybrids. *Journal of Zoology*

166:25–35.

580 Poole T.B. & Dunstone N. (1976) Underwater predatory behaviour of the American mink (*Mustela vison*). *Journal of Zoology* 178:395–412.

581 Popov V.A. (1943) [Numerosity of *M. erminea* Pall. as affected by *Skrjabingylus* invasion.] *Dokladȳ Akademii nauk SSSR* 39:160–2.

582 Potts G.R. (1980) The effects of modern agriculture, nest predation and game management on the population ecology of partridges (*Perdix perdix* and *Alectoris rufa*). *Advances in Ecological Research* 11:1–79.

583 Potts G.R. & Vickerman G.P. (1974) Studies on the cereal ecosystem. *Advances in Ecological Research* 8:107–97.

584 Pounds C.J. (1981) *Niche overlap in sympatric populations of stoats* (Mustela erminea) *and weasels* (Mustela nivalis) *in north-east Scotland*. PhD. thesis, University of Aberdeen.

585 Powell R.A. (1973) A model for raptor predation on weasels. *Journal of Mammalogy* 54:259–63.

586 Powell R.A. (1982) Evolution of black-tipped tails in weasels: predator confusion. *American Naturalist* 119:126–31.

587 Powell R.A. (1985) Possible pathways for the evolution of reproductive strategies in weasels and stoats. *Oikos* 44:506–8.

588 Powell, R.A. & Zielinski W.J. (1983) Competition and coexistence in mustelid communities. *Acta zoologica fennica* 174:223–7.

589 Price E.O. (1971) Effect of food deprivation on activity of the least weasel. *Journal of Mammalogy* 52:636–40.

590 Pulliainen E. (1981) Food and feeding habits of the pine marten in Finnish Forest Lapland in winter. In Chapman J.A. & Pursley D. eds. *Proceedings of the first worldwide furbearer conference*. Frostburg, Maryland: Worldwide Furbearer Conference Inc. pp. 580–98.

591 Pulliainen E. (1981) Winter habitat selection, home range, and movements of the pine marten (*Martes martes*) in Finnish Lapland Forest. In Chapman J.A. & Pursley D. eds. *Proceedings of the first worldwide furbearer conference*. Frostburg, Maryland: Worldwide Furbearer Conference Inc. pp. 1068–86.

592 Pulliainen E. (1982) Scent-marking in the pine marten (*Martes martes*) in Finnish Forest Lapland in winter. *Zeitschrift für Säugetierkunde* 47:91–9.

593 Pulliainen E. & Hiekkinen H. (1980) [Behaviour of the pine marten (*Martes martes*) in E Finnish Forest Lapland in winter.] *Soumen Riista* 28:30–6.

594 Räber H. (1944) Versuche zur Ermittlung des Beuteschemas an einem Hausmarder (*Martes foina*) und einem Iltis (*Putorius putorius*). *Revue suisse de zoologie* 51:293–332.

595 Ralls K. & Harvey P.H. (1985) Geographic variation in size and sexual dimorphism of North American weasels. *Biological Journal of the Linnean Society* 25:119–67.

596 Ratcliffe P.R. (1970) Occurrence of vestigial teeth in badger (*Meles meles*), roe deer (*Capreolus capreolus*) and fox (*Vulpes vulpes*). *Journal of Zoology* 162:521–5.

597 Raymond M. & Bergeron J-M. (1982) Réponse numérique de l'hermine aux fluctuations d'abondance de *Microtus pennsylvanicus*. *Canadian Journal of Zoology* 60:542–9.

598 Rees P. (1981) The ecological distribution of feral cats and the effects of neutering a hospital colony. In *The ecology and control of feral cats*. Potters Bar, Hertfordshire: UFAW pp. 12–22.

599 Reichholf J. (1983) Reagieren Bestannde des Hermelins *Mustela erminea* auf Schwankungen der Wuhlmaushaufigkeit? *Saügetierekundliche Mitteilungen* 31:69–72.

600 Rempe U. (1962) Über die Formenvermannigfaltigung des Iltis in der Domestikation. *Zeitschrift für Tierzüchtung und Züchtungsbiologie* 77:229–35.

601 Reynolds J.C. & Tapper S.C. unpublished.

602 Richards D.F. (1977) Observations on the diet of the red fox (*Vulpes vulpes*) in South Devon. *Journal of Zoology* 183:495–504.

603 Ritchie J. (1920) *The influence of man on animal life in Scotland: a study in faunal evolution*. Cambridge: University Press 550 pp.

604 Robertson P.A. & Whelan J. (1987) The food of the red fox (*Vulpes vulpes*) in Co. Kildare, Ireland. *Journal of Zoology* 213:740–3.

605 Robinson R. (1975) The red fox, *Vulpes vulpes*. In King R.C. ed. *Handbook of genetics vol. 4: vertebrates*. New York: Plenum Press pp. 399–419.

606 Robinson R. (1980) Evolution of the domestic cat. *Carnivore Genetics Newsletter* 4:46–65.

607 Roper T.J. *et al.* (1986) Scent marking with faeces and anal secretion in the European badger (*Meles meles*): seasonal and spatial characteristics of latrine use in relation to territoriality. *Behaviour* 97:94–117.

608 Ross J.G. & Fairley J.S. (1969) Studies of disease in the red fox (*Vulpes vulpes*) in Northern Ireland. *Journal of Zoology* 157:375–81.

609 Rowlands I.W. (1972) Reproductive studies in the stoat. *Journal of Zoology* 166:574–6.

610 Rowlands I.W. & Parkes A.S. (1935) The reproductive processes of certain mammals — VIII. Reproduction in foxes (*Vulpes* spp.). *Proceedings of the Zoological Society of London* 1935:823–41.

611 Ruprecht A.L. (1978) Dentition variations in the common polecat in Poland. *Acta theriologica* 23:239–45.

612 Rust C.C. (1968) Procedure for live trapping weasels. *Journal of Mammalogy* 49:318–9.

613 Ryabov L.S. (1962) [The morphological development of Caucasian pine martens and stone martens in relation to age determination.] *Zoologicheskiĭ zhurnal* 41:1731–8.

614 Sandell M. (1984) To have or not to have delayed implantation: the example of the weasel and the stoat. *Oikos* 42:123–6.

615 Sandell M. (1986) Movement patterns of male stoats

Mustela erminea during the mating season: differences in relation to social status. *Oikos* **47**:63–70.

616 Sandell M. (1989) Ecological energetics, optimal body size and sexual dimorphism: a model applied to the stoat, *Mustela erminea* L. *Functional Ecology* **3**:315–24.

617 Sandell M. (in press) Delayed implantation in mammals — an ecological explanation.

618 Satunin K. (1904) The black wild cat of Transcaucasia. *Proceedings of the Zoological Society of London* **11**:162.

619 Scales H. (1969) *Fur farm guide book.* Minnesota: American Fur Breeder.

620 Schauenberg P. (1969) L'identification du chat forestier d'Europe *Felis s. silvestris* Schreber, 1777 par une méthode ostéométrique. *Revue suisse de zoologie* **76**:433–41.

621 Schauenberg P. (1976) Poids et taille de naissance du chat forestier *Felis silvestris* Schreber. *Mammalia* **40**:687–9.

622 Schauenberg P. (1977) Longueur de l'intestin du chat forestier *Felis silvestris* Schreber. *Mammalia* **41**:357–60.

623 Schauenberg P. (1980) Note sur le squelette et la maturité physique du chat forestier *Felis silvestris* Schreb. *Revue suisse de zoologie* **87**:549–56.

624 Schauenberg P. (1981) Elements d'ecologie du chat forestier d'Europe *Felis silvestris* Schreber, 1777. *Terre et la vie* **35**:3–36.

625 Schmidt F. (1934) Uber die Fortpflanzungsbiologie von sibirischen Zobel (*Martes zibellina* L.) und europaischen Baummarder (*Martes martes* L.). *Zeitschrift für Säugetierkunde* **9**:392–402.

626 Schmidt F. (1943) Naturgeschichte des Baum- und des Steinmarders. *Monographien der Wildsäugetiere* **10**:1–258.

627 Schwalbe G. (1893) Ueber den Ferbenwechsel winterweissen Thiere. *Morphologische Arbeiten* **2**: 483–606.

628 Sealander J.A. (1943) Winter food habits of mink in southern Michigan. *Journal of Wildlife Management* **7**:411–7.

629 Segal A.N. (1975) Postnatal growth, metabolism and thermoregulation in the stoat. *Soviet Journal of Ecology* **6**:28–32.

630 Shepeleva V.K. (1957) [Responsiveness of nerve processes in the motor analysor of the Forest polecat.] *Doklady Akademii nauk SSSR, Seriya Biologiya* **106**:941–4.

631 Sherrell D.A. (1953) Raids on nest boxes by weasels. *Journal of the Forestry Commission* **23**:104–5.

632 Short H.L. (1961) Food habits of a captive least weasel. *Journal of Mammalogy* **42**:273–4.

633 Siefke A. (1960) Baummarder-Paarung. *Zeitschrift für Säugetierkunde* **25**:178.

634 Simms C. (1973) Aspects of grooming in wild mustelids in northern England. *Roebuck* **1973**:33–5.

635 Simms D.A. (1979) North American weasels: resource utilization and distribution. *Canadian*

Journal of Zoology **57**:504–20.

636 Simms D.A. (1979) Studies of an ermine population in southern Ontario. *Canadian Journal of Zoology* **57**:824–32.

637 Sjovold T. (1977) Non-metrical divergence between skeletal populations. The theoretical foundation and biological importance of C.A.B. Smith's mean measure of divergence. *Ossa, Supplement* **4**:1–33.

638 Sleeman P.D. unpublished.

639 Southern H.N. & Watson J.S. (1941) Summer food of the red fox (*Vulpes vulpes*) in Great Britain: a preliminary report. *Journal of Animal Ecology* **10**: 1–11.

640 Soutiere E.C. (1979) Effects of timber harvesting on marten in Maine. *Journal of Wildlife Management* **43**:850–60.

641 Stark R. *et al.* (1987) Gastrointestinal anatomy of the European badger *Meles meles* L. A comparative study. *Zeitschrift für Säugetierkunde* **52**:88–96.

642 Starzyk J. *et al.* (1973) Studies on the frequency of occurrence of *Toxoplasma gondii* in fur-bearing animals. *Acta biologica cracoviensia, Série zoologique* **16**:229–33.

643 Stenseth N.C. (1985) Optimal size and frequency of litters in predators of cyclic preys: comments on the reproductive biology of stoats and weasels. *Oikos* **45**:293–6.

644 Stephens M.N. (1957) *The otter report.* Potters Bar, Hertfordshire: UFAW 88 pp.

645 Stephenson R. *et al.* (1988) Heart rate and gas exchange in freely diving American mink (*Mustela vison*). *Journal of Experimental Biology* **134**:435–42.

646 Steventon J.D. & Major J.T. (1982) Marten use of habitat in a commercially clear-cut forest. *Journal of Wildlife Management* **46**:175–82.

647 Stoddart D.M. (1976) Effect of the odour of weasels (*Mustela nivalis* L.) on trapped samples of their prey. *Oecologia* **22**:439–41.

648 Stolt B.O. (1979) Colour pattern and size variation of the weasel *Mustela nivalis* in Sweden. *Zoon* **7**: 55–62.

649 Stone W.B. *et al.* (1972) Experimental transfer of sarcoptic mange from red foxes and wild canids to captive wildlife and domestic animals. *New York Fish and Game Journal* **19**:1–11.

650 Stone W.B. *et al.* (1976) Spontaneous and experimental transfer of sarcoptic mange mites from red foxes to humans. *New York Fish and Game Journal* **23**:183–4.

651 Strachan R. *et al.* (1990) *The otter survey of England 1984–86.* Peterborough: Nature Conservancy Council.

652 Stuart A.J. (1982) *Pleistocene vertebrates in the British Isles.* London: Longman Gray 212 pp.

653 Stubbe M. (1968) Zur Populationsbiologie der *Martes*-Arten. In *13th working fellowship for game and wildlife research, Gatersleben, January 1968.* Berlin: Germany Academy for Agricultural Science pp. 195–203.

654 Stubbe M. (1969) Zur Biologie und zum Schutz des

Fischotters *Lutra lutra* (L.). *Archiv für Naturschutz und Landschaftsforschung* **9**:315–24.

655 Stubbe M. (1972) Die analen Markierungsorgane der *Mustela-Arten. Zoologische Garten NF, Leipzig* **42**:176–88.

656 Stubbe M. (1977) Der Fischotter *Lutra lutra* (L., 1758) in der DDR. *Zoologischer Anzeiger* **199**: 265–85.

657 Stubbe M. (1980) Die Situation des Fischotters in der D.D.R. In Reuter C. & Festetics A. eds. *Der Fischotter in Europa — Verbreitung, Bedrohung, Erhaltung.* Oderhaus and Gottingen: Selbstverlag pp. 179–82.

658 Stuttard R.M. ed. (1986) *Predatory mammals in Britain: a code of practice for their management.* London: British Field Sports Society 94 pp.

659 Suminski P. (1962) Les caractères de la forme pure du chat sauvage *Felis silvestris* Schreber. *Archives des sciences, Genève* **15**:277–96.

660 Sumption K.J. & Flowerdew J.R. (1985) The ecological effects of the decline in rabbits (*Oryctolagus cuniculus* L.) due to myxomatosis. *Mammal Review* **15**:151–86.

661 Swire P.W. (1978) Laboratory observation on the fox (*Vulpes vulpes*) in Dyfed during the winters of 1974/75 and 1975/76. *British Veterinary Journal* **134**: 398–405.

662 Tabor J.E. & Wight H.M. (1977) Population status of river otter in western Oregon. *Journal of Wildlife Management* **41**:692–9.

663 Tabor R. (1981) General biology of feral cats. In *The ecology and control of feral cats.* Potters Bar, Hertfordshire: UFAW pp. 5–11.

664 Tadros W. & Laarman J.J. (1979) Muscular sarcosporidosis in the common European weasel *Mustela nivalis. Zeitschrift für Parasitenkunde* **58**:195–200.

665 Taketazu M. (1979) *Fox family — four seasons of animal life.* New York: Weatherhill 139 pp.

666 Talbot J.S. (1906) *Foxes at home.* London: Horace Cox 155 pp.

667 Tapper S.C. (1976) The diet of weasels, *Mustela nivalis* and stoats, *Mustela erminea* during early summer, in relation to predation on game birds. *Journal of Zoology* **179**:219–24.

668 Tapper S. (1979) The effect of fluctuating vole numbers (*Microtus agrestis*) on a population of weasels (*Mustela nivalis*) on farmland. *Journal of Animal Ecology* **48**:603–17.

669 Tapper S.C. (1982) Using estate records to monitor population trends in game and predator species, particularly weasels and stoats. *Proceedings of the International Congress of Game Biologists* **14**:115–20.

670 Tapper S.C. *et al.* (1982) Effects of mammalian predators on partridge populations. *Mammal Review* **12**:159–67.

671 Tarasoff F.J. *et al.* (1972) Locomotory patterns and external morphology of the river otter, sea otter, and harp seal (Mammalia). *Canadian Journal of Zoology* **50**:915–29.

672 Taylor J. (1968) *Salmonella* in wild animals. *Symposia of the Zoological Society of London* **24**: 51–73.

673 Taylor M.E. & Abrey N. (1982) Marten, *Martes americana,* movements and habitat use in Algonquin Provincial Park, Ontario. *Canadian Field Naturalist* **96**:439–47.

674 Taylor R.H. & Tilley J.A.V. (1984) Stoats (*Mustela erminea*) on Adele and Fisherman Islands, Abel Tasman National Park, and other offshore islands in New Zealand. *New Zealand Journal of Ecology* **7**: 139–45.

675 Tembrock G. (1963) Acoustic behaviour of mammals. In Busnel R.G. ed. *Acoustic behaviour of animals.* Amsterdam: Elsevier pp. 751–86.

676 Ternovskii D.V. & Ternovskaya Yu. G. (1978) [Potential reproductive ability in Mustelidae.] *Izvestiya Sibirskogo Otdeleniya Akademii Nauk SSSR, Seriya Biologicheskikh Nauk* **5**:88–91.

677 Ternovskii D.V. (1983) [The biology of reproduction and development of the stoat *Mustela erminea* (Carnivora, Mustelidae).] *Zoologicheskiĭ zhurnal* **62**: 1097–1105.

678 Tetley H. (1939) On the British polecats. *Proceedings of the Zoological Society of London* **109B**:37–9.

679 Tetley H. (1941) On the Scottish fox. *Proceedings of the Zoological Society of London* **111B**:25–35.

680 Tetley H. (1945) Notes on British polecats and ferrets. *Proceedings of the Zoological Society of London* **115**:212–7.

681 Thompson G.B. (1961) The parasites of British birds and mammals; the ectoparasites of the badger (*Meles meles*). *Entomologist's Monthly Magazine* **97**: 156–8.

682 Thompson G.B. (1972) Badger fleas and lice. *Entomologist's Monthly Magazine* **108**:51.

683 Thompson H.V. (1962) Wild mink in Britain. *New Scientist* **13**:130–2.

684 Thompson H.V. (1971) British wild mink — a challenge to naturalists. *Agriculture, London* **78**: 421–5.

685 Thomson A.P.D. (1951) A history of the ferret. *Journal of the History of Medicine and Allied Sciences* **6**:471–80.

686 Thomson E.H. & Fairley J.S. (1978) Notes on the Irish stoat in the Bourn-Vincent Memorial Park, Killarney. *Irish Naturalists' Journal* **19**:158–9.

687 Timofeef-Ressovsky N. (1940) Mutations and geographical variations. In Huxley J. ed. *The new systematics.* Oxford: Clarendon Press.

688 Timperley W.A. (1962) Weasel attacking tawny owl. *British Birds* **55**:276–7.

689 Tinbergen N. (1972) Food hoarding by foxes (*Vulpes vulpes* L. In *The animal in its world — explorations of an ethologist, vol. 1.* London: George Allen & Unwin pp. 315–28.

690 Tjernberg M. (1981) Diet of the golden eagle *Aquila chrysaetos* during the breeding season in Sweden. *Holarctic Ecology* **4**:12–19.

691 Todd N.B. (1978) An ecological, behavioral genetic model for the domestication of the cat. *Carnivore* **1**:52–60.

692 Tomkies M. (1977) *My wilderness wildcats*. London: Macdonald and Jane's 187 pp.

693 Toschi A. (1965) *Fauna d'Italia: Mammalia — Lagomorpha, Rodentia, Carnivora, Ungulata, Cetacea*. Bologna: Edizioni Calderini, 647 pp.

694 Trewhella W.J. & Harris S. (1988) A simulation model of the pattern of dispersal in urban fox (*Vulpes vulpes*) populations and its application for rabies control. *Journal of Applied Ecology* **25**:435–50.

695 Trewhella W.J. & Harris S. (1990) The effect of railway lines on urban fox (*Vulpes vulpes*) numbers and dispersal movements. *Journal of Zoology* **221**: 321–6.

696 Trewhella W.J. *et al.* (1988) Dispersal distance, home-range size and population density in the red fox (*Vulpes vulpes*): a quantitative analysis. *Journal of Applied Ecology* **25**:423–34.

697 Trowbridge B.J. (1983) *Olfactory communication in the European otter* Lutra l. lutra. PhD. thesis, University of Aberdeen.

698 Tumanov I.K. & Levin V.G. (1974) [Age and seasonal changes in some physiological indices of *Mustela nivalis* L. and *Mustela erminea* L.] *Vestnik Zoologii* **1974**(2):25–30.

699 Turner D.C. & Bateson P. (1988) eds. *The domestic cat: the biology of its behaviour*. Cambridge: University Press, 222 pp.

700 Turner D. & Mertens C. (1986) Home range overlap and exploitation in domestic farm cats (*Felis catus*). *Behaviour* **99**:22–45.

701 Twelves J. (1983) Otter (*Lutra lutra*) mortalities in lobster creels. *Journal of Zoology* **201**:585–8.

702 Twelves J. unpublished.

703 Twigg G.I. *et al.* (1968) Leptospirosis in British wild mammals. *Symposia of the Zoological Society of London* **24**:75–98.

704 Twigg G.I. & Harris S. (1982) Seasonal and age changes in the thymus gland of the red fox, *Vulpes vulpes*. *Journal of Zoology* **196**:355–70.

705 Universities Federation for Animal Welfare 1981. *The ecology and control of feral cats*. Potters Bar, Hertfordshire: UFAW 99 pp.

706 Vaisfel'd M.A. (1972) [A contribution to the ecology of the stoat in the cold season in the European north.] *Zoologicheskiĭ zhurnal* **51**:1705–14.

707 van Aarde R.J. (1980) The diet and feeding behaviour of feral cats, *Felis catus* at Marion Island. *South African Journal of Wildlife Research* **10**:123–8.

708 van Aarde R.J. & Blumenberg B. (1979) Genotypic correlates of body and adrenal weight in a population of feral cats, *Felis catus*. *Carnivore* **2**:37–45.

709 van Bree P.J.H. (1968) Deux exemples d'application des critères d'âge chez la loutre, *Lutra lutra* (Linnaeus, 1758). *Beaufortia* **15**:27–32.

710 van Bree P.J.H. *et al.* (1966) Skull dimensions and the length/weight relationship of the baculum as age indications in the common otter *Lutra lutra* (Linnaeus, 1758). *Danish Review of Game Biology* **4**:97–104.

711 van Rensburg P.J.J. *et al.* (1987) Effects of feline panleucopaenia on the population characteristics of feral cats on Marion Island. *Journal of Applied Ecology* **24**:63–73.

712 van Soest R.W.M. & van Bree P.J.H. (1969) On the moult in the stoat, *Mustela erminea* Linnaeus, 1758, from the Netherlands. *Bijdragen tot de dierkunde* **39**:63–8.

713 van Soest R.W.M. & van Bree P.J.H. (1970) Sex and age composition of a stoat population (*Mustela erminea* Linnaeus, 1758) from a coastal dune region of the Netherlands. *Beaufortia* **17**:51–77.

714 van Soest R.W.M. *et al.* (1972) *Skrjabingylus nasicola* (Nematoda) in skulls of *Mustela erminea* and *Mustela nivalis* (Mammalia) from the Netherlands. *Beaufortia* **20**:85–97.

715 van Wijngaarden A. & Bruijns M.F.M. (1961) De hermelijnen, *Mustela erminea* L., van Terschelling. *Lutra* **3**:35–42.

716 van Wijngaarden A. & van de Peppel J. (1970) De otter, *Lutra lutra* (L.), in Nederland. *Lutra* **12**: 3–70.

717 van Wijngaarden-Bakker L.H. (1974) The animal remains from the Beaker settlement at Newgrange, Co. Meath: first report. *Proceedings of the Royal Irish Academy C* **74**:313–83.

718 van Zyll de Jong C.G. (1987) A phylogenetic study of the Lutrinae (Carnivora; Mustelidae) using morphological data. *Canadian Journal of Zoology* **65**:2536–44.

719 Varty K. (1967) *Reynard the fox: a study of the fox in Medieval English art*. Leicester: University Press 169 pp.

720 Velander K.A. (1983) *Pine marten survey of Scotland, England and Wales 1980–1982*. London: Vincent Wildlife Trust 28 pp.

721 Velander K.A. (1985) *A study of pine marten ecology in Invernesshire*. Unpublished report, Nature Conservancy Council 49 pp.

722 Velander K.A. unpublished.

723 Venge O. (1973) Reproduction in the mink. *Kongelige Veterinaer-og Landbohoiskøles Aarsskrift* **1973**:95–146.

724 Vik R. (1955) Invasion of *Skrjabingylus* (Nematoda) in Norwegian Mustelidae. *Nytt magasin for zoologi* **3**:70–8.

725 Vogtsberger L.M. & Barrett G.W. (1973) Bioenergetics of captive red foxes. *Journal of Wildlife Management* **37**:495–500.

726 Voigt D.R. & Macdonald D.W. (1984) Variation in the spatial and social behaviour of the red fox, *Vulpes vulpes*. *Acta zoologica fennica* **171**:261–5.

727 Volobuev V.T. *et al.* (1974) [Taxonomic status of the ferret *Putorius putorius furo* by karyological data.] *Zoologicheskiĭ zhurnal* **53**:1738–40.

728 von Schantz T. (1984) 'Non-breeders' in the red fox

Vulpes vulpes: a case of resource surplus. *Oikos* **42**:59–65.

729 Waechter A. (1979) Notes sur les mammifères d'Alsace: 2. Les carnivores. *Mammalia* **43**:479–84.

730 Walker D.R.G. (1972) Observations on a collection of weasels (*Mustela nivalis*) from estates in southwest Hertfordshire. *Journal of Zoology* **166**: 474–80.

731 Walton K.C. (1964) The distribution of the polecat (*Putorius putorius*) in England, Wales and Scotland, 1959–62. *Proceedings of the Zoological Society of London* **143**:333–6.

732 Walton K.C. (1968) *Studies on the biology of the polecat* Putorius putorius (*L.*). MSc. thesis, University of Durham.

733 Walton K.C. (1968) The distribution of the polecat, *Putorius putorius* in Great Britain, 1963–67. *Journal of Zoology* **155**:237–40.

734 Walton K.C. (1968) The baculum as an age indicator in the polecat *Putorius putorius. Journal of Zoology* **156**:533–6.

735 Walton K.C. (1970) The polecat in Wales. In Lacey W.S. ed. *Welsh wildlife in trust.* Bangor: North Wales Naturalists' Trust pp. 98–108.

736 Walton K.C. (1976) The reproductive cycle in the male polecat *Putorius putorius* in Britain. *Journal of Zoology* **180**:498–503.

737 Walton K.C. & Page R.J.C. (1970) Some ectoparasites found on polecats in Britain. *Nature in Wales* **12**:32–4.

738 Wang Z. et al. (1984) Karyotypes of three species of Carnivora. *Acta zoologica sinica* **30**:188–95.

739 Warner P. & O'Sullivan P. (1982) The food of the pine marten *Martes martes* in Co. Clare. *Transactions of the International Congress of Game Biologists* **14**: 323–30.

740 Watson A. (1976) Food remains in the droppings of foxes (*Vulpes vulpes*) in the Cairngorms. *Journal of Zoology* **180**:495–6.

741 Watson H. (1978) *Coastal otters in Shetland.* London: Vincent Wildlife Trust 92 pp.

742 Wayre P. (1972) Breeding the Eurasian otter *Lutra lutra* at the Norfolk Wildlife Park. *International Zoo Yearbook* **12**:116–7.

743 Wayre P. (1979) *The private life of the otter.* London: Batsford 112 pp.

744 Wayre P. (1988) Report of Council 1987. *Journal of the Otter Trust* **1987**:1–9.

745 Webb J.B. (1975) Food of the otter (*Lutra lutra*) on the Somerset levels. *Journal of Zoology* **177**:486–91.

746 Weber D. (1987) *Zur Biologie des Iltisses* (Mustela putorius L.) *und den Ursachen seines Rückganges in der Schweiz.* PhD. thesis, Naturhistorisches Museum Basel.

747 Weber J-M. & Mermod C. (1983) Experimental transmission of *Skrjabingylus nasicola*, parasitic nematode of mustelids. *Acta zoologica fennica* **174**: 237–8.

748 Weckworth R.P. & Hawley V.D. (1962) Marten food habits and population fluctuations in Montana. *Journal of Wildlife Management* **26**:55–74.

749 Weir V. & Banister K.E. (1973) The food of the

otter in the Blakeney area. *Transactions of the Norfolk and Norwich Naturalists' Society* **22**:377–82.

750 Wiig O. & Lie R.W. (1982) Metrical and non-metrical skull variations in Norwegian wild mink (*Mustela vison* Schreber). *Zoologica Scripta* **8**: 297–300.

751 Williams T.M. (1983) Locomotion in the North American mink, a semi-aquatic mammal. I. Swimming energetics and body drag. *Journal of Experimental Biology* **103**:155–68.

752 Williams T.M. (1983) Locomotion in the North American mink, a semi-aquatic mammal II. The effect of an elongate body on running energetics and gait patterns. *Journal of Experimental Biology* **105**: 283–95.

753 Wilson P. (1982) A survey of the Irish fox population. *Irish Veterinary Journal* **35**:31–3.

754 Wise M.H. (1978) *The feeding ecology of otters and mink in Devon.* PhD. thesis, University of Exeter.

755 Wise M.H. (1980) The use of fish vertebrae in scats for estimating prey size of otters and mink. *Journal of Zoology* **192**:25–31.

756 Wise M.H. et al. (1981) A comparison of the feeding biology of mink *Mustela vison* and otter *Lutra lutra. Journal of Zoology* **195**:181–213.

757 Wlodek K. (1980) Der Fischotter in der Provinz Pomorze Zachodnie (West-Pommern) in Polen. In Reuter, C. & Festetics, A. eds. *Der Fischotter in Europa — Verbreitung, Bedrohung, Erhaltung.* Oderhaus and Gottingen: Selbstverlag pp. 187–94.

758 Woollard T. & Harris S. (1990) A behavioural comparison of dispersing and non-dispersing foxes (*Vulpes vulpes*) and an evaluation of some dispersal hypotheses. *Journal of Animal Ecology* **59**:707–20.

759 Wright M. & Walters S. (1980) *The book of the cat.* London: Pan Books 256 pp.

760 Wüstehube C. (1960) Beiträge zur Kenntnis besonders des Spiel — und Beuteverhaltens einheimischer Musteliden. *Zeitschrift für Tierpsychologie* **17**: 579–613.

761 Yalden D.W. (1982) When did the mammal fauna of the British Isles arrive? *Mammal Review* **12**: 1–57.

762 Youngman P.M. (1982) Distribution and systematics of the European mink *Mustela lutreola* Linnaeus 1761. *Acta zoologica fennica* **166**:1–48.

763 Yurgenson P.B. (1933) [Skull variation in the ermine (*Mustela erminea* L.).] *Zoologicheskiĭ zhurnal* **12**: 60–8.

764 Yurgenson P.B. (1939) [Types of habitat and the forest marten: a contribution to the ecology of the marten.] *Voprosȳ ėkologii i biotsenologii* **4**:142.

765 Yurgenson, P.B. (1956) [Determining the age of pine martens.] *Zoologicheskiĭ zhurnal* **35**:781–3.

766 Zeuner F.E. (1963) *A history of domesticated animals.* London: Hutchinson 560 pp.

767 Zima J. & Král B. (1984) Karyotypes of European mammals, part III. *Acta Scientiarium Naturalium, Brno* **18**(9):1–15.

768 Zimen E. ed. (1980) *The red fox — symposium on behaviour and ecology.* The Hague: W. Junk 285 pp.

Chapter 11 / Seals, etc.:
Order Pinnipedia

The seals and their relatives (pinnipeds) constitute a very easily recognised group of aquatic mammals often referred to the order Pinnipedia. Fossil evidence indicates that the two main subgroups of the Pinnipedia, the Otarioidea (walruses, fur seals and sea lions) and the Phocoidea (true seals) have separate geographical origins, though evidence from their chromosomes and blood proteins suggests that they share a common ancestor, close to the mustelid carnivores. Whilst it may not be correct to regard the pinnipeds as constituting a full mammalian order, they form a convenient group, and will be treated separately here.

All pinnipeds are carnivorous. They are highly adapted to aquatic life, their limbs being modified as propulsive flippers, but they come ashore (or onto ice) to give birth.

FAMILY PHOCIDAE (TRUE SEALS)

Only two species of true seals (Phocidae) are regularly found in British waters but four others, and the walrus, are occasional vagrants from the Arctic.

Seals have the body streamlined and elongated, without a pronounced neck-constriction, covered in short coarse hair with very sparse or no underfur. The young are typically born in a woolly natal coat (lanugo) differing in colour and texture from adults.

Hind limbs are principal means of propulsion in sea, but not used on land; all digits bear claws (though greatly reduced on some digits in some species), but more pronounced on forelimbs. External ear pinnae absent or very reduced. Post-canine teeth typically multicusped.

Two subfamilies: Phocinae, northern seals, comprising the genera *Phoca*, *Halichoerus*, *Cystophora* and *Erignathus* [26], all of which have been recorded from British waters, circumboreal in Arctic, Atlantic and Pacific Oceans with some adjacent seas and lakes; and Monachinae, Antarctic seals of Southern Ocean, monk seals of Mediterranean, Caribbean and Hawaiian seas, and elephant seals of sub-Antarctic and western North America.

The two species resident in Britain belong to different genera but can be difficult to distinguish, particularly in the water. The main differences are listed in Table 11.1. The vagrant species are distinctive as adults but juveniles are much more difficult to identify and juveniles are the animals most likely to wander south into British waters — see under individual species for their characteristics.

GENUS *Phoca*

In addition to *P. vitulina* the genus *Phoca* includes *P. largha*, an ice-dwelling seal from the north-west

Table 11.1. Identification of common and grey seals.

	Common seal	Grey seal
Size (nose to tip of flipper)	Up to 1.7 m	Up to 2.45 m
Spots	Small and numerous	Larger and fewer
Head	Small, crown rounded, concave 'bridge' between nose and forehead	Large, crown rather flat, no 'bridge'
Nostrils	Form V, touching below	Parallel and separated below
Post-canine teeth	Clearly tricuspid	Single-cusped, or with additional rudimentary cusps

Pacific, and three other species which are often recognised as constituting separate genera. These are *P. (Histriophoca) fasciata*, the ribbon seal of the Bering Sea and the Sea of Okhotsk; *P. (Pagophilus) groenlandica*, the harp seal from the North Atlantic and Arctic seas; and *P. (Pusa) hispida*, the ringed seal, circumpolar from the southern ice-edge to the Pole and in the Baltic Sea. Closely allied to this last form are *P. sibirica*, the Baikal seal from Lake Baikal, and *P. caspica*, the Caspian seal from the Caspian Sea. *P. groenlandica* and *P. hispida* have been reported from British coasts and are dealt with under Vagrant seals (p. 480).

Common seal *Phoca vitulina*

Phoca vitulina Linnaeus, 1758; European seas.

Harbour (harbor) seal (usual in N America); spotted seal; sand seal; selchie (selkie) (Northern Isles); black seal, tang fish (obsolete, Shetland); morlo cyffredin (Wales). Both common and grey seals may be called selchie or selkie in N Scotland.

RECOGNITION
Difficult to distinguish from grey seal, particularly when in water. When hauled out often adopt characteristic 'head-up–tail-up' attitude. Colour black to grey to sandy brown, though animals may appear white to silvery at a distance when dry; spots small and numerous, sometimes forming a network composed of small rings (cf. ringed seal, p. 480, where rings larger). Head small in relation to body (cf. grey seal) and top of head rounded; nostrils at V-angle and almost touching below [85] (Fig. 11.1). Mixed haul outs of grey and common

seals frequent though if many grey seals present these often bunch tightly on periphery of group of common seals. Inter-individual distances tend to be greater in common seals than in greys, giving common seals a more spaced-out distribution.

Skull: post-canine teeth (except first) much longer than broad and clearly tri-cusped, posterior cusps often subdivided (Fig. 11.2). Interorbital region of skull slender; palate anteriorly flat.

SIGN
On suitable substrates leave clear tracks (Fig. 11.3), width variable, adults 55–75 cm, pups 30–45 cm. New born pups leave scratch marks from long nails. Generally defaecate in water but droppings sometimes found on sandbanks or rocks; consistency very variable, but when firm, dog-like, irregularly rounded, 2–3 cm diameter, yellowish brown or, less commonly, grey. Brown faeces tend to turn grey on drying out. Occasionally fish bones, squid beaks or shell fragments recognisable. Have been known to vomit up small fish (e.g. sand eels) at basking places.

DESCRIPTION

Pelage: colour and pattern very variable. Basically a mottle of dark spots on a lighter ground (Fig. 11.4); on the back the spots coalesce to give a dark ground with paler interrupted reticulation; there may be a dark or black dorsal stripe. Males generally darker than females. Coat fades to a brownish tinge prior to moult in late summer. Pups born in first adult pelage, very rarely in white foetal coat.

Fig. 11.1. Heads of (top) grey seal (bull on left, cow in centre) and (bottom) common seal. Note the concave forehead and closely adjacent nostrils in the common seal. Also lower post-canine tooth of grey seal (left) and common seal (right).

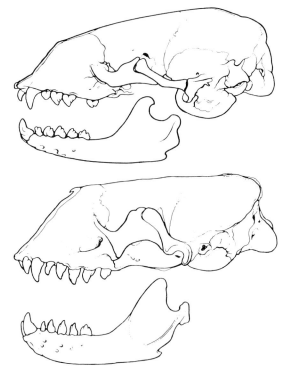

Fig. 11.2. Skulls of common seal (top) and grey seal (bottom), not to same scale (common seal *c*. 230 mm, grey seal *c*. 270 mm).

Fig. 11.3. Aerial view of common seals on a sandbank in the Wash. Note the characteristic 'head-up–tail-up' attitude and the tracks left in the sand. (Photo: Sea Mammal Research Unit, NERC.)

Fig. 11.4. Common seals: male (top), female (bottom).

Moult: undergo a complete moult each year at end of breeding season. Hair loss normally starts around the face and genitals, ends in the mid-dorsal region [67], and lasts about 3–4 weeks. Timing of moult differs with sex and age classes. Yearlings moult first, sometimes as early as June. Other seals start moulting from mid-July, with females moulting before males; in males (no data for females) immatures before matures. By late September all are fully moulted [77].

Body form: typically a rather stubby 'seal-shaped' torpedo. Forelimbs paddle shaped; digits one and two nearly equal, others shorter in order, all digits bound together in a common integument. Hind limbs fan-like with digits joined by hair-covered web; digits one and five nearly equal, two, three and four shorter. Nails present on all digits (though sometimes lost, perhaps in fighting).

Nipples: one (rarely two) abdominal pairs in both sexes; inconspicuous in males, most obvious in females during breeding season and moult. Testes in male internal, penile aperture fairly obvious even in juveniles; in female vulva and anus in common furrow (vulva swollen in adult females). Adult males with heavier build, particularly around shoulders (often scarred) but only certain way to sex in field is by view of underside.

Teeth: permanent dentition 3.1.5 (post-canines)/ 2.1.5 (post-canines). Milk teeth usually resorbed or shed before birth and permanent dentition erupted at, or shortly after, birth. Cheek-teeth much longer than broad and set obliquely in jaw. First lower post-canine usually with four cusps, second from anterior end largest. Skull with anterior part of palate shallow, posterior palatal foramen enters palate on maxilla, posterior border of palate ∧ shaped. Tendency for lacunae to be present in basioccipital and exoccipital. Nasals extend beyond posterior margin of maxillae.

Reproductive tract: male; testes inguinal, prostate immediately below bladder at junction with urethra. Simple baculum present. Female; reproductive tract bicornuate with short common uterus; vagina opening into urinogenital sinus which in turn opens to exterior by a bursa including the anus; ovaries ovulate alternately.

Chromosomes: $2n = 32$, $FNa = 60$ (as in most seals) [9].

RELATIONSHIPS
Closest relative is the largha seal, *P. largha*, an ice-breeding form in the NW Pacific with many juvenile characteristics, often regarded as a subspecies of *P. vitulina*.

MEASUREMENTS (Table 11.2).

VARIATION
The wide distribution of this species and the existence of many slightly differing local groups suggests that *Phoca vitulina* may be in a process of active differentiation [44]. Eastern Atlantic subspecies, *P. v. vitulina*, does not differ from *P.v. concolor* of the western Atlantic in consistent morphological characters and named subspecies represent geographical distinctions [61]. No consistent variation has been noted in the British Isles but there is a tendency for seals from sandy or muddy estuarine regions to have paler, more even colouring than those from rocky coasts, which generally have brighter, better marked patterning. The same tendency has been noted in N America [30].

DISTRIBUTION
Holarctic, in coastal waters mainly between 40°N and 70°N. In Europe breeds around Iceland, in Norway south from Finmark, sparsely in Baltic south of Stockholm, more abundantly in Denmark and the German Frisian coast and sparsely in Dutch Wadden Sea. Occurs sporadically along Channel coast and Biscay as far south as Portugal.
In Britain, widespread along the west coast

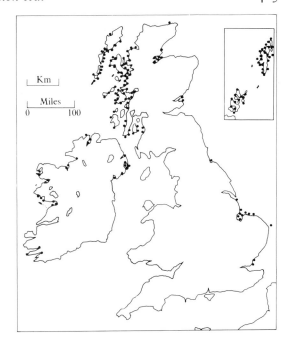

Map 11.1. Common seal (breeding distribution).

of Scotland and throughout the Hebrides and Northern Isles. On the east coast, more restricted, occurring in estuaries such as the Moray Firth, the Tay and the Wash, with smaller groups on sandbanks off East Anglia and Lincolnshire. Vagrants or remnant populations in South coast estuaries, Bristol Channel, Menai Straits. Occasionally move up inland waterways, notably Thames above Tower Bridge, East Anglian Ouse and Loch Ness [83].
In Ireland majority on shallow eastern and northeastern coast in sheltered sea loughs and estuaries. Scarce in west.

Table 11.2. Measurements of common seals.

	Males		Females	
	Range	n	Range	n
Nose to tail (cm)	130−161	26	120−155	26
Nose to tip of flippers (cm)	150−185		140−175	
Weight (kg)	55−130	22	45−106	19
Length at birth (cm) [22]*	81		79	
Weight at birth (kg) [79]	10−16		8−14	

* All data from British seals except length at birth, which was from Nova Scotia population.

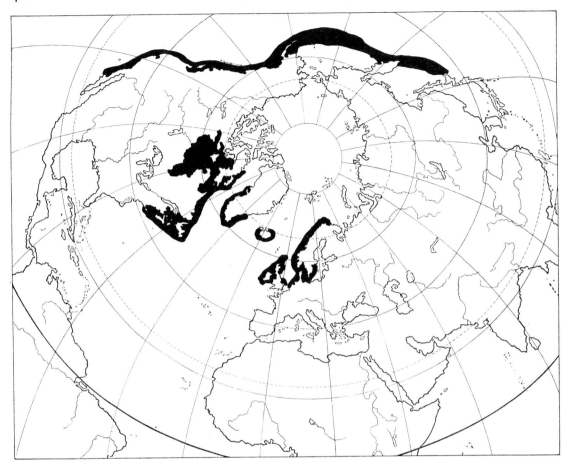

Map 11.2. Common seal.

HISTORY

Early records of seals in Britain did not generally distinguish between common and grey seals until the beginning of this century. However, it is clear that at one time common seals were more widely distributed around our coasts than at present, with colonies in, for example, the Isle of Wight in the last century, and even more recently in the Bristol Channel. Recent changes in common seal numbers in parts of Scotland and England probably relate to human activity. The decline in Shetland during the 1960s and 1970s was a consequence of hunting for skins, with a subsequent increase following protection. There has been a similar increase for the same reason in the Wash.

HABITAT

Most observations relate only to hauled-out seals and there are indications that seals may move considerable distances from habitual hauling areas. These are generally in shallow, sheltered waters, sea lochs and around island archipelagoes (Fig. 11.5). The common seal is the characteristic (though not exclusive) seal of sandbanks, mudbanks and estuaries (e.g. Wash, Abertay Sands). In such situations they use banks that allow immediate access to deep water for ease of escape. They haul out at the highest point and usually follow water as the tide recedes, leaving characteristic tracks. In Shetland, Orkney, Western Isles and west coast of Scotland found on shores of small islands (e.g.

Fig. 11.5. Common seals in the water. Note the short muzzle and closely approximated nostrils. (Photo: Sea Mammal Research Unit, NERC.)

Holm of Elsness, Orkney, Harcosay, Shetland); in remote sea-lochs (e.g. Loch Teacuis, Argyll); or on isolated skerries (Ve Skerries, Shetland). However, not restricted to remote localities when unmolested and may then haul out close to roads, piers, etc.

SOCIAL ORGANISATION AND BEHAVIOUR
Social organisation poorly understood. Size of haul-out group very variable, ranging from one to over 600. Probably solitary when feeding, though often form loose aggregations in water off haul-out sites. Tendency for there to be fewer, but larger, haul-out groups in late summer and winter [23, 47]. During the breeding season, some groups contain mostly females and pups (Fig. 11.6), while males predominate in others [45, 76]. Believed to be monogamous or promiscuous, but increasing evidence that at least a mildly polygynous breeding system exists [23, 66].

Home range: individuals return to favoured haul-out sites, exact choice depending on season and weather conditions. Seals move regularly from these inshore areas to feed in more open waters, travelling up to 50km between haul-out and feeding areas [74]. No known migratory movements, but tag recoveries indicate dispersal of pups from Wash to North Sea continental coasts [21].

Communication: not very vocal. Pups call to mothers with an almost human 'waa waa' cry. Growling threats occasionally heard on land. In water, slap surface with foreflipper to produce 'rifle-shot' sound. This, and 'snorting' at the surface, commonly used in aquatic displays between adult males. Both occur also as an element of play in juveniles [84].

Senses: vision good in both air and water, though less effective at low light intensities in air [42, 82]. As sensitive to waterborne sound as terrestrial mammals to airborne sound. Hearing not as sensitive in air, but still quite good. Auditory range to 180kHz, with directional hearing in both media [50]. Scent characteristic, and sense of smell acute. Vibrissae capable of detecting vibrations in water, such as those set up by swimming fish.

Aggressive behaviour: often subtle and rarely seen at haul-out sites. Disputes over space may lead to a series of threat gestures: growls, head thrusts and fore flipper waves [68], but rarely to a fight. Females defend area around their young pups using similar gestures. Fights on land occasionally seen during the breeding season, when oestrous females repel advances by mature bulls. Male–male competition is intense during June and July, as mature bulls are

Fig. 11.6. Common seal cow and pup. (Photo: Sea Mammal Research Unit, NERC.)

often seen with multiple bite wounds around the neck [75]. Serious fighting between males appears to occur only in the water.

Activity patterns: haul-out usually restricted to period of low tide in sandbank areas, e.g. Wash and Dornoch Firth (though may occur on marsh edges of Wash at high water). On rocky shores in Northern Isles often found hauled out at all stages of the tide. In Orkney haul-out behaviour can be diurnal, nocturnal or tidal, while some individuals may remain hauled out for periods of over 24 hours (Fig. 11.7). Variations in both pattern and frequency of haul-out occur between individuals, sexes and season, and are likely to be related to differences in feeding activity, as well as constraints of the breeding season and moult [74]. Behaviour may be less variable in those areas where site availability is constrained by the tidal cycle.

Locomotion: swim by side-to-side sweeps of hind flippers, with forelimbs used only for manoeuvring or very slow progression. On land, move by characteristic body hitching, with forelimbs on ground, hind limbs trailing or held together and lifted clear of ground. Can hitch forward with forelimbs folded against sides, or may progress in this way with one flank against ground.

Diving: dives normally last about 2–6 min, very regular, 10–20% of dive time at surface before next dive. Shorter, irregular dives when playing in the shallows. Often 'bottle', with body held vertical in the water and face above the surface, apparently asleep. When resting like this may sink down for as long as 8 min before resurfacing at the same spot. Pups can dive for up to 2 min when a few days old [45]. Adults have survived forced dives of up to 30 min and simulated depths of 206 m [35]. Deepest known dive in wild was for an adult caught in a fish trap set at over 500 m [46].

Play: pairs sometimes seem engaged in erotic rolling behaviour, particularly in the pre-pupping period and in late summer [81]. Originally thought to be pre-copulatory display, but now thought more likely to be play between immatures [75, 84]. Frequently 'porpoise', jumping repeatedly clear of the water while swimming fast, often when disturbed from, or arriving at, a haul-out site; significance of this unknown.

FEEDING

Little systematic information available but many anecdotal accounts. Appear to be opportunistic feeders, taking species which are locally or seasonally abundant or easy to catch. A wide variety of elasmobranch and teleost fish taken, as well as cephalopods, gastropods and crustaceans. In stomachs from Scotland, gadoid (particularly whiting and saithe) and clupeoid fish most abundant [56, 57], while in the Dutch Wadden Sea flounders

Fig. 11.7. Adult male common seals hauled-out at a rocky-shore site in Orkney. (Photo: Sea Mammal Research Unit, NERC.)

were the commonest species [38]. Young seals may eat considerable quantities of shrimps [16, 19].

Foraging behaviour never observed in wild. Large fish brought to the surface to be broken up by shaking, but most prey items probably swallowed whole underwater, and intact herring of up to 30 cm found in stomachs from Nova Scotia [23]. Appear not to hold prey in fore flippers (cf. grey seal).

Daily food requirement not known, but in region of 2–3 kg per day for seals in captivity [20].

BREEDING (Fig. 11.8)

Males reach sexual maturity at 5–6 years and females at 3–4 years [15, 23, 34]. Adult females normally bear a single pup each year, in June or early July, with the peak of pupping in the middle of June. Twin fetuses are known, but there are no records of twins surviving. There are no obvious regional differences in the timing of pupping around Britain (cf. grey seal). Pups are born on inter-tidal areas and possibly in the water, where they can swim and dive efficiently from birth. Gestation lasts 10–11 months, including a 2–3 month delayed implantation [32, 34]. Pups weigh 9–11 kg at birth and are 70–97 cm long.

Lactation is difficult to study as mother-pup pairs are highly mobile. In Dutch Wadden Sea, pups were suckled for 40–54 min per low tide throughout the lactation period [78]. Females remain in close contact with pups early in lactation, often diving together or carrying the pup on their backs

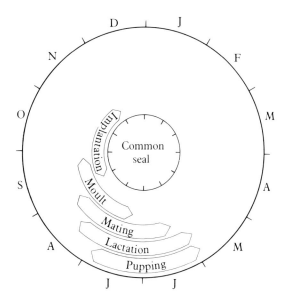

Fig. 11.8. Common seal: life-cycle.

[80]. Lactation lasts 3–4 weeks and, as weaning approaches, suckling bouts become longer but less frequent [78], and females may leave their pups for longer periods.

Young: in the Wash, male pups are larger than females and have a slightly higher growth rate [79]. Pups can more than double their birth weight during the lactation period. In Orkney, most pups are weaned by mid-July. Between late July and mid-September they are rarely seen at haul-out sites and may be spending much of their time in the water, learning to feed [74]. Pups normally lose weight during this post-lactation period. Dispersal occurs at this time and probably continues over their first winter.

Mating occurs around or soon after weaning [75]. Copulation attempts are sometimes seen at haul-out sites but few appear to be successful and it is thought that copulation normally occurs in the water [2].

POPULATION

Population size: estimates normally based on counts made at haul-out sites, but an unknown proportion of the population remains in the water. In the Wash, mark−recapture studies estimated the annual pup production equivalent to an all-age population of 6575 [71]. The maximum haul-out count was 1722, suggesting that haul-out counts substantially underestimate population size. Variations in haul-out behaviour, methodology and timing of surveys make comparison between areas difficult. The minimum population estimate for Great Britain and Ireland is 25 000−26 000, broken down by areas in Table 11.3.

Population structure: few data for British population. The following figures are from British Columbia [15].
    Annual mortality:
       Immatures (1−4 years): males 21%, females 20%.
       Matures (5+ years): males 29%, females 15%.
    Longevity: males 20 years, females 30 years.
    Pregnancy rate: 2−6 years 80%, 7−30 years 97%.

Sex ratio becomes increasingly biased towards females after sexual maturity. The estimate above of 21% for 1st year mortality is surprisingly low, and other work suggests 50−60% [58]. On Sable Island, Nova Scota, a minimum of 12% of all pups died in their 1st month of life [22]. Data are very limited for all studies.

MORTALITY

Almost nothing is known about the causes of mortality in Britain. Seals are occasionally seen with large raw lesions on their bellies or flanks, but it

Table 11.3. Population estimates of common seal.

Area	Population	Year of survey
Ireland [73]	1500−2000	1978
Inner Hebrides and W coast [70]	4500	1977
Outer Hebrides [70]	1300	1974
Orkney [63]	6600	1985
Shetland [51]	4700	1984
E coast of Scotland [70]	850−1050	1975
Wash [71]	6600	1973

is not known if this condition can be fatal. It has been suggested that similar lesions (in the Wadden Sea) are the result of infections through the umbilicus [29]. An epizootic occurred in Shetland in the 1920s [19], but no bacteriology has been described. Outbreaks of seal plague resulted in the death of several thousand common seals from the Scandinavian, German and Dutch populations in 1988 [53]. Losses were estimated at 70% of the previous population in certain areas. The disease spread to the UK in early August 1988; it is caused by a virus from the *Morbillivirus* genus which also includes viruses which cause canine distemper and rinderpest. The full impact of the disease will not be known for some time. Grey seals seem to be less affected.

There are many records (but not from British waters) of common seals found in the stomachs of killer whales [31] but this is not likely to be a significant controlling factor. There are no other known naturally occurring predators.

PARASITES

The blood sucking louse *Echinophthirius horridus* is widespread and may occur in tens of thousands all over the body. Nematode lung worms *Otostrongylus circumlitus* and *Parafilarioides gymnurus* are frequent and recognised as a serious cause of mortality in Netherlands seals. The nematode heart worms *Skrjabinaria spirocauda* also occur. Microfilaria in blood may be associated with these worms. Stomach nematodes *Contracaecum osculatum* and *Pseudoterranova* (*Porrocaecum*) *decipiens* are almost universal (for a further discussion of the latter species see p. 479). Acanthocephalian worm *Corynosoma strumosum* found in posterior part of ileum and large intestine. Cestodes, mostly *Diphyllobothrium spp.*, and trematodes recorded from both gut and liver [19].

RELATIONS WITH MAN

In the recent past has been locally regarded as a serious pest of fisheries; this view now more or less restricted to salmon fisheries, particularly those employing set nets (*see* Grey seal). Some commercial salmon fishing companies still pay bounties for killing common seals in the vicinity of their nets. The recent increase in the number of fish farms, particularly for ranched salmon, has led to more complaints about seals causing damage to fish in cages. In general, common seals are more frequently implicated than grey seals, since most establishments are found in sheltered waters. It is not clear how severe this problem is. From the seals' point of view, the fish farms and the area around them, in which seals are actively discouraged, represent a loss of habitat which may be locally significant. Most fish cages currently in use can be protected effectively by the deployment of anti-predator nets, although the type and management of the net can make a tremendous difference to its effectiveness [60]. Seals commonly play with, and puncture, plastic creel buoys, incurring the resentment of fishermen.

Local hunting of pups for skin trade in Shetland, Orkney, west coast of Scotland and Wash, common in 1960s but this trade now minimal (though common seal skin is still a traditional covering for sporrans). Important tourist attraction in several localities; the seals become very accustomed to tourist boats and allow close approach.

Legislation: protected in Great Britain by a close season from 1 June to 31 August by Conservation of Seals Act 1970, during which period seals can be killed only under licence or in the vicinity of fishing nets to protect catch. In Shetland, protected the year round under a special order. Unprotected in Northern Ireland but protected in the Irish Republic at all times by the Wildlife Act 1976.

SOUND RECORDINGS
Appendix 3: A, J, P.

LITERATURE
[20A, 44, 59A] — good general accounts of seals. [39] — now a somewhat dated account of British seals. [17] — general, but rather technical account, with emphasis on N American and Pacific forms.

NERC News gives annual updates on common (and grey) seal numbers.

AUTHORS FOR THIS SPECIES
W.N. Bonner and P.M. Thompson.

GENUS *Halichoerus*

This genus contains only the grey seal.

Grey seal *Halichoerus grypus*

Phoca grypus Fabricius, 1791; Greenland.

Atlantic seal; great seal, selkie or selchie (also used for common seal), ron mor (Gaelic); haaf-fish (obsolete, Shetland); morlo llwyd (Welsh); horse head (Canada).

RECOGNITION
Colour very variable and not useful as a field character. Spots, when distinguishable, larger and less numerous than in common seal. Head large and muzzle elongated, giving 'Roman nose' or equine appearance to face; top of head flattish (Fig. 11.9). Head shape of young grey seals similar to that of common seals. Nostrils almost parallel and separated at base (*see* Fig. 11.1).

Postcanine teeth large, usually with single conical cusp; secondary cusps when present insignificant. Interorbital region of skull wide, snout high, so that axis of nasals approximately parallel to tooth row. Anterior part of palate deeply concave.

SIGN
Faeces dog-like, 4–4.5 cm diameter, brown, black or putty colour, orange during breeding season. Rocks used regularly for hauling out may show traces of hair, particularly in spring. Characteristic musky odour. Occur on sandy beaches in some areas, leaving tracks similar to common seal, but wider.

DESCRIPTION
Marked sexual dimorphism; adult male half as large again as female, with heavy neck and shoulders, usually scarred. Head profile of male convex, with heavy muzzle compared to much flatter profile and more slender muzzle of female (Fig. 11.10). Males generally uniformly dark grey or brown background with very few pale patches,

Fig. 11.9. Grey seals: bull (top); cow (centre); pup (bottom).

Fig. 11.10. Bull grey seal. Note the long muzzle and straight profile. (Photo: Sea Mammal Research Unit, NERC.)

belly slightly paler. Females tend to be medium grey on back, shading to pale grey or cream on belly, with dark patches sparsely scattered on the lighter background. Enormous variation occurs in colour and patterning of females from very pale uniform colour with almost no spots to dark females whose patches nearly coalesce. All shades of light and dark grey, brown and silver occur; a few adults of both sexes may be completely black and some individuals may have a ginger coloration, particularly on the head. Close to the moult, worn hair gives brown or fawn coloration, especially when pelage dries.

Moult: females moult between January and March, males between March and May. Pups born in white natal fur, shed in 2−3 weeks revealing first adult coat; next moult after *c.* 15 months.

Other external characteristics much as common seal, but note long slender claws on fore flipper of grey seal.

Teeth and skull: permanent teeth 3.1.5 (often 6) (post-canines)/2.1.5 (post-canines). Milk teeth shed before birth and permanent dentition erupts shortly after. Upper incisors are larger than lower; the canines are massive and cone-shaped; post-canines undifferentiated, large and strong, some nearly circular in cross-section with single conical cusp; small secondary cusps sometimes present on fifth upper and fourth and fifth lower post-canines; first upper post-canine pushed inwards out of line in old animals.

Most noticeable feature of skull is long and wide snout with elevated frontonasal region, which is particularly marked in the male and associated with the 'roman nose' [43]. Posterior margin of palate evenly rounded, posterior palatal foramen opens on palatines, anterior part of palate strongly concave. Posterior margin of nasals approximately level with that of maxilla. Interorbital region wide.

Chromosomes: 2n = 32, FNa = 60 [9].

MEASUREMENTS (Table 11.4).

DISTRIBUTION

There are three reproductively isolated populations in the W North Atlantic, E North Atlantic and the Baltic Sea. In the west, grey seals breed on ice in the Gulf of St Lawrence and the islands off Nova Scotia; the population is distributed from Hebron, Labrador, in the north to Nantucket in the south [49]. In NE Atlantic, breeds around Iceland, Faroes, Norway from More northwards to North Cape, Murman coast of USSR, but the majority breed around coast of the British Isles (see Tables 11.5 and 11.6) [19]. The Baltic population is the smallest of the three, found mainly in Gulfs of Bothnia, Riga and Finland. Bred on Danish Coasts in 18th century, but now only occasional visitor [28]. Reliability of population estimates varies from area to area; British stock most intensively studied.

HABITAT

Typically breeds on exposed rocky coasts and caves (Fig. 11.11), but found at other times in most types of coastal habitats. Largest breeding assemblies on uninhabited islands, where seals may spread over entire top of island (e.g. Causamul), even ascending to considerable heights (e.g. 80 m at North Rona). Smaller groups in sheltered coves (e.g. Holm of Fara, Orkney) or fringing beaches (e.g. South Ronaldsay, Orkney; Monach Isles, Hebrides). Very

Table 11.4. Measurements of grey seals.		Males				Females			
		Mean	SD	Range	*n*	Mean	SD	Range	*n*
Nose to tail (cm)		207	10	195−230	25	180	7	165−195	25
Nose to tip of flippers (cm)				210−245				195−220	
Weight (kg)		233	40	170−310	25	155	24	105−186	25
Length at birth (cm)				90−105				90−105	
Weight at birth (kg)		14.5				14.5			

	E Atlantic stock	W Atlantic stock	Baltic stock
Iceland	8–10 000	71–125 000	1200
Faroes	3000		
Great Britain*	99 500		
Ireland	2000		
Norway	3000		
USSR	3000		

Table 11.5. Current population estimates for world grey seal populations.

* Numbers of grey seals breeding in Britain assessed annually by aerial photography and ground counts of pups born [e.g. 52].

Area	Number
SW Britain (Scilly Isles, Cornish coast, Dyfed coast especially islands of Skomer and Ramsey, Gwynnedd coast including Bardsey Island, Anglesey, Isle of Man)	3000
Inner Hebrides (Nave Island, Oronsay, Treshnish, Gunna)	9000
Outer Hebrides (Monach Isles, Gasker, Shillay, Coppay, Haskeir, Causamul, Deasker, North Rona)	44 500
Orkney (Greenholms, Spurness Sound, Westray Firth, Gairsay area, Pentland Firth, Auskerry)	32 500
Shetland	3500
Farne Islands and Isle of May	7000
Lincolnshire and Norfolk	< 500

Table 11.6. Numbers of grey seals breeding in Britain.

small groups in sea caves (Cornwall, Dyfed, SW Ireland), and occasionally on sandbanks (Donna Nook, Lincolnshire; Scroby Sands, Norfolk). Breeding areas rarely used by non-breeding assemblies, which are mostly on tidal rocks, reefs or sandbanks. Both breeding and non-breeding haul-outs may number several hundred animals. In Canada and Baltic, breed on ice floes.

SOCIAL ORGANISATION AND BEHAVIOUR
Outside breeding season, little known of behaviour at sea or at haul-out sites. Large post-breeding assemblies form at some sites after pupping finishes (e.g. Monachs, Deasker).

Dispersal: disperse away from breeding sites once season over, presumably to feeding areas, but stay in vicinity if rich resources available nearby (e.g. Farne Islands). Telemetry studies at Farne Islands showed some seals feeding locally, but one moved to Isle of May and up to Dundee. Individuals found far from land, e.g. feeding around oil platforms. Numbers hauling out at resting sites at any one time much lower than would be predicted from

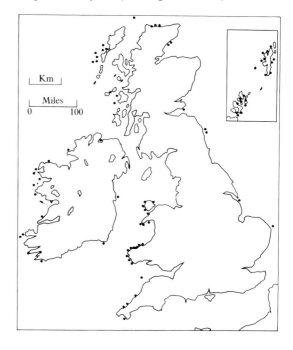

Map 11.3. Grey seal (breeding distribution).

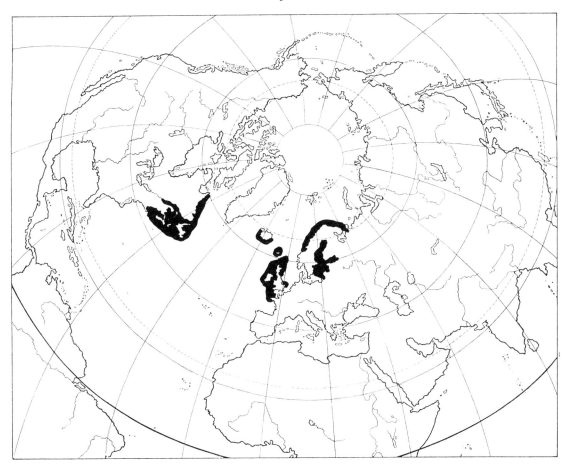

Map 11.4. Grey seal.

known populations, and remainder presumed to be at sea. Group size extremely variable; some evidence that sexes and age groups segregate. Individuals vary in hauling-out behaviour but some show pattern related to tidal rhythm [64].

From tag data pups appear to disperse from birth sites, but about 70% stay within the general area in which they were born [62]. Some pups wander far; pups tagged at North Rona found in Iceland, Ireland, Shetland; pups marked in Farne Islands found in Faroes, Minch, Norway, Denmark and Holland; pups marked at Ramsey found in Ireland, France, Spain. No known migratory movements, but general drift back to breeding sites in late summer. Evidence from branded animals of return to rookery of birth, or at least within same general area, for breeding [37, 72]. Tendency for

breeding animals to return to same site each year, and even to within metres of position occupied in previous year [5].

Social organisation during pupping season is described under 'Breeding'. Behaviour while ashore of both breeding and non-breeding seals is dominated by resting behaviour [7], but non-breeding seals spend more time being watchful. All other activities (locomotion, aggression, sexual, suckling, grooming) occupy between 1 and 5% of time.

Grooming: confined to scratching as grey seals do not groom their pelage.

Vocalisation: seals on haul-out site more tolerant of proximity of other individuals than during breeding season, but interactions still occur; these involve

Fig. 11.11. Grey seal pups in breeding colony, Orkney. (Photo: Sea Mammal Research Unit, NERC.)

open-mouth threats, flippering and hooting and moaning vocalisations. Characteristically vocal, particularly females which hiss, snarl, hoot and moan. Males snarl, hiss and growl, and can produce a throbbing sound from the back of the throat. Pups bleat and wail when hungry, hiss and snarl when frightened.

Activities largely similar both by day and night [3].

Locomotion as in common seal but not seen to porpoise and make more use of fore flippers when clambering over rocks.

Senses probably as in common seal but few data. Many records of blind grey seals in good condition and breeding successfully in consecutive seasons, so evidently can hunt without vision; vibrissae perhaps important tactile receptors. Olfactory sense much used in pup identification or in investigating unfamiliar situations. May also use sense of smell underwater as possess rhinarium external to nostrils.

FEEDING

Like common seals, grey seals are general fish feeders. Early work on diet from stomachs of seals taken near fishing nets [56] revealed gadoids and salmonids as the most important items. More recent comprehensive work on diet [63] used faecal samples from widely distributed haul-out sites at different times of the year (Table 11.7). This showed that a variety of fish are taken; proportions in diet vary from area to area and coincide roughly with abundance of prey in those areas. Composition of diet also varies seasonally. Cephalopods and crustaceans taken occasionally, but are not major items in diet. They have been known to take seabirds swimming at the surface of the sea. Average daily food requirement is about 5 kg although they may not feed every day and certainly fast during the breeding season, females for at least 3 weeks and males for up to 6 weeks. Can be pest at fishing nets, particularly salmon fishing stations.

BREEDING (Fig. 11.12)

Form polygynous breeding groups over most of

Table 11.7. Composition (% by weight) of grey seal diet from faecal analysis [63].

	Orkney	Isle of May	Farne Islands	Donna Nook
Sandeels	80	15	33	29
Cod	3	50	49	6
Saithe	6	3	6	–
Whiting	–	9	3	5
Haddock	2	7	2	–
Lemon/Dover sole	–	5	–	38
Other flatfish	5	–	3	10
Ling	–	5	–	–
Others (e.g. pout, dab, poor cod)	4	6	4	12

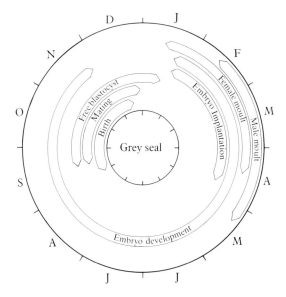

Fig. 11.12. Grey seal: life-cycle.

April. Around Britain there is a clockwise cline in the timing of pupping; September–October in the SW, October–November in west and north Scotland, and November–December at Isle of May, Farne Islands and Donna Nook [27]. Pup births reported at other times of year, particularly spring in Wales.

Large pre-breeding assemblies form at breeding grounds or nearby haul-out sites. Females come ashore to give birth, often selecting sites close to where they gave birth in previous season. Large females give birth earlier in the season than smaller females; difference in starting weight between early and late breeders may be as much as 20 kg [6]. Males come ashore as the first females pup and take up positions amongst them. No territories formed, but compete for proximity to females. They do not form a linear dominance hierarchy [5]. For large males, body size, early establishment ashore in the breeding season and high rates of weight loss are correlated.

Young: single pup produced weighing 14 kg, born in white natal coat (Fig. 11.13). Fed at 5–6 hours intervals for 16–21 days, increasing in weight at an average rate of 1.7 kg/day to reach about 45 kg at weaning [5]. Male pups larger than females at birth and grow faster (1.9 kg/day males, 1.6 kg/day females). Milk has a high fat content (54.8%) and very little lactose (0.9%); composition varies as lactation proceeds, increasing fat and decreasing water content [14]. Little maternal care apart from suckling and defence of pup against approach of other animals. Some females do not feed own pup consistently, but adopt others. Any disturbance to normal pattern appears to be disadvantageous, except to a few healthy pups which gain extra feeds.

range, but size of groups and degree of polygyny varies with nature of habitat [7]. Small beaches or caves allow space for small groups only, sandbars and tops of islands provide room for large groups to form. Sites with open access (e.g. Sable Isle, Nova Scotia) permit many males to have access to females and the sex ratio is 1 male : 2 females. Where access is restricted (e.g. by narrow gullies on North Rona) successful males can exclude others and the sex ratio is 1 male : 10 females. The degree of polygyny has marked effect on sexual success of individual males.

Timing of breeding varies in three main populations: West Atlantic, January–February; East Atlantic, September–December; Baltic, March–

Fig. 11.13. Grey seal cow and 2-day-old pup. (Photo: Sea Mammal Research Unit, NERC.)

Mating: females come into oestrus towards the end of lactation and are mated by the nearest established male [18]. Each female may be mated three times, by the same or by several males. Soon after mating, females leave the rookery, abruptly terminating the period of parental care. Some males may stay for the full duration of breeding season, up to 8 weeks. Neither males nor females feed during breeding season, but lose weight at, on average, 2.2 kg/day (males) and 3.8 kg/day (females).

Implantation delayed for 125 days; attachment of embryo occurs in early spring and gestation lasts about 214 days [24]. Occasional sexual activity in spring, and grey seals may be polyoestrous [24].

POPULATION

Females sexually mature between 3–5 years [24]; maximum recorded age of females is 46, but few live beyond 35. Males mature at about 6 years old but do not participate successfully in breeding until 10; few survive beyond 20, but maximum recorded in UK is 26 years [55]. Overall sex ratio at birth is close to unity, but sex ratio skewed towards males at start of pupping and reversed later in season [6]. Mortality of pups on beaches 14–23% [11], but may be over 40%, with topography of pupping site exerting effect on mortality rate [8]. Survival in 1st year estimated in mathematical model at 66%, up to age of maturity 93% and after

that 93.5% for females and 80% for males [36]. Grey seal numbers have increased markedly in last half century in British Isles [69]. Breeding habitat may influence the potential of populations to increase; where seals breed on narrow beaches and in caves (e.g. Wales, Cornwall and Shetland) no increase has been detected. Rate of increase varies with level of hunting or management; in undisturbed populations the rate was 7% annually (e.g. Farne Islands prior to 1972), but 3–4% where pups were hunted regularly (e.g. Orkney since 1969). Rate of increase of Scottish population between 1977 and 1984 was 4–5% annually [63].

MORTALITY

Man is the only major predator of adult grey seals, although killer whales may take seals occasionally. Off Canadian coast, great white sharks take weaned pups as they leave the rookeries. Human hunting pressure less now than in past. Causes of adult mortality not yet quantified, but diseases of the respiratory system e.g. pleurisy, pneumonia and mucous congestion, are the commonest cause of death, followed by disorders of the alimentary tract, trauma from injury and sepsis from wounds [10]. Frequent cause of death in females is disorder of the reproductive tract at or shortly after birth. Causes of death in pups better known: starvation and infections, usually initiated by failure of mother–pup bond, are most important [11, 13]. In August 1988, a viral epidemic similar or related to canine distemper and rinderpest and caused by a virus from the *Morbillivirus* genus (see Common seal) spread to British seals, and was soon detected in grey seals at the Farne Islands and on the Monach Isles. However, the evidence available at the time of writing suggests that grey seals are much less affected by the virus than common seals and show a capacity to recover from infection.

PARASITES

Recent study completed by Baker [12]. The mite *Halarachne halichoeri* found in nasal mucosa and in trachea of 36% of seals examined. The louse *Echinophthirius horridus* is found less frequently than in common seals. Gastric nematodes *Contracaecum osculatum* and *Pseudoterranova decipiens* found in 94% of stomachs examined; *Anisakis simplex* less common. Lung nematodes *Otostrongylus* sp. and *Parafilaroides* sp. were found in 57% of seals. The acanthocephalan *Corynesoma* sp. was found in the small intestine of 81% of seals examined. There is a full list of Acanthocephala, Cestoda and Trematoda [19].

Commonest bacterial pathogens are *Streptococcus* and *Corynebacterium*, but both these genera and other pathogens have a high island specificity. There is a comprehensive list of pathogens and associated diseases [11], and outbreaks of viral pneumonia are occasionally recorded [33].

Pollutants: high concentrations of mercury found in livers of grey seals in Canada [65] and off east Scotland [41], but only about 5% present as methyl mercury form, and it appears that seals may be able to demethylate mercury. Highest concentrations of organochlorines (includes PCBs, DDT and dieldrin) found in Baltic grey seals, though equally high levels found in a few individuals in UK waters. Reproductive failures and other disorders such as skull deformities may be associated with high dietary intake of organochlorines. An association has been demonstrated between high PCB levels in diet of common seals and reproductive performance [59], but no data for grey seals.

RELATIONS WITH MAN

Grey seals hunted extensively in past, perhaps resulting in numbers being kept in check. During most of 20th century, exploitation largely restricted to commercial hunting of pups for skins. Legis-lation introduced from 1914, providing close season from 1 September–31 December in Great Britain by Conservation of Seals Act, 1970 and for same period in Northern Ireland by Grey Seal Protection Act, 1932. During close season seals can be killed only under licence. Protection given in Ireland under Irish Wildlife Act.

Grey seals can be serious pests of fixed-net fisheries, particularly salmon netting stations on the east coast of Scotland. Fish may be removed from nets or seriously damaged; damage to nets now negligible due to use of man-made fibres. Levels of damage vary with season and from site to site. Spring damage level highest, as are number of seals sighted near nets, and catches lowest at this time. Levels of damage apparently unrelated to absolute numbers of seals, as damage has not increased over last 25 years while grey seal population has more than doubled. Seals also thought to attack fish outside nets, in some cases inflicting claw marks which reduce their market value. Incidence of claw damage, both in or out of nets, varies between 2.5 and 6% of catch [62]. Fixed nets for cod, lythe, saithe and hake, and long lines set for cod, are also affected by seal predation. Many attempts made to develop an effective method of seal control at nets, e.g. use of sound, poisoning with strychnine-baited fish (now illegal), but shooting is currently the only effective technique. Grey seals also cause problems at fish farms (see Common seal).

Grey seals are the definitive host to the nematode worm, *Pseudoterranova decipiens*, which passes its final larval stage in gadoid fish. Although killed by freezing or cooking, codworm reduces marketability of fish, or increases handling costs if worms have to be removed. Incidence of infestation requires presence of seals, but levels not obviously related to number of seals [54]. Another nematode found in both grey and common seals, *Anisakis simplex*, has larvae which infest herrings. Consumption of raw or lightly cured herring containing *Anisakis* larvae may result in gut lesions, leading to zoonosis known as anisakiasis. Other marine mammals, e.g. porpoises, are more important as final hosts to *Anisakis* than are either species of seal.

Seals are also thought to compete with man for fish stocks by consuming commercially valuable species of fish. Various attempts have been made to reduce seal numbers with a view to reducing damage to fisheries. Culls of pups were undertaken in Orkney in 1962, followed by setting an annual pup quota, and at the Farne Islands in 1963–65. In the late 1970s, a plan to reduce grey seal stocks in Scotland to the levels of the early 1960s, by a combination of adult and pup culls, was not effectively implemented due to protests from the environmental lobby [48]. At the Farnes, an adult cull was undertaken in 1972 and 1975 in an attempt to lessen damage by seals of fragile soil and vegetation. Management policy now directed towards keeping seals on rocky islands, away from vulnerable sites. Since the late 1970s, no licences have been issued in Britain for commercial hunting or large scale control measures.

Recent research on interactions between seals and fisheries [62] indicates that reduction in seal numbers would be unlikely to have direct effect on fish catches or levels of seal damage.

LITERATURE
[39] — general account of both species, but now rather out of date. [40] — also rather out of date. [44] — brief but comprehensive account. [4] — popular account. NERC News give annual updates on both grey and common seal numbers.

SOUND RECORDINGS
Appendix 3: A, F, J, V.

AUTHOR FOR THIS SPECIES
S.S. Anderson.

VAGRANT SEALS (Fig. 11.14)

GENUS *Phoca*

Ringed seal *Phoca hispida*

Phoca hispida Schreber, 1775: Greenland and Labrador.

DESCRIPTION
Adults grow to 140–150 cm nose to tail length, and 65–95 kg in weight; females tend to be slightly smaller than males. Very similar in shape and colouring to common seal, but perhaps generally darker. The colour is very variable, but usually a pale grey ground colour with a number of black spots, particularly on the back. Many of the spots are surrounded by ring-shaped lighter markings (hence its common name), although down the middle of the back the dark spots may be so close that they run together. The belly is silver grey.

Common seals may also occasionally have ring markings, but these are smaller than in the ringed seal.

Dentition weaker than in common seal and mandibular teeth always aligned with axis of jaw; inner side of mandible between middle post-canines concave (cf. common seal, where convex).

Ringed seals produce their pups in snow lairs from March to April. They feed on a variety of pelagic crustaceans and small fish.

DISTRIBUTION
The commonest seal in the Arctic. It is found in circumpolar Arctic coasts, wherever there is open water from near the ice edge to the Pole. Normally solitary, and rarely found in the open sea or in floating pack ice, but common in fjords and bays where the ice is firm [44]. Along Pacific Japanese coasts as far south as 35°N. Also found in the Baltic and some freshwater lakes (e.g. Lake Saimaa in Finland and Lake Ladoga in USSR).

Ringed seals do not migrate, and movements are only local. However, occasional stragglers may move south, and have been recorded from Atlantic coasts of several European countries. UK records remain rare; 1846 Norfolk coast; 1889 Lincolnshire coast; 1897 Collieston; 1901 Aberdeen; 1940 young animal Isle of Man; 1960s occasionally taken in Shetland by common seal hunters.

Harp seal *Phoca groenlandica*

Phoca groenlandica Erxleben, 1777; Greenland and Newfoundland.

DESCRIPTION
Adults grow up to 170 cm nose to tail length, and weigh about 130 kg. Sexes very similar in size. Easily recognised by the dark face and broad dark band starting on shoulders, dividing and spreading over flanks to form two roughly harp-shaped patches (hence its common name). In adult males the ground colour is a light silvery grey (almost white) and the 'harp' and face to just behind the eyes nearly black; in females the face and 'harp' are paler and may be broken into spots. There is considerable change in coat colour as the animal grows older; juvenile animals (and some adults) are covered with dark spots or blotches.

Harp seals breed in the spring on ice floes in the pack. They feed on pelagic crustaceans such as *Thysanoessa* sp. and *Themisto* sp., and fish, notably capelin (*Mallotus* sp.).

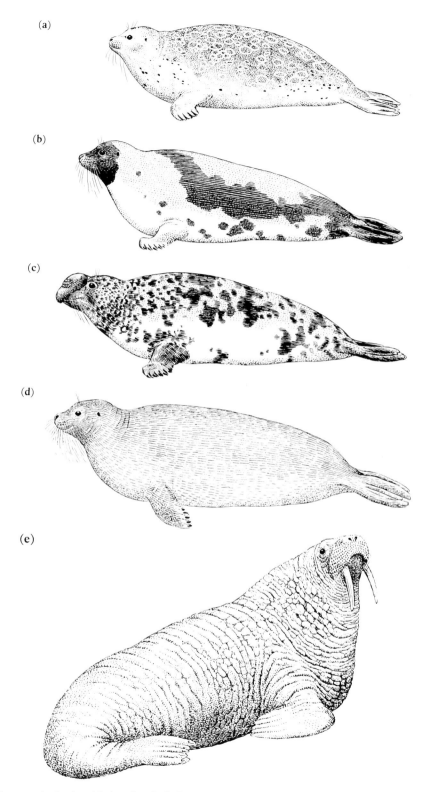

(a)

(b)

(c)

(d)

(e)

Fig. 11.14. Vagrant pinnipedes: (a) ringed seal; (b) harp seal; (c) hooded seal; (d) bearded seal; (e) walrus. Note that these are all adults — young animals are less distinctive. Not to the same scale.

DISTRIBUTION

A highly migratory and gregarious species, found in the open sea of the Arctic Atlantic; nowhere is it resident throughout the year. Its range extends north to the far open waters of the Arctic in summer and early autumn, the animals coming south in late autumn and winter in time for the spring breeding. While on migration, the seals leap and jump out of the water like dolphins [44].

There are three breeding regions: (i) off the NE coast of Newfoundland and in the Gulf of St Lawrence; (ii) in the Greenland Sea around Jan Mayen; (iii) in the White Sea. In the summer, after breeding, seals from the first region move to the west Greenland coast and the Canadian eastern Arctic, those from Jan Mayen move to the east Greenland coast and the seas west of Svalbard, and those in the White Sea move to around Novaya Zemlya. Only rarely do harp seals visit the north coast of Iceland.

Occasionally, harp seals extend their range further south in the N North Sea, occurring in large numbers along the Norwegian coasts. In such years, sightings from British coasts are more frequent. Thirty-one records since about 1800 from UK, including: 1868 one killed Lancashire; 1873 one caught in net, Argyll; 1899 two caught in net, Ayrshire; 1902 Teignmouth, Devon; 1903 Firth of Forth; 1987 one alive and one dead Shetland; 1987 adult male River Humber; 1988 male dead in Wash near Boston, Lincolnshire; 1988 one very sick near Medway, Kent; 1988 one seen off Flamborough Head, Yorkshire. One possible record from County Galway, Eire.

GENUS *Erignathus*

Bearded seal *Erignathus barbatus*

Phoca barbata Erxleben, 1777; North Atlantic.

DESCRIPTION

Adults of both sexes about 220−230 cm nose to tail length, and weight 235−260 kg; females slightly smaller than males. For their size, they have a disproportionately small head. Most characteristic feature is the great profusion of long, very sensitive, glistening white mystacial vibrissae, which make the animal recognisable from some distance. The vibrissae are unlike those of other British phocids in being straight and not beaded; they also curl, sometimes forming tight spirals at the tips, particularly when dry [44]. The 3rd digit on the fore flipper slightly longer than the others, giving a square-ended appearance to the flipper. There are four nipples (two in all other phocids except monk seals).

Colour the same for both sexes and not distinctive; usually grey ground colour, slightly darker down the mid-line, with a brownish or reddish tinge on the head, and paler grey ventrally.

Dentition very weak; teeth in adults loose-rooted and may be worn down or entirely missing. Post-canines widely spaced.

Bearded seals breed on ice-floes in April and May. They feed on bottom-living organisms, particularly molluscs.

DISTRIBUTION

Circumpolar in distribution, and found in shallow waters all along the European, Asiatic and N American coasts of the Arctic, and on all the associated islands. Not migratory, but a few animals reach the Gulf of St Lawrence and even as far south as Cape Cod. Occasional stragglers appear on northern Norwegian coasts.

In British waters few records: 1977 two records from Shetland; 1981 Mid Yell, Shetland; 1986 Ronas Voe, Shetland; 1987 two records from Shetland, one from Orkney (could be the same animal as seen in Shetland 2 days earlier); 1988 one in Orkney, two in Shetland.

GENUS *Cystophora*

Hooded seal *Cystophora cristata*

Phoca cristata Erxleben, 1777; S Greenland and Newfoundland.

DESCRIPTION

Adult males reach 220−250 cm and weigh about 400 kg, females 220 cm and 350 kg. Most conspicuous feature is the presence in adult male of an enlargement of the nasal cavity to form an inflatable crest or hood on top of the head. This starts to develop when male about 4 years old, and grows with age and increasing body size. When not inflated, the tip of the hood hangs down in front of the mouth, but when inflated forms a high cushion on top of the head, which may be twice the size of a football [44].

Ground colour grey, but lighter on the sides and belly. Many dark patches of irregular size scattered over body; these are much smaller on the neck and abdomen. Females less strongly marked than males.

Dentition distinguishable from all other seals which might be found in British waters by presence of only one incisor on each side of the lower jaw. Post-canines peg-like and widely spaced.

Pups born in March–April, when widely scattered family groups found on drifting ice floes. Pup coat slate grey on back, paler beneath. Hooded seals feed on a variety of fish and molluscs.

DISTRIBUTION

A solitary seal found in deep waters of the Arctic regions of the Atlantic on drifting ice. Occur mainly from Bear Island and Spitsbergen, to Jan Mayen, Iceland, Denmark Strait, Greenland, the east coast of Baffin Island and Labrador.

Occasional stragglers reach the British Isles: 1847 one killed River Orwell, Suffolk; 1872 one killed St Andrews, Fife; 1873 one caught Frodsham, Cheshire; 1890 one shot and another seen Sanday, Orkney; 1891 uncertain record from Benbecula, Hebrides; 1903 Elgin, mouth of River Lossie; 1980 pup seen Haaf Gruney, Shetland; 1989 Felixstowe, pup caught.

FAMILY ODOBENIDAE

GENUS *Odobenus*

Walrus *Odobenus rosmarus*

Phoca rosmarus Linnaeus, 1758; Arctic Ocean.

DESCRIPTION

One of the largest pinnipeds, second only in size to the elephant seals. Adult males 365 cm nose to tail and weigh up to 1270 kg, females 300 cm and 850 kg. Appearance distinctive; head truncated and appears rather small for the large body; large array of stiff whiskers. Skin rough, wrinkled and nearly naked in old animals but covered with short brown hair in young ones. Colour greyish or reddish. Dentition unique. Large tusks (upper canines) present in both sexes, but more slender in females. Remaining teeth (upper: incisor 3 and 3 post-canines; lower: canine and 3 post-canines) all reduced to flattened pads of dentine.

Young born in May, usually on sea-ice. Food consists mainly of clams, which are excavated from the sea-bottom at depths of up to 75 m. Some walruses adopt a habit of feeding on ringed and young hooded seals.

DISTRIBUTION

Found in shallow water around Arctic coasts. Have a preference for moving pack ice in areas where the sea is about 80–100 m deep. If no ice available, will haul out on small rocky islands. Atlantic and Pacific walruses each occur in two geographically isolated groups. Walruses still occasionally occur off Iceland, and there are 31 records on the Norwegian coast between 1900 and 1967 [25]. Occasionally found as far south as Germany, the Netherlands and Belgium.

Between 1815 and 1954, 27 records of walruses seen or killed in British waters, all of them off the Scottish coasts, except one shot in the Severn in 1839 and one seen in the River Shannon, Ireland in 1897 [44]. Since 1954 seven records; 1981 animals seen in Shetland, Arran and the Wash area; 1984 Pentland Firth; 1986 two in Shetland, one in Orkney.

AUTHOR FOR THESE SPECIES

S. Harris, with recent records from the Sea Mammal Research Unit.

REFERENCES

1 Author's data.
2 Allen S.G. (1985) Mating behavior in the harbour seal. *Marine Mammal Science* 1:84–7.
3 Anderson S.S. (1978) Day and night activity of grey seal bulls. *Mammal Review* 8:43–6.
4 Anderson S. (1988) *The grey seal.* Aylesbury: Shire Publications 24 pp.
5 Anderson S.S. & Fedak M.A. (1985) Grey seal males: energetic and behavioural links between size and sexual success. *Animal Behaviour* 33:829–38.
6 Anderson S.S. & Fedak M.A. (1987). Grey seal, *Halichoerus grypus*, energetics: females invest more in male offspring. *Journal of Zoology* 211:667–79.
7 Anderson S.S. & Harwood J. (1985) Time budgets and topography: how energy reserves and terrain determine the breeding behaviour of grey seals. *Animal Behaviour* 33:1343–8.
8 Anderson S.S. *et al.* (1979) Mortality in grey seal pups: incidence and causes. *Journal of Zoology* 189: 407–17.
9 Arnason U. (1974) Comparative chromosome studies

in Pinnipedia. *Hereditas* **76**:179–226.

10 Baker J.R. (1980) The pathology of the grey seal (*Halichoerus grypus*) II. Juveniles and adults. *British Veterinary Journal* **136**:443–7.

11 Baker J.R. (1984) Mortality and morbidity in grey seal pups (*Halichoerus grypus*). Studies on its causes, effects of environment, the nature and sources of infectious agents and the immunological status of pups. *Journal of Zoology* **203**:23–48.

12 Baker J.R. (1987) Causes of mortality and morbidity in wild juvenile and adult grey seals (*Halichoerus grypus*). *British Veterinary Journal* **143**:203–20.

13 Baker J.R. *et al.* (1980) The pathology of the grey seal (*Halichoerus grypus*) I. Pups. *British Veterinary Journal* **136**:401–12.

14 Baker J.R. (in press) Grey seal (*Halichoerus grypus*) milk composition and its variation over lactation. *British Veterinary Journal.*

15 Bigg M.A. (1969) The harbour seal in British Columbia. *Bulletin Fisheries Research Board of Canada* **172**: 1–33.

16 Bigg M.A. (1973) Adaptations in the breeding of the harbour seal *Phoca vitulina*. *Journal of Reproduction and Fertility* (Suppl.) **19**:131–42.

17 Bigg M.A. (1981) Harbour seal *Phoca vitulina* Linnaeus, 1758 and *Phoca largha* Pallas, 1811. In Ridgway S.H. & Harrison R.J. eds. *Handbook of marine mammals, vol. 2: seals*. London: Academic Press pp. 1–27.

18 Boness D.J. & James H. (1979) Reproductive behaviour of the grey seal (*Halichoerus grypus*) on Sable Island, Nova Scotia. *Journal of Zoology* **188**:477–500.

19 Bonner W.N. (1972) The grey seal and common seal in European waters. *Oceanography and Marine Biology Annual Review* **10**:461–507.

20 Bonner W.N. (1979) Harbour (common) seal. *Food and Agriculture Organisation Fisheries Series* **5**(2): 58–62.

20 Bonner W.N. (1990) *The natural history of seals.*
A London: Christopher Helm, 196 pp.

21 Bonner W.N. & Witthames S.R. (1974) Dispersal of common seals (*Phoca vitulina*), tagged in the Wash, East Anglia. *Journal of Zoology* **174**:528–31.

22 Boulva J. (1971) Observations on a colony of whelping harbour seals, *Phoca vitulina concolor*, on Sable Island, Nova Scotia. *Journal of the Fisheries Research Board of Canada* **28**:755–9.

23 Boulva J. & McLaren I.A. (1979) Biology of the harbour seal, *Phoca vitulina*, in eastern Canada. *Bulletin Fisheries Research Board of Canada* **200**:1–24.

24 Boyd I.L. (1982) *Reproduction of grey seals with reference to factors influencing fertility*. PhD. thesis, University of Cambridge.

25 Brun E. *et al.* (1968) Hvalross, *Odobenus rosmarus*, på norskekysten. *Fauna* **21**:7–20.

26 Burns J.J. & Fay F.H. (1970) Comparative morphology of the skull of the ribbon seal, *Histriophoca fasciata*, with remarks on systematics of Phocidae. *Journal of Zoology* **161**:363–94.

27 Coulson J.C. (1981) A study of the factors influencing the timing of breeding in the grey seal *Halichoerus grypus*. *Journal of Zoology* **194**:553–71.

28 Dietz R. & Heide-Jorgensen M-P. (1982) *A new breeding attempt of grey seals* (Halichoerus grypus) *in the Kattegat*. International Council for the Exploration of the Sea unpubl. report CM 1982/N: 12 (mimeo).

29 Drescher H.E. (1978) Hautkrankheiten beim Seehund, *Phoca vitulina* Linne, 1758, in der Nordsee. *Säugetierkundliche Mitteilungen* **26**:50–9.

30 Dunbar M.J. (1949) The Pinnipedia of the arctic and subarctic. *Bulletin Fisheries Research Board of Canada* **85**:1–22.

31 Eschrict D.F. (1866) On the species of the genus *Orca* inhabiting the North Sea. In Flower W.H. ed. *Recent Memoirs on the Cetacea*. London: Ray Society pp. 151–88.

32 Fisher H.D. (1954) Delayed implantation in the harbour seal, *Phoca vitulina* L. *Nature, London* **173**: 879–80.

33 Gallacher J.B. & Waters W.E. (1964) Pneumonia in grey seal pups at St Kilda. *Proceedings of the Zoological Society of London* **142**:177–80.

34 Harrison R.J. (1960) Reproduction and reproductive organs in common seals (*Phoca vitulina*) in the Wash, East Anglia. *Mammalia* **24**:372–85.

35 Harrison R.J. & Tomlinson J.D.W. (1960) Normal and experimental diving in the common seal (*Phoca vitulina*). *Mammalia* **24**:386–99.

36 Harwood J. & Prime J.H. (1978) Some factors affecting the size of British grey seal populations. *Journal of Applied Ecology* **15**:401–11.

37 Harwood J. *et al.* (1976) Branded grey seals (*Halichoerus grypus*) at the Monach Isles, Outer Hebrides. *Journal of Zoology* **180**:506–8.

38 Havinga B. (1933) Der Seehund (*Phoca vitulina*) in den Holländischen Gewässern. *Tijdschrift der Nederlandsche dierkundige vereeniging* **3**:79–111.

39 Hewer H.R. (1974) *British seals*. London: Collins 256 pp.

40 Hickling G. (1962) *Grey seals and the Farne Islands*. London: Routledge & Kegan Paul 180 pp.

41 Holden A.V. (1975) The accumulation of oceanic contaminants in marine mammals. *Rapport et procès-verbaux des réunions. Conseil permanent international pour l'exploration de la mer* **169**:353–61.

42 Jamieson G.S. & Fisher H.D. (1972) The pinniped eye: a review. In Harrison R.J. ed. *Functional anatomy of marine mammals*, vol. 1. London: Academic Press pp. 245–61.

43 King J.E. (1972) Observations on phocid skulls. In Harrison R.J. ed. *Functional anatomy of marine mammals*, vol. 1. London: Academic Press pp. 81–115.

44 King J.E. (1983) *Seals of the world*. London: British Museum (Natural History) and Oxford: University Press 240 pp.

45 Knudtson P.M. (1977) Observations on the breeding behavior of the harbor seal in Humboldt Bay, California. *California Fish and Game* **63**:66–70.

46 Kolb P.M. & Norris K.S. (1982) A harbor seal, *Phoca vitulina richardsi*, taken from a sablefish trap.

California Fish and Game **68**:123−4.

47 Krieber M. & Barette C. (1984) Aggregation behaviour of harbour seals at Forillon National Park, Canada. *Journal of Animal Ecology* **53**:913−28.

48 Lister-Kaye J. (1979) *Seal cull: the grey seal controversy.* London: Penguin Books 174 pp.

49 Mansfield A.W. & Beck B. (1977) The grey seal in eastern Canada. Environment Canada, *Fisheries and Marine Service, Technical Report* **704**:1−81.

50 Møhl B. (1968) Auditory sensitivity of the common seal in air and water. *Journal of Auditory Research* **8**:27−38.

51 NERC (1985) Seal stocks in Great Britain: surveys conducted in 1983 and 1984. *NERC Newsjournal* **3**(8):12−13.

52 NERC (1987) Seal stocks in Great Britain: surveys conducted in 1985. *NERC News* **1**:11−13.

53 Osterhaus A.D.M.E. (1988) Seal death. *Nature* **334**:301−2.

54 Parrish B.P. & Shearer W.M. (1977) *Effects of seals on fisheries.* International Council for the Exploration of the Sea unpubl. report CM 1977/M: 14 (mimeo).

55 Platt N.E. *et al.* (1975) The age of the grey seal at the Farne Islands. *Transactions of the Natural History Society of Northumberland, Durham and Newcastle-upon-Tyne* **42**(4):99−106.

56 Rae B.B. (1968) The food of seals in Scottish waters. *Marine Research* **2**:1−23.

57 Rae B.B. (1973) Further observations on the food of seals. *Journal of Zoology* **169**:287−97.

58 Reijnders P.J.H. (1978) Recruitment in the harbour seal (*Phoca vitulina*) population in the Dutch Wadden Sea. *Netherlands Journal of Sea Research* **12**:164−79.

59 Reijnders P.J.H. (1986) Reproductive failure in common seals feeding on fish from polluted coastal waters. *Nature* **324**:456−7.

59 Riedman M. (1990) *The pinnipeds: seals, sea lions and*
A *walruses.* Berkley: University of California Press, 439 pp.

60 Ross A. (1988) *Controlling nature's predators on fish farms.* Ross-on-Wye: Marine Conservation Society 96 pp.

61 Scheffer V.B. (1958) *Seals, sea lions and walruses.* Stanford: University Press 179 pp.

62 Sea Mammal Research Unit (1984) *Interactions between grey seals and fisheries.* Contract report for Department of Agriculture and Fisheries for Scotland 241 pp.

63 Sea Mammal Research Unit (1985) *The impact of grey and common seals on North Sea resources.* Final report to Commission of the European Community, Contract No. ENV 665 UK(H) 152 pp.

64 Sea Mammal Research Unit, unpublished.

65 Sergeant D.E. & Armstrong F.A.J. (1973) Mercury in seals from eastern Canada. *Journal of the Fisheries Research Board of Canada* **30**:843−6.

66 Slater L.M. & Markowitz H. (1983) Spring population trends in *Phoca vitulina richardsi* in two central California coastal areas. *California Fish and Game* **69**:217−26.

67 Stutz S.S. (1967) Pelage patterns and population distributions in the Pacific harbour seal (*Phoca vitulina richardsi*). *Journal of the Fisheries Research Board of Canada* **24**:451−5.

68 Sullivan R.M. (1982) Agonistic behavior and dominance relationships in the harbor seal, *Phoca vitulina*. *Journal of Mammalogy* **63**:554−69.

69 Summers C.F. (1978) Trends in the size of British grey seal populations. *Journal of Applied Ecology* **15**: 395−400.

70 Summers C.F. (1979) *The scientific background to seal stock management in Great Britain.* Swindon: NERC Publications Series C, **21**:14 pp.

71 Summers C.F. & Mountford M.D. (1975) Counting the common seal. *Nature* **253**:670−1.

72 Summers C.F. *et al.* (1975) Grey seal (*Halichoerus grypus*) pup production at North Rona: a study of birth and survival statistics collected in 1972. *Journal of Zoology* **175**:439−51.

73 Summers C.F. *et al.* (1980) An assessment of the status of the common seal *Phoca vitulina vitulina* in Ireland. *Biological Conservation* **17**:115−23.

74 Thompson P.M. (1987) *The effect of seasonal changes in behaviour on the distribution and abundance of common seals,* Phoca vitulina, *in Orkney.* PhD. thesis, University of Aberdeen.

75 Thompson P. (1988) Timing of mating in the common seal (*Phoca vitulina*). *Mammal Review* **18**:105−12.

76 Thompson P.M. (1989) Seasonal changes in the distribution and composition of common seal (*Phoca vitulina*) haul-out groups. *Journal of Zoology* **27**:281−94.

77 Thompson P.M. & Rothery P. (1987) Age and sex difference in the timing of moult in the common seal, *Phoca vitulina*. *Journal of Zoology* **212**:597−603.

78 Van Wieren S.E. (1981) *Broedbiologie van de gewone zeehond* Phoca vitulina *in het Nederlandse Waddengebied.* Texel: Rijksinstitut voor Natuurbeheer.

79 Vaughan R.W. (1978) A study of common seals in the Wash. *Mammal Review* **8**:25−34.

80 Venables U.M. & Venables L.S.V. (1955) Observations on a breeding colony of the seal *Phoca vitulina* in Shetland. *Proceedings of the Zoological Society of London* **125**:521−32.

81 Venables U.M. & Venables L.S.V. (1957) Mating behaviour of the seal *Phoca vitulina* in Shetland. *Proceedings of the Zoological Society of London* **128**: 387−96.

82 Walls G.L. (1942) *The vertebrate eye and its adaptive radiation.* Bloomfield Hills, Michigan: Cranbrook Institute of Science, Bulletin 19, 785 pp.

83 Williamson G.R. (1988) Seals in Loch Ness. *Scientific Reports of the Whales Research Institute* **39**:151−7.

84 Wilson S. (1974) Juvenile play of the common seal *Phoca vitulina vitulina* with comparative notes on the grey seal *Halichoerus grypus. Behaviour* **48**:37−60.

85 Wynn-Edwards V.C. (1954) Field identification of the common and grey seals. *Scottish Naturalist* **66**:192.

Chapter 12 / Ungulates:
Orders Perissodactyla
and Artiodactyla

The term 'ungulate' includes two orders of relatively large mammals which have hooves rather than claws, are capable of rapid locomotion and have a herbivorous diet.

ORDER PERISSODACTYLA (THE 'ODD-TOED UNGULATES')

This is a small order of mammals, which includes the horses, asses, zebras, rhinoceroses and tapirs. There are presently no wild representatives in the British Isles but wild horses were present in Britain during the last glaciation and as late as the Boreal phase of the post-glacial period (7000–10000 bp); there is no good evidence that they survived beyond that time. Domesticated horses have been present since the Neolithic period (5000 bp). There are no truly feral horses in Britain, but there are a number of free-ranging populations.

FAMILY EQUIDAE

Only one genus survives.

GENUS *Equus*

Seven species survive, and all have the central digit of each foot enlarged to form a hoof. In addition to the domestic horse (*E. caballus*), there is *E. ferus*, including Przewalski's wild horse of Mongolia, *E. africanus* and *E. hemionus*, the African and Asian wild asses, and *E. burchelli*, the common zebra of East Africa, *E. zebra*, the mountain zebra of SW Africa, and *E. grevyi*, Grevy's zebra of NE Africa. Dentition variable; males have canines in both jaws, but canines are absent in females. Both sexes may have variable 3 or 4 premolars in upper jaw; thus dental formula in males 3.1.3–4.3/3.1.3.3, and in females 3.0.3–4.3/3.0.3.3.

Horse *Equus caballus*

Male — stallion; female — mare; young — foal.

STATUS
Wild horses, *Equus ferus* (p. 573), were present in Britain during the last glaciation. Domestic horses have been present since the Neolithic. Within Britain and Ireland there still exist a number of free-ranging populations of relatively unimproved stock. None of these are however truly feral and self-sustaining and all are subjected to a greater or lesser degree of management.

SIGN

Dung: deposited in piles formed of discrete balls *c.* 5–7 cm diameter and dark brown in colour. When weathered can be seen to be extremely fibrous in texture. Free-ranging populations often dung in distinct sites away from preferred feeding areas, establishing distinct latrines. On favoured grasslands, a clear mosaic may become established of alternating patches of closely cropped sward devoid of any dung and ungrazed latrine patches with an abundance of dung and taller, ranker vegetation [117, 277]. Latrine sites are only grazed by horses when feed elsewhere becomes very scarce. Both grazing and latrine areas are traditional and maintained from year to year; as a result of differences in nutrient availability and grazing pressure pronounced vegetational differences develop.

Grazing: unlike other free-ranging ungulates, horses have both upper and lower incisors, and so may crop a sward more closely than many ruminant grazers. This results in a dominance of dwarf, rosette-forming or prostrate-growing species in the sward, which is also characteristically rather species-poor. Vegetational changes in grasslands and other communities in the New Forest have been described [277].

486

DESCRIPTION

All free-ranging populations are essentially of similar type: bay or dark brown ponies with thick coats and dark manes and tails, frequently lighter in colour on the belly and around the muzzle. They tend to be stockily built with short necks and rather heavy heads; ears are small and erect.

Pelage and moult: all have extremely heavy coats offering some protection from the weather. The coat grows in two phases within the year, with a thick insulatory underfur growing into the summer coat to provide a distinct winter pelage. Efficiency of insulation is remarkable: in winter ponies may be seen 'thatched' with snow because insufficient body heat is lost to melt it. It is claimed that the pattern of guard hairs in the coat maximises surface-drainage and dispersal of water away from parts of the body vulnerable to chilling: thus tail, mane, forelock and beard and a special fan of short hairs near the root of the tail all show water shedding specialisations [130].

Winter coat is shed in April or May (depending on local conditions), and regrows into the summer coat from late autumn.

Digestive system: unlike all artiodactyls the horse is monogastric and lacks the four chambered stomach of the ruminant. Instead the caecum is greatly enlarged to house the symbiotic micro-organisms required for the breakdown of cellulose.

Chromosomes: $2n = 32$ in all populations.

RELATIONSHIPS

All domestic horses are derived from the wild horse, *Equus ferus*, of which the Przewalski horse in central Asia represents the sole surviving population, or at least the minimally altered feral form.

MEASUREMENTS

Size dependent on breeding history. 'Pure-bred' Exmoors stand *c*. 127 cm at the withers (range 117–137), New Foresters up to 147 cm. Most breeds between 115–150 cm.

VARIATION

Differences in origin and extensive later attempts at breed improvement by introduction of, variously, throughbred, Hackney, carthorse, Arab and cob blood have led to extensive variation both within and between populations. Major groups can

be recognised as: Fell ponies (Lake District, Northumberland), dark colours, dark manes and tails, height up to *c*. 125–130 cm; Dartmoor ponies, bay, black or brown, height to 125 cm; Exmoor ponies, bay or dark brown with black points and pronouncedly mealy muzzle, *c*. 127 cm; Welsh ponies, dark colours, variable heights dependent on breeding history; New Forest ponies, very variable in both height and colour due to extensive 'mongrelisation' over the years. Scottish Highland ponies are now free-ranging only on the Western Isles; these populations tend to be smaller than the mainland (Garron) type: height to 134 cm, colour dun, with a dorsal stripe, usually black points and a silver mane and tail.

DISTRIBUTION

Free-ranging populations are found in the New Forest (Hampshire), Dartmoor and Exmoor (Devon), the Gower peninsula in south Wales, the Lake District, Northumberland, Shetland, certain Hebridean islands and in western Ireland.

HISTORY

It is frequently claimed that some or all of these semi-wild ponies are direct descendants of indigenous wild horses or early domestic breeds, but there is little evidence to support this and some are certainly of much more recent origin. Original Dartmoor and Exmoor stocks and those in the New Forest may, however, have more claim to ancient lineage. In a recent re-analysis of the history of domestication of the horse which emphasised behavioural relationships between the breeds the Exmoor (together with the Polish konik and Przewalski's horse) was considered a relatively direct descendant of a wild species evident in the archaeological record from 100 000 bp. Other authors also maintained that the Exmoor, and other similar 'ancestral moorland types' (Welsh mountain ponies, Hebridean ponies) are of ancient and common lineage [130, 333, 334]. Few populations however remained 'pure'. Successive introductions over the years in attempts to 'improve' the commercial quality of the breeds have resulted almost universally in a completely mongrel stock [129, 304]; other populations are, in any case, of more recent origin.

HABITAT

All British populations of free-ranging ponies occur on what is essentially marginal habitat: open moorland and rough grassland, with usually limited access to woodland cover. Actual pattern of habitat use is clearly dictated to a large degree by relative availability of different habitat types in different areas. Analysis of habitat preference by New Forest ponies [269] shows strong positive preference for grasslands throughout the year, a weak preference for woodlands and other cover communities — more evident, as might be expected, during winter months — and strong avoidance of heathland areas. Actual pattern of habitat use in New Forest reflects these preferences. Despite the low availability of favoured grasslands (which comprise less than 7% of the area available to them) the ponies spend more than 50% of their time on these communities throughout the year. Woodlands and other shelter communities are used primarily at night with more open communities occupied during the daylight: in summer there is a pronounced shift in habitat occupance at dusk as animals leave the open grasslands, where they have spent the day grazing, and seek the shelter of woodland or gorsebrake. Such a shift is less obvious during winter months when, with a greater need for shelter, the animals make more use of the cover communities at all times and emerge onto the more open communities of the Forest rather less willingly [269, 277].

SOCIAL ORGANISATION AND BEHAVIOUR

Social structure: observed social structure often far from natural, being grossly distorted by management. Studies of free-living horses elsewhere, primarily in the USA [23, 122, 360] suggest that, as in truly wild equids, the normal social 'unit' is a stallion-maintained harem of mares and sub-adults, maintained throughout the year [23, 122, 360]. Stallions are aggressively territorial and defend not only their group of mares, but also an exclusive home range [122]. Such groups are observed in many British populations although they do not always appear strictly territorial and often occupy (at least for part of the year) overlapping home ranges. However, in other areas (such as the New Forest), where populations are more closely managed, stallions may be removed from the free grazing over the winter months and only returned to free range during the summer. Under these circumstances the females develop a matriarchal social organisation of their own, with formation of permanent groups of adult mares and their followers [353]. A stallion may join up with such

a group over the summer months, but he plays little role in social structuring. The groups are not true harems and the social order is essentially matriarchal.

Group size: in those populations where harem groups are maintained, these are usually encountered as a single adult stallion with from eight to 18 mares and their offspring. Male offspring older than 2 years or so are usually excluded from the group, and female offspring too usually appear to leave the groups when they reach breeding age, to attach themselves to the harem of some other stallion.

In matriarchal groups, such as those in the New Forest, the unit most commonly observed is that of an adult mare with her offspring of the current and possibly previous year. Larger groups may be formed as associations of these basic units, but both the size and degree of persistence of these social groups varies [277, 353].

Home range little studied in Britain although extensive literature from North America, e.g. [122]. Two harem groups of Exmoor ponies had range sizes from 240–290 hectares but most activity was restricted to one area of only 45–60 hectares [129]. In the New Forest, range sizes of 125 and 140 hectares are reported for two stallion-led groups [267]; ranges of all-female units tend to be larger [277]. The size of the range seems determined by four major factors: the need to include an area of good grazing, an area for shelter, supplies of fresh water and a 'shade' (see below). Where vegetation communities occur in relatively large, homogeneous blocks (the environment is 'coarse-grained') these components of the range may be widely separated and ranges are, in consequence, much larger. Where the vegetation mosaic is of finer grain, home ranges are the more typical 100 hectares or less. Range size is also often reduced over the winter months, when ponies range less widely for forage and water is more readily available.

Social behaviour: ponies on free range are essentially group-living animals and as such display a number of behaviours designed to maintain cohesiveness of the social group. A clear dominance hierarchy is apparent amongst mares both in mare-only and in harem groups; position seems determined primarily by age [95, 134, 353]. Group-maintaining interactions are common, with group members frequently nuzzling each other or mutually grooming. Dominant females, and stallions in harem groups frequently 'cover' the dung and urine of other group members.

Aggressive interactions are relatively rare within groups, although they are more commonly displayed to individuals of other social units. Earthreats and head-threats (a movement of head towards the opponent with ears laid back) are the common postures of aggression. Teeth may be bared, and mares not infrequently bite at each other. If these displays prove ineffective a mare may turn and kick out at an opponent with hind legs. Territorial stallions show far more overt aggression; although preliminary displays are similar to those used by mares, stallions more frequently escalate to actual combat, biting at each others necks and withers, rearing onto hind legs and striking with one or both forefeet.

One further curiosity of group behaviour is 'shading' [353], when individual animals and even separate social groups come together and stand inactive in large congregations (in the New Forest commonly of 20–30 animals, occasionally up to 100). The behaviour is particularly common in mid to late summer, and the shade sites are traditional (both constant from day to day and maintained from year to year). While shading, animals stand close together and remain largely inactive, merely whisking their tails or occasionally shifting position. Such shades may be maintained for up to 6 hours. The term 'shade' is in fact a misnomer since the animals do not necessarily seek shelter from the sun, and many sites are in exposed locations; the function of the behaviour is uncertain but is believed to be an adaptation to minimise the attacks of biting insects [111].

FEEDING
Ponies are preferential grazers. Both dentition and gut physiology would suggest that they should be relatively unselective bulk-feeders. Diet has been studied in detail in two of the British populations [130, 277, 280], and supports this expectation (Fig. 12.1). There is, however, marked seasonal variation as availability of grass declines during the hot dry months of summer and during winter when the animals must compensate by increasing their intake of other forages. Almost identical changes, with increased relative emphasis of exactly the same foodstuffs at different times of year, are recorded independently for both New Forest and Exmoor

ponies. Thus in summer > 80% of the diet is made up of grass. (New Forest ponies make extensive use of purple moor-grass, *Molinia caerulea*, at this time, and in the drier months when grass production declines they feed more extensively in bogs and wetter heathlands, increasing their intake of wetland species.) As availability of grasses declines over the autumn its contribution in the diet falls to *c.* 50%; the animals compensate by increasing their intake of gorse and tree leaves. The proportion of moss in the diet also increases, and heather, which is avoided during summer, is also regularly recorded in winter. This flexibility in diet appears to be highly adaptive to changing conditions; New Forest ponies have been shown to be selecting those forages with the highest content of digestible nitrogen [277, 280].

However, most populations are susceptible to some management and in winter the diet is often supplemented with artificial feeding of hay, straw or roots.

BREEDING
Males become sexually active at 2–3 years old, but do not usually win dominance over a harem until much later. Females are receptive from about 2 years but do not necessarily breed in that year, nor do adult mares necessarily breed in every successive season; most breed 2 years in every 3. Females come into oestrus at any time from May to October, but the majority of matings are in early summer. At this period, the stallion is even more assiduous at maintaining his harem and his territory, continuously circling his mares, rounding up stragglers and herding them back to the centre of his domain. Attempted theft of oestrus mares by other stallions is, however, not uncommon, and it is at this time that most serious fights occur. Gestation period is 11 months (329–345 days) and foals may be born any time between late April and September; unless removed from their mothers by human intervention they usually continue to suckle until the following spring.

POPULATION
Both size and structure of populations of free-ranging horses in Britain are controlled by man; for example, the majority of stallions are removed from the New Forest over winter and returned to free range only between May and September. This affects not only social organisation but also the sex structure of the population. In much the

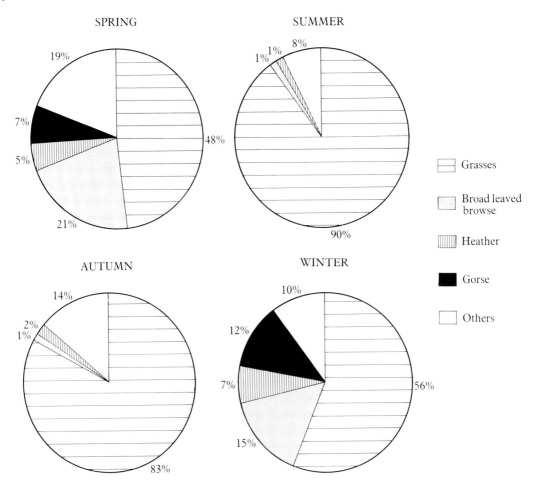

Fig. 12.1. New Forest pony diets; percentage contributions to diet.

same way, the natural age-structure is realised in few pony populations: since many, if not most, populations are commercially managed, foals or yearlings are commonly removed each autumn, for sale, and the age structure of the residual population thus grossly distorted. Finally, old animals are commonly shot or removed from common grazing. Most mares breed only 2 years out of every 3; mortality is generally low, although severe winters may occasionally cause severe losses of both adults and juveniles. In many populations (New Forest, Exmoor, Dartmoor, Gower) road accidents constitute a significant cause of death.

PARASITES

Free-ranging horse populations are susceptible to the same range of parasites and diseases as confined domestic horses. Detailed information is available only within the New Forest. Infestations by warble fly (*Hypoderma* spp.) are now fairly rare, although were once fairly common. New Forest fly (*Hippobosca equina*), locally called Crab fly or Runabout, very prevalent in the dock or between the legs; tolerated by Forest ponies but a cause of anguish to horses new to the area; also found on Dartmoor. The dipteran flies *Gasterophilus* spp. may also be common. The sucking louse *Haematopinus asini* and the biting louse *Werneckiella equi* have been recorded. Helminth parasites recorded from New Forest ponies include the following: *Taenia anoplocephalia* common and sometimes heavy infestations, hydatid cysts occasionally prevalent in livers (fox is principal host); *Ascaris equorum*, heavy infestations in foals and yearlings; *Oxyuri equi* common but infestation rarely heavy. *Strongylus, Vulgarus, Equinus* and *Edentatus* spp. all common and heavy infestations may prove fatal when grazing poor.

LITERATURE

There are few scientific reviews covering all free-range populations. Social organisation in New Forest — [277, 353] and Exmoor — [129, 130]. Food and feeding behaviour in New Forest — [269, 277] and Exmoor — [130].

AUTHOR FOR THIS SPECIES
R.J. Putman.

ORDER ARTIODACTYLA
THE 'EVEN-TOED UNGULATES'

This order includes the great majority of the large herbivorous mammals, amounting to nearly 190 species. They are predominantly terrestrial and cursorial, with long slender legs. The main common feature is the structure of the feet; the 2nd and 3rd digits are equally developed, with the axis of the leg passing between them, and the remaining digits are reduced to a variable degree. In other respects they are very diverse, occupying a wide range of habitats on all continents except Australasia and Antarctica. Three suborders are recognised: Suiformes, containing the pigs, peccaries and hippopotamuses; Tylopoda, containing the camels and llamas; and Ruminantia, containing the great majority of species, namely the giraffes, deer, cattle, antelopes, etc. Only the last suborder is now represented, but wild boar (Suiformes) were once present in Britain (p. 573).

SUBORDER RUMINANTIA
(RUMINANTS)

The ruminants are characterised especially by the presence of a complex four-chambered stomach and the habit of ruminating or chewing the cud. Food, usually herbage, is stored in the 1st chamber of the stomach, the rumen, undergoes bacterial decomposition in the 2nd chamber, the reticulum, is then regurgitated for further mastication before being again swallowed and passing into the 3rd chamber, the omasum, and finally into the 4th or true stomach, the abomasum, where acid digestion begins. The dentition is also specialised with no upper incisors, the food being cropped by the lower incisors (apparently four pairs since the lower canines are incisiform) pressing against a horny pad on the upper jaw. The cheek-teeth are high crowned with crescentic ridges of enamel — 'selenodont'. Dental formula 0.0−1.3.3 / 3.1.3.3.

The two principal families, Cervidae and Bovidae, are distinguished especially by the presence of antlers and horns respectively. Antlers are solid and bony and are cast and renewed annually; horns consist of horny sheaths on a bony core and are not shed.

FAMILY CERVIDAE (DEER)

A large family of about 40 species represented throughout Eurasia, a small area of N Africa and the Americas. Social structure in relation to habitat summarised in [96]. All but two genera (*Moschus*, which is sometimes treated as a separate family, and *Hydropotes*) have antlers and these are confined to males with one exception (*Rangifer*). The antler cycle is linked to the concentration of testosterone in the testes and blood. An increase in testosterone levels at puberty stimulates growth of the pedicles on the frontal bones of the skull, and subsequently the first antlers. Antlers are initially soft structures, highly vascular and covered in skin (velvet). High testosterone levels lead to final calcification of the antlers. The blood supply to the antlers is then stopped, the velvet 'dies' and is shed. The testes regress after the rut, and when testosterone levels are at their lowest, the antlers are cast. Sexual cycle of male deer described in [53, 54] and the antler cycle in [218].

Only two species, red and roe deer, are indigenous in Britain, but a further four species are now feral. Two others, the elk, *Alces alces*, and the reindeer, *Rangifer tarandus*, were present in Britain in the early post-glacial period but probably became extinct before Roman times. Domesticated reindeer have been introduced to the Cairngorms (p. 537) but are carefully managed and cannot be described as feral. The six wild species represent five genera. The characters of all six are detailed in Table 12.1.

GENUS *Cervus*

The largest genus of deer, with eight species. It is best represented in the Oriental region, but

Table 12.1. Some characters of the six species of deer now at large in Britain.

	Red	Sika	Fallow	Roe	Muntjac	Water deer
Maximum shoulder height (cm)	120	85	100	75	50	60
Antlers in males	+	+	+	+	+	o
Tusk-like upper canines in males	o	o	o	o	+	+
Peg-like upper canines in males	+	+	o	o	o	o
Visible tail	+	+	+	Absent but conspicuous anal tuft of hairs in females in winter	+	+
Upper surface of tail	Brown	White, with or without narrow black stripe	Long, conspicuous tail of variable colour	−	Brown	Brown
Frontal skin glands	o	o	o	Present but not conspicuous	Conspicuous	o
Metatarsal skin glands	+	+	+	+	o	o

+, present; o, absent.

one species, *C. elaphus*, considered to include the American *canadensis* [40], is found throughout much of the Palaearctic and N America. *C. elaphus* is the only indigenous species in Britain but another, *C. nippon*, has been introduced and is found in several parts of Britain and Ireland.

Red deer *Cervus elaphus*

Cervus elaphus Linnaeus, 1758; Southern Sweden.

Carw coch (Welsh); fiadh (Scottish Gaelic); fia rua (Irish Gaelic). Male — stag; craw (Welsh); damh (Scottish and Irish Gaelic). Female — hind; hydd (Welsh); eilid (Scottish Gaelic); eilit (Irish Gaelic). Mature female with calf — milk hind; without calf — yeld, blue or eild hind; young of year — calf. Other names used to describe different ages/types of animal derived from hunting vocabulary [362].

RECOGNITION
Only large red-brownish deer in Britain that does not have spots as adult. Rump patch creamy coloured extending dorsally above short, beige tail; patch not clearly marked with black as in sika and fallow deer (Fig. 12.2). Tail always shorter than ear. Antlers usually branched, not palmate as in fallow or rugose as in roe deer. First (brow) point arises at an angle >90° to main antler stem (cf. sika).

SIGN

Footprints (slots) oval, 5 cm wide in calves and 7 cm in adult males. Overlap in size and shape with other medium to large deer and sheep. Size of slot larger on snow or soft ground, or when animal is running.

Faeces variable according to diet and age of animal. In winter, droppings or 'fewmets' are acorn-shaped, up to 3 cm long and 1.5 cm in diameter; light brown to black. Deposited in groups, but may appear as a 'string' or 'runner' if the animal is moving when defaecating. In summer, especially

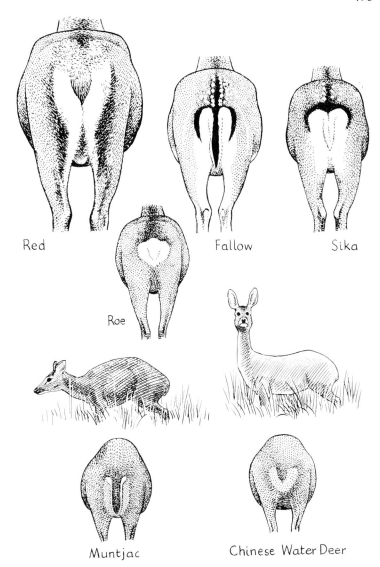

Fig. 12.2. Rump patterns of deer and characteristic profiles of muntjac and water deer.

in good habitats, stick together as 'crotties'. Size and shape of faeces overlap with those of other deer and sheep, but can generally be distinguished with experience. Number of daily defaecations varies from 24–29 in summer to 19–25 in winter [341].

Wallows used in summer by both sexes when coat is being shed, and by stags during the rut. Usually damp or boggy places, but not always so.

Marking: stags thrash or fray trees with their antlers in August when cleaning velvet, later as ritualised display during the rut. Side branches usually broken, 60–120 cm from ground. Bark also eaten from trunks of trees or exposed roots, mainly in winter and spring and from fallen branches in winter. Wound on trunk usually 80 cm from ground, but side branches unaffected.

DESCRIPTION

Pelage and moult: summer coat about 50 mm long with little or no underwool; usually reddish, dark brown or beige, rarely whitish or piebald. Belly off-white, grey or yellowish; heavily stained black or dark brown in stags during rut. Stags also develop thick dark manes at this time which are retained throughout winter (Fig. 12.3). Sometimes a dark line along neck and backbone, occasionally flanked by indistinct spots. Winter coat starts to grow in September, usually complete by December; hairs 60 mm with thick underwool 20–25 mm long. Usually brown, greyish or off-white; a few individuals whitish or piebald. Moult back to summer coat starts in late April–May, older animals and those in good condition (or non-pregnant females) moulting first; usually over by July–August. Moulting begins at the head, legs and anterior part of the body [124].

Calves' birthcoat usually reddish brown, flanked with whitish spots. Two moults, first about 2 months after birth when spots are lost, second in autumn into winter coat.

Nipples: two pairs, abdominal. Udder only conspicuous in late pregnancy and early lactation.

Scent glands: scent produced by hinds in season. Also glands on metatarsals (hock), between hooves, on ventral surface of tail and lachrymal (preorbital) in both sexes.

Skull elongated with narrow rostral region; minimum figures for condylobasal length for each sex greater than maximum of same sex in other British deer (Table 12.2).

Teeth: milk teeth 0.1.3.0/3.1.3.0. Upper canine pointed, lower canine incisiform, third lower premolar has three cusps, others one. Permanent teeth 0.1.3.3/3.1.3.3. Upper canine (tush) pear-shaped. Molars all bicuspid except third lower which usually has three cusps. After eruption, second and third premolars and all molars move forward in the jaw with age. Eruption, amount of wear on crowns [226] and annual layers in dental cement [246] used to estimate age.

Antlers can develop in calves in good habitats, but usually not before 10 months old in free-ranging deer in Britain. In poorer areas, first antlers may be no more than partially developed pedicels or

Table 12.2. Skull measurements (mm) of mature red deer hinds from Rhum.

	Mean	Range	n	Source
Condylobasal length	344	281–458	298	[229a]
Rostrum length	205	162–281	298	[229a]
Basilar length	321	260–428	298	[229a]
Palatal length	208	164–285	298	[229a]
Nasal length	122	95–175	298	[229a]
Mandible length	240	–	146	[247a]

First five measurements defined in [228]; mandible length measured from the outer edge of the socket of the 4th incisor to the heel of the jaw.

Fig. 12.3. Red deer hind and stag.

button-like antlers under skin; in better parts, short spikes occur. On deer farms, 12 points have been recorded on calves.

Antler development variable, but become progressively more branched with age (Fig. 12.4). Consist of points (tines) on a main beam, with a fork or cup of points at the top. A double brow-point is characteristic of the species, although the second (upper) of these is not always present in British red deer. Usually eight points in Scotland; up to 16 points found in native stocks, but up to 47 recorded in deer parks. Some mature stags never develop antlers (called hummels in Scotland, notts in SW England).

Cast antlers frequently chewed by deer and other mammals in Scotland; habit not so common elsewhere. Thought to be for phosphorous and possibly calcium.

Chromosomes: 2n = 48. Variable in red/sika hybrids, 64–68 recorded [165].

RELATIONSHIPS
Closely related to sika deer with which they hybridise in parts of Britain. Introgression thought to be complete in Wicklow Hills (Eire) and parts of NW England [163, 285]. Hybrids occasionally found in Scotland.

MEASUREMENTS
Weight and size very variable according to habitat and density. On open-hill land in Scotland weights considerably less than those from deer in woodlands or deer parks (Table 12.3). Stags and milk hinds are in best condition in late September, yeld hinds in late November [248]; all in poorest condition in late winter/early spring. Height at withers over

Fig. 12.4. Red deer stag with antlers in velvet but probably fully grown. (Photo: G. Kinns.)

curves in hill deer up to 122 cm in males, 114 cm in females. Length from nose to tip of tail up to 201 cm in males, 180 cm in females; variation with age shown in Table 12.4. Skull elongated with narrow rostral region; length of skull (condylobasal) in adults 300–340 mm in males, 280–335 mm in females.

VARIATION

N American and NE Asiatic races very large — wapitis, *C. e. canadensis* and *C. e. xanthopygus* respectively. British race described as *C. e. scoticus* Lönnberg, 1907 (type locality Glenquoich Forest, Inverness-shire) on basis of skull shape, but not clearly distinguishable from continental animals [228]. British race of red deer thought to be confined to Scotland, NW England and SW Ireland [228]. Other populations believed feral, established from deliberate introductions or deer escaping from deer parks including some of foreign origin.

N American wapiti introduced to various parts of Britain over last 100 years to improve 'bloodstock' for sporting purposes [362].

DISTRIBUTION

Widespread in Palaearctic from Ireland and Hebrides eastwards to Manchuria and N America. Found just south of Arctic circle in Norway (65°N) to N Africa (33°N). In Britain, main concentrations now in Scottish Highlands and Islands and SW Scotland and Exmoor. Scattered populations elsewhere with reasonable numbers in NW England and East Anglia (Thetford Chase). Found on the following islands: Arran, Bute, Islay, Jura, Mull, Pabbay, Raasay, Rhum, Scalpay, Scarba, Seil, Skye, North and South Uist, North Harris and South Lewis.

Introduced into Argentina, Chile, USA (Kentucky), Australia and New Zealand.

HISTORY

See [219, 224, 362]. Probably evolved from sika-like form, perhaps *Cervus perrieri* [219]. Occurred first in Middle Pleistocene Cromerian inter-glacial (*c.* 400 000 bp) of Europe.

Earliest deer found mainly associated with woodlands, but some evidence of them occupying treeless areas where there was topographical shelter [219].

Table 12.3. Carcase weights (kg) of red deer stags and hinds (yeld and milk) from selected areas of Britain.

Area (habitat/ population density)		Age (years)						Source
		Calf	1	2	3	4–8	>8	
Isle of Scarba, W Scotland (open country very high density)	Stags	22	35	43	49	65	74	[247]
	Yeld	21	29	38	44	49	48	
	Milk	–	–	–	39	43	42	
Glenfeshie, Central Highlands (open country high density)	Stags	26	38	50	66	83	83	[250]
	Yeld	24	36	47	51	54	53	
	Milk	–	–	–	44	47	45	
Glen Dye, E Highlands (open country very low density)	Stags	33	51	66	71	82	99	[339]
	Yeld	31	45	50	53	55	64	
	Milk	–	–	53	51	54	56	
Galloway, SW Scotland (conifer plantations low density)	Stags	38	69	74	77	103	111	[1]
	Yeld	–	61	62	55	67	70	
	Milk	–	–	65	59	72	80	
Cowal, S Argyll (conifer plantations medium–high densities)	Stags	37	55	72	82	93	106	[1]
	Yeld	38	51	55	53	56	–	
	Milk	–	56	55	59	61	61	
Strathyre, Perthshire (conifer plantations high density)	Stags	34	46	–	59	89	–	[1]
	Yeld	24	42	50	43	51	–	
	Milk	–	–	55	53	57	–	

Carcase weight = live weight minus blood and abdominal viscera. Equivalent to 67% of live weight of calves, 60% of milk hinds, 66% of yeld hinds and 56% of stags. Hind and calf weights, Oct–Feb; stags weights, July–Oct.

Table 12.4. Age-specific length (cm) for red deer on Rhum [229a].

Age	Stags				Hinds			
	Mean	SD	Range	*n*	Mean	SD	Range	*n*
1 year	–	–	–	–	142	7.2	54–58	2
2 years	163	12.7	140–178	8	155	9.2	135–168	15
3 years	169	6.7	155–180	19	160	7.0	145–178	24
4 years	174	6.5	163–185	28	161	7.3	150–178	17
5 years	181	10.3	165–198	19	167	8.3	152–180	12
6 years	179	7.8	165–193	15	165	7.8	152–180	13
7 years	175	10.5	160–188	7	168	5.7	155–178	14
8 years	183	8.2	173–193	7	167	6.4	157–180	25
9+ years	185	7.1	173–201	11	–	–	–	–

Decline in body size throughout European range since pre-historic times [224]. In Britain, decline in size since last Ice Age [224, 293] influenced initially by climatic effects on habitats, subsequently by forest destruction and disturbance by man obliging red deer to occupy treeless, poor quality, exposed hill land. Range and numbers greatly reduced in historic times becoming extinct in much of England, Wales and the Scottish lowlands by the end of the 18th century [224, 248]. Increase during 19th century due to interest in deer stalking, maintained over last 50 years through under-culling of females and colonisation of forestry plantations.

HABITAT

Highly adaptable and associated with many climatic and vegetation types from semi-arid Mediterranean areas such as Sardinia and the Atlas mountains of N Africa to the rich flood plains of the Danube, alpine meadows of Switzerland and Yugoslavia and the high snowfall areas of Norway and USSR. In continental Europe, always found associated with open woodland or woodland edge, 1000–2000 hectare of forest thought to be needed to sustain permanent population [248]. Forest types vary from pure deciduous or coniferous to mixed woodlands or plantations. Rarely occupy large tracts of dense forest [124].

In Britain, greatest concentrations found on open moorland of the Scottish Highlands and Islands. Also occupy treeless areas in some parts of Eire and in SW England, elsewhere associated with woodlands as in remainder of world range. Have colonised many conifer plantations established during the last 50 years, especially in Scotland, SW and NW England and East Anglia. Plantation age and structure important for occupation; highest densities found in open thicket (where good cover

and food are in close proximity) rather than older forests. Young stands used as feeding areas.

SOCIAL ORGANISATION AND BEHAVIOUR

Social organisation: adult males and females segregate for most of the year, in winter the areas occupied often being traditional and geographically separate [358]. Compared to adjacent male populations, hinds in winter tend to occupy areas overlying richer rocks and soils with proportionately more grassland; adjacent stag populations found

Map 12.1. Red deer.

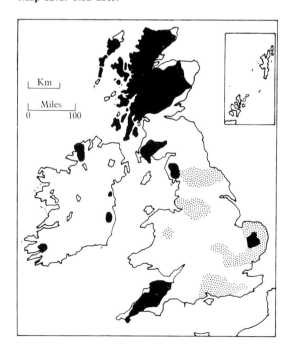

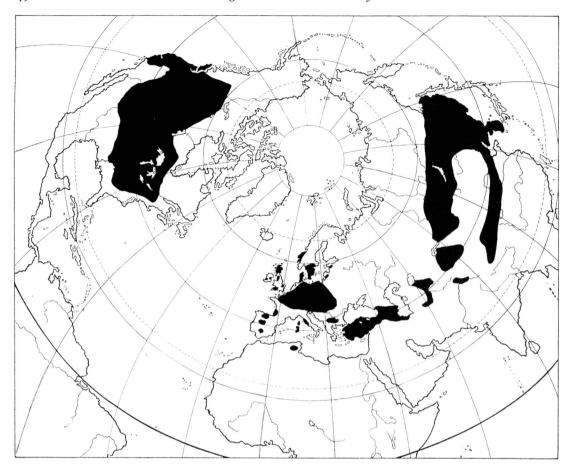

Map 12.2. Red deer.

on poorer ground often with more heather [343, 358]. Differences in habitat selection between sexes greatest at high-population densities.

Hind organisation based on matriarchy with group consisting of dominant hind and dependent offspring (Fig. 12.5). Her mature daughters and offspring have adjacent, over-lapping ranges with her; individual family groups coalesce around favourable resources [96]. Ranges of individuals or groups apparently undefended. Stag groups less stable with unrelated individuals forming semi-permanent groups for varying periods.

Group sizes vary according to habitat and weather (particularly snowfall). On open moorland, varies according to distribution and abundance of local feeding and resting areas [337]. Average around 9–11 on Rhum to around 40 in central and eastern Highlands [225]. Groups, or aggregates, of several

hundred recorded. In thick woods, most usually seen as individuals or a family group of hinds and young. Stag groups on open ground may be composed of all young, all old or of mixed ages. Within stag groups, young and subdominant animals tend to occupy peripheral positions. Hind groups sometimes composed predominantly of hinds with calves (milk hinds) or hinds without calves (yeld hinds).

Dominance hierarchy approximately linear in stag groups, related mainly to age and body size. In females, hierarchy not clearly linear. During rut, males defend harem of females and young or the area around them ('moving territory').

Home ranges: sizes vary according to habitat; largest in very open country. Vary on Rhum from 200 [225] to 400 hectares [96]; to 2400 hectares in

Fig. 12.5. Red deer hind with calf. (Photo: G. Kinns.)

eastern Highlands [338]. In forestry plantations, evidence of range size related to forest structure, being smallest (400 ha) in open parts with intimate mixtures of cover and food resources to more than 1000 hectares when ranges include more unplanted ground or blocks of older forest [52]. Marked seasonal ranges on open, hilly country with lower ground used in winter and higher ground in summer. Largely affected by weather, snow cover and food availability; may be found at altitudes over 1000 m in winter during temperature inversions [358]. As a generalisation, males found lower than females in winter, higher during July–September. No seasonal differences in range locality found in hinds in forestry plantations [52].

Dispersal: exploratory behaviour starts within 6 months of birth, being earlier in stag than in hind calves. Females establish ranges that overlap with that of dam. Strong fidelity to home area in females and no evidence of widespread or long-distance dispersal. Many young stags leave natal area, age of disperal varying from 1 year old in plantations to 2 or more on open ground, and usually occurs at rutting time or just before dam calves. Stags do not settle for several years until mature, when seasonal ranges are then established. Rutting areas of male traditional, often several kilometres from summer and wintering areas.

Activity: active throughout 24 hours. Five to nine

feeding cycles daily, two thirds during day with longest activity periods around dusk and dawn. When frequently disturbed become more nocturnal. In open, hilly country, usually found at higher elevations during the day, descending to lower levels at dusk and returning to higher ground again by dawn. These movements may cover 10 km and 750 m in altitude [107]. In forests often remain in, or close to, woodland cover during daylight, venturing onto more open areas from dusk to dawn.

Communication: best known sound is the roar, made by stags during rut. Roar sometimes preceded or followed by several grunts. Alarm calls by hinds a gruff bark or series of barks. Hinds also make a low 'moowing' sound when trying to locate young calves. The calf gives a nasal bleat or, if alarmed, a high-pitched squeal. When close together, such as at winter-feeding places, both sexes give low-pitched soft grunts when approaching each other.

Scent produced by hinds in season only detectable at short range. Role of other scent glands speculative.

Visual communication important. Rump patch flared acts as warning signal. If suddenly alarmed, may move off with series of stiff-legged jumps, sometimes all four feet together (as in sika deer). Low intensity aggressive behaviour by hinds and stags by raising chin and exposing pale chin patch with ears laid flat. Stags may tilt head and antlers on one side. If warning not heeded, hinds and stags, when in velvet, go onto hind legs and quickly box with forefeet. When antlers are hard, stags fight or spar by locking antlers together and twisting and pushing.

Movement: usually slow stride or trot when chased or disturbed, gallop for short distances; in woodlands, may lie down in cover rather than leave area when disturbed. Swim well.

FEEDING
See [209, 248] for reviews. Versatile feeders, depending on availability of plants in various habitats occupied, yet selective within these areas. Deciduous browse important in summer in some continental areas [116], but in Britain, grasses, sedges and rushes form bulk of diet (Fig. 12.6). In winter, heather, blaeberry and other dwarf shrubs very important, with brambles, holly and ivy also sought after. Ferns, lichens, shoots of deciduous and coniferous trees and, in coastal areas, seaweeds (es-

pecially kelps) eaten in autumn and winter. Can browse up to 180 cm by rearing up on hind legs. Eat bark of some trees, especially rowans, willows, Norway spruce and Lodgepole pine. Differences in food selection in stags and hinds on open ground [96, 340, 343]; in winter, stags eat more heather, hinds more grasses. Quality of winter food selected higher in hinds than in stags [340, 343]. Hind more than doubles food intake during early lactation.

BREEDING (Fig. 12.7)
Seasonal breeders, polygynous. Sexual cycle seasonal, driven by photoperiod, secondarily affected by body condition. Oestrus cycle *c*. 18 days, gestation 225−245 days. Secondary *corpora lutea* found; functions unknown.

Single young, twins very rare; sex ratio at birth about equal. Weight at birth on hill ground 6.7 kg (males), 6.4 kg (females). Weaning variable, usually over by 8 months.

Rut usually end of September−November. Stags fecund by end of 1st year and throughout the year as adults, except June. Mature stags leave bachelor groups in September and seek out hinds. Rutting areas of adult stags traditional, thought to be places where stag was first successful [96]. Stag rounds up hinds into harems which he defends against other stags. Harem size variable according to habitat; small family groups in woodlands, 10−15 usual on hill ground with more than 70 recorded. Largest and older stags rut first. Stags do not usually hold harems until 5−6 years old. Groups of non-successful adult and young stags gather around harems; on hill ground, usually found above dominant stag and his harem. All stags have greatly reduced food intake during rut and lose approximately 14% of their pre-rut body weight.

Much ritualised display during rut; wallow and spray with own urine and ejaculum, thrash vegetation and roar. Frequency and duration of roaring linked to dominance [96]. Serious fighting only between animals of comparable size. After roaring contest, animals walk side by side (parallel walk), one lowers and turns head and the pair lock antlers. Fight by pushing and twisting. Deaths and serious injuries not uncommon. Following fight, winner usually roars.

Fertility in females, and birth weight and viability of calves, depends on age coupled with body weight as affected by habitat quality and animal density [4, 96, 248, 250]. Hinds < 55 kg live weight

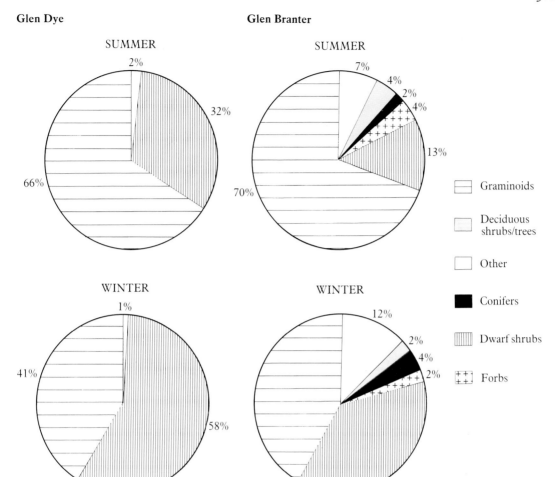

Fig. 12.6. Food of red deer in Glen Dye and Glen Branter in summer and winter.

rarely calve [27]. On much hill land, hinds reach puberty at 2 years 4 months or 3 years 4 months. Conception at 15−16 months occurs in higher quality areas or where animal density is low [4, 339]. In some woodlands, and most deer parks, majority of hinds become fertile at 15−16 months [284]; fertile calves recently found in British forests. In poor hill areas, *c.* 35% of adult hinds fail to breed each year [248].

Reproductive success of individuals studied intensively on Rhum [96]. Usual number of calves reared by females over lifetime is four (range 0−13); number sired by individual stags, six (range 0−24). Variability in hinds related to quality of

home range and group size; hinds associated with smaller groups produce more calves than those in larger groups.

Birth of young from mid-May, peaking in most northern areas during 1st or 2nd week of June; occasionally calving observed as late as December. Prior to giving birth, hind goes off on own, chasing away young of previous year, at times violently. Calf left lying alone for several days except during feeds; mother can be several kilometres away. When disturbed, newborn calves lie quite still, neck, head and ears flat out, and may remain motionless even if picked up. Accompany mother after about

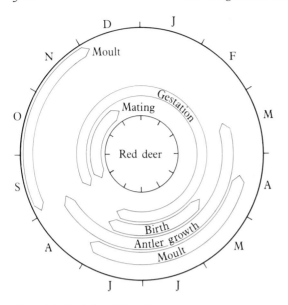

Fig. 12.7. Red deer: life-cycle.

Table 12.5. Densities of red deer in Scotland.

Area	Deer/km^2	Source
Open ground		
Rovie/Skibo (Highland)	< 1	[345]
Argyll	1.2	[345]
Skye	1.6	[345]
N Ross	6.8	[345]
Cairngorms/W Grampians	13.9	[345]
E Grampians	14.1	[345]
Glenartney (Perthshire)	26.9	[345]
Scalpay (Inner Hebrides)	31.3	[345]
Forests		
Galloway (SW Scotland)	8	[1]
Glenbranter (S Argyll)	10	[342]
Glencripesdale (N Argyll)	40	[1]

7–10 days. Young calves often form 'creches' within large hind groups, with frequent playing [107].

POPULATION

Densities variable; most reliable data from Scotland (Table 12.5). Varies with quality and structure of habitat, and management by man. Over some 30 000 km^2 of open hill land averages 9/km^2 [345]; 5–15/km^2 common in forestry plantations [284]. Density effects on reproduction and growth well documented [4, 96, 339]. High densities in wild deer associated with low growth rates, higher overwinter mortality in calves and yearlings, reduced fertility and fecundity in milk hinds, and retarded antler development in young stags [96], although this not seen in well-fed farmed deer at high densities. Scottish population of red deer increased greatly in last 40 years [341]. In 1987 estimated to be over 290 000 [94] on hill ground, with possibly 27–50 000 in woods [341].

Structure: adult sex ratio variable, averaging around 1 : 1.3 to 1 : 1.6 stags to hinds, with a range of 1 : 1 to 1 : 3.6 [94]. Population structure related to density, habitat and management. High-performance populations have greater proportion of young. In hill-land populations, calves form around 15% of

population of each sex, and animals over 8 years around 10%. Maximum longevity about 20 years.

Survival: mortality highest in calves and very old. Perinatal mortality varies annually but can be as high as 44% [339]; related to weather during calving period [94] and nutrition of mother during pregnancy [339]. Overwinter mortality varies annually from 5–65% in calves; related to initial birth weight, population density, heavy rainfall during the preceding autumn, and low late-winter temperatures and prolonged snow cover [94]. Most adult mortality in late winter, though a few hinds die giving birth. Overwinter mortality in adults related to tooth wear and associated with low winter temperatures and population density in milk hinds and yearlings of both sexes [94]. Occasional mortality due to avalanches in snow, lightning and fights during the rut.

Golden eagles predate very young calves [99]; foxes also thought to take young calves.

PARASITES

See [6, 123, 248] for reviews. Studied more in farmed situations. Of the arthropod parasites, ticks (*Ixodes ricinus*) are common; also deer ked (*Lipoptena cervi*), deer warble maggot (*Hypoderma diana*), nostril maggot (*Cephanomyia auribarbis*) a sucking louse (*Solenopotes burmeisteri*), and biting lice *Bovicola longicornis*, *B. concavifrons* and *Damalinia* spp. Effects on populations unknown but thought to be minor. Commonest helminths in Britain are liver fluke (*Fasciola hepatica*) and lung worms (particularly *Dictyocaulus* spp.). Main tape-

Fig. 12.8. Newly born red deer calf. (Photo: G. Kinns.)

worms include adult stage of *Moniezia benedini* and the cysticercus stage *Taenia hydatigena* (parasite of carnivores).

Free-ranging deer thought to be relatively free of major diseases. Serological evidence of infections with the viruses of infectious bovine rhinotracheitis, bovine virus diarrhoea, Reoviruses 1 and 2 and Adenovirus A has been recorded [216], but not likely that red deer formed an important reservoir of these diseases of cattle and sheep in the UK. Ocular disease due to bovine Herpes virus 1 has been recorded in farmed red deer calves [188]. Louping ill virus has been detected in both wild and farmed red deer but does not appear to cause clinical illness in this species [2, 292]. Farmed deer are particularly susceptible to malignant catarrhal fever, which is thought to be carried by sheep. Red deer can carry the rickettsial disease tick-borne fever.

Bacteria isolated from red deer include *Mycobacterium avium* [237], *Leptospira* spp. [101] and *Salmonella* [241]. A useful list of the diseases affecting farmed red deer [125] includes the bacteria *Yersinia pseudotuberculosis* and *Clostridium* spp.

Antibodies to the protozoan parasites *Babesia* and *Toxoplasma gondii* have been found [2]. At least seven genera of commensal intestinal ciliates are known to occur [102].

RELATIONS WITH MAN
Long association with man. Red deer remains commonest at Mesolithic and Neolithic middens [195]. Important food of early man; antlers and bones used for tools, weapons and ornaments, and skins for clothing.

In early historical times, hunting was reserved for nobility, and deer-stalking in Scotland became fashionable in the 19th and 20th centuries. Competition with livestock and forestry, especially since the first World War. Considered as having a major impact on commercial forestry and the conservation of some native plants and woodland [248]. Now being reared intensively on more than 200 deer farms in Britain, mainly for meat.

Culled annually for sport (> 1000 stags), meat and controlling populations. Currently around 40 000 carcasses per annum exported from Scotland.

Covered by four specific Acts of Parliament (and Ammendments): Deer Scotland Act 1959; Deer Act 1963; Deer Act 1980 and the Wildlife and Countryside Act 1981. These acts cover animal welfare and conservation, poaching controls, firearms and close seasons. In Scotland, the Red Deer Commission was set up especially to implement the 1959 Act and to advise on the conservation, welfare and management of red deer. This remit was later extended to other species.

LITERATURE
[107, 231, 232, 362, 364] — general information and popular accounts. [96, 248] — scientific reviews.

SOUND RECORDINGS
Appendix 3; A, C, D, E, F, G, J, P, S, T, V.

AUTHOR FOR THIS SPECIES
B.W. Staines.

Sika deer *Cervus nippon*

Cervus nippon Temminck, 1838; Japan.

Japanese or Jap deer; Fia Seapánach (Irish gaelic). Male — stag; female — hind; young of year — calf.

RECOGNITION
Medium sized, approximately intermediate in size between roe and red deer and similar to fallow. Summer coat usually chestnut red to pale yellow with pale but distinct white spots (Fig. 12.9). Winter coat, grey to almost black with spots hardly discernible except at very close quarters. Rump patch is always stark white limited on upper border by a black stripe (*see* Fig. 12.2). The tail is white or with a black line of variable thickness on the dorsal surface and hangs about half way down the tail patch (cf. fallow deer with a thick black stripe and

much longer tail). Antlers are grown by the male only and seldom have more than eight points. Bay tine absent (cf. red deer). The metatarsal glands are white and usually very distinct; unlike other deer of the genus they exude a waxy substance.

SIGN

Footprints easily confused with roe, red and fallow deer.

Faeces: similar to roe and red deer and variable in size.

Wallows: similar to red deer.

Marking: Stags thrash and fray trees with their antlers both to remove velvet and to advertise their presence to adjacent males during the rut. The antler tines are often used to score deep grooves in trunks of large trees (bole-scoring) [51, 285], a sign not normally associated with other deer species. Bark of trees is also eaten by stags and hinds, as in red deer.

DESCRIPTION

Pelage very variable between subspecies. Description here refers to type normally encountered in British free-living populations. Summer coat short, chestnut red to yellow-brown, white spots of variable intensity, arranged roughly in rows, the most distinct being either side of a dark dorsal stripe. Underparts fawn, except for inguinal region which is white. Winter coat is thicker and dark grey to almost black, and spots are absent or very faint. Rump patch is distinctly white, heart shaped and bordered by black above and on either side. Rump patch is often partially concealed in relaxed state but when alerted erection of rump hairs cause it to expand into a conspicuous heart-shaped patch.

Tail white, 15—20 cm long, with a black line of variable thickness down the dorsal surface. Metatarsal glands on hock usually white and very obvious; they produce a grey-brown waxy exudate. Facial appearance is distinct with dark lines above the eyes and a contrasting paler area between them, emphasising the anterior raised margins of the frontal bones. The head is relatively shorter than that of red deer and the ears are relatively broader and more rounded at the tips. A grey or black patch is often visible inside the ear which looks like

Fig. 12.9. Sika deer hind and stag.

a thumb print. Sika present a heavy, short-legged appearance, especially in winter coat.

Moult starts in May and is complete by July. Winter coat develops in September and is complete by early November. Stags develop thick dark manes during the rut which persist throughout the winter.

Newborn calves are of various shades of brown ranging from dark chocolate to nearly yellow-brown, and have white spots. Rump patch small and buff coloured. The 1st moult occurs from 2–3 months after birth, but is inconspicuous and calf coat is partially retained until 1st winter coat develops in October–November.

Nipples: two pairs, abdominal.

Scent glands: metatarsal (hock) and lachrymal (pre-orbital). No interdigital (pedal) gland, but the whole tail is glandular.

Skull: shorter than red deer with short pointed rostrum.

Teeth: tooth formulae and eruption sequence is identical to red deer.

Antlers: male calves grow pedicles at 6–7 months, and grow their 1st antlers, usually as simple spikes, in their 2nd year. Antler configuration is very variable but seldom exceeds eight points.

Chromosomes: $2n = 64-68$; $FNa = 68$. Number variable due to Robertsonian fusions [370]. Variable in red/sika hybrids, 64–68 recorded [165].

MEASUREMENTS
See Table 12.6. Variable according to subspecies. Most normally encountered in free-living British populations have a mean height at shoulder of 65–85 cms, males being larger than females.

Condylobasal length 235–290 mm in males and 205–245 mm in females.

VARIATION
Even within the Japanese archipelago there is considerable variation in body size, the deer on Hokkaido being as big as British woodland red deer, while those on Honshu are similar in size to sika in Britain. Subspecific status in doubt [285] and

Table 12.6. Weights of adult sika deer; weights in kg for animals with head and feet off, skin on and completely eviscerated [1].

Location	Males ($n = 20$)		Females ($n = 20$)	
	Mean	Range	Mean	Range
Sutherland	27.8	18.6–36.4	17.7	15.5–26.4
Kintyre	24.9	11.8–42.3	20.8	14.1–28.3
Great Glen	28.5	17.7–36.4	20.6	13.6–26.4
New Forest	24.4	17.3–38.6	21.1	13.6–30.5

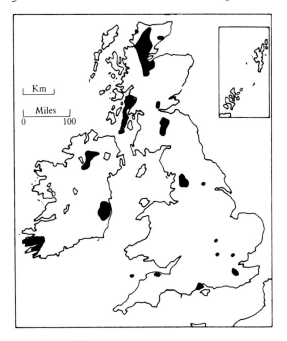

Map 12.3. Sika deer.

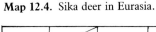

taxonomy of the genus confused. Current evidence suggest a two-way split into the Japanese Island deer (*C. n. nippon*) and the mainland asiatic deer (Manchurian and Formosan sika — *C. n. hortulorum*) [285]. Formosan and Manchurian types have been introduced to Britain, but now are probably present only in deer parks.

Hybridisation with red deer can occur and introgression is complete in Wicklow (Eire) [162, 163, 164] and parts of NW England [229]. Hybrids have been found in Scotland [285]. It has been suggested that only the Japanese island forms belong to the species *C. nippon*, all other forms being hybrids of great antiquity [229].

DISTRIBUTION

Indigenous to E Asia but now introduced to many countries including Austria, Czechoslovakia, Denmark, France, Germany, Poland, New Zealand, Great Britain, Ireland, South Africa and USA. Large populations in Sutherland, Argyll, Peebles, Ross-shire and Inverness, with smaller populations in Hampshire, Lancashire and Cumbria.

Map 12.4. Sika deer in Eurasia.

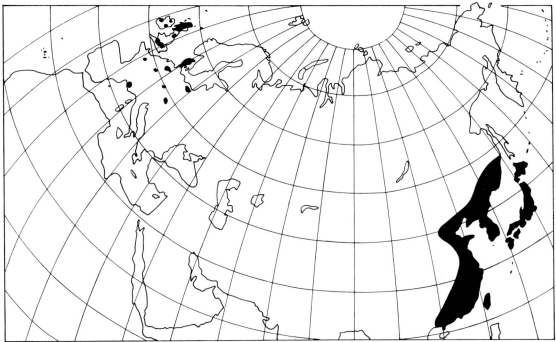

HISTORY

Considered to be primitive, being similar to *Cervus perrieri* from the Upper Pliocene from which it may have evolved [219]. Sika-like deer disappeared from Europe by the end of the Lower Pleistocene and by the middle Pleistocene were evident in eastern Asia [219]. Dispersed eastwards from Central Asia to colonise China and the Japanese islands. Asiatic forms may be the result of hybridisation with the Chinese wapiti (*Cervus elaphus xanthopygus*) in ancient times.

Introduced to several locations in Britain, mainly between 1860 and 1920. The 1860 introduction to Powerscourt in Ireland was the basis of many subsequent introductions to the British mainland. Only the Peebles population is known to come direct from Japan [285]. Currently increasing its range at most Scottish locations.

HABITAT

Usually associated with dense woodlands and scrubby vegetation. Thicket stages of commercial coniferous forests are important in Scotland. Sika are opportunists and will apparently favour dense thickets whatever the species composition. They appear to achieve their highest densities in habitats providing an intimate mix of open fields and dense woodland offering a high proportion of woodland edge. Sika seem less able to adapt to tree-less conditions than red deer have done in upland Scotland.

SOCIAL ORGANISATION AND BEHAVIOUR

Social organisation similar to red deer with stags gathering harems of hinds [211, 285], though some authors have suggested the formation of territories and the marking of rutting stands [184, 252]. If these differences really occur they may be a function of habitat type [285].

Hind groups appear similar to red deer with dominant matriarch leading a group of her recent offspring. Group size usually two to eight animals. Group size can vary almost daily with individuals leaving or joining different groups; a dominance hierarchy amongst hinds may influence this [234]. Sometimes, especially in open habitats, family groups coalesce to form large herds of up to 40 to 50 individuals, especially in autumn or winter [277, 285].

Little known of dispersal, but juvenile stags can wander widely. Range expansion led by stags, often preceding hinds by up to 10 years.

Activity: active throughout 24 hours with peaks at dawn and dusk in all seasons. Crepuscular peaks are exaggerated where human disturbance occurs.

Communication: most characteristic call is the high-pitched whistle of stags during the rut. The call begins with a groan and is repeated one to four times followed by a quiet period of 10–20 min. Sometimes it resembles a human scream. Groaning by stags is common during the rut (similar to red deer). A nasal whine is often produced from hinds with calves; calves often squeak or bleat. Both sexes have a high-pitched alarm bark of short pulse duration, which is repeated several times in quick succession [331]. Stags are less inclined to bark but when they do it is usually deeper and less prolonged.

Visual communication important; when alarmed rump patch can be flared to many times its normal size.

Gait similar to red deer and often pronks or bounces, stiff-legged, when alarmed. Can swim well, but range expansion in Scottish coastal areas suggests spread by land rather than swimming across sea lochs [285].

FEEDING

In Britain, grasses and heather dominate [234] and will eat ivy, holly, acorns and fungi when available. They become more dependent on woody browse in winter. Dietary composition in rumen samples from Scotland and S England similar, with Scottish deer taking more grasses [234]. This is likely to be influenced by availability since, like red deer, they are intermediate or opportunistic feeders [277].

BREEDING (Fig. 12.10)

Seasonal and polygynous. Seasonally polyoestrus; oestrus cycle 21 days. Gestation 220 days. Single young, twins rare. Weight at birth about 3 kg in Dorset [166].

Rut starts towards end of September or early October. Virtually all females are fecund in 2nd year; pregnant calves have been recorded [71, 184]. Thereafter hinds produce calves almost every year. Young born from early May to late June; infrequently as late as October.

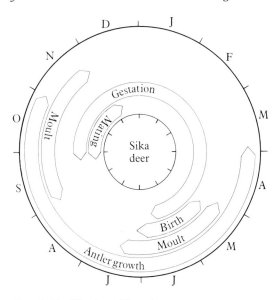

Fig. 12.10. Sika deer: life-cycle.

POPULATION

No information available for Great Britain, but probably achieve similar densities to these in Japan, where between 8 and 40 per km² [187, 207, 285]. Virtually no information available on population dynamics or structure.

In Japan they survive in harsh climatic conditions but deep snow restricts movements and influences mortality.

RELATIONS WITH MAN

Browsing of young trees and removal of bark is important to commercial forestry in Great Britain. The apparent continuing hybridisation of sika and red deer threatens the genetic integrity of native red deer. Culling for venison and trophy antlers is practiced and likely to increase in importance. Sika deer are farmed in New Zealand, England and Ireland following a long tradition (over 3000 years) of intensive husbandry in the Far East. They were the most frequently farmed species of deer until recently when red deer farming increased.

LITERATURE

[285] — Great Britain distribution and status reviewed. [124, 166, 176, 363] — general biology and habits described.

AUTHOR FOR THIS SPECIES
P.R. Ratcliffe.

GENUS *Dama*

Marginally distinct from *Cervus* and has in the past been included in that genus. Single species but two subspecies; the European fallow *D. d. dama*, and the Persian fallow, *D. d. mesopotamica*. The latter is larger and differs in antler morphology, and the two subspecies hybridise in captivity. Persian fallow survived until recently in very small numbers in the wild in only two places in Iran. In 1989 under 200 captive and wild fallow deer remained in that country. Small numbers are kept in several European zoos, in the Hai-Bar Reserve in Israel and in New Zealand.

Fallow deer *Dama dama*

Cervus dama Linnaeus, 1758; Sweden (introduced).

European fallow deer; gafrdanas (Welsh).
Male — buck; female — doe; young — fawn.

RECOGNITION

Many colour varieties ranging from white to nearly black, certain colours predominant in some geographical areas. Typical summer coat is reddish fawn with white spots along flanks and back, with black vertebral stripe extending along dorsal surface of longish (*c.* 16–19 cm) tail. In winter coat becomes greyish fawn with indistinct or no spots. (Fig. 12.11).

Only British deer with palmate antlers. Most easily confused with sika deer (of equivalent size): in summer coat, spots less apparent in sika and sika antlers are not palmate. Both have white rump patch edged with black and black line down tail: in fallow, the tail extends below the caudal patch but in sika it extends only two thirds down cauda. Hair over metatarsal gland on hock similar colour to surrounding hair and not as conspicuous as in sika.

SIGN

Footprints: cloven footprints may be confused with those of other deer or even sheep and goats but slot narrower and with stronger crescent shape than domestic stock or, for example, roe deer. Size of prints varies with age, sex and gait.

Faeces similar to those of other deer. Black, shiny, cylindrical pellets deposited in piles. Usually each

Fig. 12.11. Fallow deer doe and buck.

pellet has one end pointed and one indented: size in males *c.* 16 × 11 mm; in females *c.* 15 × 8 mm.

Rutting signs: frayed or scored bark on trees, thrashed vegetation and scrapes in the ground are indicative of rutting bucks but distinction between the species for these signs is unreliable. Bucks leave pungent urine in some scrapes, and in damp situations scrapes may resemble red deer wallows.

Play rings: in some areas, fallow create a circle of bare ground, worn clear of leaf litter, about 3 m diameter and usually centred on a decaying tree stump. Appears to be a focus for play activity: animals of various ages and of both sexes have been observed to run round the ring, but full function is unknown.

DESCRIPTION

Pelage: common colour variety has rich fawn summer coat with many prominent white spots on flanks and back (Fig. 12.12). Black vertebral stripe. Tail white underneath, black on top (cf. sika which has mostly white on top). White rump patch bordered by black curved line. In winter, coat becomes dull grey-brown with spots indistinct or absent. Menil variety is paler and lacks black border to rump patch; it retains spots in winter. Almost black variety is slightly dappled and has no white at all; many intermediate colour varieties. In all, belly is always paler than flanks. Albinos very rare but animals with white or off-white coats are common; these animals are sandy coloured at birth, becoming white when about a year old. For other colour varieties pelage of newly born similar to adult's summer coat.

Male has prominent brush of hairs from penis sheath which is visible from about 3 months and female has tuft of long (*c.* 12 cm) hairs below the vulva. Ears prominent, eyes relatively large, dew claws present.

Moult occurs May–June and late September–October in southern England.

Nipples: two pairs in both sexes. Udder prominent in lactating females.

Scent glands: suborbital, rear interdigital and metatarsal. Rutting bucks have scent gland associated with penis sheath [210]. Rear interdigital glands active within few weeks of birth and active throughout year in both sexes; odour said to resemble rancid butter.

Skin structure has been described [196] and also the sebaceous and sweat glands of the anal and circum-vulval skin [128].

Fig. 12.12. Fallow deer buck and does. (Photo: G. Kinns.)

Antlers: size very variable, depending on age, condition and genotype. Pedicles usually first noticed from 5−12 months and hard antlers present from 15 months. First antlers vary from small knobs (3 cm) to spikes up to 23 cm. Some 2nd or 3rd sets of antlers have porous tips because the velvet was shed before mineralisation of the antler was complete [80]. Size increases with age: length up to *c.* 76 cm, inside span up to *c.* 70 cm [362]. When fully developed, antlers have broad palm which distinguishes fallow from other species. Palmation may occur in 3rd year, usually later. Antlers are cast April−June, older animals casting before younger ones; regrown and clean of velvet August−September; younger animals cleaning before older ones. Pattern of antler growth related to hormonal levels and to period of spermatogenesis (August−March) [65].

Teeth: deciduous dentition 0.0.3.0/3.1.3.0, permanent dentition 0.0.3.3/3.1.3.3. Incisors and incisiform canine are spatulate; first permanent incisor twice as wide as others. Large diastema between canine and premolar. One or two incisiform teeth may be absent or one or two upper canines may be present in either dentition [59, 64]. Deciduous P_2 and P_3 and permanent P_{2-4} lophodont whereas deciduous P_4 and M_{1-3} selenodont. All lower molariform teeth quadritubercular, each with two roots, except M_3 and deciduous P_4, which are sextubercular each with three roots. Molariform teeth hypsodont, erupting throughout life, and, except P_2, undergoing well-defined mesial drift. Molar rows in mandibles closer together than in maxilla and diverge distally in slightly curved 'V'. Mandibular tooth eruption occurs by 5−6 months (M_1), 9−12 (I_1), 13−16 (M_2, I_2), 17−20 (I_3, C), 21−24 (M_3, P_4, P_3), 25−26 months (P_2) and can be used for age estimation [62].

Skeleton: skull (Fig. 12.13) described [124]. Mandibles fully developed about 3 years. Splint bones of variable length [220] present on forelegs, lateral to proximal part of metacarpal, the plesiometacarpalian condition.

Reproductive tract: uterus bicornuate with paired pea-sized ovaries. Cotyledonary placenta [159, 168]. Testes scrotal. Annual changes in weight and histology of testes [63] and the male accessory

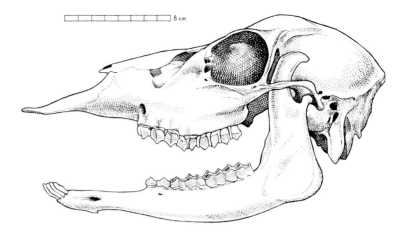

Fig. 12.13. Skull of female fallow deer.

glands (seminal vesicles, ampullae, prostate) have been described [66, 83]. Bulbo-urethal glands absent.

Chromosomes: 2n = 68, FNa = 68 [370]. Haematology [57, 73, 315]; haemoglobin types [238]; serum constituents [78, 118].

RELATIONSHIPS
Distinguished from *Cervus* by palmate antlers, lack of mane and absence of upper canine teeth, but still sometimes placed in *Cervus*.

MEASUREMENTS (Table 12.7).

VARIATION
Two subspecies, the European fallow described here and the Persian fallow *D. d. mesopotamica*. In European fallow conspicuous variation in coat colour: four main varieties but many other minor variations [65]. A long-haired variety, known only from Mortimer Forest, Shropshire, has body hairs more than twice the usual length with even larger often curly hairs on the tail, the inside of the ears and on the forehead [335]. Long hair is dominant over normal length hair and occurs in various colour varieties [330]. The hairs grow faster and over a longer period, but the character declines with age [203].

Variation in mandible size, independent of age, has been recorded [61]. Absence of one or two incisiform teeth noted in some populations: e.g. 18.7% (*n* = 107) in Richmond Park [59]. One or two upper canines may be present at birth but are

usually lost at an early age, e.g. 25% (*n* = 68) in Richmond Park [64].

Electrophoretic studies of blood proteins have failed to reveal any evidence of polymorphism in Great Britain, suggesting that any polymorphism present is far less than that observed in other species of deer [264]. Polymorphism of one enzyme (catalase) reported from W Germany [169].

DISTRIBUTION
Original range believed to have been Mediterranean zone of Europe and from Turkey to Iran. Widely introduced, now established in 38 countries between 61°N and 46°S. Most widespread species of deer in British Isles, including the islands of Anglesey, Islay, Scarba, Mull and Lambay [84].

HISTORY
A large form of fallow deer (*D. d. clactoniana*) was living in Britain during the Hoxnian period, 250 000 bp. By the Ipswichian period, 100 000 years bp, they were only slightly larger than the present-day deer. Became extinct here during the last (Würm) glaciation and survived only further south in Europe. Re-introduced to Britain, almost certainly by the Normans in 11th century when they were released in forests as highly prized quarry. By the 14th century there were many hundreds of parks where fallow were hunted. From these extensive, wild tracts of land there evolved the landscaped deer park adjacent to a stately home, many of which remain today. All the free-living fallow in the British Isles descended from a mediaeval introduction to a forest or to escapees

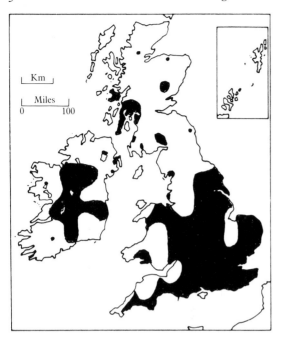

Map 12.5. Fallow deer.

from parks at various times but especially in the 20th century during the two World Wars.

HABITAT

Characteristic of mature woodland. Although sometimes colonising coniferous plantations (provided these contain some open areas) they prefer deciduous or mixed woodland with established understorey. These woodlands need not be particularly large since they are used primarily for shelter. Fallow are preferential grazers and while in larger woodlands they may feed on rides or ground vegetation between the trees, they frequently forage in agricultural or other open land outside; populations can thus equally well be supported in smaller woodlands or scattered copses in agricultural land.

Habitat use changes through the year as seasonal availability of different forages alters. Within the New Forest preference for areas of deciduous woodland from September to March/April [189, 261]. More open habitats (rides and clearings in woodland, pasture and arable land outside) were more strongly favoured from May–July (Fig. 12.14).

Map 12.6. Fallow deer (also widely introduced elsewhere).

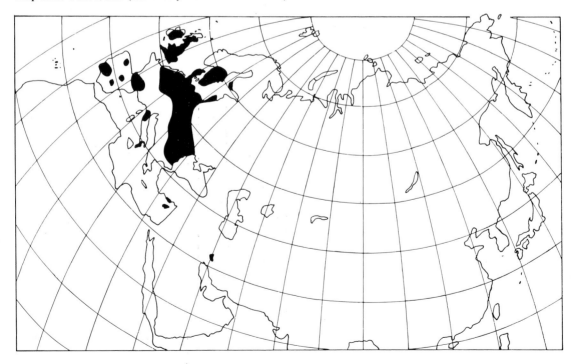

Table 12.7. Measurements of fallow deer, 2 years old and over.

	Males			Females		
	Mean	Range	*n*	Mean	Range	*n*
Weight, entire carcase (kg)						
Park (Richmond)	72	51—94	17	43	37—56	37
Wild	67	46—80	20	44	35—52	15
Live weight, new-born fawns < 24 hours old (kg)	4.6	2.5—5.9	51	4.4	2.5—5.5	42
Total length (nose—last vertebra) (cm)	166	155—179	14	149	138—157	25
Shoulder height (cm)	90	84—94	14	81	73—91	26
Girth (cm)	95	84—106	13	82	66—97	24
Hind foot (cm)	41	40—43	14	38	36—41	26
Neck (below larynx) (cm)	(seasonal variation)	39—74	14	32	25—40	21
Tail (to end of vertebra) (cm)	21	18—24	14	18	14—21	24
Ear (cm)	14	13—15	14	14	12—18	25
Skull						
Greatest length (mm)	263	241—283	47	247	231—267	46
Zygomatic width (mm)	127	115—140	69	109	102—118	54
Palatal length (mm)	101	93—117	71	98	88—106	54
Maxillary tooth row (mm)	81	73—88	71	78	68—85	55
Mandible length (mm)	200	185—216	68	191	175—203	49

SOCIAL ORGANISATION AND BEHAVIOUR

In many populations males and females remain separate for much of the year, with adult males observed together in 'bachelor' groups, and females and young (including males up to 18 months of age) forming separate herds, often in distinct geographical ranges. Males come into the female areas in autumn to breed but remain only until November–December before returning to their own ranges. Strict segregation of sexes does not, however, occur in all cases. In some populations, males remain in the female areas for longer after the rut is complete, staying with doe groups as late as April–May; in largely open habitats mixed herds containing adults of both sexes may persist throughout the year [277, 309].

In most populations males move into the female areas towards the end of September and through October; mature bucks compete to establish display grounds (rutting stands) and call to attract females. Rutting stands may be very traditional and the same buck may hold the same display ground for a number of years. Does may also be faithful to a particular rutting stand and certainly in some areas return to the area each year, frequently accompanied by their daughters; a buck

may therefore cover his own daughters and even his granddaughters. The implications of such potential inbreeding are considered by Smith [238].

Recent work has shown that there is far greater variation in fallow mating systems than had previously been suspected. Rutting stands are not always held by a single male. Although mature bucks defend their stands aggressively against potential rivals, they may tolerate the continued presence of one other, particular, male on their stand (often, but not necessarily, a younger buck). Typically, rutting stands are widely separated from each other. In some areas, however, a whole system of stands may be established very close to each other with as many as eight or nine adjacent stands in an area of only a few hundred square metres creating a communal lek [263, 310]. In other populations, usually where herds of mixed sex occur all year, males hold no display ground but merely cover receptive does when they encounter them. The type of mating system adopted by a population appears to be affected by environmental character (whether the range is open or closed, well-wooded or with scattered copses), population density, particularly the relative density of bucks to does, and local variations in distribution [311].

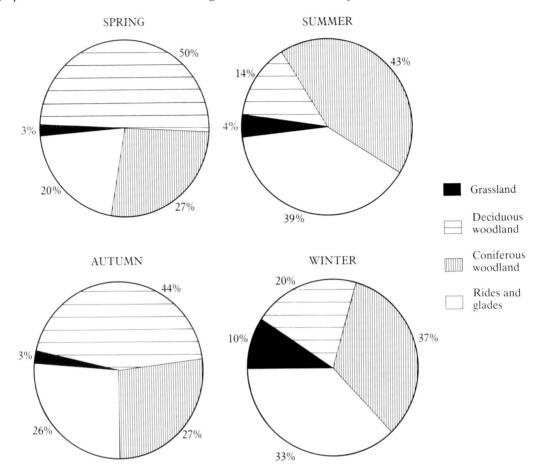

Fig. 12.14. Seasonal variation in habitat use by fallow deer in the New Forest.

Social organisation: aggregations of up to 70–100 individuals may occur when a number of individuals or smaller groups are sharing favoured feeding or resting areas. However, groups of one to five are most commonly encountered in the New Forest [189, 261] and these maintain their identity even within the larger groupings. These smaller groups are themselves far from permanent and remain open for much of the year [172, 274, 277]. Male groups are composed of individuals while female groups appear to be based on mothers with current year's young.

Group size varies with season, and stage of annual cycle (Fig. 12.15). From November to January in the New Forest, almost all males solitary or in pairs; from February to September groups of three to five become more common [189], constituting *c*. 30% of all male groups encountered. Male

groups >6 are rare at all times. Females show more variation in group size and are almost equally likely to be encountered in groups of one, two or three to five in all seasons [189]. Mean group size falls, however, from four (midwinter) to *c*. two in midsummer [261] as females prepare for the birth of their fawns in mid-June.

Group size is also clearly related to habitat. Fallow are encountered in larger groups in coniferous than in deciduous stands [273], and those in open, agricultural habitats consistently occur in larger groups than those of more closed woodland [309].

Home range: fallow are non-territorial and home ranges overlap extensively. Data on range size is limited and restricted to populations studied in the more extensive woodland environments: thus may

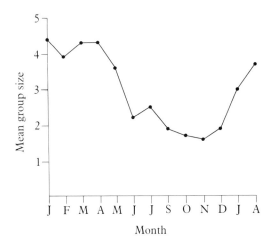

Fig. 12.15. Seasonal variation in group size in fallow deer.

be atypical and may differ markedly from that of fallow in agricultural landscapes. Preliminary results suggest summer ranges in New Forest of between 50 and 90 hectares for does (mean 70 ha), mean 110 hectares for bucks [277]. Winter ranges increase in size by about 50%.

Social behaviour: female groups are generally hierarchical and led by a dominant doe. However, the hierarchy is loose; individual animals join and leave the group freely and permanent associations between even pairs of individuals are uncommon. In consequence, social interactions such as mutual grooming are rare.

Aggressive behaviour: most obvious when males are competing for display grounds in the rut. Many contests resolved by pure display: groaning, parallel walk, displaying antlers, or thrashing antlers against vegetation. Direct fights, however, not uncommon, with head-on clashing of antlers and wrestling.

Movement: gait usually a walk or trot but when alarmed will bound stiff-legged on all four feet (pronk), stop, look around and stare and then run away. Jump well, but unless disturbed will usually go under or through a hedge or fence rather than over. Can swim well.

Activity: mainly crepuscular in habit, tending to lie up by day in vegetation that affords some degree of cover, where they drowse and ruminate. If disturbed move off quickly and quietly. At dusk they move to rides and neighbouring fields to feed. This pattern of activity seems in part imposed by disturbance. In undisturbed areas, fallow are more diurnal, grazing and lying to ruminate in the open at all hours. Older males are mainly nocturnal and rarely seen, except at height of rut. Activity rhythms change seasonally. In the New Forest, feeding was checked throughout the day in most seasons, although activity was concentrated around dawn and dusk during October–February [192] (Fig. 12.16).

Communication: usually silent for much of the year. When rutting, male repeatedly makes a deep loud belching noise called 'groaning'. Female, when suspicious of danger, especially if near young, gives short bark, sometimes repeated several times. Fawns, up to 6 months or so, bleat when disturbed or when searching for female. Female may respond with quieter bleat or whicker. Little known of non-vocal communication; when disturbed, frequently stamp a foot.

Orientation is chiefly by sight, but appear extremely short-sighted; discrimination of distant stationary objects very poor, though any movement quickly detected. Large mobile ears give acute hearing and sense of smell also acute.

FEEDING

Anatomical considerations based on the structure of the gut suggest that fallow are adapted as relatively unselective bulk-feeders [177, 178, 179]. Field studies confirm that fallow are preferential grazers. In all populations, grasses contribute > 60% of forage intake from March to September. Herbs and broad-leaf browse also make a significant contribution. Acorns, mast and other fruits are characteristic food through autumn and early winter, although importance in the diet varies from year to year with variations in fruit crop. Other major foods in winter, on which the deer rely more heavily as fruit crop is exhausted, are bramble, holly, ivy, heather and coniferous browse (New Forest) [190]. Even in winter, however, grass still contributes 20% of diet; increasing amounts of browse are taken in the autumn and winter to compensate for lack of graze material [48, 190, 278].

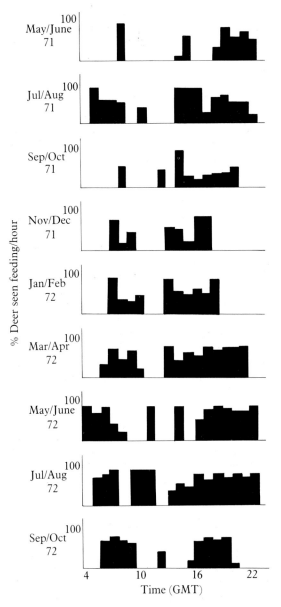

% Deer seen feeding/hour

Time (GMT)

Fig. 12.16. Seasonal variation in feeding activity of fallow deer in the New Forest [192].

BREEDING

Breeding bucks frequently herd female groups attracted to the rutting area, retaining them on the stand. When surrounded by does, the buck periodically moves among them nuzzling either neck or anogenital region. Immediately before copulation, the nuzzling is restricted to the receptive doe and

increases in intensity: the male moves his muzzle over flank and neck of the female and also nuzzles the vulva. This is accompanied by the rutting 'groan' also used for rut advertisement. Each copulation is preceded by between four and seven preliminary mountings, with no apparent erection and no attempt at intromission [356]. After intromission and ejaculation the buck dismounts and stands to emit a rapid series of deep groans.

Gestation 229 ± 2.7 days [270].

A single fawn is born in June although occasionally fawns born as late as November following a late, post-rut mating. Twin fetuses recorded rarely, e.g. two out of 326 (0.6%) uteri examined [81]. Mean birth weight 4.5 kg. Lactation sometimes lasts 9 months [65] and 90% of New Forest fallow ($n = 83$) were still lactating after 7 months [191]. Growth and development of hand-reared fawns has been described in Poland [212].

Males attain puberty at $7-14$ months but social hierarchy may prevent mating. Spermatozoa present from August to March/April but spermatogenesis reaches a peak in October/November. Antler development related to sexual cycle: casting and re-growth occur in spring and summer when bucks are sexually quiescent. Velvet is shed late summer—early autumn when spermatogenesis increasing (*see* Fig. 12.17).

Females polyoestrous; first breed at 16 months and then annually. Where food availability low, proportion of does conceiving as yearlings reduced. Breeding success of both adult and yearling does related to density in the year of birth. Fawning success related to body weight for both yearlings and adults, and it would appear that in high density populations (up to 10 animals per ha) a greater proportion fail to reach the critical threshold weight for ovulation [215]. Oestrous cycle about 21 days and does in oestrus for about 15 hours. Ovulation and fetal development have been described [10]. Reproductive biology reviewed by Sterba & Klusak [344].

POPULATION

Density: very variable and in most cases artificially controlled by man. One deer per $6-8$ ha, increasing to one per 4 ha has been estimated for parts of Essex [65].

Sex ratio: *c.* 1 : 1 at birth. In managed populations, selective culling usually aims towards one male : three females.

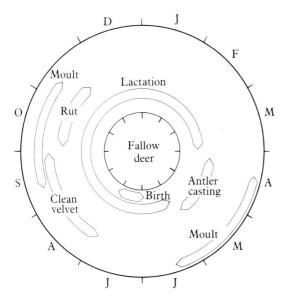

Fig. 12.17. Fallow deer: life-cycle.

Survival and age-structure: high mortality amongst neonates in first few days of life; over-winter mortality of fawns may also be heavy (*c.* 25%) dependent on severity of the weather. Natural mortality of adults usually relatively low until old age. Oldest recorded female in wild 16 years, though exceptionally may live longer (>20 years recorded in captivity). Males rarely >8–10 years. Of 87 wild deer (45 males, 42 females) killed in Essex and in Epping Forest, 21% of females were less than 1 year; 42% of males and 29% of females were less than 2 years. Of 115 deer (57 males and 58 females) killed accidentally or died in Richmond Park, 58% of males and 45% of females were less than 1 year [65].

In a study of park populations, mortality rates shown to be density dependent, and populations with a higher proportion of males suffered heavier losses. Degree of cover available was also important [279].

MORTALITY

Foxes may predate occasional neonate. Most populations managed by man who thus imposes most of adult mortality. Road-traffic accidents also serious contributor. A few males may die as result of injuries received during rut.

PARASITES

Biting louse, *Bovicola tibialis*, often numerous on debilitated animals. Deer keds (*Lipoptena cervi*) and ticks (*Ixodes ricinus*) also occur [348]. The warble fly, *Cephanomyia auribarbis*, is rare in this species; the related *Hypoderma diana* may also occur.

Endoparasites include about 18 species of gastro-intestinal nematodes but the burden is usually very slight compared with that of domestic stock [19], which are the prime host of a number of the species occurring in fallow, e.g. *Capillaria bovis*, *Tricho-strongylus vitrinus* and species of *Cooperia*, *Oesopha-gostomum*, *Ostertagia* and *Nematodirus*. *Apteragia quadrispiculata*, *Spiculopteragia spiculoptera* and *S. asymmetrica* are predominantly deer parasites. The latter was the most frequently found nematode and the most numerous abomasal worm. Wild Essex fallow whose range included cattle pastures had fewer species and smaller numbers of nematodes than a park herd which grazed with sheep and red deer [20]. Park animals aged 8–9 months dying in winter had much higher burdens than comparable animals killed at that time and clinical signs suggested parasitic gastro-enteritis was a factor contributing to mortality [78]. The bladderworm cyst (*Cysticercus tenuicollis*) of the dog tapeworm (*Taenia hydatigena*) was observed in 12.3% (*n* = 309) of fallow deer in S England [86].

Wild deer appear generally free of disease but cases have been reported of avian tuberculosis, brucellosis, tickborne fever, yersiniosis and lepto-spirosis [6]. Pasteurellosis has been described in a park herd [205]. Serological evidence of infection with bovine diarrhoea virus, reoviruses 1 and 2 and adenovirus A has been recorded [216]. Fallow from the New Forest were seropositive for *Borrelia burg-dorferi*, the causative organism of Lyme disease, a bacterial zoonosis occurring in that area [254]. Although Lyme disease is currently identified primarily in S England, it is probably more wide-spread. Fallow are also susceptible to foot-and-mouth disease but rarely show clinical symptoms.

Bone lesions similar to ringbone reported in 50% of 12 fallow sampled in Epping Forest [60] and abscess in jaws associated with erosion of bone not uncommon in older animals. High incidence (males 59%: females 21%) of deviation of at least one epiphysis of metapodial bones examined from 333 animals in one park population: also some cases of bowing of the shaft and deformity of the epiphyseal growth plate [75].

RELATIONS WITH MAN

Where fallow are established in small woodlands

in agricultural areas and feed in the surrounding farmland they may constitute a considerable pest problem. In woodland may damage young plantings or prevent regeneration of coppice [307]; bark-stripping of mature trees (both coniferous and deciduous) may also be a problem in hard winters. Severe damage to ground flora has been reported in some places, e.g. to the oxslip (*Primula elatior*) in Hayley Wood, Cambridgeshire [281]. Male fallow may also inflict considerable damage on individual trees by thrashing them with their antlers — both in aggressive display during the rut and in cleaning velvet from newly grown antlers in late summer.

In areas of high population density they may therefore be considered a pest of both agricultural and forest crops and most wild populations are thus controlled by shooting. By culling at an appropriate level the population can be managed not merely for control, but towards annual harvest of a profitable crop of venison. Production of venison has also led to the development of commercial fallow deer farms in UK and elsewhere. In addition to the venison there are also markets for the skins, antlers (when fully developed, or when in velvet), sinews, pizzle and testes. In UK, removal of growing antlers (for velvet, used as medicine in the East) is prohibited.

Legislation: fallow deer are protected by various laws relating to the capture, handling and movement of deer, types and calibres of weapons which may be used to kill deer, and the time periods when culling may take place (see Table 4.2).

Techniques for study: much important research material has been gained from simple direct observation or from analysis of carcase material. Studies of abundance and distribution of droppings may be used to estimate population density [15] or habitat use [275]; analysis of the droppings themselves has provided important information on diet [261, 277] to complement ruminal analysis.

Where individual recognition is required, e.g. for home range studies or studies of social grouping, animals may be caught and fitted with ear tags or radio collars before release. Capture with tranquilliser rifles or using special nets [297, 329] is only permitted under special licence. Individual recognition of common-coloured and menil animals is possible as the pattern of spots on the coat is unique [277].

LITERATURE
[47, 79, 85] — general introduction. [65] — a definitive review. [277] — additional material on food, social organisation and behaviour.

SOUND RECORDINGS
Appendix 3: A, C, E, F, J, P, S, V.

AUTHORS FOR THIS SPECIES
N.G. Chapman and R.J. Putman.

GENUS *Capreolus*

A distinctive genus containing a single species, although some authors argue that two species (*C. capreolus* of Europe and the Middle East and *C. pygargus* of Siberia and China) should be recognised [141].

Roe deer *Capreolus capreolus*

Cervus capreolus Linnaeus, 1758; Southern Sweden.

Male — buck; iwrch (Welsh); boc (Scottish and Irish Gaelic). Female — doe; ewig (Welsh); earb (Scottish Gaelic); earb, fearb (Irish Gaelic). Young of the year — kid, fawn.

RECOGNITION
Small to moderate sized deer, body comparatively short with long legs. Apparently tail-less except for anal tuft of hair in females in winter coat. Distinctive black nose with white chin. Distinguished from muntjac also by upright stance and pointed ears. Characteristic bounding gait when disturbed with white-cream rump patch or target flared. In male, small rugose antlers (Fig. 12.18).

SIGN

Footprints: small, up to 4.5 cm long, typical of cloven-hoofed mammals. Can be confused with other small deer and sheep.

Faeces: pellets typically elongated, cylindrical, black and shiny; size variable, in adults approximately 14 mm long and 6 mm in diameter, but overlap with other species in size and shape, even the larger red deer. In summer often stick together or when animals have been feeding on highly digestible foods. Defaecation rates vary from 17 to 23 pellet groups per day [249].

Fig. 12.18. Roe deer doe and buck.

Marking: saplings frayed or rubbed with antlers by bucks, especially in summer; usually 30–70 cm from ground and side branches broken. Ground often scraped of vegetation at base of tree. Well-trodden tracks or 'rings' around natural features such as trees, bushes or rocks found in some areas, but not of widespread occurrence.

DESCRIPTION
Summer coat reddish brown, uniform dorsally but paler underneath; hair 35 mm long. Moult into winter coat September–October; hair 55 mm long, colour variable, usually pale or olive-grey, greyish brown to almost black, especially in SW Scotland and N England [56]. Moult to summer coat mid-March to early June. Kids at birth generally pale or dark reddish brown flecked with black; dappled with white spots on sides and flanks and with a row of spots on either side of spine. Spots fade after about 6 weeks, disappearing by first moult.

Face distinctive with short muzzle. Black nose, a white rim often found above which sometimes extends onto upper part of muzzle; characteristic 'moustache stripe'; white chin. One or two pale patches on throat usual in winter coat. Rump patch very distinct, especially in winter in females, which have a white, inverted heart-shaped patch, with a backward projecting anal 'tush' of hair; in males, rump patch kidney-shaped, cream with no 'tush'. In summer, the rump patch is smaller and cream to buff in both sexes; anal tush generally absent. Ears large, prominent and rounded; eyes rounded with slanted pupils. Dew claws present; also vestigial splint bones on forelegs (teleometacarpalian condition).

Nipples: two pairs, abdominal.

Scent glands: metatarsal on outer side of hind leg just below hock; interdigital; suborbital [183]; glandular area between, and anterior to, antler pedicles in males [316].

Skull: detailed description by Flerov [124]. Small to medium sized (Table 12.8), not especially elongated in rostral or nasal regions (cf. red deer).

Alimentary system typical of selective feeders; described by Hofmann & Geiger [180].

Teeth: upper canines rare. Milk teeth usually 0.0.3.0/3.1.3.0 and permanent 0.0.3.3/3.1.3.3. Permanent teeth erupt between 8–15 months. Age determination of kids and yearlings easy due to presence of milk teeth and the obvious tripartite third premolar (three cusps). Replaced in adult dentition by a bicuspid tooth. Beyond yearling stage, annual layers in dental cement much more reliable for ageing than tooth-wear [3]. Little eruption occurs after 2 years (cf. red deer).

Antlers short, usually less than 30 cm and placed more or less vertically in a lyre-shape. Three tines on each antler usual in adults; a third central tine (the 'true' brow tine is missing) [124] faces forwards and upwards. Main beam branches dichotomously at top; posterior tine faces backwards. Lower part of antler beam covered in variable amounts of large tubercles (pearling) with well-developed burr, or coronet, at base.

Pedicles develop at about 3–4 months, with 1st

Table 12.8. Measurements of wild roe deer from S and E England.

	Males			Females		
	Mean	Range	n	Mean	Range	n
Skull (mm)						
Total length	196	174−207	7	196	190−201	4
Breadth of orbital process	90	85−95	10	82	79−88	5
Palatal length	113	92−121	7	113	107−118	4
Maxillary tooth row	58	53−66	10	56	55−58	5
Mandible length	137	127−148	2	140	−	1
Live weight (kg)						
Adult > 1 year old	23.9	18.0−28.5	44	22.3	18.0−28.0	41

antlers visible at 8−9 months; these may be buttons or simple spikes up to 10 cm long, or with one or both extra points according to habitat quality. Antlers generally fully-formed by 2 years but quality and number of tines is a poor indicator of age. Antlers cast from late October to early January, adults casting before juveniles; regrown in 'velvet' and fully formed by March (Fig. 12.19); velvet shed in April by adults, later in young or animals in poor condition. Infrequently antlers retained in velvet with the addition of further 'layers' each year (bucks called 'perruques'); thought to be due to low androgen levels, possibly caused by damage to sex organs or when testes remain in body cavity (cryptorchidism) which prevent 'cleaning' of velvet [55].

Antlers rarely observed in females. These usually remain in velvet, but not always so. These females may be true hermaphrodites or male pseudo-hermaphrodites (freemartins) [55, 183]. Antlered females, both in 'hard horn' and pregnant, known [1].

Chromosomes: 2n = 70; FNa = 68 (continental data) [370].

MEASUREMENTS
Adult size achieved at about 2 years. Mean height at shoulder 60−70 cm, males being larger than females. Body weights are given in Tables 12.8 and 12.9.

VARIATION
Two subspecies commonly accepted [219]; 'European' roe (*C. c. capreolus*), the subspecies native to Britain, and Siberian roe deer (*C. c.*

Fig. 12.19. Roe deer buck with antlers in velvet. (Photo: P. Morris.)

pygargus), which is frequently treated as a distinct species. Siberian roe introduced into various parts of Britain from the end of the 19th century with unknown success [362]. British race (*C. c. thotti*

Lönnberg, 1910; Craigellachie, Morayshire) has been described on basis of darker colour, especially of the face, but it is not generally recognised.

DISTRIBUTION

Widespread throughout Scotland and northern Britain and increasing range. In S England, present from W Kent to Cornwall, spreading north in Gloucestershire. Populations also in Essex, Norfolk and Suffolk, which are now spreading into the Midlands. Recently appeared in Wales around Llandrindod Wells. Absent from Isle of Wight and most Scottish Islands except Bute, Islay, Seil and Skye.

HISTORY

Reviewed by Lister [219] and Whitehead [364]. True roe deer first appear in the Middle Pleistocene (Cromerian) of Europe. Absent from Britain during cold stages of Pleistocene, its range probably restricted to southern Europe [219]. Absences in Britain possibly due to lack of suitable woodland cover; snow depth influences northern limits of range [127]. In historical times became extinct

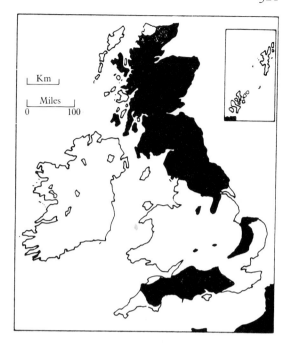

Map 12.7. Roe deer.

Map 12.8. Roe deer (including Siberian roe).

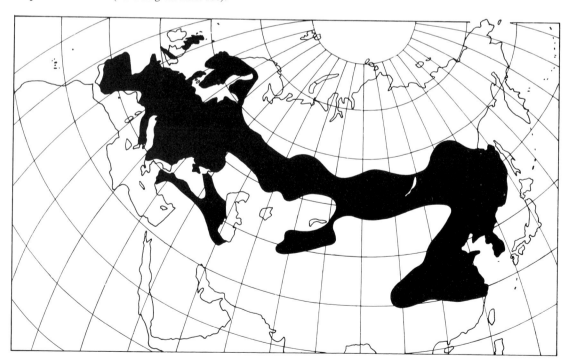

Table 12.9. Carcase weights (kg) of roe deer from selected populations in Great Britain [287].

		Kid			1			2−4			>5		
		Mean	Range	n	Mean	Range	n	Mean	Range	n	Mean	Range	n
Pickering	Bucks	15.8	11−20	20	16.3	14−19	16	18.6	14−20	20	16.4	12−21	15
(Yorks)	Does	12.8	10−15	20	16.3	13−19	13	17.3	14−20	20	14.8	16−20	17
Alice Holt	Bucks	14.4	14−16	4	14.4	12−17	5	17.9	15−19	7	16.4	−	1
(Hants)	Does	12.8	10−15	10	18.2	16−22	10	19.4	15−22	15	17.9	16−20	5
Thetford	Bucks	13.7	10−18	20	13.4	10−17	20	16.9	14−22	20	14.9	11−20	20
(Norfolk)	Does	9.9	7−13	20	14.6	12−17	20	13.8	11−17	20	15.3	11−19	15
Craigellachie	Bucks	10.6	8−16	6	13.2	8−18	17	14.5	7−18	20	15.4	6−20	14
(Morayshire)	Does	9.9	5−16	12	12.9	8−19	20	12.9	8−18	20	14.7	13−18	7

Carcase weight = live weight minus blood and abdominal and thoracic viscera. Female/kid weights, Oct−Feb; adult males, May−Oct.

throughout much of Great Britain and by the beginning of 18th century was thought to survive only in remnant woodlands in parts of the central and NW Highlands of Scotland [293]. Increase in woodlands during 18th century led to range expansion in Scotland, roe reaching Scottish Borders by 1840. Roe in southern England all considered to be derived from introductions. Roe of unknown origin introduced into Milton Abbas, Dorset, in 1800, and subsequently colonised much of SE England; deer from German stock introduced into East Anglia around 1884 [87]; roe in Lake District thought to be of Austrian origin [227].

HABITAT
Generally associated with open mixed, coniferous or purely deciduous woodland. In some parts of Scotland occupy open moorland without access to woodland cover [104]; seen up to 760 m in such areas [1]. Also occupy agricultural land in continental Europe if sufficient topographic or ground cover is available; apparently more dependent on small woods in agricultural areas in Britain. Plantation age and structure influences local density [223; 342], being highest (>25/km^2) in young stands 5−15 years old where both food and cover are abundant, falling to c. 8 deer/km^2 in 30−45 year stands and rising again to c. 16 deer/km^2 in later stages.

SOCIAL ORGANISATION AND BEHAVIOUR

Home ranges and territory: males territorial from April to August. Territories exclusive in most areas [34, 346] but not always so [204]. Territory and range size varies according to habitat (Table 12.10) but reasons for differences unclear [175, 204]. In many areas range size of males is slightly larger than that of females [204]. Non-defended winter ranges sometimes the same as summer territories [34]. Ranges of non-territorial males approximately twice size of territories and overlap with those of several bucks [34]. Territories retained year to year by same or replacement bucks; ranges of non-territorial males seldom retained, animals emigrating in spring of 2nd or 3rd year if unable to acquire a vacant area. Territorial boundaries frequently natural features such as streams, woodland rides or roads [183]. Territorial bucks seldom hold territories for more than 3 years. Maximum size that a buck can maintain thought to be in the region of 50−60 hectare [317], this varying with habitat and visibility. Males will often tolerate each other and aggregate when feeding outside their territories.

Female ranges apparently undefended but retained annually; if doe killed or removed, range 'taken-over' by young female, not incorporated into ranges of adjacent does [34]. Ranges of does overlap considerably, and can also overlap with one or several territorial males. Range size generally similar to, or smaller than, male territories [175]. Non-established young females in 2nd or 3rd year may form own ranges overlapping with that of mother, or may emigrate; mechanism of dispersal and regulation of female numbers unknown. Young males leave maternal group by their 2nd year. Territorial behaviour by female at parturition [121, 213], when ranges become smaller [202]; break-up

Table 12.10. Average range sizes (ha) of roe deer in various British habitats.

Habitat	Males	Females
Conifer plantation, Dorset* [34]	7.6 T 16.2 NT	7.5
Conifer plantation, moorland, NE Scotland [104]	35.2	—
Conifer plantation, S Scotland [221]	14.9	10.1
Conifer plantation, Dorset* [131]	11.2	20.7
Conifer plantation, Dorset* [204]	7.7	7.5
Conifer plantation agricultural land, Wiltshire [204]	15.4 T 22.3 NT	16.4
Conifer plantation, W Scotland [175]	85	67

NT, non-territorial buck; T, territorial buck.
All range sizes except those from Dorset estimated using the minimum convex polygon method.
* Same wood: Chedington, Dorset.

of mother/young associations during April–May prior to dam giving birth [24]. Does often return to same place to give birth in consecutive years [204].

Usually solitary or in small groups of male, female and young or mixed sexes. In winter, large groups may occur, especially when feeding in fields. Groups larger when living in agricultural fields, often eight to 12, but more than 60 being recorded in Scotland [1], Czechoslovakia [369] and Poland [35].

Aggressive behaviour by males includes barking, chasing, fraying and scent-marking young trees, bushes or other vegetation, and by stamping with forefeet. Fight by locking antlers and pushing and twisting; deaths may occur.

Gait usually the walk; bound when alarmed, flaring rump patch and often giving a gruff bark. If disturbed often cut-back behind source, or lie flat and hide until disturbance has passed. Will swim.

Activity: active throughout 24 hours. Nine feeding periods per day usual, with longest bouts around dusk and dawn [175]. When frequently disturbed, feed in, or close to, forest edge; venture on to more open areas or agricultural land from dusk till dawn.

Communication: both sexes give short repeated

barks, not extended as in muntjac. Male makes rasping noises, especially when courting. Females in season give high-pitched cry or squeal. Kids bleat or squeal when alarmed [183] and when hungry. Little known of non-vocal communication.

Senses of smell and hearing well developed. Visually, better at detecting movements rather than shapes.

FEEDING
Food of roe studied in E England [171], S England [185, 193], NE England [173] and Scotland [342]. Versatile and opportunistic, diet varying according to food availability in different habitats. Selective feeders [181], but buds and shoots of deciduous trees and shrubs, and non-graminaceous herbs (forbs) important throughout world range.

In S and E England, brambles (*Rubus* spp.) especially selected throughout year, with deciduous browse and forbs more important in summer; in winter, ivy, conifers, ferns and dwarf shrubs taken. In Scotland, in summer, forbs selected when available, with sorrels and rosebay willow-herb prominent; also shoots of conifers and deciduous trees, especially at bud-burst [342, 359]. In winter, heather, blaeberry and other woody browse important. Grasses eaten in small amounts throughout year; only taken in appreciable quantities in early spring or where preferred foods are not available (Fig. 12.20). Foraging on agricultural land described by Putman [276].

BREEDING (Fig. 12.21)

Breeding season (rut) occurs from mid July to end of August when males very aggressive in defence of their territories. Does are induced ovulators; probably monoestrous. The only artiodactyl to exhibit delayed implantation. After fertilisation, the blastocyst does not implant into the uterine endometrium until late December or early January when normal embryonic development proceeds [323]. Cotyledonary placentation. Females normally breed first at 14 months but pregnant kids (aged 2–3 months) have been found in a low density, high performance population in Yorkshire [289]. Twins common, especially from does aged 3 years; triplets found in good quality habitats.

Birth usually between mid-May–mid-June. Kids suckle within a few hours of birth. Young left lying alone and, if twins, usually separate. By 6–8

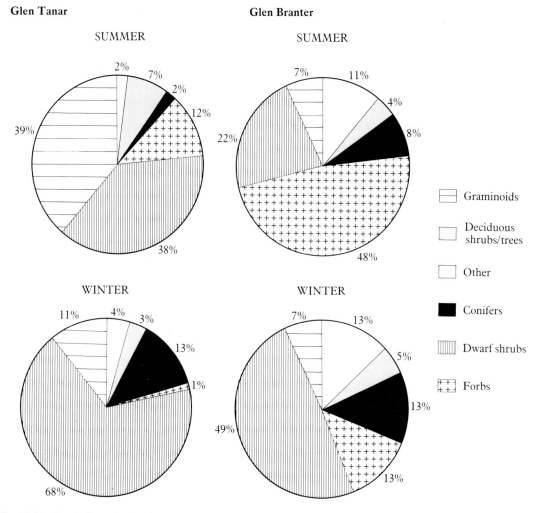

Fig. 12.20. Food of roe deer in Glen Tanar (Aberdeenshire) and Glen Branter (Argyll) in summer and winter.

weeks, kids usually accompanied and remain with mother. Lactation continues into winter although kids start to feed on vegetation within 2–4 months. Males attain puberty and will mate at 14 months. Spermatozoa present from mid-May–mid-November and testes are fully regressed by January [324].

POPULATION

Densities vary from 8–25 deer/km² in Sitka spruce forests in the Scottish Borders [222, 223] and the pine forests of East Anglia [289]. Densities related to forest structure, greatest in stands 5–15 years old reaching lowest point in close-canopy thickets but increasing again in mature stands prior to felling. In richer habitats of southern England, densities of more than 40 deer/km² have been observed in individual woods at specific seasons [201], although these areas may form only part of the animals' ranges.

Sex ratio of adults commonly two resident does to one territorial buck; number of non-territorial males variable. Counts of *corpora lutea* and of embryos *in uteri* suggest potential birth rates of 90 kids : 100 does in low-performance populations in Scotland to 210 kids : 100 does in Yorkshire [289].

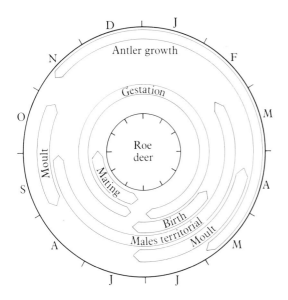

Fig. 12.21. Roe deer: life-cycle.

Age structure well documented for population at Kaló, Denmark; mean ages 2.1 years for males and 3.5 years for females; maximum age in wild roe recorded as 14 years, but most die before 8 years.

Survival: intra-uterine and high infant and yearling mortality occurs. Approximately 55–65% of kids and 50–80% of yearlings lost from populations due to mortality or emigration in summer [289]. Man main predator; over 15 000 animals culled annually. Some predation of kids by foxes and golden eagles [288].

PARASITES

Keds (*Lipoptena cervi*), the sucking louse *Solenopotes burmeisteri*, the biting louse *Damalinia meyeri* and ticks (*Ixodes ricinus*) are common in many British populations. *Cephenomyia stimulator* is a nasal bot fly specific to roe deer in Britain. Warble fly (*Hypoderma diana*) also recorded.

Lungworms (*Dictyocaulus* spp.) cause significant mortality in roe in some areas [255] and malignant catarrhal fever has been recorded [46]. Bovine and avian tuberculosis found [256, 295]. Many gastrointestinal parasites present, and liver-fluke (*Fasciola hepatica*) is very common in some areas [114]. Effects on host believed to be negligible.

Louping ill virus has been isolated from a roe deer [291]. Serological evidence of infection with bovine virus diarrhoea, reovirus 1 and 2 and adenovirus A [216]. Roe susceptible to foot-and-mouth disease under experimental conditions [126]. Antibodies to tick borne fever, *Leptospira* and *Borrelia burgdorferi* (Lyme disease) have been detected in roe from the New Forest [240, 254]. Infection with *Mycobacterium* spp. has been reported [241]. *Babesia*, a blood parasite transmitted by ticks, may cause death [367]. Lymphosarcoma was recorded in a roe deer from Dorset [368].

RELATIONS WITH MAN

Hunted from prehistoric times. Damage forestry through browsing and fraying young trees; can be very important in delaying regeneration or establishment of natural and planted forests. Pre-1960 generally treated as 'vermin' in many parts of Britain because of damage to forestry, agriculture and horticulture. Since 1970s increasing interest in exploitation as a game species and as meat. More than 13 000 culled annually by Forestry Commission in addition to those shot on private estates.

Covered by several Acts of Parliament but legislation differs between Scotland and England and Wales. Acts include the Deer Act 1973, Deer (Amendment) (Scotland) Act 1982, Roe Deer (Close Seasons) Act 1977, Wildlife and Countryside Act 1981. The various acts relate to conservation, welfare, poaching controls, firearm restrictions and close seasons.

LITERATURE

[183, 202, 271, 362, 363] — popular but detailed accounts.

SOUND RECORDINGS

Appendix 3: A, C, E, F, J, P, S, T, V.

AUTHORS FOR THIS SPECIES

B.W. Staines and P.R. Ratcliffe.

GENUS *Muntiacus*

A very distinctive genus found in SE Asia and recognised by simple, backward-pointing antlers and tusk-like canines in males. Six species are now recognised [140, 142]. Two species, the Indian or red muntjac, *M. muntjac*, and the Chinese or Reeves' muntjac, *M. reevesi*, have been kept in captivity, and the latter is now widely established in S Britain. Earlier suggestions that the muntjac found in Britain were hybrids between these two species have now been refuted [68].

Chinese muntjac *Muntiacus reevesi*

Cervus reevesi Ogilby, 1839; Kwantung, S China.

Barking deer, Reeves' muntjac.
Male — buck; female — doe; young — fawn.

RECOGNITION
Small brown deer (Fig. 12.22) with conspicuous white underside to tail which, including terminal hairs, is about 16 cm long and held vertically when animal is alarmed. Males have short simple antlers which sometimes have very small brow tines. Upper canine teeth protrude below lip in males but not as long as in Chinese water deer. Facial markings unlike any other deer in British Isles. Often stand with back hunched.

Skull distinguished at any age by size of pair of suborbital pits, almost as large as eye orbit. In male, pedicle arises from elongation of ridge on frontal bone. Skull of *M. muntjak* larger, and upper ends of premaxillae make contact with lateral margins of nasals; in *M. reevesi* skull smaller and upper ends of premaxillae do not contact nasals.

Fig. 12.22. Muntjac buck. (Photo: M: Clark.)

Footprints smaller than any other ungulate in British Isles. Outer cleave sometimes longer with tip just curved over tip of inner cleave. When walking, hind feet register on prints made by forefeet.

Faecal pellets black, shiny, striated, most weigh 0.1 g or 0.2 g and may be nearly spherical or cylindrical, length 6–13 mm, breadth 5–11 mm. Shape variable: pointed at both ends, pointed at one end and rounded or concave or flat at the other, or rounded at both ends. Deposited in heaps (mostly 20–120 pellets), sometimes some or all pellets adhering to each other. In some situations (probably high density populations) same spot used frequently so a regular latrine is formed.

Scrapes well defined (*c.* 30 cm diameter) in ground vegetation, exposing bare soil, mostly seen in habitats with high density of muntjac, where territorial disputes between adult males most likely. Scraping by vigorous pawing with forefeet is usually accompanied by aggressive behaviour to the neighbouring male.

Fraying of bark of saplings is not easily distinguished from that done by roe deer but occurs at low level — e.g. *c.* 18 to 36 cm above ground level. Mostly done by lower incisor teeth, occasionally when cleaning velvet.

DESCRIPTION

Pelage in summer rich red brown over most of body with buff belly. Extent of white on inside of thighs and chin variable. Tail rich chestnut dorsally, white below. In winter, duller, greyer brown, forelegs often almost black on front, especially in adult males. Head sandy ginger, neck of males sometimes almost golden. Males have black stripes, almost forming V, up frontal ridges and pedicles. Females have black or almost black kite-shaped pattern on forehead. Fawns have female face-pattern, males develop their characteristic pattern by about 9 months of age. Fawns born heavily spotted with buff at birth. Spots gradually fade and usually have disappeared by about 8 weeks.

Antlers: first head consists of simple spikes or knobs with no coronet. Second and subsequent heads have coronets and may have small brow tine.

Presence of brow tine one year does not necessarily mean it will be present in successive heads. In mature bucks, typically, the distal end of each antler curves backwards and usually terminates in a hooked point. Length seldom greater than 10 cm and weight greater than 17 g. Hard antlers are composed of compact bone, not spongy bone [58].

Pedicles first recognisable on head between 20–31 weeks of age. Later (32–46 weeks) small velvet-covered antlers begin to grow on the pedicles. The period in velvet is variable; cleaning occurs when the male may be 46–76 weeks old. The young males subsequently clock-in to the cycle of the adult males by casting their first antlers in May or June (median date May 26) when they may be 51–112 weeks old. Thereafter, a regular cycle [67]; new antlers grow through the summer (growing period 79–130 days, mean 106 days) clean the velvet in August–October (median date September 14) and remain in hard antler until the following casting season which ranges from the end of April to mid-July (median date May 27).

Moult in April to May is conspicuous. Usually begins on head, followed by shoulder or rump. September to October moult to winter coat is less obvious.

Nipples: two pairs.

Scent glands: a very large suborbital gland occupies pit in front of each eye. Pair of frontal glands on forehead form shallow grooves beneath the eyes, almost meeting as a small V. Hind feet have interdigital gland.

Teeth: deciduous formula 0.1.3.0 / 3.1.3.0, permanent dentition 0.1.3.3 / 3.1.3.3. All lower second and third premolars and fourth lower permanent premolars are lophodont. Deciduous lower fourth premolars, all permanent upper premolars and all molars selenodont. Permanent lower teeth erupt in order: molars, first and second incisors, premolars, third incisor and canine. Permanent upper teeth erupt in order: first molar, canine in males at 21 weeks, second and third molars, canine in females at 53–57 weeks, premolars. Full complement of functional permanent teeth attained by 83–92 weeks [77].

Marked sexual dimorphism of permanent upper canines: in male, tusk-like, curved, posterior cutting edge, sharp point and up to 45 mm long:

important as weapon. Root closed in old animals. One or both upper canines broken in 41% of 76 bucks examined over 2 years of age. In female, canine small and insignificant.

Reproductive tract: male; accessory glands comprise a disseminate prostate gland, paired seminal vesicles, ampullae and large Cowper's (bulbourethral) glands. Latter have a homologue of similar size in the female (bulbo-vestibular or Bartholin's glands). For both sexes these have been described under the name of para-urethral glands [106]. Female; bicornuate uterus. Most pregnancies occur in right horn of uterus [69].

Chromosomes: 2n = 46, all acrocentric except for small submetacentric Y chromosome. Identification of present-day feral muntjac in England confirmed by chromosome number [74].

RELATIONSHIPS

Chinese muntjac will hybridise with Indian muntjac (*M. muntjak*) [322], but the progeny are infertile [321]. Claims for hydrids in the wild in England are unsubstantiated and could only have occurred during the brief period when the two species may possibly have co-habited in the Woburn woods. Muntjac now established in England are all Chinese [68, 74].

MEASUREMENTS (Table 12.11).

VARIATION

M. reevesi has two subspecies: *M. r. reevesi* on mainland China (introduced to Britain) and *M. r. micrurus* on Taiwan which is slightly smaller.

Minor variations in pelage: some darker brown, some more ginger, rarely very pale. Forehead pattern in females variable, typically black but some are mid to dark brown. Facial stripes in males vary from jet black to less striking dark brown. Stripes usually extend the full length of the pedicles but not always. Black nape stripe present or absent in either sex. Ears may be same colour as head (golden/sandy brown) or almost black with sharp line of demarcation at base or gradually darken towards tip. Scattering of white hairs above cleaves sometimes present. Antlers occasionally with pearling at base or somewhat flattened blade-like form. Pedicles typically long but occasionally short.

DISTRIBUTION

Native to SE China and Taiwan where it inhabits scrub and dense forest between 200–400 m. Now well established over most of southern England, East Anglia and as far north as Cheshire, Derbyshire, Nottinghamshire and Lincolnshire in the Midlands. Wandering individuals, usually subadult males, not infrequently reported in urban areas, even central London.

Table 12.11. Measurements of muntjac, over 2 years old, from S England.

	Males			Females		
	Mean	Range	*n*	Mean	Range	*n*
Weight (kg)	14.8	10.5–18.3	105	12.2	9–15.8	124
Body length (nose to distal end last vertebra) (cm)	98	93–107	25	95	90–104	34
Shoulder height (cm)	49	44–52	29	47	43–52	35
Girth (cm)	58	52–61	29	53	48–61	35
Hind foot (cm)	23	22–24	30	22	21–23.5	36
Ear (cm)	8	7–8.6	30	8	7–8.6	35
Tail (to distal vertebra) (cm)	13	11–17	27	12	9–14.5	34
Tail (including terminal hairs) (cm)	17	14–20	26	16	14.5–18	17
Skull						
Greatest length (mm)	167	162–176	23	162	154–169	19
Zygomatic breadth (mm)	78	73–82	23	74	71–78	19
Mandible (greatest length) (mm)	129	123–135	23	127	122–133	19

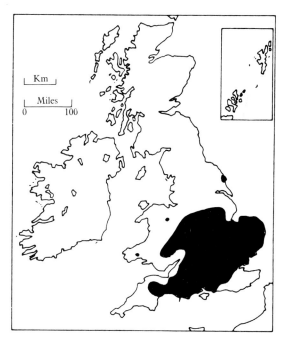

Map 12.9. Muntjac deer.

HISTORY

Introduced to Woburn Park and neighbouring woods, Bedfordshire, early in 20th century to replace the Indian muntjac which had been introduced a few years earlier. The latter was then shot out, although a few may have escaped elimination. Chinese muntjac spread from here; reports from 1922 onwards in immediate area and neighbouring counties. Some additional escapes/releases of small numbers from Whipsnade Park, Bedfordshire, Broxbourne in Hertfordshire (1930s) and Northamptonshire (1937). In first 60 years extended to a radius of 72 km from Woburn [362]; now approximately 300 km to south west, 200 km to north and north-east and 120 km to south-east.

HABITAT

Prefer dense habitat with diversity of vegetation: neglected coppice, spinneys with bramble or low ivy, scrub, young unthinned plantations, and even over-grown, undisturbed gardens are occupied. Frequently present in commercial coniferous woodlands which have some deciduous trees and ground

Map 12.10. Chinese muntjac deer.

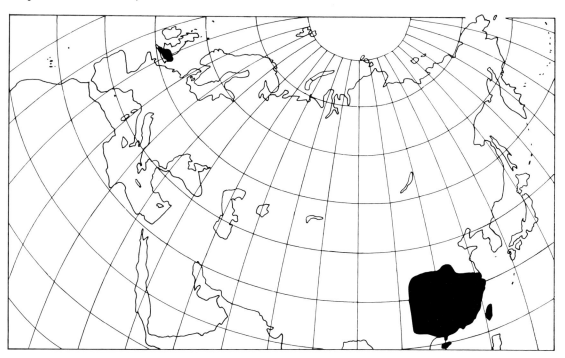

cover. Here they select areas with a variety of vegetation types, especially in the ground and shrub layers, bramble and mature nut-bearing trees [87].

SOCIAL ORGANISATION AND BEHAVIOUR
Muntjac do not form large social groups but are basically solitary animals. The vast majority of sightings are of solitary adults or subadults of either sex but sightings also occur of mature female and her most recent offspring, adult male and mature female, the latter plus the doe's latest offspring. Other combinations are much less common and seldom are as many as four seen together, but in some localities a larger number may assemble on one favoured feeding area without being a cohesive group.

For field observations the following age/sex categories have proved satisfactory. Fawns: under 8 weeks old, coat spotted or spots fading. Juveniles: indeterminate sex, 2−5 months, up to three-quarters grown. Immature females: 5−8 months, three-quarters to full-grown. Mature females: over 8 months, full size, breeding age. Subadult males: can be from 5 to 26 months; antler status varies from having only pedicle bumps to having hard 1st set of antlers. Adult males: animals enter this class between 12−26 months, after casting first head of antlers.

Observations and radio-tracking of marked animals [1] have shown that a particular mature male and adult female frequently may be together over several years but this does not indicate a life-bond as changes in associations occur, or several may occur concurrently.

Home ranges of adults in undisturbed, varied deciduous woodland stable, each of about 14 hectares, irrespective of sex or season [161]. In a longer-term study in mainly coniferous woodland most bucks had a larger range than females [91]; in both studies the ranges of several females overlapped each other and the range of each male encompassed those of several does.

Scent marking is most important means of communication. Males use facial glands more than females and dominant males more than subordinate males [17]. Suborbital glands are frequently opened, and sometimes everted to look like to a black grape, during courtship and when defecating and urinating. The deer then sometimes licks its own suborbital glands, presumably reinforcing

recognition of its own scent. The composition of the thick cream-coloured secretion is not yet known: five muscles are associated with each suborbital gland [16]. The frontal glands are frequently placed in contact with the ground. Secretion from the deep pocket of interdigital gland on hind foot must be deposited as the deer walks.

Vocalisation: loud, single barks which may be repeated a few or hundreds of times. Most usually heard after a birth, when a doe is in season or when an unfamiliar disturbance has occurred. Occasionally more a shriek than a bark. Loud scream emitted when alarmed, e.g. when caught. Young fawns squeak and doe pursued by amorous buck will give series of plaintiff squeaks.

Other communication: when alarmed, muntjac run off with the tail vertical, displaying the white underside. If unsure of a strange object, e.g. human observer, muntjac (like other deer) stamp the forefeet alternately several times. Possibly the vibrations on the ground are a signal to conspecifics.

Dispersal: age of natal dispersal is variable. Males sometimes move far away before growing their pedicles, others not until much later. Some young females remain in the mother's area and establish an overlapping range. Adults of either sex sometimes disperse from an area in which they have been established for several years.

Aggressive behaviour: fighting strategy described by Barrette [18] and Miura [253]. Sparring matches involving antler-to-antler contact, usually between unequal males, are harmless and sometimes end in mutual grooming. Fights between equally matched bucks are preceded by a slow, deliberate walk towards the opponent and often the grinding of cheek-teeth. Head-on clashing ensues, using the antlers to get into a situation where the opponent is unbalanced and can be delivered a downward blow with a tusk on the neck or face. Deep wounds from a tusk have also been seen on the rump of a male whose own upper canines were broken.

Adults of either sex will pursue a well-grown juvenile offspring, presumably driving it from its natal range.

A nursing doe in captivity will chase vigorously an intruding cat and would strike it with her hooves. Whether similar attacks are made on foxes is not known.

Activity: the main feeding periods are early morning, dusk and middle of the day but muntjac may be active at any time. After a feeding session they usually lie up, but sometimes stand, in cover to ruminate.

Fawns a few weeks old indulge in playful rushing about, mostly at dusk. A buck, particularly a subadult, occasionally has a 'bucking broncho' session lasting several minutes on the one spot during which he leaps vertically into the air, twists and almost stands on his head. He may also indulge in log pushing and lifting using his head, even rolling the log over his back. Neck fighting seen in captivity between doe and subadult offspring.

Movement: when undisturbed, usually travel at walking gait, head held low or trot purposefully. If disturbed run short distance before stopping to investigate source of disturbance; rarely bound — only if passing through extensive long grass. Occasionally stand on hind legs to reach browse.

Grooming: self grooming from 1 day of age; tongue and incisiform teeth used. Both parents will groom a fawn all over, particularly around the anus whilst being suckled. Mutual grooming is important in social behaviour and occurs between animals of the same or different sex and within the same or different age class. Mutual grooming concentrates on the neck, head and ears, especially during the spring moult, and on the antlers when in velvet.

FEEDING

Primarily browsers rather than grazers, as indicated by direct observations, rumen content analysis [194], faecal pellet analysis [167], anatomy of the alimentary tract [179], digestive studies [8] and the size of the salivary glands [208].

Analysis of faecal pellets collected over a 2-year period in a conifer forest in Suffolk recorded 85 species of plants [167]. Most important was *Rubus* (bramble and raspberry), accounting for 30–40% of the diet in all months. Other food items changed seasonally with ivy, ferns, fungi, broad-leaved trees and shrubs, nuts and other fruits all being important. Grasses were a significant part of the diet only in spring. In an Oxfordshire deciduous woodland, muntjac in summer selected rose, dogwood, blackthorn and hawthorn [161].

BREEDING

Breed throughout year, fawns born in any month with no obvious peak [76]. First conception in captive animals can occur at 5–6 months, more usually 7 months or later. Single fawn; rare reports of twin fetuses [82].

Post-partum oestrus, so female usually conceives within few days of parturition. Of 36 precisely known interbirth periods, the shortest was 211 days, 50% were 216 days and a further 31% were 220–250 days. A female can be almost continuously pregnant over many years, e.g. one captive female had 16 live births (plus one aborted fetus) in 9 years 10 months.

Testes less active in summer, but buck still capable of fertilising even when antlers just cast and while antlers are growing.

Gestation: 210 days. Mating follows period of male pursuing doe, often chasing her relentlessly, with frequent sniffing, licking of vulval area and her urine, and his exhibiting flehmen and mounting many times. Oestrous female frequently walks around with tail raised and often barking.

Sex ratio at birth *c.* 1 : 1. Of 53 captive births, 27 males : 26 females. Of 80 pregnant uteri from wild animals with sexable fetus, 42 male and 38 female. Mean weight (within 1 day of birth) 1209 g (range 900–1500 g, $n = 30$, captive animals). Lactation observed in captivity up to 17 weeks.

POPULATION

Densities vary with habitat. In a coniferous forest with some deciduous woodland, 30 muntjac (excluding fawns) in 206 hectares, a density of one per 6.8 hectares [91]. This was not optimum habitat and the density would be greater in a denser, more varied thicket woodland.

Because of the year-round breeding, at any time a population will include animals in all age categories. In one winter population of 30 animals, three were juveniles, three immature females, 14 mature females, four subadult males, six adult males [91].

Survival: potentially long-lived. Examples of longevity in captivity: 16 years for a male, over 19 for a female.

DISEASE

Generally very healthy and disease-free. Can become infected with foot-and-mouth disease but no cases recorded in wild. Erysipelas has been reported in captive muntjac in England [26]. Evidence of arthritic conditions in a few skeletons. Chronic wasting disease, including polycystic renal disease and erosion of joint surfaces, reported from Whipsnade [120]. One case of a buck with an under-shot jaw.

MORTALITY

Apart from being shot, greatest mortality is by road-traffic accidents. Dogs kill some. Occasionally carcases found have been eaten partly by foxes which may have found them as carrion. Heavy mortality reported after severe winter if prolonged periods of deep snow. Some abortions/perinatal mortality.

PARASITES

Very few endoparasites recorded. No lungworm found in 90 animals, no bladderworm cysts in 169 carcases. Incidence and numbers of gastrointestinal nematodes very low. *Nematodirus battus*, *Oesphagostomum* sp. and *Trichostrongylus* sp. (primarily parasites of sheep) recorded from eggs in muntjac faeces collected at Knebworth Hertfordshire [170]. Intestinal protozoa *Eimeria* sp. recorded [258].

Two biting lice (*Cervicola muntiacus* and *C. indica*) and one sucking louse *Selenopotes muntiacus*; *C. muntiacus* and *S. muntiacus* appear to be host specific. *C. indica* and *S. muntiacus* more common and sometimes both species on one deer, but rarely in large numbers. Tick *Ixodes ricinus* frequently present in some localities but many fewer than on roe deer in same locality. Orange larvae of mite *Trombicula autumnalis* also recorded.

RELATIONS WITH MAN

Some shooting of muntjac carried out for control. Very little if any damage is done to conifers or arable crops. The small mouth cannot bite a lump from large sugar beets or carrots. The shoots of some deciduous trees and some garden plants, e.g. roses are more vulnerable.

Road traffic takes a toll and errant muntjac in a town can create hazards.

Legislation: muntjac (at present) have no close seasons because they breed throughout the year; if females are to be culled, immature animals should be selected since they will not have a dependent fawn. Licences to catch/transport muntjac for specific purposes, as for other deer species, are at the discretion of the Nature Conservancy Council.

Techniques for study: radio-collars used to study year-round, home-range size [161]; animals individually marked with coloured collars and tags have been studied [91]. Capture method using long nets [88] and use of immobilising drugs [100] have been described.

LITERATURE

[362] — for early information on distribution in England. [332] — for a popular account of the deer which colonised a Hertfordshire garden. [90] — observations on captive and wild deer. [105] — general account.

SOUND RECORDINGS

Appendix 3: A, F, V.

AUTHOR FOR THIS SPECIES

N.G. Chapman.

GENUS *Hydropotes*

A distinctive genus with a single species, notable as one of the two species of deer without antlers. Its relationship to the other deer is discussed by Groves & Grubb [141].

Chinese water deer *Hydropotes inermis*

Hydropotes inermis Swinhoe, 1870; Yangtze River, China.

Water deer; Chinese name 'Ke'. 'Chang' also, but this is classical name for muntjac.

RECOGNITION

Reddish brown summer coat; thick, sandy colour in winter. No antlers. Adult males have long, curved upper canines. Large, rounded ears (Fig. 12.23). Black beady eyes. Slightly taller than muntjac, and differ in having a straight back (muntjac often hunched). Further distinguished from muntjac by short tail, which is never held erect, and lack of dark facial markings. Stance and movement more like those of roe, but roe taller and have a conspicuous caudal patch.

SIGN

Feet small, slots with equal cleaves, similar but larger than muntjac's. Faeces similar to muntjac's, usually longer, i.e. 1.0−1.5 cm long by 0.5−1.0 cm wide. Not usually aggregated: black or dark brown, cylindrical, pointed at one end, rounded at other.

Fig. 12.23. Chinese water deer buck. Note the wide rounded ears and protruding tusks. (Photo: M. Clark.)

DESCRIPTION

Very thick, winter coat of hollow hairs, white at base, buff near tip then black at apex giving a brindled appearance. Individuals vary in colour from pale fawn to a dark grey-brown. Muzzle white/grey when mature. Summer coat sleek and reddish brown. Transitional period from winter to summer coat between March and May; by May most have sleek, red summer coats. Fawns have pale spots in lines at birth, but lose these after 2 months. Large, rounded hairy ears held erect above head. Eyes rounded, black and button-like. Black nose with muzzle varying from brown through grey to white. Tail short, stumpy, occasionally sticks out horizontally. No caudal patch.

Scent glands: pre-orbital glands small; inter-digital glands on hind feet. Only deer with inguinal glands.

Teeth: dental formula 0.1.3.3/3.1.3.3. Long, curved, hinged upper canine (tusk) in adult male protruding well below jaw line. Upper canine small in female (*c.* 4 mm), not visible in the field. Normal tusk length for parkland animals is about 70 mm. Maximum recorded at Woodwalton Fen, Cambridgeshire, is 95 mm for extracted tooth and 66 mm (length of exposed canine in carcase). Young males have tusks intermediate in length, depending on their age.

Skeleton: skull described by Flerov [124]. Lateral metacarpals (splint bones) at distal end of cannon bone, the teleometacarpalian condition.

Chromosomes: 2n = 70; FNa = 68 [370].

MEASUREMENTS

Body measurements: Table 12.12; skull measurements Table 12.13. Data from Whipsnade Zoo, 1937: average weight of old males 11.7 kg, range 9−13 kg (*n* = 8), average weight of old females 12.9 kg, range 10−15 kg (*n* = 10), most pregnant. Some authors, e.g. Whitehead [363] state that females are lighter in weight by 2−3 kg, but measurements of wild animals at Woodwalton, Cambridgeshire (see Table 12.12) agreed with the Whipsnade observations that females are about 1−2 kg heavier, even when not pregnant. Chinese data shows no significant difference in weights of adult males (14.8 kg, *n* = 18) and adult females (15.1 kg, *n* = 21) [320]. Deer at Woodwalton are about 3 kg heavier than those at Whipsnade.

	Males			Females		
	Mean	Range	*n*	Mean	Range	*n*
Weight (kg)	14.2	12.0−18.5	8	15.6	14.0−17.4	7
Tusk length (in socket) (mm)	54.7	44.0−66.0	11	4.1	2.0−7.0	7
Body length (cm)	92.5	82.0−105.0	11	95.6	90.0−105.0	6
Height at shoulder (cm)	49.1	42.0−56.0	10	50.3	42.0−61.0	7
Ear (cm)	10.1	9.0−11.0	7	11.0	9.6−12.0	5
Tail (cm)	6.5	4.5−9.0	6	6.2	2.4−8.0	6

Table 12.12. Measurements of adult Chinese water deer from Cambridgeshire.

	Males			Females		
	Mean	Range	*n*	Mean	Range	*n*
Greatest length	167.2	163.7−171.0	5	167.0	166.5−167.5	2
Zygomatic width	70.0	68.6−71.5	5	66.1	64.0−67.0	3
Length of palate	95.0	91.6−98.2	5	96.4	96.0−96.9	2
Length of maxillary tooth row	49.7	48.4−51.4	5	49.3	48.6−50.0	3
Length of mandible	137.8	135.2−140.6	5	136.7	136.0−137.0	3
Length of canine (round outside curve, extracted)	86.9	81.5−95.1	4	16.4	15.9−17.0	2

Table 12.13. Skull measurement (mm) of adult Chinese water deer at Woodwalton Fen, Cambridgeshire [251].

Animals from various places stand about 50 cms high at the shoulder, but 60 cms also reported [124].

VARIATION

Two subspecies described — the Chinese water deer *H. inermis inermis*, the form found in Britain, and the Korean water deer *H.i. argyropus* Heude, 1884, but the latter is not recognised by Flerov [124].

DISTRIBUTION

Native range NE China and Korea. In Britain established in the wild in Bedfordshire, Cambridgeshire (including former county of Huntingdonshire) and in the Broads in Norfolk. Also introduced to France [354].

HISTORY

First kept in Britain at London Zoo in 1873, but not subsequently. First introduced into parks in early 1900s at Woburn Park, Bedfordshire. Then at Whipsnade Zoo, 1929−30, from where they have escaped and become established in the wild.

Introduced into parks including Cobham, Surrey, 1934; Basingstoke and Stockbridge, Hampshire, 1944; Ripon, Yorkshire, 1950; Bishop's Castle, Shropshire, 1950 and Ludlow, Shropshire, 1956.

First reported in the wild in 1945 from Buckinghamshire and late 1940s from Hampshire; then 1950 from Northamptonshire and Oxfordshire; early 1950s from Yorkshire; 1956 Shropshire; 1968 Norfolk [217]; 1971 Cambridgeshire; and 1976 Bedfordshire.

HABITAT

In reed beds, swampy ground and also broadleaved woodland in China and Korea. In Britain found in reed beds and woodland, where it prefers mixed vegetation with grass for grazing and scrub and woods for cover. At Whipsnade, essentially lives in open parkland with some woodland, where the species survives despite the lack of wetland. At Woodwalton Fen, the mixed fen and woodland habitat appears more similar to its native habitat; it may be significant that deer from Woodwalton are heavier than those from Whipsnade.

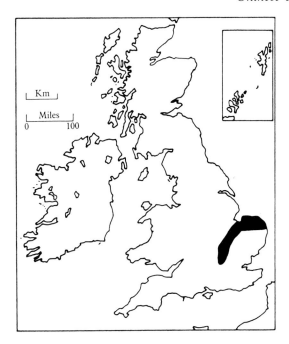

Map 12.11. Water deer.

SOCIAL ORGANISATION AND BEHAVIOUR

Usually seen alone or in pairs in China. At Whipsnade, large numbers are kept in open fields, and small groups may be observed grazing or ruminating together. In the wild, at Woodwalton Fen, they are usually observed singly. Following the rut in November–December, they are often seen in pairs until April. Does and bucks tend to separate in spring before the young are born in June or July. Sometimes seen in groups either grazing together on farmland, especially in January–February when food is scarce, or in nursery groups consisting of several does with their young in late summer. Territories are formed and defended by bucks during the rut, and young males may be driven off. In the wild at Woodwalton Fen a territory is about 4 hectare or more consisting of some open grazing land and some scrub or tree cover.

Territories are marked by scraping the ground with the forefoot and urinating, and by rubbing the head and pre-orbital glands against a tree or prominent tuft of vegetation. No noticeable fraying of saplings. Piles of faeces often found along boundaries. No known hierarchy.

Map 12.12. Water deer.

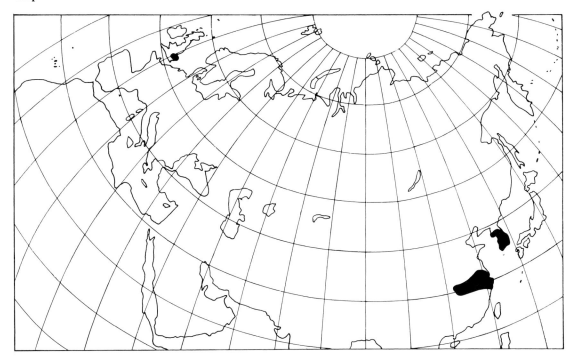

Communication mainly vocal or by scent. 'Neck-bobbing' mainly by does when disturbed. Can scent humans up to 200 m away upwind. Four different types of vocal communication recorded — barking, whickering, whistling, and screaming. Barking is the most common. This is a loud, abrupt, dog-like sound used as a warning and sound of alarm. Whickering is a rapid, medium-pitched staccato, chattering noise, usually made by the male during chases. Whistling or squeaking also part of sexual behaviour and made by buck following doe. Both sexes make a high-pitched screaming noise when chased.

Rut takes place in November–December. Pairs set up territories, defended by adult males, young males driven out and disperse. Remain in pairs until about April. Bucks thereafter usually separate from doe until the next rut. Unmated deer remain as singles and may wander from one territory to another.

Bucks parade side by side. A threat display consists of stretching out the neck, bringing the head close to the ground and shaking it from side to side. A fight ensues if a rival stands its ground. Tusks are used but generally not much damage is caused because of the protection afforded by the thick coat, although tusks may be broken and ears frayed.

Activity at any time of day or night, but main period is just before and after dusk. Usually move with a leisurely walk. When frightened run off, often flinging up hind legs. May stop, turn round and reassess danger. Other observers note squatting as hares when threatened. Good swimmers, will cross 3 m wide, deep water courses without hesitation. Also cross these on ice.

FEEDING
Mainly grasses, sedges and bramble. Feeding in open areas concentrated around dusk and dawn. At Woodwalton Fen they feed inside the nature reserve throughout the year, venturing out onto the surrounding arable land occasionally. More frequent visits to farmland during January–February when young, green vegetation is in short supply in the reserve. Eat carrot tops and weeds between the rows. Will not eat hay. Drink occasionally, obtaining most of their requirements from food and dew.

BREEDING (Fig. 12.24)
Rut takes place in November–December. Gestation period 176–210 days. Young born May–July in long vegetation in the wild, and in open fields at Whipsnade. Litters of five or six recorded in China [7], but majority of litters two or three fawns (mean = 2.53, *n* = 17) [320]. In Britain usually one or two fawns, although more embryos carried. The mean number of fawns born to 12 does at Whipsnade was 2.3 (75% twins, 25% triplets or quadruplets) [244]. Fawns weigh about 0.8 kg (range 0.15–1 kg) at birth and are spotted until about 2 months old. Young left singly in sheltered places by doe during day until she returns at regular intervals to suckle them. Weaned after 2 months but remain with doe until the autumn. Doe has two pairs of mammary glands. Capable of breeding at 5–7 months; in China reported to attain sexual maturity at 8 months [320]. Cyclical fluctuations in weight of testes [320].

POPULATION
Density at Whipsnade may be as many as 20 per 10 hectares, at Woodwalton Fen about 3 per 10 hectares. Sex ratio at Woodwalton 1:1. Deer known to live for at least 6 years.

MORTALITY
Since 1976, the remains of 56 deer found at Woodwalton Fen, 77% of these between the beginning of October and the end of March, when

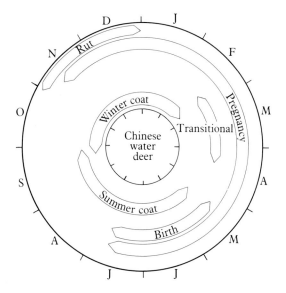

Fig. 12.24. Chinese water deer: life-cycle.

harsher weather occurs. Can suffer from starvation during hard winters, even in parkland. Young eaten by fox. Fox thought not to kill adult, but will eat carcase. Shot by man, especially on farmland. Road casualties a major cause of mortality — first identified in Norfolk from road casualties.

PARASITES
Demodex mites cause mange. Ticks (*Ixodes* spp.); keds (*Lipoptena* sp.) and lice *Cervicola meyeri* and *Dama linia* sp. all recorded. Nematode *Oesophagostomum venulosum* found in colon at Whipsnade. Haemolytic streptococci recorded in subcutaneous pustules. Suffer from pulmonary congestion and respiratory diseases. Reovirus 1 and 2 and adenovirus A recorded (serological evidence) [216].

RELATIONS WITH MAN
In China killed for commercial purposes (meat and skins) and as pests of crops; neonates killed for colostrum for folk medicine [320].

In England cause no damage to trees as they do not bark them. No great threat to crops as will only eat root crop tops when little other food available and do not exist in sufficient numbers in wild to cause much damage.

Easily raised in captivity but a tendency to escape. No statutory close seasons but British Deer Society recommends 1 March–31 October for both sexes [186].

LITERATURE
[336] — behaviour at Whipsnade. [90, 98] — brief accounts.

SOUND RECORDINGS
Appendix 3:A, P.

AUTHORS FOR THIS SPECIES
L. Farrell and A. Cooke.

GENUS *Rangifer*

A distinctive genus which is usually considered to be monospecific, although the Nearctic and Palaearctic forms are sometimes given separate specific status. Relationships between the various populations discussed in [141]. The only species of deer in which the females also have antlers.

Reindeer *Rangifer tarandus*

Cervus tarandus Linnaeus, 1758; Swedish Lapland.

HISTORY
Reindeer (Fig. 12.25) occurred in Britain during the last glacial period, and persisted into the early post-glacial, but probably became extinct before Roman times. A reference in the *Orkney Saga* to the hunting of reindeer in Caithness in the 12th century has been interpreted as evidence of their survival in Scotland to that date. However, this reference could have arisen due to confusion with red deer or from an introduction by the Vikings, and so cannot be taken as conclusive evidence of their survival to that date.

Domesticated reindeer were introduced to the Cairngorms by Mikel Utsi in 1952. The original

Fig. 12.25. Reindeer. (Photo: P. Morris.)

stock came from Sweden; after some initial difficulties they settled well, and over the years the
herd has been supplemented by Norwegian and
Russian deer. In 1988 the herd numbered 80 animals, which are free-ranging on the N slopes of
the Cairngorms. They remain on the open hill
throughout the year, never coming below the
treeline.

The rutting season takes place during 3 weeks
during the end of September and beginning of
October. Cows will often breed for the first time at
2 years old, and calves are born in May. Twins
were recorded for the first time in May 1988.

Lichens, mainly *Cladonia* spp., form the main
winter diet, becoming less important during the
summer, when the deer feed on sedges, grasses and
heather. During the autumn they have a particular
liking for mushrooms of the genus *Boletus*.

The herd is carefully managed by the Reindeer
Company Limited. Some animals are culled: the
other main causes of mortality are road-traffic accidents and dogs. There is normally a visit to the
reindeer each day, leaving Reindeer House at
Glenmore at 11 a.m.

FAMILY BOVIDAE

The largest family of ungulates, containing the
cattle, antelopes, goats, sheep, etc. Primarily an
Old World group, they are both successful and
diverse. The only species with any claim to have
been indigenous in Britain in the post-glacial period
is the aurochs, *Bos primigenius*, but domesticated
cattle, sheep and goats have been present since the
Neolithic period and have at various times given
rise to feral populations. The most distinctive
feature of bovids is the presence of horns, consisting
of permanent horny sheaths on bony cores developed from the frontal bones of the skull. They may
be present in both sexes, as in wild oxen, goats and
sheep, or only in males. Domestic breeds may lack
horns in one or both sexes. Dental formula 0.0.3.3/
3.1.3.3.

GENUS *Bos*

Contains the wild oxen of Eurasia, including the
Asiatic gaur, *B. gaurus*, banteng, *B. javanicus* and
yak, *B. mutus*, in addition to the aurochs, *B.
primigenius*. The last is extinct as a wild species but
is the ancestor of domestic cattle.

Park cattle *Bos taurus*

White Park cattle; Wild White cattle.
Male — bull; multiparous female — cow; primi-
parous female — heifer; young — calf.

STATUS
White, horned cattle with black or red ears
occur widely [262] but White Park cattle claim
descent from herds impounded in baronial hunting
parks, which date from the 13th century [282,
361]. There are many ancient accounts of white
forest cattle and the laws relating to them, but
there is no historical evidence to link them to these
park-land herds, which cannot be survivors of
undomesticated stock and are unlikely to be descended from feral woodland herds. They were
probably selected from local husbanded cattle.

At the beginning of the 20th century there were
several herds of Park cattle [361]; the principal
strains were defined as Chillingham, Vaynol,
Dynevor, Chartley and Cadzow. All are horned.
Only the Chillingham herd in Northumberland has
been kept pure (Fig. 12.26); cattle from the other
strains have been, or are being, interbred and
crossed with other breeds [5, 361], and the resulting
White Park breed must be clearly distinguished
from the pure Chillingham herd. The British
White, superficially similar to the White Park but
polled (genetically hornless), arose from another
park-land herd. Confusingly, the British White is
known in North America as the White Park. The
conformation of the White Park is that of a typical
early 20th century British beef breed, but the
Chillingham cattle resemble, skeletally, mediaeval
British cattle [92].

White Park and Chillingham cattle are freely
interfertile with other breeds [361]. Blood grouping
studies [156] show the Chillingham herd to be
remarkably homozygous, and do not reveal any
affinity with any other breed. No records have yet
been discovered of introductions to the Chillingham
herd before the 18th century and since then all
extant accounts refer to their purity [154].

DESCRIPTION
Chillingham cattle 110 cm shoulder, maximum
adult weight for bulls 300 kg, for cows 280 kg in
Chillingham Park, but 430 kg recorded for the only
mature male in the reserve herd in northern Scotland [151]. Chillingham cattle are slow growing;
18-month-old bulls weigh about 100 kg (cf. South
Devon, Britain's largest bodied native breed of

Fig. 12.26. Chillingham cattle.

commercial cattle, which weigh at least 600 kg at this age).

Both the White Park and the British White breeds are white with black ears, though some White Park calves are black and others have red ears. Chillingham cattle all have red ears, and no coloured calves have been born since the 18th century [347].

Chromosomes: 2n = 60 for all breeds. A chromosomal translocation is prevalent in the British White [119] but has not been found in the White Park [283] or in Chillingham cattle [268]. White Park cattle have a C-band chromosomal polymorphism (absence of a centromeric block of heterochromatin) [276].

DISTRIBUTION

World-wide, there are several populations of free-ranging feral cattle [157]. Most are descendants of

British beef breeds, while some are of Spanish type and a few feral Jersey dairy cattle are known in New Zealand [182]. In Britain, the only feral cattle are the Chillingham herd, and a herd on Swona, Orkney. These latter are of Aberdeen-Angus/Shorthorn mixture; they are under private ownership and there are no long-term plans for their conservation.

The Chillingham herd is held at Chillingham Park, Northumberland, with a reserve herd established in N Scotland in 1973. There is no public access to the reserve herd. The Chillingham herd was in the possession of the Earls of Tankerville until 1973, when it passed to a charity (the Chillingham Wild Cattle Association).

White Park cattle are registered by their own breed society, the White Park Cattle Association. They are mostly found in farm parks and are not currently a commercial proposition. There are fewer than 150 pure-bred breeding cows [9]. In contrast, the British White is expanding in numbers (around 450 cows) and is also securing a commercial and export market. Farm parks where these breeds can be seen include the Cotswold Farm Park (Gloucestershire), Wimpole Home Farm (Cambridgeshire), Temple Newsam (Leeds), Graves Park (Sheffield), Appleby Castle (Cumbria) and Tilgate Park (Sussex). These breeds receive extensive support from the Rare Breeds Survival Trust, and special conservation measures are being applied to the Vaynol cattle [174].

HISTORY
Skeletal studies [25] have shown that there is no exclusive relationship between Park cattle and the wild ancestor of cattle, the aurochs (*Bos primigenius*), which died out in Poland in 1627 AD [294]. No aurochs remains later than Bronze Age (i.e. pre-Roman) have been found in Britain; they were not recorded in Ireland. Historical accounts of the Chillingham cattle are lacking until the 18th century [151]. In the 19th century, the Chillingham herd was subjected to rigorous artificial selection, about half of all bull calves being castrated. The history of inbreeding in the Chillingham cattle is confirmed by their homozygosity [156], and the Vaynol cattle are also reported to be homozygous [174].

HABITAT
The two feral free-ranging herds live in very different conditions. Chillingham Park (98−235 m elevation) is ancient mediaeval pasture, with woods mostly of 18th century and early 19th century establishment [155]. Swona comprises maritime heath with abandoned arable and pasture land [157].

SOCIAL ORGANISATION AND BEHAVIOUR
Studies on many free-ranging herds, including Highland cattle on Rhum, Scotland [95], the Camargue cattle in France [313, 314], and the cattle of the New Forest [277], have shown that all-female herds are organised on the basis of a dominance hierarchy together with individual affinities. Home-range behaviour is not associated with such herds, which frequently subdivide into small groups of variable composition.

The only study of social behaviour in a herd of natural sex ratio and age distribution is that at Chillingham [154]. Here, bulls over 4 years of age live in groups of two or three, each with a home range. Cows, calves and young bulls roam apparently freely, in a group or subgroups, over the whole park, which is 134 hectares in area.

The repertoire of maintenance behaviour is similar in Chillingham cattle to that known in husbanded cattle, but year-round reproduction leads to bulls constantly being on alert for oestrous cows and rival bulls, and this is reflected in their daytime bouts of maintenance behaviour being shorter than those of cows [154].

Chillingham bulls also have distinctive vocalisations which may serve to reduce the number of dominance encounters among bulls of different home-range groups [158].

Some forms of social behaviour, well known in husbanded cattle, are rarely, if at all, seen in Chillingham cattle. These include play behaviour by adults, cow−cow mounting during oestrus, and licking of one adult by another. Social behaviour frequently takes place at night [154].

FEEDING
Cattle tend to maintain rate of intake at expense of diet digestibility, while sheep tend to maintain digestibility at expense of rate of intake [11]. Experiments have demonstrated effects of different levels and timings of grazing upon natural and semi-natural swards [136, 137], but there is little evidence so far of the factors affecting choice of sward on which to graze, although seasonal differences are clear [153].

When food is lacking, cattle coalesce into a single group [157], so the confinement resulting from localised hay feeding probably has its counterpart in nature. At Chillingham, simple dominance hierarchies, more stable from year to year for cows than for bulls, operate at such times [152] and this was also noted on Rhum [95].

BREEDING
Cattle are not seasonal breeders and their tendency to spring or summer calving is due to the lengthening effect of winter upon the post-partum anoestrus [160]. There are very few data on the mating system of herds where more than one bull is active. At Chillingham, what probably happens is that when a cow becomes receptive she is inseminated by the bull which is of highest rank in the home-range group occupying the area where she is at the time [150, 151].

At Chillingham herd records for the periods 1862−99 and 1953−85, show herd fertility (calves born per female per year) has not declined [156].

Calf survival has also remained the same with 73% of calves surviving to 1 month of age. About 50% of Chillingham calves survive to maturity. In contrast, in British upland beef herds with 'below average' performance, about 91% of calves survive from calving to marketing [243].

Onset of puberty in Chillingham bulls is at about 18–20 months of age [14]. Adult bulls have small testes, total weight being about 160 g (0.06% of body weight). In commercial dairy cattle the combined testicular weight is about 0.10% of body weight [308]. Chillingham bulls probably have rather low fertility and a short reproductive life, lasting perhaps from the onset of home-range establishment at 4 years up to 7 years, this depending on the level of competition [151].

POPULATION

Little is known of the factors affecting population dynamics in free-ranging cattle other than the Chillingham herd. In the late 19th century the size of the Chillingham herd was controlled by culling and averaged 61 [156]. Since culling stopped mortality has been correlated with number in the herd at the start of winter, and with spring rainfall [156]. After a crash to 13 in 1947 [347] numbers have recovered and after a steady rise to about 40 individuals around 1970, numbers have fluctuated between 40 and 65. Sex ratio is always biased towards females; adult survival is better in this sex [156].

PARASITES

At Chillingham, worm burden is very low [151] but on occasion young animals have been heavily infected with stomach nematodes, *Ostertagia* spp. Other parasites are as in other cattle [214]. Autopsies have never disclosed Johne's disease, TB, brucellosis or foot-and-mouth disease, but New Forest disease (infectious bovine keratitis), a fly-borne bacterial infection of the eye, was prevalent during the dry summer of 1976, leading to some bulls having impaired sight, although cows were not affected.

During the period 1977–81, about one-third of the adult bulls at Chillingham had visible injuries from fighting; loss of an eye and rupture of body wall have been observed but bulls have only rarely been killed fighting [1, 347].

RELATIONS WITH MAN

White Park cattle have potential as a beef crossing sire and are attractive members of farm park col-lections. Chillingham cows have been crossed with Shorthorn bulls [361] but commercial application of Chillingham cattle is unlikely and their conservation is justified because of their history and unique purity.

LITERATURE

[108] — review of the zooarchaeology of British cattle. [361] — history of British park cattle. [350, 351] — cattle husbandry. [149, 313, 314] — standard accounts of the behavioural repertoire of free-ranging cattle. [12] — most recent account of the ecology of such herds but needs updating.

The White Park and British White receive extensive coverage in the Ark, journal of the Rare Breeds Survival Trust.

AUTHOR FOR THIS SPECIES
S.J.G. Hall.

GENUS *Capra*

A genus with five species ranging from the Mediterranean region to the mountains of central Asia. Two wild species in Europe, *C. ibex* in the Alps and *C. pyrenaica* in the mountains of Spain. Of the three Asiatic species, the bezoar goat, *C. aegagrus*, is at least the main if not the sole ancestor of the domestic goat. The bezoar goat is still found on some Aegean islands and in Crete, but it is possible that these goats constitute relic populations of very early domestic animals [93]. There is no evidence that this or any other species of *Capra* has ever been native in Britain but feral domestic goats are well established in some areas and are generally referred to as 'wild goats'.

Feral goat *Capra hircus*

Capra hircus Linnaeus, 1758; Sweden.

'Wild goat'; gabhar fhiadhain (Scottish Gaelic); gabhar fia (Irish Gaelic).
Male — billy; female — nanny; juvenile — kid.

RECOGNITION

Only likely to be confused with certain primitive breeds of sheep. Goats (Figs 12.27, 12.28) distinguished from sheep by the presence of a callus on the knee, a beard and a potent body odour (especially in billies). Goats have flat, rather long tails

Fig. 12.27. Feral goat.

Fig. 12.28. Feral goat: an adult and young females, plus young males.

which are bare underneath. In contrast, sheep have more rounded, hairy tails. Smaller, lighter and longer haired than 'improved' (modern) goat breeds (billies usually less than 70 cm at the shoulder and less than 65 kg). Colour varies from white through to black although most individuals are grey, grey-brown or black with paler patches. Both sexes usually horned. Some ferals are polled (genetically hornless) but this is rare. Ears erect.

Skull distinguishable from sheep by convex frontals and nasals. Horn cores arise from frontals straight up rather than laterally as in sheep. Lower jaw thinner and more acutely angled than that of sheep. Distal end of metapodials (cannon bones) characterised by two converging sagittal ridges (cf. sheep which have parallel sagittal ridges) [28, 272]. In other respects, bones of goats and sheep are very similar. Precise ageing of all but nannies older than 3 years is possible by counting annual rings on horn sheaths [44]. Ring formed in winter and becomes conspicuous at the base of the horn when growth recommences in spring [138].

SIGN

Footprints very similar to sheep. Sometimes distinguishable because hoofs tend to be more splayed and smaller in goats than sheep. Goats and sheep use many of the same tracks but some goat tracks cross very steep terrain and are inaccessible to sheep.

At night and during persistent rain, use shelter such as crags, caves, rank heather and gulleys extensively.

Faeces very similar to sheep, roe deer and red deer. Pellets 1–2 cm long, cylindrical with pointed or concave ends. Tend to be more symmetrical and drier than either sheep or deer. Faeces deposited throughout home range but large accumulations occur in traditional shelter sites.

Bark-stripping signs frequent in late winter where goats have access to woodland. Bark stripped from a central vertical line splaying to either side moving up the trunk and interspersed with long rips of bark. Difficult to distinguish bark-stripping due to goats from that of red deer or sheep. Goats usually bark-strip to a maximum height of 2 m although they may climb trees and do so higher [1].

DESCRIPTION

Pelage colour variable; ranges from pure black to white with fawns and greys the most prominent colours, the latter brought about by a mixture of black and white fibres [305]. Black goats often have a fringe of long, ginger hair along the back and on hind quarters. Many Welsh ferals have dark forequarters and whitish hindquarters [38]. Dark stripe on front of forelegs frequent; some goats show a dark eel stripe, 'Jesus' saddle and brown and black pattern similar to the true wild goat. Goats from the western populations of the Southern Uplands are paler and greyer than those from the eastern populations [1].

Horns grow backwards and then outwards in a smooth curve. Wide spreading ('dorcas') horns frequent in Wales and the eastern Southern Uplands and in some Highland populations. In SW Scotland, closer set, backward sweeping horns ('scimitar') are more frequent.

Moult once a year; in late spring–early summer, the winter hair and underwool are shed. Thicker winter coat due to an increase in the length of the underwool [305].

Nipples: one pair.

Scent glands: post cornual 'musk' glands found in both sexes, and are situated immediately behind and along inside edge of the horn. These are apparently activated by testosterone and usually are only active in males [233]. Interdigital and caudal glands also present [135A].

Teeth: eruption sequence and degree of wear can be used to assign individuals to broad age classes. Incisiform teeth: in 11 nannies tracked throughout life, nine had erupted all four pairs by the age of 3.5 years. For a similar sample of nine billies, attainment of the 'full-mouthed' condition was later: three by 3.5 years, five by 4.5 years and one by 5.5 years [1]. Cheek-teeth (data from billies): deciduous premolars shed by 1.5 years. M_1 already erupted at birth, M_2 by 1.5 years, M_3 by 3.5 years. Cusps on all cheek-teeth well worn to flat surfaces by 6.5 years [45].

Excessive tooth wear and tooth loss can occur after 4 years old. By the age of 7 years goats frequently lose molars and show signs of diseased teeth. Incisiform teeth usually wear evenly and are rarely lost (although frequently fall out after death) [41].

Skeleton: in billies, frontal, nasofrontal and nasal sutures fused by 4.5 years. In nannies, fusion occurs at approximately twice this age. In billies, all postcranial epiphyses fused by the age of 6.5 years, apparently similar for nannies [45].

Reproductive tract: female: bipartite Y-shaped uterus; syndesmochorial placentation. Villi from fetal placenta clustered into groups called fetal caruncles. Male: testes and epididymides develop rapidly from 30–40 days until 140–150 days, when fully mature and weigh 90–135 g. Spermatozoa first recorded at 88–95 days. Average ejaculate into artificial vagina 0.10 to 1.25 ml [13].

Chromosomes: $2n = 60$, as other members of the genus, all of which appear to interbreed freely in captivity.

RELATIONSHIPS
Wholly or largely descended from the wild goat *Capra aegagrus* whose range extends from the Mediterranean basin eastwards to central Asia.

MEASUREMENTS (Table 12.14)

VARIATION
Goats from the SE Scotland/NE England are significantly larger and heavier than those from SW Scotland. Whilst this variation may have a genetic basis, density and range quality may also be important [41].

DISTRIBUTION
Mainly hilly and mountainous areas of Scotland, Wales and Ireland, including the following islands: Achil, Great Blasket, Bute, Cara, Colonsay, Holy Island (Arran), Islay, Jura, Lundy, Mull, Rathlin, Rhum, Skelligs. Populations often small and discrete rather than scattered over a wide area of apparently suitable ground.

Isolated feral goat populations occur elsewhere in Eurasia and Far East from southern Norway through to Japan. Australia and New Zealand have large populations. Many islands in the Pacific, Atlantic and Indian Oceans also have feral goats. A few populations in Canada and United States. World-wide, feral goats occur on at least 70 islands [302].

HISTORY
Not native. Domestic goats probably arose *c.* 9000 bp in SW Asia [108]. In Britain goats first introduced as domestic stock by Neolithic peoples [325]. Date of introduction uncertain due to confusion of goat/sheep bones in archeological sites, but earliest definite remains of domesticated goat in Britain found at a Neolithic site in Wiltshire

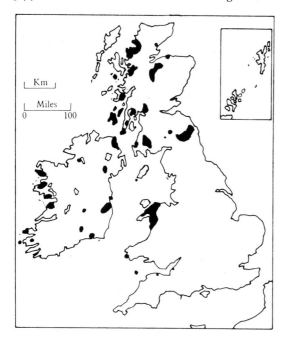

Map 12.13. Feral goat.

HABITAT
Mostly restricted to hilly or mountainous areas above 300 m where cliffs are available. Steep ground used for refuge, shelter and for feeding in associated dwarf shrub communities. Prefer dry, well-drained ground. Several populations use woodland (native and planted coniferous). Where hill sheep and goats graze the same ground, goats frequently occur on steeper, rockier ground than that used by sheep [41, 103].

SOCIAL ORGANISATION AND BEHAVIOUR
Matriarchal relationships within nanny groups. Adult billies often group together and may range separately from nanny groups. Within 'billy' groups, peers tend to associate more closely with each other than with other age classes. In the Southern Uplands, group size varies seasonally between one and 70 depending on population size. Median group size of two in spring a result of nannies near term isolating themselves from the home-range group; rises to eight in the autumn and winter when rut occurs [41]. Similar seasonal variation in group size occurs in Wales [38]. Degree of sexual segregation variable; in some populations, billy groups may be found at great distances from the nanny groups; in other populations, sexual segregation is infrequent.

Dispersion: in many populations, dispersed in home-range groups consisting of one to several matrilines and associated billies. Such groups can have clearly defined range boundaries with little overlap between neighbouring group ranges [41]. In some populations, e.g. on Rhum, billies form a separate home-range group [30]. Billies wander widely during the rut in search of nannies in

dating from 2960 ± 150 BC [206]. Majority of feral goats in Britain show characters — presence of horns, lack of neck tassles, coat pattern, prick ears and foreleg stripe — that apparently fit those of the old breeds 'Old English', 'Old Irish' or 'Old Scottish' or 'native' goat. This breed type became extinct in domestication in the early 1900s as 'improved' goat breeds were imported and sheep farming became increasingly popular. In the Southern Uplands, feral populations have been in existence since at least the 19th century [138].

	Males			Females		
	Mean	Range	n	Mean	Range	n
Head and body (cm)	129.7	118−152	10	120.9	106−136	30
Tail (cm)	11.3	8−14	10	10.7	7−14	30
Ear (cm)	10.7	9.5−11.5	20	10.8	10−11.5	29
Weight (kg)	52.4	39−65	10	41.1	29−52	30
Jaw length (mm)	174	157−198	14	172	151−190	13
Condylobasal length (mm)	226	208−241	10	221	209−243	17
Horn length (mm)	607	465−755	20	249	93−385	30
Heart girth (cm)	99.3	91−108	10	93.6	80−106	30
Height at shoulder (cm)	69.0	60−75	20	64.2	56−74	30
Beard length (cm)	26.5	26−27	2	19.6	17−22	10

Table 12.14. Measurements of adult (4 years or older) feral goats from S Scotland. Weights from late autumn−winter when goats are heaviest.

oestrus, usually returning to their non-breeding range in the summer.

Area used by home-range group between 0.3 km² and 6.5 km² (mean 3.0 km²) depending partly on the number of goats in the group (6−62), and the quality of the range [30, 37, 41].

Behaviour: few differences between the behavioural repertoires of feral and wild goats [318]. Social hierarchy exists amongst nannies and amongst billies in billy groups with dominant individuals tending to be the largest and oldest. Billies older than one year are dominant in encounters to nannies. Dominance is exerted by 'stare threat' through 'horn lowering' escalating to the 'clash' where two goats crash their heads and horns together with great force. Bouts of clashing by same-sized billies may last several hours. Dominance and mating success in billies related to pre-rut body weight and horn length [265].

Billies, in contrast to rams, urinate over forequarters; resulting odour possibly used in communicating dominance rank [97]. During the rut, billies 'test' the reproductive state of nannies by allowing her urine to flow over the vomeronasal organ whilst lipcurling (flehmen). Flehmen also given by billies in response to their own urine, and by nannies after sniffing kids [259].

Communication: contact call a series of bleats often used by dam searching for kid when it is 'hiding out'. Also used by adults when separated from group. Alarm call an abrupt, nasal snort which immediately alerts most of the group. Potentially dangerous threats cause a walking retreat or, if necessary, a run to safe ground (usually uphill to cliffs). Distress call a loud, wavering scream.

Dispersal: dispersal from known population range has never been documented. In many populations, nannies rarely disperse from their natal home-range groups. Billies may disperse to join billy home-range group or remain with natal home-range group [41, 265]. Lack of dispersal probably related to the need for known shelter sites. During severe winters, goats tend to move down hills to lower altitudes.

Activity: predominantly diurnal. Day spent alternatively feeding and ruminating (and resting). In winter, typically one long (*c.* 2 hour) rumination period, during the middle of the day. Goats in a group tend to ruminate synchronously. In summer, several rumination periods during the course of the day. May feed at dusk and at dawn during the summer and autumn. Billies feed relatively little during the rut [41].

Movement is by walking or running. Extremely agile and a good climber. Quite capable of climbing mature trees and near vertical cliff faces provided there are footholds. Frequently browses whilst on hindlegs to bring branches within reach of mouth. Apparently avoids swimming.

FEEDING
A selective but versatile ruminant adapting its diet to season and local conditions; goats may browse or graze. On British uplands, typically show a seasonal pattern of diet selection similar to that of hill sheep; in summer, grasses, sedges and rushes predominate with, in winter, increased use of dwarf shrubs, gorse and other browse. On Rhum and Holy Island, goats feed extensively on seaweed during winter [138, 266]. Goats browse more than sheep, and in areas with low availability of dwarf shrubs also select plants such as rushes, bracken and bog myrtle that are rarely eaten by sheep [38, 43]. During late winter and spring, trees may be browsed and bark-stripped. In oak woodland order of preference for bark-stripping was willow, rowan, oak, alder. Conifers, especially pines, Norway spruce and sitka spruce, are also damaged by goats [1].

BREEDING (Fig. 12.29)
Mating during autumn rut; one or two kids born between January−April. Length of oestrus cycle: 20 days in domestic dairy goats; 72% of observations fell between 15 and 24 days [13].

Gestation: 151 days in large series of goats of several breeds; 86% of observations fell between 147 and 155 days [13].

Number of fetuses: one or two; up to five recorded in domestic stock [13].

Weight at birth: 1.5−2.7 kg [139, 242].

Duration of lactation: 5−6 months; male kids suck for longer and probably obtain more milk than do female kids [265].

Main proximate cue for autumn rut is decreasing photoperiod [13]. Mating system polygynous;

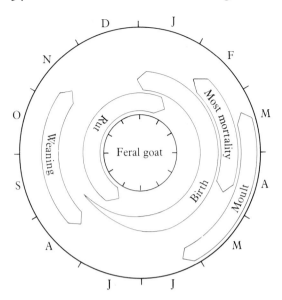

Fig. 12.29. Feral goat: life-cycle.

mating takes place following a courtship and tending period where billy guards the nanny from intrusions by other, subordinate individuals. Tending period up to 2 days. Nannies in oestrus are conspicuous: frequently bleat and lift and shake their tails. Main behavioural elements in courtship of nanny by billy are 'low stretch', 'gobble' and 'foreleg kick' [319]. These are identical to those of the wild goat [312]. Dominant billies tend and mate nannies at the peak of oestrus. Other matings attempted by young, subordinate billies occur outside peak of oestrus. These may result in successful copulations [265].

Most births in March in Southern Uplands (mean birth dates vary between 5th March–8th April in Moffat Hills) [265]. February–March in Wales [39] and January–February on Rhum [135]. Some kids born July–August in Highlands region may have been conceived in a post-partum oestrus by nannies that lost a kid in January. Alternatively, these births may be from 1st year nannies, breeding for the first time in January.

Incidence of twinning probably underestimated due to early death of one twin. In Southern Uplands and Wales proportion of nannies with twins at heel in summer varies between 1% and 20% depending on population and year [38, 41].

Sex ratio at birth 1:1 [138]. Population bias towards females is typical and arises from relatively

high mortality rates of males from 1st year onwards [41].

Young uses a hiding place for 2 to several days after birth, then follows its mother. Maternal attachment specific, rapidly formed and fairly stable. Mother labels kid via the milk or by licking it [147]. Whilst hiding out, kid is periodically suckled by mother [265, 298]. Hiding out site, which is chosen by the kid, is typically sheltered and dry, often amongst dwarf shrubs, rocks or gorse.

POPULATION

Densities (number, excluding kids, in area enclosed by outermost sightings of the population) vary between 1.5 and 11.8/km² depending on the population and the year, although typical density around 2/km². Highest densities recorded from W Eire [29] and SW Scotland [41]. Recent population estimates (mainly 1983–1985): 1700, southern Scotland/Scottish border; 355, Clyde area; 200, Rhum; 400+, Islay, Jura, Mull and west coast mainland of Scotland; 100+, central and N Scottish Highlands; 450, Wales [1, 30, 39, 133]. Population sizes in Ireland unknown. Estimated Scottish total in 1969, 4000 [138]; present Scottish total apparently little changed.

Population declines (in the absence of heavy culling) associated with severe winters, causing very high kid mortality and high adult (especially male) mortality. Population increases associated with series of mild winters which allow high survival of kids [1]. Kid mortality around birth varies between 50 and 100%. In S Scotland, kid : nanny ratio in summer inversely related to the severity of preceding winter's weather [1].

Population structure: most mortality occurs in the 1st year of life. After 1st year, survivorship relatively high for *c.* 6 years in nannies. Billies have lower survival rates. In S Scotland, after the first 6 months of life, median age at death is 3.25 for billies and 6.25 for nannies. Maximum ages recorded are 13 and 11 for a billy and a nanny respectively [41]. Records of feral goats aged 20 or more years are unsubstantiated.

MORTALITY

Kid mortality probably caused by hypothermia associated with starvation. In adults, mortality is associated with low marrow fat index [326] indicating that starvation was an important contributory cause of death. Most billies die before their teeth are particularly worn; in contrast, nannies die at an age where their teeth are heavily worn and often diseased [41].

Apart from culling by man, predators (of kids) include golden eagles and probably ravens, foxes and wild cats. Eagles use goat carrion extensively in SW Scotland [235].

PARASITES

British records from feral goats in [36, 41, 49, 103, 115, 230, 352].

Sucking louse *Linognathus stenopsis* and biting lice *Damalinia limbata*, *D. caprae* (all regularly recorded) and *D. ovis*. Ticks: *Ixodes ricinus* common. Mites: *Chorioptes bovis*.

Parasite egg counts from goat faeces in Southern Uplands and Holy Island were low and within the range found for healthy domestic sheep. Tapeworms: *Monieza expansa*. Roundworms: *Dictyocaulus filaria* in lungs; *Haemonchus contortus*, *Ostertagia circumcincta*, *O. leptospicularis*, *O. trifurcata*, *O. lasensis*, *Teladorsagia davtiani*, *Trichostrongylus axei*, *Spiculopteragia spiculoptera* in abomasum; *Bunostomum trigoncephalum*, *Cooperia* spp., *Nematodirus filicollis*, *N. battus*, *T. capricola*, *T. colubriformis*, *T. vitrinus* in small intestine; *Chabertia ovina*, *Oesophagostomum venulosum*, *Skrjabinema ovis*, *Trichuris globulosa* in colon; *Trichuris ovis*, *Skrjabinema ovis* in caecum.

Positive reactions for Louping ill, Q fever (*Coxiella burnetti*), leptospirosis (*Leptospira grippotyphosa*, *L. icterohamorrhagiae*, *L. autumnalis*), and toxoplasmosis (*Toxoplasma gondii*).

RELATIONS WITH MAN

In Britain, as elsewhere, feral goats are regarded as pests and regularly culled. Foresters claim that they cause considerable damage to plantations, and farmers claim that they compete with sheep, destroy crops and damage walls. There has been no research as yet to investigate whether goats significantly reduce the economic value of either trees or sheep. Goats in native woodlands probably prevent regeneration to a greater extent than do sheep or deer at similar density because of their greater preference for browse.

Recently, feral goats have attracted commercial interests because of their potential ability to control weed species on pasture [303] and to produce cashmere wool [306]. Exploited for food and some billies stalked for their trophy heads.

One of the few large mammals on British up-

lands; considered by many to be desirable element in the fauna. Important source of food (carrion) for few remaining golden eagles in southern Scotland [235]. Control of feral goats is usually easy: except on steep rocky ground, goats bunch together when gathered and can usually be controlled by sheep dogs. Several authors [139, 300] have stressed the value of feral goats as a 'rare breed'. Breed status of many populations is unknown but feral goats probably represent a source of genes for 'hardiness' which may in the future be exploited for crossbreeding.

Legal status of feral goats uncertain. Classified neither as a wild animal, nor as domestic stock. Readily adapts to captivity provided that a dry shelter is available and the ground is dry.

LITERATURE

[364] — a comprehensive description plus detailed distribution maps. [135] — describes feral goats on Rhum.

AUTHOR FOR THIS SPECIES

D.J. Bullock.

GENUS *Ovis*

In the Old World, wild sheep occur from Asia Minor through central Asia to NE Siberia. No wild sheep have been present in Britain or Europe in post-glacial times although wild-living sheep (mouflon) occur today on the islands of Corsica and Sardinia (*Ovis musimon*) and Cyprus (*O. ophion*). These European mouflon are the feral relic of sheep that had not long been under domestication at the time they were introduced by people in prehistoric times. Domestic sheep arose from *O. orientalis*, the Asiatic mouflon of Asia Minor and were first brought into Britain in Neolithic times.

Feral sheep *Ovis aries*

Ovis aries Linnaeus, 1758; Sweden.

Male — ram; female — ewe; juvenile — lamb.

RECOGNITION

Two forms of feral sheep occur in Britain: the Soay (Fig. 12.30) (formerly surviving only as a relic population on the island of Soay, St Kilda) is a

Fig. 12.30. Soay sheep ram.

Fig. 12.31. Boreray ewe group.

primitive breed that is more similar in many respects to wild sheep than more improved breeds in being narrow-bodied, relatively long-legged, having a short tail and narrow face. Soays are smaller than other sheep; in good condition adult rams and ewes weigh up to 35 and 26 kg respectively and stand about 50 cm at the shoulder. Unlike wild sheep, the coat of the Soay is composed mainly of wool. The Soay is only likely to be confused with certain other unimproved sheep breeds, such as the Hebridean.

The Boreray (Fig. 12.31) is a (feral) sheep confined to Boreray, St Kilda, and resembles a small Blackface sheep. The Boreray differs from the Blackface in having smaller body size, relatively larger head and, often, in having a dark collar. Both the Soay and the Boreray are highly variable in colour, the former ranging from light buff to blackish and the latter from cream-white to blackish [31, 42, 50].

Skull and skeleton: for distinctions between sheep and goats see account of feral goat. The Soay's skeleton shows characters similar to those of sheep bones from late Neolithic, Bronze Age and Iron Age sites [32]. All Boreray sheep have two horns; the majority of Soay rams and about half Soay ewes are horned, other ewes being polled or carrying distinctive horns or 'scurs' [109].

SIGN

Footprint: typical cloven hoof print very similar to feral goat.

Faeces: very similar to, but less regular than, feral goat. Deposited throughout home range but large accumulations occur in cleits, the entrances to which may become blocked by both dung and sheep carcasses [33].

Feeding remains: Soay sheep on Hirta (St Kilda) graze the grasslands to give a tussocky appearance [148].

DESCRIPTION

Pelage: colour of Soay varies from light fawn to blackish although 'light' and 'dark' phases are prevalent. Colour pattern resembles that of mouflon in having a whitish belly and scrotum/udder. The white extends to the insides of the thighs producing a distinctive rump pattern with the dark upper tail contrasting with light rump patch [109].

Colour of Boreray varies from white to blackish. In 1980, approximately 67% had cream—off white fleeces, 20% grey—grey-brown and the remainder tan or darker. Between 4% and 7% have wholly blackish coats. There is often a dark collar that extends from the nape to the front legs.

There is marked sexual dimorphism in size in both breeds. Males carry large horns in a loose spiral which in the Boreray reaches 75 cm along the curve [31, 42].

Moult: in both breeds, the fleece is cast during the summer [42, 109].

Nipples: one pair.

Scent glands: in rams, anto-orbital gland swells and opens during the rut. Caudal, circumanal, inguinal and interdigital glands also present [371]. Rams show flehmen in the same way as goats do.

Teeth: in the majority of Soays, the eruption of successive pairs of incisiform teeth is an annual event and as such can be used to estimate the age of sheep up to 4 years old [145]. Sheep can also be aged by counting cementum lines in cross-sections of the first incisor [299].

Skeleton: in Soays, the skeleton has been fully formed (including metacarpal and metatarsal fusion) by the age of 6 years [96A]. In general, the Soays on St Kilda show slower skeletal development than that of mainland improved breeds, and their dentition remains in good condition until advanced age, with very few 'broken mouths' [22].

Reproductive tract: female: bicornuate uterus; ovulation spontaneous; corpus luteum active for about 14 days; uterine epithelium frequently with black pigment; cotyledonary placenta. Male: testes and epididymes develop less quickly than in goat; mature spermatozoa first recorded at 147 days. Average ejaculate volume varies between 1.18 and 1.46 ml.

Chromosomes: $2n = 54$ as in *O. orientalis* [257]. Fertile hybrids between *O. aries*, *O. orientalis* and *O. musimon*.

RELATIONSHIPS

Domestic sheep are descended from a wild ancestor, the Asiatic mouflon *O. orientalis*, whose range extends from SW to central Asia [312].

MEASUREMENTS

See Tables 12.15, 12.16 and 12.17. Soay show a loss of appetite and weight in the winter.

VARIATION

Considerable variation in both breeds in coat colour and pattern. Soay sheep brought to mainland Britain to form flocks of 'park Soays' are mostly of the dark phase with horned females. A few fawn flocks, also with horned females, have been selected and maintained.

In the Soay (and probably the Boreray), rams can be accurately aged by counting the number of annual rings on their horn sheaths. In ewes this is either impossible (because they lack horns) or difficult owing to the small size of the horns and the small increment between rings [145].

DISTRIBUTION

Soay found on Soay and Hirta (St Kilda) and, more recently, introduced to many offshore islands; a well-known flock is on Lundy in the Bristol Channel. Boreray confined to Boreray, St Kilda.

Feral sheep also occur on *c.* 20 islands [302]. These include Arapawa, Campbell Island and Pit Islands of New Zealand [260, 301, 366], Hawaii [349] and Santa Cruz Island off California [355].

HISTORY

Sheep were first introduced to Britain as domestic stock by Neolithic peoples [325]. Date of introduction uncertain due to confusion between goat/sheep bones in archaeological sites. Sheep were first domesticated 9000 years bp in SW Asia [108]. *O. musimon* on Corsica and Sardinia and *O. ophion* on Cyprus believed to be feral relics of sheep that were imported to Mediterranean islands not long after their domestication.

Horn shape, short tail, coat colour and coat moult of Soay all suggest an affinity with wild *Ovis* species. Sheep believed to have been introduced to St Kilda in prehistoric times on the grounds that bones of Soay sheep are very like those recovered from late Neolithic, Bronze Age and Iron Age

Table 12.15. Mean live weights (kg) of Soays from Hirta in May 1963 by age and sex. Based on [109].

	Males	*n*	Females	*n*
Lambs	5.7	27	6.0	23
Yearlings	14.1	10	13.8	7
2 year olds	20.1	18	17.6	11
3 year olds	22.0	4	15.0	1
4 years and older	25.6	5	19.8	22

Table 12.16. Mean live measurements in May of Hirta Soay ewes and rams [109].

	Age (years)							
	Yearling		2		3		4+	
	Males	Females	Males	Females	Males	Females	Males	Females
Leg length (mm)	316 (38)	305 (24)	337 (31)	320 (25)	338 (6)	318 (14)	347 (11)	321 (98)
Body length (mm)	450	438	502	483	511 (5)	481	533	502
Chest depth (mm)	228	209	251	229	259 (5)	243	281	247
Pelvic length (mm)	172 (19)	167 (14)	184 (17)	173 (15)	175 (5)	175	198 (8)	179 (82)
Hip width (mm)	113	115	127	126	123 (5)	135	143 (9)	136 (93)
Wither width (mm)	125	111	135	119	141 (5)	132	161	135

Sample size in brackets.

Table 12.17. Measurements of feral sheep on Boreray mid-July 1980; data from [110].

		Females		
	Males (1 year)	4 years	7 years	Adult
Head and body (cm)	113	—	—	117
Tail (cm)	16	—	—	18
Ear (cm)	8.5	8.5	8.6	8.0
Weight (kg)	—	—	28.0	27.0
Horn length (mm)	460	—	—	285
Heart (chest) girth (cm)	86	—	—	81
Height at shoulder (cm)	63	—	—	—
Hoof length (cm)				
Fore	3.0	3.3	3+	6.3
Hind	3.0	—	3+	5.0

sites. However, the later introduction of sheep by Vikings or in Christian times is equally likely [32].

For centuries, Soay sheep were confined to Soay (St Kilda) where the population was estimated to be between 150 and 300. In 1932, following the evacuation of the St Kildans and their sheep from Hirta in 1930, 107 Soays were transferred there [50].

The Boreray represents the breed type shepherded by the St Kildans who were unable to gather their flock on this island before departing [50]. The breed represents a cross between the Blackface which reached Scotland in the 18th century, and the Old Scottish Shortwool that is now exemplified by the Orkney/Shetland type [42].

HABITAT
On St Kilda, both breeds select *Agrostis–Festuca*, *Holcus–Agrostis*, *Festuca*, *Poa* grassland and *Plantago* sward during summer. In autumn and early winter Soay on Hirta make more use of *Calluna* wet heath [245]. *Calluna* heath does not occur on Boreray.

SOCIAL ORGANISATION AND BEHAVIOUR
Soay ewes on Hirta maintain matriarchal relationships in 'ewe home-range groups'. Ram lambs leave these groups by two years of age and join, or form, separate 'ram groups'. These occupy ranges except at the rut when individual rams wander widely in search of ewes. Home-range groups occupy areas ranging in size from 0.2 to 40 hectare although individual sheep occupy a smaller area than that used by the group [146]. On Hirta, the mean number of sheep in ewe home-range groups varied between 27 and 37 between 1964 and 1967. For the same years, mean ram group size was much smaller at between one and 5.3 [143]. On Hirta, areas occupied by ewe home-range groups overlap to a variable extent, but close contact between neighbouring groups is minimised [146].

Behaviour: the behavioural repertoires of feral and wild sheep are very similar [318]. Social hierarchies develop amongst individuals in both ewe and ram groups. Rams become dominant over adult ewes in their 1st rut (as lambs). In Soay rams, high-ranking sheep form more tending bonds than lower ranking ones, and almost certainly achieve a higher mating success: they consort with ewes at the optimal time to achieve conception [200]. Dominance among rams is exerted by 'nudging' through 'blocking' escalating to 'butting' where two rams crash their heads and horns together with great force [144]. Ewes also butt one another.

Communication: contact call between lamb and ewes is the familiar bleat. Alarm call is a snort or whistle in response to danger.

Dispersal: on Hirta, all rams have left their natal ewe home-range group after 2 years of age and have joined or formed ram groups.

Activity: similar to feral goat; predominantly diurnal. In winter, most of the day spent grazing. In summer, may spend several hours lying and ruminating throughout the day but especially before noon [146].

FEEDING
Predominantly or exclusively grazers. Soay on Hirta show a marked seasonal variation in diet similar to that shown by hill sheep on the mainland of Scotland: in summer, grasses predominate with an increasing proportion of heather towards and through the winter [245]. On Boreray, sheep graze the year round [110].

BREEDING (Fig. 12.32)
Data for Soay on Hirta. Seasonally polyeostrus. One to two lambs born between March and May. Median lambing dates recorded in 6 years from 14 to 23 April [197, 198]. Survival rate of twins poorer than that of single lambs [145]. Mean length of oestrus cycle 15 days [198]. Domestic sheep have a mean oestrus cycle length of 16.5 days [13].

Gestation: 148−155 (mean 151) days for Soay ewes [198]; up to three fetuses for managed Soay sheep. Weight at birth 0.89−3.3 kg. Mean for singletons *c*. 2.0 kg. Duration of lactation not known.

Main proximate cue for autumn rut is decreasing photoperiod. On Hirta, a few ewes are in oestrus in

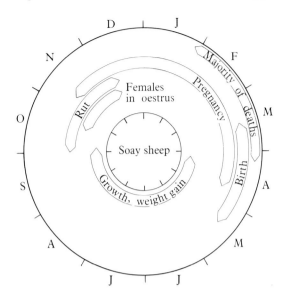

Fig. 12.32. Soay sheep: life-cycle.

late October but the majority in November [198].

Successive polygnous matings similar to the goat. Main behaviour elements in courtship of ewes by ram are 'low stretch' and 'foreleg kick', similar to those of the urial [198, 312].

Sex ratio at birth 1 : 1. Population bias towards females occurs after the 1st year of life arising from higher mortality rates of rams [145].

POPULATION

Soay: between 1952 and 1987 the total number of sheep on Hirta has fluctuated markedly from year to year showing periodic density dependent die-offs. Maximum and minimum numbers (counted in May−June and including the surviving lambs of the year) have been 1783 and 610 (corresponding to densities of 2.8/ha and 0.9/ha).

Boreray: counts of sheep from the sea between 1951 and 1980 indicate a minimum population size on Boreray of between 200−500. In 1980, the total from land counts was 699, a density of *c*. 12 per hectare. This exceptionally high density is probably maintained by the high quality pastures that are fertilised by seabird guano [42].

Population structure: lambing percentage varies greatly between years (*c*. 50 to over 100%) in an apparently density dependent manner. Survival rate of rams is less than that of ewes. In the adult segments of the population of Hirta and Boreray, the sex ratio is one ram to four to six ewes. On Hirta, all Soay rams die by the age of 10 years. On Boreray, the oldest ram recorded was 8 years old at death. The oldest Soay ewe recorded on Hirta was 15 [1, 110, 145].

MORTALITY

Most deaths occur in February–March when the nutritional value of the pastures is below the maintenance requirements of the sheep. During the rut in autumn, the rams spend much less time feeding than the ewes and this is a major factor predisposing them to higher mortality in late winter [144]. On Boreray, overgrown hooves cause 3% of adult sheep to limp [110], and such lameness may result in falls from cliffs.

PARASITES

Lice: *Damalinia ovis*. Keds: *Melophagus ovinus*. Tick: *Ixodes ricinus*, the 'sheep tick' not recorded from St Kilda; *I. rothschildi* a seabird tick occurs on Boreray [110] and may accidentally occur on sheep. Tapeworms: *Monieza* spp. Roundworms: *Nematodirus filicollis*, *Bunostomum trigonocephalum*, *Trichuris ovis* and *Chabertia ovina* (intestines). *Dictyocaulus filaria* (trachea, lungs), *Muelleris capillaris* (lungs).

No antibody for louping ill recorded for Soay sheep on Hirta. Coccidial oocysts recorded for Boreray sheep of *Eimeria weybridgensis*, *E. ninakohlyakimoriae*, *E. ovina* and *E. parva*. Detailed parasite lists in [89, 110].

RELATIONS WITH MAN

Present policy of management for Soay sheep and Boreray sheep on St Kilda is one of minimal interference whilst at the same time watching for serious damage to the ecosystem. Both sheep are classified by the Rare Breeds Survival Trust as 'Rare Breeds'. Many consider the St Kildan sheep a valuable heritage (note that the name 'St Kilda' used to be given to the four-horned breed now called the Hebridean). The Soay, in particular, is regarded as an important link with the sheep type that was first introduced to Britain in prehistoric times [32].

Both the Boreray and the Soay are hardy breeds whose lambs seem particularly well adapted to cold, wet conditions [327]. As such, these sheep may provide a useful source of genes for cross-breeding.

Sheep on St Kilda are timid but inquisitive. They flee when approached within 100 m although quickly become more confiding with regular human presence. They scatter when worked with a sheep dog and cannot be rounded up in this way.

LITERATURE

[199] — a comprehensive account of the ecology of Soay sheep on St Kilda. [110] — a comprehensive account of the natural history of Boreray, including its sheep.

AUTHORS FOR THIS SPECIES
P.A. Jewell and D.J. Bullock.

REFERENCES

1 Author's data.
2 Adam K.M.G. *et al.* (1977) The occurrence of antibody to *Babesia* and to the virus of louping-ill in deer in Scotland. *Research in Veterinary Science* **23**: 133–8.
3 Aitken R.J. (1975) Delayed implantation in roe deer (*Capreolus capreolus*). *Journal of Reproduction and Fertility* **39**:225–33.
4 Albon S.D. *et al.* (1983) Fertility and body weight in female red deer: a density-dependent relationship. *Journal of Animal Ecology* **52**:969–80.
5 Alderson G.L.H. (1982) White Park cattle. *Ark*, **9**:168–70.
6 Alexander T.L. ed. (1986) *Management and diseases of deer.* London: Veterinary Deer Society 254 pp.
7 Allen G.M. (1940) Mammals of China and Mongolia. In *Natural history of central Asia*, vol. 11(2). New York: American Museum of Natural History pp. 618–1350.
8 Anderson J.M. (1981) *Studies on digestion in Muntiacus reevesi.* MPhil. thesis, University of Cambridge.
9 Anon (1988) Rare breeds acceptance procedure. *Ark* **15**:14–15.
10 Armstrong N. *et al* (1969). Observations on the reproduction of female wild and park fallow deer (*Dama dama*) in southern England. *Journal of Zoology* **158**:27–37.
11 Armstrong R.H. & Hodgson J. (1986) Grazing behaviour and herbage intake in cattle and sheep grazing indigenous hill plant communities. In Gudmundsson O. ed. *Grazing research at northern latitudes.* New York: Plenum Publishing pp. 211–18.
12 Arnold G.W. & Dudzinski M.L. (1978). *Ethology of free-ranging domestic animals.* Amsterdam: Elsevier 198 pp.
13 Asdell S.A. (1964) *Patterns in mammalian reproduction.* New York: Cornell University Press.
14 Ashdown R.R. Personal communication.

15 Bailey R.E. & Putman R.J. (1981) Estimation of fallow deer (*Dama dama*) populations from faecal accumulation. *Journal of Applied Ecology* **18**: 697–702.

16 Barrette C. (1976) Musculature of facial scent glands in the muntjac. *Journal of Anatomy* **122**:61–6.

17 Barrette C. (1977) Scent-marking in captive muntjacs, *Muntiacus reevesi*. *Animal Behaviour* **25**: 536–41.

18 Barrette C. (1977) Fighting behavior of muntjac and the evolution of antlers. *Evolution* **31**:169–76.

19 Batty A.F. & Chapman D.I. (1970) Gastro-intestinal parasites of wild fallow deer (*Dama dama* L.). *Journal of Helminthology* **44**:57–61.

20 Batty A.F. *et al.* (1987) Prevalence of nematode parasites in wild fallow deer (*Dama dama*). *Veterinary Record* **120**:599.

21 Bennet I. (1979) The challenge of Chillingham Park. *Roebuck* **26**: 13–18.

22 Benzie D. & Gill J.C. (1974) Radiography of the skeletal and dental condition of the Soay sheep. In Jewell P.A. *et al.* eds. *Island survivors: the ecology of the Soay sheep of St Kilda*. London: Athlone Press pp. 326–37.

23 Berger J. (1977) Organizational systems and dominance in feral horses in the Grand Canyon. *Behavioural Ecology and Sociobiology* **2**:131–46.

24 Bideau E. *et al.* (1983) Note sur l'évolution de l'association mère-jeune chez le chevreuil (*Capreolus capreolus* L. 1758) étudiée par la technique du radiotracking. *Mammalia* **47**:477–82.

25 Bilton L. (1957) The Chillingham herd of wild cattle. *Transactions of the Natural History Society of Northumberland, Durham and Newcastle upon Tyne* **12**:137–60.

26 Blackmore D.K. & Gallagher G.L. (1964) An outbreak of erysipelas in captive wild birds and mammals. *Veterinary Record* **76**:1161–4.

27 Blaxter K.L. & Hamilton W.J. (1980) Reproduction in farmed red deer. 2. Calf growth and mortality. *Journal of Agricultural Science, Cambridge* **95**: 275–84.

28 Boessneck J. (1969) Osteological differences between sheep (*Ovis aries* Linné) and goat (*Capra hircus* Linné). In Brothwell D. & Higgs E. eds. *Science in archaeology*. London: Thames & Hudson pp. 331–58.

29 Bonham F.R.H. & Fairley J.S. (1984) Observations on a herd of feral goats *Capra* (domestic) in the Burren. *Irish Naturalists' Journal* **21**:208–12.

30 Boyd I.L. (1980) Population changes and the distribution of a herd of feral goats (*Capra* sp.) on Rhum, Inner Hebrides, 1960–1978. *Journal of Zoology* **193**: 287–304.

31 Boyd J.M. (1981) The Boreray sheep of St Kilda, Outer Hebrides, Scotland: The natural history of a feral population. *Biological Conservation* **20**:215–27.

32 Boyd J.M. & Jewell P.A. (1974) The Soay sheep and their environment: a synthesis. In Jewell, P.A. *et al.* eds. *Island survivors: the ecology of the Soay sheep of St Kilda*. London: Athlone Press pp. 360–73.

33 Boyd J.M. *et al.* (1964) The Soay sheep of the island of Hirta, St Kilda. A study of a feral population. *Proceedings of the Zoological Society of London* **142**:129–63.

34 Bramley P.S. (1970) Territoriality and reproductive behaviour of roe deer. *Journal of Reproduction and Fertility*, Supplement **11**:43–70.

35 Bresinski W. (1982) Grouping tendencies in roe deer under agrocenosis conditions. *Acta theriologica* **27**: 427–47.

36 Britt D. & Bullock D.J. unpublished.

37 Brown D.J. (1983) *The Rhinog goats: 2 Social and spatial organisation*. Unpublished report to the Nature Conservancy Council North Wales Region.

38 Brown D.J. & Lloyd M.G. (1981) *The Rhinog goats: 1. A survey and management review*. Unpublished report to the Nature Conservancy Council North Wales Region.

39 Brown D.J. Personal communication.

40 Bryant L.D. & Maser C. (1982) Classification and distribution. In Thomas J.W. & Toweill D.E. eds. *Elk of North America*. Harrisburg: Stackpole pp. 1–59.

41 Bullock D.J. (1982). *Aspects of the ecology of feral goats* (Capra *domestic*) *in the Southern Uplands*. PhD. thesis, University of Durham.

42 Bullock D.J. (1983) Borerays, the other rare breed on St Kilda. *Ark* **10**:274–8.

43 Bullock D.J. (1985) Annual diets of hill sheep and feral goats in southern Scotland. *Journal of Applied Ecology* **22**:423–33.

44 Bullock D.J. & Pickering S.P. (1984) The validity of horn ring counts to determine the age of Scottish feral goats (*Capra* (domestic)). *Journal of Zoology* **202**:561–4.

45 Bullock D.J. & Rackham J. (1982) Epiphysial fusion and tooth eruption of feral goats from Moffatdale, Dumfries and Galloway, Scotland. *British Archaeological Reports British Series* **109**:73–80.

46 Buxton D. (1986) Malignant catarrhal fever. In Alexander T.L. ed. *Management and diseases of deer*. London: Veterinary Deer Society pp. 86–8.

47 Cadman W.A. (1966) *Fallow deer*. London: HMSO 39 pp.

48 Caldwell J.F. *et. al.* (1983) Observations on the autumn and winter diet of fallow deer (*Dama dama*). *Journal of Zoology* **201**:559–63.

49 Cameron T.W.M. & Parnell I.W. (1933) Internal parasites of land mammals in Scotland. *Proceedings of the Royal Physiological Society of Edinburgh* **22**: 133–54.

50 Campbell R.N. (1974) St Kilda and its sheep. In Jewell P.A. *et al.* eds. *Island survivors: the ecology of the Soay sheep of St Kilda*. London: Athlone Press pp. 8–35.

51 Carter N.A. (1984) Bole scoring by sika deer (*Cervus nippon*) in England. *Deer* **6**:77–8.

52 Catt D.C. & Staines B.W. (1987) Home range use and habitat selection by red deer (*Cervus elaphus*) in a Sitka spruce plantation as determined by radiotracking. *Journal of Zoology* **211**: 681–93.

53 Chapman D.I. (1970) Observations on the sexual cycle of male deer in Britain. *Mammal Review* 1: 49–52.

54 Chapman D.I. (1972) Seasonal changes in the gonads and accessory glands of male mammals. *Mammal Review* 1:231–48.

55 Chapman D.I. (1975) Antlers — bones of contention. *Mammal Review* 5:121–72.

56 Chapman D.I. (1977) Roe deer *Capreolus capreolus*. In Corbet G.B. & Southern H.N. eds. *Handbook of British mammals*. Oxford: Blackwell Scientific Publications pp. 437–46.

57 Chapman D.I. (1977) Haematology of the deer. In Archer R.K. & Jeffcott L.B. eds. *Comparative clinical haematology*. Oxford: Blackwell Scientific Publications pp. 345–64.

58 Chapman D.I. (1981) Antler structure and function — a hypothesis. *Journal of Biomechanics* 14: 195–7.

59 Chapman D.I. & Chapman N.G. (1969) The incidence of congenital abnormalities in the mandibular dentition of fallow deer (*Dama dama* L.). *Research in Veterinary Science* 10:485–7.

60 Chapman D.I. & Chapman N. (1969) Observations on the biology of fallow deer (*Dama dama*) in Epping Forest, Essex, England. *Biological Conservation* 2: 55–62.

61 Chapman D.I. & Chapman N.G. (1969) Geographical variation in fallow deer (*Dama dama* L.) *Nature* 221:59–60.

62 Chapman D.I. & Chapman N. (1970) Development of the teeth and mandibles of fallow deer. *Acta theriologica* 15:111–31.

63 Chapman D.I. & Chapman N. G. (1970) Preliminary observations on the reproductive cycle of male fallow deer (*Dama dama* L.). *Journal of Reproduction and Fertility* 21:1–8.

64 Chapman D.I. & Chapman N.G. (1973) Maxillary canine teeth in fallow deer, *Dama dama*. *Journal of Zoology* 170:143–7.

65 Chapman D. & Chapman N. (1975) *Fallow deer: their history, distribution and biology*. Lavenham: Terence Dalton 271 pp.

66 Chapman D.I. & Chapman N.G. (1980) Morphology of the male accessory organs of reproduction of immature fallow deer (*Dama dama* L.) with particular reference to puberty and antler development. *Acta anatomica* 108:51–9.

67 Chapman D.I. & Chapman N.G. (1982) The antler cycle of adult Reeves' muntjac. *Acta theriologica* 27:107–14.

68 Chapman D.I. & Chapman N.G. (1982) The taxonomic status of feral muntjac deer (*Muntiacus* sp.) in England. *Journal of Natural History* 16:381–7.

69 Chapman D.I. & Dansie O. (1969) Unilateral implantation in muntjac deer. *Journal of Zoology* 159: 534–6.

70 Chapman D.I. & Dansie O. (1970) Reproduction and foetal development in female muntjac deer (*Muntiacus reevesi* Ogilby). *Mammalia* 34:303–19.

71 Chapman D.I. & Horwood M.T. (1968) Pregnancy in a sika deer calf (*Cervus nippon*). *Journal of Zoology* 155:227–8.

72 Chapman D.I. *et al.* (1980) Some serum constituents of fallow deer (*Dama dama*). *Research in Veterinary Science* 29:105–7.

73 Chapman D.I. *et al.* (1982) Some haematological data for fallow deer (*Dama dama*) in England. *Research in Veterinary Science* 33:205–7.

74 Chapman D.I. *et al.* (1983) Chromosome studies of feral muntjac deer (*Muntiacus* sp.) in England. *Journal of Zoology* 201:557–9.

75 Chapman D.I. *et al.* (1984) Deformities of the metacarpus and metatarsus in fallow deer (*Dama dama* L.). *Journal of Comparative Pathology* 94:77–91.

76 Chapman D.I. *et al.* (1984) The periods of conception and parturition in feral Reeves' muntjac (*Muntiacus reevesi*) in southern England, based upon age of juvenile animals. *Journal of Zoology* 204:575–8.

77 Chapman D.I. *et al.* (1985) Tooth eruption in Reeves' muntjac (*Muntiacus reevesi*) and its use as a method of age estimation (Mammalia: Cervidae). *Journal of Zoology* (A), 205:205–21.

78 Chapman D.I. *et al.* (in prep.). Observations on the incidence of gastro-intestinal nematodes and of lungworm in captive fallow deer (*Dama dama* L.).

79 Chapman N. (1984) *Fallow deer*. Oswestry: Anthony Nelson 24 pp.

80 Chapman N.G. (1986) An explanation for the porous tips of the antlers of some fallow deer (*Dama dama*). *Journal of Zoology* (A), 210:628–31.

81 Chapman N.G. (1986) Fallow deer twins. *Deer* 7:46.

82 Chapman N. (1987) More twins. *Deer* 7:103.

83 Chapman N.G. & Chapman D.I. (1979) Seasonal changes in the male accessory glands of reproduction in adult fallow deer (*Dama dama*). *Journal of Zoology* 189:259–73.

84 Chapman N.G. & Chapman D.I. (1980) The distribution of fallow deer: a worldwide review. *Mammal Review* 10:61–138.

85 Chapman N.G. & Chapman D.I. (1982) *The fallow deer*. London: HMSO 19 pp.

86 Chapman N.G. & Chapman D.I. (1987) Cysticercosis in fallow deer in England. *Acta theriologica* 32:105–13.

87 Chapman N.G. *et al.* (1985) Distribution and habitat selection by muntjac and other species of deer in a coniferous forest. *Acta theriologica* 30:287–303.

88 Chapman N.G. *et al.* (1987) Techniques for the safe and humane capture of free-living muntjac deer (*Muntiacus reevesi*). *British Veterinary Journal* 143: 35–43.

89 Cheyne I.A. *et al.* (1974) The incidence of disease and parasites in the Soay sheep population of Hirta. In Jewell P.A. *et al.* eds. *Island survivors: the ecology of the Soay sheep of St Kilda*. London: Athlone Press pp. 338–59.

90 Clark M. (1981) *Mammal watching*. London: Severn House 176 pp.

91 Claydon K. *et al.* (1986) Estimating the number of

muntjac deer (*Muntiacus reevesi*) in a commercial coniferous forest. *Bulletin of the British Ecological Society* **17**:185–9.

92 Clutton-Brock J. Personal communication.

93 Clutton-Brock J. (1981) *Domesticated animals from early times*. London: Heinemann and British Museum (Natural History) 208 pp.

94 Clutton-Brock T.H. & Albon S.D. (1989) *Red deer in the Highlands* Oxford: BSP Professional Books, 260 pp.

95 Clutton-Brock T.H. *et al.* (1976) Ranks and relationships in highland ponies and highland cows. *Zeitschrift fur Tierpsychologie* **41**:202–16.

96 Clutton-Brock T.H. *et al.* (1982) *Red deer: behavior and ecology of two sexes*. Edinburgh: University Press 378 pp.

96 Clutton-Brock J. *et al.* (1989) Osteology of the Soay
A sheep. *Bulletin of the British Museum (Natural History)* **56**(1):1–56.

97 Coblentz B.E. (1976) Functions of scent-urination in ungulates with special reference to feral goats (*Capra hircus* L.). *American Naturalist* **110**:549–57.

98 Cooke A. & Farrell L. (1983) Chinese water deer. In *Muntjac and Chinese water deer*. Warminster: British Deer Society pp. 25–44.

99 Cooper A.B. (1969) Golden eagle kills red deer calf. *Journal of Zoology* **158**:215–16.

100 Cooper J.E. *et al.* (1986) A comparison of xylazine and methohexitone for the chemical immobilization of Reeves' muntjac (*Muntiacus reevesi*). *British Veterinary Journal* **142**:350–7.

101 Corrigall W. (1978) Naturally occurring leptospirosis (*Leptospira ballum*) in a red deer (*Cervus elaphus*). *Veterinary Record* **103**:75–6.

102 Cox F.E.G. (1970) Parasitic protozoa of British wild mammals. *Mammal Review* **1**:1–28.

103 Crook I.G. (1969) *Ecology and behaviour of feral goats in North Wales*. MSc. thesis, University College of North Wales, Bangor.

104 Cumming H.G. (1966) *Behaviour and dispersion in roe deer* (Capreolus capreolus). PhD. thesis, University of Aberdeen.

105 Dansie O. (1983) Muntjac. In *Muntjac and Chinese water deer*. Warminster: British Deer Society pp. 1–24.

106 Dansie O. & Williams J. (1973) Paraurethral glands in Reeves muntjac deer, *Muntiacus reevesii*. *Journal of Zoology* **171**:469–71.

107 Darling F.F. (1937) *A herd of red deer*. London: Oxford University Press 215 pp.

108 Davies S.J.M. (1987) *The archaeology of animals*. London: Batsford 224 pp.

109 Doney J.M. *et al.* (1974) Colour, conformation, affinities, fleece and patterns of inheritance in the Soay sheep. In Jewell P.A. *et al.* eds. *Island survivors: the ecology of the Soay sheep of St Kilda*. London: Athlone Press pp. 88–125.

110 Duncan N. *et al.* (1981) *The ecology and natural history of Boreray. Report of the Boreray 1980 expedition*. Unpublished report, University of Durham.

111 Duncan P. & Vigne N. (1979) The effect of group size in horses on the rate of attacks by blood-sucking flies. *Animal Behaviour* **27**:623–5.

112 Dunn A.M. (1969) The wild ruminant as a reservoir host of helminth infection. *Symposia of the Zoological Society of London* **24**:221–48.

113 Dunn A.M. (1986) Nasal bots. In Alexander T.L. ed. *Management and diseases of deer*. London: Veterinary Deer Society pp. 70–1.

114 Dunn A.M. (1986) Gastro-intestinal parasites. In Alexander T.L. ed. *Management and diseases of deer*. London: Veterinary Deer Society pp. 88–91.

115 Dunn A.M. Personal communication.

116 Dzieciolowski R. (1969) *The quantity, quality and seasonal variation of food resources available to red deer in various environmental conditions of forest management*. Warsaw: Polish Academy of Sciences Forest Research Institute 295 pp.

117 Edwards P.J. & Hollis S. (1982) The distribution of excreta on New Forest grassland used by cattle, ponies and deer. *Journal of Applied Ecology* **19**: 953–64.

118 Eiben B. & Fischer K. (1984) Untersuchung verschiedener Blutparameter beim Damhirsch (*Dama dama* L.) im Jahresgang. *Zeitschrift für Jagdwissenschaft* **30**:235–42.

119 Eldridge F.E. (1975) High frequency of Robertsonian translocation in a herd of British White cattle. *Veterinary Record* **96**:71–3.

120 Emanuelson K. *et al.* (1987) Chronic wasting disease in muntjac and hog deer: a nephropathy and arthropathy. *Proceedings of International Conference of Zoological and Avian Medicine* **1**:495.

121 Espmark Y. (1969) Mother–young relations and development of behaviour in roe deer (*Capreolus capreolus* L.). *Viltrevy* **6**:461–540.

122 Feist J.D. & McCullough D.R. (1976) Behavior patterns and communication in feral horses. *Zeitschrift für Tierpsychologie* **41**:337–71.

123 Fennessy P.F. & Drew K.R. eds. (1985) *Biology of deer production*. Wellington: Royal Society of New Zealand, 482 pp.

124 Flerov K.K. (1952) *Fauna of the USSR. Mammals Vol. 1, No. 2. Musk deer and deer*. Moscow: Academy of Sciences of the USSR. (English translation, Israel Program for Scientific Translations, Jerusalem 1960) 257 pp.

125 Fletcher T.J. (1982) Management problems and disease in farmed deer. *Veterinary Record* **111**: 219–23.

126 Forman A.J. & Gibbs E.P.J. (1974) Studies with foot-and-mouth disease virus in British deer (red, fallow and roe) 1. Clinical disease. *Journal of Comparative Pathology* **84**:215–20.

127 Formozov A.N. (1946) *Snow cover as an integral factor of the environment and its importance in the ecology of mammals and birds*. Edmonton: University of Alberta Boreal Institute, 141 pp.

128 Frankenberger Z. (1957) (Circumanal and circumgenital glands of our Cervidae). *Československá mor-*

fologie **5**:255–65.

129 Gates S. (1979) A study of the home ranges of free-ranging Exmoor ponies. *Mammal Review* **9**:3–18.

130 Gates S. (1981) The Exmoor pony — a wild animal? *Nature in Devon* **2**:7–30.

131 Gent A.H. (1983) *Range use and activity patterns in roe deer* (Capreolus capreolus): *a study of radio tagged animals in Chedington Wood, Dorset.* BSc. thesis, University of Southampton.

132 Gibbs E.P.J. *et al.* (1975) Studies with foot-and-mouth disease virus in British deer (muntjac and sika). Clinical disease, recovery of virus and serological response. *Journal of Comparative Pathology* **85**:361–6.

133 Gibson J.A. (1972) The wild goats of the Clyde area. *Western Naturalist* **1**:6–25.

134 Gill E.L. (1980) *Aspects of the social and reproductive behaviour of a group of New Forest ponies.* BSc. thesis, University of Southampton.

135 Gordon I.A. *et al.* (1987) Ponies, cattle and goats. In Clutton-Brock T.H. & Ball M.E. eds. *Rhum: the natural history of an island.* Edinburgh: University Press pp. 110–25.

135 Gosling L.M. (1985) The even-toed ungulates: order
A Artiodactyla. In Brown R.E. & Macdonald D.W. eds *Social odours in mammals.* Oxford: Oxford University Press, pp. 550–618.

136 Grant S.A. & Hodgson J. (1986) Grazing effects on species balance and herbage production in indigenous plant communities. In Gudmundsson O. ed. *Grazing research at northern latitudes.* New York: Plenum Publishing pp. 67–77.

137 Grant S.A. *et al.* (1985) Comparative studies of diet selection by sheep and cattle: the hill grasslands. *Journal of Ecology* **73**:987–1004.

138 Greig J.C. (1969) *The ecology of feral goats in Scotland.* MSc. thesis, University of Edinburgh.

139 Greig J.C. (1977) Feral goat *Capra* (domestic). In Corbet G.B. & Southern H.N. eds. *The handbook of British mammals.* Oxford: Blackwell Scientific Publications pp. 455–9.

140 Groves C.P. & Grubb P. (1982) The species of muntjac (genus *Muntiacus*) in Borneo: unrecognised sympatry in tropical deer. *Zoologische Mededelingen* **56**:203–16.

141 Groves C.P. & Grubb P. (1987) Relationships of living deer. In Wemmer C.M. ed. *Biology and management of the Cervidae.* Washington, DC: Smithsonian Institution Press pp. 21–59.

142 Groves C.P. & Grubb P. (1990) Muntiacidae. In Bubenik A. & Bubenik G. eds. *Antlers, horns and pronghorns.* New York: Springer (in press).

143 Grubb P. (1974) Social organization of Soay sheep and the behaviour of ewes and lambs. In Jewell P.A. *et al.* eds. *Island survivors: the ecology of the Soay sheep of St Kilda.* London: Athlone Press pp. 131–59.

144 Grubb P. (1974) The rut and behaviour of Soay rams. In Jewell P.A. *et al.* eds. *Island survivors: the ecology of the Soay sheep of St Kilda.* London: Athlone

Press pp. 195–223.

145 Grubb P. (1974) Population dynamics of the Soay sheep. In Jewell P.A. *et al.* eds. *Island survivors: the ecology of the Soay sheep of St Kilda.* London: Athlone Press pp. 242–72.

146 Grubb P. & Jewell P.A. (1974) Movement, daily activity and home range of Soay sheep. In Jewell P.A. *et al.* eds. *Island survivors: the ecology of the Soay sheep of St Kilda.* London: Athlone Press pp. 160–94.

147 Gubernick D.J. (1981) Mechanisms of maternal 'labelling' in goats. *Animal Behaviour* **29**:305–6.

148 Gwynne D. *et al.* (1974) The vegetation and soils of Hirta. In Jewell P.A. *et al.* eds. *Island survivors: the ecology of the Soay sheep of St Kilda.* London: Athlone Press pp. 36–87.

149 Hafez E.S.E. & Bouissou M.L. (1980) The behaviour of cattle. In Hafez E.S.E. ed. *The behaviour of domestic animals.* London: Bailliere Tindall pp. 203–45.

150 Hall S.J.G. (1979) Studying the Chillingham wild cattle. *Ark* **6**:72–9.

151 Hall S.J.G. (1985) The Chillingham white cattle. *British Cattle Breeders Club Digest* **40**:24–8.

152 Hall S.J.G. (1986) Chillingham cattle: dominance and affinities and access to supplementary food. *Ethology* **71**:201–15.

153 Hall S.J.G. (1988) Chillingham Park and its herd of white cattle: relationships between vegetation classes and patterns of range use. *Journal of Applied Ecology* **25**:777–89.

154 Hall S.J.G. (1989) Chillingham cattle: social and maintenance behaviour in an ungulate which breeds all year round. *Animal Behaviour* **38**:215–25.

155 Hall S.J.G. & Bunce R.G.H. (1984) Vegetation survey of Chillingham Park, Northumberland. *Transactions of the Natural History Society of Northumbria* **52**:5–14.

156 Hall S.J.G. & Hall J.G. (in press) Inbreeding and population dynamics of the Chillingham cattle (*Bos taurus*). *Journal of Zoology* **216**:479–93.

157 Hall S.J.G. & Moore G.F. (1986) Feral cattle of Swona, Orkney Islands. *Mammal Review* **16**:89–96.

158 Hall S.J.G. *et al.* (1988) Vocalisations of the Chillingham cattle. *Behaviour* **104**:78–104.

159 Hamilton W.J. *et al.* (1960) Aspects of placentation in certain Cervidae. *Journal of Anatomy* **94**:1–33.

160 Hansen P.J. (1985) Seasonal modulation of puberty and the postpartum anestrus in cattle: a review. *Livestock Production Science* **12**:309–27.

161 Harding S.P. (1986) *Aspects of the ecology and social organisation of the muntjac deer* (Muntiacus reevesi). DPhil. thesis, University of Oxford.

162 Harrington R. (1973) Hybridization among deer and its implications for conservation. *Irish Forestry Journal* **30**:64–78.

163 Harrington R. (1974) The hybridization of red deer and sika deer in Northern Ireland. *Irish Forestry Journal* **31**:2.

164 Harrington R. (1982) The hybridization of red deer

(*Cervus elaphus* L., 1758) and Japanese sika deer (*C. nippon* Temminck, 1838). *International Congress of Game Biologists* **14**:559–71.

165 Harrington R. Personal communication.

166 Harris R.A. & Duff K.R. (1970) *Wild deer in Britain.* Newton Abbott: David & Charles 112 pp.

167 Harris S. & Forde P. (1986) The annual diet of muntjac (*Muntiacus reevesi*) in the King's Forest, Suffolk. *Bulletin of the British Ecological Society* **17**:19–22.

168 Harrison R.J. & Hyett A.R. (1954) The development and growth of the placentomes in the fallow deer (*Dama dama* L.). *Journal of Anatomy* **88**:338–55.

169 Hartl G.B. *et al.* (1986) Genetic variability in fallow deer, *Dama dama* L. *Animal Genetics* **17**:335–41.

170 Hawkins D. (1988) The parasitic interrelationship of deer and sheep on the Knebworth Park estate, near Stevenage. *Deer* **7**:296–300.

171 Hearney A.W. & Jennings T.J. (1983) Annual foods of the red deer (*Cervus elaphus*) and the roe deer (*Capreolus capreolus*) in the east of England. *Journal of Zoology* **201**:565–70.

172 Heidemann G. (1973) *Zur Biologie des Damwildes* (Cervus dama *Linné 1758*). Hamburg: Paul Parey 95 pp.

173 Henry B.A.M. (1978) Diet of roe deer in an English conifer forest. *Journal of Wildlife Management* **42**: 937–40.

174 Henson E. (1987) Vaynol cattle — a story of near extinction. *Ark* **14**:371–3.

175 Hinge M.D.C. (1986) *Ecology of red and roe deer in a mixed-aged conifer plantation.* PhD. thesis, University of Aberdeen.

176 Hoffmeister H. (1983) *Das Sikawild.* Hannover: Landbuch-Verlag 72 pp.

177 Hofmann R.R. (1973) The ruminant stomach — stomach structure and feeding habits of East African game ruminants. *East African Monographs in Biology* **2**:1–354.

178 Hofmann R.R. (1983) Adaptive changes of gastric and intestinal morphology in response to different fibre content in ruminant diets. *Bulletin of the Royal Society of New Zealand* **20**:51–8.

179 Hofmann R.R. (1985) Digestive physiology of the deer — their morphophysiological specialisation and adaptation. *Bulletin of the Royal Society of New Zealand* **22**:393–407.

180 Hofmann R.R. & Geiger G. (1974) Zur topographischen und functionellon Anatomie der Viscera abdominis des Rehes (*Capreolus capreolus* L.). *Zentralblatt für Veterinärmedizin C* **3**:63–84.

181 Hofmann R.R. *et al.* (1976) Vergleichend-anatomische Untersuchunger an der Vormagenschleimhaut von Rehwild (*Capreolus capreolus*) und Rotwild (*Cervus elaphus*). *Zeitschrift für Säugetierkunde* **41**: 167–93.

182 Holbrook P. (1987) Feral cattle in New Zealand. *Ark* **14**:315.

183 Holmes F. (1974) *Following the roe.* Edinburgh: Bartholomew 112 pp.

184 Horwood M.T. & Masters E.H. (1970) *Sika deer.* British Deer Society 30 pp.

185 Hosey G.R. (1981) Annual foods of roe deer (*Capreolus capreolus*) in the south of England. *Journal of Zoology* **194**:276–8.

186 Hotchkis J. (1988) Statutory close seasons for deer in the United Kingdom. *Deer* **7**:232.

187 Ikeda S. & Limura R. (1969) Ecological analysis of the environment for deer, *Cervus nippon centralis* Kishida habitat in relation to its hunting and forest utilization (mainly in the Nikko National Hunting Area). *Bulletin of the Government Forest Experiment Station, Meguro* **220**:59–119.

188 Inglis D.M. *et al.* (1983) Ocular disease in red deer calves associated with a herpes virus infection. *Veterinary Record* **113**:182–3.

189 Jackson J.E. (1974) *The feeding ecology of the fallow deer* (Dama dama *L.*) *in the New Forest.* PhD. thesis, University of Southampton.

190 Jackson J. (1977) The annual diet of the fallow deer (*Dama dama*) in the New Forest Hampshire, as determined by rumen content analysis. *Journal of Zoology* **181**:465–73.

191 Jackson J. (1977) The duration of lactation in New Forest fallow deer (*Dama dama*). *Journal of Zoology* **183**:542–3.

192 Jackson J. (1977) When do fallow deer feed? *Deer* **4**:215–18.

193 Jackson J. (1980) The annual diet of the roe deer (*Capreolus capreolus*) in the New Forest, Hampshire, as determined by rumen content analysis. *Journal of Zoology* **192**:71–83.

194 Jackson J.E. *et al.* (1977) A note on the food of muntjac deer (*Muntiacus reevesi*). *Journal of Zoology* **183**:546–8.

195 Jarman M.R. (1972) European deer economies and the advent of the Neolithic. In Higgs E.S. ed. *Papers in economic prehistory.* Cambridge: University Press pp. 125–47.

196 Jenkinson D.M. (1972) The skin structure of British deer. *Research in Veterinary Science* **13**:70–3.

197 Jewell P.A. (1988) Factors that affect fertility in a feral population of sheep. *Zoological Journal of the Linnean Society* **95**:163–74.

198 Jewell P.A. & Grubb P. (1974) The breeding cycle, the onset of oestrus and conception in Soay sheep. In Jewell P.A. *et al.* eds. *Island survivors: the ecology of the Soay sheep of St Kilda.* London: Athlone Press pp. 224–41.

199 Jewell P.A. *et al.* (1974) *Island Survivors: the ecology of the Soay sheep of St Kilda.* London: Athlone Press 386 pp.

200 Jewell P.A. *et al.* (1986) Multiple mating and siring success during natural oestrus in the ewe. *Journal of Reproduction and Fertility* **77**:81–9.

201 Johnson A.L. unpublished.

202 Johnson A.L. (1982) Notes on the behaviour of roe deer (*Capreolus capreolus* L.) at Chedington, Dorset, 1970–1980. *Forestry Commission Research and Development Paper* **130**:1–87.

203 Johnson E. & Hornby J. (1980) Age and seasonal coat changes in long haired and normal fallow deer (*Dama dama*). *Journal of Zoology* 192:501–9.

204 Johnson T.H. (1984) *Habitat and social organisation of roe deer* (Capreolus capreolus). PhD. thesis, University of Southampton.

205 Jones T.O. (1982) Outbreak of *Pasteurella multocida* septicaemia in fallow deer (*Dama dama*). *Veterinary Record* 110:451–2.

206 Jope M. & Grigson C. (1965) Faunal remains: frequencies and ages of species. In Smith I.F. ed. *Windmill and Avebury excavations by Alexander Keiller 1925–1939*. Oxford: Clarendon Press pp. 142–5.

207 Kaji K. unpublished.

208 Kay R.N.B. (1987) Weights of salivary glands in some ruminant animals. *Journal of Zoology* 211: 431–6.

209 Kay R.N.B. & Staines B.W. (1981) The nutrition of the red deer (*Cervus elaphus*). *Nutrition Abstracts and Reviews B* 51:601–22.

210 Kennaugh J.H. *et al.* (1977) Seasonal changes in the prepuce of adult fallow deer (*Dama dama*) and its probable function as a scent organ. *Journal of Zoology* 183:301–10.

211 Kiddie D.G. (1962) The sika deer in New Zealand. *New Zealand Forestry Service Information Series* 44: 1–35.

212 Krzywiński A. *et al.* (1984) Growth and development of hand reared fallow deer fawns. *Acta theriologica* 29:349–56.

213 Kurt F. (1968) *Das Sozialverhatten des Rehes* (Capreolus capreolus *L.*): *Eine Feldstudie*. Hamburg: Paul Parey, 102 pp.

214 Lancaster M.B. & Hong C. (1971) The nematode fauna of the Chillingham wild white cattle. *British Veterinary Journal* 127:113–17.

215 Langbein J. & Putman R.J. (1989) Effects of density and age on the performance of fallow deer. In Goldspink C.R. & Baxter-Brown M. eds *Management, conservation and interpretation of park deer*. British Deer Society, pp. 5–21.

216 Lawman M.J.P. *et al.* (1978) A preliminary survey of British deer for antibody to some virus diseases of farm animals. *British Veterinary Journal* 134:85–91.

217 Lever C. (1977) *The naturalized animals of the British Isles*. London: Hutchinson, 600 pp.

218 Lincoln G.A. (1984) Antlers and their regeneration — a study using hummels, hinds and haviers. *Proceedings of the Royal Society of Edinburgh* 82B: 243–59.

219 Lister A.M. (1984) Evolutionary and ecological origins of British deer. *Proceedings of the Royal Society of Edinburgh* 82B:205–29.

220 Lister A.M. & Chapman N.G. (1990) Variation in lateral metacarpals of fallow deer, *Dama dama* L. *Journal of Zoology* in press.

221 Loudon A.S. (1979) *Social behaviour and habitat in roe deer* (Capreolus capreolus). PhD. thesis, University of Edinburgh.

222 Loudon A.S. (1980) *The biology and management of roe deer in commercial forests*. Unpublished report to the Forestry Commission, Edinburgh University.

223 Loudon A. (1982) Too many deer for the trees? *New Scientist* 93:708–11.

224 Lowe V.P.W. (1961) A discussion on the history, present status and future conservation of red deer (*Cervus elaphus* L.) in Scotland. *Terre et la Vie* 1: 9–40.

225 Lowe V.P.W. (1966) Observations on the dispersal of red deer on Rhum. *Symposia of the Zoological Society of London* 18:211–28.

226 Lowe V.P.W. (1967) Teeth as indicators of age with special reference to red deer (*Cervus elaphus*) of known age from Rhum. *Journal of Zoology* 152: 137–53.

227 Lowe V.P.W. (1979) *Wild and feral deer in Great Britain*. Unpubl. NERC contract report HF3/05/43, Institute of Terrestrial Ecology Merlewood Research Station 77 pp.

228 Lowe V.P.W. & Gardiner A.S. (1974) A re-examination of the subspecies of red deer (*Cervus elaphus*) with particular reference to the stocks in Britain. *Journal of Zoology* 174:185–201.

229 Lowe V.P.W. & Gardiner A.S. (1975) Hybridization between red deer (*Cervus elaphus*) and sika deer (*Cervus nippon*) with particular reference to stocks in N.W. England. *Journal of Zoology* 177:553–66.

229A Lowe V.P.W. Personal communication.

230 MacArthur J. (1981) *A disease study of feral goats in a closed population*. Unpublished report to the Universities Federation for Animal Welfare, Potters Bar.

231 MacNally L. (1970) *Highland deer forest*. London: Dent.

232 MacNally L. (1975) *The year of the red deer*. London: Dent, 112 pp.

233 Mackenzie D. (1980) *Goat husbandry*, 4th edn. London: Faber & Faber 375 pp.

234 Mann J.C.E. (1983) *The social organisation and ecology of the Japanese sika deer* (Cervus nippon) *in southern England*. PhD. thesis, University of Southampton.

235 Marquiss M. *et al.* (1985) The numbers, breeding success and diet of golden eagles in southern Scotland in relation to changes in land use. *Biological Conservation* 34:121–40.

236 Mason I.L. ed. (1984) *Evolution of domesticated animals*. London: Longman 452 pp.

237 Matthews P.R.J. *et al.* (1981) Mycobacterial infections in various species of deer in United Kingdom. *British Veterinary Journal* 137:60–6.

238 Maugham E. & Williams J.R.B. (1967) Haemoglobin types in deer. *Nature* 215:404–5.

239 McDiarmid A. (1951) The occurrence of agglutinins for *Br. abortus* in the blood of wild deer in the south of England. *Veterinary Record* 63:469–70.

240 McDiarmid A. (1965) Some infectious diseases of free-living wildlife. *British Veterinary Journal* 121: 245–57.

241 McDiarmid A. (1975) Some disorders of wild deer in the United Kingdom. *Veterinary Record* **97**:6−9.

242 McDougall P. (1975) The feral goats of Kielderhead Moor. *Journal of Zoology* **176**:215−46.

243 Meat and Livestock Commission (1985) Beef plan results — suckler beef systems. In *Beef Yearbook 1985*. Bletchley: Meat and Livestock Commission pp. 47−68.

244 Middleton A.D. (1937) Whipsnade ecological survey. *Proceedings of the Zoological Society of London* **107**:471−81.

245 Milner C. & Gwynne D. (1974) The Soay sheep and their food supply. In Jewell P.A. *et al.* eds. *Island survivors: the ecology of the Soay sheep of St Kilda.* London: Athlone Press pp. 273−325.

246 Mitchell B. (1967) Growth layers in dental cement for determining the age of red deer (*Cervus elaphus* L.). *Journal of Animal Ecology* **36**:279−93.

247 Mitchell B. & Crisp J.C. (1981) Some properties of red deer (*Cervus elaphus*) at exceptionally high population-density in Scotland. *Journal of Zoology* **193**: 157−69.

247 Mitchell B. *et al.* (1976) Annual cycles of body
A weight and condition in Scottish red deer, *Cervus elaphus. Journal of Zoology* **180**:107−27.

248 Mitchell B. *et al.* (1977) *Ecology of red deer: a research review relevant to their management in Scotland.* Cambridge: Institute of Terrestrial Ecology 74 pp.

249 Mitchell B. *et al.* (1985) Defecation frequency in roe deer (*Capreolus capreolus*) in relation to the accumulation rates of faecal deposits. *Journal of Zoology (A)* **207**:1−7.

250 Mitchell B. *et al.* (1986) Performance and population dynamics in relation to management of red deer *Cervus elaphus* at Glenfeshie, Inverness-shire, Scotland. *Biological Conservation* **37**:237−67.

251 Mitchell-Jones A.J. unpublished.

252 Miura S. (1984) Social behavior and territoriality in male sika deer (*Cervus nippon* Temminck 1838) during the rut. *Zeitschrift für Tierpsychologie* **64**:33−73.

253 Miura S. (1984) Dominance hierarchy and space use pattern in male captive muntjacs, *Muntiacus reevesi. Journal of Ethology* **2**:69−75.

254 Muhlemann M.F. & Wright D.J.M. (1987) Emerging pattern of Lyme disease in the United Kingdom and Irish Republic. *Lancet* **8527**:260−2.

255 Munro R. (1986) *Dictyocaulus*. In Alexander T.L. ed. *Management and diseases of deer.* London: Veterinary Deer Society pp. 71−4.

256 Munro R. (1986) *Tuberculosis*. In Alexander T. L. ed. *Management and diseases of deer.* London: Veterinary Deer Society pp. 157−60.

257 Nadler C.F. *et al.* (1973) Cytogenetic differentiation, geographic distribution, and domestication in palaearctic sheep (*Ovis*). *Zeitschrift für Säugetierkunde* **38**:109−25.

258 Nelson G. (1966) A note on the internal parasites of the muntjac. *Deer* **1**:16−17.

259 O'Brien P.H. (1982) Flehmen: its occurrence and possible function in feral goats. *Animal Behaviour*
30:1015−19.

260 Orwin D.F.G. & Whitaker A.H. (1984) Feral sheep (*Ovis aries* L.) of Arapawa Island, Marlborough Sounds, and a comparison of their wool characteristics with those of four other feral flocks in New Zealand. *New Zealand Journal of Zoology* **11**: 201−24.

261 Parfitt A. (1986) Personal communication.

262 Pearson L. (1968) A note on the history of black-eared white cattle. *Agricultural History Review* **16**: 159−60.

263 Pemberton J.M. & Balmford A.P. (1987) Lekking in fallow deer. *Journal of Zoology* **213**:762−5.

264 Pemberton J.M. & Smith R.H. (1985) Lack of biochemical polymorphism in British fallow deer. *Heredity* **55**:199−207.

265 Pickering S.P. (1983) *Aspects of the behavioural ecology of feral goats* (Capra *domestic*). PhD. thesis, University of Durham.

266 Plumb J. Personal communication.

267 Pollock J.I. (1980) Behavioural ecology and body condition changes in New Forest ponies. *RSPCA Scientific Publications* **6**:1−122.

268 Pollock D. Personal communication.

269 Pratt R.M. *et al.* (1985) Use of habitat by free-ranging cattle and ponies in the New Forest, southern England. *Journal of Applied Ecology* **23**:539−57.

270 Prell H. (1938) Die Tragzeiten der einheimischen Jagdtiere (II Nachtrag). *Tharandter forstliches Jahrbuch* **89**:696−701.

271 Prior R. (1968) *The roe deer of Cranborne Chase: an ecological survey.* London: Oxford University Press 222 pp.

272 Prummel W. & Frisch H-J. (1986) A guide for the distinction of species, sex and body size in bones of sheep and goat. *Journal of Archaeological Science* **13**:567−77.

273 Putman R.J. (1980) The ecology of exploitation? *Deer* **5**:25−6.

274 Putman R.J. (1981) Social systems of deer: a speculative review. *Deer* **5**:186−8.

275 Putman R.J. (1984) Facts from faeces. *Mammal Review* **14**:79−97.

276 Putman R.J. (1986) Foraging by roe deer in agricultural areas and impact on arable crops. *Journal of Applied Ecology* **23**:91−9.

277 Putman R.J. (1986) *Grazing in temperate ecosystems: large herbivores and the ecology of the New Forest.* Beckenham, Kent: Croom Helm, 210 pp.

278 Putman R.J. (1986) Competition and coexistence in a multispecies grazing system. *Acta theriologica* **31**: 271−91.

279 Putman R.J. & Langbein J. (1989) Factors affecting mortality in deer parks. In Goldspink C.R. & Baxter-Brown M. eds *Management, conservation and interpretation of park deer.* British Deer Society, pp. 38−54.

280 Putman R.J. *et al.* (1987) Food and feeding behaviour of cattle and ponies in the New Forest, Hampshire. *Journal of Applied Ecology* **24**:369−80.

281 Rackham O. (1975) *Hayley Wood: its history and ecology.* Cambridge: Cambridgeshire and Isle of Ely Naturalists' Trust Ltd 221 pp.

282 Rackham O. (1986) *the history of the countryside.* London: Dent 445 pp.

283 Rare Breeds Survival Trust, unpublished.

284 Ratcliffe P.R. (1984) Population dynamics of red deer (*Cervus elaphus* L.) in Scottish commercial forests. *Proceedings of the Royal Society of Edinburgh* **82B**:291–302.

285 Ratcliffe P.R. (1987) Distribution and current status of sika deer, *Cervus nippon*, in Great Britain. *Mammal Review* **17**:39–58.

286 Ratcliffe P.R. (1987) Red deer population changes and the independent assessment of population size. *Symposia of the Zoological Society of London* **58**: 153–65.

287 Ratcliffe P.R. & Mayle B. unpublished.

288 Ratcliffe P.R. & Rowe J.J. (1979) A golden eagle (*Aguila chrysaetos*) kills an infant roe deer (*Capreolus capreolus*). *Journal of Zoology* **189**:532–5.

289 Ratcliffe P.R. & Rowe J.J. (1985) A biological basis for managing red and roe deer in British commercial forests. *International Congress of Game Biologists* **17**: 917–25.

290 Reed C.A. (1959) Animal domestication in the prehistoric Near East. *Science* **130**:1629–39.

291 Reid H.W. *et al.* (1976) Isolation of louping-ill virus from a roe deer (*Capreolus capreolus*). *Veterinary Record* **98**:116.

292 Reid H.W. *et al.* (1978) Isolation of louping-ill virus from red deer (*Cervus elaphus*). *Veterinary Record* **102**:463–4.

293 Ritchie J. (1920) *The influence of man on animal life in Scotland.* Cambridge: University Press 550 pp.

294 Rokosz M. (1977) History of the aurochs, *Bos taurus primigenius*, in Poland. *Chrónmyprzyrode ojczysta* **32**(5):13–25.

295 Rose H.R. (1987) Bovine tuberculosis in deer. *Deer* **7**:78.

296 Royle N.J. (1986) New C-band polymorphism in the White Park cattle of Great Britain. *Journal of Heredity* **77**:366–7.

297 Rudge A.J.B. ed. (1984) *The capture and handling of deer.* Peterborough: Nature Conservancy Council 273 pp.

298 Rudge M.R. (1970) Mother and kid behaviour in feral goats (*Capra hircus* L.). *Zeitschrift für Tierpsychologie* **27**:687–92.

299 Rudge M.R. (1976) Ageing domestic sheep (*Ovis aries* L.) from growth lines in the cementum of the first incisor. *New Zealand Journal of Zoology* **3**: 421–4.

300 Rudge M.R. (1982) Feral goats in New Zealand. *Oryx* **16**:230–1.

301 Rudge M.R. (1983) A reserve for feral sheep on Pitt Island, Chatham group, New Zealand. *New Zealand Journal of Zoology* **10**:349–63.

302 Rudge M.R. (1984) The occurrence and status of populations of feral goats and sheep throughout the world. In Munton P.N. *et al.* eds. *Feral mammals — problems and potential.* Gland: IUCN pp. 55–84.

303 Russel A.F.J. *et al.* (1983) A note on the possible use of goats in hill sheep grazing systems. *Animal Production* **36**:313–16.

304 Russell V. (1976) *The New Forest ponies.* Newton Abbot: David & Charles.

305 Ryder M.L. (1970) Structure and seasonal change of the coat in Scottish wild goats. *Journal of Zoology* **161**:355–61.

306 Ryder M.L. (1983) Will cashmere grow on Scottish Hills? *Wool Record* **September 1983**, 89, 93.

307 Sackur V. (1984) *A study of the patterns of habitat use by fallow deer* (Dama dama) *in south-west Suffolk with particular reference to coppiced woodlands.* Unpublished report, Suffolk Trust for Nature Conservation.

308 Salisbury G.W. *et al.* (1978) *Physiology of reproduction and artificial insemination of cattle.* New York: Freeman.

309 Schaal A. (1982) Influence de l'environment sur les composantes du groupe social chez le daim *Cervus* (*Dama*) *dama* L. *Revue d' Ecologie et de Biologie du Sol* **36**:161–74.

310 Schaal A. (1985) Variation of mating system in fallow deer (*Dama d. dama*). *Abstracts of the 19th International Ethological Conference, Toulouse* **1**:277.

311 Schaal A. (1987) *Le polymorphisme du comportement reproducteur chez le daim d'Europe* (Dama d. dama). PhD. thesis, Université Louis Pasteur, Strasbourg.

312 Schaller G.B. (1977) *Mountain monarchs: wild sheep and goats of the Himalaya.* Chicago: University Press 425 pp.

313 Schloeth R. (1958) Cycle annuel et comportement social du taureau de Camargue. *Mammalia* **22**: 121–37.

314 Schloeth R. (1961) Das sozialleben des Camargue-Rindes. *Zeitschrift für Tierpsychologie* **18**:574–627.

315 Schnare H. & Fischer K. (1987) Hamatokrit, Erythrozyten und Hamoglobin im Blut des Damhirsches (*Dama dama* L.) unter besonderer Berucksichtigung der Umgebungstemperatur. *Zeitschrift für Jagdwissenschaft* **33**:9–14.

316 Schumacher S. (1936) Das Stirnorgan des Rehbockes (*Capreolus capreolus capreolus* L.) ein bisher unbekanntes Duftorgan. *Zeitschrift für mikroskopish-anatomische Forschung* **39**:215–30.

317 Sempéré A. (1979) Utilisation et évolution du domaine vital chez le chevreuil mâle européen déterminées par radiotracking. *Biology of Behaviour* **4**: 75–87.

318 Shackleton D.M. & Shank C.C. (1984) A review of the social behavior of feral and wild sheep and goats. *Journal of Animal Science* **58**:500–9.

319 Shank C.C. (1972) Some aspects of social behaviour in a population of feral goats (*Capra hircus* L.). *Zeitschrift für Tierpsychologie* **30**:488–528.

320 Sheng H. & Lu H. (1985) A preliminary study of the Chinese river deer population of Zhoushan Island and adjacent islets. In Kawamichi T. ed. *Contem-*

porary Mammalogy in China and Japan. Tokyo: Mammalogical Society of Japan pp. 6—9.

321 Shi L. & Pathak S. (1981) Gametogenesis in a male Indian muntjac × Chinese muntjac hybrid. *Cytogenetics and Cell Genetics* **30**:152—6.

322 Shi L. *et al.* (1980) Comparative cytogenetic studies on the red muntjac, Chinese muntjac and their F₁ hybrids. *Cytogenetics and Cell Genetics* **26**:22—7.

323 Short R. & Hay M.F. (1966) Delayed implantation in the roe deer *Capreolus capreolus. Symposia of the Zoological Society of London* **15**:173—94.

324 Short R.V. & Mann T. (1966) The sexual cycle of a seasonally breeding mammal, the roe-buck (*Capreolus capreolus*). *Journal of Reproduction and Fertility* **12**:337—51.

325 Simmons I.G & Tooley M.J (eds) (1981) *The environment in British prehistory.* London: Duckworth 334 pp.

326 Sinclair A.R.E. & Duncan P. (1972) Indices of condition in tropical ruminants. *East African Wildlife Journal* **10**:143—9.

327 Slee J. (1981) A review of genetic aspects of survival and resistance to cold in newborn lambs. *Livestock Production Science* **8**:419—29.

328 Smith R.H. (1979) On selection for inbreeding in polygynous animals. *Heredity* **43**:205—11.

329 Smith R.H. (1980) The capture of deer for radio tagging. In Amlaner C.J. & Macdonald D.W. eds. *A handbook on biotelemetry and radio tracking.* Oxford: Pergamon Press pp. 313—17.

330 Smith R.H. (1980) The genetics of fallow deer and their implications for management. *Deer* **5**:79—83.

331 Smith S. Personal communication.

332 Soper E.A. (1969) *Muntjac.* London: Longmans, Green & Co. 142 pp.

333 Speed J.G. & Etherington M.G. (1952) The Exmoor pony — and a survey of the evolution of horses in Britain: Part I Exmoor ponies. *British Veterinary Journal* **108**:329—38.

334 Speed J.G. & Etherington M.G. (1953) The Exmoor pony — and a survey of the evolution of horses in Britain: Part II the Celtic pony. *British Veterinary Journal* **109**:315—20.

335 Springthorpe G. (1969) Long-haired fallow deer at Mortimer Forest. *Journal of Zoology* **159**:537.

336 Stadler S.G. (1988) Observations on the behaviour of Chinese water deer (*Hydropotes inermis* Swinhoe 1870). *Deer* **7**:300—1.

337 Staines B.W. (1974) A review of factors affecting deer dispersion and their relevance to management. *Mammal Review* **4**:79—91.

338 Staines B.W. (1977) Factors affecting the seasonal distribution of red deer (*Cervus elaphus* L.) in Glen Dye, north-east Scotland. *Annals of Applied Biology* **87**:495—512.

339 Staines B.W. (1978) The dynamics and performance of a declining population of red deer (*Cervus elaphus*). *Journal of Zoology* **184**:403—19.

340 Staines B.W. & Crisp J.M. (1978) Observations on food quality in Scottish red deer (*Cervus elaphus*) as determined by chemical analysis of the rumen contents. *Journal of Zoology* **185**:253—9.

341 Staines B.W. & Ratcliffe P.R. (1987) Estimating the abundance of red deer (*Cervus elaphus* L.) and roe deer (*Capreolus capreolus* L.) and their current status in Great Britain. *Symposia of the Zoological Society of London* **58**:131—52.

342 Staines B.W. & Welch D. (1984) Habitat selection and impact of red (*Cervus elaphus* L.) and roe (*Capreolus capreolus* L.) deer in a Sitka spruce plantation. *Proceedings of the Royal Society of Edinburgh* **82B**:303—19.

343 Staines B.W. *et al.* (1982) Differences in the quality of food eaten by red deer (*Cervus elaphus*) stags and hinds in winter. *Journal of Applied Ecology* **19**: 65—77.

344 Sterba O. & Klusak K. (1984) Reproductive biology of fallow deer, *Dama dama. Přírodovědné Práce ústavů Československé Akademie Věd v Brně* **18**(6): 1—46.

345 Stewart L.K. (1985) Red deer. In Murray R.B. ed. *Vegetation management in northern Britain.* Croydon: British Crop Protection Council pp. 45—50.

346 Strandgaard H. (1972) The roe deer (*Capreolus capreolus*) population at Kalø and the factors regulating its size. *Danish Review of Game Biology* **7**(1):1—205.

347 Tankerville Earl of (1978) *The wild white cattle of Chillingham.* Chillingham, Northumberland: Chillingham Wild Cattle Association.

348 Thompson G.B. (1964) The parasites of British birds and mammals. XL: Ectoparasites of deer in Britain. *Entomologist's Monthly Magazine* **99**:186—9.

349 Tomich P.Q. (1969) *Mammals in Hawaii.* Oahu: Bernice P. Bishop Museum Press 238 pp.

350 Trow-Smith R. (1959) *British livestock husbandry to 1700.* London: Routledge & Kegan Paul 286 pp.

351 Trow-Smith R. (1959) *British livestock husbandry 1700—1900.* London: Routledge & Kegan Paul 351 pp.

352 Twigg G.I. *et al.* (1973) Antibodies to *Leptospira grippotyphosa* in British wild mammals. *Veterinary Record* **92**:119.

353 Tyler S.J. (1972) The behaviour and social organization of the New Forest ponies. *Animal Behaviour Monographs* **5**:85—196.

354 van den Brink F.H. (1967) *A field guide to the mammals of Britain and Europe.* London: Collins 221 pp.

355 Van Vuren D. & Coblentz B.E. (1987) Some ecological effects of feral sheep on Santa Cruz Island, California, USA. *Biological Conservation* **41**:253—68.

356 Wallis S. unpublished.

357 Watson A. (1971) Climate and the antler-shedding and performance of red deer in north-east Scotland. *Journal of Applied Ecology* **8**:53—67.

358 Watson A. & Staines B.W. (1978) Differences in the quality of wintering areas used by male and female red deer (*Cervus elaphus*) in Aberdeenshire. *Journal of Zoology* **186**:544—50.

359 Welch D. *et al.* (1988) Roe-deer browsing on spring-

flush growth of Sitka spruce. *Scottish Forestry* **42**: 33−43.

360 Welsh D. (1975) *Population, behavioural and grazing ecology of the horses of Sable Island, Nova Scotia.* PhD. thesis, University of Dalhousie.

361 Whitehead G.K. (1953) *The ancient white cattle of Britain and their descendants.* London: Faber & Faber 174 pp.

362 Whitehead G.K. (1964) *The deer of Great Britain and Ireland.* London: Routledge & Kegan Paul 597 pp.

363 Whitehead G.K. (1972) *Deer of the world.* London: Constable & Co. 194 pp.

364 Whitehead G.K. (1972) *The wild goats of Great Britain and Ireland.* Newton Abbot: David & Charles 184 pp.

365 Whitehead G.K. (1984) Wild cattle in Wales. *Ark* **11**:307−10.

366 Wilson P.R. & Orwin D.F.G. (1964) The Sheep population of Campbell Island. *New Zealand Journal of Science* **7**:460−90.

367 Wood D.A. & Munro R. (1986) Babesiosis. In Alexander T.L. ed. *Management and diseases of deer.* London: Veterinary Deer Society p. 105.

368 Woodford M. (1966) Lymphosarcoma in a wild roe deer. *Veterinary Record* **79**:74.

369 Zejda J. (1978) Field grouping of the roe deer (*Capreolus capreolus*) in a lowland region. *Folia zoologica* **27**:111−22.

370 Zima J. & Král B. (1984) Karyotypes of European mammals, part III. *Acta Scientiarum Naturalium, Brno* **18**(9):1−51.

Chapter 13 / Marsupials:
Order Marsupialia

As indigenous mammals, marsupials are typical of the Australasian and Neotropical regions, with one species of opossum extending into N America. One species of wallaby is feral in Britain.

FAMILY MACROPODIDAE (KANGAROOS AND WALLABIES)

This family includes most of the larger herbivores of Australasia, with about 57 species in 14 to 17 genera.

GENUS *Macropus*

This genus contains most of the kangaroos and larger wallabies. The generic names *Wallabia* and *Protemnodon* have also been used for wallabies, including *M. rufogriseus*.

Red-necked wallaby *Macropus rufogriseus*

Kangurus rufogriseus Desmarest, 1817; King Island, Bass Strait.
Kangurus ruficollis Desmarest, 1817.
Macropus (Halmaturus) fruticus Ogilby, 1838; Tasmania.
Macropus bennetti Waterhouse, 1838; Tasmania.

Brush wallaby; scrub wallaby; red wallaby; Bennett's wallaby.

RECOGNITION
Only this one species of wallaby is known to be at large in Britain (Fig. 13.1). The skull (Fig. 13.2) is immediately recognisable from the combination of three pairs of upper incisors with a single pair of procumbent lower incisors. The lophodont molars are also very distinctive.

SIGN
Tracks (e.g. in snow) are unmistakeable (Fig. 13.3). Droppings are easier to observe than the animals themselves, and fairly distinctive: each pellet is ovoid, *c.* 15 × 20 mm, rounded at both ends, and composed of rather coarse fibrous material. Pellets are loosely clumped, perhaps five or six in a loose string (whereas ruminant pellets are usually in large piles and composed of finely comminuted fragments).

DESCRIPTION
Generally grizzled greyish-brown above, white below. A rusty patch over the shoulders, variable in intensity. Tail silver-grey, tipped black; the paws, feet and ears are also tipped black and the face is black in young animals. There is a pale line along the upper lip and a pale spot over each eye; these may spread in older animals to give a white face.

Chromosomes: 2n = 16 [7].

MEASUREMENTS
Males larger than females (Table 13.1). Tail length of adults *c.* 67−78 cm in males, 62−68 cm in females; hind foot *c.* 22−23 cm in males, 20−21 cm in females [4].

VARIATION
British populations derived from *M. r. rufogriseus*, the Tasmanian subspecies, which differs from *M. r. banksianus* of mainland Australia in its more sombre colour and in having seasonal breeding [7]. Fawn and silver animals have been reported in the Peak District, latter possibly very old individuals [16].

DISTRIBUTION
Native to eastern Australia from central Queensland to South Australia and Tasmania. Introduced to the South Island of New Zealand, to Germany and to various zoos and parks in Britain, notably Whipsnade (Bedfordshire).

In Britain, a feral colony in the Peak District began in 1940 with Whipsnade stock [16]. Another

Fig. 13.1. Red-necked wallaby.

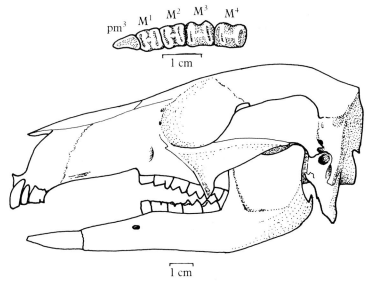

Fig. 13.2. Red-necked wallaby; skull and upper cheek-teeth.

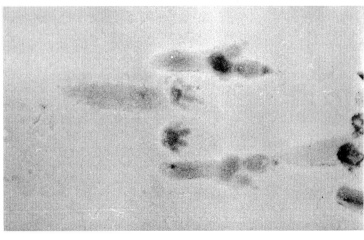

Fig. 13.3. Red-necked wallaby: tracks in snow showing hind feet, small forefeet and tail. (Photo: D.W. Yalden.)

Table 13.1. Size of red-necked wallabies related to age: mean measurements of samples in New Zealand [4].

Age (year)	Crown−tail-tip (cm)		Weight (kg)		*n*	
	Males	Females	Males	Females	Males	Females
1st	82	85	3.4	3.9	14	10
2nd	113	109	8.9	7.8	68	45
3rd	129	120	12.9	10.0	44	32
4th	136	125	15.2	11.2	25	18
5th	138	126	16.1	11.6	23	19
6th	146	130	18.7	12.2	13	7
7th	150	129	20.8	12.4	11	16

feral colony in the Weald, Sussex, survived at least from 1940–1972 but seems to have died out. A small colony around Loch Lomond has existed since at least 1975. Escapees from zoos and parks are occasionally reported in other areas. The free-ranging population at Whipsnade Zoo numbers around 400–600 [5, 6]. A small colony existed on Herm, Channel Isles, from the 1890s to about 1910.

HABITAT

This is a scrub wallaby, lying up in woodland but coming into the open to feed [2]. The Peak District population lives in scrub (mainly of pine and birch) and adjoining heather moorland [16].

SOCIAL ORGANIZATION AND BEHAVIOUR

Generally solitary, or in loose groups of up to four or five individuals, but no herd structure apparent. Usually silent, but faint growling or hissing heard when close to animals disputing food or mates [1, 6]. When alarmed, use foot-slapping (like rabbits) for first two or three bounds, presumably to warn other individuals of danger. Sight poor, but hearing acute, and ears move constantly (and independently) when suspicious.

More active towards dusk and throughout the night than during the day [5], when tend to lie-up in deep vegetation or in broken ground [17]. No permanent home site, but may favour depressions between heather tussocks or beneath young birches; in summer, often within bracken stands. No evidence of territoriality; recognisable individuals occupy home ranges of about 500 m diameter [1], comparable with 15 ha reported in Australia [17]. In fast locomotion, a bipedal jumping gait, as expected of a kangaroo (Fig. 13.4). At slower speeds, especially when feeding, the hind limbs or forelimbs

plus tail act as alternate supports (Fig. 13.3) [14]. Grooms tail, underside and hindquarters with forefeet, licking them frequently; 'comb' formed from vestigial inner hind toes used for grooming head and shoulders.

Reviews of social behaviour given by Russell [12, 13].

FEEDING

Regarded as a general grazer and browser in Australia, but no details. Peak District population feeds predominantly on heather *Calluna* (50% in summer, 90% in winter), but also on bracken, bilberry, pine and grasses [16]. Whipsnade population feeds on grasses [5]. Indulge in 'pseudorumination' [11] like other kangaroos, i.e. they have a complex stomach, in which fermentation by symbiotic bacteria and protozoa takes place, and they may regurgitate food to chew it, though less routinely than ruminants.

BREEDING

Studied in wild in New Zealand [2] and in captivity in both Australia [10] and England (Whipsnade) [6] (information in 2nd edition of *Handbook* was misleading).

Breeding seasonal, with peak of births in August–September, and peak emergence from pouch in late May–June (at Whipsnade), but breeding season spread over 6 months (births June–December in Britain, January–July in S hemisphere). Less detailed observations of feral population conform to this pattern [15]. Females breed from 1 year old, males from 2; one young per litter (twins very rare — perhaps 1%), but replacement young usually produced if first one lost from pouch early in development. Post-partem oestrous and mating results in blastocyst with delayed development; blastocyst

Fig. 13.4. A red-necked wallaby in the Peak District showing attitude when hopping slowly. (Photo: D.W. Yalden.)

stays quiescent for up to 11 months through lactation and non-breeding season. Gestation lasts usually 30 days (27–41 days recorded); pouch life lasted 275 days (264–286 days) in Australia, 247 days (185–284 days) at Whipsnade. Young stay near mother and suckle for a further 200–250 days. Mother–young relationship has been described in detail [18].

POPULATION
Peak District population increased from five in 1940 to about 50 in 1962, but then reduced by severe winter. Has varied between 10 and 20 during 1970–85 [15, 16], occupying 400 hectares of woodland and moorland. In New Zealand, population reached density of 0.6–1.3 per ha, since reduced by pest control operations. Whipsnade population reached a maximum of about 900 in 200 hectares (4.5/ha) in 1979, but then crashed in the severe 1978–79 winter.

Sex ratio of pouch young biassed, 60% male in two studies (*n* = 160); this bias also reported in adults for both Whipsnade population [6] and in wild in New Zealand [2] but difficult to interpret because females with well-grown young tend to remain in cover and are therefore under-represented in samples.

Pouch young can be aged by length of hind foot; adults can be aged post-mortem from the forward-

movement of the cheek-teeth in the skull, or from growth lines in the jaw [3, 8, 9]. Oldest feral animal so far examined was 9½ years old, but Whipsnade animals to 14 and 15 years old, and one of around 19 years in Australia [9].

MORTALITY
In Britain, New Zealand and Tasmania, suffer heavy mortality in severe snowfalls. Road casualties and other accidents also important; in Australia, an important prey of dingo *Canis familiaris*. Of 19 recent deaths of feral (Peak District) animals, six died in road accidents, seven in snowy weather, three in other accidents (drowning, falling over cliffs) and three killed by other animals (dog, fox). Suspicion that both road and other accidents result from fleeing in panic from disturbance by dogs or people; certainly timid.

RELATIONS WITH MAN
In parts of Australia, regarded as a pest of forestry, preventing natural regeneration of *Eucalyptus*. Also regarded as a forestry pest in New Zealand, where 70 000 shot in 1947–56 and many more poisoned. No likelihood of such large populations occurring in Britain. The species does well in captivity.

SOUND RECORDING
Appendix 3: P.

AUTHOR FOR THIS SPECIES
D.W. Yalden.

REFERENCES

1 Author's data.

2 Catt D.C. (1977) The breeding biology of Bennett's wallaby (*Macropus rufogriseus fruticus*) in South Canterbury, New Zealand. *New Zealand Journal of Zoology* 4:401–11.

3 Catt D.C. (1979) Age determination in Bennett's wallaby, *Macropus rufogriseus fruticus* (Marsupialia) in South Canterbury, New Zealand. *Australian Wildlife Research* 6:13–18.

4 Catt D.C. (1981) Growth and condition of Bennett's wallaby (*Macropus rufogriseus fruticus*) in South Canterbury, New Zealand. *New Zealand Journal of Zoology* 8:295–300.

5 Clarke J. & Loudon A.S.E. (1985) The effects of differences in herbage height on the grazing behaviour of lactating Bennett's wallabies (*Macropus rufogriseus rufogriseus*). *Journal of Zoology (A)* 207: 537–44.

6 Fleming D. *et al.* (1983) The reproductive biology of Bennett's wallaby (*Macropus rufogriseus rufogriseus*) ranging free at Whipsnade Park. *Journal of Zoology* 201:283–91.

7 Johnston P.G. & Sharman G.B. (1979) Electrophoretic, chromosomal and morphometric studies in the red-necked wallaby, *Macropus rufogriseus* (Desmarest). *Australian Journal of Zoology* 27:433–41.

8 Kirkpatrick T.H. (1964) Molar progression and macropod age. *Queensland Journal of Agricultural Science* 21:163–5.

9 Kirkpatrick T.H. (1965) Studies on Macropodidae in Queensland. 2. Age estimation of the grey kangaroo, red kangaroo, the eastern wallaroo and the red-necked wallaby, with notes on dental abnormalities. *Queensland Journal of Agricultural and Animal Science* 22: 301–7.

10 Merchant J.C. & Calaby J.H. (1981) Reproductive biology of the red-necked wallaby (*Macropus rufogriseus banksianus*) and Bennett's wallaby (*M. r. rufogriseus*) in captivity. *Journal of Zoology* 194:203–17.

11 Mollison B.C. (1960) Food regurgitation in Bennett's wallaby *Protemnodon rufogrisea* (Desmanest) and the scrub wallaby *Thylogale billardei* (Desmarest). *CSIRO Wildlife Research* 5:87–8.

12 Russell E.M. (1974) The biology of kangaroos (Marsupialia: Macropodidae). *Mammal Review* 4:14–59.

13 Russell E.M. (1984) Social behaviour and social organisation of Marsupials. *Mammal Review* 14: 101–54.

14 Windsor D.E. & Dagg A.I. (1971) The gaits of the Macropodinae (Marsupialia). *Journal of Zoology* 163: 165–73.

15 Yalden D.W. (1988) Feral wallabies in the Peak District, 1971–1985. *Journal of Zoology* 215:369–74.

16 Yalden D.W. & Hosey G.R. (1971) Feral wallabies in the Peak District. *Journal of Zoology* 165:513–20.

17 Johnson C.N. (1987) Macropod studies at Wallaby Creek. IV Home range and movements of the red-necked wallaby. *Australian Wildlife Research* 14: 125–32.

18 Johnson C.N. (1987) Relationships between mother and infant red-necked wallabies. *Ethology* 74:1–20.

Appendices

1 / Extinct Species

MAMMALS EXTINCT DURING THE LATE DEVENSIAN
(BEFORE 10 000 BP)

All dates are presented as 'bp', that is radiocarbon years before present.

Between 18 000 and 15 000 bp Britain was largely covered by ice sheets that enabled only a very limited arctic fauna to survive. After 15 000 bp there was a warmer phase and many mammals moved northwards, although it seems from the absence of fossils that the woolly rhinoceros (*Coelodonta antiquitatis*) and the spotted hyaena (*Crocuta crocuta*) may have become extinct in western Europe by this time. The warm phase persisted until around 11 000 bp when there was a recurrence of glacial conditions until the last retreat of the ice about 10 000 years ago. This rather arbitrary but convenient date is taken as the end of the Devensian (the last phase of the Pleistocene) and the beginning of the Flandrian (Holocene or post-glacial). After the end of the last glacial phase many species of mammal became extinct in Britain as shown by their absence in the fossil record.

The best way to assess the final period of extinction of a species is by the direct dating by radiocarbon of a series of skeletal elements, preferably from a range of sites. During the last decade the advances made in the radiocarbon dating of small samples have proved to be invaluable for the dating of skeletal remains that are too small for the conventional method, which requires about 100 g of bone. The new accelerator mass spectrometer requires only a few milligrams of bone and it is now possible to obtain a direct date from a single rabbit bone or the mandible of a vole. With a planned programme of dating it should be possible to obtain a clear definition of the times of extinction and introduction of many more members of the British fauna.

Considerable progress has already been made in this programme by the submission of critical samples to the accelerator at the Oxford University Research Laboratory for Archaeology and the History of Art.

Mammals present in Britain during the last phase of the late Devensian but which became extinct before 10 000 bp are listed in Table 14.1 with radiocarbon dates when these are available. Many of these have been published in the datelists in the journals *Radiocarbon* and *Archaeometry* and elsewhere [1, 6, 15]. In the table the individual laboratory numbers that uniquely identify each radiocarbon date are cited so that direct reference may be made to the fuller details published in the datelists.

MAMMALS EXTINCT IN BRITAIN
AFTER 10 000 BP

After the retreat of the ice at the end of the Devensian, Ireland very soon became cut off from Britain by the flooding of the Irish Channel but there was a period of around 1000 years before England was separated from mainland Europe by the breakthrough of the English Channel. During this time (the early Flandrian) a new mammalian fauna invaded Britain and mingled with those relict species that had survived the change in climate and the encroaching forestation. Many of the large mammals, however, were soon to be exterminated, probably mostly as a result of hunting by humans. These extinctions are discussed below in systematic order of the species.

LAGOMORPHA

Pika *Ochotona pusilla* Pallas

For a short period this pika was part of the late glacial fauna of southern England and it survived into the very early Flandrian [6, 15]. The radiocarbon date for two pika mandibles from Great

Table 14.1. Mammals present in Britain at the end of the last Ice Age (late Devensian) but extinct before 10 000 bp.

Species	Radiocarbon date bp	Locality	Lab. no.
Rodentia			
Dicrostonyx torquatus Arctic lemming			
Lemmus lemmus Norway lemming			
Microtus gregalis tundra vole			
Carnivora			
Alopex lagopus Arctic fox	12 400 ± 110	Gough's New Cave, Somerset	OxA−1200
Panthera leo lion			
Gulo gulo glutton			
Proboscidea			
Mammuthus primigenius mammoth	12 700 ± 160	Condover, Shropshire	OxA−1021
	12 460 ± 160	Pin Hole Cave, Derbyshire	OxA−160
Artiodactyla			
Megaloceros giganteus giant deer	11 380 ± 280	N Ireland	BM−1904
	10 920 ± 260	Ireland	BM−1840
	12 850 ± 100	Yorkshire	Birm−55
	12 180 ± 100	Devonshire	Grn−6204
Bison priscus bison			
Ovibos moschatus musk ox	18 213 ± 310	Northants.	BM−725
Saiga tatarica saiga antelope	12 380 ± 160	Gough's Cave Somerset	OxA−463

Doward Cave, Wye Valley, was 10 000 ± 120 bp (OxA−516). Today it survives only in the steppes from the Volga through northern Kazakhstan.

RODENTIA

Beaver *Castor fiber* L.

Beavers were formerly widespread throughout the Holarctic region with one species in the Palaearctic and another in N America. The preferred habitat is amongst aspen and birch woods around the shores of rivers and lakes. Its habit of felling trees and building dams has an important effect on forestation and it is probable that in the early post-glacial period, the beaver had a major influence on the growth of vegetation in the marshy areas of Britain. Its remains are fairly common in prehistoric contexts, especially in the East Anglian fens, from where two radiocarbon dates have been obtained on beaver bones: 2677 ± 123 bp (BM−722) and 3079 ± 99 bp (BM−723).

Survival of the beaver into historic times is well documented and has been described by Harting [9] who is still the authority on the extinction of mammals in Britain in the historic period. It seems that the beaver may have survived in small numbers in Wales until the 12th century. Bones of beaver have been recorded from a middle Saxon site at Ramsbury in Wiltshire [5], and recently a radiocarbon date has been obtained from a beaver bone from a site near Glastonbury, Somerset, of 1160 ± 70 bp, i.e. *c.* AD 790 (OxA−1010).

Northern or root vole *Microtus oeconomus* Pallas

The northern vole is today widely distributed throughout the tundra and taiga zones of the Palaearctic. Its remains are commonly found in Pleistocene deposits from both cold and warm periods and it survived into the early post-glacial in Britain. It has been recorded from Bronze Age levels on the Isles of Scilly [14].

CARNIVORA

Wolf *Canis lupus* L.

During the Pleistocene, before humans began to compete with the wolf, it was probably the most widely distributed of all carnivores. The wolf is the progenitor of the dog, but at the same time it has been relentlessly hunted for thousands of years. In the 1950s, the skull of a wolf was found at the Mesolithic site of Star Carr in Yorkshire, together with the very much smaller skull of a domestic dog. Despite pressure from hunting, according to historical records [9], wolves survived in England until 1500, in Scotland until 1740, and in Ireland until *c*. 1770. The history in Ireland was reviewed in detail by Fairley [7]. Although extinct in Britain, the wolf today has a widespread but sparse distribution over Europe, Asia, and N America. It is a highly social carnivore that hunts in family groups or packs, and preys on large mammals such as deer.

Brown bear *Ursus arctos* L.

Like the wolf, the bear would be a widespread carnivore if it were not hunted. The brown bear is found today in small numbers in Europe and Palaearctic Asia and in western N America. The remains of bear are occasionally found on prehistoric sites, for example at Star Carr, the Mesolithic site in Yorkshire [13], and a scapula was retrieved from a Bronze Age barrow at Ratfyn, Amesbury, Wiltshire (*c*. 3500 bp) [10]. As with most other extinct mammals, however, the final demise of the bear is recorded only in legend, for which we rely on Harting [4], but the date is made more uncertain because bears were probably brought into Britain for the sport of bear-baiting. It is very improbable that there were any wild bears in the country after the 10th century and they were never in Ireland.

Lynx *Lynx lynx* L.

The lynx is an inhabitant of mature forests with dense undergrowth. This medium-sized cat has declined over its whole range throughout Eurasia and N America with deforestation and human hunting. In Britain, the lynx appears to have become extinct during the early post-glacial. Fifteen fossil finds have been described from caves in England and Ireland [11]. The most recent of these finds that is well documented appears to be from Neale's Cave, Devonshire, which could be Mesolithic in date (pollen zone VIIa).

PERISSODACTYLA

Wild horse *Equus ferus* Boddaert

There is evidence from abundant fossil remains that the wild horse was an important member of the late glacial fauna in Britain [6, 15]. After the retreat of the ice, wild horses survived for a thousand years until the British Isles were cut off from Europe by the Channel. Then the change from the post-glacial grasslands to the forests of the Boreal period meant that there was little suitable grazing land available for herd animals, which were also under continual pressure from hunting. The latest radiocarbon date is 9770 ± 80 bp (BM−1619) obtained on a metapodial bone from the Darent gravels in Kent.

After this date the wild horse dwindled in numbers and it may have become extinct in Britain, although a few undated bones have been retrieved from early Neolithic sites and it has long been a contention that some of the races of feral pony, notably the Exmoor, are relics of the late glacial *Equus ferus*.

The earliest evidence for domestic horse comes from the site of Newgrange in Ireland [18] for which the mean of three dates obtained from charcoal is 3975 ± 40 bp (Groningen laboratory). As there is no clear-cut fossil evidence for the presence of wild horse in Ireland it is probable that the remains from Newgrange represent introduced horses that were presumably domesticated. Horse remains of around the same date have also been retrieved from a chambered tomb in Orkney (fetal elements) and from the area of the flint mines at Grimes's Graves, Norfolk, where the skull of an old mare that had been purposefully buried was dated 3740 ± 210 bp (BM−1546) [3]. The remains of domestic horse do not become frequent amongst animal remains from archaeological sites until the Iron Age.

ARTIODACTYLA

Wild boar *Sus scrofa* L.

The wild boar is an inhabitant of deciduous woodlands and it has a wide distribution over Europe and Asia. Its remains are common from Mesolithic sites in Britain and there are a few records of dubious date from Ireland [19] whilst the remains of smaller, domestic pigs are ubiquitous from early Neolithic and most later sites.

Harting [9] is yet again still the most accessible source for information on the extinction of the wild boar in historic times. It seems that it finally became extinct in England in the 17th century, but it may well have been kept going for a long while before then by introductions of new stock from the Continent and by interbreeding with domestic and feral pigs. Charles I, for example, attempted to introduce wild boar from Europe to the New Forest.

Elk *Alces alces* L.

It used to be thought that the elk was only present in Britain at the very end of the last glacial phase and the early Holocene, but recently there have been earlier records and a new radiocarbon date has been obtained on an elk bone from Kent's Cavern, Devon [12] of 31 000 ± 800 bp (OxA–1029). Three late dates have been obtained from the well-known complete skeleton of an elk from Poulton-le-Fylde, Lancashire, that had clearly been hunted as it had barbed points associated with the bones [8]. Two of the dates were obtained from detritus mud around the bones and are 12 000 ± 160 bp and 11 665 ± 140 bp (St–3832 & 3836). The third date is 12 400 ± 300 bp (OxA–150), obtained by the accelerator on bone from the skeleton.

The elk is found today in the coniferous forest zones of northern Europe and N America. Presumably at the end of the last glaciation it inhabited the same biotope and like other ungulates it was exterminated in Britain by hunting and by the change in climate. At present the latest finds of elk are those from the Mesolithic site of Star Carr, Yorkshire.

Reindeer *Rangifer tarandus* L.

Reindeer inhabited Britain throughout the Middle and Late Devensian (from *c.* 40 000 bp) to the beginning of the Flandrian, and its remains are found in the same faunal contexts as the wild horse. The suite of radiocarbon dates that has been obtained on reindeer bones suggests that this deer became extinct about the same time as the wild horse. The latest date is from a cave at Inchnadamph in Sutherland and is 8300–90 bp (SRR±2105). There are no remains of reindeer from archaeological sites to support the reference in the Orkneyinga Saga [17] that there were live reindeer in the Orkneys in the 12th century [4].

Domesticated reindeer were introduced to the Cairngorms in Scotland in 1952 and survive there as a managed herd (p. 537).

Aurochs *Bos primigenius* Bojanus

The ancestor of all domestic cattle, the aurochs or wild ox, was once as widespread as the wild boar in Europe, Asia, and N Africa. Destruction of forests and persistent hunting over thousands of years, however, led to its extinction. In Europe, the last wild aurochs was killed in Poland in 1627. In Britain, the time of extinction is not known for certain but a spectrum of radiocarbon dates points to the early Bronze Age, the latest date being from a site in Somerset which is 3245 ± 40 bp (BM–731) [2].

AUTHOR FOR THIS CHAPTER
J. Clutton-Brock.

REFERENCES

1 Burleigh R. (1986) Radiocarbon dates for human and animal bones from Mendip caves. *Proceedings of the University of Bristol Spelaeological Society* 17: 267–74.
2 Burleigh R. & Clutton-Brock J. (1977) A radiocarbon date for *Bos primigenius* from Charterhouse Warren Farm, Mendip. *Proceedings of the University of Bristol Spelaeological Society* 14:255–7.
3 Clutton-Brock J. & Burleigh R. (1983) Some archaeological applications of the dating of animal bone by radiocarbon with particular reference to post-Pleistocene extinctions. In Mook W.G. & Waterbolk H.T. eds. Proceedings of the first international symposium on C-14 and archaeology. *PACT Journal* 8: 409–19 Strasbourg: Council of Europe.
4 Clutton-Brock J. & MacGregor A. (1988) An end to Medieval reindeer in Scotland. *Proceedings of the Society of Antiquaries in Scotland* 118:23–35.
5 Coy J. (1980) The animal remains. In Haslam, J. A middle Saxon iron-smelting site at Ramsbury, Wiltshire. *Medieval Archaeology* 24:41–51.
6 Currant A.P. (1986) The late-glacial mammal fauna of Gough's Cave, Cheddar, Somerset. *Proceedings of the University of Bristol Spelaeological Society* 17: 286–304.
7 Fairley J.S. (1975) *An Irish beast book*. Belfast: Blackstaff Press, 201 pp.

8 Hallam J.S. *et al.* (1973) The remains of the late-glacial elk associated with barbed points from High Furlong, near Blackpool, Lancashire. *Proceedings of the Prehistoric Society* **39**:115–21.

9 Harting J.E. (1880) *British animals extinct within historic times*. London: Trübner 258 pp.

10 Jackson J.W. (1935) In Stone J.F.S. Some discoveries at Ratfyn, Amesbury and their bearing on the date of Woodhenge. *Wiltshire Archaeological and Natural History Magazine* **47**: 55–80.

11 Jenkinson R.D.S. (1983) The recent history of northern lynx (*Lynx lynx* Linné) in the British Isles. *Quaternary Newsletter* **41**:1–7.

12 Lister A.M. (1984) The fossil record of elk (*Alces alces* (L.)) in Britain. *Quaternary Newsletter* **44**:1–7.

13 Noe-Nygaard N. (1983) A new find of brown bear (*Ursus arctos*) from Star Carr and other finds in the late glacial and post glacial of Britain and Denmark. *Journal of Archaeological Science* **10**:317–26.

14 Pernetta J.C. & Handford P.T. (1970) Mammalian and avian remains from possible Bronze Age deposits on Nornour, Isles of Scilly. *Journal of Zoology* **162**:534–40.

15 Stuart A.J. (1982) *Pleistocene vertebrates in the British Isles*. London and New York: Longman 212 pp.

16 Sutcliffe A.J. (1985) *On the track of ice age mammals*. London: British Museum (Natural History) 224 pp.

17 Taylor A.B. (1938) *The Orkneyinga Saga. A new translation*. Edinburgh: Oliver & Boyd 445 pp.

18 Wijngaarden-Bakker L.H. van. (1974) The animal remains from the Beaker Settlement at Newgrange, Co. Meath: first report. *Proceedings of the Irish Academy* **74C**:313–83.

19 Woodman P.C. (1978) *The Mesolithic in Ireland*. Oxford: BAR British Series 58 360 pp.

2 / Ephemeral Introductions and Escapes

Historically, additions to the British native mammal fauna have been both deliberate and accidental. The acclimatisation of exotic species became a subject of particular interest from the middle of the 19th century and as a result various foreign mammals were turned out on private estates around Britain. Well-established exotics, such as the sika deer, date from this time. The accidental introduction of musk rats during the 1930s precipitated legislation to prevent the liberation of potentially damaging exotic species. The Ministry of Agriculture, Fisheries and Food now maintains a register detailing new instances of free-living exotics, including animals found in cargo at ports of entry and escapes from zoos. The potential for accidental introduction of new species is considerable.

In 1986 there were 54 zoos and safari parks registered with the National Federation of Zoological Gardens of Britain and Ireland, plus more than a hundred other licenced collections of varying size, between them exhibiting many hundreds of different mammal species from all parts of the world. In addition, numbers of valuable fur-bearing mammals are ranched in Britain and although there are now stricter legal controls for keeping dangerous mammals many unusual exotic pets exist in private homes as well as the more numerous though less varied small species kept as children's pets and laboratory stock.

Most escapes are unable to survive for long or are quickly recaptured. This chapter deals only with those species that have bred or have lived in the wild for more than a year, other than single individuals. Brief mention is also made of some species which may qualify but without satisfactory confirmation. Long-established exotics such as red-necked wallaby and coypu, now considered naturalised species, are dealt with more fully in the main text. The history of all introduced species has been reviewed by Roots [30], Lever [22, 25], and more recently by Baker [5].

Canadian beaver *Castor canadensis* (Rodentia, Castoridae)

NATURAL RANGE AND HABITAT
Forested parts of temperate N America. The closely related European beaver *Castor fiber* was formerly part of the native British fauna. There has been a recent campaign to persuade the Government to permit their reintroduction but legal objections have so far prevented any liberations of this species [21, 23, 33].

STATUS IN BRITAIN AND IRELAND
The Canadian species is that most commonly kept in zoological collections in Britain. In the past several captive colonies have been established, living under seminatural conditions, on various private estates: at Sotterley Park, near Beccles, Suffolk in 1870; on the Island of Bute, Strathclyde, Scotland in 1874; and at Leonardslea, Horsham, Sussex, in 1890. A thriving colony existed on Bute for many years, while at Leonardslea there were still beaver present in 1938 some 50 years after the initial foundation, although two new animals were added in 1917 [7, 26]. The small group of beaver at Sotterley Park escaped confinement soon after their arrival and were at liberty in the park for two seasons during which time they bred. Their offspring attempted to establish themselves on Benacre Broad, some 7 km from the park but were eventually all either captured or killed [15]. More recently escaped beaver have been recorded in Essex and in Somerset, the latter animal having survived in the wild for at least 8 years [6].

Golden hamster *Mesocricetus auratus* (Rodentia, Muridae, Cricetinae)

RECOGNITION
Soft-furred, plump, blunt-faced rodent with a very short, scarcely visible tail and capacious cheek pouches. Larger than a field vole but smaller than

a rat (head and body *c.* 150 mm). Common coloration a bright golden brown, with contrasting white undersides; dark cheek stripes, collar mark and white pouch patches are variable. Selective breeding in captivity has produced a wide variaty of coat types and colour variants, including long-haired, rex-coated, white, cream and parti-coloured individuals.

NATURAL RANGE AND HABITAT
M. a. auratus, from which all domestic stock is derived, is known only from N Syria. Very few wild-caught specimens recorded, all from Aleppo and nearby localities. Other subspecies occur in the steppes of Asia Minor and the S Caucasus; and other species of *Mesocricetus* north of the Caucasus and in Bulgaria and E Rumania.

STATUS IN BRITAIN AND IRELAND
The first live specimens imported from Aleppo in 1880, by retired British Consul, J.H. Skere, were taken to Edinburgh where a small stock flourished in captivity for *c.* 30 years before dying out. All current domestic hamsters are descendents of a single adult female and her 12 young captured in Aleppo in 1930 and taken to Jerusalem University. [1, 14]. This initial group increased to *c.* 150 in a single year; today hamsters are one of the commonest and most popular children's pets and are widely kept in private homes, schools and laboratories. There are undoubtedly frequent escapes; as a result several feral populations have been established in protected semiurban environments such as basements, under floors and in out-houses. Several infestations have been recorded [4, 24, 31, 32]: Bath, Avon, 1958 — 52 caught in basement from six that had escaped in 1957; Finchley, N London, 1962 — 25 caught in a shop from four that escaped in 1960; Boothe, Lancashire, 1962—17 trapped in a florist shop; Bury St Edmunds, Suffolk, 1964—65 — 230 caught in a colony under shops; Burnt Oak, Barnet, N London, 1980—81 — 150 caught around houses, sheds and allotment gardens on a council housing estate.

Mongolian gerbil *Meriones unguiculatus* (Rodentia, Muridae, Gerbillinae)

RECOGNITION
A sleek, yellowish-brown rodent with a well-haired, black-tipped tail and white underparts. Feet pale with black claws, soles of the hind feet almost entirely covered with fur. Eyes large, upper incisor teeth grooved. Larger than a wood mouse but smaller than a rat (head and body *c.* 120 mm, tail *c.* 100 mm). Several colour varieties have been bred, including black, white, grey and pale fawn.

NATURAL RANGE AND HABITAT
Arid steppe and desert in Mongolia and adjacent regions of China and USSR. Lives in small colonies in burrow systems.

STATUS IN BRITAIN AND IRELAND
First bred in captivity in Japan; 11 pairs from there formed the foundation stock imported into the USA in 1954 [2]. They reached Britain during the 1960s and soon gained popularity as a children's pet because of their gentle nature and ease of maintenance. They are more social than hamsters and are consequently often kept in pairs or groups; escapees readily establish themselves under the floors of houses and out-buildings but have also survived in less protected environments. There are several records for Yorkshire [17, 18, 19]: two from isolated areas on Thorne Moor and at Swinfleet Moor early in 1971; at Bradford in 1975 three animals were found in a burrow under tree-roots in woodland near a housing estate. During March 1987 gerbil remains were recovered from a fresh long-eared owl pellet, collected at a roost near Mexborough, South Yorkshire [20]. In a more typical incident gerbils were found living under sheds at a school in Armthorpe between 1972 and 1973. More escaped from the school science laboratory in 1975 and this colony was still in existence in 1977. The best documented population existed in burrows in and around a woodyard, under sheds and houses at Fishbourne, Isle of Wight, Hampshire. A colony of over 100 animals was estimated in 1976, all descendants of a few gerbils used in a children's TV programme and left behind in 1973 [22].

Short-tailed porcupines *Hystrix* spp. (Rodentia, Hystricidae)

NATURAL RANGE AND HABITAT
Eight species occur in Africa and S Asia, in forest and (in African and SW Asia) in steppe and savanna.

STATUS IN BRITAIN AND IRELAND
Easily maintained in captivity and commonly kept in zoological collections. Considerable burrowing

and gnawing ability can lead to escapes. A well-documented instance of a feral population of the Himalayan porcupine, *H. brachyura*, occurred near Okehampton, Devon, during the 1970s, originating from a single pair which escaped from a wildlife park in 1969. There were a number of records within a 16 km radius of Okehampton but the colony centred in an area of woodland of about 3 km² just south of the town. When they were found to have caused extensive damage to a spruce plantation in 1973, the Ministry of Agriculture were alerted and a live-trapping programme instigated. By 1980, a total of five adults and one sub-adult had been accounted for [12, 13].

In 1972 a pair of African crested porcupines *H. cristata* escaped at Alton Towers, near Stoke-on-Trent, Staffordshire. Subsequently the animals were sighted or signs found from an area of 7 km² around Alton Towers for at least 2 years. Other records occurred near Market Lavington in Wiltshire [22] where porcupines were reported on three occasions during 1974, from Rye, Sussex where quills were found in nearby woodland between 1979 and 1981 [35] and from County Durham where a specimen of *H. cristata* was at large for over a year [5].

Muskrat *Ondatra zibethicus* (**Rodentia, Muridae, Arvicolinae**)

NATURAL RANGE AND HABITAT
River systems, lakes, ponds and swamps in Canada and USA.

STATUS IN BRITAIN AND IRELAND
Imported to several localities in England and Scotland from 1927 until 1932 as stock for fur-farms, marketing the commercially valuable pelts known as musquash. Escapees soon established viable wild population. By 1932 muskrats inhabited rivers and marshes in 14 counties, the largest concentrations being in Shropshire, Sussex and Perthshire. Further introductions were halted by the Destructive Imported Animals Act implemented in 1932. This was followed by an eradication campaign by the Ministry of Agriculture. Three years of concerted trapping accounted for some 4500 animals and by 1937 the total wild population had been eliminated [16, 36, 37].

In Ireland, three individuals imported in 1929 to Annaghbeg, County Tipperary, escaped and by 1933 muskrats were established over an area of 50

square miles from Lough Derg south to Nenagh. An extermination campaign initiated late in 1933 harvested nearly 500 specimens, and the last individual was killed in 1935 [11]. There is no evidence that this species has recurred in Britain or Ireland since these dates.

Raccoon *Procyon lotor* (**Carnivora, Procyonidae**)

RECOGNITION
Distinctive looking carnivore about the size of a cat (head and body *c.* 550 mm). It has a plump, grey furred body, hunched back, pointed nose and ears and a black mask across the eyes. The tail is fairly short and bushy, ringed with a series of black bands, *c.* 300 mm.

NATURAL RANGE AND HABITAT
North and Central America; prefers woodland near water.

STATUS IN BRITAIN AND IRELAND
An appealing animal, frequently kept in small zoos and as an exotic pet. It has an inquisitive nature and dexterous forepaws which combine to make an expert escape artist. An opportunistic feeder able to survive in a wide variety of different habitats, this species is already well established in parts of France, Germany and the Netherlands [25, 29]. There is no evidence of a breeding population in Britain; however, there have been some 20 records of free-living individuals from many different regions, e.g. Brecon, Powys, Wales, 1977; Strathclyde, Scotland, 1981; Haywards Heath, Sussex, 1978. More recently there have been records from Norfolk, two from Yorkshire, including a pair of wild-born cubs from near Sheffield in 1984 (a pregnant female was known to have escaped in the area earlier) and three captured in different localities in Somerset during 1985 [34]. Some animals are known to have been at liberty for over a year; one individual recaptured after 4 years [5, 6].

Wild Boar *Sus scrofa* (**Artiodactyla, Suidae**)

NATURAL RANGE AND HABITAT
Widespread throughout the Palaearctic region from W Europe and N Africa to China, Japan, India, Sri Lanka and Indo-China. Prefers woodland, scrub or reedbeds.

STATUS IN BRITAIN AND IRELAND

Extinct as a native species since the late 17th century but the subject of a number of deliberate reintroductions on private estates particularly during the 19th century. There have also been some more recent inadvertent liberations. Breeding groups were kept at Cherborough Park, Dorset, from 1840, and on Sir Francis Darwin's Derbyshire estate between 1826 and 1837 [15]. Another population existed at Drummond Castle, Perthshire, where six were shot between 1800 and 1810 and boars continued to be recorded until 1830 [3]. About 1820, two boars were at large in woodland south of Colchester, Essex. More recently, a pair kept on a private estate at Ardwall, Kirkcudbrightshire, escaped to nearby woodland, where they produced eight piglets. In 1976, a young boar was killed by a vehicle on a road near Cawdor Castle, Nairn. Evidence suggests this was a recent escapee but its origins have not been traced [9, 28]. In 1977 several escaped from Chilham Castle, Kent; most were eventually shot or killed but some are still unaccounted for as is one escapee recorded in Norfolk *c.* 1983 [6].

Père David's deer *Elaphurus davidianus*

RECOGNITION

A large, rather inelegant deer similar in size to the red deer (shoulder height *c.* 1300 mm). Head rather long, hooves large and splayed; the distinctive tail is longer than that of any other deer (*c.* 500 mm) with a dark tassled tip. The summer coat is tawny with a dark dorsal stripe, in winter the coat consists of coarse, wiry, buff-coloured hair. Males carry antlers composed of two shafts one almost vertical with one or more branches, the other backward pointing and simple.

NATURAL RANGE AND HABITAT

Formerly in the marshy lowlands of NE China; thought to have been extinct in the wild for more than 2000 years. Preserved by successive Chinese emperors in the Imperial Hunting Park south of Peking (Beijing) where they were 'discovered' by Père Armand David in 1865. During extensive flooding in 1894 the park walls were breached and many of the animals perished; the survivors were destroyed during the following years of civil unrest.

STATUS IN BRITAIN AND IRELAND

A few years before the loss of the Peking herd a number of animals had been procured by various European zoos. During the 1890s, the 11th Duke of Bedford acquired the surviving deer from Paris, Berlin and Cologne to form the nucleus of a successful breeding herd. Their descendants can be seen today in the deer park at Woburn Abbey, and Whipsnade Zoo in Bedfordshire, as well as many other zoos and parks [8]. Some individuals have escaped to the wild. An animal seen near Aston Abbotts, Buckinghamshire, between 1963 and 1964 probably came from Woburn [10]; another single deer noted at Balmaha, near Loch Lomond during 1952 and 1953 was probably one of several deer which escaped from a zoo near Strathblane a few years earlier [27]. Another group of about 12 strayed from a farm near Swindon, Wiltshire, in 1981 and several were known to be still at large over a year later [6].

AUTHOR FOR THIS CHAPTER
D. Hills.

REFERENCES

1 Aharoni B. (1932) Die Muriden von Palestina und Syrien. *Zeitschrift für Säugetierkunde* 7:173.
2 Aistrop J.B. (1968) *The Mongolian gerbil.* London: Dennis Dobson 78 pp.
3 Ancaster, Earl of. Personal communication.
4 Baker S.J. (1986) Free-living golden hamsters (*Mesocricetus auratus*) in London. *Journal of Zoology* 209: 285−96.
5 Baker S.J. (1987) Irresponsible introductions and reintroductions of animals into Europe with particular reference to Britain. *International Zoo Yearbook* 24/25:200−5.
6 Baker S.J. Personal communication.
7 Barrett-Hamilton G.E.H. & Hinton M.A.C. (1921) The beaver. In *A history of British mammals.* London: Gurney & Jackson pp. 681−2.
8 Beck B.B. & Wemmer C.M. eds. (1983) *The biology and management of an extinct species, Pere David's deer.* Park Ridge, New Jersey: Noyes 193 pp.
9 Cawdor, Earl of. Personal communication.
10 Cowdy S. (1965) Mammal report 1958−1965. *Middle Thames Naturalist* 18:8.
11 Fairley J.S. (1982) The muskrat in Ireland. *Irish Naturalists' Journal* 20:405−11.
12 Gosling L.M. (1980) Reproduction of the Himalayan porcupine in captivity. *Journal of Zoology* 192:546−9.
13 Gosling L.M. & Wright M. (1975) Feral porcupines. *Report, Pest Infestation Control Laboratory* 1971−73: 160−1.
14 Harrison D.L. (1972) *Mammals of Arabia*, vol. 3. London: Ernest Benn.

15 Harting J.E. (1880) *British mammals extinct within historic times.* London: Trübner 258 pp.

16 Hinton M.A.C. (1932) The muskrat menace. *Natural History Magazine* 3:177–84.

17 Howes C.A. (1973) *Annual Report, Yorkshire Naturalists' Union* 1972:4–7.

18 Howes C.A. (1983) An atlas of Yorkshire mammals. *The Naturalist* 108:41–82.

19 Howes C.A. (1984) Free range gerbils. *Bulletin of the Yorkshire Naturalists' Union* 1:10.

20 Howes C.A. Personal communication.

21 Jarvis P.J. (1980) Beavers and bustards. *Ecos* 1(4): 24–6.

22 Lever C. (1977) *Naturalized animals of the British Isles.* London: Hutchinson 600 pp.

23 Lever C. (1980) No to the beaver. *Ecos* 1(2):22–3.

24 Lever C. (1983) The golden hamster in the London area. *London Naturalist* 62:111.

25 Lever C. (1985) *Naturalized mammals of the world.* London: Longman 487 pp.

26 Loder E. (1898) On the beaver-pond at Leonardslea. *Proceedings of the Zoological Society of London* 1898: 201–2.

27 Mitchell J. (1983) Strange beasts on bonny banks. *Scottish Wildlife* 19(3):20–4.

28 Morris P. ed. (1976) *Newsletter, Mammal Society* 27:2.

29 Neithammer G. (1963) *Die Einburgerung von Säugetieren und Vögeln in Europa.* Hamburg: Paul Parey 319 pp.

30 Roots C. (1976) *Animal invaders.* Newton Abbot: David & Charles 203 pp.

31 Rowe F.P. (1960) Golden hamsters *Mesocricetus auratus* living free in an urban habitat. *Proceedings of the Zoological Society of London* 134:499–503.

32 Rowe F.P. (1968) Further records of free-living golden hamsters. *Journal of Zoology* 156:529–30.

33 Sage B. (1981) Conservation and introduced species. *Discussion Papers in Conservation* 30:46–9.

34 Seddon C. Personal communication.

35 Tweedie W.F. Personal communication.

36 Warwick T. (1934) Distribution of the muskrat in the British Isles. *Journal of Animal Ecology* 3: 250–67.

37 Warwick T. (1941) Contribution to the ecology of the muskrat in the British Isles. *Proceedings of the Zoological Society of London* 110:165–201.

3 / Sound Recordings

While sound recordings are essential for the detailed study of mammalian vocalisations, and are often useful aids for field identification and public education, they are frequently difficult to obtain. Nonetheless, voices of most British mammals have been recorded and many may be heard on commercially issued tapes and gramophone records. The main sources of recordings of species found today in the wild in Britain are given below. Each source has been assigned a letter which is referred to, where appropriate, at the end of each species account.

A Unpublished recordings in the collections of the British Library of Wildlife Sounds (BLOWS), National Sound Archive, 29 Exhibition Road, London SW7 2AS. Includes material submitted by many sound recordists, and copies of the BBC Natural History Sound Archives recordings. Many of the older publications listed below are no longer produced but all are available for listening in BLOWS.

B W.E. Schevill & W.A. Watkins (1962). Whale and porpoise voices. One 30 cm 33.3 rpm disc with 24 pp booklet. Oceanographic Institute, Woods Hole, Massachusetts, USA. Eighteen species, of which 13 occur in British waters.

C C. & L. Weismann (1962). Voice recordings of Scandinavian mammals. Two 10 cm tape reels at 19 cm/s, numbers 14 and 15. C. Weismann, Skeltofte, Pederstrupvej 125, DK-4953 Vesterborg, Denmark. Eight British and one other mammal species.

D J. Roedle (1965). Röhrende Hirsche-rotwild in der Brunft. One 17 cm 45 rpm disc, 09901−6. Kosmos Verlag, Stuttgart, West Germany. Red deer.

E J-C. Roché (1965). Guide sonore du náturaliste 3. Mammifères sauvages. One 17 cm 45 rpm disc, P030. L'Oiseau Musicien, La Haute Borie, St Martin-de-Castillon, 84750 Viens, France. Six British and three other mammals.

F E. Simms (1969). British mammals and amphibians. One 30 cm 33.3 rpm disc, BBC RED 42M.

BBC Records, London. Thirty-eight species of mammals (including three domestic and three now extinct in Britain), and six amphibians.

G A. Klapper (c. 1970). Hirschbrunft. One 30 cm 33.3 rpm disc. Verlag Paul Parey, Hamburg, West Germany. Red deer. With German commentary.

H R.S. Payne (1970). Songs of the humpback whale. One 30 cm 33.3 rpm disc, Capitol ST-620. Capitol Records, California, USA.

I J.C. Lilly (1973). Sounds and the ultrasounds of the bottle-nosed dolphin. One 30 cm 33.3 rpm disc, FX6132. Folkways Records, New York, USA.

J S. Palmér and J. Boswall (1975). A field guide to the mammal voices of Europe. Two 30 cm 33.3 rpm discs, RFLP 5016−17. Swedish Broadcasting Corporation, Stockholm, Sweden. Forty-one British and 28 other species. With detailed sleeve notes.

K R.S. Payne (1977). Deep voices — the second whale record. One 30 cm 33.3 rpm disc, Capitol ST 11598. Capitol Records, California, USA. Three species.

L M.C. & D.K. Caldwell (1978). Sound communication by the bottle-nosed dolphin. One 30 cm 33.3 rpm disc, Leprechaun-1. Biological Systems, Inc., Florida, USA. With detailed commentary on natural history, sonar and communication.

M R. Margoschis (1978). The fox. One cassette. R. Margoschis, 80 Mancetter Road, Atherstone, Warwickshire. A variety of calls. Detailed notes on inlay card.

N K. Mizne and A. Komori (1979). Dolphin's world (Japanese). One 30 cm 33.3 rpm disc, Columbia XZ-7006. Nippon Columbia Ltd, Japan. Includes eight cetaceans found in British waters. Japanese commentary and illustrated pamphlet.

O P. Ouellet (1979). Northern whales. One 30 cm 33.3 rpm disc, Music Gallery Editions no. 19. Music Gallery Editions, Ontario, Canada. Three whale species and bearded seal.

P H. Lütgens (1979). Zooführer fur Säugetierstimmen. Six cassettes, Arno Graul C-7925/1−6. Arno Graul, Mühlacker, West Germany. Three hundred and thirty-six mammal species, including 28 on the British list, all recorded in zoos.

Q I. Ahlén (1981). Identification of Scandinavian bats by their sounds. One cassette, with 56 pp report. Department of Wildlife Ecology. Sveriges Lantbruksuniversitet, Box 7002, S-750-07 Uppsala, Sweden. Ultrasounds converted by bat detector of 12 species. Four of these also heard as slowed-down tape recordings.

R P. Spong (1982). Songs and sounds of *Orcinus orca*. One 30 cm 33.3 rpm disc, TRC 926. Total Records, Vancouver, Canada.

S S. Palmér & N. Linnman (1982). Däggdjursläten. One cassette, Esselte Studium 3149−030. Esselte Studium, Stockholm, Sweden. Twenty-four European mammals (including 12 British species), with commentary in Swedish.

T O. Mihály (1982). Animal sounds of Hungary. One 30 cm 33.3 rpm disc, Hungaraton LPX 19151. Budapest, Hungary. Six mammals (all on British list) and 41 other animal species.

U P. Richardson (1985). The bat tape — identification of British bats using the QMC 'mini' detector. One cassette with 9 pp leaflet. Northants Bat Group, 10 Bedford Cottages, Gt Brington, Northampton NN7 4JE. Ten species.

V R. Margoschis (1985). Mammal haunts. One cassette. R Margoschis, 80 Mancetter Road, Atherstone, Warwickshire. Sixteen species including feral horse.

W S. Elliott (1986). The sounds of Britain's endangered wildlife. One cassette, NSA C3. Available from the British Library of Wildlife Sounds. Seven mammals and 25 other species.

X I. Ahlén (1987). European bat sounds. One cassette. I Ahlén, Department of Wildlife Ecology, Sveriges Lantbruksuniversitet, Box 7002, S-750 07 Uppsala, Sweden. Ultrasounds of 25 species (including all those found in Britain) made audible with bat detectors and 'time expansion' instruments.

Y D. Macdonald & K. Jackson (1987). Running with the fox. One cassette, SN856. Sounds Natural, Upper End, Fulbrook, Oxford OX8 4BX. An interview with D. Macdonald interspersed with various fox calls.

AUTHOR FOR THIS CHAPTER
R. Ranft.

Glossary and Abbreviations

Agonistic Competitive (behaviour).

Alveolus The socket or cavity in a jaw bone occupied by the root or roots of a tooth.

Anoestrus A state of quiescence of the sexual organs in the female, seasonal or between oestrous cycles.

Apocrine glands Secretory glands in which the cells themselves constitute part of the secretion, as in sebaceous and mammary glands.

Aspect ratio Of a wing, the ratio of length to mean width.

Baculum The bone found in the penis of some mammals, also known as the *os penis*.

Blastocyst A stage in the development of a fertilized egg after cell-division has begun but before firm attachment to the wall of the uterus. Development may be delayed for a considerable time at this stage.

BM(NH) British Museum (Natural History).

bp Before the present (capital letters indicate a date determined by radiocarbon dating).

Brachycardia Having a very slow heart-beat, e.g. during hibernation.

Calcar A cartilaginous or bony rod arising from the ankle of a bat, supporting the trailing edge of the tail membrane (Fig. 6.1, p. 82).

Carnassials The teeth of carnivores that are specialised for shearing flesh — the last upper premolars and the first lower molars.

Chromosomes The thread-like elements in the nucleus of a cell, carrying the genetic material. The number is usually characteristic of a species and is expressed as the *Diploid number* (*2n*), being the number in normal somatic (as distinct from reproductive) cells. Each chromosome may consist of one or two arms and the number of arms may be more constant in a species than the number of chromosomes. It is called the *Fundamental number* (FN) more often expressed as Fundamental number of autosomes (NFa), i.e. excluding the sex chromosomes.

Cline A kind of geographical variation within a species where there is a gradual and progressive change in one or more characters over a large area. The rate of change is not always constant and areas of more abrupt change may demarcate subspecies.

Cohort In analysing age-structure and longevity in population a cohort is a group simultaneously recruited to the population whose subsequent fate is followed through.

Commensal An animal that derives benefit by living in close association with another species without directly harming it as a parasite does.

Condylobasal length One of the most frequently used measures of the length of a skull, from the occipital condyles behind to the anterior points of the premaxillary bones in front.

DDT A persistent organochlorine insecticide.

Diastema A natural gap in a row of teeth, especially that between the incisors and the premolars or molars when canines are absent.

Dioestrus Sexual quiescence between two oestrous cycles.

Diptera Two-winged flies.

Drey A squirrel's nest.

Epigenetic polymorphism Variability in a population caused by the interaction of genetic constitution and development processes.

Epiphyses The terminal parts of a long bone or vertebra that ossify separately from the main shaft of the bone and only become fully fused with it on reaching adult size. The degree of fusion can sometimes be used to estimate age.

Erythrism A condition of the pelage in which red pigment (phaeomelanin) predominates due usually to absence of the black pigment (eumelanin).

Feral Denoting an animal or population that has reverted to the wild from a state of domestication.

Flehmen Behaviour involving raising of the upper lip, shown especially by male ungulates in response to female odours and possibly connected with the detection of scent by Jacobson's organ in the roof of the mouth.

FM Frequency modulated (of a bat's ultrasonic voice).

FNa Fundamental number of autosomes — see *Chromosomes*.

Holarctic Region The biogeographical region comprising the Nearctic Region (North America) and the Palaearctic Region (northern Eurasia).

Home range The area normally utilized by an individual animal.

Hymenoptera The order of insects including bees, wasps and ants.

Hypsodont Of teeth, high-crowned (in extreme cases ever-growing) and therefore able to withstand considerable wear by abrasion.

Karyotype The set of chromosomes in a cell, especially when arranged in sequence for description.

Ked A parasitic fly of the family Hippoboscidae.

kHz Kilohertz: in measuring the frequency of sound, one thousand cycles per second.

Kinaesthetic Sensitive to one's own movement or position.

Leptospire A spirochaete bacterium causing the disease leptospirosis affecting especially the liver and kidneys of many species of mammals.

Life span The maximum age to which an animal can live (physiological longevity).

Longevity Mean longevity is the average age lived by members of a population under natural conditions. Often given as 'expectation of further life'.

Lophodont Of a tooth, with the cusps elongated to form narrow ridges.

Machair Lime-rich, sandy coastal pasture, especially in the Outer Hebrides.

Melon In whales, a fat deposit above the upper lip, sometimes forming a conspicuous rounded protuberance.

Merocrine glands Those in which the secretory cells remain intact during secretion as in most sweat glands (cf. *Apocrine*).

Molar The posterior chewing teeth that are not represented by precursors in the milk dentition.

ms Millisecond, i.e. a thousandth of a second.

n Number of items in a sample.

Nearctic Region The biogeographical region comprising North America.

Oedema A pathological condition involving the excessive accumulation of serum in a tissue.

Orthodont Of rodent upper incisors, pointing downwards, i.e. the most usual situation (cf. *Pro-odont*).

Palaearctic Region The biogeographical region comprising Europe, North Africa and Asia north of the Himalayas.

Paratenic host One that is not essential for a parasite's life-cycle.

Parturition The process of giving birth.

PCBs Polychlorinated biphenyls: industrial hydrocarbons which are persistent pollutants in water.

Pelage The hairy coat of a mammal (cf. plumage).

Pheromone An aromatic secretion that has a specific effect on another animal of the same species.

Polyoestrous Having a number of oestrous cycles per year or per breeding season.

Polymorphic In genetics, describing a population in which a number of discrete variants of one character are found in considerable numbers (as distinct from one normal condition and rare variants).

Post-partum, post-parturient Immediately after birth (but referring to the mother, not the offspring).

ppm Parts per million.

Pro-odont Of rodent incisors, projecting forwards (cf. *Orthodont*).

Refection The habit of an animal eating its own faeces as a normal nutritional stratagem.

Rostrum The anterior part of a skull, in front of the orbits (i.e. the skeleton of the muzzle).

SD Standard deviation: a statistical measure of the dispersion of measurements about the mean value.

SE Standard error (of a mean): a statistical measure of the accuracy of the mean value of a sample. The true mean of the population is likely to fall within the range represented by the mean of the sample $\pm$ one SE.

Selenodont Of teeth, with a crown pattern of longitudinal, crescentic ridges.

Stenopaic Of an eye, with a narrow slit-like pupil.

Sympatric Of two species, with overlapping ranges.

Thermogenetic Able to generate heat by metabolic means.

Tragus A lobe developed from the lower rim of the ear, extending upwards across the conch (especially developed in many bats).

Unicuspid Of teeth, having a single cusp or biting point (especially the simple conical teeth in the upper jaws of shrews).

Vibrissae Whiskers, i.e. specialised sensory hairs, usually best developed on the face but also found on other parts of the body.

Index